HANDBOOK OF RES ENT AND RELIGION

Handbook of Research on Development and Religion

Edited by

Matthew Clarke

Deakin University, Melbourne, Australia

Edward Elgar

Cheltenham, UK • Northampton, MA, USA

Published by
Edward Elgar Publishing Limited
The Lypiatts
15 Lansdown Road
Cheltenham
Glos GL50 2JA
UK

Edward Elgar Publishing, Inc.
William Pratt House
9 Dewey Court
Northampton
Massachusetts 01060
USA

A catalogue record for this book
is available from the British Library

Library of Congress Control Number: 2012943185

MIX
Paper from
responsible sources
FSC® C018575

ISBN 978 0 85793 356 0 (cased)

Typeset by Servis Filmsetting Ltd, Stockport, Cheshire
Printed and bound by MPG Books Group, UK

Contents

List of contributors vii

1 Understanding the nexus between religion and development 1
Matthew Clarke

PART I RELIGIOUS FAITH AND DEVELOPMENT

2 Islam as aid and development 17
Peter Riddell
3 Buddhism and development 31
Emma Tomalin and Caroline Starkey
4 Christianity and international development 51
Séverine Deneulin
5 Judaism – a cry for justice 66
Matthew Clarke
6 Hinduism and development 79
A. Whitney Sanford
7 Sikhism and development: a perfect match? 97
Darshan S. Tatla
8 Daoism and development 113
James Miller
9 Confucianism 124
Xiangshu Fang and Lijun Bi
10 Indigenous religions and development: African traditional religion 138
Namawu Alhassan Alolo and James Astley Connell
11 Name it and claim it: Prosperity Gospel and the global Pentecostal reformation 164
Matthew Sharpe

PART II DEVELOPMENT ISSUES/THEMES AND RELIGION

12 Gender, religion and development 183
Emma Tomalin
13 Moral power at the religion–development–environment nexus 201
Cynthia Moe-Lobeda with Frederica Helmiere
14 Corruption, religion and moral development 220
Heather Marquette
15 Islamic education: historical evolution and attempts at reform 238
Masooda Bano
16 Religion, conflict and peacebuilding in development 252
Shawn Teresa Flanigan

17 Religion in the policy domains of international financial institutions 268
John Rees

18 A sustainable Islamic microfinance model in poverty alleviation 286
Aimatul Yumina

19 Religion and post-disaster development 305
Ismet Fanany and Rebecca Fanany

20 Religious symbolism and the politics of urban space development 326
Yamini Narayanan

21 Cultural heritage and development in South East Asia 338
Jonathan Sweet and Jo Wills

PART III FAITH-BASED ORGANIZATIONS AND MISSION

22 'Do not turn away a poor man': faith-based organizations and development 359
Michael Jennings

23 'Pan-Islamism' as a form of 'alter-globalism'? Hizb Ut-Tahrir and the Islamic Khilafah State 376
Bruno De Cordier

24 Religion and development: prospects and pitfalls of faith-based organizations 402
Gerhard Hoffstaedter and David Tittensor

25 Mission, missionaries and development 413
Steve Bradbury

26 Why Western-based, Pentecostal mission organizations undertake community development in South East Asia 430
Vicki-Ann Ware, Anthony Ware, Matthew Clarke and Grant Buchanan

PART IV CASE STUDIES

27 Religion, development and politics in Nigeria 453
Insa Nolte

28 Religion and development in Brazil, 1950–2010 472
Rowan Ireland

29 FBOs in Tanzania 491
Michael Jennings

30 Partnership through translation: a donor's engagement with religion 505
Jane Anderson

31 The (in)visible hand of Muhajirat: a field observation on labour migration, social change and religion in the Vakhsh Valley, Tajikistan 521
Bruno De Cordier

32 Where shadows fall patchwork: religion, violence and human security in Afghanistan 540
James Astley Connell

33 Australian development FBOs and NGOs 570
Lindsay Rae and Matthew Clarke

Index 585

Contributors

Namawu Alhassan Alolo, University of Birmingham, UK

Jane Anderson, Australian National University, Australia

Masooda Bano, University of Oxford, UK

Lijun Bi, Monash University, Australia

Steve Bradbury, Tabor College Victoria, Australia

Grant Buchanan, Harvest Bible College, Australia

Matthew Clarke, Deakin University, Australia

James Astley Connell, University of Birmingham, UK

Bruno De Cordier, Ghent University, Belgium

Séverine Deneulin, University of Bath, UK

Ismet Fanany, Deakin University, Australia

Rebecca Fanany, Deakin University, Australia

Xiangshu Fang, Deakin University, Australia

Shawn Teresa Flanigan, San Diego State University, USA

Frederica Helmiere, University of Washington, Seattle, USA

Gerhard Hoffstaedter, University of Queensland, Australia

Rowan Ireland, La Trobe University, Australia

Michael Jennings, School of Oriental and African Studies (University of London), UK

Heather Marquette, University of Birmingham, UK

James Miller, Queen's University, Canada

Cynthia Moe-Lobeda, Seattle University, USA

Yamini Narayanan, Deakin University, Australia

Insa Nolte, University of Birmingham, UK

Lindsay Rae, World Vision Australia

John Rees, University of Notre Dame, Australia

Peter Riddell, Melbourne School of Theology, Australia

A. Whitney Sanford, University of Florida, USA

Matthew Sharpe, Deakin University, Australia

Caroline Starkey, University of Leeds, UK

Jonathan Sweet, Deakin University, Australia

Darshan S. Tatla, independent scholar, based at the University of Birmingham, UK

David Tittensor, La Trobe University, Australia

Emma Tomalin, University of Leeds, UK

Anthony Ware, Deakin University, Australia

Vicki-Ann Ware, Deakin University, Australia

Jo Wills, Queensland Museum, Australia

Aimatul Yumina, Deakin University, Australia

1 Understanding the nexus between religion and development

Matthew Clarke

INTRODUCTION

Eighty per cent of the world's population profess religious belief. The world's 2.1 billion Christians, 1.3 billion Muslims, 950 million Hindus, 400 million Buddhists, 13 million Jews and millions holding other traditional spiritual beliefs suggests that religious belief is a common human characteristic. Religious practice of these adherents generally involves 'the worship of a personal supernatural deity, a revealed scripture, a divinely ordained code of laws, and an assortment of institutions and communal structures in which the religion is observed' (Segal, 2009, p. 4). Whilst religion is primarily concerned with a personal relationship with an unseen order, rightful relations with this unseen order is most often dependent upon ensuring rightful relations with fellow humans and our immediate community. Religion and religious beliefs and practices[1] therefore have a material dimension that results in a high level of relevance to 'day-to-day' living. Those with religious beliefs interpret their own circumstances and make decisions on how to act and interact within wider society based on religious teachings that contain precepts on how to live a righteous life, including responding to those who are materially poor. This is particularly important when we consider that (using the most common World Bank measure of poverty), over 1 billion of the world's population live in poverty and exist on less than US$1 a day (and nearly 3 billion live on less than US$2 a day). More than 1 billion people around the globe do not have access to safe water, 115 million children do not attend primary school and 10 million children die each year of preventable illness (World Bank, 2011). Religion therefore is not simply concerned with the private circumstances of an individual and their rightful relationship with a supernatural deity, but rather it has a social realm that has relevance for wider society.

Religion is an important aspect of culture and lived experience (of the poor and non-poor). However, it has not yet been fully appreciated within the development studies literature or within mainstream development practice. Development itself is a contested term. It is contested in both its meaning and its means of achievement. There is no single measure of development and assessment of development requires a range of indicators. To ensure that benefits of development are sustained, the environment must also be a central priority. However, it is clear that the overriding intrinsic goal of development is to advance human dignity, freedom, social equity and self-determination. A lack of development is characterized by social exclusion, poverty, ill-health, powerlessness and shortened life expectancy. Good development outcomes are best achieved when communities have ownership of the goals and processes of development and where there are participatory representation, transparency and accountability mechanisms. Good development outcomes must also explicitly consider the importance of gender and diversity. Development occurs in all societies. It involves processes that require an appreciation of existing endogenous strengths and (often) exogenous interventions. Successful development requires critical analysis, mutual learning and acceptance of its paradoxes and dilemmas. Development interventions must therefore not only be cognisant of the culture and experiences of the communities in which they are aimed, they must also be prepared, designed and implemented with this culture and experience as a driving force.

This volume considers the value and central role religion plays in the culture and lived experience of the majority of the world's population and calls for a greater understanding of the nexus between religion and development. Just as gender (initially 'women in development') was found in the 1970s and 1980s to be core to implementing 'better' development interventions, and the environment was similarly 'discovered' along with the notion of community participation in the 1980s and 1990s, it is suggested throughout this volume that while religion is not the answer to development, understanding its place in the personal and social lives of people may well enhance development outcomes.

DEVELOPMENT: A BRIEF PRIMER

Improving the lives of the poor is a worthy pursuit that is difficult to argue against. However, as an international priority, it is a relatively recent phenomenon dating back to the end of World War II. Following the successful reconstruction of war-devastated Europe under the largely US-funded Marshall Plan, the international community focused attention on the newly emerging states resulting from the winding back of past colonialization of Asia, Africa and Latin America. President's Truman's 1949 Inauguration Speech is largely recognized as the starting point of the international community's commitment to improving the lives of the poor. Within Truman's speech, the United States was set the task of:

> embark(ing) on a bold new program for making the benefits of our scientific advances and industrial progress available for the improvement and growth of underdeveloped areas . . . More than half the people of the world are living in conditions approaching misery. Their food is inadequate. They are victims of disease. Their economic life is primitive and stagnant. Their poverty is a handicap and a threat both to them and to more prosperous areas . . . Our aim should be to help the free peoples of the world, through their own efforts, to produce more food, more clothing, more materials for housing, and more mechanical power to lighten their burdens.[2]

Altruism was, of course, not a sole driver of this new-found determination to improve the material lives of the poor. Quite quickly, 'development' was mired in Cold War politics with both the West and East supporting political and social development throughout the globe as a strategic aspect of their own international interests. That notwithstanding, it is clear that aid flows and other financial and technical support was made available in sums greater than previously.[3]

Development occurs at all levels of society – from the macro to the micro. However, early efforts of the international community were primarily concerned with improving macroeconomic conditions and centred largely on improving economic growth. The policies implemented to enhance economic productivity included a focus on building significant infrastructure and import substitution industries. The premise of these 'modernization' policies were that if these undeveloped countries could resemble Western (i.e., the United States) economies, they would quickly industrialize and rapidly increase their economic development.

There were five stages to this 'modernization' approach, likened as it were to an airplane taking off. The first was the 'traditional' stage whereby the poor countries were in a state of poverty going about traditional ways of living. The second was the 'pre-take-off'. Here the poor were beginning to shed their traditional modes of living for more 'modern' methods. The analogy of this was a plane slowly moving down the runway. The third stage was 'take-off' whereby the plane or economy slowly began to gain momentum and escape the situation of poverty. Fourth was the 'drive to maturity' where the poor would increasingly resemble wealthy countries with rapid industrialization and modern economies. The final stage would be the achievement of the goal of 'mass consumption'. These five stages of growth were encapsulated by Rostow (1960), whose book *Stages of Economic Growth* was not so subtly subtitled, *A Non-Communist Manifesto*. Certainly, modernization theory viewed capitalism as the only means to improve the lives of the poor.

This overt focus on capitalism as the appropriate response to poverty had as a result the downplaying of religion as a constitutive force for positive change. Religion was understood by modernists in one of two ways – it was, at best, a private affair that had little or no social benefits or consequences or, at worse, it acted as a bottleneck to economic growth along with other bottlenecks of traditional economic systems (non-cash economies, bartering) and traditional relationships (kinship ties, feudal ties, extended family) that again was limiting optimal economic productivity. Ultimately, the view of religion was its irrelevance to the modern state, which would wither quickly away or retreat to a private realm and thus its redundancy to the development project. This irrelevance or redundancy meant that explicit consideration of religion was non-existent.

The exclusion of religion within this modernist discourse and practice was not unexpected or unusual. Rather, the exclusion of religion as a factor of development in the modernization approach could best be understood as a continuation of the economic and social secularization experienced in developed countries over the previous few hundred years (Juergensmeyer, 2010). Weber's ([1904] 1930) Protestant work ethic both linked the rise of capitalism to religious belief, but also sowed the seeds for the eventual secularization of the economic sphere. It is no longer widely argued that Weber's thesis on the causal relationship between Protestantism and capitalism is direct and linear (see Robertson, 1959 for an early critique of this position). Rather, it is more reasonable to argue that capitalism was supported by the Protestant work ethic, but in turn, the Protestant work ethic became so visible and identifiable because of the conditions of an expanding capitalist system. Thus, in this instance, a religious and an economic system were self-supporting. Without spending too much time re-working this hypothesis, the conflation of the Puritan ascetic and capitalist entrepreneur was self-supporting. Wilber and Jameson capture this endogeneity well:

> To the Puritan, life was long spiritual combat, with battles all fought alone. Thus, the Puritan character esteemed hard work, frugality, sobriety and efficiency. Self-reliance became the symbol of this world of asceticism. In the development of the capitalist spirit as embodied in the person of the inventor and engineer and captain of industry, the Puritan character played an important formative role. (Wilber and Jameson, 1980, p. 470)

The impact of Puritanism on the secularization of the economy (capitalism) goes further though. Puritanism is a very private affair, with individuals having an individual relationship with God. Grace, by which one is saved, is a direct gift of God and cannot be intermediated by earthly institutions. Thus, an externalization of this relationship with God only diminishes it. Salvation is not derived through good earthly works or deeds and therefore Puritans reject the notion of having a social role in society. This individualism of religious belief enhanced and supported the role of individualism across all realms of society – including the economic. Having aided the success of capitalism through mutual characteristics (those noted above of hard work, frugality, sobriety and efficiency), capitalism was able to break away from any dependency it may have had on this religious basis and became dominant both socially and individually as society sought to grow and individuals pursued their own wealth. As capitalism's influence over society grew, so the impact of religion withered. Secularization of society and the hegemony of capitalist structures grew out of the previous sectarian base but fulfilled the same role of providing a structure and set of rules and aspirations around which to build and sustain societies and communities. However, religion did not wither and in fact outlasted the modernist approach to development.

In response to the perceived inequities and failures these early development policies wrought, a backlash against modernization occurred, originating in Latin America. The perception grew that rather than improving the lives of the poor, engaging within the modern economy actually worsened the lives of the poor. Drawing on analysis of long-term economic activity in Latin America, an opposing theory – dependency – was formed (Gunder Frank, 1971). Within this understanding, the poor of the world were poor precisely because the rich of the world were rich. Development and underdevelopment were different sides of the same coin and the relationship between poor and rich was causal and linear. The term 'underdevelopment' was used instead of 'undeveloped' (favoured by modernists who viewed the circumstances of poor countries as inert) because underdevelopment was a verb that described what had happened to the poor – a very specific outcome of modernist policies. The policy then that the dependency school called for was the retreat from the world capitalist economy completely. Only by removing themselves completely from the West could these poor countries experience true development. As with modernization though, there was no acknowledgement that religion had any role to play or any value to add in righting the circumstances of the poor.

Without any practical policies, the influence of dependency as an approach to achieving development waned quickly. The dominant approach to development again reflected the dominance of capitalism and whilst the goals of expansion growth being the driver of development reflected that of modernization, a new set of policies reflected the domestic policies being implemented in the United States under Reagan and the United Kingdom under Thatcher. The 'market' gained prominence in the allocation of scarce resources and so government spending was stripped back, government assets were privatized, labour laws were weakened, protectionism was dismantled and markets deregulated. Many developing countries (note this aspirational term to describe poor countries) received World Bank and International Monetary Fund support to implement structural adjustment programmes that would unfetter the domestic markets and achieve economic growth. These policies were known as the Washington Consensus and when later implemented with less rigour (but with the same intent) became known as the post-Washington

Consensus. As with modernization and dependency though, the primary focus remained on economic growth first and foremost with no inclusion of religion (or other aspects of culture and social practices) in consideration of effective policies.

As a macro exercise, the pursuit by the international community to improve the lives of the poor through economic expansion has excluded consideration of religion over the past seven decades. Organizations that are more interested in micro- or community-level development, such as non-governmental organizations (NGOs) have also been relatively blind to the intersection of religion and development. While NGOs have increasingly understood the need for community inclusion and moving from interventions that are welfare based to those that are community inspired and implemented (see Korten, 1990),[4] there remains a very strong hesitancy to practically engage with the spiritual or religious beliefs of communities.

Again, much of this aversion can also be ascribed to the secular nature of development as described above, in which religion is considered as being either socially irrelevant or personally redundant. So whilst the value – indeed necessity – of understanding and championing local culture and practices is now commonplace and 'mainstream' this has not yet incorporated the religion and religious beliefs of individuals and their communities. No doubt that part of this is explained by the actions of individuals and organizations undertaking evangelization under the guise of development. It is of central importance to be vigilant regarding the vulnerability of the poor. Those with resources can exploit this vulnerability quite easily and take advantage of people's apparent desperation for material improvements in their lives. Recent experiences in Aceh and Haiti following natural disasters demonstrate how religious goals of certain organizations can pollute wider humanitarian efforts. So deep-seated is this concern, that many faith-based organizations undertaking development work as expressions of their ministries are also fearful of being seen to be 'mixing' development work with evangelical activities (see Clarke, 2012 for a series of case studies). This nervousness of working in the intersection of religious and development activities has the result that again the constitutive force of religion is ignored.

BRINGING RELIGION INTO THE DEVELOPMENT SPACE

This volume does not seek to purport or support a proposition that religion is the 'answer' to development. Such a position is untenable and is without merit. It is important to acknowledge that religion, religious institutions, religious beliefs and religious faith can negatively affect the lives of the poor. For example, the negative impact of religion on world conflict (Fox and Sandler, 2006), security issues (Seiple and Hoover, 2004), extremism in international politics (Haynes, 2007 and Juergensmeyer, 2008) have all been recently considered. Certainly these critiques should not be ignored. Indeed, persuasive arguments can be made that religion has contributed to many of the issues that bolster poverty, including gender inequity, the doctrine of predestination, religious spending on sacred buildings, emphasis on non-temporal salvation, protecting vested interests of those in authority, and so on. Whilst not denying these problematic issues, this volume holds the view that religion must also be considered as an important constitutive force that requires proper consideration (see Barr, 2010 for the use of religion in international politics). In this sense, religion should be considered 'exotic' but a normal part of the social context considered when investigating 'development' (see Durkheim [1915] 1976).

More than 30 years ago, a special edition of the leading development studies journal *World Development* on 'Religion and Development' was published. The Guest Editor of this special edition wrote, 'most development authors and practitioners have simply assumed that religious beliefs incarnate a superstitious or retrograde approach to knowledge and reflect an uncritical cast of mind incompatible with the demands of modern rationality' (Goulet, 1980, p. 483). At that time, a common view of those supporting further study of the nexus between religion and development included the idea that 'having a meaningful existence' (Goulet, 1979, p. 49) was the most basic of human needs and a meaningful existence by definition requires having a spiritual belief. More explicitly, that 'the future prospects of the human species depend upon internalizing an essentially religious perspective, sufficient to transform secular outlooks that now dominate the destiny of the planet' (Falk, 1978, p. 134). Again, this is not the view predominantly held by contributors to this volume. Rather, what is proposed is that as 80 per cent of the world's population profess religious faith, ignoring it will result in sub-optimal development outcomes. Contributors to this volume argue that as religious belief and religious structures are a reality in many billions of people's lives and inform people's private and social behaviours as well as providing an understanding of why the world exists and a normative view of how it should be, this necessitates greater investigation of the intersection of religion and development. As such, religious belief cannot be ignored by those seeking to achieve material improvement in living standards of these people.

Certainly, there is little doubt of the importance of religion to those professing religious faith. Within the largest survey of poor people around the world by the World Bank it was evident that worldviews were based in religious terms: 'When asked why there are rich and poor, they answered, "Destiny", "That's the way God created the earth", and "The rich are of the devil and the poor of God"' (Narayan et al., 2000, p. 229). Regardless of religious faith or geographical location, a common view held was that overcoming poverty required faith and prayer. The survey also indicated that well-being is closely aligned to spirituality and religious observance: 'Tranquillity and peacefulness are important to poor people, even when poverty does not decrease. Maintaining social traditions, hospitality, reciprocity, rituals, and festivals is central to poor people's self-definitions as humans' (ibid., p. 267). While the development specialists might be non-believers or agnostic about the role of religion, their intended 'recipients' are not. It is odd, therefore, that this disjunction around the place and importance of religion in development exists. The exclusion of religion from consideration severely constrains efforts and compromises the ability to improve the lives of the poor. Religious identity is integral to a community's culture and the exclusion of religious consideration will limit successful development interventions and therefore it is necessary to conflate examination of religion and development to enhance efforts aimed at improving the lives of the poor. Of course, it is not necessary for organizations involved with development interventions to themselves ascribe to these views, but it makes little sense to ignore them. If these views are genuine, then seeking to engage with them will result in greater understanding of the communities that development organizations are working to assist and therefore reduce the barriers to successful and persistent benefits of interventions.

More widely than just these individual worldviews, religion is increasingly becoming more visible in the public arena. First, there has been an increase in the role that religious groups and religion have assumed in social movements. For example, the global Jubilee 2000 and the subsequent Make Poverty History campaigns had religious geneses. Second, religion has become increasingly important in terms of civic culture. Religious groups are becoming increasingly important in providing 'identities' for people and communities. Third, the process of globalization has enhanced the reach of religion and religious groups. Religious groups are able to connect across the globe in ways that were not possible until only recently, resulting in a stronger sense of identity and wielding a greater sense of influence. Finally, participation in religion and commitment to religious values is seen as a rational choice, with many religious groups actively seeking to 'grow' their congregations (Ebaugh, 2002). Politics and religion continue to be closely intertwined in many environments (both North and South). While development actors are largely secular, this secularism causes tensions when dealing with constituents or communities (both in the North and South) that are linked to religious groups. A primary purpose of this volume is to provide a sense of these points of contention and provide various examples of how these points of contention can be or have been avoided.

SEEKING AN AUTHENTIC ENGAGEMENT BETWEEN RELIGION AND DEVELOPMENT

Accepting that there is a valid need for better understanding the intersection of religion and development, it is important that this engagement of development organizations be genuine or authentic. Again, the point is made that it is not necessary for those implementing development initiatives to share the same religious belief as those they are targeting or indeed hold any religious beliefs or convictions. What is necessary is a willingness to accept that if people to whom such development interventions are targeted do have such beliefs, that this affects both their social and personal understanding of poverty and their response to it. Further, whilst this is not the only factor that affects people's worldview, it can be one of significance that ought not be ignored or be sidelined. As discussed, the secularization of the development process has meant that religion has long been excluded from mainstream discussions of international development. The argument presented throughout this volume though is that religion should not be seen as something *apart* from development processes, but rather it should be seen as *a part* of these processes.

Certainly there is some way to go in the 'normalizing' of religion within development discourse and practice. Paying lip service or using rhetoric to suggest engagement is, of course, insufficient. Therefore, it is not about 'taking advantage' of religion as it is not the 'answer'. Rather it is about recognizing that religious beliefs:

> harbour within them a latent dynamism which, when properly respected, can serve as the springboard for modes of development which are more humane than those drawn from outside paradigms. When development builds from indigenous values it extracts lower social costs and imposes less human suffering and cultural destruction then when it copies outside models. This is so because indigenously-rooted values are the matrix whence people derive meaning in their lives, a sense of identity and cultural integrity, and the experience of continuity with their environment and their past even in the midst of change. (Goulet, 1980, p. 485)

This harnessing of local values can be either authentic or unauthentic (or instrumental or non-instrumental to use Goulet's phrases). Indeed, it is not uncommon to see development practitioners enculturate their interventions to make them more palatable to their targeted beneficiaries. It is recognized that behaviour change programmes addressing the transmission of HIV, for example, should be targeted to particular social cohorts if they are to be effective. Commercial sex workers require different information in different languages and presented in different ways from that of high school students or illegal migrants (see Clarke, 2002 for further discussion on this and the evolution of the different 'generations' of approaching behaviour change programmes). It makes sense to incorporate local conditions and values in this way. But, these examples are in fact inauthentic. They are simply co-opting or 'clothing' pre-existing interventions or predetermined activities in local garb. There is no genuine or authentic engagement with the local circumstances. In more blunt terms, this is simply window dressing.

Authentic engagement requires much more than simply trying to 'sell' development interventions that have already been determined by presenting them in local language, flavours and colours. Rather, authentic engagement means drawing on existing values in the first instances to determine these development goals. Authentically engaging with existing value systems will result in development goals that are relevant and appropriate to existing needs and that will resonate with the local population. Local values therefore provide a dynamism that supports new and innovative ways to approach development. An authentic engagement with the affected communities will necessarily be more effective than interventions that are unauthentic and simply clothed in local 'dress'. For example, following the Indian Ocean tsunami and the overwhelming international response (see Clarke et al., 2010) there was an influx of international aid agencies offering assistance. One of the major criticisms of non-Islamic NGOs was their inability to fully appreciate the religious sensitivity required. Staff found it difficult to abide by Islamic laws on appropriate dressing and fraternizing between men and women. In turn, local communities would use these examples of 'inappropriate' behaviour against these NGOs and withhold cooperation from them. As a result, there was much inefficiency within the tsunami reconstruction (Telford and Cosgrave, 2006). Authentic engagement with the local communities by these non-Islamic NGOs would have highlighted not just the views held by those affected by the tsunami as to its cause (see Fanany, 2010 for a fuller explanation of why it was widely thought Allah sent the tsunami) and how this would affect responses to reconstruction efforts, but also to the importance of other non-humanitarian activities of aid workers, such as dress codes, and so on that affected their ability to access and engage with communities.

CONTENTS OF THIS HANDBOOK

It is not expected that this volume be read in its entirety or in a single sitting. Rather, this volume should be used as a reference work to which a reader might refer for information regarding a range of issues related to the intersection of religion and development. This book is therefore divided into four parts, each of which pulls together a series of chapters with a connecting theme.

Increasing religious literacy is a key task of those seeking to enhance the understanding between religion and development. Part I therefore discusses key tenets and beliefs and histories of religions as well as describes how these religions view key aspects of religion. The religions covered include: Islam (Chapter 2 by Riddell), Buddhism (Chapter 3 by Tomalin and Starkey), Christianity (Chapter 4 by Deneulin), Judaism (Chapter 5 by Clarke), Hinduism (Chapter 6 by Sanford), Sikhism (Chapter 7 by Tatla), Daoism (Chapter 8 by Miller) and Confucianism (Chapter 9 by Fang and Bi). Each of these religions has very explicit views as to both the cause and response to poverty and development that affect the private and social realms in which adherents live. The definition of religion that supports the inclusion of each of these belief systems is that of Geertz (1973). This pragmatic approach defines religion as evoking an overarching explanation of existence that is presented in a factual and realistic manner through a series of symbols that evoke certain feelings and motivations amongst adherents. Belief systems vary greatly as to the reason for existence and the relationship between humankind and the divine. There are also great differences in the symbols and ceremonies used to communicate the relationships between the temporal and otherworldly. These chapters have not been prepared to a 'formula' and so differ as to their emphasis and focus. It is clear though that each religion provides very firm teaching around behaviour of and towards the poor. Whilst this teaching predominantly focuses on responses at the individual level, the expectations of behaviour can be extrapolated to encompass both community and national responses and expectations. In this sense, these religions speak to both individual believers but also provide a framework for how 'Christian' or 'Islamic' countries, among others, should also respond to and address poverty and associated development issues. It is unusual for a single volume to present such a survey of religion and development (see Clarke, 2011 as an exception).

Two additional chapters are included due to the particular view they cast upon development. The first additional chapter within this first part addresses traditional African religions (Chapter 10 by Alolo and Connell). Given the poverty within Africa and its colonial (Christian) history, this chapter provides interesting insights into how a traditional religion is responding to contemporary pressures of poverty and development. The second chapter (Chapter 11 by Sharpe) concerns the rise of Prosperity Gospel congregations in both developed and developing countries as an interesting recent phenomenon. It has been included to present a very specific instance of a denomination (of Christianity) responding to the spiritual needs of both those with wealth and those without wealth.

The second part of this volume includes a range of thematic studies. These thematic studies consider how religion responds to key issues within development. Gender is, for example, a key cross-cutting development issue that affects all aspects of planning and implementing development interventions at both the micro and macro levels. It is no longer feasible to ignore how women and men relate within society and the influence this has on the experience of poverty and development. Perhaps one of the most striking criticisms of all religions concerns how men and women are viewed and the expectations placed upon each in their private and social lives. As this chapter (Chapter 12 by Tomalin) argues, while religion has often subordinated the role and position of women to men, it does contain great potential to reverse this outcome and so holds common goals with mainstream development views around gender. It is the harnessing of this potential that requires a greater engagement between development and religion.

In a similar manner, a range of other development issues are also discussed within this part's chapters. The environment (Chapter 13 by Moe-Lobeda with Helmiere) and education (Chapter 15 by Bano) are both important issues – along with gender – that must also be considered across a range of development initiatives. A functioning environment is a requirement for a sustained economic development (see Clarke and Islam, 2006) and education is a springboard for both individual and national progress (see Clarke and Feeny, 2007). Again, various religions provide very clear precepts regarding these issues drawn from both their sacred texts and social teaching. Similarly, corruption (Chapter 14 by Marquette) constrains development as it occurs at the local and national levels. Overcoming (at least minimizing) corruption requires a raft of strategies, but reliance on religious edicts against corruption alone will not be sufficient. Authentic engagement with religion in addressing these development issues requires an understanding of both the limits of religion to 'control' human behaviour that is detrimental to the individual as well as society – but also its potential to leverage more positive private and social responses to poverty. As this chapter of corruption (and indeed all these thematic chapters) indicates, religion should be considered neither the divine answer to all development issues nor an ethereal redundancy. Rather, an appreciation of its role in the lives of 80 per cent of the human population must be understood, for example, understanding how microfinance (Chapter 18 by Yumina) can be affected through Islamic tenets of charity and how lending can influence current development practices utilized to reduce poverty – particularly amongst the poorest. Similarly, whilst religion is a cause of conflict (Chapter 16 by Flanigan), it also has the potential to resolve conflict and perhaps, more importantly, assist with reconciliation following periods of conflict. Excluding from analysis the positive role religion can play in these fraught environments is to minimize the opportunities for effective outcomes. The role that religion plays in humanitarian assistance (Chapter 19 by Fanany and Fanany) is also discussed. Natural disasters wrought both physical and psychological destruction. Making sense of these complex humanitarian emergencies often involves invoking religious explanations. Failing to understand or appreciate this aspect can again result in sub-optimal development outcomes. Urban planning and addressing the needs of the urban poor (Chapter 20 by Narayanan) is also a significant problem – hence its inclusion in the Millennium Development Goals. Religion can assist with harnessing local responses to slum living. Certainly donors (Chapter 17 by Rees) are increasingly becoming aware of the potential benefits that can be gained from engaging more directly with religious bodies and networks. They are realizing that they are innovative delivery mechanisms of aid and other development activities. This part of the book, finally, also considers how religious congregations and buildings can also work collaboratively with local communities to preserve cultural traditions and enhance tourism opportunities (Chapter 21 by Sweet and Wills).

The third part of this book considers the role of faith-based organizations (FBOs) and missionaries in the wider development context. Missionaries can perhaps be considered the forerunners of modern development workers. The focus of both is to bring about improvements in the material circumstances of the poor. Whilst this may not have been a primary goal of missionaries, there are numerous examples of where missionaries provided welfare services in the absence of any state-provided assistance. Such care and provision of services has occurred both in their own countries of origin but also in 'mission' countries (see Williams, 1972; Harnetty, 2001; Wetherell, 2005; Gardner, 2006, 2008). Chapters in this part of the book specifically look at FBOs and how they are different from NGOs (Chapter 22 by Jennings) as well as their strengths and weaknesses (Chapter 24 by Hoffstaedter and Tittensor). The roles of both Christian missionaries (Chapter 25 by Bradbury) and Islamic mission organizations (Chapter 23 by De Cordier) are also discussed, as is the changing mode of behaviours of some missionaries in South East Asia (Chapter 26 by Ware, Ware, Clarke and Buchanan).

Practical case studies considering how the intersection of religion and development is playing out across various countries are presented in the fourth part of this volume. These case studies are broad-ranging and cover Africa (Chapter 27 by Nolte and Chapter 29 by Jennings), Latin America (Chapter 28 by Ireland), the Pacific (Chapter 30 by Anderson), Southern Eurasia and Southwest-Central Asia (Chapter 31 by De Cordier and Chapter 32 by Connell respectively), and the developed world (Australia) (Chapter 33 by Rae and Clarke). These case studies provide evidence that the intersection of religion and development is neither new nor static.

CONCLUSION

If religion is important to individuals and social constructs (as is the premise of this volume), development effectiveness requires a better understanding of what adherents to different religions understand about poverty, charity, inequality and so on. There is also value in more clearly understanding religious teaching on related issues such as gender, environment, economic prosperity and so forth throughout this volume. It will become clearer that there are divergent views on these matters both between different religions but also within the same faith traditions. It will also be clearer that religions are by definition neither conservative nor radical. Whilst it is easy to locate examples of stereotypes of religions being male-dominated and hierarchical, this volume will also provide examples of where religious faith stands firmly in the corner of the oppressed and disadvantaged and where social justice is a core tenet.

It may be unusual to conclude the introductory chapter to a significant volume of research to call for further research, but given the current infancy of this field of study, such a call is reasonable. As discussed, this volume contains a large survey of the interesting work that is being done by scholars from a range of disciplines, countries and religious affiliations (or not). It is, however, research that is coming from a small base. More empirical evidence is required to support the proposition that religion is a constitutive force for positive development outcomes. There is insufficient evidence to fully understand how religion and development intersect. For example, more work is required to understand:

- the theologies of development in different religious traditions;
- what faith-based development is and how it differs from development undertaken in the absence of faith communities;
- how FBOs differ from NGOs in their operations and the persistence of benefits of these interventions;
- how missionaries incorporate 'development' interventions within their mission and how this might differ from NGOs undertaking similar sectoral activities;
- the role (good and bad) religion plays in community conflict resolution.

Of course, there are many more areas of study that are necessary. The exciting aspect of being within this field is that it is in its infancy. Just as the work of Boserup (1970) gave rise to a substantial literature concerning gender, a similar literature is waiting to be written regarding this issue. Already the literature is being built up, and whilst there are small pockets of collaboration and funded research (such as the Religion and Development project at the University of Birmingham, the Berkley Center for Religion, Peace and World Affairs at Georgetown University, the International Development and Religion stream within the American Academy of Religion, the annual Deakin Religion and Development Roundtables at Deakin University, and the Knowledge Centre Religion & Development in the Netherlands), much work is occurring in isolated pockets and without connection to a larger international community of scholars. The goal of this volume is to bring together much of the exciting research on religion and development to assist in consolidating and codifying the present state of play in this field. Ideally, an expansion of research and changes to professional practice within the development sector will quickly follow, demanding further handbooks, book series and journals in this field.

While religion is not the answer to development, it is certainly true that nor is its exclusion. Religious belief is observable in all societies and thus can be considered pervasive, persuasive and persistent. The values and attitudes associated with religious beliefs within countries can affect both public policy settings as well as social behaviours (with both positive and negative consequences possible). As one shaper of human society, religious belief is a deep and protean aspect of human life. Yet, consideration of the impact of religion has been poorly understood in international development. It is now time for this to be remedied and reversed.

NOTES

1. For the remainder of this chapter, religion, religious belief and religious practices will be used largely as synonyms referring to the holding and expression of religious faith.
2. http://www.trumanlibrary.org/whistlestop/50yr_archive/inagural20jan1949.htm; accessed 16 July 2012.
3. Of course, earlier efforts including the establishment of national and later the International Federation of the Red Cross and Red Crescent Societies and the British and Foreign Anti-Slavery Society indicate earlier desire to address human misery outside of national boundaries. Similarly, the League of Nations in 1934 called for universal primary education (which remains one of the Millennium Development Goals set by the international community in 2000). However, these efforts were not of the scope of that which followed World War II.
4. See Clarke (2010) for an alternative view on the value of welfare-orientated development interventions.

REFERENCES

Barr, M. (2010), 'Religious nationalism and nation-building in Asia', *Australian Journal of International Relations*, **64**(3), 255–61.

Boserup, E. (1970), *Women's Role in Economic Development*, London: Allen & Unwin.

Clarke, M. (2002), 'Achieving behaviour change: three generations of HIV/AIDS programming and jargon in Thailand', *Development in Practice*, **12**(5), 625–36.

Clarke, M. (2010), 'Re-imagining capacity building when participation is constrained: illegal Burmese migrants in Thailand', in S. Kenny and M. Clarke (eds), *Challenging Capacity Building*, London: Palgrave.

Clarke, M. (2011), *Development and Religion: Theology and Practice*, Cheltenham, UK and Northampton, MA, USA: Edward Elgar Publishing.

Clarke, M. (2012), *Mission and Development: God's Work – Good Works*, London: Continuum Books.
Clarke, M. and S. Feeny (2007), *Education for the End of Poverty: Implementing ALL the Millennium Development Goals*, New York: Nova Science.
Clarke, M. and S. Islam (2006), 'National account measures and sustainability objectives: present approaches and future prospects', in *Sustainable Development*, **14**(4), 219–33.
Clarke, M., I. Fanany and S. Kenny (2010), *Post-Disaster Reconstruction: Lessons from Aceh*, London: Earthscan.
Durkheim, E. ([1915] 1976), *The Elementary Forms of the Religious Life*, translated by J. Swain, London: Allen and Unwin.
Ebaugh, H. (2002), 'Presidential address 2001, return of the sacred, reintegrating religion in the social sciences', *Journal for the Scientific Study of Religion*, **43**(3), 385–95.
Falk, R. (1978), 'Satisfying human needs in a world of sovereign states: rhetoric, reality and vision', in J. Gremmillion and W. Ryan (eds), *World Faiths and the New World Order*, Washington, DC: Interreligious Peace Colloquium.
Fanany, I. (2010), 'Reconstructing the invisible landscape', in M. Clarke, I. Fanany and S. Kenny, *Post-Disaster Reconstruction: Lessons from Aceh*, London: Earthscan.
Fox, J. and S. Sandler (eds) (2006), *Religion in World Conflict*, London: Routledge.
Gardner, H. (2006), *Gathering for God: George Brown in Oceania*, Dunedin: University of Otago Press.
Gardner, H. (2008), 'The "faculty of faith": evangelical missionaries, social anthropologists and the claim for human unity in the nineteenth century', in B. Douglas and C. Ballard (eds), *Foreign Bodies: Oceania and Racial Science 1750–1940*, Canberra: ANU Press.
Geertz, C. (1973), 'Thick descriptions: towards an interpretive theory of culture', in C. Geertz (ed.), *The Interpretation of Cultures*, New York: Basic Books.
Goulet, D. (1979), 'Strategies for meeting human needs', in C. Wilber (ed.), *Growth with Equity*, New York: Paulist Press.
Goulet, D. (1980), 'Development experts: the one-eyed giants', *World Development*, **8**(6–7), 481–9.
Gunder Frank, A. (1971), *Capitalism and Underdevelopment in Latin America*, London: Penguin.
Harnetty, P. (2001), 'The famine that never was: Christian missionaries in India, 1918–1919', *The Historian*, **63**(3), 555–75.
Haynes, J. (2007), *An Introduction to International Relations and Religion*, Harlow: Pearson and Longman.
Juergensmeyer, M. (2008), *Global Rebellion: Religious Challenges to the Secular State, from Christian Militias to Al Qaeda*, Berkeley: University of California Press.
Juergensmeyer, M. (2010), 'The global rise of religious nationalism', *Australian Journal of International Affairs*, **64**(3), 262–73.
Korten, D. (1990), *Getting to the 21st Century: Voluntary Action and the Global Agenda*, West Hartford, CN: Kumarian Press.
Narayan, D., R. Patel, K. Schafft, A. Rademacher and S. Koch-Schulte (2000), *Voices of the Poor. Can Anyone Hear Us?*, Washington, DC: World Bank and Oxford University Press.
Robertson, H. (1959), *Aspects of the Rise of Economic Individualism: A Critique of Max Weber and his School*, New York: Kelley and Millman.
Rostow, W.W. (1960), *The Stages of Economic Growth: A Non-Communist Manifesto*, Cambridge: Cambridge University Press.
Segal, E. (2009), *Introducing Judaism*, London: Routledge.
Seiple, R. and D. Hoover (eds) (2004), *Religion and Security: The New Nexus in International Relations*, Lanham, MD: Rowman and Littlefield.
Telford, J. and J. Cosgrave (2006), *Joint Evaluation of the International Response to the Indian Ocean Tsunami: Synthesis Report*, London: Tsunami Evaluation Coalition.
Weber, M. ([1904] 1930), *The Protestant Ethic and the Spirit of Capitalism*, London: Butler and Tanner.
Wetherell, D. (2005), 'The Anglicans in New Guinea and the Torres Strait Islands', in P. Herda, M. Reilly and D. Hilliard (eds), *Vision and Reality in Pacific Religion*, Canberra: Pandanus Books.
Wilber, C. and K. Jameson (1980), 'Religious values and social limits to development', *World Development*, **8**(7–8), 467–79.
Williams, R. (1972), *The United Church in Papua New Guinea and the Solomon Islands*, Rabaul Papua New Guinea: Trinity Press.
World Bank (2011), *World Development Indicators*, Washington, DC: World Bank.

PART I

RELIGIOUS FAITH AND DEVELOPMENT

2 Islam as aid and development

Peter Riddell

INTRODUCTION

Muslims are increasingly prominent in the discourse of international development assistance. Population projections foresee that by 2050, three of the six most populous nations in the world will have Muslim majorities (Indonesia, Pakistan, Bangladesh), with the largest nation in terms of numbers, India, hosting a Muslim minority larger than most Muslim-majority countries.[1] According to the Pew Research Center Report (2011, p. 13):

> Globally, the Muslim population is forecast to grow at about twice the rate of the non-Muslim population over the next two decades – an average annual growth rate of 1.5% for Muslims, compared with 0.7% for non-Muslims. If current trends continue, Muslims will make up 26.4% of the world's total projected population of 8.3 billion in 2030, up from 23.4% of the estimated 2010 world population of 6.9 billion.

But numbers are merely the tip of the iceberg; the question of poverty is far more central to our discussion. Many of the world's poorest societies have Muslim-majority or substantial Muslim-minority populations. In 2008, Muslim-majority countries made up five of the top seven recipient countries of humanitarian aid: Sudan, Afghanistan, Palestine, Somalia, and Iraq, with another, Ethiopia, having a large Muslim minority (Global Humanitarian Assistance, 2011). Poverty and deprivation in Muslim societies is compounded by political instability, with the result that Muslims have long constituted around 80 per cent of the refugees and victims of war and disaster in the world (Bellion-Jourdan, 2000). The United Nations High Commissioner for Refugees *Global Trends 2009* report counted 16 million refugees and asylum seekers and 26 million internally displaced people uprooted within their own countries, with major countries of origin including Muslim-majority Afghanistan (2.8 million) and Iraq (1.9 million), which together account for 45 per cent of all refugees under UNHCR's responsibility.[2]

RICH AND POOR IN SOCIETY IN ISLAM

What does the Islamic faith of these communities have to say about such a parlous social and economic situation? The primary Muslim sacred text, the Qur'an, recognizes that some people are wealthy and some are poor. Not only that, it sees this situation as part of the divine plan:

> *An-Nahl* 16: 71: And Allah hath favored some of you above others in provision. (Ali, 1995)

If social inequity seems to be the result of God's creative work, Muslims consider that the solution can also be found in the faith of Islam, which offers several mechanisms for alleviating this situation:

Zakat

Islam is based on five core duties, or pillars, with the third pillar, charity or *zakat*, tackling the problem of poverty. *Zakat* is mentioned over 30 times in the Qur'an, and is often linked with prayer, the second of the pillars:

> *Al-Baqara* 2:43: And be steadfast in prayer; practise regular charity; and bow down your heads with those who bow down (in worship).[3]

The secondary body of sacred text in Islam, the Prophetic Traditions or Hadith, go into considerable detail about how *zakat* should be calculated, who should receive it and so forth. Like the Qur'an, the Hadith collections draw a link between charity and prayer, two key pillars of Islam:

> Narrated by Abu Huraira: . . . Abu Bakr said, 'By Allah! I will fight those who differentiate between the prayer and the *zakat* as *zakat* is the compulsory right to be taken from the property (according to Allah's orders). By Allah! If they refuse to pay me even a she-kid which they used to pay at the time of Allah's Apostle I would fight with them for withholding it'.[4]

The adith collections provide the core of the *fiqh* (jurisprudence) texts, which systematized the payments of *zakat*. In the modern period, *zakat* is calculated on all of an individual's assets at the end of each year, with a fixed rate of 2.5 per cent per annum being set. This system provides many of the welfare requirements of the needy in Muslim communities.

Islam allows wealth accumulation; there is not the same jaundiced view of wealth that is held in some parts of Christianity. But non-payment of *zakat* on one's wealth is forbidden, with dire consequences specified in the Hadith:

> Narrated by Abu Huraira: Allah's Apostle said, 'Whoever is made wealthy by Allah and does not pay the *zakat* of his wealth, then on the Day of Resurrection his wealth will be made like a bald-headed poisonous male snake with two black spots over the eyes. The snake will encircle his neck and bite his cheeks and say, "I am your wealth, I am your treasure"'[5]

And further:

> Inform those who hoard wealth, that a stone will be heated in the Hell-fire and will be put on the nipples of their breasts till it comes out from the bones of their shoulders and then put on the bones of their shoulders till it comes through the nipples of their breasts; the stone will be moving and hitting.[6]

Those entitled to receive a share from the *zakat* are mentioned in the Qur'an at *Sura* 9:60:

> Alms are for the poor and the needy, and those employed to administer the (funds); for those whose hearts have been (recently) reconciled (to Truth); for those in bondage and in debt; in the cause of Allah; and for the wayfarer: (thus is it) ordained by Allah, and Allah is full of knowledge and wisdom.

Finally on *zakat*, the collection can be done in various ways. Some governments assist with *zakat* collection, such as Saudi Arabia, Pakistan, and the Sudan. In Malaysia, *zakat* payments can now be made online via a government website.[7]

Sadaqa

Apart from *zakat*, Islam also calls on the rich to provide other monetary assistance for activities such as relatives' maintenance, good hospitality, feeding the poor, assisting the distressed, providing medical care for the sick and rendering assistance during calamities, like wars, starvation, and so forth. Such voluntary gifts over and above the obligatory *zakat* are known as *sadaqa*. This form of giving represents a symbol of individual piety. It is not timetabled like the annual *zakat*. In some locations *sadaqa* has become more significant than *zakat* in terms of providing support for causes seen as worthy, including the in the West. Burr and Collins observe that 'private donations of *sadaqa* provided an essential means by which mosques and their outreach programs in support of Muslim communities were able to survive in North America' (Burr and Collins, 2006, p. 19).

Waqf

A third key instrument for implementing the Qur'anic call to undertake charity is *waqf*, or perpetual endowments. This serves as ongoing charitable giving beyond death, meaning that the deceased giver will continue to earn merit. *Waqf* is not mentioned in the Qur'an but finds support in the Hadith:

> Umar had acquired land in Khaybar and came to the Prophet to consult him in this matter saying: 'O Messenger of God, I have acquired land in Khaybar which is more precious to me than any property I have ever acquired'. He [Muhammad] said: 'If you want, make the land itself unalienable and give [the yield] away as alms (*in shi'ta habbasta aslaha wa-tasaddakta biha*)'. He (Ibn 'Umar) said: Thereupon 'Umar gave it away as alms [in the sense] that the land itself was not to be sold, inherited or donated. He gave it away as alms for the poor, the relatives, the slaves, the jihad, the travellers and the guests. And it will not be held against him who administers it if he consumes some of it[s yield] in an appropriate manner or feeds a friend who does not enrich himself by means of it.[8]

Peters (2002, p. 59) defines *waqf* in the following terms: 'a person, with the intention of committing a pious deed, declares part of his or her property to be henceforth unalienable . . . and designates a person or public utilities as beneficiaries of its yields'. Burr and Collin (2006, p. 19) argue that 'the most notable *waqf khayr* (charitable trust) is the Islamic Cultural Foundation established by [Saudi] King Faisal shortly before his death to support the Islamic Center in Geneva and thus the spread of Islam in Europe'.

The fruit of such charitable endowments are directed to diverse causes, including poverty alleviation, the costs of building maintenance, mosque staff, madrassas, religion schools, Sufi hospices, hospitals, and public fountains (Campo, 2009). In some Islamic countries governments take responsibility for managing the *awqaf*. Overall, there are three kinds of *waqf*: religious *waqf* for mosque construction and support; philanthropic *waqf* supporting education, health services, parks, and so on; and poverty alleviation *waqf*.

What is striking in the discussion in preceding paragraphs is the extent to which charitable giving and religious duty and piety are inextricably intertwined: generous giving earns merit points in the Hereafter, whereas a shirking of the duty of charitable giving will incur terrifying punishments after death. In such a context, it is little wonder that Muslim aid and development activities around the world typically carry a heavy religious overlay.

ISLAMIC RELIEF AND DEVELOPMENT: ARAB OFFICIAL DEVELOPMENT ASSISTANCE (ODA)

The generosity of Arab aid donor countries is well known. Three governments lead the way among Arab nations in terms of providing development assistance: Saudi Arabia, the United Arab Emirates, and Kuwait, in that order. Arab foreign aid was negligible before the quadrupling of real oil prices in 1973–74. Although Arab government aid has ebbed and flowed over the years according to varying oil prices, between 1974 and 1994 Arab governments gave 13.5 per cent of world assistance, with Saudi Arabia being one of the world's largest single bilateral donors (Villanger, 2007). In 2008 in the list of top 40 donors of humanitarian aid, Saudi Arabia appeared at no. 10 (US$727.2 million), the United Arab Emirates at no. 30 (US$110.6 million), and Kuwait at no. 32 (US$95.6 million) (Global Humanitarian Assistance, 2011).

The extent of Saudi involvement in development assistance can be gauged from the proportion of its bureaucratic operations involved in this field of activity. Burr and Collins (2006, p. 27) note that 'of the nineteen ministries that manage the government of Saudi Arabia, eight are involved, directly or indirectly, in charitable giving'.

However, this substantial programme of development support is very focused in terms of its goals and targets. A key consideration is the building of Arab, and Muslim, solidarity, with Villanger (2007, p. 9) observing that 'of the cumulative development finance from the eight major Arab donors[9] as of 31 December 2005, almost 60 percent went to Arab countries'.

Over a decade earlier, Bellers (1993) was similarly pointing out that Saudi Arabian development assistance was granted predominantly to non-revolutionary Arab and Muslim countries, with the principal beneficiaries being Egypt, Syria, Turkey, Bangladesh, the Sahel zone in Africa, and Morocco.

While Bellers' report from 1993 observed that most Saudi money was disbursed as budget subsidies rather than to specific projects, almost two decades later mega-projects in Muslim locations had assumed a significant role in Saudi development policies, with some US$511 million being channelled through the Islamic Development Bank for projects including the US$222.70 million Tirana-Elbasan Road in Albania, the US$107.81 million Schools Development Programme in Turkey, and the US$95 million Grain Steel Silos in Pakistan.[10]

This sense of prioritizing Arab or Muslim beneficiaries is also reflected in figures pertaining to humanitarian assistance. In 2009 Saudi Arabia gave 79 per cent of its humanitarian aid to Palestine, Pakistan, and Ethiopia; UAE gave 98 per cent of its humanitarian aid to Pakistan, Palestine, and Yemen, and Kuwait gave 100 per cent of its humanitarian aid to Palestine (Global Humanitarian Assistance, 2011, p. 33).

Neumayer illustrates the contrast well, by commenting that 'a typical Arab recipient country received 22 (6) times more bilateral (multilateral) Arab ODA as compared to a typical non-Arab recipient country in the period 1974–1997'.[11] Although Arab ODA is mostly bilateral – some 86 per cent of all Arab government aid was channelled bilaterally between 1995 and 2004 – nevertheless, the huge amounts available in ODA means that multilateral agencies still received generous quantities for disbursement among their various beneficiaries. The main Islamic multilateral aid agencies are the Gulf Organization for the Development of Egypt (GODE), the Arab Fund for Economic and Social Development (Arab Fund), the OPEC Fund for International Development (OPEC Fund), the Arab Monetary Fund, the Islamic Development Bank (IDB)[12] and the Arab Bank for Economic Development in Africa.

It is important to consider why Islamic relief organizations generally prioritize Arabs and Muslims as beneficiaries. The reasons are threefold, according to Bellion-Jourdan (2000, p. 15):

- Political reasons – there are Islamic causes where the victims are Muslims (Bosnia, Kashmir, Palestine).
- Pragmatic reasons – over 80 per cent of refugees are Muslims.
- Dogmatic – *zakat* should be directed towards the Muslim community.

Implied but not stated directly in these reasons is the merit to be earned by charitable giving to fellow believers, thereby avoiding some of the punishments in the Hereafter, mentioned previously.

But there is a second key priority for Arab ODA, in addition to Arab and Muslim solidarity. It has to do more specifically with promotion of the faith of Islam. Muslim governments do not share the reluctance of Western governments to fund religious activity. In the early twenty-first century, Saudi Arabia was reportedly spending US$4 billion annually on international aid, 'with two-thirds of that sum devoted to strictly Islamic development' (Dowd-Gailey, 2004). The Islamic Development Bank's operations bring this notion into stark relief. Again we quote from Villanger's important study (2007, pp. 19–20):

> The Islamic Bank, which is the single biggest Arab donor agency measured by cumulative disbursements up to the end of 2005 and is funded mostly by official aid from the Arab countries, is restricted to lending only to member countries of the Organisation of the Islamic Conference . . . One of the most important tasks for the [Islamic Development] Bank is to provide financial means through different modes of Islamic financing that are compatible with Sharīʿah.

It should be noted at this juncture that funding support for faith activities is not simply sourced from governments and multilateral agencies. Indeed, aid support originating from the Saudi royal family is primarily directed towards religious and educational institutions (Bellers, 1993). No doubt such priorities and preferences in part point to one eye of Muslim aid and development policy-makers being firmly fixed on eschatological promises and warnings.

THE RISE OF THE INGO SECTOR

From the mid-1970s vast funds became available for Islamic aid and development. Large numbers of Islamic non-government organizations (INGOs) emerged in a short space of time. Between 1980 and 2000, there was rapid growth of the numbers of INGOs in African countries: Ethiopia (0–13); Kenya (8–23); Nigeria (54–523); Sudan (5–29); Uganda (8–37). Overall, in 17 African countries surveyed by Yaylaci (2008), INGO numbers grew from 138 to 891.

Petersen attributes the rise of Muslim NGOs from the 1970s to, first, a general increase in international NGOs since World War II, and second, to Islamic resurgence around the world since the 1970s. These conditions were facilitated by famine in the Horn of Africa in the 1980s, wars in Afghanistan and Bosnia where Muslims were seen as victims, and the rise in oil prices and availability of huge funds as a result. At the same time, Petersen (2010, p. 4) reminds us of the importance of seeing Muslim NGOs as a heterogeneous group:

> the aid field contains several different kinds of Muslim NGOs, each presenting different understandings of Islam and different ways of Islamizing aid. Some promote a pervasive, all encompassing Islam, others an almost secular, invisible Islam.

Several of the emerging INGOs became particularly prominent. In the following paragraphs we will survey some of the most influential INGOs, examining their policies and priorities and assessing their place within the broader Islamic aid and development landscape. Inevitably, the INGOs, accessing their funds predominantly from Arab governments and Muslim multilateral agencies, reflect the same twin-pronged priorities of supporting fellow Muslims and promoting Islam, though sometimes in different ways.

The Muslim World League

Perhaps the best example of the dual-function Islamic approach to aid and development is provided by the Saudi Arabia-based charity Rabita al-Alam al-Islami, or the Muslim World League (MWL), which serves as a kind of INGO mother-ship. Founded in Mecca in 1962 and one of the largest INGOs, its status as an NGO is subject to debate. In the words of Burr and Collins (2006, p. 34):

> although a considerable portion of funding for MWL now comes from contributions by wealthy businessmen and *zakat*, the Saudi royal family remains the most substantial and steady donor both as private individuals and as representatives of the Saudi government. . . . It [is] . . . very difficult to maintain the façade that MWL was a non-government organization as conceived in the West when in fact it is an agency of the Saudi government.

The MWL has many international arms, including the Rabita Trust, Pakistan founded in 1988,[13] and the Rabita Bangladesh, which started in Bangladesh with relief operations in 1978. The priorities of Rabita Bangladesh serve as a useful point of focus in understanding the way that Islamic development agencies mix development work with religious activity.

In a detailed study of Rabita Bangladesh, Kalimullah and Fraser (1990, p. 86) noted that 'a large part of its work is the provision of financial and material support for evangelical Islamic organizations'. So the activities that they encountered were diverse: medical care, establishment and maintenance of hospitals and nurse training centres, village health worker training, mobile dispensaries, a model agricultural farm, and provision of water supplies. But hand in hand with these were activities of a religious kind:

the renovation of mosques and schools, distribution of religious books, training courses to hospital patients on the Qur'an, Hadith, and hygiene, with copies of the Qur'an being distributed to patients in the hospitals. Also, part of the activities of Rabita Bangladesh was the establishment of vocational colleges, teaching vocational subjects and Islam.

Support for Rabita Bangladesh came from diverse sources: the Bangladesh government, via one of its ministries, the Islamic Foundation; foreign governments (Saudi Arabia, Kuwait, Libya), and local political parties, especially the Islamist Jamaat-e-Islami.

So this agency prioritized both development and evangelism by thoroughly intermixing the two, and in the process, received substantial support from governments.

Islamic Relief Worldwide

Providing a study in contrasts is Islamic Relief Worldwide (IRW), the largest Muslim relief agency. Established in 1984 by Egyptian immigrants in Birmingham, UK, within 25 years this agency had an annual budget of US$60 million, with 1500 staff worldwide, fundraising offices in 13 countries and operating in all in 28 countries, with its largest programmes being in Pakistan, Indonesia, Lebanon, and Palestine.

A sense to which this body engages with Muslim beneficiaries can be gleaned from its 2006 annual report, which lists the countries that receive most of the organization's aid: *Afghanistan*, *Albania*, *Bangladesh*, *Bosnia-Herzegovina*, China, *Egypt*, Ethiopia, India, *Indonesia*, *Iraq*, *Jordan*, Kenya, *Kosovo*, *Mali*, Malawi, *Niger*, *Pakistan* (including Pakistan-administered Kashmir), *Palestinian Territories*, Russian Federation (*Chechnya/Ingushetia*), *Somalia*, *Sudan*, *Yemen* (Islamic Relief Worldwide and Subsidiary Undertakings, 2006). The italicized countries (17 of 23) are those that have at least 50 per cent Muslim populations.

However, IRW's approach to Islam in development sets it apart from many other INGOs. Petersen's research into this agency concluded that IRW first and foremost embraces the discourse of mainstream aid and development, rather than Islam: poverty reduction, empowerment, human rights, and the Millennium Development Goals. Its Islamic identity is based on values, not formal expression through preaching. Petersen (2010) cites an IRW project manager who explained that 'When we work, we don't go to the Qur'an to see what to do. We work from a development perspective'.

Petersen herself comments that 'Islamic Relief explicitly dissociates itself from missionary activities, rejecting traditions of mixing *da'wa* and aid' (ibid.). She terms this 'invisible Islam', contrasting it with an approach of 'embedded Islam', which characterizes the work of some other INGOs.

International Islamic Relief Organization

The International Islamic Relief Organization (IIRO) was established in 1975 and by 2010 it had activities in 95 countries, with its largest programmes in Saudi Arabia, Jordan, Egypt, Sudan, Nigeria, and Somalia (Petersen, 2010). Its stated mission from its establishment was to 'provide relief and aid to Muslims as peoples and groups wherever they are, should they face disasters endangering their being, their religious beliefs or their freedom' (Abuza, 2003, p. 24). IIRO thus embodies the idea of building Muslim solidarity with mixed humanitarian and religious functions. It is an affiliate of the Muslim

World League, as well as being a member of the International Islamic Council for Da'wa and Relief (IICDR).

Burr and Collins (2006, p. 35) note the dual humanitarian/religious function of the IIRO in observing that 'as an appendage of MWL, the humanitarian mission of IIRO included the protection of Muslim minorities and the sponsoring of programs for teaching and memorizing the Quran'.

Petersen's research (2010) bears out Burr and Collins' observations. She observed that 'the IIRO promotes an understanding of Islam as all-encompassing and pervasive, influencing all aspects of aid provision – what we may call an *embedded Islam*' (p. 10; original emphasis). This is a very different approach to aid than that embraced by IRW. Petersen further observes:

> The provision of aid is explained and legitimated with reference to Muslim traditions and concepts such as zakat, sadaqa and hadiths rather than the Millennium Development Goals, the Universal Human Rights Declaration or the Human Development Index . . . Thus in IIRO we find an Islamization of almost all aspects of aid. (Ibid.)

Al-Haramain Islamic Foundation

Another prominent Islamic NGO is the Al-Haramain Islamic Foundation. It was established in 1988 with headquarters in Riyadh, as a branch of the MWL. In 2006, Burr and Collins (2006, p. 39) note that Al-Haramain:

> achieved considerable respect for building and restoring mosques and in constructing and funding Quranic schools in impoverished villages. It has printed nearly 15 million copies of Islamic books, established more than 1,100 mosques, schools, and centers, and has dispatched more than 3,000 'missionaries' to spread Islam abroad.

Clearly its method of operations provides echoes of the 'embedded Islam' approach described above.

Islamic Foundation for Ecology and Environmental Sciences

This spirit of using aid to strengthen the Islamic identity of Muslim recipient communities can be seen in far flung Muslim populations at some distance from the Arab world. For example, the Islamic Foundation for Ecology and Environmental Sciences (IFEES), a Muslim conservation organization established in the 1980s, ran environmental ethics workshops based on the Qur'an in 1998 and 2001 in fishing villages on the East African coast. 'Mosque leaders and Qur'an schoolteachers attended the workshops alongside leaders of the fishermen. The core message was that dynamite fishing was illegal according to Islam, and the fishermen responded by ending this practice immediately' (Gambrill, 2011, p. 9).

Muslim Aid

Muslim Aid was founded in 1985 by Yusuf Islam when leading British Muslim organizations jointly responded to the endemic humanitarian crisis in Africa.[14] In subsequent years

Muslim Aid directed its operations to crises in Sudan, Bangladesh, Somalia, Mozambique, and Chad. In 1989–90 it established health centres in Rostamabad and Loshan, Iran; provided food, medicines, and shelter in Kashmir; and funded schools, orphanages, and health centres in Palestine. At the time of writing, Muslim Aid field offices were located in *Indonesia*, Cambodia, Sri Lanka, India, *Bangladesh*, *Pakistan*, *Somalia*, *Sudan*, *Jordan*, *Lebanon*, *Iraq*, *Bosnia*, *Gambia*, Kenya (Muslim-majority countries in italics).

Muslim Aid offices in First World countries include a growing operation in Australia. Annual Reports of Muslim Aid Australia (MAA) referred to diverse projects in *Yemen*, China, *Pakistan*, *Gaza*, *Bangladesh*, Cambodia, *Somalia*, *Indonesia*, *Afghanistan*, and *Lebanon*. In 2008–09 the bulk of MAA disbursement went in Food Aid. Activities that year included relief supplies for Pakistan earthquake victims; medical/healthcare inputs to Gaza, Somalia, and Indonesia; drinking water projects in Gaza, Bangladesh, Cambodia, Somalia, and Indonesia; education projects in Pakistan and Afghanistan; support for orphans in Gaza and Yemen; and US$50 000 raised for the Victorian bushfire appeal and handed over to Red Cross Australia. Again, the clear focus of MAA activities was among diverse Muslim communities.

NOT ONLY MUSLIMS, BUT ALSO NON-MUSLIM COMMUNITIES TARGETED

Islamic relief and development work can also be found in certain locations and circumstances among non-Muslim communities. Bellion-Jourdan (2000) offers three reasons for this, as follows:

- *da'wa* (mission outreach) – aid is an instrument of conversion;
- genuine compassion for human misery regardless of creed;
- promotion and marketing issues.

Again, these reasons hint at a key motivating factor, without discussing it at length. Given the understanding of charitable work as necessarily both physical and spiritual, according to the fundamental texts and doctrines of Islam, it is to be expected that development work by Muslim agencies among non-Muslims would have a missionary dimension to it.

Researcher after researcher reports that Muslim development work among non-Muslims is carried out for purposes of *da'wa*. Burr and Collins (2006, p. 38) undertook a detailed study of Islamic aid activities and, after considering the work of hundreds of Saudi charities, commented that 'most of these charities were . . . committed to assisting the destitute, supporting education, health, and refugees, and furthering Islam by *da'wa* and the construction of mosques'.

A Saudi agency of relevance to this discussion is the Benevolence International Foundation founded in Saudi Arabia in 1992. Its stated purpose at its foundation was to 'provide humanitarian assistance to those afflicted by natural disasters'. However, agency directors in interview stated that relief and development was subsidiary to *da'wa*: by 1999 its mission statement declared that the organization's purpose was 'to make Islam supreme on this earth' (ibid., p. 46).

The final INGO that we will consider is the Islam Prochar Samity (IPS), established in Bangladesh by a group of new converts to Islam, mostly ex-Hindus. Like the Rabita Bangladesh, it received considerable funding support from the Jamaat-e-Islami, the fundamentalist political party in Bangladesh. It also received funding assistance from the Bangladesh Rabita branch of the MWL.

IPS projects included the Savar Neo-Muslim Training Centre and various Neo-Muslim Rehabilitation Centres across Bangladesh. The agency integrated development work with the teaching of Islam, provided temporary hostel accommodation, training in various skills, charitable dispensaries – and ran Qur'an correspondence courses. Kalimullah and Fraser (1990, p. 85) commented that the agency 'concentrates its activities on converting non-Muslims to Islam'.

MUSLIM AID WITH A DIFFERENCE: THE GRAMEEN BANK

Although the Grameen Bank is not technically an INGO, it was established by Muslims, in a Muslim-majority country with the vast majority of its staff and beneficiaries being Muslims. However, there the similarities with most INGOs ends[15] as the Bank does not intentionally prioritize Muslims as beneficiaries, nor does it seek to consolidate or promote the Islamic faith in its various activities.

The Bank was established by Muhammad Yunus (1997), who, after studying and teaching economics at university in the USA, returned to his native Bangladesh in 1972. He was appalled by the widespread poverty in his country, and witnessed the Bangladeshi poor crippled by exorbitant interest rates on loans and locked in a cycle of debt. He surveyed a particular village and discovered that 42 people could initiate small-scale income-generating projects with an outlay of only US$27. He then sought funding from local and national banks and was ridiculed, with the response that poor people were not 'creditworthy', reflecting the widespread belief that the extreme poor would not pay back loans.

Yunus established the Grameen Bank on 2 October 1983. Its purpose was to make small-scale loans to the poor in Bangladesh. The results have been astounding. By 2010 the Bank had 2564 branches and worked in 81 362 villages.[16] The total staff was 22 807 and the total number of borrowers was 8.28 million, of whom 97 per cent were women.

In fact, the focus on women was to become a key priority for the Grameen Bank, which observed that families benefited more if wives borrowed than if husbands borrowed.[17] There was initial difficulty in recruiting women as beneficiaries, with the women wary of their husbands' response. To address this, Bank officials persuaded women to borrow in groups. In time, the women involved began to take a greater interest in decisions about family size, nutrition, sanitation, and housing.

The bank has had a significant international impact and within 15 years of its establishment some 56 countries had initiated Grameen Bank-type programmes.[18] However, it has not been all plain sailing for the Grameen Bank. Periodic backlashes from fundamentalist Muslim groups (Sider, 1997, p. 234; Yunus and Jolis, 1998, pp. 153–5) took the form of microcredit banks being burned down, microcredit being condemned as unIslamic, and women borrowers being beaten and threatened (Jolis, 1997, p. 7). This backlash was connected with a perception by the perpetrators of a redefining of women's traditional roles through Grameen Bank activities. A likely further factor is that the Bank did not wear an Islamic identity on its sleeve, as do most INGOs, nor did it target Muslim communities specifically, unlike other agencies such as Rabita Bangladesh. Muhammad Yunus comments:

> We make loans to Muslim, Hindu, Christian and Buddhist women alike, all religious and cultural groups are represented in our board of directors. There is no reason for religious or cultural wars if the poorest can, through their own self-help, their own micro-capital, develop and become independent, active, thinking and creative human beings. (Yunus and Jolis, 1998, p. 154)

THE FINANCING OF TERRORISM DEBATE

This chapter should not ignore a controversial issue that has been raised regarding certain Islamic humanitarian aid activities. The following statement by US-based Muhammad Hisham Kabbani, a leader of the Naqshbandiyya-Haqqaniyya Sufi movement, is pertinent:

> there have been many non-profit organisations established in the United States whose job is only to collect money and to send it . . . to extremists outside the United States. This is a big dilemma that is facing us here, because you don't know where the money is going, and it is more than hundreds of millions of dollars that have been sent to extremist parties in the Middle East and the Far East, as well as Afghanistan and the Caucasus now. Our sources say that many, many millions of dollars have been collected and sent. They send it under humanitarian aid, but it doesn't go to humanitarian aid . . . some of it will go to homeless people and poor people but the majority, 90 per cent of it, will go into the black markets in these countries and buying weapon arsenals.[19]

In the context of such concerns, a number of Muslim NGOs have been subject to close scrutiny in recent years. Several Muslim NGOs were deregistered in Kenya in 1998 on suspicion of involvement in the bomb attack on the US embassy in Nairobi:[20] Help Africa People; Mercy Relief International; Al-Haramain Islamic Foundation; IIRO; and Ibrahim al-Ibrahim Foundation (Versi, 1998).

As Petersen (2012) observes: '[t]he focus on Muslim NGOs, increasingly seen as de facto accomplices in radical Islamist terrorism, intensified with the 9/11 attacks on the Twin Towers and Pentagon in 2001'. In December of that year the US government froze the assets of the Holy Land Foundation for Relief and Development, a Muslim charity based in Texas, accusing it of directing financial support to Hamas, the Palestinian Islamist movement. In early March 2002, the US government froze the assets of al-Haramain Islamic Foundation branches in Somalia and Bosnia-Herzegovina, alleging that they provided financial support for terrorist activities.[21]

In the context of such developments, the US think tank, the Council on Foreign Relations, established an Independent Task Force on Terrorist Financing. Its 2004 report commented:

> Through the support for madrassas, mosques, cultural centers, hospitals, and other institutions, and the training and export of radical clerics to populate these outposts, Saudi Arabia has spent what could amount to hundreds of millions of dollars around the world financing extremism. (Independent Task Force on Terrorist Financing, 2004, p. 21)

And further:

> Such Saudi financing is contributing significantly to the radicalization of millions of Muslim in places ranging from Pakistan to Indonesia to Nigeria to the United States. (Ibid.)

As of 2010, 31 Muslim NGOs had been designated by the US State Department as having links with radical Islamist groups, 13 by the United Nations, and one by the European Union (Petersen, 2010). The Saudi government has not been immune to these pressures, announcing in June 2004 the creation of the National Commission for Relief and Charity Work Abroad to monitor private Saudi funding for charitable activities overseas (Clarke, 2007).

Anthony Bubalo and Greg Fealy (2005, p. 55) highlight the difficulty of dealing with the role of the Saudis in this issue:

> Saudi Arabia has provided considerable legitimate humanitarian and development assistance to Muslim causes around the world. The difficulty is trying to disentangle genuine charity from the funding of terrorist groups and the propagation of ideas that cross the line between purely religious and a more political activism. This difficulty is reinforced by the lack of Saudi transparency.

These statements remind us that even in this issue, religious considerations play a part, with aid activities motivated to some degree by a particular take on religious piety and duty – even if such a take is specific to a limited number of highly literalist, activist groups.

CONCLUSION

This survey of Islamic aid and development activities has highlighted a fascinating crossover between aid and faith. The Islamic primary texts both explain the context of social disadvantage and provide mechanisms for addressing it. At the same time, Muslims are exhorted to see aid as part of their religious duty, which will pay dividends in the Hereafter. It is little wonder then that most expressions of Islamic aid – government, organizational, individual – are underpinned by religious considerations: helping fellow Muslims and consolidating Islam. This call finds justification in the fact that Muslims are so heavily represented in terms of the world's poor.

NOTES

1. US Bureau of the Census, International Data Base (18 June 2008), available at: http://www.geohive.com/earth/population3.aspx; accessed 15 July 2010.
2. 'UNHCR annual report shows 42 million people uprooted worldwide', Press Release, 16 June 2009, available at: http://www.unhcr.org/4a2fd52412d.html; accessed 15 July 2010.
3. See also 98: 6, 73: 21.
4. *Sahih Bukhari*, Volume 2, Book 23, Number 483.
5. *Sahih Bukhari*, Volume 2, Book 24, Number 486.
6. *Sahih Bukhari*, Volume 2, Book 24, Number 489.
7. http://www.malaysia.gov.my/EN/Relevant%20Topics/MoneyTaxInvestment/Citizen/TaxationAndCollections/zakat/Pages/zakatTax.aspx; accessed 14 August 2011.

8. Peters (2002) citing Ibn Hadjar al-'Askalani (n.d.), *Bulugh al-maram*, Cairo, no. 784.
9. Villanger (2007, p. 19) notes that 'These are . . . the Islamic Bank, the Abu Dhabi Fund, the OPEC Fund, the Saudi Fund, the Arab Fund, the Kuwait Fund, the Arab Bank and the Arab Monetary Fund'.
10. Ahmed Rashid (1 March 2011), 'Saudi Arabia: Islamic Development Bank approves $511 million for mega projects', available at: http://www.english.globalarabnetwork.com/201103011034/Related-news-from-Saudi/saudi-arabia-islamic-development-bank-approves-511-million-for-mega-projects.html; accessed 4 August 2011.
11. Cited in Villanger (2007, p. 18).
12. The IDB was established in 1973 with headquarters in Jeddah, and at the time of writing had 56 shareholding member states, of which the main shareholders were Saudi Arabia, Libya, Iran, Egypt, Kuwait, Turkey, Qatar, and the UAE.
13. 'No light at the end of the tunnel for stranded Pakistanis', *Arab News*, 17 December 2004, available at: http://archive.arabnews.com/?page=7&section=0&article=56195&d=17&m=12&y=2004; 'The great tragedy!!!', 15 December 2006, available at: http://www.paktribune.com/news/index.shtml?163175; accessed 14 August 2011.
14. http://www.muslimaid.org/index.php/about-us/history/the-beginning-of-muslimaid; accessed 14 August 2011.
15. In its avoidance of intentional *da'wa*, the Grameen Bank resembles Islamic Relief Worldwide, which nevertheless adopts a subtle Islamic values approach that distinguishes it from the Bank.
16. http://www.grameen-info.org/index.php?option=com_content&task=view&id=26&Itemid=0; accessed 6 June 2010.
17. For the rationale of the Grameen Bank's decision to target women, cf. Yunus and Jolis (1998, Chapter 10).
18. For details on international replications of the Grameen Bank, cf. Yunus and Jolis (1998, Chapter 24).
19. Speech on 7 January 1999 at the US Department of State, cited in Cox and Marks (2003, p. 67).
20. 'US freezes Saudi charity assets', *BBC News Online*, 12 March, 2002, available at: http://news.bbc.co.uk/2/hi/americas/1868306.stm; accessed 5 August 2011.
21. 'US freezes Saudi charity assets', op cit.

REFERENCES

Abuza, Zachary (2003), 'Funding terrorism in Southeast Asia: the financial network of Al Qaeda and Jemaah Islamiyah', *NBR Analysis*, **14**(5), 24.

Ali, Abdullah Yusuf (ed.) (1995), *The Holy Qur'an: English Translation and Commentary*, Chicago: Kazi Publications Inc.

Bellers, Juergen (1993), 'Aiding their Moslim friends: Saudi Arabia's development policy', *Development and Cooperation*, No. 4, 28–9.

Bellion-Jourdan, J. (2000), 'Islamic relief organizations: between "Islamism" and "Humanitarianism"', *ISIM Newsletter*, May, 15.

Bubalo, Anthony and Greg Fealy (2005), *Joining the Caravan? The Middle East, Islamism and Indonesia*, Lowy Institute Paper No. 05, Sydney, 55.

Burr, J.M. and R.O. Collins (2006), *Alms for Jihad*, Cambridge: Cambridge University Press, p. 9.

Campo, J.E. (2009), *Encyclopedia of Islam*, New York: Facts On File Inc, pp. 96–7.

Clarke, Gerard (2007), 'Agents of transformation? Donors, faith-based organisations and international development', *Third World Quarterly*, **28**(1), 89.

Cox, C. and J. Marks (2003), *The 'West', Islam and Islamism*, London: Civitas, p. 67.

Dowd-Gailey, J. (2004), 'Islamism's campus club: the Muslim Students' Association', *The Middle East Quarterly*, **XI**(2), available at: http://www.meforum.org/603/islamisms-campus-club-the-muslim-students; accessed 14 August 2011.

Gambrill, Amy (2011), *From Practice to Policy to Practice: Connecting Faith and Conservation in Africa*, Washington, DC: USAID, p. 9.

Global Humanitarian Assistance (2011), *Global Humanitarian Assistance Report 2010*, Wells, Somerset: Global Humanitarian Assistance, p. 148.

Independent Task Force on Terrorist Financing (2004), *Update on the Global Campaign Against Terrorist Financing*, Task Force Report No. 40B, New York: Council on Foreign Relations Press, 21.

Islamic Relief Worldwide and Subsidiary Undertakings (2006), *Annual Report*, 16, available at http://www.islamicrelief.com/WhoWeAre/Files/report2006_3iuytezi.kaz.pdf; accessed 5 July 2012.

Jolis, Alan (1997), 'Microcredit: a weapon in fighting extremism', *International Herald Tribune*, 19, 7.

Kalimullah, N.A. and C.B. Fraser (1990), 'Islamic non-government organisations in Bangladesh with reference to three case studies', *Islamic Quarterly*, **XXXIV**(2), 86.
Peters, R. (2002), 'Wakf', *Encyclopaedia of Islam, New Edition, Volume XI*, Leiden: Brill, p. 59.
Petersen, Marie (2010), 'Islamizing aid: Muslim NGOs after 9.11', paper presented at 60th Political Studies Association Annual Conference, 29 March–1 April 2010, Edinburgh UK, available at: http://www.psa.ac.uk/journals/pdf/5/2010/1375_1229.pdf; accessed 12 January 2012.
Pew Research Center (2011), *The Future of the Global Muslim Population: Projections for 2010–2030*, Washington, DC: Pew Research Center Publications, p. 13.
Sider, R. (1997), *Rich Christians in an Age of Hunger* (4th edition), London: Hodder & Stoughton.
Versi, Shabbir (1998), 'Kenya bans Muslim NGOs', *The Muslim News*, No. 113, 25 September, 8.
Villanger, Espen (2007), *Arab Foreign Aid: Disbursement Patterns, Aid Policies and Motives*, Bergen: Chr. Michelsen Institute.
Yaylaci, Ismail (2008), 'Communitarian humanitarianism: the politics of Islamic humanitarian organizations', paper presented at the Workshop on 'Religion and Humanitarianism', American University of Cairo, 3–5 June, p. 3.
Yunus, Muhammad (1997), 'Soul from the ground up', *Noetic Sciences Review*, Spring.
Yunus, Muhammad and Alan Jolis (1998), *Banker to the Poor*, London: Aurum Press.

3 Buddhism and development*

Emma Tomalin and Caroline Starkey

INTRODUCTION

Whether or not Buddhism is a religion is always open to question. Scholars of religion typically include Buddhism within their inquiry since it shows many of the characteristics of what a religion is understood to be: systems of belief, institutional organization around belief and ritual practices, religious specialists in its monastic system and an ethical discourse based upon its teachings and beliefs. However, the fact that Buddhism does not teach belief in a transcendental deity or supernatural being(s) does differentiate it from most other religious systems. While the figure of the Buddha and various *bodhisattvas*[1] do, at the popular level, more or less, fulfil the role of transcendental deities, and often Buddhists will combine local animistic beliefs in the supernatural within their Buddhist practice, the 'orthodox' view is that a reliance upon the divine is an obstacle to the individual taking responsibility for their own journey towards enlightenment.

Buddhist teachings begin with the fact of human suffering (Pāli: *dukkha*/Sanskrit: *duhkha*),[2] which is caused by craving and desire (*tanha*/*trsna*) for things external to the individual self. The Buddha expressed this within the Four Noble Truths, the teaching delivered at his first sermon. These truths are:

1. The truth that suffering (*dukkha*) exists.
2. The truth that the arising of suffering has an origin, which is craving (*tanha*).
3. The truth that *dukkha* has a cessation (*nirodha*).
4. The truth that there is a path leading to the cessation of *dukkha* (the Noble Eightfold Path of Right View, Right Intention, Right Speech, Right Action, Right Livelihood, Right Effort, Right Mindfulness and Right Concentration).[3]

The Buddha taught that craving for things in the world are a source of *kamma*/*karma*,[4] which means we continue to be reborn each time we die as *kamma* 'binds' us to future rebirth. To those unfamiliar with Buddhist teaching, the doctrine of *kamma* may appear to be similar to fatalism, which within the context of thinking about development could seem to be non-conducive to social ethics that encourage people to consider ways that they can improve their situation. However, the Buddha intended to gesture towards explanations for social difference rather than to establish fixed roles and social situations. Harvey argues that the emphasis is upon what the individual can do to improve his or her situation, even if certain aspects of it have been conditioned by actions in a previous life, including your social class, your general characteristics (including gender), 'crucial' good and bad things that happen, and the way in which you see the world (2000, p. 23). Nevertheless, there is an important sense in which Buddhism teaches an individual to 'live patiently with a situation' (ibid.).

Anatta

Alongside the implications of *kamma*, the Buddha taught that the belief in a discrete permanent individual 'self', to which we are attached, is itself a fundamental mistake or delusion that must be recognized in order to escape *samsara* (the cycle of rebirths). The teaching of *anatta/anatman* ('no self') is at the very core of the Buddha's second sermon, which he gave following his own realization of the causes of human suffering (Harvey, 1990). While this teaching may seem highly esoteric, the Buddha taught the practical means to overcome craving and attachment through the 'eightfold path'. Hence, ethics with respect to how one acts, thinks or talks, for instance, are crucial to the ultimate goal of Buddhism. Morality is:

> part of a spiritual path which largely consists of cultivating a more wholesome character by undermining moral/spiritual defilements and cultural counteractive virtues. This process of transformation is seen to culminate in a state of liberation from all traces of greed/attachment, hatred and delusion, and their consequent suffering, through the experience of Nirvana. (Harvey, 2000, p. 58)

Buddhists are guided in this quest by what are called the three refuges: Buddha, *dhamma* and *sangha*. We will now briefly explore the third of these refuges, *sangha*, which we feel is particularly relevant within a discussion of development.

Sangha and the Spread of Buddhism

From the very beginning in Northeast India (dates of the Buddha's life are taken as circa 485–405 BCE, following Gombrich, 1992) the Buddha envisaged the need for a 'fourfold *sangha*' (community) consisting of fully ordained men and women (*bhikkhus/bhiksus* and *bhikkhunis/bhiksunis*) as well as laymen and women (*upasaka* and *upasika*). Hence, a system emerged whereby some Buddhists renounced the world in order to join the monastic *sangha/samgha* where they could more fully live within an environment that was conducive to meditation practice and living by the eightfold path in order that they might achieve enlightenment (the state where one is freed from *samsara*), whereas others remained in the world and supported the monastic community through the giving of alms.[5] Despite the seeming emphasis here upon choosing the religious life in order to satisfy a personal commitment to gain release from *samsara*, the monastic *sangha* has also served the community. For instance, as Pongsapich (1993, p. 1) tells us: 'from the earliest times, monks and their monasteries provided refuge for the needy and the sick, their schools offered education to the public, and their precincts were used for communal activities in all localities'.

As Buddhism developed and spread to different regions of the world, different schools of thought emerged. Today there are three main extant traditions: Theravada, found in Sri Lanka, Thailand, Burma, Cambodia and Laos; Mahayana, found in Korea, China, Japan and Vietnam; and Vajrayana, found in Tibet, Nepal and parts of Northern India.[6] There are important differences between the Buddhist teachings in the different schools, but these differences represent attempts to improve explanations of reality in order to improve upon the means to achieve enlightenment. For instance, the later Mahayana and Vajrayana schools emphasize the concept of *sunyata* (emptiness) rather than no-self (*anatta/anatman*) in order to express the notion of impermanence and non-duality.

Buddhist Precepts and Rules

Lay Buddhists and monastics pledge to keep certain precepts or rules. There are five precepts that are kept by lay Buddhists (although some may opt to keep eight[7]): non-injury to all living beings (*ahimsa*); avoiding theft and cheating; avoiding sexual misconduct; refraining from lying and other forms of wrong speech; and retaining sobriety. The ethical conduct of monastics, by contrast, is governed by the *vinaya* (monastic code), which includes the maintenance of complete celibacy. In the Theravada tradition, for instance, there are 227 rules for monks, which include, elaborate upon and add to the lay precepts. On the whole, the Buddha considered that living in the world created obstacles that made it difficult to eradicate 'greed, hate and delusion'. Hence, the rules governing the monastic way of life were intended to create the optimum conditions for Buddhist practice.

Dana ('Giving') and Philanthropy

It is important to note the centrality of giving (*dana*) within Buddhism as an action that is 'karmically fruitful' (Findly, 2003). Linked to the idea of giving is the sharing of the karmic fruits of action. In the Theravada tradition a boy who is ordained as a novice monk, for instance, will share the fruits of this auspicious action with his mother who has enabled him to enter the monastic *sangha*. In the Mahayana tradition we find this idea in the transference of karmic fruits to 'all sentient beings', particularly in the figure of the *bodhisattva* (Harvey, 2000, p. 66). The most prominent aspect of giving is with respect to the alms offered to the monastic *sangha*.[8] According to Pongsapich, 'philanthropy in Thailand has a very long tradition . . . To witness rows of Thai monks begging for food from citizens who give alms every morning is to observe a ritual dating back to the dawn of Buddhism in the country' (1993, p. 1).

However, while this is evidence of a culture of giving (philanthropy), it is to the monks rather than to the needy in the community. Thus, whether this culture of giving ever extends to support for development projects (not linked to the monastic community) is not made clear (Pryor, 1991). Many monasteries do, however, provide shelter, food, health care and education, so in giving to monks people are supporting the social service dimension of the temples. For instance, there are examples of the involvement of Buddhist monks in HIV/AIDS palliative care and prevention awareness.[9] However, the primary motivation for *dana* may be the religious merit accrued, rather than the desire to help the poor.

Yet, while some Buddhists may give to Buddhist temples/monks to increase their religious merit regardless of what activities the temples/monks are involved in, we can also find examples of Buddhists giving specifically to development-related projects. In particular, the important Buddhist values of loving kindness (*metta*) and compassion (*karuna*), whereby the Buddhist endeavours to overcome the apparent distinction between their own self and others, would seem to support concern for the needy. The largest civic organization in Taiwan, for instance (giving away well over US$20 million in charity a year) is a Buddhist organization called Ciji/Tzu-Chi. Whilst this suggests that some Buddhists are motivated to give to development organizations as a fulfilment of the Buddhist ethic of *dana* (Laliberte, 2004) it would be interesting to ascertain whether Buddhists are more likely to give to Buddhist organizations than secular ones.

BUDDHIST ETHICS OF SOCIAL JUSTICE

Within the context of international development, it is useful to consider what Buddhism has to say about social ethics (Kalupahana, 1995). A good place to start is the Buddhist attitude towards the caste system in India (a system of social ethics that is modelled on hierarchy rather than social equality). In Buddhism, equality is valued as a social good and according to the Buddha: 'Not by birth does one become an outcaste, not by birth does one become a brahmin. By (one's) action one becomes an outcaste, by (one's) action one becomes a brahmin' (*Sutta Nipata*: 136, cited in Harvey, 2000, p. 110). Thus, although one is born into a particular social class, he or she is considered to be able to move from within this if their talents and efforts allow. Although Buddhism emerged from within a Hindu philosophical world-view, from the outset it was sharply opposed to the caste system and instead considered that anyone was capable of reaching *nirvana* (enlightenment). Hence, the monastic *sangha* was open to all regardless of social standing, and Buddhism continued to thrive and grow during the centuries following the death of the Buddha, throughout India and beyond.

However, by the tenth century CE, Buddhism was in decline in its homeland, only to eventually die out. Yet its more recent revival in India owes its success to precisely these radical notions of social equality, particularly as a result of Dr Babasaheb Ambedkar, who worked to outlaw untouchability for the Dalit[10] caste. While Ambedkar (1891–1956) was born as an 'outcaste' or 'untouchable', he managed to pursue higher education in the USA and the UK and to become a lawyer and Bahujan[11] political leader, as well as the main author of the Indian constitution after independence. However, his pursuit of Dalit rights was not confined to politics: instead, he converted to Buddhism in 1956 and then converted an estimated 380 000 of his followers to the tradition. This conversion was, on the one hand, a symbolic rejection of Hinduism, which was considered through its sanction of the caste system to justify the oppression of outcastes. On the other hand, the conversion to Buddhism has proved to be an important means of enabling Dalits to enhance their self-worth and, to a degree, their social standing in a society that continues to exercise discrimination against what are now called, for classification purposes, Scheduled Castes and Scheduled Tribes (SC/ST) (Omvedt, 2004; Jaffrelot, 2005).[12] This is relevant as studies on Dalit communities indicate consistently low levels of education, health and income compared to higher castes (Robb, 1996).

If we broaden the discussion of social equality to considerations of human rights it is important to note that although Buddhism does not talk directly about 'rights' in the modern Western sense, there is much within the tradition that appears supportive of rights-based thinking (Keown, 1992; Husted et al., 1998). Harvey suggests, however, that some Buddhists may object to the language of rights because it can come across as aggressive and self-centred, and that moreover, it goes against the Buddhist understanding of the impermanence of the individual self. He argues that, on the whole, notions of 'universal human duties' are seen as more suitable within a Buddhist framework, which would seem to fit well with our earlier discussion of the Buddhist precepts. With respect to negative rights (i.e., the right to not be subject to something), Harvey suggests that these are strong within the tradition because of the emphasis upon others having a duty not to harm other living beings. Support for positive rights (i.e., the right to be entitled to something), however, is less strong as the tradition sees them 'more as something that it is good for others to choose to provide' (2000, p. 121) rather than as an inalienable right.

The above discussion has provided a brief overview of some key Buddhist teachings, beliefs, practices and values, including social and political values. In the following section we will briefly consider the movement of 'Engaged Buddhism' and then move on to look at the relationship between Buddhism and particular development concerns.

BUDDHISM AND DEVELOPMENT

Engaged Buddhism

While some branches of Buddhism (e.g., Zen, a branch of Mahayana Buddhism) have typically stressed the meditative and other-worldly, there have been recent shifts in Buddhist thinking across its different traditions, whereby the tradition has responded to many of the concerns that occupy international development. James (2004), for instance, shows that over the past century there have been developments in Zen Buddhism that seek to transform the meditative into critical action, especially with respect to concern for the environment. Queen's (2000) edited volume *Engaged Buddhism in the West* points to the emergence of a new style of Buddhism that has come to be called 'Engaged Buddhism', which promotes movements that relate to issues of poverty, the environment and social and political justice.

The term Engaged Buddhism is modern, first used by the Vietnamese monk Thich Nhat Hanh in 1963 (Eppsteiner, 1988; Queen and King, 1996; Hanh, 2002). Some scholars consider that the roots of Engaged Buddhism go back to transformations during the colonial period, particularly in Sri Lanka where there was a Buddhist resurgence in the face of the Protestant critique of what was considered to be the socially passive and transmundane nature of traditional Buddhist thought and practice (Harvey, 2000, p. 112). Others claim, however, that Engaged Buddhism, as a style of socially active and reformist Buddhism, predates the colonial era, and that the *sangha* in Asia, for instance, is actually reviving modes of practice that were suppressed by the colonialists. Yarnall (2000) divides Engaged Buddhists into two types: the traditionalists (who consider that social engagement is inherent to the Buddhist tradition: it is nothing new) and the modernists (who see Engaged Buddhism as a contemporary response to social problems). The traditionalists (who are both Asian and Western, whereas the modernists are predominantly Western) argue that the image of Buddhism as other-worldly and uninterested in social issues is a Western orientalist construction (e.g., beginning with Max Weber's depiction of Buddhism) (Macy, 1988, p. 173).

The range of issues that concern Engaged Buddhism share many parallels with those of international development. For instance, on the 'DharmaNet International' website[13] there are Engaged Buddhism resources that include: consumerism, environmental issues, gender, peacemaking and non-violence. However, although organizations such as the Buddhist Peace Fellowship are based in the USA, it is not the case that Engaged Buddhism is only driven by Western Buddhists. Within all Buddhist countries there are groups and organizations that consciously consider themselves 'Engaged Buddhists', but there are also instances of Buddhist social activism, social service provision or humanitarian assistance that exist without explicitly locating themselves as 'engaged'. Well-known examples of this include: Tzu Chi (a Taiwanese organization; see Huang and Weller, 1998); Sarvodaya (a Sri Lankan organization; see Macy 1985; Bond, 2004); 'development monks' in Thailand (see Darlington, 1997, 2000a, 2000b); Sulak Sivaraksa (Thai Buddhist social activist and scholar; Sivaraksa, 1999, 2002, 2005); the Santi Asoke Buddhist Movement, Thailand (Essen, 2005); International Network of Engaged Buddhists (with its headquarters in Bangkok); Maha Ghosananda (Cambodian monk; Ghosananda, 1992); Soka Gakkai (Japanese organization; see Stone, 2003); Dr Ambedkar (India; Ambedkar [1957] 1984); and the Dalai Lama (Tibet; Dalai Lama, 1999).

It is, however, also important to consider how 'ordinary' Buddhists would also respond to development concerns and issues. This is also relevant since most Buddhists are not explicitly involved in movements for social change yet do hold beliefs and participate in practices that have an impact upon social change and development. In the following sections, we will relate this discussion to concerns about 'Buddhism and ecology', 'Buddhist economics', 'Buddhism and gender' and 'Buddhism and peace-building'. While this discussion will aim to look at these issues without filtering them through the lens of Engaged Buddhism, this can be quite difficult to do since much explicit thinking about development concerns within Buddhism has been shaped by the thinking of so-called Engaged Buddhists.

BUDDHISM AND ECOLOGY

Discussions about Buddhism and the environment are typically found within Engaged Buddhist literature. The literature stresses the positive ways in which Buddhist thought and practice can influence care for the natural world and has a normative agenda in calling for a greater recognition of this potential within environmental initiatives across the globe. This is to be distinguished from another, smaller, genre of literature that would be concerned to look at the ways in which Buddhist thought and practice influences people's relationship to the natural world. This influence may not always be positive, in terms of how it translates into 'environmentally friendly' behaviour (Harris, 1991).

The website of the Forum on Religion and Ecology at Yale has a useful bibliography on Buddhism and ecology.[14] Rather than review this literature, our aim here is to map out some of the key themes arising within a Buddhist approach to the environment; to deal briefly with some critiques; and to give some details of environmental organizations working within a Buddhist framework.

In his overview of Buddhism and ecology, Swearer (1998) points to several features of the tradition that are conducive to ecological thought. For instance, he draws attention to the importance of compassion in the tradition and argues that 'out of a concern for the total living environment, Buddhist environmentalists extend loving-kindness and compassion beyond people and animals to include plants and the earth itself'. Moreover, the teaching of *kamma* and rebirth applies to all sentient beings and, at times, also to plants and trees (ibid.).

Critiques of this ecological interpretation of Buddhism point out that the tradition can also be seen to go against ecological thinking. For instance, central to Buddhist soteriology (theory of salvation) is the idea that the material world is a source of suffering and attachment that makes it difficult to realize the impermanence of notions of individual selfhood (Harris, 1991). This, it is argued, would hardly seem to support an attitude conducive to environmental conservation. Moreover, the idea of 'no self' (*anatta/anatman*) or emptiness (*sunyata*) may be incompatible with ecological awareness (a criticism Swearer highlights), since it would seem to 'undermine human autonomy and the distinction between self and other, essential aspects for an other-regarding ethic' (Swearer, 1998). However, this reading of the doctrine of *anatta* is arguably problematic, since such an understanding of the lack of distinction between self and other would also seem to mean it would be impossible for a person to operate at all on a day-to-day level. This is surely not how we should understand the teaching of *anatta*, since it would seem to render it useless. Instead, Buddhism makes a distinction between two levels of truth: conventional (*sammuti sacca*) and ultimate (*paramatta sacca*). Teachings about *anatta* are taught as *paramatta sacca* whereas environmentalism is taught in the sphere of *sammuti sacca*. On the conventional level we do, of course, consider ourselves to be discrete selves; however, the purpose of Buddhist practice is that at the ultimate level this distinction is invalid.

Yet, it cannot be assumed that Buddhism is inherently environmentalist, since Buddhist environmentalism is a modern phenomenon and, as such, is the product of a particular interpretation of the tradition. However, there are very many environmentalist organizations across the globe that quite successfully draw upon Buddhist teachings as the foundation for their ecological thought and action (see the example of the 'development monks' in Thailand, below). For instance, the website of the Forum on Religion and Ecology at Yale has a list of 'engaged projects' within the Buddhist tradition[15] and UK-based Alliance of Religions and Conservation is working with a number of Buddhist organizations across the globe.[16]

Development Monks in Thailand

The work of Parnwell focuses upon a case study from Northeast Thailand of the role played by a local abbot and 'development monk', Than Phra Khruu Supajarawat, in promoting sustainable development based on Buddhist principles and involving a local 'faith community'. Since the early 1980s, Than Phra Khruu has mobilized his local community to reverse ecological destruction through the resuscitation of traditional healing and herbal medicines, reforestation, soil rehabilitation and the development of organic rice farming. These efforts have gone hand in hand with community-centred initiatives such as the construction of a community rice mill, the introduction of a community currency system and the operation of community markets. Some of these activities have also involved national NGOs who have been attracted to the area by a practical example of the grassroots and community culture-focused forms of development that they philosophically follow (Parnwell, 2005a, 2005b, 2006):

> Drawing on Buddhist principles and practices, ecology monks have adapted traditional rituals and ceremonies to draw attention to environmental problems, raise awareness about the value of nature, and inspire people to take part in conservation efforts. Ceremonies such as tree ordination rituals (*buat ton mai*), in which trees are blessed and wrapped in saffron robes to signify their sacred status, are part of a larger effort to foster a conservation ethic rooted in Buddhist principles and bolstered by Buddhist practices.[17]

The idea, as Parnwell implies, is that by appealing to Buddhist 'principles' through respected religious practitioners such as monks, development concerns garner increased support from the (Buddhist) populace (Parnwell, 2005a; see also Ekachai, 1994; Darlington, 1997, 2000a, 2000b; Udomittipong, 2000).

BUDDHIST ECONOMICS

The term 'Buddhist economics' first appeared in an essay by E.F. Schumacher, published in *Asia: A Handbook* (Wint, 1966), published in 1969 in *Manas Journal* and later collected with other essays in Schumacher's famous volume *Small is Beautiful: Economics as if People Mattered* (1973). He begins the essay with the observation that: 'Right Livelihood' is one of the requirements of the Buddha's Noble Eightfold Path. It is clear, therefore, that there must be such a thing as Buddhist economics' (Schumacher, 1969, p. 1). Whereas the modern economist, he argues, sees human labour as 'an item of cost, to be reduced to a minimum if it can not be eliminated altogether, say, by automation' (ibid.), the Buddhist takes a different view: 'to give man [sic] a chance to utilise and develop his faculties; to enable him to overcome his ego-centredness by joining with other people in a common task; and to bring forth the goods and services needed for a becoming existence' (ibid., p. 2).

One arguably problematic conclusion that Schumacher draws is that a Buddhist economics is 'needs based', rather than maximizing production or employment, and therefore he concludes that 'women, on the whole, do not need an "outside" job, and the large-scale employment of women in offices or factories would be considered a sign of serious economic failure' (ibid.). Their role instead is to care for children in the home. The 'economic failure' he alludes to consists of an economic system that puts profit and consumption above individual need and Buddhist practice. Thus, if we rewrite this from a more enlightened perspective that does not employ a biological essentialism about women's natural roles as mothers and carers, the more important point to be made about Buddhism is that it would support an economic system based upon 'the Middle Way between materialist heedlessness and traditionalist immobility, in short, . . . "Right Livelihood"' (ibid., p. 6).

Schumacher also draws attention to 'production from local resources' (ibid., p. 3), 'simplicity and non-violence' (ibid.) and the sustainable use of natural resources as fundamental to a Buddhist economics. While he is suggesting that the basis for such an economic system exists conceptually within Buddhist contexts, his vision does seem romantic and nostalgic. How would such a system fit within a broader global economic framework not based upon Buddhist principles? How could the will to implement and sustain such a system be generated in poor Buddhist contexts where people are already bound up in capitalistic economics and where their route out of poverty seems to be contingent upon greater incorporation into the capitalist system?

In order to begin to address these questions it would be necessary to find examples of Buddhist economics in practice, or at least to look at the writings of Buddhists about economics and development that are grounded in grassroots experience. Pryor, in two articles (1990, 1991), looks at the attitudes towards economics in Buddhist texts. In his first paper ('A Buddhist economic system – in principle') he concedes that his 'discussion of ideas in the formal Buddhist canonical sources does not tell us anything very specific about how Buddhism is actually practiced today' (1990, p. 340). His second paper ('A Buddhist economic system – in practice'), despite its title, continues with this emphasis. While it is important to understand what 'tradition' tells us about a Buddhist view(s) of economics, this traditional view has been formulated within particular socio-economic-cultural contexts, and it is also important to investigate the articulation of traditional Buddhist ideas within the contemporary era (Dehejia and Dehejia, 1993; Payutto, 1994). However, we will begin with a brief discussion of Pryor's articles and will then move on to look at work by Zadek (1993) that attempts to locate such interpretations of the Buddhist texts within a modern context, with particular reference to the Savodaya Shramadana Movement in Sri Lanka. We will finish by discussing an article by David Loy on the topic of Buddhism and poverty (1999).

Pryor begins his discussion with the observation that 'the notion of Buddhist economics may seem a contradiction in terms' (1990, p. 339).[18] For instance, 'its doctrines of nibbana (nirvana) appears to both deny the importance of economic activity and to encourage withdrawal from the world' (ibid.). However, contemporary Buddhist scholars (in both Asia and the West), he notes, are increasingly interested in examining the links between the tradition and economic systems. Pryor focuses upon the '" . . . worldly actions" of the laity' (ibid., p. 343), since the monastic community does not engage in economic activity. While:

> property per se for the layman [sic] is not despised . . . First, the owner of such wealth should not be unduly attached to it, nor must he [sic] accumulate it by immoral means. To cultivate this non-attachment, a person must be generous and give large parts of it away, specially to the monks. (Ibid., pp. 344–5)

In his second article, Pryor is interested to understand how the economic principles expounded in the Pali Canon (the Theravada Buddhist set of texts), influenced actual economic behaviour. He begins by pointing out that Theravada Buddhism does not have a system of giving to the poor since it was primarily the monks who were the recipients of donations. He does suggest, however, that it is not indifferent to the poor, since the moral virtues of compassion and generosity are regarded as one way of increasing merit. Moreover, the revered Buddhist kings were known for the financial aid that they gave to the poor and donations to the monastic orders did then place the monks in a position of being able to provide refuge to the destitute or helping the poor. Thus, 'although there is little discussion of distributive justice, redistribution of income, either through the public, private, or monastery sectors, is certainly regarded in a favorable light' (Pryor, 1991, p. 1).

Zadek (1993) writes that his work takes 'the debate beyond his [Pryor's] focus upon the canonical texts and into the heartland of Buddhism, into "practice" itself' (p. 433). He discusses the Sarvodaya Shramadana Movement in Sri Lanka as a 'community organization working to improve the situation of people in rural areas throughout Sri Lanka'

(p. 436). He continues, 'important here is that the philosophy and imagery through which Sarvodaya's aims and approach are articulated are drawn from a combination of Gandhian and Buddhist principles' (ibid.; Ariyaratne, 1978–91; Macy, 1985; Batchelor and Brown, 1992). While the extent of the successes of Sarvodaya has been a subject of considerable debate Zadek suggests that his paper does 'illustrate the types of actions and forms of organization that might arise from people rooted in Buddhist perspectives, and the kind of tensions that can built up around such approaches' (1993, p. 437).

Sarvodaya Shramadana Movement

Founded by A.T. Ariyaratne, in 1958, the Sarvodaya Shramadana Movement is an organization based upon Buddhist and Gandhian principles that provides development projects for Sri Lankan villages (Ariyaratne, 1978–91, 1979, 1980a, 1980b, 1982, 1988a, 1988b, 1990, 1996; Ariyaratne and Macy, 1992; Zadek and Szabo, 1993). It is the largest indigenous organization working in reconstruction following the 2004 tsunami. As Zadek tells us:

> The critical feature of Sarvodaya's method is embodied in its approach to village-level consultation and mobilization. Sarvodaya has evolved a process of decision-making at village level which would in secular 'development vocabulary' be called participative decision-making (Chambers, 1992; Max-Neef, 1991). This includes, for example, meetings of the entire village in family gatherings, and the formation of groups within the village (women, youth, elders, etc), who are then encouraged to articulate their own needs and the path by which those needs might be achieved (usually with some technical, organizational or material help from Sarvodaya). (1993, p. 436)

While the movement considers itself to be founded upon Buddhist principles, its website stresses that it 'actively engages people of all religions and ethnic backgrounds'.[19] Its strategic development plan is divided into three interlocking dimensions: 'consciousness goal'; 'economics goal'; and 'power goal'.[20] The 'consciousness goal' involves the 'transformation of human consciousness through spiritual, moral and cultural awakening, and deepening societal commitment to non-violence'. The 'economics goal' involves 'transformation of the society through the creation of a full engagement economic system that creates sustainable village economies which meet the 10 basic needs of all Sri Lankans through social, economic and technological empowerment'. And the 'power goal' involves the 'transformation of the political system to establish community self governance (*gram swaraj*), participatory democracy and good governance through political and legal empowerment'.[21]

Buddhism, Poverty, Debt and Borrowing

Loy, in his article 'Buddhism and poverty' (1999) is interested in modern application of traditional Buddhist thinking about economics to an understanding of poverty (see also Loy [n.d.]; Sizemore and Swearer, 1990). He provides a critique of the neoliberal economic approach of the contemporary development project and argues that Buddhist teachings can provide both alternative models of development that do not have as many negative consequences as the neoliberal model, and resources to deal with those negative consequences. He suggests that 'development projects that aim to end poverty by "developing" a society into an economy focused on consumption are grasping the snake by the wrong end' (Loy, 1999, p. 4) since the:

> [s]ingle-minded pursuit of material wealth will not make human beings happy or even rich. A world in which envy (issa) and miserliness (macchariya) predominate cannot be considered one in which poverty has been eliminated. This follows from the second noble truth of the Buddha: the cause of dukkha is tanha 'craving'. When human beings gain an intense acquisitive drive for some object, that object becomes a cause of suffering. (Ibid.)

Being in a situation of poverty also 'leads to borrowing and increasing debts and thus ever-increasing suffering' (ibid., p. 1). However, this is not just a consequence of being 'poor' but also because humans tend to be attached to material goods and sensory pleasure. So the eradication of poverty is not just a matter of more provision of material wealth but should go hand in hand with a process of transformation within the individual where he or she realizes that material wealth (beyond the satisfaction of basic needs) is a cause of attachment and suffering. Moreover, in one text from the Pali Canon, the *Anguttara Nikaya*, Loy tells us that 'the Buddha speaks of the four kinds of happiness (sukha) attained by householders: possessing enough material resources, enjoying those resources, sharing them with relations and friends, and not being in debt' (ibid., p. 4). As Sizemore and Swearer write: 'to be non-attached is to possess and use material things but not to be possessed or used by them' (1990, p. 2).

However, the Buddha did not consider that avoiding personal debt and poverty was the responsibility of the householder alone (i.e., poverty is not just a consequence of greed for material possessions that leads to borrowing, debt and poverty). Instead, rulers must do their best to prevent poverty amongst their people. The consequences of avoiding this duty are outlined in the following quotation:

> Thus from not giving of property to the needy, poverty became rife, from the growth of poverty, the taking of what was not given increased, from the increase of theft, the use of weapons increased, from the increased use of weapons, the taking of life increased – and from the taking of life, people's lifespan decreased, their beauty decreased. (*Digha Nikaya*, III. 68, cited in Harvey, 2000, p. 197)

Our final sections consider the relationship between Buddhism and gender, and Buddhism and peace-building, two key development issues.

BUDDHISM AND GENDER

While the central teachings of Buddhism can be considered as gender neutral (since they concern the ways in which the individual – regardless of sex – may overcome *dukkha* [suffering]) the actual practice of the tradition has not been gender equal. In many instances, women have been denied equal ordination rights with men, and pervasive across Buddhist traditions is the idea that women are a lesser rebirth than men. The Buddhist texts tell us that the Buddha established a male religious order (*bhikkhu sangha*) as well as a female religious order (*bhikkhuni sangha*), yet this tradition has only survived continuously in Mahayana Buddhist countries, having died out within Theravada and Tibetan Buddhism by the eleventh century. The Buddha apparently had to be asked three times before he reluctantly agreed to allow women to enter the *sangha* and the first woman to be ordained was his step-mother Mahapajapati. The extent to which his reluctance to ordain women indicates a genuine concern that they are not capable of leading a renunciate life, has been debated (Owen, 1998). It can be suggested, on the one hand, that he was not free from social conditioning about women's capabilities (Gross, 2001, p. 7), or, on the other hand, that his reluctance was based upon doubts that women ordinands would be accepted by the broader society. Whereas today it is believed that women can only be fully ordained in the presence of both male and female ordinands (the dual ordination), Mahapajapati was ordained by the Buddha through receiving the eight *garudhammas*, or eight 'special rules', which fully ordained nuns are expected to keep to this day. However, many are critical that these place restrictions on *bhikkhunis* and support the lower status of women, since even the most novice monk is deemed more senior than the most senior female monastic, who must bow in his presence (Tsomo, 1999). Owen suggests that the giving of the *garudhammas* were a reflection of the Buddha's initial reluctance to allow women to be ordained since he did not believe they were capable of joining the *sangha* (1998, pp. 20–26) and others have argued that they were later additions to the tradition and do not reflect the Buddha's intentions (Kabilsingh, 1991, pp. 29–30; Kusuma, 1999, p. 20; Tsomo, 1999, p. 27).

The marginalization of women within the Buddhist tradition, particularly within Theravada and Tibetan Buddhism where women have not been able to fully ordain as *bhikkhunis*, has led some to make links between the gender hierarchies in Buddhism and wider socio-cultural discrimination against women (for example, see Peach, 2000 and Tomalin, 2006). One way of strengthening women's position within the tradition as well as within society, it is argued, is to allow women the same ordination rights as men. Even in contexts where women are allowed full ordination rights they still often suffer discrimination both within Buddhism and society. Thus, some women within these contexts are also campaigning for improved conditions and a transformation in gender-oppressive ideologies supported by Buddhism that have an impact upon social attitudes towards women. Nonetheless, with women in positions of leadership in Buddhism they are more likely to be able to challenge negative stereotypes held about women as well as to provide positive role models. For instance, the *bhikkhuni* ordination has been recently revived in Sri Lanka and there is a movement in Thailand to do the same there (but it faces fierce opposition). A strong theme within this movement is the argument that gender hierarchies within Thai Buddhism have a broader cultural impact upon social attitudes that disempower women. As van Esterik writes, Buddhism is a 'key component of Thai identity' providing 'a way of viewing the world, a sense of reality, moral standards, and a shared language and metaphors for analyzing their existing life situation' (2000, pp. 65–6; Peach, 2005, p. 124). Buddhism reinforces the understanding that women are a lower rebirth than men because of *kamma* acquired in previous lives (Owen, 1998) and 'women are socialised to be relational, socially embedded and family oriented rather than independent, autonomous, self-determining individuals' (Peach, 2005, p. 124). This intrinsic inferiority of women is reinforced within the structure of everyday public Buddhist practice and custom:

> Men perform all the public roles of Buddhism, ordained as monks or as lay officiants, leading the chanting, conducting rituals, and participating as members of the *wat* (temple) committee.

> In addition, the organization of space in the meeting hall clearly denotes the differential status distinctions between monks and lay persons, elders and younger people, and women and men. Monks sit upon a raised platform, denoting higher status. Elderly men sit closest to the monks, followed by younger men. Women sit around the perimeter. The elderly men make merit by placing food in the monks' bowls first, followed by the younger men. Not until the youngest boy has made his offering will the most elderly woman lead the other women to make their offerings. (Klunklin and Greenwood, 2005, p. 48)

Many advocates of the *bhikkhuni* ordination consider that there is a very direct relationship between the low status of women in Thai Buddhism and the inferior status of women in Thai society, which places them at risk of abuses such as domestic violence and sex trafficking, as well an increased vulnerability to HIV/AIDS. There is a body of literature that examines the relationship between Thai Buddhism and women's oppression in Thailand, particularly with respect to the issues of sex trafficking and HIV (Thitsa, 1980; Peach, 2000, 2005; Klunklin and Greenwood, 2005). For instance, as the activist and writer Khuankaew suggests:

> One of the core causes of violence against women has not yet been touched upon – the beliefs, attitudes, traditions, and values that come out of a patriarchal society influenced by Buddhism itself . . . in the discussions at the local, national and international meetings of women organizations the root causes of prostitution have always been poverty, western models of development and modernization . . . Hardly mentioned as a cause of prostitution is the lack of leadership roles for women in Buddhism. (Khuankaew, 2002, p. 16)

In Thailand the only formal religious option available to women is life as a white robed *mae chi*. The *mae chi* institution is not mentioned in the Buddhist texts, in fact its exact origins are unclear (Lindberg-Falk, 2000, p. 45), and many are critical that it is a poor substitute for the *bhikkhuni* ideal. The living conditions of a *mae chi* are often inadequate, they have little opportunity for study of the *dhamma* (Buddhist teachings) and the majority live in temples, where they cook and clean for the monks (Muecke, 2004).[22] As Puntarigvivat argues 'the replacement of mae chi by a bhikkhuni institution would greatly raise women's status at the core of Thai culture and would begin to address many of women's problems in Thailand – including poverty, child abuse and prostitution' (2001, p. 225).

The reasons that girls and women enter prostitution in Thailand are complex, and researchers are likely to point to the lack of educational and economic opportunities for poor females, as well as the demands of a profitable sex-tourism industry. However, the tendency of Buddhist teachings not to view sex work as immoral or degrading, removes much of the stigma associated with similar work in many other cultures (Peach, 2005, p. 125). In Thai culture, prostitutes are not viewed with universal negativity and in the Buddhist texts we find stories about prostitutes, often as friends of the Buddha. Moreover, as Peach tells us, one popular attitude towards prostitution in Thailand is that is enables women to earn money that they can give as donations to monks. This provides them with an opportunity to earn merit in order to improve their *kamma* for a better rebirth in the next life (i.e., as a man), implying that women are considered to be less important than men (ibid., p. 125). Thus, 'traditional Thai Buddhist culture functions to legitimate the trafficking industry, and thereby deny the human rights of women involved in sexual slavery' (Kabilsingh, 1991, p. 67; Muecke, 1992; Satha-Anand, 1999; Peach, 2000, p. 65; Puntarigvivat, 2001, p. 227).

Some women within Tibetan Buddhism are also campaigning for full ordination rights as an important means of transforming the status and opportunities for other categories of nuns (e.g., *mae chis*) as well as lay women. There is an interesting transnational aspect to these campaigns. For instance, the women involved in the *bhikkhuni* movement in Thailand are linked to broader networks of Buddhist women in both Thailand and abroad (Tomalin, 2009). On an international level, the Thai and Tibetan *bhikkhuni* movements reflect a broader campaign to secure equal ordination rights and status for women across Buddhist traditions. For instance, in July 2007 in Hamburg 'The First International Congress on Buddhist Women's Role in the Sangha: Bhikshuni Vinaya and Ordination Lineages' was held; since 2002 there has been an annual award ceremony for 'Outstanding Women in Buddhism' on International Women's Day in Bangkok; and there is an international Buddhist women's organization called Sakhyadhita that holds a conference every other year. In contexts where religious beliefs, discourses and practices continue to have a strong public appeal, strategies to empower women within these traditions have relevance for development.

Moreover, in Buddhist contexts, nuns (both fully ordained and other types) are involved in important forms of welfare and service delivery. In Cambodia, for instance, a country ravaged by war and political violence, a category of female monastic (*donchee*), akin to the Thai *mae chi*, is playing a role in education linked to social development. Cambodian women are under-represented in the public sphere, face high rates of maternal mortality and HIV infection, and experience high levels of domestic violence (Surtees, 2003, p. 30; United Nations, 2006, p. 8). However, Khemacaro (1998) argues that 'Buddhism is the sole institution which cuts across the deep political divisions separating Cambodians today' (see also Suksamran, 1993) and it is increasingly recognized that there is a social and educational role for religious practitioners, particularly with and for women (Loschmann, 2000, p. 93). In recognition of this, a collaboration between international NGOs and Buddhist practitioners has been fostered in Cambodia, through the 'Nuns and Wat Grannies' Breast Feeding programme. In this development project, which was internationally funded by RACHA (The Reproductive and Child Health Alliance) and supported by the Heinrich Boll Foundation, Buddhist nuns (*donchee*) were trained to publically disseminate information to women on healthy breast-feeding practices. According to RACHA, the benefit of working with Buddhist nuns is that the information they provide is more likely to be trusted and followed by other Buddhist women as a result of their status as religious practitioners, and the programme increased the number of women likely to take up early breast-feeding practices (Suksamran, 1993, p. 102; Kong et al., 2002; Crookston et al., 2007).

BUDDHISM AND PEACE-BUILDING

Although Buddhism is typically associated with peace and non-violence (Edwards, 1998), Buddhist countries have not been immune to outbreaks of war. Nevertheless, support for violence is difficult to find within the Buddhist texts and the tradition holds many resources that can support peace-building endeavours (Hanh, 2005; Chodron and Boucher, 2006; Sachs, 2006; Topmiller, 2006; Khong, 2007).[23] However, as Harvey writes:

> These resources and ideals must sometimes be better known and applied more fully . . . The post-colonial period has left a legacy of instability and social readjustment in several Buddhist lands, and it is clear that, in certain quarters, there has been a danger of religious revival degenerating into exclusion of non-Buddhist ethnic groups (Sri Lanka), egalitarianism degenerating into hatred (Cambodia), and anti-colonial nationalism degenerating into zenophobia (Burma). (Harvey, 2000, p. 283)

Puri's (2006) book about Engaged Buddhism and the Dalai Lama, discusses the latter's thought on issues such as non-violence, human rights and the political autonomy of Tibet. The Dalai Lama is a particularly good example of a Buddhist figure combining attention to the pressing socio-political issues of the current era with traditional Buddhist teachings. However, other figures such as A.T. Ariyaratne (Sri Lanka), Aung San Suu Kyi (Burma), Sulak Sivaraksa (Thailand), Dr Ambedkar (India), Thich Nhat Hanh (Vietnam), Maha-Ghosananda (Cambodia), Nichidatsu Fujji, Daisaku Ikeda and Nikkyo Niwano (Japan) have also sought to transform situations of violence into peace through employing Buddhist principles.

CONCLUSION

In this chapter, our aim has been to provide an introduction to key Buddhist teachings, beliefs, practices and values and to relate these to issues that are relevant to development. It is not a comprehensive study, and as such does not take adequate account of the diversity that exists both between and within different Buddhist cultures, or of the gulf that exists between textual and lived religion. However, it presents an overview that individual researchers can use as a starting point for more focused research in this area.

NOTES

* This chapter was initially published in an extended form as Tomalin, E. (2007) 'Buddhism and development: a background paper', Religions and Development Working Paper No. 18, Religions and Development Project, International Development Department, University of Birmingham.

1. Within Mahayana and Vajrayana (Tibetan) Buddhism we find figures called *bodhisattvas*. *Bodhisattva* means 'being-for-enlightenment'. These are individuals who take vows (the '*bodhisattva* vows'), including to work towards the enlightenment of all beings while at the same time progressing their own development towards full Buddhahood (the '*bodhisattva* path'). This contrasts with the aim within the earlier tradition of Theravada Buddhism, where the emphasis is upon one's own enlightenment without the compassionate focus upon helping others also to become enlightened. Popular *bodhisattvas* include Maitreya and Guanyin/Avalokitesvara.
2. Pāli is the original language of Indian Theravada Buddhism and Sanskrit of Indian Mahayana Buddhism. The early texts have also been translated into other languages.
3. *Samyutta Nikaya*: LVI, 11, available at: www.buddhanet.net/4noble.htm; accessed 25 October 2011.
4. In Sanskrit, for example, *karma* is a noun derived from the verbal root 'kr', which means 'to do', 'to make'. However, in addition to meaning action or work, it also refers to the results or 'fruits' of one's actions. In Indic religions it is *karma* that keeps the individual bound to future rebirths and that influences the nature of the particular rebirth.
5. For lay Buddhists this is a positive source of merit – *punna/punya* – which can improve their chances of a better rebirth in the future.
6. See Skilton (1994) for an historical account of spread and emergence of different schools. These schools also spread to the West, beginning in the eighteenth century (see Baumann, 1995).
7. The additional three precepts are: not eating after midday; not engaging in entertainment; and abstaining from high or large beds.

8. Thus *dana* also has a gendered dimension since, in practice, it is believed that more merit can be generated through giving to male mendicants rather than female. In Thailand, for instance, the white-robed nuns (*mae chis*) typically receive less alms than the orange-robed male monks (*bhikkhus*), thereby adding to the precariousness of their existence. The implications for gender and development will be discussed later in this chapter.
9. Examples include the following: 'Buddhist monks provide HIV/AIDS care', http://cambodia.usaid.gov/node/321; 'Buddhist monks raise AIDS awareness in Laos', http://www.unaids.org/en/resources/presscentre/featurestories/2006/november/20061114undplaoen/; and 'the Sangha-metta project', http://www.buddhanet.net/sangha-metta/project.html; all accessed 25 October 2011. See also Bechtel and Apakupakul (1999); Kubotani and Engstrom (2005). The annual conference of the International AIDS Society typically has presentations on this topic (see http://www.iasociety.org/Default.aspx?pageId=7 to search past conference abstracts).
10. Mahatma Gandhi gave the name *harijan* ('born of god') to those who stood outside the caste system and were otherwise known as 'outcastes' or 'untouchables'. Today the term Dalit is used and preferred in self-designation, variously translated as 'crushed', 'stepped on' or 'oppressed'.
11. A political party in India, representing Dalits.
12. As a direct response to Ambedkar's call for a '*dhamma* revolution' – in which the Buddha-*dhamma* is (quite untraditionally) used as a basis for social projects to uplift the Dalits – different organizations have emerged with this as their goal. One such organization in Maharashtra, Bahujan Hitay, works closely with the Karuna Trust, a UK-based NGO, linked to Triratna (formerly the Friends of the Western Buddhist Order).
13. http://www.dharmanet.org/lcengaged.htm; see also 'Resources for socially engaged Buddhists', Buddhist Peace Fellowship – http://www.bpf.org/what-buddhists-are-saying/resources-for-socially-engaged-buddhists; accessed 25 October 2011.
14. http://fore.research.yale.edu/religion/buddhism/bibliography.html; accessed 6 July 2012.
15. http://fore.research.yale.edu/religion/buddhism/projects/index.html; accessed 25 October 2011.
16. http://www.arcworld.org/; accessed 6 July 2012.
17. 'Buddhist engaged projects: Thai ecology monks', available at: http://fore.research.yale.edu/religion/buddhism/projects/thai_ecology.html; accessed 25 October 2011.
18. The focus of his discussion is upon Theravada Buddhism, practiced in Burma, Cambodia, Laos, Sri Lanka and Thailand.
19. http://www.sarvodaya.org/about/faq; accessed 25 October 2011.
20. http://www.sarvodaya.org/about/strategic-goals/; accessed 25 October 2011.
21. Ibid. See also Hewage (1973); Kantowsky (1980); Goulet (1981); Moore (1981); Wismeijer (2000); Colletta (1982); Dasgupta (1982); Arrindell (1983); Williams (1984); Bobilin (1988); Dissanayake (1991); Perera et al. (1992); Perera (1995); Bond (1996).
22. Whilst there are high profile *mae chi* (and lay Buddhist women) in Thailand (see Seeger, 2009), they are still numerically less significant than male monastics and their opportunities for spiritual development are hampered by their lack of educational, financial and legal structures of support.
23. See bibliography on 'war, violence, conflict, non-violence' on the Buddhist Peace Fellowship website: http://www.bpf.org.

REFERENCES

Ambedkar, B.R. [1957] (1984), *The Buddha and His Dhamma*, Bombay: Siddharth Publications.

Ariyaratne, A.T. (1978–91), *Collected Works, Volumes 1–5*, Moratuwa, Sri Lanka: Sarvodaya Press.

Ariyaratne, A.T. (1979), *Intellectual and Cultural Environment of Child in the Family*, Moratuwa, Sri Lanka: Sarvodaya Press.

Ariyaratne, A.T. (1980a), *Sarvodaya and Development*, Moratuwa, Sri Lanka: Sarvodaya Press.

Ariyaratne, A.T. (1980b), 'The role of Buddhist monks in development', *World Development*, **8**(7–8), 587–9.

Ariyaratne, A.T. (1982), *In Search of Development: The Sarvodaya Shramadana Movement's Effort to Harmonize Tradition with Change*, Moratuwa, Sri Lanka: Sarvodaya Press.

Ariyaratne, A.T. (1988a), 'The desired Sarvodaya socio-economic order', in R. Bobilin (ed.), *Revolution from Below: Buddhist and Christian Movements for Justice in Asia: Four Case Studies from Thailand and Sri Lanka*, Lanham, MD: University Press of America, pp. 38–42.

Ariyaratne, A.T. (1988b), 'The social philosophy of the [Sarvodaya Shramadana] Movement and tradition', in R. Bobilin (ed.), *Revolution from Below: Buddhist and Christian Movements for Justice in Asia: Four Case Studies from Thailand and Sri Lanka*, Lanham, MD: University Press of America, pp. 43–8.

Ariyaratne, A.T. (1990), 'Does development education in the more developed world make a difference in the less developed world?' (A Third World Perspective), Calgary, Canada: International Centre, Division of International Development, University of Calgary.
Ariyaratne, A.T. (1996), 'Buddhism and Sarvodaya', Delhi: Indian Books Centre.
Ariyaratne, A.T. and J. Macy (1992), 'The island temple and tank: Sarvodaya: self-help in Sri Lanka', in M. Batchelor and K. Brown (eds), *Buddhism and Ecology*, London: Cassell, pp. 78–86.
Arrindell, N.J. (1983), 'A comparative analysis of two rural development programs: Sri Lanka's Sarvodaya Shramadana Movement and Thailand's Functional Literacy Program – a participant and expert profile', PhD thesis, University of Maryland.
Batchelor, M. and K. Brown (eds) (1992), *Buddhism and Ecology*, London: Cassell.
Baumann, M. (1995), 'Creating a European path to nirvana: historical and contemporary developments of Buddhism in Europe', *Journal of Contemporary Religion*, **1**(1), 55–70.
Bechtel, G.A. and N. Apakupakul (1999), 'AIDS in Southern Thailand: stories of *Krengjai* and social connections', *Journal of Advanced Nursing*, **29**(2), 471–5.
Bobilin, R. (1988), *Revolution from Below: Buddhist and Christian Movements for Justice in Asia: Four Case Studies from Thailand and Sri Lanka*, Lanham, MD: University Press of America.
Bond, G.D. (1996), 'A.T. Ariyaratne and the Sarvodaya Shramadana Movement Sri Lanka', in C.S. Queen and S.B. King (eds), *Engaged Buddhism: Buddhist Liberation Movements in Asia*, Albany, NY: State University of New York Press, pp. 121–46.
Bond, G.D. (2004), *Buddhism at Work: Community Development, Social Empowerment, and the Sarvodaya Movement*, Bloomfield, CT: Kumara Press.
Chambers, R. (1992), 'Rural appraisal: rapid, relaxed and participatory', Institute of Development Studies Working Paper No. 311, Brighton: IDS.
Chodron, P. and S. Boucher (eds) (2006), *Practicing Peace in Times of War: A Buddhist Perspective*, Boston, MA: Shambhala Publications.
Colletta, N.J. et al. (1982), 'Cultural revitalization, participatory nonformal education, and village development in Sri Lanka: the Sarvodaya Shramadana Movement', *Comparative Education Review*, **26**(2), 271–86.
Crookston, B.T., K.A. Dearden, K. Chan, T. Chan and D.D. Stoker (2007), 'Buddhist nuns on the move: an innovative approach to improving breastfeeding practices in Cambodia', *Maternal and Child Nutrition*, **3**(1), 10–24.
Dalai Lama (1999), *Ethics for the New Millennium*, New York: Riverhead Books.
Darlington, S. (1997), 'Not only preaching – the work of the ecology monk Phrakhru Nantakhun of Thailand', *Forest, Trees and People Newsletter*, **34**, 17–20.
Darlington, S. (2000a), 'Rethinking Buddhism and development. The emergence of environmentalist monks in Thailand', *Journal of Buddhist Ethics*, **7**, 1–14.
Darlington, S. (2000b), Tree ordination in Thailand', in S. Kaza and K. Kraft (eds) *Dharma Rain: Sources of Buddhist Environmentalism*, Boston: Shambhala Publications, pp. 198–205.
Dasgupta, S. (1982), *Placing the Poor at the Centre of the Stage and the Gathering Storm: An Evaluation Study of the Sarvodaya Shramadana Movement of Sri Lanka*, Calcutta: Jayaprakash Institute of Social Change.
Dehejia, V.H. and R.H. Dehejia (1993), 'Religion and economic activity in India: an historical perspective', *American Journal of Economics and Sociology*, **52**(2), 145–53.
Dissanayake, W. (1991), 'Ethics, development, and communication: a Buddhist approach', in F. Casmir (ed.), *Communication in Development*, Norwood, NJ: Ablex, pp. 319–37.
Edwards, D. (1998), *The Compassionate Revolution: Radical Politics and Buddhism*, Totnes: Green Books.
Ekachai, S. (1994), 'People and forests', in S. Ekachai, *Seeds of Hope: Local Initiatives in Thailand*, Bangkok: Thai Development Support Committee, pp. 72–83.
Eppsteiner, F. (ed.) (1988), *The Path of Compassion: Writings on Socially Engaged Buddhism*, Berkeley: Parallax Press.
Essen, J. (2005), *Right Development: The Santi Asoke Buddhist Reform Movement of Thailand*, Lanham, MD: Lexington Books.
Findly, E.B. (2003), *Dana: Giving and Getting in Pali Buddhism*, Delhi: Motilal Banarsidass.
Ghosananda, M. (1992), *Step by Step: Meditation on Wisdom and Compassion*, Berkeley: Parallax Press.
Gombrich, R. (1992), 'Dating the historical Buddha: a red herring revealed', in H. Bechert (ed.), *The Dating of the Historical Buddha Part 2*, Göttingen: Vandenhoeck & Ruprecht, pp. 237–59.
Goulet, D. (1981), *Survival with Integrity: Sarvodaya at the Crossroads*, Colombo: Marga Institute.
Gross, R. (2001), *Buddhism After Patriarchy: A Feminist History, Analysis, and Reconstruction of Buddhism*, Albany: State University of New York Press.
Hanh, T.N. (2002), 'The fourteen precepts of engaged Buddhism', *Social Policy*, **33**(1), 39–40.
Hanh, T.N. (2005), *Peace Begins Here: Palestinians and Israelis Listening to Each Other*, Berkeley: Parallax Press.

Harris, I. (1991), 'How environmentalist is Buddhism?', *Religion*, **21**(2), 101–14.
Harvey, P. (1990), *An Introduction to Buddhism: Teachings, History and Practices*, Cambridge: Cambridge University Press.
Harvey, P. (2000), *An Introduction to Buddhist Ethics*, Cambridge: Cambridge University Press.
Hewage, L.G. (1973), 'The role of religious institutions in Asian development'(mainly based on the Sarvodaya experience in Sri Lanka), in *Religion and Development in Asian Societies: Papers Presented at the Seminar Organized by the Marga Institute, at the Fatima Retreat House, Lewella, Kandy, 9–16 December 1973*, Colombo, Sri Lanka: Marga Publications, pp. 35–63.
Huang, J.C. and R.P. Weller (1998), 'Merit and mothering: women and social welfare in Taiwanese Buddhism', *The Journal of Asian Studies*, **57**(2), 379–96.
Husted, W.R., D.V. Keown and C.S. Prebish (1998), *Buddhism and Human Rights*, London: Curzon Press.
Jaffrelot, C. (2005), *Dr. Ambedkar and Untouchability: Analyzing and Fighting Caste*, New Delhi: Permanent Black.
James, S.P. (2004), *Zen Buddhism and Environmental Ethics*, Aldershot: Ashgate.
Kabilsingh, C. (1991), *Thai Women in Buddhism*, Berkeley: Parallax Press.
Kalupahana, D.J. (1995), *Ethics in Early Buddhism*, Honolulu: University of Hawaii Press.
Kantowsky, D. (1980), *Sarvodaya: The Other Development*, New Delhi: Vikas.
Keown, D. (1992), 'Bibliography on Buddhism and human rights', *Journal of Buddhist Ethics*, **2**, available at: http://blogs.dickinson.edu/buddhistethics/files/2010/04/A-BIBLIOGRAPHY-ON-BUDDHISM-AND-HUMAN-RIGHTS.pdf; accessed 25 October 2011.
Khemacaro, Y.H. (1998), 'Steering the middle path: Buddhism, non-violence and political change in Cambodia', Conciliation Resources, available at: http://www.c-r.org/accord-article/steering-middle-path-buddhism-non-violence-and-political-change-cambodia; accessed 6 July 2012.
Khong, C. (2007), *Learning True Love: Practicing Buddhism in a Time of War*, Berkeley: Parallax Press.
Khuankaew, O. (2002), 'Buddhism and domestic violence', *The World Fellowship of Buddhists Review*, **34**(3–4), 22–6.
Klunklin, A. and J. Greenwood (2005) 'Buddhism, the status of women and the spread of HIV/AIDS in Thailand', *Health Care International for Women*, **26**(1), 46–61.
Kong, K., T. Savery and M. Stewart Titus (2002), 'Member voices: EngenderHealth makes creative strategies in low-resource settings', *HealthLink* No. 114.
Kubotani, T. and D. Engstrom (2005), 'The roles of Buddhist temples in the treatment of HIV/AIDS in Thailand', *Journal of Sociology and Social Welfare*, **32**(4), 5–21.
Kusuma, Bhikkhuni (2000), 'Inaccuracies in Buddhist women's history', in K.L. Tsomo (ed.), *Innovative Buddhist Women: Swimming against the Stream*, Richmond: RoutledgeCurzon, pp. 5–12.
Laliberte, A. (2004), *The Politics of Buddhist Organizations in Taiwan: 1989–2003: Safeguard the Faith, Build a Pure Land, Help the Poor*, London and New York: Routledge.
Lindberg-Falk, M. (2000), 'Women in between: becoming religious persons in Thailand', in E.B. Findly (ed.), *Women's Buddhism, Buddhism's Women*, Boston: Wisdom Publications.
Loschmann, H. (2000), 'The revival of the Don Chee Movement in Cambodia', in K.L. Tsomo (ed.), *Innovative Buddhist Women: Swimming Against the Stream*, London: Curzon Press, pp. 91–5.
Loy, D. (n.d.), 'Shall we pave the planet, or learn to wear shoes? A Buddhist perspective on greed and globalization', available at: http://www.inebnetwork.org/thinksangha/tsangha/loy-globo.html; accessed 25 October 2011.
Loy, D. (1999), 'Buddhism and poverty', available at: http://www.buddhachannel.tv/portail/spip.php?article3707; accessed 25 October 2011.
Macy, J. (1985), *Dharma and Development: Religion as Resource in the Sarvodaya Self-help Movement*, West Hartford, CT: Kumarian Press.
Macy, J. (1988), 'In Indra's net: Sarvodaya and our mutual efforts for peace', in F. Eppsteiner (ed.), *The Path of Compassion: Writings on Socially Engaged Buddhism*, Berkeley: Parallax Press, pp. 170–81.
Max-Neef, M. (1991), *Human Scale Development: Conception, Application and Further Reflections*, London: Apex Press.
Moore, C. (1981), *Para-Professionals in Village-level Development in Sri Lanka: The Sarvodaya Shramadana Movement*, Rural Development Committee, Center for International Studies, Cornell University.
Muecke, M.A. (1992), 'Mother sold food, daughter sells her body – the cultural continuity of prostitution', *Social Science and Medicine*, **35**(7), 891–901.
Muecke, M.A. (2004), 'Female sexuality in Thai discourses about Maechii (lay nuns)', *Culture Health and Sexuality*, **6**(3), 221–38.
Omvedt, G. (2004), *Ambedkar: Towards an Enlightened India*, New Delhi: Penguin Books India.
Owen, L.B. (1998), 'On gendered discourse and the maintenance of boundaries: a feminist analysis of the Bhikkhuni order in Indian Buddhism', *Asian Journal of Women's Studies*, **4**(3), 8–60.
Parnwell, M.J.G. (2005a), 'The power to change: rebuilding sustainable livelihoods in North-East Thailand',

The Journal of Transdisciplinary Environmental Studies (TES), **4**(2), available at: http://www.journal-tes.dk/vol_4_no_2/NO4_MI_l.PDF; accessed 25 October 2011.

Parnwell, M.J.G (2005b), 'Crowding out and clawing back: local institutions and sustainable livelihoods in North-East Thailand', *International Development Planning Review*, **27**(2), 143–68.

Parnwell, M.J.G (2006), 'Eco-localism and the shaping of sustainable social and natural environments', *Land Degradation & Development*, **17**(2), 183–95.

Payutto, Venerable P.A. (1994), *Buddhist Economics: A Middle Way For The Market Place*, available at: http://www.kusala.org/pdf/Buddhist_Economics.pdf; accessed 25 October 2011.

Peach, L.J. (2000), 'Human rights, religion and (sexual) slavery', *Annual of the Society of Christian Ethics*, **20**, 65–87.

Peach, L.J. (2005), '"Sex slaves" or "Sex workers"? Cross-cultural and comparative religious perspectives on sexuality, subjectivity, and moral identity in anti-sex trafficking discourse', *Culture and Religion*, **6**(1), 107–34.

Perera, J. (1995), 'In unequal dialogue with donors: the experience of the Sarvodaya Shramadana Movement', *Journal of International Development*, **7**(6), 869–78.

Perera, J. et al. (1992), *A People's Movement Under Siege*, Moratuwa, Sri Lanka: Sarvodaya Publishing Services.

Pongsapich, A. (1993), 'Defining the nonprofit sector: Thailand', Working Paper of the Johns Hopkins Comparative Nonprofit Sector Project.

Pryor, F.L. (1990), 'A Buddhist economic system – in principle: non-attachment to worldly things is dominant but the way of the law is held profitable', *American Journal of Economics and Sociology*, **59**(3), 339–49, available at: http://ccbs.ntu.edu.tw/FULLTEXT/JR-ADM/pryo.htm; accessed 25 October 2011.

Pryor, F.L. (1991), 'A Buddhist economic system – in practice', *American Journal of Economics and Sociology*, **50**(1), 17–33, available at: http://ccbs.ntu.edu.tw/FULLTEXT/JR-ADM/pryor.htm; accessed 25 October 2011.

Puntarigvivat, T. (2001), 'A Thai Buddhist perspective', in J.C. Raines and D.C. Maguire (eds), *What Men Owe to Women: Men's Voices from World Religions*, New York: State University of New York Press.

Puri, B. (2006), *Engaged Buddhism The Dalai Lama's Worldview*, New Delhi: Oxford University Press.

Queen, C.S. (ed.) (2000), *Engaged Buddhism in the West*, Boston: Wisdom Publications.

Queen, C.S. and S.B. King (eds) (1996), *Engaged Buddhism: Buddhist Liberation Movements in Asia*, New York: SUNY.

Robb, P. (1996), *Dalit Movements and the Meanings of Labour in India*, New Delhi: Oxford University Press.

Sachs, R. (2006), *The Buddha at War: Peaceful Heart, Courageous Action in Troubled Times*, London: Watkins Books.

Satha-Anand, S. (1999), 'Looking to Buddhism to turn back prostitution in Thailand', in J.R. Bauer and D.A. Bell (eds), *The East Asian Challenge for Human Rights*, Cambridge: Cambridge University Press.

Schumacher, E. (1969), 'Buddhist economics', *Manas Journal*, **22**(33), 1–5.

Schumacher, E. (1973), *Small Is Beautiful*, New York: HarperCollins.

Seeger, M. (2009), 'The changing roles of Thai Buddhist women: obscuring identities and increasing charisma', in *Religion Compass*, **3**(5), 806–22.

Sivaraksa, S. (1999), *Global Healing: Essays and Interviews on Structural Violence, Social Development and Spiritual Transformation*, Boston: Wisdom Books.

Sivaraksa, S. (2002), 'Engaged Buddhism: selections from the speeches and writings of Sulak Sivaraksa', *Social Policy*, **33**(1), 41–6.

Sivaraksa, S. (2005), *Conflict, Culture, Change: Engaged Buddhism in a Globalizing World*, Boston: Wisdom Books.

Sizemore, R.F. and D. Swearer (1990), *Ethics, Wealth, and Salvation: A Study in Buddhist Social Ethics*, Columbia, South Carolina: University of South Carolina.

Skilton, A. (1994), *A Concise History of Buddhism*, Birmingham: Windhorse Publications.

Stone, J.I. (2003), 'Nichiren's activist heirs: Soka Gakkai, Rissho Kosekai, Nipponzan Myohoji', in C.S. Queen, C. Prebish and D. Keown (eds), *Action Dharma: New Studies in Engaged Buddhism*, London and New York: RoutledgeCurzon, pp. 63–94.

Suksamran, S. (1993), 'Buddhism, political authority and legitimacy in Thailand and Cambodia', in T. Ling (1993) (ed.), *Buddhist Trends in Southeast Asia*, Singapore: Institute of Southeast Asian Studies.

Surtees, R. (2003), 'Negotiating violence and non-violence in Cambodian marriages', *Gender and Development*, **11**(2), 30–41.

Swearer, D. (1998), 'Buddhism and ecology: challenge and promise, available at: http://fore.research.yale.edu/religion/buddhism/;accessed 25 October 2011.

Thitsa, K. (1980), *Providence and Prostitution: Image and Reality for Women in Buddhist Thailand*, London: Change International Reports.

Tomalin, E. (2006), 'The Thai bhikkhuni movement and women's empowerment', *Gender and Development*, **14**(3), 385–97.
Tomalin, E. (2009), 'Buddhist feminist transnational networks, female ordination and women's empowerment', *Oxford Development Studies*, **37**(2), 81–100.
Topmiller, R.J. (2006), *Lotus Unleashed: The Buddhist Peace Movement in South Vietnam, 1964–1966*, Lexington: University Press of Kentucky.
Tsomo, K.L. (1999), 'Mahaprajapati's legacy: the Buddhism women's movement: an introduction', in K.L. Tsomo, *Buddhist Women Across Cultures: Realizations*, New Delhi: Sri Satguru Publications, pp. 1–44.
Udomittipong, P. (2000), 'Thailand's ecology monks', in S. Kaza and K. Kraft (eds), *Dharma Rain: Sources of Buddhist Environmentalism*, Boston: Shambhala Publications, pp. 191–7.
United Nations (2006), *United Nations Development Assistance Framework (Cambodia) 2006–2010*, available at: http://web.undp.org/execbrd/pdf/Cambodia%20UNDAF%202006-10%20%20final.pdf; accessed 7 August 2012.
Van Esterik, P. (2000), *Materializing Thailand*, Oxford: Berg Books.
Williams, J.R. (1984), 'Religion, ethics and development: an analysis of the Sarvodaya Shramadana Movement of Sri Lanka', *Canadian Journal of Development Studies*, **5**(1), 157–67.
Wint, G. (ed.) (1966), *Asia: A Handbook*, New York: Praeger.
Wismeijer, H. (2000), 'Diversity in harmony: a study of the leaders of the Sarvodaya Sharamadana Movement in Sri Lanka', PhD dissertation, Department of Cultural Anthropology, University of Utrecht, Netherlands.
Yarnall, T.F. (2000), 'Engaged Buddhism: new and improved!(?) made in the USA of Asian materials', *Journal of Buddhist Ethics*, **7**, available at: http://www.thezensite.com/ZenEssays/CriticalZen/Engaged_Buddhism.htm; accessed 25 October 2011.
Zadek, S. (1993), 'The practice of Buddhist economics?', *American Journal of Economics and Sociology*, **52**(4), 433–45.
Zadek, S. and S. Szabo (1993), 'Buddhist organisation: the case of the Sarvodaya Shramadana Movement', Value-based Human Organisation Working Paper Series No. 2, London: New Economics Foundation.

4 Christianity and international development

*Séverine Deneulin**

INTRODUCTION

'Before the white man came, we had the land and they had the Bible; now we have the Bible and they have the land'. So goes an African saying. Development studies has long been suspicious of religion, and rightly so. The evangelization of the Americas was mixed with the greedy motives of the Kingdoms of Spain and Portugal to plunder the continent of its resources. Bringing Christianity to Africa and the colonization of the continent were not very distinguishable enterprises. The evangelization of Africans and the expansion of the Empire went hand in hand. The technology and skills of the colonial powers made Christianity appealing and served to justify its superiority (Hastings, 1994).

On the other hand, the Christian religion has paradoxically been a powerful force for defending human dignity. When the exploitation of indigenous people was widespread in Latin America during colonization, Bartolomé de las Casas, a Dominican friar, became the pioneer of human rights and defended freedom of conscience and of religion. In Africa, at the time of independence, a large proportion of educational and health services were provided by Christian missionaries. Today, so-called 'faith-based organizations' provide more than half of all health care services in sub-Saharan Africa (see Clarke et al., 2008).

It is difficult for anyone working or researching in the field of international development not to avoid confronting Christian beliefs and practices, not only given the numbers – an estimated 2.1 billion Christians worldwide[1] – but also given their influence in social, economic and political life. This invites a reassessment of the way religion has been researched and taken into account in development studies so far (Deneulin and Rakodi, 2011). A major step in that direction is to understand religion from within and grasp the language through which it apprehends international development.[2] The object of this chapter is to enable this with regard to Christianity.

The chapter is divided into two main sections. The first discusses the fundamentals of Christianity and its social, economic and political implications. It emphasizes that Christian beliefs are inseparable from a community of people who follow Jesus Christ and aim at continuing his mission of revealing God in the world. The chapter then describes the defining beliefs of this community, their principal Creed, and what this affirmation of faith implies for social and political engagement. Christianity is what those who belong to the global Christian community believe and do in light of these beliefs. The Christian religion is therefore characterized by heterogeneity, for different members have diverse interpretations of these core beliefs. There is no unified interpretation of Christian doctrine. Given that the Catholic Church has the largest number of adherents among the Christian community and the most unified interpretation of doctrine, the chapter will present a Christian perspective from within the Catholic tradition. The second section outlines three major features of this perspective on international development:

1. Human dignity and the inseparability of the material and spiritual dimensions of human life.
2. Humans are called to live in communion with each other and with God, therefore human dignity is inseparable from solidarity and concern for the good of all.
3. Human actions are marked by sin, therefore the struggles for justice and human dignity are inseparable from conversion to God.

THE CHRISTIAN FAITH: THE CREED

Discipleship and Community

The word 'Christian' was first used at Antioch to refer to the followers of Jesus, a Jewish man born in Palestine circa 6 BC and who claimed to be Messiah of the people of Israel, the Christ.[3] His mission was to reveal the face of God. His birth already challenged the political and religious establishment of the time. The Gospel of Luke relates that some shepherds, one of the most marginalized professions at the time, were the first to recognize him, in his childhood, as the Messiah, God's messenger to the world. The synoptic Gospels (Matthew, Mark and Luke) report that it is at his baptism in adulthood that Jesus began to reveal God publicly. The prologue of St John's Gospel writes that Jesus is the Word of God who came into the world.

According to the Gospel accounts, Jesus chose disciples to accompany him and witness to his life. They were chosen so that, by living closely to his ministry, they would in turn reveal God in the world by acting like Jesus. This dynamic reaches its climax at the Last Supper when Jesus washes his disciples' feet (John 13) – a gesture that prefigures his imminent self-giving and death – and summons them to do the same: to serve one another and reveal the face of a servant God. This may risk death, for revealing the face of God is often at odds with religious and political authorities (see below).

The early disciples whom Jesus chose to witness his ministry went on to continue his works of revelation after his death, and made other disciples. As the number of disciples grew, they met in small assemblies at the end of the Sabbath day in a disciple's house to re-enact the Last Supper and remember Jesus's life, death and resurrection, and so instituting the church (*ekklesia* or 'assembly' in Greek). Divisions and disagreements about how to live the Jesus way were, however, not uncommon. As time went by and direct witnesses of Jesus's life died, these assemblies put in writing the story of Jesus. These became the Gospels, each named after the disciple around whom the assembly was gathered.

As the number of Jesus's followers grew in the first centuries after his death, disagreements among the Christian community widened further. Some denied the human nature of Jesus; others denied the resurrection of the body of Christ. In the face of mounting disagreements and fragmentation, which threatened the unity of the newly officially Christian empire, the emperor Constantine called a meeting of Church leaders in Nicea in 325, the first Council of the Church (Johnson, 2003, pp. 32–6), to set some fundamentals. Departing from these ran the risk of being excluded from the Christian community.[4] The Council of Nicea declared that Jesus was both fully human and fully divine. The leaders of the church met again in 381 in Constantinople, declared the doctrine of the Trinity (that God was a communion of three persons, the Father, Son and Holy Spirit), and agreed on a profession of faith, the Creed, which would define belonging to the Christian community.

From this account of origins of Christianity, one can observe that beliefs and community are closely intertwined. It is the profession of faith of the first disciples who recognized Jesus as the Messiah, which established the Christian community, but it is through that community that people come to believe and profess the Christian faith. Because there is a community of disciples who continue Jesus's work of revealing God in the world, people can profess a Christian faith and believe in God. The Christian faith and Christian community are inseparable. Christianity started with a few people who recognized Jesus as Messiah, and who responded to his invitation to follow him and live like he did. Faith and discipleship, that is, following Jesus through words and actions, go hand in hand. This has considerable implications for understanding the role of Christianity in international development: Christianity is not only a set of beliefs one adheres to, but also a way of life. Proclaiming Jesus as the Son of God through prayer and worship is inseparable from actions that aim at revealing the face of God in economic, social and political structures. The next sub-sections discuss the Creed in its version known as the 'Symbol of the Apostles'.

God the Creator

'We believe in God, creator of heaven and earth'. The starting point of the affirmation of Christian faith is the belief that all creation and creatures do not exist at random, but have been created by God's gratuitous love. The Gospels narrate some of Jesus's miracles to manifest that God has power over creation, and that creation belongs to God.

For those who profess that God is the creator of all that exists, not respecting creation implies not respecting God. Humans have been given the natural environment as God's gift to provide for their needs, but it is a gift they have to cherish and protect. They are stewards, not owners, of creation. Therefore, material goods are not the property of humans, but ultimately belong to God and serve God's glory. This may imply limits on private property to serve the good of all (cf. section two).

If one believes that God created the world out of love to manifest His/Her glory, all created life is called to share in God's glory, for this is why creation exists. Human beings are called to reflect the glory of God in their body, in their relations with each other, and their relation with the natural environment. Christians believe that all human beings have been created in the image of God and are called to manifest God's love in the world. When social, political and economic processes distort the capacity of humans to live in the image of God, Christians believe that restoring right relationships between people and the environment is part of affirming their belief in God the creator.

When economic, social and political structures deny a 12-year-old girl education because she is a girl and force her to work as a sex worker to feed her siblings because she is an orphan and has no other work opportunities, these structures obstruct the glory of God. This is not to say that the girl's life does not reflect God's glory, for nothing can stop the Creator from manifesting His/Her love for creation, but the structures of the country in which she lives, and one may add the wider global structures of distribution of power and assets, fail to give glory to God by not providing conditions for the girl to live well. Working at making economic, social and political structures more conducive to human flourishing is constitutive of evangelization, of bringing the good news of God's revelation to the world. As a document of the Catholic Church, *Evangelii Nuntiandi*, published in 1975 by Pope Paul VI, states:[5]

> [E]vangelization involves an explicit message, adapted to the different situations constantly being realized, about the rights and duties of every human being, about life in society, about international life, peace, justice and development. . . . The Church, as the bishops repeated,[6] has the duty to proclaim the liberation of millions of human beings. . . . This is not foreign to evangelization. Between evangelization and human advancement there are in fact profound links. These include links of an anthropological order, because the person who is to be evangelized is not an abstract being but is subject to social and economic questions. (Paragraph 6)

Divine and Human

The Creed continues, 'We believe in Jesus Christ, God's only Son, who was conceived by the Holy Spirit and born of the Virgin Mary'. Christians believe in a God who is one in a communion of three persons, the Father, the Son and the Holy Spirit. God is not an undifferentiated monad but a differentiated unity of three persons in relation. If humans are made in the image of God, then the human being is fully human when living in communion with other people and at the service of each other. Belief in a triune God implies that the good of oneself and of the communion of people one participates in are mutually self-implicating, a point we shall return to in the second main section. Christianity's relational anthropology is ill at ease with political traditions that emphasize the primacy of the individual, such as social contract theory and political liberalism, or ideological traditions that prioritize the pursuit of self-interest and individual utility maximization as in neoclassical economics.

By affirming belief in a triune God, Christians hold that the provision of individual rights cannot be separated from the set of relationships in which people live, and which are constitutive of their lives. Restoring right relationships, restoring communion among human beings and readjusting the creation to its purpose, is the reason why God became human. The Nicea-Constantinople version of the Creed adds that Jesus became human for the forgiveness of sins. When humans lose sight of God, relationships are distorted away from the Creator's intentions. A search for power and domination takes precedence over service to one another, with all the consequences that sin entails: people going hungry because an economic structure allows financial speculation on basic commodities, making food prices shoot up, or forces them to grow one single export crop that is vulnerable to price volatility; people dying at a young age because a political structure makes it possible for political leaders to buy weapons instead of invest in basic infrastructure (cf. section two). But Christians believe that Jesus came to reconcile human beings to God, and inaugurate a new Creation, a new world no longer corrupted by sin.

For God to share the human condition, beginning from life in the womb to death, the cooperation of a woman was needed. God asked a poor, young and unmarried Jewish girl if she would agree to bear the Son of God (Luke 1: 26–38), to be the channel through which God could become human (John 1: 14). Mary accepted and was asked to name her son 'Jesus'.[7] God needed the agency of a human being in order to be revealed. Christians believe that, because God became flesh through Mary's yes to God, followers of Jesus are likewise called to make the Word of God flesh in their lives, be totally open to God and let their lives be transformed by the power of God.

Soon after accepting to bear the Son of God, Mary sings the Magnificat (Luke 1: 46–56),[8] which proclaims that God sends the rich away empty, throws down the mighty from their thrones, and scatters the proud-hearted. Accepting God in one's life reverses power relations and questions the existing economic, social and political order (Johnson, 2003, p. 160). Being a Christian, accepting God's revelation to the world through Jesus, implies making a judgement on the existing economic, social and political arrangements and the extent to which they reflect God's glory.

Death and Resurrection

The Creed jumps from Jesus's birth to his death: 'He suffered under Pontius Pilate, was crucified, died and was buried; he descended to the dead. On the third day he rose again; he ascended into heaven, and is seated at the right hand of the Father, and he will come to judge the living and the dead'. The Creed is silent on Jesus's public ministry, and goes straight to its consequence: Jesus's revelation of God to humankind enters in conflict with worldly authorities. His ministry has disturbed authorities of the Jewish Temple. He has performed miracles on a Sabbath day, is not observing Jewish purification practices, eats in the houses of publicans and prostitutes, has thrown merchants out of the Temple and criticized some Pharisees for being hypocrites. Jesus is a threat to the religious establishment, which subsequently accuses him of blasphemy, an offence condemnable by death in Jewish law.

The Jewish authorities bring Jesus to Pilate, the Roman governor who has the power to condemn or release Jesus, but Pilate finds no basis for condemnation – Jesus is not a rebel whose kingdom will overthrow the Roman occupation – and offers to release him. But some of the religious leaders have manipulated the crowd to demand Jesus's crucifixion (crucifixion was the most shameful way of dying at the time). Pilate fears for his own career, and the rebellion that might erupt should he release Jesus. He lets the crowd decide and washes his hands of the matter (Matthew 27: 24).

It is no coincidence that Mary, Pilate and Jesus are the only three human beings named in the Creed (Johnson, 2003, pp. 159, 168). Mary and Pilate offer the two contrasting responses that humans can give to God: Mary, a poor and marginalized woman, accepts God and gives birth to Jesus; Pilate, a wealthy and powerful man, rejects God and kills Jesus. We can see here a glimpse of the 'option for the poor', which is a key feature of a Christian perspective on development (cf. section two). God is on the side of the oppressed and marginalized.

The opposition between Jesus and Pilate narrates a key aspect of Christian discipleship: following Christ and proclaiming God's reign may bring conflict with political authorities, sometimes to the point of death. One of the most well-known examples is that of Oscar Romero.

Oscar Romero was appointed archbishop of El Salvador in 1977. He had never been heard making political statements about the social conflict that was engulfing the country. He was considered psychologically weak and easy to manipulate to suit the interests of the religious and political elite. But Romero did not continue to be as he had been before his appointment. A few weeks after becoming archbishop, a friend of his, a Jesuit priest, was murdered because of his support for land reform, along with two children and a man to whom he was giving a lift. It was the first time that the military dictatorship had killed a priest. The event profoundly transformed Romero. He began to make regular radio broadcasts critiquing the military dictatorship. How could Catholic soldiers kill their brethren? How could the Salvadorian elite go to Mass, say they love God and deny food, shelter and basic human needs to their brothers and sisters? That was a message too hard for some to listen to. Romero, like Jesus, was troubling the existing social and moral order, and had to be silenced. He was murdered whilst saying Mass on 25 March 1980.

The Creed professes that Jesus died and was buried. He lived fully a human life. However, Christians believe that death is not the end because Jesus has risen from the dead. The Resurrection is the core of the Christian faith. St Paul wrote that if Jesus is not resurrected, faith is without substance (1 Corinthians 15: 13–19). Jesus now shares the glory of God and his resurrection prefigures the new creation, when all will be one in God. Christians live in the hope that justice, a world of communion between God and all creation, will come about at the end of times, when 'Jesus will come again to judge the living and the dead', as the Creed affirms. Until this happens, Christians are accountable to Christ (Johnson, 2003, Chapter 6). The standard to assess whether their lives have been good or not is whether they have reflected God's glory, whether they have worked at making relations among people and with the environment more just, more in tune with their created purpose.

The Church

Those who profess the Christian faith often fail to live up to the standard described above. Some abuse children or hurt their spouse through unfaithfulness, neglect or lack of respect. Some fail to speak out against injustice. Some live lives that are more resource-intense than the environment can sustain. This names only a few of the many discrepancies that one can observe between what Jesus taught and lived and the way Christians live. Related to this failure of Christians to be disciples and to re-enact Jesus's life in their own, the Creed continues: 'We believe in the Holy Spirit, the holy catholic Church, the Communion of Saints, the forgiveness of sins, the Resurrection of the body, and the life everlasting'. The Holy Spirit brings human beings into communion with God. Christians believe that God's revelation did not end with Jesus's death, but continues in the world through the Holy Spirit, who ceaselessly renews the human 'spirit' and transforms it in the likeness of God (Johnson, 2003, Chapter 7).

When the human spirit understands Scriptures as a justification of human dominion over creation, of slavery, of women's subordination to men, God sends the Spirit so that human beings may interpret Scriptures in a way that better conforms to God. In its Catholic interpretation, Christian doctrine holds that the Holy Spirit can speak through each human being, irrespective of faith, for God speaks through the human conscience.[9] Thus, an atheist young man who refuses to join the draft in a war he sees as unjust, at the risk of imprisonment, or an agnostic person who makes public a case of corruption at the risk of losing her job, can be examples of the Spirit of God at work through conscience.

Even if in many respects the community of people who profess the Creed fails to reflect God's glory, the church, or the assembly of people gathered to proclaim their belief in the triune God and to remember the life of Jesus who revealed God, is a sign of God's presence and redemption in the world. Christians believe that it is through the church, although not exclusively, that God continues the work of revelation. When Christians profess in the Creed their belief in the 'holy catholic Church', they do not believe in the Catholic Church headed by the pope in the Vatican, but believe that God works through the whole of the community –'catholic' means in Greek 'throughout the whole' (Johnson, 2003, pp. 268–73).

The church may be called 'holy' because it springs from God's revelation to humanity but it remains sinful because its members are sinners. This is why Christians believe in the role of the Holy Spirit in continuing God's work, transforming the human spirit to become more Christ-like. God was revealed in Jesus, but humans will only ever grasp a fraction of that revelation, and will grasp it through their own narratives, contexts, social norms, and all sorts of influences, whether consciously or unconsciously. God continues the work of revelation throughout history to open people's eyes to sin through the action of the Holy Spirit.

The interpretation of what it means concretely to be a disciple of Christ may be as diverse as there are Christians. However, the Catholic Church, headed by the Pope, has developed over the centuries a set of principles that are expounded in numerous encyclicals, or papal documents, which analyse various situations such as labour exploitation, injustice, inequality, nuclear deterrence, financial speculation, political authoritarianism, global trade, from the perspective of God's revelation to the world. This body of teachings is known as Catholic Social Teaching, and is addressed not only to Catholics and Christians from other denominations but 'all people of goodwill'.[10] The second part of the chapter examines the specific understanding of international development found in that teaching.

A CHRISTIAN PERSPECTIVE ON INTERNATIONAL DEVELOPMENT

Integral Human Development: Material and Spiritual

For Christians, 'development' is the process through which people reach their fulfilment in God and live the purpose for which they have been created: to reflect the image of God.[11] As the encyclical *Populorum Progressio*, published by Pope Paul VI in 1967, stated: 'To be authentic, [development] must be well rounded; it must foster the development of each person, and the whole person' (paragraph 14). The human being and his or her well-being should be the end of all economic, social, and political processes. This implies that human dignity, giving people what is their due as human beings, is a key principle in a Christian perspective on development.

If a child dies of an easily preventable disease because of lack of adequate public health provision, human dignity is violated. If a girl is unable to pursue secondary education because of lack of adequate public education provision or is forced to stay at home to care for younger siblings, human dignity is violated. If a woman is unable to take time off work when ill and risks dismissal because of inadequate labour rights, human dignity is violated. If workers are prevented from being union members because their country fails to respect freedom of association and freedom of expression, human dignity is violated. If people are denied the right to vote for the person of their choice and protest against policy decisions they disagree with, human dignity is violated. In other words, promoting human rights is a central feature of respect for human dignity, and Christians have a duty to protect economic, social, civil and political rights and to speak out whenever they are violated.[12]

With its affirmation of the centrality of human dignity and respect for human rights, a Christian perspective on international development bears many similarities with what is known as the human development paradigm, publicized by the UNDP in its annual *Human Development Reports* and conceptually rooted in the works of Amartya Sen. It considers development as 'a process of expanding people's real freedoms – their valuable capabilities – and empowering people as active agents of equitable development on a shared planet' (Alkire, 2010). The end of development is to provide opportunities for people to reach their potential as human beings: to be educated, to be healthy, to be creative, to participate in the life of the community, to engage in relationships, to live in a peaceful environment, to enjoy nature, to express themselves, to make decisions about their lives, and so on.[13]

Despite the many similarities between a Christian and human development perspective on development, there is one fundamental difference. Christians affirm that the human being finds ultimate fulfilment in God. The pursuit of social and economic well-being is essential to human development, but not sufficient. To recall the above definition, economic and social development should have the development of each and the *whole* person as its end. Christians believe that humans become more human when they are closer to God. To reflect this reality, Catholic Social Teaching refers to integral human development.[14] The development of the whole person is not complete without spiritual considerations.

One could argue that the human development perspective is open to the transcendental or spiritual dimension of life, for respect for human rights includes respect for freedom of religion (Article 18 of the Universal Declaration of Human Rights). However, by affirming that humans find their ultimate fulfilment in God, a Christian perspective does much more than adding another dimension to development alongside the social, economic, cultural or political or dimensions. It introduces a different anthropology that leads to a different understanding of the very concept and meaning of development.

For Christians, the spiritual and material dimensions of life are inseparable. Christians believe that eternal life, when humans will be with their Creator, is the end of human progress. As the latest document of Catholic Social Teaching, *Caritas in Veritate*, issued by Pope Benedict XVI in 2009, puts it:

> Without the perspective of eternal life, human progress in this world is denied breathing-space. . . . Institutions by themselves are not enough. . . . Development requires a transcendent vision of the person, it needs God: without him, development is either denied, or entrusted exclusively to man, who falls into the trap of thinking he can bring about his own salvation, and ends up promoting a dehumanized form of development. (Paragraph 11)

This inseparability of the material from the spiritual dimension of life introduces a fundamental difference between a Christian and non-Christian perspective on international development at two levels: humans are called to be in communion with each other and God, and human actions are marked by sin.

The Call to Communion: Solidarity and Responsibility

Christians believe that God is a communion of three persons, the Father, Son and Holy Spirit, and that humans have been created in the image of God. As a consequence, they believe that human well-being will reflect an analogous communion. The good of each person depends on the good of their communion, which in turns depends on the good of each person. The principle of the common good is another key feature of a Christian perspective on international development.

The common good is a good shared in by all those who are forming a certain community. It is the good constituted by the relationships of people with each other. The principle of the common good holds that the good of the community formed by these relationships and the good of each individual are mutually implicating (Hollenbach, 2002).[15] The Catechism of the Catholic Church, issued by Pope John Paul II in 1992, affirms that the common good is the end of political authority, the reason for which it exists (paragraph 1910). The role of government is to provide the conditions through which the good of all and each can be secured.[16] Christians are called to speak out whenever a government fails to fulfil its role of providing the conditions in which the good of all can be secured.

A country that fails to have a minimum wage legislation or sets it so low that parents have to keep two jobs to afford food and housing, not only violates the principle of human dignity (by failing to give decent employment, which enables a decent living) but also the principle of the common good (for long working hours do not facilitate family relations and leave much time for workers to participate in the life of the community). A country that encourages a work culture of long working hours through tax incentives, violates the principle of the common good too (for it discourages people to spend more time with family and friends or participate in community matters). A government that has a regressive tax structure and makes basic social services provision according to the ability of users to pay violates the common good (for it undermines the duties of solidarity citizens have with each other).

The common good is best realized in a context of subsidiarity, that is, a context in which decisions and actions are taken at the most local level whenever possible. The principle of subsidiarity was first asserted in the encyclical *Quadragesimo Anno*, published in 1931, 40 years after the first papal social encyclical:

> [I]t is an injustice and at the same time a grave evil and disturbance of the right order to assign to a greater and higher association what lesser and subordinate organizations can do. For every social activity ought of its very nature to furnish help to the members of the body social, and never destroy and absorb them. (Paragraph 79)

The latest encyclical *Caritas in Veritate* defines subsidiarity as 'first and foremost a form of assistance to the human person via the autonomy of intermediate bodies' (paragraph 57). Christians thus neither support an all-encompassing state that denies people the freedom to act for themselves and others in civil society, nor do they support a state that leaves it up to individuals to do what higher associations do best such as providing public goods. Waste collection may be organized by a local association of neighbours because of state failure to provide such services, but this goes against the principle of subsidiarity for the municipal government is the entity best responsible for providing such public good. Homeless care may be taken charge of by state-run organizations but the state should not prevent community initiatives from providing shelter and companionship to homeless people. Doing so would go against the principle of subsidiarity.

The principle of the common good is bound up with solidarity and responsibility. Commitment to the common good is synonym for solidarity. The encyclical *Sollicitudo Rei Socialis*, issued by Pope John Paul II in 1987, defines solidarity as 'this firm and constant determination to work for the common good; that is, for the good of all and each because we are all responsible for all' (paragraph 38). Christians, by virtue of following Christ who throughout his life spoke up for the poor, oppressed and marginalized of his time (such as women, publicans, tax collectors and blind people) and restored their dignity as full members of God's people, have a special responsibility in building structures of solidarity in the world and ensuring a better distribution of power and resources. The Jubilee 2000 campaign for debt relief was an illustration of this Christian commitment to solidarity. The campaign brought together a large coalition, mainly of churches and other Christian bodies, demanding the cancellation of the debt of heavily indebted countries so that more resources could be freed to provide basic services instead of servicing the debt and enriching Western banks. The pastoral land commission in Brazil is another example of the involvement of Christians in constructing a world more in harmony with God's creation through demanding a fairer distribution of land.

Solidarity is a virtue that is obviously not specific to the Christian faith. Many seek to build a more equitable world without reference to God. There is, however, a distinct aspect of a Christian perspective on solidarity. Christians justify solidarity in their belief in the existence of God. God is the creator and ultimate end of human life. Humans are united in a common origin and destiny and share a universal brotherhood (or sisterhood!) in Christ. Goods are destined to be enjoyed by all, and those who have goods have a duty to share with those in need. From the principle of the common good, a Christian perspective on development affirms the principle of the universal destination of material goods. Christians hold that private ownership of goods is not absolute, as the 1967 encyclical on international development, *Populorum Progressio*, stated:

> Every one has the right to glean what he needs from the earth. . . . Created goods should flow fairly to all. [Therefore] the right to private property is not absolute and unconditional. . . . The right to private property may never be exercised to the detriment of the common good. . . . When private gain and basic community needs conflict with one another, it is for the public authorities to seek a solution of these questions, with the active involvement of individual citizens and social groups. (Paragraphs 22–23)

The papal document *Octogesima Adveniens*, issued in 1971, even advocates that those who have goods in abundance should give them up:

> In teaching us charity, the Gospel instructs us in the preferential respect due to the poor and the special situation they have in society: The more fortunate should renounce some of their rights so as to place their goods more generously at the service of others. (Paragraph 23)

While a Christian perspective on development shares a lot with the human development approach, its conception of the human person as reaching fulfilment in God introduces a more 'integral' or 'wholesome' vision of human development. For the human development approach, the good of each human person is determined by a process of public reasoning and democratic deliberation (Sen, 2009). The end of development is to enable people to live a life they have reason to value, to promote valuable freedoms, and it is up to deliberative processes to determine what these valuable freedoms could be. The human good, what constitutes the development of a person, is what people decide through a public reasoning process.

For Christians in contrast, the human good is sharing God's life. The process of public reasoning is oriented towards this. From a Christian perspective, the exercise of human freedom (for example, in democratic participation) cannot be dissociated from the horizon of the common good and the purpose for which humans have been created, to reflect God's glory. The 1987 encyclical by Pope John Paul II, *Sollicitudo Rei Socialis*, conceives of freedom and responsibility as two sides of the same coin: 'In order to be genuine, development must be achieved within the framework of solidarity and freedom, without ever sacrificing either of them under whatever pretext' (paragraph 33). The human being is fully free to the extent that he or she is responsible for others. Thus, one could imagine a deliberation process where people come to the agreement that a valuable life is one that is chosen and that the government should provide the conditions for people to live a life of their choice, whether it means working 15 hours a day in a business and enjoying a lavish lifestyle or taking early retirement and spending one's life surfing on a beach. This political liberal account is perfectly compatible with the human development approach (see Nussbaum, 2011). However, from a Christian perspective, a deliberation process that leads to that outcome violates the common good and de-links freedom from responsibility towards others. A life oriented to the satisfaction of one's own good only is not a Christian one.

This articulation of human freedom towards the horizon of the common good characterizes a Christian perspective on international development. This brings us to a second difference of an anthropological order between a Christian and non-Christian perspective on development: human freedom may have been given by God to manifest His/Her glory, but humans often fail to orient their freedom towards God.

Sin: Transformation and Hope

Human freedom is not always exercised for the purpose of the common good. Christians might use their freedom against the principle of the common good and failed to share what they have with those in need. This is why a Christian perspective on development does not ignore the reality of sin, of humans using their freedom against God and their own fulfilment, and connects the reality of injustice and material poverty to sin. That some people lack the material conditions to live well is connected to other people lacking of openness to God and failing to love God and live in solidarity with fellow human beings. The moral poverty of some has consequences for the material poverty of others, as the 1967 encyclical on development by Pope Paul VI, *Populorum Progressio*, states: 'What are less than human conditions? The material poverty of those who lack the bare necessities of life, and the moral poverty of those who are crushed under the weight of their own self-love' (paragraph 21). Because some are 'crushed under their self-love' and fail to love God and live in solidarity, others suffer. Because rich landowners refuse to redistribute their land, millions of landless peasants suffer.

The human being is a unity of body and soul, and the transformation of the material world is bound up with moral transformation, as the latest Catholic encyclical by Pope Benedict XVI, *Caritas in Veritate*, affirms:

> The question of development is closely bound up with our understanding of the human soul. . . . Development must include not just material growth but also spiritual growth, since the human person is a 'unity of body and soul', born of God's creative love and destined for eternal life. The human being develops . . . when he enters into dialogue with himself and his Creator. . . . There cannot be holistic development and universal common good unless people's spiritual and moral welfare is taken into account, considered in their totality as body and soul. (Paragraph 76)

That poverty and injustice are the result of sin, or more specifically structural sin, has been a key point made by liberation theology. Gustavo Gutierrez (1971, p. 174) writes that 'sin is evident in oppressive structures, in the exploitation of humans by humans, in the domination and slavery of peoples, races and social classes. Sin appears, therefore, as the fundamental alienation, the root of situations of injustice and exploitation'. The numerous sinful actions of individual human beings create a structure of sin, which in turn influences the behaviour of individuals. When numerous individuals are motivated by the prospect of maximum profit and returns on their capital investment and not the well-being of workers, this creates an economic structure in which the logic of profit-making has priority over the well-being of workers, often leading to their exploitation for the sake of maximum profit-making. The sinful actions of individuals have created a structure of sin, which then imposes a sinful behaviour on economic actors who support the structure. It is very difficult for anyone who has a bank account not to have money invested in an economic structure that privileges profits at the expense of the well-being of workers.

The notion of structural sin advanced by liberation theologians has become part of official Catholic Social Teaching, notably in the 1987 encyclical *Sollicitudo Rei Socialis* by Pope John Paul II:

> Structures of sin are rooted in personal sin, and thus always linked to the concrete acts of individuals who introduce these structures, consolidate them and make them difficult to remove. And thus they grow stronger, spread, and become the source of other sins, and so influence people's behaviour. (Paragraph 36)

Structural sin differs from individual sin in three respects (Deneulin et al., 2006). First, structures of sin generate the experience of an impossible choice. The person who lives in structural sin is driven to undertake actions that he or she may disapprove of (it is difficult to avoid having a bank account in a bank which invests in companies that subordinate the well-being of workers to the profit-making). Second, structures of sin may generate a sense of blindness (is one aware of the fact that holding an account in a high street bank contributes to a structure of sin?). Third, structures of sin are persistent and difficult to change (as a small customer, how can one change the investment portfolio of a bank?). A single individual action is not sufficient to change the structure (my individual action put my money in a cooperative bank that only invests in cooperative enterprises is not likely to make the global economic system oriented to the well-being of workers). Overcoming structural sin requires a collective turning away from sin and coming back to God – although the action of one single individual can be prophetic and be an inspiration for others, such as single individuals buying shares in a bank in order to attend the general assembly and confront the senior management with their sinful investment practices.

A Christian perspective on international development emphasizes the interconnectedness of human actions. What some people do has a considerable effect on the lives of others. This is especially manifest in the case of environmental degradation. The 1991 encyclical *Centesimus Annus* issued by Pope John Paul II underlines this:

> Equally worrying is *the ecological question* which accompanies the problem of consumerism and which is closely connected to it. In his desire to have and to enjoy rather than to be and to grow, man consumes the resources of the earth and his own life in an excessive and disordered way. At the root of the senseless destruction of the natural environment lies an anthropological error, which unfortunately is widespread in our day. Man, who discovers his capacity to transform and in a certain sense create the world through his own work, forgets that this is always based on God's prior and original gift of the things that are. . . . Instead of carrying out his role as a co-operator with God in the work of creation, man sets himself up in place of God and thus ends up provoking a rebellion on the part of nature, which is more tyrannized than governed by him. (Paragraph 37)

A Christian perspective on international development does not reduce development to a material project of changing structures, for development is 'integral'. As important as it is, establishing structures more conducive for people to live well has to be accompanied by moral transformation, by a 'change of heart'. Development is also about people being more Christ-like. This lengthy quote from the latest Catholic encyclical, issued by Pope Benedict XVI in 2009, *Caritas in Veritate* summarizes this best:

> Man is constitutionally oriented towards 'being more' (paragraph 14) . . . [W]hat does it mean 'to be more'? Paul VI answers the question by indicating the essential quality of 'authentic' development: it must be 'integral, that is, it has to promote the good of every man and of the whole man'. Amid the various competing anthropological visions put forward in today's society, . . . the Christian vision has the particular characteristic of asserting and justifying the unconditional value of the human person and the meaning of his growth. In promoting development, the Christian faith does not rely on privilege or positions of power . . . but only on Christ, to whom every authentic vocation to integral human development must be directed. *The Gospel is fundamental for development*, because in the Gospel, Christ, in the very revelation of the mystery of the Father and of his love, fully reveals humanity to itself. Taught by her Lord, the Church examines the signs of the times and interprets them, offering the world what she possesses as her characteristic attribute: a global vision of man and of the human race. . . . Integral human development on the natural plane, as a response to a vocation from God the Creator, demands self-fulfilment in a transcendent humanism which gives [man] his greatest possible perfection. . . . The Christian vocation to this development therefore applies to both the natural plane and the supernatural plane; which is why, when God is eclipsed, our ability to recognize the natural order, purpose and the 'good' begins to wane. (Paragraph 18; italics in original)

Economic, social, political or technological means are not sufficient promote development. Development cannot be reduced to a man-made enterprise. It is also a journey of conversion, of coming back to God, for there is a causal relationship between sin and injustice. Working at providing the conditions in which each human being can live in dignity, at guaranteeing the respect of human rights, is a moral task. A vision of development that ignores the transcendental dimension of life, risks being dehumanizing.

CONCLUSION

Religion is unavoidable in development. Yet, engaging with it brings serious challenges. A Christian anthropological vision of the human is at odds with a secular anthropology. For the former, being human is being open to God, and the exercise of freedom is set within that horizon. For the latter, being human is to exercise freedom and reason without God. However, conflict need not be the outcome of two different visions. Openness to the other, and therefore entering the other person's point of view and understanding of what it means to be human, is of paramount importance when engaging with religion in international development.[17]

A Christian vision of development does not separate the material from spiritual dimension of life. Christians believe that humans are made in the image of God and only reach their fulfilment in God. Development, working for social justice and protection of the environment, goes hand in hand with conversion of the heart. From a Christian perspective, the origin of injustice, inequality, exploitation and destruction of the environment lies in human beings turning away from God. It lies in failure to love; it lies in lack of solidarity, in greed, in search for power and domination over creation, in lack of respect for the dignity of each human being.

From a Christian perspective, the aim of development is not make the world Christian but to reveal the face of God and restore communion between human beings and creation. Non-Christians do show solidarity with fellow human beings, serve them, respect God's creation and live a life turned to God (often even more than professing Christians!). This is why the Christian perspective on international development outlined here is not only relevant for Christians. It is universal and holds for every person of goodwill (to whom the documents of Catholic Social Teaching are addressed).

NOTES

* I thank Matthew Clarke for the invitation to write this overview, and Joe Devine, Helen Stawski and Nick Townsend for their comments on an earlier draft.

1. See the World Christian Database at http://www.worldchristiandatabase.org.
2. See especially Chapter 6 'Dialoguing traditions' in *Religion in Development* (Deneulin, 2009).
3. *Kristos* is the Greek translation of the Hebrew word 'Messiah', the anointed one. In the Hebrew Scriptures, prophets and kings were anointed to symbolize that they had a mission from God (Johnson, 2003, p. 115).
4. Symbolizing membership to the Christian community through profession of faith derives from the Jewish tradition of the 'Shema Yisrael' (Deuteronomy 6: 4), where affirmation of belief in the one God defined the Jewish community against polytheism (Johnson, 2003, pp. 11–13).
5. The document can be found at http://www.vatican.va/holy_father/paul_vi/apost_exhortations/index.htm; accessed 1 July 2012.
6. This refers to the 1971 Synod of Bishops: 'Listening to the cry of those who suffer violence and are oppressed by unjust systems and structures, and hearing the appeal of a world that by its perversity contradicts the plan of its creator, we have shared our awareness of the Church's vocation to be present in the heart of the world by proclaiming the good news to the poor, freedom to the oppressed, and joy to the afflicted' (paragraph 6). The document can be accessed at http://www.osjspm.org.
7. The name Jesus comes from the Hebrew Yaheshua or 'God saves' (Johnson, 2003, p. 114).
8. The Gospels were written after the experience of the Resurrection. By echoing the Song of Hannah (1 Samuel 2: 1–10), Luke insists on the radical transformation implied by letting God enter one's life.
9. The Pastoral Constitution of the Catholic Church, *Gaudium et Spes*, issued at the Second Vatican Council in 1965 states that it is in their conscience that humans are 'alone with God', that it is 'in fidelity to

conscience' that 'Christians are joined with the rest of men in the search for truth, and for the genuine solution to the numerous problems which arise in the life of individuals from social relationships' (paragraph 16).

10. For a pedagogical introduction to Catholic Social Teaching, see www.virtualplater.org.uk. All the documents of the Catholic Church cited in this chapter can be accessed on the Vatican website at www.vatican.va.
11. For the international development implications of the creation of human beings in the image of God, see the report *Wholly Living* by theology think tank Theos and evangelical and Catholic development agencies Tearfund and CAFOD at http://www.cafod.org.uk/resources/policy/wholly-living-report2; accessed 11 July 2012.
12. The *Compendium on the Social Doctrine of the Church* writes that human rights are 'one of the most significant attempts to respond effectively to the demands of human dignity' (paragraph 152).
13. See Sen (1999), Nussbaum (2000, 2011), Alkire (2002) and Alkire and Deneulin (2009).
14. Other Christian denominations tend to refer to 'integral mission'. The evangelical development organization Tearfund defines integral mission as the 'indivisible proclamation and demonstration of the Gospel that results in the transformation of the whole person'. See http://www.tearfund.org.
15. For a discussion of the common good, see Deneulin and Townsend (2007).
16. For an account of the role of the government from a Christian perspective, see Townsend (2009).
17. Cf. Chapter 6 'Dialoguing traditions' in *Religion in Development* (Deneulin, 2009).

REFERENCES

Alkire, S. (2002), *Valuing Freedoms*, Oxford: Oxford University Press.

Alkire, S. (2010), 'Conceptual overview of human development', background paper for 2010 *Human Development Report*, available at: http://hdr.undp.org/en/reports/global/hdr2010/papers/HDRP_2010_01.pdf; accessed 7 July 2012.

Alkire, S. and S. Deneulin (2009), 'The human development and capability approach', in S. Deneulin (ed.), *An Introduction to the Human Development and Capability Approach*, London: Earthscan, also available at http://www.idrc.ca/en/ev-143029-201-1-DO_TOPIC.html; accessed 7 July 2012.

Clarke, G., M. Jennings and T. Shaw (eds) (2008), *Development, Civil Society and Faith-based Organizations*, Basingstoke: Palgrave Macmillan.

Deneulin, S. with M. Bano (2009), *Religion in Development: Rewriting the Secular Script*, London: Zed.

Deneulin, S. and C. Rakodi (2011), 'Revisiting religion: development studies thirty years on', *World Development*, **39**(1), 45–54.

Deneulin, S. and N. Townsend (2007), 'Public goods, global public goods and the common good', *International Journal of Social Economics*, **34**(1/2), 19–36.

Deneulin, S., M. Nebel and N. Sagovsky (eds) (2006), *Transforming Unjust Structures*, Dordrecht: Springer.

Gutierrez, Gustavo (1971), *A Theology of Liberation*, reprinted in 2000, London: SCM Press.

Hastings, Adrian (1994), *The Church in Africa: 1450–1950*, Oxford: Clarendon Press.

Hollenbach, David (2002), *The Common Good and Christian Ethics*, Cambridge: Cambridge University Press.

Johnson, Luke Timothy (2003), *The Creed: What Christians Believe and Why It Matters*, London: Darton, Longman and Todd.

Nussbaum, M. (2000), *Women and Human Development*, Cambridge: Cambridge University Press.

Nussbaum, M. (2011), *Creating Capabilities: The Human Development Approach*, Cambridge, MA: Belknap Press.

Sen, Amartya (1999), *Development as Freedom*, Oxford: Oxford University Press.

Sen, Amartya (2009), *The Idea of Justice*, London: Allen Lane

Townsend, Nicholas (2009), 'Government as social infrastructure', in N. Spence and J. Chaplin (eds), *God and Government*, London: SPCK.

5 Judaism – a cry for justice

Matthew Clarke

INTRODUCTION

Key Jewish figures are familiar to many as they also appear in the sacred texts of Christianity and Islam. However, the exact dates, and indeed the historical authenticity, of the existence of many of these key figures are less clear than that of the key figures of Christianity and Islam and indeed Buddhism.

The sacred text of Judaism includes the Torah (the first five books, also known as the Pentateuch, or the 'Law'), the Nevi'im (Prophets) and the Ketuvim (Writings). Tradition holds that Moses wrote the first five books and in it describes the pre-history that resulted in the Israelites being a nation seeking God's Promised Land. The Torah contains five books with content addressing two primary issues: (1) the history of the creation of humanity and evolution of a specific nation and people; and (2) divine laws delivered to these specific people. This text presents God's relationship with the Jews. The first book – Genesis – is a 'historical' account that sets out the relationship between the Jews and God, whereas the remaining four books are more 'contemporary' accounts.

The starting point of Genesis is creation. However, this event is followed by human failure to act according to God's will, the eventual cleansing of earth by God, and the new Covenant between God and a new people that He has called to be His own. The importance of Genesis is less with its scientific description of the beginning of time or its pragmatic qualities as a creation story, but more so with its providing a direct heritage of the Jewish people to be God's chosen race. The first event described in Genesis is that of God creating heaven and earth followed by the creation of all living things, the most important of which are humans (Adam and Eve) to enjoy the fruits of his work. Yet, the frailty of human nature soon became apparent with Adam and Eve disobeying God, resulting in the second event – their banishment from the Garden of Eden and subsequent experience of pain and shame and living lives of hard toil.

Noah is the central figure in the third key event of the first book – the destruction of humankind. By this time, humans had become evil and violent. So offended was God by this that He determined to destroyed humankind:

> The LORD was grieved that he had made man on the earth, and his heart was filled with pain. So the LORD said, 'I will wipe mankind, whom I have created, from the face of the earth – men and animals, and creatures that move along the ground, and birds of the air – for I am grieved that I have made them. (Genesis 6: 6–7)

God's destruction came in the form of a flood. However, God was able to find one virtuous family and chose Noah and his family to survive this destruction. God charged Noah and his family with the task of preserving a pair of each kind of animal so that following the water receding after the flood, the earth would again be abundant with life.

The fourth event that unites Jews with God is the singling out of Abraham from Noah's descendants to father a nation that would be God's chosen people: 'The LORD appeared to Abram and said, "To your offspring I will give this land"' (Genesis 12: 7). It is this Covenant that binds the Jewish people so closely to God as God chose this people above all others. Following the description of the Abrahamic Covenant, the Book of Genesis then describes other key Jewish figures, including Isaac, Jacob and Joseph.

The remaining four books of the Torah further strengthen the link between God and His chosen people. The Book of Exodus tells the story of Moses leading his people from slavery in Egypt to find God's Promised Land. It was during the 40 years of wandering the desert that God revealed the Ten Commandments to Moses. The third book, Leviticus, describes the role of the priests (Levites) in teaching the Israelites how to live holy lives, and different sets of laws around sacrifices, purity and atonement. There are over 600 laws in these first five books of the Torah, whereas there are only seven set out for Gentiles[1] (Leaman, 2006). The fourth book – Numbers – describes in greater detail the wandering of the Israelites for 40 years as they search for God's Promised Land. This inability to find this land was due to their disobedience (though God continued to provide for them during this time). The final book is Deuteronomy and describes the final phase of the Israelites' wanderings, Moses' death,[2] the appointment of Joshua as the new leader, and the final entering of the Promised Land. This final event renewed God's Covenant with the Jews.

Unlike the historical figure of Jesus, who only led a very small number of believers, with few expectations that he would rise up against the occupying Romans, the majority of key Jewish figures were both concurrently religious and political leaders – much in the manner of Mohammed. Moses was clearly the first of these great leaders. Following his death and having entered the Promised Land and defeated the Canaanites (who were occupying his land), a great nation was built by Joshua, which was subsequently governed by various great monarchs, including Saul, David and Solomon who successfully ruled over Israel for approximately 100 years, from 1025 to 928 BCE.

The remainder of the sacred texts are a mixture of history, prophecies and praise to God. The Nevi'im has eight books that record the often poetic and florid writings of historical prophets. The final division is that of the Ketuvim, which comprises the miscellaneous writings of prophets written before the building of the Second Temple (Segal, 2009). Collectively, these texts are known as the Tanakh as the initial letters of these three divisions, Torah, Nevi'im and Ketuvim (T, N and K) combined formed the acronym TaNaKh (ibid.).[3] However, the Tanakh is best understood through commentaries:

> and in particular the Mishnah and Talmud, the two main texts that mediate on aspects of Jewish law and practice and so provide us with a concrete set of ideas about how we might act in accordance with the Bible and with what accompanies the Bible, that is, the oral tradition in Judaism. (Leaman, 2006, p. xiii)

This focus on action is very important to the practice of Jewish faith and Judaism is often labelled a very legalistic religion as a result. The interpretation of various laws accounts for much religious dialogue (and argument) about and within Judaism. Indeed, Hegel (1977) argued that this focus on laws pushed God away from humankind by 'denying humanity any direct connection with God' (Leaman, 2006, p. 19). Probably a more helpful and accurate interpretation, though, is to understand Judaism as a religion based on orthopraxis (correct action, or right practice), compared with Christianity as being based on orthodoxy (right belief or faith). Christianity was founded on a call to faith in Jesus Christ as the means of salvation; hence while practice is not unimportant, the primary focus of scholars throughout history has been to define right belief, that is, orthodoxy. In Christianity, right practice flows out of right belief. Indeed, the very idea of a religious 'faith' is derived from this Christian understanding. Judaism, on the other hand, was founded from a call by God to enter into a Covenant where God promises blessing in return for obedience. The focus of Jewish scholars throughout the ages has therefore been to define right practice, that is, orthopraxis. Right practice itself informs and teaches right belief.

BASIC JEWISH BELIEFS

Defining Judaism by what it believes is therefore, not surprisingly, difficult. There is no doubt that one of the greatest contributions Jewish belief has made is that of monotheism. Unlike its contemporary communities, the people of Moses and Abraham recognized one God above all others. It is upon this foundation of monotheism that all else within Judaism stands. Having said this though, unlike Christianity, Judaism does not have an official creed setting out its beliefs. The closest that exist might be the Thirteen Principles of Faith as set out by medieval Jewish scholar Maimonides. These precepts (see Steinberg [1945] 1975) are:

1. The existence of God.
2. The oneness and uniqueness of God.
3. The immateriality of God.
4. The eternalness of God.
5. Prayer must be directed to God alone.
6. The words of the prophets are true.
7. Moses was the greatest prophet.
8. The Torah was given to Moses by God.
9. There will be no other Torah.
10. God knows all.
11. God will punish the wicked and reward the good.
12. The Messiah will come.
13. The dead will be resurrected.

As can be seen, the centrality of God is critical to Jewish belief, but beyond this monotheistic belief, Judaism is characterized as a religion defined more by practice than by beliefs. 'One evidence of this is that Jews have never promulgated an official creed that must be accepted to belong to this faith' (Smith, 1991, p. 300). This practice is guided by both the laws set out in the Tanakh – over 600 of them – as well as the reflection and consideration of these laws contained within commentaries, known as Oral Law. Despite its name, the Oral Law consists of various written texts by various scholars on the Tanakh as well as reflections on how to reconcile different interpretations of the Tanakh by these thinkers. As a body of work, it is much longer than the Tanakh and requires language skills in both Hebrew and Aramaic. This body of opinion and counter-opinion is complex and difficult to navigate. However, it forms a large part of Jewish culture and law. Indeed, 'the Oral law in the shape of the Mishnah, Talmud, and many other works is the real object of interest of many Jews' (Leaman, 2006, p. 77). Its importance lies in the fact that while the Tanakh is sacred, some interpretation and explication is required.

The most well-known laws amongst the more than 600 edicts contained with the Tanakh are the ten given to Moses by God on Mount Sinai. The *Aseret ha-Dibrot*[4] provides a structure around which society can effectively operate. The first six commandments are related to the relationship between humanity and God, while the final four are more temporally focused and make a social world functional (Smith, 1991). These 'Ten Sayings' are found twice in the Tanakh, first in the Book of Exodus (20: 2–14) and second in the Book of Deuteronomy (5: 6–18):

> I am HaShem thy God, who brought thee out of the land of Egypt, out of the house of bondage. Thou shalt have no other gods before Me.
>
> Thou shalt not make unto thee a graven image, nor any manner of likeness, of any thing that is in heaven above, or that is in the earth beneath, or that is in the water under the earth; thou shalt not bow down unto them, nor serve them; for I HaShem thy God am a jealous God, visiting the iniquity of the fathers upon the children unto the third and fourth generation of them that hate Me; and showing mercy unto the thousandth generation of them that love Me and keep My commandments.
>
> Thou shalt not take the name of HaShem thy God in vain; for HaShem will not hold him guiltless that taketh His name in vain.
>
> Remember the sabbath day, to keep it holy. Six days shalt thou labour, and do all thy work; but the seventh day is a sabbath unto HaShem thy God, in it thou shalt not do any manner of work, thou, nor thy son, nor thy daughter, nor thy man-servant, nor thy maid-servant, nor thy cattle, nor thy stranger that is within thy gates; for in six days HaShem made heaven and earth, the sea, and all that in them is, and rested on the seventh day; wherefore HaShem blessed the sabbath day, and hallowed it.
>
> Honour thy father and thy mother, that thy days may be long upon the land which HaShem thy God giveth thee.
>
> Thou shalt not murder.
>
> Thou shalt not commit adultery.
>
> Thou shalt not steal.
>
> Thou shalt not bear false witness against thy neighbour.
>
> Thou shalt not covet thy neighbour's house; thou shalt not covet thy neighbour's wife, nor his man-servant, nor his maid-servant, nor his ox, nor his ass, nor any thing that is thy neighbour's. (Exodus 20: 2–20)

As noted, the second half of these commandments are not specifically religious, but are common to social mores across time. As Segal (2009) notes: 'Many of them were of an ostensibly prosaic character, not very different from the ones that we would expect to find in any civilized society' (p. 228). Indeed, the development of a just society based upon fair rule and law is one of the seven laws for Gentiles contained within the Noachide Laws (see above and note 1).

However, as stated, these are not the only prescribed behaviours within the Tanakh. In addition to the over 600 laws for Jews, the Book of Psalms lists various attributes that humans should aspire to should they wish to dwell in God's sanctuary:

> He that walketh uprightly, and worketh righteousness, and speaketh truth in his heart;
>
> That hath no slander upon his tongue, nor doeth evil to his fellow, nor taketh up a reproach against his neighbour;
>
> In whose eyes a vile person is despised, but he honoureth them that fear HaShem; he that sweareth to his own hurt, and changeth not;
>
> He that putteth not out his money on interest, nor taketh a bribe against the innocent. He that doeth these things shall never be moved. (Psalms 15: 2–5)

Motivation to undertake good works or to live a righteous life are less overtly linked to an afterlife than might be found in Christian or Islamic adherents. Indeed, the promise of an afterlife to motivate good work occurs late in the Tanakh (and was mostly likely written during a period of Jewish persecution when devotion may have waned under this Hellenistic assault; Segal, 2009):

> And many of them that sleep in the dust of the earth shall awake, some to everlasting life, and some to reproaches and everlasting abhorrence. And they that are wise shall shine as the brightness of the firmament; and they that turn the many to righteousness as the stars for ever and ever. (Daniel 12: 2–3; also see 2 Maccabees)

Thus, unlike Christianity, perhaps which has a stronger focus on life after death that may be a motivation for some temporal good works, there is less of an emphasis within Judaism.

JUDAISM AND DEVELOPMENT

It could be said that there are several reasons for the possible unsuitability of the inclusion of Judaism in a book seeking to understand how development is understood within the world's major religions. These reasons might include the relatively small number of the Jews in the world, the religion's close association with a distinct ethnic group and geographical location, resulting in a lack of a wider interest in the developing world, the acculturation of Jewish teaching in subsequent sectarian as well as secular social systems, and finally that it is yet to be completely fulfilled as a religion (in the sense it is still waiting for its Messiah). These combined arguments suggest that the relevance of

Judaism for the conditions of the world's poor is minimal and little can be gained from an exploration of its sacred texts and social teaching. However, such a position is not entirely persuasive when we expand our consideration of the Jewish belief to incorporate the Jewish experience.

Perhaps in contrast to other religions, it is the lived experience of the Jews that directly speaks to key development issues: hope for justice and care for others. While other religions will rely more heavily on sacred texts and social teaching to inform approaches to development, it is the direct historical experience of Jews that shapes their understanding of these concepts. The remainder of this chapter will consider how Judaism enhances our understanding of a cry for justice within a developmental context.

Judaism and a Cry for Justice

A reasonable manner by which to summarize the (ancient and contemporary) historic experience of the Jews is that of persecution. As a small tribe of people, they were easy prey for their larger more developed neighbours. Over the millennia, the story of Judaism is heavy with violence. Following some hundreds of years of low-level conflict with other nearby tribes, the Israelites were enslaved by the Egyptians in approximately 1700 BCE. They had to wait for over 400 years[5] before Moses – under God's direction – freed them and they entered the Promised Land. However, their Kingdom fell again six to seven centuries later and they were exiled in Babylon and later conquered by the Romans. Persecution continued with the Muslim conquest in CE 638, massacres by Crusaders in 1096, expulsion from England in 1290 (followed by expulsion from Spain in 1492), pogroms throughout the eighteenth and nineteenth centuries, and the Holocaust between 1933 and 1945.

Of course, the early Israelites were not only those being persecuted and there is no doubt that the Tanakh contains many graphic depictions of violence and war. For example, the Book of Esther takes great delight in describing the number of Persians that were killed when the Jews undertook a pre-emptive strike against them. The Tanakh also contains numerous accounts of the slaughter of newborn babies, the slaying of entire peoples, and various accounts of other war-time behaviours we would today label as atrocities (for example, see the conquest of Canaan described in Joshua). 'The Bible is full of rape, murder, incest, cheating and so on, and sometimes these acts are carried out by the heroes in the text' (Leaman, 2006, p. 132), although these are not always condoned and sometimes included in the story as object lessons of rebuke and moral failure, and in honesty about human weakness. Military or bellicose terms are widely utilized within the Tanakh (see Exodus 15: 3; Joshua 17: 1; Judges 20: 17; I Samuel 17: 33; II Samuel 17: 8; Ezekiel 39: 20). However, it is the periods of persecution that left the most indelible mark upon the Jewish character. Because of the violence of this early history, Judaism contains within it a longing for peace and a hope that justice and more compassionate times will evolve. Not only is peace a significant theme through the Tanakh, it is clear that this is God's desire for us (see Isaiah 2: 1–4; Job 25: 2; Micah 4: 1–5; Psalms 96; Proverbs 3: 17).

Judaism contains two notions: that God directly intervenes in the world at crucial times and that Jews are God's chosen people. As His chosen people, the Jews are recipients therefore of both His love and challenges – challenges especially in that God chooses repeatedly to use what happens to the Jews as a object lessons to the world. Throughout their history, the most powerful event that encapsulates their hope for justice was the Exodus from Egypt:

> The Exodus, that incredible event in which God liberated an unorganized, enslaved people from the mightiest power of the age, was not only the event that launched the Israelites as a nation. It was also the first clear act by which Yahweh's character was made known to them. (Smith, 1991, p. 304)

It was by God's grace that the Jews were delivered from the Egyptians (Exodus 12: 50; Deuteronomy 33: 29). God was powerful, but also good and loving. He was a God that provided hope.

Thus, while it is common to characterize the God of the Torah as harsh, unforgiving, militaristic, blood-thirsty, demanding, and so on, this depiction is in fact hollow. Rather, the times were harsh, unforgiving, militaristic, blood-thirsty, and demanding, but Yahweh (or Jehovah) cared for widows and orphans, lifted His people out of slavery, and seeks righteous behaviour and justice:

> It was I who taught Ephraim to walk, taking them by the arms; but they did not realize it was I who healed them. I led them with cords of human kindness, with ties of love; I lifted the yoke from their neck and bent down to feed them. How can I give you up, Ephraim? How can I hand you over, Israel? How can I treat you like Admah? How can I make you like Zeboiim? My heart is changed within me; all my compassion is aroused. (Hosea 11: 3–4, 8)

Understanding the evolution of this hope for justice requires initial consideration of the role of prophecy and prophets within Judaism. Unlike other religions, God's relationship with this people has been intermediated by numerous prophets who have spoken on behalf of God. While Jesus was the central figure of Christianity, Mohammed the primary figure of Islam, and Buddha the focus of Buddhism, Judaism has a long list of figures – many of whom we know and many of whom we no longer know by name – who have spoken for God.

Smith (1991) identifies three distinct prophetic movements. The first was the Prophetic Guilds in which prophecy was a result of a mass ecstatic state brought about through music and dancing (reminiscent of Dervish dancers). Pronouncements were not the primary purpose of these guilds, rather it was to lose one's own sense of self to a divine emotion:

> After that you will go to Gibeah of God, where there is a Philistine outpost. As you approach the town, you will meet a procession of prophets coming down from the high place with lyres, tambourines, flutes and harps being played before them, and they will be prophesying. The Spirit of the LORD will come upon you in power, and you will prophesy with them; and you will be changed into a different person. Once these signs are fulfilled, do whatever your hand finds to do, for God is with you. (I Samuel 10: 5–7)

The second movement was that of the Pre-Writing Prophets (known as this because while we know many of their names, they did not author any books). These prophets receive their divine visitations while alone (as compared to the Prophetic Guilds) and the message given to them is clear and specific. Speaking for God, these prophets began the cry for justice. God sent *ordinary* people to decry the actions of kings, those in power and whole cities.[6] This demand for justice was revolutionary and unprecedented:

> Then the word of the LORD came to Elijah the Tishbite: 'Go down to meet Ahab king of Israel, who rules in Samaria. He is now in Naboth's vineyard, where he has gone to take possession of it. Say to him, "This is what the LORD says: Have you not murdered a man and seized his property?" Then say to him, "This is what the LORD says: In the place where dogs licked up Naboth's blood, dogs will lick up your blood – yes, yours!"'. (I Kings 21: 17–19)

As Smith (1991) points out, this story is quite unique and has 'revolutionary significance' for humankind. An ordinary man confronts a powerful king on behalf of someone who has been wronged. Elijah has no official position in society – he is neither a priest, merchant nor politician. He is simply a man called upon by God to denounce the wrong actions of the king. His authority to speak against the injustice being meted out was entirely based on speaking on behalf of God. And it was indeed this divine authority resting within Elijah that allowed him to speak so courageously, but importantly, to have his message heard and accepted as 'just'. Rather than being immediately struck down by the king's guards, Elijah was heard and his message accepted by the king.

The third movement was the Writing Prophets. These prophets extended the challenge of individual corruption or wickedness to corrupt social order and unjust institutions. Prophets such as Amos, Hosea, Isaiah and so forth lived in a period of great social inequity, even in Israel. Power and wealth was concentrated in the hands of the few and the lives of the ordinary were traded cheaply:

> It was a world in which masters punished their slaves at will, women were subjugated to men, and unwanted children were abandoned to die in lonely places . . . Stated abstractly, the Prophetic Principle can be put as follows: The prerequisite of political stability is social justice, for it is in the nature of things that injustice will not endure. Stated theologically the point reads: God has high standards. Divinity will not put up forever with exploitation, corruption and mediocrity. (Smith, 1991, p. 291)

As children of God, even the most lowly widow and child must be afforded basic dignity and rights. In this short historical epoch, this relatively small number of prophets set out in no uncertain terms God's demand for justice.

However, justice is not easily delivered. Suffering often precedes justice and again, the Jewish history shows a spirit of optimism that is relevant for contemporary development. As a small nation, the Israelites were often subjugated by their foes since Moses delivered this new people. Following Assyria's conquest of the Northern Kingdom in 721 BCE and the capitulation of the Southern Kingdom to Babylon in 586 BCE, it would have been reasonable for the Israelites to question God's plan for them and perhaps even reject Him. Rather, they saw this suffering as an opportunity to learn the value of freedom, but more importantly to be a redemptive act for the world (Smith, 1991). When they were finally free from Babylon after nearly 50 years they sang of their joy: 'Leave Babylon, flee from the Babylonians! Announce this with shouts of joy and proclaim it. Send it out to the ends of the earth; say, "The LORD has redeemed his servant Jacob"' (Isaiah 48: 20–22). It was not just a lesson for the Israelites to learn. God meant for their captivity and subsequent release to be a lesson for all humanity down the ages:

> God was using them to introduce into history insights that all peoples need but to which they are blinded by ease and complacency. God was burning into the hearts of the Jews through their suffering a passion for freedom and justice that would affect all humankind . . . Stated abstractly, the deepest meaning the Jews found in their Exile was the meaning of vicarious suffering: meaning that enters lives that are willing to endure pain that others might be spared it. (Smith, 1991, p. 295)

> I, the LORD, have called you in righteousness; I will take hold of your hand. I will keep you and will make you to be a Covenant for the people and a light for the Gentiles, to open eyes that are blind, to free captives from prison and to release from the dungeon those who sit in darkness. (Isaiah 42: 6–7)

Turning to recent history, the Jews see the Holocaust as a significant defining event; some suggest it is on par with the Exodus and the Exile (Berkovits, 1977). While there have been a variety of responses and the debate continues, many have responded in terms similar to during the Exile. While there is no sense that the Holocaust was a punishment for breach of the Covenant, many choose to interpret it as part of God's redemptive message to the world (despite the enormous cost to his chosen people). They argue that the very survival of the Jews is argument for God's existence and care, and evidence of a reason to hope in even the worst circumstances.

It is not a far leap then from this role of carrying the inequities of the world to that of setting foundations of hope and progress, which are fundamental to modern development processes. Despite the long history of oppression, dispossession and apparent abandonment, the Israelites of the Talmud, an ancient central text of Judaism, and perhaps even in more contemporary times, have not forgone hope. It is perhaps this inherent sense that things will improve that Judaism has bequeathed current development thinking. This is not simply a hope tied to material comfort, but has a broader more spiritual element and social aspect. Indeed, the Judaic wait for their Messiah sits at the centre of this hope. Messianic tradition within Judaism is both very complex and fluid. Different sects have at different times conflated political as well as spiritual freedom within their expectations. Depending on their historical conditions, the importance of political freedom over spiritual enlightenment shifts and changes (Klausner, 1955). 'In periods when the Israelites were still living an independent political life in their own land, ethical perfection and earthly bliss were emphasized; whereas in periods of subjugation and exile the yearning for political freedom was more prominent' (Smith, 1991, pp. 298–9). That said though, the experience of persecution overlaid by the experience of the Exodus remained dominant touchstones within Judaism, which impacts their approach to life and provides insights into how the downtrodden must continue their cry for justice. Again, this is only furthered by the emphasis on the practice of the religion (orthopraxis) over correct belief (orthodoxy).

While this cry for justice is heard by God, it is not simply enough for humankind to pass all responsibility to God. Jews recognize that while there are over 600 laws set out in the Torah by which to live a righteous life, it is not simply enough to follow laws at the personal level – there is also a requirement to act in the best interests of one's society and community. There is thus a recognition that social responsibilities exist and any cry for justice must also involve the individual acting to improve the circumstances of their community. Thus, it is reasonable to argue that Judaism is primarily about deed, and it is only through appropriate actions that a righteous relationship with God can be realized.

According to Levinas (1990), it is not appropriate for a Jew to retreat into himself to pray to God, because it is only in society that God can be found: 'For Judaism, one can live a religious life if one responds to God by trying to bring about justice, if one responds to God by helping other human beings, which will result in his response to us being *hineni* (here I am) as in Isaiah 58: 8–9' (Leaman, 2006, p. 47). This 'mixed life' encourages scholarly devotion alongside manual labour. Thus, many great historical rabbis were also labourers, carpenters, and so on, and did not eschew *ordinary* day-to-day tasks for the monastic dedication to study.

Jews know that temporal existence is short-lived (see Psalm 103: 14; Job 4: 19; Ecclesiastes 3: 18–19), but because we are created by God, life is blessed. 'To speak of the hallowing of life in Judaism is to refer to its conviction that all life down to its smallest element can, if rightly approached, be seen as a reflection of the infinite source of holiness, which is God' (Smith, 1991, p. 301). Life though is also dependent on a social connection and this working together and undertaking collective action is life affirming. Life should be a celebration, but one that has God at its centre. The good that life may bring must be shared with God, for this sharing augments our joy.

Charity

As with other religions, charity is considered a virtue in Judaism. The most evident demonstration of God's charity is that of the Exodus and subsequent period of 40 years during which He provided food and water. Yet how humans might act in charitable ways is not explicitly defined in the Tanakh. Thus, we turn to the commentaries to gain a clear understanding of how to understand charity. One such commentary (by Maimonides) provides eight levels of charity:

1. The highest level . . . is that of one who assists a poor person by providing him with a gift or a loan or by helping him find employment – in a word, by putting him in a situation where he can dispense with other people's aid.
2. A step below this stands the person who gives alms to the needy in such a way that the giver does not know to whom he gives, and the recipient does not know from whom he takes. This is doing a good deed for its own sake.
3. One step lower is where the giver knows to whom he gives but the poor person does not know from whom he receives. Thus the great sages would go and secretly put money in the doorways of poor people.
4. A step lower is where the poor person knows from whom he is taking but the giver does not know to whom he is giving.
5. Lower than this is where someone gives a person a gift before he asks.
6. Lower still is one who gives only after the poor person asks.
7. Lower than this is one who gives less than is fitting, but does so with a friendly life.
8. The lowest level is one who gives ungraciously. (Maimonides, 1982 – *Hilkhot Matanot l'Ani'im* 10.1.7–14, cited in Leaman, 2006, pp. 12–13)

The hierarchy of charity is interesting as it suggests responsibilities of behalf of both those giving and receiving charity. As is reminiscent of the view of charity in Islam, it is clearly better to give charity than receive it, as the highest form of charity results in moving the recipient out of the situation that requires assistance in the first instance. In this sense there is no problem with someone becoming wealthy or owning and enjoying material possessions. This focus on moving people out of a dependent relationship on someone else approximates strongly with best practice in humanitarian assistance and development aid. Korten (1990) long ago noted the importance of community ownership of development interventions in his four typologies of non-governmental organizations (NGOs). Within Korten's stylized typologies, the continuum of (northern) NGO practice begins with the provision of relief and welfare services, progresses to the delivery of community development, moves from that to sustainable systems of development and then finally to become a people's movement. The implicit assumption within this continuum is that community participation increases throughout this progression and this is inherently right and proper. Community ownership within development interventions has now become widely accepted as the minimum requirement for successful and sustained development outcomes (see Chambers, 2005):

> It is interesting to speculate on why this is so significant and at the same time note that a good deal of Jewish charity has a very practical bent. The Society for Trades and Agricultural Labour (OTL) system was very effective in training Jews to learn an occupation from which they could support themselves. (Leaman, 2006, p. 13)

Not only is this practical in the sense of allowing someone to acquire the skills to find gainful employment, more importantly it also enhances the dignity of that person who is now working and supporting themselves (and perhaps their family and community). This at the same time allows those with less to keep their dignity (often preserved through anonymity), which is very important. Dignity is an important part of our well-being, often more important than wealth, and so it is important that the maintenance of dignity be stressed at all times. However, it is also important to note that being poor is not of itself a noble position. While taking advantage of the poor is expressly refuted in the Torah, it is also noted that the poor should NOT receive any specific favour in judgements.

Another example by which Jews are required to provide for others is the concept of the Jubilee year. Leviticus describes the year of Jubilee in which the fiftieth year is set aside as holy and in which debts are cancelled and liberty is provided to all:

> And if thy brother be waxen poor, and his means fail with thee; then thou shalt uphold him: as a stranger and a settler shall he live with thee. Take thou no interest of him or increase; but fear thy God; that thy brother may live with thee. Thou shalt not give him thy money upon interest, nor give him thy victuals for increase. I am HaShem your God, who brought you forth out of the land of Egypt, to give you the land of Canaan, to be your God. And if thy brother be waxen poor with thee, and sell himself unto thee, thou shalt not make him to serve as a bondservant. As a hired servant, and as a settler, he shall be with thee; he shall serve with thee unto the year of jubilee. Then shall he go out from thee, he and his children with him, and shall return unto his own family, and unto the possession of his fathers shall he return. For they are My servants, whom I brought forth out of the land of Egypt; they shall not be sold as bondmen. Thou shalt not rule over him with rigour; but shalt fear thy God. (Leviticus 25: 35–43)

This, of course, was the biblical source inspiring the recent Jubilee 2000 campaign,[7] which called for debt relief for the world's poorest countries.

Judaism and Gender

The issue of gender within Judaism is also worthy of brief discussion. It is possible to say that while some women have been very visible within the Tanakh, the role they have played has largely been secondary (Fonrobert, 2000). How this is mirrored in Jewish cultural and social practices depends largely on the Jewish tradition being considered (Segal, 2009). Within traditional practices (originating during the Talmudic period and now reflected within current Orthodox practices), women continue to hold roles that can be considered secondary to those of males: inability to fully participate in the synagogue, exclusion from scholarly study of the Tanakh and Talmud,[8] presumed responsible for primary family needs, and given a lesser expectation of ritual compliance around prayer. That said, there were certain rituals that were given to women, such as the kindling of Sabbath lamps and preparing the dough offering. Overall though, women in the Orthodox tradition hold a far more passive role compared with the active role assigned to males.

That being said, much of this lower status within religious lives reflects the social manifestation of community life in traditional times. 'The society that emerges from ancient Jewish texts is based on heterosexual, polygamous families' (Segal, 2009, p. 260). Marriage was a social convention that both protected women and promulgated community. Indeed, unlike Buddhism, Hinduism and Christianity, a preference for a monastic, celibate life is eschewed (for both men and women) within Judaism.[9] In some ways – akin to the discussion of marriage within Islam – women benefited from marriage. A pre-nuptial agreement (*ketubah*) guaranteed the rights of women throughout (and after) their marriage and divorce was understood as a legitimate option that would not carry stigma for either party. In non-orthodox or reformed tradition, the distinction between male and female is less evident. Women and men can both be called upon to read from the Torah in the synagogue, women can train as rabbis and marital roles reflect those of the secular society more than a religious tradition.

CONCLUSION

Judaism is the bedrock upon which Christianity and Islam have been built and it was the monotheistic nature of Judaism that changed the nature of how God is conceived by much of the world's population today. While we may question the contemporary influence of Judaism on the lives of the world's poor, there is no doubt that it has played a important role in emphasizing a cry for justice that is evident in both Christian and Islamic thinking, which is so relevant to all the world's poor regardless of religious belief or otherwise. The desire for change and the knowledge that injustice is ultimately unsustainable can provide succour for the oppressed. Whilst current circumstances may appear hopeless, the story of Judaism is hope based on justice that is God's desire. So while the importance of Judaism on the current circumstances of the world's poor might be less obvious than the other world religions, it has played a significant role in forming and shaping the understanding of the nature of hope and justice that are core to contemporary development thinking.

NOTES

1. Gentiles are those who are not of the Jewish chosen people. These seven laws are called the Noachide Laws and were given to Noah by God. Adherents must not worship idols, commit murder, steal, be sexually promiscuous, blaspheme, or eat flesh of animals while they are alive. Moreover, communities of adherents must themselves fashion their own just laws.

2. Moses' death is described in this book – 'And Moses the servant of the LORD died there in Moab, as the LORD had said' (Deuteronomy 34: 5) – even though Moses is said to have written this book himself.
3. In Hebrew, vowels were not originally written (Segal, 2009).
4. These are widely known as the Ten Commandments, but a more accurate translation would be the Ten Sayings, the Ten Statements, the Ten Declarations, the Ten Words or even the Ten Things.
5. Scholars are divided as to whether the 400 years is measured from the time of being enslaved or the time of Joseph and the emigration to Egypt (which would make the enslavement significantly shorter).
6. Of course, not all those called willingly accepted God's missive (though eventually they do): 'The word of the LORD came to Jonah son of Amittai: "Go to the great city of Nineveh and preach against it, because its wickedness has come up before me." But Jonah ran away from the LORD and headed for Tarshish. He went down to Joppa, where he found a ship bound for that port. After paying the fare, he went aboard and sailed for Tarshish to flee from the LORD' (Jonah 1: 1–3).
7. Jubilee 2000 evolved into the Make Poverty History campaign after 2000. Perhaps the greatest success of these two campaigns has been that of advocacy and lifting the issue of debt to international attention (see Barrett, 2000 and Make Poverty History and Micah Challenge, 2009).
8. There were, of course, exceptions to this. Two examples include the daughter of the Gaeon Rabbi Samuel ben Hohni who reportedly lectured on the Talmud to male students in the eleventh century, and a woman called Dulcie who gave public lectures on the Sabbath in the thirteenth century.
9. The only exception to this within Judaism are the Essenes 'who eschewed marriage out of misogynistic motives' (Segal, 2009, p. 260).

REFERENCES

Barrett, B. (ed.) (2000), *The World will Never be the Same Again*, London: Jubilee 2000 Coalition.
Berkovits, E. (1977), *Faith After the Holocaust*, New York: Von Nostrand.
Chambers, R. (2005), *Ideas for Development*, London: Earthscan.
Fonrobert, C. (2000), 'To increase Torah is to increase life', in J. Runzo and N. McMartin (eds), *The Meaning of Life in the World Religions*, Oxford: Oneworld.
Hegel, G. (1977), *Faith and Knowledge*, trans. by W. Cerf and H. Harris, New York: State University of New York Press.
Klausner, J. (1955), *The Messianic Idea in Israel*, New York: Macmillan.
Korten, D. (1990), *Getting to the 21st Century: Voluntary Action and the Global Agenda*, West Hartford, CT: Kumarian Press.
Leaman, O. (2006), *Jewish Thought*, New York: Routledge.
Levinas, E. (1990), *Difficult Freedom: Essays on Judaism*, trans. by S. Hand, Baltimore: John Hopkins University Press.
Maimonides, M. (1982), *Mishneth Torah*, Yale Judaic Series, New Haven, CT: Yale University Press.
Make Poverty History and Micah Challenge (2009), *Millennium Development Goal 8 Review Australia 2009*, Canberra: Make Poverty History and Micah Challenge, available at http://www.makepovertyhistory.com.au/getdoc/1c187606-9904-4b7a-8354-92e48ee19c4e/Goal8_report_web.aspx; accessed 29 January 2010.
Segal, E. (2009), *Introducing Judaism*, London: Routledge.
Smith, H. (1991), *The World's Religions*, San Francisco: Harper.
Steinberg, M. ([1947] 1975), *Basic Judaism*, Orlando: Harcourt Brace.

6 Hinduism and development

A. Whitney Sanford

INTRODUCTION

Hinduism is one of the world's oldest religious traditions and is the third largest tradition, following Christianity and Islam. The greatest population of Hindus live in the Indian subcontinent, comprising India, Pakistan, Sri Lanka, Nepal, and Bangladesh, although India is home to the vast majority of Hindus. Hindus comprise approximately 84 percent of India's population; Muslims approximately 13 percent, with the remainder a mixture of Buddhists, Sikhs, Jains, Christians, and Parsis. A significant, and growing, Hindu diaspora now resides in regions such as the Caribbean, Africa, Great Britain, and the United States.

This chapter illustrates the central texts, practices, and concepts of Hinduism, highlighting categories and concepts meaningful for Hindus. This discussion presents a broad overview of the tradition but focuses on those concepts that have or might shape attitudes towards development, for example, ethics and sacred geographies. Given these constraints, this chapter will not focus on areas such as the chronological development of Hinduism or its rich theological and philosophical traditions. To pursue any of these concepts in more depth or from alternate perspectives, the following works are excellent sources: Flood (1996), Mittal and Thursby (2004), Rinehart (2004), and Hawley and Narayanan (2006).

DEFINING HINDUISM

Encapsulating any religious tradition into a single chapter is always a challenge, but the sheer breadth and diversity of Hinduism complicate this task even more. The term Hinduism incorporates a remarkably broad and diverse collection of texts, theologies, rituals, and devotional practices that have developed over a period of at least 4000 years. Further, Hinduism has no singular definitive text, authority, or historical founder. While the Vedas (composed circa 1500–1200 BCE), a set of scriptures 'heard' by seers approximately 2500 years ago, contain the earliest teachings and ritual practices and are considered authoritative, the intervening centuries have produced theological, ritual, geographical, and caste differences that render any unifying description problematic. For this reason, some scholars prefer the term 'Hindu traditions' to convey this pluralism and to avoid reifying or privileging a particular set of practices or population.

Part of the confusion stems from the term 'Hinduism' itself. Originally, the term Hindu was a geographic designation, denoting the religious practices of the residents of the Indus Valley. Later, it designated Muslims from non-Muslims, and eventually, under British rule, 'Hinduism' became commonplace and the primary means to identify a set of religious practices (Rinehart, 2004, p. 1). Today, some practitioners use the term

Sanatana Dharma (Eternal Religion), but Hinduism continues as the term of popular usage. What we refer to today as Hinduism, in reality, describes a broad array of practices, deities, and philosophies, yet nonetheless, a set of shared vocabulary and practices provides coherence and unity. Similarly, despite Hinduism's theological pluralism, most of Hinduism's theologies and philosophies describe an essential unity that underlies the range of deities as well as material phenomena.

Hinduism, along with other non-biblical traditions, presents scholars with a secondary challenge – that many categories derived to explain the Abrahamic traditions, that is, monotheistic traditions tracing a lineage from the patriarch Abraham, for example, Judaism, Christianity, and Islam, do not adequately describe traditions such as Hinduism. The range of activities and concepts contained within the term Hinduism have altered how scholars understand the term religion itself. Early studies on comparative religion used concepts derived primarily from Christian and Protestant thought and privileged issues of faith and belief. For example 'What do Hindus believe?' was the central question. These studies did not consider 'religious' aspects of life, such as food, that are central to Hindu practice. In response, scholars and Hindus themselves often argued that 'Hinduism is not a religion, but a way of life' because Hindu thought and practice governs and shapes virtually all aspects of life, from theology to food practices. Exploring traditions such as Hinduism, Buddhism, and indigenous traditions has led scholars to expand concepts of what counts as religion, and this expansion has, in turn, shaped scholarship about the Abrahamic traditions.

TEXT, PRACTICE, AND ORALITY

Many of those curious about Hinduism ask about Hindu texts, for example, 'What is their book?' because text and scripture are central to the Abrahamic traditions, for example, the Bible and the Qu'ran. No one single book holds the pride of place in the Hindu tradition. The Vedas, the oldest and most authoritative texts, hold the greatest authority, but they are less relevant to daily devotional practices than are texts such as the tenth-century Bhagavata Purana, which details the life of and proper worship of the deity Krishna. The Upanishad, the latest of the Vedic texts (circa 800–400 BCE) are discussions that speculate about the nature of the soul (*atman*) and ultimate reality (*brahman*), and most subsequent Hindu theological and philosophical thought is grounded in explications of these ideas. Today, however, while these texts maintain a ritual authority, later works such as the Hindu epics or treatises dedicated to specific deities play far greater roles in Hindus' lives.

Hindus have emphasized orality and sound over the written text. For example, many texts are most efficacious when heard and performed, not read silently. 'Heard' and 'remembered' exist as two categories of Hindu sacred literature. Texts that were heard are considered revelatory and hold more authority than 'remembered' texts. The Vedas were 'heard' by ancient sages and were memorized and passed down orally. The Ramayana (fourth to fifth century BCE), a Hindu epic that illustrates the triumph of good over evil, is often chanted by groups of Brahman priests in temples on significant holidays. Although many temple-goers might not understand the original Sanskrit of the text, they do know the stories, and hearing the text brings merit. Chanting of works such as the epic Ramayana represents one aspect of orality; in this case, exact repetition of the words is critical, and many will memorize such works in their entirety. Oral narrative and performance, which allows for improvization and contextualization represents another facet of oral culture.

Scholars and others coming from the Abrahamic traditions have typically underestimated the importance of oral culture and have privileged the written word. However, many practices, norms, and values are not written in texts but are part of village or regional custom, for example, norms regulating marriage or women's behavior often derive from regional culture and are passed orally. Similarly, practices such as land and water use were governed by local custom that could be adapted to changing circumstances. Typically these rights were accorded to communities, not individuals (Hardiman, 2007, pp. 43–4).

This privileging of scripture and the written word has not only led to misunderstandings about non-Western religious traditions, but has reshaped these traditions in some notable cases. For example, the British sought to rule Hindus according to Hindu law, and the Laws of Manu (CE 100–200), a text that prescribes regulations for social living, gained great importance as the foundation of Indian law. Although this text and its commentaries were relevant for jurisprudence, custom, dictated by relevant caste and geographic factors, was also significant in guiding mores and behavior, but the British emphasis on text had a disproportionate effect on the Indian legal system. I echo the warnings of others regarding the 'mining' of texts for approaches to development or other issues. While texts have and can be used by Hindus and others to think through salient issues, the number of texts and the lack of any one central text should caution us to avoid privileging one text (Patton, 2000, p. 45; Narayanan, 2003, p. 131). With this caveat in mind, I will discuss concepts and texts that have provided a moral and legal framework for Hindu social thought.

BASIC CONCEPTS OF HINDUISM

Dharma

The concept of *dharma* is foundational for Hindu ethics and practice and provides theoretical and metaphorical structures for considering humans in relation to the cosmos, the divine, and other human beings. The concept of *dharma* does not have a parallel in English or in any Western religious or theological system:

> *Dharma* is propriety, socially-approved conduct in relation to one's fellow men or to other living beings (animals or superhuman powers). Law, social usage, morality, and most of what we ordinarily mean by religion, all fall under this head. (Creel, 1977, p. 2)

Dharma translates loosely as law, duty, and truth and denotes the moral, cosmic, and social order that humans are obligated to maintain. In that context, *dharma* also connotes 'the active realization of truth', and indicates the action of striving for or performing the truth. Humans and deities exist within the cosmic order and are bound through mutual obligation (Jamison and Witzel, 2002, pp. 67–9). *Dharma*, a nominalization of the verb 'to sustain', maintains and protects the moral and physical order.

According to the Hindu understandings of *dharma*, the universe functions in a predictable, cyclical order. That is, when things go well, seasons change, the sun rises and sets, and crops grow and later die. The moral, social, and cosmic orders are linked, and maintenance of the moral and social orders determines, in part, the continuation of the cosmic or natural order. When the moral order disintegrates, then the physical landscape deteriorates. This linkage persists in contemporary explanations for environmental degradation.

The moral, social, and physical realms are linked, meaning that moral and righteous behavior is necessary to sustain agricultural and earthly processes. While the concept of *dharma* is the subject of much theological and philosophical discussion, the most common use of the term indicates the duties incumbent on individuals, fulfillment of which holds together the physical and moral fabric of society (Dwivedi, 2003, p. 125). Dwidevi, who has written broadly on environmental stewardship in India, writes that:

> *dharma* can be considered an ethos, a set of duties, that hold the social and moral fabric together by maintaining order in society, building individual and group character, and giving rise to harmony and understanding in our relationships with all of God's creation. (Ibid., p. 123)

Dharma then includes not only duties and obligations within the social realm, but also those within the biotic community and so all beings are subject to moral consideration.

How does one determine what is dharmic and what would be the appropriate course of action in a given situation? Hindus draw upon a range of sources, including text, custom, narrative, and rules of conduct, that comprise what religion scholar Leela Prasad describes as a dynamic 'fluid text' that shapes ethical considerations (Prasad, 2007, pp. 118–19).

Themes of *dharma* and morality appear in most Hindu texts, but the *dharma* texts provide the most concentrated discussion of these norms. The dharma texts, the Dharmashastras and Dharmasutras (CE 100–200), and their subsequent commentaries provide the most comprehensive discussion of the principles of *dharma*. It is important to note that these texts were never actual laws, but prescriptive texts describing an ideal society, primarily from the point of view of Brahman males (Zelliot, 2004, pp. 245–6). These texts, including the Laws of Manu, detail behavioral rules and norms for virtually all aspects of life, including production of food, relations between men and women, and funerary rituals. In particular, these texts describe rules for different social units (the precursor of the caste system); men and women; and norms appropriate to one's stage of life, for example, student or householder. *Varnashramadharma* refers to the idea that one's *dharma* depends on both one's social role and stage of life. The term *varna* alludes to a four-fold social structure based on a division of labor first mentioned in the earliest Vedic texts, and each of these groups had specific duties and norms of behavior, for example. Brahmans – priests; Kshatriyas – kings and warriors; Vaishyas – merchants, artisans, and farmers; and Shudras – servants. *Dharma* was upheld by each of these groups, fulfilling their obligations. Over time, through inter-marriage, Hindu social structure became much more complicated, with exponentially more social units that are not uniform across India. When the Portuguese arrived in the fifteenth century they used the word '*casta*' (the derivation of the word caste) for India's social structure. While many in India do use the English word 'caste', the terms *jati* and *varna* are the indigenous terms. *Jati* is the more specific term and describes a social unit held together by common customs and food practices, in-group marriage, and usually occupation (Zelliot, 2004, p. 248).

Some Hindus cite *yamas* and *niyamas*, or restraints and observances, as providing a code of conduct for an ethical life and are foundational for spiritual progress. These rules first appeared in the Vedas, the earliest of the Hindu texts, but were expounded upon in later texts, including Patanjali's Yogasutras (circa 100 BCE–CE 500). The *yamas*, the 'don'ts', are balanced by the *niyamas*, 'the dos'. The *yamas* include: non-violence; truth; non-coveting; abstinence from inappropriate sexual behavior; patience; perseverance; compassion; honesty; appropriate diet; and purity. The *niyamas* include: modesty; satisfaction with what one has; charity; faith; study of the Vedas; developing spiritual knowledge; fulfilling sacred vows; recitation of mantras; and performing austerities. The *yamas* and *niyamas*, along with *dharma*, provide a flexible set of guidelines for religious practice as well as daily life that enable the individual to determine an appropriate course of action. Determining the right course of action is contextual, depending on the specifics of the situation itself and the individuals involved; for example, as noted above, *dharma* differs depending on conditions such as gender and age.

Dharma and Narrative Ethics – Hindu Epics

The contextual nature of *dharma* is strikingly different from most Western ethical systems, which have tended to focus on abstractions and universal principles. Story and narrative rather than abstract rules provide venues for deliberating the proper course of action, closer to the narrative ethics of philosophers Alisdair MacIntyre and Martha Nussbaum (Prabhu, 2007, p. 333; Sanford, 2012, p. 48) While Hindus draw guidance from a broad range of stories and myths, Hinduism's two epics, the Mahabharata (circa 400 BCE–CE 400) and the Ramayana (circa 4–500 BCE), are particularly instructive for considering issues of *dharma* and appropriate behavior.

These epics are often described as representing the battle between good and evil, but, in general, good and evil are understood as relative terms. Hinduism does not construe an absolute good or evil; theodicy has not been an issue in Hindu thought. Instead, these epics illustrate what the Hindu tradition sees as central human tensions: choosing to fulfill one's *dharma* vs. *kama*, or desire. The stories contained in the epics demonstrate how dilemmas of *dharma* are resolved in the context of specific situations.

The Mahabharata narrates the events surrounding the devastating war between the two families, the Pandavas and the Kauravas. The stories contained in the Mahabharata illustrate human emotions and actions and their consequences in the context of specific narratives, and the appropriateness of action is framed through those specifics. Over 100 000 verses, this rambling epic discusses the goals of human life and ruminates on human guilt and responsibilities while telling the stories of those involved in the war. This war leaves massive death and destruction and ushers in the Kaliyuga, the fourth of Hinduism's four cosmic time periods, the period in which we are in today. The Kaliyuga is characterized as a time of moral decay when humans are unable to uphold *dharma*, and Hindus consider our contemporary events in the context of the Kaliyuga.

The Ramayana narrates the story of the King Rama, an incarnation of the deity Vishnu, and Rama's wife Sita and brother Lakshman. This epic illustrates King

Rama's triumph over the demon Ravana, an illustration of good over evil. Like the Mahabharata, the Ramayana details views of the cosmos as well as theological and philosophical ideals. Perhaps most important for many Hindus, this epic sketches out ideals for behavior in the context of specific roles and relationships. Rama is considered an ideal king; his rule was just and fair, and he placed fulfilling his duty to his family and subjects over all considerations. The rule of King Rama, or Ram-rajya, is valorized as a golden era of kingship. His wife Sita's steadfast devotion to Rama renders her an icon for spousal devotion. These stories provide models for evaluating how one's behavior fulfills their particular *dharma*.

Karma

The rules of *dharma* are closely linked with the concept of *karma*, or action and its repercussions. Hindu thought, as well as Buddhist and Jain thought, has emphasized that human action typically results from desire for things like relationships or material goods. The bulk of human desire and the subsequent action is a result of attachment to one's own ego, for example, much of human action emerges from desire to assuage pride. Acting upon desires leads to a karmic debt that traps humans in an endless cycle of death and rebirth, or reincarnation. Further, *karma* determines the conditions of one's next birth, for example, the *jati* or gender into which one is born. Much Hindu thought and practice has focused on means to reduce desire and eliminate one's karmic debt. Yoga, for example, is a set of practices and philosophies designed to reduce desire and attachment to ephemeral things and attachments.

The Bhagavad-Gita (The Song of the Lord) is a central Hindu text, interspersed into the epic Mahabharata, composed between 200 BCE and CE 200, and is particularly important for Vaishnavas, those Hindus who worship the deity Vishna in his multiple descents to earth. It explicates *karma-yoga*, the path of action to spiritual liberation, and presents teaching on reducing ego attachment, and devotion to Krishna, a descent of Vishnu. The Bhagavad-Gita's teachings regarding selflessness and reducing ego attachments were particularly influential for Mohandas K. Gandhi and complemented his Jain values, for example, non-possessiveness and non-violence that also shaped his thought. The Bhagavad-Gita recounts the dialogue between the warrior Arjuna and his charioteer, the deity Krishna, on the eve of the great war between two families that both brings massive death and destruction and ushers the earth into the Kaliyuga, the era of immorality and decay. Arjuna asks how it could possibly be right to fight his family members on the battlefield, and Krishna offers a discourse about duty, selfless action, and devotion to god. For many Hindus, this text provides a guide to fulfilling one's various duties and acting in the world without selfishness. Further, these concepts offer resources to balance one's needs with the demands for consumption promised by global capitalism.

Renunciation and Reincarnation

Much Hindu thought has been dedicated to how one might avoid or eliminate accruing the karmic debt that traps one in the cycle of rebirth. Beginning in the sixth century BCE, scholars and others developed philosophies and practices of yoga and ascetic practices designed to reduce physical and mental attachments to things and ideas that were impermanent. These debates and discussions that comprise the Upanishads convey the realization that humans suffer because we become attached to ephemeral ideas and things and that these attachments urge us to act, thus accruing the karma that causes rebirth. Recognition that desire and attachments cause suffering brings wisdom about the true nature of the self and reality and prompts the individual to reduce these attachments. Reducing one's karmic debt, the individual achieves enlightenment or release, or *moksha*, from rebirth.

The Hindu tradition contains a significant ascetic strain, and some renunciants, or *sannyasins*, abandon society to pursue religious goals. Only a small percentage of Hindus take vows of *sannyas*, and most *sannyasins* take these vows when they have completed their household responsibilities, that is, when their sons have sons. The vows of *sannyas* are serious and permanent. The renunciant's family performs the necessary funerary rituals, and the renunciant is 'dead' to family and society. While themes of renunciation, yoga, and austerities have played a significant role in Hindu thought and practice, they have received a disproportionate share of scholarly attention, leading some to label Hinduism a 'world-denying' tradition. The philosophies and practices of yoga and renunciation are foundational for Hindu thought and practice, but devotion to deities, ritual practice, and festivals comprise a far greater proportion of Hindu religious life than do meditation and asceticism.

Devotion, Ritual, and Practice

One of the most important aspects of Hindu life and practice is devotion (*bhakti*) to the gods and goddesses of Hinduism. In answer to 'how many deities?', the stock answer of 330 million can be understood to suggest the effulgence and pervasiveness of divinity, that divinity overflows and cannot easily be contained. The Hindu cosmos contains a range of divine beings, including major divinities of the Hindu pantheon, for example, Siva, Krishna, and Ganesha; local village gods and goddesses; and semi-divine beings such as *nagas* (serpents) and *yakshas* (tree spirits). While most Hindu philosophies and theologies emphasize that an essential unity underlies these multiple representations of the divine, different deities are subjects of their own mythological, ritual, and theological traditions. Hindus can be broadly grouped into Saivas (those who worship Shiva), Vaishnavas (worshippers of Vishnu and his descents, for example, Ram and Krishna), and worshippers of Devi, the Goddess in her multiple forms. Worshipping one deity in the Hindu tradition does not mean denying the existence or power of other deities; typically, Hindus choose one deity over another through personal or family choice. Altars in homes and temples usually contain several different deities. Deities chosen for home altars reflect regional and familial preferences as well as individual choice.

Hindu ritual practices vary widely according region, caste, and social status, chosen deity, gender, and stage of life. Three generations living within the same household might each have different patterns of devotional ritual practice. The Hindu tradition reveals an enormous flexibility and adaptability to individual and community circumstances and thus no single authoritative text or body dictates ritual practice. Although there are numerous ritual manuals that describe and suggest how rituals should be performed, most are not obligatory.

The Ritual Calendar

Hindu ritual practices occur according to daily, monthly, and annual cycles; this circular view of time aligns with the Hindu concept of cosmic time. We might consider these elements as a series of concentric rings, or cycles, each of which determines specific elements of Hindu ritual life. The Hindu ritual calendar provides a guide as one goes through life. For example, the calendar provides a guide for when it is appropriate to perform life cycle rituals, for example, a child's naming ritual, marriage, and death rituals. Each moment is significant, and, depending on whether it is considered auspicious or inauspicious, guides the devotee in what activities are appropriate for any given time. This calendar informs Hindu ritual life from the public temple-based festivals such as those observed by scores of devotees to the private home and family-based rituals and vows primarily observed by women.

The Hindu ritual calendar largely follows the lunar calendar, which is based upon the cyclical waxing and waning of the moon. Since India adopted a solar calendar for civil use in 1957, most festival dates are now determined in both the more traditional lunar calendar as well as the solar calendar. Solar calendars reflect the lunar cycle as well; many temples, for example, each year publish pamphlets that provide both lunar and solar dates for festivals and events specific for that temple.

Each lunar month is divided into two parts: the light half (*shukla paksha*) when the moon is waxing and the dark half (*krishna paksha*) when the moon is waning. Typically, the bright half is considered auspicious or favorable, while the dark half of the month is less favorable or inauspicious. Many days of each month, such as the full moon day (*purnima*) and new moon day (*amavasya*), are significant for the ritual calendar as well. Most of these days each month are associated with a festival or ritual observance. Divali, for example, falls upon the *amavasya* or new moon day of the month Ashvin, the darkest night of the year. On this night, Hindus invite Lakshmi, Vishnu's consort and the goddess of prosperity, into their homes and businesses to gain prosperity in the coming year. Devotees keep rows of candles lit through the night to guide her way (Sanford, 2004).

Ritual Practice

Puja/seva

The smallest cycle of the ritual calendar is the daily one, and many Hindus perform daily rituals at home on an individual basis. Some of these rituals are done according to personal motivation and individual proclivities, while other rituals are prescribed according to one's social, caste, and gender status. For example, many Hindu families start the day with *puja* at home, worshipping the family's chosen deities. *Puja* (worship or offering) or *seva* (service) as many Hindus refer to it, is one form of honoring the divine. This ritual is performed on a daily basis by Brahman priests in temples and by ordinary people in their homes. The ritual occurs throughout the whole of India on behalf of the gods and goddesses of that country. It is based on the appropriate treatment of a guest in one's home. For the duration of the ritual, the deity is, in fact, a guest in one's home or temple. The following is a list of offerings that would be appropriate in a home or temple:

- offering flowers;
- offering food and water;

- offering water for a bath;
- a fresh change of clothes;
- washing the feet;
- offering light (*āratī*).

After the ritual is finished, devotees are offered *prasad*, the consecrated offerings. So, if a devotee has given flowers, the flowers will first be offered to the image then given back to the devotee. Many devotees will only eat food that has first been offered to a deity. When the devotee performs *seva* for an image of a deity, Krishna or Siva, for example, the devotee hopes to 'see', or take *darshan*, of the deity. This means that the image is not merely a symbol of divine, but the deity becomes manifest in the image when invoked by the devotee. So, some devotees have an actual vision of the divine at this time.

The incarnation of the deity in material form points to an important distinction between Hindu thought and that deriving from the biblical traditions. In Hindu thought, it is possible for the divine to manifest in the material world; divinity is both immanent and transcendent. Indeed, some Hindu theological traditions posit creation as an emanation of the divine, as opposed to *creatio ex nihilo*, that is, the world is not different from the divine. This tradition of sacred immanence in the world influences how Hindus view the material world both in religious and environmental terms.

Fasting

Certain days are also designated for fasting, depending on individual choices and on one's chosen deity. For example, Hindus may fast on certain days of the month such as *purnima* (full moon) and *ekadashi* (the 11th day of the fortnight). Fasts are an important aspect of Hindu ritual life, and there are many different types. In some cases, fasting simply means abstaining from certain types of foods, such as grains. Devotees fast for a variety of reasons. Some fast to honor a particular deity, while others fast to obtain a specific end, such as an end to a child's illness or to gain a child. Many women, in particular, fast to maintain the well-being of their family and to insure domestic tranquility. Fasts are considered efficacious, that is, fasting brings results. While fasts are a significant part of Hindu devotional life (especially for women), their importance is not reflected in the formal textual tradition of Hinduism. Instead, much of the information about fasts is passed down orally or through pamphlets available at temples and pilgrimage centers.

Festivals

Hindus follow a yearly cycle and observe a variety of festivals and holidays. This section will describe some of the major festivals as the year cycles through the changing seasons. Most festivals commemorate events from Hinduism's rich mythology. India was and still is largely based on an agrarian lifestyle and economy. Even in urban regions, festivals reflect their rural roots.

Nag Panchami

The festival Nag Panchami, or Snake's Fifth, is an annual ritual that has agricultural significance, hence its inclusion in this discussion. In the Hindu cosmos, *nagas* (serpents) belong to a class of semi-divine beings, or *devatas*. They reside in the subterranean waters and help move water according to the agricultural cycle. They are also known to be capricious and petulant, and devotees must take pains to placate them. Many Hindus will make offerings to these beings throughout the year; it is particularly important on Nag Panchami.

Ritual practice during Nag Panchami makes peace with snakes on the fifth day of the dark half (the fortnight in which the moon is waning) of the lunar month of Shravan (August–September). Shravan falls within the rainy season when most of India is lush and green. On Nag Panchami, farmers do not plow the land to avoid inadvertently harming a snake. They offer snakes milk and crystallized sugar – known favorites – to avoid being bitten by a snake for the coming year (Singh and Nath, 1999, p. 118). This reflects the reality that snakebite is a significant cause of death in India and also that agricultural activities such as plowing can harm or kill snakes. Many lakes or ponds have a resident *naga* deity to whom propitiatory peace offerings can be made when necessary. Supplicants leave offerings such as milk at anthills because anthills are believed to be the entrances to serpents' dwelling places (Alter, 1992, p. 137; Sanford, 2012, p. 66). In South India, Hindus build images of snakes out of cow dung on either side of the entrance to the house to welcome the snake god. Some go to anthills, a place where snakes reside, to worship the snake. Others build a five-hooded snake out of substances including turmeric powder, sandalwood and saffron (Alter, 1992, p. 137).

Dussehra

Dussehra, the tenth day of the bright half of Ashvin (September–October), honors Rama's victory over the demon Ravana. This day is marked by large-scale dramas known as Rama Lila, which enact the hero god Rama's life. The highlight of the day is when devotees explode effigies of the demon Ravana and his brother and son, which have been stuffed with firecrackers. Thousands of spectators cheer the demise of the demons.

Divali

Divali (or Dipavali), the festival of lamps, is a highlight of the fall season, with celebrations lasting for five days. Divali is truly a festival of the home, and most *pujas* and festivities occur within the home and family. Families and friends exchange gifts and sweets, and firecrackers explode continuously for the duration of the festival. Everyone wears new clothes. Divali itself falls on the *amavasya*, or new moon day of Ashvin. Like many festivals, the Divali period celebrates events significant to different parts of India and different deities. For example, Divali commemorates Rama's return to Ayodhya after slaying the demon Ravana and his coronation as king, as well as honoring Lakshmi, the goddess of wealth.

Pilgrimage

Many Hindus consider pilgrimage to sacred sites or personages an extremely important aspect of the tradition. Some pilgrimages might be undertaken annually, dictated by the ritual calendar, and others might be a once in a lifetime experience. The Indian subcontinent is dotted with pilgrimage destinations, and the concept of sacred geography is important within the Hindu tradition. The region of Braj, for example, a cultural and linguistic region southeast of Delhi, is considered the home of the deity Krishna when he lived upon the earth 5000 years ago. Devotees travel from all over India to visit sites and temples that commemorate his time upon the earth.

The land of India (Bharat) is itself sacred, and each of India's four cardinal points is a pilgrimage destination. Pilgrims might visit these four sacred sites (*char-dham*) of Rameshwaram in the south, Puri in the east, Dwarka in the west, and Badrinath in the north. Badrinath is also one of the four pilgrimage destinations in the Himalayas that are considered the home of the deity Shiva. Pilgrims visit Badrinath, Yamunotri (the source of the Yamuna River), Gangotri (the source of the Ganges River), and Kedarnath in the summer months when the snows have melted.

While all four of these sites are important, Yamunotri and Gangotri are particularly significant because they are the sources of two of India's most important rivers. Materially, the Yamuna and Ganges rivers provide much of the water for north India and are thus critical for agriculture, among other things. Theologically, however, according to Hindu thought, rivers are considered the incarnation of the Goddess, and visiting the sources of these great rivers is an act of great religious significance. Many Hindus also start the day with a ritual bath in a sacred river such as the Yamuna or the Ganges. Water absorbs and washes away impurities, and so this bath is believed to wash away one's transgressions.

Purity–Pollution/Auspicious–Inauspicious

The axes of purity and pollution and auspicious and inauspicious play critical roles in shaping social relations, food and hygienic practices, and timing of events and rituals. The details of applying these concepts differs according to region and social status, but the importance of purity and auspiciousness cannot be underestimated for both religious and social practice. Imagine a Cartesian diagram with purity–pollution as the x-axis, and auspicious–inauspicious as the y-axis. Events might be plotted anywhere on this diagram, depending on the specifics of the event and the individuals involved.

Purity/pollution

India's hierarchical social structure determines the inherent purity of an individual. Brahmans, the priestly class, for example, are more pure than the other classes, in descending order. Similarly, males are inherently more pure than females. Many aspects of life, including food preparation and hygienic practices, revolve around maintaining purity and not coming into contact with pollution. Rules of purity determine what foods can be eaten and how they should be prepared and with whom one might eat. Brahmans, for example, will only eat food prepared by a cook of similar status. Norms of commensality (eating at the same table) have traditionally been strict, although modern social structures and the blend of people in urban contexts has softened these rules. Traditionally, in rural regions, a village might have three wells – one each for Brahmans, the three lower castes, and 'untouchables', those outside the social structure. Water's permeability makes it a vehicle for washing away and transferring pollution. Pollution can also be a transitory phenomenon, resulting from events such as illness or death, childbirth, and menstruation. Typically, individuals remain in seclusion during and/or after these occurrences for a prescribed period of time.

Auspicious/inauspicious

It is equally important to maintain a state of auspiciousness. Similar to the purity and pollution dichotomy, auspiciousness can either be a prolonged state or can refer to the timing of events and rituals. Marriage is considered an auspicious state, especially once a woman has born a son, and for women, there is little more important than preserving this auspicious state. In the Hindu tradition, it is a woman's responsibility to maintain her family's health, particularly that of her husband, and she is considered to have the power to do so. Women have a considerable power, or *shakti,* and, according to the Hindu tradition, this power is auspicious when a woman is married because she can use this power to maintain her family. Women gain this power through practices such as fasting observances or *vrats*. Her power only becomes inauspicious or threatening when she is not in the state of marriage. A widow is considered inauspicious and is viewed with great suspicion because she did not protect her husband. Women have power to create life, and this power, when not subject to control, can be dangerous to social stability and so is perceived as demonic (Gold, 2000, pp. 212–13).

Similarly, all dates for rituals, festivals, and life cycle rituals must be calculated according to a complicated set of criteria if they are to be auspicious and efficacious. Each day has a planetary association, reflecting the importance of astrology within Hindu practice. Additionally, most days of the week are considered auspicious or inauspicious for any given activity. While these prohibitions are not specifically 'religious', they structure devotees' lives and daily activities in a variety of areas. It is important to know these days – or to consult someone who does – because specific times of the day, month, and year are often either auspicious or inauspicious for any given activity. For example, the day of the new moon is inauspicious for marriages (Raheja, 1988, p. 41).

HINDU PERSPECTIVES ON DEVELOPMENT THEMES

Like most religious traditions, it is impossible to designate a single approach to any given topic – gender or charity, for example. Positions on broad themes differ both according to one's sectarian perspective and also according to one's social position within the tradition. Nonetheless, we can start with one Hindu definition of development provided by ICOREC (International Consultancy on Religion, Education, and Culture) that resonates with contemporary discussions of the triple bottom line of sustainability: 'A process of enabling sustainable livelihood in harmony with natural resources as the foundation for spiritual progress' (Tyndale, 2005, p. 84).

Tyndale cites Indian development expert Kamla Chowdry echoing the necessity of a paradigm shift, that ethics, not simply economics, should guide development. Chowdry states that:

> eradication of hunger and poverty is not merely an intellectual exercise of science, technology, or economics, but also involves an inner change. To alter the system, it is necessary to alter the paradigm of development, and to take cognizance of the spiritual, of the inner voice, of the ethics and values that promote sustainable development. (Ibid.)

Her words reflect the values and practices of Mohandas (Mahatma) Gandhi and his follower Vinoba Bhave, both of whom integrated religious values into their work with the poor and marginalized populations of India. They set up educational centers and programs designed to provide economic and social opportunities in the context of village life. Gandhi and Bhave both described their work as *seva* and understood this work in a context of humility and reciprocity (Kumar, 2005, p. 35). As activist Satish Kumar notes, the word 'development' connotes patronage or one-sidedness whereas *seva*, or service, indicates relationship and mutual benefit (ibid.). Similarly, Rebecca Klenk argues that much development literature identifies categories such as 'peasants' and 'women' as problems to be solved rather than assessing the lived experiences of the people in these categories (Klenk, 2004, p. 61). Rebecca Klenk's work with Gandhian activists demonstrates that rural women contested both descriptions of 'development' and the nature of their problems (ibid.).

Social Justice and Equity

Hindu thought, with its traditional underpinnings of *varna/jati* and *dharma*, exists in tension with modern and contemporary goals of social equity and justice, especially those enshrined in India's Constitution (Coward, 1989, pp. 33–4; Prabhu, 2007, p. 332). Indian society is hierarchical and highly stratified, and many Hindus attribute their role in society to meritorious behavior and adherence to *dharma* in previous circumstances. Traditionally, the laws of *karma* have been used to justify the situation of women and the lower classes. Further, the goals of *dharma* are social and cosmic stability, sustaining order by performing one's duty in the context of a pre-existing 'order of right'. This framework has prevented India from developing systemic notions of distributive justice (ibid.).

This tradition means that contemporary India has had to balance traditional social concepts with modern concepts such as equality of all beings and the individual. Numerous modern Hindu thinkers, including Swami Vivekananda, have argued that *karma* instead offers a freedom and agency to the individual (Coward, 1989, pp. 31–2). Discussions over women's rights in the Indian Constitution exemplify this tension. In pre-Independence India, many women argued for a uniform civil code that would deal with matters such as divorce, inheritance, and marriage, equally for the entire population. However, bowing to pressure primarily from religious conservatives, the Hindu Code Bill created separate civil codes such that Muslims, Hindus, and Christians would each be governed by their respective religious laws, thus effectively enshrining the most conservative views (Jain, 1986, pp. 256–7).

Throughout history, India has certainly seen numerous movements towards broader social inclusion and equity. The Hindu devotional movement that spread throughout India from the tenth through the sixteenth centuries emphasized an equality of all before the divine, and, in the process, opened up space for women and those of lower social status to participate. Devotional thought was transmitted in the different vernaculars, rather than Sanskrit, accessible only to Brahman males, and rituals could be performed in homes by lay people. Importantly, myths and songs emphasized the preference of the divine for the humble piety of the dispossessed.

In the twentieth century, Mohandas K. Gandhi championed the strength of women, the poor, and the marginalized, and interpreted his work with these populations in the context of *seva* (Kumar, 2005, p. 36). He blended aspects of Hindu tradition with modernity's emphasis on the efficacy and responsibility of the individual. Gandhi himself never renounced the caste system, unlike his contemporary Ambedkar, and while many consider him an icon of social justice, others have heavily criticized Gandhi for this lapse. The Indian Constitution, enacted in 1949, declared illegal both discrimination based on caste as well as the status of untouchability (Zelliot, 2004, p. 267).

Gender, Education, and Health

In India's highly stratified society, women have typically been subordinated to men in most aspects of life. Certainly many women, especially those of higher social rank, do have great access to power and means, but, in general, women have had less access to education and control of property and resources. We cannot, though, look at women as a homogeneous category; women's situations differ according to a range of factors including social status, wealth, and stage of life. For example, a Dalit woman is likely to experience at least two levels of exclusion from basic needs, such as water and education (Ahmed, 2005, p. 2).

By and large, India has demonstrated a marked preference for sons over daughters. This preference results, in part, from the eldest son's predominant role in Hindu funerary rituals. The son's ritual actions that insure his ancestors do not go to a form of hell elevate his status relative to his sisters.

In the economic sphere, daughters have come to be viewed as a drain on family income. First, a daughter is considered to be part of her husband's family, thus investing in a son provides continued benefits. A common saying likens caring for daughters to watering flowers in a neighbor's yard. Additionally, over time Indian weddings have become increasingly lavish, and one or more of these weddings brings on enormous expense. Further, grooms' families have come to expect larger gifts, cars or scooters, depending on the wealth of the family, often pushing the bride's family into debt. These expenses lead some families to put money towards the culturally required dowry rather than education.

In India, scholars such as Ann Gold (2000) and Bina Agarwal (1995) have documented women's songs and practices of resistance to male authority and property ownership. Gold notes that she, among other scholars, has observed women's resistance to their scripted roles, but that these women's practices – and research documenting them – are marginalized in social and academic contexts (Gold, 2000, pp. 208–10). Some of this academic marginalization resulted from reliance on Sanskrit texts and male Brahmans as authorities on Hindu religious practices, but scholarship over the past 20 years has been much more open to oral culture and narrative as well as ethnographic explorations of women's rituals, practices, and social roles. This contemporary scholarship has opened up women's worlds and provided a more balanced understanding of Hindu thought and practice.

Exploring local customs, rather than over-reliance on prescriptive texts such as the Dharmashastras, illustrates women's roles and practices. While this has no textual reference, many Hindu women partake in a form of seclusion, or *purdah*, especially those of higher castes or rural women. This form of seclusion is especially incumbent on newly married women in their new villages who are most likely to live in extended multi-generational households. In her new home and village, a married women is expected to show shame, or *lajj*, in front of her new family, especially her in-laws. This behavior includes refraining from speaking, especially in front of one's father-in-law and casting one's eyes downward. Over time, as she becomes integrated into her new family, these restrictions will ease. At least for her early years, the new bride is the most subordinate member of the family. The combination of seclusion and subordinate status affects women's access to health care, including family planning.

Women, especially daughters and daughters-in-law perform a disproportionate percentage of the family's labor, and most of this work falls into the domestic, unpaid category. For example, young women are responsible for obtaining water for daily needs, including water for food, agriculture, and sanitary/health needs. This economic necessity makes many families unwilling or unable to send their daughters to school (Ahmed, 2005, pp. 18–21). The young bride performs much of the family's labor, including getting water from the village well, if necessary, and rising early to make food for the family. Understanding women's roles in the family sheds light on specific vulnerabilities as they change over time (Adato and Meinzen-Dick, 2007, pp. 28–32, 332). In discussions regarding development and economic opportunities, women critiqued both the familial and transnational structural inequities that denied them access to wider markets and caused economic hardship (Klenk, 2004, pp. 68–9).

Environment

The natural world plays a large role in Hindu thought and practice, and both Hindus and scholars of Hinduism have cited the mythological and ritual role of plants and animals as evidence of an appreciation of the environment. In practice, however, regardless of sacred text, India's rivers have become polluted, and the mountains deforested. For example, by the time the Yamuna River reaches the pilgrimage city of Vrindavan, her waters have been sadly depleted by agriculture, and the remaining flow is toxic with pollutants from upstream Delhi (Haberman, 2006, pp. 14–15). The case of rivers is particularly instructive because it demonstrates the adaptability and flexibility of Hinduism.

As noted above, rivers are considered the embodiment of the Goddess and are thus sacred; rivers are the equivalent of the mother, a highly esteemed position in the family. One line of argument asks how one could pollute one's mother, that one's mother deserves respect. Vasudha Narayanan cites an apt agricultural metaphor in her discussion of devotion to the River Kaveri as a mother. When the Kaveri River is swollen with the monsoon rains that will feed the new crops, devotees say she is pregnant and indulge her 'pregnancy food cravings' when they picnic on the banks of the river and consider that Kaveri Amman (the mother) is their guest (Narayanan, 2003, pp. 136–7). Devotees respond to the river's needs, and the river maintains agricultural productivity. However, although rivers are also seen as purifying, the theme of the indulgent mother who cleans up after her (polluting) children is not particularly helpful ecologically. This idea has emerged in efforts to clean up the Ganges River in Varanasi, India, where the idiom of river as mother is a double-edged sword. While many devotees claim that dirtying one's mother is wrong, others maintain that Mother Ganga is eternally tolerant and will clean up after her errant children (ibid.; Alley, 2003, pp. 143–4).

The scope of environmental degradation in India, however, has led to great concern both from religious perspectives as well as health perspectives. The Yamuna's pollution has made it difficult for Hindus to take ritual baths, and massive deforestation in the Himalayas has led to landslides that have killed those on pilgrimage. In response, numerous movements have emerged to save India's rivers, trees, and forests. The Clean Ganga Campaign in Varanasi works closely with the head priest of Sankat Mochan Temple, one of the most important temples in that city; this priest is also an engineer at nearby Benares Hindu University (Alley, 2003, p. 153). In Vrindavan, priests, devotees, and activists have worked to restore the Yamuna's flow and clean her waters, and devotion to the deity Krishna provides the impetus for their actions (Haberman, 2006, pp. 149–56). Additionally, many temples or sacred sites have developed programs to preserve their local waters and trees. That the land, plants, and trees surrounding temples are considered sacred provides a rationale. Venkateswara, one of the wealthiest temples in India, offers saplings as *prasad* so that devotees can plant a sacred remnant at home and offers special treatment for devotees who donate for the purchase of trees and plants (Narayanan, 2003, pp. 132–5). Further, this new activism demonstrates possibilities for the involvement of priests.

Charity, Poverty, and Gifts

Practices of charity and gifts lie in the balance between Hindu notions of compassion and *dharma*. Compassion is a principal theme of the Hindu tradition, and it is incumbent on Hindus to act compassionately towards all living beings. Gifts (*dana*), and how one gives gifts, also play a central role in the Hindu moral universe (Heim, 2007, p. 192). First, the Hindu laity is responsible for gifts to monks, nuns, and Brahman priests, and these gifts bring the donor merit. Merit is, in part, determined by the perceived worthiness of the recipient, so gifts to recipients such as Brahmans have greater merit than those directed to the poor, who are not considered worthy of such gifts. According to the karmic system, the poverty results from moral failings (Heim, 2007, pp. 194, 198). *Dana* flows upward, is not a reciprocal exchange, and does not include gifts made based on compassion rather than worthiness. For example, the epic Mahabharata states that 'the lame, the blind, the deaf, the mute, and the diseased should be maintained but not given formal gifts' (ibid., p. 199). Outside this formal theory of gifts, Hindus are enjoined to care for the weakest and most vulnerable.

Hindu texts have not addressed poverty as a broad theme. The Hindu system of karmic justice has led some to consider poverty a trap of one's own making, but the shifts of the twentieth century have weakened the power of the karmic system as sole explanation for one's fate. Mohandas K. Gandhi's campaign to help India's poor helped many to understand the social and economic structures that trapped these large numbers in crushing poverty. Prior to the modern period, poverty was seen as inevitable, an outcome of the traditional system of *dharma* and the social order. The twentieth century brought much social dislocation, but also the possibility that humans could control social conditions (Creel, 1977, p. 37).

CONCLUSION

This chapter has stressed the diversity and flexibility of the Hindu tradition, and it should not be surprising that assessing whether Hinduism is in harmony or contradiction with concepts and practices of development would be extremely difficult, if not impossible. Watching India's rise from Independence to today, where India boasts the world's largest middle class and is on the forefront of scientific discovery, it seems clear that Hinduism has adapted to modern challenges and opportunities. While Hindus retain many traditional values, they have also embraced new opportunities and the mobility that has led to changes in most sectors, including transportation, health, and education. In making ethical decisions, Hindus weigh the different factors and address the issue in its context, and questions of development will likely be addressed in situ and according to the specifics of the situation. In considering the issue of genetically modified (GM) foods, for example, Hindus might accept GM foods out of compassion for the needs of the hungry but consider them unacceptable in religious ritual. Similarly, the dharmic requirements of begetting ten sons has eased, given population pressures (Crawford, 1995, p. 195). The Hindu tradition holds rich resources for decision-making and considering the merits of specific development projects.

REFERENCES

Adato, Michelle and Ruth Meinzen-Dick (eds) (2007), *Agricultural Research, Livelihoods, and Poverty*, Baltimore: The Johns Hopkins University Press (published in cooperation with the International Food Policy Research Institute).

Agarwal, Bina (1995), *A Field of One's Own: Gender and Land Rights in South Asia*, Cambridge, UK: Cambridge University Press.

Ahmed, Sara (2005), 'Why is gender equity a concern for water management', in *Flowing Upstream: Empowering Water Management Initiatives in India*, Ahmedebad: Centre for Environmental Education.

Alley, Kelly (2003), 'Idioms of degeneracy: assessing Ganga's purity and pollution', in Richard C Foltz (ed.), *Worldviews, Religion and the Environment*, Belmont, CA: Wadsworth/Thompson, pp. 143–60.

Alter, Joseph S. (1992), *The Wrestler's Body: Identity and Ideology in North India*, Berkeley: University of California Press.

Coward, Harold. G. (1986), 'Purity in Hinduism', in Harold G. Coward (ed.), *Hindu Ethics: Purity, Abortion, and Euthanasia*, New York: SUNY Press, pp. 71–130.

Crawford, S. Cromwell (1995), *Dilemmas of Life and Death. Hindu Ethics in North American Context*, New York: SUNY Press.

Creel, Austin (1977), *Dharma in Hindu Ethics*, Columbia, MO: South Asia Books.

Dwivedi, O.P. (2003), 'Dharmic ecology', in Richard C. Foltz (ed.), *Worldviews, Religion and the Environment*, Belmont, CA: Wadsworth/Thompson, pp. 119–29.

Flood, Gavin (1996), *An Introduction to Hinduism*, Cambridge, UK: Cambridge University Press.

Gold, Ann Grodzins (2000), 'From demon aunt to gorgeous bride: women portray female power in a North Indian festival cycle', in Julie Leslie and Mary McGee (eds), *Invented Identities: The Interplay of Gender, Religion and Politics in India*, Delhi: Oxford University Press, pp. 203–30.

Haberman, David (2006), *River of Love in an Age of Pollution: The Yamuna River of Northern India*, Berkeley: University of California Press.

Hardiman, David (2007), 'The politics of water scarcity in Gujurat', in Amita Baviskar (ed.), *Waterscapes: The Cultural Politics of Natural Resources*, Uttaranchal: Permanent Black, pp. 40–64.

Hawley, John S. and Vasudha Narayanan (eds) (2006), *The Life of Hinduism*, Berkeley, CA: The University of California Press.

Heim, Maria (2007), '*Dana* as a moral category', in Purushottama Bilimoria, Joseph Prabhu and Renuka Sharma (eds), *Indian Ethics: Classical Traditions and Contemporary Challenges*, Farnham, Hampshire: Ashgate Press, pp. 192–209.

Jain, Devaki (1986), 'Building a common foundation for social change', in Diana L. Eck and Devaki Jain (eds), *Speaking of Faith*, New Delhi: Kali for Women, pp. 255–70.

Jamison, Stephanie and Michael Witzel (2002), 'Vedic Hinduism', 65–113, available at: www.people.fas.harvard.edu/~witzel/vedica.pdf; accessed 10 July 2012.

Klenk, Rebecca (2004), '"Who is the developed woman?": women as a category of development discourse, Kumaon, India', *Development and Change*, **35**(1), 57–78.

Kumar, Satish (2005), 'Development and religion: cultivating a sense of the sacred', in Makarand Paranjape (ed.), *Dharma and Development. The Future of Survival*, New Delhi: Samvad India Foundation, pp. 33–42.
Mittal, Sushil and Gene Thursby (eds) (2004), *The Hindu World*, New York: Routledge.
Narayanan, Vasudha (2003), 'Wood, wind and wisdom: ecological perspectives from the Hindu tradition', in Richard C. Foltz (ed.), *Worldviews, Religion and the Environment*, Belmont, CA: Wadsworth/Thompson, pp. 130–43.
Patton, Laurie L. (2000), 'Nature romanticism and sacrifice in Rgvedic interpretation', in Christopher Key Chapple and Mary Evelyn Tucker (eds), *Hinduism and Ecology: The Intersection of Earth, Sky and Water*, Cambridge, MA: Harvard University Press, pp. 39–58.
Prabhu, Joseph (2007), 'Reflections of moral ideals and modernity: Gandhi and nonviolence', in Purushottama Bilimoria, Joseph Prabhu and Renuka Sharma (eds), *Indian Ethics: Classical Traditions and Contemporary Challenges*, Farnham, Hampshire: Ashgate Press, pp. 329–37.
Prasad, Leela (2007), *Poetics of Conduct Oral Narrative and Moral Being in a South Indian Town*, New York: Columbia University Press.
Raheja, Gloria Goodwin (1988), *The Poison in the Gift. Ritual, Prestation and the Dominant Caste in a North Indian Village*, Chicago: University of Chicago Press.
Rinehart, Robin (2004), 'Introduction. The historical background', in R. Rinehart (ed.), *Contemporary Hinduism: Ritual, Culture, and Practice*, Santa Barbara, CA: ABC-CLIO, pp. 1–66.
Sanford, A. Whitney (2004), 'The ritual calendar', in R. Rinehart (ed.), *Contemporary Hinduism: Ritual, Culture, and Practice*, Santa Barbara, CA: ABC-CLIO, pp. 123–54.
Sanford, A. Whitney (2012), *Growing Stories from India: Religion and the Fate of Agriculture*, Lexington, KY: University Press of Kentucky.
Singh, Chitralekha and Prem Nath (1999), *Hindu Festivals, Fairs and Fasts*, New Delhi: Crest Publishing House.
Tyndale, Wendy (2005), 'Poverty and development: is religion relevant?', in M. Paranjape (ed.), *Dharma and Development. The Future of Survival*, New Delhi: Samvad India Foundation, pp. 82–93.
Zelliot, Eleanor (2004), 'Caste in contemporary India', in R. Rinehart (ed.), *Contemporary Hinduism: Ritual, Culture, and Practice*, Santa Barbara, CA: ABC-CLIO, pp. 243–72.

7 Sikhism and development: a perfect match?*

Darshan S. Tatla

INTRODUCTION

This chapter examines how Sikhism has influenced the economic outlook and social ethos of its followers by examining relevant literature. At its most general level, the review raises the question of whether the Sikh tradition is compatible with or hinders development, as generally understood in the mainstream 'development discourse' (Nkurunziza, 2007). This question is discussed by examining the nature of Sikhism, its evolution over time and the values, beliefs and practices of its adherents. Religious values, beliefs and practices not only affect economic life, they also influence social relationships at family, community and societal levels. For example, membership of a religious group can and does affect livelihood decisions, a person's sense of social inclusion or exclusion, and the ways and means of social and political engagement. Given the social composition of a particular community, the question arises of whether and how some groups are discriminated against, how various social groups feel about their social position and the reactions of those who feel marginalized. Ideas of inclusion or exclusion within a religious tradition are particularly relevant, given the dominance of Jat Sikhs.

The chapter outlines Sikh religious values and beliefs that influence the actions of both individuals and the various social groups that make up Sikh society. The chapter notes how in recent times the Punjab economy, especially its agrarian sector, has undergone a form of capitalist development. Many observers have attested that the Sikh peasantry was largely responsible for the success of this 'green revolution'. While this transformation has invited many commentaries, especially from economists, the role of religion in agrarian change and the developmental process has attracted little attention. Nevertheless, the developmental phase of Punjab's economy provides enough data and field studies to see how Sikhism has provided a particular understanding of 'development' and how far the 'work ethics' of its adherents are relevant to the economic changes observed.

SIKHISM AND ITS FOLLOWERS

Sikhism has been described in various ways. However one decides to define it, Sikhism, has over the course of its 500 years' history, acquired all the ingredients of what sociologists recognize as a religion: a system of belief centred on a sacred book, religious institutions known as *gurdwaras*, a set of beliefs and ritual practices, and an ethical discourse based upon its teachings and beliefs. As such, Sikhism is now generally acknowledged as the youngest religion on the world scene, with Punjab as the homeland of its followers, the Sikhs.

Although, like most other religions of the world, Sikhism is predominantly concerned with people's quest for God, it departs radically from other Indic religions, which invariably advocate some degree of renunciation of the world to achieve the spiritual ideal. Sikhism, in contrast, situates salvation in this world. Its theology, the essence of which is captured in the statement: 'those who serve in the world, only they attain salvation' ('*vich duniya sev kamayie, tan dargah baisan jaiye*'), and an ethical discourse flowing from this theological imperative, has had profound implications for its followers in terms of their outlook, generating beliefs, practices and values that foster proactive and positive participation in social life and the affairs of the world.

Sikhism's influence and geography is centred in Punjab. However, an exercise that focuses on evaluating the role of religious values in development in Punjab can also be of comparative use, for example in examining the influences of Sikhism and Hinduism in other Indian states. As a comparative exercise, this discussion can draw out parallel and contrasting features with the Hindu and Buddhist traditions of the Indian subcontinent in particular. It can also highlight how adherents of Sikhism – a significant number of people, although a small minority of India's population – have been influenced by their beliefs to carve out a distinct economic and social life in the Punjab state.

According to the 2001 Census of India, Sikhs constitute 1.9 per cent of the country's 1 billion plus population. Of the Sikh population of over 19 million, more than 80 per cent live in Punjab, the rest being either settled in India's large metropolitan cities of Delhi, Mumbai and Kolkata and or scattered across the country. In Punjab, the Sikhs constitute a majority community. The main constituent of Sikh society consists of Jats – a landowning social class from rural Punjab. The second largest group comprises Ravidasi and Mazhabi Sikhs, a landless class generally dependent upon Jats. They are followed by Ramgarhias – artisans, carpenters and others – and finally there is small group of urbanized Khatri Sikhs. Historically, several sects have been prominent – among them Nirmalas and Udasis constituted a priestly class. Currently, three sects, Namdharis, Nirankaris and Radhasoamis, all of which began during the colonial rule, have a considerable number of followers. There are also Sant traditions in rural Punjab – the Nanaksar, Rarewala, Bhindaranwala, Akhand Kirtani Jatha and others. Each is headed by a lineage of saints, usually lasting three or four generations, who developed a distinct pattern of worship or some other distinguishing characteristics, and often had considerable local influence and spiritual authority.

A noteworthy characteristic of Sikh demography since the 1960s has been the emergence of a global Sikh diaspora, currently estimated at 2 million people, of whom a majority is settled in three major Western countries – Canada, the United States and the United Kingdom (Tatla, 1999). It is mainly the Sikh diaspora that has helped to gain the community's international recognition, as many individual Sikhs have asserted their right to be 'different', by campaigns for the right to wear the turban, and challenging host states' conventions and policies on integration and multiculturalism. At the same time, members of the new generation of overseas Sikhs have raised many uncomfortable questions regarding their religious heritage by contending prevalent interpretations of Sikh ethics and theology and offering alternatives in the light of many issues they face in the contemporary world.

SIKH TEACHINGS, BELIEFS AND PRACTICES

Guru Nanak, as the founder of the new faith, set out an alternative vision after examining and rejecting the prevailing Indic religious traditions, distilling his philosophy in a stanza that begins the religious text of Sikhism, Adi Granth (AG) or Sri Guru Granth Sahib (AG: 1):

> ਸਤਿਨਾਮੁ ਕਰਤਾ ਪੁਰਖੁ ਨਿਰਭਉ ਨਿਰਵੈਰੁ ਅਕਾਲ ਮੂਰਤਿ ਅਜੂਨੀ ਸੈਭੰ ਗੁਰ ਪ੍ਰਸਾਦਿ (There is One God, Truth by name, Primal creator, Without fear, Without enmity, Timeless in form, Unborn, Self-existent, The gift of the Guru)

This passage has been treated as the most fundamental to Sikh teaching, with numerous commentaries, including recent feminist interpretations. Most commentators agree that the core of Sikh doctrine consists of a belief in one formless divine God, immanent, ever-present and all-powerful, and that this world is His creation, with no particular aim other than His pleasure or will. The human being is regarded as the highest form of life bestowed by the divine, and the main aim of this life is to attain liberation (*mukti*), from the fate of perpetual suffering through reincarnation.

In pursuing the spiritual ideal of salvation, what is the distinctive contribution of the Sikh religious tradition over other Indic religions? The most significant aspect is Sikh gurus' rejection of the prevailing notion of asceticism (*sannyasa*). This stance was in sharp contrast to contemporary religious thought in medieval India, where the Hindu religious tradition in its dominant manifestations, the Nathpanthis, Jogis and the Bhakti movements emphasized renunciation as the main means of man's salvation. Two other major religious traditions, Buddhism and Jainism also advocate a degree of renunciation as an essential ingredient of people's religious quest. In contrast, the Sikh doctrine emphasized social life (*grihast*), amidst the world while remaining unsullied by worldly temptations. The founder, Guru Nanak, provided an example of such a fusion of spiritual and social life by settling down to the life of a householder at Kartarpur, a new town he established on the banks of the Ravi after visiting major religious centres, including those at Hardwar, Baghdad, and, according to tradition, Mecca.

For the congregation, a building known as *dharamsala* was reserved (later called *gurdwara*), where his followers gathered to share in the spiritual life, not as a monastic order, but as individuals with different capacities working in a cooperative spirit. Nanak's nine successors added to the foundation through more verses and precepts, as well as establishing appropriate institutions and towns for the growing number of followers. Amritsar and Goindwal emerged as two major Sikh centres, the former acquiring holy status for its temple surrounded by a pool built by the fourth and fifth gurus. The second guru, Angad, started the institution of a community kitchen, which provided free meals (*langar*), and was initiated to break caste barriers and pool devotees' earnings in kind and cash to provide welfare for the needy and hungry. Women worked in the *langar*, their admission into both the common kitchen and the congregation removing any doubt about their equal status in spiritual pursuits. The fifth guru then took this further when he decided to include in the Guru Granth the works of 'low caste' poets (Kabir, Namdev and Ravidas), whose verses strongly denounced the caste hierarchy. Sikhism was forced into political history when the fifth guru, Arjan, was executed on the orders of the

Mughal emperor Jahangir. As a reaction to the martyrdom of the fifth guru, his son, the sixth guru, started wearing weapons and constructed a fortress-type structure, the Akal Takhat (literally immortal throne), facing the Harmandir (God's home). He also devised new rules for public life, propagating a judicious mix of 'righteous politics directed by religious ethics' (*miri-piri*).

The organizational structure of early Sikh society was given a decisive shape by the tenth and last guru, Gobind Singh. He ended personal guruship in favour of the Guru Granth – the sacred composition compiled by the fifth guru, which has been placed at the centre of the Sikh temple in Amritsar (Harmandir), since 1604. Gobind formally transformed, by and large, what was still a pacifist society of Sikh followers into a more close-knit religious community through a formal initiation ceremony called *amrit*. He called the new order of Sikhs the Khalsa Panth (brotherhood of the pure), and specified that their personal attire should include '5 Ks'[1] to reflect their identity as a true Sikh.

SOURCES OF SIKH ETHICS

There are four separate sources for Sikh ethical practices. The first and foremost is the Guru Granth Sahib, the most sacred Sikh scripture, which is revered as the living embodiment of the ten gurus and that sits at the centre of every *gurdwara* as the focal point of worship and prayer. The second source is the sacred Sikh literature. Among them, *vars* (heroic ballads) of Bhai Gurdas, the scribe of the original Guru Granth, are considered a 'key' to the Guru Granth's ethical message. The Dasam Granth, compiled by Mani Singh, contains the compositions of Guru Gobind Singh as well as writings by the guru's court poets (*durbari kavi*). Within the sacred literature genre, there are also *hukamnamas* (orders), presumed to be written by some of the gurus, especially the ninth and tenth gurus. These are distinguished from a later set of *hukamnamas* issued by the head of Akal Takhat, Amritsar (Sarbrah or Jathedar), in the late nineteenth and twentieth centuries. The third source of Sikh ethics is prescriptive literature, known as *rahitnamas* (codes of belief and practice). There are several, varying in content and size. These tracts or manuals contain 'dos' and 'don'ts' of social conduct, with relevant quotes from the Guru Granth. Matters covered include details of the initiation ceremony; rules of social life; ceremonies regarding birth, marriage and death; prohibitions on gambling and smoking; the expectation that Sikhs will fight valiantly in battle; and how a Sikh must not make a distinction between the rich and poor, the high and low status. *Rahitnamas* are thus rules for an ideal life of ethical purity and spiritual aspiration.

However, in practical terms, most ordinary Sikhs look for moral and political guidance to the Akal Takhat, although some proclamations issued by its Jathedar have run into difficulties since the June 1984 tragedy when the Indian armies invaded the Golden Temple in Amritsar, resulting in a massacre of pilgrims and what the Indian government called 'extremists'. In the 1930s, faced with diverse religious practices within Sikh society, the elected Shiromani Gurdwara Parbandhak Committee (SGPC) initiated a long process of consultation within the community and published a standard *Sikh Rahit Maryada* (SGPC, 1953). The 'Rahit' provides a succinct outline of what it means to be a Sikh, setting out the definition and essence of the religious, social and ethical framework within which the religion's followers were expected to live.

Writing to draw the attention of English language readers in the Western world, M.A. Macauliffe, a colonial officer who undertook the first systematic exploration of Sikhism, summed up Sikh ethics in 1909 in the following:

> To sum up then the moral and political merits of the Sikh religion; it prohibits idolatry, hypocrisy, caste distinctiveness, the con-cremation of widows, the immurement of women, the use of wine and other intoxicants, tobacco-smoking, infanticide, slander, pilgrimage to sacred rivers and tanks of the Hindus; it inculcates loyalty, gratitude for all favours received, philanthropy, justice, impartiality, truth, honesty, and all the moral and domestic virtues known to the holiest citizens of any country. (Macauliffe [1909] 1963, vol. 1, p. xxiii)

Much later, Niharranjan Ray (1975, p. 61), concluded his study of Sikhism with its impact upon its followers:

> Guru Nanak's genius lay in the fact that he tore away from the atmosphere of negation and declared himself positively in favour of worldly life, of acceptance of the duties and obligations of the human individual to the temporal and the material, and at the same time of equal importance of the duties and obligations of religious discipline and spiritual quest for the ultimate. After long centuries, he gave back to the people of India the idea and ideal of a balanced life.

Adding Macauliffe's enumeration of Sikh social ethics to what Ray calls the rejection of an 'atmosphere of negation', it seems fair to conclude that the Sikh religious tradition did not accept the 'fatalism' associated with the karmic theory of Indic religions, according to which human beings' actions were of little use since their fate is predetermined by the *karma* of their previous lives. The Sikh tradition qualified this fundamentally, regarding people's situation as subject to change by conscious human action in this life. Indeed, according to Sikh theology, a guru can bestow *nadar* (grace or bliss) on an earnest person in return for rightful conduct and thus wipe out his or her karmic fate altogether. Fatalism had no place in the new Sikh theology. In addition, neither caste nor gender was a barrier to spiritual pursuits.

This is significant in the context of thinking about development, as people were prompted to improve their situation. Nor was it necessary to abandon the world to attain spiritual ideals. Rather than rejecting the world, Nanak's vision emphasized the social aspect of emancipation, that is, spiritual perfection can only be attained through engaging with the world. And the task was to be accomplished through *sangat* – the congregation of well-intentioned people. The Sikh vision rejected extremes of both austerity and over-indulgence and instead advanced what has been called a 'life-affirming doctrine'.

Beyond these two fundamental precepts, the Sikh scriptures provide an ethical discourse on several aspects of social life. Human behaviour, according to the scriptures, is motivated by *kam* (lust), *krodh* (anger), *lobh* (greed), *moh* (materialism), and *ahankar* (ego), which are 'learnt dispositional activities rather than biological characteristics' (Singh [1970] 1996, p. 54). An ideal is to achieve *sahaj*, a balanced equilibrium in human life, by disciplined individual use of each of the above traits. The essence of social and spiritual life is to live amidst the world positively but in a disinterested way, being aware of the world's avarice, falsehoods and temptations. The human body is to be treated as the temple of God (Bala, 1999, p. 177), not regarded as something evil to be tortured, as Jogis do, but disciplined through austere living and spiritually purified through God's name.

Avtar Singh ([1970] 1996), elucidates four precepts arising from the Sikh scriptures, namely universal brotherhood (*ek pita eks ke ham barak*), social equality (*age jaat na hai*), seeking the well-being of all (*sarbat da bhala*), and an obligation to social service (*seva*). The above theology translates into concrete social ethics in the following manner. First, a Sikh must endeavour to dwell on God's name (*nam japo*); second, a person must earn a living through earnest means (*kirt karo*); and third, earned surplus should be shared (*vand chakna*). The imperative of earnest living through work and sharing of earnings with the needy can easily translate into active pursuit of economic activities and allocating a share of one's earnings for social welfare schemes for the less capable or disabled, or indeed in building other institutions of community welfare. The notion of altruism (*seva*), was translated into an obligation: a tenth of one's wealth to be donated for the welfare of the poor or other charitable causes (*daswandh*). While the concept survives, Sikhs have lacked any institutional arrangement for translating it into a viable contemporary practice.

Individuals were prompted to a life of virtuous and engaged living. Verses written in the language spoken by common people extolled them to rise in the morning and undertake mundane tasks with enthusiasm, thus creating an ethics of 'infectious living' while remembering God's name:

> He who considers himself a disciple of the true guru
> Arises early in the morning to recite God's name
> Then go to earn livelihood enthusiastically working hard
> Lo, you are ready for a bath in God's pool of nectar
> Such is the blessing of the guru. (AG: 305)

Through such prompting, a spirit of individualism was fostered, freeing Sikhs from supposedly pre-assigned places in society. In addition, much of the sacred literature was thought to inspire individuals with a cheerful disposition in adversity (*chardhi kala*), and a spirit for 'passionate living'.

What is more reasonable to say is that Sikh ethical discourse lends itself easily to a social ethos that fosters positive and active roles for individuals, encouraging people to take the initiative in building their lives rather than passively accepting their destiny and place in society – what Sen (1999) calls an essential role of religion to ensure 'quiet and contentedness' in the face of life's incapacitating hardships. The Sikh tradition thus fosters individual spirit while repudiating the debilitating effects of caste, which binds people's fate to their previous incarnations. At the same time, the tradition emphasizes collective action for the welfare of the needy and weak. Thus, an individual's mind is to be nourished through his or her membership of the congregation (*sangat*), while obligations to the less fortunate are to be fulfilled by contributing towards caring for fellow beings.

SIKHISM AND ECONOMIC DEVELOPMENT

According to the development economist Arthur Lewis (1989), a religious system can be regarded as consistent with the requirements of economic development if it lays stress upon material values, work and productivity, thrift and productive investment, honesty in commercial relationships, experimentation and risk-bearing and equality of opportunity. Judging by these criteria, the Sikh religious tradition would seem eminently suitable for economic development. With much of its ethical discourse emphasizing a work ethic, albeit through honest means, and rationality helped through discouraging any beliefs in popular cults or magic and superstition, it seems that the social psychology of Sikh peasants should be geared towards worldly achievements.

Along with economists, sociologists have also debated the role of religious values upon individuals and societies. In this context, Max Weber's thesis on Indian religion has been the subject of much debate. Put in its simplest form, Weber asked 'does religion impede or advance development'? He compared the economic ethic of different creeds in his essay 'The social psychology of world religions' ([1915] 1946), and concluded that ascetic Protestantism was particularly adapted to the development of capitalism, a thesis he elaborated in his influential title *The Protestant Ethic and the 'Spirit' of Capitalism* ([1905] 2002). Applying Weberian analysis to India's slow growth, Singer (1956), Bauer (1961) and Lewis (1989), in their bid to identify the cultural and religious factors in economic growth, observed how Hindus 'disdain' manual labour. In their view, this, coupled with Jaini attitudes to animals, could well have held up Indian's economic development. Kapp (1963), a sociologist, also concluded that the 'other-worldliness' of 'Hindu culture and Hindu social organization are determining factors in India's slow rate of development'.

However, given the record growth rate of the Indian economy since the 1990s, following the federal government's trade liberalization, a straightforward relation between cultural or religious practices as unambiguously retarding or aiding economic development is difficult to sustain. Indeed, as Arvind Sharma (1980) has argued, in the case of a tradition as complex as the Hindu religion, there might be a positive relationship in spite of apparent contradictions, especially as caste stratification could very well be suitable for sustaining trades and the associated skills of entrepreneurship required for the accumulation of financial and human capital.

Sikhism has occasionally been labelled the 'Protestant ethic of South Asia'. Unshackled by caste restrictions on occupations, Sikhs could choose (or change), their occupations and livelihoods. With an emphasis on manual labour and a number of elements in its theology that aid individual rationalism, the followers of Sikhism seemed well adapted to economic development. Elaborating this thesis further, Marian Smith (1948), noted, 'The characteristic feature of Sikhism is the affirmation in it of the opposites, the synthesis of the worldly and other-worldly, of the temporal and the spiritual. . . . In Sikhism, effectual religious devotion is fully compatible with ordinary duties of life'.

How does the record of the Sikh peasantry stand up in the light of the above remarks? Although there are scattered small-scale studies of economic achievement by Sikhs during colonial times, there is none that covers the entire span of their history. However, two recent studies, Dass (1988) and Kaur (1990), can help in understanding 'Sikh economics'. Examining economic ideas contained in the Sikh sacred writings, Dass found many verses directly relating to issues of trade, wealth, capital, commerce, savings and wages, as well as commentaries on various occupations. He found that several of such verses were constitutive of a positive attitude towards economic life. Dass draws attention to the often-cited Sikh precepts of honest labour (*kirt karna*) and sharing earnings (*vand chakna*), contrasting them with the general Indian religions' emphasis on renunciation (*moksa*). The gurus, he noted, 'preferred the life of a householder to that of a wandering holy man (*sadhu*)', reminding men and women to strive for better lives through work. The scriptures endorse no distinction between occupations per se, nor do they restrict mobility or travel. As a result, Sikhs have not refused any occupation as inherently 'bad' or 'polluted' and have travelled far and wide in search of livelihoods, crossing the seas when such a journey was taboo among a section of the Indian population. Although aware that a multi-cast of factors play a part in moulding people's attitudes towards economic life, in the case of Sikhs, Dass (1988, p. 1), asserts that 'one important element appears to be their religion' and goes on to observe that 'Close examination of the Sikh people reveals that their bent of mind, their physical frame, their religious fervour, their enterprising quality, and their life-style are different from the majority of other Indians'.

While Dass's study is concerned mostly with the scriptural and prescriptive ideas that might have constituted Sikhs' behaviour towards the economic aspects of life, Kaur analyses how such ideas were translated into practice by the faithful. In particular, she explores the role of religion in the economic development of Punjab, where a majority of the Sikh population live and work. Starting with the view of Marshall, a Cambridge economist, that the 'two great forming agencies of the world's history have been the religious and the economic' (1949, p. 1), Kaur states her hypothesis: 'Sikh religion has imparted to its followers values which have greatly fostered their moral and material progress. It has encouraged worldly success and fulfillment of one's social responsibilities' (Kaur, 1990, p. 57). Kaur tests her hypothesis by undertaking a brief survey of Sikhs' economic history. She starts in the 1880s, when the British administration launched a major agrarian project aiming to convert Punjab's western wastelands into farmlands by diverting river water through digging new canals. Thousands of Sikh peasants were persuaded to colonize the newly irrigated areas. In less than a generation, 'bar colonies' as these lands were popularly known, grew into highly productive farms. At one stage, Punjab's surplus wheat was exported to several countries, including the United States. Malcolm Darling, the British administrator and keen observer of the agrarian scene, noted how Sikh farmers converted the 'ugliest and dreariest part of India . . . [into the] breadbasket of India' and applauded the Sikh farmer 'as the backbone of the colonies, as he is of the Punjab' (Darling, 1937).

Kaur then turns to the postcolonial era. She notes how the Sikh peasantry, due to the partition of Punjab, had to abandon highly developed irrigated lands but recovered remarkably from the tragedy in less than a decade. This was an outstanding feat, as farmers were, as a rule, allocated smaller areas than the farms they had left behind (Randhawa, 1974), with the result that several thousands migrated further, to other parts of India, the Terai region in Uttar Pradesh (now Uttaranchal Pradesh). Both within and outside Punjab, Sikhs have shown greater mobility in the pursuit of economic opportunities than other communities affected by the partition. In a real sense, the uprooting of 1947, rather than breaking the 'Sikh spirit', energized it (Randhawa, 1974; Nair, 1979).

Then as the Indian government tried to boost agricultural production through the promotion of new technology and high-yielding varieties of wheat and rice in the 1960s, Sikh farmers implemented this 'green revolution' strategy with enthusiasm. Kaur finds in Sikh farmers' outlook and work ethos the inspiration of Sikh religious values.

WEALTH, POVERTY AND DEBT

On wealth and its accumulation, Nanak condemned 'the business that is carried on without truth and a sense of piety'. However, he also recognized that accumulation of wealth always involves exploitation, calling it sin: 'Without sins one cannot accumulate wealth, on death, it accompanies not' (AG, 15). The gurus were also acutely aware of economic inequalities and offered explanations largely in terms of excessive greed (AG, 182). If there were a choice, the scriptures say, the Sikh way must be to avoid indulgence:

> If world were to be encrusted with the diamonds and rubies,
> My bed studded with rubies,
> And if there were an alluring damsel
> Her face glistening with jewels tempting me with seductive gestures,
> Forbid it, O Lord, that beholding such temptation,
> Lest I should forget thy name. (AG, 14)

Thus, blind pursuit of wealth and riches must expect ruin unless rich people pause to reflect and think. The scriptures contain stark reminders of the fate of those who lived a life of indulgence in palaces and amassed wealth at the cost of others:

> Where are those sports, those stables and horses, those trumpets and clarions?
> Where are those sword-belts, those chariots and those scarlet tunics?
> Where are those mirrors and those handsome faces?
> They are nowhere to be seen. (AG, 415)

Wealth, it is averred, must be earned through earnest means, not as a result of exploiting the poor. With respect to Sikh attitudes towards poverty, it is noteworthy that in a land where begging as a profession has survived all social influences to the contrary, no Sikh is found as a beggar. Even in the dire circumstances following the partition of Punjab, when over a million Sikhs became refugees, no Sikh was seen begging. Unlike Hindu ascetics, as noted above, poverty is not regarded as a sign of holiness or as essential to spirituality. Instead the emphasis of Sikh teachings is on earning through honest means and sharing wealth with the needy. The Sikh religious tradition provides spiritual dignity to the poor and exhorts them to improve their lot, while identifying with those who are struggling against the rich.

There is no scriptural injunction against usury. It contrast, it has been part of folklore and administrators' persistent complaints about the Punjab peasantry that it has a long legacy of living beyond its means – borrowing in lean times and consuming with abandon with the harvest in sight (Darling, 1937). During the colonial era, indebtedness among Punjab peasants was a recurrent issue, as frequent reports by British administrators confirm (van den Dungen, 1972). In the 1890s, the issue of a debt-ridden peasantry became so serious that the colonial state passed the Land Alienation Act of 1900, which barred the transfer of land to non-farming classes, thereby penalizing the money-lender urbanite class of *banias*.

In the post-independence period, the expansion of banking services into rural areas, providing comparatively cheap credit to farmers, has ensnared many peasants into the debt trap again. More recently, with stagnant or declining agricultural productivity, many peasants have fallen behind with repayments. In the last decade, many farmers have committed suicide. The Punjab government has acknowledged at least 2116 suicides since 1986, while commentators believe the numbers are just the 'tip of an iceberg', as many cases remain unreported (*Tribune*, Chandigarh, India, 10 August 2005; B.P. Singh, 2010). Summarizing the results of several studies relating to farmers' suicides, Gill and Singh (2006), conclude that:

> Suicides were attributed to a number of reasons, ranging from poverty to crop failure, indebtedness, marital discord and alcoholism, but in our view it [the rise in suicides] was mainly due to the economic crisis that the peasantry, in Punjab, in general, is facing and which has led them to borrow heavily.

It might be argued that many peasants have forgotten the balance between exploitation and conservation so clearly stated by the Sikh tradition in other aspects of social life. Although it is unclear why such an imperative can so easily be forgotten, the clue might be to look for other factors. In this case, a farmer with a small landholding is easily tempted by the state's incentives in the form of cheap finance, while also being forced to use excessive amounts of chemical fertilizers and pesticides (many of them unregulated and dangerous), to maintain production. This process may take such a small farmer into the debt trap and is contributing to an economic crisis that many consider is threatening the fabric of contemporary Punjabi social life.

ECOLOGICAL AND SOCIAL CRISIS

While the Sikh work ethic has helped in raising agricultural production, the net impact of the 'green revolution' has led to severe environmental crisis: over-exploitation of underground water for irrigation and farm land has brought about an ecological crisis in Punjab. Besides decreasing productivity, there is soil degradation and the appearance of a variety of environment-related diseases. The indiscriminate use of pesticides and chemical fertilizers has contributed to this ecological disaster (Shiva, 1991; World Bank, 2004). Several Sikh economists, the most eminent of whom is S.S. Johl, have strongly advocated switching to more ecologically sustainable farming practices, including rotation of diversified crops (such as sunflowers and other oil-yielding varieties), organic farming, horticulture and re-forestation.

During the last three decades Punjab has rapidly been integrated into the Indian economy. For all practical purposes, the region resembles a specialized colony geared to the primary production of food grains, with few incentives for diversification or industrialization. The initial gains of Punjab's agrarian economy did not result in balanced development of the countryside and instead have led, as noted above, to lopsided development of agrarian sector alone. This raises questions about the Indian government's regional policy and the implications of Indian federalism, but there are as yet few studies on this topic (see Rao and Singh, 2005; B.P. Singh, 2010). The role of the Sikh religion assumes great importance in the developmental process, not only in terms of the beliefs and value system of its adherents, but also as an instrument of political mobilization by Sikh leaders seeking a fair distribution of both economic and non-economic resources from the Indian federal government.

Punjab's recent development experience raises a further serious question: has the Sikh ethical understanding of 'development' proved adverse in the long run even if it aided economic development in the short term? The answer might be a qualified yes. Insofar as religious values made Sikh peasantry economically active, the ethical discourse has played a positive role. However, Sikh teachings provide little guidance on how to deal with the resulting unforeseen consequences. Currently, attempts are being made to search relevant passages for guidance, for example, on ecological matters. Referring to possible technological solutions, Chahal (2005, p. 133), argues that 'theologically, genetic engineering cannot be justified from the Sikh perspective', and that the search for improving or perfecting nature through such manipulation is doomed. On a practical plane, only the Namdhari sect, members of which adhere to strict vegetarianism and homespun clothes, are dedicated to conserving the 'mother planet' for all.

SIKH SOCIETY AND SOCIAL EXCLUSION

Peculiar to the Indian subcontinent, one of the most notable causes of social differentiation is caste – an indigenous Hindu religious philosophy that justifies a hierarchy (*varna-ashram*), of four social groups. By virtue of one's birth into a particular *varna*, a person belongs to that social group, the particular caste group. In this scheme, the top social strata is assigned to Brahmans, followed by Kshatriyas and Vaishyas, with the lowest being Sudras (or Shurdras). Each person's status is predetermined through previous incarnations.

Like many reformist movements within and independent of Hindu religion, Sikhism severely criticized the practice of social exclusion on the basis of caste. Indeed, this was one of the defining characteristics of Guru Nanak's message, which offered emancipation to all, irrespective of the caste in which they found themselves. Nanak repudiated the caste hierarchy and its associated notion of pollution:

> Worthless is caste and worthless an exalted name
> For all mankind there is but a single refuge. (AG: 83)

This message was reinforced by third Guru Amar Das who, as already pointed out, built on the concept of spiritual equality through initiating a common kitchen (*langar*), for the congregation (*sangat*), thus promoting commensurability through sharing food together (*pangat*). The fifth guru built the Harmandir with four doors open to all (*updes chaun varna ko sanjha* – preaching to all four castes in common). Guru Arjan, in compiling the Guru Granth, decided to include the writings of Bhagats who were Sudra: Ravidas, Namdev and Kabir being the three most prominent. Finally, the idea of equality was given full institutional legitimacy through the initiation ceremony of *amrit* or '*khande ki pahul*' introduced by the tenth guru – nectar drunk from the same bowl. The doctrine of distinction based upon caste was ultimately buried, along with the notion of 'pollution', by this ceremony of initiation into Sikhism. How was this new Sikh religious tradition of inclusion translated into actual practice by its new followers, who were largely drawn from Hindu society with its caste distinctions?

Despite Sikh rejection of caste, contemporary Sikh society consists of some 30 caste-like social groups, of which Jats form a large majority, almost two-thirds of the total population (Marenco, 1974). The next largest category is Ramgarhia or Rahitia Sikhs, largely drawn from the artisan classes, who form about one-tenth of the total. The 'Dalit Sikhs' constitute more than 15 per cent, while the Khatris, formerly the dominant constituent of the community, are about 5 per cent. The 'untouchables', also classified as Scheduled Castes (SCs), in the Indian constitution and increasingly known as Dalits, a term that has gained currency over all others, form more than a quarter of contemporary Punjab's population, far above the Indian average of 16 per cent. The majority of Dalits are either working tenants or labourers for peasants, with fewer than 5 per cent being cultivators, owning a negligible proportion of the farm land (0.4 per cent). Their landlessness is partly attributed to the 1900 Land Alienation Act, whereby the British administrators barred non-agricultural classes from owning farms. This measure was felt to be necessary to stop the usurpation of land by the commercial classes, mostly Banias.

Given Sikh doctrine's prohibition of caste distinctions, how can caste-type differences and differentials within Sikh society be accounted for? McLeod (2007) points out how Sikh practical behaviour falls short of this ideal. In terms of marriage and social mixing of different social groups, a large majority of Sikhs follow *jati* and *gotr*[2] regulations and commensurability restrictions are also observed, although supposedly without damaging adherence to egalitarian principles. Sikh commentators argue that the Sikh social system offers a radical rupture with the Hindu caste system, asserting that Western historians' and social scientists' insistence upon caste as integral to all South Asian societies only underlines their ignorance of Sikh society, which in their view is an exception to the rule (see J. Singh, 1981).

In a wide-ranging review of Dalits' status in contemporary Sikh society, Puri (2003), an academic at Guru Nanak Dev University in Amritsar, found contradictions in the Sikh rhetoric of equality and widespread discrimination against 'Sikh low castes'. He alleges that Jats' political domination through the Akali Dal in Punjab is responsible for blocking land reforms that would have benefited Dalits. He also sees double standards amongst the Sikh leadership, in pleading the case for Sikh Dalits' inclusion in the 'Scheduled Groups classification' offered by the government of India while 'pretending that Sikhism is egalitarian' (Puri, 2003, p. 2697). Ram (2007), also underlines the failure of the Sikh tradition in devising a casteless society, citing cases of Jat Sikh and Dalit confrontation in some Punjab villages. Another sociologist, Jodhka (2002, 2006), who undertook extensive fieldwork among Punjab's Dalits, has offered a more balanced evaluation. Jodhka interprets cases of discriminatory practices by the landowning class of Jats against landless Dalits as economic, social or cultural rather than religious in nature. Thus, the issue seems not so much to be a case of the Sikh religious tradition failing to reorder oppressive social relations, as of new developments and potentialities presented by the new Indian regime of a democratic power structure.

Sikhism and Gender Inequality

Sikh theologians have credited the Sikh religious tradition with a very positive attitude to the gender question. They have pointed out how the scriptural literature lauds women as equal to men in the spiritual sphere. With this scriptural backing, practical steps were taken to invite women to participate in public life. In both congregations (*sangat*) and community kitchens (*langar*) women were invited to play a role – serving one and all just as expected of men. The *gurdwara* was open to them just as it was for men and they could take part in its upkeep and management. Amar Das, the third guru, advocated marriage based on equality; stressing fidelity, he condemned *purdah* (the veil covering women's faces), and female infanticide. He also spoke against the practice of *sati* (immolation of the widow on the pyre of her husband), and encouraged the remarriage of widows. Historians also record 22 *manjis* (preaching centres), established by him to collect offerings from followers far and wide followers, who included four women. Today, women are initiated into the faith just as men through the ceremony of *amrit*, they read scriptures both at home and in the *gurdwaras*, they can serve as *granthi*[3] and they can participate in all religious activities outside the home including the management of religious institutions.

Apart from biological differences, women are considered to be equal to men before God and all men or women are to be judged by their deeds, regardless of sex, creed and birth. More significantly, woman's traditional role in Indian society as elucidated in Hindu scriptures was seen to have been radically reversed by Sikhism. A well-known couplet of Guru Nanak is often quoted in support of this thesis:

> Of woman are we born, of woman conceived, to woman betrothed and wedded?
> Woman we befriend, by her continues the human race;
> When woman dies, woman is sought for; it is she who maintains the world order.
> Why revile her of whom are born the great?

Besides scriptural references, more injunctive proclamations against denigrating women or subordinating them as inferior human beings are found in *rahitnamas*: one such injunction cautions against the custom of *sati*, *purdah* is discouraged, and another commands a social boycott of those indulging in female infanticide (*kurhi-mar nal na varto*).

In contrast to this rather celebratory discourse advanced by Sikh theologians, Jakobsh (2003), a Canadian scholar, offers a far more critical assessment of the position of Sikh women through history. While not discounting that the Sikh religious tradition did make a clear break from Islamic and Hindu traditions, she contends that the empirical reality of the subordinate role of Sikh women continues today. In the words of an American-born Sikh girl (Kaur, 2005) who expressed her frustration at the hypocrisy in the Sikh community:

> Why haven't Sikh women risen up a long time ago in protest against such treatment, reciting the words of the gurus? Why did we not endeavor long ago to realize fully the freedom and equality the gurus preached for all human beings, regardless of gender?

In a major effort to explain the discrepancy between the scriptural and practical position of women in Sikh society, Singh (1993), has evolved what has been called a neo-orthodox position, arguing how Sikh scriptures have been systematically interpreted from a male viewpoint. This, she asserts, is the chief reason why Sikh women's subordinate position is maintained and they are consigned to marginality. Insisting on a revised reading of the Sikh scriptures, Singh sets out an agenda for women to contest the established structures of power as well challenge theological practices in the light of a 'true' interpretation of the scriptures.

While the theoretical discussion continues to use the religious tradition as a cultural resource, the focus of the debate is shifting to popular culture and its effect on Punjabi women. Basarke (1996), for example, argues 'how can women expect equality when the Sikh community seems unable to distinguish between religious tenets and culture imposed by the majority community which engulfs them?' It is thought that much of the Sikh cultural ethos has accepted ideas, roles and practices from Hindu culture and that in practice, Sikh women's rights are governed by the more regressive legal framework of the Hindu social system. Thus, it is argued that property inheritance laws, also laws governing divorce and annulment of marriage, have been framed without fully taking account of the Sikh tradition.

It is pertinent to note the influence of the cultural values of Punjabi society. Some Punjabi parents, especially from the upper classes, consider a daughter a liability, as her marriage entails a considerable dowry and wife-givers have a low status. For such cultural reasons, neglect of female children and in some cases female infanticide became a common practice almost a century ago (Panigrahi, 1972). Indeed, such was the wide acceptance of female infanticide in Punjab that newly-born female children were starved to death by being denied their mother's milk with a ritual incantation:

> *Gurh khayin puni katin, Aap na aain, bhai nu ghattin* (Eat sweets, spin the thread; don't come again, send your brother).

The first census in 1881 proved colonial administrators' worst fears right, as the figures showed just 847 females per 1000 males. In the Punjab states, this ratio was even lower at 828 females per 1000. In the post-independence period, Punjab continues to trail behind other Indian states. The 2001 census found just 793 girls per 1000 boys, the lowest among the Indian provinces.

Since the 1980s, the figures suggest that another factor or rather facility has assisted in killing girl children – the availability of the new technology of abortion, has led to an increase in 'foeticide'. In contrast to former times, when infanticide was largely confined to richer sections of society, the new technique has 'democratized' the practice to include the peasantry, with only the poor and God-fearing families remaining immune from the menace of such 'modernity'. Although in the Prenatal Diagnostic Act the government has banned the sex-determination test, non-stringent implementation of the legislation has meant that the test is widely available and used. Alarmed by the sex imbalance among Sikhs, the Jathedar of Akal Takhat in 2001 issued a dictum against female foeticide.

CONCLUSION

This chapter shows Sikhs' understanding of 'development' has been facilitated by ethical values derived from the religious tradition, which provide them with a generally rationalistic, this-worldly and individualistic outlook. As a result, Sikhs have competed with each other and others to improve their own lot and the situation of their families, as well as contributing in a characteristic way to various collective ventures and welfare activities inspired by the Sikh religious tradition of *vand chakna* (sharing) and *seva* (service).

Understanding development as an individual enterprise, seeing one's well-being as related to one's own endeavours, the religion's adherents have utilized their skills, abilities and resources through a strong work ethic that shuns begging and includes a 'here and now' attitude and an enthusiasm for all things economic and material, based on an expectation of 'whatever you sow, so shall you reap'.

It would be fair to conclude that this this-worldly approach has contributed to the economic development of Punjab, where the pace of development has generally been ahead of other Indian regions, during both the colonial and postcolonial periods. Imbued with a competitive spirit, the Sikh peasantry made a success out of the 'green revolution' strategy adopted by the government of India in the 1960s. However, by the 1990s, the green revolution had exhausted its potential, with Sikh farmers having reached the limits of production of wheat and rice and over-exploitation of pesticides, fertilizers and underground water, especially for the rice crop. Trapped by governmental incentives, the Punjab countryside today is a scene of ecological crisis, with the water table dropping fast and the productivity of both rice and wheat cultivation falling while mechanized agriculture is unable to absorb a large pool of educated Sikh youngsters.

On some of the wider issues arising from developmental concerns, it can be suggested that the record of the Sikh tradition's influence on its followers seems to be mixed. The case of gender equality is a prime example of this, with the religious tradition advocating equality, while the inertia of cultural factors prohibits women from participating equally in public life. Similarly, those for whom caste has been a debilitating factor in their personal lives and a source of stigma for social groups have found much solace in the Sikh tradition's emphasis on social equality and equal entitlement to a spiritual life and religious institutions. However, Sikhism as a basis for a Sikh society without caste distinctions has different meanings for different economic classes, Jats being politically, socially and economically favoured and other groups remaining disadvantaged.

NOTES

* This chapter is a much shorter version of a paper arising from a project on 'Religion and Development' based at the University of Birmingham. The project was funded by the Department for International Development (DFID), UK. The views expressed are not necessarily those of DFID or the University of Birmingham.

1. The 5 Ks are five physical symbols worn by Sikhs who have been initiated into the Khalsa: *Kesh* (uncut hair); *Kara* (a steel bracelet); *Kanga* (a wooden comb); *Kaccha* – also spelt, *Kachh, Kachera* (cotton underwear); *Kirpan* (steel sword).
2. *Jati* means caste groupings; *gotr* indicates within a particular subgrouping a lineage of kinship. For example, a Tatla would not marry into Tatla *gotr* as all those of Tatla *gotr* are supposed to have originated from a common ancestor.
3. A *granthi* is a priest within a *gurdwara* – a person employed by the management committee for the upkeep of the *gurdwara* who performs common religious ceremonies and other chores.

REFERENCES

Bala, Shashi (1999), *Sikh Metaphysics*, Amritsar: Singh Brothers.
Basarke, A. (1996), *Where are the Women? Current Thoughts on Sikhism*, Chandigarh: Institute of Sikh Studies.
Bauer, Peter (1961), *Indian Economic Policy and Development*, New York: Praeger.
Chahal, S.K. (2005), *Ecology, Redesigning Gene: Ethical and Sikh Perspectives*, Amritsar: Singh Brothers.

Darling, M.L. (1937), *The Punjab Peasant in Prosperity and Debt*, New Delhi: Manohar (reprinted 1977).
Dass, J.R. (1988), *Economic Thought of the Sikh Gurus*, New Delhi: National Book Organization.
Gill, Anita and Lakhwinder Singh (2006), 'Farmers' suicides and response of public policy: evidence, diagnosis and alternative from Punjab', *Economic and Political Weekly*, 30.
Jakobsh, D. (2003), *Relocating Gender in Sikh History: Transformation, Meaning and Identity*, New Delhi: Oxford University Press.
Jodhka, S.S. (2002), 'Caste and untouchability in rural Punjab', *Economic and Political Weekly*, 11 May, 1814–23.
Jodhka, S.S. (2006), 'Caste and democracy: assertion and identity among Dalits of rural Punjab', *Sociological Bulletin*, **55**(1), 281–99.
Kapp, K.W. (1963), *Hindu Culture, Economic Development and Economic Performance*, Delhi: Sage.
Kaur, Upinder Jit (1990), *Sikh Religion and Economic Development*, New Delhi: National Book Organization.
Kaur, Valerie (2005), 'Equality of women in Sikh ideology and practice', available at: http://www.sikhwomen.com/equality/ideology_vs_practice.htm; accessed 12 July 2012.
Lewis, Arthur (1989), *The Theory and Experience of Economic Development*, London: Allen and Unwin.
Macauliffe, M.A. ([1909] 1963), *The Sikh Religion*, New Delhi: S. Chand and Co.
Marenco, Ethne K. (1974), *The Transformation of Sikh Society*, Portland: HaPi Press.
Marshall, Alfred (1949), *Principles of Economics*, London: Macmillan.
McLeod, W.H. (2007), 'Sikhs and caste', in T. Ballantyne (ed.), *Textures of the Sikh Past*, Delhi: Oxford University Press, pp. 104–31.
Nair, Kusum (1979), *Blossoms in the Dust: The Human Element in Indian Development*, Chicago: University of Chicago Press.
Nkurunziza, E. (2007), 'An overview of development studies: background paper for the religions and development research programme', WP 2, Religions and Development, Birmingham University.
Panigrahi, Lalita (1972), *British Social Policy and Female Infanticide in India*, Delhi: Munshiram Manoharlal, pp. 2761–8.
Puri, Harish (2003), 'Scheduled castes in Sikh community: a historical perspective', *Economic and Political Weekly*, 28 June, 2693–701.
Ram, Ronki (2007), 'Social exclusion, resistance and *deras*: exploring the myth of casteless Sikh society in Punjab', *Economic and Political Weekly*, 6 October, 4066–73.
Randhawa, M.S. (1974), *Green Revolution: A Case Study of the Punjab*, Delhi: Vikas.
Rao, Govinda M. and Nirvikar Singh (2005), *The Political Economy of Federalism in India*, Delhi: Oxford University Press.
Ray, N. (1975), *The Sikh Gurus and the Sikh Society: A Study in Social Analysis*, New Delhi: Munshiram Manoharlal (revised edition).
Sen, A.K. (1999), *Development as Freedom*, Oxford: Oxford University Press.
SGPC (Shiromani Gurdwara Parbandhak Committee) (1953), *Sikh Rahit Maryada*, Amritsar.
Sharma, Arvind (1980), *The Hindu Scriptural Value System and India's Economic Development*, New Delhi: Heritage Publications.
Shiva, Vandana (1991), *The Violence of Green Revolution*, London: Zed Books.
Singer, Milton (1956), 'Cultural values in India's economic development', *The Annals of the American Academy of Political and Social Science*, **305**(May), 81–91.
Singh, Avtar ([1970] 1996), *Ethics of the Sikhs* (3rd edition), Patiala: Punjabi University Press.
Singh, Birinder Pal (ed.) (2010), *Punjab Peasantry in Turmoil*, Delhi: Manohar.
Singh, Jagjit (1981), *The Sikh Revolution: A Perspective*, New Delhi: Kendri Singh Sabha.
Singh, Nikky G. Kaur (1993), *The Feminine Principle in the Sikh Version of the Transcendent*, Cambridge: Cambridge University Press.
Smith, Marian (1948), 'Synthesis and other processes in Sikhism', *American Anthropologist*, **50**(3), 457–62.
Tatla, Darshan S. (1999), *The Sikh Diaspora: The Search for Statehood*, London: Routledge.
Van den Dungen, P.H.M. (1972), *The Punjab Tradition; Influence and Authority in Nineteenth-century India*, London: Allen and Unwin.
Weber, M. ([1905] 2002), *The Protestant Ethic and the 'Spirit' of Capitalism and Other Writings*, edited, translated, and with an introduction and notes by Peter Baehr and Gordon C. Wells, Harmondsworth: Penguin Books.
Weber, M. ([1915] 1946), 'The social psychology of the world religions', in Hans Gerth and C. Wright Mills (eds), *From Max Weber: Essays in Sociology*, New York: Oxford University Press.
World Bank (2004), *Resuming Punjab's Prosperity: The Opportunities and Challenges Ahead*, Washington: World Bank.

8 Daoism and development

James Miller

INTRODUCTION

Daoism, also spelled Taoism, is China's organized, indigenous religious system. Daoists take as their focus the goal of obtaining the Dao, or Way, the unnameable source of generative vitality in a universe of constant transformation. The methods for realizing this goal have been revised and reinvented throughout Daoism's 2000-year history but can be generally understood in terms of mediating between the fluid energies of the body, the community and the cosmos. Daoists pay attention to the subtle energies of the inner body and engage in meditative cultivation practices that aim to restore and enhance the functioning of the body with the goal of bringing about long life and spiritual transcendence. They also worship a complex hierarchy of sacred powers that includes at its apex the Three Pure Ones, impersonal instantiations of the Dao itself, and also a wide variety of personal gods who were once human beings but who, over the course of their lives, achieved transcendence, sometimes understood as immortality.

From the perspective of an outside observer, Daoism has two distinct characters: an elite tradition of monks and priests who are dedicated to the quest of obtaining the Dao, and a communal tradition integrated into local society and patronized by non-initiated lay people. The elite tradition is focused on maintaining and transmitting the teachings of the various lineages to a relatively small number of initiates who are deemed to be suitably qualified by virtue of their religious commitment. This elite tradition is esoteric, in that the contents of its teachings are not generally transmitted to non-initiates, and it generally has a hierarchical structure so that initiates must demonstrate their accomplishment at a lower level of teaching before receiving transmissions of a higher level of teaching. This elite tradition is by definition somewhat obscure and tends to jealously guard its distinct identity and sacred authority.

At the same time, however, Daoism also embraces the common Chinese religious tradition that pays little heed to religious distinctions. In this tradition, non-initiated lay people patronize temples to pray for good fortune, to mark the changing of the seasons, and to conduct rituals for the departed. The patrons of such temples and services may not be aware whether their temple is run by Daoists, Buddhists or other local religious traditions. The main thing is that they regard the temple as having spiritual efficacy. Within this common religious framework, however, there are specifically Daoist rituals for funerals and exorcisms that call upon distinctively Daoist gods and have specific Daoist characteristics that can be easily detected by the trained observer. The most distinctive Daoist ritual is the *jiao*, generally a complex multi-day event aimed at restoring the balance between the community and the cosmos. The most lavish of these is the rite of cosmic renewal, staged only once every 60 years, to mark the beginning of a new cycle of the Chinese calendar.

From an internal perspective, however, Daoists generally categorize themselves according a variety of distinct lineages, each with its own genealogy of sacred authority. Daoists are initiated into a tradition by a master, receiving sacred texts and teachings into the methods taught by that tradition. Historically these various traditions were often centred on particular sacred mountains, and are frequently referred to by the name of the mountain. For this reason, some Daoist lineages tended to have strongholds in distinct regions of China and, at times these affiliations have maintained their various historical and geographic distinctions. In the modern period, however, all lineages and forms of Daoism have been increasingly subjected to mechanisms of centralization, nationalization and bureaucratization under the aegis of a single organizational framework, known as the Chinese Daoist Association (CDA). The CDA is based at the White Cloud Monastery in Beijing, which is one of the most important monasteries associated with the Complete Perfection (Quanzhen) tradition of monastic Daoism that dominates northern China. For this reason contemporary Daoism at the national level tends to reflect this elite monastic form, though, historically, this is a relatively late Daoist movement that does not really represent the whole of the tradition. The CDA is itself supervised by the State Administration for Religious Affairs (SARA).

MODERNITY, HARMONY AND DEVELOPMENT

The concepts of development (*fazhan*) and, in particular, scientific development (*kexue fazhan*) are key terms in the ideology espoused by China's modernizers since the beginning of the twentieth century. Such revolutionary terms were developed, however, in direct opposition to earlier conceptual frameworks regarding the basic functioning of human society, its relationship to the natural environment and the cosmos. The modern concept of development is, essentially, predicated on a linear theory of time, in which human activity contributes in a cumulative, meaningful way towards some final goal or purpose. This was not the generally received view of traditional Chinese governance, set in place some 2000 years earlier in the dominant theory of Han dynasty Chinese scholar Dong Zhongshu, which held that the relationship between the three realms of humanity, earth and heaven should ideally be one of reciprocity or mutual resonance (*ganying*; see de Bary, 1960, p. 208). The sacred duty of the emperor in this view was to conduct rituals to ensure the positive correlation between humanity, earth and heaven so as to bring about the most optimal flourishing. Indeed, the success of the empire was thought to depend in part upon the ritual activity of the emperor, which sought to correct periodic imbalances in the relationship between humans and the cosmos (see Miller, 2012). In such a view, the function of religion was a mediating one: to bring everything back into alignment so as to create a balanced, homeostatic organism. This cyclical view can even be seen in the traditional Chinese system for measuring time based on the 12 animals of the Chinese zodiac and the five elements, according to which the clock is reset every 60 years.

It is entirely understandable, therefore, that China's modernizers should see 'development' as a revolutionary concept that aimed not towards the continuous cyclical alignment of humanity, earth and heaven, but rather the relentless transformation of the same towards some positive goal. This view placed progress in opposition to Chinese traditional views, especially Confucianism and Daoism, and was one reason why these traditions were particularly scorned by revolutionary modernizers. A prime example of this can be see in the work of Chen Duxiu (1879–1942), a founder of the Chinese Communist Party (CCP) who, in a now-famous essay ('Call to youth', 1915), advocated four chief characteristics among China's revolutionaries: that they be independent, not servile; progressive, not conservative; aggressive, not retiring; and cosmopolitan, not isolationist (Lawrance, 2004, pp. 2–3). In all four cases, Chinese religions in general, and Daoism in particular, were found wanting.

Daoism, like all religions, contains a conservative element within it. While, from a spiritual perspective, Daoists might believe they advocate independence rather than servility, the institutional structures of Daoism are designed along a hierarchical basis in which students cannot simply 'think' their way into enlightenment, but must generally be guided by teachers and have their progress validated by the religious community. Second, Daoist elites aim to preserve their authority through the transmission of classic scriptures, and seek to indoctrinate new generations with values and beliefs developed centuries ago. From this perspective it can hardly be regarded as a 'progressive' movement. Third, Daoists are noted for seeking sanctuary in remote mountain areas and in withdrawing from the conventions of ordinary human society. At the same time, Daoists explicitly deprecate aggression and value non-interventionist ways of acting in the world. Finally, Daoists tend to value the inner, spiritual life. They are not missionaries, nor generally do they seek to transform the external world. Doubtless Chen Duxiu would regard them as isolationist in attitude. In all four aspects that he enumerates, it is easy to see how Daoism can easily be classified in the negative of the binary pairs. From Chen's perspective, therefore, it is well nigh impossible to imagine how Daoism might contribute something to development.

The classification of religion as a hindrance to development was only made worse by Marx's view of religion as a narcotic. From this point of view, Daoism, like other religions, is not simply a set of values and beliefs that may be regarded as ideologically opposed to the values of social development. Rather, religions also have the social function of hindering historical progress. Given the widespread adoption of these views of religion by China's modernizers, it is not surprising that they came to view religion as an enemy in the goal of political revolution, social and economic progress and scientific development. It is also hardly surprising, therefore, that Chinese communist revolutionaries engaged in iconoclastic campaigns to destroy temples, denigrate Confucius and eradicate all forms of what they perceived to be superstitious thinking that was opposed to scientific materialism.

Such anti-religion thinking was by no means confined to communist modernizers. Duara (1991) details how nationalist aspirations conflicted with the local networks of religious power in the first half of the twentieth century. Chinese general and second President of the Republic Yuan Shikai, for instance, 'sought to systematically dismantle the institutional foundations of popular religion' by appropriating local temple property and establishing schools and government offices in their stead (Duara, 1991, p. 76). Nationalist modernizers further made use of the political distinction between religion and superstition in their attempt to centralize the power of the newly emerged Republican state. The anti-superstition campaigns of the late 1920s and early 1930s proscribed popular religious practices such as geomancy and physiognomy while simultaneously advocating the cult of national figures such as Confucius and Laozi. As Duara

(1991, p. 80) demonstrates, the effect of this was to consolidate national power over local society by bringing 'legitimate' religious activities under state control while at the same time excluding from the definition of religion those popular practices that it could not easily control. 'Superstitious' practices involving charms and talismans were also associated with secret societies and local religious organizations, which had also historically functioned as networks of dissent against central state power.

The ideological distinction between legitimate religious organizations and popular 'superstitious' activities was maintained in the Deng Xiaoping era after the hard-line leftist policies associated with the Cultural Revolution (1966–76) came to an end. National religious associations were revived and placed under the oversight of the Religious Affairs Bureau, now the State Administration for Religious Affairs. More recent times, however, have seen the emphasis placed on pragmatic, rather than ideological, considerations regarding the role of religious activities in China's continued development. Religious leaders now form part of the Central People's Political Consultative Conference (CPPCC) and the Communist Party has instead formed a broad coalition of ruling elites, including religious figures, on whom it depends for its continued legitimacy. This has led to a renewed understanding of religion from a broad socio-cultural perspective rather than in purely ideological terms, and a rethinking of what religion might positively contribute to social development. Following Marxist thinker Gramsci in recognizing the value of the 'cultural' sector (Zeng, 2011, p. 773), China's leaders have reconsidered the value of traditional Chinese culture, rehabilitated Confucius, and permitted the overt functioning of authorized religion, while maintaining an ever closer watch on undesirable religious and cultural phenomena. The resultant 'religious boom' has cost the government considerable sums of money in terms of vacating and restoring confiscated religious properties and subsidizing the operating expenses of authorized religious organizations (ibid., p. 768).

At the same time, the goal of rapid economic development has come to be supplemented once again with 'back-to-the-future' virtues such as 'harmony' (*hexie*) and 'spiritual civilization' (*jingshen wenming*). Such emphases on spirituality and culture are designed to help ensure broad social stability, and crack down on official corruption and dissident social movements.

COMMUNITY WELL-BEING

Putting aside the dominant narratives that have come to frame Daoism in the modern period, it is possible to examine the ways in which Daoists have historically interacted with local communities in terms of social and economic development. The earliest Daoist community of which we have a clear understanding was known as the Way of the Orthodox Unity (*Zhengyi dao*), and functioned as a theocracy in south-west China for about 70 years from 142 CE. Common to most traditional Chinese communities it operated on a collective basis, collecting an annual tax from each household and imposing regulations governing the upkeep of the communal environment, such as not wantonly felling trees, picking flowers, digging holes or drying marshes (Schipper, 2001, p. 81). Such concern for the common spaces was no doubt advantageous for the well-being of the community as a whole and may be regarded as characteristic of Chinese society in which the interests of the group are accorded a high priority. In Schipper's (2001, p. 89) analysis, however, these injunctions draw on an older tradition 'rooted in the rejection of the feudal society and the ritual practices of the public cults of the city-states'. That is to say, the ethical foundation for the community was one predicated on a sense of being a different kind of society with a different kind of ritual life. These earliest Daoist communities thus tended to be in this sense peripheral communities, predicated on a rejection of the conventional social order and embracing a life based on simple communities and natural sacred spaces.

As Daoism became more integrated into mainstream Chinese society, however, it tended to merge with local religious organizations and embedded itself in the common religious life of Chinese people. In a later publication, Schipper (2008) makes the argument for understanding Daoism as the primary framework within which Chinese religious life takes place. In its transition from the periphery to the mainstream, however, it brought about a change in the relationship between local communities and religious institutions. In particular, the 'covenants of purity' (*qingyue*) specified that Daoist gods were not to be offered animal sacrifices and Daoist priests were not to receive salaries. As a result of the latter, temples came to be owned and funded by the collective rather than by priestly lineages. Thus, in contrast to affiliation-based religions in which people pay tithes to a religious organization that is distinct from secular society and governed by a special class of religious professionals, Chinese people founded community associations (*hui*) or common management organizations (*gongsi*, now the term for 'corporation') in order to manage their collective religious lives. As a result, the gap between 'religious' activities and other local economic, educational or charitable activities becomes harder to discern. These communal associations, for instance, became significant managers of local wealth held in trust for the benefit of the community. In keeping with their originally religious motives, some of these funds are typically devoted to religious activities, but in many cases a significant proportion could be channelled into local enterprises or educational activities.

Despite the attacks against local religions and 'superstitious' activities throughout the twentieth century, local religious collectives are still important drivers of development in rural China. Tsai (2002), for instance, provides evidence of how rural development projects at the village level in mainland China are actively initiated and managed by temple or lineage organizations. At one research site in Fujian Province, for instance, a village temple committee took over the responsibility of building roads. From the 400 000 yuan in annual donations to the temple in 2000, the temple committee paid for four roads to be paved, and village basketball courts to be constructed (ibid., p. 11). Tsai makes the positive conclusion that 'the use of community social institutions to provide village services makes coercive strategies unnecessary while empowering citizens to participate in civic life' (p. 24). Where religious institutions are owned by the community as a whole they are able to play a role in local development. In these cases, government authorities do not wish to condemn such local religious organizations as 'superstitious' but rather bring them under the wing of the state as officially authorized 'venues for religious activities (*zongjiao huodong changsuo*)' (Chau, 2005, p. 245).

The positive effect of local religious activities perhaps goes against traditional theories of the social function of religious activities, whereby religious rituals are most commonly associated with 'festival time' in Chinese rural society. As Tam (2006, p. 78) explains, the rhythms of rural Chinese life are traditionally divided into an 'ordinary time' where labour and commerce are paramount, and a 'festival time' that emphasizes play, theatre and social exchange. From the perspective of economic development, therefore, the ritual activities of local festivals might seem to function in opposition to significant economic development. Festival time does not produce a vast amount of direct economic activity, except for the expense of mounting religious rituals, staging operas and hosting lavish banquets. The traditional Chinese understanding of the value of these times of relative economic inactivity was that they were a time to 'keep the bow unstrung' (ibid., p. 79), that is to say, times of quiet and passivity rather than intense economic activity.

Chau (2005), however, challenges this traditional view of religious activity as economically otiose. His fieldwork in northwest China demonstrates how the local temple association used community donations to engage in a wide range of economic, philanthropic and educational activities:

> Besides being a site of both individual and communal worship, a temple is also a political, economic, and symbolic resource and a generator of such resources. A beautifully built temple and a well-attended temple festival attest not only to the efficacy of the deity but also to the organizational ability of the temple association and the community. (Chau, 2005, p. 238)

As Laliberté et al. (2011, p. 148) note, although it might seem that festival activities such as opera troupes and folk music performances organized by local temples are not directly related to philanthropic endeavours, the money spent on candles and incense, plus the funds left in donation boxes during these times can generate substantial revenues. In the case of the area studied by Chau, these funds were used to build a primary school and launch a reforestation project that attracted international acclaim. In these cases, 'temples are like enterprises that generate prosperity for the local economy (especially if they are regional pilgrimage centers) and income for the local state. It is thus in the interest of the local state to protect local temples as they would local enterprises' (Chau, 2005, p. 245).

Although it is important to pay attention to the 'hard' economic value contributed by Daoist and other Chinese community religious associations to local development, the 'soft' value of such organizations should also not be underestimated. Tam (2006) emphasizes the way in which religious activities play an important role in creating and performing networks of interaction within and between local communities, and notes, for instance, how religious festivals in south-east China contribute to a broader sense of community by bringing together various extended family networks and local ethnic groups, even to the extent of overloading local cellphone networks (Tam, 2006, p. 71). From this example, we can see that Daoist ritual activity functions as a kind of social lubricant, orchestrating and coordinating the mutual interaction of various communities. The work of contemporary anthropologists such as Chau and Tam, therefore, plays an important part in demonstrating the significance of Daoism for development not only in economically quantifiable terms, but also in terms of the development of social capital.

In both these cases the value that religion brings to the table is not characterized in terms of values or beliefs, but rather in the way that ritual activities serve the social function of maintaining healthy networks of community association. There is, however, an underlying set of values that reinforce Chinese religious approaches to community organization, and which deserves further explanation. In this regard it is important to understand that Daoists have not tended to regard the communities with which they engage as monolithic, unchanging entities. Rather, the normative model for understanding community has been that of the body, that is, an organism whose well-being is constituted by the proper functioning of its internal systems as much as external or environmental factors.

In the Daoist view, the outward health of the body is determined by a complex internal system in which *Qi*, or vital energy, is distributed via a network of meridians, each associated with the major organs or viscera: heart, liver, lungs, spleen and kidneys. Health obtains when *Qi* flows smoothly through the entire system and all the organs are in communicative reciprocity with each other. This view of the body is the foundation for Chinese medicine and also for Daoist meditation practices. It relies on a theory of well-being defined as optimal harmony that obtains within a system. In principle, this theory can be applied to define what is good and bad in a wide range of analogous systems: good can be defined as what brings about the flourishing of the whole system; evil can be defined as deviations of *Qi* that produce negative effects upon the whole system. From this systems perspective, good is a function of the relationships between the various actors, and is something that is distributed across the network rather than isolated in one particular area.

As an example of this, we can turn to ancient Chinese political theory in which the operations of the state were understood by analogy with the body. Just as the health of the body depends on the free flow of the various fluids, so also the health of the state was thought to depend on the free circulation of power and knowledge among the various ranks of government. In the view of the third century BCE document, known as the *Springs and Autumns of Mr. Lü* (*Lüshi Chunqiu*), the 'virtue' of the ruler is viewed as a kind of fluid that circulates throughout the organism of the state:

> When the ruler's virtue does not flow freely [i.e., if he does not appoint good officials to keep him and his subjects in touch] and the wishes of his people do not reach him, a hundred pathologies arise in concert and a myriad catastrophes swarm in. The cruelty of those above and those below toward each other arises from this. The reason that the sage kings valued heroic retainers and faithful ministers is that they dared to speak directly, breaking through such stases. (Sivin, 1995, p. 6)

Here we can see clearly a notion of what disorder consists of, namely, the 'hundred pathologies' and 'myriad catastrophes' that 'swarm in' when the fluid, charismatic virtue of the ruler does not flow smoothly throughout the nation. Conversely, communal well-being obtains when the ruler's virtue flows unhindered throughout the nation.

Throughout Chinese history, Daoists have consistently emphasized the well-being of the individual body and the communal body in these terms, seeking to bring about healing within the body (of the individual or the community) and also to defend the body from negative environmental factors characterized in Chinese mythology as demons and ghosts. Thus as Laliberté et al. (2011, p. 142) explain, 'Daoist priests were expected to provide protection against diseases and demons through rituals, exorcism, and healing. The most common form of Daoist charity was to provide free medicine and medical care to the needy'. Daoists have thus undertaken significant work in the area of health care, regarding it not so much as an adjunct charitable activity directed towards helping the needy, but as a part and parcel of their worldview in which health and long life are regarded as fundamental virtues.

To give two examples of the involvement of Daoists in healing arts and science, the first general classification of Chinese herbs was undertaken by the Daoist Tao Hongjing (456–536). This work, the *Divine Farmer's Materia Medica* (*Shennong Bencao Jing*) contains 365 recipes for drugs classified in three levels (Kohn, 2005, p. 171). Tao's work drew on a long tradition of Daoist preoccupation with herbs, fungi, minerals and animal parts whose properties were thought to aid the promotion of long life and even immortality. Similarly, the later physician and Daoist master, Sun Simiao (601–693) compiled an even more extensive compendium, *Beiji Qianjin Yaofang* (*Essential Prescriptions Worth a Thousand, for Urgent Need*), and is widely revered in Daoist temples across China as the God of Medicine. Daoism and health are thus firmly intertwined in the popular imagination in China, and in the West, so much so that there is often much confusion about whether various concepts or practices ought to be understood as 'Daoist' or 'medical' or 'religious' (Kohn, 2005, pp. 7–8). This confusion is indicative of the fact that the Western category of religion does not always make sense out of the Chinese cultural situation, in which the lines between what we would call religion, culture, economy, politics and medicine are often drawn in different ways than in the West. Thus, Daoists are not known for establishing hospitals as discrete centres of medical treatment in which the body is treated separately from an emphasis on religious or spiritual matters. Rather, community temples and temple associations form nodes in the networks through which Chinese people deal with health issues.

This interconnection of Daoism and health continues to play a role in shaping Chinese people's values in regard to public policy. Using data from the 2006 Taiwan Social Change Survey, Chang (2010) performed a statistical analysis of religious values and preferences for various redistributive social policies in contemporary Taiwan. Part of the impetus for conducting this research was that although spending on social care has grown substantially in Taiwan, the country has also been facing increased economic inequality as the result of globalization and economic liberalization (ibid., p. 102). In such a context, understanding the motivations for public attitudes towards redistributive social policies becomes all the more important. The key finding was that Protestant Christians tended to favour social insurance and welfare programmes, whereas Buddhists and Daoists favoured the government's role in providing health care (p. 81). While Chang's article does not offer any specific evidence about Daoism, it does conclude that inheriting the values of Confucianism, Daoism and Buddhism 'leads to differences in preferences for redistributive policies [compared] with those of Western Christian societies' (p. 102). There is at least initial evidence for supposing that in a modern East Asian society, Daoists continue to hold identifiable values regarding these key aspects of public policy, and that health care is a particular focus for them.

SUSTAINABILITY

Cyclical models of economic activity have once again come to the fore as linear models of economic development push up against the ecological limits imposed by the natural carrying capacity of the earth. Prominent ecological economists such as Daly (1996) argue for 'steady state economics' (SSE) rather than conventional growth economics. For now, however, international work towards climate change mitigation has pushed China to focus not on limiting growth in absolute terms, but in reducing the intensity of carbon emissions per unit of economic activity. The climate change policies promoted in China's twelfth Five Year Plan (2011–15) call for the development of 'circular economies' in which the waste product of one economic process becomes a valued input for another process (Information Office of the State Council, 2011). Typically, two or more enterprises are co-located so as to facilitate this economic synergy. China's Vice Minister of Environmental Protection argues that although industrialization broke through the 'static, circulating economic pattern' of traditional agriculture, this model is ultimately unsustainable as it demands high energy consumption and produces massive pollution (Pan Yue, 2007, p. 11). He continues:

> Human beings obtain materials and energy from nature, and they must return them to the circulating system and do their best to reduce waste and destruction. Such an energy circulating system operating in line with the law of nature is exactly what was put by ancient Chinese as 'round and round goes the divine order of things'.

This is a paraphrase of Chapter 16 of the classic Daoist text, *The Way and Its Power* (*Daode jing* or *Laozi*, after its author), which articulates a fundamental insight of the Daoist worldview, namely, a basic cosmic pattern of emergence and decay, activity and stillness, *yang* and *yin*. Daoists regard this pattern as natural, and derived it from the observation of the rotations of heavenly bodies through the sky. If Daoist philosophy has anything to contribute to notions of development, it is from within this circular perspective, in which the functioning of a system is basically understood not as a simple linear growth but as continuous exchange. Translated to an economic sphere this invites a theory of development rooted not in Christian or post-Christian faith in continuous linear development towards some ever-unattainable utopian ideal (see Gray, 2004), but rather a more realistic and holistic view that pays attention to the overall health and well-being of the community.

Given the political realities in contemporary China, however, it is not surprising that the Chinese Daoist Association (CDA) has avoided the role of critiquing China's economic policies. This does not mean, however, that it has completely avoided the issue of the environment as a key religious question. Such efforts go back to at least 1995 when the CDA issued a 'Declaration on Global Ecology'. The final page of this declaration summarizes the whole in three bullet points:

- We shall spread the ecological teachings of Daoism, lead all Daoist followers to abide in the teachings of self-so or non-action, observe the injunction against killing for amusement purposes, preserve and protect the harmonious relationship of all things with Nature, establish paradises of immortals on Earth, and pursue the practice of our beliefs . . .
- We shall continue the Daoist ecological tradition by planting trees and cultivating forests. Using traditional hermitages as an organizational base, Daoists will conscientiously plant trees and build forests, thereby making the natural environment beautiful and transforming our hermitages into the paradise worlds of the immortals.

- We shall select some famous Daoist mountains as exemplars of the systematic task of environmental engineering. We expect to reach this goal by the early years of the new century. (Zhang, 2001, p. 370)

While this goal may have been hopelessly optimistic, there is no doubt that the seeds sown in 1995 continue to bear fruit in the present, with ongoing attempts by the CDA to preserve Daoist sacred spaces as paradigmatic locations for contemporary urban Chinese to encounter China's 'lost' nature. The CDA's Maoshan Declaration (2008) and its accompanying Eight Year Plan advocate that Daoist sacred sites be regarded not simply as places where religious activities take place but also as sites of environmental significance and locations for environmental education (Miller, 2013). Moreover, in a partnership with the Alliance for Religions and Conservation (ARC), the CDA established a small Daoist ecology temple in a conservation site near Taibaishan, Shaanxi. While it is perhaps too soon to be able to measure the practical effects of such policies and activities, it is at least worthwhile noting that a major national religious organization in China has embraced the preservation of specific environments as a central religious value.

Duara (2011, p. 24) speculates that what we may be seeing here is the embrace of sustainability as 'an emergent ideal, a new type of transcendence and sacrality with the capacity to motivate and mobilize persons and groups'. From this perspective, Daoism may be regarded as contributing to the development of an alternative to the conventional paradigms of secular modernization and economic development, namely, ecological sustainability. In so doing, whether it realizes it or not, the CDA is playing a certain role in contributing to a national conversation in China about what development and modernization should look like. In contrast to the Maoist 'utopian urgency' of 'Let's attack here!/Drive away the mountain gods/Break down the stone walls/To bring out those 200 million tons of coal' (quoted in Shapiro, 2001, p. vii), there is now a sense that the preservation, rather than destruction, of natural environments has not just a positive effect on the well-being of the community, but is rather one component of a transcendent value that demands attention in its own right and to which other values must ultimately be subordinate.

REFERENCES

Chang, Wen-Chung (2010), 'Religion and preferences for redistributive policies in an East Asian country', *Poverty & Public Policy*, **2**(4), 81–109.

Chau, Adam Yuet (2005), 'The politics of legitimation and the revival of popular religion in Shaanbei, North-Central China', *Modern China*, **31**(2), 236–78.

Daly, Herman E. (1996), *Beyond Growth: The Economics of Sustainable Development*, Boston: Beacon Press.

de Bary, William Theodore (1960), *Sources of Chinese Tradition*, New York: Columbia University Press.

Duara, Prasenjit (1991), 'Knowledge and power in the discourse of modernity: the campaigns against popular religion in early twentieth-century China', *The Journal of Asian Studies*, **50**(1), 67–83.

Duara, Prasenjit (2011), 'Sustainability and the crisis of transcendence: the long view from Asia', keynote address, Conference on Asian Modernities and Traditions, Leiden University, 9 September, available at: http://media.leidenuniv.nl/legacy/duarapresentation.pdf; accessed 11 July 2012.

Gray, John (2004), 'An illusion with a future', *Daedalus*, **133**(3), 10–17.

Information Office of the State Council (2011), *China's Policies and Actions for Addressing Climate Change*, issued on 22 November 2011, available at: http://www.gov.cn/english/official/2011-11/22/content_2000272_10.htm; accessed 15 January, 2012.

Kohn, Livia, in cooperation with Stephen Jackowicz (2005), *Health and Long Life: The Chinese Way*, Cambridge, MA: Three Pines Press.

Laliberté, André, David A. Palmer and Keping Wu (2011), 'Religious philanthropy and Chinese civil society', in David A. Palmer, Glenn Shive and Philip L. Wickeri (eds), *Chinese Religious Life*, Oxford: Oxford University Press, pp. 139–51.

Lawrance, Allan (ed.) (2004), *China Since 1919: Revolution and Reform. A Sourcebook*, New York: Routledge.

Miller, James (2012), 'Nature', in Randall Nadeau (ed.), *The Wiley-Blackwell Companion to Chinese Religion*, Oxford: Blackwell.

Miller, James (2013), 'Monitory democracy and ecological civilization in the People's Republic of China', forthcoming in Nina Witoszek and Lars Trågårdh (eds), *Civil Society in the Age of Wikileaks: Challenges to Monitory Democracy*, Oxford: Berghahn Books.

Pan Yue (2007), *Thoughts on Environmental Issues*, Beijing: China Environmental Culture Promotion Association.

Schipper, Kristofer (2001), 'Daoist ecology: the inner transformation. A study of the precepts of the early Daoist ecclesia', in N.J. Giradot et al. (eds), *Daoism and Ecology: Ways Within a Cosmic Landscape*, Cambridge, MA: Harvard University Center for the Study of World Religions, pp. 79–94.

Schipper, Kristofer (2008), *La Réligion de la Chine*, Paris: Fayard.

Shapiro, Judith (2001), *Mao's War Against Nature: Politics and the Environment in Revolutionary China*, Cambridge: Cambridge University Press.

Sivin, Nathan (1995), 'State, cosmos, and body in the last three centuries BC', *Harvard Journal of Asiatic Studies*, **55**(1), 5–37.

Tam Wai Lun (2006), 'Local religion in contemporary China', in James Miller (ed.), *Chinese Religions in Contemporary Societies*, Santa Barbara, CA: ABC-CLIO, pp. 57–84.

Tsai, Lily Lee (2002), 'Cadres, temple and lineage institutions, and governance in rural China', *The China Journal*, No. 48, 1–27.

Zeng, Chuanhu (2011), 'Coalition and hegemony: religion's role in the progress of modernization in reformed China', *Brigham Young University Law Review*, No. 3, pp. 759–82.

Zhang Jiyu (2001), 'A declaration of the Chinese Daoist Association on global ecology', in N.J. Girardot et al. (eds), *Daoism and Ecology: Ways Within a Cosmic Landscape*, Cambridge, MA: Harvard University Press, pp. 361–72.

9 Confucianism

Xiangshu Fang and Lijun Bi

INTRODUCTION

Confucianism, which draws its name from the ancient Chinese scholar Confucius, has long influenced Chinese social and political institutions with the concepts of a hierarchical moral order. As Confucianism rose to dominance in Chinese society, Confucius became respected as a sage, and temples dedicated to Confucius were built across China. The main tenets of Confucianism were derived from Confucius himself, his early disciples, and later the Confucian school of philosophers and scholars. It has also absorbed important contributions from other religious and philosophical sources, both from within China and from outside.

Confucianism (儒教, *rujiao*)[1] has shaped the Chinese people's outlook and behaviour from the Warring States period (403–221 BC) to the present day. Based on the concepts of the family and state that predated Confucius, the Confucian Classics defined precise details of social behaviour and especially exalted the notion of filial piety. Particular emphasis was placed on the social obligations enshrined in the five human relationships of father and son; ruler and minister; elder brother and younger brother; husband and wife; and friend and friend. During Confucius' life (551–479 BC) the imperial rule of the Zhou dynasty (1046–256 BC) was weak, and the feudal princes vied for supremacy, each having their own form of government. Confucius dreamed of restoring the social order according to the rules of propriety (*li*) in the early Zhou dynasty. He never denied that he was 'believing in and loving the ancients', and was 'fond of antiquity and earnest in seeking it' (*Analects* 7: 1 and 7: 19).[2] His teachings are rich with nostalgia for the golden era of antiquity. Confucianism was first espoused by rulers of China's early Han dynasty (206 BC–AD 9). This political philosophy of Confucianism was the interpretation and crystallization of the principles and ideas attributed to Confucius by scholars and officials such as Mencius (372–289 BC), Xunzi (298–238 BC) and Dong Zhongshu (179–104 BC). It emphasized the ruler's duty to set a moral example and govern in the interest of the populace, and has developed characteristics beyond anything conceived by Confucius himself.

Of all conservative systems in human history Confucianism has been the most successful. This success explains why the notions of passivity, compliance, submissiveness, acceptance of fate and maintenance of the status quo have always been highly valued in China. These features continue to be main attributes of Chinese culture, with the notable characteristics of alertness to hierarchic differences and the demand of obedience to proper authority. The influence of Confucius did not end in China. From China it spread throughout East Asia. Confucianism has had a salient influence on the neighbouring societies and cultures of Korea, Japan, Vietnam and Singapore, which have developed ways of living and thinking derived from the wisdom of the sage.

LIFE AND CORE TEACHINGS OF CONFUCIUS

'Confucius' is a seventeenth-century Jesuit Latinization of Kong Fuzi (孔夫子 – Master Kong), as he was known by his followers. His personal name was Qiu (邱) and his courtesy name (given at his attainment of adulthood) was Zhongni (仲尼). He is said to have been born in 551 BC in the State of Lu, in the modern Shandong Province of China. His father was a district magistrate and died when he was only three, leaving his care and education to his mother. During his youth he was remarkable for his grave demeanour and knowledge of ancient learning, which gained him respect among his countrymen. At the age of 20, he was entrusted with the duties of being a subordinate officer at the revenue department, and was later appointed a supervisor of fields and herds. When he was 24, his mother passed away. In conformity with the ancient practice, which was no longer observed, he immediately resigned from all his employment to mourn for his mother for a period of three years. During this time, he devoted himself to study.

His examination of the ancient writings made him determined to teach his countrymen the doctrines of the former sages and to revive the ancient rites. When he was 30 he was already reputable amongst the educated and influential men of the court of the State of Lu as a teacher. He visited the imperial capital Luoyang, in current Henan Province. Here, together with his disciples, he examined documents of the past and the present with close scrutiny. When he returned home, his respect for the ancients became even greater. His admirers increased and fame followed. His disciples came from all parts of the land, and public opinion began to be influenced by his words and actions.

In 500 BC, Confucius was appointed as the local magistrate. He was now 50 years old, and began to carry out the best rule he could in his position. For three years, he administrated state affairs with an extensive mixture of zeal, prudence and severity. However, he did so with regard for the rights and wants of all classes. This resulted in the State of Lu becoming the envy and dread of all other states. His precepts had fairly been put into practice and his influence increased with the acknowledgement of his success. He moved to the State of Wei and began to travel with his disciples into adjoining states to extend his doctrines. He returned to his native state at the age of 68 and devoted his time to compiling his edition of the Classics and teaching his now large band of students. He died in 479 BC, aged 71, leaving behind a single grandson, Zisi. Through Zisi, succession has been transmitted to the present day.[3]

Confucius is credited with having edited what were to become the Chinese Classics, a collection of poetry, music, historical documents, and an extensive commentary on the *Book of Changes* (*I Ching* or *Wu Jing*). The *Spring and Autumn Annals* is the only Classic entirely attributed to Confucius, though there is no evidence, which beyond reasonable doubt proves the sage's genuine compilation, except for Mencius' (372–289 BC) claim that it was the sage's work. Confucius' aim is believed to be the construction of a narrative of events in continuation with the *Classic of History* (*Shu Jing*). With the assistance of his pupils, he is said to have drawn up a history of his own state, extending from the reign of the Duke Ping of Lu to about the period of his birth (722–480 BC). The title *Spring and Autumn* is generally understood by many scholars as a term for chronological annals. The connotations are that the sage evaluated these events through his sanctions, which are life-giving like spring, and his disapprovals, which are life-withering like autumn. The focus is on various states' diplomatic relations, alliances and military actions, as well as births and deaths among the ruling families. The chronicle also takes note of natural disasters such as floods, earthquakes, locust plagues and solar eclipses, as these events were seen to reflect Heaven's influence on the human world. The annalistic structure is followed strictly, to the extent of listing the four seasons of each year even when no events were recorded. The original text was substantiated by later Confucian scholars, Zuo Qiuming, Gongyang and Guling, who filled the gaps between the meagre sentences and added both flesh and life to the skeleton.

The *Analects* of Confucius is conceivably the most important of the entire Confucian canon. It is a collection of the sage's words and actions as recorded by his disciples. Divided into 20 chapters, the book is not arranged chronologically. This book discloses Confucius' shrewd insight into his countrymen's characteristics, and knowledge of the manner in which they could best be approached and influenced. The central concerns in this book are his life-long dream of reviving the doctrines of the ancients, his tenets of benevolence, filial piety and truthfulness, and his firm belief in education. Among the most remarkable passages in Confucius' *Analects* are the following:

> Zi Gong asked, saying, 'Is there one word which may serve as a rule of practice for all one's life?' The Master said, 'Is not RECIPROCITY such a word? What you don't want done to yourself, do not do to others'. (15: 23)
>
> The Master said, 'Governing with morality resembles the North Star, which is fixed, and all other stars surround it'. (2: 1)
>
> The Master said, 'Learning without reflection will profit nothing; reflection without learning is dangerous'. (2: 15)
>
> The Master said, 'Knowledge produces pleasure clear as water; complete virtue brings happiness solid as mountain; knowledge prevails all things; virtue is tranquil and happy; knowledge is delight; virtue is long life'. (6: 23)
>
> The Master said, 'The superior man does not promote a man simply on account of his words, nor does he put aside good words because of the man'. (15: 23)
>
> The Master said, 'Without recognizing the ordinances of Heaven, it is impossible to be a superior man. Without an acquaintance with the rules of Propriety, it is impossible for the character to be established. Without knowing the force of words, it is impossible to know men'. (20: 3)[4]

A marked feature of the *Analects* is its prescriptive rather than descriptive emphasis on the ideal man, which he called *junzi* – a true gentleman or a superior man. Moral superiority could be acquired by all men who were willing to learn. The character of *junzi* was the possession of *ren* (benevolence), a virtue in which the individual and society were harmonized. The *Analects* of Confucius contains numerous references to the qualities of *junzi*, who 'considers righteousness to be essential in everything. He performs it according to the rules of propriety. He brings it forth in humanity. He completes it with sincerity. This is indeed a superior man' (15: 18). 'In his conduct to himself, he was humble; in serving his superiors, he was respectful; in nourishing the people, he was kind; in ordering the people, he was just' (5: 16). 'The faults of the *junzi* are like the eclipses of the sun and moon. He has his faults, and all men see them; he changes again, and all look up to him' (19: 21).

Often Confucius spoke in a manner that highlighted his own impression that Heaven had conferred on him a special commission to instruct the world. For example, once he said:

> At fifteen, I had my mind bent on learning. At thirty, I stood firm. At forty, I had no doubts. At fifty, I knew the decrees of Heaven. At sixty, my ear was an obedient organ for the reception of truth. At seventy, I could follow what my heart desired, without transgressing what was right. (*Analects*, 2: 4)

On another occasion, when looking at a stream, he compared its current to the transmission of good doctrines throughout succeeding generations, but often he only seemed to entertain faint hopes that his doctrines would be received by future generations.

MENCIUS

Mencius emerged as a sage a century after Confucius died. He had the advantage of the example, fame and teaching of his master, Confucius. Nevertheless, in many respects, he displayed an originality of thought, firmness of purpose and extensive views superior to Confucius, and therefore must be regarded as one of the greatest men China has ever produced.

Mencius was born in 371 BC in a place not far from Confucius' native district. His father died early, leaving the guardianship of the boy to his widow, Zhang Shi. Mencius' caring and thoughtful mother has been cited for centuries as a model for all virtuous parents in China. Mencius sought to defend the doctrine of Confucius against other influential thinkers of the time, such as Mozi (479–381 BC) and Yang Zhu (440–360 BC). He is probably best known for the view that 'human nature is good', a view based on the defence of Confucian ideals, which developed a self-cultivation process. His view was subsequently challenged by Xunzi (298–238 BC), another major Confucian thinker, who advocated the alternative view that 'human nature is evil'.

Confucian thinkers of the Han dynasty (206 BC–AD 220) were influenced by the teachings of both Mencius and Xunzi, but by the late Tang dynasty (AD 618–907), influential intellectuals such as Han Yu (AD 768–824) began to regard Mencius as the true transmitter of Confucius' doctrine. This view was shared by the Song dynasty scholar, Zhu Xi (AD 1130–1200), who selected the *Mencius* as one of the *Four Books*, which became canonical texts of Confucian teachings. From then on, Mencius came to be regarded as the greatest Confucian thinker subsequent to Confucius himself, and his teachings have been very influential on the development of Confucian thought in China.

The *Mencius* consists entirely of Mencius' teachings. Most scholars nowadays think that the *Mencius* was almost certainly compiled by his disciples or disciples of his disciples. The text was subsequently edited and shortened by Zhao Qi in the second century AD with a commentary on the text. This version of the text was used by subsequent scholars and is also the most current version.

The book makes reference to a number of key philosophical terms in early Chinese thought, as well as to ideas associated with the teachings of Confucius as recorded in the *Analects*. The three most important terms and concepts in the book are *tian* (天– Heaven), *ming* (命 – mandate, decree, destiny), and *de* (德 – virtue, power). Mencius made it clear that the king retained the authority to rule only if he respected *tian ming*, the mandate from Heaven to rule. Here his preservation of the Mandate of Heaven should depend on his *de*, which refers to qualities such as generosity, self-sacrifice, humility, receptiveness to instruction, as well as to powers associated with these qualities. These powers include the recipient's compulsion to respond to generous acts and a non-coercive power of attraction and transformation.

Similar to his idol Confucius, Mencius travelled broadly, offering his advice to rulers of various states. He repeatedly tried to convert them to the belief that any ruler able to win over the people through benevolent government could succeed in unifying 'all under Heaven' (天下). He advocated detailed and specific proposals concerning political and financial measures in order to ease tax burdens and reduce military escalation. He argued that the pursuit of military dominance would backfire because it would turn the world against the ruler of such domination, whereas those who were benevolent would have no enemies.

Mencius expanded Confucius' social and economic ideas and stressed people's well-being as one of the government's most important objectives. He argued that '(t)he people are the most precious and venerable thing. The spirits of the grain come second. The princes are of the least importance' (*Mencius*, 14: 14). The most important contribution that Mencius made to the development of Chinese history, particularly in terms of power transition, was his innovative elucidation of the 'Mandate of Heaven' notion. He developed this notion into the principle that bad rulers would lose their right to rule. When an emperor no longer possessed virtue, the Mandate of Heaven could be withdrawn and the dynasty could be replaced. This interpretation of the emperor's responsibility afforded the Confucian school broad popular appeal. In the eyes of the Chinese peasant population, the emperor's suitability could easily be judged based on decisions and performance. Natural catastrophes, civil war, disorder, famine and suffering all became indications of lack of virtue and Heaven's discontent. Celestial signs such as comets and earthquakes were heavenly warnings. When things went wrong and the heavenly mandate had expired, rebellion was justified in order to replace the old dynasty with a new one. The ramifications of this were far-reaching. In more recent Chinese history, foreign forces such as Mongol and Manchu conquerors were accepted as possessing the Mandate of Heaven to rule China.[5]

CONFUCIANISM AS A STATE CULT

It was during the Han dynasty (202 BC–AD 220) that much of China's cultural, political, administrative, and indeed ideological frameworks, were formed. The features of these frameworks that emerged during the Han dynasty affected China until the middle of the twentieth century. It was the Han emperors who established the legitimacy and effectiveness of centralized authority. This authority would become a ruling governmental norm for all future regimes. The acceptance of the central authority of a single ruler, as a norm, involved the acceptance of certain ideas concerning the function, duties and place of the emperor and his subjects.

The Han emperor who had the greatest impact on Chinese culture and society was Emperor Wu (156–87 BC). In 140 BC, Emperor Wu of Han conducted an imperial examination of over 100 young scholars recommended by officials, most of them commoners with no noble background. This event would prove to have a major impact on Chinese history, as it was the official origins of the establishment of Confucianism as the sanctioned imperial doctrine. This came about because a young Confucian scholar, Dong Zhongshu, was evaluated to have submitted the best essay, in which he advocated the establishment of Confucianism. Dong Zhongshu's thought integrated *yin-yang* cosmology into a Confucian ethical framework. He emphasized the importance of the *Spring and Autumn Annals* as a source for both political and metaphysical ideas, which were based on the tradition of the *Gongyang Commentary*, namely, seeking hidden meanings from a text. He laid down rules that regulated the legitimacy of a monarch as well as providing a set of checks and balances for a reigning monarch.

During Emperor Wu's reign, highly centralized administration needed a large number of bureaucrats. But where and how did the regime find so many workers to staff its extensive bureaucracy at various levels? Emperor Wu was the one who accepted Dong Zhongshu's advice and took decisive measures to solve the problem. In the capital city of Chang'an, an imperial academy was established and each year it produced two kinds of graduates: the first group being the sons and nephews of high-ranking officials; the second group consisted of the sons and nephews of those who were not so high-ranking, including commoners. The first group was titled 'members of imperial guards' and served as a manpower reserve from which all ministries and commissions recruited their officials. The recruits were usually placed at the lowest level. The second group, on the other hand, returned to their native provinces and districts to serve as local officials. The imperial academy was founded with five faculties, each specializing in one of the five canonical Classics – *Classic of Changes* for divination, the *Classic of History*, the *Classic of Poetry*, which was a collection of ancient folk poems, the *Classic of Rites*, and the *Spring and Autumn Annals* – chronologies of Confucius' own State of Lu. According to tradition, they were compiled or edited by Confucius himself. These five ancient Chinese books were used as the basis for Confucianism studies. The force of these *Five Classics* is their ethical rather than their theoretical or metaphysical content, and these elements delineate the main moral principles of Confucianism.[6]

Ranging to the Song dynasty (AD 907–1279), Confucian texts with commentaries by famous Confucian scholars exceeded a canon of 13 Classics, in total filling an estimated 120 volumes today. In order to simplify this unwieldy corpus of ancient texts, a Song dynasty Confucian scholar Zhu Xi (AD 1130–1200) selected the famous *Four Books* – the *Analects* of Confucius, the *Mencius*, the *Doctrine of the Mean* and the *Great Learning*. With these books, it was more realistic that any potential candidate for the scholar-gentry class would be able to master them in a reasonably short period of time.

At the beginning of the nineteenth century, most Chinese people did not doubt the long-held belief that China was the central kingdom of the world. No other country had a greater population than China, Chinese products were in great demand in foreign countries and its territories had been expanded under the rule of the Manchu Qing dynasty. However, from the mid-nineteenth century onwards Western warships and guns began to shatter Chinese confidence. This was most pertinent when China suffered numerous humiliating setbacks after it was defeated by Western powers and Japan, and had to cede territories such as Hong Kong, Macau and Taiwan and open up treaty ports where foreigners could set up their 'concessions'.

Leading figures of the Chinese literati in conjunction with Manchu rulers began a reform movement to strengthen China's position by imitating Western devices and Western institutions. The government began to send students overseas, mainly to Britain and other European countries, the United States and Japan. This so-called 'self-strengthening' reform movement was based on the attractive but fallacious slogan 'Chinese learning as the fundamental structure; Western learning for practical use'. It appeared as if Western arms, gunboats, steamships, science and technology could be used to preserve Confucian values, instead of destroying them. In 1905, a more drastic and monumental step was taken in order to abolish the imperial civil service examination system altogether. This system had established the framework for relations between the government and elite literati for nearly 2000 years. It was, however, too late for the Qing dynasty, which collapsed in 1911.

In the May Fourth New Culture Movement a few years later, young intellectuals began to challenge the long-standing Confucian value of holding high esteem for elders. They called upon fellow young people to be aware of the incompatibility of Confucianism and modernity. They claimed that filial piety, loyalty, chastity and righteousness were nothing but slavish morality. This period was marked by the advent of a wave of new revolutionary ideas. Many Chinese intellectuals questioned the role and suitability of the dominating ideology of Confucianism, which was seen as the main obstacle to China's modernization. They began to seek new ideological remedies from the West, and eventually adopted Marxism and Leninism.

In the later years of the Cultural Revolution (1966–76), Confucius became the official target of a campaign of criticism and was condemned as being representative of all reactionaries in Chinese history. However, since the 1980s, Confucianism has made a spectacular comeback in China. Although the majority of proponents for the revival of Confucianism came from the tertiary sector, the party-state leadership found that neo-Confucian views were quite in tune with their own goals. The neo-Confucians argued that modernization did not mean Westernization and that the seeds of modernization could also be found in Chinese history and values, especially in Confucianism. They insisted that Confucianism, instead of being an obstacle to modernization as was purported by the May Fourth intellectuals and Maoist ideologues, could be conductive to China's progress. Citing the dynamic economies of other Confucian-shaped East Asian societies as an example, they asserted that a revived sense of Confucianism could provide the intellectual and cultural substance for China's rapid economic growth. In addition, this could also help China avoid Western capitalist immorality and individualism. The party-state leadership agreed with these views. However, Confucian authoritarian values were stressed rather than the sage's teaching, which stated that the literati had an obligation to criticize officials who abused power or engaged in any unfair treatment of the population.

CONFUCIANISM AND EDUCATION

Although Confucius was referred to by his peers as a man of wisdom and knowledge, he described himself modestly as an avid student who loved learning more than anything else. During his life, he attracted a large number of young and able students. As a teacher, Confucius demanded students' total commitment to learning. He was a tolerant and inclusive instructor who did not consider any distinction in terms of socioeconomic background when selecting his students. He would take only what they could afford as payment for his services, but he set high standards, and if his students did not demonstrate seriousness and enthusiasm towards his lessons, Confucius would not put up with them. He established a school with the explicit purpose of educating subsequent generations about political leadership. His curriculum encouraged personal articulation and refinement and was more directed at developing students' moral characteristics than teaching any one practical skill set. Confucius had various disciples who came from the central states of China. They were devoted to their master and responded to him with reverence. There is no better evidence of this unwavering respect than the fact that they meticulously recorded their master's criticism of themselves, and then went on to establish branch schools based on these records to perpetuate their master's teachings.

Confucians believe that 'from the Son of Heaven down to mass of the people, all must consider the cultivation of the person the root of everything besides' (*Great Learning*, 6).[7] Confucius formulated the following for a youth:

> A youth, when at home, should be filial, and, abroad, respectful to his elders. He should be earnest and truthful. He should overflow love to all, and cultivate the friendship of the good. When he has time and opportunity, after the performance of these things, he should employ them in polite studies. (*Analects*, 1: 6)

Training in Confucian Classics was essential to ensure that the educated man would acquire the moral qualities and the strength of character that would enable him to fulfil his duties, both as a filial son at home and as a loyal subject in society. He was expected to have a high sense of respect for public responsibilities and was even anticipated to commit suicide and perish with his emperor if the dynasty were defeated. Though in reality many shifted their allegiances, some did choose to die. The ideal of the scholar-gentry was summarized by a Song dynasty scholar-gentry official Fan Zhongyan, who wrote in his famous essay 'Yueyang Pavilion': 'First to sense every care that is under Heaven, Last to know the joy that is free to all others'.[8]

This ideal was not always practised, but it was believed to be a standard for the scholar-gentry's behaviour and it provided a moral ground for the literati to act in times of crisis. Members of this elite group were educated moralists and moral educators. They had the responsibility, as described in Confucian Classics, to even educate rulers about the best way to govern through moral cultivation.

CONFUCIANISM AND DEVELOPMENT

Confucius advocated active participation in business and social activities, and always attached importance to production. During the Spring and Autumn period of Chinese history (771–475 BC), named after the *Annals* of the same name, social productive forces rapidly developed. In order to meet their increasing greed, the rulers ruthlessly exploited labourers, who carried out large-scale construction, which included building roads and city walls and fighting wars. In view of this situation, Confucius advocated that rulers should show compassion for the people, and only draw on their labour in a sustainable manner. Sustainability, at this time, meant only using peasant labour during the slack season of the year. This was important to ensure that peasants had enough time for ploughing and sowing – thus increasing the production of grain (see *Analects*, 1: 5).[9]

Confucius' ideas about ensuring 'sufficient food, sufficient military equipment and the confidence of the people in the ruler' originated in a conversation between him and his disciple Zi Gong:

> Zi Gong then asked, 'If it cannot be helped, and one of the three must be dispensed with, which of the three should be forgone first?'
> 'The military equipment,' said the Master.
> Zi Gong again asked, 'If it cannot be helped, and one of the remaining two must be dispensed with, which of them should be forgone?'
> The Master answered, 'Part with the food. From old, death has been the lot of all men; if the people have no faith in their rulers, there is no standing for the State'. (*Analects*, 12: 7)

'Food' is the most basic material. Without it, both civilians and soldiers cannot live and the country will cease to exist. A strong army and sufficient military equipment are the basic guarantees for the country's existence. Without them, there is no guarantee for the people's safety and it may prove difficult to remain independent. The people are the 'roots' of the country. Everything produced by the country comes from the people. If the people have no confidence in the ruler of the country, it will collapse from within.

With regard to the military dimension, this largely referred to provision for security against attack, as in ancient times nomadic raids on the cultivated central regions of China had been an ever-present threat to the security of the central regions. Hence the provision of security from physical attack constitutes a measure of good governance. The following dialogue indicates Confucius' thoughts on the issue:

> When Confucius set off on a journey to the State of Wei, Ran You, his disciple, drove the carriage for him. When they arrived at Wei, Confucius saw a lot of people there and exclaimed, 'How numerous are the people!'
> Ran You said, 'Since there are thus numerous, what more shall be done for them?'
> 'Enrich them,' was the reply.
> 'And when they have been enriched, what more should be done?'
> The Master said, 'Educate them'. (*Analects*, 13: 9)

Indeed, during the Spring and Autumn period, anyone with breadth of vision realized that human beings were valuable resources and an important factor in the development of production. If there were more people, more grain could be produced, and the country would become prosperous and strong. Confucius did not think it would be enough to simply 'enrich them'. He perceived that it would be necessary to develop education and skills for the common people upon their rise to comfort. Confucius believed that in order to raise the cultural level of the common people, productive forces had to be promoted. The Confucian development formula pattern places emphasis on the role of education:

Thorough investigation of all things → complete knowledge → sincere thoughts → rectified hearts → cultivated persons → regulated families → rightly governed states → the whole kingdom being made tranquil and happy

Confucius placed stress on morality and justice, disparaged personal gains and combined justice with interests. In other words, the economy could not benefit from the profit motive alone, rather it benefits from a society that values morality. Confucius once reflected, 'Riches and honours acquired by unrighteousness are to me as a floating cloud' (*Analects*, 7: 16).

CONFUCIANISM AND THE ENVIRONMENT

Confucian thinkers characteristically regard nature in a holistic manner; all things in nature depend on each other and form an organic whole. They also consider human beings to be part of nature. Emphasis is also placed on the fact that people and nature are closely bound in a harmonious primary relationship. The pre-Qin (i.e., pre-221 BC) Confucian thinkers developed these ideas into the theory of the unity of man and Heaven or nature.[10]

The traditional Chinese theory concerning oneness of Heaven and man can be traced back to the records and decrees of the early Western Zhou dynasty (1027–771 BC). The first Zhou kings (King Wen, King Wu, and particularly the Duke of Zhou) believed that their legitimacy to rule was based on *tianming* (the Mandate of Heaven). Thereafter, every king or emperor of later dynasties called himself *tianzi* (Son of Heaven). The 'Son of Heaven' was the only person entitled to preside over state rituals for serving Heaven. According to Confucian canonical *Classic of History* and *Classic of Poetry*, *tian* (Heaven) consisted of four functions:

1. Dominator. *Tian* (Heaven) governs all creatures.
2. Creator. All things originate from *tian* (Heaven).
3. Sustainer. After creating myriad things, *tian* (Heaven) does not leave them alone without its control and support.
4. Revealer. The function of *tian* (Heaven) is not confined to the appointment of a ruler. It reveals its endorsement or withdrawal of support through natural phenomena.

Another Confucian Classic, the *Doctrine of the Mean*, states: 'What Heaven conferred is called NATURE; an accordance with this nature is called THE PATH *of duty*; the regulation of this path is called INSTRUCTION' (Chapter 1), and '(a)ll things are nourished together without their injuring one another' (Chapter 30).[11] Heaven, Earth and humans are not considered in isolation. On the contrary, the three are placed within a larger system and are taken as a whole. The change and development of humans and nature are regarded as a related, harmonious and balanced movement.

To understand the meaning of Heaven, rendered from the Chinese *tian*, it is worth noting that neither 'Heaven' nor 'Nature' fully articulates the connotation of *tian*. Tian encompasses various notions that include the sky, weather, the natural order, and also a human moral order. According to Confucius' disciple, Xunzi (310–219 BC) '*tian* represents a natural order, operating according to unchanging principles, not intervening in extraordinary ways in human affairs but, rather, providing the context within which all living things exist' (as cited in De Bary et al., 2000, p. 170).

When attempting to understand the spectrum of meaning attached to *tian*, it is possible to appreciate why nature is equated with Heaven (*tian*) rather than Earth, as is often the case in today's environmental discourse. Therefore, 'saving' the environment requires more than simple physical preservation. It calls for reverence and duty to the environment's greater self, nature. This extension of humanity carries ethical concerns for the environment.

In advocating the concept of the unity of Heaven and man, Confucian thinkers do not purport that there is no difference between the two. Rather, they consider that Heaven is the same as nature, which runs its own course, and human acts of transforming nature need to be based on the understanding and observation of the laws of nature, otherwise, the human habitat will be damaged and endangered. Hence the Confucian view holds humans to be part of nature, meaning that they should respect and act in accordance with the laws of nature.

CONFUCIANISM AND HEALTH CARE

Confucianism also informs practices on health and longevity in China. Confucius did not refrain from the pleasures of life, such as eating and sex. However, he sought to achieve a balance between extremes, and to avoid excess. He proposed the idea that life fulfilment could be achieved through associating with others, first in family life, and subsequently in community life. He stressed the importance of social order and an active life, focusing on the individual behaving in accordance with the concept of nature consisting of Heaven, human beings and the Earth.

Confucianism fundamentally conceives people to be members of social groups – specifically, the family, the clan, the community and the state – not as atomic individuals as is commonly perceived in modern society. Confucianism is family oriented and virtue-oriented. It takes the family as humans' primary moral community as well as being the centre of individual health care and well-being. The family-oriented model of Confucianism offers an alternative way of considering what constitutes a community and common good. The Confucian approach to ethics is relevant to health care today, especially in terms of aged care, where family plays a larger role by drawing on family savings accounts.

Confucianism in general can be viewed as a theoretical expression and a systematic justification of traditional family values in ancient China. *Xiao* (filial piety), which primarily defines a child's moral duty to his or her parents, has been understood in the 2500-year-long Confucian tradition as the 'root' of morality (*Analects*, 1: 2). Confucius' emphasis on filial piety with regard to adult children, ensuring respectful care for their aged parents, has had a tremendous influence on shaping Chinese understanding of morality. On the one hand, taking good care of one's parents is often seen as a cardinal virtue of a moral person and constitutive of being a good citizen. On the other hand in Chinese tradition, ensuring that all parents and elderly people receive good care from their children is taken as proof of a good society and government. Mencius said that in a good society 'a son and a younger brother should be taught their obligation of taking good care of their aged parents. The people with grey hair should not be seen carrying burdens on the street' (*Mencius*, 1: 7). If they were, it would be a matter of shame for the children as well as for the government.

The Confucian approach affirms the integrity and responsibility of the family. When families need to save and take risks together regarding health care, they are encouraged to recognize the limitations of individual lives, while affirming the larger social reality of the family. This approach challenges the stream of modern individualism that encourages the fragmentation of families into isolated individuals. It indicates the possibility of enduring bonds of human love and mutual concern, and offers an insight into an authentic Confucian appreciation of the family's role in confronting human suffering and finitude.[12]

GENDER IN CONFUCIANISM

Confucianism is heavily based on ancient cosmology derived from early agricultural activities along the Yellow River valley. This ancient cosmology is characterized by its deep belief that the world is the product of two interacting complementary elements, *yin* and *yang*. *Yin* was the attribute of all things female, dark, weak, and passive, whereas *yang* was the attribute of all things male, bright, strong and active. While male and female were both necessary and complementary, one by nature was passive towards the other. Based on this belief, Confucians constructed an ideology that drew on the Classics to indoctrinate their concept that the harmony of society was built upon hierarchical structure that reflected superior and inferior human relationships.

Ever since the Han dynasty, Confucian moralists regulated the moral requirements for girls and women. These requirements originated from the *Classic of Rites*: 'to be a woman means to submit'. In an ideal Confucian home, women were expected to demonstrate obedience at every stage of life. As children, girls were required to obey their fathers; as wives, women were required to obey their husbands; and as widows, women were required to obey their grown-up sons. At no point in her life was a woman, according to the traditional Confucian view, expected to function as an autonomous being free of male control. The mechanism of subordination reduced women to a state of economic dependence, physical subservience and sexual servitude (Croll, 1978, p. 13).

From the Confucian point of view, male children were regarded as the continuation of the family. To find a wife for a son was to ensure this continuation. But for a girl, it was different. Her parents married her to another family to secure their posterity, and often accepted some goods in return. She was received by her husband's family as a chattel. Here, the issue of virginity became crucial in order to preserve a pure blood line. For the girl's own parents and family, virginity was a matter of reputation and honour. Preventive measures to ensure chastity finally reached an extreme with women having their feet bound in order to limit freedom of movement. Separation of sexes and placement of unmarried girls in inner chambers were based on the Confucian rule that 'males and females shall not allow their hands to touch in giving or receiving anything' (*Mencius*, 7: 17). This also became a significant norm.

Despite the fact that in Dynastic China's patriarchal and polygamous society men had multiple wives and concubines, women were not allowed to see men other than their close relatives, husbands, or masters. Male sexual desire and fantasy could be indulged in based on endless excuses without being condemned as having breached Confucian ethics. Women's sexual needs and satisfaction were never recognized, despite Confucius' earlier statement that human nature demanded food, drink and sex, a claim that appeared to apply to both genders.[13]

CONCLUSION

Confucianism essentially envisages man as a social creature who is bound to his fellows by *ren* (benevolence), a term often rendered as sympathy, human-heartedness, benevolence, mercy or kindness. This *ren* is believed to be expressed through five human relations – sovereign and subject, parent and child, elder and younger brother, husband and wife, and friend and friend. Of these, the filial relationship is stressed. These relations can only function smoothly with the exact adherence to *li* (propriety), a term denoting the combination of etiquette and ritual. In at least four out of the five relations, a person may be superior to some but inferior to others. If in his subordinate status he wishes to be treated properly he must treat his inferiors with propriety. Correct conduct cannot be forced by compulsion, but rather by a sense of virtue obtained by observing suitable models of deportment. Confucianism's rationale for organizing society began with the cosmic order and its hierarchy of superior–inferior relationships. Parents are superior to children, men to women, rulers to subjects. Each person has a role to perform. If everyone performs their role, social order would be sustained.

Another important Confucian belief is that men by nature are good and have an innate moral sense. They can be led to the right path by education, especially through their own efforts of self-cultivation. However, they can also be guided by the emulation of models. The individual, in their own effort to do the right thing, can be influenced by the examples of sages and superior men who have succeeded in placing correct conduct ahead of all other considerations. This ancient Chinese stress on the moral educability of men has persisted to the present and continues to inspire the government to pursue moral education.

Taking the people as the 'root', food as the 'basis', and soldiers as the 'pillar', Confucianism combined the integrity of the three aspects of state survival, namely, the development of economic production, the strengthening of military training, and the improvement of the people's quality of being. Confucianism does not give humans dominion over nature, nor does it sacrifice human development at the altar of pristine nature. Confucians maintain the oneness of humankind and nature, the harmony and unity between the two. The *Doctrine of the Mean* says: 'Let the states of equilibrium and harmony exist in perfection, and a happy order will prevail throughout heaven and earth, and all things will be nourished and flourish' (Chapter 1). In handling relations between the human and natural worlds, people need to observe the principle of 'equilibrium', so that the vitality and harmony of nature, the ecological balance of the natural environment, can properly be maintained. Contemporary Confucianism calls for the engagement with the serious moral enterprise of restructuring social institutions and reformulating public policies in accordance with fundamental Confucian moral concerns and commitments to family and virtue.

NOTES

1. The character 儒 (*ru*) existed before the Confucius era. It consists of two parts: 人 (*ren*) and 需 (*xu*). Together, they imply 'the weak people'. The people of *ru* were descendants of aristocratic families of early Zhou times, who were in decline. These people had an affluent cultural background, which would qualify them to serve as assistants in various rituals. Because the special robe of such assistants was called *ru*, it

was most likely that the group *ru* had already been developed into a profession. After some lengthy learning and practice, Confucius became a specialist in rituals, working as an assistant at sacrificial and funeral rites in the early stage of *ru*.

2. Collection of sayings and ideas attributed to the Chinese philosopher Confucius and his contemporaries. For the English translation, see Legge (1971).
3. The main sources for Confucius' life are Zhang Bingnan (1989) and Williams (1965).
4. The English translation of these quotes and those discussed in this section below is taken from Legge (1971) with the alteration of a few words.
5. The main sources for the discussion on Mencius are Nivison (1996) and Shun (1997).
6. The main source for the discussion on the Han Confucianism is Fang (2011).
7. The English translation of this and the following quotes is taken from Legge (1971).
8. The English translation is taken from Fang and Hay (1992).
9. The main source for the discussion in this section is Zhang Youmin and Li Tianchen (2000). The English translation is taken from Legge (1971), with the alteration of a few words.
10. This section draws heavily on Li Tianchen (2003) and Fu (2003).
11. For the full English translation, see Legge (1971).
12. The main source for the discussion in this section is Fan (2002).
13. The main source for the discussion in this section is Fang (2011).

REFERENCES

Croll, E. (1978), *Feminism and Socialism in China*, London: Routledge.
De Bary, W.T. et al. (2000), *Sources of Chinese Tradition*, New York: Columbia University Press.
Fan, Ruiping (2002), 'Reconstructionist Confucianism and health care: an Asian moral account of health care resource allocation', *Journal of Medicine and Philosophy*, **27**(6), 675–82.
Fang, X. (2011), *The Rise of Ancient China: Fragmentation and Amalgamation*, Saarbrücken, Germany: LAP.
Fang, X. and T. Hay (1992), *East Wind, West Wind*, Melbourne: Penguin.
Fu, P. (2003), '*Tian* (*T'ien*): Heaven', in A. Cua (ed.), *Encyclopaedia of Chinese Philosophy*, New York: Routledge, pp. 726–8.
Legge, J. (1971), *The Chinese Classics*, Taipei: Wenshizhe chubanshe.
Li Tianchen (2003), 'Confucian ethics and the environment', in *Culture Mandala: The Bulletin of the Centre for East-West Cultural and Economic Studies*, **6**(1), available at: http://epublications.bond.edu.au/cm/vol6/iss1/4; accessed 12 July 2012.
Nivison, D.S. (1996), *The Ways of Confucianism: Investigations in Chinese Philosophy*, La Salle, IL: Open Court.
Shun, K. (1997), *Mencius and Early Chinese Thought*, Stanford, CA: Stanford University Press.
Williams, S.W. (1965), *The Middle Kingdom*, Taipei: Ch'eng-wen Publishing Company.
Zhang Bingnan (1989), *Kongzi zhuan* (*The Biography of Confucius*), Changchun: Chilin wensi chubanshe.
Zhang Youmin and Li Tianchen (2000), 'Economic lessons from Confucius for the new century', in *The Culture Mandala*, **4**(1), available at: http://www.international-relations.com/cm4-1/Zhang.htm; accessed 12 July 2012.

10 Indigenous religions and development: African traditional religion*

Namawu Alhassan Alolo and James Astley Connell

INTRODUCTION

The recent resurgence of interest in the significance of religion for development has of yet provided little illumination of traditions described as 'indigenous', 'traditional', 'folk', or 'ethnic' religions, and the ways in which they influence development. Unsurprisingly, given the number of these traditions, such neglect remains problematic. Although portrayed as marginal, these religions underpin the spiritual identities of many Africans, and they collectively constitute the majority of the world's religions (Harvey, 2000). While globalization, modernization and the rapid growth of the 'missionary religions' may have precipitated the decline of some, in a number of regions, such as South America, China, and parts of Africa, indigenous religions have experienced revival, or have been adapted and incorporated alongside these new faiths (Olupona, 2004). The historical significance of such revival is revealing in its own right, but the fact that these religions are so often clustered around the social, political and economic 'margins' of society should more immediately signify their salience for development, particularly in light of concerns over social difference and exclusion, indigenous rights and rural development. If the need to understand the role of religion in development is justified, the place of indigenous religions may prove especially important.

This chapter explores the role and significance of African traditional religion (ATR) for development. While rich in variant practices and traditions, ATR forms one of the world's largest indigenous belief systems, with an estimated 100 million adherents across the continent.[1] Although empirical research is scant, broader research into religion and development, and the contributions made by other disciplines, suggest that ATR may hold considerable importance for the lives and well-being of people across Africa. Religious values, morals, institutions, organizations and leaders, we now know, are not only of importance to individual and communal notions of identity, but have wide-ranging, irregular, and yet tangible influences on a range of critical development concerns. Despite extraordinary progress in development in many African countries, poverty and conflict remain but two of a litany of issues affecting human well-being. The relevance of understanding how such a historically important belief system may intervene in development is clear.

Such understanding is nevertheless complicated by a shortage of empirical research and a number of definitional concerns. Whether ATR can in any way, for instance, be considered a homogeneous religion – or indeed in any way 'traditional' – will immediately provoke impassioned debate amongst scholars of various disciplines. This is a debate that in the interests of clarity and brevity we shall, for the most part, skirt around, and refer to ATR in the singular – if parenthetically. Our chapter is intended as an explorative background piece, the purpose of which is to shed light on how ATR frames certain development concepts, as well as to provide an overview of the tradition to readers who may be unfamiliar with it. Given that 'development' has many meanings, we draw from a constellation of the most frequently discussed issues, and consider the ways that ATR may intervene upon and within them. First, we shall situate our discussion within the broader debate on religion and development, and more specifically that of indigenous religions and development, drawing attention to the shared history of malignment and marginalization of these traditions. We shall explore how various historical interests have influenced the way ATR has been represented, before moving on to consider conceptions of the human and spirit realms, and notions of morality.

'INDIGENOUS' RELIGIONS AND DEVELOPMENT

Over recent years there has been a rekindling of scholarly interest in the role and significance of religion for development. Research has illuminated religion's embedded influence in everything from conflict and conflict resolution, to health, the environment, gender equality, ideas of justice, governance and poverty alleviation. In spite of such illumination very little insight into the rich and poorly understood universe of indigenous and folk religions has been provided. Indeed, compared with the 'world religions', there has been a sense of disinterestedness in these religions by both researchers and research institutions (Olupona, 2004). However marginal these religions may be, they remain decidedly important for millions of people – particularly at the social 'margins'. While difficult to determine precisely, 'indigenous' or 'traditional' religions are believed to sustain over 400 million people worldwide. Also, as with the 'world religions', fears that indigenous religions are in any way dying out may be presumptuous. Worldwide there has been a perceptible and often politically spirited resurgence of indigenous religions. In South America the so-called Andean 'indigenous resurgence' (Cleary and Steigenga, 2004) is vividly coloured with pre-Columbian spiritual symbolism, and in China, rapid economic development has not led to:

> total disenchantment with beliefs concerning magic in the cosmos. On the contrary, the revival of folk religions in the Delta region is serving as a countervailing re-embedding force from the local cultural context, leading to the coexistence of the world of enchantments and the modern world. (Law, 2005)

The little research conducted concerning these belief systems suggests their continued salience to many communities world-wide and their profound bearing on key development issues. Scholars have drawn attention to an intervening role on gender (Kendall, 1984; Law, 2005); health (Bever, 2000; Shoko, 2007); conflict and social relations (Brain, 1982); and conservation and development (Richards, 2000). The apparent revival of folk religion in some parts of rural China, for instance, may play a critical role in reinforcing gender inequalities in the Pearl Delta region (Law, 2005, p. 105), while a similar revival of 'indigenous' religion across the Andes has been cited as a critical factor in the extraordinary Andean 'indigenous resurgence' and consequent issues of political identity and representation, indigenous rights, governance, and environmental management (Cleary and Steigenga, 2004). A similar pattern of resurgence is also evident across the African continent, and has indicated important links between African traditional religion and development issues such as conflict (Richards, 2002; Jackson, 2010), environment, governance and social exclusion (Richards, 1996), health (Shoko, 2007), and gender and fertility (Adongo et al., 1998).

The reasons why these belief systems have failed to gain greater attention demands examination. The sheer number of these traditions generates a variety of logistical problems, particularly as they are often found at the social peripheries. Scholarship too 'often follows the flag' (Levine, 1986), and limited research resources in both the broader political sciences and development studies have been more urgently required for understanding how religion affects conflict, governance and peace-building in regions such as Afghanistan. This neglect, however, may also be due to a variety of discourses that have historically worked to eclipse and discredit indigenous religions. Indeed, although diverse in geography, practice and cosmogony, indigenous and folk religions tend to share histories of marginalization and malignment by foreign political, religious and intellectual institutions. The social and political sciences, informed partly by intellectual currents such as evolutionism and partly by the prejudices of the societies from which they emerged, expected 'primitive' or 'primal' religions to reveal the nature of religious practice as it was at the birth of human history (Cox, 2007). Whether dissected by those hoping to prove the evolutionary superiority of Christianity or by anti-Christian scholars attempting to reveal the irrational and superstitious nature of all religion, the result was the same: a series of tendentious accounts that framed indigenous belief systems as primitive, arcane and archaic – living archaeologies of modern, sophisticated faith systems (ibid., p. 9).

While the adoption of the term 'indigenous' has helped assuage these problems, a number of pejorative terms and assumptions remain. 'Primal' or 'archaic', for instance, which replaced the offensive 'primitive', but still cast indigenous religion and culture as ethnographic artefact (Harvey, 2000), remained in use until the 1990s (Cox, 2007). Other terms serve to stress the 'strangeness' of these religions and the cultures that practised them. 'Totemism', 'animism', and 'fetishism' reflect an almost prurient obsession with indigenous cultures, and helped reinforce imaginings of their otherworldliness. Even reference to 'traditional' in ATR is ambiguous, easily suggestive of the 'backward' (Harvey, 2000) or anti-modern nature of indigenous beliefs, and, of course, 'indigenous' is itself not without problem, threatening to subsume a diversity of beliefs and peoples under normative understandings of primacy, legitimacy and the politics of marginalization.

It is noteworthy that indigenous religions are not only themselves marginal in an 'academic' sense, but frequently sustain those politically, geographically and socially marginalized – those least represented within prevailing political and economic orders. From this perspective, terminology is perhaps indicative of deeper political processes working to maintain and justify asymmetrical power relations over the subaltern. The very tension between 'modernity' – defined by openness to secular values, scientific progress and technology – and the 'traditional' focus of indigenous religions may, for some world-systems analysts, represent less a conflict of values and more the tension of globalized neo-liberal agendas and the division of labour – a struggle between core and periphery (Olupona, 2004). In this case, interventions designed to overcome the 'primitiveness' of the developing world, may be understood as attempts to facilitate markets, rather than as truly humanitarian efforts to improve human rights, good governance or poverty alleviation.

Such analyses may go too far. At the same time they remind us that terminology frequently has a political function. Through using such terms, some modern scholars, who often conflate essentialist notions of religion and culture with vague notions of 'tribalism' and 'progress' contribute to a broader discourse that frames the perpetuity of conflict, poverty or social failure in a region such as Africa, as due to a fundamental incompatibility between 'Africanness' and modernity, rather than the vagaries of the global economic system or the exploitation of the South by the North. The portrayal of a system such as African traditional religion as 'strange' and 'irrational' helps reinforce a perspective of an Africa lost deep down the rabbit hole. It is a region benighted by belief in ghosts, spirits and witchcraft, and bound by taboos and fetishist practices that underpin its social and political 'anarchy'.[2] Rather than 'strange', however, it is the ordinariness of indigenous beliefs that should be realized. As with all religions, 'It is the very ordinariness and unexceptional regularity of (religious) lifeways that make them powerful or empowering' (Harvey, 2000, p. 3). Religions are, after all, human activities. For Harvey (ibid.), it is not the perception that indigenous religions are in some way stranger or less complex than other religions that makes them important for study, but the very fact that they are as 'similarly human' as any other religious tradition.

As is true with other religions, the processes of 'political liberalization' (Rakodi, 2011, p. 35), that have allowed religious actors, organizations and institutions a seat at the table in development also brings risks regarding indigenous religion. The recognition of religious interests, while positive, can be a double-edged sword. 'Spirituality and religion have often been sources of conflict and oppression rather than development and liberation' (Van Beek, 2000, p. 32) and they are not, it should be noted, in the same way accountable as political actors. The wave of positivity that follows arguments for the 'empowerment' of indigenous people and societies must not distract from questions over what and who constitutes 'indigenous', or from the potential that these belief systems institute practices oppositional to development and human well-being – for example, the likely exaggerated, but still disturbing reports of *muti* ('medicine') killings in contemporary African communities. The de-politicization of taken-for-granted development panacea such as *inclusion* or *indigenous rights* tends to suspend the often contentious meanings and problematic consequences of such concepts. If recognition, inclusion and engagement are to be pursued, it should be with greater understanding.

AFRICAN TRADITIONAL RELIGION: A HISTORY IN SCHOLARSHIP

African traditional religion forms the predominant religion for an estimated 100 million people across the continent and is one of the world's largest and perhaps best known indigenous religions. While Christianity and Islam today comprise the largest religious denominations, ATR nevertheless remains highly influential, and even more so if considering the number of 'syncretic' fusions of ATR, Christianity and Islam. However, despite the religion's clear importance in the lives of African people, empirical research attempting to trace the ways in which the religion intervenes within political, social and economic development is scarce. More importantly, where ATR has been considered in scholarship or the media, portrayals are often stereotypical and misrepresentative. As with Africa itself, the religion bears a paradoxical reputation: on the one hand seen as mysterious and timeless, on the other as irrational and anarchistic. Both portrayals serve not only to perpetuate myths about ATR, but also to depoliticize the religion, removing it from its social and historical context. Yet the way in which ATR has been historically framed is in itself illuminating, providing not only a reflexive means by which to deconstruct the prejudices inherent to modern treatment of the religion, but also how these prejudices have served to shape ATR's reception in contemporary Africa.

A number of historical currents including evolutionism, colonialism, the functionalism of British and French anthropological schools and African nationalism, have influenced the study of African traditional religion. Ray (1976, pp. 2–14) outlines three distinct phases of the study of ATR. The initial phase, starting in the eighteenth and nineteenth centuries, comprised mostly written accounts by early missionaries, travellers and colonial agents; their accounts of the religion, for the most part, were neither objective nor scholarly, but were subjective and largely based on unsystematic 'collections of random observations and superficial opinions designed to appeal to the popular European mind' (ibid, p. 2). Although many of these authors did not stay long enough to observe and acquaint themselves with the beliefs and practices of Africans in any depth, African religion was portrayed as a bizarre, savage and primitive collection of beliefs and practices. Frobenius, writing in 1931 (p. xiii), recalled a passage in a Berlin journal:

> Before the introduction of genuine faith and a higher standard of culture by the Arabs, the natives [sic] have no political organization, nor, strictly speaking any religion . . . In examining the pre-Muhammedan condition of Negro races [we should] confine ourselves to the description of their fetishism, their brutal and often cannibalistic customs, their vulgar and repulsive idols. None but the most primitive instincts determine the lives and conduct of the Negroes, who lacked any kind of ethical inspiration.

In 'Sources, with particular reference to the Southern Sudan', Evans-Pritchard (1971, pp. 144–5) also recounts how travel reports from the region painted ATR as the beliefs of a savage and primitive people. They were, he noted, characterized by:

> a reference to cannibalism, a description of pygmies (by preference with a passing reference to Herodotus), a denunciation of the inequities of the slave trade, the need for the civilizing influence of commerce, something about rain-makers and other superstitions, some sex (suggestive though discreet), add snakes and elephants to taste; bring slowly to the boil and serve.

It is likely, as Mbiti (1969, pp. 2–8) argues, that these descriptions forged ATR's association with derogatory terminology such as fetishism and animism. According to Evans-Pritchard (1965, pp. 231–3), two prominent explorers, Sir Samuel Baker (1867) and Sir Richard Burton, contributed significantly to the propagation of ATR as a crude or primitive religion. Baker argued in 1867 (see Evans-Pritchard, 1965, p. 231), that:

> without any exception, they [Africans] are without a belief in a Supreme Being, neither have they any form of worship or idolatry nor is the darkness of their minds enlightened by even a ray of superstition. The mind is as stagnant as the morass which forms its puny world.

Similarly, Sir Richard Burton (quoted in Evans-Pritchard, ibid.) suggests, 'the negro is still at that rude dawn of faith fetishism – and he [sic] has barely advanced to idolatry . . . He has never grasped the idea of a personal Deity, a duty in life, a moral code or a shame of lying'.

Beliefs in the amoral and benighted nature of ATR left a deep imprint on the study of the religion and have done much to entrench perceptions of its apparent primitivism. While such sources may make uncomfortable reading they nevertheless require situating vis-à-vis the emerging modernist paradigm and social evolutionary theory. Social evolutionary theorists were concerned with tracing religion from its most primitive form to its highest level of development – considered to be monotheism. Ikenga-Metuh (1987) contends that this phase in the study of ATR was characterized by an emphasis on the study of the religion, not least because they believed their mission was to find examples of primitive forms of religion that were considered to have survived in Africa, and were actually evident in ATR. Central to evolutionary approaches was the view that all 'higher forms' of beliefs, concepts, institutions, art or any aspect of culture were not endogenous to Africa, but imported from outside. The result was a series of theories established to explain how religious traits had found their way into Sub-Saharan Africa from Western Europe, Egypt or the Middle East.

The popularity of evolutionary theory as an explanatory model for social and cultural development declined in the twentieth century. According to Ray (1976, p. 6), this was partly attributable to the discovery that certain non-literate people, particularly hunter-gatherer communities in Australia and North America, were capable of conceiving a 'genuine notion of a supreme being despite their status as technologically primitive people'. Furthermore, as Ikenga-Metuh (1987, pp. 5–8) argues, a growing suspicion that monotheism predated polytheism undermined the logic of evolutionary theory. Nevertheless, while evolutionary approaches to understanding ATR gave way, embedded notions of ATR as a 'primitive' faith system have endured, and are reflected by a similar treatment of African culture and society more broadly. In Robert Kaplan's 'The coming anarchy' (1994), the tenacity of such prejudice is apparent. Kaplan's article betrays a bleakly pessimistic view of a West Africa rented by tribalism, social anarchy and overpopulation. A quote he includes from a West African minister implies that such problems stem, in part, from a 'resistance' to Western religion:

> 'In the poor quarters of Arab North Africa,' he continued, 'there is much less crime, because Islam provides a social anchor: of education and indoctrination. Here in West Africa we have a lot of superficial Islam and superficial Christianity. Western religion is undermined by animist beliefs not suitable to a moral society, because they are based on irrational spirit power'.

In the early twentieth-century, evolutionist approaches to the study of ATR gave way to the burgeoning field of anthropology. Ikenga-Metuh (1987, pp. 5–8) argues that the colonial establishment created an environment in which anthropologists could undertake extensive fieldwork and documentation of the traditions, customs, beliefs and practices of Africans before these beliefs and practices could be 'contaminated' by foreign influences. Anthropological approaches to the study of ATR evolved in two distinct schools or national lines: British and French. This, according to Ray (1976, p. 7), unfortunately 'slanted fieldwork studies according to the nationality of the author, and thus imposed a "colonialist" structure upon the study of African social and religious systems'. While British anthropologists were largely concerned with the sociological aspect of culture, kinship systems and political organization, French anthropologists were much more concerned with illuminating African cosmological systems and their implicit philosophical assumptions. For British ethnographers, the study of ATR aimed to understand its function in the social system – how religion was used to legitimate socio-political institutions, how rituals were used to sustain the social order, and how religious underpinnings highlighted the social structure – an approach that would later shift with Evans-Pritchard's approach to understanding and explaining the meaning of African systems of ideas within their own universe. By contrast, the French school of anthropology was more concerned with understanding African religious systems in their own right not as mere 'reflections of socioeconomic relations but [as] coherent and autonomous spheres of thought and action' (Ray, 1976, p. 10).

Towards the latter part of the twentieth century, a number of African scholars started to turn their attention to the study of ATR. While overdue, many of these contributions – particularly amongst the earlier anthropological and theological studies – have nevertheless been criticized for their political proximity to African nationalist movements that attempted to de-emphasize difference and encourage unity amongst Africa's diverse peoples (Platvoet, 1996). Defiant of the colonial 'stigma' of anthropology (ibid., p. 121), a small number of both amateur, nationalistically inspired, Western-educated intellectuals, and professional African anthropologists, for example, pioneered a number of ethnographies in African societies. On the Gold Coast, intellectuals such as J.H. Mensah Sarbah (1968) and J.B. Danqah (1968) considered Fante and Akan traditional society, institutions and culture, while professional anthropologists such as Jomo Kenyatta (1961) and Kofi Busia (1968), completed studies of religion and culture amongst the Kikuyu and Akan societies. Unfortunately, despite constituting a milestone in the discipline, these studies were seen as derivative and highly de-contextualized, drawing heavily on the authors' personal 'Christian' world-views.

A more extensive body of research serving to canonize ATR as the indigenous religion of Africa have been provided by African theologians such as John Mbiti (1970–91), Bolaji Idowu (1962–75), Ikenga-Metuh (1987) and Magesa (1998). Their cultural function, according to Platvoet (1996, p. 124) was the:

> restoration of a respectable past, thereby uplifting the self-respect and dignity of educated Africans vis-à-vis the dominant Western colonial culture . . . [their] political function was to help bring national unity in Africa's ethnically plural societies which were rife with tensions, by de-emphasizing the differences between the religions and by highlighting the theistic beliefs they had in common.

These authors envisaged ATR as a pan-Africanist ideology of a 'common Africanness' (a cultural unity), an interpretation heavily influenced by Christian notions of a single, omnipresent God. Such a belief, Idowu argues (1975, pp. 103–4), forms the 'real cohesive factor . . . [and] the ground [on which] we can speak of the religion of Africa in the singular'. It is an argument shared by John Mbiti (1970), who like Idowu, has been criticized for his portrayal of the autonomous recognition of a Supreme God in Africa as 'attempting to lay the basis of a distinctively African theology by blending the African past with the Judeo-Christian tradition' (Ray, 1976, p. 15).

More recently, a small but increasing number of African historians have started to engage ATR in research. Such work is particularly welcome given the lack of historical knowledge of ATR and indigenous religions more generally. Despite important contributions made by African historians such as Mainga (1972), Kimambo and Omari (1972) and Gwassa (1972) however, they have nevertheless attracted similar criticism for a propensity towards broader ideological narratives. Yet while such contortions and (re)imaginings of ATR may provide complications for 'purist' disciplines, they are nonetheless of importance for development studies, for they allow an insight into how religions such as ATR may be re-appropriated by communities to express identities and interests.

This brief introduction to the historical treatment of ATR, hopefully, underlines the importance of historical reflexivity when considering the contemporary role of ATR in development. While transcendent in cosmology, religions are nonetheless inescapably political and intimately intertwined with history and identity narratives. Those considering the contemporary relevance of ATR, and its role in African development, should bear in mind the hermeneutic effects such narratives may have on how people value the religion individually and collectively.

ATR IN CONTEMPORARY AFRICAN SOCIETY

So what distinguishes African traditional religion? What practices, beliefs and institutions underpin its spiritual cosmology? How possible is it to treat such a diverse and geographically diffuse number of traditions as a single religion, and just how 'traditional' is ATR? The following section attempts to provide insight into these fundamental questions, beginning with a short consideration of the deeply problematic question of whether ATR constitutes a single belief system, or whether it is a collection of several distinct religions, and a discussion of what it is that makes ATR 'traditional'.

'Unity in Diversity' – Tradition and Plurality in ATR

A number of compelling arguments back the claim that ATR is, in fact, a multiplicity of belief systems. 'We speak of African traditional Religions in the plural' argues African theologian John Mbiti (1969, p. 1), 'because there are about one thousand African peoples, and each has its own religious system'. For Mbiti, that African people have different religious rituals, ceremonies and leaders warrants a pluralistic understanding of ATR. Similarly Booth (1977, p. 3) argues:

> Our reading and observation turn up a profusion of phenomena to which we may attach such labels as supreme gods [sic], nature spirits, ancestor rituals, initiation practices . . . and demons with considerable variety from place to place. Perhaps we will decide there is no such thing as 'African Religion', but 'African Religions'.

The considerable diversity of practice and belief in ATR across Africa lends weight to arguments that the religion should be considered in the plural. Driven in part by contemporary post-modern concerns for difference and suspicion of meta-narratives these arguments are appealing, and inject scepticism into theories that treat religion and religious identities as in any way hermetic or primordial. The notion that ATR may still claim an underlying unity has, however, recently enjoyed a revival. Magesa (1997, p. 6) for instance, maintains that ATR may be treated as a single belief system, and notes that this was recognized as early as the 1920s at a study conference of missionaries in Le Zoute, Belgium. Though the Le Zoute conference recognized the diversity marking Africa geographically, linguistically, and sometimes in the physical appearance of its people, it concluded that there was an 'essential unity: "underlying all the divergence that marks the pagan . . . Negro tribes, there is a fundamental unity of belief and outlook upon the world . . . Africa is a unity – a unity in diversity"' (ibid., p. 6). More recently, several scholars claiming to study ATR from the 'inside', including John Mbiti himself (1990), tend to conclude that ATR *should* be considered a single religion with the same basic world-view, despite innumerable variant expressions. The varying elements in the religion, it is argued, are variations in expression rather than variations in the basic belief system (Parrinder, 1962; Maquet, 1972; Idowu, 1973). In a later publication, *Introduction to African Traditional Religion*, Mbiti (1991a) advocates the study and conception of ATR as a single religion, arguing that the belief system cuts across the African sub-region and shares remarkable features with respect to the basic world-view of Africans.

These scholars contend that the existence of diversity within ATR is in no way incommensurable with its underlying unity – a credible proposition when considering the substantial intra-religious difference within the world religions. The reasons for why this contention remains so important it is suggested, and why it is important for development, is that it is inescapably political. Following decolonization, enthusiasm for the pan-African nationalist movement drove a need to find common ground on which to unite the disparate peoples of the continent. As Pobee and Mends (1977, pp. 10–11) note, such political appropriation of traditional religion was, however, counter-productive, a 'betrayal of African culture by African nationalism'. Modern scholars, eager to provide more nuanced understanding of Africa and redress past wrongs, have consequently over-emphasized the difference within Africa's spiritual fabric. While we treat ATR as a single religion for its underlying beliefs and common institutions, we do so parenthetically and in recognition that all religions, while drawing on common reservoirs of myth, symbols and traditions, are highly pluralistic and subject to interpretation.

The notion of 'tradition', which, by definition, seems adversative to 'development' is also interesting. For some, especially post-development theorists, the privilege accorded 'modern' Western values and institutions over the 'traditional' values of many developing communities is problematic, assuming as it does that the values of Western development agencies are somehow universally recognized. To some extent, the 'traditional' aspect of ATR is similarly located to the question of plurality in that, for many, 'traditional' carries connotations of historicity, and legitimacy (Olupono, 2004). In the context of the African nationalism, the re-appropriation of traditional religion represented a 'quest for African personality' (Pobee and Mends, 1977, p. 10), and provided symbolic means by which to construct historical legitimacy. While some have viewed this with derision, arguing that 'Africans have assumed acquaintance with authentic tradition often with no real basis', and often promoted as African what has been the 'artefact of Europeans' (ibid.), others have defended the idea that traditions provide a deeper sense of unity and sense of cultural meaning against alienating forces of modernity (Uwah, 2010). Tradition, it is argued, bears a spiritual as well as political significance, and resonates with belief in the relationship between humanity, ancestors and ghosts. '"Traditional"', notes Harvey (2000, p. 9), 'clearly labels something of significance to many indigenous religions, i.e. those that honour what previous generations did as formative and of abiding significance'. Uwah (2011, p. 81) adds that ritual can 'create solidarity in the form of subjective experiences of sharing the same meaningful world . . . Traditional religion is one ritual that despite the influence of Westernization and scientific developments in Africa, still holds meaningful implications in people's everyday life'.

Beliefs, Customs and Practices in ATR

'Religion', argues Mbiti (1969, p. 29), 'is the way of life of Africans', it is an all-encompassing force that pervades every aspect of life.[3] For all its myriad forms of expression, various commonalities of belief and practice nonetheless suggest a deeper cohesiveness to ATR: there is a common attitude, a common spirit woven into the social fabric of Africa. Though we treat the religion as singular here, this neither precludes the extent of diversity nor the potential that contemporary ATR may have a number of 'roots'.[4] Nevertheless, Stamer (1995, pp. 121–5) writes that ATR represents:

> a global framework of life, encompassing every human situation and governing the whole of society. It is closely linked to the ancestral soil and places each African both in the succession of the generations (the ancestors), in his [sic] relationship with his fellow creatures and in his productive activities. Everything is religious! The direct relation with God is rarely explicit but the belief in one God, Who is Creator . . . underlies everything else. God does not intervene in the day-to-day affairs of life. These are governed by other invisible forces, good or evil, from whom it is possible to win favours through the ritualized experience of the ancestors.

As implied, perhaps more fundamental than the number of common rituals, institutions and practices underpinning various manifestations of ATR, is the widespread belief in the intimate relationship between the spirit world, the community and the environment – both geographically and throughout time. This relationship is characterized by a spiritual hierarchy that underpins the wide spectrum of African religious practice, a hierarchy constituted of belief in one supreme God, deities, various spirit forces, and the living dead – or the ancestors. There are, according to Ikenga-Metuh (1987, p. 17), 'institutionalized patterns of beliefs and worship practiced by various African societies from time immemorial in response to the "Supernatural" as manifested in their environment and practice'. Similarly pervasive is a religious ontology that is fundamentally 'anthropocentric', in that everything is perceived in terms of its relationship with humanity (Mbiti, 1969). For instance, God is the creator and maintainer of humankind; spirits oversee the destiny of humankind; while the animals, plants and other natural phenomena provide the environment to support humanity's existence and with whom humanity establishes a mystical relationship. For Africans:

> this anthropocentric ontology is a complete unity which nothing can break up or destroy. To destroy or remove one of [the above structures] is to destroy the whole [of] existence including the destruction of the creator, which is impossible. One mode of existence presupposes all the others, and a balance must be maintained so that these modes neither drift too far apart from one another nor get too close to one another. (Mbiti, 1969, p. 16)

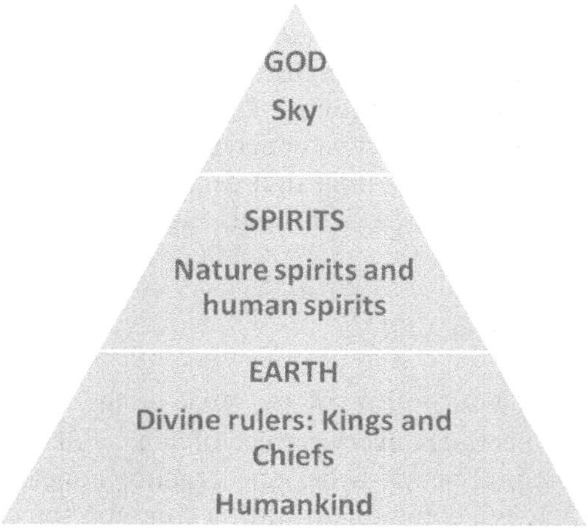

Figure 10.1 Spiritual hierarchy in African traditional religion

At the highest level of the spiritual hierarchy (Figure 10.1) in ATR, belief in God, known variously as Ngewo (Mende), Nyame (Ashanti), or Nzambi, Nyambe in Central and Southern Africa (Parrinder, 1974, p. 33) may be seen as the 'golden thread running through the heart of the religion' (Imasogie, 1985, p. 22). The Supreme Being has many attributes: omnipresent, omnipotent, transcendent and immanent, among others. For the Mende, God is the author of all life, including the spirit world; for the Kono people, God represents the omnipresent and the eternal, living in the sky but also living 'through all the generations of man' (Parrinder, 1974, p. 33). The supposed gender of God varies between and sometimes within societies. While some writers on the Ashanti of Ghana speak of God as female – the Great Mother, symbolized by the moon – others speak of God among the Ashanti as having a duality of sex, Father-Mother God, symbolized by the sun. According to an Ashanti myth, Nyame rules over the sky, a goddess of creation over the earth, and Old Mother Earth over the underworld, that is over the dead who lie buried in her pocket (in their graves) (ibid.). Whether the masculinization of God in the literature is an accurate reflection of the way Africans conceive God or whether it is a conception of God interpreted through the Judeo-Christian lens, remains a question outside the scope of our discussion.

Belief in spirits forms an important dimension of traditional belief. According to Mbiti (1990) and Ikenga-Metuh (1987), spirits are creations of God, and occupy a status between God and humans, though they are not identical to either. Adherents of ATR will communicate with spirits primarily because they are considered powerful enough to bring harm or good to a given people: 'If, as many Africans believe, both human suffering and human prosperity have their origins in relations with the spirit world, cultivating that relationship assumes great importance' (Ellis and Ter Haar, 2004, p. 51). So the living must constantly endeavour to win the favour of the spirit world, and to avert its wrath. Communication may be achieved via prayer, divination, dreams, visions, or possession – although it is believed some are more capable of communion than others. For Ellis and Ter Haar (ibid., p. 52), 'In African religious traditions, the representation of spirits as real beings emphasizes the personal rather than the metaphorical aspect of relationships between the visible and invisible worlds'.

The spirit world consists of both 'nature' and 'human' spirits. The former, more popular in Western rather than in Central or Southern Africa, may be broadly divided into those spirits that inhere in the sky – such as the sun, the moon, stars, rainbows, rain, storms and wind – and those that inhere in the earth – in hills, mountains, boulders, trees (such as the Baobab), forests, metals, animals, sources of water, and certain diseases. Spirits from both sources – sky and earth – are believed to have substantial influence over human well-being. Amongst the Ashanti, storm spirits are considered particularly powerful, and are frequently held responsible for calamities; amongst the Yoruba, the Ibo and the Ewe, these spirits are similarly feared as the most dreadful, and accordingly worshipped for their power (Parrinder, 1974, p. 51; Ray, 1976, pp. 23–85). For the Ashanti, the earth itself is considered a powerful spirit capable of exacting punitive sanctions against humankind. In the African cosmology, myths, symbols and legends are used to illuminate the origin, activities and relationships of the spirits to human beings. Offerings and sacrifices are often made to them either asking for their direct help or as intermediaries to relay the people's requests to God.

Human spirits, by contrast, are thought to have a direct physical relationship with the living (Mbiti, 1991a, pp. 75–7). These spirits were once ordinary people living on earth, and since death have been worshipped, venerated, invoked and revered. Human spirits comprise both the long dead, who are frequently known as ghosts and whose stories are often told in myths, legends, folk lore and possessions (ibid.), and the living dead, often synonymous with 'ancestors', and who represent more recently deceased. Belief in the living dead in particular is pervasive. The spirits of the living dead are regarded as ever-living, ever-watchful beings that possess the power to both help and harm their living relatives (Parrinder, 1962, p. 24; Mbiti, 1991, pp. 75–6; Ashanti, 1997, pp. 10–14).

Humankind represents the lowest level of the spiritual hierarchy. Humans perform rites and rituals to invoke the Supreme God, the deities and the ancestors in the hope that this will avert calamities and bring them fortune. People have constant contact with the divinities, including the ancestors, at every stage of their life cycle, and rites of passage are commonly undertaken to mark major life transitions. Rites associated with pregnancy, birth, puberty, marriage and death, all form important periods of transition where the spirit world may be of assistance. These rites form a bond between 'temporary processes and archetypal patterns in order to give form and meaning to human events. This is done according to a three-fold pattern consisting of rites of separation, transition, and reincorporation' (Ray, 1976, pp. 90–91).

Although God is the creator and controller of the divine force, energy or power that permeates the universe, the spirits have access to this power, and are believed to be capable of using it. Some human beings – and to a lesser extent animals and plants (Parrinder, 1962) – may also, however, be gifted with, or acquire spiritual power. Medicine men and women, witches, priests and priestesses, are believed capable of tapping into and manipulating this power for their own purposes – good or ill. In many parts of Africa, rulers, kings or chiefs may be viewed as imbued with spiritual power. In the hierarchy of belief, kings and chiefs are perceived as God's representatives on earth. For instance, the Bantu people of South Africa perceive their chiefs as symbols of tribal unity, the 'Zulu, in the time of famous Chaka, raised their king to a godlike eminence'

(Parrinder, 1974, p. 67), while the Swazi perceive the 'king and his mother as the head of the hierarchy of mortals' (ibid., p. 69).

An important issue concerns how ATR allows for understanding of the self, particularly given the strong community spirit that pervades social life in Africa. Ray (1976, p. 133) argues that Africans conceive personhood as a process of mediation between individual self and collective identity as a member of society. A person is thought of as a constituent element of a community, by which 'the individual is conscious of himself [sic] in terms of "I am because we are, and since we are, therefore I am"'. Traditional religion forms 'a major tenet of communalism in African traditional life' (Uwah, 2011, p. 87), a focus reinforced temporally, it is suggested, as well as spatially, through the inclusion of ancestors and other human spirits in everyday life. Despite the collectivist nature of African societies, however, Ray argues that there is nevertheless recognition of individuals as unique persons endowed with distinct personalities and capabilities by God, and motivated by personal needs. To this extent:

> African thought acknowledges the transcendence of individuals over their own socio-cultural conditions. However, the emphasis on a person's individuality and freedom is always balanced against the social and historical context. It never approximates the Western notion of individualism – the idea that men [sic] are essentially independent of their social and historical circumstances – [as] the African traditional worldview is too systematic for such a doctrine, too logically and dynamically integrated. (Ray, 1976, p. 132)

Evil Spirits, Witchcraft and Sorcery

In as much as African traditional religion is concerned with the quest for good, so too is it concerned with the quest to ward off evil. For Africans, evil is both physical and moral. While the former is regarded as any misfortune that befalls an individual or community, the latter is conceived of as 'any voluntary anti-social behaviour or any infringement of the decrees of God, the deities, or the ancestors' (Ikenga-Metuh, 1987, p. 161). Within certain African cosmologies, however, evil, misfortune and unusual events are often attributed to mystical agencies: evil spirits, witches or sorcerers. Some evil spirits, for instance, are believed to be disincarnate human spirits, while others are non-human spirits who attack individuals, families and communities. The Igbo have three classifications of evil spirits: evil spirits of children (*Umo Aro*); evil spirits of deceased young men (*Ogbonuke*); and evil spirits of adults (*Akalogeli*) who died without offspring (ibid., p. 167). Lucas (1970, p. 168) argues that evil spirits of young children are feared most by young mothers, as the spirits of these children form a 'confraternity of spirits who visit the world in incarnate form for short periods . . . The spirits are born into babies who die in infancy or boyhood [sic]'. Idowu (1962, p. 80), however, describes these spirits as 'wandering spirits who specialize in the sadistic mischief of finding their way into wombs to be born to die'. While some Africans attribute misfortune to the work of evil spirits, witches or sorcerers, others associate misfortune with the evil eye, broken taboos, perjured oaths or even God (p. 161). Ikenga-Metuh (1987) notes that though most African societies regard God, deities and ancestors as good and just, these mystical agencies are capable of inflicting physical evil as a premonitory, corrective or punitive measure. Human agents, such as witches and sorcerers, are also commonly believed capable of causing misfortune. Witches, for one, are usually, although not uniquely, believed to be women, and, unlike sorcerers who achieve their ends through knowledge of magic, may exact their will supernaturally through an innate power. Witches are broadly 'considered to be slaves of aberration and addiction, and thus conceived [of as] weird, sometimes tragic figures' (ibid., p. 170).

Belief in evil spirits, magic, and especially witchcraft, is often disparaged. As has been true elsewhere, accusations of witchcraft, often used to scapegoat, inflict revenge, or attain self-advancement, have dramatic personal, social and political consequences in the form of assault, murder or expulsion (Ellis and Ter Haar, 2004). However misunderstood, reports of the continued persecution of individuals imagined to be witches across Africa (Caplan, 2010) as well as of *muti* killings, and child sacrifice amongst various communities, provide cause for concern. There also appears to be a marked relationship between such institutions and conflict. In the wake of the brutal war in the Democratic Republic of Congo, various media reported the abuse, murder and disownment of 'thousands' of child witches, or '*enfants sorciers*' (Dowden, 2006). During the conflict extremely violent ritualistic acts were also carried out against – purportedly magical – pygmy groups. Despite these events, coverage of witchcraft in Africa remains something of a straw-man, reflecting more entrenched public prejudices of Africa's 'strangeness', and a range of recycled myths (Caplan, 2010). This is not to deny that such practices occur, but rather to act as reminder of the mythologies and ignorance perpetuated in part by a 'failure to distinguish between ideas of witchcraft and actual manifestations' – that is, between 'discourse and empirical reality' (Caplan, 2010, p. 7).

A wealth of contributions from other disciplines suggest that beliefs in magic and witchcraft may form psychological structures that 'transcend contextual differences' (Briggs, 1996, cited in Bever, 2000, p. 573), and serve a broad range of respective functions for communities and/or individuals. Such functions may be useful in understanding how beliefs such as these intervene on development. Evans-Pritchard's seminal study amongst the Azande, for instance, suggests that belief in witchcraft and magic exist as a kind of 'natural philosophy by which the relations between men and unfortunate events are explained' (1937, p. 63). For James Brain (1982), drawing on the principle of the 'limited good', witchcraft needs to be understood as a mechanism for explaining and mediating socioeconomic tensions within and between environmentally vulnerable agricultural communities (p. 379).

AFRICAN TRADITIONAL RELIGION AND CONCEPTS OF DEVELOPMENT

The following section explores a number of current development concepts vis-à-vis African traditional religion – that is, how ATR frames, conceptualizes and influences these concepts. It should be reiterated that, with the exception of a few sources concerning morality, there is a general dearth of literature that directly examines the relationship between ATR and development. ATR's treatment of these issues is consequently revealed indirectly, through ideas about how conflict can be handled and justice secured; notions of political authority and ethical behaviour; and ideas of gender roles and relations. A series of implicit questions underpinning our discussion ask, 'What is the role, place and influence of African traditional religion for well-being and development in

Africa?', 'Does African traditional religion, more than other religious traditions, contribute to, or impede the broader goals of development?', and, finally, 'What does this mean for development?' Throughout, we emphasize the fundamental need for greater research to redress the considerable shortfall in knowledge.

Morality

A consideration of morality in ATR is important for understanding how the religion views wider development concepts, as well as how Africans perceive and express themselves as individuals and collective groups. It is often taken for granted that religion plays an important role in the formation and maintenance of individual and public moral and ethical values. It is also assumed that such values may facilitate development goals in governance, gender relations, conflict resolution, justice or environmental stewardship. 'There are growing calls', Marquette (2010, p. 1) argues, for instance, 'for religion to be used in the fight against corruption, based on the assumption that religious people are more concerned with ethics than the non-religious'.

According to Mbon (1991, pp. 101–9), ethics in Africa encompass every aspect of life. They govern individuals' understanding of themselves and their relationships with others. Ethics are expressed in the daily conversations of individuals, group proverbs, myths, folklore and names, which spell out people's ideas, aspirations and life philosophies. For Africans, ethics are manifest in the norms that regulate relationships between individual members of society and their social groups. Ikenga-Metuh (1987, p. 243) contends that the concept of morality in African societies can be identified 'from the sanctions or commendations attaching [to] the infringement or observance of [social] norms'. Thus, African concepts of morality emerge from humans' relationship with God and the ontological order. Myths of creation explain how God created humans and they in turn betrayed God by either revealing God's secret of creation (a Tutsi myth) or eating God's food (a Mende myth), which subsequently disrupted the ontological order and resulted in both moral evil and physical evil becoming permanent features of the world (ibid.).

Mbiti (1991a, p. 174) also argues that morality in ATR deals with conceptions of what is right and wrong, good or evil, and is based on a belief in many African societies that morals are given by God. Two forms of moral conduct may be identified: personal and social. The latter, according to Mbiti (1991a, p. 174), is of greatest importance, 'since a basic African view is that the individual exists only because others exist'. Sawyer (in Mbon, 1991, p. 102) agrees, asserting that moral norms hold that 'the behaviour of the individual without exception is right or wrong according as it affects the group – sometimes a closer, nuclear family group; at other times, a wider circle of extended families and friends'. This was particularly so if the 'act of the individual was one that offended the gods [sic] or ancestral spirits. [Such acts] included stealing, cheating, murder, incest or any of the ancestor-sanctioned rules governing and guiding the social and religious life of the community' (ibid.).

As noted, some historical discourses have sought to frame ATR as fundamentally *amoral*. There has long been contention over whether Africans have a moral sense that reflects a perception of good or evil rather than mere adherence to individual norms or prohibitions, and whether that perception has any religious basis. Some, such as Krige and Krige (1954. p. 72), have argued that 'the African moral view' is governed not by the dictates of conscience or any deeply internalized divine law, but by blind conformity to custom and tradition, including taboos or prohibitions by the ancestors. Despite the often prejudicial nature of these arguments, even those who argue *for* a moral foundation within ATR recognize that this is a challenging position. Green (1983) illustrates this difficulty through contrasting notions of 'God' in ATR and 'Western theism'. Contrary to Christian beliefs, for instance, where God represents an unwavering moral standard against which 'in some eschatological domain' (p. 3) humans will be accordingly judged, in ATR, while considered caring of humanity and morally good, he is rarely concerned with human moral trespass – being, amongst the Lugbara, for instance, 'far away' and 'morally otiose' (p. 3). Amongst some societies he can also be inexplicably cruel, and is therefore frequently requested to *refrain* from intervention in human life (Green, 1983). Green cites a Dinka hymn that is illustrative of this ambiguity, and notes that it is the apparent lack of a 'retributive eschatology' (p. 4) in ATR that explains why some understand the belief system as one 'devoid of moral purpose' (p. 5).

Such arguments, however, occlude and distort the nature of African morality (Ikenga-Metuh, 1987, p. 244). For Green (1983), they reflect a Western theological bias that assumes the universality of 'God' as moral adjudicator. Africans, conversely, live in a 'morally saturated religious universe . . . a world in which all really significant interpersonal relationships, including relationships between humans and spiritual beings, have moral content and are governed by moral considerations' (p. 5). Instead of 'God', spirits, ancestors, and ghosts are instrumental in the maintenance of morality. Ray (1976, p. 147) concurs, arguing that it is the *ancestors* that 'constitute the basic categories of moral and legal thought. This raises them above the transitory human level and invests them with sacred significance . . . the rights and duties sanctioned by the ancestors both define and regulate basic [moral behaviour that governs] social and political relations'.

'Moral conscience' amongst Africans is also evident within language – particularly myths and proverbs. According to Idowu (1962, p. 154), for example, the Yoruba word for 'consciousness' is *ifa aya* (the oracle of the heart), which is believed to be inserted into humans by God to enable them to live moral lives. Whether one lives a morally good or bad life is contingent on how the individual responds to their *ifa aya*, and one who behaves wickedly or shamelessly is told 'he [sic] has no sense of shame, he has no oracle of the heart' (ibid.).

Yet assumptions as to the positive relationship between religion and morality are nevertheless problematic, and it is crucial to ask whether 'morality and religion [are] so precisely and narrowly related' (Green, 1983, p. 5) as is often assumed. Countries with high levels of religiosity, for example, often also score highest in terms of corruption (Marquette, 2010, p. 1), and as Marquette notes, despite popular assumptions to the contrary, 'the evidence for a causal relationship between religion . . . and either higher or lower levels of corruption is in no way convincing'. This is not to argue that a relationship between religion, morality and ethics does not exist, rather, this relationship is fluid and discursive (ibid., p. 5).

Conflict

Renewed interest in the role of religion for human development and well-being has been especially keen at the nexus with conflict and its aftermath. Conflicts, whether on a small or large scale, often draw on religious justifications and symbols, even where religious difference is not evident. Indeed, while the extent to which religion influences conflict remains contested, it is difficult to entirely dismiss its importance as an 'intervening variable' (Hasenclever and Rittberger, 2000) in the course of either conflict or peace-building. For many African countries, conflict remains a serious threat to human well-being. Despite an abundance of general research, however, explorations of the religious dimension of African conflicts is scarce, and for this reason knowledge of how African traditional religion intervenes, and to what effect, is wanting. In part, this is because African conflict has served as something of an intellectual testing space for theories of political violence. Some, keen to emphasize the 'irrationality' of African society, point to the 'hyper-violence' of many African conflicts as symptomatic of a form of 'New Barbarianism', a model of political violence based on cultural – or tribal – difference largely alien to classical 'ideological' [sic, justifiable] 'warfare' seen in the West. Others (Collier and Hoeffler, 2001) have instead stressed the instrumental nature of African conflict, arguing that its origins and perpetuation lie with resource competition and economic inequality. And a further group of 'New Wars' (Kaldor, 2006) theorists, interpret African conflict as symptomatic of the postmodern condition – facilitated by international markets and processes of globalization, and driven by an identity politics based on inclusion and exclusivism (Kaldor, 2006, p. 10). All approaches tend to neglect the value of local conflict rationales, and the potential role of religion.

Greater illumination of what conflicts *mean* to people who are actually involved within them and the role ATR may play in defining these needs is certainly required. Despite the popular perception that African conflicts lack the same degree of religiosity in evidence elsewhere, elements of the spiritual are nevertheless evident. During the conflicts in Northern Uganda, the Democratic Republic of Congo, and in Sierra Leone, traditional leaders, institutions, practices and beliefs including the use of sorcery, belief in spirit possession, and secret societies have left a perceptible imprint on the course and nature of political violence. During the Great African War of 1997–2004, the systematic murder, rape and mutilation of pygmy communities, believed by many as having 'magical' status, remains one of the most invisible humanitarian tragedies of the early twenty-first century.

Some attempts to better understand this relationship have already been made. At the broader, conceptual level, Magesa (1997, pp. 268–70) argues that conflict in the African context is perceived and sanctioned vis-à-vis the preservation of life. 'Whether it takes the form of a feud, a raid for cattle, the acquisition of land or other property, or repulsion of attack – in other words, whether [it] is acquisitive or redistributive – its ethical validity is established within that context'. Even within societies that abhor war, such as the !Kung, war and blood sharing is justified in terms of the preservation of life, and is usually followed by elaborate rituals. This perception is similar to that of more warlike societies, such as the Zulu of South Africa and the pastoralists of East Africa. In much of Africa, in addition to civil conflicts (and the occasional conflict between states), much of the social conflict is between what may be termed militias or vigilante groups, which according to Ellis and Ter Haar, 'whether large or small, defensive or aggressive, [all] have in common . . . a spiritual component, expressed in the use of ritual and the use of medicines' (2004, p. 110).

In addition to the relationship between conflict and religion, Gluckman (1965), argues that ideas of conflict *resolution* are also interwoven with African traditional religion and its associated system of ethics and morality. Magesa (1997, pp. 271–2), acknowledges the role of the legal system but claims that in resolving conflict, such institutions are inseparable from moral values, as:

> both are founded on kinship, lineage, joking and clan relationships. The purpose of both is essentially the same: to protect and enhance life in the universe. Similarly, resolution of conflict is connected to the religious system and is inseparable from it. To speak of law and reconciliation is to speak of morality and ritual at the same time.

For example, the traditional Gacaca system of community justice, currently being used as part of the post-conflict transformation and reconciliation process in Rwanda, has so far been successful in bringing peace, however fragile, to the country. Greater illumination of how traditional institutions draw on and are informed by the broader tenets of traditional religious belief, may allow for greater understanding of *why* institutions function the way they do and the reasons for why they may agitate conflict, but also allow recognition of their unfulfilled potential for peacemaking.

Local-level analysis by Jackson (2010), however, complicates the picture. Jackson's study, which examines the role of religion amongst Acholi members of the Lord's Resistance Army (LRA) in Northern Uganda, focuses on the role played by religion in providing a teleological explanation, or a fundamental logic, to actors involved in political violence. He argues that while religion – in this case a mish-mash of ATR, Christianity and Islam – certainly acted as a means of generating fear and loyalty between Acholi insurgents, the idea that it was nothing more than a superficial control mechanism is misplaced, for both the foot soldiers, and probably Kony himself, actually believed it (Jackson, 2010, p. 18). Kony's belief system framed the Acholi not only as victims of the Ugandan government, but also of the spirit world. The traditional Acholi spirits, and the Acholi people themselves, had failed, and only through purifying acts of extreme violence could they be redeemed. The obsession with redemption and purification explains for Jackson not only the range of bizarre quasi-religious battlefield practices of the LRA, but also the extraordinary violence perpetrated against Acholi people themselves – a practice that amounted to 'auto-genocide'. The value of Jackson's analysis allows not only for understanding of how people rationalized the extreme acts of violence they committed, but also for a glimpse of actors' own motivations for perpetuating conflict; in this case fear – fear of marginalization and annihilation.

Crime and Justice

According to Shorter (1977), the conception of justice in ATR is intricately interwoven with conceptions of society and its purpose. In much of the sub-region, 'the experiences of society as a clearly bounded group strongly outweigh the experiences of ego-centred networks of personal relationships' as communities prioritize their stability, existence and continuity over the rights of the individual (ibid., p. 3). Price (1975, pp. 70–79) reinforces this point by his argument that an individual's identity is carved from her or his group identity, which may be the family, clan, lineage, tribe or community. Individual rights in many communities are often subordinate to and subsumed under community rights. In essence, there is a very limited sense of individuality, as allegiance is owed to the group. Even within societies where individuals enjoy greater freedoms and rights (i.e., individual rights that are not subsumed under community rights), such as some pastoralist societies, the 'individual . . . is extremely limited in the degree of social support he [sic] could expect to help reinforce [these rights] against other individuals' (ibid., pp. 70–90).

In many parts of the sub-region, codified or written law did not exist prior to colonialism, which meant that any decisions pertaining to social control and collective decisions were addressed on a case-to-case basis or in the light of precedents, typically using drawing on religion as a guide. Shorter (1977, p. 4) argues that the concept of justice in pre-colonial systems of governance:

> was devoid of vindictiveness, and there was scarcely an idea of retributive or deterrent justice. Persons caught *in flagrante delicto*, in the act of theft, or in the act of adultery, might receive immediate punishment, but past crimes were rarely followed up and there were hardly any penal institutions.

Generally, although the idea of crime as an anti-social act existed, the emphasis was how to maintain social cohesion and restore and promote social relationships acceptable to the deities of the community. The priority is therefore to ensure social stability and cordial relationships among members of a group, which implies that 'reconciliation and the restoration of social harmony [are] the objects of judicial proceedings, not retribution' (ibid., p. 6).

On the practice of law, Magesa (1997) argues that the conception and purpose of the practice of law in the African sense is the maintenance of relationships between individuals and their communities:

> Just as in the moral order, wrongdoing from a 'legal' point of view concerns the disturbance of these relationships. A breach of law, in this sense, is more likely to constitute a tort or delict rather than a crime, if the concept of crime refers to the violation of a formal legislation of the state. Torts and delicts, by contrast, are wrongs against norms and customs, and the punishment of these wrongdoers involves compensation, to be determined by those structures in society that may, in this sense, be called 'courts'. (Magesa, 1997, p. 273)

In fact, the most important part of the judicial process is the act of listening, by the judges, to all parties, both the litigant and the plaintiff. According to Gluckman (1965), the Barotse of Zimbabwe, for instance, have a system in which each party is allowed to narrate their story without interruption, which, it is hoped, will ensure the peaceful and just settlement of the case.

Gibbs (1967, p. 284) argues that in the African context, judgements are meant to serve both reconciliatory and therapeutic purposes. The Kpelle people of Liberia, for instance, use them to 're-educate the parties [and the community at large] through a type of social learning brought about in a specially structured interpersonal setting'. Magesa (1997) however, cautions that the reconciliatory function of judgements does not imply that punishment is not meted out to the 'convicted'. On the contrary, punishment is sometimes meted out, but may take the form of a reprimand, in accordance with which the accused will issue an apology to the complainant. Gibbs (1967, p. 287) contends that the Kpelle Moot court in Liberia, for instance, has one of its most important rewards in group approval 'which goes to the wronged person who accepts an apology and to the person who is magnanimous enough to make one'. As a sign of restored harmony, there is usually a material offering that the court distributes among the litigants to welcome renewed cordial relations.

Gender

Gender, of course, is a field with an important social and intellectual history of its own, yet issues of gender equity, and particularly the rights of women in development nevertheless form the vanguard of many 'rights-based' programmes. In Africa, as elsewhere, various concerns about the representation of women politically and in the workplace, the access of girls to education, and women's critical role in ensuring child health, have been stressed as imperatives for effective political, social and economic development The relationship between gender and various religious institutions forms a key area for concern – more often than not in terms of the barriers religions may put on women's interests.

In ATR, concepts of gender and gender roles are perhaps best understood in relation to four primary sources: mythology, proverbs, prayers and religious practices. These are fundamental sources in ATR, not only to understand gender, but also to appreciate and explain the religion as a whole. Myths, for instance, provide an explanation of some aspects of society that history does not fully explain. Proverbs, on the other hand, are expressions of wisdom acquired through experience, reflection, observation and general knowledge, while prayers are sources of knowledge that illustrate the spirituality of the people praying, the inner person (Mbiti, 1991b, pp. 67–9). Religious practices in turn illustrate the actual manifestation of religion in activities. These four sources are drawn upon to explain the way women are perceived and their status within African cosmogony.

There are several myths involving women in African societies, yet it is those concerning creation in which women feature most prominently. Baumann (1964)[5] presents myths that explain the existence of an original mother of mankind, from whom all people originated. The Akposso of Togo, for instance have a myth that explains how Owoluwu (God) created a woman as his first creation on earth and sired a child (the first human being) with her. Amongst the Ibibio of Nigeria, Baumann (1964) notes a myth that recounts human origins from the divinity Obumo, who was the son of mother-divinity Eka-Abassi. The Tutsi of Rwanda hold a myth that God's first creations – a woman and a man – did not have children, but after several pleas for children, God mixed clay with saliva to form a human figure. The figure was placed in a pot that was to be kept for nine months, with the woman pouring milk into the pot every day. The woman was instructed by God to bring out the figure only when its limbs had formed. This instruction was followed dutifully and after nine months, the woman pulled out a full human being (Baumann, 1964). Mbiti (1970, p. 61) suggests that some African myths seek to explain women's adeptness in the domestic sphere. Women are often attributed the invention of fire, or for the discovery of various food-stuffs and their preparation. 'Thus the cooking skills of the woman are attributed to her from mythological times. She is thus not only the bearer of human beings, but also their cook who provides them with nourishment'.

Immediately recognizable is that though these myths seem to place women at the forefront of creation, they also serve to reinforce and legitimize gender roles. It would appear that these myths even seek to link human life to God through the women's reproductive role. The Tutsi pot, for instance, symbolizes a mother's womb, where a baby takes shape and from which it is born after nine months. Although important for the way they directly connect women to God, these myths tend also to assume a specific reproductive – or domestic – function for women, and can perhaps be used to illuminate the embedded cultural narratives that constitute gender stereotypes. As with the major religions, Mbiti (1970, pp. 171–7) also highlights several myths that associate women with temporal suffering, death and alienation from God. An abundance of such myths describe how mankind was punished with mortality and suffering for failing God's test – failure that is often laid at the feet of women. Amongst the Ashanti, Mbiti describes a myth where a woman pounding *fufu* (the national food) disturbs God, who retreats further into the heavens. The woman persists, and builds an ever higher tower that finally topples, killing many people. Amongst the Bambuti pygmy of Zaire, he describes a further myth where God forbade the first man and woman from eating a specific fruit. The woman, however, tempted by pregnancy cravings, persuaded the man to retrieve the fruit – and mankind was consequently punished with death.

For Mbiti (1991b), women are valued highly within traditional African societies, 'Not only do they bear life, but they also nurse, they cherish, they give warmth, they care for life since all human life passes through their own bodies'. Proverbs, which form a rich resource for understanding concepts of gender in traditional society, appear – at times somewhat obliquely – to stress this value. A Kikuyu proverb says, 'Wives and oxen have no friends' to illustrate that the value of a wife is so high that she must not be given away. Another proverb warns 'A woman must not be killed', emphasizing the role of women as mothers and implying that to kill a woman is to kill her existing or potential children, and thus the whole of humanity (Barra, 1960, p. 62). Even at birth there are proverbs that link girls to their future sexual and reproductive roles. Dalforo (1984, p. 214), points to a Logbara proverb 'A baby-girl means beautiful cows', noting the implication that a woman is believed destined for marriage and the wealth that will bring the family in terms of a bride price, food stuffs and other services.

Once again the reinforcement of gender roles is, however, clear, and raise a series of important questions. What happens, for instance, if a woman remains unmarried? Or, if sexual and reproductive roles are as crucial to women's roles in African societies as the proverbs imply, what happens if a married woman is unable to bear children? Mbiti (1991b, p. 64) argues that 'the woman who is not married has practically no role in society, as far as traditional African worldview goes'. Dalforo (1984, p. 286) complements this argument by citing proverbs that illustrate the expectation that all women get married to ensure the continuity of society. For instance the Lugbara (Uganda) use the proverb 'An ugly girl does not become old at home', to mean that, regardless of a girl's comeliness she is expected to get married, lest she will bear no children and will thus be deprived of womanhood. For the childless woman, a Kikuyu proverb sums up her sorrow in traditional African societies: 'The woman whose sons have died is richer than a barren woman' (Barra, 1960, p. 61). Note that the emphasis in this proverb is on sons, not daughters, in itself speaking to the importance attached to boys in comparison with girls in many African societies. This proverb explains the fact that, while a woman might be excused for losing her 'precious' sons, there is hardly any excuse for a woman to be barren. Hence 'A barren wife never gives thanks', because children are the greatest gifts for which thanks are given (ibid.).

Many prejudices about women are also contained within proverb. 'This woman is fire', one proverb states, 'This woman is a deceitful crocodile', says another, and 'Do not desire a woman with beautiful breasts if you have no money', warns a third (Mbiti, 1991b, p. 66). Barra (1960) notes a Kikuyu proverb that additionally frames women as indiscreet: 'Women have no secure gourds', it argues, 'but only leaking, upside down ones'. Massek and Sidai (1974, p. 32) also point to a Maasai proverb that demonstrates the idea that women ruin men: 'The prostitute can make you useless', it states, blaming the woman, rather than the solicitor of sex, for this danger. Finally Bannerman (1974), points to a Ghanaian proverb that articulates that 'When a woman increases in wealth, they are silent. But when they fall into trouble, the whole world gets to know'. This proverb, according to Bannerman, explains the complaints of African men that women are very complex creations, whom they (African men) fail to understand.

In ATR, though both women and men generally participate in religious activities and make contributions to the spiritual welfare of their lives, families and societies, women's roles are generally subordinate to those of men, and often confined to private prayer in the domestic sphere. In the public sphere, while priestesses do exist in some societies, the principal intercessor with the spirits is almost invariably a male priest (Kilson, 1976). While a few African societies such as the Mende and the Swazi may give primary ritual responsibilities to women in communal cults, these roles are often shared with men. For instance, 'among the Swazi, the queen mother shares a dual monarchy with her son and together they serve the royal ancestors and make rain magic' (ibid., p. 138). Despite their subordinate role to men however, women nevertheless play a vital role in personal rituals associated with status transformation, such as childbirth, puberty and death. For instance, Mbiti (1991b, p. 68) argues that 'almost everywhere in Africa, the mediums (who are so important in traditional practices) are nearly always women. In most cases, it is also the women who experience spirit possession'. Though the role of women in traditional healing is also significant, it is often the case that women traditional healers are confined largely to the treatment of children and other women's medical needs, while male healers are able to practise on men, children and sometimes even women.

In ATR, sexual relations in ritual are interwoven with those in secular life as they tend to be connected to vitality through reproductive functions. Women are perceived as the force of life, crucial for the continuity of the community. At the same time they are regarded as a source of danger, as expressed in certain religious rituals. Blood associated with menstruation and childbearing is regarded as polluted in many African societies, hence rituals are conducted to separate women from others. 'Women' Mbiti (1991b, p. 136) argues 'therefore are anomalous creatures – intimately associated with the well-being of society through their life-giving attributes and deeply threatening through their polluting qualities'. One will note the paradoxical position of women in ATR, while on the one hand they are regarded highly for their reproductive roles, on the other they are disdained for their sexuality.

Three basic principles are evident in ATR's construction of gender relations: first, is the notion that women are, in general, subordinate to men; second, that various essential differences exist between the sexes; and third, that men and women, nevertheless, complement one another. Despite the vital mutual dependency of the sexes however, the primary association of women with the domestic sphere, fertility and social continuity reinforces their 'domestic and inferior orientations in society'. In and of themselves, therefore, Kilson (1976, p. 140) argues therefore 'African traditional religious ideologies do not promote social change'. How intractable this conflict between ATR and such a vital development objective may be, remains to be seen.

CONCLUSIONS: ATR AND DEVELOPMENT IN CONTEMPORARY AFRICA

This chapter has provided an overview of ATR and some of the ways in which the religion may intervene with various concepts of development. There is, of course, a veritable mountain of issues left uncharted. We have been unable, due to space limitations, to discuss the relationship between ATR and the prevailing human rights discourse, for instance, or how the religion frames notions of land ownership, health, education or the environment. Similarly, we neglect a significant and interesting relationship with public authority, governance and emerging African political philosophies such as Ubuntu. Each of these topics deserves far greater consideration than is possible within these pages. While we have attempted to provide a brief consideration of morality, conflict, justice and gender vis-à-vis ATR, this has been more for illustration than conclusiveness. We have instead attempted to illuminate the conceptual contours of this vast and under-researched area and tried to emphasize first the historic marginalization that ATR – and other indigenous religions – have experienced and that still shapes the way they are understood and treated today, second, the continued salience of these traditions for African people regardless of their persistent marginalization, and third, perhaps most critically, the need for greater, and more nuanced, research.

Of course, for some, concerns will still remain over actively engaging ostensibly undemocratic religious actors and institutions in development. This is understandable. Religion and religious values are complex and 'undecided'; the belief that secular development can somehow capture and control religions, picking and choosing those elements most attractive to development is arrogant and reckless. There are also countless issues of representation. *Should* religion be involved in decisions that affect non-believers or believers of other faiths – particularly where people's lives and well-being are at stake? Pobee and Mends (1977, p. 10), for instance, caution claims over the 'pervasiveness' of ATR, noting that for some people, participation in religious practices and ritual serve more communal than spiritual functions, and 'the sacral role of the traditional rulers has become for some mere ceremony'. Empowering unrepresentative religious actors may in such cases be in danger of unduly interfering with processes of social change. It is not the place here to provide answer for these questions, and our point is a far more humble one. As we discuss above, both indigenous peoples and the belief systems that sustain them have been historically marginalized. While for some groups, these belief systems have been lost or have blended with other religious traditions, for others they remain clearly important but little understood by scholars or the wider public. A significant fear is that increased recognition of the 'world religions' in development may somewhat ironically serve to further marginalize these traditions – particularly as those same – mostly negative – historical discourses still seem to remain popular. Uncritical and stereotypical media reports of witchcraft and sacrifice in Africa, for instance, do little to dispel people of their prejudices about the traditional beliefs of the continent, and have barely advanced in sophistication since the nineteenth century. Our argument is not to deny that ATR may contain many undesirable practices – most religions have at some point in their histories – but rather to re-emphasize that indigenous religions such as ATR are not 'strange' or otherworldly, but remarkable in their 'ordinariness' (Harvey, 2000), locally meaningful, and historically conditioned. The prevailing interest in indigenous rights and of the social margins provides a perfect opportunity for a renewed programme of research exploring the important interface between these long-neglected belief systems and human well-being.

NOTES

* The views expressed in this chapter do not necessarily reflect the religious beliefs or otherwise of the authors.

1. Given the geographical distribution, relative diffuseness of the tradition and the number of fusions of ATR with Christianity and Islam, determining the number of adherents of ATR is understandably complex. This figure was extrapolated from *The World Christian Encyclopaedia* (Barrett et al., 2001).
2. The use of 'anarchism' alludes to Robert Kaplan's (1994) contentious article 'The coming anarchy', which portrays a West Africa plagued by tribal conflict, resource scarcity and overpopulation.
3. Caution should be exercised here – the extent of adherence to religion is notoriously difficult to gauge – see Pobee and Mends (1977) and below.
4. Indeed, in his treatise of African history, Christopher Ehret (2002, p. 15) traces a number of distinct religious traditions on the continent, noting that religion comprised a variety of 'monotheistic, henotheistic, nontheistic and even polytheistic' forms.
5. In Mbiti (1988, pp. 69–82).

REFERENCES

Adongo, P., J.F. Phillips and F. Binka (1998), 'The influence of traditional religion on fertility regulation among the Kassena-Nankana of Northern Ghana', *Studies in Family Planning*, **29**(1), 23–40.

Ashanti, K.F. (1997), 'Taking back our Ptahra gods and holy temples', paper presented at Association of Black Psychologists Annual Convention, Washington, DC, available at: http://afgen.com/ptahra.html; accessed 12 July 2012.

Bannerman, J.Y. (1974), *Mfantse-Akan Mbusem* (*Ghanaian Proverbs*), Accra: Ghana Publishing Corporation.

Barra, G. (1960), *1000 Kikuyu Proverbs*, Nairobi: East African Literature Bureau, and London, Macmillan and Co.

Barrett, D., G. Kurian and T. Johnson (2001), *World Christian Encyclopaedia Second Edition: A Comparative Survey of Churches and Religions in the Modern World, Volume 1: The World by Countries: Religionists, Churches, Ministries*, Oxford: Oxford University Press.

Baumann, H. (1964), *Shopfung und Urzeit des Menschen im mythus der Afrikanischen Volker* (2nd edition), Berlin: Reimer.

Bever, E.W.M. (2000), 'Witchcraft fears and psychosocial factors in disease', *Journal of Interdisciplinary History*, **30**(4), 573–90.

Booth, J.S. (1977), 'An approach to African religion', in J.S. Booth (ed.), *African Religions, A Symposium*, New York: NOK Publishers.

Brain, J. (1982), 'Witchcraft and development', *African Affairs*, **81**(234), 371–84.

Busia, K. (1968), *The Position of the Chief in the Modern Political System of Ashanti: A Study of the Influences of the Contemporary Changes on Ashanti Political Institutions*, London: Frank Cass.

Caplan, P. (2010), '"Child sacrifice" in Uganda? The BBC, "witch-doctors" and anthropologists', *Anthropology Today*, **26**(2), 4–7.

Clearly, E.L. and T. Steigenga (2004), *Resurgent Voices in Latin America: Indigenous Peoples, Political Mobilization and Religious Change*, New Brunswick, NJ: Rutgers University Press.

Collier, P. and A. Hoeffler (2001), 'Greed and grievance in civil war', World Bank Policy Research Paper No. 2355.

Cox, J.L. (2007), *From Primitive to Indigenous: The Academic Study of Indigenous Religions*, Aldershot: Ashgate.

Dalforo, A.T. (1984), *Logbara Proverbs*, Rome: MCCJ.
Danquah, J.B. (1968), *The Akan Doctrine of God: A Fragment of Gold Coast Ethics and Religion*, London: Frank Cass.
Dowden, R. (2006), 'Thousands of child "witches" turned on to the streets to starve', *The Observer*, 12 February 2006.
Ellis, S. and Ter Haar, G. (2004), *Worlds of Power: Religion Thought and Political Practice in Africa*, London: Hurst and Co.
Pritchard, E.E. (1937), *Witchcraft, Magic and Oracles Among the Azande*, Oxford: Clarendon Press.
Evans-Pritchard, E.E. (1965), *Theories of Primitive Religions*, Oxford: The Clarendon Press.
Evans-Pritchard, E.E. (1971), 'Sources, with particular reference to the Southern Sudan', *Cahiers d'Etudes Africaines*, **11**(41), 144–5.
Frobenius, L. (1931), *The Voice of Africa*, London: Oxford University Press.
Gibbs, J.L. (1967), 'The Kpelle Moot', in P. Bohannan (ed.), *Law and Warfare: Studies in the Anthropology of Politics*, New York: The Natural History Press.
Gluckman, M. (1965), *Politics, Law and Ritual in Tribal Society*, Chicago: Aldine Publishing Company.
Green, R. (1983), 'Religion and morality in the African traditional setting', *Journal of Religion in Africa*, **XIV**(1), 1–23.
Gwassa, C.G.K. (1972), 'Kinjikitile and the ideology of Maji Maji', in T.O. Ranger and I. Kimambo (eds), *The Historical Study of African Religion, with Reference to East and Central Africa*, London: Heinemann, pp. 202–17.
Harvey, G. (2000), *Indigenous Religions – A Companion*, London: Cassell.
Hasenclever, A. and V. Rittberger (2000), 'Does religion make a difference? Theoretical approaches to the impact of faith on political conflict', *Millennium: Journal of International Studies*, **29**(3), 641–74.
Idowu, E.B. (1962), *Oldsmar: God in Yoruba Beliefs*, London: Longman.
Idowu, E.B. (1973), *African Tradition Religion: A Definition*, London: SCM Press Ltd.
Idowu, E.B. (1975 edition), *African Traditional Religion: A Definition*, London: SCM Press.
Ikenga-Metuh, E. (1987), *Comparative Studies of African Traditional Religions*, Onitsha, Nigeria: IMICO Publishers.
Imasogie, O. (1985), *African Traditional Religion*, Ibadan, Nigeria: Oxford University Press Nigeria.
Jackson, P. (2010), 'Politics, religion and the Lord's Resistance Army in Northern Uganda', Working Paper No. 43 from the Religions and Development Research Programme at the University of Birmingham, United Kingdom, available at: http://www.religionsanddevelopment.org/files/resourcesmodule/@random454f80f60b3f4/1274702557_Working_Paper_43_complete_for_web.pdf; accessed 12 July 2012.
Kaldor, M. (2006), *New and Old Wars: Organized Violence in a Global Era* (2nd edition), Cambridge: Polity Press.
Kaplan, R. (1994), 'The coming anarchy – how scarcity, crime, overpopulation, tribalism and disease are rapidly destroying the social fabric of our planet', *The Atlantic Magazine*, February, available at: http://www.theatlantic.com/magazine/archive/1994/02/the-coming-anarchy/4670/1/; accessed 12 July 2012.
Kendall, L. (1984), 'Korean shamanism: women's rites and a Chinese comparison', *Senri Ethnological Studies*, **11**.
Kenyatta, J. (1961), *Facing Mount Kenya: The Tribal Life of the Kikuyu*, London: Mercury Books.
Kilson, M. (1976), 'Women in African traditional religions', *Journal of Religion in Africa*, **8**(2), 133–43.
Kimambo, I.N. and C.K. Omari (1972), 'The development of religious thought and centres among Pare', in T.O. Ranger and I. Kimambo (eds), *The Historical Study of African Religion, with Reference to East and Central Africa*, London: Heinemann, pp. 111–21.
Krige, J.D. and E.J. Krige (1954), 'The Loved of the Transvaal', in Daryl Forde (ed.), *African Worlds: Studies in the Cosmological Ideas and Social Values of African Peoples*, London: Oxford University Press, pp. 55–82.
Law, P. (2005), 'The revival of folk religion and gender relationships in rural China: a preliminary observation', *Asian Folklore Studies*, **64**(1), 89–109.
Levine, D. (1986), *Religion and Political Conflict in Latin America*, Chapel Hill, NC: University of North Carolina Press.
Lucas, J.O. (1970), *Religion in West Africa and Ancient Egypt*, Lagos: National Press.
Magesa, L. (1997), *African Religion: The Moral Traditions of Abundant Life*, Mary Knoll, NY: Orbis Books.
Magesa, L. (1998 edition), *African Religion: The Moral Traditions of Abundant Life*, Mary knoll, NY: Orbis Books.
Mainga, M. (1972), 'A history of Lose religion to the end of the nineteenth century', in T.O. Ranger and I. Kimambo (eds), *The Historical Study of African Religion, with Reference to East and Central Africa*, London: Heinemann, pp. 95–107.
Maquet, J.J. (1972), 'The kingdom of Ruanda', in D. Forde (ed.), *African Worlds*, London: Oxford University Press, pp. 164–89.

Marquette, H. (2010), 'Whither morality? "Finding God" in the fight against corruption', Working Paper No. 41 from the Religions and Development Research Programme at the University of Birmingham, United Kingdom, available at: http://www.religionsanddevelopment.org/files/resourcesmodule/@random454f80f60b3f4/1274702441_Working_Paper_41_complete_for_web.pdf; accessed 12 July 2012.
Massek, A. and J.O. Sidai (1974), *Envenom too Lamasery – Wisdom of Massa*, Nairobi: Tran Africa Publishers.
Mbiti, J. (1969), *African Religions and Philosophy*, London: Heinemann.
Mbiti, J. (1970), *Concepts of God in Africa*, London: SPCK.
Mbiti, J. (1988), 'The role of women in African traditional religion', *Cahiers des Religions Africaines*, **22**, Kinshasa, Congo: Centre d'Etudes des Religions Africaines, Université Louvain de Kinshasa, 69–82.
Mbiti, J. (1990), *African Religions and Philosophy*, London: Heinemann.
Mbiti, J. (1991a), *Introduction to African Religion*, London: Heinemann.
Mbiti, J. (1991b), 'Flowers in the garden: the role of women in African religion', in J. Olupona (ed.), *African Traditional Religions in Contemporary Society*, New York: Paragon House, pp. 67–72.
Mbon, M.F. (1991), 'African traditional socio-religious ethics and national development: the Nigerian case', in J.K. Olupona (ed.), *African Traditional Religions in Contemporary Society*, New York: Paragon House, pp. 101–10.
Olupona, J.O.K. (2004), *Beyond Primitivism: Indigenous Religious Traditions and Modernity*, London: Routledge.
Parrinder, G. (1962), *African Traditional Religion*, London: Sheldon Press.
Parrinder, G. (1974 edition), *African Traditional Religion*, London: Sheldon Press.
Platvoet, J. (1996), 'From object to subject: a history of the study of the religions of Africa', in J. Platvoet et al. (eds), *The History of Religions in Africa: Past, Present and Prospects*, Cambridge: Roots and Branches.
Pobee, J.S. and E.H. Mends (1977), 'Social change and African traditional religion', *Sociological Analysis*, **38**(1), 1–12.
Price, David (1975), *Society and Bureaucracy in Contemporary Ghana*, Berkeley: University of California Press.
Rakodi, C. (2011), 'Inspirational, inhibiting, institutionalized: exploring the links between religion and development', Working Paper No. 66 of the Religions and Development Research Programme at the University of Birmingham, available at: http://www.religionsanddevelopment.org/files/resourcesmodule/@random454f80f60b3f4/1315399922_working_paper_66_complete_for_web.pdf; accessed 12 July 2012.
Ray, B.C. (1976), *African Religions: Symbol, Ritual and Community*, Englewood Cliffs, NJ: Prentice-Hall, Inc.
Richards, P. (1996), *Fighting for the Rainforest: War, Youth and Resources in Sierra Leone*, Oxford: James Currey.
Richards, P. (2000), 'Chimpanzees as political animals in Sierra Leone', in J. Knight, *Natural Enemies: People–Wildlife Conflicts in Anthropological Perspective*, London: Routledge.
Richards. P. (2002), 'Green Book millenarians? The Sierra Leone war from the perspective of an anthropology of religion', in Niels Kastfelt (ed.), *Religion and Civil War in Africa*, London: C. Hurst & Co Ltd.
Sarbah, Mensah (1968), *Fante Customary Laws*, London: Frank Cass.
Shoko, T. (2007), *Karanga Indigenous Religion in Zimbabwe: Health and Well-being*, Aldershot: Ashgate.
Shorter, A. (1977), 'Concepts of social justice in traditional Africa', *Pro Dialogo Bulletin*, **12**, 32–51, available at: http://www.afrikaworld.net/afrel/atr-socjustice.htm; accessed 12 July 2012.
Stamer, J. (1995), *Islam in Sub-Saharan Africa*, Estella: Editorial Verbo Divino.
Uwah, I.E. (2011), 'The representation of African traditional religion and culture in Nigeria's popular film', *Politics and Religion Journal*, **1**(5), 81–102.
Van Beek, K.A. (2002), 'Spirituality: a development taboo', in D. Eade (ed.), *Development and Culture*, Oxford: Oxfam, pp. 60–77.

11 Name it and claim it: Prosperity Gospel and the global Pentecostal reformation

Matthew Sharpe

INTRODUCTION

Since the 1980s, Prosperity Gospel has been the fastest-growing strand of Pentecostal Christianity. The global growth of Pentecostalism meanwhile, particularly in the developing nations, has been so rapid as to amount to what critics have variously called a 'restructuring of Christianity', 'the fourth great age of Christian expansion' (Poloma, 2000), or even a 'reshaping [of] the religion of the 21st century' (Cox, 1996). Known variously as the Gospel of Heath and Wealth, Word of Faith, Prosperity Theology, Name It and Claim It, Seed-Faith, Abundant Life and 'Neo-Pentecostalism', the Prosperity Gospel centres around two key ideas. The first is that God is a benevolent deity who wants believers in His son Jesus Christ to be socio-economically prosperous, as well as healthy in body and soul. Second is the idea that believers can actively claim as a kind of covenanted *right* this-worldly abundance. The means to do this is through 'positive confession' and the power of the spoken word (*rhema*), coupled with financial offerings or 'tithes' to their churches, and unwavering faith that God will provide.

While Prosperity Gospel shapes, in increasing numbers, churches like the African Victory Bible Church, Conquerors Church, Chapel International, Hillsong in Australia, and global denominations like the Universal Church of the Kingdom of God, Prosperity is better described as an inter-denominational, inter-national movement: 'a relational community of believers, voluntary organizations, fellowships, conferences, and ministries loosely defined by a shared doctrine, a network without definite leader or governing body' (Harrison, 2005, p. 14). Central to its remarkable growth first in the United States, then in the global South, is Prosperity's embrace of mass media and many of the characteristic features of postmodern, consumerist capitalism. Commentators stress the centrality of the televangelical Trinity Broadcast Network and related networks (plus promotional videos, CDs and DVDs, and now web-stores) to the proselytizing of Prosperity, together with its often stadium-based or 'megachurch', rock music and light-filled, forms of worship.

Prosperity's core ideas, and its growing global influence, are both highly contentious, with leading ministers being repeatedly subject to scandal and charges of economic misconduct. Christian critics, often from within Pentecostalism, depict the Prosperity movement as a heretical betrayal of the *theologia crucis* (theology of the cross) central to Christianity, an idolatry of money and self at the expense of love and charity (e.g., Harrison, 2005, pp. 12–14; Bruggerman, 2007; Asamoah-Gyadu, 2010). Political and sociological criticisms variously depict Prosperity as a theological mystification of the neoliberal emphasis on acquisitive individualism; a desperate exercise in wishful thinking that distracts the vulnerable from addressing the structural causes of their disadvantage;

if not a kind of American-led conspiracy to propagate capitalism, and break down forms of traditional, indigenous forms of life, in the global South (Coleman, 2002; Robbins, 2004; Adogame, 2010).

This chapter will examine the ideas and worship of Prosperity Gospel (hereafter also simply 'Prosperity'), then Prosperity's history and spread into Africa, Latin America and Asia. The causes of Prosperity's stunning growth in the developing world will then be considered, drawing on the growing literature on the movement, as well as the wider debates on the extraordinary growth of Pentecostalism in the global South. Finally, we will examine the effects of Prosperity, and Pentecostalism more widely, on the communities in which it takes hold, weighing more critically against more sanguine accounts of its political, social and economic influences, or what one commentator has called the 'Pentecostalization' of parts of the developing world.

PROSPERITY: IDEAS AND WORSHIP

The first perplexity about Prosperity for outsiders is: how can the Christian religion, founded on the suffering of the sad and sorrowful 'lamb of God' – a prophet who kept company with the socially disenfranchised, who announced that his kingdom 'was not of this world', and who proclaimed the insurmountable difficulty for the rich man to go to heaven – be held to glorify the unabashed pursuit of economic wealth?

Prosperity theology has a powerful set of responses to these questions. These responses both inherit and markedly alter the much older connection famously identified by sociologist Max Weber between 'the Protestant ethic and the spirit of capitalism'. Prosperity's claims to Christian legitimacy are rooted in a selective reading of the Bible as providing a series of decisive 'proof texts' of the vision that, in the words of one preacher: 'I must tell you boldly: God wants to make you rich' (Robert Tilton, in Alexander, 2009, p. 61). Key proof-texts of this kind from the New Testament are 3 John 1: 2: 'Beloved, I wish above all things that thou mayest prosper and be in health, even as thy soul prospereth' and John 10: 10: 'I am come that they might have life, and that they might have it more abundantly'. Christ's famous Parable of the Talents (Matthew 25: 14–30) is also important to Prosperity, with its conclusion that: 'to everyone who has more will be given, and he will have abundance, but from him who doesn't have, even that which he has will be taken away. Throw out the unprofitable servant into the outer darkness'. Prosperity teachings also place great significance on certain Old Testament sayings, notably from the Book of Malachi: 'Bring ye all the tithes into the storehouse, that there may be meat in mine house, and prove me now herewith, saith the LORD of hosts, if I will not open you the windows of heaven, and pour you out a blessing, that there shall not be room enough to receive it' (Malachi 3: 10).

Some Prosperity preachers additionally claim that the traditional images of Jesus as living an ascetic life, indifferent to material wealth, are false – the product of an outdated Christianity too preoccupied with negativity, suffering and asceticism. They argue that Jesus and his disciples were in fact very wealthy. This wealth is attested by their ability to travel around as they wished, biblical references to the apostles' previous business activities and to Judas' role as a kind of treasurer for the apostolic group, and Jesus' ability to command audiences from the highest echelons of Judean society (e.g., Blake,

2009). According to several Prosperity teachers, Christ even wore a 'designer coat' in a way that anticipates and justifies the often lavish, ostentatious aesthetics of today's Prosperity Gospel teachers, decked out in expensive suits or coats of many colours: many of their elite flying first class or on private jets between international conference centres, enormous, lavishly endowed megachurches, and televangelical commitments (Perriman, 2003, p. 146; Hladky, 2012, p. 11).

Prosperity Gospel books then bear titles that sound every bit like 'New Age' or 'Self Help' manuals: *You Can Win!*, *Reaching Your Potential*, *God's Will is Prosperity*, *Biblical Keys to Financial Prosperity*, and *God's Success Formula*, or E.E. Allen's *The Secret to Scriptural Financial Success.* Prosperity Churches regularly involve sermons or group classes on financial responsibility and entrepreneurship, and other aspects of prospering economically in the contemporary world. Unlike earlier modes of Protestant sanctification of capitalist accumulation, however, the emphasis here falls much more on the unashamed achievement and consumption of economic goods, than on the inner virtues and self-denials necessary to achieve it (Lingenthal, 2012, p. 55). The testimony of Nigerian Winners' Chapel Bishop David O. Oyedepo on his conversion is here illustrative:

> There was a time in my life when I was known as a failure . . . The only car my family had before then was stolen . . . But to the glory of God in October 2000, He gave me a Mercedes Benz car. I have also been able to dedicate a new mansion God blessed me with to the glory of His Name. To crown it all, another car was recently added to my family. I have every reason to celebrate the faithfulness of God. (In Asamoah-Gyadu, 2010, p. 3)

Yet critics can be too rash by focusing exclusively on Prosperity's sanctification of the pursuit of economic wealth. This is only one, albeit the most unusual, feature of Prosperity Gospel's teachings, and one part of the operative understanding of 'prosperity' amongst believers. In fact, this understanding is typically much more holistic than critics imagine. Central to Prosperity's particular species of Christian theology is its controversial interpretation of the meaning of Christ's atonement on the cross. The crucial argument is that Christ's sufferings atoned not only for humans' spiritual sins, but also for our bodily sufferings: 'Surely he hath borne our griefs [*kholee*] and carried our sorrows [*makob*] away' (Isaiah 51; cf. Matthew 8: 17). Prosperity shares with other strands of Pentecostal Christianity an emphasis on the miraculous healing, through faith, of bodily infirmities (e.g., Alexander, 2009) – indeed, it is highly sceptical of a strong separation of mind or spirit and the flesh, sin and bodily infirmities. Prosperity claims that Christ's power of miraculous healing both spirit and flesh, which he bestowed upon his apostles, is not a thing of the distant biblical past. It is an ever-renewed and renewing power the Lord bestows upon all his believers, which can be reclaimed by worshippers in the present of twenty-first-century reality. For Prosperity believers, we live today, still, in a world of signs and wonders, and we must only relearn how to see and to produce them (Anderson, 2000, pp. 2–3). It is this sense of living in a still-enchanted world, in stark contrast to the perceived depthlessness of secular ideologies – and the real miseries of the impoverished South – that shapes Pentecostals' ecstatic megachurch ceremonies. In another distinctive mark of this contemporary neo-Pentecostalism, these ceremonies are characterized by bringing together large numbers of worshippers (in some megachurches upwards of 40 000 (Hartford Seminary, 2000–06; Gramby-Sobukwe and Hoiland, 2009). These huge public events have many of the features of modern rock concerts, from spectacular lighting to loud, contemporary styles of musical performance, which are interspersed with call-and-response-style sermonizing, episodes of spirit healing and, often, of speaking in tongues (Hollenweger, 1972; Cox, 1996, p. 259; Kramer, 2005).

Indeed, Prosperity teachings characteristically claim that the Bible aims to set out the good news of a kind of covenant or contract between God and His believers, mediated through the Son. In Genesis 12 and 17, God promises Abraham that He will make his name great, give to his 'seed' a great nation, and make them 'fruitful', if Abraham keeps the faith. According to Prosperity teachings, Christians became heirs to that Abrahamic covenant by identification with Abraham's descendants through Christ, his ministry and his passion (cf. Galatians 3: 29). In Prosperity teachings, God is accordingly depicted as bound by a kind of contract not to withhold His grace, and fruits, from His believers. Another way this thought is sometimes expressed is to argue that the universe – and God – is governed by a set of 'spiritual laws', alongside material laws of nature, which believers can rely unfailingly upon (Perriman, 2003, p. 2; Hagin, 2007, pp. 118–19; Hladky, 2012, p. 4). Believers' prosperity is in this way *already there*, if only they learn how to access this divine beneficence. We note that this is one more notable point of contrast with earlier forms of (especially Calvinist) Protestantism, which differently sanctified economic accumulation. The idea here is that one can, quite literally, 'bank upon' God's blessings if one knows how to access them, rather than needing to agonize continuously over whether one may or may not have been chosen by His inscrutable will (Miller, 2007, pp. 163–4).

The means believers can draw upon to access this never-depleting source of divine prosperity are equally distant from Calvinist species of inner-worldly asceticism. These means are twofold. First is the practice of 'positive confession', the teaching that believers may claim whatever they desire from God, simply by speaking it in faith (Perriman, 2003, p. 137; Hagin, 2006, pp. 3, 111–14). This practice is amongst the most apparently bizarre features, for outsiders, of Prosperity's distinctive ways of worship: with believers encouraged to proclaim out loud what it is they want or *are expecting* by God's supernatural grace: 'I'll never be broke another day in my life'; 'I am expecting supernatural increase this week'; 'I am expecting supernatural debt-cancellation this week' (examples in Harrison, 2005, p. 4). Underlying the belief in positive confession (or 'name it and claim it', as it is sometimes called) is a particular understanding of the importance of the spoken word (*rhema*), in contrast to what is written (*logos*). The Prosperity movement's largest American teaching centre for prospective ministers is called the Rhema Ministerial Association International, and its leading magazine *The Word of Faith* (ibid., p. 16). The key theological notion here draws on the observation that God's creative power in Genesis is one of *speaking things into being*. Just so, since humans are made in the image of God, and moreover, believers are parties to the covenantal relation with Him through Christ, Prosperity argues that the human capacity to speak – when this speech proceeds from true faith – allows believers to co-participate in the work of creation, exercising dominion over physical and spiritual realities (e.g., Hanegraaf, 1993; Dollar, 2002). This emphasis on the primary, living and creative importance of the spoken word accessible to all believers, incidentally, marks one important difference between Prosperity and forms of fundamentalist Christianity. In the latter, emphasis falls on the unwavering importance of the 'It is written . . . ' of the Bible, rather than the ecstatic spoken word – however much commentators often conflate Pentecostal evangelism with 'Christian fundamentalism' (Adogame, 2010, pp. 503–4).

The second, more controversial means the Prosperity believer has available to them to access their invisible potential for God-graced prosperity is the practice of tithing. This involves paying one-tenth of their gross income weekly to their church. The promise is that, in return, God will bless them with all the wishes that they profess in their positive confessions. Believers are encouraged, in a sermon before the offering on the importance of giving, to give additional 'love offerings' to the church when they can. Sometimes, as in the teaching of prominent Minister Oral Roberts, the kind of supernatural gift economy involved here is depicted in agricultural metaphors. Believers plant 'seeds' by giving their earnings, which shall because of God's grace and faithfulness yield a harvest later on, 100 or 1000 fold. Roberts is famous for the 1950s' 'blessing pact', in which subscribers who bequeathed US$100 to his work were promised a refund, should they not receive an equivalent gift from an unexpected source within one year (Lofton, 2011, p. 46). In a different way, controversial Bishop Edir Macedo of the Universal Church of the Kingdom of God in Brazil depicts 'the miracle of the tithe' as a 'putting [of] God to the test', as much as a test of the faith of the believer: 'God orders us to test Him so that blessing can descend upon us' (Garrard-Burnett, 2007, p. 221).

PROSPERITY: CRITICISM, HISTORY AND DEVELOPMENT

Almost all aspects of the Prosperity Gospel's teachings and practices have been the subject of intense scrutiny and criticism as the movement has continued to grow. The movement has been marked by a series of scandals, with prominent preachers subject to allegations of financial misconduct and mismanagement, nearly wherever Prosperity has reached (Jenkins, 2006, p. 106; Alexander, 2009, p. 68; Lingenthal, 2012, p. 52). Christian theologians of differing denominations have attacked its conception of a contract-bound God as based in faulty, over-simplistic readings of scripture. A key point of Christian criticism is Prosperity's implied theodicy (understanding of the nature of God's justice, and the problem of evil). The teachings of positive confession, with its background teachings of the world-forming power of faithful speech and man's powers of co-creation are seen as deeply unable to explain the persistence of evil and poverty in people's lives (Harrison, 2005, p. 13; Bruggerman, 2007, pp. 132–6; Alexander, 2009, pp. 67–9). Or else, it is observed, Prosperity Gospel comes close to the deeply uncompassionate position of blaming the victim for his or her suffering, since it is held that humans can through faith and words master their own destinies: 'wealth as God's will and blessing and poverty as curse' (Oral Roberts, in Kalu, 2008, p. 256). Theologians contest the Christian provenance of some Prosperity preachers' teaching that Christ died on the cross, not only physically, but also spiritually. In addition, the so-called 'little-gods' scandal surrounding Prosperity teachings calls into question whether Prosperity's *theologia gloriae* (theology of empowerment or glory) is deeply gnostic, underplaying the significance of the Fall and the abiding reality of physical illness, instead promoting the heretical idea of *theosis:* that human beings become as gods in this life (Hanegraaf, 1993; Bowman, 2001, Chapter 9; Peters, 2006; Asamoah-Gyadu, 2010).

These theological criticisms of Prosperity Gospel merge closely into questions concerning the movement's origins and historical development. The last two decades have seen a series of polemical works on this topic (Hanegraaf, 1993, 2009; Bowman, 2001), presenting Prosperity as a cult-like sect, with deeply non-Christian roots. The key work here is perhaps Daniel McConnell's *A Different Gospel* (1988). McConnell's work was ground-breaking in its claim that the recognized founding father of the Prosperity Gospel in the United States, Kenneth Hagin Senior, leaned heavily on the ideas of Essek William Kenyon. This debt is significant, for Kenyon is directly indebted to the nineteenth-century American New Thought movement, closely associated in its turn with 'Christian science' and parapsychology. According to New Thought teaching, all of reality, including human beings, are in some sense God (a kind of pantheism), but in God there can be no sickness. It follows that physical illness, and other forms of human suffering, cannot be fully real; and that human beings can heal themselves almost instantaneously, when they come to know the true reality or 'science' of their condition. Today, significantly, non-Christian versions of this teaching flourish, in books like *The Secret,* widely publicized on the *Oprah Winfrey Show* (Lofton, 2011).

Leading Prosperity or Word of Faith teachers and televangelists Kenneth Hagin, Oral Roberts, Frederick Price, Kenneth Copeland, Don Gassett and others are held by critics then to have inherited their decisive theological convictions from E.W. Kenyon and the New Thought movement. However, these assessments need to be balanced against the deeper roots of the development of the Prosperity Gospel movement in the longer history of Protestant engagements with, and promotion of, capitalist economic and cultural forms. Other commentators have pointed to the roots of Prosperity ideas, particularly concerning the god-like empowerment of believers, in the tradition of Christian perfectionism coming out of nineteenth-century Wesleyan Methodism (Towns, 2008). It is also notable that nearly all of the key figures in the movement began their confessional lives within the wider Pentecostal churches, before breaking with these often on the strength of experiencing a miraculous healing or revelation. The spiritual universe of the Prosperity movement, a still-enchanted universe in which the supernatural has not fled, and in which faith alone can work miracles and physical healings, is unmistakably close to that of other Pentecostal denominations (e.g., Poloma, 2000, pp. 2–3; Alexander, 2009). The Prosperity emphasis on *rhema* (or spoken word) intersects closely with the importance of speaking in tongues or *glossolalia* as a sign of God's transformative power in older Pentecostal churches. In terms of organizational structure, Prosperity's non- or cross-denominational, flexible network of churches and preachers, without a centralized, hierarchical governing body again mirrors features of the wider Pentecostal movement, which scholars have seen as important in explaining Pentecostalism's incredible expansion over the last decades (Robbins, 2004, p. 125; Adogame, 2010, p. 501). Finally, the energetic, music-filled and enthusiastic nature of Prosperity Gospel worship, encouraging the direct, mass participation of the congregation in the ceremony, and a lived sense of ecstatic participation in the Holy Spirit, situate Prosperity very much within the Pentecostal orbit, as the widespread label of 'neo-Pentecostal' given to the movement reflects.

While disagreement persists concerning the theological genealogy of Prosperity, there is wider consensus concerning the founding moment of the Prosperity Gospel or Word of Faith movement in the United States, in the 'healing revivals' of the immediate post-war period. In 1949, Kenneth Hagin began mission work around the United States, soon joining forces with revivalists Oral Roberts, A.A. Allen and Gordon Lindsay, each of whom were moving towards recognizably Prosperity-style ministries. In the African American community after the war, as Stephanie Mitcham has examined (2007), preachers such as Johnnie Coleman, Sweet Daddy Grace and Reverend 'Ike' Eikerenkoetter began to gain adherents, initiating the still-continuing growth of Prosperity in the black American community (Harrison, 2005, pp. 135–6). Commentators have furthermore noted the paradoxical 'fit' between the Pentecostal emphasis on lived, experiential and ecstatic religiosity and the wider embrace of the 'experiential, affective, emotive, practical, personal, activist, and behavioural in intent and expression' by the 'baby boomer' generation, soon to be embraced by mainstream media and marketing: 'in fact, during the 1960s, Pentecostalism and American culture took steps towards each other. The Pentecostals became more mainstream while American culture became more experiential, subjective, and less cognitive in its outlook' (Kyle, 2006, pp. 148–9). Prosperity's unique combination of this subjective, experiential religiosity, with a theological justification of the pursuit of wealth, placed it uniquely well to compete in the emerging world of consumerist, corporate capitalism (cf. Lyon, 2000).

The 1960s and early 1970s were certainly decisive years for the emerging Prosperity movement in the USA, situating the Gospel as ready to undertake its more recent, international career. In 1963, the Oral Roberts University was founded, its syllabuses built around Prosperity teachings and values; in 1967, Hagin began broadcasting his 'Faith Seminar of the Air' radio programme; and in 1974, RHEMA Bible College was founded, which would teach over 10000 new ministers by the mid-1990s. However, perhaps the defining feature of Prosperity Gospel, and the key to its extraordinary proselytizing dynamism, is the advent of televangelism, which its leading figures have been instrumental in promoting in America, then around the globe. Televisual programming allows the Prosperity Gospel to reach out to huge numbers of people, every day and night, in their own homes. Hollywood-style production values, together with the charismatic personae of Pentecostal preachers, the alluring promises of Prosperity, its powerful, uplifting music, and the ability to selectively present favourable subjective testimony, each contribute to the extraordinary success of this medium of preaching. Prosperity's Trinity Broadcasting Network (or TBN) was founded in 1973 (as Trinity Broadcasting Systems). It began nationwide cable distribution in 1978. It has since provided a forum for nearly all of the leading Prosperity preachers: Joel Osteen, Nasir Siddiki, Steve Munsey, Benny Hinn, Rod Parsley, Creflo Dollar, Joyce Meyer, Eddie L. Long, Jesse Duplantis, Paula White and Kenneth Copeland. The network presently (February 2012) boasts 35 full-power television stations serving larger metropolitan areas in the USA alone. Globally meanwhile, TBN is carried on over 5000 TV stations, 33 international satellites, cable systems all over the globe, and, of course, the internet – another modern medium Prosperity has enthusiastically embraced. Every day, Word of Faith broadcasts screen in Europe, Russia, the Middle East, Africa, Australia, New Zealand, the South Pacific, India, Indonesia, Southeast Asia and South America (Bruce, 1990; Robbins, 2004, p. 137; Harrison, 2005, pp. 14–18; Walton, 2009; Lingenthal, 2012, pp. 51–5).

THE PENTECOSTAL REFORMATION: PROSPERITY GOES GLOBAL

The spread of Prosperity Gospel, particularly after 1980, into Asia, Africa and Latin America is one part of a much larger story, the extraordinarily rapid spread of Pentecostal

Christianity in the global South since 1970. The figures attesting to this spread, a kind of 'second reformation' of Christendom, are arresting. According to David Barrett, whereas in 1970 there were 74 million 'Pentecostal/charismatic' Christians globally, by 1997 this figure had reached nearly 500 million, over a quarter of the world's Christians (in Poloma, 2000, p. 1; cf. Pew Foundation, 2006, p. 1). While sociologist David Martin is more conservative about the figures, he agrees that the growth of Pentecostalism globally represents 'the largest shift in the religious marketplace over the last 40 years' (at Miller, 2007, p. 19). Strikingly, while numbers of Pentecostals in first world countries have largely plateaued, by 2002 it was widely estimated that over two-thirds of all Pentecostals live outside the developed West (Adogame, 2010, p. 498). According to the World Christian Database, whereas in Africa in 1970 less than 5 per cent of the population was Pentecostal, by 2005 Pentecostals represented over 12 per cent of the continent's population, well over 100 million. The growth in Latin America is even more spectacular: from 12.6 million Pentecostal and charismatics in 1970, to an estimated 157 million by 2005 (75 million Pentecostals alone, or 13 per cent of population), prompting some concern amongst Catholics that Latin America is becoming evangelical (Stoll, 1990; Adogame, 2010, p. 503). As of 2006, the Christian Database estimated that Pentecostals constituted 73 per cent of all Latin American Protestants, from less than 50 per cent in 1980.

This extraordinary growth of Pentecostalism outside the developed nations is an extremely diverse, diffuse phenomenon. Numbers of converts and rates of growth vary from country to country, and in each local context, new churches are situated within, and obliged to negotiate, vastly diverging political, economic, cultural, post-colonial and wider religious contexts (cf. Coleman, 2002, pp. 12–13). A ten-country Pew Foundation survey of Pentecostals spanning Africa, Asia and the Americas in 2006 confirmed only some very general characteristics: notably, that (despite expectations) the levels of both income *and* education amongst Pentecostals in the developing nations (in contrast to the USA) was not significantly lower than those in the wider population, that the age and gender profiles of Pentecostals again matched wider national populations, while Pentecostals across all nations unsurprisingly tended to be more conservative on social issues (like alcohol consumption and homosexuality) than their contemporaries (Pew Foundation, 2006).

Statistical data concerning global numbers of Prosperity believers, and the growth of the Word of Faith movement are currently (February 2012) harder to find. Nevertheless, studies on Pentecostalism in both Latin America (particularly Brazil) and Africa (particularly Nigeria) closely associate Prosperity or Word of Faith ministries with a contemporary, 'third wave' of Pentecostal evangelization, beginning around 1980. This, the most quantitatively spectacular wave, supersedes earlier, more 'classical' Pentecostal revivals, characterized as it is by growing access of indigenous populations to electronic and print media, the advent of national and international seminars, outreaches, and aggressive, marketing-backed projects of evangelization (Adeboye, 2003–04; Kalu, 2008, p. 259). A sense of the rising proportion of Prosperity Gospel movements within African Pentecostalism is given by the Pew Foundation's 2006 survey, in which 85 per cent per cent of Kenyan Pentecostals, 90 per cent of South African Pentecostals and 95 per cent of Nigerian Pentecostals agreed that God would 'grant material prosperity to all believers who have enough faith' (Pew Foundation, 2006; Phiri and Maxwell, 2007, p. 1). While numbers in other South American nations are not on the same scale,

Brazil's neo-Pentecostal Universal Church of the Kingdom of God had grown to over 2 million members in 2000, an increase of 1.8 million new members in the 1990s alone, and presently commands a following of over half a million Argentineans (Gooren, 2010, pp. 355–6). In Asia, Pentecostalism has made significant inroads in the Philippines, India and China. The South Korean Yoido Church, which preaches its own distinctive brand of Prosperity Gospel, presently boasts 1 million members, making it the largest single congregation in the world (Lee, 2004).

Over the last decade, a vast but divided literature has appeared concerning the extraordinary growth of Pentecostal and neo-Pentecostal or Prosperity Churches. Broadly, two theoretical tendencies are discernible in this literature.

The first, springing predominantly from Western scholars, depicts the growth of Pentecostalism and Prosperity in the South as the result of an exporting of capitalist, or specifically American, values into the developing nations (e.g., Brouwer, et al., 1996; Kyle, 2006). Prosperity Gospel, in Paul Gifford's paradigmatic work for example, is in effect a new phase of colonialism at the hands of Western evangelical missionaries, facilitated by the rapid spread of TBN and global televangelism. 'In this strain of religion', Gifford has claimed, 'things like "democracy", free enterprise, individual liberty, "a strong dollar", and American military superiority acquire almost divine status' (Gifford, 1987, p. 85). Taken to its extremes, the evangelical advocates of Prosperity are depicted as 'unscrupulous manipulators greedy for wealth and power' (Anderson, 2000, p. 12). This is in short a kind of conspiratorial, neo-Voltairian depiction of one more, this time trans-European, episode of 'priestly corruption', which of course draws support from the scandals surrounding Prosperity Preachers in the USA, Brazil and Africa. But it has failed to convince all commentators.

As critics have noted, this type of account, by itself, says little to how the Prosperity Gospel has managed to successfully convert millions of followers to these foreign values. The response of Gifford and like scholars to this question generally involves a 'deprivation and disorientation' model of explanation (Anderson, 1979; Chesnut, 1997; Corten, 1999). The widespread embrace of Prosperity and Pentecostalism amongst the most insecure and economically impoverished is seen here as a compensatory response to socioeconomic helplessness. To paraphrase Marx's memorable words, Pentecostal Christianity is an opiate for the poor, disinherited and the displaced of the earth, inevitably created by the rapid export of dynamic, multinational capitalist economies into the developing world. Despite some conflicting evidence concerning appeal in some rural communities (Oskarsson, 1999; Adogome, 2010, p. 511), Prosperity and Pentecostalism are aligned in these accounts with the urban centres, the sites of the growing numbers of churches and megachurches, and populations of newly displaced rural migrants, often living in slums or beneath the poverty lines (Martin, 1990, pp. 190–91; Robbins, 2004, p. 123). To people thus cut free from traditional communities, kinship and family structures, Pentecostal churches proffer a kind of substitute social, almost quasi-familial network, which at the same time promises a unity with believers of all races and places globally (Robbins, 2004, pp. 125, 136; Miller, 2007, p. 23; Adogame, 2010, p. 511). This network is built around a high-intensity, time-consuming ritual life, a collective, well-defined or simplistic worldview and moral code, and the promises of millennial redress. In Prosperity's case, as we have seen, these promises are of a miraculous, this-worldly liberation (Robbins, 2004, p. 124).

The problems these accounts of Prosperity's growth face are of at least three kinds. First, the correlation between the most extremely impoverished and all denominations of Prosperity and other Pentecostal churches does not hold without exception. Prosperity in particular attracts converts from across the social classes, including significant numbers of well-educated, middle class Africans and Latin Americans (Anderson, 2000, p. 12; Pew Foundation, 2006; Miller, 2007, p. 21). Second, critics have argued that this type of account is falsely Western-centred, and effectively denies autonomy, creativity and agency to the indigenous cultures and peoples at the heart of today's Pentecostal Christian reformation (e.g., Hackett, 1995; Veer, 1996, p. 7; Coleman, 2002, pp. 11–13; Martin, 2002; Robbins, 2004, p. 126; Adogame, 2010, p. 503). Notably, it has been observed that Pentecostalism within the USA itself, from the Azusa Street revival (the famous 1905–15 revival in Los Angeles) to today, has always been a distinctively African strand of Christianity, mediated through African American culture (MacRobert, 1988). Hollenweger (1994) stresses the 'black roots' of the distinctly ecstatic, experiential mode of Pentecostal worship: with its music, its stress on the orality of worship, the inclusion of dreams and visions in worship, and acceptance of the deep connection of body and spirit. From the side of the developing countries – this being the second, countervailing strand in the literature on Prosperity and Pentecostalism – authors like Ogbu Kalu have stressed that African Pentecostalism and neo-Pentecostalism are in no way simple 'transplants' of a ready-made American product onto a blank, receptive cultural soil (Adogame, 2010, p. 509; Clarke, 2010, p. 114). Rather, new forms of worship emerge from the confrontation between imported, religious ideas and indigenous traditions, negotiated in highly specific cultural and political circumstances. 'African Pentecostalism did not originate from Azusa Street and is not an extension of the American electronic church . . . it is one of the ways that Africans responded to the missionary structures and appropriated the message' (Kalu, 2008, p. viii). Prosperity's vision of a physically healthy and ostentatiously prosperous life, Kalu notes, speaks to traditional African beliefs associating blessing by the gods with 'a life of peace and tranquillity, especially peace with God, the spirits, kinsfolk, neighbours', as in the Akan's notion of *Nkwa* (signifiying a spirit of vibrant life, fertility, prosperity) (Kalu, 2008, pp. 262–3). It also marks a transformation of the traditional idea of the 'big man of the village' into 'the big man of the big God', capable of bestowing such worldly blessings and warding off evil spirits (ibid., pp. 103–22). Commentators also point to the continuity between Pentecostalism's 'enchanted' worldview – one populated by good and evil forces, both accessible to believers – with indigenous traditions in both Africa and Latin America (Miller, 2007, pp. 24–5). As Robbins comments, Pentecostalism:

> preserves these beliefs in the sense of accepting their cognitive claims concerning the existence of spiritual forces, but it does not retain the 'normative presuppositions' about the moral value of the spiritual world that often accompany them . . . By a process of demonization, [Pentecostalism] makes indigenous spirits representatives of the devil . . . then leads people to devote much of their energy to struggling against it, an activity that has the effect of further proving its existence and demonstrating its relevance to post-conversion life. (Robbins, 2004, pp. 128–9)

Sceptical depictions of the spread of neo-Pentecostalism as the importation of a fully formed Western ideology to the global South have a third shortcoming. They also overlook the organizational specificity of these religious forms, which position them from the start as 'religion made to travel' (Dempster et al., 1999; Adogame, 2010, p. 499). Pentecostalism from its beginning has placed a great emphasis on evangelization: the Azusa Street revival itself brought together white and African Americans, Asians and Latinos all charged and inspired to spread the word of the Holy Spirit. Commentators also note in this connection the egalitarianism written deep into Pentecostal beliefs. These appeal explicitly and equally to men and women of all races, and are characterized by a marked anti-elitism and anti-intellectualism (Miller, 2007, pp. 177–8). Anyone inspired by the Spirit is capable of evangelizing, regardless of educational or other qualifications. This is part of the empowerment message these churches bring to their converts (Willems, 1967, p. 136; d'Epinay, 1969, p. 75; Stoll, 1990, p. 13; Anderson, 2000, p. 10).

We have mentioned above the organizational peculiarities of the Pentecostal churches, and their acentric network without a single bureaucratic and institutional centre, instead 'held together by their publications and other media productions, conferences, revival meetings, and constant travel' of leading preachers (Robbins, 2004, p. 125). This almost 'postmodern' organizational form situates Prosperity and kindred Pentecostal movements peculiarly well to negotiate the dynamic world of neoliberal, global capitalism (Coleman, 2002, p. 12; Martin, 2002, pp. 15–17). The combination of a theological egalitarianism, together notably with the foundational, maligned importance placed on tithing, combine to quickly make local churches financially and organizationally autonomous, their organizational roles peopled by local converts, even when they are initially founded by an international pastor on an imported model (Robbins, 2004, p. 131; Adogome, 2010, pp. 511–12).

Finally, it is worth underlining that critics can be too cynical in weighing the existential power, and importance, of the exuberant, spectacular, and miracle-promising mode of worship to Prosperity Gospel in explaining the cause of its growth. As Miller has put it: 'the engine of Pentecostalism is its worship' (2007, p. 23). Set against the backdrop of often extraordinarily difficult life circumstances, as Blumhofer comments, experience of these services, revivals, and other ritualized gatherings readily generates a 'spiritual acquisitiveness' in believers, driving them 'relentlessly on to the next experience' of the presence and power of the Holy Spirit (Blumhofer, 1993, pp. 210–11; Hunt, 1998; Kramer, 2005; Miller, 2007, pp. 169, 176).

PROSPERITY AND ITS DISCONTENTS: EFFECTS AND SIGNIFICANCE

Whilst everyone can agree on the unquestioned significance of the growth of Prosperity and the spread of Pentecostalism globally, people are divided on *what* this significance *amounts to* in debates surrounding development, economics, politics and society. Critical theological and social-scientific perspectives express concern that Prosperity exploits growing numbers amongst the world's most vulnerable populations, taking in tithes from the poorest and offering in exchange only false hope and inflated promises of miracle healings and untold economic abundance. Faced with collective social problems demanding a structural analysis and concerted political action, Prosperity is charged with promoting self-centred individualism, and diverting converts' attention away from the lasting causes of their social deprivation (e.g., Asamoah-Gyadu, 2010). Politically, the close connection between Pentecostalism in the United States and political conservatism is noted. The key role of charismatic pastors and celebrity preacher figures in the Pentecostal churches has been charged with enforcing an authoritarian 'patron/client' style of worship. Pentecostal churches are notable for having in some instances having supported oppressive political regimes, notably including the Pinochet regime in Chile (d'Epinay, 1969; Martin, 1990, 2002; Bastian, 1993). Nevertheless, the emerging scholarly consensus again significantly qualifies any too one-sided, Cassandrist depictions of Prosperity and the globalization of Pentecostal Christianity. Politically, empirical studies do not bear out a necessary connection between Pentecostals in different contexts and far-right conservative parties. Instead, studies have found that church members tend to vote in ways closely paralleling other members of their social classes (Martin, 1990, p. 240; Smilde, 1998; Gill, 2002, p. 214; Robbins, 2004, p. 135; Pew Foundation, 2006). Pentecostal religion's deep-set egalitarianism and organizational flexibilities, some commentators argue, suggest a deeper affinity between Pentecostalism and democratization, with church communities constituting a kind of 'free space' or 'protective social capsule' in which believers can gain experience in egalitarian social relations, public speaking, organization and self-help (Martin, 1990, pp. 108, 234, 284; Burdick, 1993, p. 226; Marshall, 1993, pp. 224–5; Dodson, 1997, p. 34; Robbins, 2004, p. 134). One necessary condition for the remarkably rapid spread of neo-Pentecostalism in both Latin America and Africa since the mid-1970s has, of course, been the near-contemporaneous democratization in nations across those continents (Pew Foundation, 2006).

Defenders of Prosperity Gospel point first of all to the effects of empowerment and hope that its ministry produces in believers. Where critics see a teaching of untold Prosperity in a world where a billion people live on less than US$1 a day as quixotic or callous (e.g., Alexander, 2009, p. 69), Prosperity teaching sees its message as one of deep compassion, speaking to the pressing desire of these people to transform their condition. As Carol Alberto of Brazilian Universal Church of the Kingdom of God explains: 'when you have someone in your audience with four hungry children, it's hard to tell them to wait for their reward in the next life' (at Alexander, 2009, pp. 70–71). In an article advocating Word of Faith, Vinson Synan asks readers to imagine three sermons delivered on the 'smoky mountain' of some outer-city slum in the third world, and to consider which will most likely inspire an audience: one preaching soulful resignation to the unchanging oppressive realities of poverty; the second, a 'social gospel' sermon preaching the need for government-led economic changes; and a third, Prosperity sermon preaching:

> If you will believe the gospel, the Lord will immediately break the power of sin in your life and you can be filled and empowered by the Holy Spirit to speak in tongues, cast out devils and evangelize the world. You can be instantly set free from your addictions to alcohol, tobacco, sexual promiscuity and drugs, and Jesus will make you into a healthy, honest member of society. God is not against you. There is no virtue in being poor just for the sake of being poor. So God will also bless you materially as you work hard, live honestly, save your money and give a portion of your own income to others. (Synan, 2008–12; Alexander, 2009, p. 73)

Commentators observe that Prosperity's teachings help promote self-worth in converts (often an extremely scarce resource amongst the structurally disadvantaged), just as the sermons, group classes and publications on entrepreneurship engender new skills of economic management in believers (Miller, 2007, pp. 174–7). The work of evangelization, in which converts are encouraged to participate, itself resembles a type of religious entrepreneurship, gathering and persuading new clients into the church network. While critics hence document many cases of disappointed hopes and economic exploitation, studies also attest to large numbers of Prosperity converts whose lives have been turned around decisively by their joining the movement (Robbins, 2004, p. 136; Miller, 2007, p. 176). Prosperity's emphasis on entrepreneurship and learning the secrets of financial management, and the general Pentecostal promotion of social virtues, can make many subjects more reliable employees, able to be integrated into the 'flexible' post-Fordist workplaces of the new global economy (Robbins, 2004, p. 136). The very emphasis Prosperity places on physical and economic flourishing, while it downplays the realities of structural oppression (Martin, 1990, p. 266; Robbins, 2002) differentiates the movement from older, more other-worldly forms of Pentecostalism and Christianity. Miller notes that, even when the high hopes the Prosperity Gospel inspires in many are dashed, the very raising of subjects' this-worldly hopes can have a beneficial effect, animating in them a sense that this economic and political world can be changed for the better (Miller, 2007, pp. 1–32).

A similarly ambiguous harvest concerning Pentecostalism and gender awaits the reader in the literature. On the one hand Pentecostalism is strongly anti-homosexual and traditionally Western in its attitude to gender relations (Pew Foundation, 2006). On the other hand, commentators have noted the importance women have in the movement as bearers of spiritual authority, and differently, of the beneficial effect for women of the Pentecostal promotion of social and economic virtues in combating indigenous machismo culture, notably in Latin American countries (Robbins, 2004, pp. 132–3; Chesnut, 2003; Gooren, 2010, pp. 364, 372). For all its characteristic emphasis on individualist self-empowerment, finally, Prosperity Churches in the USA and the Southern nations have a record of contributing to programmes of social education and assistance, often in conditions characterized by a wider 'institutional deficit' wherein the state and other institutions in civil society are inoperative, or unable to provide these services (Miller, 2007, p. 169).

CONCLUSION

While theological and secular critics of Prosperity are hence surely justified in raising deep concerns about this remarkable historical movement's teachings and practices, its growing presence and contribution to the developing world cannot be ignored. In a study of the Latin American countries, Gooren has argued that rather than simply questioning the effects of Pentecostalism on pre-existing sociopolitical contexts and institutions, we need to begin to speak of a 'Pentecostalization' of these societies: one measured in terms of a growing presence of conversion stories in the mass media, the evidenced need of politicians to actively court the Pentecostal vote; changing attitudes towards gender roles, including a growing challenge to machismo; and growing valorization of economic entrepreneurialism consistent with Prosperity teachings (Gooren, 2010). In the same vein, the last decade has seen the emerging phenomenon of 'reverse mission' (Adogome, 2003–04; 2010, p. 507), with African Prosperity Churches and the Latin American

Universal Church of the Kingdom of God themselves 'going global', opening churches and evangelizing in developed wealthy nations (Burgess, 2011). Whether secular and mainline Christians in the developed world like it or not, the dynamic, ambiguous and prodigal reality of Prosperity Gospel is one that will only become more present in the twenty-first century, demanding understanding and enlightened response.

REFERENCES

Adeboye, Olufunke (2003–04), 'Pentecostal challenges in Africa and Latin America: a comparative focus on Nigeria and Brazil', *Afrika Zamani*, Nos. 11 & 12, 136–59.

Adogome, Afe (2003), 'Betwixt identity and security: African new religious movements and the politics of religious networking in Europe', *Nova Religio: The Journal of Alternative and Emergent Religions*, **7**(2), 24–41.

Adogame, Afe (2010), 'Pentecostal and charismatic movements in a global perspective', in Bryan S. Turner (ed.), *The New Blackwell Companion to the Sociology of Religion*, Hoboken, NJ: Wiley-Blackwell.

Alexander, Paul (2009), *Signs and Wonders: Why Pentecostalism is the World's Fastest Growing Faith*, Hoboken, NJ: Jossey-Bass.

Anderson, Robert M. (1979), *Vision of the Disinherited: the making of American Pentecostalism*, Peabody, MA: Hendrickson.

Anderson, Allan (2000), 'Evangelism and the growth of Pentecostalism in Africa', available at: http://artsweb.bham.ac.uk/aanderson/Publications/evangelism_and_the_growth_of_pen.htm; accessed February 2012.

Asamoah-Gyadu, Kwabena (2010), 'From 'Calvary Road' to Harvesters International': an African perspective on the cross and gospel of Prosperity', advance paper for 2010 Lausanne Global Conversation Cape Town Conference, available at: http://conversation.lausanne.org/en/resources/detail/10573; accessed February 2012.

Bastian, J-P. (1993), 'The metamorphosis of Latin American Protestant groups: a sociohistorical perspective', *Latin American Res. Rev.*, **28**(2), 33–61.

Blake, John (25 December 2009), 'Passions over "Prosperity Gospel": was Jesus wealthy?', *CNN*, available at: http://articles.cnn.com/2009-12-25/living/RichJesus_1_jesus-prosperity-gospel-teachings?_s=PM:LIVING; accessed February 2012.

Blumhofer, E.L. (1993), *Aimee Semple McPherson: Everybody's Sister*, Grand Rapids, MI: Eerdmans.

Bowman, Robert M. Jr (2001), *The Word-Faith Controversy: Understanding the Health and Wealth Gospel*, Grand Rapids, MI: Baker Books.

Brouwer, Steve, Paul Gifford and Susan D. Rose (1996), *Exporting the American Gospel: Global Christian Fundamentalism*, London: Routledge.

Bruce, Steve (1990), *Pray TV: Evangelism in America*, London & New York: Routledge.

Bruggerman, Walter (2007), *Mandate to Difference: An Invitation to the Contemporary Church*, Louisville, KY: Westminster John Knox Press.

Burdick, J. (1993), *Looking for God in Brazil: The Progressive Catholic Church in Urban Brazil's Religious Arena*, Berkeley: University of California Press.

Burgess, Richard (2011), 'Bringing back the Gospel: reverse mission among Nigerian Pentecostals in Britain', *Journal of Religion in Europe*, **4**(3), 493–522.

Chesnut, A. (1997), *Born Again in Brazil: The Pentecostal Boom and the Pathogens of Poverty*, New Brunswick, NJ: Rutgers University Press.

Chesnut, A. (2003), *Competitive Spirits: Latin America's New Religious Economy*, Oxford: Oxford University Press.

Clarke, Clifton R. (2010), 'Ogbu Kalu and Africa's Christianity: a tribute', *Pneuma*, **32**(1), 107–20.

Coleman, S. (2000), *The Globalisation of Charismatic Christianity: Spreading the Gospel of Prosperity*, Cambridge: Cambridge University Press.

Coleman, S. (2002) 'The faith movement: a global religious culture?', *Culture and Religion: An Interdisciplinary Journal*, **3**(1), 3–19.

Corten, A. (1999), *Pentecostalism in Brazil: Emotion of the Poor and Theological Romanticism*, New York: St Martin's.

Cox, Harvey (1996), *Fire From Heaven: The Rise of Pentecostal Spirituality and the Reshaping of Religion in the Twenty-first Century*, London: Cassell.

Dempster, M., B. Klaus and D. Petersen (eds) (1999), *The Globalization of Pentecostalism: A Religion Made to Travel*, Oxford and Irvine: Regnum.

D'Epinay, C.L. (1969), *Haven of the Masses: A Study of the Pentecostal Movement in Chile*, London: Lutterworth.

Dodson, Michael (1997), 'Pentecostals, politics and public space in Latin America', in Edward L. Cleary and Hanna W. Stewart-Gambino (eds), *Power, Politics and Pentecostals in Latin America*, Boulder, CO: Westview Press, pp. 25–40.
Dollar, Creflo (2002), *Made After His Kind* (DVD), 15 September 2002.
Garrard-Burnett, Virginia (2007), 'Stop suffering? The Iglesia Universal del Reino de Deos in the United States', in Timothy J. Steigenga and Edward L. Cleary Tugers (eds), *Conversion of a Continent: Contemporary Religious Change in South America*, New Brunswick, NJ: Rutgers University Press.
Gifford, P. (1987), '"Africa shall be saved": an appraisal of Reinhard Bonnke's pan-African crusade', *Journal of Religion in Africa*, **17**(1), 63–92.
Gill, A. (2002), 'Religion and democracy in South America: challenges and opportunities', in T.G. Jelen and C. Wilcox (eds), *Religion and Politics in Comparative Perspective: The One, the Few, the Many*, New York: Cambridge University Press, pp. 195–211.
Gooren, Henri (2010), 'The Pentecostalization of religion and society in Latin America', *Exchange*, **39**(3010), 355–76.
Gramby-Sobukwe, Sharon and Tim Hoiland (2009), 'The rise of megachurch efforts in international development: a brief analysis and areas for further research', *Transformation: An International Journal of Holistic Mission Studies*, **26**(2), 104–17.
Hackett, R. (1995), 'The gospel of prosperity in Africa', in R. Roberts (ed.), *Religion and the Transformation of Capitalism*, London: Routledge.
Hagin, Kenneth (2006), *Mountain-moving Faith*, Tulsa, OK: Faith Library Publications.
Hagin, Kenneth (2007), *Biblical Keys to Financial Prosperity*, Tulsa, OK: Faith Library Publications.
Hanegraaf, Hank (1993), *Christianity in Crisis*, Eugene, OR: Harvest House.
Hanegraaf, Hank (2009), *Christianity in Crisis: The 21st Century*, Nashville: Thomas Nelson, Inc.
Harrison, Milton F. (2005), *Righteous Riches: The Word of Faith Movement in Contemporary African American Religion*, Cary, NC: Oxford University Press.
Hartford Seminary, Hartford Institute for Religion Research (2000–06), 'Database of megachurches in the US' available at: http://hirr.hartsem.edu/megachurch/database.html; accessed February 2012.
Hladky, Kathleen (January 2012), 'I double-dog dare you in God's name! Claiming Christian wealth and the American Prosperity Gospel', *Religion Compass*, **6**(1), 82–96, available at: http://onlinelibrary.wiley.com/doi/10.1111/j.1749-8171.2011.00325.x/full; accessed February 2012.
Hollenweger, W. (1994), 'After twenty years' research on Pentecostalism', *Theology*, No. 87: 403–12.
Hunt, Stephen (1998), 'Magical moments: an intellectualist approach to the neo-Pentecostal faith ministries', *Religion*, **28**(3), 271–80.
Jenkins, Philip (2006), *The New Faces of Christianity: Believing the Bible in the Global South*, Oxford/New York: Oxford University Press.
Kalu, Ogbu (2008), *African Pentecostalism: An Introduction*, Oxford/New York: Oxford University Press.
Kramer, Eric W. (2005), 'Spectacle and the staging of power in Brazilian neo-Pentecostalism', in *Latin American Perspectives*, **32**(1), 95–120.
Kyle, Richard G. (2006), *Evangelicism: An Americanized Christianity*, New Brunswick, NJ: Transaction Publishers.
Lee, Young-Hoon (2004), 'The life and ministry of David Yonggi Cho and the Yoido Full Church Gospel', *AJPS*, **7**(1), 3–20, available at: http://www.apts.edu/aeimages/File/AJPS_PDF/04-1-YHLee.pdf; accessed February 2012.
Lingenthal, Lukas (2012), 'Pentecostalism in Brazil: churches, businesses, and political parties', *Kas International Reports*, 19 January 2010, available at: http://www.kas.de/wf/en/33.29975/; accessed July 2012.
Lofton, Kathryn (2011), *Oprah: The Gospel of an Icon*, Berkeley: University of California Press.
Lyon, D. (2000), *Jesus in Disneyland: Religion in Postmodern Times*, Cambridge: Polity.
MacRobert, I. (1998), *The Black Roots and White Racism of Early Pentecostalism in the USA*, London: Macmillan.
Marshall, Ruth (1993), '"Power in the name of Jesus": social transformation and Pentecostalism in Western Nigeria "Revisited"', in T. Ranger and Olufemi Vaughan (eds), *Legitimacy and the State in Twentieth Century Africa: Essays in Honor of A.H.M Kirk-Green*, London: Macmillan, pp. 213–46.
Martin, D. (1990), *Tongues of Fire*, Oxford: Blackwell.
Martin, D. (2002), *Pentecostalism: The World Their Parish*, Oxford and Malden, MA: Blackwell.
McConnell, Daniel (1988), *A Different Gospel: Biblical and Historical Insights into the Word of Faith Movement*, Peabody, MA: Hendrickson Publishers.
Miller, Donald E. (2007), *Global Pentecostalism: The New Face of Christian Social Engagement*, Berkeley: University of California Press.
Mitchem, Stephanie (2007), *Name It and Claim It?: Prosperity Preaching in the Black Church*, Cleveland: Pilgrim Press.
Oskarsson, G.N. (1999), 'African Pentecostalism', *Swedish Missiological Themes*, **87**(3), 405–18.

Perriman, Andrew (2003), *Faith, Health, and Prosperity*, Waynesboro, GA: Paternoster Press.

Peters, Justin (2006), *A Call for Discernment* (an online seminar series) available at: http://www justinpeters.org/index.php?option=com_content&view=article&id=5&Itemid=5; accessed February 2012.

Pew Foundation (2006), *Spirit and Power: A 10-Country Survey of Pentecostals*, POLL, 5 October 2006, available at: http://www.pewforum.org/Christian/Evangelical-Protestant-Churches/Spirit-and-Power.aspx; accessed February 2012.

Phiri, Isaac and Joe Maxwell (2007), 'Gospel riches', *Christianity Today*, available at: http://www christianity-today.com/ct/2007/july/12.22.html; accessed February 2012.

Poloma, Margaret (2000), 'The spirit bade me go: Pentecostalism and global religion', paper prepared for presentation at the Association for the Sociology of Religion Annual Meetings, 11–13 August 2000, Washington, DC, available at: http://hirr.hartsem.edu/research/pentecostalism_polomaart1.html; accessed February 2012.

Robbins, Joel (2002), 'My wife can't break off part of her belief and give it to me: apocalyptic interrogations of Christian individualism among the Urapmin of Papua New Guinea', *Paideuma*, **48**, 189–206.

Robbins, Joel (2004), 'The globalization of Pentecostal and charismatic Christianity', *Annual Review of Anthropology*, **33**, 117–43.

Smilde, D.A. (1998), '"Letting God govern": supernatural agency in the Venezuelan Pentecostal approach to social change', *Soc. Relig.*, **59**(3), 287–303.

Stoll, David (1990), *Is Latin America Turning Protestant? The Politics of Evangelical Growth*, Berkeley: University of California Press.

Synan, Vincent (2008–12), 'Word of Faith Movement has deep roots in American History', available at: http://www.believersstandunited.com/word_of_faith_movement.html; accessed February 2012.

Towns, Joe (2008), 'The origin of Prosperity Gospel: Part II: perfectionism', *Talking Pentecostalism*, available at: http://talkingpentecostalism.blogspot.com.au/2008/04/origin-of-prosperity-doctrine-in.html; accessed February 2012.

van der Veer, Peter (1996), 'Introduction', in P. van der Veer (ed.), *Conversion to Modernities. The Globalization of Christianity*, New York: Routledge.

Walton, J.L. (2009), *Watch This! The Ethics and Aesthetics of Black Televangelism*, New York: NYU Press.

Willems, E. (1967), *Followers of the New Faith: Culture Change and the Rise of Protestantism in Brazil and Chile*, Nashville, TN: Vandebilt University Press.

PART II

DEVELOPMENT ISSUES/ THEMES AND RELIGION

12 Gender, religion and development

Emma Tomalin

INTRODUCTION

Gender analysis of religions as well as of the development process has radically transformed our understanding of both. Feminist studies of religion have existed since the 1970s (Daly, 1973; Mernissi, 1975; Reuther, 1983; Ahmed, 1992; Singh, 1993). Literature has emerged from within feminist theology, religious studies and, increasingly, in feminist work within the social sciences that draws attention to the negative impacts of religions that often support patriarchal values that have the potential to oppress women and limit their life chances, as well as to the potential of religion to empower women (Aquino, 1993; Peña, 1995, 2007; Sleboda, 2001; Dube and Kanyoro, 2004; Foley, 2004; Bradley, 2006; Phiri and Nadar, 2006). From the early 1970s we also find the beginnings of a critique of the development process from a feminist perspective, with the publication of Ester Boserup's book *Women's Role in Economic Development* (1970). In this text she emphasized the centrality of women to the development process, yet their subordinate position in most societies meant that unless this was addressed, poverty was unlikely to be overcome. While neither of these traditions of feminist critique would consider their work done and remain as important today as 40 years ago, both have developed with vigour and influence, representing a crucial voice against the male bias inherent both within religions and the development process.

Nonetheless, due to the secularist and materialist leanings of both development studies and the style of feminist thinking that has shaped 'gender and development' (GAD) approaches, it is only recently that these feminist critiques have begun to intersect in a direct way, despite shared concerns about female marginalization and discrimination. 'Gender and development' has, on the whole, not taken that seriously the impact of religious values, beliefs and organizations upon gender relations, despite the clear link between religious values and women's status (Seguino, 2011). Religion is often cited as an impediment to women's access to employment, health care or education, but the dynamics of this interaction less often become the research focus. In the mainstream literature there has been a failure to engage with the ways in which some feminists across the globe seek to transform gender relations through engaging with feminist interpretations of their traditions, as well as a lack of interest in the ways in which religion can inform alternative, sometimes more culturally appropriate, understandings of development. Over the past decade, this neglectful attitude towards religion in development has begun to recede. The 'resurgence of religion' globally (which has become particularly visible since 9/11), and the accompanying importance of religion as a marker of identity, underscores the need for development to consider religion as a relevant factor (Thomas, 2005). Religious issues are receiving more consideration in development as a result of the direct engagement of donors with faith-based organizations (FBOs) and religious leaders. Moreover, a wider range of GAD-related programmes now directly engage with religion through forming partnerships with organizations that pursue women's rights within a religious framework (Bradley, 2006, 2010; Tadros, 2010, 2011).

My aim in this chapter is to explore the recent intersection between feminist critiques of religion and of development, and the implications for women. While religions can be considered to play a role in shaping social attitudes about gender that contribute towards women's subordination, it is also the case that religions are diverse and often internally contested. We find a range of expressions of 'religious feminisms' across the globe that argue for gender-equal interpretations of religious traditions as a means of countering conservative religiosity that tends to consider women as secondary to men. This can be expedient in highly religious contexts, but also of crucial importance to women who value their religious identity and for whom it is personally desirable to find ways of strengthening this identity while at the same time challenging their religions when they deny their rights. However, engagement with religions must be undertaken with sensitivity to the context, considering the great potential for religion to discriminate against women. There is some concern that donors are now in rather a hurry to partner with religious leaders and FBOs without adequate consideration of the gender consequences (Tadros, 2010; Tomalin, 2011). As Pearson and Tomalin have noted 'there is an anxiety that in the rush to engage with a hitherto neglected group of stakeholders, the painful journey over the last 35 years to mainstream development gender equity objectives into overall development strategy is being sidelined' (2008, p. 47).

'GENDER AND DEVELOPMENT' (GAD) AND RELIGION

From the 1970s onwards, 'women in development' (WID) approaches aimed to bring women into the development process through focusing on increased economic and educational opportunities. However, there was little attention to the cultural or religious impediments to achieving this. Moreover, it was assumed that if women were given similar opportunities to men then their situation would improve. WID was criticized for failing to account for the underlying structural reasons for gender inequality and critics argued that it relied upon the assumption that increasing women's opportunities (e.g., educational or employment) would be sufficient to end gender discrimination (Rathgeber, 1990; Moser, 1993; Hedman et al., 1996; Jackson and Pearson, 1998; Pearson, 2000). Neither, they argued, did it challenge the Western and gender bias inherent within the development project itself.

By the 1980s, we find a shift in focus to thinking about 'gender and development' (GAD). As Moser writes:

> The WID approach . . . is based upon the underlying rationale that development processes would proceed much better if women were fully incorporated into them (instead of being left to use their time 'unproductively'). It focuses mainly on women in isolation promoting measures such as access to credit and employment as the means by which women can be better integrated into the development process. In contrast, the GAD approach maintains that to focus on women in isolation is to ignore the real problem, which remains their subordinate status to men. In insisting that women cannot be viewed in isolation, it emphasized a focus on gender relations when designing measures to 'help' women in the development process. (Moser, 1993, p. 3)

Moser (1993), drawing upon the earlier work of Molyneux (1985), makes a distinction between women's 'practical' and 'strategic' gender needs. She argues that while development ought to cater for practical needs, such as access to employment, education or health care, this alone will not necessarily enable women to enhance their strategic position within the gender hierarchy. Thus:

> strategic gender needs are the needs women identify because of their subordinate position to men in their society . . . They relate to gender divisions of labour, power and control and may include such issues as legal rights, domestic violence, equal wages and women's control over their bodies. (Ibid., p. 39)

By contrast:

> practical gender needs do not challenge the gender divisions of labour or women's subordinate position in society. Practical gender needs are a response to immediate perceived necessity . . . and are often concerned with inadequacies in living conditions such as water provision, health care and employment. (Ibid., p. 40)

Despite these shifts to considering women's subordination as related to unequal gender relations (which cannot simply be addressed by attempting to give women similar opportunities to men) the extent to which religion contributes towards maintaining gender difference has received little attention. This has led some to criticize GAD approaches for being informed by Western materialist and secular feminist models that fail to account for the different ways that religion shapes women's oppression as well as the strategies they employ to deal with it (Ahmed, 1999). Moreover, involvement in religious traditions is an important aspect of many people's lives and contributes to their well-being, despite its potential to discriminate against women. The fact that the Western development project has tended to measure progress and well-being in terms of material factors has been critiqued for overlooking the 'spiritual' dimensions of human life (Tyndale, 2006; Deneulin and Banu, 2009). The assumption underpinning the materialist view of human existence, that religion is primitive and will disappear as societies modernize and become more like the West, reflects neither the evidence presented by the contemporary resurgence of religion nor the experience and attitudes of many people in developing contexts.

While it is important neither to reduce the subordination of women to religious or cultural causes, nor to essentialize poor women as particularly religious/spiritual, religio-cultural factors are relevant to many of the concerns that 'gender and development' typically addresses. A critique of the absence of religion as an important aspect of thinking about the roots of gender inequality was part of a wider critique that began to emerge from the margins of development studies in the 1990s (Eade, 2002; Selinger, 2004; Tyndale, 2006). Predating this, in 1980, the journal *World Development* published a special issue on the topic of religion, arguing that development was unlikely to be successful unless it worked with the 'moral base' of a society (Wilber and Jameson, 1980). Nonetheless, this special issue 'fell largely on deaf ears' (Deneulin and Rakodi, 2011, p. 45) and it is only now, 30 years later, that considerations of religion are beginning to be included within development research, policy and practice. At the grassroots many women's organizations have been grappling with the implications of religion for far longer, and have incorporated considerations of religion into their work, either in terms of strategies to resist the implications of conservative religiosity or working with religious leaders and organizations to improve women's lives.[1] However, such strategies have only recently become part of the mainstream development agenda.

In this chapter I suggest that a consideration of the role that religion plays in women's lives in developing contexts can be important in understanding ways of approaching their 'strategic gender needs' (Moser, 1993) but that this view of empowerment has 'not grown out of some theoretical debate, but primarily out of the experiences of women working at the grassroots level in many parts of the world' (Rowlands, 1998, p. 17). There has been criticism that the notion of 'empowerment' has become a 'buzzword' (ibid., p. 11) or a 'motherhood' term (Parpart, 2002, p. 41) and that 'the appropriate meaning will be understood without being explained' (Rowlands, 1998, p. 11). Others have been critical that the force behind the term has been undermined through its use by a range of actors, from the World Bank to grassroots women's organizations in developing countries, and often for different purposes. While it is important not to ignore the ways in which the idea of empowerment may have become rhetorical and weakened in some settings, Rowlands' definition of empowerment as 'women increasing their ability to act, to perceive themselves as capable, to hold opinions, to use time effectively, to control resources, to interact with others, to initiate activities, to respond to events' (1998, p. 23) arguably captures the goal of much feminist activism across the globe. The ways in which religion can stand in the way of this as well as offer resources to support it – concerns that have shaped feminist studies of religion over the past 40 years – is also now increasingly becoming of interest to work within 'gender and development'.

RELIGION AND GENDER INEQUALITY: NEGATIVE AND POSITIVE OUTCOMES

A recent study by Seguino analyses cross-country data on gender attitudes from the World Values Survey and relates these to levels of religiosity (2011). Her analysis demonstrates that religiosity 'is positively associated with gender inequitable attitudes' (p. 1309) and 'that the effect of religiosity extends beyond attitudes to negatively impact several measures of gendered well-being outcomes' (p. 1319). While it is impossible for a large-scale survey to adequately capture the diversity within religions as well as between religions, this study does demonstrate that 'no major religious denomination stands out as being significantly more strongly associated with gender inequitable attitudes than the others' (p. 1313). These patterns were also observed even once GDP and level of development were controlled for. Seguino concludes that these results debunk assumptions that Islam is particularly problematic for gender equality, although the bulk of studies on this topic would seem to suggest that this is the case (therefore suggesting that other factors are at play in this focus on Islam). She also, however, suggests that we should scrutinize the 'impact on gender equality of aid funneled through religious organizations. Donors may find that religious non-governmental organizations have a weaker record in improving women's relative well-being than non-religious organizations' (p. 1317).

While the statistics might suggest that at a macro-level the negative impact of religiosity on gender-unequal attitudes, as well as outcomes, means that we should avoid engagement with religions in pursuit of women's empowerment, Seguino also notes that at a micro-level, 'religious institutions themselves are susceptible to change, albeit slow, and internal groups show evidence of advocating for progressive change' (ibid.). There are increasing numbers of women (and men) across the globe who are deeply critical of the gender-inequitable attitudes promoted by their religious traditions and the real impact that these have both in society and within their religious traditions. Thus, the importance of transforming religion from within is seen as both necessary for religious reasons but also because it can have a broader impact on gender attitudes that limit women's life chances, particularly in deeply religious contexts. Moreover, in strongly religious contexts, particularly where the state and/or political parties are influenced by conservative religious attitudes and is wary of secular feminism as a Western imposition, it can be expedient to approach gender issues within a religious framework.

Earlier predictions about secularization and the eventual disappearance of religion as societies modernized are now widely discredited for being overly simplistic. Thus, any assumptions that the negative influence of religion on gender inequality would cease to be a problem, with increased economic and educational opportunities for both women and men (and therefore there was little point in engaging with religion in the short term), are now being revised. Explanations of the reasons for the contemporary global 'religious resurgence' are complex and debates are ongoing, but what they do indicate is that there is no straightforward relationship between economic development and a lessening of religiosity. This suggests the importance of building considerations of religion into the development process, not least with respect to considerations of the causes of and strategies to ameliorate gender inequality.

In the remainder of this chapter I explore in more detail three areas raised by Seguino's quantitative study (2011): the evidence that religions are problematic for gender-equal attitudes and outcomes; the need to be cautious about the current wisdom to channel funds through FBOs or other religious organizations; and the extent to which 'religious feminisms' could/should be considered within development, including 'gender and development'.

THE NEGATIVE IMPACT OF RELIGION ON WOMEN'S HUMAN RIGHTS: CHALLENGES FOR 'GENDER AND DEVELOPMENT'

The extent to which religious traditions teach that men and women are different and therefore afford them different human rights has been widely explored in the literature, particularly with respect to Islam (e.g., Afary, 1997; Moaddel, 1998, 2002; Gerami and Lehnerer, 2001; Lachenmann, 2004 [Senegal]; Rawi, 2004 and Helie, 2004 [Afghanistan]; Jamal, 2005 [Pakistan]; Soares, 2006 [Mali]). Differences between men and women, often reduced to women's biological capacity to bear children, also result in understandings of different roles and responsibilities between the sexes. Such biological determinism has been strongly rejected by feminists since the 1960s, yet is a feature of many versions of religious traditions, which consider that such differences are immutable and divinely sanctioned. The fact that the renewed public visibility of religion across the globe tends to be associated with styles of religiosity that emphasize such conservative values is of concern to women's rights activists. In the following discussion I will examine two areas that have been raised as areas of concern by feminist critics of religion and of development: reproductive rights and religious fundamentalism. In each case we can see the crucial role of effective secular legislation to protect women, but also the importance of better understanding the ways that religious values contribute to women's subordination and the extent to which the feminist transformation of religion could play a role in securing women greater access to rights.

Reproductive Rights

One of the most worrying issues facing women's rights activists is the opposition of such conservative religious actors to reproductive rights. As Razavi writes, this:

> has been evident in the alliance forged between some Islamist states and the Vatican (in the context of the United Nations conferences of the 1990s) in opposition to the demands of global women's movements for gender equality, and most explicitly in reproductive and sexual rights. (2009, p. v)

Since the 1994 United Nations 'Population and Development Conference' in Cairo, the idea of reproductive rights has increasingly dominated discussions about issues around family planning (Grimes, 1998; Smyth, 1998). There was a shift to 'a new and broader reproductive rights approach that is fundamentally different from the prevailing family planning and demographic approach to population' (Bandarage, 1998, p. 7). However, Bayes and Tohidi (2001) observe the emergence of a strategic Muslim–Catholic alliance, which was particularly visible at the 1995 Beijing women's conference and continues to be suspicious of current approaches to reproductive rights. An analysis of religious speeches that were made during the 1995 Beijing conference was undertaken by Couture (2003) and she expresses concern with the way that a number argued that women's reproductive choices should be defined by religious values. This points to a tension within the international women's movement, represented at the Beijing conference by both secular and religious actors, between universal rights and cultural/religious particularisms (Vuola, 2002).

Powerful North American voices have also been instrumental within this conservative religious backlash against reproductive rights through the 'Mexico City Policy' (more recently reincarnated as the so-called 'global gag rule'). The evangelical 'religious right' in North America was influential in former President George Bush's reinstatement of the 'Mexico City Policy' on his first day in office in January 2001 (Crane and Dusenberry, 2004). First introduced by the Reagan Administration in 1984, it was overturned by the Clinton Administration in 1993 and again repealed by President Obama in 2009. It not only prohibited any organization in receipt of US funds – both domestically and internationally – from providing abortions (except in the cases of pregnancy from rape, incest or when a woman's life is in danger), but also extended to advice and information about abortion services, and any lobbying activity for the legalization of abortion. This policy has had a detrimental affect on the provision of reproductive and health services for women that goes far beyond the apparent curtailment of abortion-related services (Cohen, 2001; Rose, 2005, p. 1211; Center for Reproductive Rights, no date).

Women's rights activists have expressed concern about the ways in which 'conservative' religious traditions influence women's access to reproductive services, such as contraception and abortion (Obermeyer, 1994; Amin and Hossain, 1995; Bowen, 1997; El Dawla, 2000; Hasna, 2003; Kazimov, 2003; Borland, 2004). This can be in terms of the ways in which religion influences the availability of reproductive services through its impact upon broader social values and legal frameworks, as well as the impact that religious values have upon the reproductive 'choices' that women make. Kane (2008), for instance, explores the influence of the Catholic Church on recent changes in abortion policy in Nicaragua, Colombia and Mexico City (see also Sánchez Fuentes et al., 2008). In all three contexts, women's activism for abortion rights intensified in the wake of the United Nations women's conferences of the 1990s. However, this activism took place against the backdrop of opposition from the Catholic Church, with support from growing numbers of evangelical Protestants. In Nicaragua, an alliance between Catholics and evangelical Protestants was influential in achieving an outright ban on abortion in 2006, resulting from a change of heart by the former Sandinista president, Daniel Ortega. During his reign in the 1980s he had supported abortion, but during his 2006 election campaign he opposed abortion in order to gain Catholic votes.

By contrast, the barriers that the Catholic Church erected for legal abortions in Columbia and Mexico City via shifting 'the discourse from health, gender, and rights to religious considerations' (Kane, 2008, p. 366) were more successfully dismantled. In Columbia there was modest success, resulting in legislation in 2006 to permit 'therapeutic abortions'. In Mexico City in 2007 all abortions in the first trimester became legal. Thus, in some contexts, religious opposition can be effectively met by the use of international (secular) law to support arguments about reproductive health and rights. However, the need to be vigilant and to protect even limited access to abortion is underscored by the case of Nicaragua. Political considerations may often trump support for women's rights in contexts where the church is powerful.

In terms of reproductive choice, the issues of 'son preference' and the 'reversed sex ratio' in India and China have received attention. In both countries we find 'reversed sex ratios', where the sex ratio is 'masculine' (there are more men than women), whereas in most other parts of the globe it is 'feminine'. As Amartya Sen argued in his famous article, 'More than 100 million women are missing' (1990):

> It is often said that women make up a majority of the world's population. They do not. This mistaken belief is based on generalizing from the contemporary situation in Europe and North America, where the ratio of women to men is typically around 1.05 or 1.06, or higher. In South Asia, West Asia, and China, the ratio of women to men can be as low as 0.94, or even lower, and it varies widely elsewhere in Asia, in Africa, and in Latin America. How can we understand and explain these differences, and react to them? (Sen, 1990, p. 61)

While these differences can be at least partially explained in terms of the level of care that women receive within the particular societies (i.e., in terms of diet and access to health services), Sen also wrote in 2003 that:

> Another more important and radical change has occurred over the past decade There have been two opposite movements: female disadvantage in mortality has typically been reduced substantially, but this has been counterbalanced by a new female disadvantage – that in natality – through sex specific abortions aimed against the female fetus. (p. 1297; see also Klasen, 1994; Klasen and Wink, 2003)

Female infanticide and now increasingly the sex-selective abortion of female foetuses, particularly in India and China, has been given an economic explanation. In China the one child policy, since 1979, has given rise to a marked preference for boys, in a culture where males are more economically productive and are expected to care for parents in their old age. In India, the reversed sex ratio is considered to be linked to the practice of female infanticide and sex-selective abortion of female foetuses due to the spread and intensification of dowry, where money and/or gifts are given by the bride's family to the groom's family at marriage similarly supports a preference for male children (Basu, 1999; Banerjee, 2002). What was once a practice largely confined to upper caste Hindus in the north of India, spread to other castes, religions and regions of South Asia (see Rozario, 2009). The reasons for this are complex and are, at least partially, dependent upon a combination of 'Sanskritization' (upper caste emulation), neo-liberalization and rise of cash incomes (Banerjee and Jain, 2001; Banerjee, 2002). There is also some perception that the size of dowries has grown in recent decades, putting increasing pressure on families to prefer sons to daughters (Sen, 1992, 1993; Basu, 1999; Banerjee, 2002; Drèze and Sen, 2002; Sunder Rajan, 2003; Jayaraj and Subramanian, 2004; Bradley et al., 2009). The pressure on females in respect of dowry, however, not only begins before birth but extends after the time of marriage. Demands for dowry often continue after a bride is married and can result in violence or even murder of women if they are unable to meet them.

While the practices of sex-selective abortion and female infanticide have been given economic explanations and legal solutions have been set in place, which have not managed to ameliorate the problem, cultural or religious factors (which advocate a preference for sons) should also be considered. Neither the one child policy nor dowries are religious practices, yet the extent to which economic explanations dovetail with religious and cultural understandings about the role of women has been noted. In China, for instance, the strong Confucian preference for boys would seem to add to female disadvantage when coupled with the one-child policy. The Confucian tradition has a strong emphasis upon sons above daughters, for both cultural and economic reasons: sons are necessary to perform rituals to the ancestors and there is a cultural and economic expectation that sons will care for their parents in old age (Li, 1995; Feng, 1996; Greenhalgh, 2001; Junhong, 2001).

In India, where notions of female roles and responsibilities are engrained in and supported by many people's religious belief and practice, the interfaces between religion, gender and dowry need investigation, as they might be important in understanding the interconnecting factors that sustain abusive dowry practices. This could help us understand the religio-cultural underpinnings of the dowry problematic, as well as influence forms of activism to curb dowry practices. In particular, it is important to understand the ways in which religion helps shape and sustain gender hierarchies in India and its potential to challenge patriarchy. There are features of Hinduism, for instance, that sustain views about women that play a role in shaping social institutions that can serve to normalize discrimination as well as violence against women. For example, scholars within the study of religion argue that religion plays a part in both sustaining discriminatory heterosexual marriage practices and also normalizing violence against women (Hawthorne, 2004; King and Beattie, 2004; Bradley, 2006, 2009; McIntosh, 2007). King (2005, p. 3298) argues that religion must, therefore, form part of the critical analysis of all forms of oppression against women, since religions are predominantly, if not exclusively, shaped by male perspectives and experiences. She writes that:

> Religion and gender are not simply two parallel categories that function independently of each other; they are mutually embedded within each other in all religions, suffusing all religious worlds and experiences. It is because of this deep hidden embeddedness that gender is sometimes so difficult to identify and separate out from other aspects of religions until one's own consciousness is trained into making a gender critical turn. (Ibid., p. 3299)

What this discussion suggests is that to oppose the religious obstacles to women's rights through the use of secular legal strategies may not be appropriate in every situation. Instead, to engage with 'feminist' or 'gender-equitable' interpretations of religious texts and traditions, through supporting influential individuals or organizations that undertake this approach, can be a more effective way of transforming attitudes and diminishing gender inequality. For instance, dowry has been illegal in India since 1961, but continues to spread and intensify. While this suggests that the legal system is not performing as well as it should, it is also the case that dowry practices rely upon and reinforce the inferior status of women and better understanding the role that religion plays in this could make a useful contribution (Bradley and Tomalin, 2010). This underscores the important point that religion in societies functions intersectionally with other social forms. It is part of a nexus of factors that shapes people's opinions and values, including those relating to gender. To reduce social phenomena to religious causes is likely to limit our analysis, yet to ignore the role that it plays alongside economic or political influences is also limiting.

Religious Fundamentalism

As Howland has noted, we increasingly find the rise of tendencies within all religions in which 'vigorous promotion and enforcement of gender roles whose explicit intent entails the subordination of women' (Howland, 2001, p. xi). These styles of religiosity are frequently denoted as 'fundamentalist', although such terminology is problematic, not least because the term is not normally employed by those it is used to describe and tends to be used by Westerners in a negative sense, typically with reference to Islam (Hawley and Proudfoot, 1994). As Hawley and Proudfoot suggest, it is frequently used to describe those who 'crudely contrast to the even-handed, pluralist, liberal approach *we* would prefer to take' (ibid., p. 18; emphasis added). Attention has also been drawn to the way in which the plight of women within 'fundamentalist' contexts has been used to justify military campaigns by the West against Muslim countries and that such women 'figure in imperialist agendas in a thoroughly orientalist manner' (Ahmed, 1992; Stabile and Kumar, 2005, p. 765). Nonetheless, many also consider that it is a useful term pointing towards a modern phenomenon with shared characteristics, including the control and subordination of women, that manifests across different religious traditions (Hawley and Proudfoot, 1994, pp. 27–30). Religious fundamentalists tend to hold conservative attitudes about the different roles and rights of women and men, backed up by reference to 'tradition', specifically textual tradition. Their goals are largely incompatible with those of Western feminism and are sometimes articulated in direct opposition to feminist ideas.

Women's human rights in religion have been most explored with respect to Islamic contexts, where many are concerned with the increasing Islamization in some Muslim areas. In Nigeria, for instance, the adoption of Shari'ah law in the north of the country, since 2000, has been shown to act to women's disadvantage. Kalu (2003), for instance, discusses well-publicized cases where women found guilty of adultery have been sentenced to death by stoning (this has been adopted as an Islamic response to adultery). Other studies focus on the links between Islam and domestic violence, including so-called 'honour killings', as well as the relationship between Islam and 'forced marriage' (Hajjar, 2004; Ali, 2008; Patel and Gadit, 2008; Sookhdeo, 2008; Fernandez, 2009). While secular legal instruments clearly play an important role in enabling women to protect themselves against the impact of fundamentalism, others have argued that this may not be sufficient. This may be the case particularly in highly religious contexts and ones where there is suspicion of gender programmes (e.g., amongst male religious elites) being a product of Western, secular values. Ahmed explores the consequences that the rise of 'Islamic extremism' or 'fundamentalism' in Somalia since the early 1990s has had for women. She notes an increase in certain practices under the influence of fundamentalism, such as a rise in early marriage and polygamy, a desire for larger families, a decline in women's power in formal politics, and an increased obligation to veil. She considers that the lack of religious education amongst the public means that they are unable to oppose the use of Islamic texts to oppress women and moreover that Islamic extremists consider that women's movements are 'the central enemy', since fundamentalism is 'built upon the oppression of women'. While this indicates that the work on women's organizations must be significant, since it causes such concern to religious extremists, 'their work is hindered by the lack of a coherent shared policy, and lack of access to the growing literature by Islamic scholars of both sexes, which challenges the denial of women's rights using religious texts' (1999, p. 72). However, she argues that strategies to eradicate these practices must come from within Islam, but the potential for this is limited by a lack of religious education, which places women at the mercy of 'religious fundamentalists' and means that they are not able to oppose the use of Islamic texts to oppress them (1999, pp. 70–72).

Gender Implications of Engaging with Religion

The above analysis lends support to the findings of the quantitative study carried out by Seguino discussed earlier in the chapter (2011). Using data from the World Values Survey she demonstrates a positive correlation between religiosity and gender inequality and questions the current trend within development to channel funds to faith-based organizations. While not all FBOs support gender inequality (indeed, many pursue religious feminist strategies) the evidence from her analysis suggests that more often than not FBOs and male religious leaders are likely to negatively influence gender relations and to engage with them without adequate consideration of the gender consequences, or perhaps indeed at all, which will not promote women's empowerment.

This conclusion reflects a broader concern that many development actors now seem to be in rather a hurry to engage with religion, sometimes even actively seeking to support their work above that of secular actors. For instance, former US President George Bush, in his January 2003 State of the Union Address, promised US$15 billion for the

'President's Emergency Plan for AIDS Relief' (PEPFAR) and by 2005 a quarter of all PEPFAR partners were FBOs. This is a trend that reflects PEPFAR's explicit position that 'faith-based groups are priority local partners'.[2] The fact that 20 per cent of these funds were for HIV prevention, of which at least a third was to be spent on 'abstinence until marriage' programmes (which are more likely to be delivered by FBOs), has gender consequences. Women in developing countries have a higher incidence of HIV/AIDS than men and are likely to benefit from the promotion of consistent condom use.[3]

Regarding this recent 'turn to religion' by development, others are also concerned that there is often an assumption that 'a feminist re-engagement with religious texts within a religious framework is a panacea for altering gender bias in laws, policies and practices' (Tadros, 2011, p. 9). Bartelink and Buitelaar, for instance, evaluate a project run by the Dutch government in Yemen that aimed to understand how women 'draw on religious and cultural resources to claim rights to reproductive health and education' (2006, p. 352) and to incorporate Muslim women's experiences into policy. They conclude that the project set out to prove the assumption that Islam could empower women rather than to test it. For instance, they found that women were reluctant to use feminist interpretations of the Koran when presented with them – perhaps as a reaction against perceived Western interference – and that they stuck to 'traditional' interpretations as often as men. Marshall and Taylor (2006) also pick up on this theme in an article that discusses two workshops held by Oxfam in 2004 and 2006 that aimed to encourage members of its staff to explore their work on gender issues in 'Muslim contexts', and to 'understand the impact of religious, political, and other identities on gender equality' (2006, p. 23). The participants, who were mostly Muslim, promoted the view that religion should be considered, since there is a need to respond to local knowledge when approaching women's rights. However, they also argued that it was crucial not to prioritize religious identities over other identity markers or to assume that Muslim women were particularly religious. Moreover, they stressed that when talking about 'Muslim contexts' 'we should bear in mind that contexts are constantly evolving, and that our understanding of context is both time- and place-specific, and subjective' (ibid., p. 426). Comparisons between the 2004 and the 2006 workshops demonstrate how quickly the terrain can shift, with participants highlighting the ways in which the increasing politicization of Islam and Western military action placed further pressure on many Muslim women. Strategies for engagement need to be ever more sensitive, cautious and contextual, and 'key allies' (e.g., religious leaders or faith-based groups) must be carefully identified to ensure that they are committed to diversity and gender equality.

Very little research has been carried out to date on the gender-related implications of current development policies and practical initiatives that actively engage with religion (those that explicitly engage with gender as well as those that do not). For instance, it is often the case that it is the male leaders in religious traditions that are engaged by development agencies, with the effect of marginalizing women's voices. The highly patriarchal nature of most traditions means that women are unlikely to occupy positions of authority in religious institutions and FBOs. Balchin gives an example:

> I recall the fury of a women's rights activist from the Mindanao region in the Philippines in the 1990s. A foreign bilateral agency had apparently gathered local ulema [Muslim legal scholars] in order to produce a statement supporting women's reproductive rights from an Islamic

> perspective. Although this was not a normal sphere of the local ulema's concern, the statement was duly issued, but more importantly, the gathering facilitated networking among the ulema that subsequently contributed to the formation of a political grouping that promoted a fundamentalist vision of Islam. In other words, a development approach reinforced conservative interpretations of religion and strengthened the power of those who do not have pluralism and equality at heart. (2011, p. 17)

Others have cautioned that while religion can provide women with coping strategies and concrete support services, this may also involve gender costs where access to services or assistance may be conditional 'on conforming to the FBO's interpretation of religiously appropriate gender roles and behaviour' (Tadros, 2010, p. iii). It is also often assumed that FBOs and religious leaders are closer to the grass roots, thereby being in a 'better' position to reflect and meet women's needs. This may be the case in some situations, but secular organizations may also have these qualities and not all FBOs are local or embedded within the community. This points to the importance of grounding engagement with religion (in terms of organizations or leaders) in empirical knowledge of the location, and not ignoring the gender politics of particular religious institutions or FBOs and the broader social, political and economic context in which they are embedded.

THE ROLE OF RELIGIOUS FEMINISMS

When looking at the 'big picture', as illustrated by Seguino's study (2011), it is tempting to conclude that religions are more likely than not to be bad for women and that engagement with religions by development are unlikely to deliver greater gender equality. While the 'big picture' may be compelling, there also seems to be good reason for considering the role of religious feminisms in the pursuit of gender equality. However, this must be approached with sensitivity and caution and it must not be assumed that engaging with religious feminisms is always best for women.

While some studies are critical of the ways in which religion can be used to restrict women's rights and advocate a secular approach instead, others emphasize the potential benefits of finding correlates for rights within religious traditions (Afkhami and Friedl, 1977; Afkhami, 1995; Ali, 2000; Nussbaum, 2000; Donno and Russet, 2004; Drumbl, 2004; Engineer, 2004; Sechzer, 2004; Kardam, 2005). Thus, religion is seen as a barrier to women's human rights but also as an important vehicle for changing attitudes, which obstruct the realization of rights. In this 'religious feminist' discourse we frequently find the argument that religious traditions were more gender equal in earlier periods before they succumbed to the influence of patriarchy (Cooey et al., 1991; Holm and Bowker, 1994). Whether or not this view can be strictly justified is debatable, the challenge for 'religious feminists' today is how to disentangle patriarchal values from their justification as religious, and to promote alternative (many would argue 'authentic') interpretations of religious traditions that are supportive of women's human rights and empowerment. 'Feminist' organizations, such as Sisters of Islam in Malaysia, a group of feminist Shari'ah lawyers, are undertaking such interpretive work as well as working at the grassroots level to transmit more egalitarian versions of Islam to women (Sleboda, 2001; Foley, 2004). Thus, while religion clearly acts against women's interests in many contexts, particularly when its control is in the hands of a conservative male elite, to engage with 'religious feminisms' may be more effective than secular strategies in certain circumstances. Adamu, for instance, writing about Nigeria, argues that 'because gender issues are both religious and political concerns in many Muslim societies . . . any attempt to reform gender relations that excludes religion is likely to fail' (1999, p. 56). She suggests that because international donors have not incorporated Islam into their gender policies and programmes there is a perception that 'GAD' is a tool of the West and that some of the principles adopted in international documents, such as CEDAW (The United Nations 'Convention on the Elimination of all forms of Discrimination Against Women'), are seen to be at odds with Islamic values about the family. While there are Muslim feminists in many Islamic contexts who are committed to the pursuit of women's rights within an Islamic framework, they tend to find themselves trapped between conservatives in their own tradition and critics from the West who believe that in using Islam as a framework from which to approach rights they are ultimately 'accepting or supporting their own subordination' (ibid., p. 57). Adamu points out that by the 1990s Western donors were beginning to fund Islamic NGOs working on women's rights, but that relationships between the different actors remained tense.

One of the hurdles facing this approach is the fact that visions of what counts as 'female empowerment' may differ since religious feminisms do not necessarily map neatly onto GAD goals. Arguably there is a need for a better understanding of what constitutes notions of women's empowerment in different contexts and an openness to include a diversity of views and strategies even when they might seem to conflict with secular feminisms premised on female and male equality in all spheres of life. Deneulin and Bano (2009) draw a contrast between secular women's rights NGOs in Pakistan, which tend to stress 'individual liberty, including sexual liberty, and participation of women in economic and political affairs' (2009, p. 160), and female madrasas [places of learning], for which the focus is on women's interests being 'best served in a stable family unit . . . [where] the emphasis is not on equality but on equity' (ibid.). They argue that Western NGOs have tended to engage with the secular Westernized elite feminists in Pakistan and have marginalized the female 'Islamic leadership' (ibid., p. 285) in the madrasas. These different understandings of empowerment suggest the need for 'dialogue', where each group attempts to understand the other's point of view. Moreover, research that addresses both tensions and successes in interactions between secular and religious actors in relation to gender concerns could be useful in highlighting areas where there is likely to be agreement, as well as potential flashpoints that need to be carefully negotiated or even avoided.

CONCLUSION

This chapter has explored the ways in which the feminist studies of religion and 'gender and development' have recently begun to intersect in ways that potentially offer greater opportunities for women's empowerment in different contexts. The recent 'turn to religion' in development is potentially positive for women, since it opens up space for different sorts of religious feminisms in GAD work, recognizes that FBOs are often important providers of services accessed by women, and acknowledges the importance of the 'spiritual' as well as the 'material' in people's lives (UNFPA, 2005, 2008). However, it may also have negative gender-related consequences, which have yet to be adequately considered by development practitioners and policy-makers. Development donors seem in rather a hurry to engage with religious leaders and faith-based organizations, thereby running the risk of colluding with dangerous forms of essentialism about poor women and cutting off the possibility of pursuing potentially more useful 'secular' strategies.

NOTES

1. See in particular the Oxfam journal *Gender & Development*, which published two special issues (**7**(1) 1999 and **14**(3) 2006) on the topic of religion, gender and development (Tomalin, 2011).
2. *PEPFAR: Community and Faith-based Organizations* (September 2005), Report to Congress, available at: http://www.pepfar.gov/progress/76864.htm; accessed 26 October 2011.
3. See *UNAIDS Report on the Global Aids Epidemic* (2010), 25, available at: http://www.unaids.org/global-report/Global_report.htm; accessed 26 October 2011.

REFERENCES

Adamu, Fatima (1999), 'A double-edged sword: challenging women's oppression within Muslim society in Northern Nigeria', *Gender and Development*, **7**(1), 56–61.

Afary, Janet (1997), 'The war against feminism in the name of the almighty: making sense of gender and Muslim fundamentalism', *New Left Review*, No. 224, 89–110.

Afkhami, Mahnaz (ed.) (1995), *Faith and Freedom: Women's Human Rights in the Muslim World*, London: Tauris.

Afkhami, M. and E. Friedl (eds) (1997), *Muslim Women and the Politics of Participation: Implementing the Beijing Platform* (Gender, Culture & Politics in the Middle East) Syracuse, New York: Syracuse University Press.

Ahmed, Leila (1992), *Women and Gender in Islam: Historical Roots of a Modern Debate*, New Haven and London: Yale University Press.

Ahmed, Sadia (1999), 'Islam and development: opportunities and constraints for Somali women', *Gender and Development*, **7**(1), 69–71.

Ali, Sameem (2008), *Belonging*, London: John Murray.

Ali, Shaheen Sardar (2000), *Gender and Human Rights in Islam and International Law: Equal Before Allah, Unequal Before Man?*, The Hague/London: Kluwer Law International.

Amin, Sajeda and Sara Hossain (1995), 'Women's reproductive rights and the politics of fundamentalism: a view from Bangladesh', *The American University Law Review*, **44**(4), 1319–43.

Aquino, Maria Pilar (1993), *Our Cry for Life: Feminist Theology from Latin America*, translated by D. Livingstone, Maryknoll, New York: Orbis Books.

Balchin, Cassandra (2001), 'Religion and development: a practitioner's perspective on instrumentalisation', *IDS Bulletin*, **42**(1), 15–20.

Bandarage, Asoka (1998), *Women, Population and Global Crisis: A Political Economic Analysis*, London: Zed Books.

Banerjee, N. (2002), 'Between the devil and the deep blue sea: shrinking options for women in contemporary India', in K. Kapadia (ed.), *The Violence of Development: The Politics of Identity, Gender and Social Inequalities in India*, London: Zed Books, pp. 43–68.

Banerjee, N. and D. Jain (2001), 'Indian sex ratios through time and space: development from women's perspective', in V. Mazumdar and N. Krishnaji (eds), *Enduring Conundrum: India's Sex Ratios*, New Delhi: Centre for Women's Development Studies, pp. 73–119.

Bartelink, Brenda and Marjo Buitelaar (2006), 'The challenges of incorporating Muslim women's views into development policy: analysis of a Dutch action research project in Yemen', *Gender and Development*, **14**(3), 351–61.

Basu, A.M. (1999), 'Fertility decline and increasing gender imbalance in India, including a possible South Indian turnaround', *Development and Change*, **30**(2), 237–63.

Bayes, Jane H. and Nayreheh Tohidi (eds) (2001), *Globalization, Gender, and Religion. The Politics of Women's Rights in Catholic and Muslim Contexts*, Basingstoke: Palgrave.

Borland, Elizabeth (2004), 'Cultural opportunity and tactical choice in the Argentine and Chilean reproductive rights movements, *Mobilization*, **9**(3), 327–40.
Boserup, Ester (1970), *Women's Role in Economic Development*, London: Allen & Unwin.
Bowen, D.L. (1997), 'Abortion, Islam, and the 1994 Cairo Population Conference', *International Journal of Middle East Studies*, **29**(2), 161–84.
Bradley, Tamsin (2006), *Challenging the NGOs: Religion, Western Discourses and Indian Women*, London: IB Tauris.
Bradley, Tamsin (2009), 'Physical religious spaces in the lives of Rajasthani village women the ethnographic study and practice of religion in development', *Journal of Human Development and Capabilities*, **10**(1), 43–62.
Bradley, Tamsin (2010), *Religion and Gender in the Developing World: Faith-based Organizations and Feminism in India*, London: IB Tauris.
Bradley, Tamsin and Emma Tomalin (2010), 'The contemporary dowry problematic: exploring the role of the study of religion in bridging the gap between theory and practice', *Religions of South Asia*, **3**(2), 251–74.
Bradley, Tamsin and Emma Tomalin with Mangala Subramaniam (2009), *Dowry: Bridging the Gap Between Theory and Practice*, London: Zed.
Center for Reproductive Rights Factsheet: 'The global gag rule's effects on NGOs in 56 countries', available at: http://reproductiverights.org/en/document/the-global-gag-rules-effects-on-ngos-in-56-countries; accessed 26 October 2011.
Cohen, Susan A. (2001), 'Global gag rule: exporting antiabortion ideology at the expense of American values', *The Guttmacher Report on Public Policy*, **4**(3), available at: http://www.guttmacher.org/pubs/tgr/04/3/gr040301.html; accessed 26 October 2011.
Cooey, Paula M., William R. Eakin, Jay B. McDaniel (eds) (1991), *After Patriarchy: Feminist Transformations of the World Religions*, Maryknoll, New York: Orbis.
Couture, D. (2003), 'Women's rights and religion: an analysis of some Islamic and Catholic discourses', *Studies in Religion–Sciences Religieuses*, **32**(1–2), 5–18.
Crane, Barbara B. and Jennifer Dusenberry (2004), 'Power and politics in international funding for reproductive health: the US global gag rule', *Reproductive Health Matters*, **12**(24), 128–37.
Daly, Mary (1973), *Beyond God the Father: Towards a Philosophy of Women's Liberation*, Boston: Beacon Press.
Deneulin, Séverine with Masooda Bano (2009), *Religion in Development: Rewriting the Secular Script*, London: Zed Books.
Deneulin, Séverine and Carole Rakodi (2011), 'Revisiting religion: development studies thirty years on', *World Development*, **39**(1), 45–54.
Donno, D. and B. Russett (2004), 'Islam, authoritarianism, and female empowerment – what are the linkages?', *World Politics*, **56**(4), 582–607.
Drèze, J. and A. Sen (2002), *India: Development and Participation*, Oxford: OUP.
Drumbl, M.A. (2004), 'Rights, culture, and crime: the role of rule of law for the women of Afghanistan', *Columbia Journal of Transnational Law*, **42**(2), 349–90.
Dube, Musa W. and Musimbi Kanyoro (eds) (2004), *Grant Me Justice! HIV/AIDS and Gender Readings of the Bible*, Maryknoll, New York: Orbis Books.
Eade, Deborah (2002), 'Preface', in Deborah Eade (ed.), *Development and Culture*, Oxford: Oxfam GB in Association with World Faiths Development Dialogue, pp. ix–xiv.
El Dawla, Aida Seif (2000), 'Reproductive rights of Egyptian women: issues for debate', *Reproductive Health Matters*, **8**(16), 45–54.
Engineer, Asghar Ali (2004), *The Rights of Women in Islam*, Elgin, IL: New Dawn Press.
Feng, W. (1996), 'A decade of one child policy: achievements and implications', in A. Goldstein and W. Feng (eds), *China, the Many Facets of Demographic Change*, Boulder, CO: Westview Press, pp. 97–120.
Fernandez, S. (2009), 'The crusade over the bodies of women', *Patterns of Prejudice*, **43**(3–4), 269–86.
Foley, Rebecca (2004), 'Muslim women's challenges to Islamic law: the case of Malaysia', *International Feminist Journal of Politics*, **6**(1), 53–84.
Gerami, Shahin and Melodye Lehnerer (2001), 'Women's agency and household diplomacy – negotiating fundamentalism', *Gender and Society*, **15**(4), 556–73.
Greenhalgh, S. (2001), 'Fresh winds in Beijing: Chinese feminists speak out on the one child policy and women's lives', *SIGNS*, **26**(3), 847–86.
Grimes, Seamus (1998), 'From population control to "reproductive rights": ideological influences in population policy', *Third World Quarterly*, **19**(3), 375–93.
Hajjar, L. (2004), 'Religion, state power, and domestic violence in Muslim societies: a framework for comparative analysis', *Law and Social Inquiry, Journal of the American Bar Foundation*, **29**(1), 1–38.
Hasna, Fadia (2003), 'Islam, social traditions and family planning', *Social Policy and Administration*, **37**(2), 181–97.

Hawley, John S. and Wayne L. Proudfoot (1994), 'Introduction', in John S. Hawley (ed.), *Fundamentalism & Gender*, New York and Oxford: Oxford University Press, pp. 3–44.
Hawthorne, S. (2004), 'Rethinking subjectivity in the gender-orientated study of religions: Kristeva and the subject in process', in U. King and T. Beattie (eds), *Gender, Religion and Diversity: Cross Cultural Perspectives*, London and New York: Continuum, pp. 40–50.
Hedman, Birgitta, Francesca Perucci and Pehr Sundström (1996), 'Gender issues', in *Engendering Statistics: A Tool for Change*, Stockholm and Orebro: Statistics Sweden, pp. 13–15.
Helie, Anissa (2004), 'Holy hatred', *Reproductive Health Matters*, **12**(23), 120–24.
Howland, Courtney W. (2001), *Religious Fundamentalisms and the Human Rights of Women*, Basingstoke: Palgrave.
Jackson, Cecile and Ruth Pearson (eds) (1998), *Feminist Visions of Development: Gender Analysis and Policy*, London: Routledge.
Jamal, Amina (2005), 'Feminist "selves" and feminism's "others": feminist representations of Jamaat-e-Islami women in Pakistan', *Feminist Review*, **81**(1), 52–73.
Jayaraj, D. and S. Subramanian (2004), 'Women's wellbeing and the sex ratio at birth: some suggestive evidence from India', *The Journal of Development Studies*, **40**(5), 91–119.
Junhong, Chu (2001), 'Prenatal sex determination and sex selective abortion in rural Central China', *Population and Development Review*, **27**(2), 259–81.
Kalu, O.U. (2003), 'Safiyya and Adamah: punishing adultery with sharia stones in twenty-first-century', *Nigeria African Affairs*, **102**(408), 389–408.
Kane, Gillian (2008), 'Abortion law reform in Latin America: lessons for advocacy', *Gender & Development*, **16**(2), 361–75.
Kardam, Nüket (2005), *Turkey's Engagement with Global Women's Human Rights Norms*, London: Ashgate.
Kazimov, Necva B. (2003), 'Egypt's reservations to the United Nations Convention on the Elimination of Discrimination against Women and women's rights in Egypt', *The American Journal of Islamic Social Sciences*, **20**(3–4), 1–45.
King, Ursula (1995), *Religion and Gender*, Oxford and Malden, MA: Blackwell Publishers.
King, U. and T. Beattie (eds) (2004), *Gender, Religion and Diversity: Cross Cultural Perspectives*, London and New York: Continuum.
Klasen, S. (1994), 'Missing women reconsidered', *World Development*, **22**(7), 1061–71.
Klasen, S. and C. Wink (2003), 'Missing women: revisiting the debate', *Feminist Economics*, **9**(2–3), 263–300.
Lachenmann, Gudrun (2004), 'Female spaces in Muslim West African societies', *Peripherie*, **24**(95), 322–40.
Li, J. (1995), 'China's family planning program: how well has it worked? A case study of Hebei Province 1979–1988', *Population and Development Review*, **21**(3), 563–85.
Marshall, Mandy and Nigel Taylor (2006), 'Tackling HIV and AIDS with faith-based communities: learning from attitudes on gender relations and sexual rights within local evangelical churches in Burkina Faso, Zimbabwe, and South Africa', *Gender & Development*, **14**(3), 363–74.
McIntosh, Esther (2007), 'The concept of sacrifice: a reconsideration of the feminist critique', *International Journal of Public Theology*, **1**(2), 210–29.
Mernissi, Fatima (1975), *Beyond the Veil: Male–Female Dynamics in Modern Muslim Society*, Cambridge, MA: Schenkman Publishing Company.
Moaddel, Mansoor (1998), 'Religion and women: Islamic modernism versus fundamentalism', *Journal for the Scientific Study of Religion*, **37**(1), 108–30.
Moaddel, Mansoor (2002), 'The study of Islamic culture and politics: an overview and assessment', *Annual Review of Sociology*, **28**(1), 359–86.
Molyneux, Maxine (1985), 'Mobilization without emancipation? Women's interests, states and revolution in Nicaragua', *Feminist Studies*, **2**(2), 227–54.
Moser, Caroline (1993), *Gender Planning and Development: Theory, Practice and Training*, London: Routledge.
Nussbaum, M. (2000), *Women and Human Development: The Capabilities Approach*, Cambridge: Cambridge University Press.
Obermeyer, Carla Makhlouf (1994), 'Reproductive choice in Islam: gender and state in Iran and Tunisia', *Studies in Family Planning*, **25**(1), 41–51.
Parpart, J. (2002), 'Lessons from the field: rethinking empowerment, gender and development from a post-(post-?) development perspective', in K. Saunders (ed.), *Feminist Post-development Thought*, London: Zed Books, pp. 41–56.
Patel, S. and A.M. Gadit (2008), 'Karo-Kari: a form of honour killing in Pakistan', *Transcultural Psychiatry*, **45**(4), 683–94.
Pearson, Ruth (2000), 'Rethinking gender matters in development', in Tim Allen and Alan Thomas (eds), *Poverty and Development into the 21st Century*, Oxford: The Open University in Association with Oxford University Press, pp. 383–402.

Pearson, Ruth and Emma Tomalin (2008), 'Intelligent design? A gender sensitive interrogation of religion and development', in Gerard Clarke and Michael Jennings (eds), *Development, Civil Society and Faith-based Organizations*, Basingstoke: Palgrave, pp. 46–71.
Peña, Milagros (1995), 'Christian women in Latin America: other voices, other visions', *Journal of Feminist Studies in Religion*, **11**(1), 81–94.
Peña, Milagros (2007), *Latina Activists Across Borders: Women's Grassroots Organizing in Mexico and Texas*, Durham, NC: Duke University Press.
Phiri, Isabel Apawo and Sarojini Nadar (2006), *African Women, Religion and Health: Essays in Honor of Mercy Amba Ewudziwa Oduyoye (Women from the Margins)*, Maryknoll, New York: Orbis Books.
Rathgeber, Eva M. (1990), 'WID; WAD; GAD: trends in research and practice', *The Journal of Developing Areas*, **24**(4), 489–502.
Rawi, Mariam (2004), 'Betrayal', *Reproductive Health Matters*, **12**(23), 116–19.
Razavi, Shahra (2009), 'Foreword', in Jose Casanova and Anne Philips, 'A debate on the public role of religion and its social and gender implications', Gender and Development Programme Paper No. 5, UNRISD, pp. iii–v.
Reuther, Rosemary Radford (1983), *Sexism and God Talk: Towards a Feminist Theology*, Boston: Beacon Press.
Rose, Susan (2005), 'Going too far? Sex, sin and social policy', *Social Forces*, **84**(2), 1207–32.
Rowlands, Jo (1998), 'A word of the times, but what does it mean? Empowerment in the discourse and practice of development', in Haleh Afshar (ed.), *Women and Empowerment: Illustrations of the Third World*, Macmillan: Basingstoke, pp. 11–34).
Rozario, S. (2009), 'Dowry in rural Bangladesh: an intractable problem?', in Tamsin Bradley and Emma Tomalin with Mangala Subramaniam, *Dowry: Bridging the Gap Between Theory and Practice*, London: Zed, pp. 29–58.
Sánchez Fuentes, María Luisa, Jennifer Paine and Brooke Elliott-Buettner (2008), 'The decriminalization of abortion in Mexico City: how did abortion rights become a political priority?', *Gender & Development*, **16**(2), 345–60.
Sechzer, J.A. (2004), 'Islam and woman: where tradition meets modernity: history and interpretations of Islamic women's status', *Sex Roles*, **51**(5–6), 263–72.
Seguino, Stephanie (2011), 'Help or hindrance? Religion's impact on gender inequality', *World Development*, **39**(8), 1308–21.
Selinger, Leah (2004), 'The forgotten factor: the uneasy relationship between religion and development', *Social Compass*, **51**(4), 523–43.
Sen, A. (1990), 'More than 100 million women are missing', *New York Review of Books*, **37**(20), available at: http://ucatlas.ucsc.edu/gender/gratio.html; accessed 26 October 2011.
Sen, A. (1992), 'Missing women', *British Medical Journal*, **304**(6827), 587–88.
Sen, A. (1993), 'The economics of life and death', *Scientific American*, **268**(5), 40–47.
Sen, A. (2003), 'Missing women – revisited', *British Medical Journal*, **327**(7427), 1297–8, available at: http://www.bmj.com/content/327/7427/1297.full; accessed 26 October 2011.
Singh, Nikky-Guninder Kaur (1993), *The Feminine Principle in the Sikh Vision of the Transcendent*, Cambridge: Cambridge University Press.
Sleboda, Jennifer (2001), 'Islam and women's rights advocacy in Malaysia', *Asian Journal of Women's Studies*, **7**(2), 94–136.
Smyth, Ines (1998), 'Gender analysis of family planning: beyond the "feminist vs. population control" debate', in C. Jackson and R. Pearson (eds), *Feminist Visions of Development: Gender Analysis and Policy*, London and New York: Routledge, pp. 217–38.
Soares, Benjamin F. (2006), 'Islam in Mali in the neoliberal era', *African Affairs*, **105**(418), 77–95.
Sookhdeo, Rosemary (2004), *Secrets Behind the Burqa*, McLean, VA: Isaac Publishing.
Sookhdeo, Rosemary (2008 edition), *Secrets Behind the Burqa*, McLean, VA: Isaac Publishing.
Stabile, Carole A. and Deepa Kumar (2003), 'Unveiling imperialism: media, gender and the war on Afghanistan', *Media, Culture and Society*, **27**(5), 765–82.
Sunder Rajan, R. (2003), *The Scandal of the State: Women, Law, and Citizenship in Postcolonial India*, Durham, NC: Duke University Press.
Tadros, Mariz (2010), 'Faith-based organizations and service delivery: some gender conundrums', UNRISD, Gender and Development Programme Paper No. 11.
Tadros, Mariz (2011), 'Introduction: gender, rights and religion at the crossroads', *IDS Bulletin*, **42**(1), 1–9.
Thomas, Scott M. (2005), *The Global Resurgence of Religion and the Transformation of International Relations: The Struggle for the Soul of the Twenty-first Century*, New York/Basingstoke: Palgrave Macmillan.
Tomalin, Emma (2011), *Gender, Faith and Development*, Rugby: Practical Action Publishing.
Tyndale, Wendy (ed.) (2006), *Visions of Development: Faith-based Initiatives*, Aldershot: Ashgate.

UNFPA (2005), *Culture Matters – Working with Communities and Faith-based Organizations: Case Studies from Country Programmes*, New York: UNFPA, available at: http://www.unfpa.org/public/publications/pid/1430; accessed 26 October 2011.

UNFPA (2008) *Culture Matters: Lessons from a Legacy of Engaging Faith-based Organizations*, New York: UNFPA, available at: http://www.unfpa.org/public/pid/1353; accessed 26 October 2011.

Vuola, Elina (2002), 'Remaking universals? Transnational feminism(s) challenging fundamentalist ecumenism', *Theory, Culture & Society*, **19**(1–2), 175–95.

Wilber, Charles K. and Kenneth P. Jameson (1980), 'Religious values and social limits to development', *World Development*, **8**(7–8), 467–79.

13 Moral power at the religion–development–environment nexus

Cynthia Moe-Lobeda with Frederica Helmiere

INTRODUCTION

To the Catholic Maryknoll sisters of Northern Luzon, in the Philippines, the connection between religion and ecology is robust, self-evident, and urgent. Situated outside of smog-ridden Baguio City, the sisters have witnessed the environmental degradation of the city resulting from urban and economic development. Their response? Convert the convent school into a center for alternative environmental education, start a biodynamic garden, create the 'Stations of the Earth' and reconnect local Filipinos and visitors with an earth-centered spirituality.

The Maryknoll sisters exemplify an emerging nexus between development, religion, and the environmental dimensions of development theory and practice. But how exactly is it that these three fields speak to one another? And why might development studies require a deeper understanding of religion's intersection with environmental concerns? The questions lead into confounding, uncharted, and shifting terrain.

The problems begin with terminology. Each term – religion, development, environment – has multiple and contested connotations and denotations. Elsewhere in this volume, readers will encounter conundrums inherent in the concepts of 'development' and 'religion'. 'Environment' is no less vexing. Chief among its problems is the inherent anthropocentrism implied in the term. Using 'environment' to signify what is commonly called the 'natural world' suggests that it is, before all else, 'environment' for the human species. This assumption places humans *apart from* rather than *a part of* earth's web of life – the planet's systems of water, air, and soil and its diverse, interconnected life forms. That perceived separation is a taproot of the earth crisis. The term 'environment' perpetuates this anthropocentric worldview. Changing it, over the long term, means changing language used to describe the earth–human relationship. Hence, we prefer minimal use of 'environment'. Herein we use the term because it has currency in the public discourse, but where appropriate, we substitute 'ecological'.[1] This alternative situates humans within earth's web of life rather than above it.[2]

PRESENTING QUESTIONS AND PREVIEW OF RESPONSE

What insights and resources might religion bring to ecological concerns as they appear in development theory, planning, and practice? What problems may ensue if religion is ignored in examining the ecological dimensions of development? Our response, in summary form, is this:

Local and global ecological phenomena impact development work everywhere. The communities, peoples, and nations whom development purports to serve – namely those most devastated by poverty and imposed powerlessness – are, in general, those most threatened and ravaged by ecological destruction. Ecological destruction is rooted in human beings' impact on their environments, and religious beliefs and practices influence human beings' relationship to their environments in both conscious and subconscious ways. (To the extent that religions shape societal assumptions and worldview, the influence of religion pertains even to people who disavow religious allegiance.) Thus, to address the roots of ecological degradation, for the sake of curtailing and reversing it, requires consideration of religious factors.

Said differently, development to the point where all people – and in particular those who find themselves on the receiving end of development projects – may thrive depends upon reversing the massive ecological destruction that now threatens life on earth. Religious factors have undeniably contributed to the earth crisis we now face. Moreover, religion may serve as a powerful force for radically reorienting human–earth relations toward sustainability and radically reshaping social relations toward justice within and between nations.

To flesh out these connections fully would require volumes. Our intent in these few pages is far more modest: to touch upon the role of Christianity in fostering ecological degradation and in promoting ecological healing, as related to development work. We proceed in four steps. The first summarizes the fused terrain between development, religion, and ecology. The second introduces the emerging understanding that religion as a whole plays a role in the well-being of earth's web of life. The third focuses on the part Christianity has played in fostering ecological degradation as related to development. The fourth and final step, the chapter's largest portion, explores Christian traditions as the root of ecological healing.

Before all, however, it is important to clarify our disciplinary approach and the presuppositions undergirding all that follows. Theological ethics functions as our primary disciplinary lens. Since both theology and ethics within it are disciplines in rapid change, methodological presuppositions matter.

APPROACH AND PRESUPPOSITIONS

Theo-ethical Presuppositions

Our decision to view religion through the lens of Christian traditions does not imply the claim that Christianities hold moral wisdom superior to that of other religions or spiritual traditions. On the contrary we are convinced that all of earth's religious traditions are called to contribute their wisdom and resources to the work of forging sustainable earth–human relations marked by justice. We focus on Christianity because it bears a unique moral burden. Inseparably wound up in the philosophical, ideological, and cosmological assumptions of modernity, it has contributed disproportionately to the earth crisis and to the development paradigm that is so closely connected to that crisis. This of course, is because Christianity more than other religious traditions, informed the worldviews and epistemology of the Euro-Western world out of which 'development' was constructed. And Christianity, through its missionary movements and theological justification of European superiority, has historically paved the way for the Western, neo-colonial development paradigm. Having played these historic roles, Christianity bears a tremendous responsibility to bring its resources to the pan-human tasks of rebuilding earth's health, and of building equitable relations between the global South and the global North.

A second presupposition concerns the plurality of Christian traditions. We speak not of Christianity but of Christianities, not of Christian tradition but traditions. The assumption that there is one Christian tradition has subordinated the vast diversity within Christian traditions and within the spectrum of people and peoples who have identified as Christian. As a result, countless forms of Christianity have been lost, subordinated, or ignored.

A third methodological assumption is that Christian traditions (beliefs, practices, texts) have been forces of both oppression and liberation from oppression, begetting death and destruction as well as life and healing. The great paradox of Christian history is that the tradition has cultivated both the worst and the best of human being and culture. Christianity is complicit in the conquest of the Americas, slavery, colonization, fascism, and gender-based oppression. Yet Christianity also helped to produce the civil rights movement, the abolitionist movement, resistance to fascism, liberation in the face of colonization, and other movements toward social justice and liberation from oppression.

Fourth, we presuppose that theology is a critical discipline and as such its tasks include critique, retrieval, and reinterpretation or reconstruction. *Critique* discloses where Christian symbols, images of God, convictions, and practices have served the causes of domination, oppression, and destruction rather than the causes of life, liberation, and healing. Images of God and other religious symbols are culturally and historically contingent. Many Christian symbols developed in the context of patriarchy, empire, and a Hellenistic assumption of hierarchical dualism in which spirit reigned over matter. Thus emerged a God who was Father, King, distant from the world, and head of a chain in which men are closest to God and the earth is furthest. *Retrieval* rediscovers and reclaims aspects of the tradition that have been ignored, suppressed, denied, overlooked, or domesticated, and that could engender social and ecological healing and liberation. Reforming Christian symbols, theologies, images, and theological constructions is the task of *reconstruction* or *reinterpretation*. The Protestant Reformation is a prominent illustration of these three tasks of theology at work. All three are necessary in bringing religion to the cause of ecological healing.

Finally, the greatest shift in theology in the last 50 years is the recognition that all theological work is contextual. Beliefs, convictions, truth claims, and sacred texts are shaped by context and must respond to it. The overwhelming contextual factor for any examination of the development–religion–environment nexus in early twenty-first century is that humankind, or at least certain segments of humankind, pose a threat to the rest of life on earth, with calamitous consequences for the world's most impoverished people.

Social Theoretical Presuppositions

Climate imperialism and environmental racism[3]

A grave intellectual and moral fault line of the environmental movement, at least in the United States, has been the failure to connect earth's degradation to the pernicious forms of social injustice madly eating away at humankind (yet largely unseen by people who benefit from systems of power and privilege). In general, descendants of the tribes of Europe have a greater chance of protection from the impacts of global warming and toxic waste than do many of the earth's peoples. Efforts to address climate change and other aspects of the earth crisis may either exacerbate or reduce existing injustice based on race/ethnicity and class. This chapter assumes that social injustice and ecological destruction are inseparable.[4,5] The connections are apparent and multifarious. They take many forms, two of which are climate imperialism and environmental racism.[6] Both illustrate the significance of environmental concerns for the development field.

'Climate imperialism' refers to the imbalance between nations responsible for climate change and the nations suffering or predicted to suffer from its effects. The people of industrialized nations produce far more greenhouse gasses per capita than do the people of less industrialized lands. Yet the latter suffer first and foremost from the consequences.[7] The over 600 million environmental refugees whose lands will be lost to rising seas if Antarctica or Greenland melt significantly will be disproportionately people of color, as are the 25 million environmental refugees already suffering the consequences of global warming. So too are the people who will starve if climate change significantly diminishes crop yields of the world's three staples – corn, rice, and wheat. The 40 percent of the world's population whose lives depend upon water from the seven rivers fed by rapidly diminishing Himalayan glaciers are largely not white people. Coastal dwellers in the global South lose their food supplies and livelihoods at a higher rate to rising sea levels and the increasing fury of storms. Economically impoverished countries are less able to implement adapting strategies than are we of the industrialized world. In short, the climate crisis is powerfully shaped by both economic privilege and white privilege.

The social inequity and ecological degradation nexus takes a second form, known as 'environmental racism'. The term refers to 'institutional rules, regulations, and policies of government or corporate decisions that deliberately target certain communities for least desirable land uses, resulting in the disproportionate exposure of toxic and hazardous waste on communities based upon race/ethnicity or class'.[8] 'Environmental racism', while initially referring to environmental discrimination based on race alone, has come to denote the disproportionate distribution of environmental dangers not only in communities of color but also communities of economically marginalized people. Illustrations of environmental racism are countless.[9]

Climate imperialism and environmental racism demand holding social justice and ecological well-being together in the quest for a sustainable relationship between the human species and the planet. Eco-justice is a term for that linkage. Eco-justice calls forth morally and politically challenging questions, such as the rights of each nation to the earth's 'environmental space',[10] or the manner in which the over-consuming countries of the global North are to account for the 'ecological debt' owed to those who are suffering most from, but contribute least to, ecological degradation.

Critique of development

This chapter presupposes a critique of the relatively recent and remarkably powerful concept of *development*, meaning Northern 'experts' helping Southern governments and communities transform their country toward a modern, industrial, capitalist economy or the myriad projects intended to raise standards of living 'through the mediation of western technology, institutions, and practices'.[11] Development, in this sense, has been traditionally understood by its proponents as a morally faultless force for positive change whose absence is a problem for the countries labeled by the capitalist industrialized world as 'underdeveloped'.

Development is, of course, far from monolithic; development theories, approaches, practices, and practitioners across the decades and continents have been as varied as the individuals involved. It is difficult to reject or replace the term because, as James Ferguson argues, it is in itself a central value that 'forms the very framework within which argumentation takes place' and serves as the 'interpretive grid' through which we understand roughly two-thirds of the world.[12] The term 'development' is used also by theorists and practitioners who reject 'development' in its traditional sense, yet use the term to indicate their own work to support historically exploited peoples' struggles for their rights and lives.

Challenges to the development discourse and practice have been leveled from numerous camps.[13] The neo-Marxist critique argues that the development apparatus[14] seeks to aid capitalistic exploitation in countries by 'incorporating new territories into the world system, or working against radical social change, or bribing national elites or mystifying the *real* international relations' – rendering development programs by organizations such as the World Bank and USAID mere efforts to promote imperial capitalism.[15] A post-modern deconstructive critique argues that aid projects reinforce the systems that cause poverty in the first place because poverty is not a symptom of scarcity but of powerlessness, and aid organizations fail to bring about radical structural changes in political and economic systems.[16] Development projects, therefore, especially those rooted in a capitalist framework, are more likely to *cause* poverty than cure it[17] and critics argue that most development projects fail to meet their own stated goals.[18]

'Post-development theory', born of postcolonialism and poststructuralism, rejects development as a neo-colonial project 'produced discursively by the West to continue its imperial project, disguised as humanitarian and philanthropic interventions'.[19] The West, and in particular the USA, invented the term, classifying the world's majority an 'underdeveloped' minority to be developed by a benevolent Western world.[20] The great danger of development, posits Christian ethicist George Zachariah, is its insidious corroding of the moral agency and political will of the people it purports to serve.[21] This point reappears later in the chapter.

Theorists on many fronts, ourselves included, argue that development is fundamentally flawed due to its largely unquestioned correlation with economic growth. Economic growth is inadequate and deceptive as a measure of economic well-being.[22] It often masks as good, projects that have devastated communities that are already impoverished. These include flooding by dams that do not provide energy to communities demolished by them, forceful displacement of subsistence communities from their commons and homelands, toxification of water supplies, depletion of biomass for commercial fishing, spread of genetically modified seeds, and more.[23]

Liberation theologies too have criticized and in some cases denounced development, along with neo-liberal economic globalization. Much liberation theology recognizes that development projects grounded in neo-liberal economic policies are complicit in the oppression of already impoverished people.[24] Liberation theology rejects political, economic, and social projects that increase the gap between rich and poor, impoverish people, or degrade the natural goods upon which they depend.

As environment enters the discourse, the grounds for questioning development as constructed and imposed by Western industrialized nations expand. Development, in particular through the World Bank, the IMF, and USAID, has devastated ecosystems and natural goods upon which impoverished people depend for life.[25] Moreover, the myth that 'growth has no limits' underwrites development theory. Earth's ecological limits falsify that principle. Growth, on the contrary, has impenetrable limits. They are the limits of the planet's resources, its capacity for waste absorption, and its many essential services such as climate regulation, soil regeneration, water purification, and carbon sequestration.

We presuppose the validity of the aforementioned critical stances and locate ourselves most fully with the liberation theological perspective, and with the critiques of growth and of neo-liberalism. However, we add an additional critique that is central to the argument that follows. Development, as traditionally constructed and conducted, *disables the moral agency of the common citizen of the global North* in a particular sense. It is our agency to carry out what some Christian traditions consider a central dimension of the human vocation: embodying the love of God in the world by working to dismantle systemic injustice. These presuppositions – both theo-ethical and social theoretical – undergird all that is to come in this chapter.

DEVELOPMENT, RELIGION, AND ENVIRONMENT

That development must be concerned with ecological issues is indisputable. Human well-being, purportedly the aim of development, depends on ecological well-being. Unchecked, environmental degradation, in the forms of climate change and water issues alone, will render impossible the aims of development at its best: that all people have the necessities for life with dignity including relative social equity and power to participate in the decisions that shape the terms of social life.[26] Human beings cannot live and thrive without the essential services provided by the rest of nature.[27] The ecological crisis, therefore, is inherently a crisis for development work in any particular locale, whether affected by local or global phenomena. Communities are affected by environmental degradation caused by forces operating in their locale – be those forces indigenous to the area or imposed – as well as degradation caused by distant forces. The latter refers in particular to climate change caused disproportionately by societies of the global North, and the drought, flooding, disease and agricultural disasters that come in its wake. This chapter is concerned largely with this latter form of environmental damage.

Likewise, development and religion share a complex history that lingers to this day. That which Foucault calls 'pastoral power' was introduced to the West by Christianity, and took on an institutional form.[28] Strong ideological ties between American Protestantism and the national government 'found practical expression in the missionary efforts to further the national purpose and in the close relations many of the missions enjoyed with the government'.[29] But as missionary activities came under increasing criticism and the Western project of international development entered the scene, faith-based development organizations slowly replaced them, functioning in some cases as de facto development workers.

The historical correlation of development with economic growth renders a weighty connection between development, environment, and religion.[30] Development aimed at economic growth has repeatedly destroyed natural systems upon which many already impoverished people depended for life. Short-term economic growth figures, as a measure of development, externalize and thereby hide sometimes terrible environmental costs to be borne by people who may have gained nothing from the economic growth. To consider development issues fully, requires considering environmental and religious factors.

Religion plays yet another role in linking environmental concerns with development. Humanly caused environmental destruction is, by definition, a result of how humans relate to their environments. Human societies' relationships to their environments are shaped, often unconsciously, by religiously influenced worldviews, cosmologies, and value systems. Said differently, environment destruction is a matter of earth–human relations.

RELIGION AND EARTH–HUMAN RELATIONS

The last third of the twentieth century witnessed an unprecedented shift in earth–human relations. One young and dangerous species now threatens earth's capacity to sustain life as we know it. Every field of human endeavor has a role to play in what Thomas Berry calls the 'great work' of our day – to forge a sustainable relationship between the human species and its planetary home. As we enter the 'Ecozoic era',[31] the world's religions are called to 'eco-reformation'.[32] This is a call to become earth-honoring religions capable of furthering the human shift into a sustainable relationship with our planetary home. Doing so entails two basic movements. One is to uncover and name the religious traditions' contributions to ecological degradation. The purpose of this self-critical investigative work is to end those contributions and open the door to reshape religious traditions such that they serve the well-being of earth and its life systems. The second movement is that very reformation. It entails retrieving earth-affirming aspects of the traditions that may have been obscured or suppressed over the centuries, and imaginatively reinterpreting or reconstructing religious beliefs, symbols, and practices.

Both movements require acknowledging the profound but often unrecognized role of religion in shaping how human beings relate to the material world around them. Religions provide belief systems, cosmological stories, rituals, moral vision and norms, ethical behaviors, relationships, symbol systems, institutional arrangements, and historical legacies 'premised on an understanding of human beings as other than or more than simply their purely social or physical identities'.[33] Religious resources link humans to the 'matrix of mystery from which life arises and unfolds'.[34] They mediate experience of God, the numinous, or the transcendent, and help us live with a sense of identity, meaning, and purpose.

These functions of religion raise the fundamental cosmological and moral questions of human life. According to a given religious tradition, how did the material world come into being and why does it exist? What is its destiny? Where does matter end and spirit begin? How do humans fit in to the story of the earth? What is our destiny and purpose? What ways of being and acting are good, right, and true? Who and what is to be valued, who and what eschewed? Who has the power to establish these norms and values?

What social arrangements are to be valued and sought? How are relations of power and privilege to be ordered?

Such questions are as ancient as the religious traditions themselves. The given answers – conscious or not – powerfully shape how human individuals and societies *understand the nature of the world around them*, its value, why it has value or does not, and how humans are to live in relationship to the rest of the natural world. Who we think we are matters. Are we divinely mandated to have dominion over the earth and use it for our good alone? Or are we Adamah (Adam), 'mud creatures' made of dust and moisture, here to live in communion with all that is, and to cultivate and protect the soil?[35] Religions, notes moral theologian, Daniel Maguire, are 'those swirling, symbol-packed movements . . . the main source of moral attitudes that emerge as the basal assumptions of laws, politics and economics'.[36] These basal assumptions are deeply intertwined with the current status of the earth. Herein lies the historical power of religion in determining how human beings relate to the other-than-human parts of nature.

Until recent decades, the impact of religion on earth–human relations went largely unrecognized. However, in 1967, historian of medieval technology Lynn White published a seminal essay accusing Christianity of bearing tremendous responsibility for the worldviews and ways of life that have led modern societies into environmentally dangerous and degrading modes of living. This accusation and widespread discussion of it over the following decades, together with the raging earth crisis, brought religions' impact on earth's well-being into both environmental and religious discourse.

To be sure, the roles of different religious traditions in relationship to ecological well-being have been as different as night and day. For example, some traditions value the search for otherworldly rewards solely, while others affirm one's terrestrial experience; each perspective impacts the value of earthly matter. Religious ritual has the potential, through signs and symbols, to reveal and prescribe a kinship with the environment or dominance over it. Traditions vary in their recognition of nature's intrinsic worth or instrumental worth alone. As eco-feminist theology attests, often the religious worldviews that valorize dominance over the 'natural world' valorize a corresponding dominance over women.

Because of the tremendous potential in religious traditions to guide people's way of understanding and relating to the natural world, these traditions bear great moral responsibility. If the people faithful to particular religious traditions do not uncover and draw upon the resources offered by their traditions, then those life-saving and life-sustaining resources remain dormant. Tremendous gifts of power for life and for the good are left untapped. 'Great religions', writes Daniel Maguire, 'are born in imaginative power and can shift the tectonic plates of attitude and worldview'.[37] The environmental crisis calls urgently for that transformative power.

Secular bodies, including networks of renowned scientists, have called for religious wisdom to enter the quest for ecological sustainability. Increasingly the earth crisis is seen as a matter not only requiring political will and techno-fixes but also spirituality and morality. Science has shown that human behavior is threatening earth's capacity to sustain life as we know and love it. Yet, this knowledge does not appear to be producing the change that it demands. Societies of the global North, though they possess the wealth and technology to make the requisite radical changes (for instance, in carbon emissions) are blatantly failing to do so, barreling forward instead with reprehensible climate imperialism. Religion may offer the moral and spiritual power for the fundamental reorientation of life that is required if humans are to live sustainably within earth's ecological systems. Without that shift, the world's impoverished people and nations – those whom development claims to serve – will continue to bear the brunt of climate change and other forms of ecological devastation.

All of earth's great spiritual traditions are called upon to plumb their depths for the wisdom to meet the moral challenges of our day. The wisdom from any religious tradition is richer and fuller when placed in dialogue with others. Moreover, religious wisdom will bear yet more fruit in collaboration with other bodies of human knowledge, and in particular, the sciences.

Today, beliefs, practices, values, and symbols in many religious traditions are being rediscovered and reconstructed to evoke earth-honoring forms of human society. The hope lies in the unique power and energy of religions to morally denounce biocide and geocide, to be countercultural and subversive, to claim the story of humans as part of the natural world and utterly dependent upon it, to re-envision the sacred as including the earth, and to reawaken the underestimated power of relatedness in earth's web of life. We turn now to one set of religious traditions, Christianities, and its relationship to the earth crisis. The next two steps examine Christianity first as a cause of ecological degradation, and then as a source of ecological healing.

CHRISTIANITY AS A ROOT OF ECOLOGICAL DEGRADATION

The 'case against Christianity' as a main culprit responsible for the ecological crisis has been well developed, and is now commonplace in the discourse of religious environmentalism. A cursory summary is provided here, and the link to development is established.

The Judeo-Christian tradition has powerfully influenced attitudes, both religious and secular, that 'teach disregard for non-human species and that look upon the natural world as primarily, or solely, at hand for human exploitation'.[38] Lynn White's groundbreaking essay argued that humans' identity in relation to the land is rooted in religious heritage. That identity shapes the way human societies perceive and treat their natural environments.[39] According to White, the anthropocentric Judeo-Christian tradition historically licensed the exploitation of nature by granting humans dominion over the earth and by infusing Western society with that fundamental assumption. It constituted the common sense understanding of the world and humans' place in it during the formative period of Christian doctrine, and thereafter for centuries. White's essay initiated the 'dominion' controversy, convincing many emerging eco-theologians that a divine mandate for human dominion decreed in the first creation story of Genesis (1: 26–30) has profoundly influenced the development of Western civilization, resulting in abusive patterns of behavior regarding the earth. This attitude of control and entitlement emerging from Genesis is unconscious, White argued, manifesting itself in major Western societal developments such as the Industrial Revolution and market capitalism, and, in turn, our current ecological crisis. These developments, of course, have furthered Western exploitation of what some have called the 'developing world', and have shaped the course of development work in those places.

Subsequent theologians deepened the critique, arguing that the Christian tradition stripped nature of its sacredness. The God of Christianity was a transcendent deity who created the world but was not to be confused or associated with it, and certainly did not dwell within it. Humankind's true and spiritual home is in heaven; we are but sojourners on this earth. Salvation frees the soul from earth for ascent into heaven, and human destiny is dissociated from earth's destiny. This desacralization, together with dominion theology, paved the way for unmitigated technical manipulation of nature. Today, modern manifestations of these messages and a society immersed in Western scientific discourse and the market economy perpetuate ecological exploitation.

White's thesis has been fiercely debated for decades. With many other eco-theologians, we hold that the 'case against Christianity' is valid and invaluable to the extent that it holds Christianity responsible for the earth-degrading orientation of Western culture. Yet the case is faulty to the extent that it holds Christianity *solely* responsible for that orientation or rigidly intractable with regard to earth's well-being. Other worldviews also played a part. For instance, the elevation of spirit over matter, which is so central to the dominion and desacralization perspective (and is attributed by many exclusively to Christianity) was, in fact, found in Platonic philosophy long before the dawn of Christianity.

Furthermore, the 'case against Christianity' is weak whenever it portrays Christian scriptures as *singularly* earth degrading. As Paul Santmire notes, there is an ambiguous ecological promise in scriptures and many biblical texts revere nature.[40] Some portray nature as imbued with divine presence, participating in God's work, and praising God. Moreover, in the Bible's second creation story (Genesis 2: 4–25), God calls humans not to dominion over the earth, but rather to till and protect it. Thus, while dominant traditions within Christianity have tended to ignore the earth-affirming face of the scriptures, that face is decidedly present.

CHRISTIANITY AS A ROOT OF ECOLOGICAL HEALING

The damage wrought by Christianity is matched by the potential within it for helping to build ways of living marked by equity among people and mutually enriching earth–human relations. Christian traditions, including their scripture, are replete with vital resources to be retrieved, reinterpreted, and reclaimed in the service of earth's well-being and earth-affirming ways of living. The last 25 years have seen a vital faith-based environmental movement emerging within Christian traditions around the world. This movement is diverse, widespread, growing rapidly, and burgeoning with creativity. It is blooming in the academy, institutional church structures, and popular expressions of everyday religion. The extent to which this movement brings about change – in behaviors, beliefs systems, values, and social structures – is the extent to which it contributes to ecological healing and to development at its best.

Loci of Earth-affirming Christianities

In the academy, both graduate and undergraduate programs in theology and religious studies are developing programs in 'ecology and religion' under various rubrics. A Green Seminary Initiative provides networking opportunities for seminaries committed to greening Christianity. A five-volume *Earth Bible* series proposes hermeneutics of scripture from perspectives of earth. The American Academy of Religion's unit on religion and ecology is vibrant, and the Yale-based Forum on Religion and Ecology is exploring the varied resources of world religions in order to foster an interdisciplinary approach to complex environmental concerns.

National and international church bodies have accompanied academic theology in the dawning awareness that Christian faith calls for allegiance to earth's well-being. The World Council of Churches (WCC) was a forerunner. Its 1974 General Assembly in Nairobi called member churches and the world to establish 'just, sustainable, and participatory' societies. In 1983 the WCC urged its members and the international community to recognize and support the 'integrity of creation' along with peace and justice. Since that time, every major denomination in the United States (with the exception of the Southern Baptists) has issued statements calling Christians to care for creation, to 'earth-keeping', or to 'allegiance to earth' as inherent in allegiance to God.

Particularly noteworthy is the leadership role that the church has played within the global community in relating environmental concerns to social justice issues, and thereby to concerns of development. Incidents of this role are countless. One example is the World Council of Churches, which, as James Martin-Schramm points out, was one of the early voices to articulate the social justice–environment nexus and warn of its dangers. The 1994 publication *Accelerated Climate Change: Sign of Peril, Test of Faith* referred to nature as 'co-victim with the poor'. 'Earth and people will be liberated to thrive together, or not at all', declared the text.[41]Voices from the global South have led the way in correlating the oppression of the earth with the oppression of women and subaltern communities the world over, and in linking these to development initiatives. Leonardo Boff, one of Latin America's pre-eminent liberation theologians, published the manifesto of that connection in his 1995 *Cry of the Earth, Cry of the Poor*. Latin American eco-feminist Ivone Gebara (2002) linked the structural evil of ecological destruction with the structural evil of gender injustice. Numerous others have followed. Particularly relevant to the religion–development–environment nexus is the recent work of Indian Christian ethicist, George Zachariah. His *Alternatives Unincorporated: Earth Ethics from the Grassroots* (2011) attributes environmental destruction to colonization by Western-oriented development and neo-liberal globalization. The earth, Zachariah argues, is objectified, commodified, and otherized just as human beings are objectified, commodified and otherized in much development discourse. Development, together with globalization, he says, has brutalized the earth and its subaltern human communities in the same sweep, and can be overturned only if the voices and agency of courageous social movements in those communities are heard and respected.

As is the case with many new theological shifts, Christian environmentalism is taking hold in the lives of everyday Christians and their worshiping communities more slowly. To many it is unknown. Others however, embrace 'greening Christianity' with tremendous energy, hope, creativity, and tenacity.[42]

All of these loci of Christianity – the academy, the institutional church at national and international levels, local faith communities – are nurturing change toward earth-honoring, justice-making forms of Christianity. They seek to contribute religious resources to the profound social, political, and cultural changes required to put the brakes on the ecological devastation that threatens the lives of all, but especially of those who are already impoverished. Here we consider two of those resources, ethics and theology, building on the methodological perspectives identified earlier in this chapter. Those perspectives presuppose critique, retrieval, and reconstruction as central tasks of theology and theological ethics.

Moral-spiritual Power for Justice and Ecological Well-being

Christian theology and ethics may be a source of moral-spiritual power for the work of reshaping earth–human relations along the lines of ecological sustainability and justice. At the outset of this chapter, we concurred with post-development theorists' claim that development has often tended to disable the moral and political agency of the people it claims to serve. We added an additional critique that development, generated from the USA, may also subtly disable the moral agency of the common US citizen to challenge structural injustice. Here we elaborate on that critique.

Where poverty exists, structural injustice is at work, especially in the form of economic structures that create wealth for some at the cost of impoverishing others and threatening earth's life systems. Those systems include the neo-liberal global economy, climate injustice, the legacy of colonialism, and many aspects of the 'development' imposed by the West on the peoples that it labeled 'developing'. Garnering the moral-spiritual agency to confront these asymmetries of power and privilege is the moral challenge of the global North. Meeting this challenge calls for *political* engagement in the classic sense of the term: the processes whereby the ordering of society is determined.

Development, however, is frequently a depoliticized force for people of the global North. For the most part, development does not challenge the structures that impoverish people and devastate eco-systems. Development discourse convinces us that what 'poor people' need is technical assistance, humanitarian aid, and resources. That assumption obscures the reality that people are poor because political-economic structures make them poor while making others rich.

In this sense, *development contributes to the moral and political oblivion of economic privileged people of the global North.* It enables us to hide from our own complicity in the systemic exploitation of countless communities. We can ignore these as causes of vast human subjugation and suffering, and hide under the cloak of private virtue by supporting development work and projects. They are considered adequate. Through them, we assume, we have met our moral duty to help people in need.

A familiar Chinese proverb illustrates the inadequacy of this stance: 'Give a man [sic] a fish and you feed him for a day. Teach a man to fish and you feed him for a lifetime'. This adage has been understood to mean that development is better than charity. However, teaching someone to fish will not provide food if the fish supply is rapidly drained because a large dam was built upstream to benefit elite interests, or multinational corporations over-harvest fish from the waters, or toxic waste is dumped nearby, or climate change decimates fish habitat, or a fence is built around the fish pond to privatize the resource. Teaching a person to fish and providing technical assistance to enable fishing can obscure the need to address those larger systemic issues.

Christian theology and commitments are a source of moral agency for recognizing structural injustice and confronting it. We consider here three broad theological claims: the moral norm of neighbor-love reconceived as a political-ecological vocation, an understanding of God indwelling the created world, and a theological anthropology that situates human beings *within* rather than outside of earth's natural matrix of life. All three resources retrieve under-recognized aspects of ancient Christian traditions and reinterpret Christian beliefs, symbols, and practices. All are rooted deeply in Christian scripture and tradition, especially as they have been reinterpreted by liberation theological movements stemming from the global South and by eco-feminist theologies. This sampling of theological resources heralds forms of Christianity that subvert the assumed human right to dominion over the earth and acclaim the sacredness of earth and its life forms.

Neighbor-love as an ecological vocation

Christians, along with Jews and Muslims, claim that the sacred Mystery (so lamely called 'God') loves this creation with a love beyond human reckoning, a love that 'will not cease in all the endless ages to come' (Hadewijch of Brabant, 1981). This ancient claim of Christian tradition, manifested throughout the centuries in different theological streams, holds that human beings are given by God a lifework, a calling. It is to receive God's love and then live it into the world. This call is iterated in the commandment to 'love your neighbor as yourself' (Matthew 22: 39). 'Neighbor-love' is widely regarded as the fundamental moral norm of Christian life. 'Love', as a religious moral norm, does not refer primarily to a feeling or an affection, but rather to a steadfast commitment to serve the well-being of whomever or whatever is loved. And it bears particular obligation to serve those in need.

More often than not in Christian traditions, neighbor-love has been interpreted as pertaining to interpersonal relationships; it is seen as an interpersonal virtue bearing no obligation to political engagement aimed at confronting and changing social structural relationships. Thus, to serve the well-being of people who are suffering from poverty has meant to provide aid and development assistance that alleviates the suffering and enables escape from poverty, but not to challenge the systemic injustices that cause poverty. Christians are more likely to provide shelter to the homeless than to confront the wage structures, taxation policies, and health and education inequities that render people homeless. Thus, the moral power to challenge systemic causes of poverty is diminished.

This has not always been the case, however. Countless streams of Christian theology have perceived political implications of neighbor-love, and have seen in neighbor-love a mandate to seek justice in the face of unjust power structures and social orders. The abolitionist movement in nineteenth-century England and the United States, the Social Gospel movement of early twentieth-century United States, Catholic Social teaching regarding economic justice beginning in the late nineteenth century, political theology, and the various forms of liberation theology[43] have all embraced the idea that God's love, embodied in human beings, calls us to struggle for the liberation of all people from oppression and from whatever thwarts life's full flourishing. These Christian traditions maintain that the love of God and the neighbor-love to which people are called is a justice-making love, a love that tenaciously subverts all powers of domination and oppression. Said otherwise, neighbor-love is a *political* virtue as well as an interpersonal one. The claim is solidly rooted in both First and Second Testaments of the Christian Bible.[44]

In the last three decades, ecological theology has reclaimed the idea – also firmly grounded in the Bible but repressed by dominant Christian traditions for many years – that God's love and human neighbor-love extend *beyond the human* to encompass the entirety of creation. The God of liberation is also the God of creation. Eco-theology asserts that this God seeks redemption of the entire cosmos from all forces that thwart the aim of abundant life for all, not merely the redemption of individual human beings. This love is hungering for all of creation to flourish. Neighbor-love, therefore, is reinterpreted as a political-*ecological* vocation.

Any theology of love worth its salt must constantly recognize the bottomless and treacherous fallibility with which Christians throughout the centuries have betrayed and distorted the call to neighbor-love. The Inquisition and the Crusades, the theological justifications of chattel slavery, Christian entanglement with colonialism, and Christian denigration of the earth and of human sexuality are but a few examples. Methodologically speaking, the critical task must accompany the reconstructive task of theology. Nevertheless, the claim that God calls people to a justice-making love that embraces the entire world with all of its elements and creatures is a powerful resource for motivating social change toward ecological sustainability and justice.

God indwelling

The second theological affirmation considered here is that this force of divine love and life is coursing throughout all of creation, including its human creatures. While not all streams of Christian traditions profess God's presence within all people and within the other-than-human parts of nature, many do. The claim is most striking where it has been largely ignored. The Lutheran tradition, for example, does not commonly celebrate divine presence 'flowing and pouring through all things', yet Luther himself did. 'The power of God', he wrote, 'must be essentially present in all places even in the tiniest leaf'.[45] God 'is in and through all creatures, in all their parts and places, so that the world is full of God and [God] fills all'.[46] Lutheran theology, increasingly aware of earth-care as a mandate of faith, is re-exploring and reclaiming this aspect of Luther.

This notion of God within all things is known as 'panentheism', meaning God in everything.[47] The idea is firmly rooted in what may be the central distinctive Christian claim, that the Holy One is immanent within the material world as well as transcending it. Immanence comes from the Latin '*immanere*' – to remain within. Historically in Christian theology, God 'within us' implies God 'among us'. We presuppose this two-dimensional sensibility.

God's immanence, as a concept and a faith claim, has a centuries-long and contested history. We cannot here engage the theological and philosophical debate regarding the term and its referents. Suffice it to say that different schools of Christian theology have emphasized God's immanence, or transcendence, or a 'balance' between the two. That 'balance' has also been understood in varied ways. Most Christian traditions assume some form of dialectic between God's immanence and God's transcendence in relationship to the world.

An historical shift in modernity vis-à-vis the issue is relevant here. Theological liberalism (eighteenth through early twentieth centuries) tended to emphasize God's immanence. Neo-orthodoxy then critiqued this emphasis and emphasized God's transcendence. More contemporary theologies, especially some feminist and eco-feminist theologies, reclaim the legacy of an immanent God. They assert crucial moral import in the claim that God indwells bodies, relationships, and the earth. We stand within this theological tradition and suggest that it holds immense potential for moral power on behalf of sustainability and justice.

One root of moral power is the strength, courage, hope, and moral will that humans may derive from the conviction that the sacred Spirit, in the form of indomitable justice-making and earth-honoring love, dwells within human beings and all of nature, and as such is present fully in struggles for ecological well-being and social justice. Another root of moral power arises in the act of confronting a rather horrific question. This question is based on the Christian faith claim that one particular form in which God has manifest Godself in history is the form of Jesus of Nazareth who was executed by the Roman Empire as a threat to its hegemony.[48] Human beings – in this case imperial Rome – crucified the One whom Christians have claimed to be God. If this God dwells within the earth, and if the earth is being brutalized at human hands, *are we once again crucifying God?* To take seriously this question might result in challenging the ongoing exploitation of earth. Finally, if earth and its elements and creatures are the dwelling place of God, then they are sacred.

Humans as part of nature

A third theological resource is a dramatic reform in theological anthropology. We have noted already that a fundamental set of questions to which religions respond are the questions of moral anthropology. Who are we? What does it mean to be moral beings? How do we fit into the story of all that is? Early Christianity, wrought as the mixture of Hellenistic and Hebrew traditions in a cauldron of competing versions of each spawned multiple theological anthropologies. Over time, the emerging dominant renditions taught human superiority over the rest of creation, and defined the material world as either ephemeral and spiritually inconsequential or evil.

Eco-theology has rigorously critiqued these tenets. Reinterpreting biblical texts and theological traditions, this new movement in theology fosters ecologically attuned moral anthropologies that take many forms and have varied biblical foundations. For example, rather than finding humans to be set apart by God to have dominion over the rest of the created world, some ecological interpretations argue that human beings are situated integrally *within* the rest of nature; humans are crafted from soil (humans from *humus*, Adam from *adamah*), and it is the same soil from which other animals are made.[49] Humans are, moreover, called to protect and cultivate the soil.[50] As noted at this chapter's outset, the social construction of who humankind is in relationship to the rest of earth's matrix of life shapes how we live in relationship to it.

Held together, these three theological claims may engender moral-spiritual power for confronting systemic oppression and for reconstructing how humans relate with the rest of nature. Neighbor-love as a political-ecological virtue calls for defying exploitation of earth and of other human beings. God's presence indwelling all of nature renders it sacred and vulnerable to crucifixion at human hands. And humans as *a part of* nature rather than *apart from* it call for situating human economies within the limits of earth's economy of life. These resources, while relevant to Christian communities, may also bear power beyond their boundaries. The notion that an indefatigable force of love and life is at play in the world, indwells material reality, and empowers humans to join in its life-giving work does not require adherence to Christian doctrine or creed.

Christian traditions, as they are developing in the academy and the church at all levels, may play a significant role in motivating and guiding people to reshape earth–human relations and North–South relations along lines of ecological sustainability and social justice. In this manner, Christian traditions contribute to the aims of development at its best – that all people have the necessities for nurturing health, wholeness, and meaningful participation in the earth community.

CONCLUSION

We began with a question: 'Why bring religion into the picture when addressing ecological issues in development theory, planning, and practice?' Our response stems from the paired realities that human well-being, especially the well-being of people furthest from the centers of power and privilege, depends upon ecological well-being, and ecological well-being is determined largely by how humans treat their environment. Religious factors influence human beings' relationship to their environment. Thus, to consider the environment in its fullness requires consideration of religious factors. Religion, and Christianity in particular, has played a causal role in the ecological degradation that now haunts the planet. Yet religion, and again, Christianity in particular, also offers a unique constellation of resources for building sustainable earth–human relations that are marked by justice within and between societies.

NOTES

1. This is not to suggest that the two terms are always interchangeable. Such is not the case. Both have multiple uses depending upon disciplinary perspective, theoretical stance, and other contextual factors.
2. In like manner, we replace the term 'humans and nature', with 'humans and other-than-human parts of nature' or 'humans and the rest of nature'.
3. This section is adapted from the forthcoming book by Cynthia Moe-Lobeda, *Christian Ethics for the 'Uncreators': Morality in the Face of Systemic Evil* (2013).
4. For elaboration of this connection, see Agyeman et al. (2003).
5. It is noteworthy that the World Council of Churches was one of the early voices to articulate that nexus and warn of its dangers, doing so nearly two decades ago.
6. Julian Agyeman et al. (2003) eloquently summarize the moral impact of environmental racism and climate injustice: 'While the rich can ensure [at least for the time being] that their children breathe cleaner air . . . and that they do not suffer from polluted water supplies, those at the bottom of the socio-economic ladder are less able to avoid the consequences of motor vehicle exhausts, polluting industry and power generation or the poor distribution of essential facilities. This unequal distribution of environmental "bads" is, of course, compounded by the fact that globally and nationally the poor are not the major polluters. Most environmental pollution and degradation is caused by the actions of those in the rich high-consumption nations, especially by the more affluent groups within those societies . . . [Yet] affluent countries in the North are avoiding or delaying any real reduction in their greenhouse gas emission through the so-called "flexible mechanisms" [in the Kyoto Protocol]: emissions trading, the Clean Development Mechanism and Joint Implementation' (ibid., pp. 1–2).
7. A statement by the National Council of Churches of India (2002, p. 2) articulates it well: 'the powerful nations and the powerful within the developing nations continue to extract from the atmospheric common disproportionately. In that process they have emitted and continue to emit greenhouse gases beyond the capacity of the planet to withstand. However the subaltern communities with almost zero footprint are forced to bear the brunt of the consequences of global warming'.
8. United Church of Christ Commission for Racial Justice (1987). I would add that the understanding of environmental racism in the report encompasses not only 'deliberate targeting' but also decisions and actions that are not deliberately targeted. The definition in this report has been augmented in varied ways. Earth Justice Legal Defense Fund at its oral intervention at the 55th Session of the United Nations

Commission on Human Rights, refers to environmental racism as: 'institutional, or industry action, or failure to act, that has a negative environmental impact which disproportionately harms – *whether intentionally or unintentionally* – individuals, groups, or communities based on race or colour' (italics mine).

9. Widely known examples such as the 1984 disaster in Bhopal and Hurricane Katrina are but the tip of the iceberg. The ongoing grind of 'hidden' environmental racism is ubiquitous. Our food, clothing, transportation, housing, and consumption, as we now live, are built on it. The production chain of textiles is a sequence of poisons: 'cotton fields are sprayed with chemical cocktails to which the workers are also exposed without protection and which subsequently contaminate the soil. In the spinning and weaving factories, workers are exposed to dust just as the dyers are to fumes from the dyeing process' (Boesak and Hansen, 2010, p. 188). The Coca Cola plant in India consumes vast quantities of water daily and pollutes more, effectively destroying the water supply and agricultural livelihoods of the surrounding people. The razing of rainforests and export of lumber strips livelihood and homes from many of the world's 350 million forest dwellers. The beneficiaries are the corporations responsible who bear none of the environmental and human costs, and 'us', the consumers of lumber and Coca Cola made cheap by the theft or destruction of water supplies, land, and food supplies. The victims are disproportionately not white.
10. 'Environmental space' is a rights-based and equity-based tool for measuring and comparing different populations' environmental impact developed in 1982 by German economist Horst Siebert. It was popularized in Europe in the early 1990s. The tool portrays eco-justice in terms of all people having equal right to consumption of earth's resources and use of earth's services, limited by the planet's carrying capacity. The earth's total environmental space is 'the total amount of pollution, non-renewable resources, agricultural land and forests that can be used globally without impinging on the access by future generation to the same resources' (Friends of the Earth Netherlands, 1992). Each country has a right to the same amount of environmental space per capita, which implies eliminating at least international inequities in aggregate resource consumption and carbon emissions.
11. Zachariah (2011, p. 17). Theorist of radical democracy Douglas Lummis argues in a similar vein that economic development is 'anti-democratic in that it is a process of establishing and strengthening an undemocratic form of rule over a central aspect of people's lives – their work – and also in that it generates inequality in wealth and power' (1996, p. 48).
12. Ferguson (1994, p. xiii).
13. Arturo Escobar (1995, p. 6), citing Michel Foucault, explains that discourse analysis creates the possibility of 'stand[ing] detached from [the development discourse], bracketing its familiarity, in order to analyze the theoretical and practical context with which it has been associated. It gives us the possibility of singling out 'development' as an encompassing cultural space and at the same time of separating ourselves from it by perceiving it in a totally new form'.
14. The 'apparatus' for Foucault, referred to the mixed and varied collection of institutions, discourses, laws, statements, programs, propositions, silent justifications – basically knowledge structures – that maintain and strengthen the exercise of power.
15. Ferguson (1990, p. 11).
16. Scott (1998). Also, Lappe and Collins, as cited in Ferguson (1994, p. 11).
17. Kathleen Nadeau (2002) argues that state sponsored neo-liberal development projects, especially its economic policies, are complicit in the oppression of the poor.
18. Ferguson (1994, p. 8).
19. Zachariah (2011, p. 22).
20. Gustavo Esteva (1992, p. 6) cites Harry Truman's 20 January 1949 address as the point of invention. 'We must embark', declared Truman, 'on a bold new program for making the benefits of our scientific advances and industrial progress available for the improvement and growth of underdeveloped areas'.
21. Zachariah (2011). James Ferguson also argued that development's great damage is in 'de-politicizing both poverty and the state' (1990, p. 256).
22. See Moe-Lobeda (2004, Chapter 3).
23. George Zachariah (2011, p. 11).
24. Nadeau (2002).
25. For example, the construction of the Aswan dam is cited as a near-environmental disaster, resulting in massive soil erosion, soil salinity, destabilization of fisheries, loss of soil fertility, water pollution from fertilizers, algae blooms and introduced aquatic species. Many rural development programs (RDPs) imposed upon the rural poor have included technology transfers that were maladapted to local environmental limitations. High-yielding varieties of cash crops have likewise been urged upon rural farmers in the global South, bringing with them the need for heavy use of chemical fertilizers and pesticides and diminishing biodiversity in many areas.
26. Clearly the perceived relationship between environment and development has shifted along with Western constructions of 'development' and along with the increasing social implications of environmental

degradation. Wolfgang Sachs traces that relationship from the early 1970s when 'environmentalism was regarded as inimical to the alleviation of poverty' (1992, p. 29).

27. Ecosystem services refer to resources and processes supplied by natural functioning ecosystems. Services include the production of food and water, regulating climate and disease, filtering toxins, decomposition of dead matter, supporting nutrient cycles and crop pollination and carbon sequestration, and providing recreational and spiritual benefits.
28. Michel Foucault (1997, p. 68).
29. Clymer (1986, p. 53).
30. Growth, of course, has been not only in nations of the global South, but also in nations of the global North who benefit economically from 'development' in the global South.
31. According to a Thomas Berry film (1996), 'In the sequence of biological periods of Earth development we are presently in the terminal phase of the Cenozoic and the emerging phase of the Ecozoic era. The Cenozoic is the period of biological development that has taken place during these past 65 million years. The Ecozoic is the period when human conduct will be guided by the ideal of an integral earth community, a period when humans will be present upon the Earth in a mutually enhancing manner'.
32. Term first used, to the best of our knowledge by Christian ecological ethicist Larry Rasmussen.
33. Gottlieb (2009).
34. Mary Evelyn Tucker, unpublished paper delivered at a conference at Yale University sponsored by Yale Divinity School and Yale School of Forestry and Environmental Studies, 2006.
35. Both understandings are claimed as the primary or a primary message of the creation stories in the Hebrew Bible (known by Christians as the Second Testament or the Old Testament). 'Mud creatures' is the interpretation of the Hebrew word commonly translated as Adam, by second-century theologian and church leader, Irenaeus of Lyons.
36. Maguire (2000, p. 1).
37. Ibid., p. 6.
38. Kinsley (1994, p. 2).
39. White (1967, p. 1205).
40. Santmire (1985).
41. World Council of Churches (1994) Martin-Schramm (2010, p. 24).
42. For examples see websites of the World Council of Churches, National Council of Churches in the USA, Interfaith Power and Light, National Religious Partnership for the Environment, Green Faith, Lutheran Earthkeeping Network, and partner organizations to be found on these websites.
43. These begin with Latin American liberation theology and spread as black liberation theology; womanist, Mujerista, and feminist theologies; Minjung theology; Dalit liberation theology; and more.
44. The biblical foundations of neighbor-love as a call to justice are far too extensive to summarize here. Countless volumes elaborate. One of the more comprehensive is Bruce Birch (1991).
45. Luther, 'That These Words of Christ, "This is My Body," etc. Still Stand Firm Against the Fanatics' (Fischer, 1961, p. 57).
46. Luther, the *Weimar Ausgabe* 23.134.34, as cited by Paul Santmire (1985, p. 129).
47. Panentheism is sorely misunderstood by some who conflate it with pantheism. In fact the two are distinctly different; panentheism stands firmly within historic Christian claims, while pantheism does not.
48. Crucifixion, the way in which Jesus of Nazareth is said to have been killed, was in fact a form of execution reserved by imperial Rome of his day for rebels or others perceived by the empire as a threat to its power.
49. *Adam* and *adamah* are the Hebrew words in Genesis' second creation story translated respectively as 'Adam' and 'soil'.
50. The Hebrew words are *shamar* and *abad*, translated as 'protect' or 'keep' and 'cultivate' or 'till'.

REFERENCES

Agyeman, Julian, Robert Bullard and Bob Evans (2003), 'Joined up thinking: bringing together sustainability, environmental justice and equity', in *Just Sustainabilities: Development in an Unequal World*, Cambridge, MA: MIT Press, pp. 1–16.

Berry, Thomas (1996), Film: *The Ecozoic Era: Our Hope for the Future*.

Birch, Bruce C. (1991), *Let Justice Roll Down: Old Testament, Ethics and Christian Life*, Louisville, KT: John Knox Press.

Boesak, Allan and Len Hansen (2010), *Globalisation II – Global Crisis, Global Challenge, Global Faith*, Stellenbosch: SUN Press.

Boff, Leonardo (1995), *Cry of the Earth, Cry of the Poor*, Maryknoll, NY: Orbis Books.

Clymer, Kenton J. (1986), *Protestant Missionaries in the Philippines, 1898–1916*, Urbana and Chicago: University of Illinois Press.
Escobar, Arturo (1995), *Encountering Development: The Making and Unmaking of the Third World*, Princeton: Princeton University Press.
Esteva, Gustavo (1992), 'Development', in Wolfgang Sachs (ed.), *The Development Dictionary*, London and New Jersey/Johannesburg: Zed Books/Witwatersrand University Press.
Ferguson, James (1990), *The Anti-politics Machine: 'Development', Depoliticization, and Bureaucratic Power in Lesotho*, Cambridge: Cambridge University Press.
Ferguson, James (1994 edition), *The Anti-Politics Machine: 'Development', Depoliticization, and Bureaucratic Power in Lesotho*, Minneapolis: University of Minnesota Press.
Fischer, Robert (ed.) (1961), *Luther's Works, Volume 37: Word and Sacrament III*, Minneapolis: Augsburg Fortress Press.
Foucault, Michel (1997), 'History of governmentality', in Paul Rabinow (ed.), *Ethics, Subjectivity and Truth. The Essential Works of Foucault 1954–1984, Volume I*, New York: The New Press.
Friends of the Earth Netherlands (1992), *Sustainable Netherlands Action Plan*, available at: http://sd-cite.iisd.org/cgi-bin/koha/opac-detail.pl?biblionumber=5222; accessed 6 August 2012.
Gebarra, Ivone (2002), *Out of the Depths: Womens' Experience of Suffering and Evil*, Minneapolis: Fortress Press.
Gottlieb, Roger (2009), *A Greener Faith: Religious Environmentalism and Our Planet's Future*, New York: Oxford University Press.
Hadewijch of Brabant (1981), *The Complete Works*, translated by Mother Columba Hart, Mahwah, NJ: Paulist Press.
Kinsley, David R. (1994), *Ecology and Religion: Ecological Spirituality in Cross-cultural Perspective*, Englewood Cliffs, NJ: Prentice Hall.
Lummis, C. Douglas (1996), *Racial Democracy*, Ithaca and London: Cornell University Press.
Maguire, Daniel C. (2000), 'Introduction', in *Visions of a New Earth: Religious Perspectives on Population, Consumption and Ecology*, Albany: State University of New York.
Martin-Schramm, James (2010), *Climate Justice*, Minneapolis: Fortress Press.
Moe-Lobeda, Cynthia (2004), *Healing a Broken World: Globalization and God*, Minneapolis: Fortress Press.
Moe-Lobeda, Cynthia (2013), *Christian Ethics for the 'Uncreators': Morality in the Face of Systemic Evil*, Minneapolis: Fortress Press.
Nadeau, Kathleen M. (2002), *Liberation Theology in the Philippines: Faith in a Revolution*, Westport/Manila: Praeger/De La Salle University Press.
National Council of Churches of India (2010), 'Policy on Indian churches: engagement in eco-justice ministries', adopted by Resolution No. EC: 2010.28(9) of the Honorable Executive Committee of the NCCI on 16 September 2010.
Sachs, Wolfgang (1992), 'Environment', in W. Sachs (ed.), *Development Dictionary*, London: Zed Books.
Santmire, Paul H. (1985), *The Travail of Nature: The Ambiguous Ecological Promise of Christian Theology*, Philadelphia: Fortress Press.
Scott, James C. (1998), *Seeing Like a State: How Certain Schemes to Improve the Human Condition have Failed*, New Haven: Yale University Press.
Truman, Harry S. Inaugural Address ([20 January 1949] 1967), in *Documents on American Foreign Relations*, Connecticut: Princeton University Press.
United Church of Christ Commission for Racial Justice (1987), *Toxic Wastes and Race: A National Report on the Racial and Socio-Economic Characteristics of Communities with Hazardous Waste Sites*, available at: http://www.ucc.org/about-us/archives/pdfs/toxwrace87.pdf; accessed 19 July 2012.
White, Lynn jr. [sic] (1967), 'On the historical roots of our ecologic crisis', *Science*, **155**(3767), 1203–7.
World Council of Churches (1994), *Accelerated Climate Change: Sign of Peril, Test of Faith*, Geneva: WCC Publications.
Zachariah, George (2011), *Alternatives Unincorporated: Earth Ethics from the Grassroots*, London: Equinox.

14 Corruption, religion and moral development*

Heather Marquette

INTRODUCTION

Interest in fighting global corruption has increased significantly since the former head of the World Bank, James Wolfensohn, famously spoke out against the 'cancer of corruption' in 1996. Since then, international organizations, bilateral donor agencies, charities, multinational corporations, individual activists, government watchdogs and so on have struggled to explain why corruption occurs, let alone to formulate clear strategies for its eradication. The World Economic Forum's Global Agenda Council on Anti-Corruption estimates that 'the cost of corruption equals more than 5% of global GDP (US$ 2.6 trillion) with over US$ 1 trillion paid in bribes each year'.[1] The consequences of corruption, particularly for developing countries, are hard to underestimate:

> The consequences of corruption are not limited to economic inefficiencies; it also reduces the provision of welfare in society, undermines democracy and political institutions, contributes to social inequalities and conflict, can have a potentially devastating impact upon the environment, and constitutes a violation of human rights. (Marquette et al., 2011, p. 17)

Millions of dollars have been spent by donor agencies on anti-corruption programmes and several well-known attempts to measure corruption to inform better policy-making have been made, such as Transparency International's Corruption Perception Index (TI-CPI)[2] and the World Bank Institute's Worldwide Governance Indicators.[3] Despite this, many perceive corruption to be on the increase globally and new and innovative ways to fight corruption continue to be sought.

Much time has been spent by the World Bank, among others, in establishing corruption as a symptom of institutional failure, while cultural aspects of corruption have been deliberately underplayed (Marquette, 2003), although a growing body of work is emerging that explores the potential of cultural explanations for corruption (see, for example, Putnam, 1993; La Porta et al., 1997; Della Porta and Vannucci, 1999; Treisman, 2000; Warren, 2001; North and Gwin, 2004 among others). Of particular interest are those studies that use religion as a proxy for culture and attempt to establish a link between religion and corruption at the national level (see, for example, Paldam, 2001; Gatti et al., 2003; Norris and Inglehart, 2004; Beets, 2007).[4] It has been argued that:

> in countries where religion plays a vital role in the lives of most people, many, including public servants, are likely to derive their ethical framework at least in part from their religion. Religion is said to provide many with a language of ethics and, often, an actual set of rules to live by, some of which can be interpreted as being of particular importance to fighting corruption. (Marquette, 2012, p. 14)

The increasing attention given to the religion–corruption nexus stems from the argument that fairness and honesty are basic to the teachings of many religions, and that they can therefore be used in attempts to reduce corruption (Luxmoore, 1999). All the major world religions attempt to define humans' relationship with a sole or dominant deity, but also served as sources of institutions used in managing early societies. Thus, they all address the issue of honesty (see, for example, Reisman, 1979; Armstrong, 2007). According to Beets, two apparent assumptions underlie attempts to enlist the support of religious leaders and groups in the fight against corruption. The first is that:

> faithful adherents to religion will refrain from corruption because of the inherent theft, dishonesty, illegality, and mistreatment of others [it implies]. The second, related assumption is that those who are not faithful adherents of religions are more likely to engage in corruption because of an absence of religious guidance. (Beets, 2007, p. 72)

However, in apparent contradiction to these assumptions, many of the most corrupt countries in the world (according to the TI-CPI) also rank high in terms of religiosity (using indicators such as those used by the Pew Global Attitudes Project).[5] On this basis, there would appear to be little evidence to support the above assumptions.

I have argued elsewhere that the evidence for a causal relationship between religion (or types of religion) and either higher or lower levels of corruption is in no way convincing (Marquette, 2010, 2012). The methodologies being employed thus far are insufficient for proving – one way or another – a causal relationship. The literature is largely quantitative, with a dearth of empirical, fieldwork-based evidence. The results are often contradictory, depending upon which international dataset has been used, which points to significant methodological concerns. The findings are tentative at best, offering comparisons between various datasets and pointing towards possible explanations, sometimes rooted in theory, sometimes not. The data used are often flawed, making the explanations that are put forward problematic. Data are aggregated at the country level and cannot tell us anything about how individuals' attitudes towards corruption are formed, the impact of religious (and other socio-cultural influences) on attitude formation, or the ways that individuals condemn or justify corrupt behaviour using the language of religion.

In this chapter I argue that the methodologies used in many current studies are not adequate to study what are ultimately individual decisions, which are at least in part informed by individuals' own ethical and moral standpoints. As such, starting research with the mindset that particular types of activities are corrupt, and thus 'wrong', may prevent researchers from uncovering why people develop particular attitudes towards corruption, or why they choose to behave in a way that some would label as corrupt. I do not posit here a 'correct' ethical or moral standpoint on corruption. As Migdal (2001, pp. 19–20) points out:

> What may be easily labelled as corruption or criminality, such as nepotism or smuggling, can also be looked at, for instance, as a morality favoring kinship ties over meritocracy or one expressing the right of movement of people and goods across the boundaries arbitrarily imposed by state law.

Whether an individual agrees or not with Migdal's characterization of the nature of corruption, what is lacking from much of the current research on religion and corruption is a sense that there may be alternative ways that people view corruption, which in their minds may be moral. It is argued in this chapter that, if a valid understanding of how religion influences people's attitudes and behaviour towards corruption is to be developed, it is necessary to start from a critical and interpretive perspective and from an individual level of analysis.

There are currently few, if any, published studies that approach the study of religion and corruption in this way. If corruption research is to explore some of these issues at the individual level, as well as at the regional and national levels, it is important to look at the literature on how attitudes are formed, in relation to religion, and the impact that religion has on attitudes towards moral issues and on moral reasoning. This chapter reviews a number of studies, few of which deal specifically with corruption, in order to establish useful ways forward for corruption researchers. These studies focus on 'deviant behaviour', defined by Clinard and Meier as, 'a violation of a norm' (2011, p. 6). They go on to explain that norms are 'expectations of conduct in particular situations' that 'regulate human social relations and behaviour' (p. 10). A number of studies have shown that people who live in highly corrupt countries tend to almost universally condemn corruption (see, for example, Gatti et al., 2003; Armah-Attoh et al., 2007; Persson et al., 2010; Marquette, 2012). This then suggests that although corrupt behaviour may be widespread, it is not 'normal', thus making it 'deviant' behaviour.

Unlike the majority of the studies to date on corruption and religion, which tend to be largely economics and political science based and use large-N international datasets, this literature is largely sociological and psychological. Although studies generally focus on the individual level of analysis, some do use global survey data, such as the World Values Surveys. Many of the studies are empirical in nature, although some are rooted within the theoretical literature, and most are quantitative, rather than qualitative (i.e., structured survey based rather than semi-structured interview based).

Importantly, it has not been possible to identify any literature that examines these issues in developing country contexts, with the overwhelming bulk of the studies based on US population surveys and a smaller number focusing on the Scandinavian and Benelux countries. Much of the current interest in global corruption arises from its impact on development and developing countries in particular; as such, the available studies may provide a useful guide for future research on corruption, but it is important to consider the significance of context to their findings. There is no reason to assume a priori that results of surveys of college students in the USA will be replicated by surveys or interviews with public servants and others in developing countries; nevertheless, there is still much to be learned methodologically from exploring the theoretical and explanatory issues raised by this literature. This chapter is thus both a methodological exploration and an original contribution to a rich literature that delineates links (or the lack thereof) between religion and moral decision-making, by extending it to the context of the study of public sector corruption, particularly in the developing world.

RELIGION AND ATTITUDES TOWARDS MORAL ISSUES

Increasingly, the influence of religion on attitudes towards corruption is becoming of interest to a wide range of actors. The World Bank has a Development Dialogue on Values and Ethics; the World Faiths Development Dialogue works on corruption;

several international faith-based organizations, such as Christian Aid, Tearfund and Islamic Relief, have undertaken anti-corruption work, and so on. Making links between religion and corruption seems common sense in many ways. It may be reasonable to assume that many people derive their ethical framework from their religion. Certainly those people who consider themselves to be religious are likely to do so, but even those who describe themselves as secular, humanist, agnostic or atheist may be influenced by the religion that forms a significant part of their cultural heritage, even if its influence is not acknowledged. Many early studies (and some contemporary ones) by theologians and other 'religionists' seem to assume that there is a clear, measurable, positive relationship between religiosity and morality. Even David Nussbaum, the Chief Executive of Transparency International, referred to a study by the Federal Reserve Bank of St Louis, which concluded that:

> A belief in hell tends to mean less corruption and less corruption tends to mean a higher per capita income . . . Combining these two stories . . . suggests that, all else being equal, the more religious a country, the less corruption it will have and the higher its per capita income will be. (Cited in Nussbaum, 2006, p. 14)

However, the bulk of the literature shows that the impact of religion on attitudes towards moral issues is not clear-cut. Sometimes religion has a measurable influence and sometimes it does not. Sometimes religious people take a more 'moral' position on issues and sometimes they do not. In addition, as noted above, the data used and analysis conducted is often subject to challenge. For example, the original article cited by Nussbaum has since been updated to take out the conclusion quoted above because errors in the data used to arrive at it were subsequently detected (Kliesen and Schmid, 2004).

Furthermore, as we will see, many factors come into the formation of attitudes towards moral issues – age, education level, gender, engagement with a wider community, the nature of the religious community(ies) involved, the nature of the moral issue itself, and so on. What is clear is that religion itself, in terms of theology or religious teachings, appears to have very little influence on attitudes towards moral issues related to corruption, with socialization being a much more significant factor in determining individuals' attitudes towards corruption. Thus, one of the problems identified is that the influence of religion lies less in what the texts say than in how they are interpreted and also in how their relevance and importance to collective social behaviour is understood.

Much of the literature seeks to explain 'deviant' behaviour, often in the context of increased secularization and the (perceived) decline in moral values. Ter Voert et al. (1994), for example, conclude from their review that the literature suggests that:

> the decline of religion and the decline of an 'absolutist' perspective on moral values go hand in hand. Secularization has led to moral breakdown, and interaction is based on self-interest rather than on any more charitable notions . . . Empirical research indicates that religious people are more likely to express strong disapproval of behaviours like cheating on taxes and welfare than nonreligious people. (Ter Voert et al., 1994, p. 302)

In another example, Cortes (1965) claims that 'Most acts of delinquency are amoral, and the roots of morality are either principally or exclusively religious. Delinquents, therefore, should be lower than nondelinquents in religiosity or religiousness' (p. 122).

A highly influential study by Hirschi and Stark (1969) called this claim into question. Their own survey of young people in California showed that the alleged relationship is not the case. Respondents were asked to disclose both their own actual deviant acts (such as stealing, getting into fights, and so on). In addition, the authors examined police reports on delinquency. They found that attendance at church did not impact either actual delinquent acts or attitudes towards delinquency, even amongst respondents who believed in a literal hell and devil. This research ran counter to what many saw as a 'common sense'[6] approach to delinquency and undermined a number of public and social programmes in the USA that encouraged increased religious attendance as a deterrent to delinquent behaviour.

However, a number of empirical studies emerged in the following two decades that showed just the opposite effect, confirming Cortes' original hypothesis. One of the most interesting is that by Tittle and Welch (1983), who sought to find theoretical explanations to oppose Hirschi and Stark's surprising findings. In order to test the hypotheses, the authors undertook a multi-state (US) survey, including respondents of different ages, education levels, income, religious affiliations, gender, and so on. They included questions on deviant behaviour, including small theft, large theft, pot (marijuana) smoking, illegal gambling, assault, lying to an intimate, tax evasion and not standing for the national anthem. They label the two hypotheses proven valid by their research 'normative dissensus' and 'perceived conformity'. Based on Parsons' work on social systems (1937, 1951), 'normative dissensus' is defined as a state in which 'disagreement about the badness of various behaviours prevails', and their hypothesis states: '*The extent to which religiosity influences conformity varies directly with (a) general normative dissensus in a given context . . . or (b) with normative dissensus concerning specific offences*' (p. 659, emphasis in original). In other words, religion is more likely to impact attitudes towards those moral offences specific to that religious context. As such, religiosity may help to predict 'conformity to rules uniquely prohibited by religious institutions but not to rules prohibited by society as a whole, [which] actually reflects the effect of normative dissensus' (ibid.). According to Tittle and Welch:

> The fundamental idea is that social order rests on collectively held values . . . To the extent that people internalize moral commitments reflecting consensual values, they will probably not contemplate deviance, or if they do consider rule breaking, moral revulsion or potential feelings of guilt will restrict action. Religion presumably aids internalization by linking supernatural sanctions to moral precepts, many of which correspond to behaviour norms of the larger society. Moreover, participation in religious activities and institutions continually reinforces and strengthens internalized moral commitments – therefore, according to functional thinking, religious training and active participation should be highly predictive of conformity to social rules – at least those social rules which religious groups define as having moral components. (Tittle and Welch, 1983, pp. 656–7)

In terms of 'normative dissensus':

> '[t]he statistics support the idea that involvement in religious activities has a strong constraining effect on deviant behaviour in contexts characterized by relative normative ambiguity. Apparently when secular moral guidelines are unavailable, in flux, or have lost their authority and hence their power to compel, the salience of religious proscriptions is enhanced. (Ibid., p. 672)

They found that there was little to no difference between religious and non-religious respondents when it came to behaviour that is condemned by society as a whole, particularly large theft, assault and tax evasion. However, they found considerable differences when it came to behaviour that society generally does not condemn widely, such as pot smoking and not standing for the national anthem. The implication for research on corruption is that, if their hypothesis holds, religion may have more of an impact on attitudes concerning corrupt behaviour that society generally does not condemn widely than it does for behaviour that is condemned more widely. In corruption parlance, this could mean the difference between 'low-level corruption', also known as 'petty corruption' – cutting red tape, engagement in clientelistic networks, and so on, that is, the sort of corruption that many engage in – as opposed to 'high-level corruption', also known as 'grand corruption' – political corruption, state capture, and so on, that is, the sort of corruption engaged in by the powerful alone.

'Perceived conformity' is based on work in criminology by Sutherland and Cressey (1978). It asserts that where:

> deviance is directly related to excess exposure to social definitions (or message inputs) favourable to deviance . . . [it] seems to suggest that the greater one's religiosity, the less likely the person will be exposed to an excess of favourable deviant definitions; hence, the greater the likelihood of conformity. (Tittle and Welch, 1983, p. 657)

Tittle and Welch's 'perceived conformity' hypothesis states, '*The extent to which religiosity influences conformity varies directly with the aggregated religiosity displayed in a given context*' (p. 660, emphasis in original). It would be expected to work best where messages are both widespread and consistent with religious messages. In terms of 'perceived conformity':

> boundary maintenance and moral differentiation may become most salient when substantial variation is perceived in the moral conduct of contemporaries. In such contexts the perceived rarity of virtuous behaviour may enhance its value and motivate religiously active people to distinguish themselves from the mass of sinners through conspicuous conformity to social norms. (Ibid., p. 673)

This is a very interesting finding for corruption research. It contradicts much earlier research by arguing that 'religiosity inhibits deviant propensity most effectively in contexts where the proportion of people who are non-religious is greatest' (p. 674). In other words, it may work best when religious people feel that not engaging in corruption demonstrates their own religiosity in contrast to the corrupt behaviour engaged in by 'the mass of sinners'. However, in countries where few people are non-religious, corruption is widespread, and those who are known to engage in corrupt behaviour are also known to be religious, it is difficult to see how religious people can seek to differentiate themselves in the way suggested by this hypothesis. As Tittle and Welch conclude, 'religiosity has the greatest effect on conformity when each of the four contextual conditions prevail: general normative ambiguity, low social integration, generalized perception of low peer conformity, and a relatively high proportion of people who are not religious' (ibid.). This may be useful for researchers in helping to explore why countries with high levels of religiosity often have high levels of corruption.

Throughout the 1970s and 1980s, US studies produced findings that both contrasted with and confirmed those of Hirschi and Stark, leading to theoretical and empirical bewilderment. In 1996, over 25 years on from the original study, Stark sought to explain why such differences in findings might exist. He argued that subsequent studies showed a strong sociological impact, in that young people in other parts of the country than the West Coast, where the original study was conducted, seemed to behave differently and have different attitudes. It is widely agreed that people on either coast in the USA generally demonstrate lower levels of religiosity than those in the middle states, and most of the studies with contrasting findings took place away from either coast. Stark explained:

> I suspect that what counts is not only whether a particular person is religious, but whether this religiousness is, or is not, ratified by the social environment. The idea here is that religion is empowered to produce conformity to the norms only as it is sustained through interaction and is accepted by the majority as a valid basis for action. (Stark, 1996, p. 164)

He thus explains the differences by concluding, 'Religious individuals will be less likely than those who are not religious to commit delinquent acts, *but only in communities where the majority of people are actively religious*' (p. 164, emphasis in original). This is interesting, especially as it directly contradicts Tittle and Welch's findings on 'perceived conformity'. In Stark's analysis, based on a number of empirical studies, widespread membership in religious communities provides a disincentive to engage in delinquent behaviour. Although these studies are all based in the United States, and generally consist of surveys of teenagers and college students, the contradictory findings may be important for corruption research more generally because, no matter what the outcome, the research seems to point towards membership in religious communities as having a significant impact on attitudes towards moral issues, although only where the social environment condemns delinquent behaviour.

White (1968) reviewed theories contemporary at the time that suggested that theology should be seen as the primary source of differences between religions and between those that are religious and those that are not. These suggested 'that individuals who "believe" seek a consonance between . . . theological tenets and their attitudes and behaviour in other spheres of life' (p. 24). However, White himself disagreed with these theories, identifying instead with work by Lenski (1961) that showed how communalism and associationalism, as aspects of religious involvement, are much more significant than theology, leading to what White called the 'interaction model of religious influence' (1968, p. 25).[7] Partly the significance of communalism and associationalism could, he asserted, be explained by the way that interaction is backed both by sanctions (e.g., loss of status or position within the community, public condemnation) and by the reinforcement of community norms. Harris and Mills (1985) concur with White, and 'further suggest that measures of religious *participation* will better explain the impact of religion on . . . attitudes than will religious preference, belief, or intensity measures' (pp. 139–40, emphasis in original).

Membership in religious communities comes through as a significant factor in another study by Scheepers and Van Der Slik (1998) in the Netherlands. They argue that previous research is flawed because it isolates individuals and neglects important sources of socialization, including the role of parents, spouses and members of the individuals' religious communities, 'with whom they might discuss all kinds of everyday problems as well as moral issues' (p. 679). Although they support the hypothesis that 'moral attitudes are primarily affected by one's individual characteristics, that is, more specifically by religious involvement, religious beliefs, one's education level, and personal income', they see the need to look at theories that suggest that social interaction in religious communities is particularly significant, because 'the influence of religion on a variety of moral issues might operate through moral community formation' (pp. 679–80). Referring to work by Stark (1996), for example, they reflect that the research seems 'to imply that people take roles in a community, (re-)define social situations, deliberate upon specific issues, and adjust their responses to each other. As a result, specific subcultural patterns, that is, values, norms, and behaviours prevail' (p. 680).

Going back to the study by Ter Voert et al. (1994), the effect of religion on 'self-interest morality', including in pecuniary issues (e.g., tax evasion, insurance fraud, selling goods without disclosing problems), is examined, which brings us closer to research on corruption in terms of public moral issues. They helpfully begin by reviewing previous research, explaining that:

> Several studies indicate that in European countries and the United States respondents who are less likely to describe themselves as religious or to engage in religious practice are more inclined to have a permissive moral outlook towards actions involving pecuniary dishonesty . . . one possible explanation for the relationship between religion and self-interest morality is that religion carries a certain set of absolute moral values. (Ter Voert et al., 1994, p. 303)

As the main religious communities in the Netherlands are Protestants and Catholics, they try in their research to assess whether there is a difference between adherents of these two communities, as well as between the religious and the non-religious. Referring to work by Greeley (1989), they suggest that the two denominations are differentiated in the following ways:

> Protestants value the virtues of initiative, integrity, honesty, and thrift more than Catholics because Protestants are individualists and have an imagination of society as 'sinful and God-forsaken'. Protestants have a dialectical imagination; they picture the individual as struggling for his or her personal freedom over against the sinful oppression of social networks, and they stress those values of behaviours that contribute to the strengthening of personal freedom and independence from group control. Catholics, on the other hand, are communitarian because they have an imagination of society as sacramental, that is, revelatory of God – the Catholic analogical imagination pictures humans as integrated into social networks – networks which in fact reveal God – and stresses those values and behaviours which contribute to the building up and strengthening of those networks. (Ter Voert et al., 1994, pp. 303–4)

Their findings suggest that Catholics are more permissive of pecuniary issues than Protestants, but conclude that denomination matters less than church involvement. Indeed:

> We conclude that Christian belief and church involvement both had moderate effects on self-interest morality. Strong Christian believers were more likely to have a strict moral outlook than those low on Christian belief . . . our results indicate that the decline of religion and the decline of a strict attitude toward self-interest morality go hand in hand . . . and this difference exists irrespective of nonreligious background characteristics. The decline of religion seems to bring about a process of uncertainty about morals. (Ibid., pp. 317, 320)

However, it is very important to note that they found that non-religious people still rated highly on disapproval ratings, so the difference between religious and non-religious respondents is at the high end of the disapproval scale.

Ter Voert et al. (1994) also argue that their findings dispute Greeley's claims about the differences between Protestants and Catholics, because pecuniary issues have community-damaging impacts (pp. 318–19). This conclusion seems to be based on quite a simplistic understanding of community and social networks: it assumes, for example, a single Catholic vision of 'society' and that the nature of 'religious belief' is clear. However, not only are there variations within worldwide Catholicism[8] but also the nature of religious belief is far from clear. It is well known that in some instances people are 'born into' religious traditions, whereas adherence to others requires a conscious individual choice. Thus, self-declaration of religious denomination amongst certain groups (notably Catholics) does not act as a particularly good guide to how members act, nor how their religiosity influences their day-to-day behaviour. The significance for corruption research is that the religious communities under study need to be understood and differentiated, in terms of their overall 'vision' of society, as members of global religious communities, and in terms of their own national and regional contexts.

In a similar vein, Middleton and Putney (1962) differentiate between different types of moral standards in order to explain differences between various theoretical and empirical studies. Previous studies, they explain, 'have failed to find relationships between measures of religiosity and ethical behaviour, nondelinquency, humanitarianism, and altruism. In contrast, several studies have found the religious less likely to violate certain moral standards' (p. 142). The difference, once again, seems to be between private moral standards, such as sexual morals, and public moral standards, such as cheating. It is worth citing them at some length:

> We believe that this particular confusion, and much of the confusion surrounding the relation between religion and morality, derives from failure to distinguish two different types of ethical standards – the ascetic and the social. Social standards proscribe actions which in general are harmful to the social group, and, we hypothesize, tend to be shared by the religious and nonreligious alike as part of a general social ideology. The fact that religious ideology may also proscribe these actions is incidental; we would hold with Durkheim that religion is more a reflection of social morality than a source of it. Cheating, then, is a violation of a social standard, and it is not surprising that the nonreligious engage in it no more often than the religious. In contrast, ascetic standards – abstinence from sensual indulgences, gambling, and the like – derive primarily from an ascetic religious tradition. Within the context of religion violations of ascetic standards may be held spiritually harmful to the perpetrator. But since such violations are usually not directly or obviously harmful to the social group – at least in moderation – ascetic standards have less persuasiveness to the secularly oriented individual. He is therefore more likely to violate them. In short, we hypothesize that differences in behaviour between the religious and the nonreligious are confined to specific areas and are a product of differences in standards rather than a differential upholding of standards. (Middleton and Putney, 1962, pp. 142–3)

Their own study, which asked about both attitudes and actual actions, corroborates this: the religious are more likely to believe that anti-ascetic actions are wrong and are less likely to engage in them. However, when it comes to anti-social actions, the study found that there was no difference between the religious and the non-religious, in terms of either attitudes or violating their own standards by engaging in anti-social actions (p. 151). Interestingly, while women were found to be much stricter in terms of moral standards related to anti-ascetic actions, particularly sexual behaviour, there was little difference between men and women in terms of anti-social actions, and in one action particularly – stealing from hotels – women were much more permissive than men. Differentiating between different types of moral attitudes, therefore, seems to be important for research. It is interesting that many of the studies reviewed here took place after Middleton and Putney's study in 1962, yet they continued to fail to make this distinction.[9]

It is useful to conclude this section by looking at a study that tries to differentiate between values and attitudes. Harris and Mills (1985) explain that they propose a theory in which values partially determine attitudes, quoting Rokeach: 'While an attitude represents several beliefs focused on a specific object or situation, a value is a single belief that transcendentally guides actions and judgements across specific objects and situations . . . value is a determinant of attitude as well as of behaviour' (Rokeach, 1968, pp. 160; cited in Harris and Mills, 1985, p. 138). In this context, they state, 'we regard broadly specified attitudinal orientations, such as civil liberties or on deviant behaviour, as indicators of a general value such as self-determination' (Harris and Mills, 1985, p. 138).

Looking at value conflict is important when trying to understand the impact of religion and belief on attitudes towards morally complex and controversial subjects. Harris and Mills further explain:

> To this premise of inner ambivalence yielding unified preference, we add two corollaries. First, competing values and norms not only create inner conflict in the deciding person but also generate a substantial amount of autonomy and flexibility in decision-making . . . Second, many such contrasting values and interests are structurally rooted in each person's roles and statuses, making the ambivalence sociological because it is rooted in social structure . . . The anchorage of conflicting values in simultaneously held roles (or a single role) provides a degree of legitimacy to one's behaviour regardless of how the decision comes out. One can both contain and express inconsistent views without losing role or status, since group life is predicted upon such inconsistency and supports it through sociological ambivalence. (Ibid.)

Because of this, they argue that it is important to control for the effects of value conflict in studies looking at the impact of religion on attitudes, and they identify the two main value conflicts as 'responsibility for others (RFO)' and 'self-determination (SD)'. In their own study on attitudes to abortion, they found that individual respondents needed to deal with their own internal value conflict between RFO and SD in order to come to a view on abortion, and that the sources of conflict came from both within their own religious communities and outside. They refer to these variables as 'additive', or existing socially, outside religious involvement, and 'interactive', or legitimized within religious groups (Harris and Mills, 1985, p. 141). This again brings us back to Tittle and Welch's 'normative dissensus' and 'perceived conformity' hypotheses and reminds us of the need to try to identify 'messages' that respondents receive from both within their religious communities and outside them, and to identify possible sources of value conflict regarding corrupt behaviour.

RELIGION, CORRUPTION AND MORAL REASONING

The previous section looked at literature that has examined the relationships between religion and attitudes toward deviant behaviour, basically looking at the outcome of religion's influence on attitudes. This section, in contrast, looks at literature that examines the relationships between religion and moral reasoning, that is, basically looking at processes rather than outcomes. It is obvious from the previous section that religion has an impact on attitudes towards moral norms of behaviour, even if there is not much of a consensus about what this impact is. The same lack of consensus can be found in the literature on moral reasoning. Much of the literature reviewed here focuses on the sophistication of moral reasoning processes, concluding that the type of religiousness is significant to how an individual processes messages about moral issues. What is meant by 'type' is not the religion itself but the way it is expressed and understood by the individual.

A study by Duriez and Soenens (2006) is particularly useful and is discussed in some detail here. They begin by summarizing some key studies regarding moral action choices:

> moral behaviour is the result of at least four component processes: (1) identifying a situation as a moral problem, (2) figuring out what one ought to do and evaluating possible plans of action, (3) evaluating how the various courses of action serve moral and nonmoral values and deciding which action will be pursued, and (4) executing the plan of action . . . there are several interpretive systems by which moral action choices can be generated. People may rely on justice reasoning or so called moral reasoning . . . but they may also rely on concepts of care . . . social norms and conventions . . . or religious prescriptions. (Duriez and Soenens, 2006, p. 76)[10]

Duriez and Soenens highlight Kohlberg's arguments regarding moral reasoning as particularly significant. According to them:

> Kohlberg (1981) has argued that religiosity and moral reasoning are inherently unrelated because they constitute two distinct areas of human concern: whereas moral decision making is grounded in rational arguments of justice and is influenced by level of cognitive development (e.g. education) and exposure to socio-moral experiences (e.g. role-taking opportunities), religious reasoning is based on revelations by religious authorities. Whereas the primary function of morality is to resolve competing claims among individuals, the primary function of religion is to affirm morality. In other words, whereas moral reasoning provides moral prescriptions, religious reasoning affirms moral judgement as meaningful. (Duriez and Soenens, 2006, p. 76)

This is not to suggest, of course, that religious persons are incapable of rational arguments based on justice, nor that those making such arguments must do so without reference to religious texts or arguments. It depends, they assert, on how individuals process moral action choices, based upon the type of religious or non-religious person they are and their stage of moral development. By 'type', Duriez and Soenens mean the 'extent [to which] people accept the existence of God or some other transcendent reality and . . . being religious or not and being spiritual or not' (p. 77). They call this the 'inclusion or exclusion of transcendence'.[11]

Individuals may process religious contents either literally or symbolically, but in this interpretation the inclusion or exclusion of transcendence is significant. A person may interpret transcendence literally, what Duriez and Soenens refer to as 'literal affirmation', in which 'the literal existence of the religious realm is affirmed' (as in religious fundamentalism), or 'literal disaffirmation', in which 'the existence of the religious realm is rejected and in which the possibility is lost out of sight that religious language has a

Table 14.1 Moral decision-making

Levels	Stage number	Description of stage
Pre-conventional	Stage 1	Avoid punishment
	Stage 2	Satisfy one's needs
Conventional	Stage 3	Be a nice person
	Stage 4	Maintain the social order
Post-conventional	Stage 5	Focus on the moral principles upon which social norms are based
	Stage 6	Focus on abstract ethical principles, such as equality and respect for the dignity of human beings

Source: Based on discussion in Duriez and Soenens (2006, p. 78).

symbolic meaning. Religious language is understood in a literal way, but this time religion is rejected' (p. 77).[12] Similarly, individuals may interpret religious contents symbolically, but this may result in either 'symbolic disaffirmation', in which 'the existence of the religious realm is rejected, but where the possibility is taken into account that religious contents might refer to a hidden symbolic meaning', or 'symbolic affirmation', where 'the existence of the religious realm is affirmed, and in which one tries to encompass and transcend reductive interpretations in order to find a symbolic meaning in the religious language which has personal relevance' (ibid.).

The significance of this way of looking at how individuals interpret religious contents in terms of moral decision-making is evident when comparing Duriez and Soerens' model with their discussion of Kohlberg's (1984) six stages of moral development (Table 14.1).

Kohlberg's stages, Duriez and Soerens say, should be understood in terms of the level of sophistication each stage requires. It does not imply that those at Stage 6, say, will make 'better' decisions than those at Stage 3, but that they demonstrate more consistency in their approach. As they explain:

> When there is a conflict between conventions and moral principles, a conventional reasoner will judge by convention rather than by moral principle, whereas a post-conventional reasoner will judge by principle rather than by convention. However, this does not imply that individuals at the post-conventional level are also more moral. (Duriez and Soerens, 2006, p. 78)

These two models help to link religiosity and morality. In religious communities where principled reasoning is valued (Stages 5 and 6), members will have higher preferences for this than in those communities where principled reasoning is not part of the teaching. However, what also needs to be taken into consideration is where the stages of moral reasoning fit with respect to Duriez and Soerens' literal/symbolic and the inclusion/exclusion of transcendence models. It is the combination of the two that is significant in terms of predicting the quality of outcome, that is, how moral a decision will be. In other words, 'The moral reasoning of religious persons depends on the seriousness of their religious commitment and on the moral stage which is normative for their religious community' (ibid.).

Their own study, mainly of Belgian university students and their parents, confirms this. Those respondents who were more religious and processed religion in a literal sense had lower moral reasoning scores. Duriez and Soerens conclude:

> although religious people tend to be conservative and submissive, they are neither more or less happy, good-natured and tolerant. This suggests that the impact of being religious or not on individuals' lives is limited when it is separated from the impact of the way people process religious contents. The impact of the way people process religious contents, on the other hand, seems vitally important, with people processing religious contents in a literal way not only showing less advanced moral reasoning abilities but also less psychological well-being, less empathy and more prejudice. (2006, p. 81)

A related point is, of course, that the way a particular religious community approaches principled reasoning is also very important. In an earlier study, Duriez (2003) suggests that Roman Catholic churches attract people with literal affirmation values, so people with low moral competence may be attracted to the Roman Catholic Church, presumably because of its emphasis on literal orthodoxy.

These ideas may also have relevance for the policy-making community. Encouraging moral development education programmes, for example, in literal-orthodox religious communities that do not value principled reasoning is unlikely to produce more principled moral reasoning. The nature of particular religious communities needs to be taken into account. As Duriez and Soerens conclude:

> There is a consensus among researchers that educational programs targeted at stimulating moral development should be aimed at learning to translate one's ethical principles to solutions for specific problems with which one is confronted in real life, even under those circumstances where factors like prejudice, authority or the so-called moral majority try to prevent people from thinking about the different aspects that are part of the problem. (2006, p. 81)

Another study that contributes to our understanding of how religion may or may not contribute to an individual's moral reasoning is by Sapp and Jones (1986). Like Duriez and Soerens, they suggest that 'religiosity is not a crucial determinant of situational honesty . . . [and that] religious people can be more intolerant, more prejudiced and lacking in humanitarian concern than non-religious people' (p. 208). They are quick to point out, however, that other studies do show contrasting results and that 'the relationship between religiosity and moral reasoning may be curvilinear', especially for children who go to religious schools, for whom early conventional moral reasoning may be more sophisticated than their peers. However, studies do show that such children do not seem to move towards post-conventional reasoning (p. 209), again suggesting that the religious community in which people are located is significant.

Sapp and Jones refer to Allport (1966), who makes a 'distinction between the intrinsic orientation (a religious sentiment in which faith is both the supreme value and the master motive) and the extrinsic orientation (a utilitarian, self-serving attitude providing self-justification and endorsement of one's way of life)' (p. 209). This seems to refer to whether or not religion is seen as an end in itself or a means to bring meaning to one's life. However, in Allport's work it means the difference between someone who goes to church regularly and who bases his or her life around religion and someone who goes to church more sporadically and is more secular – or at least less religious – in outlook (Allport, 1966, pp. 454–5).

However, Sapp and Jones identify weaknesses in Allport's model, which make further research based upon it difficult. Referring to work by Batson (1976) and Batson and Raynor-Prince (1983), they point out that Allport's model seems to assume that an intrinsic orientation is a more mature orientation, whereas it is not necessarily so. Indeed, 'it may indicate a fanatical devotion to orthodoxy' (Sapp and Jones, 1986, p. 209). Extrinsic orientation can also be either negative (e.g., religion as a means of providing status, networks and even wealth) or positive (e.g., religion as a framework for articulating a position on social justice). So rather than assuming that an intrinsic orientation will be a more moral orientation, an intrinsic orientation can have both positive and negative effects on moral reasoning.

Further, as Sapp and Jones go on to say:

> as Allport's definition of mature religiosity was translated into operational concepts, several components were omitted . . . These were: 1) mature religious sentiment is integrative and accepting of complexity; 2) mature religious sentiment is self-critical and doubting; and 3) mature religious sentiment emphasizes a continuing, tentative search for more knowledge about religious questions. (Sapp and Jones, 1986, p. 209)

Again, we can see the relevance of Duriez and Soenens' model and Kohlberg's levels of moral development here. It is the openness to principled reasoning, the ability and desire to approach moral issues from a self-critical perspective and an emphasis on religion as a 'quest', or 'an endless process of probing and questioning generated by the tensions, contradictions, and tragedies in their own lives and in society' (Batson, 1976, p. 32) that leads to more mature moral reasoning. It could certainly be argued that the skills required for mature moral reasoning are just the sorts of skills needed by someone faced with a decision about whether to behave corruptly or not.

Sapp and Jones' study is far too narrow to draw meaningful conclusions, as it is simply a survey of 97 undergraduate students at one conservative US university, all of whom were taking a module on educational psychology. However, their findings may still be applicable to corruption research: those who see religion as a quest to find existential meaning tend to be more principled in moral reasoning, but 'intrinsic religiosity and principled moral reasoning are not highly related . . . the evidence also suggests that intrinsic religiosity may have more in common with conformity and a devotion to orthodoxy than it does with an introspective concern with social justice' (p. 213). The implications of this are that religion experienced intrinsically, as an end in itself, may not play a role in attitudinal formation regarding corruption, while the opposite may be true for religion experienced extrinsically.

CONCLUSION

The studies on religion and deviant behaviour discussed here are all based in either the United States or the Benelux countries, but the language used will be familiar to anyone engaged in research in developing countries – traditional, rational, modern, secular, orthodox, and so on. However, the current Western research on religion and corruption, and on religion and deviant behaviour more generally, seems to reproduce the public/private distinction between the secular and religion, between public and private moralities. Work in public administration by Ekeh (1975) and Hellsten and Larbi (2006) question the relevance of this dichotomy in a developing country context. In Nigeria, for example, Smith (2007, p. 5) argues that:

> when Nigerians talk about corruption, they refer not only to the abuse of state offices for some kind of private gain but also to a whole range of social behaviour in which various forms of morally questionable deception enable the achievement of wealth, power, or prestige as well as more mundane ambitions. Nigerian notions of corruption encompass everything from government bribery and graft, rigged elections, and fraudulent business deals, to the diabolical abuse of occult powers, medical quackery, cheating in school, and even deceiving a lover.

Thus, in many developing countries, public and private morality are said to overlap, making the public/private distinction a false dichotomy. This is particularly important when it comes to applying the approach taken by Middleton and Putney (1962), for example, that distinguishes between anti-ascetic and anti-social behaviour. From anthropology, writers such as Bloch (1977), Sperber (1975) and Boyer (1994), for example, emphasize the cognitive process and how ultimately 'moral systems' in many developing countries are often worked out in terms of an 'applied ethics', which may or may not incorporate 'religious' or transcendent elements. This points to the need for real caution in assuming that the application of the methodologies described in this chapter in a developing country context, and in the context of corruption, will produce similar results. They may, of course, but they also may not.

Still, there is much here that may assist researchers looking to understand how and why corrupt behaviour occurs. Research on religion and attitudes towards deviant behaviour suggests that individuals' interpretation of messages on moral behaviour is significant in terms of determining their acceptance or rejection of deviancy, but there is little evidence to suggest that the religious will reject behaviour that is 'anti-social' any more than the non-religious. Indeed, there is little evidence to suggest that religion, in terms of religious content, impacts upon individuals' attitudes towards public morality. Membership of a religious community that rejects behaviour seen as being 'corrupt' seems more likely to have an impact, but a lot depends upon the way in which members of the community are encouraged (or discouraged) to engage in principled reasoning.

In either case, the individual on his or her own, or as part of a religious community, is likely to face conflicting messages in terms of behaviour that is deemed to be 'deviant', particularly where corruption is widespread – systemic even – and involves individuals known to be religious (Marquette, 2012; see also Persson et al., 2010). Because of this, it is important to approach the study of corruption with an open mind in terms of defining what constitutes corruption. Individuals exist within multiple communities – religious, family, friends, colleagues, professional and personal networks and so on. Although messages from these various communities may very well conflict, it is clear that the communities will all, in some way or another, impact upon individual attitudes towards corruption. The same can, of course, be said about those individuals who conduct research on corruption or design policies to combat it: all go through similar processes of socialization. No matter what the economic impact of corruption is upon development and developing countries, it is becoming increasingly clear that to really understand why corruption occurs, it may be necessary to put aside prior assumptions about what corruption is and why people engage in it.

NOTES

* This chapter is an output from the Religions and Development research programme funded by the UK Department for International Development (DFID) for the benefit of developing countries. The views expressed are not necessarily those of the DFID.

1. See http://www.weforum.org/content/global-agenda-council-anti-corruption-2011; accessed 18 July 2012.
2. The TI-CPI is a 'survey of surveys' that looks at perceptions of corruption and then ranks countries according their score. It can be found at www.transparency.org, along with an explanation of its methodology.
3. See http://info.worldbank.org/governance/wgi/index.asp; accessed 18 July 2012.
4. I explore this literature in more detail in Marquette (2012).
5. Religiosity, although not formally defined in the Pew Global Attitudes Project (http://pewglobal.org/) is defined by the *Oxford English Dictionary* as 'religiousness, religious feeling or sentiment' or 'affected or excessive religiousness'. Measures of religiosity focus on self-definition as a member of a religious community, regular participation in religious services and rituals, and regular prayer.
6. Polzer warns that corruption policies are often based on what Schaffer called the 'common sense policy fallacy' (Schaffer, 1984; Polzer, 2001, p. 22; see also Marquette, 2012).
7. White explains that the interaction model of religious involvement contains two principles: 'The first of these principles is that religion is first and foremost a group phenomenon . . . The second basic principle . . . is that the religious group, like any other group, has a particular *normative* structure' (1968, p. 25, emphasis in original).
8. Guiso et al. (2003) argue that their study shows that Catholics raised after Vatican II are less likely to break legal norms than pre-Vatican II Catholics. They do not provide much in the way of evidence or explanation for this claim, but it certainly highlights the danger of seeing religious communities as homogeneous masses. It may also point to the role of normative values concerning principled reasoning within religious communities, but without evidence, it is not possible to make a definite claim in this regard.
9. Middleton and Putney raise another very interesting methodological issue in their paper, one that surprisingly does not often come up in the literature – the issue of social desirability bias, or the proclivity of respondents/interviewees to present themselves in such a way that others will see them favourably, although they do not refer to it as such. At the end of their survey, they asked a simple question: 'How frank have you been in your responses – very frank, partially frank, not frank at all?' They found that this question led many respondents to go back to the survey to revise their answers in order to be more honest. Considering that corruption research involves behaviour that is socially (and often ascetically) undesirable, social desirability bias must be taken into account, and Middleton and Putney's question may be one way to deal with the issue.
10. They refer to studies by Kohlberg (1976); Gilligan (1977); Lawrence (1979); Rest (1983); Turiel (1983); Nisan (1984); and Thoma et al. (1991).
11. Based on early work by Wulff (1991).
12. Richard Dawkin's recent work in *The God Delusion* (2006) is a good example of this.

REFERENCES

Allport, G.W. (1966), 'The religious context of prejudice', *Journal for the Scientific Study of Religion*, **5**(3), 447–57.

Armah-Attoh, D., E. Gyimah-Boadi and A.B. Chikwanha (2007), 'Corruption and institutional trust in Africa: implications for democratic development', Afrobarometer Working Paper No. 81, December.

Armstrong, K. (2007), *The Great Transformation: The World in the Time of Buddha, Socrates, Confucius and Jeremiah*, London: Atlantic Books.

Batson, C.D. (1976), 'Religion as prosocial: agent or double agent?', *Journal for the Scientific Study of Religion*, **15**(1), 29–45.

Batson, C.D. and L. Raynor-Prince (1983), 'Religious orientation and complexity of thought about existential concerns', *Journal for the Scientific Study of Religion*, **22**(1), 38–50.

Beets, S.D. (2007), 'International corruption and religion: an empirical examination', *Journal of Global Ethics*, **3**(1), 69–85.

Bloch, M. (1977), 'The past and the present in the present', *Man*, **12**(2), 278–92.

Boyer, P. (1994), *The naturalness of religious ideas: a cognitive theory of religion*, London: University of California Press.
Clinard, M. and Meier, R. (2011), Sociology of Deviant Behavior, 14th ed., Belmont, CA: Thomson Higher Education.
Cortes, J.B. (1965), 'Juvenile delinquency: a bio-social approach', in A. D'Agostino (ed.), *Family, Church, and Community*, New York: P.J. Kennedy, pp. 114–55.
Dawkins, R. (2006), *The God Delusion*, London: Bantam.
Della Porta, D. and A. Vannucci (1999), *Corrupt Exchanges: Actors, Resources, and Mechanisms of Political Corruption*, New York: Walter de Gruyter.
Duriez, B. (2003), 'Religiosity, moral attitudes and moral competence: a research note on the relation between religiosity and morality', *Archiv für Religiouspsychologie*, **25**, 210–21.
Duriez, B. and B. Soenens (2006), 'Religiosity, moral attitudes and moral competence: a critical investigation of the religiosity–morality relation', *International Journal of Behavioral Development*, **30**(1), 76–83.
Ekeh, P. (1975), 'Colonialism and the two publics in Africa: a theoretical statement', *Comparative Studies in Society and History*, **17**(1), 91–112.
Gatti, R., S. Paternostro and J. Rigolini (2003), 'Individual attitudes towards corruption: do social effects matter?', XV Conferenza Società Italiana di Economia Pubblica (SIEP), Università di Pavia.
Gilligan, C. (1977), 'In a different voice: women's conceptions of self and morality', *Harvard Educational Review*, **49**(4), 481–517.
Greeley, A. (1989), 'Protestant and Catholic: is the analogical imagination extinct?', *American Sociological Review*, **54**(4), 485–502.
Guiso, L.P., P. Sapienza and L. Zingales (2003), 'People's opium? Religion and economic attitudes', *Journal of Monetary Economics*, **50**(1), 225–82.
Harris, R.J. and E.W. Mills (1985), 'Religion, values and attitudes toward abortion', *Journal for the Scientific Study of Religion*, **24**(2), 137–54.
Hauk, E. and M. Saez-Marti (2002), 'On the cultural transmission of corruption', *Journal of Economic Theory*, **107**, 311–35.
Hellsten, S. and G. Larbi (2006), 'Public good or private good? The paradox of public and private ethics in the context of development', *Public Administration and Development*, **26**(2), 135–45.
Hirschi, T. and R. Stark (1969), 'Hellfire and delinquency', *Social Problems*, **17**(2), 202–13.
Kliesen, K.L. and F.A. Schmid (2004), 'Fear of hell might fire up the economy', *The Regional Economist*, July, available at http://stlouisfed.org/publications/re/articles/?id=383; accessed 18 July 2012.
Kohlberg, L. (1976), 'Moral stages and moralization: the cognitive developmental approach', in T. Lickona (ed.), *Moral Development and Behavior: Theory, Research and Social Issues*, New York: Rinehart and Winston, pp. 31–53.
Kohlberg, L. (1981), *Essays on Moral Development, Vol. 1: The Philosophy of Moral Development*, San Francisco, Harper and Row.
Kohlberg, L. (1984), *The Psychology of Moral Development: The Nature and Validity of Moral Stages* (Essays on Moral Development, Volume 2), San Francisco: Harper and Row.
La Porta, R., A. Lopez-de-Silanes, A. Shleifer and R. Vishny (1997), 'Trust in large organizations', *American Economic Review*, **87**(2), 333–8.
Lawrence, J.A. (1979), 'The component procedure of moral judgment making', *Dissertation Abstracts International*, **40**(896B).
Lenski, G. (1961), *The Religious Factor*, New York: Doubleday and Co., Inc.
Luxmoore, J. (1999), 'Churches urged to help fight global corruption', *Catholic New Times*, **23**(2), 12–13.
Marquette, H. (2003), *Corruption, Politics and Development: The Role of the World Bank*, Basingstoke: Palgrave.
Marquette, H. (2010), 'Whither morality? "Finding God" in the fight against corruption', Birmingham: Religions and Development Working Paper No. 41, available at http://www.religionsanddevelopment.org/index.php?section=1; accessed 18 July 2012.
Marquette, H. (2012), '"Finding God" or "moral disengagement" in the fight against corruption in developing countries? Evidence from India and Nigeria', *Public Administration and Development*, **32**(1), 11–26.
Marquette, H., R. Flanary, S. Rao and D. Morris (2011), 'Supporting anti-corruption reform in partner countries: concepts, tools and areas for action', EuropeAid Concept Note No. 2, October, available at: http://capacity4dev.ec.europa.eu/t-and-m-series/document/concept-paper-nr-2-supporting-anti-corruption-reform-partner-countries-concepts-tools-and-a; accessed 18 July 2012.
Middleton, R. and S. Putney (1962), 'Religion, normative standards, and behavior', *Sociometry*, **25**(2), 141–52.
Migdal, J. (2001), *State in Society: Studying How States and Societies Transform and Constitute One Another*, Cambridge: Cambridge University Press.
Nisan, M. (1984), 'Social norms and moral judgment', in W. Kurtines and J. Gewirtz (eds), *Morality and Moral Development*, New York: Wiley, pp. 208–24.

Norris, P. and R. Inglehart (2004), *Sacred and Secular: Religion and Politics Worldwide*, Cambridge: Cambridge University Press.

North, C. and C. Gwin (2004), 'Religion's role in the rule of law', paper presented to the Society for the Scientific Study of Religion/Association for the Study of Religion, *Economics and Culture*, Kansas City, Missouri, October.

Nussbaum, D. (2006), 'Money versus morality: is corruption just a matter of misaligned incentives?', London: London School of Economics, STICERD and DESTIN Public Lecture, 18 October.

Paldam, M. (2001), 'Corruption and religion: adding to the economic model', *Kyklos*, **54**(2–3), 383–414.

Parsons, T. (1937), *The Structure of Social Action*, New York: McGraw-Hill.

Parsons, T. (1951), *The Social System*, New York: Macmillan.

Persson, A., B. Rothstein and J. Teorell (2010), 'The failure of anti-corruption policies: a theoretical mischaracterization of the problem', Quality of Government Institute Working Paper 2010:19, available at: http://www.sida.se/PageFiles/39460/Failure%20Anti_Corruption%20policy%20%282%29.pdf; accessed 18 July 2012.

Polzer, T. (2001), 'Corruption: Reconstructing the Bank's Discourse', DESTIN Working Article No. 18, December.

Putnam, R. (1993), *Making Democracy Work: Civic Traditions in Modern Italy*, Princeton, NJ: Princeton University Press.

Reisman, W.M. (1979), *Folded Lies: Bribery, Crusades, and Reforms*, New York: Free Press.

Rest, J.R. (1983), 'Morality', in P. Mussen (ed.), *Manual of Child Psychology*, Volume 3 (4th edition), New York: Wiley, pp. 556–629.

Rokeach, M. (1968), 'Beliefs, attitudes, and values: a theory of organization and change', San Francisco: Jossey-Bass.

Sapp, G.L. and L. Jones (1986), 'Religious orientation and moral judgment', *Journal for the Scientific Study of Religion*, **25**(2), 208–14.

Schaffer, B. (1984), 'Towards responsibility: Public policy in concept and practice', in E.J. Clay and B. Schaffer (eds), *Room for Manoeuvre: An Exploration of Public Policy in Agriculture and Rural Development*, London: Heinemann Educational Books, pp. 142–90.

Scheepers, P. and F. Van Der Silk (1998), 'Religion and attitudes on moral issues: effects of individual, spouse and parental characteristics', *Journal for the Scientific Study of Religion*, **37**(4), 678–96.

Smith, D.J. (2007), *A culture of corruption: everyday deception and popular discontent in Nigeria*, Princeton, NJ: Princeton University Press.

Sperber, D. (1975), *Rethinking symbolism*, Cambridge: Cambridge University Press.

Stark, R. (1996), 'Religion as context: hellfire and delinquency one more time', *Sociology of Religion*, **57**(2), 163–73.

Sutherland, E.H. and D.R. Cressey (1978), *Criminology* (10th edition), Philadelphia: Lippincott.

Ter Voert, M., A. Felling et al. (1994), 'The effect of religion on self-interest morality', *Review of Religious Research*, **35**(4), 302–23.

Thoma, S.J., J.R. Rest and M.L. Davison (1991), 'Describing and testing a moderator of the moral judgment and action relationship', *Journal of Personality and Social Psychology*, **61**(4), 659–69.

Tittle, C.R. and M.R. Welch (1983), 'Religiosity and deviances: toward a contingency theory of constraining effects', *Social Forces*, **61**(3), 653–82.

Treisman, D. (2000), 'The causes of corruption: a cross-national study', *Journal of Public Economics*, **76**(3), 399–457.

Turiel, E. (1983), 'Domains and categories in social-cognitive development', in W. Overton (ed.), *The Relationship Between Social and Cognitive Development*, Hillsdale, NJ: Erlbaum, pp. 69–106.

Warren, M. (2001), 'Social capital and corruption', paper presented at the EURESCO Conference on 'Social Capital', 15–20 September, University of Exeter.

White, R.H. (1968), 'Toward a theory of religious influence', *The Pacific Sociological Review*, **11**(1), 23–8.

Wulff, D.M. (1991), *Psychology of Religion: Classic and Contemporary Views*, New York: Wiley.

15 Islamic education: historical evolution and attempts at reform

Masooda Bano

INTRODUCTION

Madrasas (Islamic schools) have become a focus of global attention since 9/11. The system of Islamic education has, in view of some, become synonymous with *jihad* and Islamic militancy. Madrasas are argued to indoctrinate children from poor families with radical ideals. However, what does the madrasa education really involve? And, why have the attempts by colonial and post-colonial ruling elites to reform Islamic education failed? Madrasas are one of the oldest institutions of learning in the Islamic world. While schools for Quranic learning, normally referred to as *muktabs*, and mosque-based study circles started in Prophet Muhammad's time, the evolution of these Quranic schools into madrasas designed to interpret and understand the Quranic and other religious texts started in the eleventh century in Iran (Hefner and Zaman, 2007). The tradition spread to Baghdad in 1063, Damascus in the 1090s, Cairo in the 1170s, and by the thirteenth century had also spread to India, where the madrasa system consolidated under the Mughal Empire (ibid.). Unlike the mosques, the madrasa system allowed for the residence of teachers and students and provided a library. Normally drawing on permanent sources of income, such as a *waqf* (religious endowment) property, the madrasa provided for salaries of the faculty and scholarships for students. The main objective of madrasas was to prepare scholars of Islam with a special emphasis on the teaching of *fiqh* (Islamic jurisprudence).

These madrasas taught both transmitted subjects (those reliant on the religious texts) as well as the rationalist subjects (those focusing on logic) (Robinson, 2007). The transmitted subjects included Quranic recitation, Arabic grammar, Quranic interpretation, jurisprudence, the sources of law and didactic theology, while maths, logic and science featured prominently within the rationalist subjects. Under the Muslim empires such as Mamluks and Seljuqs in the Middle East and Mughals in South Asia, madrasas trained officials for the court and for the judiciary. Further, Muslim rulers patronized the madrasas to win moral legitimacy in the eyes of the public. Thus, in most contexts, *'ulama* (Islamic scholars) in the madrasas worked out a cooperative relationship with the state to provide both spiritual and professional education and train officials to run affairs of the state.

This close collaboration between the state and the madrasas across the Middle East and South Asia, however, faced a serious setback with the ascendancy of the European system of education, science and technology in the eighteenth and nineteenth centuries (Robinson, 2007). As the Ottoman Empire started to crumble in late eighteenth century and many Muslim countries came under Western colonial rule, madrasa education came to be seen as irrelevant to the needs of modern society (Hefner and Zaman, 2007). In India, for instance, with the displacement of the Mughal Empire by British colonial rule, the official sources of support to madrasas dwindled. The British withdrew the support extended by the Mughal rulers to the Muslim institutions through the policy of *Madad-i-Ma'ash*, a policy of allocating revenue-free lands to ensure income for the working of the madrasas (Nizami, 1983). More importantly, due to the changes in the administration and economy introduced by the colonial rulers, madrasa education lost its economic relevance.

The result was that whereas earlier Muslim education had relevance to both religious and secular needs, gradually it became increasingly otherworldly. Though Middle Eastern states such as Egypt and Syria had limited exposure to colonial rule as compared to the Indian subcontinent, even in these societies Islamic educational institutions got sidelined in favour of Western education (Hefner and Zaman, 2007). Even in Turkey, which was never formally colonialized, the recognition by the Ottoman rulers of their declining powers vis-à-vis the European states, especially their failure to compete with the latter's advances in military technology and warfare, by the late nineteenth century had resulted in attempts aimed at replicating the Western educational institutions and initiating reforms within the madrasa system. The process was dramatically accelerated under Kemal Ataturk, who in his bid to reform and modernize the Turkish state and society, ordered closure of madrasas in Turkey: 439 madrasas and Quranic schools were closed in 1924 and only eight were allowed to remain open – a measure whose severity could not be matched by the states in any other Muslim majority country (Agai, 2007).

While colonial rule led to displacement of madrasas from mainstream society and economy in the Muslim world, the onset of colonial rule also brought changes within the internal working of the madrasas. Some Muslims, who attended modern educational institutions, transferred principles of these Western institutional models to religious education. The concept of having formal classes and a fixed syllabus that was introduced in the Islamic school, Dar-ul Uloom Deoband (a madrasa tradition that evolved in India under British rule and that today has the largest madrasa network in South Asia) as opposed to the informal teaching practices pursued in earlier madrasas, was itself a result of the exposure of *'ulama* of this madrasa to Western educational institutions established under the colonial rule (Metcalf, 1982).

In order to compete and survive in this changed environment, the madrasas were required to dramatically reorganize themselves. In Turkey, for instance, Ataturk did order closure of most madrasas but the state move did not result in entirely suppressing the popular demand for Islamic learning and *'ulama*'s determination to respond to that. A tradition of informal study circles started and formalized in the years following the forced closure of the established madrasas, eventually compelling the state to take over the responsibility of providing Islamic education in an attempt to regulate it (Agai, 2007).

This very brief overview of the changes in the working of madrasas in the Middle East and the South Asia in response to exposure to Western educational institutions and the different degree of experience of colonial rule shows that the rules established by the state institutions and the socioeconomic and political incentives have played a key role in shaping the nature of activities of the madrasas. Before looking at the different responses to state-led attempts at madrasa reform in the two regions, it might be worthwhile to look in detail at the evolution of a madrasa system in one context to better understand its traditional features and teaching practices.

MADRASA EDUCATION SYSTEM IN SOUTH ASIA

The madrasa system evolved in South Asia from the twelfth century. Its emergence across the subcontinent was a response to two developments: conversion to Islam through the preaching of the Sufis who had started migrating to India as early as the eighth century, and the establishment of Muslim rule in India beginning in the twelfth century. Prominent madrasas were already in place by the early thirteenth century: Mu'izzi Madrasa in Delhi established in 1211, Madrasa Faerozia established by Nasir Ahmad Kabacha in 1224 in Uch and Madrasa Nasiria in Delhi established by Sultan Altutmush are some of the prominent madrasas from earlier period (Ali, 1963). With the consolidation of Muslim rule in South Asia, the madrasa system came to exercise great influence in shaping the public interpretation of Islam. The close link between development in the madrasas and the changes in public understanding of Islam is a much noted fact in scholarship on Islamic studies, causing scholars to argue that it was the *'ulama* within the madrasas 'that made men Muslim and their communities Islamic' (Robinson, 2000, p. 178). At the individual level they defined what it was to be a good Muslim; at the official level they supported the Muslim rulers in establishing a system of judiciary and administration based on Islamic principles. The *'ulama* thus staffed the various levels of the judiciary, oversaw the whole charitable establishment of the empire, acted as prayer leaders at town mosques, and became most influential among the courtiers (Metcalf, 1982). In addition, they educated the entire nobility. Much of this authority extended beyond the period of Muslim rule; even during the colonial period, the *'ulama* exercised what Metcalf (1982) dubs the 'concentric circles of influence', whereby their authority trickled through multiple levels, including links with students and disciples, occasional solicitation of judicial decisions, public attendance at their sermons, writing and publication of religious literature, and public preaching and debate. As Zaman (1999, p. 302) argues, 'The decline of the madrasa is a familiar theme in modern Muslim analyses of the decline of Islam'. The *'ulama* have thus been viewed as critical players in the interpretation of Islam in South Asia.

It is, however, important to acknowledge here that, though the *'ulama* have traditionally exercised maximum authority in interpreting the religious texts, this authority has not been entirely uncontested. The power to shape the actions of Muslims in South Asia has also been shared by the Sufis, who established mystical Sufi orders. The *'ulama* and the Sufis share a common interest in making believers adhere to Islamic principles in their day-to-day practices. However, they differ on many counts, the most significant of which is their approach towards worldly concerns. The Sufis are primarily concerned with the cleansing of the inner self, and seek to distance themselves from the formal sphere of state; the *'ulama*, on the other hand, actively engaged with the Muslim courts. Many of the madrasas in South Asia were actually established by the Muslim rulers to meet the official and stately needs of the time and thus the madrasas were often based in the main cities. The Sufis, on the other hand, because of the emphasis on spiritual dimensions preferred to stay away from the basis of power. They therefore based themselves in the rural areas, often deep in the interior of the country (Nizami, 1983); even when forming their hospices in the cities they preferred to build them at the city's boundaries.

This has led to differences in the basis of authority of the two groups: the *'ulama* draw their authority mainly through demonstrating knowledge of the religious texts;

the Sufi, on the other hand, often draw followers on the basis of personal charisma.[1] Thus, though it is important not to over-stress the differences between the two groups and to recognize that the two did not operate in complete isolation – there were always strong intellectual and spiritual bonds between the Sufis and the *'ulama* in South Asia. For example, the prominent Delhi madrasa of Shah Waliullah was mainly connected to Naqsh Bandi Sufi order, and the Farangi Mahall, the other prominent madrasa, had affiliation with the Chishti and Qadiri Sufi orders (Nizami, 1983) – the difference in the extent of their engagement with the state and the formal public sphere did have an impact on their working. The *'ulama*'s direct engagement with the Muslim courts was one of the important factors consolidating their authority over interpretation of the Islamic texts. The influence of the *'ulama* in shaping public interpretation of Islam, even in present-day South Asia, is visible in government attempts to modernize the madrasas across Bangladesh, India and Pakistan in the hope of this leading to an interpretation of popular Islam more in line with the demands of modernity (Malik, 1997). The policy reports that hold *'ulama* within the madrasas responsible for sustaining the recruitment of young madrasa students for Islamic *jihad* also seem to attribute similar authority to the *'ulama* to shape popular understanding of Islam. There is thus a strong argument for studying the changes in public interpretation of Islam through a focus on changes in madrasas in South Asia.

It might also be worth noting that the twentieth century also saw the rise of another set of contenders to the authority of the *'ulama*, namely, the modern Islamic scholars, trained in Western-style colleges and universities rather than in the madrasas. A prominent example from this group is Jamaat-i-Islami, a prominent Islamic movement in South Asia, whose founder, Maulana Maududi, was not trained in a madrasa. While such scholars did win adherents from the Muslim classes, they did not displace the power of the *'ulama* or the role of the madrasas from the Muslim societies. Rather, Jamaat-i-Islami came to run its own madrasas, and currently runs one of the state-recognized madrasa boards in Pakistan.

The other point that needs to be clarified at the outset about the conceptualization of madrasas is the controversies about perceiving madrasas to be formal organizational structures. There is evidence that, for a long time, the madrasa system had no formal organizational structure, that is, the teaching was not organized by classes and it did not offer a sequential curriculum, or formal degree certificates (Metcalf, 2002), though these formal features are an integral part of the madrasa network in present-day South Asia. While the causes of this shift in themselves make an interesting subject of analysis, it is important to make clear that not having a fixed curriculum or formal class structure does not imply that the madrasas were not formally recognizable organizations in the earlier period. Many of the madrasas from the very earlier period were established by Muslim rulers with the clear purpose of imparting certain basic core teachings to the future officials of the Muslim courts (Ali, 1963). These madrasas had many paid teachers and many students. Within this formal structure the *'ulama* within the madrasas covered certain core texts, though the teaching was highly personalized and revolved around the teacher (Nizami, 1983). Especially in the madrasas established around specific religious families, there was often no attendance register, no degree-awarding system, and no fixed curriculum. The respect accorded to an *'alim* (Islamic scholar) was based not on a degree certificate or on the name of the madrasa in which he studied but on the recognition of being the student of a well-known *'alim*. Students flocked around eminent scholars known for their expertise in teaching certain subjects or core books. On completion of these books, students were issued with an *ijaza* (certificate) stating the subject studied and the name of the teacher who had taught them. Thus, while the nature of teaching in madrasas did remain relatively informal, the formal organizational structure of the madrasa education system emerged in South Asia from the twelfth century as soon as the Muslim invaders started to establish their hold in the area.

This informality in actual structure and methods of teaching remained the hallmark of the madrasa education system in South Asia till the rise of Dar-ul-Uloom Deoband in 1866; this was to become the most influential madrasa during the twentieth century.[2] While a movement towards formation of a consolidated standard curriculum for madrasas began under the *'ulama* of Farangi Mahall (a prestigious madrasa of the sixteenth and seventeenth centuries), it was only in Dar-ul-Uloom Deoband that the system of a set curriculum, formal classes, a set examination system and a formal degree-awarding system was introduced (Metcalf, 2002). In terms of teaching content, however, the *'ulama* of Dar-ul-Uloom drew heavily upon scholarship developed within the Farangi Mahall and Madrasa-i-Rahimia, another prestigious madrasa of the seventeenth and eighteenth centuries. The reason for this easy transfer of knowledge from one madrasa to another is that, while the innumerable madrasas dotting the Indian landscape were not under any central control and not even the most prominent madrasas from the early period had survived in their individual capacity till the twentieth century, the Islamic scholarship produced in the prominent madrasas of each period was systematically transmitted to the next generation through the very deep but informal bonds of a teacher–student relationship.[3] Most pupils considered it their moral obligation to follow in the path of their teachers and advance their teachings:[4] scholarship produced within influential madrasas of the time was thus successfully transmitted to the next generation, even when the madrasa itself faced decline.[5]

That the concerns about present-day madrasas' disengagement from modern intellectual inquiry are not attributable to the core principles of Islam whereby it restricted free thought is clear from a number of factors, most importantly in the balance of the curriculum taught in the leading madrasas of the seventeenth and eighteenth centuries. Tracing the evolution of madrasas in South Asia makes it clear that the madrasas, as well as the institution of Islam, has not trodden a linear path. Rather there have been major shifts in the working of madrasas, as well as in the interpretations that the *'ulama* within the madrasas have accorded to the Islamic texts. The heavy focus on the teaching of religious subjects in the traditional madrasas in South Asia (minus the state-supported Aliya madrasas in Bangladesh and Karzai madrasa in West Bengal) does not find support in much of the history of madrasa teaching in South Asia. Leading madrasas placed prime emphasis on the teaching of theology but, in addition, covered all the critical subjects of the time; in particular they shared a similar emphasis on the use of logic. From the very beginning the curriculum in the madrasas in India had two categories of subject: rational subjects (*maqulat*) and transmitted subjects (*manqulat*, reliant exclusively on the religious texts). The former included subjects based on reason, including *mantaq* (logic), *hikmat* (philosophy), *tibb* (medicine), *riyazi* (mathematics), and *hai'at* (astronomy); the latter focused on religious texts like *tafsir* (exegesis), *hadith* (tradition) and *fiqh* (jurisprudence).

The actual balance of rationalist and transmitted subjects taught varied among madrasas, but from early on all madrasas covered both: for instance, a series of madrasas established by Firuz Shah Tughluq (1351–88) during the fourteenth century had medicine, metaphysics, natural sciences and mathematics in the curriculum (Nizami, 1983). Central to Islamic learning was the Quran and the great books, most of which had been written by the end of the eighth century of the Islamic era (Robinson, 2000). Scholars relied on a series of commentaries, super-commentaries, and notes to understand these texts. The sixteenth and seventeenth centuries marked new trends within the madrasa system in South Asia as they opened up to the study of new subjects. Scholarship within the madrasas of South Asia made a major shift towards rationalist subjects in this period. The trigger for this shift was Fadl Allah Shirazi, an Iranian scholar who arrived at the Mughal Emperor Akbar's court in 1583, and became acclaimed for his excellence in rational sciences, such as philosophy, astronomy, geometry, astrology, geomancy, arithmetic, and so on (Robinson, 2000). He was equally learned in Arabic, *hadith*, interpretation of the Quran and rhetoric. Shirazi encouraged the widespread study of the rational subjects within South Asian madrasas, culminating in the rise of Dars-i-Nizami, a formal madrasa curriculum that spread across the South Asian madrasas during the eighteenth century. This period drew the sons of the elite to the leading madrasas, as the madrasas had gradually acquired the status of grooming the elite (Nizami, 1983).

The seventeenth and eighteenth centuries were periods of superior rationalist scholarship within the leading madrasas. For the leading South Asian madrasas, this was a period of constant expansion and innovation within rationalist scholarship. The scholars at Farangi Mahall, which became a major intellectual centre of rationalist inquiry, engaged with European sciences: one translated Newton's *Principia* into Persian. A senior scholar of Farangi Mahall, Mulla Nizam-uddin (died 1748), consolidated the Dars-i-Nizami during this period, providing instruction in grammar, rhetoric, philosophy, logic, scholasticism, *tafsir*, *fiqh*, *hadith* and mathematics. The teaching method also recorded a shift towards argumentation and discussion to encourage the use of reasoning, and it discouraged concentration on textual matters. That, at the time of the British takeover of India, the bigger madrasas of South Asia excelled in education, was noted in the observations of British officers as well as those of Indian scholars:

> They learn through the medium of Arabic and Persian languages, what young men in our colleges learn through those of Greek and Latin – that is grammar, rhetoric and logic. After his seven years of study, the young Muhammedan binds his turban upon a head almost as well filled with the things which appertain to these branches of knowledge as the young man raw from Oxford – he will talk as fluently about Socrates and Aristotle, and Hippocrates and Galen and Avicenna – and what is more to his advantage in India, the languages in which he has learnt what he knows are those which he most requires through life.[6]

After a visit to Farangi Mahall in 1896, Maulana Shibli Nomani, a leading Muslim scholar, declared with a touch of hyperbole: 'this is the very Cambridge of our India' (Robinson, 2001).

While the Farangi Mahall *'ulama* dominated the religious discourse of the time, a noticeable group of *'ulama* had gathered around Shah Wali Ullah (died 1762), an influential Islamic scholar, at Madrasa-i-Rahimia. As opposed to the emphasis on philosophy within Dars-i-Nizami, Shah Wali Ullah's teachings focused more on the traditional subjects revolving around the Quran and *hadith*. This curriculum better suited the students,

Table 15.1 Representation of traditional and rationalist sciences in Madrasa-i-Rahimia and Dars-i-Nizami

Subjects	Madrasa-i-Rahimia No. of books	Dars-i-Nizami No. of books
Exegesis (*tafsir*)	2	2
Hadith (traditions of the Prophet)	3	1
Philosophy (*falsafa*)	1	3
Logic (*mantiq*)	2	11
Scholasticism (*kalam*)	3	3
Rhetoric (*balaghat*)	2	2
Etymology and syntax	2	12
Medicine (*tibb*)	1	
Astronomy and mathematics (*ha'at aur hisab*)	A few small brochures	5
Jurisprudence (*fiqh*)	2	2
Principles of jurisprudence (*usul-i-fiqh*)	2	3
Mysticism	5	

Source: Nizami (1983).

especially those interested purely in religious subjects; it did not completely ignore logic and philosophy but it did emphasize the importance of going back to the 'literal word' (Robinson, 2000).

The different emphasis on rationalist and traditional sciences in the two madrasas can be seen in Table 15.1.

What is ironical is that, under the period of Muslim leadership, it is rationalist scholarship within Farangi Mahall that thrived in the madrasas of South Asia. Here they boasted of vibrant intellectual debate and excellence in rationalist subjects. With the onslaught of colonial rule, which in principle brought with it modern scientific education, the rationalist scholarship led by the *'ulama* of Farangi Mahall started to be superseded by the emphasis on revealed subjects as shown in Shah Wali Ullah's madrasa, manifested in the rise and dramatic expansion of the Dar-ul-Uloom Deoband established in 1866. Colonial rule, however, brought an end to this era of rationalist scholarship within madrasas. Deprived of state support, and having to compete with Western education institutions introduced by the British, the madrasa education system became exclusively focused on study of Islamic texts and inculcating personal piety within the believers.

ATTEMPTS AT REFORM OF MADRASA EDUCATION

In the post-colonial period, the popular demand for Islamic education continued, though the platforms through which that demand was met varied across the Middle Eastern and South Asian states. The leaders in the Muslim countries, following in the footsteps of their colonial predecessors, tried to regulate the working of the madrasas to lead to a renewed interpretation of Islamic text, which could prove more amicable to their modernization agenda than the orthodox conceptions of those principles. However, across the Middle East and South Asia, the state tried to regulate the religious education in different ways. In the Middle East, the state has been more inclined to bring religious education within the domain of state responsibility. In South Asia, on the other hand, the state has been more tolerant of private ownership of madrasas despite making attempts to reform them. The resulting relationships have thus been different.

Accurate data on total numbers of madrasas are difficult to find for any country mainly because even in countries where governments have banned or restricted private madrasas, it has proved impossible to check the emergence of unregistered madrasas, study circles, or Islamic educational movements. As noted above, in Turkey the forced closure of madrasas by the government of Mustapha Kemal Ataturk did not result in complete surrender of popular demand for Islamic education. Neither did the *'ulama* stop themselves from continuing to seek new avenues to impart that education. Informal Islamic study circles, referred to as *cemaats*, replaced the madrasas banned by the Turkish state, with the result that in order to retain control of religious learning, the state was forced to open state-owned schools of Islamic education to train prayer leaders and Islamic scholars (Agai, 2007). Departments of theology were also established in Turkish universities. Later, study of Islam as one of the subjects was also reintroduced in the state curriculum. In addition, the state has been tolerant of an influential educational movement that has grown out of these informal study circles that emerged as one of the responses to state closure of the madrasas. Led by Fethullah Gülen, the movement establishes elite schools for secular education but builds into the teaching a strong Islamic moral code of behaviour based on conservative Islamic discourse (ibid.).

In Egypt the state has also attempted to systematically control the platforms for imparting Islamic education but unlike Turkey here the state tried to take control of the existing institutions of Islamic education rather than replacing them with new ones. In other words, in Egypt, the state from the very beginning attempted to harness the moral authority exercised by the *'ulama* within the public by co-opting them into the state system rather than attempting to eradicate their power (Zeghal, 2007). One reason for this clarity in approach was that the structure of religious authority in Egypt had over time become centralized in one leading institution of Islamic learning, namely Al-Azhar University. Representing a long tradition of independent Islamic scholarship, the *'ulama* of Al-Azhar had acquired a mass public following. To regulate the interpretation of Islamic texts and to ensure that religious authority is not channelled towards forces attempting to pose a political challenge to the secular Egyptian regimes, respective governments opted to gradually bring Al-Azhar within state control rather than forcing it to close.

The state therefore nationalized Al-Azhar in 1961 and gradually established a carefully calculated relationship with the religious authorities. The Sheikh of Al-Azhar was given the rank of a minister in return for ensuring that his *fatwas* (Islamic rulings) do not dramatically compromise state interests (ibid.). However, the university was also allowed a certain level of autonomy to ensure that it retains the religious authority with the public and is not reduced to being viewed as a rubber stamp for legitimizing state orders. The Sheikh of Al-Azhar thus has to constantly play a balancing act to protect the state interests but also to ensure that he does not provide so dramatic an interpretation of a text that he loses all public credibility, which has been in question ever since the forging of alliance between the state and the senior ranks at Al-Azhar (ibid.). The institution to date, however, remains the primary provider of Islamic education in Egypt. In the academic year, 2000–01, 483 981 female students and 836 753 male students attended the Egyptian Azharites institutes (ibid.).

Even in Syria, the state attempted to closely regulate the provision of Islamic education. Religious education is primarily a responsibility of the Ministry of Religious Affairs though a selected number of private Islamic foundations are allowed to impart Islamic education, the most prominent of which is Al-Noor Foundation in Damascus followed by Al-Fateh Islamic Institute.[7] The Syrian state, unlike its counterparts in Egypt and Turkey, has for the most part dealt with these Islamic schools more cautiously. It has neither tried to completely suppress them nor has it tried to borrow their moral authority by trying to actively co-opt them. The Syrian state has tried to regulate the public interpretation of Islam by running its own religious education programmes to train preachers and provide for higher study of theology through its highly influential Ministry of Awqaf. However, it has also allowed a selected number of prominent Islamic scholars to run their own charitable foundations for spreading Islamic education. These foundations have traditionally had a strong student following even from foreign countries such as Turkey, Pakistan, and so on.[8] In the post-9/11 context though, the Syrian government has introduced strict monitoring mechanisms to regulate the presence of foreign students at these foundations.

In Syria the state also therefore established a careful model to closely coordinate with the Islamic foundations to ensure that they are allowed certain space so that the leading *'ulama* do not resort to extreme measures to protest, but at the same time it keeps close watch over the working of these foundations to ensure that their leaders do not pose a threat to their government or the state's modernization agenda. To check any signs of radicalization in Syrian Islamic schools, in recent years the state has worked to establish a unified government-approved curriculum in consultation with the heads of these foundations, removing all books that are viewed to spread sectarian discord. Since the end of 2008, the government also requires that comprehensive, detailed accounts be submitted to a government committee for audit. The government is also trying to gain greater control over school staff by bringing the teachers at these foundations onto the government payroll. The main incentives offered to the leaders of these foundations to accept these reforms is the promise of granting state recognition to the degree certificates issued by their educational institutions.

As opposed to the Middle Eastern context, in South Asia the states have been more tolerant of private ownership of madrasas. Even in the context of South Asia, the estimates of madrasas remain contested due to large number of informal and unregistered madrasas in these countries. The estimates for madrasas across the three countries range from 10000 to 30000 or more (Ahmed, 2005). The governments in all the three countries are currently trying to compile more reliable data in order to better monitor and regulate the madrasas. Recent government estimates record 16000 registered madrasas in Pakistan, with an estimated population of 1.5 million students (Ministry of Education, 2006). Other studies argue that the total number of madrasa students in Pakistan constitutes less than 3 per cent of the total school age population in Pakistan (Andrabi et al., 2005; Cockcroft et al., 2009).

Estimates for India are even less reliable. According to the Centre for the Promotion of Science at the Aligarh Muslim University in India in 1985 there were 2890 madrasas in country. In 2002 the Union Minister for Home Affairs claimed the number stood at 31 857. In 2003, a leading Muslim paper claimed that there were some 125 000 madrasas in India, catering to around 3 million students (Nair, 2009). The Justice Rajindar Sachar Committee, appointed by the prime minister to study the social, educational and economic status of Muslims in the country, however, shows that only 4.3 per cent of Muslim children are studying in madrasas (Sachar, 2006).

Bangladesh has by far seen the most rapid spread of madrasas in South Asia. The number of secondary madrasas in Bangladesh has increased at a phenomenal pace. Today 33 per cent of all secondary-level students and 15 per cent of all post-secondary students enrolled in the state education system are in Aliya (reformed) madrasas (Bano, 2008a).

The state's willingness to allow the private ownership of madrasas should not be interpreted to mean that the state in these countries has not attempted to regulate the madrasas or has not had the aspirations to make them a partner in the modernization process through introduction of secular subjects. In Bangladesh in 1979, the government undertook a scheme to modernize the madrasa education system, whereby secular subjects such as English, Bengali, science and mathematics were to be taught along with religious subjects and languages. Another important aspect of the reform was the replacement of Urdu with Bangla as a medium of instruction in the madrasas. Madrasas engaging with the reforms received government recognition and subsequently qualified for aid money to finance teachers' salaries (ibid.). In India, the main attempt at implementing these reforms was made by the Ministry of Human Resource Development in 1993–94. The focus was on introducing teaching of science, maths, social studies, Hindi and English in order to provide education comparable to the national system of education. The scheme supported appointment of qualified teachers in madrasas to teach secular subjects and assisted with funds for developing book banks and some related material (Nair, 2009).

The outcome of these attempts by the state to make madrasas partners in advancing the state conception of modernity has been different across the three countries. As opposed to India and Pakistan, a much larger proportion of madrasas in Bangladesh accepted the reform programme: a clear Aliya and Qaumi (unreformed) madrasa system has evolved in the country (ibid.). In India, acceptance of the state programme has been more restricted and has varied across the states. Today, seven states (Assam, Bihar, Madhya Pradesh, Orissa, Rajasthan, Uttar Pradesh and West Bengal) have set up state-sponsored madrasa education boards and some states, such as West Bengal, have been able to convince leaders of a noticeable number of madrasas to join the reform programme: up to 1977 there were 238 official madrasas in West Bengal and since then the number of the registered madrasas has doubled (Nair, 2009). Today there are 500 madrasas registered with the West Bengal Madrasa Board as opposed to 550 with the Karzai (traditional) Madrasa Board (ibid.). In Pakistan, on the other hand, the reforms have had least acceptance within the madrasas: as late as 2008, only 250 out of the 16 000 registered madrasas had entered the government reform programme introduced in 2001 (Bano, 2007b). The difference is revealing because the predominant number of madrasas across the three countries belong to the Deoband school of thought. This shows that the differing ability of the state to make madrasas cooperate in the state modernization agenda is not entirely a product of madrasa ideology but has strong bearing on the socioeconomic context in which the negotiations for these partnership arrangements are taking place.

The six country experiences thus can be grouped into three types of relationships: co-optation (Bangladesh and Egypt), collaboration (Syria and India) and confrontation (Pakistan and Turkey). The reason for drawing these distinctions is that they reflect different levels of autonomy enjoyed by the madrasas and therefore reflect the different natures of relationships that can emerge between the two sides. In Bangladesh the reformed madrasas are today attempting to produce students who can compete with the children of secular schools rather than aiming to take up religious positions. The graduates of these reformed madrasas don't attempt to claim religious authority, which remains in the hands of the unreformed traditional madrasas (Bano, 2008a). Given that the state has been able to establish a very large number of reformed madrasas, where the leaders of these madrasas are willing to work within the state-developed framework, the Bangladesh model can be classified as a co-optation model as in the case of Al-Azhar in Egypt, where the state ideology has become more dominant in shaping the relationship.

The same holds true in the case of reformed madrasas in West Bengal (Nair, 2009). However, in India as a whole the state has not been able to ensure this large-scale reform of madrasas. The Indian model thus sits closer to the Syrian model where the state and the religious scholars are keen to ensure that both sides stay within clearly defined limits to prevent any hostility. Madrasas in India and Islamic foundations in Syria work strictly within their approved religious education mandate, staying clear of politics so that the state gets no excuse to tighten its regulatory framework (ibid.). This model is thus that of coordination where both sides know of their underlying differences in ideological positions and engage only to the point to ensure that they can maintain smooth coexistence.

In Pakistan and Turkey, the relationship between the state and madrasas has, on the other hand, been marked with confrontation. In Pakistan, the main reason for that has been the lack of trust between the two sides. Since 9/11, the state has tried to regulate the madrasas and has launched a programme to introduce secular subjects in madrasa curriculum. The programme has, however, failed to win cooperation of madrasa leaders because of the state's close association with the US 'war on terror'. The reform programme was even funded by the US government, further strengthening the *'ulama*'s suspicions about the state intent. Thus, the relationship between the two sides is that of confrontation. The Turkish experience was also marked with a highly confrontational approach under the regime of Ataturk, who closed all madrasas with a few exceptions. However, the Turkish experience at this point in time is better classified as that of coordination. Now the state has a well-established state-owned Islamic education system and at the same time allows for running of parallel Islamic education movements as represented in the emergence of Fethullah Gülen's movement. Thus, the Turkish experience also shows that relationships are dynamic and that their complexity is better understood by studying them over a period of time rather than looking at them at one point in time.

The above categories of relationships emerge due to different characteristics of the state as well as the madrasas in the six countries. The question is, however, is it possible to identify certain underlying factors that play a key role in shaping the nature of relationship between the state and madrasas?

FACTORS SHAPING THE STATE–MADRASA RELATIONSHIP

The responses of the madrasas to state-led attempts at reform in the two regions show the importance of three factors: financial incentives, trust of the state and embeddedness in the community.

Financial Incentives Matter

The state–madrasa engagement across the six countries shows that the state's willingness to make a financial commitment to support the proposed intervention is critical for winning the cooperation of the madrasas. The countries where the state has had relative success in establishing a relationship with the madrasas, such as in Bangladesh, the state of West Bengal in India, Egypt, Turkey, or Syria, are the ones where the state either made serious financial investments in establishing a state-owned Islamic education programme or provided strong incentives to the leaders of the madrasas to introduce secular subjects in the madrasa curriculum. In Bangladesh and West Bengal, the state covers all the salaries of the teachers whether teaching religious or secular subjects. In Pakistan and India (at the national government level), one major reason that the state has failed to make the programme appeal to the madrasa leadership is its unwillingness to make a serious financial commitment to the programme. The states in both only offered to cover salaries of the secular subject teachers, leaving the main financial burden intact on the madrasa leadership. Further, it offered lower salaries for these teachers than offered to those in secular schools. The incentives were thus not compelling enough for the madrasa leadership to engage with the state, especially given that the relationship in both these contexts also suffered from an inherent trust deficit.

Trust of the State

In Pakistan and India, apart from the fact that the state has offered weak incentives, the reason madrasas have refused to adopt reforms is that the context in which the incentives were being offered inherently suffered from a trust deficit. In Pakistan in the post-9/11 context where the government had become an active ally of the US in the 'war on terror', the *'ulama* remained very suspicious of the reform programme. In India, on the other hand, because they represented a minority, the *'ulama* have always been inherently suspicious of any state attempts to engage with the madrasas (Nair, 2009). This has made the leading madrasas resistant to accepting state funding. The primary requisite for establishing this trust is indeed a shared ideological vision. However, trust can also be evolved even among parties with competing ideologies if an interactive process is evolved. It is because of this that despite shared ideological resistance to state-led madrasa reforms by the *'ulama* in most Muslim societies, the state has been successful in advancing the integrated agenda in some contexts, such as seen in the nature of engagement between the Sheikh of Al-Azhar and the Egyptian state.

Embeddedness in the Community

Finally, the existence of the madrasa system and demand for Islamic education despite efforts by the state to regulate it across the six countries verifies the popular assumption that madrasas are deeply embedded in the communities. Even in Turkey, despite use of force and despite evolution of a well-respected and well-funded state supported system of Islamic education, the tradition of informal study circles has continued and has led to establishment of a movement of Islamic education, which not only operates within Turkey but also now runs 250 educational institutions internationally (Agai, 2007). This deep-rooted support for Islamic education shows the need to take religion seriously in understanding development processes.

More specifically, the research also shows that madrasas sacrifice their popular following if they become too close to the state and are seen to have compromised on their core principles. This is the challenge faced by the reformed madrasas in Bangladesh and West Bengal (Bano, 2008a; Nair, 2009). They have adjusted so completely with the state demands that they have in the process lost their public legitimacy – a challenge also partially faced by *'ulama* of Al-Azhar (Zeghal, 2007).

CONCLUSION

A systematic assessment of the factors shaping the reform agenda and responses of the *'ulama* requires a much closer examination of the state and madrasa engagement in the two regions. However, what this chapter has attempted to establish is that madrasas also respond to incentives and can end up forging different types of relationships with the state, ranging from cooperation to outright resistance. Strong financial incentives and mutual trust are two critical factors in ensuring smooth cooperation between the two sides. Trust is most easily established if the two sides share an ideological worldview but it can also be cultivated if the state is willing to engage in a consultative process.

Finally, the chapter also argues that making madrasas accept reforms or co-opting them by offering very strong financial incentives where they lose their core values is counterproductive. Madrasas that agree to record too dramatic a shift away from the established principles of the faith they represent, such as demonstrated by the reformed madrasas in Bangladesh and West Bengal, lose their moral authority (Bano, 2008a). Such madrasas lose popular following, making the community shift its religious allegiance to another religious-based organization.

NOTES

1. For a good review of the differences between the nature of authority exercised by the *'ulama* and the Sufi saints, see Kraemer and Schmidtke (2006).
2. In Pakistan, out of a total of 16000 registered madrasas, 10000 belong to the Deobandi school of thought; in Bangladesh all Qaumi (unreformed) madrasas, estimated to be around 9000 are Deobandi; the same is the case for India, which hosts the parent Deobandi madrasa. Since 9/11, Deobandi madrasas have attained international notoriety for promoting orthodox Islam since most Taliban leaders were trained in Deobandi madrasas in Pakistan.
3. The bigger madrasas generally had a large number of smaller madrasas under their direct influence in the neighbouring *qasbats* (small towns) and towns, which extended their influence beyond the big cities (Nizami, 1983).
4. Shaikh Nizamuddin Auliya, the famous thirteenth-century Sufi and scholar, even quoted a *hadith* (practice of the Prophet Muhammad), which was not found in standard collections, on the authority of his teacher – thereby revealing his trust in the knowledge of his teacher (Nizami, 1983).

5. Madrasas could decline within one or two generations or even after nurturing religious scholarship for centuries either due to loss of calibre of *'ulama* with successive generations or because of the changing fortunes of the Muslim rulers who patronized them.
6. Observations of a British colonial officer noted in Nizami (1983).
7. http://www.abunour.net/?lan=4; accessed 19 July 2012.
8. Interviews with officials in Al-Fatah Institute and Abu-Noor Foundation Damascus, 2010.

REFERENCES

Agai, B. (2007), 'Islam and education in secular Turkey: state policies and the emergence of Fethullah Gulen Group', in R.W. Hefner and M.Q. Zaman (eds), *Schooling Islam: The Culture and Politics of Modern Muslim Education*, Princeton, Princeton University Press.

Ahmed, S. (2005), 'Testimony of Samina Ahmed to US Senate Foreign Relations Committee: combating terrorism through education – the Near East & South Asian experience', Washington, DC, 19 April 2005, available at: http://www.crisisgroup.org/en/publication-type/speeches/2005/testimony-of-samina-ahmed-to-us-senate-foreign-relations-committee.aspx; accessed 19 July 2012.

Ali, N. (1963), Musalaman-i-Hind-ki Tareekha Ta'leem. Karachi: Suleman Academy.

Andrabi, T., J. Das, A.J. Khawaja and T. Zajonc, 'Religious school enrollment in Pakistan: a look at the data', World Bank Working Paper Series No. 3521, The World Bank.

Bano, M. (2007b), 'Contesting ideologies and struggle for authority: state–madrasa relationship in Pakistan', WP No. 14, DFID Religions and Development Research Consortium, University of Birmingham.

Bano, M. (2008a), 'Allowing for diversity: state–madrasa relationship in Bangladesh', WP No. 13, DFID Religions and Development Research Consortium, University of Birmingham.

Cockcroft, A. et al. (2009), 'Challenging the myths about madaris in Pakistan: a national household survey of enrolment and reasons for religious schools', *International Journal of Educational Development*, **29**(4), 342–9.

Hefner, R. and M.Q. Zaman (eds) (2007), *Schooling Islam: The Culture and Politics of Modern Muslim Education*, Princeton: Princeton University Press.

Kramer, G. and Schmidtke, S. (2006), 'Introduction', in G. Kramer and S. Schmidtke (eds), *Speaking for Islam*, Leiden: Brill.

Malik, J. (1997), 'Dynamics among traditional religious scholars and their institutions in contemporary south Asia', *The Muslim World*, **LXXXVII87**(3–4), 199–220.

Metcalf, B. (1982), *Islamic Revival in British India: Deoband, 1860–1900*, Princeton: Princeton University Press.

Metcalf, B. (2002), '"Traditionalist" Islamic activism: Deoband, Tablighis, and Talibs', Leiden: International Institute for the Study of Islam in the Muslim World.

Ministry of Education (MOE) (2006), *National Education Census*, Government of Pakistan, Islamabad: Academy of Educational Planning and Management.

Nair, P. (2009), 'The state and madrasas in India', Working Paper No.15, DFID Religion and Development Project, University of Birmingham.

Nizami, F. (1983), 'Madrasahs, scholars, saints: Muslim response to the British presence in Delhi and Upper Doab 1803–1857', unpublished DPhil dissertation, University of Oxford.

Robinson, F. (2000), *Islam and Muslim History in South Asia*, New Delhi: Oxford University Press.

Robinson, F. (2001), 'Islam and the West: clash of civilisations?', *Asian Affairs*, **33**(3), 307–20.

Robinson, F. (2007), *Islam, South Asia, and the West*, New Delhi: Oxford University Press.

Sachar, R. (2006), *Prime Minister's High Level Committee on Social, Economic and Educational Status of the Muslim Community of India*, Delhi: Govt. of India.

Zaman, Q. (1999), 'Religious Education and Rhetoric of Reform: The Madrasa in British India and Pakistan', *Comparative Studies in Society and History*, **41**(2), 294–323.

Zeghal, M. (2007), 'The "recentering" of religious knowledge and discourse: the case of Al-Azhar in twentieth-century Egypt', in R.W. Hefner and M.Q. Zaman (eds), *Schooling Islam: The Culture and Politics of Modern Muslim Education*, Princeton: Princeton University Press.

16 Religion, conflict and peacebuilding in development

Shawn Teresa Flanigan

INTRODUCTION

A considerable amount of development work takes place in contexts of conflict, both current or past, often with the goal of facilitating recovery from the devastating effects of war. In these settings religion can prove to be a problematic source of tension and a criterion for exclusion, as well as a tool for promoting peace and service. Referred to by Little and Appleby (2004) as 'the ambivalence of the sacred' (p. 2), religion has the ability to stimulate militancy on behalf of the other, as well as militancy aimed against the other. In other words, religion may promote intolerance and hatred, but also may encourage tolerance, non-violence and a readiness to appreciate and respect difference (Little and Appleby, 2004). As Coward and Smith (2004) note, 'Whether upholding universal human rights or denying them to "heretics" or "infidels", religious actors, of course, always believe that they are doing God's will and thus serving the common good of humanity, properly understood' (p. 2).

This chapter gives a broad overview of a variety of roles religious actors may play in conflict and peacebuilding. I will begin by briefly discussing the role of religion in sowing or intensifying conflict, as well as how faith promotes peace in a variety of world religions. I will then examine various roles religious actors may play in the peacebuilding context, followed by a discussion of the ways religious identity can create conflict in the practice of service provision by organizations engaged in development work.

RELIGIOUS ROOTS OF CONFLICT AND PEACE

As Little and Appleby (2004) note, 'the genius of religiously inspired social welfare and peacemaking activism is rooted in the same zeal for holiness powering the holy wars and religiopolitical crusades' (p. 2). The ideologies of the world's major religions advocate principles of peace and non-violence, but historically religious teachings have also been influential contributors to intolerance, discrimination, and violence (Swearer, 2010).

As early as Weber (1963) and Durkheim ([1912] 1954), sociologists studying religion have recognized the role religious belief plays in encouraging certain kinds of human behavior and giving rise to communal activity; faith and group loyalty are often motivators for altruistic behavior (Simon, 1993). Just as religious identity and beliefs are often an incentive for charity and altruism in general, research has shown that faith plays an important role in motivating the employees and volunteers of faith-based non-profit service providers. As Nichols (1988) noted in his examination of non-profits providing humanitarian relief, 'it was religious motivation that inspired relief workers to travel halfway around the world and serve their fellow human beings' (p. 234).

However, religion has also served as a rationale for violence in all major religious traditions (Treverton et al., 2005). Like the religious motivation for charity and service provision, the religious underpinnings of violence and the growth of religious terrorism have been discussed by a number of scholars (Hoffman, 1998; Stern, 1999; Cronin, 2002; Juergensmeyer, 2003). Juergensmeyer (2003) notes that religion often provides the motivation, justification, organization, and worldview that allow for public acts of violence. In fact, religious ideology may indeed make violence more severe; some scholars argue that terrorist organizations with religious ideology are more lethal than other terrorist organizations (Hoffman, 1998; Asal and Rethemeyer, 2008). As Hoffman (1998, p. 26) notes:

> For the religious terrorist, violence is a sacramental act or divine duty, executed in direct response to some theological demand or imperative and justified by scripture. Religion therefore functions as a legitimizing force, specifically sanctioning wide-scale violence against an almost open-ended category of opponents (i.e., all peoples who are not members of the religious terrorists' religion or cult).

As scholars at the RAND Corporation note:

> Increasingly, religion is both an identifiable source of violence around the world and simultaneously so deeply interwoven into other sources of violence – including economic, ideological, territorial, and ethnic sources – that it is difficult to isolate. While certainly not a new phenomenon, religiously motivated violence has become a pervasive element of modern conflicts. (Treverton et al., 2005, p. 1)

Given the important role that religion plays in both conflict and altruism, and given the prevalence of organizations conducting development work in contexts of conflict, there is little doubt that an understanding of the role of religion in violence and peacebuilding is important for development scholars and practitioners. It is beyond the scope of this chapter to discuss the numerous theological underpinnings for violence and peacebuilding in the world's major religious traditions, though such a discussion undoubtedly would be interesting. Rather, this chapter focuses on how religion can serve as both a tool and a barrier for individuals and organizations working 'on the ground' in contexts of conflict, exploring the roles that religious actors can play as peacebuilders and the conflict that religion can create in service settings.

ROLES OF RELIGIOUS ACTORS AS PEACEBUILDERS

According to Marty (2002, p. 19), 'So preoccupied have we become in asking why religion has been so central to killing that most of us have neglected to explore the potential for people acting in its name to heal'. While one could spend a great deal of time reviewing the ways in which various world religions are construed as justifying the use of violence, it is likely more useful for development policy and practice to focus on the teachings and tools religions offer their followers regarding peacebuilding. The world's major religions share roughly similar scriptural and spiritual values, and this has the potential to reinforce their ability to contribute to peacebuilding. In recent years increasing numbers and types of religious peacemakers have worked to build peaceful coexistence in religiously diverse societies (Haynes, 2009).

Religious actors are well situated to play an important role in peacebuilding. Religious actors are very often long-term players in their communities who live among the people and groups involved in conflict, often belonging to those very groups (Coward and Smith, 2004). This social position grants religious actors a great deal of relevant cultural and political knowledge. This advantage is enhanced by the fact that, in many contexts, religious leaders and organizations hold a position of authority and trust. As Sampson (1994) notes, in some communities where the state is weak or non-existent, religious groups may be the only institutions that hold some degree of credibility for the population at large.

However, the act of peacebuilding is complex and may not be a simple charge for even the most savvy and experienced of religious leaders. Coward and Smith (2004) differentiate between the act of peace*making* and the act of peace*building*. While many leaders may be prepared for the act of peacemaking, or promoting peace and tolerance through the art of moral persuasion, peacebuilding is a much more complex process of non-violent social change (ibid.). Coward and Smith describe peacebuilding as 'the range of activities performed by religious actors and institutions for the purpose of resolving and transforming deadly conflict, with the goal of building social relations and political institutions characterized by an ethos of tolerance and non-violence' (ibid., p. 5). The authors suggest that even skillful religious leaders may be poorly prepared for this complex and long-term process (Coward and Smith, 2004).

Religious actors are intricately involved in the day-to-day welfare provision that makes survival and recovery possible in many contexts of conflict. These undertakings are of critical importance, but do not fall within the realm of peacebuilding roles that will be discussed here. Little and Appleby (2004) describe a variety of different roles that religious actors may play in peacemaking and peacebuilding. Among others, these include heralds, advocates, observers, educators, and mediators. In this section these roles are discussed, as well as the roles religious actors play in reconciliation and institution building, with examples from contexts of conflict and development around the world.

Heralds

One role Little and Appleby (2004) identify that religious actors may play in contexts of conflict is that of 'herald', or a messenger or bearer of news. Because religious actors often are deeply rooted in local communities, these actors may have a sense of growing divisions and impending conflicts in advance of others. In addition, religious actors may also serve as messengers promoting peace and peacebuilding activities.

The Inter-Religious Council of Sierra Leone (IRCSL) is given credit as a herald of upcoming conflict in the case of the coup against President Tejan Kabbah in 1997. In the early 1990s, the Revolutionary United Front, formed ten years prior by a well-intentioned group of dissatisfied teachers and students, was taken over by Foday Sankoh who led the organization in a campaign of horrific violence. Employing tactics learned from other African warlords, Sankoh led his soldiers, often drugged youth, in dreadful acts such as the systematic chopping off of civilians' hands and legs. Religious leaders mobilized against this common enemy, forming the IRCSL. Founding members included prominent Muslim organizations and Catholic, Pentecostal, and Protestant Christian organizations. A delegation from the IRCSL met President Kabbah just prior to the 1997 coup to warn him about the worsening security situation in the country and urge him to take action. Due in part to this warning, troops were able to fly the president out of the country just as the coup began (Penfold, 2005).

When considering religious actors as heralds of peace, oft cited is the role that Buddhist leader Maha Ghosananda played in Cambodia's *Dhammayietra* or 'Pilgrimage of Truth' in the early 1990s. These 45-day walks by monks and lay people covered hundreds of kilometers in areas that were still violently divided following the Khmer Rouge regime and the Vietnamese invasion. Buddhist leader Maha Ghosananda directed walkers to move 'step by step' towards peace, stating:

> Each step is a prayer, each step is a meditation, each step will build a bridge . . . We must find the courage to leave our temples and enter the temples of human experience, temples that are filled with suffering. If we listen to the Buddha, Christ or Gandhi, we can do nothing else. The refugee camps, the prisons, the ghettos and the battlefields will then become our temples. (Haynes, 2009, p. 70)

Residents of local communities saw the marches as a sign that peace was becoming consolidated, which helped to overcome popular fear of political participation and build confidence in upcoming elections (Morris, 2004; Haynes, 2009). The 'Pilgrimage of Truth' was largely credited with generating 90 percent participation in Cambodia's first free elections (Morris, 2004).

Advocates

In contexts of conflict, religious actors may also play a role as advocates, pushing for government reform, stronger civil society, and better social conditions (Little and Appleby, 2004). Such examples are numerous. Vietnamese Buddhist monk Thich Nhat Hanh, though perhaps better known in the West as a Zen meditation teacher and author of a multitude of self-help books, began as a peace activist who was involved in post-Vietnam War recovery in Saigon, assisted political refugees, and actively formulated peace proposals for consideration by the US government (Swearer, 2010). In Thailand, Buddhist liberationist Sulak Sivaraksa became an advocate of non-violent social change and major figure in the development of intellectual concern over the social, economic, and political problems facing the country. In addition to creating a number of NGOs to address various social and political issues, Sivaraksa was a vocal critic of the monarchy and the subsequent military coup that took power in 1991, publicly criticizing their lack of democratic reform. His emphatic public advocacy for reform in Thailand's governing bodies resulted in Sivaraksa's imprisonment and political exile (Little and Appleby, 2004; Swearer, 2010).

Another often cited example of Buddhist peace advocacy is the work of A.T. Ariyaratne and the Sarvodaya Shramadana movement in Sri Lanka. Ariyaratne founded Sarvodaya Shramadana, which means 'Awakening of All Through the Gift of Labor', as a rural development program. Sarvodaya has since become the largest welfare organization in Sri Lanka, but in addition to providing relief and development services, Ariyaratne advocates reform in political and economic structures by targeting Sri Lankan institutions with a Buddhist critique. He characterizes Sri Lanka's politics as ruled by *chanda* (alienation based on a variety of communal divisions); *dvesha* (propaganda based on rumors and lies that encourages violent conflict); and *bhaya* (a spirit of fear and mutual suspicion). Ariyaratne also criticizes the Sri Lankan economy for promoting the material well-being of only a small minority of society, in contrast to Buddhist economics, which seeks, among other things, a cooperative rather than competitive system (*kalayamittata*), and a healthy, sustainable lifestyle (*samajivakata*). Ariyaratne appeals to Buddhist principles while consciously emphasizing the common values shared by Sri Lanka's multiple religious traditions (Neumaier, 2004; Swearer, 2010).

Observers

Religious actors may also act as observers, serving as a physical and moral presence that works to actively monitor and discourage violence, corruption, and human rights violations (Little and Appleby, 2004). Rather than taking on the passive role that the word 'observer' might suggest, these actors maintain a physical presence in zones of active conflict, risking their safety and even their lives due to their religious commitment.

Peace Brigades International (PBI) was founded with the intent of internationalizing the idea of Shanti Sena, a Gandhian-inspired Peace Army. PBI initially placed volunteer peace teams in Guatemala and Nicaragua to provide protective accompaniment of local human rights activists living under threat of abduction or assassination, thus providing international witnesses that discouraged disappearances and unlawful executions. PBI now operates in 17 countries, sponsoring monitoring projects, accompanying the return of refugees, and helping to develop programs of non-violent, civilian-based defense (Moser-Puangsuwan, 1996). The ecumenical Christian group Witness for Peace engages in similar work, organizing a permanent border and conflict monitoring program on Nicaragua's borders during the 1980s, documenting human rights violations, and accompanying Guatemalan refugees from Southern Mexico (Moser-Puangsuwan, 1996; Little and Appleby, 2004). Christian Peacemaker Teams sponsored by the Mennonites and the Church of the Brethren Churches first acted abroad to seek hostage release in Iraq in 1990. These teams have also served to document human rights violations and provide a protective presence to targeted communities in Haiti, Iraq, Israel and Palestine, Canada, and the United States (ibid.).

Educators

Religious actors play an important role as educators, engaging in long-term efforts at conflict transformation in classrooms, seminars, and training groups. Religious actors may be instrumental in educating individuals and groups about others' religious values, thereby promoting greater multicultural understanding. Religious actors may also educate their own followers about various ideas and structures by couching those discussions in the teachings of their own faith, as is the case in a number of Muslim peacebuilding organizations in Africa, Europe, and the United States (Abu-Nimer and Kadayifci-Orellana, 2008), and in the work of Thai Buddhist leader Sulak Sivaraksa (Swearer, 2010).

An example of an organization involved in education aimed at interreligious understanding and conflict transformation is the Interreligious Coordinating Council in Israel (ICCI). The ICCI works to promote mutual understanding among all faiths in Israel and the Palestinian territories through education about the ways in which their religions all preach peace and can contribute to a solution to the Israeli–Palestinian conflict (Kronish, 2008). The ICCI states its mission is 'to harness the teachings and values of the three monotheistic religions and transform religious leaders in Israel into sources of reconciliation and coexistence for Jews, Christians, and Muslims who share the same land' (Kronish, 2008, p. 227). Made up of more than 60 Jewish, Christian, Muslim, ecumenical and interreligious organizations, the ICCI engages in a wide variety of activities including facilitating dialogue groups in which the members study each other's sacred texts. The ICCI sees interreligious text study as an important tool that brings people closer together by allowing individuals to 'see the divine image in the other' (ibid., p. 228). The coalition particularly works to target influential religious and cultural leaders and opinion-makers with its programs, carefully selecting participants based on their potential to influence multiple individuals in their own communities. In this way the ICCI maximizes its impact, with a focus on communities rather than individuals, and engagement in long-term programs and relationship-building (Kronish, 2008).

The ability to educate communities while remaining centered in a religious perspective can be central to an initiative's effectiveness in some communities. Abu-Nimer and Kadayifci-Orellana (2008) explain that a variety of Muslim peacebuilding organizations have been effective at promoting democracy and human rights in their communities because they have involved Muslim religious leaders or successfully grounded their claims on religious texts, values, and principles. In addition to the quality of their work and the respect they have earned in their communities, the ability to legitimize ideas of democracy and human rights from a specifically Muslim perspective is crucial (ibid.). Similarly, Thai Buddhist leader Sulak Sivaraksa has been involved in the founding of numerous organizations, including the Thai Inter-religious Commission for Development, which encourages Buddhist student associations to participate in social change programs and promote educational projects for slum-dwelling children, and the Santi Pracha Dhamma Institute (SPDI), or Peace Democratic Institute. The SPDI has a number of projects including the Thai Forum Program, which educates the mass media on alternative approaches to peace and justice; and Sekiyadhamma, a network of socially engaged monks developing a constructive Buddhist challenge to social and environmental problems (Swearer, 2010). Sivaraksa's creative reinterpretation of traditional Buddhist teachings has been instrumental in increasing Buddhist involvement in social and political activism.

Negotiators

Yet another role that religious actors may play in contexts of conflict is that of 'negotiator' or mediator (Little and Appleby, 2004). Religious individuals, often as representatives of faith-based organizations, have engaged in mediation in an effort to resolve conflicts for many decades (Haynes, 2009). In this role, third-party faith-based actors may act as a go-between among warring parties, or may facilitate conversations with the parties physically present. According to Bercovitch and Kadayifci-Orellana (2009), negotiation efforts by faith-based actors differ from those of secular actors in that they explicitly emphasize spirituality; often use religious texts, values, and vocabulary; and may use religious or spiritual rituals during the process of mediation. Religious mediators may have some benefits to offer the negotiation process that secular actors lack, including greater perceived credibility and legitimacy by the parties involved, an ability to leverage their distinct moral and spiritual influence, and access to a large spectrum of community members through religious institutions. Additionally, many religious actors have long-term involvement in the community that extends beyond the date when a peace agreement is signed, which allows these actors to help monitor the agreement and assist with healing, building social institutions, and seeking justice (ibid.).

In some cases religious negotiators themselves are from the communities embedded in a local conflict. Such was the case with the Inter-Religious Council of Sierra Leone (IRCSL), discussed earlier in the chapter. Made up of key figures from a variety of the country's Christian and Muslim communities, the IRCSL's religious affiliation was one of the critical factors leading to its success, as this faith identity caused the organization to be viewed as credible both by the government and the Revolutionary United Front (RUF) (Penfold, 2005; Bercovitch and Kadayifci-Orellana, 2009). While the IRCSL could not prevent the coup in 1997 or stop the violence completely, they actively pursued dialogue with the coup leaders, pressuring the government to give the public an opportunity to hear the RUF and its allies' demands (Penfold, 2005; Abu-Nimer and Kadayifci-Orellana, 2008). While always condemning the coup and the RUF's human rights abuses (Abu-Nimer and Kadayifci-Orellana, 2008), the IRCSL delegation also told RUF leader Sankoh that they recognized him as one of the key players in the peace process and provided humanitarian aid to his troops in the field (Penfold, 2005). The IRCSL's engagement with the both sides is credited as preventing greater abuses against civilians, and earned the respect of both the government and the rebels (Penfold, 2005; Abu-Nimer and Kadayifci-Orellana, 2008). The IRCSL's approach was to remain impartial and act as a facilitator, with Council members acting as go-betweens during impasses. During moments when the parties were unable to agree, Council members relied upon prayer and preaching (Penfold, 2005). When a peace agreement was finally signed in 1999, the IRCSL was seen as valuable enough a peacemaker that the accord called for the establishment of a 'Council of Elders and Religious Leaders' to mediate disputes (however, the Council was never established). The IRCSL also played a pivotal role in convincing a skeptical public that the rebels' peace was sincere, in part by marketing the peace agreement from the religious pulpit (Penfold, 2005). In the case of Sierra Leone, the IRCSL's religious identity and religious motivations and practice all played a critical role in the organization's success as a peacemaker.

In other cases the involvement of religious 'outsiders' can be more effective for negotiation. While the intricate cultural and political knowledge possessed by local religious leaders is often invaluable, in some contexts of conflict an outsider status allows a position of even-handedness and neutrality that is useful in the mediation process. The work of Quakers in Nigeria, the Mennonites in Nicaragua and the lay Catholic movement Sant'Egidio in a variety of contexts including Mozambique all provide examples of this. In each of these cases it is not only the impartiality of the negotiators but the infusion of religion in their methods that is important for their success.

In Nigeria, the Quakers were the only third party able to win the trust of both parties in the civil war in 1967 (Sampson, 1994). Because religious identity had been used to promote divisions in Nigeria, many were suspicious of religious institutions, so the Quakers' unofficial status and lack of denominational affiliation were important factors in gaining this trust. However, not only neutrality but the Quakers' religious motivations were critical to the parties of the conflict. Both parties were aware of the Quakers' pacifist beliefs, and believed their spiritual convictions were what motivated them to endure the hardships and dangers of working in war zones. Their readiness to face such hazards for no motive other than religion earned the respect of both parties (Bercovitch and Kadayifci-Orellana, 2009). The Mennonites in Nicaragua and Sant'Egidio in Mozambique, in addition to benefiting from their neutral status, were able to use a variety of Christian themes as a framework for negotiation. In the mediation process between the Nicaraguan government and native peoples during the civil war in the 1980s, Mennonite negotiators focused on Christian ideals such as service, acceptance of suffering, the harvest of righteousness that awaits those who sow in peace, and the holy role of the peacemaker. Throughout negotiations, both sides turned to this religious symbolism to create bridges between the groups and bring focus to shared goals rather than individual concerns (Nichols, 1994). In the Mozambique peace talks in the early 1990s, Sant'Egidio leaders drew upon Christian symbols of brotherhood and a shared status as children of God to unite the Mozambican people during the negotiations (Bartoli, 2004; Bercovitch and Kadayifci-Orellana, 2009). In addition to Sant'Egidio's welcome neutrality and a compassionate outlook (Smock, 2004), this strategy helped bring about the signing of a general peace accord in October 1992.

Reconciliation and Institution Building

Haynes (2009) argues that peacemaking should not only focus on the short-term attainment of peace, but also must seek to develop restorative justice, facilitate acknowledgment and acceptance of accountability among conflicting groups, and address the structural problems that make future conflict more likely. Religious actors have the potential to play an important role in building institutions that can lead to reconciliation.

Truth and Reconciliation Commissions have emerged in many post-conflict contexts, particularly in Africa and Latin America (Botman, 2004), and in numerous instances religious actors have played an important role in the creation and function of these institutions. The Parliament of Sierra Leone explicitly referenced religious leaders' assistance in facilitating reconciliation. Understanding that the religious community had played a crucial role in the peace process, the Parliament appointed a Methodist bishop as their Truth and Reconciliation Commission's head and involved religious leaders in all its undertakings. Religious leaders were present to offer guidance and advice during sensitive activities such as collection of statements and testimonies, and truth telling and conflict resolution sessions (Penfold, 2005). In other cases, such as in South Africa, Truth and Reconciliation Commissions have presented a venue for religious bodies to acknowledge their own culpability in community conflicts and violence, which serves as an important starting point for building healthy relationships in communities (Botman, 2004).

Institutions that promote interreligious dialogue can be of extreme importance as well, particularly in circumstances of religious conflict or in communities where religion and other identities like ethnicity have become inextricably linked. Nigeria's

Muslim–Christian Dialogue Forum (MCDF) is an oft-cited example. As of the early 1990s, violence among Muslim and Christian communities became a common occurrence in Nigeria, with communities in the northern state of Kaduna suffering acutely. In 1995 the MCDF was formed by two former enemies and revered members of their religious communities, Christian pastor James Movel Wuye and Muslim imam Muhammad Nurayn Ashafa. Though each man attempted to have the other killed only three years prior, both men believed God had beckoned them to correct their mistakes and turned their efforts toward non-violence, reconciliation, and the advocacy of peaceful relations. In 1999 they co-authored a book entitled *The Pastor and the Imam: Responding to Conflict*, which discusses both the Bible's and the Quran's obligations for peaceful coexistence, and in 2003 they enrolled together in an annual peacebuilding institute at the School for International Training in Vermont. The MCDF has facilitated a variety of dialogue workshops with Christian and Muslim youth leaders, knowing that Muslims and Christians from this age group have been guilty of a great deal of the recent religious violence in Nigeria. The inaugural workshop concluded with participants agreeing to a 17-point declaration recommending, among other things, that Christians and Muslims should love each other unconditionally as brothers and sisters; that both communities should show goodwill to each other at all times; and that each religious community should better inform its members of the other faith's beliefs (Haynes, 2009).

RELIGION AS A SOURCE OF CONFLICT WITHIN DEVELOPMENT ACTIVITIES

Considering various religions' justification of violence and the ways in which religious actors may engage in peacemaking and peacebuilding is important. However, equally important but often overlooked are the ways that religious conflicts may manifest themselves within the micro-context of service provision. Important concerns may arise when faith-based actors such as NGOs provide services in countries that have experienced religious violence (Flanigan, 2010). Tilly (2003) asserts that certain mechanisms promote, inhibit, or channel collective violence; among these mechanisms are polarization and boundary activation. Polarization involves a widening of social or political space between claimants in a contentious episode, and promotes collective violence by making us–them boundaries more salient. As boundaries between groups become more salient, social interactions increasingly organize around these boundaries, and actors increasingly differentiate between within-boundary and across-boundary interactions (ibid.). Tilly (2003) calls this process 'boundary activation' (p. 21). The same boundary activation that promotes collective violence can also influence the behavior of faith-based actors operating in communities that have experienced violent religious conflict. Research shows that faith-based NGOs in some contexts of conflict serve fewer community members of other ethnic and religious identities for reasons related to both the behavior of the organization and the behavior of potential service recipients. First, boundary activation may cause faith-based NGOs to overtly discriminate against community members with another ethno-religious identity, or may cause faith-based NGOs to do less outreach to community members of other religions and ethnicities. Second, boundary activation may cause potential service recipients of other religions and ethnicities to be apprehensive about seeking services from the faith-based NGO, even if the organization might be willing to provide services to them (Flanigan, 2010).

Whether real or merely misconceptions, perceptions of discrimination and evangelism by faith-based development NGOs can also raise suspicion and heighten tension in communities (see the case study on Sri Lanka in this chapter for a detailed example). In his study of religious NGOs in Bangladesh, Ahmad (2004) studied Islamic, Christian, Buddhist, and Hindu NGOs, finding that all of the NGOs were subjects of the suspicions of community members. While the Christian NGO was widely suspected of evangelism, the Muslim NGO was suspected of supporting terrorist activities and obstructing projects that promoted women's work outside the home. Meanwhile, the Buddhist and Hindu organizations were criticized for only targeting services to members of their own faith (ibid.). In his study of NGOs in West Africa, Anheier (1994) notes that competition for believers by religious NGOs in Nigeria created conflict between religious and secular NGOs as well as between NGOs of different faiths. He asserts that the dual goal structure of Nigerian NGOs – both providing development assistance and gaining adherents – was a significant constraint that was detrimental to the impact of the organizations' work (ibid.). Pul's (2004) study of NGOs in northern Ghana illustrates the potential role that non-profit organizations can play in creating and exacerbating division and conflict. In a study that sought to understand why certain locales experience higher degrees of violent conflict than others, Pul (ibid.) found that NGOs created along ethnic lines have intensified longstanding battles between groups over citizenship rights.

These studies show the possible implications that religious and ethnic identity may have for non-state provision of development services in the developing world. Equity guarantees are important in societies where political rights are often fledgling and poorly defined, and where religious, ethnic, or other sectarian divisions exist. In addition to these concerns, one must also consider the role of power in these service settings. There are unique power dynamics at play in service settings where the individuals served are poor and their basic needs are unmet (Handler, 1973, 1979). According to Hasenfeld (1987), the amount of power a service provider has over the recipient is a direct function of the recipient's ability to obtain aid elsewhere. When a service recipient is dependent on a single entity for certain types of aid, as is often the case in the developing world (van Tuijl, 1999), the recipient lacks power, liberty, and true choice. This lack of power and choice makes service recipients especially vulnerable in instances of discrimination, evangelism, and other forms of coercion or exclusion (Flanigan, 2010).

CASE STUDY: FAITH-BASED DEVELOPMENT SERVICES AND SRI LANKA'S ANTI-CONVERSION MOVEMENT

Sri Lanka is a tropical island in the Indian Ocean, sometimes wistfully described as a teardrop hanging from the chin of India. Sri Lanka is home to more than 20 million people, and its population is ethnically, religiously, and linguistically diverse. Decades of discrimination against Sri Lanka's ethnic Tamil minority by the ethnic Sinhalese majority gave rise to the well-known terrorist organization, the Liberation Tigers of Tamil Eelam (LTTE), also called the Tamil Tigers (Reuter, 2002). In 1983 the LTTE began a military offensive designed to create an independent state for Sri Lanka's Tamil minority, and the ensuing 20-plus year civil war has been described as 'one of the deadliest and most protracted ethnic conflicts of our time' (DeVotta, 2004, p. 2).

Although Sri Lanka had a vibrant voluntary sector even before the country's independence from British rule in 1948 (Wanigaratne, 1997; DeVotta, 2005), much of Sri Lanka's NGO sector emerged as a response to this violent conflict, with the sector's activities strongly shaped by the needs created by the war. In addition to addressing those needs, both local and international NGOs were heavily involved in coping with the aftermath of the 2004 Asian tsunami. The tsunami killed nearly 40 000 Sri Lankans, and led to near-immediate rise in the number of NGOs working on the island.

In Sri Lanka following the tsunami there was strong anti-NGO sentiment present both in the political sphere and in the realm of public opinion, due in part to the fact that a large proportion of foreign aid was channeled through NGOs (DeVotta, 2005; Orjuela, 2005). This was not new; since the 1950s, suspicion has permeated political and bureaucratic attitudes towards NGOs, their activities, and their supporting donor agencies in Sri Lanka (Hodson, 1997; Wanigaratne, 1997). Sri Lanka's anti-NGO sentiment has taken a violent, and at times deadly, turn. By far the most notable act of violence against the NGO community was the execution of 17 ethnic Tamil aid workers from the French NGO Action Against Hunger in August 2006. While this incident was extreme, NGO workers in Sri Lanka's north and east were frequently the target of grenade attacks, attacks by angry mobs, and threats (Senanayake and Sengupta, 2006). During field research conducted by Flanigan (2010) in 2006, the majority of interview participants from Sri Lankan NGOs indicated that their NGO had been the target of violent actions or threats at some point during their operation.

Anti-NGO fervor in Sri Lanka has been driven by tales of NGO mismanagement and corruption (DeVotta, 2005), and a belief that the NGO community unfairly favored the Tamils and the LTTE in the civil war (DeVotta, 2005; Renner, 2006). But a third and perhaps even more incendiary source of anti-NGO sentiment following the 2004 tsunami was fear of religious conversion by faith-based NGOs (Flanigan, 2010).

In post-tsunami Sri Lanka there was a strong fear that faith-based NGOs, particularly international organizations, had come to the island for the purpose of converting Sri Lankans of all religious groups to an evangelical Protestant form of Christianity (ibid.). Christian fundamentalists were accused of using NGOs as a disguise for their evangelical activities (Wanigaratne, 1997), with some contending that Christians took advantage of social problems such as poverty, war, and lack of education in order to engage in aggressive evangelism (United States Department of State, 2005). This fear was not entirely unfounded, as some evangelical Christian FBOs used tsunami aid to spread their religious message (DeVotta, 2005; Flanigan, 2010). While certainly not true of the majority of employees of faith-based NGOs, several employees of Christian NGOs reported evangelism as a specific aim of their humanitarian work (Flanigan, 2010). One interview participant, who mentioned that his organization receives substantial funding from the United States government, describes his NGO's evangelic mission as follows:

> [Our NGO's] mission is relief and evangelism, even though in Sri Lanka the evangelism mandate is dealt with lightly due to the social dynamics that are present here right now. In the south there is a strong anti-Christian element with the Buddhist parties, and the national legislature is currently considering an anti-conversion bill, so things are tense for us. So [our NGO's] goal is to show God's love through action. We don't have any direct evangelistic campaign here.

Interviewer: But in other countries where you work, would you be more direct about evangelizing people?

Yes, if the situation permits it then we can be more direct. But this varies on a country-by-country basis. We have to be careful of the social and religious context. In other countries we could talk to people more openly about the gospel, but not here. So in Sri Lanka we hope that those touched by our work will ask questions about our faith, and then want to learn more about Christian teachings. In that way, they open the door for us. But we really want to live our faith by helping people, all people, regardless of what they believe. Conversion is a need of the hour, but (our NGO) focuses on compassionate, unconditional relief. (Flanigan, 2010, p. 99)

Other NGO staff indicated that their organizations did not engage in evangelism, but then described activities that many would consider forms of proselytization. For example, one NGO employee explained how service recipients end up joining his church after receiving trauma counseling following the tsunami:

We don't do evangelism. But we always take care of the spiritual side of the person, and we did this during the trauma counseling, as part of the tsunami response. What we did is we shared Christ's love at the end of the counseling. Some people, they accepted Christ, and then their life is definitely changed. And now we have joined the people to our church, they are coming to Sunday services. And you can see the effects of it, because they have stopped drinking, they have stopped smoking, and so you can see a difference in their life, in the way they live, in how they take care of their house and take care of their children.

Interviewer: I'm curious, if you don't do any direct evangelism, what do you think makes the people start coming to your church?

Well, some people they ask, 'Why are you coming and doing this for us?' Then we share Christ's love, we say, 'Christ loves us and we will show Christ's love to you through us'. So this makes them understand what we're doing.

Interviewer: So usually they would ask you?

Yes, because they are surprised. They think, 'Why is this man doing things for us when he doesn't have to?' So they always have this question on their mind. (Flanigan, 2010, p. 92)

Reports of forced conversion to Christianity by missionaries and faith-based NGOs sparked several movements to pass anti-conversion legislation in the Sri Lankan Parliament. The proposed laws typically criminalized conversion, requiring new converts to register with the government when they changed their religion, and imposing fines or jail sentences on anyone convicted of 'unethically' converting another person to their religion. Legislation usually included harsher penalties for conversion of vulnerable groups such as children, prisoners, people with disabilities, and refugees (Parliament of Sri Lanka, 2004; United States Department of State, 2005). The humanitarian activities of FBOs were specifically targeted by the anti-conversion legislation as a form of 'allurement'. One proposed bill defined allurement as 'any temptation in the form of: (1) any gift or gratification whether in cash or kind; (2) grant of any material benefit, whether monetary or otherwise; (3) grant of employment or grant of promotion in employment' (Parliament of Sri Lanka, 2004, p. 1).

It is easy to imagine that many of the humanitarian activities of faith-based NGOs could be construed as falling within this definition of allurement. Christians counter that their humanitarian work is sincere and not targeted at conversion (United States Department of State, 2005), and Sri Lanka's Catholic Bishops' Conference and the National Christian Council reminded political leaders that all religions compel their followers to do charitable works and it would be wrong to label all such acts as efforts at conversions (Balachanddran, 2004). Many staff members from Christian NGOs felt endangered by this movement, particularly anti-conversion legislation, as they believed it would limit their freedom of expression and their ability to assist the poor. Several staff members believed that anti-conversion legislation, if passed, would allow officials to depict many forms of humanitarian relief as efforts at allurement and therefore would give officials even greater ability to force NGOs out of the country. And while the majority of staff members from faith-based NGOs did not indicate that evangelism was a goal of their organization, several interview participants indicated that they had been accused of conversion at various points during the organizations' history (Flanigan, 2010). As one interview participant from a Christian FBO describes:

> In Sri Lanka faith-based NGOs are very stigmatized, especially if they aren't Buddhist NGOs. This makes it difficult to work, especially in the south where there is more Buddhist nationalist sentiment. The faith-based NGOs are always criticized in media, and actually (our NGO) was accused of conversion by the newspapers just based on our name, even though at this point we are almost secular and we certainly don't have any religious activities. (Flanigan, 2010, p. 90)

Those interview participants from NGOs that were not engaged in evangelism typically reported that, over time, local communities would come to see that they were not engaged in conversion and trust would begin to build (Flanigan, 2010). As one interview participant notes:

> They [non-Christian NGOs and community leaders] were willing to work with us because they saw that we had no ulterior motives. They saw that we were not there to convert, which some churches do, but we have made a very strong effort never to do that. So we ended up being approached by people who had never approached us before, which is very good. And now we are working with them to do other projects. (Flanigan, 2010, p. 95)

While many allegations of evangelism by faith-based NGOs in Sri Lanka are certainly untrue, fears of conversion are not entirely unfounded. Concern regarding conversion is tied to an awareness that people experiencing poverty and other related problems can be subtly pressured to change religions when faith-based NGOs offer financial and other incentives (Thiagarajah and Ropers, 2005). These apprehensions are quite rational given that scholars indicate that recruiting adherents is a possible goal of faith-based social service providers (James, 1989; Rose-Ackerman, 1996; Anheier and Salamon, 1998). Bearing in mind the fact that social service providers hold notable power over service recipients, particularly the poor and vulnerable, one can see how ethical concerns might arise (Hasenfeld, 1987). In Sri Lanka there is an additional perception that, while faith-based NGOs may offer aid to everyone, more and better aid is offered to those who formally join their church (Thiagarajah and Ropers, 2005). Highly publicized incidents of faith-based NGOs engaging in conversion, particularly post-tsunami, have given Sri Lankans a negative perception of the NGO community at large and undoubtedly make it more difficult for faith-based NGOs to conduct their work (ibid.).

CONCLUSION: POTENTIAL UNFULFILLED

Despite the challenges just described, the potential role of religious actors as peacebuilders should be heartening. Many examples exist of the successful peacebuilding efforts of religious actors, and the various roles they may assume are numerous. A single individual or organization may themselves assume several roles, as becomes apparent with the multiple mentions of the Interreligious Council of Sierra Leone and the work of Thai Buddhist leader Sulak Sivaraksa in this chapter. As Haynes (2009) notes, religion's role in helping to resolve conflicts and build peace can be a critical element in achieving human development more generally. The abundance of peacebuilding assets that religious actors have to offer communities is a resource that can be utilized by development practitioners and peacemakers worldwide.

However, this resource has largely gone untapped. Numerous scholars describe the peacemaking and peacekeeping roles of religious actors as missed opportunities (Little and Appleby, 2004). The role of religious leaders in these efforts is often critical, and as Appleby (2006) notes, religious leaders often fail to understand or enact their potential peacebuilding roles and many religious leaders lack the ability to 'exploit their strategic capacity as transnational actors'. Abu-Nimer and Kadayifci-Orellana (2008) note that the role that Muslim leaders must play in peacebuilding is heightened because many Muslim communities have limited access to the wide range of religious interpretations of Islam, which increases their dependence on clergy. In addition, many Muslims lack access to original Islamic texts such as the Quran because illiteracy is high in many communities, especially among women, and the majority of the world's Muslims do not speak Arabic even when literate. This dependence on religious leadership further complicates peacebuilding efforts because texts used in the Islamic educational institutions typically do not highlight the peacemaking values of Islam (ibid.).

Additionally, the very aspects that often make religious leaders appealing as peacebuilders, such as their rootedness in local communities and their position as respected leaders, can also cause them to be deeply rooted in the conflict and reluctant to engage in bold peacemaking measures. Internal divisions between moderates and conservatives within individual faith communities and the influence of religious extremists can dissuade leaders' engagement in peacebuilding roles (Clark, 2010).

Clark (ibid.) argues that in Bosnia and Herzegovina religious actors are doing little to facilitate reconciliation, and are 'seemingly not fully aware of their own latent capacity as peace-builders' (p. 691). Rather than engage in honest discussion about the past, many religious actors deny or dismiss their own groups' war crimes and human rights abuses. This reinforces each community's adherence to their own separate and divisive narrative of the history of the region and its conflicts. In some cases religious actors do not actually want peace and are obstructing the peace process, using religious symbols such as the erection of crosses in divided communities to maintain and intensify inter-ethnic divides (ibid.).

Nonetheless, the resources religious actors can offer the peace process and their various roles as advocates, observers, educators, mediators, and institution builders must be valued. Strategic and thoughtful religious leaders, faith-based organizations, and development practitioners can capitalize upon these skills, networks, and cultural assets to work to prevent conflict and promote peace.

REFERENCES

Abu-Nimer, Mohammed and S. Ayse Kadayifci-Orellana (2008), 'Muslim peace-building actors in Africa and the Balkan context: challenges and needs', *Peace & Change*, **33**(4), 549–81.

Ahmad, M. (2004), 'Roots of funding, roots of trust: the struggle for survival and credibility among religious NGOs in Bangladesh', paper presented at International Society for Third Sector Research Sixth International Conference, Toronto, ON.

Anheier, H. (1994), 'A comparative analysis of institutional development and NGOs in West Africa', in E. Sandberg (ed.), *The Changing Politics of Non-governmental Organizations and African States*, Westport, CT: Greenwood Publishing.

Anheier, H. and L. Salamon (1998), *The Nonprofit Sector in the Developing World*, Manchester: Manchester University Press.

Appleby, R.S. (2006), 'Building sustainable peace: the roles of local and transnational religious actors', Paper presented at the Conference on New Religious Pluralism in World Politics, Washington, DC.

Asal, Victor H. and R. Karl Rethemeyer (2008), 'The nature of the beast: organizational structures and the lethality of terrorist attacks', *Journal of Politics*, 70(2), 437–49.

Balachanddran, P.K. (2004), 'Lanka's anti-conversion law targets evangelical movements', *Hindustan Times*, 1 July.

Bartoli, Andrea (2004), 'Christianity and peacebuilding', in Harold Coward and Gordon S. Smith (eds), *Religion and Peacebuilding*, Albany: State University of New York Press.

Bercovitch, J. and S.A. Kadayifci-Orellana (2009), 'Religion and mediation: the role of faith-based actors in international conflict resolution', *International Negotiation*, **14**(1), 175–204.

Botman, H. Russel (2004), 'Truth and reconciliation: the South African case', in Harold Coward and Gordon S. Smith (eds), *Religion and Peacebuilding*, Albany: State University of New York Press.

Clark, Janine Natalya (2010), 'Religion and reconciliation in Bosnia & Herzegovina: are religious actors doing enough?', *Europe-Asia Studies*, **62**(4), 671–94.

Coward, Harold and Gordon S. Smith (2004), *Religion and Peacebuilding*, Albany: State University of New York Press.

Cronin, I. (2002), *Confronting Fear: A History of Terrorism*, New York: Thunder's Mouth Press.

DeVotta, Neil (2004), *Blowback: Linguistic Nationalism, Institutional Decay, and Ethnic Conflict in Sri Lanka*, Stanford, CA: Stanford University Press.

DeVotta, Neil (2005), 'Civil society and non-governmental organizations in Sri Lanka: peacemakers or parasites?', *Civil Wars*, **7**(2), 171–82.

Durkheim, E. ([1912] 1954), *The Elementary Forms of the Religious Life*, New York: The Free Press.

Flanigan, Shawn (2010), *For the Love of God: NGOs and Religious Identity in a Violent World*, Sterling, VA: Kumarian Press.

Handler, J.F. (1973), *The Coercive Social Worker: British Lessons for American Social Services*, Chicago: Rand McNally College Publishing Company.

Handler, J.F. (1979), *Protecting the Social Service Client: Legal and Structural Controls on Official Discretion*, New York: Academic Press.

Hasenfeld, Y. (1987), 'Power in social work practice', *Social Service Review*, **61**(3), 469–83.

Haynes, Jeffrey (2009), 'Conflict, conflict resolution and peace-building: the role of religion in Mozambique, Nigeria and Cambodia', *Commonwealth & Comparative Politics*, **47**(1), 52–75.

Hodson, Roland (1997), 'Elephant loose in the jungle: the World Bank and NGOs in Sri Lanka', in D. Hulme and M. Edwards (eds), *NGOs, States and Donors: Too Close for Comfort?*, London: Macmillan Press, pp. 79–92.

Hoffman, B. (1998), *Inside Terrorism*, New York: Columbia University Press.

James, E. (1989), *The Nonprofit Sector in International Perspective: Studies in Comparative Culture and Policy*, New York: Oxford University Press.

Juergensmeyer, M. (2003), *Terror in the Mind of God: The Global Rise of Religious Violence*, Berkeley: University of California Press.

Kronish, Ron (2008), 'Interreligious dialogue in the service of peace', *Crosscurrents*, **58**(2), 224–46.

Little, David and Scott Appleby (2004), 'A moment of opportunity? The promise of religious peacebuilding in an era of religious and ethnic conflict', in Harold Coward and Gordon S. Smith (eds), *Religion and Peacebuilding*, Albany: State University of New York Press.

Marty, Martin E. (2002) 'Is religion the problem?', *Tikkun Magazine*, **17**(2), 19, as cited by Ron Kronish (2008), 'Interreligious dialogue in the service of peace', *Crosscurrents*, **58**(2), 224–46.

Morris, Catherine (2004), 'Case studies in religion and peacebuilding: Cambodia', in Harold Coward and Gordon S. Smith (eds), *Religion and Peacebuilding*, Albany: State University of New York Press.

Moser-Puangsuwan, Yeshua (1996), 'Grassroots initiatives in unarmed peacekeeping', *Peace Review*, **8**(4), 569–76.

Neumaier, Eva K. (2004), 'Missed opportunities: Buddhism and the ethnic strife in Sri Lanka and Tibet', in Harold Coward and Gordon S. Smith (eds), *Religion and Peacebuilding*, Albany: State University of New York Press.
Nichols, Bruce (1994), 'Religious conciliation between the Sandinistas and the East Coast Indians in Nicaragua', in Douglas Johnston and Cynthia Sampson (eds), *Religion, the Missing Dimension of Statecraft*, New York: Oxford University Press.
Nichols, J. (1988), *The Uneasy Alliance: Religion, Refugee Work, and U.S, Foreign Policy*, New York: Oxford University Press.
Orjuela, Camilla (2005), 'Civil society in civil war: the case of Sri Lanka', *Civil Wars*, **7**(2), 120–37.
Parliament of Sri Lanka (2004), *A Bill on Prohibition of Forcible Conversion of Religions*, Colombo: Parliament of Sri Lanka.
Penfold, Peter (2005), 'Faith in resolving Sierra Leone's bloody conflict', *The Round Table*, **94**(382), 549–57.
Pul, H. (2004), 'Belonging and not belonging: citizenship and the new forms of exclusion, association and conflicts in Northern Ghana', paper presented at International Society for Third Sector Research Sixth International Conference, Toronto, ON.
Renner, Michael (2006), 'Politicization of aid in Sri Lanka turns deadly', Worldwatch Institute.
Reuter, Christoph (2002), *My Life is a Weapon: A Modern History of Suicide Bombing*, Princeton, NJ: Princeton University Press.
Rose-Ackerman, S. (1996), 'Altruism, non-profits and economic theory', *Journal of Economic Literature*, **34**(2), 701–26.
Sampson, Cynthia (1994), 'To make the real bond between us all: Quaker conciliation during Nigerian Civil War', in Douglas Johnston and Cynthia Sampson (eds), *Religion, the Missing Dimension of Statecraft*, New York: Oxford University Press.
Senanayake, Shimali and Somini Sengupta (2006), 'Aid agencies stymied by war in Sri Lanka', *The New York Times*, 17 August.
Simon, H. (1993), 'Altruism and economics', *American Economic Review*, **83**(2), 156–61.
Smock, David R. (1995), *Perspectives on Pacifism: Christian, Jewish, and Muslim Views on Non-violence and International Conflict*, Washington, DC: United States Institute of Peace.
Stern, J. (1999), *The Ultimate Terrorists*, Cambridge, MA: Harvard University Press.
Swearer, Donald K. (2010), 'Religion, world order, and peace: Buddhist responses', *Cross Currents*, **60**(3), 314–18.
Thiagarajah, J. and N. Ropers (2005), *An Annotation to the 'Principles of Conduct for the International Federation of Red Cross and Red Crescent Societies/International Committee of the Red Cross and NGOs in Disaster Response Programmes'*, Colombo: Consortium of Humanitarian Agencies and Berghof Foundation for Conflict Studies – Sri Lanka Office.
Tilly, C. (2003), *The Politics of Collective Violence*, New York: Cambridge University Press.
Treverton, G., H. Gregg, D. Gibran and C. Yost (2005), *Exploring Religious Conflict*, Santa Monica: RAND Corporation.
United States Department of State (2005), *International Religious Freedom Report 2005*, Washington, DC: United States Department of State.
van Tuijl, P. (1999), 'NGOs and human rights: sources of justice and democracy', *Journal of International Affairs*, **52**(2), 493–512.
Wanigaratne, Ranjith (1997), 'The state–NGO relationship in Sri Lanka: rights, interests, and accountability', in D. Hulme and M. Edwards (eds), *NGOs, States and Donors: Too Close for Comfort?*, London: Macmillan Press, pp. 79–92.
Weber, M. (1963), *The Sociology of Religion*, Boston: Beacon Press.

17 Religion in the policy domains of international financial institutions

John Rees

INTRODUCTION

This chapter considers the issue of religion and development via the growing relations between religious groups and international financial institutions (IFIs). A specific focus will be to analyse the engagement with faith institutions and communities by the World Bank, arguably the most influential IFI in world politics. Specifically, the chapter will examine four issues. First, on the issue of method, a rationale is offered for why religion is an important focus in development theory and practice, and by extension, why placing religion at the forefront of the analysis offers unique insights into development discourse. Second, on the issue of development institutions, this approach is modelled by understanding the central policy platforms of the World Bank through the terms of religion previously established. Third, on the issue of policy, we examine the multiple and varying influences that allowed religion to enter the discourse and domain of World Bank activity in the 1980s and 1990s. Fourth, on the implications of these events going forward, strengths and limitations of the World Bank's faith engagement to date are considered.

THE INTERSECTION OF RELIGION AND DEVELOPMENT

What is development and why is it imperative that any consideration of development practice take seriously the issue of religion? Moreover, how can religion be employed at the conceptual level to provide new understandings of the development sphere? Our first section will explore these questions.

The Legitimacy of Religion in Development Studies

Development is a highly contested term 'concerning how "developing countries" can improve their living standards and eliminate absolute poverty' (Kingsbury, 2004, p. 1). Development in practice is constituted by a broad range of priorities from crisis relief to long-term reconstruction, from environmental sustainability to gender empowerment, from good governance at the international level to community consultation at the local level.

Why is it important that we add the consideration of religion to this already substantial list? One answer is that the inclusion of religion helps us to resolve what Harcourt calls a central paradox in development practice and theory, namely, 'the denial of religion at the heart of modern development, yet at the same time its strong value claims for greater good that many religious organizations share' (Harcourt, 2003, p. 3). Let us consider both elements of the paradox. On the one hand, development is a practical consequence of the rise of modernization and secularization, leading Peet to suggest that development 'is a founding belief of the modern world', which holds that '(p)rogress has long since replaced God as the icon of our age' (1999, p. 1). Rist goes further to suggest that because development 'distinguishes modern societies from those that have gone before' (2008, p. 13) it has thus become 'an element of modern religion' (p. 23). These brief statements emphasize the secular subordination of religion by the forces of modernity. On the other hand, not only do development ethics resonate with many fundamental axioms of religion, the development sphere is characterized by the primacy of religious belief. Religious actors, whether as faith institutions or religious communities, feature prominently in development contexts. As Tyndale observes, 'belief that there can be no true development without spiritual advancement . . . is, in one form or another, still the belief of the majority of people in the world today' (2002, p. 45). In other words, what we might term the 'sacral' dimensions of life are normative for many, if not most, of the agents and subjects of development action. Thus, any general discourse that excludes or ignores the question of religion remains unable to answer the paradox of development.

A second answer to why we add the consideration of religion to development is that the exclusion of religion leaves important understandings and resources underutilized in the formation and contestation of development policy. Whilst the importance of religion in development is rapidly gaining credence (Haynes, 2007; Clarke and Jennings, 2008), it still falls outside established development norms. Despite a movement towards holism in development discourse, key sources of ideas on development theory and practice still reflect the marginalization and problematization of religion without the balancing perspectives on centrality and utility (McDuie-Ra and Rees, 2010). Thus, Ver Beek argues that despite 'the evident centrality of spirituality to such decisions, the subject is conspicuously under-represented in the development discourse' (2002, p. 60). Such a tension is reflected across many dimensions of the development field. For example, in the domain of international crisis relief, Pfanner notes that religion 'largely remains taboo in humanitarian action', yet also acknowledges that '[m]uch of international humanitarian action consists of intercultural work, in which the religious dimension is an important factor' (2005, p. 240). This tension is also reflected in the academic study of development. Clarke suggests two reasons for this neglect: '"secular reductionism" – the neglect of religious variables in favour of other sociological attributes such as class, ethnicity and gender – [and] "materialistic determinism" – the neglect of nonmaterial, especially religious, motivations in explaining individual or institutional behaviour' (2008, p. 17). Thus, there is scope to better situate the complex interaction between the secular and sacral factors in development toward a broader conceptual engagement to the benefit of both theory and practice.

Situating Religion at the Forefront of Development Studies

A central approach in the continued re-evaluation of religion and development concerns the conception of religion itself. Speaking of the study of international relations more broadly, Thomas warns that 'it will not be sufficient . . . to simply add religion . . . to our existing concepts and theories' (2005, p. 79). Thomas instead calls for an understanding of religion as 'a type of social tradition' that 'cannot be separated from specific social and cultural context' (p. 88). In other words, religion becomes an ever-present element of the social world made manifest in different ways depending on the practices and behaviours of people in particular contexts.

One immediate consequence of this approach is a challenge to the secular–sacral dichotomy that exists at the foundation of the development tradition. As Asad poignantly argues, '[I]f the secularization thesis seems increasingly implausible to some of us this is not simply because religion is now playing a vibrant part in the modern world of nations. In a sense what many would anachronistically call "religion" was always involved in the world of power' (2003, p. 200). Such a rationale helps us go beyond the mere inclusion of religion in development and anticipates another progression in our thinking: why placing religion at the *forefront* of the analysis yields new insights in our thinking about development.

I wish to suggest that maximizing the study of religion in development means taking seriously the ubiquity of religion in the development sphere. By ubiquity I am not suggesting that 'everything is religious', but rather, that development activity can be interpreted through a lens that views both secular and sacral aspects of the development sphere as involving religion. The distinction between 'secular' and 'sacral' is important and worth exploring further.

Understanding Development in 'Secular' and 'Sacral' Terms

We begin with arguably the most important idea in the re-conception of religion in the theory and practice of international relations and development: *secularism is not the absence of religion, but rather, the subordination of extant religious interests to other agendas in the public sphere* (see Rees, 2011, pp. 1–12). Therefore, a secular perspective of development will deduce how and in what ways existing religious organizations and interests become subordinate to the processes of more dominant actors and agendas.

For example, a secular perspective can be seen in the way religious actors are involved in adding ethical legitimacy and accountability to mainstream approaches to economic development. Saul (1997) has argued that nineteenth-century industrialization only produced social progress once civil society groups began to agitate against the Dickensian conditions first produced by the new modern cities. Stiglitz (2003) has argued for a similar role of civil society groups and institutions to produce a new paradigm of development in a rapidly globalizing world. For some theorists religion plays an important role in this process to produce a more ethical framework for the global market economy. Dunning calls the end product 'Responsible global capitalism (RGC) . . . a means of providing a richer, healthier and more meaningful life style for individuals and their families; and of advancing the economic objectives and social transformation of societies' (2003, pp. 11–12). The RGC project includes religious actors as part of 'non-market institutions within which the market is embedded and which, together, characterize a global society' (ibid., p. 13). Within this approach, religious perspectives are included to inform the broadening set of development measures such as the Human Development Index

(HDI) of the UN, thereby becoming embedded in the 'value-adding activities of RGC' (ibid., pp. 15, 17). Within the discourse divergent religious traditions are viewed as an important source of moral standards required to uphold a coherent ethical framework of globalization (Ahmad, 2003; Griffiths, 2003; Sacks, 2003). In this way we see religion employed as a source of moral legitimacy for development orthodoxy united under a project of moral improvement for economic globalization. This is a secular expression of religion because even though religious traditions are active (and indeed important) in this development discourse, they are also subordinate to a larger more primary economic agenda.

In contrast to the secular perspective of religion, *a sacral understanding conceives and observes ways in which religious actors and interests act as primary agents in the public sphere* (see Rees, 2011, pp. 12–18). Therefore, a sacral perspective of development will deduce how and in what ways existing religious organizations and interests shape and even create development practices and priorities.

A sacral perspective of religion can be seen in the way faith-based organizations play a primary and often indispensible role in achieving core development objectives. For example, the Community of Sant'Egidio, a lay Catholic organization founded in Rome in 1968 on a platform of service to the poor and working for peace, is a noted actor in the area of conflict mediation (Appleby, 2000, pp. 288–92; Haynes, 2007, pp. 91–4). Sant'Egidio's efforts in political mediation extend to contexts as diverse as Algeria, Burundi and Guatemala. Sant-Egidio's contribution is sacral because the primary motivation for action grows out of the religious tradition to which it belongs. Two prominent examples of this work are Sant'Egidio's central role in the successful resolution in 1992 of the civil war in Mozambique (Haynes, 2007, p. 92) and its role as a central mediator in the unsuccessful peace negotiations between Serb, Albanian and Kosovar leaders prior to the international war between NATO forces and Serbia in 1999 (Appleby, 2000, pp. 290–91). Based on these kinds of efforts and achievements, Appleby describes Sant'Egidio as an 'exemplary' institution evidencing 'the ability of religious NGOs to collaborate fruitfully with secular government and non-governmental organizations' (ibid., p. 290). In the same way that secularism does not mean the absence of religion, sacralism does not negate the importance of secular interests. For the Community of Sant'Egidio, secular actors and interests are incorporated into the more primary framework of the Catholic peace tradition.

To summarize, I have offered a rationale for why religion is an important focus in development theory and practice, and why placing religion at the forefront of the analysis offers unique insights into development discourse. More specifically, the demarcation of secular religion (as subordinate) and sacral religion (as primary) is important because it means that the full range of institutions and interests shaping development can now be analysed through the religious lens. Therefore, such an approach fundamentally recasts studies of religion in development, once driven by the basic question 'What is religion and does it have a role in development?', to a new agenda motivated by the more productive question 'Where is religion and what is it doing in the development sphere?' As an example, the latter question allows us to study the secondary (secular) and primary (sacral) dynamics of religion at play in the policy domain of development institutions. So it is that we now turn to a brief analysis of the world's premier development IFI from a religious perspective.

THE DEVELOPMENT POLICIES OF THE WORLD BANK GROUP

Having laid the conceptual ground for a new approach to religion in development, we can now analyse development institutions according to this approach. This will be operationalized by studying the policy dynamics of the World Bank Group (WBG) through the religious lens. The importance of the WBG in our analysis is established, followed by secular and sacral interpretations of WBG approaches to development over time.

The Power and Influence of the WBG

It has been argued that knowledge underpins the setting of the development agenda and is concentrated in IFIs, particularly the World Bank and regional development banks, as well as influential bilateral aid donors. Since the shift away from state-led development towards market-led development in the 1970s the power of IFIs has increased as they control knowledge to set development priorities and the material capacity to implement them (Bøås and McNeill, 2004, pp. 3–6). One clear and significant outcome of this process is that IFIs have opened a space for other actors to negotiate and set the development agenda (Guttal, 2006, p. 27). The opening of the development space has led to a greater role for civil society in setting, negotiating, and implementing development priorities (Carbone and Lister, 2006, p. 7). Whilst we are principally concerned to analyse this 'opening' process at the WBG from a religious perspective, a brief introduction to the institution is required.

At the close of World War II and the beginning of the modern development era, the World Bank and the International Monetary Fund (IMF) were established to stabilize international currencies and facilitate post-war reconstruction (Woods, 2001, p. 279). Along with the General Agreement on Tariffs and Trade (GATT) these institutions were also created to align free-market economies and deal with problems that had arisen in the international economy in the 1930s (O'Brien and Williams, 2004, p. 118). Analytical perspectives of the WBG vary from conceptions of an (often malign) hegemonic power (Murphy, 2000, pp. 789–80) to an (often ineffective) development bureaucracy (Einhorn, 2001; Woods, 2001; Stiglitz, 2003) to a pluralistic institution of ongoing importance and (often unrealized) potential to better development practice (St. Clair, 2006).

The WBG consists of five distinct but interrelated parts: the International Bank for Reconstruction and Development (IBRD), the International Finance Corporation (IFC), the International Development Association (IDA), the Multilateral Investment Guarantee Agency (MIGA) and the International Centre for the Settlement of Investment Disputes (ICSID). Each of these constituent parts performs distinct functions and, more importantly, can be potentially understood according to varying procedural values. Thus, the World Bank Group is at once a single organization and what may be legitimately called an IGO cluster. The reader will have observed that I at times abbreviate the proper noun World Bank as WBG. On no occasion shall I use the shortened form 'the Bank', even though it is a common usage in secondary literature and also the World Bank's own abbreviation. The preference for WBG is a way to emphasize the view of the World Bank as both a plural and a unitary entity. As a related aside, such an approach also reflects what is needed in thinking about religions – though united by a unique tradition, each religion is also internally diverse.

There are several reasons why the World Bank is the subject of considerable attention by development studies, and is therefore an appropriate focus for our study of religion. First, the WBG is the largest multilateral development institution in the global political economy (GPE) with a constituency that is equally global. As noted by Nobel Prize winner and founder of the Grameen Bank in Bangladesh Muhammad Yunus, 'the World Bank's influence is global and total' (cited in Benjamin, 2007, p. xi). Most WBG loans are part of larger packages that involve regional development banks and UN agencies (such as the UNDP). In 2008, the WBG committed US$38.2 billion in loans, grants, equity investments and guarantees to its members and private businesses in member countries (World Bank, 2008, p. 2). Its focus is to fund investment in infrastructure, reduce poverty and help countries adjust their economies to the demands of the GPE. The most significant international organizations to affect disparities in global economic development belong to the WBG (Rittberger and Zangl, 2006, p. 50).

Second, the WBG wields a relative though not insignificant autonomy from the constituent states that govern it. In financial terms, the World Bank is creditworthy on private capital markets and can conduct its core operations without the constant ratification of states (ibid., p. 173). The World Bank is also an independent agency within the United Nations system (Pease, 2003, p. 22). Barnett and Finnemore appealed to seven major studies that 'consistently [identified] an independent culture and agendas for action' (1999, p. 705) to conclude that IOs (international organizations) such as the World Bank are diffusers of norms – understood as collectively held views or standards of behaviour (Finnemore, 1996) – that simultaneously serve, inform and create the interests of states.

Third, the WBG has undergone numerous missional changes and its operations have over time come under increased and often intense scrutiny (Agarwala, 1983; Einhorn, 2001; Woods, 2001). Forman and Segaar (2006) describe the global political economy as operating within rapidly 'changing dynamics of mutilateralism' that are, in turn, created by the conditions of 'accelerated globalization'. As a result, WBG operations have been characterized by often radical shifts in development priorities. Shifts in WBG policy reflect (and sometimes create) shifts in the global development agenda. We shall now interpret the shifts in WBG development policy through the heuristic lens of religion.

The Dynamics of the WBG Policy in Religious Perspective

As Pincus and Winters note, 'the World Bank as we know it bears little resemblance to the institution envisaged at the Bretton Woods conference in 1944' (2002, p. 2). Rittberger and Zangl summarize the evolution of the World Bank's development from its creation to the present through four phases (2006, pp. 175–6). What follows is a brief description of some of the secular and sacral dynamics of religion at work within the phases of WBG operations so described.

The subordination of religion: modernization to poverty eradication

Given the modern secular origins of development practice, it is unremarkable to suggest that the first two phases of WBG policy were characterized by the strong subordination of religion. The question 'Where is religion?' in the policy domain of the WBG in this period is answered in the negative.

The first phase (1946–68) of the WBG was characterized by modernization and focused on monumental state development projects (Kapur et al., 1997, pp. 85–137). During this period, 'the standard view of an underdeveloped country saw it as one with a predominantly large population characterized by the absence of modern values' (O'Brien and Williams, 2004, p. 268). In the 1950s and 1960s the view that 'modernization necessarily leads to a decline of religion, both in society and in the minds of individuals' (Berger, 1999, p. 2) was an uncontested axiom of the West. Remenyi observes, with notable exceptions, that development theorists in the period, 'regarded the improvement of people's livelihoods as little more than by-products of the building blocks of modernization' (2004, p. 25; see also pp. 25–26). Simultaneously, the global development agenda was established within a theory of economic dualism whereby modern dynamic political economies were contrasted to traditional stagnant society of the Third World (O'Brien and Williams, 2004, p. 268). The subordination of religion, generally considered as belonging to a pre-modern cultural layer, was an automatic consequence of this view in development. As such, there appears to be no emphasis on religion within the WBG agenda.

Whilst the WBG would begin to move toward a broader philosophy in the late 1960s, religion was no less subordinate. One general reason for this may be that post-colonial demands being formulated by Third World coalitions such as the Non-Aligned Movement and Group of 77, and formalized in the United Nations Conference on Trade and Development (UNCTAD), were driven by secular-critical ideological positions. For instance, in 1974 the proposed New International Economic Order marked an ideological clash between critical development approaches (i.e., contesting liberal capitalism) and liberal approaches that favoured Western modernization models (Cohn, 2005, pp. 105–6). The driving forces for change in this context were therefore secular-critical ideologies that argued exclusively within a materialist framework.

In this context, the second phase of WBG operations (1968–79) under the Presidency of Robert McNamara marked a significant shift toward a basic needs approach combined with an economistic emphasis on growth and distribution (Rittberger and Zangl, 2006, pp. 175–6). Poverty eradication and a focus on 'poverty projects' became the central objectives of the World Bank at this time (Kapur et al., 1997, p. 331; see also pp. 269–330). During this phase, in important contexts such as Africa, the WBG became a 'leading aid coordinator, analyst, and source of technical assistance' rather than a direct deliverer of aid (ibid., p. 710). It should therefore be noted that significant and dynamic debate characterizes this period when understood from the perspective of broader WBG operations. However, it is equally true that this dynamic process subordinated religion to a negligible status at the institutional level of the WBG. There was much movement within the secular sphere of development, but few openings existed for sacral influence.

Subordination and resistance: the shift to structural adjustment

In the third phase of the WBG's evolution (1979–94), religion remained a subordinate element to secular development orthodoxy. However, the sacral agency of religious actors did begin to play a role in contesting and broadening the development agenda. The third phase of the World Bank's development is characterized by a strategy of structural adjustment programmes (SAPs) (Rittberger and Zangl, 2006, p. 176). First articulated in 1979 (ibid., p. 506; see also pp. 505–11), structural adjustment operated when the WBG and the IMF 'linked the allocation of loans initially to macroeconomic conditions and later even to political conditions' (ibid., p. 175) favourable to neoliberal assumptions and interests. In development terms, this phase can be seen as the dominance of market-led economistic development orthodoxy, and gave birth to the phrase 'Washington Consensus' in international politics.

The third phase is marked by increased and at times intense conflict between the WBG and an array of dissenting actors in the international system, and not without justification. Although described as the 'most powerful of the public institutions of global governance' (Murphy, 2000, p. 791) the World Bank was also perceived by many as having malign interests, seeking patronage from hegemons and bestowing structural injustice upon lesser actors. The 1980s marked a period of intense protest toward World Bank policy. Since the shift away from state-led development towards market-led development in the 1970s the power of IFIs increased as they began to control both knowledge to set development priorities (Bøäs and McNeill, 2004, pp. 3–4). The development agenda espoused by IFIs came under heavy criticism in the 1980s and 1990s and the response of IFIs has been referred to as a 'new kind of synthesis' (Stiglitz, 2003; Öniş and Şenses, 2005, p. 273) that has opened a space for other actors to negotiate and set the development agenda (Guttal, 2006, p. 27; see also McDuie-Ra and Rees, 2010). Religious actors played a role in this process, contesting the development agenda set by the WBG. Marshall and Van Saanen observe aspects of this critique from the vantage of religious actors in development: 'Conflicts around dam building and displacement of indigenous people, in particular, resonated deeply with many faith institutions, as did the mounting indebtedness of many poor countries, and perceived links between economic growth and environmental damage' (Marshall and Van Saanen, 2007, pp. 2–3).

Mihevc (1995) describes the increased agency of religious actors in Africa responding to the conditions generated by the ideology of SAPs. In the mid-1980s the All African Conference of Churches (AACC) commissioned a long-term study to examine the root causes of drought and famine in the continent. The report observed that 'the economic mechanisms of exploitation and oppression once set in motion are difficult to reverse and this is the problem that all Africa is facing' (quoted in Mihevc, 1995, p. 227). Such observation led to the Luanda Declaration of 1989, formulated by a network of economists, theologians, social scientists and grassroots community activists to decry SAPs ideology (ibid.). Thus, Mihevc observes a significant change in the broad-based agency of the churches of Africa from the 1980s onwards, becoming 'far more outspoken in criticising the national elites who . . . actively participated in a model of development that have led to greater impoverishment and the repression of basic human rights' (ibid., p. 229). He continues:

> The grace period indicative of the 1960s and 1970s where churches . . . subordinated issues like democracy and human rights to the more pressing problem of development has given way to a spate of harsh indictments of the political elites who have profited from this model of development at the expense of the poor. (Ibid.)

The changed posture described above did not go unnoticed by the WBG, and as we shall explore, would influence WBG strategy and development. In summary, the third phase of WBG operations can be understood as the continuing secular subordination of religion via the economistic philosophy of the SAP regime. Yet simultaneously, the third phase is characterized by sacral elements of resistance as religious actors emerged both in coalitions opposed to SAPs and as distinct respondents to the legacy of SAPs.

From subordination and protest to the integration of religion: the Comprehensive Development Framework

The turbulence of the third phase led to transformations of development orthodoxy (Stiglitz, 2003). This new period (1995–2005) saw the emergence of religious groups from the status of secondary players in development advocacy against SAPs to development partners within a new development framework.

The transition beyond structural adjustment policy-lending was partly internal, via a re-dedication to poverty reduction and internal reviews such as the *Wapenhans Report* of 1992. Yet other reports held to a firm ideological commitment to the SAP regime. 'The Bank's 1994 Adjustment in Africa report concluded that the fruits of adjustment had not yet been borne in Africa [because of] the inadequate and half-hearted adoption of reforms' (Kapur et al., 1997, p. 797). Significantly, policy change was also the result of advocacy for change by civil society actors such as development NGOs (Rittberger and Zangl, 2006, p. 175). Thus, the fourth phase is marked by a range of broader initiatives, most significantly formulated in the Comprehensive Development Framework (CDF) submitted in 1999 during the Presidency of James D. Wolfensohn (1995–2005). According to Pincus and Winters, the WBG 'internalized the logic of its critics to a surprising degree' (2002, pp. 175–6) and with this came the transition to a broader development agenda.

Under WBG President James Wolfensohn, the CDF was established as a response to the failures of structural adjustment, predicated on the concept of partnership between the WBG and the borrowing government, with the former playing 'the repositioned institutional role of "Knowledge Bank"' (ibid.). Alongside this, and in a radical shift from the top-down agenda of structural adjustment, was the WBG's adoption of a bottom-up 'human poverty' approach emphasizing a liberal democratic concept of 'capabilities', defined as 'the overall freedoms people have to live the kind of lives they have reason to value' (Sen, 1999, p. 10). The emphasis on human capabilities also placed a high priority on increasing the WBG commitment to democratization in development, and to partnership with civil society actors such as trade unions, small business and, of course, religious communities.

The impact upon WBG relations with religious actors was therefore immediate. We continue the example drawn from the African churches to illustrate the kind of expectations and approaches held by religious actors toward the CDF. In March 2000 a conference was jointly organized by the WBG and the Council of Anglican Provinces of Africa. Held in Nairobi, the conference on 'Alleviating Poverty in Africa' was designed to explore closer collaboration between the participants 'especially at the grassroots level' in anticipation of future meetings 'involving the full range of faith communities in Africa and other important actors, such as governments and the private sector' (Belshaw et al., 2001, p. viii). The exchanges identify issues of responsibility, accountability, contribution and caution, within a development dialogue where the WBG and the churches were considered equals. Samuel observes that the world's largest development agency brings to religious organizations 'enormous resources, professionalism, an understanding of markets, and finances' (2001, p. 242). One consequence is that the World Bank brings a professionalism of reporting that challenges the practice of religious actors and makes them more accountable to donors. Yet the WBG also 'brings its own vulnerability and its interest in refashioning itself so that it can serve developing countries more effectively' (ibid.). These elements combine to reinforce the perception of the WBG as dynamic, and from the perspective of at least some religious actors such as Samuel, open to change and transformation in the implementation of development partnerships. To adopt Christian religious parlance in keeping with the current example of prospective partnerships with African churches, the World Bank could also bring a degree of penitence for past mistakes to new partnerships with religious actors. Mihevc parallels the religious zeal for SAPs in the 1980s with missionaries of previous generations (1995, pp. 10–19; see also George and Sabelli, 1994). Thus, the burdens of the past seem to be a *shared* challenge for religion and the WBG. For instance, the African church must face a legacy of both missionary imperialism and the concomitant role as pacifier, on religious grounds, of populations against their own political interests (Mihevc, 1995, pp. 226–32).

These elements lead to perhaps the most important instrumental role attributed to the WBG by Samuel, namely, that of an advocate for religious actors in their relations with states: 'Could the World Bank lean on governments and ask them to work with the Church? [To say to governments]: If you want to work with the World Bank, work with the Church also' (2001, p. 242). The advocacy role so described is important and complex. Not only does it equate with the conventional challenge of representing the weak in the face of the powerful. In terms of the present study, it also embodies an expectation that the WBG will represent the interests of sacral agents in their relation to secular state actors. It is a crucial litmus test on the issue of partnership that takes seriously the secular–sacral dynamics of religion. Could the WBG meet this expectation? Early indications through the third and fourth phases of WBG operations were positive and led to the creation of a religion and development programme at the WBG.

Whilst the example we have used is that of dialogue between the WBG and Christian leaders, the ensuing engagements by the WBG were broadly based across multiple faiths. We turn now to consider select dynamics of religion that influenced the World Bank across the third and fourth phases of its policy development.

HOW RELIGION ENTERED THE POLICY DOMAIN OF THE WBG

Aside from the general impetus created by the CDF, how did religion enter the policy domain of the WBG? We shall attempt to answer this question by identifying secular and sacral dynamics of religion that emerged over two decades and laid the foundation for the creation of the faith and development framework of the WBG. The following details are indicative of a larger story of which I have written elsewhere (see Rees, 2011).

Secular Religion and World Bank Policy

We begin by categorizing two dynamics that helped to bring religion into the development discourse of the WBG as secular. As in previous applications, secular factors are understood to hold religion as a secondary element in the development process. These dynamics are the policy approaches of comparative IOs toward religion and the motivations of WBG President Wolfensohn (1995–2005).

Policy developments on religion in comparative IOs

NGO advocacy against World Bank policy in the 1980s suggest that external actors can influence ideological posture and practice of IFIs to some extent. Scholars have observed the effect of socialization processes upon IO behaviour. As a recent study on the WBG and culture summarizes, 'the World Bank ought to be understood as a cultural as well as an economic institution . . . economics and economic systems are culturally constituted frameworks, both productive of and reproduced by complex networks of social relations (Benjamin, 2007, p. xii). To this extent, the WBG's faith and development thinking is part of a broader collective process of engagement by IOs on the question of religion. For example, Thomas observes that at the same time the WBG was beginning to face the issue of religion in its policy framing, the World Health Organization (WHO) 'started to redefine health, well-being and quality of life to include spiritual health' (2004, p. 25). Similar engagements with religion were also being made by the International Labour Organization (ILO) (Peccoud, 2004) and the Inter-American Development Bank (Wolfensohn, 2004, pp. 21–2). These examples portray an IO sector responding to the instrumental pressures of religion in contemporary world politics and potentially the legitimacy dividends that such engagements could yield. It is the socialization process between IOs that is to be emphasized here rather than the primary agency of religious actors. As such, it is a secular factor where religion plays an important secondary role in the policy development process.

WBG President James Wolfensohn

It is hard to imagine a faith and development programme at the World Bank without the influence of key leaders and relational networks among them. However, by far the most significant personal influence upon the increased agency of religion at the World Bank goes to its President, James D. Wolfensohn. Throughout the volumes of World Bank documents that bear his name, religion seems nowhere explicit in a personal sense. His biographer mentions little of religion, nor of Wolfensohn as a gatekeeper for faith and development (Mallaby, 2004). Nevertheless, it remains the case that 'the systematic attempt to engage the worlds of religion' is directly attributable to him (Marshall and Van Saanen, 2007, pp. 5–6). It is Marshall, who worked for several years as a counsellor to the President and was heavily involved in the WBG religion initiative, who explicitly identified a religious motivation to Wolfensohn's pursuit of faith partnerships (2006, p. 4). However, Marshall is equally clear that beyond religious conviction, three other factors of an instrumental nature were guiding Wolfensohn forward:

> A negative one was that we were hearing a lot of criticism from faith institutions about the Bank . . . This was one reason to engage, whether to explain ourselves better or to understand better why there was this opposition . . . The second reason was that Jim saw religious or faith organizations as the largest distribution system in the world . . . The third was that he was very impressed by specific data about the role of faith organizations in education and health. (Marshall, 2006, p. 5)

On the weight of argument, therefore, the agency of ideas and interests affecting Wolfensohn on religion was secular instrumental more than it was sacral.

Sacral Religion and World Bank Policy

We shall now suggest two sacral factors that helped to bring religion into the development discourse of the WBG. As in previous applications, sacral factors hold religious actors and interests to be a primary force in political dynamics. The dynamics are an informal forum on ethics held among WBG staff, and the Jubilee 2000 debt campaign.

The Friday Morning Group

The first sacral factor is situated in the individual religious motivations of WBG staff that led to a small group with a disproportionate influence. Institutions can be understood in operational, historical and also personal ways. The latter approach might include characterizations of an organization's members, such as cultural background, education, and also religious belief. According to Marshall and Van Saanen: 'a small but not insignificant number of Bank staff members have some training in theology, and many more are members of faith communities or are inspired and motivated by the values that have drawn them to development work' (2007, p. 5). In 1981 some of these staff members based at the WBG headquarters in Washington DC began to meet every Friday morning. So it was that the Values for Development Group, more popularly known as the Friday Morning Group (FMG) began (see Beckmann et al., 1991b).

What role might such a group have played in steering the WBG toward religion? First, the FMG became a place where the topic of religion could be explicitly interwoven with World Bank policy discourse, and this had an implicitly broadening effect on policy discourse. It is no coincidence that the same David Beckmann, who in 1981 helped found a holistic forum like the FMG, also warned the institution in 1983 that 'the Bank's activities have become markedly less focused on reducing poverty' (Kapur et al., 1997, p. 349). Such internal discourses were to become important for the holistic developments that ensued in subsequent years. Beckmann for instance, would go on to lead Bread for the World, one of the Christian NGOs who linked with the WBG's new Environmental Department in 1987. Second, it could be argued that the FMG provided the concept (and nomenclature) of 'values' that would, subsequently, help create an institutional space for engaging religion called 'the DDVE' (Development Dialogue on Values and Ethics). The concept of 'values' may have thus allowed both informal and formal discourses on religion to flourish without being collapsed into, or lost inside, more generic discussions of 'culture' in development. At the FMG, 'values' translated into topics such as 'Hindu philosophy in action' (Agarwala, 1991), development and Christian hope (Beckmann, 1991a), relations between faith and science (Burmester, 1991), and Islamic views of a just society (Serageldin, 1991). Third, the longstanding presence of the FMG provided the idea of religion-as-values with a longevity beyond any particular evolution of the WBG. Ownership of the FMG by the institution constitutes de facto a small but not insignificant ownership of the importance of religion as part of its historical and ideological identity. Each of these factors alludes to the agency of religion to shape aspects of WBG culture and policy, thereby encouraging the view that the FMG embodies a sacral dynamic that helped bring religion into the WBG.

Jubilee 2000 and debt advocacy

One of the most important religious actors to emerge in the development sphere in the past decade has been the Jubilee 2000 movement. The concept of Jubilee originates in the biblical concept of debt forgiveness laid out in ancient Hebrew Law, and is specifically referred to in the biblical text of Leviticus 25. Jonathan Sacks describes the Jubilee principle from its original meaning in the contemporary context of development activism:

> The Bible is acutely aware that the workings of the free market can create, over time, inequalities so great as to amount to dependency and which can only be removed by periodic redistribution. Hence the sabbatical year in which those who had sold themselves into slavery through poverty were released, and all debts cancelled . . . This was the biblical legislation behind the successful campaign, Jubilee 2000, to provide international debt relief to developing countries and underlies Chancellor of the Exchequer Gordon Brown's proposal for a 'modern Marshall Plan' for the developing world. (Sacks, 2003, pp. 223–4)

Whatever hermeneutical merits and pitfalls may exist in the transfer from ancient to modern situations, in terms of agency the concept of Jubilee became an undoubtedly prime influence behind one of the most significant global advocacy movements of recent decades. In the post-Cold War period Third World debt became one of the leading points of contestation between and among civil society actors, states and IFIs. Debt remained critically high in sub-Saharan Africa, for instance, and the African churches advocated for change on this and the effects of structural adjustment since the 1980s (Mihevc, 1995, pp. 225–72). Building on this foundation, Jubilee – both the concept and the advocacy movement of the same name – seemed to act with gravitational force to pull this energy into a larger global protest phenomenon and 'resulted in a global social movement that altered popular and official views of debt relief and enabled civil society to participate in development decisions' (Marshall and Keough, 2004, p. 44; see also Busby, 2007).

The power of the Jubilee movement was not lost on the incoming World Bank President. Marshall and Keough write:

> When James Wolfensohn became President of the World Bank in 1995, one of his earliest acts was to pose demanding and far-reaching questions about the approach to debt and highly indebted countries . . . Thus the Jubilee 2000-inspired movement . . . helped to encourage and accelerate alternative mechanisms to relieve the debt of the world's poorest countries. (2004, p. 40)

The resulting strategies included the Heavily Indebted Poor Countries initiative (HICP) and Poverty Reduction Strategy Papers (PRSPs), both designed to manage debt reduction in the context of sustainable and structural development.

As important as the connections generated by Jubilee were, the tensions it created with the WBG as the campaign progressed are also worth noting. Wolfensohn had misgivings about a second round of debt relief, which created conflict with a coalition of actors including Oxfam, Jubilee and governments such as in Uganda (Mallaby, 2004, p. 44). Moreover, the Jubilee push to debt cancellation was not met, and the prescriptions for its advancement were deemed too slow. Thus, whilst the 'Jubilee organizers generally came to recognize that the World Bank . . . had become more inclusive', dissatisfied with the HIPC-PRSP initiatives, the successor movement to Jubilee 2000 'continues in its critique of the World Bank and works to mobilize popular support in favour of alternative solutions' (Marshall and Keough, 2004, p. 44). Thus, Jubilee 2000 became a key learning ground for the simultaneous connections and disconnections that sacral development partnerships could bring to IFIs.

OBSERVATIONS

Through this indicative sample we can observe that the dynamics that animated the WBG's initial engagement with religion were spread across the secular–sacral spectrum (for extended analysis see Rees, 2011, pp. 88–99). This is significant because it suggests that the locus of religion as it was introduced to the WBG is to be found neither in secular motivations alone nor purely in WBG strategy. To the contrary, the religious factors involved in the account leave development analysts and policy-makers with a complex array of issues to consider. I shall name just two. First, *secular and sacral factors outside the WBG domain* seem to play a role in influencing the WBG on religion: the socialization process among other predominantly secular IOs and the sacral concept of Jubilee. Whilst Jubilee 2000 involved action on the equally secular issue of debt reduction for the Third World, without the sacral concept of the biblical Jubilee, the impetus behind this specific campaign action would not have existed at all. Second, *secular and sacral factors inside the WBG domain* also play a role: President Wolfensohn engaged faith actors and interests mainly from an instrumental motivation, and the FMG was created from the vestiges of religious belief in the lives of World Bank staff.

The introductory analysis of secular and sacral dynamics of religion therefore suggests that both elements of religion were at play to influence the policy formation of the world's largest and most power development IFI. Without the prior reconsideration of how religion should be understood in development discourse as both secular and sacral, the nuanced understanding of religion in WBG policy would have remained either unnoticed or merely interpreted through a secular-instrumental grid. There is, of course, much more to the story to explore than present space allows (see Pallas, 2005; Marshall and Van Saanen, 2007; McDuie-Ra and Rees, 2010; Rees, 2011, pp. 103–37), however, we now turn to more general themes that arise from the arguments that have been laid.

IFIs and the Faith Engagement

I conclude the chapter with two questions of importance in the consideration of IFI policy toward religion going forward. Each question deals implicitly with secular and sacral dynamics of religion. The first concerns development policy from above (i.e., at the macro-level of the international system). The second concerns development from below (i.e., at the micro-level of international society). Each question is relatively simple, and yet is indicative of the complexities opening up to researchers in religion and development studies.

How will IFIs respond to the ongoing interests of religions compared to the embedded interests of nation-states?

Of all the details one could include in the subsequent story of the World Bank's faith and development programme, one story stands out both for its drama and its implications. In late 2000, the WBG Executive Board met to consider President Wolfensohn's proposal for the establishment of a small 'Directorate on Faith', which was modelled on a successful programme of the Inter-American Development Bank. The plan was vetoed by a margin of 24 votes to zero (Tyndale, 2003, p. 25; Clarke, 2007, pp. 81–2). What is to explain the complete rejection of the President's own proposal? The Directorate on Faith may have been perceived by key stakeholders to be the outer edge of an already worrying expansion of the IFI's mandate, what would subsequently be called the 'World Bank's mission creep' (Einhorn, 2001). Yet what appears more central in interpreting the decision is the long-held issue of sacral agency in international relations. This is certainly Wolfensohn's own perspective:

> our Board, including the United States, and other members of the Board, have vigorously opposed the mixing of faith and the work that we do. They say that the faith-based organizations – it's the old story of church and state. You don't want to mix the running of the country with any sort of infection from the faiths . . . national governments do not give homes to faith-based organizations typically in their own administrative set-ups, and they're just not prepared to let us do it. (Wolfensohn, 2004, pp. 21–2)

Thus, the veto represents a classic strategy of Westphalian control where nation-state stakeholders contain the energies of culture and religious interests for reasons of operational stability. At a time when religion and development research is burgeoning, religion and IFI research may therefore have reawakened the age-old problematique of state-centricity.

Can (and should) IFIs extend their work with faith-based organizations (FBOs) and reach out to faith communities (FCs)?

One of the studies co-written by the author on religion and development concluded that 'formalized religious organizations seem to have a different capacity than informal religious groups and communities in relations with IFIs as they have access to the political spaces where the international development agenda is negotiated and set' This view was reached after analysing the type of religious organizations that the WBG worked with against the three categories (McDuie-Ra and Rees, 2010, p. 28):

- formal organizations in the North: setting the development agenda;
- formal organizations in the South: access to the development agenda;
- informal actors in the South: limited access to the development agenda.

Those WBG programmes least successful were with informal communities in the South. What remains unclear is whether this conclusion tells us about the limits of IFI capacity or the inadequacy of IFI policy at the grassroots level. At a time when religion and development research is concentrating on FBOs, the development priorities of FCs might serve as a litmus test for whether IFI policy reflects a commitment to development partnerships at the ground level of development practice.

CONCLUSION

I have introduced the issues above with the intention of provoking further enquiry – and scrutiny where it is needed – into the growing relations between religious groups and IFIs. We have done so attempting to work within clear and controllable assumptions about how the different dynamics of religion can be employed as analytical tools in development studies. This has been modelled in the first instance via an introductory study of religious impacts upon World Bank policy. Understanding the ubiquity of religion in the development sphere, and the utility of secular and sacral understandings of religion at work in development theory and practice, creates new possibilities for analysing religion in development at the conceptual, institutional and policy levels.

REFERENCES

Agarwala, R. (1991), 'A harmonist manifesto', in D. Beckmann, R. Agarwala, S. Burmester and I Serageldin, in *Friday Morning Reflections at the World Bank: Essays on Values and Development*, Washington, DC: Seven Locks Press, pp. 1–16.

Ahmad, K. (2003), 'The challenge of global capitalism: an Islamic perspective', in J.H. Dunning (ed.), *Making Globalization Good: The Moral Challenges of Global Capitalism*, Oxford: Oxford University Press, pp. 181–209.

Appleby, R.S. (2000), *The Ambivalence of the Sacred: Religion, Violence, and Reconciliation*, Lanham, MD: Rowman and Littlefield.

Asad, T. (2003), *Formations of the Secular: Christianity, Islam, Modernity*, Stanford, CA: Stanford University Press.

Barnett, M.N. and M. Finnemore (1999), 'The politics, power and pathologies of international organizations', *International Organization*, **53**(4), 699–732.

Beckmann, D. (1991a), 'Sober prospects and Christian hope', in D. Beckmann, R. Agarwala, S. Burmester and I. Serageldin, *Friday Morning Reflections at the World Bank: Essays on Values and Development*, Washington, DC: Seven Locks Press, pp. 17–36.

Beckmann, D., R. Agarwala, S. Burmester and I. Serageldin (1991b), *Friday Morning Reflections at the World Bank: Essays on Values and Development*, Washington, DC: Seven Locks Press.

Belshaw, D., R. Calderisi and C. Sugden (2001), *Faith in Development: Partnership Between the World Bank and the Churches of Africa*, Oxford and Washington, DC: Regnum Books and The World Bank.

Benjamin, B. (2007), *Invested Interests: Capital, Culture, and the World Bank*, Minneapolis, MN: University of Minnesota Press.

Berger, P. (1999), 'The desecularization of the world: a global overview', in P. Berger (ed.), *The Desecularization of the World: Resurgent Religion and World Politics*, Grand Rapids, MI: Eerdmans, pp. 1–18.

Bøås, M. and D. McNeill (2004), 'Introduction, power and ideas in multilateral institutions: towards an interpretive framework', in M. Bøås and D. McNeill (eds), *Global Institutions and Development: Framing the World?* London and New York: Routledge, pp. 1–12.

Burmester, S. (1991), 'Can the twilight of the gods be prevented?', in D. Beckmann, R. Agarwala, S. Burmester and I. Serageldin, *Friday Morning Reflections at the World Bank: Essays on Values and Development*, Washington, DC: Seven Locks Press, pp. 37–54.

Busby, J. (2007), 'Bono Made Jesse Helms Cry: Jubilee 2000, debt relief, and moral action in international politics' *International Studies Quarterly* 51 (2), 247–75.

Carbone, M. and M. Lister (2006), *New Pathways in International Development: Gender and Civil Society in EU Policy*, Aldershot: Ashgate.

Clarke, G. (2007), 'Agents of transformation? Donors, faith-based organisations and international development', *Third World Quarterly*, **28**(1), 77–96.

Clarke, G. (2008), 'Faith-based organizations and international development: an overview', in G. Clarke and M. Jennings (eds), *Development, Civil Society and Faith-based Organizations: Bridging the Sacred and the Secular*, New York: Palgrave Macmillan, pp. 17–45.

Clarke, G. and M. Jennings (eds), *Development, Civil Society and Faith-based Organizations: Bridging the Sacred and the Secular*, New York: Palgrave Macmillan.

Cohn, T.H. (2005), *Global Political Economy: Theory and Practice*, New York: Pearson Longman.

Dunning, J.H. (2003), 'The moral imperatives of global capitalism: an overview', in J.H. Dunning (ed.), *Making Globalization Good: The Moral Challenges of Global Capitalism*, Oxford: Oxford University Press, pp. 11–40.

Einhorn, J. (2001), 'The World Bank's mission creep', *Foreign Affairs*, **80**(5), 22–37.

Finnemore, M. (1996), 'Norms, culture, and world politics: insights from sociologies institutionalism', *International Organisation*, **50**(2), 325–47.
Forman, S. and D. Segaar (2006), 'New coalitions for global governance: the changing dynamics of multilateralism', *Global Governance*, **12**(2), 205–25.
George, S. and F. Sabelli (1994), *Faith and Credit: The World Bank's Secular Empire*, London: Penguin Books.
Griffiths, B. (2003), 'The challenge of global capitalism: a Christian perspective', in J.H. Dunning (ed.), *Making Globalization Good: The Moral Challenges of Global Capitalism*, Oxford: Oxford University Press, pp. 159–80.
Guttal, S. (2006), 'Challenging the knowledge business', in P. Utting (ed.), *Reclaiming Development Agendas: Knowledge, Power, and International Policy Making*, Basingstoke: Palgrave Macmillan/UNRSID, pp. 25–42.
Harcourt, W. (2003), 'Editorial: clearing the path of collective compassion', *Development*, **46**(4), 3–5.
Haynes, J. (2007), *Religion and Development: Conflict or Cooperation?*, New York: Palgrave Macmillan.
Helleiner, E. (2002), 'Economic nationalism as a challenge to economic liberalism', *International Studies Quarterly*, **46**(3), 307–29.
Kapur, D., J.P. Lewis and R. Webb (1997), *The World Bank: Its First Half Century, Vol. 1.*, Washington, DC: Brookings Institution Press.
Kingsbury, D. (2004), 'Introduction', in D. Kingsbury, J. Remenyi, J. McKay and J. Hunt (eds), *Key Issues in Development*, Sydney and New York: Palgrave Macmillan.
Mallaby, S. (2004), *The World's Banker*, Sydney: University of New South Wales Press.
Marshall, K. (2006), 'Interview: religion and international development', *Pew Forum*, 6 March, available at: www.pewforum.org/Government/Religion-and-International-Development.aspx; accessed 24 May 2008.
Marshall, K. and L. Keough (2004), *Mind, Heart and Soul in the Fight Against Poverty*, Washington, DC: The World Bank.
Marshall, K. and M. Van Saanen (2007), *Development and Faith: Where Mind, Heart and Soul Work Together*, Washington, DC: The World Bank.
McDuie-Ra, D. and J.A. Rees (2010), 'Religious actors, civil society and the development agenda: the dynamics of inclusion and exclusion', *Journal of International Development*, **22**(1), 20–36.
Mihevc, J. (1995), *The Market Tells Them So: The World Bank and Economic Fundamentalism in Africa*, London: Zed Books.
Murphy, C.N. (2000), 'Global governance: poorly done and poorly understood', *International Affairs*, **76**(4), 789–804.
O'Brien, R. and M. Williams (2004), *Global Political Economy*, New York: Palgrave Publishing.
Öniş, Z, and F. Şenses (2005), 'Rethinking the emerging post-Washington Consensus', *Development and Change*, **36**(2), 263–90.
Pallas, C.L. (2005), 'Canterbury to Cameroon: a new partnership between faiths and the World Bank', *Development in Practice*, **15**(5), 677–84.
Pease, K-K.S. (2003), *International Organizations: Perspectives on Governance in the Twenty-first Century*, Upper Saddle River, NJ: Pearson Education Inc.
Peccoud, D. (ed.) (2004), *Philosophical and Spiritual Perspectives on Decent Work*, Geneva: International Labour Office.
Peet, R. (1999), *Theories of Development*, New York: The Guildford Press.
Pincus, J.R. and J.A. Winters (2002), 'Reinventing the World Bank', in J.R. Pincus and J.A. Winters (eds), *Reinventing the World Bank*, Ithaca, NY: Cornell University Press, pp. 1–25.
Pfanner, T. (2005), 'Editorial', *International Review of the Red Cross*, **87**(858), 237–41.
Rees, J.A. (2011), *Religion in International Politics and Development: The World Bank and Faith Institutions*, Cheltenham, UK and Northampton, MA: Edward Elgar.
Remenyi, J. (2004), 'What is development?', in D. Kingsbury, J. Remenyi, J. McKay and J. Hunt (eds), *Key Issues in Development*, New York: Palgrave Macmillan, pp. 22–44.
Rist, G. (2008), *The History of Development: From Western Origins to Global Faith*, trans. by P. Camiller, London and New York: Zed Books.
Rittberger, V. and B. Zangl (2006), *International Organization: Polity, Politics and Policies*, New York: Palgrave Macmillan.
Sacks, J. (2003), 'Global covenant: a Jewish perspective', in J.H. Dunning (ed.), *Making Globalization Good: The Moral Challenges of Global Capitalism*, Oxford: Oxford University Press, pp. 210–31.
Samuel, V. (2001), 'The World Bank and the churches: reflections at the outset of a new partnership', in D. Belshaw, R. Calderisi and C. Sugden (eds), *Faith in Development. Partnership between the World Bank and the Churches of Africa*, Oxford and Washington, DC: Regnum Books/TheWorld Bank, pp. 237–43.
Saul J.R. (1997), *The Unconscious Civilization*, Harmondsworth: Penguin.
Sen, A. (1999), *Development as Freedom*, New York: Knopf.
Serageldin, I. (1991), 'The justly balanced society', in D. Beckmann, R. Agarwala, S. Burmester and

I. Serageldin, *Friday Morning Reflections at the World Bank: Essays on Values and Development*, Washington, DC: Seven Locks Press, pp. 55–74.

St. Clair, A.L. (2006), 'The World Bank as a transnational expertised institution', *Global Governance*, **12**(1), 77–95.

Stiglitz, J.E. (2003), 'Towards a new paradigm of development', in J.H. Dunning (ed.), *Making Globalization Good: The Moral Challenges of Global Capitalism*, Oxford: Oxford University Press, pp. 76–107.

Thomas, S.M. (2004), 'Faith and foreign aid, or how the World Bank got religion and why it matters', *The Review of Faith and International Affairs*, **2**(2), 21–30.

Thomas, S.M. (2005), *The Global Resurgence of Religion and the Transformation of International Relations*, New York: Palgrave Macmillan.

Tyndale, W. (2002), 'Faith and economics in "development": a bridge across the chasm?', in D. Eade (ed.), *Development and Culture: A Development in Practice Reader*, London: Oxfam GB/WFDD, pp. 45–59.

Tyndale (2003), 'Idealism and practicality: the role of religion and development', *Development*, **46**(4), 22–8.

Ver Beek, K.A. (2002), 'Spirituality: a development taboo', in D. Eade (ed.), *Development and Culture: A Development in Practice Reader*, London: Oxfam GB/WFDD, pp. 60–77.

Wolfensohn, J. (2004), 'Millennium challenges for faith and development: new partnerships to reduce poverty and strengthen conservation', Third Annual Richard Snowdon Lecture, Interfaith Conference of Metropolitan Washington, 30 March, Trinity College, Washington, DC, accessed 25 May 2006 from the website of the Development Dialogue on Values and Ethics (DDVE, World Bank) http://web.worldbank.org. Statements by President Wolfensohn used in this research are from the transcript of the Q&A that occurred following the Snowdon Lecture. Details of the Q&A are no longer included in the lecture transcript available on the World Bank website at http://go.worldbank.org/OAX42ODDR0.

Woods, N. (2001), 'Making the IMF and the World Bank more accountable', *International Affairs*, **77**(1), 83–100.

18 A sustainable Islamic microfinance model in poverty alleviation

Aimatul Yumina

INTRODUCTION

The UNDP *Human Development Report 2010* notes that based on the Multidimensional Poverty Index (MPI), there are 1.7 billion people living in poverty. Of these, 51 per cent live in South Asia; 28 per cent in sub-Saharan Africa; 15 per cent in East Asia and the Pacific; 3 per cent in Latin America and the Caribbean; 1 per cent in the Commonwealth of Independent States (CIS); and 2 per cent in the Arab states.

Islamic societies comprise 20 per cent of the world population or 1.3 billion Muslims worldwide. Nearly 70 per cent of all Muslims live in Asia (including the Middle East), while just over a quarter live in Africa. Poverty and destitution is widespread in Muslim countries. The report of the Islamic Development Bank (IDB) in 2008 reveals that its five member countries, Indonesia, Bangladesh, Pakistan, Nigeria and Egypt account for over half a billion (528 million) of the world's poor with incomes below US$2 a day or national poverty line. Those countries are Muslim dominated, except Nigeria. Based on the Human Development Index, majority Muslim countries are ranked very low, for example Mali at 101 and Burkina Faso at 102 out of 120 countries in the world (Obaidullah and Khan, 2008).

Accordingly, the access to financial services in the Islamic world is also very limited. The IDB reveals that only one-fifth or less of the adult population has access to financial services based on the data available in 17 member countries. In Saudi Arabia, Lebanon and Malaysia, more than half of its population has access to financial services, while the others such as Pakistan, Sudan, Palestine, Nigeria and Mozambique and Sierra Leone only less than 15 per cent of its population are financially included.

Concrete action to reduce the poverty and destitution problem is the implementation of one of the UN Millennium Development Goals (MDG), to cut by half the people living in poverty by 2015. Providing access to financial services is a critical factor in the achievement of the MDG. The evidence shows that access to financial services enables people to increase their household income, build assets and reduce their vulnerability to crisis; specifically, it has significant impact on improving health, nutrition intake, education and empowering women (Littlefield et al., 2003).

This chapter is interested in one aspect of poverty alleviation: microfinance. In particular it is interested in understanding how microfinance as a poverty alleviation tool aligns with poverty alleviation as understood within Islamic religious teaching. This chapter is set out as follows. Section two will discuss how poverty alleviation is understood and responded to within Islamic religious teaching. Section three describes Islamic microfinance as a poverty alleviation strategy. An integrated model of Islamic microfinance is introduced in the fourth section before this is illustrated by an Indonesian case study in section five. Section six concludes this chapter.

ISLAM AND POVERTY ALLEVIATION

Poverty in Islamic Perspective

Islam is a very practical religion. Muslim teaching is not just concerned with religious or spiritual practice (belief in one God, prayer, charity, fasting and pilgrimage), but also with social etiquette. 'For example, the Qur'an advises Muslims not to visit people when they are resting and provides guidelines on how to greet one another, dress appropriately and how to interact with the Prophet' (Saeed, 2008, p. 73). It also sets out very detailed legal directives addressing marriage, divorce and custody of children. In Islam, faith is closely linked to action. The Arabic term for righteousness is *birr*, which also translates as social justice and love. Therefore, a righteous Muslim is also a Muslim who loves others and seeks social justice for the poor and disempowered. Very early in the Qur'an, help for the poor is made a central tenet of Muslim faith:

> Righteousness is not to turn your faces towards the East and the West; the righteousness is her who believes in Allah, the Last Day, the angels, the Book and the Prophets; who gives of this money, in spite of loving it, to the near of kin, the orphans, the needy, the wayfarers and the beggars, and for the freeing of slaves; who performs the prayers and pays the alms-tax. Such are those who keep their pledges once they have made them, and endure patiently privation, adversity and times of fighting. (Qur'an 2: 177)

In this sense, Islam requires more than faith; it requires action based upon that faith. The underlying principle of Islamic social teaching that is most relevant to development is that of equality (Shepherd, 2009). This sense of equality is clearly evident in its approach to the allocation of scarce resources, and it is argued that Islam is:

> directed towards the creation of a meaningful and positive equality among human beings. As such the Islamic purpose cannot be realised until genuine freedom to human beings is restored and freedom from all forms of exploitation – social, spiritual, political and economic – assured. (Rahman, 1967, p. 103)

Just before his death, Muhammad made it clear that all Muslims are equal and deserving of respect: 'You know that every Muslim is the brother of another Muslim. You are all equal' (Qur'an 107: 1–3). The very marked shift in social relations during Muhammad's rule is a clear indication of how powerful this sense of equality was. Moreover, the Qur'an specifically relates the neglect of the poor with the neglect of religion: 'Have you observed him who denies religion? That is he who repels the orphan, and urges not the feeding of the needy' (Qur'an 107: 1–3). The importance of meeting basic needs was very evident to the desert-dwelling Arabs of this time. Water, food and shelter are necessary for subsistence and so access to these goods was vital. It was also evident that people had to work hard to be able to gain these goods. Life was hard and living conditions difficult; hard work was required to survive. Certainly, the personal experiences of the Prophet, working as a shepherd and then a merchant, reflected the importance of a work ethic. The Qur'an makes it clear that hard work is required: 'Man will get nothing but what he strives for' (Qur'an 53: 39). As Yasien Mohamed suggested, 'Islam is a world-affirming religion' (Mohamed, 2006, p. 416). If Islam is to be characterized in any way, it is its practical nature that most differentiates it from the other world religions.

Islamic Approach to Poverty Alleviation

Muhammad was a political leader as well as Prophet. Thus, from Islam's genesis, religious beliefs and faith have been grounded in the day-to-day circumstances of its adherents. It is this practical and political focus that Islam has much to engage with in terms of modern development concepts, such as poverty. The problem of poverty and destitution though is not new and has been faced by all civilizations. Qardhawi (2009) examines the position of the poor before Islam in ancient civilizations such as Egypt and Babylon, and notes their poverty was a result of their having no access to the land and productive activities. In fulfilling their basic needs, the poor often sold themselves as slaves to the rich. Modern poverty also remains largely a function of a lack of access to productive capital. Islam directly addresses this issue by establishing the importance of social justice, social insurance and social solidarity within the Qur'an and in the *sunnah* of His Messenger (ibid.).[1]

The importance of equality within Islam is clearly evident in the focus of resource redistribution through Islamic charities such as *zakat*, *awqaf* and *shadaqa*. Fighting for the poor is considered as fighting for Allah's cause and is equivalent to fasting and prayer (Leaman, 2006). The obligation of paying *zakat* in the Qur'an is stated 30 times and most of them associated with the obligation of prayer (*salat*) in the same verse. Hence, we may note that Islam is very concerned with poverty and equality.

In Islam, poverty is defined as the inability of individuals to meet the five basic requirements in life, consisting of religion, physical self, intellect or knowledge, offspring and wealth (Hassan, 2010). There are two terms in the Qur'an to express the condition of poverty: *faqr* and *maskanah*. 'The *shadaqa* (*zakat*) are only for the *fuqara* (poor) and al *masaakin* (the needy)' (Quran 9: 60). *Fuqara* is the plural form of *faqr*, indicating the condition for those who are unable to adequately provide for their own basic needs, while *al masaakin* is plural for *maskanah*, which are those people who are destitute and extremely needy. Although Islamic scholars have long debated which group is most in need in their lives, the Qur'an states that both the *faqr* and *maskanah* are eligible as Islamic charities recipients. Islamic charities ensure the poor obtain sufficient basic material necessities of life by wealth transfer and income distribution.

Poverty Alleviation Tools in Islam

Islamic charities are major instruments that have central roles in poverty alleviation. The broad term of charity is called *shadaqa*, when it is compulsory it is called *zakat* and when its benefits are expected to be permanent, it is called *shadaqa jariah* or *waqf* (Obaidullah, 2008). *Zakat* and *shadaqa* engage in poverty alleviation through income distribution and wealth transfer. On the other hand, the *waqf* – the perpetual charity, is used for long-term investment to improve the non-income aspect of the poor such as

Table 18.1 Comparison of poverty alleviation tools in Islam

	Zakat	*Shadaqa*	*Waqf*
Compulsory/Voluntary	Compulsory	Voluntary	Voluntary
Rate	Fixed rate	Any amount	Any amount
Spend	Generally spent in one year	Generally spent in one year	Generally capitalized
Investments	Generally not invested – needs to be discharged as soon as possible	Generally not invested – may be discharged according to need and mandate	Invested in social or economic asset
Time for payment	Generally paid in Ramadan	Can be paid at any time	Can be paid at any time
How payment is made	Generally paid in cash or stocks	Can take the form of any asset	Can take the form of any asset – cash, land, coins, jewellery

Source: Hassan (2010).

health, education, physical resources and employment (Hassan, 2010). Since Islamic charities include various types that have distinctive characteristics, Hassan (2010) provides a comparison of Islamic charities as poverty alleviation tools as shown in Table 18.1.

Zakat

The word *zakat* in Arabic means to grow or to increase and when referred to people it means to improve or to become better (Qardhawi, 2009). In Sharia law, the word *zakat* refers to the determined share of wealth prescribed by God to be distributed among deserving categories. Islam considers that all things belong to God, therefore possessions are purified by setting them aside for those in need. Many Islamic scholars argue that *zakat* will create cleanliness of the inner soul, increase wealth and help the poor to grow (ibid.).

Although *zakat* is compulsory charity in Islam to fight poverty, the awareness of Indonesian Muslims of paying *zakat* is very low. The amount of *zakat* collected per year is far behind the potency of *zakat*. For example, the largest *zakat* institution in Indonesia only collected US$2.6 million in 2010, where the national potency of *zakat* on household income reaches US$61 trillion.[2]

Depending only on *zakat* as microfinance also poses additional problems since the majority of *zakat* is paid during Ramadan, while the poor require help throughout the year. To solve this problem, several *zakat* institutions in Indonesia have developed a partnership with business enterprises to deduct *zakat* from employees' salaries directly before being paid every month. Furthermore, the effect of *zakat* fluctuation can be minimized by creating *zakat* funds that can be used the whole year (Chalikuzhi, 2009).

Shadaqa

The word *shadaqa* comes from the root word *sidq*, which implies giving away goods and funds for the sake of God in expression of faithfulness and in realization of the belief in resurrection and afterlife (Qardhawi, 2009). In current times, *shadaqa* is usually a charitable donation for God's sake for those in need. Obaidullah (2008) notes that *shadaqa* may include various forms of charity, such as *tabarruat* (donations), *heba* (gifts), *infaq* (charitable spending) and may indicate any act of kindness and charity.

Since it is voluntary, the total amount of *shadaqa* collected through institutions/organizations is very low. It is more common to give the *shadaqa* to the poor directly, instead of through institutions. *Shadaqa* is usually given to the closest relative or neighbours who are in need. Due to its cultural value, it can be argued that the institutionalization of *shadaqa* faces more challenges than *zakat*. However, the increasing awareness of corporate philanthropy and corporate social responsibility in the form of services to the community creates a potential to generate more *shadaqa* from commercial business rather than personal *shadaqa*.

Waqf

In Arabic, *waqf* means to stop, to contain or to preserve. In Sharia law, *waqf* is holding certain physical assets and preserving them for the long-term benefit of society. The objectives of *waqf* include the provision of religious services, socioeconomic relief to the needy and the poor segments of society, education, and environmental, scientific and other purposes (Ahmed, 2007).

The forms of *waqf* asset are mostly land or buildings that are used for religious/social purposes. However, there is significant growth in cash *waqf* worldwide. The nature of *waqf* spending that can be capitalized is potentially utilized to increase the capital base of microfinance. Ahmed (2007) notes the return of *waqf* funds is important to provide the subsidized microcredit or even interest-free credit such as *qard hassan* without reducing sustainability of the institution.

ISLAMIC MICROFINANCE'S ROLE IN POVERTY ALLEVIATION

The Concept of Microfinance and its Problems

Microfinance is an important intervention to reduce poverty. Microfinance offers basic financial services for the poor. The Consultative Group to Assist the Poor (CGAP) defines microfinance as the supply of loans, savings and other basic financial services for the poor. Providing financial services for the poor is neglected by formal financial institutions as this group of people are inherently high risk due to their inability to meet the standards and requirements of formal financial institutions. Zeller and Meyer (2002) argue that the lack of access to financial services constrains the ability of poor people to acquire assets, start a business, finance their emergency needs and increase their welfare. Improving access to financial services through microfinance is believed to solve these problems to some extent. As a financial institution, microfinance has to pursue dual objectives: obtaining financial sustainability and serving the poor as a social objective.

The success factors of microfinance are the application of the group-lending mechanism and focusing on women clients. The group-lending mechanism consists of a number of microfinance clients, in which every member of the group guarantees the loan repayment of all members. As the poor cannot provide asset-backed guarantees, this mechanism is powerful in reducing non-performing loans (Armendáriz and Morduch, 2005). In addition, the application of the group-lending mechanism will reduce the transaction cost in credit delivery by transferring the roles of information acquisition, loan monitoring and loan enforcement from banks to groups of borrowers (Dusuki, 2008). This functions as social capital. Furthermore, in its early development, microcredit focused on serving women (Yunus and Jolis, 1998; Helms, 2006). Women were willing to work harder to get out of poverty since they suffered the most. Women would use their money for family purposes and to prepare their children for better lives. The literature notes that women are more reliable than men in loan repayment. In practice however, conventional microfinance has faced many problems (Ahmed, 2002), such as:

- High non-performing loan rates due to asymmetric information problems. The microfinance loan is usually provided to women, however, in practice, men take control of the loan and use it for consumption purposes rather than productive activities.
- Lack of economic viability of the institution due to high operational costs since poor people usually live in rural areas with lack of infrastructure and require intensive loan monitoring.
- Low rate of return on investment since microenterprises usually engage in low-risk business.
- Only targeting the upper level of the poor and leaving out the extremely poor since the extremely poor have inherently chronic problems such as severe illness, illiteracy and lack of skills.

Given the drawbacks of microfinance, this chapter offers an alternative model of microfinance based on Islamic finance principles. Islamic finance principles can potentially be applied to enhance microfinance practice since both concepts basically share the similar values. Both have a social mission to fight poverty, promote entrepreneurship and risk sharing as well as ensure the capital is equally distributed to the society. The next subsection will describe the concept of Islamic microfinance and provide a comparison between conventional and Islamic microfinance.

The Concept of Islamic Microfinance

Islamic microfinance is a new area in the literature that combines both Islamic finance and microfinance. Islamic finance is the concept of finance based on Sharia – the Islamic law. Its core belief is that money is not an earning asset, thus it cannot traded as a commodity. This implies that all financial transactions must be representative of real transactions or sale of goods, services or benefits (Ayub, 2007). The general principles of Islamic finance (Khan, 2008) include the following:

- Islamic finance involves risk sharing between all parties in a transaction.
- Financial transactions must be asset backed, therefore they are linked with tangible assets instead of financial speculation.
- There must be a clear contract about the product sold between the seller and the buyer.
- Islam forbids all economic activities that are morally and socially harmful such as business that deals with alcohol, gambling and prostitution.
- Financial risk must lie solely with the owner/lender of the capital not with the manager or agent who works with the capital.
- Any predetermined interest rate is prohibited.
- It is not permitted to sell what one does not own, thus short selling is not allowed in Islam.

All these concepts confirm that Islamic finance is an ethical finance system that promotes the equal distribution of income or wealth, and provides social justice for society. Theoretically, microfinance institutions can take the advantage of Islamic finance principles to potentially increase their viability and sustainability. They might benefit by implementing the Islamic scheme of transactions, targeting the family rather than focusing only on women clients, using religion as social capital as well as obtaining other sources of financing from Islamic charities.

Implementation of Islamic finance instruments

Islamic finance has great potential to provide various schemes and instruments suitable for microfinance practice (Abdul Rahman, 2007). Dhumale and Shapcanin (1998) describe that *mudarabah*, *musyarakah* and *murabahah muajjal* are three basic principles of Islamic finance that can be applied to build viable microfinance institutions (MFIs). In *mudarabah* and *musyarakat* contracts, micro-enterprises and MFIs may develop a partnership in conducting projects under a PLS (profit and loss sharing) mechanism. This mechanism can be applied either in savings mobilization or in the project financing. In the case of success, the profit will be distributed at the predetermined rate but when the project fails the losses will be taken on by the MFIs. Here MFIs take the role of monitoring and providing entrepreneurs with sufficient skill to avoid failure of the investment. This scheme would also encourage the role of microfinance as social development vehicles. *Murabahah* is another scheme that it is possible to apply in MFI practices. *Murabahah* is similar to the trade contract in the working capital loan and similar to leasing in the context of long-term investment in fixed assets. This is the asset-backed transaction that would reduce the possibility of diverting funds other than those being requested. In summary:

- *Mudarabah* is a partnership between banks as the investor who provides capital to other parties who provide entrepreneurial skill. Generated profit will be shared between banks and the entrepreneur on the predetermined rate and any losses will be borne by banks as an investor. However, if the losses are caused by mismanagement, the entrepreneur will be responsible for the losses.
- *Musyarakah* is an equity participation contract where the bank is not always the only provider of capital. There are two or more parties who share capital

and expertise. Profit and losses will be share based on the amount of capital invested.

- *Musaqat* is specific type of *musyarakah* contract for orchard and crop growing. In this case the harvest will be shared among the equity partners based on their contribution.
- *Murabahah-Muajjal* is acquiring goods based on the demand of the customers and selling them at mark-up price. The clients pay the asset at the future date on the instalment scheme.
- *Qard hasan* is an interest-free loan as suggested by Sharia law that every wealthy Muslim should help others. In this case, banks are permitted to charge administrative fees for loan management.
- *Ijarah* is a leasing contract when clients use the asset by paying the rent. One specific type of *ijarah* is the lease purchase scheme (*ijarah wa iqtina*) in which the instalment includes the acquiring price of the product. By the end of instalment period, the possession of goods will be transferred to the clients.

Islamic schemes of transaction guarantee and encourage the participation of every segment of society. In particular, the implementation of the Islamic participatory approach in fund mobilization and financing promotes justice, brotherhood, social equality and financial inclusion of the poor (Dusuki, 2008).

Family targeting rather than focus on women clients

One success factor of the Grameen Bank in increasing repayment rates is focusing on women clients. Women are more reliable in loan repayment and will use the money for family purposes. However, Ahmed (2002) argues that focusing on women as target clients might raise several problems. Asymmetric problems might occur when men take the loans and control the use of the funds received by female members of family (Rahman, 1999). Furthermore, targeting women might also create tension in the family as men put pressure on women to obtain credit because it is easier for women to receive credit, but the men use the fund for their purposes. In addition, many studies have found that credit given to women generates low rates of return since women engage in low-risk and low-productive activities (Rahman and Khandker, 1994). In addition, Obaidullah (2008) notes that focusing only on women is a sensitive issue in Islam. Therefore, Islamic MFIs prefer to target the family rather than women in the family. By doing this, Islamic MFIs would reduce the moral hazard and adverse selection problem in giving a loan as the risk is being shared by the whole family.

The importance of religion as social capital

The group-lending mechanism is often applied by MFIs to reduce the risk of high non-performing loans. This mechanism is well known as being introduced by the Grameen Bank and is now widely applied around the world. This mechanism utilizes the concept of social capital by enforcing the share norm, value and behaviour through formation of the peer guarantee mechanism to replace the physical collateral in lending practice. Dusuki (2008) notes that the group-lending mechanism is not alien in Islam and has been known as the concept of *as sabiyah*. He argues that both *as sabiyah* and social capital share the same positive values such as teamwork, sense of belonging, cooperation and

Table 18.2 Differences between conventional versus Islamic microfinance

Issues	Conventional Microfinance	Islamic Microfinance
Source of funds	Donor funds, commercial funds and savings mobilization	Donor funds, commercial funds, savings mobilization and Islamic charity (*zakat*, *shadaqah* and *awqaf*)
Mode of financing	Interest-based financing	Islamic finance instruments
Financing the poorest	The poorest have been left out	The poorest can be served using Islamic charities
Target clients	Women	Family
Funds transferred	Cash given	Goods transferred
Approach to loan repayment	Group pressure and joint liability	Group pressure and joint liability and religious value

Source: Adapted from Ahmed (2002).

trust. If this concept is based on the religion paradigm it would be beneficial for the success of the application of the group-lending mechanism. This idea is supported by Ahmed (2002) who notes that Islamic MFIs may take advantage of this from a religion perspective as loan repayments are an obligation for Muslims.

The availability of various sources of financing

Another important advantage of Islamic MFIs is the availability of various sources of financing. Incorporating Islamic charities as the MFI's source of financing will be beneficial since this fund is non-interest bearing. Islamic MFIs may use this fund as complementary funds to finance the non-investment activities such as assisting the poor in their basic needs, conducting training to enhance the skill and capability of the borrower, and other community development activities. In addition, these complementary funds will reduce the possibility of using the loan obtained for non-productive purposes (Ahmed, 2002). As a result, the default rate can be minimized.

Therefore, it is argued that Islamic microfinance schemes do differ from traditional approaches in terms of their client focus, understanding of social capital and accessing various forms of capital. The summary of different practice between conventional and Islamic microfinance is presented in Table 18.2.

THE ROLE OF THE ISLAMIC MFI IN POVERTY ALLEVIATION

Hassan (2010) notes that the Islamic approach to poverty alleviation ideally involves comprehensive approaches including (1) increasing income levels with pro-poor programmes, (2) achieving an equitable distribution of income and (3) providing equal opportunities for all social segments. Microfinance with its social objective can support the achievement of those approaches. The role of microfinance in poverty alleviation has been drawn by Zeller and Meyer (2002) in three pathways by improving income generation through providing production credit for savings and asset accumulation, decreasing risk through selecting more efficient assets and liabilities, and smoothing consumption by providing consumption credit (Zeller and Meyer, 2002). Practically, microfinance will contribute to the poverty alleviation agenda through supporting micro-credit, micro-saving, micro-entrepreneurs and constraining the practice of informal money lenders. Furthermore, microfinance can be used as a strategy to distribute *zakat* and Islamic charities for better outcomes in poverty alleviation.

The graduation model of microfinance has been developed to help the poor move out from poverty:

> The graduation model targets the 'ultra poor' – people who have no assets and are chronically food insecure. The graduation program combines support for immediate needs with longer term investments in training, financial services, and business development so that within two years ultra poor people are equipped to help themselves 'graduate' out of extreme poverty. (CGAP, 2012, online)

The graduation model, however, requires extra cost and high dependency on the donor funds in order to provide the non-financial services for the clients. As noted previously, one of the advantage of Islamic microfinance is the availability of various sources of funding, including Islamic charities as interest-free financing. Hence, Islamic microfinance has a greater potential to achieve the poverty alleviation objective by offering both social and commercial services.

Social Services

Social services are specially created for the extremely poor, the unserved clients in conventional microfinance practice. These clients face multiple constraints on income generation. They often lack skills and education and deal with chronic health problems. Hence, microfinance has to identity the non-financial constraints of their clients and provide them with various social services to enhance their ability in income generation (Zeller and Meyer, 2002).

The objectives of social services are to improve the well-being of the extremely poor and to equip them with sufficient skills and knowledge. After obtaining adequate skills, it is expected that some of the extremely poor can conduct small enterprises and finally lift themselves to the wealthier group of the poor – the economically active poor. This is a very important intervention.

These services are not the profit centre of the institution while it requires high operational costs. Therefore, the most appropriate source of financing for these services is interest-free funds such as donor funds and Islamic charities. Islamic microfinance has the advantage of being able to access various Islamic charities including *zakat*, *shadaqah* and *waqf*. The utilization of Islamic charities in providing financial services would not jeopardize the future profitability and sustainability of the institutions.

Commercial Services

Commercial services may offer various financial services for the whole poor segment of the population, especially the economically active poor. Commercial services include the

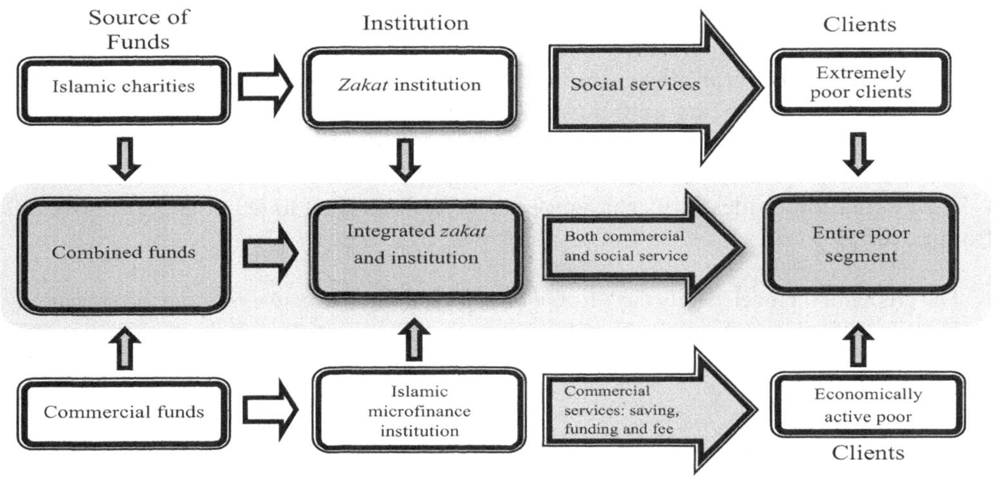

Source: Author's own work.

Figure 18.1 Integrated model of microfinance

provision of micro-saving, micro-credit and other services. In designing the commercial services, microfinance can apply the various Islamic finance instruments such as *murabahah*, *mudharabah* and others. Offering commercial services is very crucial for microfinance to achieve self-sustainability and to serve wide outreach. These services might be financed using commercial sources of funds such as savings mobilization or profit from investment.

It can be noted that by combining two sources of funds in microfinance, the institution may offer both commercial and social services without reducing the sustainability of the institution. More importantly, it can increase the outreach of microfinance and increase the role of microfinance in poverty graduation.

The integration of the microfinance model that utilizes both commercial and Islamic charities source of funds is presented in Figure 18.1. This model offers an integrated model of two institutions: the institution of *zakat* and Islamic charities with the institution of Islamic microfinance. The integrated institution utilizes combined sources of funds: *zakat* and Islamic charities as well as the commercial source of funds. In the context of Indonesia, the integrated institution might be developed into two types of institutions. *Zakat* is the institution that has authority from the government to collect *zakat* and Islamic charities. They may use these funds for developing microfinance programme. The second alternative form is Baitul Maal wat Tamwil (BMT). This is a special microfinance institution in Indonesia that consists of two organizations, the social and the commercial organization. BMT is operated under supervision and regulation of the Cooperative Department of Indonesia. Like the formal rural bank, BMT in Indonesia has the opportunity to mobilize funds through offering savings to the public and offering credit products to their clients.

The model offers various advantages:

- It provides adequate services for the extremely poor clients and shifts some of them to the economically active poor client group.
- It is possible to create sustainable microfinance since it does not only depend on the donor fund to provide the microfinance. Having a licence as regulated microfinance, the institution might offer various financial services including provision of savings, credit and other fee-based financing services.
- It increases the accountability of both institutions since they need to report to *zakat* and Islamic charity payers and its potential payers, Sharia compliance finance as well as the microfinance institution supervisory board. By increasing the accountability of the institutions, it will increase the willingness of those people to pay *zakat*.
- It will create sustainable microfinance with lower default rates and reduce the possibility of misuse of loans since the microcredit is only for skilled people who conduct income-generating activities.
- It will reduce the agency problems since both institutions engage in the same values and objectives.
- It will solve the debate of best practice of microfinance by *welfarist* and *institutional* schools. On one side, the institution will use the donor funds as the supporting funds for non-investment activities and on the other side it will use commercial microfinance that may obtain sources of funds from the commercial market.

EXAMPLES OF THE INTEGRATED MODEL OF MICROFINANCE

The implementation of the application of Islamic finance to the microfinance practice has been applied widely in the last decade. Indonesia is the main representative example of its application. As the biggest Muslim population in the world, the application of Islamic finance is widely applied in Indonesia to meet the high demand for Islamic financial services. In terms of market share, Islamic finance in Indonesia is less than 3 per cent of the total market, however, it has high outreach in rural areas, consisting of ten Islamic banks, 23 Sharia commercial bank units (Bank Syariah), 145 Islamic rural banks and 1000 Islamic cooperative units (Karim, 2010).

Two programmes will be discussed: the economic empowerment programme of Baitul Maal Muamalat Indonesia (BMMI) and Baitul Qiradh of Badan Amil Zakat Nasional. Both programmes focus on the microfinance initiative and utilize *zakat* and Islamic charities as sources of funding for microfinance practice. The major difference between them is that Baitul Qiradh has moved ahead by developing microfinance projects as strategic business units, which require formal regulation as Islamic microfinance.

Baitul Maal Muamalat Indonesia (BMMI)

Baitul Maal Muamalat Indonesia (BMMI) is a licensed *zakat* organization in Indonesia that can collect Islamic charities (*zakat*, *shadaqa* and *waqf*) and disburse the funds for social purposes. BMMI has been engaged in various projects including education, emergency aid for natural disasters, and direct support for the poor as well as economic empowerment programmes.

As a social organization that focuses on economic empowerment, BMMI has built a partnership with various organizations including Islamic Development Bank, Ford Foundation and several commercial institutions such as PT Telkom Indonesia and Newmont Indonesia. Its main sources of funds to finance all the programmes are various Islamic charities including *zakat*, *shadaqa*, *waqf* and donor funds from its partners.

The BMMI economic empowerment programme is named Komunitas Usaha Mikro Muamalat Berbasis Masjid (KUMMM), a mosque-based Muamalat Community Micro Enterprise programme. This programme is designed to provide revolving working capital credit for low-income micro-entrepreneurs who actively participate in mosque activities. This programme is supported by continuous technical assistance, mentoring and monitoring as well as formation of a group support system.

The philosophic background of this programme is integrating economic empowerment with developing the religious beliefs of society. Three basic principles of this programme are *zakat* disbursement for eligible targets based on Sharia, building the religious capacity of the *zakat* recipient, and encouraging *zakat* recipients to develop their business with modern management systems.

Recently, KUMMM has served 4697 low-income micro-entrepreneurs based in 185 mosques in 24 major cities in Indonesia. Total funds disbursed are approximately US$1069 million. This figure is very low compared with many potential clients to be served. The data from the Indonesian Ministry of Religious Affairs shows that in 2004 the number of mosques in Indonesia was 643 834. From the brief survey of BMMI, only four out of 100 mosques are involved with the economic empowerment of their society. KUMMM encourages mosques to take part in this programme by providing revolving working capital credit for street vendors, peddlers and hawkers who conduct trade around the mosques. The credit recipients will get the revolving credit (approximately US$75–200) as interest-free loans in three instalments (*qard hassan*) to develop their business. The second loan will be give after the first loan is fully paid, and the third loan is the final loan and will be given after the second loan is paid.

The management of BMMI has developed a blueprint for the expansion of the KUMMM programme in order to develop more formal microfinance institutions. In the first phase, the programme is only financed by *zakat* and Islamic charity to provide *qurd hassan* for low-income people who are not bankable. In the second phase, BMMI will provide credit for micro-entrepreneurs who have assets less than IDR50 million using the profit and loss sharing mechanism (PLS). In this step the programme will be financed either by Islamic charities or the PLS. In further phases, the institutions will become more commercial by offering not only credit but also savings products. Funds generated from savings can be used as alternative sources of financing. Each phase will run over three years, however, at present the programme depends only on *zakat* and Islamic charities for the programme's funding. By implementing this approach, the programme is expected to support the microfinance programme and at the same time increase the religious beliefs of society.

Baitul Qiradh of Badan Amil Zakat Nasional

Badan Amil Zakat Nasional (BAZNAS) is a *zakat* organization owned by the Indonesian government. As a social organization, BAZNAS has created several programmes including education, health, economic and aid for natural disasters.

Indonesia Makmur is the economic empowerment programme that utilizes *zakat* and Islamic charities as the only source of funds to assist the poor in the agriculture, animal husbandry and fishery sectors. BAZNAS offer *qurd hassan* schemes of financing and provides technical assistance for small enterprises in several areas in Indonesia including Nusa Tenggara Barat, Nusa Tenggara Timur, West Sumatra and West Java.

Moving forward in their economic empowerment programme, BAZNAS has built a partnership with BMT ONE, which has been engaged in Islamic finance in Indonesia for more than 20 years to develop strategic business units in a microfinance initiative that is known as Baitul Qiradh. Baitul Qiradh aims to assist the poor by improving welfare by providing loans under the *qurd hassan* mechanism as well as profit and loss sharing financing. The source of funds to provide *qurd hassan* loans is *zakat* and Islamic charities, while the institution also offers savings and financing products under the profit and loss sharing mechanism.

Recently, BAZNAS and BMT ONE have developed three Baitul Qiradh in Indonesia, with on average assets valued at US$250 000–860 000. Baitul Qiradh Baiturahman is one of the Baitul Qiradh's branches that is located in Aceh Province. The institution has assisted many poor people in Aceh after the tsunami disaster in 2008. Its target clients are micro-traders, micro-entrepreneurs and the informal sector, especially in around the Ulee Kareng market area. It provides various savings products under the *mudharabah* and *wadiah*[3] mechanism as well as financing products under *mudarabah*, *murabahah*, *bai bisaman ajil*[4] and *ijarah* schemes. Its finance ranges from US$50–750, which can be installed over six months to three years.

In addition, 20 Baitul Maal have been developed in Jogjakarta and East Java Province. Baitul Qiradh has implemented a modern management system with integrated technology and online transactions in all its branches in Indonesia using the BAZNAS card, thus all transactions can be made in all areas of Indonesia. Utilizing both Islamic charity and commercial funds may facilitate Baitul Qiradh to increase its outreach in many areas of Indonesia.

EVALUATING THE PROGRAMMES

Learning from the existing programmes like BMMI and Baitul Qiradh BAZNAS, we may draw an evaluation based on the theory of microfinance and Islamic finance from several dimensions: their target clients, their sources of financing and their products and lending schemes as summarized in Table 18.3.

The Target Clients

The central debate of microfinance practice now is whether the programme has reached the poorest groups of the population. As noted, microfinance is a suitable tool for

Table 18.3 Evaluation of existing programmes

Programme	KUMMM of BMMI	Baitul Qiradh BAZNAS
Target clients	Street vendors, peddlers, hawkers and micro-entrepreneurs surrounding the mosques	Poor in the agriculture, animal husbandry and fishery sectors
Source of fund	*Zakat* and Islamic charities	*Zakat*, Islamic charities and commercial sources of funds
Products and lending schemes	*Qurd hassan*	*Qurd hassan*, savings and financing under *mudarabah* and *murabahah* schemes
Loan disbursed	US$1069 million	More than US$0.5 million[a]

Note: [a] Only based on Baitul Qiradh Baitur Rahman Aceh.

Source: Authors' own work.

poverty reduction for the economically active poor (Robinson 2001). This idea is supported by Hulme and Mosley (1996) who said that the microfinance contributing to poverty reduction is particularly effective in improving the status of middle and upper segments of the poor. However, clients below the poverty line were worse off after borrowing (ibid.).

Both programmes offered by BMMI and Baitul Qiradh BAZNAS are only targeted at poor/low-income clients who have some form of employment or skills in conducting micro-enterprises. BMMI for example, focuses its programme only on the street vendors, peddlers and hawkers surrounding the mosques. Ahmed (2002) notes that one reason the extremely poor have been left out is that they usually divert the funds received for the consumption purposes rather than productive activities. Furthermore, the extremely poor who have a lack of skills only generate the lowest investment returns, which makes it difficult to repay the loans. Ideally, economic empowerment programmes will provide training and skill development to equip the poorest of the poor to take part in income-generating activities. Here, *zakat* and other forms of Islamic charities can be used as alternative financing to provide training and skill development of the extremely poor, so that some of the extremely poor can shift to the higher group – the economically active poor who are most targeted by microfinance (Obaidullah, 2008).

The Source of Funds

The KUMMM of BMMI in Indonesia and the Baitul Qiradh BAZNAS have integrated the use of Islamic charities and microfinance for the purpose of economic empowerment and poverty alleviation. The BMMI microfinance initiative only utilizes funds from the Islamic charities to finance its operation. The major issue in utilizing *zakat*, *awqaf* and *shadaqa* as financing sources in microfinance is the uncertainty over the amount of funds being mobilized (Obaidullah, 2008). The funds have been fluctuating from some time since it is purely voluntary and depends on the willingness of Muslims to pay charity. Evaluating this practice based on the microfinance theory, this programme is based on the old paradigm of the *welfarist* school, where donor funds are the only funding of microfinance. Depending only on this type of funding will not create sustainable microfinance with sound financial performance and high outreach. From an Islamic perspective, the main function of *zakat* and other Islamic charities is to ensure the poor receive the basic material necessities of life and to function as a safety net for the poor. However, the future plans of BMMI will combine several sources of financing: Islamic charities, public savings, and returns from funding services, although the implementation of the programme at the moment is still using *zakat* and other Islamic charities as the only source of financing. It is argued that the low number of clients up to now is due to lack of source of financing.

Baitul Qiradh as the strategic business unit of BAZNAS and BMT ONE has built into formal Islamic microfinance that combined *zakat* and Islamic charities as well as mobilizing funds through public savings and generating income through the profit and loss sharing mechanism. Baitul Qiradh has been developed into a commercial institution by integrating its system in all branches in Indonesia. This practice has adopted the *institutional* view that to serve large numbers of clients the institution has to be financial sustainable and cannot depend to the donor funds in the long run.

PRODUCTS AND LENDING SCHEMES OF THE PROGRAMMES

Another similarity between KUMMM BMMI and Baitul Qiradh BAZNAS is providing the interest-free loan scheme for target clients. This mechanism is called *qurd hassan*, which is a kind of loan returned at the end of the agreed period without any interest or share in the profit or loss of the business (Chapra, 1995). From a narrow perspective, the objectives of this scheme are to help the poor and to establish a better relationship between the poor and the rich, while, in broader perspective, the implementation of *qurd hassan* encourages wealth transfer, increases the money supply and reduces poverty by providing facility for the poor to create employment and business ventures.

In the *qurd hassan* scheme any extra amount of loan repayment is considered as *riba* (usury). The scheme provides no profit for the institutions, however, service and management fees are lawful in Islam (Wilson, 2007). Islamic banks usually charge a 2–3 per cent service fee additional to the loan. As a charitable loan, *qurd hassan* is designed for the personal use of the needy. Microfinance practice is very high cost but the microfinance institution can maintain its sustainability by charging adequate interest spreads and by practising secure loan management (Ayayi and Sene, 2010). Since interest is prohibited in Islam, it is suggested that instead of only offering *qurd hassan*, microfinance practice should establish profitable Islamic schemes of transaction to finance the project such as *murabahah* and PLS schemes.

Baitul Qiradh BAZNAS as an Islamic microfinance institution has offered various Islamic schemes of transaction such as *mudharabah* and *murabahah* in various products of savings, financing and long-term investment. By being commercial institutions, the MFIs might access diversified sources of funds and reduce the possibility of liquidity shortage (Campion and White, 2001), therefore, MFIs can grow continuously and meet the increasing demand for loans. Additionally, by offering savings services, MFIs can expand their client base and serve their social objectives by providing financial services for large numbers of low-income clients. Sharing the same arguments, Claudill et al. (2009) maintain that commercialization has a positive impact on increasing the efficiency of MFIs. Their study shows that MFIs that are more reliant on subsidy are less efficient than those that depend on deposit and are less reliant on the subsidy donor.

To sum up, the economic empowerment programme offered by BMMI has integrated the use of *zakat* and other Islamic charities for microfinance by offering interest-free loans or *qurd hassan* for micro-entrepreneur based around mosques in Indonesia. However, with regard to the issue of sustainability, it is suggested that the programme should offer various products under the profit and loss sharing mechanism. In this way, *zakat* and Islamic charities can be used only for providing non-profitable services for the extremely poor.

The second programme, Baitul Qiradh, is an example of integrated institution of *zakat* and Islamic charities with the microfinance initiative. As the strategic business unit of BAZNAS, Baitul Qiradh has developed into a formal Islamic microfinance institution under licence as BMT. As a formal institution, it could offer both savings and credit products by implementing Islamic schemes of transaction. Additionally, the institution also provides *qurd hassan* using *zakat* and Islamic charities as the source of funds.

However, since the basic function of *zakat* and Islamic charities is to create the equal distribution of income in society, both institutions are expected to target not only the economically active poor but also the extremely poor clients. To be successful in poverty alleviation, microfinance has to be supported by non-financial services along with financial services. The combination of commercial funds and interest-free funds in microfinance will be beneficial to serving a wide outreach and achieving sustainability.

CONCLUSION

Poverty and financial exclusion are widespread in Islamic society. Islam, however, has lucid objectives and directions in addressing and assisting the poor. The concern over poverty is clearly evident in resource distribution through Islamic charities. Furthermore, this chapter also reveals the possibility of integrating Islamic charities into microfinance practice. It also shows that Islamic finance principles can provide a constitutive force for microfinance. By integrating Islamic financial principles and microfinance activities with Islamic charity, this chapter has shown it is possible to pursue the dual objectives of increasing outreach and enhancing sustainability.

NOTES

1. The Arabic meaning of *sunnah* is habit or usual practice. It is the second fundamental law of Islam that consists of the Prophet Muhammad's lifetime sayings, deeds, and tacit approval on different aspects of life (Baderin Mashood, 2009, p. 197).
2. Data collected and analysed by FEM Institut Pertanian Bogor, Indonesia, 2011.
3. Safekeeping of a deposit. The depositors do not share any profit or losses from the investment. However, microfinance can provide gifts for the depositors.
4. The deferred contract in which the bank as seller of a product accepts deferred payments in instalments or in a lump sum. The price is agreed on between the buyer and seller.

REFERENCES

Abdul Rahman, Abdul Rahim (2007), 'Islamic microfinance: a missing component in Islamic banking', *Kyoto Bulletin of Islamic Area Studies*, **1**(2), 38–53.

Ahmed, Habib (2002), 'Financing microenterprises: an analytical study of Islamic microfinance institutions', *Islamic Economic Studies*, **9**(2), 27–64.

Ahmed, Habib (2007), '*Waqf*-based microfinance: realizing the social role of Islamic finance', Integration of Awqaf in the Islamic Financial Sector Conference, 6 March, Singapore.

Armendáriz, Beatriz and Jonathan Morduch (2005), *The Economics of Microfinance*, Cambridge, MA: MIT Press.

Ayayi, Ayi Gavriel and Maty Sene (2010), 'What drives microfinance institution's financial sustainability', *Journal of Developing Areas*, **44**(1), 303–24.

Ayub, Muhammad (2007), *Understanding Islamic Finance*, Chichester: John Wiley and Sons Ltd.

Baderin, Mashood (2009), 'Understanding Islamic law in theory and practice', *Legal Information Management*, **9**(3), 186–90.

Campion, Anita and Victoria White (2001), *NGO Transformation*, Bethesda, MD: Microenterprise Best Practices Development Alternatives Inc.

CGAP (2012), 'Graduate program overview', available at: http://www.cgap.org/p/site/c/template.rc/1.26.1467/; accessed 22 July 2012.

Chalikuzhi, Azad (2009), 'Problems and prospects of contemporary *zakat* management: a qualitative embedded case studies investigation', Ecole Superieure de Commerce de Lille.

Chapra, Umer M. (1995), *Towards a Just Monetary System*, Leicester: The Islamic Foundation.

Claudill, Steven B., Daniel M.Gropper and Valentina Hartaska (2009), 'Which microfinance institutions are becoming more cost effective with time? Evidence from a mixture model', *Journal of Money, Credit and Banking*, **41**(4), 651–72.

Dhumale, Rahul and Amela Shapcanin (1998), *An Application of Islamic Banking Principles to Microfinance*, United Nation Development Programme and The World Bank.

Dusuki, Asyraf Wajdi (2008), 'Lifting barriers in financing the small and poor entrepreneurs: lessons from group-based lending scheme and Ibn Khaldun's social solidarity', in M.a.L. Obaidullah and Hajah Salma Haji (eds), *Inclusive Islamic Financial Sector Development: Enhancing Islamic Financial Services for Micro and Medium Sized Enterprises*, Brunei Darussalam: Islamic Research and Training Institute of the Islamic Development Bank and the Centre for Islamic Banking, Finance and Management of Universiti Brunei Darussalam.

Hassan, M. Kabir (2010), 'An integrated poverty alleviation model combining zakat, awqaf and microfinance', 7th International Conference – The Tawhidy Epistemology, *Zakat* and *Waqf* Economy, Bangi, Bangladesh.

Helms, Brigit (2006), *Access for All: Building Inclusive Financial Systems*, Washington, DC: Consultative Group to Assist the Poorest, The World Bank.

Hulme, David and Paul Mosley (1996), *Finance Against Poverty*, London: Routledge.

Karim, Adiwarman (2010), 'The real market leader', *Republika Online*.

Khan, Ajaz Ahmed (2008), *Islamic Microfinance: Theory, Policy and Practice*, Birmingham: Islamic Relief Worldwide.

Leaman, O. (2006), 'Money', in O. Leaman (ed.), *The Qur'an: An Encyclopaedia*, London: Routledge.

Littlefield, Elizabeth, Jonathan Morduch and Syed Hashemi (2003), 'Is microfinance an effective strategy to reach the Millennium Development Goals?', Focus Note No. 24, available at: http://www.cgap.org/gm/document-1.9.2568/FN24.pdf; accessed 21 July 2012.

Mohamed, Y. (2006), 'Wealth', in O. Leaman (ed.), *The Qur'an: An Encyclopaedia*, London: Routledge.

Obaidullah, Muhammad (2008), *Introduction to Islamic Microfinance*, India: International Institute of Islamic Business and Finance.

Obaidullah, Muhammad and Tariqullah Khan (2008), 'Islamic microfinance development: challenge and initiative', Policy Dialogue Paper, Islamic Development Bank.

Qardhawi, Yusuf (2009), *Fiqh Al Zakat, Vol. 1*, translated by M.D. Kahf, Jeddah, Saudi Arabia: Scientific Publishing Centre.

Rahman, Aminur (1999), 'Microcredit initiatives for equitable and sustainable development: who pays?', *World Development*, **27**(1), 67–82.

Rahman, F. (1967), 'Some reflections on the reconstruction of the Muslim society in Pakistan', *Islamic Studies*, **6**(9), 103–20.

Rahman, R.I and S.R. Khandker (1994), 'Role of targeted credit programmes in promoting employment and productivity of the poor in Bangladesh', *The Bangladesh Development Studies*, **22**(2), 49–92.

Robinson, Marguerite S. (2001), *The Microfinance Revolution: Sustainable Finance for the Poor*, The World Bank.

Saeed, A. (2008), *The Qur'an: An Introduction*, London: Routledge.
Shepherd, W. (2009), *Introducing Islam*, London: Routledge.
Wilson, Rodney (2007), 'Making development assistance sustainable through Islamic microfinance', *IIUM Journal of Economics and Management*, **15**(2), 197–217.
Yunus, Muhammad with Alan Jolis (1998), *Banker to the Poor: Micro-Lending and the Battle Against World Poverty*, London: Aurum Press.
Zeller, Manfred and Richard L. Meyer (2002), *The Triangle of Microfinance: Financial Sustainability, Outreach and Impact*, Baltimore, MD: Johns Hopkins University Press.

19 Religion and post-disaster development*

Ismet Fanany and Rebecca Fanany

INTRODUCTION

This chapter explores the role religion and religious organizations can play in development in a post-disaster context. Special attention will be given to the development efforts in Aceh, Indonesia, following the 2004 Indian Ocean tsunami. This province of Indonesia was disproportionately affected by the disaster, both in terms of loss of life and physical destruction. This chapter begins with an overview of the place of religion in development and how scholars and practitioners view it. Development and the Islamic world specifically and the way religion is currently seen in the context of post-disaster aid will also be discussed. An overview of Acehnese society around the time the tsunami occurred is provided as background for a consideration of religion and development in post-tsunami Aceh. How the Acehnese view the disaster and the role of their religious faith in shaping their perceptions of the event and post-tsunami development efforts are described, with the chapter closing with a discussion of what this might mean for future development efforts, especially in the context of natural disaster.

RELIGION AND DEVELOPMENT

The aim of international development is to foster economic growth and reduce poverty. In this context, the importance of culture has long been acknowledged in producing the desired results, but religion, which is a central aspect of culture, is often overlooked or avoided (Marshall, 2001). Ver Beek (2000) suggests that religion is consciously avoided by development agencies and scholars of development studies. Selinger (2004) reached a similar conclusion based on the online articles and materials made available by the United Nations, World Bank, and other major development organizations. When religion does figure in the development discourse, it is usually not applied to the development of strategies or programs.

Religion is generally conceptualized in one of three ways by development scholars. It may be seen as a societal structure or institution that might be used to support the aims of a development program. Alternatively, religion is sometimes seen as an aspect of culture that is often viewed as impeding development efforts. Finally, religion may be seen as a form of personal motivation that is a means to support the ideological aims of a development program (ibid.). Religion is not generally seen as a positive structural factor that might be useful in the implementation of development programs or strategies or in development theory. The reasons for this have been suggested to be fear of imposing an outside perspective, fear of creating conflict, lack of precedent relating to the issue in question, and the separation of religion from science that dominates Western sociological and political approaches (Ver Beek, 2000). Marshall (2001) proposes similar reasons and suggests that the separation of religion and state, where religion addresses spiritual issues and the state material ones, has institutionalized the gap between religion and development.

If religion has been missing from the development activities of governments and international aid organizations, it has been significantly more important in the practical activities of some religious NGOs, even though recent literature on development has tended to overlook the specifically religious organizations operating in this field (Lunn, 2009). The term 'faith-based organization' has come into use to distinguish these religiously based NGOs from others with a different orientation (Clarke, 2006). In fact, religious organizations have a long history of participation in charity activities. Christian missions have been active in various parts of the world for centuries and sometimes provided services on behalf of the colonial powers. Similarly, Islamic charitable funds (*waqfs*) have an equally long history and have funded the constructions of schools, hospitals, and other public institutions (Lunn, 2009).

Religious organizations have a number of strengths relevant to participation in the development field, as well as weaknesses. The fact that they tend to work at every level of society and exist in every community has given them a very significant ability to reach rural areas and even those experiencing conflict or social upheaval. This has meant they have been very effective in distributing aid, especially in the context of emergencies or disasters (Mayotte, 1998; Tomalin, 2006). Further, religious organizations often exhibit a high level of motivation and are seen as working for the public good to a greater extent than government agencies. They also tend to be more sensitive to local need and more flexible in their programs and initiatives (Mayotte, 1998; Smith and Sosin, 2001; Goody, 2003). However, religious organizations are often viewed more warily because humanitarian aid and development activities have been used to legitimize evangelism and conversion (Lunn, 2009). Examples of this are presented in the literature, such as when the real aim of literacy programs is to allow participants to read scripture (Goody, 2003; Salemink, 2004).

It has been argued that religious organizations are specially placed to participate in development because the major religions all have principles and values that relate to issues like poverty, inequality, charitable giving, respect for others, and compassion and assistance for those in need. On the one hand, these values and moral precepts may provide a strong foundation for sustainable and appropriate development not focused on economic factors (see, for example, Tyndale, 2006). On the other hand, it has also been suggested that such values may be too idealistic to serve as a basis for practical development activity (Tinbergen, 1989). At present, there is growing interest in a more holistic approach to development that recognizes religion as an integral aspect of people's lives (Ver Beek, 2000; Ter Haar and Ellis, 2006). This view that seeks to integrate religion with other development approaches is seen as having the potential to succeed where secular programs have failed (Verhelst and Tyndale, 2002). Several frameworks have been proposed for this holistic approach to development (see, for example, Norgaard, 1994; Haverkort et al., 2003), but other scholars (Singh, 1999; Jechoutek, 2004) suggest that this approach is merely a return to a more traditional, pre-modern worldview.

In this context, it has been noted that there seems to be a growing interest in religion in the context of development. This is a recognition of the central role faith plays in the lives of many individuals as well as in structuring the group dynamic and communal life of many societies (Clarke, 2011). Interestingly, this rediscovery of religion as a motivating factor in a whole range of human behaviors is also observable in other fields and areas of scholarly investigation, such as psychology (see, for example, Lavretsky, 2010), health (see Seybold and Hill, 2001), and social behavior (see Ebstyne King and Furrow, 2008; Lim and Putnam, 2010). It is not coincidental that these aspects of the human experience are also significant in influencing the outcomes of development programs, suggesting that religion cannot be ignored as an important force in understanding how people see themselves, interact with others, and create the social structures in which their lived experiences occur.

DEVELOPMENT AND THE ISLAMIC WORLD

As described above, religion has not been a major factor in development studies, which, like many other fields, has been strongly influenced by what has been called 'secular reductionism' (Clarke, 2006), which has led to a great deal of attention being paid to sociological characteristics (ethnicity, class, gender, etc.) and little to religious issues. This situation has gradually begun to change with a 'deprivatization' of religion (Cassanova, 1994), which has coincided with the emergence of religious nationalism in several parts of the world (Juergensmeyer, 1993). At the same time, a polarization between the West and the Islamic world has emerged that is deeper than immediate development concerns and relates as well to a conflict between cultures that have and have not benefitted to the same degree from the current state of globalization (De Cordier, 2009).

This issue is of particular importance in light of the fact that countries with a large Muslim population have historically been underdeveloped compared to the West and have earned a significantly lower share of world income than their population would indicate (Kuran, 1997). Further, high population density and geographic location have made many of these nations particularly susceptible to natural disaster, which is often the occasion for relief efforts and aid programs, often from the West. For example, of the 55 members of the Islamic Development Bank, 27 are categorized as low-income countries (IDB, 2004). The UN Office for Humanitarian Affairs has disbursed 27 percent of funds raised in various humanitarian appeals in countries where most of the population is Muslim (IRIN, 2007). Similarly, about 48.5 percent of persons registered by the UN High Commissioner for Refugees are Muslim (UNHCR, 2006). This is not to say, however, that Muslim countries are always on the receiving end of aid programs or are the only regions of the world that experience poverty and social upheaval. Nonetheless, the significant level of need, coupled with the dominance of Western organizations and donors in the aid sector, makes for a special situation.

Part of the problem seems to have come from a perceived failure of Western approaches to social development to create lasting change in many Islamic (as well as non-Islamic) societies. A particularly problematic aspect of such approaches has been the trend towards secularism inherent in most Western development initiatives (Wigger, 2005). This has been associated with religious resurgence in the Muslim world that has a number of separate components. The first of these is a change in the nature of Western influence from a physical presence (through colonialism) to a cultural domination. A second is a selective desire for Western products and technologies with a concurrent rejection of things viewed as culturally 'Western'. Finally, a third force is the re-emergence of traditional, cultural practices resulting from the long process of decolonization (De Cordier, 2009). At the same time, both Islamic and non-Islamic nations are experiencing rapid social change, urbanization, modernization, conflict, spread of technology, collapse of traditional cultural identities, and the emergence of new identities along religious lines.

The Pew Global Attitudes Project (2011) provides some interesting insight into these issues. When asked whether they saw themselves as a Muslim first or as a citizen of their nation, 94 percent in Pakistan, 65 percent in Jordan, 49 percent in Turkey, and 40 percent in Indonesia saw themselves as Muslims first. In terms of attitudes towards Christians, 6 percent in Turkey, 48 percent in Egypt, 52 percent in Indonesia, and 16 percent in Pakistan report favorable views. When asked specifically about the reasons for a lack of prosperity in Muslim countries, 53 percent of Muslim publics attributed this to US and Western policies, 49 percent to their own governments' corruption, 42 percent to a lack of democracy, and 12 percent to Islamic fundamentalism. The Western public had starkly contrasting views, with 14 percent identifying US and Western policies as the cause, 54 percent government corruption in the locations in question, 50 percent a lack of democracy, and 32 percent Islamic fundamentalism. These figures highlight the sense of mistrust of Western institutions among members of many Muslim societies as well as the perception that Western policies are unfavorable to them.

In the specific context of development practice, De Cordier (2009) identifies several factors that may indicate how significant religion is likely to be in the practical implementation of programs. These include: the presence of conflict that involves religious identities and actors; horizontal and vertical social mobility (such as rural–urban migration or international movement); the role of religion and religious figures in society, especially where religious identity is confused or unclear; situations where social divisions coincide with religious ones (such as wealth differences between Muslims and non-Muslims); the nature of the state and civil society; and the nature of public opinion and the extent to which local and global media frame coverage of events with a religious dimension.

All of these, as well as general sentiments among the receiving public, take on increased importance if the aid program of interest concerns disaster response where the emergency nature of the situation is likely to produce increased stress, which, in turn, may lead to a heightening of social tensions (see, for example, Palinkas et al., 1993; Adams et al., 2002; Norris et al., 2002; Jacobs and Williams, 2011). Disaster relief takes place in contexts of high stress in which those affected may turn strongly to traditional and cultural means of adapting, in which religion often figures significantly.

RELIGION AND POST-DISASTER AID

Religious organizations and faith-based aid agencies have long been involved in disaster relief, among their other activities. It happens that many of these groups have been active in regions vulnerable to natural disaster and hence have been well placed to respond when unusual events occur. Further, it is likely that, in some situations at least, the spiritual principles on which these organizations were founded provide a philosophical basis from which to approach the problem as well as to provide insight into a conceptualization of the suffering of those affected.

The 1998 Aitape tsunami was one of the most significant natural disasters to affect Papua New Guinea in recent history. More than 2000 people were killed, many thousands suffered physical or psychological trauma, and some 10000 were displaced. The people of the worst affected region were predominantly Roman Catholic, with the church having been established there approximately 100 years before. The area was unprepared for such an event and had to rely heavily on the extensive aid that was rapidly made available (Fountain et al., 2004). It is estimated that major NGOs raised about 20 million kina for disaster relief (Nelson, 1999). Government response to the event was weak, and the majority of aid work and coordination was carried out by the Aitape Catholic Diocese Relief Committee. This extended to rebuilding roads and bridges, infrastructure that was normally managed by the government. This was possible largely because the organization became the main group to receive and channel disaster relief funds from the national and international donors who felt the national and provincial governments were not reliable. Nonetheless, the government did not relinquish its role in coordinating disaster relief, which led to considerable conflict between the Catholic diocese and government authorities. Another group, the Combined Churches Organization, was also involved in the relief effort, although to a lesser extent, and worked in the area through its network of pastors, in some cases, for very long periods following the tsunami. The etiology of this event, as understood by aid workers in contrast to local people affected directly, is especially interesting. Aid personnel along with scientists and scholars interested in the tsunami saw the event as a natural one that occurred as a result of explainable, physical forces. In this context, they tended to view disaster aid as an altruistic gift that should be accepted by the people affected as a manifestation of Christian charity. Among those affected by the tsunami, a rumor circulated that the event had been caused by a bomb that had been planted in the ocean by foreigners for some ulterior motive (suggested to relate to supposed oil deposits in the area) and that the aid was a pay off or 'blood money' for the losses that occurred. The distribution of aid was fraught with problems from the local perspective, including favoritism towards certain groups (largely by Catholic organizations), unequal distribution of resources, and corruption, which were exacerbated by the differences in understandings about the nature of the event (Fountain et al., 2004).

Perceptions about aid in the context of natural disaster have been observed to be related to religious affiliation in Fiji, a region prone to hurricanes. The nation's population is made up of Christians, Hindus, and Muslims with at least 95 percent of people identifying themselves as a member of one of these faiths. Following Hurricane Nigel in 1997, Gillard and Paton (1999) reported that 94 percent of Fijian Christians were confident of aid and assistance from their church. Substantial foreign aid from overseas Christian organizations was, in fact, available to support reconstruction of houses, relocation, food, medical assistance, and limited financial aid. There were no demands placed on recipients, and the church was seen as creating an 'assistance environment'. By contrast, Hindus and Muslims had lower expectations of aid from their religious institutions and were expected to provide manual labor (those whose occupations were in trades fields), food (for mosque and temple committees and poorer members of the community), and building supplies (for mosques and temples) as well as financial aid to needy community members. In contrast to Christians, Fijian Hindus and Muslims were expected to contribute to the repair and maintenance of their religious institutions in a 'demand' scenario of post-disaster relief. As a result, Hindus and Muslims were more likely to be dissatisfied with the post-disaster aid they had access to than Christians and often reported financial/material demands being made on them.

A similarly prominent role was played by local churches following Hurricane Katrina in the US city of New Orleans in 2004. Following this disaster, churches acted as 'first responders', providing food, clothing, and temporary housing (Cain and Barthelemy, 2008). Despite some concern about religious institutions being involved in services usually understood to be a government responsibility in the USA, the ability and willingness of local churches to provide aid and social services placed these organizations at the forefront of aid efforts. Despite the legal separation of church and state, the role of religious organizations as providers of social services is well-established in the USA (Chaves and Tsitsos, 2001). Different from some parts of the world, religious response to Hurricane Katrina came largely from individual churches in the affected community, rather than from the diocese or central administrative unit of any one denomination. The public generally supported the role of churches in disaster relief and were grateful for what they felt was immediate and effective assistance to anyone who needed it without obligation on the part of the recipient (Cain and Barthelemy, 2008). Many churches found their resources greatly stretched following the disaster (Cabrera et al., 2006), bringing to light the question of whether religious institutions should have access to public funding available to secular organizations for disaster relief (Cain and Barthelemy, 2008).

These three examples highlight the role and experience of various religious organizations and institutions may play in disaster relief. Several important issues are discernable that manifest in different ways, depending on the social context. These include the appropriate role of government and its relationship to religious institutions, the requirements or lack of requirements for those receiving assistance, the level at which involvement of religious organizations occurs, and the intersection of religious or organizational goals with the aim of alleviating suffering. These are all important elements in understanding the place of religion in development activities and will be considered below in the specific context of Aceh following the 2004 Indian Ocean tsunami.

ACEH AND THE 2004 TSUNAMI

At the time of the tsunami, Aceh had a population of about 4 million, consisting of members of a number of Indonesian ethnic groups, and was almost entirely Muslim. Sometimes referred to as 'The Veranda of Mecca', the province is religiously conservative and fundamentalist and, when the tsunami occurred, had already begun to express these views in its local laws. Regional Autonomy became law in Indonesia in 2001[1] and led to a large-scale program of government decentralization that resulted in devolution of responsibility for a wide range of public services to the regions. Regional Autonomy also gave new momentum to the Gerakan Aceh Merdeka (GAM) (Free Aceh Movement), which had been in a state of rebellion against the government of Indonesia since the 1970s. This movement, which demanded independence for Aceh, was widely supported by the public through the 1990s. Following the tsunami, however, a ceasefire was declared, and the parties resolved to end the conflict. A peace agreement was signed in 2005, giving Aceh special autonomy status and mandating the withdrawal of a majority of the Indonesian troops in exchange for the disarmament of GAM. Former GAM members remain active in regional politics and administration, however, along with representatives of various national parties from other backgrounds.

The armed conflict with the government of Indonesia contributed in some ways to how the Acehnese viewed the tsunami. Many Acehnese, especially in the areas around the provincial capital Banda Aceh, blamed what they perceived as decadent, non-Islamic behavior of government forces in Aceh as one of the factors that prompted God to send the tsunami to their region. During the early stages of the recovery period, stories circulated among the Acehnese in this part of the province of how, on the evening before the disaster, members of the military were celebrating in their barracks, drinking and engaging in inappropriate acts with women who were not their wives. Rumor held that, not only were they all killed in the disaster, but that they and their barracks were swallowed up by earth. In fact, the location of their former post became part of the ocean floor that ended up underwater following subsidence of the coastline. Whether the party in question really occurred is not clear, but the Acehnese still express their moral interpretation of the disaster and the religious overtones they ascribe to the event in stories of this kind, which have become a kind of oral history of the tsunami.

The people of Aceh are almost entirely Muslim. As is the case throughout the Malay world, of which Aceh is a part, adherence to Islam is a characteristic element of identity and is required of anyone who is a member of the Acehnese ethnic group. The Acehnese people are native to the northernmost part of the island of Sumatra and speak a local language that is linguistically related to Malay. They make up approximately 50 percent of the province's population, with the rest being drawn from the Javanese, Gayo, Alas, and other ethnic groups, who are also almost entirely Muslim. In total, about 99 percent of the province's population is thought to be Muslim (BPS, 2009). The province's full name, Nanggroe Aceh Darussalam, reflects both Acehnese culture and Islamic influence, and local scenery is characterized by the presence of mosques in every occupied location, large or small. Other manifestations of Islamic culture and society are easily observable and include the widespread wearing of Islamic dress, the use of Arabic script on buildings and in political and public information campaign slogans, decorative arts reminiscent of those of the Middle East, and more recently the implementation of Syariah (Sharia) (Islamic) law at the local level.

Islam in Indonesia is usually described as syncretic, drawing on a range of sources including older, pre-Islamic religious beliefs common in the region (see Cederroth, 1999). In some parts of the nation, this aspect of the religion is taken to be a moderating influence, and religious expression in certain areas, such as in Java, is viewed as considerably less orthodox than in other parts of the world and often includes a strong element of pre-Islamic belief (see, for example, Beatty, 1996). In Sumatra, however, there are several areas that are seen as religiously conservative and more fundamentalist in their views of Islam. These include the province of West Sumatra, inhabited almost entirely by members of the Minangkabau ethnic group; some parts of eastern and southern Sumatra, including the province of Riau, inhabited largely by Malay; and of course Aceh, at the northern tip of the island. Islam seems to have come to this region with traders, was adopted by choice, rather than imposed by force, and incorporates many elements of Sufi beliefs (McAmis, 2002). Sufism (or *tasawwuf*) represents the inner, mystic dimension of the religion and places strong emphasis on hospitality (*zihkr*), ritualized acknowledgement of God (*ziarah*), and divine determinism (*takdir*) (Howell, 2001). In Aceh, these elements of belief lie at the core of individual and group response to disaster and tragedy. An Acehnese proverbial saying derived from the Quran states that, in times of trouble, people should 'hold fast to the rope of God'.[2]

THE ACEHNESE VIEW AND UNDERSTANDING OF THE TSUNAMI

Almost without exception, the Acehnese public ascribed the undersea earthquake and resulting Indian Ocean tsunami of 2004 to an act of God. In the West, this expression is usually used to refer to a natural event that is outside people's control and often carries the connotation that no blame can be laid on human agents for any resulting damage. To the people of Aceh, however, an act of God means something quite different for they do not perceive acts of God to be random, and such events are believed to occur deliberately for a purpose known only to God but that may be deduced by humans. To the people of Aceh, this means that it is not possible for human beings to understand or know God's plan for them, but it may be possible to discern certain aspects of God's intent and to respond to them through their religious and moral actions.

Following the tsunami, it was obvious to many people in Aceh that the disaster resulted from laxity in their own moral and religious attitudes as well as to un-Islamic activities that occurred in their area, regardless of who was involved. To many, the evidence suggesting this was overwhelming and was easily visible in many locations where mosques had been spared when every other building around them was destroyed by the tidal wave. This occurred in Banda Aceh, Lampuuk, Baet, Kaju, Meulaboh, and many others and was reported by the media across the region (see, for example, *ChannelNewsAsia*, 2005). Many residents who sought refuge in mosques survived the tsunami, further strengthening the idea that the disaster was a form of divine commentary on the community's religious behavior. A number of observers, including several from international aid agencies, saw a more prosaic explanation for this phenomenon, ascribing the phenomenon to the fact that mosques were more strongly built because of their social importance and were frequently located at the highest point available as a sign of reverence. Survivors often accepted this judgment, saying that these facts were equally a sign of God's participation in the affairs of humans as surely it was He who caused people to build their mosques in this way and in these locations.

To many people in Aceh, the need for a divine warning in the form of a tsunami was a result of a perceived slackening of religious observance and declining moral standards that resulted from a number of social factors. To many people, these included the long period of conflict between the Acehnese and the government of Indonesia, which distracted the public from its religious life; a growing interest in material objects and a corresponding weakening of traditional communal institutions; and the increasingly secular nature of the public sphere, possibly as a result of integration into Indonesian national culture. To many Acehnese, the tsunami was viewed as a divine pronouncement about the social change that had been observed by many people for some time and that had accelerated in recent years. The verdict seemed to be overwhelmingly negative to the majority of those affected.

One woman with a university degree, who served as chair of the provincial branch of a national Islamic women's organization, expressed this general idea in a very personal and vehement manner. She recounts watching television at her home in Banda Aceh on Christmas Eve 2004 and being shocked to find a national Christmas variety program was being broadcast by the Aceh affiliate of TVRI, the Indonesian national television station. She was affronted, as this program contained references to the religious nature of the holiday even though it also featured entertainment acts of a secular nature. She says that, seeing the program, she prayed to God, asking that He just destroy the world if even Aceh was now showing Christmas programming to its Muslim population. The next day, the tsunami struck; this woman and two of her daughters were at home and took refuge on the second floor of the house. As the building began to fill with water and she realized they were going to die, she changed her mind and began to pray that God would save them. The water receded after a time, sparing the woman and one of the daughters but killing the other as well as many friends, relatives, and colleagues. When interviewed after the disaster, this survivor was convinced both her prayers had been answered and was proud to relate this story of what she believes is God's direct response to her prayers. She seems to feel no internal conflict at the idea that, if she is correct, her prayers were directly responsible for the deaths of hundreds of thousands of people in her town and elsewhere, as well as widespread destruction across South and Southeast Asia.

While extreme in nature and intensely personal, this survivor's perception of the disaster is by no means unique in Aceh. A majority of survivors have the same kind of view about their importance to God and see the tsunami as a reasonable warning about their behavior. While they, of course, feel the loss of loved ones, property, livelihood, and cultural institutions, they believe that this was their fate (*takdir*) and there is no point fighting God's will. It is worth noting that a similar response is often seen in religious Muslims elsewhere in Indonesia as a response to natural disasters, most recently in Padang, West Sumatra, which experienced a large and very destructive earthquake on 30 September 2009.

Interestingly, some elements of the Muslim community in Indonesia outside of Aceh also saw a divine origin in the tsunami and agreed that it was triggered by the behavior of the Acehnese. In West Sumatra, for example, another strongly Islamic region in Indonesia that was hit by a strong earthquake in 2009 that killed hundreds of people and caused extreme damage, natural disasters are also seen and understood in the same way. Many people in West Sumatra attributed the 2009 earthquake to God who intended to punish non-Islamic behavior and warn the public of what He could and would do if they did not behave in a religiously appropriate manner. It is interesting to note that, in West Sumatra, which has a local popular culture in the Minang language, both the 2004 tsunami and the 2009 earthquake have been immortalized in pop songs. As is the case in other forums, these songs call for listeners to move closer to God and make themselves more submissive to His will, these actions being seen as directly called for as a response to natural disaster.

Returning to the 2004 tsunami, some observers outside of Aceh placed a different kind of religious interpretation on the event. They noted that the Acehnese were extremely arrogant about the quality of their religious observance and piety, and the tsunami had been intended as a warning from God to be more humble and stop placing themselves above the rest of the Indonesian Muslim community (see, for example, al-Bustom, 2010). Some Indonesian bloggers even suggested the reason so many young people were killed by the tsunami was because their excessive religious zeal would lead them to become terrorists in the future, and God wished to prevent this before it happened (see, for example, JockoThinker, 2009).

Generally, however, there was wide agreement among the public in Aceh that the tsunami had been a warning sent by God and that the appropriate response required rebuilding and re-establishing their culture and society but also a re-evaluation of their own behavior and attitudes in the context of Islamic law and theology. It was this understanding that led to the rejection of foreign aid that was viewed as coming from organizations thought to have a 'Christianizing' mission or that seemed to impose requirements that were incompatible with traditional social patterns and lifestyle. The issue of missionary activity (*Kristenisasi*) in Aceh has been widely discussed in Indonesia and led directly to demands by the Acehnese public that certain aid agencies be expelled from the region (see Artawijaya et al., 2006 for complete documentation of this issue as it was discussed in the Indonesian media).

ISLAM AND POST-TSUNAMI DEVELOPMENT IN ACEH

Post-disaster development is different from other types of development in at least one important respect: it is preceded by an unanticipated event that leads to destruction. The people for whom the development is intended, therefore, are already disadvantaged in terms of their emotional state and available resources during the planning and implementation of the development program. The worse the disaster, the more disadvantaged they may be, relative to their pre-disaster state. The 2004 tsunami, for example, was one of the worst natural disasters in modern history. Hundreds of thousands of people were killed, communities were completely destroyed, and material loss and destruction were enormous.

In the case of the Aceh, the destruction caused by the disaster can be grouped into two categories: (1) destruction to the visible landscape and (2) destruction to the invisible landscape. The first type includes the loss of houses, schools, hospitals, mosques, and other buildings; roads, bridges, power generators, and other infrastructure; and loss of life. These are easier to quantify. Some of the physical elements of society, like buildings and infrastructure, can be replaced even though the experience of Aceh disaster has shown that more is involved in replacing schools than simply rebuilding. Loss of human capital – teachers and students – has been much more difficult to replace, as human beings are not interchangeable and there are strong affective elements associated with missing individuals. The destruction to the invisible landscape is much harder to assess and even harder to repair. In the case of Aceh, this has been equally serious and relates to the loss of community and the accumulated knowledge it contained. The survivors of the disaster experienced personal loss, taking a range of forms, and also had to reorient themselves in a post-disaster landscape that lacked, not just their own loved ones, but also a significant portion of the pre-disaster community whose skills and abilities were instrumental in the functioning of society. In other words, the social structures that formed a backdrop for their pre-disaster experience and that provided the affective context in which they lived had been altered so as to be almost unrecognizable.

How survivors view and understand the effects of natural disaster will have a significant impact on their perceptions about appropriate reconstruction. Their acceptance of development efforts will also be determined to a significant degree by this view and understanding. And as described above, the Acehnese, for example, saw the tsunami as an undeniable message from God, as a warning or punishment or both. They have no doubt that God will send a similar or worse disaster in the future if they do not heed this warning.

The role religion plays in post-disaster development, then, depends on the extent to which it plays a role in the way people view and understand natural disaster. In the case of Aceh, religion provides a complete etiology of disaster. To many Acehnese, faith is, in fact, the only explanation. This religious conviction in Aceh has played a much greater role in the development of the invisible landscape than of the visible one. The influence of religion in physical development can be seen, for example, in the insistence of survivors that the aid donors who proposed to rebuild their houses should also rebuild their mosque or repair it if it was not destroyed. There was no opposition to non-Muslim aid organizations constructing houses and mosques. But when rumors began to spread among the Acehnese that Christian organizations might be in Aceh, not just to help, but also to proselytize, there were strong reactions from the community; at one point certain groups were asked to leave Aceh even though this was never enforced (for examples of this problem, see Behn, 2005; Cooperman, 2005; Endonesia, 2005; Gartland, 2005; Powell, 2005; *The Australian*, 2005).

The religious views of the Acehnese and their understanding of the disaster had two main effects in the impact of the disaster on the invisible landscape in Aceh. First there is evidence to suggest that their religious faith lessened the impact of the disaster. Members of the public almost invariably state that they accept the tsunami and its aftermath. Some have noted that, despite the loss, pain, and suffering it caused, the disaster had an important and beneficial result, in that it showed that God still loves them and cared enough to warn them that they had strayed too far from their religion. This may explain, at least partly, the conclusion of the WHO, in its recommendations about mental health services in Aceh, that Western constructs of community development were misguided and unwelcome (WHO, 2005).

The second role of the religious views and understanding of the disaster of the Acehnese lies in development and reconstruction of their invisible landscape. To the extent that this landscape was damaged by the disaster, its reconstruction has been shaped much more by faith than by the restoration of buildings and infrastructure. The precepts of Islam, as understood and applied by the Acehnese public, provided a source of resilience and also dictated a socially acceptable response that included, as noted, a strengthening of religious institutions and practices in the public sphere.

Survivors of the tsunami overwhelmingly did not experience the emotional distress and trauma reaction that would have been expected in a Western setting and which relief agencies had prepared for. In fact, survivors were observed to be surprisingly resilient given the scope of the disaster and level of loss and did not themselves feel in need of any kind of psychological support. Perceptions of need centered on housing, the means of making a living, and being reunited with friends and family members in an attempt to return to a normal life. This is not to suggest that individual survivors were not distressed at all, but the level of emotional disturbance seemed to be well within the capacity of sufferers, as well as the community, to absorb. Their faith provided a meaning for the disaster and this meaning was viewed as applying to everyone in the community, and this perception of a shared lot grounded in religious etiology came to be a source of strength in adapting to loss.

In this context, it is worth considering how some affected individuals compared the emotional and psychological impact of the devastation caused by the tsunami and that resulting from armed conflict with the Indonesian army, which was seen as a worldly problem without specific religious connotations. A high ranking provincial government official with an overseas postgraduate degree (interview 5 August 2010), for example, noted that, while the severity of the tsunami was many times greater than the conflict in terms of loss of life and material damage, the trauma and emotional impact of the conflict was much greater than the tsunami. He could accept what he saw as the wrath of God but not the cruelty of other human beings. He also found he could easily understand that God might warn or even punish the Acehnese with a natural disaster and believed that God always acted in their best interest. The Indonesian army, however, clearly did not have the interests of the Acehnese at heart. He wondered why there had been no counseling available during the conflict when some Acehnese might have needed it and did not comprehend why foreign aid providers, in particular, insisted on offering this service when the Acehnese felt quite relaxed and accepting about the tsunami. Similar views were expressed repeatedly by many individuals and illustrate the depth of the Acehnese belief in God's will and their acceptance of even extremely severe events that they attribute to this cause.

The importance of community in the emotional response and ability of tsunami survivors to adapt and to develop the post-tsunami invisible landscape cannot be ignored. Malay culture tends to be highly sensitive to social norms; a very high premium is placed on consensus and conformity, and it is generally not considered desirable to stand out or go against the group. There is a religious basis for this cultural feature of the Malay. In Islam, people are seen as all the same to God, and the only thing that allows one individual to stand out from others to God is *taqwa* (obedience to God's will). An example of this attitude was observed in the town of Lampuuk, which was almost totally destroyed (except for its mosque) by the tidal wave. One of the most pressing needs of survivors in this area following the disaster was housing as most of the village had been destroyed. They quickly formed a group to represent the interests of residents and began negotiating with aid agencies for assistance replacing their lost dwellings. Eventually, the residents' committee decided to accept aid from the Turkish Red Crescent. After many delays during which survivors had to live in emergency accommodation, all 700 promised dwellings were ready for them to move into in April 2007. Even though many houses had been available long before this and there had been serious disagreements about how these houses should be allotted, the Lampuuk survivors all waited to move in until everyone could be accommodated because of their desire to preserve their community structure and maintain the traditional orientation of their village. Many new houses remained empty, however, as the residents preferred to live in groups and chose to occupy certain buildings only. Many of them had lost all or most of their family members and did not want to live in relatively empty houses or by themselves. This reaction is typical in the Malay world where support networks, based first on extended family ties and then on community or group affiliation, are the main social structure in coping with adverse situations. In better times when more opportunities are available, this behavior is not usually seen, with individuals generally acting in their own interests. The reversion to a group mentality fostering mutual dependence among individuals who are related through family or geographical ties is an important emotional strategy among the Malay that serves to promote emotional resilience and support a return to normal life that maintains social norms including religious behavior.

This group mentality has a strong religious aspect as well. Many required observances in Islam are best performed in a group. The most important of these observances is *shalat*, the five daily prayers that have a specific form and timing. Islam in Indonesia holds that it is best, in terms of religious virtue, if prayers are carried out communally, with family members when performed at home or with other people when performed at mosques or community prayer houses. Fasting during the month of Ramadhan, another pillar of Islam, also has a strong communal element. Breaking the fast in a group at sunset is an important ritual during this holy month, and fast breaking is an opportunity to entertain at home as well as to be a guest in other people's homes. In Aceh, as well as elsewhere in Indonesia, the group orientation of these religious rituals serves to strengthen a communal mentality and foster a strong sense of belonging to the group. Shared religious faith forms the basis for social groupings at various levels, from the family at the lowest and expanding to include the whole Muslim population of Indonesia or the world.

Another example of the importance of communal religious experience in the emotional response of the Acehnese can be seen in the quick re-emergence of *pengajian* or religious discussion groups. *Pengajian* are normally held at mosques or community prayer houses, usually once a week, but there is no requirement for timing. Anyone can attend, and the usual format is for a religious scholar to discuss some topic of interest to the group from a religious perspective. In some cases, there may also be discussion between the scholar and the audience. The *pengajian* functions as a forum for religious study as well as to strengthen a sense of community and to reinforce religious and social norms. For this reason, *pengajian* are normally attended by people who live in the local area near the mosque or prayer house, even though residents of other places may attend.

Following the disaster, discussion at *pengajian* was dominated by theories about the etiology and meaning of the tsunami. Much of this has stemmed from the survival stories of individuals, often tempered by time and latter day interpretations. People seem to experience a form of emotional release by telling and retelling these same stories that serve to reinforce the idea of shared lot and divine intervention in their lives. There can be no doubt that having these opportunities to talk about their experience has provided a sense of comfort and has helped many Acehnese to give meaning to the events they witnessed by offering their own perceptions for comment by others.

The value of activities of this kind to the Acehnese is their role in reinforcing the idea of a shared lot and common experience that has now become part of the cultural fabric of this region. Every member of the larger ethnic group has some kind of personal involvement in the tsunami, either directly or through the experiences of a family member, distant relative, friend, co-worker, or other from the same village or region. The disaster has become a bond shared by this entire generation of Acehnese and is one of the main formative experiences of the current generation of youth. The process of communal interpretation and the meaning ascribed to the event through this process has created a new narrative for the Acehnese community that has served as an important source of community resilience as well as personal adaptation.

It is clear that the re-establishment of religious and social structures of this kind have been very important in adjustment to post-disaster reality. The traditional institutions of the community provided a framework and a starting place to re-establish communal life with the facilities available. The most central of these institutions is religion, because of its importance in driving group experience and encouraged perhaps by the survival of many mosques, as noted above. As a religious significance was ascribed to the event itself, it seemed appropriate to most survivors that the solution to their dilemma be sought in religion as well. To most of them, this meant restoring the means of religious observance and a moral lifestyle as quickly as possible, on both a personal as well as community level.

The cognitive rationale for this centered on the idea of *takdir*, that the fate of many Acehnese was to experience and survive the tsunami, just as it was the destiny of others to die at this time. As their fate lay in God's decision for them and was part of His overall plan for creation, there was no point in opposing an inevitable outcome. Similarly, many survivors felt there was no reason to be distraught, beyond a manageable emotional response to loss, because this type of reaction amounts to doubting God's judgment about the proper unfolding of events. This kind of rationale is often employed by Indonesian Muslims in other contexts and provides considerable support that results in observed high levels of resilience that is often observed in individuals as well as communities in the Malay world. This type of worldview, which has been criticized in the Malay world since colonial days as a kind of passive fatalism and was even commented negatively upon by former Malaysian Prime Minister Mahathir Mohamad (see Mahathir, 1970), nonetheless has great value in encouraging an acceptance of misfortune and allowing individuals to cope in situations of great stress. It is often the case that Indonesian Muslims, including those in Aceh, are observed to react much less strongly to events that are considered extremely distressing in the West. This reaction tends to be genuine and is not generally a suppression of distress; the individuals involved do not believe themselves to be experiencing unusual stress as their attribution of events to a divine source, and their resulting acceptance of them, makes such a reaction unnecessary in their eyes. It was for this reason that counseling efforts offered to tsunami victims in Aceh were met with such dissatisfaction and rejection (see, for example, Miller, 2005; WHO, 2006; Zulkarnain, 2006), and survivors were particularly adamant about the inappropriateness of these services.

To survivors, there was no reason to be upset about the tsunami and its results. In fact, they tended to be completely calm and matter of fact in discussing what had happened in general, as well as what they had personally experienced. Their belief in the infallibility of God's decisions seems to underpin this reaction, and, in this sense, even the most extreme loss of life and possessions seemed reasonable and acceptable as survivors believed that God must have had a good reason for His actions. For this reason, there was no sense that the disaster was unfair, represented an insurmountable burden, or should result in inconsolable grief. The fact that God permitted something of this magnitude to occur seemed to offset any personal emotional trauma that might be expected to result from such a loss, as the whole experience was rooted in deeply held religious convictions.

For this reason, for survivors of the tsunami in Aceh, the experience often served to renew their interest in religious practice and identification. It is important to note, however, that outward expressions of faith – such as attendance at religious services and events, modes of dress, fasting at appropriate times, and so on – are not necessarily an indication of personal feelings or belief, but these visible aspects of religion were considered extremely important following the tsunami as part of the new, reconstructed society in Aceh. In other words, the visible manifestation of religious observance took on even greater importance as part of a newly re-established social norm. The widely held view that it was necessary to restore Islamic culture and institutions in the region meant to many people that this would have to include conformity to certain aspects of religious practice in daily life. If people were not inclined to conform to more rigorous social norms, many survivors felt it would be appropriate to require such behavior by law.

As a result, there has been a strong and undeniable trend towards and demand for the implementation of Syariah law in Aceh in the years since the tsunami. This movement began prior to that event, around the time Regional Autonomy took effect in 2001, but gained momentum following the disaster. *Qanun*, as Syariah laws are referred to in Aceh, have been passed by the Regional Parliament (*Dewan Perwakilan Rakyat Daerah*) as allowed by Indonesian Law No. 11 of 2006 on Governance in Aceh (*Undang-Undang Nomor 11 Tahun 2006 tentang Pemerintahan Aceh*). Most recently, *Qanun* have been passed calling for severe punishment, including public lashing, imprisonment, and punitive fines, for offenses like homosexuality, adultery, rape, and pedophilia, which are seen as detrimental to the public's morals. Earlier rulings addressed Islamic dress for women, mandatory completion of the five daily prayers, mandatory fasting during Ramadhan, mandatory almsgiving, and prohibition of gambling and alcohol. Although these new rulings have been heavily criticized in the Indonesian media, especially in the context of what has been viewed as bizarre punishment for moral offences, several of Aceh's political parties have taken the implementation of Islamic law as their main platform issue and have enjoyed considerable public support (*Kompas*, 2009). Despite the fact that laws with penalties of this kind are not considered appropriate in Indonesia's legal system, many people in Aceh are anxious that their region become an 'Islamic state' by implementing the *Qanun*. In the period leading up to the passing of the *Qanun Jinayat* (Islamic Criminal Code) laws described above, the local media reported that the public held the view that delay in passing the full spectrum of Islamic law would be detrimental to society and that such delays were the result of a few Acehnese individuals acting as agents of outside interests (see, for example, *Rakyat Aceh*, 2009). Once these laws took effect on 14 September 2009, speculation began to surface that this action taken by the Regional Parliament in the last weeks of its term was an effort to bring Aceh closer to the Islamic society desired by many religious leaders and members of the public (see Rina, 2009). The fact that such laws might violate the Indonesian Constitution and, as such, may be declared invalid by the Minister of the Interior has not served to lessen the public's desire to establish a more religious society run on Islamic principles.

The dichotomy of perception visible in Acehnese society is a very interesting after-effect of the tsunami and reconstruction of the affected area. There are many Acehnese who believe on a personal level that the disaster was an instance of divine judgment and feel a resulting need to create a more religious society that runs along the lines defined by their religious beliefs. Many of these individuals, as well as others who perhaps do not share the same interpretation of the meaning of the tsunami, nonetheless do not wish to live under rigorous Islamic law, and complaints about the enforcement of the *Qanun* are common. Even so, support for what is perceived as a more moral state is strong, and this view continues to color local perceptions about cultural and social issues. For example, news of a beauty contest that resulted in Qory Sandrioriva, Miss Aceh 2009, being crowned Miss Indonesia was met with criticism by religious and social leaders. Their objections centered on the fact that the contest follows the Western pattern for such events that they view as being in complete opposition to Islam and that Ms. Sandrioriva should not be allowed to represent the Acehnese people as she does not embody the characteristics they feel are important (*Antara News*, 2009).

Additionally, while there is a strong evidence to suggest that religion is most influential in the way the Acehnese view the tsunami and the devastation it caused and that religion has had an equally strong impact on post-disaster development in the region, there are equally strong reasons to suggest that the influence of religion in Aceh has significant limitations. For example, one of the most common complaints among members of the community is that corruption in the context of post-disaster development has been a serious problem. It was well known, for example, that officials or other well-connected individuals were able to obtain new houses built for tsunami survivors, even though they themselves did not experience any loss as a result of the event. Similarly, the fact that roads and other infrastructure built to replace that destroyed by the tsunami did not conform to specifications, with contractors cutting corners and using inferior materials. At the same time, every Acehnese agrees that corruption is prohibited by their religion and those in positions of authority, in particular, should act for the best interests of the community. They have no answer for the question of why their strong religious faith has failed to check corruption of this kind. Some feel that only God can devise a punishment sufficient to end corruption in Aceh. As corruption is endemic in Indonesia and is an inevitable part of doing business of any kind, it may be worth investigating further the relationship of this practice to religious belief in Aceh and elsewhere in the country.

RELIGION AND DEVELOPMENT IN FUTURE DISASTERS

The experience in Aceh following the 2004 Indian Ocean tsunami provides ample evidence of the importance of religion in the understanding and interpretation of such events by the people who experience them. It is difficult, however, to predict in advance exactly how the religious views of any given population might shape their response to disaster and even more difficult to apply such knowledge in designing development programs intended to address their needs. Disaster, by its nature, generally cannot be anticipated, even in parts of the world prone to natural events like floods or earthquakes. It is for this reason that the need for more in-depth cultural, including religious, knowledge of groups who are to be the recipients of development aid is frequently noted in the literature (see, for example, Powell, 2006; Jager, 2007; Lunn, 2009).

Because a large portion of development aid for disaster relief is provided by Western agencies whose guiding principles derive from the philosophical views of their societies of origin, it is likely, if not inevitable, that there will exist fundamental differences of perception between them and the communities in which they wish to operate. In particular, the Western social/political paradigm separates religion from the public sphere; when religious organizations provide social services, they tend to model their activities after secular agencies working in the same field. That is, in the West, the religious orientation of an aid-providing organization generally remains far in the background and often is only evident in the stated basis of the group in question. This has been noted in the context of religious or faith-based organizations providing disaster relief in Western countries, such as following Hurricane Katrina in the USA (see, for example, Cain and Barthelemy, 2008). In many non-Western countries, however, religious expression is considered appropriate and expected in the public sphere, as in the case of Aceh and in Indonesia in general. In the Islamic world, this may be a special problem, exacerbated perhaps by events in the political arena that suggest a natural opposition between the West (and its assumed Christian orientation) and Islam.

For this reason, disaster aid, whether from an international organization or from within the country itself, must be seen as according with local interpretation and local expectations. Following the Indian Ocean tsunami in Aceh, for example, aid that was clearly associated with the dominant religion of the area, in this case Islam, was clearly preferable to that that came from sources that were locally associated with other religions (even if religion played no part in the proffered aid). It was for this reason that the development efforts of the Turkish Red Crescent were greatly preferred to those of other secular groups and especially to those of groups believed to be Christian in orientation. In this case, it was the perception of religious orientation that seemed to be more significant than any actual religious principles that may have directed the activities or the organizations in question. The Acehnese, for example, had no particular knowledge of the nature of Islam in Turkey or any specific information about the Red Crescent itself. Rather, they were reacting to a perception that any group affiliated with their own religion was preferable to one of unknown, potentially conflicting, origin. This highlights the observation that response to disaster may include an intensification of identity issues and in-group–out-group distinctions (see, for example, Deeny and McFetridge, 2005; Dugan, 2007; Gunn, 2007). Religion, then, may color aid recipients' perception of the value and appropriateness of development programs in a manner that has little relationship to the content of that aid, which, in most cases, is in fact neutral and consists of the physical necessities required for survival.

The religious beliefs of the target population also relate closely to their perception of what aid is required and the direction development should take. In Aceh, for example, tsunami survivors felt little need for psychological counseling and support. Their requirements centered on housing, food, and medical aid immediately following the disaster and restoration of infrastructure and community structures in the longer term. They felt capable of providing for their own emotional recovery and did demonstrate a notable level of long-term community and individual resilience. As described above, this resilience seemed to derive almost wholly from their religious faith and the interpretation and meaning of the event their particular beliefs ascribed it. This meaning-related resilience has been shown to be extremely important in coping with adverse events and is one of the major benefits religious faith may provide, regardless of the specific religion or the location and population of interest (see Pargament and Cummings, 2010). In practical terms, development programs that do not fit with this perception of need are likely to be viewed as irrelevant by potential recipients, pointing up the dilemma of Western paradigms that have largely excluded the role of religious faith and may fail to take it into account in other cultural contexts. In fact, Western models of human response to disaster and other kinds of adversity that are deeply rooted in enlightenment philosophy are increasingly seen as culture bound and unable to address the cognitive and affective needs of people in non-Western cultures (see, for example, Von Peter, 2008; Kortmann, 2010).

Finally, and perhaps most important, the religious beliefs of a community may define the meaning they give to a natural disaster, as in the case of Aceh. This, in turn, may have important implications for what is seen as acceptable and desirable. In practice, it may be difficult to determine in advance what specific elements of assistance are seen locally as being of first priority and, conversely, which are seen as expendable or have not even been thought of. The desire of the public in Aceh to have mosques rebuilt or repaired first is an example of the former, while the perceived lack of need for counseling services is an example of the latter. The ability of aid providers to accommodate these perceptions in their programs may mean the difference between being seen as welcome assistance or as an unwanted intruder. The problem, of course, is how to identify such perceptions and respond to them in the short timeframe available following natural disaster, a situation complicated by the fact that many donor organizations operate around the world based on need and do not necessarily have a great deal of insight into local culture. Again, using Aceh as an example, the prolonged period of conflict preceding the tsunami combined with the comparatively closed nature of the community meant that potential aid providers knew little about the pre-disaster nature of the communities they planned to assist. This all points to a growing need for greater insight into religion and cultures around the world where development activities of all kinds take place and suggests there may be great value in incorporating some of the knowledge base available in other disciplines, such as anthropology, sociology, psychology, and other related fields, into the planning of development programs, especially in the special context of post-disaster aid where more appropriate efforts are of even greater significance.

NOTES

* The data in this chapter come from the field work in Aceh conducted by I. Fanany in the second half of 2010. The author wishes to acknowledge the time and funding provided by Deakin University through its Outside Study Program scheme that made this field work possible.

1. Regional Autonomy, as defined by the 1999 and 2000 laws concerning the nature of the resulting decentralization, changed the structure of government administration from a highly centralized system under the New Order government (which ended in 1997) to one where county-like divisions of provinces and municipal governments (*kabupaten* and *kotamadya*, respectively) became the main administrative centers. This change removed the provincial governments from the decision-making process, except at the highest policy level, as most services, including health, education, and commerce, were now run in the regions.
2. This idea, expressed in Indonesian as *berpegang pada tali Allah* (hold onto the rope of God), appeared widely in Aceh in news and opinion reports, mosque sermons, and even blogs as the tsunami and the resulting devastation began to be addressed in public forums shortly after the event.

REFERENCES

Adams, R.E., E.J. Bromet, N. Panina, E. Golovakha, D. Goldgaber and S. Gluzman (2002), 'Stress and well-being after the Chernobyl Nuclear Power Plant accident', *Psychological Medicine,* **32**(1), 143–56.

al-Bustom, A.G. (2010), 'Fungsi dan Peranan Agama dalam Bencana, Pancaniti' Blog, available at: http://ngamumule-islam.blogspot.com.au/2010/06/fungsi-dan-peranan-agama-dalam-bencana.html; accessed 1 August 2012.

Antara News (2009), 'Ulama: Qory Bukan Cerminan Putri Aceh', *Antara News*, 10 October 2009, available at: http://antaranews.com/berita/1255152537/ulama-qory-bukan-cerminan-puteri-aceh; accessed 23 July 2012.

Artawijaya, H.A. Bastoni and E. Mulyatman (2006), *Serambi Mekkah Dihempas Tsunami, Diterjang Kristenisasi: Liputan Langsung Wartawan Sabili*, Jakarta: Qalammas.

Badan Pusat Statistik (BPS) (2009), 'Statistik Nanggroe Aceh Darussalam', BPS, Banda Aceh, available at: http://aceh.bps.go.id/; accessed 23 July 2012.

Behn, S. (2005), 'Indonesia ousts Christian groups', *The Washington Times*, 17 March.

Beatty, A. (1996), 'Adam and Eve and Vishnu: syncretism in the Javanese Slametan', *Journal of the Royal Anthropological Institute*, **2**(2), 271–88.

Cabrera, F., B. Richards and G.R. Stevenson (2006), 'Katrina's aftermath: the role of the rapid mobilization action plan', *Illness, Crisis and Loss*, **14**(4), 373–86.

Cain, D.S. and J. Barthelemy (2008), 'Tangible and spiritual relief after the storm: the religious communities' response to Katrina', *Journal of Social Service Research*, **34**(3), 29–42.

Cassanova, J. (1994), *Public Religions in the Modern World*, Chicago: University of Chicago Press.

Cederroth, S. (1999), 'Indonesia and Malaysia', in D. Westerlund and I. Svanberg (eds), *Islam Outside the Arab World*, New York: St Martins Press, pp. 253–77.

ChannelNewsAsia (2005), '"Miracle" mosques defy tsunami onslaught', available at: http://muslimvillage.com/forums/topic/10424-miracle-mosques-defy-tsunami-onslaught/; accessed 1 August 2012.

Chaves, M. and W. Tsitsos (2001), 'Congregations and social services: what they do, how they do it and with whom', *Non-Profit and Voluntary Sector Quarterly*, **30**(4), 660–83.

Clarke, G. (2006), 'Faith matters: faith-based organisations, civil society and international development', *Journal of International Development*, **18**(6), 835–48.

Clarke, M. (2011), *Development and Religion: Theology and Practice*, Cheltenham, UK and Northampton, MA, USA: Edward Elgar.

Cooperman, A. (2005), 'Tsunami orphans will not be sent to a Christian home', *The Washington Post*, 14 January 2005.

De Cordier, B. (2009), 'The "humanitarian frontline", development and relief, and religion: what context, which threats and which opportunities?', *Third World Quarterly*, **30**(4), 663–84.

Deeny, P. and B. McFetridge (2005), 'The impact of disaster on culture, self, and identity: increased awareness by health care professionals is needed', *Nursing Clinics of North America*, **40**(3), 431–40.

Dugan, B. (2007), 'Loss of identity in disaster: how do you say goodbye to home?', *Perspectives in Psychiatric Care*, **43**(1), 41–6.

Ebstyne King, P. and J.L. Furrow (2008), 'Religion as a resource for positive youth development: religion, social capital, and moral outcomes', *Psychology of Religion and Spirituality*, **S**(1), 34–49.

Endonesia (2005), 'Juwono: LSM Kristen Silakan Keluar dari Aceh', available at: http://www.dataphone.se/~ahmad/050326.htm; accessed 1 August 2012.

Fountain, P.M., S.L. Kindon and W.E. Murray (2004), 'Christianity, calamity, and culture: the involvement of Christian churches in the 1998 Aitape tsunami disaster relief', *The Contemporary Pacific*, **16**(2), 321–55.

Gartland, M. (2005), 'Banda Aceh invites Christians' aid, but not their proselytizing', *The Post and Courier*, 26 December.

Gillard, M. and D. Paton (1999), 'Disaster stress following a hurricane: the role of religious differences in the Fijian Islands', *Australian Journal of Disaster and Trauma Studies*, No. 1999-2, available at: http://www.massey.ac.nz/~trauma/issues/1999-2/gillard.htm; accessed 23 July 2012.

Goody, J. (2003), 'Religion and development: some comparative considerations', *Development*, **46**(4), 64–7.

Gunn, F.X. (2007), 'Spiritual issues in the aftermath of disaster', *Southern Medical Journal*, **100**(9), 936–7.

Haverkort, B., K. Van't Hooft and W. Hiemstra (eds) (2003), *Ancient Roots, New Shoots: Endogenous Development in Practice*, London: Zed Books.

Howell, J.D. (2001), 'Sufism and the Indonesian Islamic revival', *The Journal of Asian Studies*, **60**(3), 701–29.

IRIN (2007), 'A clash of ignorances: relief aid and the Arab and Islamic world', available at: http://www.irin-news.org/fr/reportfrench.aspx?reportid=70771; accessed 22 July 2012.

Islamic Development Bank (IDB) (2004), *Annual Report 29 1424h (2003–2004)*, Jeddah: IDB.

Jacobs, K. and S. Williams (2011), 'What to do now? Tensions and dilemmas in responding to natural disasters: a study of three Australian state housing authorities', *International Journal of Housing Policy*, **11**(2), 175–93.

Jager, S.M. (2007), *On the Uses of Cultural Knowledge*, Washington, DC: Strategic Studies Institute.

Jechoutek, K.G. (2004), 'Through the eye of the needle: tradition, spirituality and human development', in A. Shutte (ed.), *Humanity in Science and Religion: The South African Experience*, Pietermaritzburg: Cluster Publications.

JockoThinker (2009), Blog posting, available at: http://newsgroups.derkeiler.com/Archive/Soc/soc.culture.indonesia/2009-01/msg01587.html; accessed 1 August 2012.
Juergensmeyer, M. (1993), *The New Cold War? Religious Nationalism Confronts the Secular State*, Berkeley, CA: University of California Press.
Kompas (2009), 'Syariah jadi Isu Utama: Kampanye Dari Pintu ke Pintu', *Kompas*, 17 March, available at: http://bisniskeuangan.kompas.com/read/xml/2009/03/17/09452622/syariah.jadi.isu.utama; accessed 23 July 2012.
Kortmann, F. (2010), 'Transcultural psychiatry: from practice to theory', *Transcultural Psychiatry*, **47**(2), 203–23.
Kuran, T. (1997), 'Islam and underdevelopment: an old puzzle revisited', *Journal of Institutional and Theoretical Economics*, **153**(1), 41–71.
Lavretsky, H. (2010), 'Spirituality and aging', *Aging Health*, **6**(6), 749–69.
Lim, C. and R.D. Putnam (2010), 'Religion, social networks, and life satisfaction', *American Sociological Review*, **75**(6), 914–23.
Lunn, J. (2009), 'The role of religion, spirituality and faith in development: a critical theory approach', *Third World Quarterly*, **30**(5), 937–51.
Mahathir, M. (1970), *The Malay Dilemma*, Singapore: Asia Pacific Press.
Marshall, K. (2001), 'Development and religion: a different lens on development debates', *Peabody Journal of Education*, **76**(3&4), 339–75.
Mayotte, J.A. (1998), 'Religion and global affairs: the role of religion in development', *SAIS Review*, **18**(2), 65–9.
McAmis, R.D. (2002), *Malay Muslims: The History and Challenge of Resurgent Islam in Southeast Asia*, Cambridge: Wm B. Eerdmans Publishing.
McAmis, R.D. (2002), *Malay Muslims: The History and Challenge of Resurgent Islam in Southeast Asia*, Cambridge: Wm B. Eerdmans Publishing.
Miller, G. (2005), 'The tsunami's psychological aftermath', *Science*, **309**(5737), 1030.
Nelson, H. (1999), 'Crises of God and man: Papua New Guinea political chronicle 1997–1999', *Journal of Pacific History*, **34**(3), 259–64.
Norgaard, R.B. (1994), *Development Betrayed: The End of Progress and a Co-Evolutionary Revisioning of the Future*, London: Routledge.
Norris, F.H., M.J. Friedman, P.J. Watson, C.M. Byrne, E. Diaz and K. Kaniasty (2002), '60,000 disaster victims speak: part I. An empirical review of the empirical literature, 1981–2001', *Psychiatry*, **65**(3), 207–39.
Palinkas, L.A., M.A. Downs, J.S. Petterson and J. Russell (1993), 'Social, cultural, and psychological impacts of the *Exxon Valdez* oil spill', *Human Organization*, 52(1), 1–13.
Pargament, K.I. and J. Cummings (2010), 'Anchored by faith: religion as a resilience factor', in J.W. Reich, A.J. Zautra and J.S. Hall (eds), *Handbook of Adult Resilience*, New York: The Guilford Press, pp. 193–212.
Pew Global Attitudes Project (2011), *Common Concerns About Islamic Extremism: Muslim–Western Tensions Persist*, Pew Research Center, Washington, DC, available at: http://www.pewglobal.org/2011/07/21/muslim-Western-tensions-persist/; accessed 23 July 2012.
Powell, M. (2006), 'Which knowledge? Whose reality? An overview of knowledge used in the development sector', *Development in Practice*, **16**(6), 518–32.
Powell, S. (2005), 'Christian groups "proselytizing" Muslims', *The Australian*, 24 December.
Rakyat Aceh (2009), '15 Ormas Islam Desak DPRA Sahkan Qanun Hukum Jinayat', Rakyat Aceh Online, 9 September 2009, available at: http://www.rakyataceh.com/index.php?open=view&newsid=13254&tit=BANDA%20ACEH%20-%2015%20Ormas%20Islam%20Desak%20DPRA%20Sahkan%20Qanun%20Hukum%20Jinayat; accessed 23 July 2012.
Rina (2009), 'Dewan Didesak Sahkan Qanun Jinayah', AcehKita.com, 8 September 2009, available at: http://www.acehkita.com/berita/dewan-didesak-sahkan-qanun-jinayah/; accessed 1 August 2012.
Salemink, O. (2004), 'Development cooperation as quasi-religious conversion', in A.K. Giri, A. van Harskamp and O. Salemink (eds), *The Development of Religion/The Religion of Development*, Delft: Eburon, pp. 121–30.
Selinger, L. (2004), 'The forgotten factor: the uneasy relationship between religion and development', *Social Compass*, **51**(4), 523–43.
Seybold, K.S. and P.C. Hill (2001), 'The role in religion and spirituality in mental and physical health', *Current Directions in Psychological Science*, **10**(1), 21–4.
Singh, R.P.B. (1999), 'Rethinking development in India: perspective, crisis and prospects', in D. Simon and A. Narman (eds), *Development as Theory and Practice*, Harlow: Addison Wesley Longman, pp. 55–75.
Smith, S.R. and M.R. Sosin (2001), 'The varieties of faith-related agencies', *Public Administration Review*, **61**(6), 651–70.
Ter Haar, G. and S. Ellis (2006), 'The role of religion in development: towards a new relationship between the European Union and Africa', *The European Journal of Development Research*, **18**(3), 351–67.
The Australian (2005), 'Aid groups warned against preaching', 11 January.

Tinbergen, J. (1989), 'Development cooperation and religion', in J.S. Augustine (ed.), *Strategies for Third World Development*, New Delhi: Sage Publications, pp. 11–15.
Tomalin, E. (2006), 'Religion and a rights-based approach to development', *Progress in Development Studies*, **6**(2), 93–108.
Tyndale, W. (2006), *Visions for Development: Faith-based Institutions*, Aldershot: Ashgate.
United Nations High Commissioner for Refugees (UNHCR) (2006), *The State of the World's Refugees: Human Displacement in the New Millennium*, Geneva: UNHCR.
Ver Beek, A.K. (2000), 'Spirituality: a development taboo', *Development in Practice*, **10**(1), 31–43.
Verhelst, T. and W. Tyndale (2002), 'Culture, spirituality and development', in D. Eade (ed.), *Development and Culture: Selected Essays from Development in Practice*, London: Oxfam, pp. 1–24.
Von Peter, S. (2008), 'The experience of "mental trauma" and its transcultural applications', *Transcultural Psychiatry*, **45**(4), 639–51.
Wigger, A. (2005), 'Encountering perceptions in parts of the Muslim world and their impact on the ICRC's ability to be effective', *International Review of the Red Cross*, **87**(8585), 346–7.
World Health Organization (2005), *Manual for the Community Level Worker to Provide Psychosocial Care to Communities Affected by the Tsunami Disaster*, WHO, New Delhi, available at: http://www.searo.who.int/LinkFiles/List_of_Guidelines_for_Health_Emergency_ community_level-workers.pdf; accessed 23 July 2012.
World Health Organization (2006), *WHO Recommendations for Mental Health in Aceh*, Geneva: WHO, available at: http://www.who.or.id/eng/contents/aceh/WHO_Recommendations_Mental_Health_Aceh.pdf; accessed 23 July 2012.
Zulkarnain (2006), 'Client values in the counselling process', *Prosiding Persidangan Antarabangsa Pembangunan Aceh*, Bangi: Universiti Kebangsaan Malaysia, 26–27 December, 117–23.

20 Religious symbolism and the politics of urban space development

Yamini Narayanan

INTRODUCTION

Considerable scholarship has been devoted to the study of the transformation of religion in urban spaces, the growth and influence of urban religious movements, issues of multiculturalism and pluralism, and religion and migration. Robert Levy's seminal work *Mesocosm* (1990), for instance, exhaustively studies the anthropology of urban Hinduism in Bhaktapur city in Nepal. However, religion's substantive historical and ongoing influence on the process of urbanization itself, urban design and planning and sustainable urban development, has been comparatively less rigorously understood. Peter Hall, Clara Greed and Aaron Wildavsky have all argued that the religious urge has been tremendously influential in urban planning, and has thus been a critical determinant of the social, political and spatial processes of urbanization.

These critiques place the rapidly burgeoning cities of the developing world, particularly South Asia, in an interesting light. Asia undoubtedly has several of the largest and the fastest growing cities and in the world, and the highest concentration of human population density, especially in South Asia or the Indian subcontinent. In examining the strategies for a sustainable urban future in South Asia, a theological critique of some of the major religions of the region would be invaluable in locating and understanding the ethics and values that have shaped and continue to shape the built environment in the large megapolises and urban areas of South Asia. Several South Asian cities are also hotbeds of international religious extremism and terrorism, and undoubtedly have an influence in shaping and being shaped by powerful religious forces. Space is a loaded 'ideology' (Lefebvre, 1976) and sifting through the various ideological discourses that shape urban space in South Asia is one of the first steps in understanding the ideological politics of urban space in a region where it is increasingly at an unprecedented premium.

My aim in this chapter is to consider how contemporary and emerging forms of Hinduism conceptualize the urban space and mediate the development of the city/a city, using a very specific case of a new urban goddess, the Manushi Swachha Narayani or the Goddess of Cleanliness, who was created in 2005 as a divine mascot to mobilize the cause of street vendors in Delhi city for their right to hawk in the urban space. This goddess was conceived of by the efforts of *Manushi*, a leading Indian socio-academic journal on women and society with a strong social conscience, and Madhu Kishwar, the editor-in-chief of the journal and a social activist. *Manushi* had taken on the activist task of representing and agitating for the rights of street vendors in Delhi to hawk in clearly demarcated public spaces, arguing that they too had a right to earn their livelihood. These small-scale businesses are, however, treated as illegal encroachment by antiquated laws, in spite of the fact that Delhi, like any developing city, needs its small vendors for cheap goods and food to be available to its large working-/lower-class populations (Kishwar, 2005). The Swachha Narayani is presented as a 'secular goddess' (ibid.); and yet, the human form of the goddess is inspired by the image of the ten-armed goddess Durga. Indeed, the two goddesses have starkly similar aims – to enable the triumph of righteousness over evil.

I use this case to study the influence of one particular form that contemporary Hindu religion has taken on the urban development of the 'secular' cities in India rather than explicitly Hindu pilgrimage cities. Several Indian cities are key sites of Hindu pilgrimage and can clearly demonstrate the influence of the Hindu worldview on the urban environment; what, however, of the modern megapolises and large cities whose contemporary planning worldview claim the influence of rationality and secularity? How can we see the influence of the religious worldview on the urban design and the urbanization process of such cities? Can the Hindu religious worldview contribute to moral order in the city, while co-existing with a multi-religious as well as a modernity worldview? And what does this mean for sustainability in general/of a city? How are religious symbols evocative of modern development issues such as urban planning and space utilization?

The chapter is structured as follows: I first present an overview of the issues on the use of Delhi's public spaces by street vendors (particularly in the decade leading to the Commonwealth Games in 2010), and the ideological conflict over the use of the city's urban space. I then present the case of the Swachha Narayani, a divine mascot created by the journal *Manushi* as a symbol of empowerment for the street vendors. Next, I make a religious anthropological critique of the goddess and her impact in determining the outcome of spatial politics in Delhi. Lastly, I offer some conclusions, bringing the critical themes of this chapter together.

THE STREET HAWKING ISSUE IN DELHI

The growing tensions around the use, allocation and development of urban space in Indian cities is strongly characterized by competing claims to it by the city's upper/middle and poor/working classes. The policy of economic liberalization by the Congress government in 1991 set in motion sweeping changes in mobilizing middle-class consumption and lifestyles of affluence (Varma, 1998), and in the process, also privileging cities, the nerve centres of capital consumption, over the rural regions. The aspiration to remake Delhi into a 'world city' or a developed Asian city like Singapore or Hong Kong drove the sweeping changes in the urban landscape, as witnessed by the rapid mushrooming of large shopping malls and multiplex cinema complexes across the capital city (Jain, 2001). Such urban redevelopment further removes the middle classes from the lower classes, for they are beyond the affordability of the latter. Paradoxically, while this has led to an increased clamping down on the street hawkers who do serve the needs of the working class such as providing cheap food, the shopping malls have started to provide street food to the middle classes – in albeit 'sanitary' conditions and at exorbitant prices that defeat one of the main purposes of street cuisine, that is, affordability (te Lintelo, 2009).

Delhi is home to approximately 300 000–600 000 street hawkers, the majority of whom are women, according to NGO and scholarly estimates (*Manushi*, 2001; SPA, 2004). Clear government estimates are unavailable as street hawkers are not recognized as such in population statistics (te Lintelo, 2009). These vendors engage in a variety of small-scale businesses on pushcarts, footpaths, or in makeshift stalls selling clothes, cooking vessels, plastic household items, fruit and vegetables, small electronic goods, and food. However, only about 5 per cent of the vendors have been provided with trading licences and in 1999, the Municipal Corporation of Delhi (MCD) sharply escalated the fees from Rs.500 to Rs.5000 for hawking without a permit (Vinod, 2005). However, this defeats an earlier Supreme Court ruling that stated that pedestrian paths in India have more uses than just serving as walkways and that street vendors must be allowed their fundamental right to work and livelihood and use the footpaths for this, as long as it did not obstruct other uses (ibid.).

In the decade leading to the Commonwealth Games in Delhi in 2010, the MCD redoubled its eviction drive to chase out the hawkers who were 'encroaching' on government land in order to 'beautify' the city. Vinod (ibid.) notes, 'When asked where these "illegal encroachers" would go once they are beaten and chased out of their livelihood space, Madan Thaplial, PRO of NDMC summed up his government's attitude to these poor street entrepreneurs: "Let them go anywhere!"'

One of the main accusations against the street vendors is that they dirty the surrounding areas, block the walkways for pedestrian and even vehicular traffic, and they peddle unsanitary food, leading to disease by contamination and adulteration (Kishwar, 2001). Middle-class values such as health and cleanliness (Baviskar, 2003) drive the urban development planning, but in a manner that excludes the welfare of the lower classes. Varma (1998) notes that the Indian middle classes have access to knowledge and bureaucratic power that is disproportionate to the lower classes' access to it; however, they are unlikely to use it to advance the social and political development of the lower classes. Moreover, studies of the food samples of street food and food served in middle-class establishments hardly show variation, if any, in the sanitary standards of food preparation or the food itself (Kishwar, 2001; te Lintelo, 2009). Further, the power of middle-class aspirations behind the street vendors' eviction are clear in the fact that while the MCD clamps down on street vendors, it is, however, willing to allow street food in a 'global avatar' at 'al fresco tables', in the manner of wealthy Asian cities like Singapore and so on (Gautam, 2007) or allow only pre-packaged food, in spite of the fact that this enormously raises costs for the vendor as well as the typically lower-class consumer.

In 2009, the Delhi Mayor Kanwar Sain announced the MCD's intention to introduce the idea of mandatory bio-cryptic registration of hawkers and street vendors to maintain a database of all the 'legal' licensed vendors in the city. The hawkers would be 'required to pay Rs.400 to cover the cost of survey, registration, record creation, issuance of bio-cryptic photo identity cards, coded number plate and three-dimensional photographic survey', all of which would be shared by the Delhi Police to additionally address any 'security concerns' associated with street vendoring (*The Hindu*, 2009). However, as early as 2005, this had proved to be a potential death-knell for the largely illiterate 8000 female street vendors and a large number of illiterate male vendors in the city as they have no reliable means of procuring the required permits (Serrill, 2005). As is typically the case when government regulations threaten the collapse of poor livelihoods, the SEWA (Self-Employed Women's Association) has taken up the cause of preserving poor female entrepreneurs' incomes and livelihoods, and provides loans and political representations to these women. However, the SEWA has managed to take only 2000 women under its protection.

The MCD and a series of Delhi Master Plans, including the Vision 2021 has neglected to design vendoring zones in the city, in spite of repeated petitions by the hawkers and the NGOs acting as their representatives, chiefly SEWA and *Manushi*. The spaces currently occupied by the hawkers come at a premium cost to the hawkers for they are forced to pay several million rupees worth of bribes to the police and MCD henchmen annually (Kishwar, 2001); legalizing the hawkers zones and expeditious issue of licences in a fair manner would be more cost effective for the hawkers (Vinod, 2005).

In August 2010, shortly prior to the launch of the Commonwealth Games, the National Association of Street Vendors of India (NASVI), with a membership base of 300 000 members in 20 states, organized a large protest near the Jawaharlal Nehru Stadium, the location of the Games (Indo-Asian News Service, 2010). The NASVI had requested the state Chief Minister Sheila Dikshit for the city's street vendors, especially the food hawkers, to be part of the city's urban tourism experience and hosting strategy; however, their goods and push-carts continued to be routinely confiscated by the MCD and the NDMC (New Delhi Municipal Council) immediately prior to, and even beyond the staging of the Games (ibid.).

In 2011, the Municipal Corporation of Delhi commissioner, New Delhi Municipal Council chairperson, Delhi Development Authority vice-chairperson, the State Urban Development secretary and Madhu Kishwar of the advocacy group and journal *Manushi* formed a special committee to draft the much-awaited legislation on the protection of the rights of the vendors, based on the Model Street Vendors (Protection of Livelihood and Regulation of Street Vending) Bill 2009. Madhu Kishwar has long been involved in representing the rights of the street vendors through *Manushi* and in working directly with the street workers to restore their sense of safety, empowerment and confidence in the city where they have been denied livelihood rights. Kishwar was centrally involved in the conceptualization of the divine mascot created to ensure the protection of the street vendors, the *Manushi* Swachha Narayani, or the Goddess of Cleanliness. The Goddess is an intriguing symbol for the ideological conflict over Delhi's public space, and I provide an overview in the next section.

MANUSHI SWACHHA NARAYANI: THE GODDESS OF CLEANLINESS

In March 2005, a new goddess was born to add to Hinduism's already exhaustive pantheon of colourful divine images through the efforts of *Manushi*. *Manushi* had taken on the crusade to protect the Delhi street vendors and small-scale pavement businesses from 'routine human rights abuses, humiliation, assaults on their livelihood and huge extortion rackets legitimized by archaic laws which treat this legitimate occupation as an "illegal activity" despite the fact that the city cannot function without street vendors' (Kishwar, 2005, p. 7). In addition, this large section of the poor urban self-employed does the government a double favour by saving them the disgrace of unemployed citizens, as well as by removing the burden of their unemployment from their shoulders (Kishwar, 2005).

However, these citizens face extortion and violations of their dignity and human rights on a daily basis (Kishwar, 2001). *Manushi* has been involved with the task of safeguarding the interests of street vendors for several years now, against demonic practices of corruption (ibid.). These practices include confiscation of their goods upon non-payment of extortion or bribe, imposing a fine for 'encroachment' when there are no other legal spaces provided for their businesses, and beatings (ibid., p. 4). These citizens fall way below the minimum tax threshold and technically earn non-taxable income; however, Kishwar (2001) writes that approximately 5 million street sellers are forced to pay up nearly 40 million rupees a month to corrupt officials as bribes!

An important part of *Manushi*'s efforts to empower the street vendors against this sort of brutality was to inculcate a sense of self-esteem and power through a cleanliness drive. A particular challenge, writes Kishwar (ibid.), was to remove the prejudice of influential citizens and the officials that the street vendors were responsible for the squalor, filth and chaos in Delhi. In the process of motivating the hawkers to take responsibility for maintaining cleanliness and cultivating respect for their physical and natural environment, *Manushi* started the practice of revering and worshipping the lowly broom in December 2001 (Kishwar, 2005). The broom signified both the determination to clean the physical and natural environment and create surroundings where the human spirit can thrive, as well as a community's resolve to cleanse the government, which had acquired all the ugly colours and taint of corruption, arrogance, sloth and oppression. The worship of the broom was conducted in accordance with the typical worship of the other members of the Hindu pantheon, with *bhajans* (devotional music), *dholak* (drums) and with the waving of the sacred fire around the broom deity (Kishwar, 2012).

The deity acquired a divine-human form over the next four years, resembling Goddess Durga, with ten arms, each holding a symbol of development, both for the individual and the community. The deity represents a combination of the three major Hindu goddesses – Lakshmi, the goddess of wealth, Saraswati, the goddess of learning and Durga, for 'the requisite strength and power to combat the forces of evil that engulf the lives and livelihoods of street hawkers' (ibid.). The transition of the deity from a broom to a gendered human form is natural in Hindu society. Anthony Good notes (2000, p. 273), 'In Hindu cosmology, the materialization of divinity – a prerequisite for worship – is inseparably linked not only to the emergence of time but also to the devolution of divinity into gendered forms'. This provides a basis for human kinship that is central to Hindu worship (Good, 2000). Named Manushi Swachha Narayani, her worship involves more than just a tribute to cleanliness. The other symbols (and their significance as they pertain to various aspects of sustainability) in her ten hands include the following:

1. The broom to represent reverence for a clean, natural environment, and the determination to clean up corruption.
2. A clock to symbolize the need to change through the new lens of introspection, to keep up with the changing times and to remove archaic laws and customs that cause the continued exploitation of the people, particularly the poor.
3. A coin in her palm emphasizes that all people should be allowed to earn a livelihood with dignity.
4. A weighing-balance that communicates commitment to social justice.

5. A video camera, since this equipment was used to capture several instances of municipal harassment of the vendors on tape. Kishwar credits video footage for many of their successful campaigns.
6. A *diya* or an earthen lamp to dissipate the darkness and hopelessness from the lives of the vulnerable.
7. An account book that symbolizes maintaining honest accounts.
8. A pen to emphasize the resolution to spread literacy and education, as well as to communicate the message that the pen is mightier than the sword.
9. A conch shell to represent purity, as well as to serve as a clarion call to citizens for collective self-organization, so that they can truly participate in a democratic system of governance.
10. Barley stalks to indicate prosperity as well as the spread of the message of the Broom Goddess. Just as one seed reaps innumerable grains, it is hoped that this initiative would launch numerous others.

The debut worship of the Broom Goddess was at Sewa Nagar in Delhi, where *Manushi* had established a Model Market to demonstrate how street vendors and pavement businesses can be integrated with the local economy in an efficient and aesthetic manner (Kishwar, 2005). The statue of the Goddess was taken to Sewa Nagar with joyous celebrations and fanfare marking the journey, to the sounds of the *shehnai* (wind instruments) and the *dholak* (drums). Kishwar (2005, p. 4) writes: 'This proved a tremendous morale boost for the terrorized vendors. Call it coincidence or a miracle, the situation started improving rapidly after Devi Swachha Narayani positioned herself in Sewa Nagar'.

A female mascot for the vendors who are overwhelmingly women was also reassuring in the male-power-dominated arena of claiming and withholding urban space, and by her powers to build a growing sense of community, which is important for women. Kishwar writes (2012):

> The impact of her presence was far greater than we had anticipated. It not only energized the members of the pilot project but also became a live link with local residents. They began to come and express solidarity with our project by coming with floral offerings and joining in the evening *aarti* [worship].

In keeping with the secular spirit of the worship of the Swachha Narayani, a Muslim was appointed the chief priest and presides over her daily worship (ibid.). Several of the chief followers of the Goddess are Muslim vendors, who refer to the centuries of joint worship by Hindus and Muslims in India to common deities (ibid.).

Furthermore, the Swachha Narayani also offered, in a highly tense situation where the *Manushi* workers were being abused and harassed by the local thugs who resented the fact that the Sewa Nagar market was increasingly a safe and bribe-free zone for the vendors, the possibility of reconciliation with the local goons and violent gangs sponsored by the local political parties (ibid.). The corrupt beat constables as well as the hostile thugs asked to be able to come and make a pilgrimage to see her. Significantly, *ahimsa* or non-violence is a central principle behind the symbolism of the Broom Goddess. She has ten arms like the fierce Durga (goddess of power); however, none of the symbols she carries are suggestive of violence. Manushi Swachha Narayani stands for the peaceful resistance to oppression of the vulnerable.

Thus it was that within a year of her conception, the Sewa Nagar Model Market was transformed from a filthy vending zone to one of the most vibrant, colourful and clean street markets in Delhi (ibid.). Through the Broom Goddess, who stands for the moral and legitimate rights for a section of the road users who are vulnerable to tyrannical 'government controls', *Manushi* also hopes to cause a shift in consciousness in the urban middle classes who depend on the street vendors, and to 'move out of the Third World mindset that accepts dirt and squalor as the inevitable fate of our citizens' (Kishwar, 2005, p. 11). The Broom Goddess is also a reminder that Indian cities have to be sensibly and sensitively planned in accordance with 'the actual requirements of our citizens and their income levels' (ibid.).

However, in the face of increased aggression from some of the local political gangs and personal assaults upon Kishwar (who narrowly avoided being fatally lynched three times since 2007) and other *Manushi* workers, the Sewa Nagar project had to be closed down. The Swachha Narayani temple, which had become 'an emotional centre point for the project' came under threat (Kishwar, 2012). The goons threatened to start a communal riot on the basis that the Goddess offended Muslim sensibilities, however, the Iman of the local mosque refused to be drawn into the politics. The thugs then claimed that the Goddess was insulting Hindus because of the worship of the unclean broom, and insisted that the 'imaginary' goddess was an affront to the 'real' goddesses (ibid.).

In spite of its eventual shutdown, the Sewa Nagar project has been widely acknowledged to be a success. The United Nations Commission for the Legal Empowerment of the Poor sponsored a documentary film on the Goddess and the Sewa Nagar Market 'advocating it as an international role model for the legal empowerment of the urban poor' (ibid.). The worship of the Broom Goddess evolved into a full-scale 'Manushi Swachha Narayani Clean Governance' civil society movement. In 2006, *Manushi* signed a Memorandum of Understanding with the MCD, agreeing that the vendors would pay their *tehbazari* or license fee to the MCD through *Manushi*. The Ministry of Urban Development in the Indian Government asked *Manushi* to submit an Action Plan for Delhi's street hawkers, based on the Sewa Nagar Model, which would also provide a blueprint for urban street vendors across India (Bhaneja, 2010). While the MCD has tried to block the Ministry's support several times, the Manushi Swachha Narayani campaign has stepped up in Delhi to respond to an issue of urban space conflict that has intensified elsewhere in the major cities of India as well (ibid.). Kishwar has set up partnerships with other NGOs in cities such as Kolkata and Mumbai, so that this issue may be treated as a matter of national urban importance.

MANUSHI SWACHHA NARAYANI AND THE RELIGIOUS INFLUENCE ON DELHI

The Manushi Swachha Narayani is an unexpected symbol of emancipation for the urban poor. The use of a goddess symbol – and a Hindu goddess in form, even as she is ostensibly a secular goddess – in representing the rights of the marginalized to their share of the urban space in an Indian city and as a mascot for urban development reform is mired in several problematic historical and religious ideologies and assumptions. First, religious symbols – classical, pagan, or neo-creations – have been traditionally meaningful in the villages and rural regions in India (Foulston and Abbot, 2009, p. 223). Modernization with its accompanying twin corollaries of secularization and urbanization was believed to herald the demise of religion and the site of this gradual dissolution was to be the city. Second, reformers in India for the last 150 years – Baptist evangelists in nineteenth-century India and rationalist social reformers like Raja Rammohan Roy and Swami Dayanand – were emphatic that idol worship was one of the paramount problems of Indian society, leading to blind faith and superstition, and they strove to prevail upon the masses to form a more secularized society where the forces of truth and reason would overcome. Third, use of the goddess symbol itself in an Indian context is intriguing. While Western feminists have eulogized the goddess for her feminine strength, purity and power, Indian feminists have, until very recently, spurned the goddess as a patriarchal symbol, associated as she typically is with the embodiment of wifely and womanly virtues (McDermott, 2005). However, environmental and social activism in India has started to return to the goddess symbol as a means of self-determination and agency.

The Hindu pantheon of gods and goddesses can be understood as a 'system of signs, constructed and limited so that they can be both understandable and directive to the city's inhabitants' (Parish, 1997, p. 451). The deities of the pantheon represent morality and power, both of which are central to the construction and legitimization of any social organization. The symbolism of the Swachha Narayani as a righteous figure provided the contrast for the hooligans to be seen, as Kishwar (2012) refers to them, as the 'modern demons'. The Goddess provided an impetus to social and political mobilization in a manner reminiscent of the dove and the olive branch as a mascot by the nuclear disarmament movement in Europe – a clear biblical reference initiated by church groups (who had quite a prominent role in the campaign), yet neutral enough to not be regarded as a symbol of religious doctrine and thus appealing to secular/atheist members of the movement as well. In the Indian context, the explicitly religious attributes of the Goddess, and her very Hinduness would make her an object of appeal.

As Indian public intellectual Asis Nandy explains (2001, p. 126):

> a crucial identifier of Hinduism – as a religion, a culture and a way of life – has been the particular style of interaction humans have had with gods and goddesses. Deities in everyday Hinduism, from the heavily Brahminic to the aggressively non-Brahminic, are not entities outside everyday life, nor do they preside over life from outside; they constitute a significant part of it.

These interactions are human, familial and individualized (Roland, 1988), rather than solely (if at all) transcendental. Furthermore, 'these gods and goddesses not only populate the Hindu world but regularly visit and occasionally poach on territories outside it' (Nandy, 2001, p. 126). The pantheon fills a gaping sacral void and offers the opportunity to resacralize human lives and inspire humans with confidence as regards their deities (Nandy, 2001). The Hindu pantheon is pervasive, even invasive, and forces engagement or at least acknowledgement with atheists, agnostics and believers of other faiths in the South Asian (and even international) context (ibid.). That a member (even a newly admitted one) of the pantheon should be a subject of interest in a development study should then not be so surprising.

Among the Hindu pantheon, the female goddesses have particularly aroused the interest of feminist and areal studies scholarship. Feminism has typically taken on the cause of empowerment of women as well as other marginalized, downtrodden groups; hence the question 'Is the Hindu goddess a feminist?' begs itself (Rajan, 1998). The examples of Sita, the embodiment of a model wife, or fierce and uncontrollable Kali seem to either reinforce patriarchal values or flaunt black rage as a means of assertion, neither of which are particularly empowering. The goddess form has also been arrogated by Hindu nationalist parties such as the BJP and RSS as 'Mother India' or 'Bharat Mata', and the 'Ashtabhuja', a goddess form specifically created by the women's wing of the RSS 'to provide women with an anti-Muslim rallying symbol' (McDermott, 2005, p. 3610).

However, environmental activists have begun to return to the goddess symbol as a way of stimulating movements and action for ecological and social justice. With its resonances with motherhood, the goddess image can be elevated to the status of the ever-compassionate carer and protector of the wronged and the weak. This revival has occurred mainly in the villages and rural areas where the goddess was traditionally celebrated. For instance, a Science schoolteacher in Menasikhyathana Halli village in rural Karnataka erected the shrine of 'AIDS-Amma' on 1 December 1997, the World AIDS Day, to educate and spread AIDS awareness among the villages to arrest the spread of the disease as well as deal with the social stigma associated with AIDS. The Swachha Narayani signifies the possibility of supreme empowerment and strength, represented as she is by the combination of the holy trinity of Hindu goddesses.

Moreover, the Swachha Narayani was seen as a source of enormous emotional strength for Kishwar and the other *Manushi* workers, several of whom were female, and the wronged vendors to carry through their protest and assertion of their vending rights, even in the face of vandalism, terrorism and physical intimidation. When the project collapsed at Sewa Nagar, a new space was won in Nehru Place, and Kishwar (2012) wrote:

> Finally, the fact that we are still alive and fighting it out for overall policy reform for street vendors proves that we enjoy Her protection. I feel grateful that the Goddess gave us the wisdom not to make Sewa Nagar into our be-all-and end-all issue. Our Goddess has given us the required patience and resilience not to expect instant results, not to get demoralized when the going gets tough, to accept defeat with equanimity and not let victories give an exaggerated sense of achievement.

While the small project in Sewa Nagar failed, the attention that this brought to the movement ensured that Kishwar was invited to the highest levels of law and urban policy reform to allow vendors the right to peaceful livelihood.

The Manushi Swachha Narayani is also unique in that that she is an urban creation and a significant determinant in the resolution of the politics of ownership and use of urban space and development. She marks critical points of intersection and difference between theology and secular urban space design theory. Her physical presence, her human form and her temple are reminiscent of the demarcation of space in Hindu pilgrimage cities (Good, 2000). Parish (1997, p. 453) writes, 'The city is part what the Hindu pantheon makes it. Urban space, form, and action are shaped, known and experienced in terms of religious meanings'. Religion, politics and development are intimately intertwined in India (Larson, 1995), and the Swachha Narayani provides a moral force for a longstanding issue of equitable and just space allocation to its poorer citizens in Delhi. In Sewa Nagar, prior to her abolishment by the vandalizing goons, her presence and ritualistic worship provided the energy and inspiration to make it one of the best practice vending areas, through the peaceful sharing of urban space in a manner that promoted local economic development, alleviated poverty and promoted a sense of community. Through religious symbolism influencing urban space use, the city itself can become sacralized and 'layered in religious meaning . . . expressed in art and iconography . . . [and] constituted in action by way of rituals, processions and festivals' (Parish, 1997, p. 453).

Does this potentially mean a sacralization – or some might even have it – a resacralization of urban space in Delhi? Does the Swachha Narayani foretell of ways in which theology might intersect with urban planning in the future in Delhi and other 'secular' Indian cities? This leads to the grave question of what forms of religion would lead to the most profitable outcomes for good sustainable development. Christianity triumphed over paganism, which allowed the Genesis to be interpreted in its most authoritative form (Gorringe, 2002). Does the Brahminical Hinduism, with its emphasis on the 'self', and low tolerance for 'social pollution' through the caste system and the eschewing of the lower classes bear a greater responsibility for social and ecological destruction in India? Can the Swachha Narayani be interpreted as a new attempt at the greening of Hinduism? Gorringe notes (ibid., p. 222) that a 'theory of the built environment' must ultimately be a 'theory of salvation'. The Swachha Narayani stands for equitable access to urban space, social and ecological justice, and awareness. In standing for democracy, she also stands for the values that shape the community, its architecture, economics and development.

The longevity and the impact of socially created goddesses are questionable. The AIDS-Amma, for instance, eventually became seen as a danger rather than succour since the villagers might be inclined to pray for deliverance rather than proactively and scientifically approach the disease. In fact, her worship itself became a source of social stigma in some instances (Foulston and Abbot, 2009, p. 223). The Swachha Narayani, on the other hand, has advanced well into her seventh year in human form; her previous incarnation as a broom takes her to over a decade. It appears that with the Clean Governance Movement and Kishwar's involvement in policy reform, her symbolic value as a divine mascot for the urban poor and the cause she stands for will be further recognized in Delhi and eventually in the other major cities of India. However, the greater concern for symbols and metaphors is not whether they endure; it is that they work. The Manushi Swachha Narayani reinforces the carrying power of religious symbolism and its ongoing influence in sustainable urbanization – a project that is purportedly rationalist, secularist and techno-scientific.

CONCLUSIONS

Paraphrasing Finnish city planner Seppo Kjellberg, Gorringe (2002, p. 2) describes the purpose of theology in urban planning as 'a science of reconciliation, promoting interdisciplinary dialogue, bringing all concerned with questions of the built environment together, but offering as its own perspective an understanding of the overall purpose of humankind with creation'. Religion on its own can offer no comprehensive authority on ecologically and politically just and equitable urban planning; it may play, however, a vital role in animating human lives and fulfilling human purpose, which might be ultimately critical in enabling an authentic sustainable development. The task of studying religion and its impact and influence in cities, which is where a growing majority of the planet's citizens now live, is thus important.

The case of Manushi Swachha Narayani in Delhi city is symbolic not only of the street hawkers' right to vend, but also of the possibility of pragmatic integration of religion and urban planning. The ongoing movement to secure the rights of poor street vendors to hawk in the public spaces of Delhi (and the other cities of India) is one of the longest enduring battles over the use and allocation of space in the city. This is also a battle between unequals as the poor neither have the access to information about their political rights as do the middle/upper classes, nor do they have the means to resist the unfair oppression of their fundamental rights and the terrorization of their lives by corrupt politicians and police on a daily basis. The righteousness, sense of justice and deliverance that the Swachha Narayani stood for was critical in reinforcing a sense of confidence, morale and strength in the vendors to fight for their rights. The ability and the willingness to resist oppression is vital for equitable development and true democracy.

The case of the Swachha Narayani also demonstrates that it is indeed possible for a religious worldview on urban space usage to coexist, and in fact, work effectively with modernity and a techno-scientific view of development. The Goddess was the single clearest clarifier of the fact that improper land use in Delhi, the perpetuation of filth and squalor in the built environment, and the urban poverty was not because of the street vendors, but the corrupt MCD and police officials, as well as the local goons, who had a vested interest in maintaining the status quo to ensure the flow of bribe and blackmail moneys to them (Kishwar, 2012). As Kishwar notes, the Goddess and her temple had become the 'emotional centres' for mobilization of the vendors, as well as educating them on cleanliness, their rights and proper space usage in Sewa Nagar, however, the corruption of the MCD officials, police and continuous harassment and death threats by local gangs led to the eventual shutdown of that project. Nevertheless, the vendors' resistance achieved sufficient momentum that Madhu Kishwar and other *Manushi* workers were invited to the country's highest forum on urban policy reform to investigate the possibilities of a democratic and just use of public space for the street vendors.

Importantly, the Swachha Narayani confirms that the Goddess symbol in India can indeed be an important figure for peaceful ecological and social activism and movements. While theological constructs of some Hindu goddesses like Sita can be seen to pander to patriarchy, activist constructs of the goddess inevitably draw upon the all-encompassing motherly strength, and the attributes of power and righteousness, learning and wisdom, and wealth from strong goddess figures like Durga, Saraswati and Lakshmi to mobilize for their cause. The nurturing and protective qualities of these goddesses can provide the reassurance and self-confidence required to challenge the ugly forces of corruption and fear-mongering. Furthermore, a goddess figure inspired by the Hindu pantheon is enormously served by the familiar connections, which are already an intrinsic part of everyday negotiations and meaning-making mechanisms to most Indians, both Hindu and non-Hindu (Nandy, 2001).

The Manushi Swachha Narayani confirms that religion is not merely an ideology but a lively force that shapes the urban experience in the architecture, politics, society and administration and governance of a city. With the renewed interest in scholarship in the interface between religion and urban planning, the urbanization process of the future may be defined by a holistic inspiration for human development that fully includes appropriate models of scientific and technical planning but does not exclusively rely on it, to provide an enabling context for the flourishing of the human spirit.

REFERENCES

Baviskar, A. (2003), 'Between violence and desire: space, power and identity in the making of metropolitan Delhi', *International Social Science Journal*, **55**(175), 89–98.

Bhaneja, Balwant (2010), 'Quest for Gandhi: a nonkilling journey', Center for Global Nonkilling: Creative Commons, available at: http://nonkilling.org/pdf/volume_gandhi.pdf; accessed 15 March 2012.

Foulston, Lynn and Stuart Abbot (2009), *Hindu Goddesses: Beliefs and Practices*, Sussex: Sussex Press.

Gautam, V. (2007), 'From the streets to the food courts', *The Times of India*, 6 June 2007.

Good, Anthony (2000), 'Congealing divinity: time, worship and kinship in South Indian Hinduism , *Journal of the Royal Anthropological Institute*, **6**(2), 273–92.

Gorringe, T.J. (2002), *A Theology of the Built Environment: Justice, Empowerment, Redemption*, Cambridge: Cambridge University Press.

Greed, Clara H. (1994), *Women and Planning: Creating Gendered Realities*, London: Routledge.

Hall, Peter (1988), *Cities of Tomorrow: An Intellectual History of Urban Planning and Design in the Twentieth Century*, Oxford: Basil Blackwell.

Indo-Asian News Service (2010), 'Delhi street vendors oppose eviction drive', 10 August 2010.

Jain, M. (2001), 'The happening city', in P.K. Varma and B.P. Singh (eds), *The Millennium Edition on New Delhi*, Oxford and New Delhi: Oxford University Press.

Kishwar, M.P. (2001), 'Jhadu Pooja at Sewa Nagar: Manushi's Campaign for Cleansing Governance, *Manushi*, 127, 3–11.

Kishwar, M.P. (2005), 'Emergency avatar of a secular goddess: Manushi Swachha Narayani descends to protect street vendors', *Manushi*, 147, 4–17.

Kishwar, M.P. (2012), *The Making and Unmaking of a Model Market for Street Vendors: Avatār of Goddess of Good Governance and Citizenship Rights*, available at: http://www.Manushi.in/articles.php?articleId=1586; accessed 20 March 2012.

Larson, G.J. (1995), *India's Agony Over Religion*, Albany: State University of New York Press.

Lefebvre, H. (1976), 'Reflections on the politics of space', *Antipode*, **8**(2), 30–37.

Levy, R. (1990), *Mesocosm: Hinduism and the Organization of a Traditional Newar City in Nepal*, Berkeley: University of California Press.

Manushii (2001), 'In danger of sabotage: historic intervention by the prime minister', *Manushi*, 125, 11–14, July–August.

McDermott, Rachel Fell (2005), 'Goddess worship: the Hindu goddess', in Lindsay Jones (ed.), *The Encyclopedia of Religion Vol. 6* (2nd edition), Detroit: Macmillan Reference USA, pp. 3607–11.

Nandy, A. (2001), 'A report on the present state of health of the gods and goddesses in South Asia', *Postcolonial Studies*, **4**(2), 125–41.

Parish, S.M. (1997), 'Goddesses dancing in the city: Hinduism in an urban incarnation – a review article', *International Journal of Hindu Studies*, **1**(3), 441–84.

Rajan, R.S. (1998), 'Is the Hindu goddess a feminist?', *Economic and Political Weekly*, **33**(44), 225–32.

Roland, A. (1988), *In Search of Self in India and Japan: Toward a Cross-Cultural Psychology*, Princeton, NJ: Princeton University Press.

Serrill, Michael (2005), 'An angel for Delhi's street vendors', *Business Week Online*, March, 1.

SPA (School of Planning and Architecture) (2004), *Role of Hawkers in the Urban Informal Sector and Internalizing Hawking Activities and Spaces in the City Planning and Development Process* , Report Commissioned by the Ministry of Urban Employment and Poverty Alleviation, Government of India, New Delhi, pp. 169.

te Lintelo, Dolf, J.H. (2009), 'The spatial politics of food hygiene: regulating small-scale retail in Delhi', *European Journal of Development Research*, **21**(1), 63–80.

The Hindu (2009), 'Now bio-cryptic I-cards for Delhi hawkers, street vendors', 31 November 2009.

Varma, P.K. (1998), *The Great Indian Middle Class*, New Delhi: Penguin Books India.

Vinod, R. (2005), 'No space for street hawkers', *Business Standard*, 23 August 2005, available at: http://www.ccsindia.org/ccsindia/pdf/no%20sapce%20for%20street%20hawkers.pdf; accessed 9 March 2012.

Wildavsky, Aaron (1973), 'If planning is everything, maybe it's nothing', *Policy Sciences*, **4**(2), 127–53.

21 Cultural heritage and development in South East Asia

Jonathan Sweet and Jo Wills

INTRODUCTION

This chapter discusses research undertaken into the developmental role of museums and heritage sites in Thailand and the Greater Mekong Subregion, a geographical area that also includes Cambodia, Laos PDR and Myanmar. It contextualizes an international project, the Lampang Temples Project, to explore the potential role that museums and heritage sites can play in place-based development work, particularly in an Asian context where sacred places are simultaneously valued by local members of the community and as destinations for religious pilgrims and international tourists.

The discussion of the Lampang Temples Project is located within an understanding of the international discourse concerning the roles of museums in development, including those contributions to this discourse that have originated in the Asia-Pacific region. It is also situated within an understanding of the role of international agencies and local governments in the promotion of programmes and infrastructure for the preservation of Buddhist heritage and the relationship of this development strategy with tourism.

Furthermore, due to the participatory and observational experience of the authors in the Lampang Temples Project, the chapter also considers the issues involved in applying cross-cultural pedagogies to the management of cultural tourism sites, including United Nations Educational, Scientific and Cultural Organization (UNESCO) World Heritage Sites. The results of the Lampang Temples Project support the contention that collaborative training models and pedagogies can be adapted, provided that differing cultural contexts and suppositions are appropriately articulated and integrated. Further, it suggests that this type of collaborative approach to the management of cultural tourism sites has the potential to play an important role in Buddhist heritage development processes.

The Lampang Temples Project was undertaken in Lampang, Northern Thailand to assist Buddhist monks with their desire to 'develop' their understandings of the roles sacred sites and cultural material of spiritual and social significance play within a tourism system. A tourism system is understood as multi-tiered and includes the activities of a range of individuals, community stakeholders, organizations and consumers, including government tourism offices, travel agencies, tour operators and service providers. The system may cater for a broad spectrum of visitor needs across a range of destinations and activities.[1] In these fields of activity, secular and religious heritage sites (including a wide range of museums) have become key destinations in South East Asia, and their preservation has often been viewed as a means of contributing to community development. However, while the saffron-robed monks of Northern Thailand are key stakeholders in this system and feature prominently in tourist literature, in their traditional religious roles they have largely remained somewhat disengaged from tourist processes and marketing.

The Lampang Temples Project sought to bridge this gap through learning and cross-cultural development. By expressing an interest in benefiting more directly from the specialty tourism markets of cultural and heritage tourism, the monks (and their associated communities) chose to explore the process of enhancing and developing interpretive 'museum-like' programmes at their monasteries. The project was interesting because it brought local and foreign heritage experts into a close-knit cross-cultural dialogue that at once challenged and broadened individual and community capacity. Cross-cultural learning opportunities enable participants both to broaden their understanding of their discipline and enhance their own skills. In this case, the temples project challenged museology from the outset, because the Buddhist temples of Northern Thailand are, of course, not strictly museums. In the Thai context, however, the temples are heritage sites that act as community centres and living repositories for community culture and memory – therefore a rich subject for museological exploration and reflection about the relationships between heritage practices and community development.

The Lampang Temples Project was a six-day museology workshop that took place at Wat Pongsanuk, Lampang, in Northern Thailand (16–21 June 2009). The main workshop participants were 22 Buddhist monks from temples around the Lampang region, which is located to the east of Chiang Mai. They were of various ranks and ages, and they represented a number of temples from the Lamphun district of Northern Thailand, particularly in Chiang Mai and Lampang. These principal participants are custodians of a diverse range of material culture that has been donated by community members over time, only some of which is on display at their temples. Secondary participants were post-graduate students from Chiang Mai University, who were keen to develop their knowledge of museology. It is important, too, to mention that the local Lampang community, particularly from Wat Pongsanuk, were intimately involved in the workshop preparation, catering and support.

The process of developing and delivering the project provided opportunities to gain insights into the role of cultural heritage sites and their relationship with economic and social development in the region. Thus, the project became an innovative and transformational space, one in which investigations into how theology can influence heritage practices and the relevance of Western museum practices and approaches to cultural tourism in South East Asian heritage sites of spiritual, social and historical significance could be explored.[2] The chapter, therefore, reflects on the issues raised by the relationships between these matters and considers how religion and community development can be assisted by innovative, heritage-based participatory practices and activities that are cross-cultural in design, delivery and evaluation.

The Lampang Temples Project was informed by a number of issues that are discussed in this chapter. It is most relevant that museums and cultural heritage agencies have a long history of working in a development context, in both Western and Asian cultures. In the Greater Mekong Subregion, the recent history of cultural heritage practice advanced by UNESCO and its partner organization the International Centre for the Study of the Preservation and Restoration of Cultural Property (ICCROM) has provided resources for a model of collaboration between the staff of local governments, international agencies and regional universities that are active in specialist discipline areas.[3] Within this strengthening matrix, the Lampang Temples Project offered an opportunity for a group of specialists to investigate the appropriateness of applying Western concepts of museology within Buddhist monasteries. Some aspects of this process have been reported on by project partners from the Fine Arts Department of Chiang Mai University.[4] The project also offered an opportunity to apply and assess the value of some evaluation techniques.

THE STATUS OF HERITAGE PROJECTS IN THE GREATER MEKONG SUBREGION

In Thailand and the Greater Mekong Subregion, cultural and heritage tourism is especially noticeable at high-profile UNESCO World Heritage Sites, such as the Historic Town of Sukhothai and Associated Towns, and the Town of Luang Prabang. The popularity of these places with international visitors has created substantial commercial opportunities and, in some cases, local people have profited through direct involvement in the provision of services, including heritage site management and interpretation. Evaluation of the management of these sites by UNESCO has suggested that sustainable development benefits from the involvement of local communities in the planning and driving of heritage projects. It is, after all, community heritage that is being preserved and interpreted.[5]

The relationships that have developed between World Heritage designation and tourism at the highest government levels have also informed interest in the synergies between heritage development of places of national and local significance.[6] Thus, in the Greater Mekong Subregion recent cultural heritage practice has contributed to various kinds of heritage projects, some in less prominent and more challenging environments. For example, a project informed by a 'pro-poor tourism' paradigm was recently undertaken to assist with the research and drafting of a heritage interpretation plan for foreign visitors to Viengxai, a remote town in Houphan Province in North East Laos that is home to an extensive and complex cave site that was the wartime stronghold of the communist political movement Pathet Lao.[7] These kinds of development heritage projects often share similarities in design and methodologies that are built on the articulation of heritage values and community consultation. In contrast, however, the Lampang Temples Project can be distinguished by its focus on sustainable development in a Buddhist religious context. It aimed to enhance the capacity of monks (and local people associated with temples) to better provide for the heritage and cultural needs of their local communities and to more effectively engage the interests of Buddhist pilgrims and international cultural tourists.

MUSEUMS, HERITAGE AND DEVELOPMENT

Museums and heritage agencies have increasingly sought to broaden their influence in society since the mid-1960s. An assessment of contemporary museology and cultural heritage literature, therefore, highlights the great potential for museums and cultural heritage agencies to contribute to development activities. It is important, too, to recognize the broad definition of museum in both a Western and South East Asian context. Many religious institutions in Western society have significant collections without specifically identifying as museums – in this way they have many similarities to the temple collections through South East Asia.

Since the 1990s, institutions and agencies have increasingly embraced the social inclusion and community engagement rhetoric and developed much closer connections to their constituent communities. This shift in practice is significant; it has seen a move away from object-focused work to more people- and issues-related work. The evolution of this shift – in both a Western and Asian museological context – is important. By refocusing the idea of museums and cultural heritage work, it has been possible for these museums and heritage agencies to be more actively involved in capacity building and learning-related community development work.

Museums in the Service of Society and the New Museology

The International Council of Museums' (ICOM) definition of museums evolved between 1946 and 1973, but centred on collecting and exhibiting activities. Yet the socio-political atmosphere of the 1960s and 1970s that focussed on issues such as race relations, ecology, drug abuse, poverty and warfare also influenced the museum industry in England, Europe, America and Australia. This social change inspired French and Canadian museologists to radically review the state of museum practice and call for museums to work more collaboratively with communities in a manner that was responsive, inclusive and participatory.[8] Others influenced by this discourse called for the model of museums as ivory towers to be dismantled and for museum work to reflect the issues and changes in society not as reflections of the past, but as representative and inclusive of the present.[9]

By 1974 a radical shift in the definition of museums occurred when ICOM declared that museums should be 'first and foremost in the service of all mankind'.[10] This change in operational intent moved museums away from their inward focus on things towards a future focus on people and community, and constituted a major step towards museums working in a more developmental context. Since this time, the idea of museums being 'in the service of all mankind' has evolved to museums being 'in the service of society and its development', yet another definitive statement about museums' potential as participants in social change and development frameworks.[11] The notion of service suggests that the museums can use their collecting activities in both a representational and transformational capacity. However, it may be argued that being 'in the service of its society and development' carries an implicit sense of reciprocity, one in which relationships and dialogue become an integral component of museum work. In this scenario, museums can actively learn from and engage with the individuals, communities and societies that they actively seek to inform and support. Until the end of the twentieth century, this reciprocity was overridden by public perception of museums as providers and generators of information.[12] Changes wrought by this shifting definition, however, have provided more scope for integrated community and development work within the museum milieu.

The changing focus from objects to people and relationships was embraced by new museologists from the 1980s onwards.[13] This meant that concepts such as 'community', 'interpretation' and 'intangible cultural heritage' became as important as the traditional museum practices of collection and documentation.[14] Radicalization of this concept saw the emergence of different models of museums embedded within communities such as the 'inclusive museum' and 'eco museum' models.[15] Complex as these models were, they were all underpinned by common principles: placing the public and local community at the centre of museum work instead of the collection and reversing the traditional approach to disseminating knowledge. Further, these were models that were perhaps best enacted at the local and community level. It is pertinent today that many inclusive forms of museum practice that integrate development principles, such as the Lampang Temples Project, occur at the local level because they are not as entrenched in institutional hierarchy as larger, more traditional museums.

Social Inclusion – Capacity Building and Engagement

The advent of the new museology made way for significant changes within museum practice. At the turn of the twenty-first century the Western museum industry underwent a form of millennial musing in which both academics and museum workers speculated on the social relevance and role of museums.[16] Extended understandings about audience research, evaluation and learning have been explored, all based on the notion of museums working with the public.[17] Further, the rise in use of technology has also made a significant impact on the capacity for publics to engage with museum work, a change inspired by philosophical development, and deliverable via technology.

An increasingly competitive entertainment and leisure industry has begun to compete with museums for the public's recreational time, an issue that is prevalent in both Western and South East Asian communities. This has given rise to museums having to address issues of social sustainability in the face of increased financial pressures and accountability (although one can argue that the focus on financial accountability alone explicitly undervalues the social impact of museum work).[18] Again, this issue has resonance with the experience of changing markets and social structures within the South East Asian context. Further, museum activities have been analysed in relation to the broader sustainability agenda in which social, economic and environmental representation, education and internal institutional policies sit side by side and demand greater consideration of the ways in which museums impact, influence and contribute to society. In 1995, for example, UNESCO's declaration on cultural diversity stated that 'development divorced from its human or cultural context is growth without a soul', a position that underlined the importance of equal representation within the museum sector.[19] It is relevant, too, that the Lampang Temples Project was situated within UNESCO's Museums Capacity Building Programme. It was a pilot project in a broader programme designed to help identify a range of needs and to articulate priorities for museums and collecting organizations in the Asia-Pacific region and to provide guidance for the development of relevant programmes in specialized spiritual contexts.

Social and political changes within the broader museological industry, therefore, can be seen to have had a significant impact on the potential for museum work and development work to co-exist and be infused by the principles of participatory community development.

In South East Asia

Another outcome of the new museology has been a shift in attitude in the relationships between museum organizations and indigenous people. Museums in Australia and Canada, for example, have been more willing to engage more profoundly with non-Western systems of knowledge, including those that have spiritual foundations. Furthermore, there has been a concern to understand indigenous forms of 'curatorship' and conservation in South East Asia and to incorporate traditional and local practices into the international museological and heritage discourses.[20]

Within the Asia-Pacific region local professionals have also advocated for the prioritization of local knowledge relevant to heritage preservation. For example, in 1995 Nepalese archaeologist, Uddhav Acharya, addressed a conference in Nara, Japan, which was focused on the problems of international cooperation in heritage conservation. Although he saw benefits in international cooperation, he had experienced a range of problems and argued that 'foreign experts had no knowledge of indigenous and traditional technology'.[21] Furthermore, he argued they were often not familiar with the geographical and climatic situations, had no idea of the availability and quality of construction materials, and adopted, at times, an air of supremacy that he found offensive and unfounded. Acharya argued that experts needed to be 'open minded and broad minded', in other words to learn more about the cultures in which they were going to participate and to truly work in a cooperative manner with local professionals.

As these concerns reverberated, the anthropologist Christina Kreps advanced a new paradigm that embraced the apparent connections between traditional indigenous cultural practices and museum-like activities.[22] Increasingly, this recognition of diversity was formalized in specific development programmes. From 2004 to 2010 ICCROM actively promoted local preservation practices within the Association of Southeast Asian Nations (ASEAN) group of countries through its CollAsia 2010 capacity building programme.[23] These shared concerns with understanding conservation in South East Asia, particularly the appropriate management and interpretation of material culture that was held in community collections. This was also something central to the Lampang Temples Project.

Kreps' research explored the similarities between Western museology and the traditional preservation of cultural heritage by the Dayak people of Indonesian Borneo.[24] Despite the cultural differences between these people and the Thai Buddhist monks, the research had implications for the cross-cultural practice that was played out in the Lampang Temples Project. The methodology she used of 'comparative museology' was defined as: 'the systematic study and comparison of museological forms and behaviour in diverse cultural settings. Its aim is to show that although the museum is generally construed as a modern Western cultural form, museological-type behaviour is a long-standing, cross-cultural phenomenon'.[25]

As an anthropologist Kreps recognized 'museological-type behaviour' as a more universal trait across cultures, and there is no doubt that the preservation of cultural material was broadly practised before the articulation of the modern museum. In South East Asia, Buddhist temples performed preservation functions too, something that had been recognized in the discourse. For example, in 1977 Sri Lankan museologist, S. Bandaranayake, reported that deeply held preservation practices in Sri Lanka had historically existed in palaces, temples and monasteries, and village communities. He identified these 'traditions, which involved the collection and preservation of cultural objects, [as] . . . an organic part of our civilization from early historic times'.[26]

The promotion of critical reflection is a highly regarded characteristic of contemporary museology, and through the championing of alternative preservation practices Kreps was an active agent in an international museological discourse. This was intended to aid 'the liberation of culture from the hegemony of the management regimes of Eurocentric museology . . . to contribute to the continual reappraisal of museums and museological practice'.[27] In recent years this rhetoric has helped to drive the open, more inclusive discourse of museology promoted by UNESCO and ICCROM in the Asia-Pacific region. The Lampang Temples Project applied and investigated some of these ideas and offers a paradigm of collaborative development practice that was informed by a concept of complementary cross-cultural interaction in a specific spiritual context.

HERITAGE TOURISM AND DEVELOPMENT AGENDAS

The roles of ESCAP and Government

In the Greater Mekong Subregion, intergovernmental organizations have been influential in promoting development goals through heritage projects. The Economic and Social Commission for Asia and the Pacific (ESCAP) is a regional development organization headquartered in Bangkok that was established by the United Nations in 1947.[28] It is a multi-lateral organization with 62 member countries that specifically aims to reduce poverty and manage the erosive effects of globalization on local cultures. In 2003 ESCAP promoted the potential benefits of linking cultural heritage with tourism as a means of stimulating development in South East Asia. This was encapsulated in a published research report titled the 'Promotion of Buddhist tourism circuits in selected Asian countries'.[29] In part the report recognized the advantages of delineating tourist routes that were built upon the traditional religious practice of Buddhist pilgrimage.[30] It argued, idealistically, perhaps, that the linkage of Buddhist sacred sites across the region though a modern tourism system could potentially provide a number of important benefits. First, the circuits would give tourists and local people a better understanding of the Buddhist heritage and its associated values; second, the circuits would strengthen regional cooperation; and third, the routes would contribute to sustainable social and economic development.[31]

It is critical that the ambitious recommendations in the report reflected a top-down international development paradigm that seemed to ignore ideological differences and local hostilities between neighbours.[32] In reality, the relationships between Buddhist heritage and tourism have been negotiated in more organic ways. In part this resulted from Thailand's distinction in the region due to its long-standing tourist industry, which was considered to be the country's biggest earner of foreign exchange and a major contributor to development infrastructure.[33] Although much of this tourism is focused on the country's many beach resorts, by 2000 heritage was becoming an increasingly important and utilized asset.

Early infrastructure development that supported heritage tourism included a domestic airport especially built to precipitate visitation to the archaeological park of Sukhothai, the site of the ancient Siamese capital, north of Bangkok.[34] Sukhothai was organized as a heritage park in 1988 and designated as a UNESCO World Heritage Site in 1991. The designation of the site as World Heritage underscored the integration of Buddhism and the monarchy in Siam. The inscription of the site's significance unites aesthetical and spiritual values with national interests. It describes architectural elements that have survived, and includes the statement that, 'The great meeting rooms with the massive chevet decorated with a monumental portrait of Buddha [which] are specific to Sukhothai architecture and subsequently influenced all Thai art'.[35] This added symbolic legitimacy to the current Constitution of Thailand, which stipulates that Thai kings be practising Buddhists. Paradoxically, the universal acknowledgment of these values through the UNESCO World Heritage list, also gives buoyancy to the state's desire to support the linkages between the representation of the nation state, Buddhism, heritage preservation and tourism.

The synergies that have been exploited between Buddhist, Khmer and Thai heritage with national representation and tourism have continued to be considered a strong alliance for regional development. In 2008 the Prime Minister of Thailand built on the earlier recommendation of Buddhist circuit routes, when he addressed the ESCAP. On that occasion he said that the Thai government had proposed 'a tourist route initiative' within the Greater Mekong Subregion. This, he said, was linked to the need to continue to improve transportation and communication among people of the region and was designed to complement existing economic corridors and other related cooperative frameworks. The aims of the plan were reported in the ESCAP Annual Report: 'the proposed route would connect major cities and tourist destinations across the subregion, in particular World Heritage Sites. It would promote economic activities, create local opportunities and bridge the subregion with China, India and beyond'.[36] Such is the perception of the enormous potential of heritage tourism in the region.

Heritage tourism offered a vision of regional unity and mutual material benefit (in a sometimes tense political context). The success of the enterprise would depend to a large extent on the preservation of heritage values and their long-term sustainability in the face of competing opportunities. The ESCAP report in 2003 noted the 'strong awareness' amongst participants that there was a real need to 'preserve the [Buddhist] heritage for future generations'.[37] These were issues of some urgency in South East Asia where the cultural heritage in some countries was perceived to be at risk from rapid urbanization (and Westernization).[38] Urban development issues were compounded by poor planning in the tourism industry and this was accompanied by the increased exposure of many Buddhist sites, continuing to place artefacts of spiritual significance (Buddha images) at risk of removal from their temples through the unethical practices.

In 2006, the risks to cultural heritage provoked a new ESCAP resolution drawing on the evolving paradigm of sustainable tourism. This resolution invited member states to 'take measures to minimize sociocultural and environmental impacts of tourism . . . as well as . . . the promotion of green tourism and the preservation of cultural heritage by, amongst other measures, promoting an adequate regulatory framework'.[39] By 2008 ESCAP had also recognized the importance of capacity building in professional approaches to heritage management and directly funded the production of a curriculum for trainers in cultural tourism site management in the Greater Mekong Subregion.[40]

The 2003 ESCAP report was a very significant navigational publication. While it focused on Buddhism it also recognized cultural and spiritual diversity in the region.

Thus it advocated a balance between the benefits and opportunities from tourism based on cultural, religious and artistic heritage, and social and aesthetic issues and 'the need to maintain cultural integrity, respect diverse ways of life and preserve the heritage for future generations'.[41] It also stressed that it was 'clear that issues of sustainability would require active participation by all stakeholders in order to address the formidable challenges involved'.[42] At its heart, however, the report promoted the idea that Buddhist theology had much more to offer heritage preservation and could also make an economic and development contribution to tourism: first, through developing 'a better understanding of the history, culture, religion and aesthetics associated with the Buddhist heritage throughout Asia', and second, through providing 'a guiding philosophy, aesthetic, and approach to progress that tourists, local communities, planners and policy makers can use in their approach to tourism in Asian countries'.[43] In its promotion of Buddhist theology in a period of heightened sensitivity to globalization, the ESCAP report charted an agenda for building strong alliances between key stakeholders, heritage preservation and the development of cultural tourism in the region.

UNESCO and LEAP and Professional Training

In recent years the importance of intangible heritage values and practices was promoted through the articulation of the *Nara Document on Authenticity* (1994+) (and later the UNESCO Convention for the Safeguarding of the Intangible Heritage).[44] The *Nara Document* represented the concerns of some countries in the Asia-Pacific region (led by Japan) that Western approaches to heritage conservation were not necessarily appropriate in Asian cultures, where the continuity of spiritual practice is of higher significance than the preservation of degraded built heritage. There was perceived to be a fundamental problem with the notion of universal conservation criteria and values.[45] This position can be profoundly linked to the practices of Buddhism, which offers its own history of preservation activity and a meditation on revival. It has also given rise to a concerted campaign to raise the status of local community involvement in heritage conservation in what is a professionally dominated field of practice.[46]

Furthermore, the tensions between the rapid urbanization of Asian cities and the preservation of historic environments often disenfranchized local people and threatened their cultural traditions. UNESCO and ICCROM argued that a strategy to deal with this threat was by through assisting local people to directly participate in the preservation of their cultural heritage. This was taken up through the LEAP programme – 'LEAP, Integrated Community Development and Cultural Heritage Preservation Through Local Effort in Asia and the Pacific'. Between 1995 and 1998 the LEAP programme was rolled out to promote and facilitate the involvement of local people in the preservation of cultural heritage sites. The Advisor for Culture at UNESCO Bangkok, Dr Richard Engelhardt, elaborated on the rationale in 1997 at the seminar 'Heritage for the Future, The World Cultural Heritage in Asian Countries: Sustainable Development and Conservation', Kyoto-Tokyo, Japan. In particular, he emphasized the direct link between heritage preservation and sustainable development, saying that government policies and efforts ought not be restricted to managing a small number of internationally significant heritage sites. Through his experience in Asia he understood the generational connections that people had to places. In his words, 'it is particularly important to [draw] upon the traditional cultural heritage of each locality if future economic and social development is to prove acceptable and sustainable in the long-run'.[47] In his role at UNESCO Bangkok, Engelhardt was adept at influencing political decision-making on heritage issues at the highest government levels but he was also acutely aware that authenticity in heritage was dependent on the continuity of local 'grassroots' participation.

Critically, the LEAP programme was designed to produce practical outcomes that were underpinned by the belief that the sustainability of heritage preservation was linked to *meaningful* job creation, including employment generated by needs of the tourism industry. Thus, the programme sought to teach people in local communities skills that were directly relevant to heritage preservation, including heritage interpretation, conservation monitoring, and preservation maintenance. Through participation in the training programme it was intended that local people would learn marketable skills relevant to heritage management and would also benefit socially and spiritually from contributing to the preservation of their own heritage. According to Engelhardt, it was ultimately the aim of the LEAP programme to help to 'develop the means through which [local people] benefit financially from the enhanced conservation of the monuments and sites while maintaining their social and spiritual tradition intact'.[48]

One focus of the LEAP programme was in Laos PDR, where problems concerning the relationships between heritage preservation and tourism were emerging after the designation of Luang Prabang as a World Heritage Site in 1995. The practice of Buddhism is particularly visible in Laos PDR in the cities of Vientiane and Luang Prabang, the attractive northern town that is situated on the banks of the Upper Mekong River. It occupied a strategic location and was connected by long-standing pilgrimage and trade routes, including the Silk Route, to other regional centres such as Chiang Mai and Lampang in Northern Thailand. The dense constellation of richly decorated Buddhist temples located in Luang Prabang retained an important spiritual role in this region following the communist revolution of 1975, although the traditional fine arts capacity with which these monasteries were associated had became degraded. Nevertheless, the description of the heritage significance of Luang Prabang praises the highly preserved townscape and finds universal significance in the architectural values of the place, recognizing the coexistence of traditional Lao structures and French colonial architecture and urban planning.

Since its designation as a World Heritage Site, the atmosphere and beauty of the town has attracted many Western tourists, many extending their visits to Thailand and flying in directly from Chiang Mai. This has led to a substantial growth in French colonial-style facilities to accommodate their needs. So much so that in the view of the regional officers of UNESCO the preservation of the heritage values that in part gave the town its distinction and prominence were perceived to be at risk. It was evident that poor tourism practices overseen by a secular government were bringing into sharp focus the need to more effectively negotiate the tensions between heritage values and national interests.[49]

The linkage of Buddhist heritage with tourism offered an alternative means through which local people could benefit meaningfully from heritage tourism-associated occupations. These included the involvement of local people in the preservation of sacred Buddhist sites and temples, places and organizations with which they may have profound spiritual connections. UNESCO explained the relationship between religious practice and preservation:

> In accordance with Buddhist beliefs, communities and individuals in Luang Prabang traditionally make merit by providing temples with much-needed support for undertaking building projects – through donations of time, labour and funds. Therefore the management and preservation of temples also has an economic function – providing artisans with a form of income.[50]

The approach can be linked to Buddhist teaching where 'labour' is valued because it 'provides an opportunity to use and develop one's skills' and to assist 'individuals in overcoming their own ego by working collectively with others'.[51] Thus, as Clarke has observed, the development process is incorporated into an individual's enlightenment path.[52]

In an aligned attempt to balance the demands of tourism with the needs of the community, UNESCO sought to address preservation and management issues through an educational publication designed to facilitate cooperation and understanding between tourist planners and operators and heritage managers and local residents.[53] As the Buddhist temples of Luang Prabang are central to the town's identity and to the provision of engaging visitor experiences, Buddhist monks were identified as key stakeholders in the tourist system and critical to the preservation of the signature temples. As the authors wrote in *IMPACT*:

> The monks of Luang Prabang traditionally held a pivotal role in the preservation of Luang Prabang's heritage. In addition to their role in creating an intimate spiritual bond between the communities and their temples, they are responsible for constructing, decorating, maintaining and restoring temples.[54]

Across the region Buddhist monks have traditionally shared this common responsibility for the preservation of their temple buildings and their collections, a process that in recent times has been most emphatically demonstrated by the restoration works undertaken at Wat Pongsanuk, where the Lampang Temples Project was located.

THE LAMPANG TEMPLES PROJECT, THAILAND

Project Planning: Collaboration, Communication and Community Engagement

As noted in the introductory section, the Lampang Temples Project had multiple partners and different types of participants. The observations and comments in this section of the chapter draw specifically on the experiences of Deakin University staff during the development and delivery of the project.[55]

In terms of understanding the capacity for heritage projects to inform development processes, it is important to recognize that the Lampang Temples Project comprised a series of key set-up phases/activities prior to the delivery of the workshop itself. The first of these phases was actually a precursor to the Lampang Temples project. It comprised a heritage conservation project run by Chiang Mai University at Wat Pongsanuk in 2008 to preserve built cultural heritage features of the temple. The Viharn Phra Chao Pun Ong Conservation Project was designed to revive the spirit of cooperation between artisans and community in the restoration of the temple.[56] The process of raising awareness of heritage issues and reviving traditions meant that discussions about the value of heritage were already part of the communities' consciousness when the Lampang Temples Project was conceived. This prior interest and local engagement in related issues cannot be underestimated as a key factor contributing to the successful delivery of development projects.

Another key preliminary activity involved Deakin University sending Dr Jo Wills to liaise with staff at the UNESCO Bangkok office, and to meet Chiang Mai University staff and community representatives on location in Lampang. Information gleaned from this preliminary 'reconnaissance' phase provided vital contextual background and ensured that the needs of participants and local stakeholders remained central throughout the project as it was advanced. It also highlighted the importance of opening communication channels between international project partners. The shared experience of visiting different sites (each with different issues) and discussing the project in an applied setting allowed the project partners to collaboratively identify key points of interest and need. It allowed the Thai project partners to direct Deakin staff regarding principles and protocols required to run the project. Further, it also provided opportunities to meet with consulate staff from the United States of America, including the US Embassy, to secure additional funding.

Following this meeting, representatives from Chiang Mai University continued with the logistical planning for the project and engaging with the local community and prospective participants. They organized a selection process for the monks and a 'pre-training session' with participants before the workshop to ensure that monks had a basic understanding of museums and could be confident participants in the programme. The ability to have local representatives continuously liaising with local participants was critical to maintaining project momentum up until its delivery, ensuring the project was on track to meet their desired outcomes, and in ensuring that the infrastructure and materials were available.

This direction and onsite support allowed staff from Deakin University to concentrate on devising a draft workshop manual and programme and considering the cross-cultural pedagogical issues. The Lampang programme needed to investigate ways to help the Buddhist monks, as cultural custodians, achieve a level of confidence in museological disciplines, and to make informed decisions about the long-term management of the artefacts that are in their care. These include many items of aesthetic, spiritual and historical significance. One of the challenges for Deakin staff working on this project was, therefore, to consider how to apply their own culturally formed learning to a new and different cultural context. This opportunity for the 'trainers' to reflect on cultural learning, and in so doing refine their own practice, was invaluable. It required recognizing the specific cultural and spiritual needs of the participant communities, whilst integrating best-practice methods of museological knowledge into a flexible and engaging learning programme.

Of particular interest was discussion regarding the use of the Australian devised 'significance' methodology, a process designed to assist museum workers in Australia to better understand and manage their collections. It is also used to assist museums be more systematic in terms of what it is they accept into their collections. The use of this methodology was considered at once critical and problematic. While the use of a system to classify, understand and manage the temple collections was critical, the criteria had a different meaning in Thailand than in Australia. The criterion that considers an object's social or spiritual significance was at once redundant and critical. To recognize the items' value because of their spiritual significance was important in terms of communicating the region's cultural diversity to a broad cultural tourism market. Yet for the Buddhist monks and local community it was a moot point. The item, by its very existence as an offering to the temple, had spiritual significance. In this context, therefore, the comparative criteria of provenance, interpretative potential, condition and rarity became critical tools in the process of understanding an item's and collections' importance.

Once the key topics were identified, preliminary readings sourced and a draft programme finalized, the material was given to Chiang Mai University staff who arranged for the material to be translated into Thai and distributed to the participants.

Delivering the Workshops

As noted above, the workshops were delivered in the *viharn* (assembly hall) at Wat Pongsanuk. This ornate facility, complete with a number of sacred Buddha images, was an appropriate space for the workshops as *viharns* are designed for interaction between monks and the laity. Further, it allowed for the monks to perform morning and afternoon prayers before sessions began.

Following the formal opening procedures, the *viharn* was quickly turned into a classroom. Deakin staff rearranged the more formal learning layout of rows of desks into clusters whereby participants formed small groups. This layout set the precedent for the most of the participatory and group-based learning activities within the formal classroom setting. This basic difference in learning styles was an important point of difference, and was noted by monks at the end of the workshops as a good way of learning and interacting.

The workshop programme was broken into key topics, and structured around applied group work activities. Most mornings consisted of more theoretical discussions and afternoons were spent on activities and practical sessions. There was also one morning of site visits, to provide monks with the opportunity to see a couple of different temple examples.

To address the language barriers for participants and trainers, a trained interpreter was used for each session. Despite the time-consuming nature of this process, this was most successful. Care was required, however, in the sharing of the microphone between female Deakin staff and the monks – it always required an intermediary to adhere to cultural protocols.

The Thai students were critical participants in the project and contributed directly to its success. They became involved in many logistical aspects of the workshop and they worked alongside the monks, providing additional English language skills and some technical assistance. In some cases, these participants also provided important specialist knowledge, particularly concerning local approaches to the cataloguing of artefacts and the design of displays. This integration of local people and local knowledge into the programme was therefore critical, and invaluably increased the ultimate benefits for all who participated.

Deakin staff went into the workshops under the misconception about the technical capabilities of the participants. The monks, and the associated Chiang Mai university students, had a high level of technical literacy and were actively engaged in compiling detailed presentations as part of the workshop requirements. This demonstrates the importance of technology as a cross-cultural learning tool in a range of different settings, including development settings.

Applied learning was critical to the workshop. Deakin staff sought to use specific items from the Wat Pongsanuk collection as learning tools to facilitate group learning. At the end of the workshop, each group presented their findings integrating their understanding of the key concepts learned throughout the week.

Discussing the Benefits of Collaborative Workshops

During the workshop, an evaluation form was designed by representatives from UNESCO Bangkok, with assistance from Deakin University and Chiang Mai University staff. Monks were given this form to complete and return by the end of the workshop.

Deakin University staff also facilitated a feedback session at the end of the workshop. This involved asking participants to identify three key things they had learned during the week that they would take back to their temples. This focus-group-style feedback session allowed participants to hear how others had learned during the week. The majority of positive comments focused on an appreciation of the information gleaned from their participation in the programme. This was interesting because participation had been mandatory for a number of the monks; these monks, in particular, noted their experience was enhanced by the collaborative learning dynamics of the workshop format. There was general agreement about the benefits of group learning and potential for future collaboration between participants' temples.

Other comments pointed towards the benefits of undertaking this type of learning, and clearly demonstrate the role that museum work can play in a development context. One participant met a fellow monk who could assist him with translation of ancient texts, a skill he had not expected to find at the workshop. This, he suggested, will allow translation of hitherto unexplored texts and thus enable a new understanding of their spiritual heritage. Another articulated his experience of the programme in the context of promoting Buddha's teachings – by having a better understanding of the artefacts, he reasoned, he was both inspired and empowered to convey this message to members of his community.

Cautionary comments were also offered during this session. Although one monk valued the information he had gleaned from participation, he warned that individuals needed to ensure they did not develop an unhealthy sense of their own importance in relation to their acquisition of knowledge. Despite this hesitation, the participant identified a way that he could rationalize his participation in future types of activity. By assisting temples outside his immediate community and area of responsibility, he reasoned, such work could become part of the merit-making process and thus rationalize participation. Interestingly, this can be seen in the context of Clarke's assertion that the development process should be incorporated into an individual's enlightenment path.

In terms of sustainable development practices, the monks expressed an interest in developing a supportive network through which they could disseminate information, use to solve problems and issues as they arose, and to be the basis for future training activities.

CONCLUSION

In the Greater Mekong Subregion the linkages between Buddhist heritage, tourism and development can be witnessed in a number of ways. At the historical park at Sukhothai there is a strong resonance between the archaeological built heritage and Thai national identity, with local people benefitting directly through employment as official heritage interpreters for the site. At the living town of Luang Prabang there is a strong connection between long-held artistic practices represented in Buddhist temples and the viability of local contemporary craft industries. The Lampang Temples Project should be seen alongside these examples. It reflects the concerns of local heritage experts, UNESCO and ICCROM, to foster sustainable heritage preservation through local participation and the continuity of traditional cultural and spiritual practices, and the concerns of ESCAP and local government to develop the foundations of sustainable cultural tourism through developing understanding of the relationships between heritage management and the tourism system.[57] As a part of a continuous development process, the Lampang Temples Project is significant because it responded to the interest of the monks themselves to reflect on the appropriate use of their heritage resources. The project utilized an innovative cross-cultural pedagogy and recognized the centrality of Buddhist theology and above all illustrates that sacred places can integrate museum work and be development spaces.

NOTES

1. The World Tourism Organization (UNWTO) has two definitions of cultural tourism. In the narrow sense, cultural tourism includes 'movements of persons for essentially cultural motivations such as study tours, performing arts and cultural tours, travel to festivals and other cultural events, visits to sites and monuments, travel to study nature, folklore or art, and pilgrimages'. In the broader sense it is defined as 'all movements of persons, because they satisfy the human need for diversity, tending to raise the cultural level of the individual and giving rise to new knowledge, experience and encounters'. Cited in Pedersen (2002, pp. 23–4).
2. Reflecting 'a values based' approach to heritage significance that was developed in the Burra Charter and has been adopted by the UNESCO World Heritage assessment process. The application of this to religious and spiritual contexts in underdeveloped countries and its usefulness has been questioned. See Poulios (2010).
3. For example, through the establishment of The Asian Academy for Heritage Management, see: http://asian-academy.org/.
4. Boonyasurat and Srisomwongwathana (2010).
5. See Bandarin (2010).
6. It has been noted that there may be a conflict between national and universal values and interests.
7. Partners in the Viengxai project were the Kaysone Phomvihane Memorial Caves Office (KPMCO), the Netherlands Development Agency (SNV), the United Nations World Tourism Organization (UNWTO) and Deakin University, Australia. See Wills et al. (2007).
8. Hauenschild (1988).
9. Noble (1971).
10. Van Mench (1992).
11. Article 2, Clause 1 of the ICOM statutes (ICOM, 2001, http://icom.museum/).
12. Weil (1995).
13. Hauenschild (1988).
14. Mayrand (1985, p. 200); Hauenschild (1988); Vergo (1989).
15. Riviere (1985); Varine (1985); Van Mench (2003).
16. Hein (2000); Delarge (2001); Weil (2002).
17. Silverman (1995); Hein (1998); Falk and Dierking (2000).

18. Scott (2002, 2003).
19. UNESCO (1995).
20. See also, Kreps (2009).
21. Acharya (1995, p. 8).
22. Kreps (2003, p. 5).
23. ICCROM and SPAFA, *CollAsia 2010*, available at: http://www.collasia2010.org/aboutus.htm; accessed 11 February 2012.
24. Kreps (2003, p. 36).
25. Ibid., p. 4.
26. Bandaranayake (2000, p. 141).
27. Kreps (2003, p. 5).
28. http://www.unescap.org/about/index.asp; accessed 24 July 2012.
29. ESCAP (2003).
30. Ibid., p. ii.
31. Ibid., p. 2.
32. Note, for example, the long-standing border dispute between Cambodia and Thailand that led to conflict over the possession and management of Preah Vihear, a Khmer heritage site designated a UNESCO World Heritage Site in 2008. See Silverman (2011).
33. Nimmonratana (2000, p. 65).
34. Ibid.
35. http://whc.unesco.org/en/list/574; accessed 11 January 2012. Chevet in this case refers to a decorated semicircular form at one end of the temple.
36. ESCAP (2008a, p. 7).
37. ESCAP (2003, p. 3).
38. Logan (2002).
39. ESCAP (2006).
40. ESCAP (2008b).
41. ESCAP (2003, p. 3).
42. Ibid.
43. Ibid.
44. See http://whc.unesco.org/uploads/events/documents/event-833-3.pdf for the *Nara Document* (accessed 25 July 2012); see also Smith and Akagawa (2009) on intangible heritage.
45. Gamini (2000, p. 108).
46. Poulios (2010, pp. 173–4).
47. Engelhardt (1997, p. 8).
48. Ibid., p. 11.
49. Long and Sweet (2006).
50. UNESCO (2004, p. 18).
51. Clarke (2011, p. 67).
52. Ibid., p. 71.
53. UNESCO (2004, p. 9).
54. UNESCO (2004, pp. 17–18.
55. A number of reports were compiled during the development of the Lampang Temples Project and these have been used to inform the comments within this section. Further, Deakin staff made observational notes and conducted a range of informal interviews with project partners throughout the workshop. Notes taken during the participatory monk's evaluation session at the end of the workshop also form an important part of the material referred to in this section.
56. UNESCO (2011).
57. ESCAP (2003, p. 63).

REFERENCES

Acharya, Uddhav (1995), 'Technological problems in the international co-operative activity for monument conservation in Nepal', Fifth Seminar on The Conservation of Asian Cultural Heritage, 17–19 October, Nara, Agency for Cultural Affairs, Japan, and Tokyo National Research Institute of Cultural Properties, in cooperation with Tokyo National Museum, Nara National Museum, Nara National Cultural Properties Research Institute, Japan Foundation, and The Nara International Foundation Commemorating the Silk Road Exposition, Nara.

Bandaranayake, S. (2000), 'The role of the museum in the preservation of the national cultural heritage – some theoretical notes', in P.H.D.H. De Silva, *Colombo Museum 100 Years 1877–1977* (2nd edition).
Bandarin, Francesco (2010), 'Preface', in Nao Hayashi Denis (ed.), *Community-based Approach to Museum Development in Asia and the Pacific for Culture and Sustainable Development*, Paris: UNESCO.
Boonyasurat, Woralun and Angela Srisomwongwathana (2010), 'Wat Pongsanuk Community based Museum', in Nao Hayashi Denis (ed.), *Community-based Approach to Museum Development in Asia and the Pacific for Culture and Sustainable Development*, Paris: UNESCO, pp. 70–83.
Clarke, Matthew (2011), *Development and Religion, Theory and Practice*, Cheltenham, UK and Northampton, MA, USA: Edward Elgar.
Delarge, A. (2001), 'People involvement changes the museum', available at: http://www.osservatorioecomusei.net; accessed 6 December 2004.
Engelhardt, Richard (1997), 'The challenge of preserving historic environment in the rapidly modernizing context of Asia. An introduction to UNESCO's "LEAP" Programme for Integrated Community Development and Cultural Heritage Site Preservation Through Local Effort in Asia and the Pacific', *Proceedings of the Seventh Seminar on The Conservation of Asian Cultural Heritage. Heritage for the Future. The World Cultural Heritage in Asian Countries: Sustainable Development and Conservation*, October 13–18, 1997, Kyoto-Tokyo, Japan, Tokyo: National Research Institute of Cultural Properties.
ESCAP (2003), 'Promotion of Buddhist tourism circuits in selected Asian countries', *ESCAP Tourism Review*, No. 24, New York.
ESCAP (2006), 'Resolutions of the Economic and Social Commission for Asia and the Pacific 2000–2006', *Volume IV – Compendium of Resolutions, 2000–2006*, United Nations, pp. 131–2.
ESCAP (2008a), *Annual Report 24 May 2007–30 April 2008*, p. 7, available at: http://www.unescap.org/EDC/English/AnnualReports/2008%2864%29.pdf; accessed 24 July 2012.
ESCAP (2008b), *Cultural Tourism Site Management. A Training Manual for Trainers in the Greater Mekong Subregion*, United Nations.
Falk, J. and L. Dierking (2000), *Learning from Museums: Visitor Experiences and the Making of Meaning*, Walnut Creek, CA: AltaMira Press.
Hauenschild, A. (1988), 'Claims and reality of new museology: case studies in Canada, the United States and Mexico' [online], Hamburg University, available at: http://museumstudies.si.edu/claims2000.htm; accessed 24 July 2012.
Hein, G.E. (1998), *Learning in the Museum*, London: Routledge.
Hein, H.S. (2000), *The Museum in Transition: A Philosophical Perspective*, Washington, DC: Smithsonian Books.
Kreps, C. (2003), *Liberating Culture: Cross-cultural Perspectives on Museums, Curation and Heritage Preservation*, London: Routledge.
Kreps, C. (2009), 'Indigenous curation, museums, and intangible cultural heritage', in L. Smith and N. Akagawa, *Intangible Heritage*, London: Routledge, pp. 193–208.
Logan, William (ed.) (2002), *The Disappearing Asian City: Protecting Asia's Urban Heritage in a Globalizing World*, New York: Oxford University Press.
Long, Colin and Jonathan Sweet (2006), 'Globalization, nationalism and world heritage: interpreting Luang Prabang', *South East Asia Research*, **14**(3), 445–69.
Mayrand, P. (1988), 'The new museology proclaimed', *Museum International*, **37**(4), 200–201.
Nimmonratana, Taksina (2000), 'Impacts of tourism on a local community: a case study of Chiang Mai', in K.S. (Kaye) Chon (ed.), *Tourism in Southeast Asia. A New Direction*, New York: The Haworth Hospitality Press.
Noble, J.V. (1971), 'Museum prophecy: the role of museums in the 1970s', *Curator: The Museum Journal*, **14**(1), 69–74.
Pedersen, Arthur (2002), *Managing Tourism at World Heritage Sites: A Practical Manual for World Heritage Site Managers*, Paris: UNESCO World Heritage Centre, pp. 23–4.
Poulios, Ioannis (2010), 'Moving beyond a values-based approach to heritage conservation', *Conservation and Management of Architectural Sites*, **12**(2), 170–85.
Riviere, G.H. (1985), 'The ecomuseum – an evolutive definition', *Museum International*, **37**(4), 182–3).
Scott, C.A. (2002), 'Measuring social value' in Richard Sandell (ed.), *Museums, Society and Inequality*, London: Routledge, pp. 41–55.
Scott, C.A. (2003), 'Museums and impact', *Curator – The Museum Journal*, **46**(3), 293–310.
Silverman, Helaine (2011), 'Border wars: the ongoing temple dispute between Thailand and Cambodia and UNESCO's World Heritage list', *International Journal of Heritage Studies*, **17**(1), 1–21.
Silverman, L. (1995), 'Visitor meaning making in museums for a new age', *Curator*, **38**(3), 161–9.
Smith, Laurajane and Natsuko Akagawa (eds) (2009), *Intangible Heritage*, London and New York: Routledge
UNESCO (1995), *Our Creative Diversity: Report of the World Commission on Culture and Development*, Paris: UNESCO.

UNESCO (2004), *IMPACT: The Effects of Tourism on Culture and the Environment in Asia and the Pacific: Tourism and Heritage Site Management in Luang Prabang, Laos PDR*, UNESCO Bangkok.
UNESCO Bangkok (2011), 'UNESCO Asia-Pacific Awards for Cultural Heritage Conservation', UNESCO Bangkok, available at: http://www.unescobkk.org/culture/world-heritage-and-immovable-heritage/asia-pacific-heritage-awards-for-culture-heritage-conservation/previous-heritage-awards-2000-2010/2008/award-winners/wat-pongsanuk/;accessed 5 February 2012.
Van Mench, P. (1992), 'Towards a methodology of museology', available at: http://www.utoronto ca/mouseia/papers.html; accessed 6 May 2005.
Van Mench, P. (7 December 2003), 'Museology and management: enemies or friends? Current tendencies in theoretical museology and museum management in Europe', paper presented at the 4th Annual Conference of Japanese Museum Management Academy, Tokyo.
Varine, H. de (1985), 'The word and beyond', *Museum International*, **37**(4), 185.
Vergo, P. (1989), *The New Museology*, London: Reaktion Books.
Weil, S. (1995), *A Cabinet of Curiosities: Inquiries into Museums and their Prospects*, Washington, DC: Smithsonian Institution Press.
Weil, S. (2002), *Making Museums Matter*, Washington, DC: Smithsonian Books.
Wijesuriya, Gamini (2000), 'Conserving the Temple of the Tooth Relic, Sri Lanka', *Public Archaeology*, **1**(2), 99–108.
Wills, Jo, Colin Long, Jonathan Sweet and Simon Wilmot (2007), 'Transformative learning in the hidden city: writing an interpretation plan at the Viengxai Field School in northern Laos', *Proceedings, ICOMOS 2007: Extreme Heritage: ICOMOS Conference held at James Cook University, Cairns, 19–21 July 2007*, pp. 1–12, Cairns, Queensland: James Cook University.

PART III

FAITH-BASED ORGANIZATIONS AND MISSION

22 'Do not turn away a poor man'*: faith-based organizations and development

Michael Jennings

INTRODUCTION

Despite the long trajectory of development and humanitarian action undertaken by faith- and religious-linked organizations in developing countries, the role of such organizations in development remains controversial amongst donors and academics. Accused of propagating teachings that undermine efforts to reduce and eliminate poverty, of expounding faith tenets that serve to disempower marginalized groups (especially women), of focusing on fellow faith adherents to the exclusion of others, or propagating discrimination and violence, faith and religious-linked organizations are believed by some not just to be problematic development actors, but outright dangerous in their impact and effect.

Whilst donors have since the late 1990s sought to engage with faith-based organizations, especially those that lie outside their normal field of vision (a trend sped up, but not created, by post-9/11 politics and the wars that followed), that engagement remains patchy and controversial within donor organizations. In part this reflects the failure of understanding of how FBOs work in development, and upon sets of assumptions as to the role of religion and religious identities in fermenting divisions, tensions, conflict and discrimination.

Yet despite concerns over their role, FBOs and organizations situated within a religious tradition do not just have a long-standing role in development and humanitarian activity, they are major actors in terms of scale of activity, resources (human and capital) they bring, and their involvement in the lives of the poor across the developing (and even the developed) world. The question as to whether faith-based and religious institutions should have a role in 'development' appears parochial to many living in developing countries: not just ahistorical, but ignoring the very real presence these organizations have in the day to day lives of the poor. At the international level, faith-based organizations wield a political and economic power (as well as social and cultural power within their respective faiths) that belies efforts to portray them as at best minor actors. World Vision International, for example, spent US$2.48 billion in 2010 (World Vision International, 2011, p. 5). This is more than net overseas development assistance spent by countries such as Switzerland (US$2.29 billion), Finland (US$1.36 billion), Austria (US$1.2 billion) and Ireland (US$895 million) during the same year (OECD, 2011). A World Bank study looking at the experiences and views of over 60 000 people from 60 countries found FBOs emerged as critically important institutions, especially for the rural poor (Narayan et al., 2000, p. 222). To suggest that FBOs should not, or are not, playing a key role in development is to ignore the realities of immense spending power and global activity in efforts to eradicate poverty.

This chapter considers the role that faith-based organizations (FBOs) play in development, challenging some of the critiques that are raised against them. That is not to dismiss the criticisms, nor to suggest that FBOs as a categorical type are unproblematic. But the role FBOs have and are playing is more nuanced, more widespread, and in some cases more attuned to local concerns and discourses than the fiercest critics of faith-based action have allowed for.

JUST WHAT IS A DEVELOPMENT FBO?

One obvious criticism that might be levelled at the terminology used in this chapter is over the use of the term 'faith-based organization'. Why not refer to 'faith-based development organizations' (FBDOs) rather than seek to create a broad category that might be less amenable to definitional capture? FBDOs are an important category of FBOs engaged in development and humanitarian activity, but they are not the sole means through which religious and faith institutions engage in this area. Individual parish churches, missions, mosques, temples, and so on, as well as national-level religious hierarchical authorities also engage in what would be defined as development interventions. The deliberate use of FBO (rather than focus on a subset of FBOs who are also development actors in their own right) is to seek to capture the variety of forms of engagement, and implications this has for broader understandings of how religion functions in a development context. Indeed, by purposely not focusing on organizations that most resemble orthodox development actors, the chapter argues that it is precisely this lack of resemblance of many FBOs to traditional development organizations that gives the faith sector a potential area of competitive advantage.

In their definition of the non-governmental organization Lester M. Salamon and Helmut J. Anheier specifically excluded religious organizations (NGOs) (1995, pp. 14–15). The definition seems overly constrictive, and many would not agree with such an exclusion. But not all faith-based organizations are NGOs, and even amongst those that might be seen as such, the religious links of the organization demand analytical acknowledgement. At the risk of essentializing the religious/faith element of such organizations over their development objectives and principles, the FBO can nonetheless be considered as a categorical term, even if there are considerable overlaps with the NGO. Nor should such a taxonomic distinction imply that the NGO must inherently be, as Salamon and Anheier suggest, secular. It is possible, indeed it happens in practice, for organizations to straddle more than one type, evading the analysts' efforts to simplify and categorize.

Moreover, the question as to what exactly is an FBO is central to engagement with the critiques of FBO development and humanitarian work. For whilst some FBOs may be problematic as regards gender, or democracy, say, that is not true for all. In other words, the character and typology of the FBO must be taken into account in understanding how it is likely to engage in development, and in seeking to explore how donors can best work with certain categories of FBO (and, of course, when they should choose not to).

Gerard Clarke and Michael Jennings define the FBO 'as any organization that derives inspiration and guidance for its activities from the teachings and principles of the faith or from a particular interpretation or school of thought within the faith' (Clarke and

Table 22.1 Points of difference for FBOs

	Passive	Active	Persuasive	Exclusive
Representative orgs and apex bodies				
Charitable development orgs				
Missionary orgs				
Socio-political orgs				
Radical, illegal or terrorist orgs				

Source: Matrix adapted from Clarke (2008, p. 34).

Jennings, 2008, p. 6). However, the generic and generalized nature of this definition, whilst capturing the broad sweep of organizational forms that fall under this category, fails to adequately differentiate important points of difference. Accordingly, Clarke (2008) breaks down this broad definition by type of organization, and by its approach to engagement in development activity in Table 22.1.

Along the vertical line, the main types of FBO move from umbrella organizations; through organizations that look like, and might be considered as NGOs in terms of their key functions (Christian Aid, CAFOD, Muslim Aid, the Aga Khan Foundation, for example); next come organizations whose primary objective is missionary work, but who also undertake development activity within that task; and finally the more problematic areas of FBOs who are engaged in socio-political activities and advocacy, and radical and/or illegal (possibly terrorist) organizations. Precisely where an organization fits along this line reflects its own internally defined objectives: Christian Aid, for example, sees itself as an NGO, its formal link to the Church of England not being a determining factor in who it works with or the projects it undertakes. But external definitions can complicate that positioning. Hezbollah might, for example, primarily define itself as a socio-political organization, but it is considered by the US government as a terrorist organization (and by others who reject that label, certainly as 'radical'). The difference between legitimate socio-political and radical is blurred at the edges of both, and often subject to external perceptions.

The horizontal axis describes the place of religious beliefs and response to non-believers in the activities of the organization. Whilst 'passive' implies that faith does not act as a key driver, 'active' suggests that faith and religious teachings play a more important role in shaping the activities of the organization. Persuasive organizations seek to advance the interests of the faith (by, for example, conversion), whilst exclusive organizations focus solely on those who share the religion, or particular branch of that religion.

The matrix is useful in outlining the main characteristics of different organizational types and the various key ways in which they function in relation to working with particular communities. It also helps in understanding how donors perceive different FBO organizations in seeking to engage (or disengage) with them. But there are also problems with the matrix. One is that it fails to sufficiently account for the ways that individual organizations might straddle different categories (a problem of all matrices, of course, and a problem of literal usage rather than intention). But, if one argues that an important aspect of the FBO is the context in which it operates (i.e., its local position and power within the local community, its role within local and national government structures, etc.), the matrix in seeking to understand how the organizational type shapes its activity does not fully account for how this context might shape the organization in turn.

Turning to the multiple places occupied by a single organization, and individuals within that organization, even in so-called 'passive' organizations, faith may play a more significant role than is apparent at first glance. Christian Aid, for example, has a Chief Theological Officer, seeking to map the organization's activities within a broader understanding of Christian ethics and morality. Ingie Hovland's (2008) work on the Norwegian Lutheran Mission, for example, demonstrates the complexity of understanding how 'faith' operates within an organization. Not only are those engaged in the 'non-religious' development activity motivated by their faith, but officially secular projects are imbued with practices, principles, discourses and symbols of faith, intended or not. At times, an individual FBO might be passive in its activities, at others active or even persuasive. But it can also be all of these at the same time.

How can one really distinguish between passive and active when those terms are subject to differing interpretations within a single organization? For example, is a faith-based hospital that treats those of any (or no) faith equally, is explicit in its policy of not seeking to convert those attending for treatment or care, but which holds regular public prayers in wards, and which invokes God as part of the healing process, passive or active (Hovland, 2008)? Is it both? And such definitional problems become increasingly hard to make (or, rather, increasingly subject to the perspective of the individual making the assessment) when considering differences between 'active' and 'persuasive'.

Context is also a key element in understanding the nature of the FBO and how it engages in development and humanitarian activity. For example, where does a parish within Roman Catholic hierarchy fit into the matrix? Is it a 'representative body'? It may function as such within the local parish context, but not within the national or international. But neither can it be considered as belonging to the other strands of FBO types: it is not a 'charitable development organization', even if it undertakes a considerable amount of what might be considered charitable development activity. It is not a missionary organization, but an established church. Neither could it be considered a socio-political nor radical organizational type.

Moreover, in many developing countries, religious institutions have local power beyond the spiritual realm, functioning as temporal power actors, often in collaboration, and sometimes in conflict, with the state and other official development actors. So to return to the parish church outlined above, how to consider development activity that is designed to support official government policy, or has been 'contracted' by the state? Is this 'faith-based' activity, or should it be considered as part of the wider 'voluntary sector private service provider' type? Does it represent the extension of faith values into the public sector, or the co-option of the independent agency of religion by the state?

Looking at faith-based organizations engaged in development and humanitarian activity from the perspective of both the context in which it operates, as well as seeking to understand how FBOs might operate with several different objectives at once, a revised matrix might look something like Table 22.2.

Table 22.2 How FBOs operate in different contexts

	Policy Setting & Advocacy Function	Financial (Fund-raising & Disbursement)	Development & Humanitarian Interventions	Religious Pastoral Care & Conversion
Institutional religious hierarchies				
Apex/umbrella organization				
National religious authority				
Local religious institutional hierarchies				
Dedicated institutional development organizations				
Missionary organizations				
Non-institutional religious organizations				
Faith-based development organizations				
Faith-based socio-political organizations				
Missionary organizations				
Individual religious leaders				

Source: Author.

The new matrix divides FBOs into two main types: those belonging to an institutional hierarchy, and those who are independent actors (although these may ally themselves to a particular authority, even if they are not bound to it by formal rules and systems). Under the first type, institutional religious hierarchies, 'apex organizations' reflect the senior institutional hierarchy of a religious organization, responsible (in terms of their development engagement) for policy matters, setting out guidelines for general direction and objectives, and holding ultimate authority over elements within the overall hierarchy. They may also play a financial role, allocating funds to elements lower down the chain. At the national level, religious institutions also play policy and advocacy roles (the former within the parameters set by the overall authority, and the latter mostly at the national level), but may also have dedicated 'development-focused' organizations, which would not be considered 'faith-based development organizations', which operate outside official authority structures of the faith. Local religious institutions – the parish church – are primarily engaged with pastoral care. However, they will also run projects under their own authority, as well as raise and mobilize funding at parish level. 'Types' therefore tick multiple boxes, operating in several areas at once, or at different times but within the same agency.

Missionary organizations (here used in a very loose sense, bringing together faith organizations that define themselves as missionary, but also those that do not, but who do seek to convert people to their particular faith or branch of teaching) straddle the two. Some organizations are under the authority of an apex organization (the Vatican, for example). Others may be independent of such authority, and thus fall into the second section. Whilst they are likely to be primarily concerned with religious teaching and proselytizing, they may also undertake development and humanitarian activities, although this is not their main driver. Faith-based development organizations (FBDOs), on the other hand, are primarily concerned with development and humanitarian interventions. However, some might also engage with conversion and proselytizing, where such activity is seen as allied or linked somehow to this core function. Some FBDOs might actively seek to hide, or downplay, their faith status, identifying primarily as an NGO rather than be linked to more overtly religious types. This raises an interesting question as to whether the 'FBO' emerges from within (a conscious decision to make visible the faith foundations), or from without (an external assessment based on analysis of the organization and those who work for it). Missing from Clarke's matrix (Table 22.1), are individual religious leaders, both from world religions, but also (and importantly) local prophets, leaders from non-recognized branches of world religions, and those from indigenous religious traditions, all of whom may be engaged in development in some capacity.

FBOs: THE CASE AGAINST

The place of the FBO in development is both assured by the scale of its activity; and contested, with concerns and opposition over the place of faith and religion in the 'secular' development project. Unlike the NGO (often assumed to be a secular organization) whose role in development relief and social welfare provision is rarely fundamentally challenged in the orthodox literature (even if aspects of its practice are), the place of FBOs and other institutional types linked to religion and spirituality is indeed questioned by some who see in their role dangers to development process and principles.

For the most ardent critics of faith engagement, the implicit assertion is that development is an inherently secular project, and any engagement of religious and faith organizations in that project is inevitably damaging. Amartya Sen, a prominent champion of the development as secular approach, thus cautions governments and donors not to collaborate too closely with religious groups (Sen, 2006, pp. 12–19). Moreover, he cautions against interpreting political and social action through the religious lens: doing so, he suggests 'downgrades' what in effect are political and social initiatives, albeit carried out by those who happen to be religious (ibid., p. 78). At the heart of this argument is an assertion that the realm of the spiritual is antithetical and in opposition to the objectives of modern, rational developmentalism and its counterpart, democracy. Such views have found their way into broader development thinking. The UNFPA (United Nations

Population Fund), for example, in setting out guidelines for how it might work with FBOs in promoting development, sets up two distinct development spheres: the 'international development' sector, populated by 'largely "secular" agents'; and 'an important parallel faith-based universe of development', the edges of both only recently blurring and merging as the two bubbles encounter each other (UNFPA, 2009, p. 1).

But as Chapter 29 (this volume) has demonstrated, the reality is that religion has long been an integral player in development and humanitarian activity, pre-dating the state in regions such as colonial Africa. FBOs in former British colonial Africa, in this instance in the form of missionary organizations, assisted in the construction of the welfare infrastructure of the African state. The passing of empire led to a redefining of the relationship between religion and state, and the increasing encroachment of the secular state into welfare provision. But it did not end the work of FBOs – now broadening out in type and religious background – in development. Nor have religious leaders sought to present their actions in secular terms. The pro-democracy movements across Africa in the late 1980s and 1990s, led frequently by church leaders, relied explicitly on the moral authority of the *religious* institution from which those leaders emerged (Gifford, 1994, p. 513). The 1995 Pastoral Letter from Kenya's Catholic bishops, lambasting President Moi's regime for its human rights abuses, was similarly overtly religious in its format and language (Jennings, 2008, pp. 111–12).

More serious, perhaps, are criticisms that focus on potential and actual tensions that emerge between religious teaching and development practice and policy. Most notably, of course, is the question of human rights. Maxine Molyneux and Shahra Razavi argue that the ability of FBOs to act as impartial brokers between donors, governments and communities is undermined by their failure to give due place to fundamental freedoms and rights: 'When religious authorities become the spokespeople for nations and ethnic communities, and where no guarantees exist for equality, democracy or human rights protection within the political context, there is little scope for contestation and dialogue' (Molyneux and Razavi, 2006, p. 18). Institutions who look to the ultimate authority of God, or the equivalent spiritual being, are (it is suggested) more equivocal in their relationship and commitment to human-made laws such as the Universal Declaration of Human Rights, and the body of rights, entitlements and laws that emerge from that document. Is it reasonable to assume, where a clash exists between official religious teaching and a human-made law, FBOs will tend to look to the former as representing the 'truth'?

Equally problematic is the approach to gender, gender equity and gender justice in religious teachings, and in the day-to-day workings of religious organizations. As Ruth Pearson and Emma Tomalin note:

> By ignoring dissenting or different voices within religious traditions and/or by failing to deconstruct representations of dominant 'culture and tradition' espoused by religious leaders, women's voices will be silenced and the progress towards gender equality will be set back. (Pearson and Tomalin, 2008, p. 65)

How can organizations, one might reasonably ask, who fail to put their own house in order in terms of gender relations, participate fully in development interventions that must at their heart recognize gender power as a major factor in creating, sustaining and perpetuating poverty and vulnerability? FBO interventions may be, Mariz Tadros notes 'used overtly or more subtly as a means of seeking to inculcate religious values and ideologies. Often, controlling women's behaviour becomes a symbol of conformity to religious ideology' (2010, p. iii). The conservative teachings of many religions as regards women, their role in society, and especially (in the context of development) on reproductive rights, clashes with the aims and objectives of many development interventions, and with best practice approaches in relevant areas. The workings of the Mexico City Policy and the Bush-era PEPFAR programme, which reflect the influence of the Christian Right on successive Republican governments, have clearly undermined sexual and reproductive health (including work in HIV and AIDS), as well as putting at risk programmes working with specific categories of women such as commercial sex workers.

There is a need not to assume women are passive in the face of conservative moral teachings. Tadros continues: 'While women are the targets of many such processes, they are not simply repositories of doctrines and ideologies and often engage in acts of subversion as well as covert and overt forms of contestations' (ibid.). And as Naila Kabeer shows, conservative religious and social teachings and practices can act as both protector and cage for women, but this does not prevent some women (and men) from being able to challenge and counter religious teachers who seek to demonize women's greater independence (Kabeer, 2011). Nonetheless, the extent to which FBOs may participate in propagating teachings and values that undermine gender equality, equity and women's empowerment is highly problematic. It is also a particular challenge for donors, who may have to explain why they are engaging with organizations whose values so diametrically oppose their own.

Whilst there are real dangers of reconciling the place of rights within religions (who accord ultimate authority to the spirit world, not the physical) to that within secular authorities (who look to the 1948 Universal Declaration of Human Rights and the international instruments that followed) those differences can be over-stated. Not least because the framing of the 1948 Universal Declaration owed much to the advocacy of an alliance of Protestant American, European and Lebanese Christians, and a Jewish lobby, a detail lost in the subsequent 'secular' version of its creation (Linden, 2008, p. 72). And although the questions raised by Pearson and Tomalin are important, their criticisms might be applied equally to the male-dominated cultural worlds of many donor governments, their official development agencies, and other secular development actors, including 'secular' NGOs. The dangers, then, are very real, but not universal within, or even particular to, 'religion' in general (even if religion is an important area in which these tensions play out).

Another significant criticism of FBOs stems from the analysis of the role of religion in creating and sustaining conflict. Perspectives building on Samuel Huntington's 'clash of civilizations' hypothesis (1993) in particular see religion as a potent force in dividing communities and the wider world. Shawn Flanigan, for example, looking at the role of FBOs in conflict zones, sees them as 'particularly problematic in contexts of religious and ethnic conflict', where 'FBOs may mirror, reinforce, and reproduce societal tensions that are present in the cultures in which they operate' (Flanigan, 2010, pp. 2–3). The binary nature of religious faith (one is either a believer or a non-believer) tends towards the exclusion of those who do not share the faith, and carried over into development terms, donors are necessarily reluctant to engage with FBOs who overtly pursue such sectarian policies. World Vision International, for example, has been seen as problematic for some European donors as a result of its linking of proselytizing and development interventions, which are seen as potentially divisive and potentially linked to conflict.

In reality, many FBOs (and especially those who are constituted specifically as development organizations) do not practise such exclusion. Or at least, the exclusion is more subtle than simply turning away those who do not share a faith. This partly reflects the multiple revenue streams secured by many larger FBOs (if they are in receipt of donor funds, it is hard for them to establish a clinic, say, that only treats those of a single religion); but it also reflects the broader objectives, albeit framed within a religious discourse, that underlies the work of many of these organizations.

Whilst sectarian organizations clearly do exist, the question as to whether an FBO focuses on one particular faith community alone is not necessarily a challenge to development and donor values. Hezbollah, for example, provides welfare, development and humanitarian services in areas it controls, but only for those who subscribe to both its faith and political values. Similarly, the Hindu-nationalist Rashtriya Swayamsevak Sangh (RSS) organization in India is sectarian in its welfare activities, seeking to promote the Hindu faith and identity. This is obviously problematic for donors. But FBOs might also choose to work within a single faith community, because this is where they can have their best impact. Few would argue, for example, that efforts to use religious teaching to reduce HIV-related stigma, can only really be carried out by an organization who shares that faith and who can persuade others that religious teaching demands compassion. A Muslim (or Buddhist, or Hindu, etc.) organization might not be considered sectarian, in such cases, even if it works solely with Muslims (Hindus, Buddhists, etc.) in this way.

A greater problem is likely to be where an FBO is the single service provider in a district, and where those outside the religion are unwilling to access services or resources because they feel excluded from the overt or covert faith symbolism and discourse that permeates such provision. In this sense, FBOs become problematic because of what they represent, not necessarily because of what they are. This is not, of course, particular to the FBO: in areas of contested political space, government services may also function in such a way – excluding those who distrust or fear the state.

WHAT MAKES FBOs DISTINCTIVE?

But if FBOs are not unproblematic in their engagement with and place in development and humanitarian interventions, as a category they do have characteristics that mark them out as different from secular NGOs, even with FBDOs who consciously choose to downplay their faith element to better resemble secular NGOs. These characteristics result specifically from the intersection of faith with development concerns, although the extent to which they are realized will differ according to type, underlying driver, and the use to which those characteristics are put. Central to this area of competitive advantage is the notion of 'trust', and the extent to which FBOs engaged in development have higher levels of trust than other development actors, which might enable them to engage in particular ways in which less trusted organizations might struggle. In particular, organizations that are trusted to speak for the best interests of individuals and communities may be more effectively able to address individual behaviour and cultural issues, inter- and intra-community tensions and conflicts, and wider moral economy underpinnings of poverty, vulnerability and marginality. However, whilst much analysis of the FBO focuses on the organizational structures, and the competitive advantages that follow, the question of the extent to which religion itself is a critical factor is less addressed. This might, of course, be the most important aspect: does the 'faith' component of an FBO make it substantially different in the effect it can have compared to a secular NGO?

'Sticky Trust'

The question of the extent to which institutions – public and private – are trusted by citizens to have their best interests at heart underpins debates on the effectiveness of the state, on whether social capital can build such trust and the implications of declining social capital (see especially Putnam, 2000), and how these in turn feed into trust between communities (as individuals and in groups). This is not the place to debate the extent to which a lack of trust is an important factor in undermining good governance, and in turn development progress. Nor is this a wider consideration of the extent to which religions engender trust, how they do it, and how that trust can in turn be lost or damaged. But within the confines of the perspective of this chapter, the extent to which an institution is trusted – in the sense that it is perceived to care for the lives, wishes, needs and aspirations of those who interact with it – appears to be an important one for that institution's ability to engage with development, and persuade people of its intentions and objectives, and secure willing engagement by those people in development interventions.

Hardin (2006) identifies three conceptions of 'trust' (although he makes the point that the literature is really dealing with a related, but separate concept of 'trustworthiness' – the characteristics and actions of an institution or individual that lead others to place trust in it/her. First, 'trust as encapsulated interests': trust, in this sense, reflects the extent to which interests are 'encapsulated in the interests of the trusted' (Hardin, 2006, p. 18):

> A more general account simply includes a requirement that the trusted be trusted because . . . she might be supposed to take the truster's interests into account in her choice whether to do what would fulfil the trust. Her reason might be moral concern or self-interest, either directly or indirectly.

The second conception regards trust as 'a matter of moral commitment'. The third looks to questions of 'character or disposition' (ibid., p. 23). Hardin again reiterates that here, questions of morality and character are reflective of the inherent qualities of trustworthiness rather than trust, an important distinction when applying this back to the characteristics of the FBO.

All three conceptions might be said to apply, in differing ways, operating in different contexts, and at different times, within the FBO. The extent to which FBOs might be considered trustworthy clearly builds on the sense amongst faith adherents (but also amongst many who do not share the denominational or even any faith) that FBOs in their activities are guided by a sense of the interests of the communities within which they live and work. Moreover, trustworthiness, certainly within faith communities, and in many cases as a more general rule, is defined in strongly religious-moral terms.

Discussions on trust/trustworthiness also differentiate between 'strong' and 'weak' trust, again, an important distinction when considering the potential competitive advantage of the FBO in relation to other development actors. Thinking about trust as 'sticky' or 'non-sticky' offers another way of conceptualizing how institutions interact with communities and individuals, and the extent to which they are granted trust. Many development actors might be considered to have high levels of strong trust, but that trust is not necessarily given across all areas. Trust might be considered to be sticky where it covers a broader area, and where the bonds are less likely to be broken if an intervention fails, or an individual leader or official is seen to break that trust. It is here that FBOs again might be seen as having a strong competitive advantage, having high levels of sticky trust.

The trust with which many FBOs engaged in development are imbued in part reflects the religious character of the institutions, and the belief of faith adherents in those religious teachings and those responsible for elucidating those teachings and guiding the faithful. However, one can point to more concrete aspects that contribute to establishing FBOs as trustworthy, and endowed with high levels of sticky trust. The three most important are, first, the level at which FBOs operate, with few other organizations capable of straddling the immediate local-ness, whilst at the same time engaging internationally through global faith networks. Second, the 'faith' platform of the FBO contributes to a high degree of authority and power held by the organization. Third, the shared language and worldview of the FBO, especially in conceptions of well-being, what it means to be fulfilled, and 'developed', marks it out as distinctive from other secular development actors. None of these characteristics are inevitably positive in their outcomes, and in some cases can be highly problematic. But they do allow us to see where FBOs perhaps have their greatest influence.

Perhaps the main difference between the FBO and secular development actors (be they state, NGO or other forms) is that FBOs and religious institutions that undertake development interventions are part of the community in which they are based: physically sharing the same space; spiritually sharing a common worldview. The dual nature of this community (geographically bonded and spiritually diffuse) makes the FBO at once a local and a global institution, tapping into multiple identities.

The 2003 World Bank survey of 60000 people across 60 countries found that faith-based organizations emerged as vitally important institutions for the rural poor in particular. FBOs, the report noted:

> emerge frequently in poor people's lists of important institutions. They appear more frequently as the most important institutions in rural rather than in urban ones. Spirituality, faith in God and connecting to the sacred in nature are an integral part of poor people's lives in many parts of the world. Religious organizations are also valued for the assistance they provide to poor people. (Narayan et al., 2000, p. 222)

Moreover, it concluded, 'religious organizations feature more prominently than any other single type of state institution' (although it also noted FBOs 'do not disappear when ineffective institutions are mentioned'; ibid.).

The importance of the FBO in this regard lies particularly in the fact that religious institutions are far more likely to be present within a community than almost any other form of organization. Development-oriented FBOs, particularly those based in institutional religious hierarchies, are intensely local in their relationships with communities, physically present and engaged in the minutiae of the lives of its adherents. Moreover, the relationships of some FBOs may have been more long-standing than even state bodies. In many areas in sub-Saharan Africa, for example, the parish church and especially the mosque are likely to pre-date the institution of the colonial state. And where colonial states were not established – Ethiopia, for instance – the Christian Church has a claim to be as old an institution as the state, both at a national and especially at a local community level.

Longevity is not a sufficient explanation to account for the relative success of FBOs in reaching the poor and vulnerable. Established churches, based on former missionary organizations, or Islamic structures in East and West Africa may have this advantage, but the success of other, newer forms of faith institutions, notably the Pentecostal movement, suggests it is the local, rather than long-standing, character that makes a difference.

At the same time as existing in a physical form at the level of the community, FBOs are also frequently linked to global faith networks, making them a significant force politically and economically. The Protestant World Council of Churches, for example, help mobilize funding, devise and advise on policy as regards key issues related to development, and provide training and other supports for local church members. The Muslim Brotherhood, currently playing a critical role in post-Mubarak Egypt, links through its own organization and affiliates Muslims from across the world. The Islamic Gulen movement has established educational institutions in over 90 countries, working through local Muslim faith-based institutions.

Global faith networks give access to capital, allowing FBOs to draw on resources that cannot be accessed by secular NGO counterparts, the source of which is less likely to cause potential frictions between the ideals and principles of the organization and the donor (a potential consequence for secular NGOs in relying on donor funding). It also brings human capital in the form of volunteers, experts and other people who can be drawn on in various ways. The global level of operation also gives FBOs substantial clout in dealing with national governments, international organizations and donors through the lobbying and advocacy power of such networks.

Such networks also allow for deeper relationships to emerge between individual FBOs from different countries, and through this establish more personalized links between individuals belonging to such churches. Hefferan's study (2009) of the Parish Twinning Program of the Americas (PTPA) shows how linkages between North American Catholic parishes, and those in Haiti, have mobilized not just capital, but other forms of support, as well as highlighting the real problems of power balances, ownership and control over development processes that can be a feature of such programmes.

The power held by religious institutions and FBOs grants them high levels of control over the outer, as well as inner, lives of their faith communities. Religious leaders have spiritual power. But as a result many also have temporal power, and more so than leaders of secular NGOs, government officials and many other authority figures, religious leaders potentially carry greater force within communities. Spiritual power comes from speaking with, or representing, the voice of the spiritual realm. Temporal power stems from the elite status of many religious leaders, whether local or national elites. As members of village or district committees and councils, leaders within civil society movements, members of formal or informal faith advisors to heads of state, they carry political weight. The 1994 Kenyan Catholic bishops' Pastoral Letter condemning the

Kenyan government for human rights abuses, for example, saw senior Catholic clergy using the protection their positions granted them to speak out in a public and highly political way. Similarly, Jesuit priests heading anti-government protest marches in the Philippines combine spiritual authority with significant temporal power (the hope being that state security officials will be less willing to use extreme force against priests). The current spate of immolations in Tibet by Buddhist monks, whilst couched in religious terms, makes use of the wider temporal authority enjoyed by the spiritual elite.

The authority of FBOs and religious institutions is given greater resonance from a worldview that embraces the secular and the spiritual world, recognizing the influence of the latter on the former. 'Religious thought provides believers with a cosmology able to provide a comprehensive explanation of the world, including theories as to why things happen the way they do', write Ellis and Ter Haar (2004, p. 14). 'That fact alone makes religion of great political importance in any society where the overwhelming majority of people holds some sort of religious belief' (ibid.). It also means that FBOs who engage with the spiritual dimension share (as well as help shape) the ways communities understand the world and how it works.

The stickiness of the trust placed in FBOs is especially reflective of this shared holistic understanding of the person: the environment in which they live, work and socialize; the meaning of what it means to 'be developed', to be safe and secure; what 'health', 'success' and 'well-being' mean to people.

Other development actors may have trust, may even have high levels of 'strong trust'. Nonetheless, their organizational underpinnings mean they are not necessarily trusted across all aspects of an individual's life. An NGO may be more trusted than the state to deliver funding without siphoning off aid money, to ensure an intervention meets the needs of the community as a whole (or the more vulnerable members of that community) rather than elite interests, but its focus is limited to that intervention, or to a wider commitment to poverty reduction, empowerment, or some tangible, physical gain. The state may be trusted to look to the longer-term interests of its citizens, as well as wider concerns that fall outside the 'development' sphere, but as long as people remain law abiding, the state's concern with inner morality is limited or non-existent. The state is responsible for, and sees only, a part of the individual – the public, the civic, the taxable and productive unit.

Religious leaders and FBOs are assumed to care for more than the physical life of the individual and wider community. Their interests span the immediate now and the metaphysical next. A community does not just consist of clients or recipients, or economic units to be taxed or improved, but whole people whose physical lives represent but a part of their total existence. 'Development' therefore is more than just providing for the immediate physical needs of people, but also their spiritual needs. True, secular organizations might also frame their development vision in such terms (empowerment, capacities, and so on), but the terms used rarely reflect the language and discourse of those they are working with. The language of FBOs speak much more readily to these. Thus, in the case of HIV and AIDS prevention activity, a secular organization might provide advice on how to protect against HIV infection using the ABC model (abstain where possible, be faithful, and use a condom). An FBO would frame the message not just about protecting against infection, but about the responsibility of being a good, moral person – one does not remain faithful just for prevention, but for broader well-being. This does not make FBOs necessarily better in such interventions – where, for example, they ignore the 'C' part of the equation, they may in fact put lives at risk – but it can give them the potential to be more effective in motivating, in this case, behavioural change.

Clearly, not all FBO types will share all of these features to the same extent. An overseas FBDO, albeit likely to work with a local partner, may have less 'sticky trust' than the local place of worship that also undertakes development interventions. FBDOs that suppress the language of faith and religion less so. But nonetheless, the spiritual underpinning of the FBO, regardless of type, places it somewhere on this continuum.

The Place of 'Religion'

A more difficult question as to the competitive advantage of the FBO is the place of religion itself. Are FBOs able to engage in particular ways, reach particular communities and have particular impacts because their organizational form and method of engagement gives them an advantage, or is there something about the 'faith' character itself that is critical?

In the area of HIV and AIDS, some have attempted to answer this question, looking at prevalence rates amongst certain faith communities and seeking to correlate this to the message and approach taken by that religion. Some research has suggested a positive correlation between religiosity and lowered susceptibility to infection with HIV. Trinitapoli and Regnerus (2006), for example, suggest that research in Malawi demonstrates that religious 'commitment' (marked by attendance of a weekly service) is a significant factor in predicting HIV risky behaviour. Those who define themselves as committed are less likely to report having either extra-marital sexual partners, or having had an STD. Whilst Trinitapoli and Regnerus looked to the level of commitment, Robert Garner's research in South Africa pointed towards denomination as the critical factor. Pentecostal churches showed a significant reduction in (reported) extra- and pre-marital sex amongst members (perhaps helping to explain the success of Pentecostalism amongst women in particular in sub-Saharan Africa). 'Mainstream' Anglican and Catholic churches reported little significant change in behaviour, and higher numbers of reported extra- and pre-marital sex (Garner, 2000). Studies by Addai (1999) in Ghana show similar results for evangelical churches (especially for women). Whilst some studies on Islam and HIV have identified practices such as Islamic-approved polygamy as increasing risks of infection, others have shown a link between active Islamic faith and lower levels of infection. Teachings on alcohol and extra-marital sex, practices such as the emphasis on cleanliness through ritual washing, and especially male circumcision provide a degree of protection (Gray, 2004). However, other research has also shown lower awareness and less behaviour change amongst Muslim women in comparison to women in Christian churches (Takyi, 2003), further complicating the assumed relationships between faith and HIV.

Such micro-studies may not be capable of demonstrating a positive link between extent of faith and lowered risk of infection (not least because the research is often contradictory across different contexts and faiths). However, they do allow for some tentative hypotheses. Whilst some have suggested that religious proscriptions and teachings condemning certain practices (notably, in relation to HIV, sex outside marriage) have a role, it is clear that these have had impact in some cases, but not in many. What appears to be more important is the broader context in which these teachings, religious advice and exhortations are undertaken. In the case of South Africa, Garner (2000, pp. 48–50) noted four key aspects to the apparent success of Pentecostalism in changing the behaviour of its adherents: indoctrination (through the emphasis on teaching and bible study); religious experience (through high levels of participation in church life); 'exclusion' (the emphasis on boundaries between the saved and the non-saved); and 'socialization' (Pentecostals being more likely to socialize solely with other Pentecostals, thus reinforcing the power of the church over daily lives, and behaviour).

If there is a correlation between religious adherence and lowered risk (and this is a very big if), it is likely that it is not just the religious aspect of the message, but the context in which this message is occurring. This has wider implications across development interventions, for example with efforts to address gender inequity, or efforts to promote particular behavioural responses to new challenges or opportunities. The framing of those messages within a broader framework (i.e., one remains faithful not just to protect against HIV and AIDS, but to be a good person; religious 'texts' demand that adherents respect women not just because the law and human rights instruments demand it, but as a sign of respect for God) strengthens them and aids acceptance. The social reinforcement of these messages, backed by clear sanctions for transgressions, further embeds them. In other words, faith matters not necessarily solely because of the religious teaching itself, but because of the particular context, which would be difficult if not impossible for secular organizations to adopt, in which messages are transmitted, interpreted and acted upon.

CONCLUSIONS

These characteristics have implications for the role of FBOs in development and humanitarian interventions. On the one hand, the proximity to the people with whom they work, and the ability to tap into globalized faith networks (and the resources those networks can mobilize) create very powerful institutions. Combined with the spiritual and temporal authority held by religious leaders and FBOs, and their framing of teachings and advice within a discourse shared by many of the communities in which they operate, FBOs are powerful institutions at the local, national and international level. But this can make the potential problematic aspects described earlier more powerful in their impacts. In the case of HIV and AIDS, there is little doubt that the capturing of US HIV and AIDS and family planning policy by Christian evangelical groups has undermined international best practice models of interventions in these areas. The contributions of successive popes and the Vatican as to whether the condom is a legitimate disease prevention tool, or a sinful device that goes against the right to life (a position shared by many other religious denominations and faiths) has put people at risk of infection with HIV. Given the type and level of trust afforded to religious institutions and leaders, what they say matters, and when they perpetuate stigma, poor science, power structures that marginalize women or other groups, they can become a significant part of the problem.

Yet that authority and trust also enables them to defend the poor, the persecuted, the marginalized, to argue why certain groups should be cared for and respected as demanded by religious teachings (not vaguely articulated and, from the perspective of communities, distant human rights laws and language). FBOs can help gain acceptance for interventions that from other development actors might be seen as interference, disruptive and dangerous. Certain types of FBOs are capable of standing up to the state (although, where they choose to ally with the state, they can reinforce authoritarianism), acting as civil society actors and leaders.

Faith retains a controversial place in development. But that controversy perhaps reflects the lack of understanding of the faith world by donors and other secular development actors. The issues that cause concern (sectarianism, questionable approaches to rights and towards women and other marginalized groups, role in catalysing social tensions and conflict) may be particularly pronounced in the faith sector, but are not particular to it. Moreover, whilst not avoiding the critique of faith engagement in development, nor can their current and past role be dismissed or written out of history. FBOs have a vital role to play in development because this is a role they are already playing to a substantial degree, and have been doing so as a sector long before secular NGOs emerged, and in some cases the state itself. In the end FBOs matter because the poor themselves tell us that they do.

NOTE

* 'Do not turn away a poor man . . . even if all you can give is half a date' (Al-Tirmidhi, Hadith 1376).

REFERENCES

Addai, I. (1999), 'Does religion matter in contraceptive use among Ghanaian women?', *Review of Religious Research*, **40**(3), 259–77.

Clarke, G. (2008), 'Faith-based organisations and international development: an overview', in Gerard Clarke and Michael Jennings (eds), *Development, Civil Society and Faith-based Organisations: Bridging the Sacred and the Secular*, London: Palgrave Macmillan, pp. 17–45.

Clarke, G. and M. Jennings (eds) (2008), *Development, Civil Society and Faith-based Organisations: Bridging the Sacred and the Secular*, London: Palgrave Macmillan.

Ellis, S. and G. Ter Haar (2004), *Worlds of Power: Religious Thought and Political Practice in Africa*, London: Hurst.

Flanigan, S. (2010), *For the Love of God: NGOs and Religious Identity in a Violent World*, Sterling: Kumarian Press.

Garner, R. (2000), 'Safe sects? Dynamic religion and AIDS in Africa', *The Journal of Modern African Studies*, **38**(1), 41–69.

Gifford, P. (1994), 'Some recent developments in African Christianity', *African Affairs*, **93**(373), 513–34.

Gray, P. (2004), 'HIV and Islam: is HIV prevalence lower among Muslims?', *Social Science and Medicine*, **58**(9), 1751–5.

Hardin, R. (2006), *Trust*, Oxford: Polity.

Hefferan, T. (2009), 'Encouraging development "alternatives": grassroots church partnering in the US and Haiti', in Tara Hefferan, Julie Adkins and Laurie Occhipinti (eds), *Bridging the Gaps: Faith-based Organizations, Neoliberalism, and Development in Latin America and the Caribbean*, Lanham, MD and Plymouth UK: Lexington, pp. 69–82.

Hovland, I. (2008), 'Who's afraid of religion? Tensions between mission and development in the Norwegian Mission Society', in Gerard Clarke and Michael Jennings (eds), *Development, Civil Society and Faith-based Organisations: Bridging the Sacred and the Secular*, London: Palgrave Macmillan, pp. 171–86.

Huntington, S. (1993), 'The clash of civilizations?', *Foreign Affairs*, **72**(3), 22–49.

Jennings, M. (2008), 'The spirit of brotherhood: Christianity and Ujamaa in Tanzania', in Gerard Clarke and

Michael Jennings (eds), *Development, Civil Society and Faith-based Organisations: Bridging the Sacred and the Secular*, London: Palgrave Macmillan, pp. 94–116.
Kabeer, N. (2011), 'Between affiliation and autonomy: navigating pathways of women's empowerment and gender justice in rural Bangladesh', *Development and Change*, **42**(2), 499–528.
Linden, I. (2008), 'The language of development: what are international development agencies talking about?', in Gerard Clarke and Michael Jennings (eds), *Development, Civil Society and Faith-based Organisations: Bridging the Sacred and the Secular*, London: Palgrave Macmillan, pp. 72–93.
Molyneux, M. and S. Ravazi (2006), *Beijing Plus 10: An Ambivalent Record on Gender Justice*, Occasional Paper No. 15, Geneva: United Nations Research Institute for Social Development (UNRISD).
Narayan, D. Robert Chambers, Meera K. Shah and Patti Petesch (2000), *Voices of the Poor: Crying Out for Change*, New York: Oxford University Press.
OECD (2011), 'Aid statistics online', available at: http://www.oecd.org/document/35/0,3746,en_2649_34447_47515235_1_1_1_1,00.html; accessed 24 October 2011.
Pearson, R. and Emma Tomalin (2008), 'Intelligent design?: A gender-sensitive interrogation of religion and development', in Gerard Clarke and Michael Jennings (eds), *Development, Civil Society and Faith-based Organisations: Bridging the Sacred and the Secular*, London: Palgrave Macmillan, pp. 46–71.
Putnam, R. (2000), *Bowling Alone: The Collapse and Revival of American Community*, New York: Simon and Schuster.
Salamon, L. and Helmut K. Anheier (1995), *The Emerging Non-profit Sector: An Overview*, Manchester: Manchester University Press.
Sen, A. (2006), *Identity and Violence: The Illusion of Destiny*, London: Allen Lane.
Tadros, M. (2010), 'Faith-based organizations and service delivery: some gender conundrums', UNRISD Gender and Development Programme Paper No. 11.
Takyi, B.K. (2003), 'Religion and women's health in Ghana: insights into HIV/AIDS preventive and protective behaviour', *Social Science and Medicine*, **56**(6), 1221–34.
Trinitapoli, J. and Mark D. Regnerus (2006), 'Religion and HIV risk behaviours among married men: initial results from a study in rural sub-Saharan Africa', *Journal for the Scientific Study of Religion*, **45**(4), 505–28.
UNFPA (2009), 'Guidelines for engaging faith-based organizations (FBOs) as agents of change', available at: http://www.unfpa.org/culture/docs/fbo_engagement.pdf; accessed 25 July 2012.
World Vision International (2011), *2010 Annual Review*, available at: http://www.wvi.org/wvi/WVIAR2011.nsf/; accessed 24 July 2012.

23 'Pan-Islamism' as a form of 'alter-globalism'? Hizb Ut-Tahrir and the Islamic Khilafah State

Bruno De Cordier

> If they can have the European Union, why can't we have a Caliphate?
> (Mushahid Ullah, Pakistani senator, 2011)

INTRODUCTION

Development as well as conflict are intrinsically linked to past and ongoing processes of globalization, and to attempts by different centres and actors to maximize their space and position in the reality of globalization, and steer the social and economic changes and opportunities that globalization brings.[1] The inevitable collision of interests, goals and norms and values therein leads to various forms of contestation of globalization or at least of certain of its impacts and directions that it is taking. What is commonly known as the anti-globalization movement – but has been more adequately called 'alter-globalism' for a number of years – for instance, typically opposes globalization dominated or felt to be dominated by neo-liberal capitalism and development models, international financial institutions, transnational corporations, military interventions, and cultural and governance Westernization, all of which further consolidate the domination of OECD economies and centres of power to the detriment of the global periphery.

BETWEEN OPPOSING AND REDIRECTING

Eddy Fougier defines alter-globalism as:

> currents and movements that belong to civil society that denounce the neo-liberal nature of the current process of globalization, aspire for other forms of globalization and try to link this goal to different struggles that these movements and currents carry out at the local and national level.[2]

For Leszek Gawor, the alter-globalist movement is 'no longer aimed against globalization but rather against its heartless, purely economic version, devoid of social sensitivity. Therefore, it does not take a hostile stance towards modernity but only wishes to have "globalization with a human face"'.[3] In other words, alter-globalism does not oppose globalization, global interaction and cooperation per se, but what is called corporate-led globalization and the economic and social inequalities that come with it. Fougier furthermore observes that the alter-globalist movement, by its composition, organization and mode of action, groups a wide variety of Western (Marxism, Christianity, ecology, trade unionism, feminism) as well as non-Western (anti-imperialism, indigenism) modes of resistance and alternatives.[4]

Despite a common dislike for imperialism, for the neo-liberal capitalist character of the current phase of globalization and the latter's cultural and social impact on the wider Muslim world – much of which is situated in the global periphery – the position of explicitly Islamic movements and opinion leaders in the alter-globalist movement as well as the relationship between the two is uneasy at best. And the presence of Islamic faith-based groups in the alter-globalist movement is limited as compared to the size of the Muslim world and its share in the impact of globalization and conflict.[5] One major explanation for this is the ideological orientation of the groups that traditionally dominate alter-globalism and its incompatibility with Islamic views on a number of issues. Another, in our opinion, can be found in a number of fundamental characteristics and interpretations of globalization of radical Islamic movements that offer political resistance against the current way of globalization and its negative social and cultural effects, and propose faith-based alternatives that, in their view, are able to achieve social justice, at least in a space that is defined by both religious affiliation and a common historical predicament.

At times, when some observe an increasing role for religious actors and movements in the contestation of or response to globalization or at least its negative impacts and its current nature,[6] there is an increasing and ever more explicit use by several political Islamic movements of an anti-imperialist and anti-capitalist discourse and terminology that was long considered to be the exclusive domain of militant Marxism and 'classical' alter-globalism, yet reflect certain concepts of social justice and solidarity in Islam that existed long before Marxism and alter-globalism came into being. The question is now whether Islamic faith-based concepts are, or are becoming, a form of alter-globalism too, and perhaps one that even reflects realities and issues in the Muslim world better than 'classical' alter-globalism.

One typical aspect of the alter-globalist movement is its wide and at times chaotic diversity of groups, ideologies and approaches that it encompasses. Nonetheless, Leszek Gawor distinguishes seven common traits and aims within the movement. First, he finds, 'as a matter of policy, alter-globalism opposes the globalist practice of reducing the description and evaluation of reality only to the economic dimension, amounting to recording growth, deficit or inflation indicators on a macro-scale' (Gawor, 2008, pp. 129–30). Second, alter-globalism 'expresses opposition to "the end of politics" – to surrendering all areas of social life to the market, especially the spheres of education, culture, social security and welfare' (ibid.). In Gawor's view:

> neo-liberal globalization and lack of social security lead to an increase in crime all over the world, hence the alter-globalist defence of the state as the institution that is to represent the interest of members of this community on the one hand, and on the other the demand for global, legal and political regulations aimed at controlling financial markets. (Ibid.)

Third, for Gawor, alter-globalism:

> accepts closer interaction between economies and societies. Global coordination of exchange of goods and services is necessary. An institution responsible for this area must, however, take into consideration a broad range of social goals, such as provision of basic economic rights to all people (fair wages and working conditions), environmental protection and, finally, the promotion of the model of sustainable development in the Third World countries. (Ibid.)

Fourth, it:

> readily recognizes the results of 'the information revolution'. The movement of information not only determines the possibilities (used by neo-liberalism) of managing economy on a global scale but it is also a condition for building civic society, forming structures of direct democracy, and indirectly controlling all economic–political projects. Moreover, alter-globalists regard this free movement of information as the main mode of social influence. (Ibid.)

Fifth, alter-globalism:

> rejects the radically determinist vision of the world, assuming the possibility of real influence on social reality by even informal social movements (especially NGOs). For this reason, it firmly rejects the alternative imposed by the neo-liberal doctrine: either the market and globalization in its contemporary version, or populism and economic disaster. (Ibid.)

Sixth, alter-globalism opposes:

> social uniformity, which is manifested in practice by the support of all local movements. . . . Although it does not distance itself from globalization processes, alter-globalism promotes the catchphrase 'Think globally, act locally' and opts for 'local community'. It uses the term 'glocal(ism)' to define such a model of community, which, while making use of the opportunities offered by globalization processes (for example fast information communication), does not lose its local (regional) colour. In this interpretation, 'glocal' communities are the most desirable form of social organization, guaranteeing the use of modernity with the simultaneous preservation of traditional local (regional, ethnic, national) models and values. (Ibid.)

Finally, Gawor believes that:

> this outline of the main points of the alter-globalist program presents a definite vision of society in the age of globalization. This is to be a society that makes use of globalization but can also control these globalization processes. Hence the necessity also arises: the only response to the globalization of capitalism must be to create a global civil society.[7](Ibid.)

We will treat the question whether Islamic faith-based movements and concepts are, or are becoming, a form of alter-globalism against Gawor's characteristics, through a case study of the pan-Islamic party Hizb Ut-Tahrir. This is a transnational movement that advocates the unification of the Muslim countries in an Islamic state under the restored Caliphate, a political leadership for the Ummah, the worldwide community of believers. The group is much talked about in specialized literature as well as media reports for its alleged ties with, and direct as well as indirect role in, violent radicalism. The group is often portrayed by some neo-conservative, right-wing Zionist and libertarian circles in the USA and the EU as a vanguard of what these circles see as 'a totalitarian Islamic super-state' that will sooner or later replace the USSR as the enemy and 'empire of evil'. In several majority Muslim successor states of the USSR, Hizb Ut-Tahrir has also acquired a quasi-official status of a public enemy whose presence and activities serve as a justification for regular rounds of repression and purges while selling these internationally as 'war on terror'.[8]

Yet little is known about the party's developmental views and to what extent these views are anchored in, or reflect, certain realities and aspirations in the Muslim world. A section on why there is a need to restore the Caliphate on *Al-Badil* (Arabic for 'The

Alternative'), a web portal connected to Hizb Ut-Tahrir, opens with a number of statistics that illustrate economic and social inequality and injustice in today's world economy. '(Remember that) we live in a world where . . . one percent of the richest hold 95 percent of all wealth', the text starts, and continues:

> One billion people have no access to running water; where 1.5 billion have no access to basic health care; the 200 richest individuals in the world doubled their annual revenue, and the overall sum of these equals the resources of 2.5 billion of the poorest; 3 billion individuals live with less than 2 dollars and 1.3 with less than one dollar per day; and where 20 percent of the population of so-called developed countries consume 86 percent of the globe's wealth.[9]

Whether these statistics are exact or what their actual source is, is not the point for now. The relevance of this passage, and the reason why we quote it, is that global social and developmental indicators are raised as an opening argument to advance a faith-based alternative that is inspired by entities that existed in earlier phases of globalization, against capitalism, which dominates the current phase of globalization.

THE PERCEIVED HISTORICAL FRAMEWORK OF THE FUTURE

The Hizb Ut-Tahrir Al-Islami or Islamic Liberation Party, as the group is called in full, is, in its own parlance:

> a political party whose ideology is Islam, so politics is its work and Islam is its ideology. It works within the Islamic Ummah and together with her, so that she adopts Islam as her cause and is led to restore the Khilafah (Caliphate) and the ruling by what Allah revealed. Hizb Ut-Tahrir is a political group and not a priestly one. Nor is it an academic, educational or a charity group. The Islamic thought is the soul of its body, its core and the secret of its life.[10]

As such, its aim is:

> to resume the Islamic way of life and to convey the Islamic Call to the world. This objective means bringing the Muslims back to living an Islamic way of life in (the domain of Islam) and in an Islamic society such that all of life's affairs in society are administered according to the Shar'iah rules, and the viewpoint in it is the Halal (lawful) and the Haram (prohibited) under the shade of the Islamic (Khilafah) State. The party, as well, aims at the correct revival of the . . . Ummah through enlightened thought. . . . It also strives to bring her back to her previous might and glory such that she wrests the reins of initiative away from other states and nations, and returns to her rightful place as the first state in the world, as she was in the past, when she governs the world according to the laws of Islam.[11]

The party was founded in Al-Quds (Jerusalem) in 1952–53 by the Islamic scholar and activist Taqiuddin An-Nabhani (1909–77) and four of his companions, with the original dual purpose of establishing an Islamic state and liberating Palestine. The Al-Azhar-educated An-Nabhani and most of the party's other founders were Jordanians of Palestinian origin. As such, they were directly and personally confronted with the consequences, including displacement, of the demise of the Ottoman state and Caliphate in 1924, the subsequent carve-up of the Middle East, and the foundation of the State of

Israel and partition of Palestine in 1948.[12] This deeply affected the party's worldview in the sense that it explains many of the Bilad Al-Islam's (the area of Islam or the Muslim world) modern ills and woes back to Western imperialist conspiracies, as well as competition and rivalry between imperialist powers, that pervade the modern history of the Muslim Ummah from as early as the eighteenth century and explain its predicament up to the present day.[13]

In the party's view, nationalism and separatism were propagated by the Western powers and missionaries to divide the Ummah, prevent the return of an Islamic power like the Ottoman and other empires, and leave the Muslim world vulnerable to Western conquest and domination. For An-Nahbani, the demise of both the Ottoman state and of the Caliphate form a culminating point in this process, since the fact that the Muslims hardly responded to the event or were unable to appreciate its gravity, showed the success of alien ideologies spread by cultural imperialism, as it was a cumulative affect of centuries of faulty understanding of Islam. The hopes to transfer the Caliphate from the Ottomans to the Arabs again were dashed after the promised unified Arab state that was to arise on the ruins of the Ottoman Empire did not materialize and instead gave way to a carve-up of the Ottoman and Arab territories in various national states.[14] The fact that the cities of Medina, Mecca and Al-Quds, Islam's three most sacred cities and the first three major urban centres to be integrated in the early Islamic sphere in the years 622, 630 and 638 respectively, are now either occupied by non-Muslims (Al-Quds by the State of Israel) or under the control of a 'vassal regime of the West' (Mecca and Medina by Saudi Arabia) stand symbol for an overall humiliation.

The Ummah's present division into what Hizb Ut-Tahrir calls '56 statelets', which mostly came into being through colonialism, occupation and imported secular ideologies (nationalism, socialism and later neo-liberalism), and the 'criminal rulers' of these 'statelets', enforces a convenient status quo for the sake of the West and, to a lesser extent, other non-Islamic powers and thwarts the Ummah's large economic, political and human potential.[15] Hizb Ut-Tahrir's ideology thus suggests not so much geographic expansion of the Islamic world as the liberation and re-unification of the Islamic world in its present shape under the rule of a unifying institution anchored in that area's common and comprehensive ideological-religious identity: the Caliphate. This unification cannot be done within the framework of existing regional or global platforms of Muslim countries like the Arab League, the Organization of the Islamic Conference or the Economic Cooperation Organization.

The reason for this is that these organizations are perceived as unable to bring about real change in this field, because they largely gather the very same corrupt 'puppet governments' and 'anti-Islamic' regimes that basically pursue national and great power agendas and are, as such, considered the crux of the Islamic world's chief problem. 'After people's independence was taken away from them, they were given all sorts of surrogates as long as it was not the new Caliphate', a spokesperson of Hizb Ut-Tahrir explained:

> The same applies to the UN and so on. These are nationalist confederations with an anarchic space and no legitimacy. The governments of the Muslim member states use some aspects of Islam or see Islam as a source of morality. But at the same time they rely on extraneous social and economic models despite the fact that Islam provides a transnational social and economic model itself.[16]

Additionally, individual leaders like Libya's Gaddafi and Iraq's Saddam Hussein, who once tried to rally pan-Islamic solidarity, had little credibility due to the secular nature of their regimes and the opportunistic nature of their respective pan-Islamic turns.

Hizb Ut-Tahrir's hallmark is the re-establishment of the Caliphate. This is a system of governance by Caliphs, who are successors to the Prophet Muhammad as the leader of the Muslim community.[17] Even though the concept may seem utopian, it bases itself on periods of Islamic history where entities under the rule of the Caliphate did exist, hence Hizb Ut-Tahrir's emphasis on its *re*-establishment rather than *establishment*. The major Caliphates that existed in Islamic history were those of the four Patriarchs of Medina (632–661), the Umayyad Caliphate of Damascus (661–750), the Abbasid Caliphate of Baghdad (750–1258) and finally the Ottoman Caliphate (1517–1923). The Patriarchal Caliphs of Medina were chosen by consensus of the Muslim community's elders and were known as leaders of the believers. After them, the Caliphate became hereditary and dominated by dynasties. The last, the Ottoman Caliphate, was abolished in early 1924, leaving the Ummah without a Caliph thereafter.[18]

None of the above-mentioned Caliphates ruled over the Muslim world in its present geographic scope nor were they states or super-states in the modern sense of the term.[19] Yet these periods of Caliphate rule coincide to a large extent with periods of remarkable advances in Muslim political, cultural and scientific power. The expansion of the Bilad Al-Islam in these periods of history was also a phase of globalization in its own right. Even if the enormous size and socio-cultural diversity of the geographic area that was affected unavoidably contained existing and new fault lines, according to Maurice Lombard:

> a crucial fact between the invaded West (the . . . Migration Period) and the invading West (the Crusades) was the creation of a vast politico-religious but especially economic domain from Central Asia to the Iberian Peninsula: the Muslim world. Its rapid creation was assorted with commercial expansion in the vast 'common market' that thus emerged. This commercial expansion was shored up by an immense influx of monetary metal, efficient systems of coin issuance and circulation, and the development of credit systems . . . as well as urban development either through the emergence of new cities or the rapid growth of ancient ones.[20]

The expansion of the land of Islam and its frontier securitization under different Caliphates increased the connectivity between a wide range of regions and centres, and integrated different economic systems in an entity defined by ideology and the institution of the Caliphate rather than by ethnicity and language. The rehabilitation and expansion of the old Roman postal system, the emergence of a renewed monetary system based on the gold standard and, especially, the (re)integration and (re)connection of agricultural core areas (Andalusia, the Nile basin, Mesopotamia), urban centres, continental and maritime (the Mediterranean, the Persian and Arabian Gulf, and the Caspian) trade route systems, and the presence of major poles of demand in Frankish Europe, the Byzantine Empire, Kievan Rus and the African kingdoms consolidated a sphere that dominated and had the initiative in that phase of globalization.[21] It is not that the Caliphates initiated all these realities and achievements all by themselves. Their merit was rather that their political project connected, revitalized and put to use realities and achievements that in many cases existed long before they arose. The Muslim world, both as an actual and virtual cultural sphere, did not disappear with the Umayyad and Abbasid Caliphates as political entities.

THE BELEAGUERED UMMAH AS A DEVELOPMENT PARADIGM

The Islamic Khilafah State as envisioned by Hizb Ut-Tahrir aims at the restoration of a state that existed in a previous phase of globalization. The historical precedent of the Islamic Golden Age, held against the present global position and predicament of the Ummah and the belief that Islamic evidences dictate that the Caliphate is the correct solution, define a space for an alternative political system and development model grafted on a common identity through both religion and the said position and predicament of the Ummah and the Bilad Al-Islam. In that respect, and in our opinion, Hizb Ut-Tahrir's pan-Islamic worldview and the development space that it defines have to be understood against four realities: the demographic share of adherents of Islam or at least populations associated with Islam in the overall world population; the global position of the Muslim world in the world economy; the presence and evolution of conflict in the Muslim world; and an opinion climate in Muslim societies that is, at least according to certain sources, favourable towards the goal of the unification of all Muslim countries and the re-establishment of the Caliphate.

As said, first, the development space is demographically defined. The actual and foreseen share of Muslims, or at least of populations who identify themselves or are associated with Islam to one extent or another, in the world population and in the global religious landscape in particular, has grown both naturally and through conversion from 13.1 per cent in 1900 over 19 and 21.7 per cent in the years 2000 and 2025 respectively, to an estimated 23.4 per cent in 2050. This is one of the largest growth rates after Pentecostal and non-denominational Christianity whose increase is predominantly fuelled by conversion. Even if Islam is not foreseen to overtake Christianity, the numerical size and its clear concentration in a largely continuous geographic area gives it the necessary critical mass on which to base ideological claims for a proper position and fair share in the global sphere.

Second, the development space is defined in terms of a predicament and position of the Muslim world in the global economy, and this at the socioeconomic and conflict level. This position is rather peripheral, with a share in the world economy (GDP, DFI, imports and exports) that is well below the Ummah's demographic share in the world population, and shares of extreme poverty, refugees and internally displaced persons that are clearly above it. Of course, these statistical averages say little about regional and sub-regional differences and are also determined by the presence of a number of low-income countries in sub-Saharan Africa as well as a number of large Complex Political Emergencies. At the same time, the Bilad Al-Islam has an impressive share of the world reserves in strategic resources like oil, natural gas and uranium, to name but three examples, and also shows a GDP growth slightly above the world average and well above that in OECD countries. This is partly explained by the presence of raw materials and their price dynamics, and the presence of a number of economic growth centres. Yet the nature, social impact and uneven horizontal as well as vertical spread of this growth is giving ground for various forms of contestation of the status quo.

The general level of warfare in Muslim majority contexts during the period 1946 to 2007 is about double the level in the non-Muslim and Muslim minority contexts when considered on a per capita basis. Until 1971–73, the armed conflict trend for Muslim majority contexts runs at about one-half of the magnitude for the non-Muslim contexts, with sudden increases around the foundation of the State of Israel, the start of the Indo-Pakistani conflict, and the zenith of both the Cold War and the decolonization wave in Africa and the Arab world. The trend in Muslim majority contexts increases sharply in 1979–83 and rapidly surpasses the level for non-Muslim countries in the wake of the Iranian revolution, the Iran-Iraq war and what is sometimes called the 'Second Cold War', which started with the USSR's invasion and occupation of Afghanistan. Armed conflict in the Muslim minority contexts is substantially lower than that in the non-Muslim contexts until 1989–91 (the unravelling of the USSR and Yugoslavia and the beginning of the civil wars in West Africa) even though they are roughly comparable in population.

Armed conflict and forthcoming Complex Political Emergencies are certainly not unique or limited to majority Muslim contexts. Yet the convergence of great power rivalry and proxy warfare, the proliferation of national states on the political world map and frontier securitization imply that a substantial number of armed conflict zones are indeed situated in a geographical area that largely overlaps that of what is known as the Muslim world. One of the causes lies in patterns of colonialism and neo-colonialism in combination with local social hierarchies and political power systems that deepen social tension. More importantly, the area of the Muslim world largely overlaps regions the physical geography of which is characterized by an abundance of strategic raw materials, oil and natural gas in the first place. This causes geopolitical competition and resource wars for control of these resources. Throughout its modern history – the imperial–colonial era, the Cold War and the present competition between established and emergent powers and centres for assets that increase their chances of survival in the global economy – this region has always found itself locked between colliding spheres of influence. Finally, the area also has a physical geography that is more vulnerable to natural disasters, earthquakes, regular droughts and deltaic floods in particular, which explains the sizeable number of humanitarian emergencies and affected populations.[22]

Hizb Ut-Tahrir's pan-Islamic worldview does not consider the above situations to be a fatality nor a matter of resources or capacity, since the Bilad Al-Islam has the necessary geostrategic position, the urban and agricultural core areas, the natural resources, the economic and industrial potential, the military strength, the demographic share in the world population, the intellectual legacy and the common ideological framework to become a superpower in the new global order that shall emerge from what the organization perceives as the ongoing decline of the long-dominant West.[23] The crux of the problem is rather of a political nature, that is, the lack of political unity and dominance of non-Islamic development models in the Islamic world, and an interest by various actors outside as well as inside the Bilad Al-Islam to keep the situation as such.

The fourth reality against which Hizb Ut-Tahrir's worldview and the development space that it defines have to be understood against is an opinion climate in Muslim societies that is favourable to the goal of the unification of all Muslim countries and the re-establishment of the Caliphate. The existence of such a positive opinion climate is not only something propounded by Hizb Ut-Tahrir itself, it is also suggested by a number of opinion polls. In a survey conducted by the Program on International Policy Attitudes by the University of Maryland in early 2007 in four majority Muslim societies it is suggested that if not clear majorities then at least substantial parts of the respondents agree with the objective of unifying the Muslim countries under a Caliphate. According to the survey data, averages of 36 per cent agreed strongly and 29 per cent agreed somewhat with this goal, while country-wise support stood at 74 per cent in Pakistan, 71 per cent in Morocco, 67 per cent in Egypt and 49 per cent in Indonesia. Although the study discusses the unification of the Islamic world under the Caliphate as one of Al-Qaeda's and not Hizb Ut-Tahrir's goals, it is frequently quoted in the latter's publications and communications to argue that there exists a large support base for the idea of re-establishing the Caliphate in general.[24] Similarly, a survey conducted by the Pew Forum on Religion & Public Life in 2010 indicates that an average of 52 per cent of the Muslim respondents in sub-Saharan Africa expect the Caliphate, as the golden era of Islamic rule, to be re-established during their lifetime.[25] This does not mean that the respondents actually support the idea, but that they have at least expectations about it and do not consider it absurd or utopian.

RECLAIMING GLOBALIZATION?

Hizb Ut-Tahrir's world and development views do not contest globalization and modern technological achievements and resources per se, but rather its direction of globalization dominated as it is or perceived to be by the USA and the OECD sphere and by neo-liberal capitalism. At first glance, this is very similar to the alter-globalist movement. This is not the way the group sees itself though. 'Since capitalism is dominant in this phase of globalization it has become intertwined with it, yet both are separate', a party member who we interviewed said:

> Globalization has been going on for centuries even before capitalism arose, so what we have now is a collision between Islam and capitalism which appropriated globalization, rather than one between Islam and globalization. Alter-globalists, for their part, often equate capitalism to globalization. They feel pressure from neo-liberal globalization, they see an erosion of the national level, and so they retreat to either the local or global level in reaction. They don't want to replace power with power but are rather disappointed by the apathetic masses and maximalize a space for themselves. It's essentially anti-political. By contrast, Islam and Muslims do rather want to replace power with power and bring in a uniform ideology rather than just contest and resist or focus on local issues, since liberation cannot go through individual space but through an authority.[26]

By stressing the role of the state in that process, Hizb Ut-Tahrir's ideology and discourse actually reflect a reality noticed by Olivier Roy, who states that while regimes and rulers may be despised in much of the Muslim world, the state as a re-distributor of wealth and power, and defender of common interests is not.[27] 'The biggest problem of alter-globalism is that it is lacking in solutions', added another party respondent. 'It's one thing to have an analysis and a critique, another to have a solution. And this ultimately gets us into ideology'.[28] What it comes to is reclaiming the initiative in globalization. What Islamic alternative to capitalism is foreseen then? In order to have an answer to this question, we took a model developed by Leslie Sklair that compares capitalist globalization with Sklair's proposed socialist and human rights-based alternative to capitalist globalization that pretty much reflects that put forward by mainstream alter-globalism, and added a third column to define Hizb Ut-Tahrir's alternative, the economy under the Islamic Khilafah State, as compared to the two others. The result is shown in Table 23.1.

Table 23.1 Hizb Ut-Tahrir's Islamic globalization against capitalist and socialist globalization

Capitalist Globalization[a]	Socialist globalization[a]	The Islamic Khilafah State[b]
Export-orientation	Revival of local economy	Localism preferred based on a general policy of self-sufficiency; domestic economy to drive growth; trade based on strategic and national interests, without tariffs and dependence on reciprocity; export-orientation, on the condition that revenue from the export of public goods such as natural resources serve the public good; revival of the local economy as per speciality and possibility
Foreign borrowing to service debt	Renegotiate foreign debt	Live within means as foreign debt brings foreign dependency; renegotiate foreign debt and make it compliant with Shar'iah (no interest) in parts of the IKS that have debt; reduce or eliminate regional and sub-regional imbalances within the IKS to reduce the need for external loans; maximum self-sufficiency
Austerity measures to pay the debt	Local economic expansion	Repay use of public goods (energy), borrow from domestic citizens and tax rich citizens (from surplus assets); create space and possibility for local economic expansion and eliminate the base for inflation through economic policies based on Islam and Shar'iah (gold/silver standard), smaller taxed footprint through an Islam- and Shar'iah-based taxation system (wealth not income and consumption oriented); focus on the family and individual charity as the core responsible unit of social protection, and social protection by the state in extreme cases
Shrinking state	Community control of the local economy	Strong welfare safety net for the weak and vulnerable; all other male adults are obliged to work; role of state defined and fixed based on ideology not expediency; alleviation of absolute poverty is an important economic goal; *Zakaat* (Islamic solidarity tax) irrespective of need ensures that the state always has a role; well-defined roles and responsibilities of the state as per Shar'iah, IKS does not go below or beyond these roles; family and faith as core elements of the social tissue and social-economic organization
Export zones processing imported components	Exports linked to local economy	Export zones: a means to an end; prohibition of certain imports and exports as per Shar'iah; emphasis on export and processing zones or local economy as per local conditions and comparative advantages
Race to the bottom for wages and conditions to attract investment	Increased wages to stimulate the local economy	Wages determination reflects the requirements of the highly productive domestic economy based on the policy of self-sufficiency; wage setting prohibited but fair wage encouraged through active God-conscience behaviour; rights of workers guaranteed by the state; natural conditions in the IKS and Islamic rules to protect investment; prohibition of certain imports, exports and investments as per Shar'iah; Shar'iah rulings around wages; the state does not interfere in matters of price setting

Table 23.1 (continued)

Capitalist Globalization[a]	Socialist globalization[a]	The Islamic Khilafah State[b]
Transnational corporation (TNC) and finance-driven economy	Economy driven by producers and consumers' cooperatives	Strong domestic economy driven by firms owned by state citizens, irrespective of religion; profit and non-profit-driven companies and partnerships encouraged by minimum taxation and low regulation; limited scope for TNCs under Shar'iah; anti-monopoly legislation in Shar'iah; economy definitely not finance driven, but low tax (wealth not income tax oriented) – and ownership law driven – high velocity in the circulation of wealth
Transnational capitalist class (TCC)-driven competing state system	Democratic unions of producer–consumer cooperatives	Wealth circulation actively promoted ensures greater economic parity; distribution of wealth actively promoted by God-conscience behaviour and pro investment tax system; state guarantees rights of workers, resolving industrial disputes; Islamic anti-monopoly legislation; anti-nationalism: within the IKS, the existence of the supra-state itself eliminates the need for TCC-driven competition between states; cooperation is based on need and regulated by Islamic regulation of trade
Culture-ideology of consumerism	Culture-ideology of human rights on a global scale	Consumption based on living within one's means – distinction between satisfaction of basic needs for all, then enablement of satisfying more luxurious needs; prohibition of industries relating to vices: drugs, alcohol, gambling; God-conscience behaviour pervades all aspects of the economy and impacts how needs and wants are satisfied by goods and services; rights and duties inherent to Islam and Shar'iah law (protection of honour, mind, wealth, beliefs); culture of meeting the needs of the people and maximizing their potential (social, economic, spiritual)

Notes:
[a] As defined in Sklair (2002).
[b] See note 32.

Sources:
Table compiled by the author on the basis of Sklair (2002), Table 11.1, p. 311.
Interview with Jamal B. Harwood, member of the Executive Committee of Hizb Ut-Tahrir, London, 5 April 2011 and e-mail exchanges with the same respondent on 6 and 12 April 2011.
An-Nabhani (1990–97).
Al-Badil (undated).

The antithesis to Islamic globalization and economic development as it is proposed above is not so much 'the West' per se as extraneous development models copied by elite groups in Muslim countries and heralded, or perceived to be heralded, as a new economic model for the Muslim World in general. One case that is brought forward in Hizb Ut-Tahrir's development-related discourse and literature in this regard is the Gulf city-state of Dubai, which, with its rapid modernization and 19 free economic zones, its reorientation from an extractive oil economy to a service hub, grandiose urban development, and a cosmopolitan and libertine air brought by a population that consists of more than 85 per cent of expatriates and immigrant workers, came to symbolize capitalist globalization.[29] 'For many, Dubai indeed physically symbolizes the present phase of globalization, and it's what some would like to see happen for the Muslim world in general', a party cadre and specialist on economic and development issues told the author:

> But it's a fake model that is not sustainable. Most of Dubai's development is based on white elephants – impressive skyscrapers, artificial islands, theme parks and tax-free shopping centres – and prestige events. Wealth is not prohibited in Islam. But if natural resources like oil, on which Dubai's wealth was initially based, are sold out to multinational companies and prop up tyrants, and if one bases development on a bubble instead of following Islamic economic principles then one becomes extremely vulnerable to the flaws of the capitalist system, as was shown after the debt crisis of 2008. They reap as they sow, as they follow a failed, unsustainable model. Moreover, Dubai's development is based on social inequities that are forbidden by Islam: the massive import of cheap labour that is harshly treated and is subject to salary gaps depending on its origin and gender.[30]

Dubai's perceived collapse is also caused by a complete lack of industrialization and self-sufficiency in what the party calls real, tangible goods and services, the almost complete dependence on unsteady transnational companies, imported human resources and foreign cash lines, and the abandonment of Islamic economic principles that advocate the opposite.[31]

Another case that, for Hizb Ut-Tahrir, illustrates the impact of non- or anti-Islamic economic development policies is Pakistan. 'Land and the feudal system are the crux there', the same party respondent found:

> In Islam, land, except for public lands with natural resources like oil and gas, public waterways and public roads, can be privately owned and owned by companies. But it cannot be monopolized nor leased, except in a few well-defined areas. The monopolization by a few families of large tracts of land is not accepted in Islam. But that's what happens in Pakistan, by the landowners and absentee landlords, by agro-industrial companies from the Gulf who buy up land to grow food, and so on. The crux of the country's and society's problem is the land issue and neo-feudalism.[32]

In Pakistan, two-thirds of the population is rural and two-thirds of these work in agriculture. The negative effect on chronic poverty in Pakistan of the high degree of inequality in land ownership and the exploitative practices attached to it, is indeed something recognized by large international development institutions.

According to one study of 2002, some 65 per cent of the large and very large land estates in Pakistan were owned by 7 per cent of the rural households, while 49 per cent of rural households had no land at all. Likewise, 64 per cent of the poorest households were landless and held less than 10 per cent of the land.[33] Land inequality and feudalism also increase vulnerability to the effects of natural disasters, as became evident in some parts of the country during the floods in 2010.[34] Many large land owners are also politicians or otherwise connected with the bureaucratic establishment. For Hizb Ut-Tahrir, the situation is exacerbated by what it sees as the complicity and convergence of interests between corrupt national and local elites, and external centres of power who use these elites to implement their policies at the detriment of large parts of the population. Examples that the party mentions in its publications are the impact of the debt crisis on Pakistan, the IMF-driven elimination of government subsidies for basic social services and agriculture, high external debt, Pakistan's costly involvement in the US-led global war on terror that drains substantial resources for what is seen as a war against Islam and Muslims and the abysmal corruption among Westernized elite groups and the current civilian government in particular. The fact that these corrupt elites are entrenched in power through a Western-style, parliamentary democratic system that is based on man-made and not divine laws, and which is brought to power by elections that were declared free and fair by international observers, show for Hizb Ut-Tahrir that democracy is no prerequisite or catalyst for development as some development theorists claim.[35, 36]

THE PRACTICE OF 'PAN-ISLAMISM'

What is shown by the above is that, rather than bemoan moral decay and loss of traditions as alleged consequences of globalization, Hizb Ut-Tahrir formulates critiques on existing situations that indeed do contain elements that one also finds in critiques by alter-globalists, but that serve as a base to formulate what the group and its followers see as the Islamic alternative and solution to these situations, thereby basing itself on historical examples when spheres and entities defined by Islam hold the initiative in globalization. Now what are the characteristics of Hizb Ut-Tahrir's organization and political methodology, and do these meet (some of) the characteristics of the alter-globalist movement as they were identified by Gawor at the beginning of this chapter? Olivier Roy describes Hizb Ut-Tahrir as a movement that started in reality and for the liberation of a national context (Palestine) yet, contrary to other initially pan-Islamic movements like the Muslim Brotherhood, evolved into a fully transnational and de-territorialized movement. Like Salafism, Roy says, it belongs to a category of neo-fundamentalist or second-generation Islamist movements that propagate a 'true Islamic' alternative cleansed of cumbersome and corrupted cultural factors and in which belonging is not defined in terms of nationality, ethnicity and race, language, kinship or descent, but of ideology and membership of the Ummah.[37]

Hizb Ut-Tahrir's globalist and pan-Islamic character first come forward in its ideology. This ideology is Islam, without mentioning whether it follows Sunnism or Shiism or any particular current or school of law therein. 'Despite their absolute condemnation of the current situation in the so-called Muslim world, Hizb Ut-Tahrir's members do not at all see themselves as the only true Muslims', Jean-François Mayer remarks:

> In fact, despite the current conditions in the Muslim world, they would not label ordinary Muslims as bad Muslims, but rather see themselves as the vanguard of the reformation of the Muslim world and, most of all, as the bearers of a fully Islamic political solution. This contrasts strongly with the views of some radical Islamic groups, which justify their violent actions by claims of a general state of apostasy.[38]

A controversial issue is the group's alleged orientation towards Salafism, a puritanical Sunni current along with which Hizb Ut-Tahrir is mentioned by Roy as an example of de-territorialized neo-fundamentalism.[39] 'It all depends on how one defines Salafism', a party spokesman said:

> It has multiple meanings and conceptions to people. Many people equate Salafism to Wahhabism, which is the official doctrine in Saudi Arabia. If it's what that they think, well, in that case we are definitely not inspired by it. The house of Saud and the Wahhabi establishment were imperialist agents who contributed to the destruction of the Ottoman Caliphate. Wahhabism legitimizes a tribal monarchy. This is not what Islam stands for. Salafism, however, means to be led by the example of the Salaf As-Salih, the companions of the Prophet and the first generations of Muslims as you know. Muslims respect them and so do we.[40]

As such, the group certainly has a Salafist orientation. 'But in fact', the respondent continued:

> Islam is Islam. We do not follow one particular thought or school of law. For example, in Sunnism, there are four major schools of law which are centred around authoritative scholars to which people turn to know what the law is when they are faced with certain issues. From our objective of re-establishing the Islamic Khilafah State, we consult scholars from different schools and we use the views and arguments from the strongest Islamic sources.

A factor that sets Hizb Ut-Tahrir apart from more extreme if not violent forms of Salafism is the absence of a virulent discourse against Shiites and Sufism, although some observers see this as a mere tactical move to widen the party's support base. 'We do not attach significance to sectarian identities. Even if we do not agree with the Shiites on a number of points, we still recognize them as Muslims and part of the reality of the Ummah', another of the party's cadres explained. 'Those who want to fan sectarian strife want to divide the Ummah, which, in turn, serves the interests of the enemies of Islam'.[41] Regarding its stance towards Sufism, the party criticizes attempts by the USA and Britain as well as by the regimes in Uzbekistan and Pakistan to co-opt Sufism as an ideological tool against 'extremism'. It thereby argues that they use a travesty of Sufism that does not reflect 'moderate Sufism' and the role it played in Islamic history at all, thereby pointing at authoritative Sufi scholars, the importance of Sufis under the Caliphates and the leadership of Sufi leaders in anti-colonial uprisings in the nineteenth century.[42]

Hizb Ut-Tahrir's globalist and pan-Islamic character further comes forward in its organizational structure and geographic scope. The movement is active, or has at least been manifesting itself in one way and to one extent or another, in some 40 countries, yet hardly any reliable figures exist on its actual membership. Party cadres themselves remain vague about the issue when asked. 'If our aim is to convince people to re-establish the Islamic Khilafah State, what criteria of success do we use?' one of the party's spokesmen explained:

> It's not that we want everyone to become Hizb Ut-Tahrir members, but rather that there is an opinion climate and that the key ideas circulate in interaction with society. The party is not an aim in itself, like the Islamic Khilafah State is. We also do not believe in a ruling party system in Islam. The party is rather a channel of ideas.[43]

The attendance at its activities has ranged from two dozen at seminars on specific topics in various European cities to over an estimated 10000 at a rally for the re-establishment of the Caliphate in El-Bireh on the West Bank in 2010, to the some 80000 people at the International Khilafah Conference that was organized by the party's Indonesian chapter in Jakarta in 2007. Likewise, of the estimated 8000 political prisoners in Uzbekistan in 2003, more than half were believed to be arrested on charges of belonging to the group.[44]

In terms of organization, Hizb Ut-Tahrir is not a global network of different, more or less like-minded organizations, but a movement with a global pyramidal structure. This structure, set up by An-Nabhani in the movement's early days, is quite similar to and likely inspired by that of revolutionary movements that were active in the Middle East in those days, more specifically the Pan-Arabic nationalist Baath and, to a lesser extent, communist parties. Three main levels of party work are evident from the party's hierarchy and organization.

First, although Al-Quds is set to be the capital of the future Islamic Khilafah State, the movement has no clear headquarters or global capital. Many analysts and journalists who cover the group believe that Hizb Ut-Tahrir's global headquarters and nerve centre are situated in London, but that is probably a misperception. The party's branch there is indeed one of the most vocal and also most eye-catching internationally, first, since London is one of the centres of the English-speaking world, second, because of the global influence of the English language that it uses, and third, because of the multinational (Pakistani, Bangladeshi, Arab and African) immigrant origins of its members and cadres there. Citing security concerns, party or party-associated respondents remain vague about the whereabouts of Sheikh Ata Abu Rashta, an engineer who is Hizb Ut-Tahrir's third global leader since he was elected in 2003, limiting answers to 'somewhere in the Middle East' when the question is asked.[45]

Second, according to Suha Taji-Farouki, the gravity centre of movement de facto lays at the provincial level and with the provincial committees for reasons of security (that is, to avoid the movement collapsing at once in case of 'decapitation') as well as manageability.[46] The provinces, which are a purely administrative given for the party, mostly coincide with existing countries and national states (for example, the Wilayah of Pakistan) although in certain cases, party provinces cover only a part of a country (for instance, the Wilayah of the Crimean Peninsula, which is a southern part of Ukraine). Hizb Ut-Tahrir makes a distinction between two sorts of provinces: the Majal or specific Muslim areas and societies that were previously within the Khilafah State, which are capable of becoming an Islamic Khilafah State at this time and where the party wants to change society; and provinces outside the Majal, which include Muslim areas that do not have the necessary conditions as well as non-Muslim countries and societies (the European Union, the United States, Australia, the non-Muslim parts of Russia) where immigration and other historical and personal circumstances brought Muslims to live but are neither targeted for societal change nor for integration in the Islamic Khilafah State. Outside the Majal, the party limits its work to educating the Muslims who live there so that they remain with Islam and support the establishment of the Caliphate.[47] In practice, this approach delivers what, in alter-globalist terminology, is called a 'North–South interaction', which is shown in the Table 23.2.

Third, rather than being based on a network of civil society organizations like alter-globalism is, Hizb Ut-Tahrir is embedded and has expanded in a transnational space created by both horizontal mobility and migration, and the rapid growth of global communication.[48] Second-generation Muslim immigrants in the West have been key players in the party's development and activity of the last two decades, while in some cases like Pakistan, sections of Hizb Ut-Tahrir have been established by 'returnees' with roots in the country but who grew up in immigrant communities abroad.[49] The party makes maximum use of modern communication technologies and media, the internet in the first

Table 23.2 Hizb Ut-Tahrir's North–South interaction

Hizb Ut-Tahrir in the Muslim World	Hizb Ut-Tahrir in the West
Main focus and main space for change: bears the brunt of the modern global paradigm	Was not under Islamic rule: has therefore no space and no theatre for change
Struggle with and against the incumbent secular regimes or monarchies	No struggle for the overthrow of governments there, yet critical of and hostile towards the support given by Western democracies to regimes and monarchies in the Muslim world
Re-establishment of the Islamic way of life that once existed there	Muslim minorities face pressure to abandon their Muslim identity; hence the main struggle in the West consists of making Muslims keep, or return to, Islamic identity and values and keeping Muslim minorities connected to the wider Islamic world

Source: Table compiled by the author on the basis of interviews with Taji Mustafa, Media Representative of Hizb Ut-Tahrir in Great Britain, and Hassan Choudhury, member of Hizb Ut-Tahrir and contributor to *New Civilisation Magazine*, London, 5 April 2011.

place.[50] It does this to advocate the re-establishment of the Caliphate and discuss a wide range of issues, from current affairs to developmental and social topics like environment and gender, from that perspective. It does so through its official section portals as well as a wide range of non-official sites that largely reflect the movement's views (*Al-Badil*, *Qirim Vilayeti*, *Expliciet*) and official (*Al-Wayi*, *Khilafah Magazine*) and associated journals (*New Civilisation Magazine*, *Vozrozhdenie*, *Halifat*, *Expliciet* . . .) in over a dozen languages.[51] Despite the variety of publications, portals and the differing degrees to which they are connected to Hizb Ut-Tahrir, the views and issues that are raised do often show a striking uniformity. The party's communication approach wants to confront Muslims in different parts of the world with the predicaments and challenges faced by co-religionaries in other parts of the world as well as with the causes thereof. It advances Islamic perspectives and alternatives, thereby taking up issues that were long thought to be issues confined to alter-globalism.[52]

This brings us at once to the local level of organization, which consists of two sub-levels: the major urban centres, which are targeted in their capacity of economic and political centres and are historically places from where Islam spread, and the most basic level (the 'grassroots level' in development parlance), which consists of cells in neighbourhoods or institutions, and of individuals.

What interaction is there between the local and global level, and are there symbolic causes of Hizb Ut-Tahrir that symbolize the connection between local situations and global power structures, as the Zapatista insurgency and the predicament of the native population in the Mexican state of Chiapas were for the alter-globalists at one time?[53]

We obviously interact with and work at the local level because Muslims and party members live in daily realities and local environments', a party spokesman believed. 'As such we try to

> explain to people that the local situations that they are confronted with are, in fact, the result of a wrong global order of things, of the capitalist system, and that Islam has an answer. As for symbolic causes, plenty are found in the daily reality and in current affairs. The border situation between Gaza and Egypt, and Mubarak's rcle in the embargo against Gaza, for example, show the effect of artificial borders and nationalism. Or take the Arab revolutions, which showed that the Muslims were weary with the corrupt tyrant and neo-liberal capitalism that were imposed on them. Many situations are recognizable from Islamic history too. The persecution of Muslims in Uzbekistan, for instance, reminds one of the Prophet Muhammad and his companions in Mecca in the early days of Islam.[54]

A fourth factor that comes forward from Hizb Ut-Tahrir's organization is, that unlike Hamas or the Muslim Brotherhood, to name but two examples, Hizb Ut-Tahrir has no formal social or charitable wing, even though members of the party's Indonesian section have been involved in humanitarian work and operated three health centres after the earthquake in West Sumatra in late 2009.[55] The absence of a social and charitable wing is not accidental yet a conscious choice integrated in Hizb Ut-Tahrir's political methodology, which states that:

> the organizations which are established for welfare activities, such as building schools, hospitals, helping the poor, the orphans and the needy, . . . although they are of the things which Islam encourages Muslims to carry out, do not have any relationship with the vital issue for Muslims and they would not achieve the goal for which Muslims must work to achieve . . . and distract the group to work to establish (the Caliphate). Moreover . . . the permanent caring for the affairs (of the people) is a duty which belongs to the states not the . . . individuals.[56]

'The struggle for the Caliphate is a political and intellectual struggle, not a social or humanitarian one', a party cadre explained:

> The Prophet Muhammad carried out a political and intellectual struggle. The work against poverty only arose after the foundation of the Islamic State, whose role it is. What happened in West Sumatra was an initiative of our Indonesian members but not of the party. There are party obligations and there are individual obligations, and helping people in need is one of the individual obligations in Islam. Our members live in communities and interact with the people there. After the earthquake, they could not sit passively and do nothing. So as such, this is what they did. We live in a society and have to care after people's interests but link that to a political goal. So social and charitable work with a political message for the sake of vital issues is possible, for example campaigns against drugs and offering Islam as an alternative.[57]

Finally, a fifth remark is that despite regular attempts by law enforcement and intelligence agencies and think tanks to link the group to terrorism or, at least, to consider it an advocate of armed struggle or what is considered to be terrorism, there are no credible indicators that Hizb Ut-Tahrir as such has been involved in acts of terrorism or that it has a paramilitary wing like Hamas, to name but one example.[58] Hizb Ut-Tahrir condemns indiscriminate suicide bombings, sectarian violence and attacks against minorities (Shiites, Christians) and often considers terrorist attacks to be either part of an imperialist plot implemented by agents and mercenaries to discredit Islam and divide the Ummah, or acts by the corrupt regimes to deviate popular attention from their policies or to justify repression or military operations.[59] At the same time, even if it is not involved in armed struggle itself, Hizb Ut-Tahrir believes that in certain cases, armed resistance by Muslims against Kafir (non-Muslim) aggressors and occupants and oppression by Taghut (tyrant) rulers who collaborate with the infidel agressors and leave no possibility for non-violent opposition is that of Jihad ad-Daf (defensive Jihad).[60,61]

Rather than social and charitable work or armed struggle, Hizb Ut-Tahrir's political methodology is, in its own words, based on the struggle of the Prophet Muhammad, which consists of three stages: the stage of culturing or finding the individuals who are or can be convinced by the thought and method of the party so as to establish a vanguard group; the stage of interaction with the Ummah in order for it to work for Islam in life, state and society, adopt the interests of the Ummah, and challenge the current rulers in Muslim countries; and finally the stage of taking the government, implementing Islam completely and taking its message to the world.[62] The party is not so much directed toward seizing the state and then forcing what is seen as a truly Islamic alternative upon society, but rather directed at persuading society, or segments thereof, to accept its ideas, which would then lead to a change in regime. A key element herein is the concept of Ahl An-Nusrat (People of Support). Historically, this refers to the support that the Prophet Muhammad rallied among a number of Arab tribes while establishing control over Medina in the year 622.

In the modern meaning, Ahl An-Nusrat refers to existing groups and institutions in society that are technically or militarily capable of removing the present authorities through a coup d'état and establishing, securing and maintaining the Islamic alternative.[63] 'The Ahl An-Nusrat are people who influence key players', a party member found. 'When one moves, the others move. They have a choice to make. Either they go with the regime or they go with the people who are struggling and this includes serious risks'.[64] These actors and institutions vary from context to context but most often refer to the armed forces since in several large and strategic Muslim countries like Pakistan, Indonesia and Egypt the military are the backbone of the state *and* also control, to one degree or another, key sectors and assets of the economy.[65] Ideological activity is therefore often concentrated on the armed forces. 'The support of Ahl An-Nusrat is indeed vital for the Islamic project', confirmed a party cadre. 'We have to avoid a repetition of the Algerian tragedy between 1991 and 1994, where the army did not support the Islamic change and the country slipped into civil war. This is not the aim'.[66]

Hizb Ut-Tahrir's hopes in the military are particularly clear in its discourse on Pakistan. In Bangladesh, where historically the army also has large political clout, the party supported a heavily repressed mutiny of a border guard unit in Dhaka against the 'corrupt and treacherous' civilian government in early 2009, while more recently it called, in vain, on the Egyptian army to intervene in Libya to stop the civil war, depose Gaddafi and prevent the intervention of foreign powers.[67] The foreseen role for the military, both as major stakeholders in the state and in the economy in several parts of the Majal, therefore also has development relevance just as it is a far cry from the engagement of civil society in alter-globalism. Despite its 'internationalist' character and the presence of issues in its discourse that one also finds in that of alter-globalists, Hizb Ut-Tahrir does not want to be seen as an element of global civil society, which Gawor identifies as one of the key characteristics of alter-globalism.

'To start with', an earlier-quoted party respondent stressed:

> we are a global political party with a uniform ideology, and not a loose confederation or mosaic of all sorts of non-governmental organizations and associations who do have a number

> of common issues and a common opponent perhaps, but no clearly defined, common and comprehensive alternative to the capitalist order. Civil society is the third sphere in a society, positioned directly between the private individuals and the state. It is made up of private individuals working for the public good. Civil society is variable in its potency and strength since some states compress the available public space and prevent individuals from entering it unless they act in line with the state's aims. However, this does not mean civil society does not always exist. It does but it can be incredibly weak . . . [68]

> . . . Civil society as it is defined nowadays is rather a recent discussion whereas in Islam, to be critical of unjust rulers has been a prescription and a natural fact for centuries. Civil society is only a reality at the meeting point or junction of the individuals and a state. By definition, it cannot exist if there are no individuals and state to exist in between. It definitely cannot exist outside a state since it can only exist in between individuals and a state. And since there is no global state there can be no global civil society. There can only be civil societies within national states. The same goes for the role of the local. For alter-globalists 'going local' is a reaction, whereas for us, it's a natural habitat. Civil society, non-governmental organizations and other elements of alter-globalism cannot be Ahl An-Nusrat since they don't have the position or the weight to be so. They often have an extremely negative stance towards the state and especially the military, whereas we don't.[69]

CONCLUSION: BREAKING THE LIMITS OF 'ALTER-GLOBALISM'

This brings us back to the initial question of this chapter: are Islamic movements, in this case the transnational movement Hizb Ut-Tahrir and its concepts of restoration of the Caliphate, a form of alter-globalism? If we look at Fougier's definition of alter-globalism at the beginning of this chapter, then we see that Hizb Ut-Tahrir indeed denounces the neo-liberal nature of the current process of globalization, aspires to other forms of globalization and tries to link this goal to different struggles that are at the local and national level. The difference with alter-globalism is that it does so from a fixed and comprehensive worldview and as a global vanguard party rather than a civil society network. The purpose is to regain the initiative and the upper hand in globalization for a specific group and development space that is defined by religious and ideological affiliation.

In terms of Gawor's characteristics of alter-globalism, Hizb Ut-Tahrir and its pan-Islamic alternative do oppose the globalist practice of reducing the description and evaluation of reality only to the economic dimension, yet considers economics, just like society, to be defined and led by a comprehensive religious framework. Likewise, it also opposes the surrendering of all areas of social life (education, culture, social security and welfare) and defends the state 'as the institution that is to represent the interest of members of this community on the one hand, and on the other the demand for global, legal and political regulations aimed at controlling financial markets'[70] at least in those areas where Islam defines a role and responsibility for the state. Similarly, since both society and the economy are regulated by Islam, closer interaction between economies and societies come natural in the group's view, whereas the necessary coordination of exchange of goods and services and provision of basic economic rights, environmental protection and, finally, the promotion of the model of sustainable development is set in the institution that is to apply Islam in all its aspects.

The recognition of the results of 'the information revolution' by Hizb Ut-Tahrir is obvious through its political methodology and the intensive use of the internet to spread its message, expand its virtual presence and use free movement of information as the main mode of social influence. The use of modern communication technology and other technological achievements to propagate a concept that was defined in the early years of Islam is not seen as contradictory but rather a way to reclaim globalization in this phase of history. Hizb Ut-Tahrir believes that values, norms, and the organizations of society and economy must be anchored in Islam and in comprehensive divine laws than are not subject to changes, no matter what the historical circumstances are.[71] While for Gawor, alter-globalism opposes social uniformity and supports all local movements, and uses the opportunities offered by globalization processes to guarantee the simultaneous preservation of traditional local (regional, ethnic, national) models and values and build a 'glocal' social order, Hizb Ut-Tahrir and the Islamic political alternative that it advances see the local as a natural working and living environment that is affected by wider global processes. As such, the local and local struggles are both a base and links in a project of uniformity as a reaction against another uniformity, at least in the targeted development space defined by religious affiliation. Finally, as was made clear in the previous section of this chapter, Hizb Ut-Tahrir does not believe in global civil society nor does it want to be part of it.

So there are similarities as well as fundamental differences between Hizb Ut-Tahrirs pan-Islamism and alter-globalism. Where does it fit in the contestation of the current form of globalization then? Fougier distinguishes four types, which are represented in Figure 23.1.

At first glance, Hizb Ut-Tahrir fits best into the category of radical contestation, in the sense that it completely rejects the existing economic system and its principles, mindset, institutions and actors, aims less at social revolution than at defining and promoting utopian alternatives and, even if it has no paramilitary wing and remains non-violent, considers certain armed struggles against what it sees as oppression as 'defensive Jihad'. Some interviewed party cadres seem to look in the same direction. 'We are radical in the sense that we want a complete change but with an outlined alternative that can be applied. We are not reformist and do not believe in social revolution and violent resistance but in change that is people-led and that has the support of the Ahl An-Nusrat'.[72] So far, Hizb Ut-Tahrir's proposed alternative has not been put into experimental practice among certain groups or in certain spaces, but in our view, this may not remain the case. Depending on the evolution of the situation in some parts of the Muslim world, an entity, parallel or in actual power, in a limited geographic area can emerge that considers itself a 'core Caliphate'.[73] Likewise, the 'utopian' character of Hizb Ut-Tahrir's alternative is relative, for what is utopian in current historical circumstances might be less so once these circumstances change. Predictions in say, 1980, that a fledgling European super-state would one day include portions of Yugoslavia and the USSR were considered utopian as well, whereas now it is reality.

Hizb Ut-Tahrir's Islamic alternative applies in the first place to the Bilad Al-Islam more than to the world in general. As such, it also contains elements of contestation for alternative governance in the sense that it wants to counterbalance existing institutions and centres by its own alternative, the Islamic Khilafah State, and rejects cooperation with international organizations, international financial institutions and multinational corporations that embody the unjust order of things. Party members we spoke to

Ethical contestation Denunciation based on ethical values and norms of the social inequalities, environmental damage and the non-democratic character of, or caused by, 'corporate-led globalization' and of the policies of global organizations and structures that propagate it Rehabilitation of the role of the state as a protector against and counterweight to 'corporate-led globalization' Focuses on moral pressure, watchfulness and denunciation (cf. the 'watchdog groups')	*Reformist contestation* Economic system reform through the acceptation and application of social, environmental and democratic norms by multinational corporations as well as governments Strategy of dialogue and cooperation with international organizations, international financial institutions and multinational corporations Mostly by traditional NGOs
Radical contestation Complete rejection of the existing economic system and its principles, mindset, institutions and actors Aims less at social revolution than at defining and promoting utopian alternatives that are sometimes put into experimental practice among certain groups or in certain spaces Often, though not always, violent or at least sympathetic to armed struggle that is considered justified	*Contestation for alternative governance* Transformation of the economic system and its principles, mindset, institutions and actors Wants either to counterbalance existing institutions by strengthening others (e.g., ILO, UNCTAD), put existing institutions under 'genuine democratic control' or dismantle them and create alternative institutions and structures Stresses importance of 'global fiscality' Rejects cooperation with international organizations, international financial institutions and multinational corporations

Source: Table compiled by the author on the basis of Fougier (2002).

Figure 23.1 Fougier's typology of globalization contestation

propose to put Hizb Ut-Tahrir and like-minded movements in a category not included in the typology above: ideological contestation:

> We are indeed radical, but the four categories are still in the capitalist framework. We see contestation differently. We do not contest globalization; we contest capitalism and seek to remove the nation states and the continuation of the colonial order through the nation-state. In the end it's about the question: who makes the law: man or God?[74]

To conclude, in our opinion, Hizb Ut-Tahrir and its pan-Islamic worldview are alter-globalist in a way that challenges the definitions and characteristics of alter-globalism at times when alter-globalism ceased to be a, real or claimed, 'comparative advantage' of the left.

NOTES

1. For a discussion of earlier phases and patterns of globalization, see, for instance, Kennedy (1989, pp. 3–38), Osterhammel and Petersson (2007) and Blancheton (2008).

2. Fougier (2008, p. 5). The translations from quotes in languages other than English are the author's. For the original text, refer to the source.
3. Gawor (2008, p. 129).
4. Ibid., p. 35.
5. For more on the relationship between the alter-globalist movement and Islamic movements and opinion leaders and the different attitudes within the first toward the latter, see Fougier (2008, pp. 95–100).
6. Mayer (2007, p. 62).
7. Gawor (2008, pp. 129–30).
8. Filiu (2008, p. 15). For a semi-official perception from the region of Hizb Ut-Tahrir in the former USSR, see Rabbimov (2004).
9. *Al-Badil* (undated). A similar discourse can be found in the online analytical manifesto by Khan (2008, pp. 29–31).
10. Hizb Ut-Tahrir Media Office web portal, category 'Hizb Ut-Tahrir', available at: www.hizb-ut-tahrir.info/info/english.php/category_en/categ_415; accessed on 3 April 2010.
11. Ibid.
12. Following the Arab-Israeli war of 1948, East Jerusalem and Cisjordan (the West Bank) were then still occupied and administered by Jordan, which is why Hizb Ut-Tahrir is sometimes considered to be a group of Jordanian origin.
13. Commins (1991, p. 159).
14. Taji-Farouki (1996, p. 78). See Zallum (2000, pp. 30–34) and *Al-Badil* (2003).
15. In the group's view, this process still continues up to the present with the recent Western-supported secession of South Sudan as the latest example. See also Khan (2011) and the special South Sudan issue of the Russian version of *Al-Wayi* (2010), *Yuzhnii Sudan – spetsvypusk*, No. 286.
16. Interview with Taji Mustafa, Media Representative of Hizb Ut-Tahrir in Great Britain, London, 5 April 2011.
17. It may be tempting to compare the person of the Caliph and the institution of the Caliphate with that of the Pope and the Vatican in Roman Catholicism. Although throughout history the Caliph had a popular aura similar to that of the Pope, the two are fundamentally different. First, the Caliph is not a cleric, is no single religious authority and is more a political and military than a religious leader of a global community of believers. Second, unlike the Pope, he is not appointed by an equivalent of the papal conclave, but is elected (at least in Hizb Ut-Tahrir's view) by the Ummah Council, which is itself a periodically and popularly elected assembly that assumes the tasks of popular representation and of the state council. The Caliph rules according to a *Bay'ah* (oath of allegiance), a sort of governance contract with the Ummah, which lays the foundation for his ultimate authority. Third, the Caliph is not the leader of one particular current within Islam as the Pope is for Roman Catholics and the other Christian churches that recognize his authority, but of the entire Ummah as well as the Dhimmi or non-Muslims who fall under his responsibility (and with which the Caliph also has a governance contract). Fourth, the Caliph is a human and not a theological state. Finally, the intended Islamic Khilafah State is physically more than a city-state like the Vatican, which has no design to suppress national states and unite as much Roman Catholic lands as possible in a single entity under the Pope. See Hizb Ut-Tahrir (1996, esp. Chapter 4) and e-mail exchange with Okay Pala, Media Representative of Hizb Ut-Tahrir in the Netherlands, 10 March 2011. Also, for the sake of completeness, the Caliph is not the Mehdi (the Messiah).
18. Esposito (2003, p. 301). The time span between the end of the Abbasid Caliphate after the destruction of Baghdad and execution of the Caliph by the Ilkhan Mongols in 1258 and the beginning of the Ottoman Caliphate upon the Ottoman conquest of Cairo in 1517 is known as the 'Shadow Caliphate' (or the Abbasid Caliphate of Cairo). During this period, members of the Abbasid dynasty who survived the Mongol onslaught and their descendents were given refuge by the Mamluk Sultanate of Cairo and continued to bear the title of Caliph for ceremonial and religious but not political matters. Other dynasties that had the title of Caliph at one time were the Fatimids of Cairo (909–1171, the only Shiite Caliphate) and the Umayyads of Cordoba (929–1031), which both split from the Abbasid Caliphate.
19. At its zenith during the reign of Harun Ar-Rashid (786–809) and Abu Jafar Al-Mamun (813–833), the Abbasid Caliphate of Baghdad ruled, in one form or another, over an area that stretched from the Iberian Peninsula in the west to Multan and Al-Mansura in what is now Pakistan in the east, with North Africa and parts of the Sahara, the lower Nile basin, the Levant and the Arabian Peninsula, Mesopotamia, Persia, the southern Caspian basin, greater Khorassan and Transoxiana (the southern part of what used to be the USSR) in between. Not included was most of present-day Turkey, which was still part of the Byzantine Empire, and Sudan, then still the Christian Kingdom of Dongola. For a detailed account of the pattern of expansion, consolidation and eventually secession and collapse, see Kennedy (2004).
20. Lombard (1972, pp. 95–6).
21. Ibid., pp. 41–5, 210–11.
22. De Cordier (2009, p. 671).

23. This thesis is extensively elaborated in party publications like Abu Abdullah (2010) and Khan (2009a, 2009b).
24. Kull (2007, pp. 15–16).
25. The Pew Forum on Religion & Public Life (2010, pp. 13 and 31).
26. Interview with Hassan Choudhury, member of Hizb Ut-Tahrir and contributor to *New Civilisation Magazine*, London, 5 April 2011.
27. Roy (2007, p. 54).
28. Interview with Jamal B. Harwood, member of the Executive Committee of Hizb Ut-Tahrir, London, 5 April 2011.
29. For a description and comment of Dubai's development, see Lavergne (2009).
30. Interview with Jamal B. Harwood, member of the Executive Committee of Hizb Ut-Tahrir, London, 5 April 2011. For an examination of the vulnerability of the Dubai boom, see Davidson (2008).
31. Khan (2008, pp. 60–61; 2009c).
32. Interview with Jamal B. Harwood, member of the Executive Committee of Hizb Ut-Tahrir, London, 5 April 2011. See also An-Nabhani (1990–97, pp. 118–31).
33. World Bank (2002, pp. 84–5).
34. *IRIN Humanitarian News and Analysis*, 'Pakistan: floods uncover evidence of feudalism's impact on poor', available at: www.irinnews.org; accessed 20 May 2011.
35. Salahuddin (2010). See also Khan (2008, pp. 5–8). This also fits into a general rejection of Western-style democracy. See *Al-Badil* (2009).
36. For a discussion of the relationship between democracy and development in development theory, see Menocal (2007).
37. Roy (2002, pp. 157, 163 and 217–18). For a party-affiliated view, see F. Khan (2004).
38. Mayer (2004, p. 19). The requirement for the party and its members not to consider itself as an entity separate from the Ummah it lives with, to approach and involve the Ummah as it is, and not to undertake any actions that alienate the party from the Ummah is also evident from the writings of Taqiuddin An-Nabhani, for example, An-Nabhani (undated, pp. 70–71).
39. Roy (2002, Chapter 6).
40. Interview with Taji Mustafa, Media Representative of Hizb Ut-Tahrir in Great Britain, London, 5 April 2011. Zallum (2000, pp. 5–16). For a concise explanation of the complex differences and relationship between Salafism and Wahhabism, see Stanley (2005).
41. Interview with Okay Pala, Media Representative of Hizb Ut-Tahrir in the Netherlands, Breda, 13 September 2010. Although there are no statistics, some of Hizb Ut-Tahrir's cadres in Lebanon are Shiites. See Abedin (2010).
42. Abdullah (2009).
43. Interview with Taji Mustafa, Media Representative of Hizb Ut-Tahrir in Great Britain, London, 5 April 2011.
44. International Crisis Group (2003, p. 33).
45. Interviews with Okay Pala, Media Representative of Hizb Ut-Tahrir in the Netherlands, Breda, 17 November 2009 and Taji Mustafa, Media Representative of Hizb Ut-Tahrir in Great Britain, London, 5 April 2011. Some researchers believe that 'somewhere' to be Jordan, the party's cradle. For a discussion, see Ruder (2006, p. 29).
46. Taji-Farouki (1996, pp. 117 and 119).
47. E-mail exchange with Okay Pala, Media Representative of Hizb Ut-Tahrir in the Netherlands, 15 and 17 May 2011, and Hizb Ut-Tahrir Pakistan Q&A section, available at: www.hizb-pakistan.com/home/spokesman/qa; accessed on 24 May 2011.
48. Roy (2002, pp. 217–18).
49. Rana (2010, pp. 3–4).
50. For the importance of the internet in the contemporary development of political Islam, see Roy (2002, pp. 179–91).
51. Here also, the way communication is organized reflects an adaptation to a security situation, since publications and portals that are not party organs can continue to appear when and where sections of Hizb Ut-Tahrir are outlawed.
52. One example is a document developed by Hizb Ut-Tahrir members in Denmark on environment and climate change. Hizb Ut-Tahrir (2009).
53. Fougier (2008, pp. 14 and 35).
54. Interview with Taji Mustafa, Media Representative of Hizb Ut-Tahrir in Great Britain, London, 5 April 2011.
55. Hizb Ut-Tahrir Indonesia, 'Statement of Hizb Ut-Tahrir Indonesia on the earthquake disaster in West Sumatra', available at: http://www.hizb-ut-tahrir.info/info/english.php/contents_en/entry_4856; accessed 5 November 2009. This earthquake, which took place on 30 September 2009, had an

eventual death toll of over 1100. For details, see Office for the Coordination of Humanitarian Assistance (2009).

56. Hizb Ut-Tahrir (1999, pp. 16–17).
57. Interview with Okay Pala, Media Representative of Hizb Ut-Tahrir in the Netherlands, Breda, 17 November 2009.
58. Karagiannis and McCauley (2006, p. 326).
59. See, for example, Hizb Ut-Tahrir Pakistan, 'The current spate of bomb blasts is an attempt of the American and Pakistani governments to pave the way for the military operation in North Waziristan', Press Statement No. 10015, 13 March 2010, available at: http://www.khilafah.com/index.php/analysis/asia/8984-the-current-spate-of-bomb-blasts-is-an-attempt-by-the-american-and-pakistani-governments-to-pave-the-way-for-the-military-operation-in-north-waziristan and Hizb ut-Tahrir's open letter to the Ulema of Pakistan, Press Statement No. 09060, 17 December 2009, www.hizb-pakistan.com/home/prs/press-statement-hizb-ut-tahrirs-open-letter-to-the-ulema-of-pakistan; both accessed on 22 April 2011; *Al-Wayi*, 'Christians and Muslims in Egypt need the return of the Khilafah', available at: www.khilafah.com/index.php/the-khilafah/non-muslims/10966-christians-and-muslims-in-egypt-need-the-return-of-the-khilafah; accessed 7 April 2011), and Hizb Ut-Tahrir of Indonesia, 'Statement on mosque suicide bomb at police sation', Press Statement No. 199, 16 April 2011, posted on the portal of Hizb Ut-Tahrir Media Office, available at: hizb-ut-tahrir.info/info/english.php/contents_en/entry_12625; accessed on 28 April 2011. The author had the content of the English versions of the statement checked against the Urdu and Bahasa versions for their uniformity in the condemnations.
60. Interviews with Okay Pala, Media Representative of Hizb Ut-Tahrir in the Netherlands, Breda, 17 November 2009 and Hassan Choudhury, member of Hizb Ut-Tahrir and contributor to *New Civilisation Magazine*, and Taji Mustafa, Media Representative of Hizb Ut-Tahrir in Great Britain, London, 5 April 2011. For an examination and discussion of the various allegations of links between Hizb Ut-Tahrir and armed militants, see Mayer (2004).
61. This line reminds the author somewhat of that of Western left-wing activists who, though not involved in or even prone to violent action, did show sympathy for movements waging a guerrilla war against oppressive regimes, like the FMLN in El Salvador (1981–92) for example.
62. An-Nabhani (undated, p. 69) and Hizb Ut-Tahrir (1999, pp. 32–5).
63. Karagiannis and McCauley (2006, pp. 326–7).
64. Interview with Hassan Choudhury, member of Hizb Ut-Tahrir and contributor to *New Civilisation Magazine*, London, 5 April 2011.
65. For a thorough case study on the role of the military in the economy of Pakistan, see Siddiqa (2007); pp. 30–58 also refers to other examples like Indonesia.
66. Interview with Jamal B. Harwood, member of the Executive Committee of Hizb Ut-Tahrir, London, 5 April 2011.
67. See, for instance, Rana (2010, pp. 4–5); Hizb Ut-Tahrir Pakistan's address to 'the sincere officers' of the armed forces of Pakistan, 'Rid yourselves now of the traitor rulers', available at: http://www.hizb-ut-tahrir.info/info/english.php/contents_en/entry_13052, *Al-Wayi*, 'Egyptian army must intervene in Libya to end the bloody massacres and prevent intervention by foreign powers', available at: http://www.khilafah.com/index.php/activism/middle-east/11409-egyptian-army-must-intervene-in-libya-to-end-the-bloody-massacres-and-prevent-intervention-by-foreign-powers and 'Hizb ut-Tahrir to the Supreme Council of the Egyptian Armed Forces: the second Camp David protector has fallen!', http://www.khilafah.com/index.php/analysis/middle-east/11249-hizb-ut-tahrir-to-the-supreme-council-of-the-egyptian-armed-forces-the-second-camp-david-protector-has-fallen, and Hizb Ut-Tahrir Bangladesh, 'Sheikh Hasina is handing you over to crusader America and polytheist India. Overthrow her treacherous government before she succeeds', http://www.hizb-ut-tahrir.info/info/english.php/contents_en/entry_7774; all materials accessed on 24 May 2011.
68. Interview with Hassan Choudhury, member of Hizb Ut-Tahrir and contributor to *New Civilisation Magazine*, London, 5 April 2011. See also Choudhury (undated).
69. Ibid.
70. Gawor (2008, p. 129).
71. F. Khan (2004).
72. Interview with Jamal B. Harwood, member of the Executive Committee of Hizb Ut-Tahrir, London, 5 April 2011.
73. Hizb Ut-Tahrir Pakistan's manifesto seems to suggest that Pakistan ('the starting point for Khilafah') has a number of conditions to become so, given the importance of the armed forces in the state. See Hizb Ut-Tahrir Pakistan, *Pakistan, Khilafah and the Re-Unification of the Muslim World. Manifesto of Hizb Ut-Tahrir for Pakistan*, http://www.khilafah.com/images/images/PDF/Books/manifesto-english.pdf; accessed 25 July 2012. Pakistan is a country that was specifically founded for Muslims, which makes it the only modern state specifically founded for a religious community besides the State of Israel.

74. Interview with Hassan Choudhury, member of Hizb Ut-Tahrir and contributor to *New Civilisation Magazine*, London, 5 April 2011.

BIBLIOGRAPHY

Abdullah, H. (2009), 'Sufism and the revival of the Ummah', available at: http://www.khilafah.com/index.php/comment/6741-sufism-and-the-revival-of-the-ummah; accessed 17 March 2011.

Abedin, M. (2010), 'Hizb Ut-Tahrir's new drive in the Levant', available at: http://religion.info/english/interviews/article_474.shtml; accessed 17 February 2011.

Abu Abdullah, J.M. (2010), *The Emerging World Order and the Islamic Khilafah State*, Dhaka: Hizb Ut-Tahrir Bangladesh.

Abu Al-Rashta, A.B.K (2009), *Economic Crises: Their Reality and Solutions from the Viewpoint of Islam*, Beyrouth: Hizb Ut-Tahrir.

Al-Badil (undated), 'Comment l'Etat Islamique peut vaincre la pauvreté', available at: http://albadil.edaama.org/index.php?option=com_content&view=article&id=217:comment-letat-islamique-peut-vaincre-la-pauvrete&catid=41:khilafah&Itemid=59; accessed 27 April 2011.

Al-Badil (2003), 'Les origines du nationalisme dans le monde musulman', available at albadil.edaama.org; accessed 6 April 2011.

Al-Badil (2009), 'Opposition entre le système démocratique et le système du pouvoir en Islam', available at: http://albadil.edaama.org/index.php?option=com_content&view=article&id=194:opposition-entre-le-systeme-democratique-et-le-systeme-du-pouvoir-en-islam&catid=48:publications&Itemid=62; accessed 26 March 2011.

An-Nabhani, T. (1990–97), *The Economic System in Islam*, London: Al-Khilafah Publications.

An-Nabhani, T. (undated), *Concepts of Hizb Ut-Tahrir (Mafahim Hizb Ut-Tahrir)*, London: Al-Khilafah Publications.

Blancheton, B. (2008), *Histoire de la Mondialisation*, Brussels: Editions De Boeck Université.

Choudhury, H. (undated), 'Can we have a "global civil society"?', *New Civilisation Magazine*, available at: http://www.newcivilisation.com/index.php/main/newciv/views/can_we_have_a_global_civil_society/58; accessed 25 March 2011.

Commins, D. (1991), 'Taqi Al-Din An-Nabhani and the Islamic Liberation Party', *The Muslim World*, LXXXI(3–4), 194–211.

Davidson, C. (2008), *Dubai: the Vulnerability of Success*, New York: Columbia University Press.

De Cordier, B. (2009), 'The "humanitarian frontline", development and relief, and religion: what context, which threats and which opportunities?', *Third World Quarterly*, **30**(4), 663–84.

Della Porta, D. (2008), 'L'Altermondialisme et la recherche sur les mouvements sociaux', *Cultures et Conflits*, **70**, Altermondialisme(s) oublié(s), 13–31.

Esposito, J.L. (ed.) (2003), *The Oxford Dictionary of Islam*, Oxford: Oxford University Press.

Filiu, J.P. (2008), 'Ranimé par de petits groupes islamistes. Le spectre du califat qui hante les Etats-Unis', *Le Monde Diplomatique*, **5**(MMVIII).

Fougier, E. (2002), 'Le mouvement de contestation de la mondialisation', *Annuaire Français de Relations Internationales*, **III**, 847–51.

Fougier, E. (2008), *L'Altermondialisme*, Paris: Le Cavalier Bleu.

Gawor, L. (2008) 'Globalization and its alternatives: antiglobalism, alterglobalism and the idea of sustainable development', *Sustainable Development*, **16**(2), 126–34.

Hizb Ut-Tahrir (1996), *The Ruling System in Islam*, London: Al-Khilafah Publications.

Hizb Ut-Tahrir (1999), *The Methodology of Hizb Ut-Tahrir for Change*, London: Al-Khilafah Publications.

Hizb Ut-Tahrir (2009), *The Environmental Problem. Its Causes and Islam's Solution*, Copenhagen: Hizb Ut-Tahrir Denmark.

International Crisis Group (2003), *Radical Islam in Central Asia: Responding to Hizb Ut-Tahrir*, ICG Asia Report No. 58, Osh and Brussels: ICG.

Karagiannis, E. and C. McCauley (2006), 'Hizb ut-Tahrir al-Islami: evaluating the threat posed by a radical Islamic group that remains nonviolent', *Terrorism and Political Violence*, **18**(2), 315–34.

Kennedy, H. (2004), *The Prophet and the Age of the Caliphates*, Harlow: Pearson.

Kennedy, P. (1989), *The Rise and Fall of Great Powers. Economic Challenge and Military Conflict from 1500 to 2000*, London: Fontana Press.

Khan, A. (2008), *Geopolitical Myths*, available at: http://www.khilafah.com/index.php/multimedia/books/4078-book-geopolitical-myths; accessed 17 March 2011.

Khan, A. (2009a), *The Khilafah's Energy Policy*, pp. 16–23, available at: http://www.khilafah.com/index.php/the-khilafah/khilafah/7534-report-the-khilafahs-energy-policy; accessed 27 March 2011.
Khan, A. (2009b), 'Islam and industrial development', pp. 1–8, available at: http://www.khilafah.com/index.php/the-khilafah/economy/6557-islam-and-industrial-development; accessed on 27 March 2011.
Kahn, A. (2009c), 'The collapse of Dubai's economic dream: a consequence of abandoning the Islamic economic system', available at: http://www.khilafah.com/index.php/the-khilafah/economy/8390-the - collapse-of-dubais-economic-dream-a-consequence-of-abandoning-the-islamic-economic-system; accessed 19 March 2011.
Khan, F. (2004), 'Redefining the globalisation debate', available at: http://www.newcivilisation.com/home/ideas-philosophy/redefining-the-globalisation-debate; accessed 25 March 2011.
Khan, S. (2011), 'The Sudan referendum', *Khilafah Magazine*, March, 6–7.
Kull S. (ed.) (2007), *Muslim Public Opinion on US Policy, Attacks on Civilians and Al-Qaeda*, World Public Opinion Survey No. 3/07, Program on International Policy Attitudes, College Park: University of Maryland.
Lavergne, M. (2009), 'Dubaï, utile ou futile? Portrait d'une ville rêvée à l'heure de la crise', *Hérodote*, **2**(133), 32–57.
Lombard, M. (1972), 'Espaces et réseaux du haut moyen-age', *Le Savoir Historique* No. 2.
Mayer, J.F. (2004), 'Hizb ut-Tahrir. The next Al-Qaida, really?', PSIO Occasional Paper No. 4/2004, Geneva: The Graduate Institute – Programme for the Study of International Organizations.
Mayer, J.F. (2007), 'Les courants religieux à l'horizon 2037', *Futuribles. Analyses et Prospective*, No. 332, 55–69,
Menocal, A.R. (2007), 'Analysing the relationship between democracy and development: defining basic concepts and assessing key linkages', ODI Background Notes, available at: http://www.odi.org uk/resources/details.asp?id=1342&title=analysing-relationship-democracy-development-defining-basic-concepts-key-linkages; accessed 23 May 2011.
Office for the Coordination of Humanitarian Assistance (2009), *West Sumatra Earthquake. Humanitarian Response Plan in Coordination with the Government of Indonesia*, available at: http://reliefweb.int/report/indonesia/west-sumatra-earthquake-humanitarian-response-plan-2009-coordination-government; accessed 7 November 2009.
Osterhammel, J. and P.P. Petersson (2007), *Geschichte der Globalisierung. Dimensionen, Prozessen, Epochen*, Munich: Verlag C.H. Beck.
Rabbimov, K. (2004), 'Hizb ut-Tahrir: flagman antidemokraticheskoi kampanii islamizma', *Rossia i musulmanskii mir*, **12**, 78–89.
Rana, M.A. (2010), *Hizbut Tahrir in Pakistan: Discourse and Impact*, Islamabad: Institute for Peace Studies.
Roy, O. (2002), *L'Islam Mondialisé*, Paris: Editions du Seuil.
Roy, O. (2007), *Le Croissant et le Chaos*, Paris: Hachette.
Ruder, D.J. (2006), *The Long War in Central Asia: Hizb-Ut-Tahrir's Caliphate*, Fort Leavenworth: United States Army Command and General Staff College – School of Advanced Military Studies.
Salahuddin, A. (2010), 'A radical approach to Pakistan's economic crisis', available at: http://www.khilafah.com/index.php/the-khilafah/economy/10084-a-radical-approach-to-pakistans-economic-crisis; accessed 20 May 2011.
Siddiqa, A. (2007), *Military, Inc. Inside Pakistan's Military Economy*, Oxford: Oxford University Press.
Sklair, L. (2002), *Globalisation: Capitalism and its Alternatives*, Oxford: Oxford University Press.
Stanley, T. (2005), 'Understanding the origins of Wahhabism and Salafism', *The Jamestown Foundation Terrorism Monitor*, **3**(14).
Taji-Farouki, S. (1996), *A Fundamental Quest. Hizb Al-Tahrir and the Search for the Caliphate*, London: Grey Seal.
The Pew Forum on Religion & Public Life (2010), *Islam and Christianity in Sub-Saharan Africa*, Washington, DC: The Pew Research Center.
World Bank (2002), *Poverty in Pakistan: Vulnerabilities, Social Gaps, and Rural Dynamics*, Poverty Assessment Report No. 24296-PAK, Washington, DC: The World Bank Group: Poverty Reduction and Economic Management Sector Unit.
Zallum, A.Q. (2000), *How the Khilafah was Destroyed*, London: Al-Khilafah Publications.

24 Religion and development: prospects and pitfalls of faith-based organizations

Gerhard Hoffstaedter and David Tittensor

INTRODUCTION

For a long time international development and religion were seen to be mutually exclusive – a somewhat ironic turn of events, considering that many of the largest secular aid and development agencies today owe their beginnings to some aspect of faith and/or religious ideals, and that much of the reconstruction efforts in Europe after World War II were undertaken by Christian organizations. Indeed, such was the ubiquity of Christian aid groups that a research report in 1953 found that 90 per cent of the post-war relief was provided by religious agencies (Ferris, 2005). This about turn took place in the 1960s and 1970s with the emergence of many countries from colonial rule, particularly from Africa and Asia. For these countries the notions of modernity and development – and how to achieve them – took centre stage. As a result some countries looked to Europe and North America, which represented the Western development model, whilst others turned to the communist East in Russia, East Germany and Hungary for inspiration (Anderson and Woodrow, 1998). Yet, while these camps represented two starkly different approaches to obtaining the 'developed state', they contained a couple of important commonalities: (1) both believed in the primacy of the state in governing and improving society; and (2) both expressed that there was no role for religion. In the post-World War II period, communism sought to replace orthodox Christianity (and in some cases Islam) with militant atheism, while the West became enthralled by the 'secularization theory', which proposed that religious institutions and actors were losing their social significance. The net result of these trends was the view that development could only be provided by government policy and programmes that were material and technical in their orientation.

In the academy, then a driving force for government policy, this led to what could be classified as the 'sociologization' of development studies (De Larrinaga and Doucet, 2008; Barrs, 2010) with academics and practitioners building on thinkers such as Weber and Durkheim, which produced a series of dualistic models of development that relied on positivist methodological techniques and statistics. The thrust of these models was that the global South could be developed through major state investments in infrastructure, heavy industries and the like that would shift their economies from agrarian to industrialized economies, a move that would ultimately lead to prosperous modern states (Barrs, 2010). This developmental view held sway up to the 1980s and was replaced, after lacklustre results, by neo-liberal strategies that went in the opposite direction, in that they asked the countries to reduce public spending. Led by the International Monetary Fund (IMF), Structural Adjustment Programmes (SAPs) were introduced for economies that were struggling to service their debt (Mexico, Argentina, Brazil etc.), which mandated the privatization of public utilities, marketing boards and other state enterprises, and the liberalization of almost all domestic markets (Maclellan, 2006).

However, rather than rectifying the situation, these liberalizing policies created service shortfalls that had to be picked up by civil society. Both secular NGOs (non-government organizations) and faith-based organizations (FBOs) experienced a boom as a result. Such was the growth in the aid sector, particularly of the FBOs, that the World Bank found by the beginning of the 2000s that around half of the education and health care needs of SAP-affected countries were undertaken by FBOs. Yet, despite this proliferation of FBOs in the last 20 years there has been little recognition of their efforts by academics (McDonald, 2002; Mohamad, 2010), governments or international organizations. For example, in the USA it was not until the combined effect of the 1996 Welfare Act's Charitable Choice provision and the subsequent 2001 Faith Based and Community Initiative that removed active discrimination against FBOs from obtaining government contracts. Further, it was not until 2004 that USAID's (US Agency for International Development) longstanding funding doctrine that barred organizations from receiving funding if they engaged in sectarian practices, such as worship and proselytization, was overturned by the Supreme Court, a provision that many countries, like Australia, still adhere to and that precludes many religious aid organizations from government assistance (*BBC News*, 2008). Similarly, both the UK and Norway have begun to include FBOs as significant players in their aid programmes. In 2004 the United Kingdom's aid agency, the Department for International Development (DFID), established the Programme Partnership Arrangements (PPAs) scheme, which includes, amongst others, four FBOs – Christian Aid, the Catholic Fund for Overseas Development (CAFOD) and Progressio (formerly the Catholic Institute for International Relations), and Islamic Relief – with a total funding stream of £25 million. Alongside this, DFID instituted a £3.5 million research programme on 'Faiths and Development' in partnership with Birmingham University in 2005 (Clarke, 2007). In the same year, Norway established its own research programme under the Norwegian Research Council and the country's aid agency NORAD. By 2006 Norway had set aside 20 per cent of its NGO budget for FBOs (Mohd Roslan Mohd Saludin, 2007; Tonnessen, 2007).

This increased recognition and activism on the part of governments to provide funding to FBOs has been welcomed by some commentators who see it as the missing element in the development puzzle. Lunn (2009) and Marshall (2001), for instance, extol FBOs' virtues, explaining that they are better placed to deliver services due to their unrivalled reach in rural areas via their strong social networks and religious values, which engender greater trust. On account of these strengths Mayotte (1998, p. 66), speculates 'they may prove to be the most effective and lasting of the development agencies'. However, others are more cautious in their assessment of the benefits that religion brings to the development sector. Rakodi (2007), worries that the current interest by development agencies to work more closely with FBOs may just be the latest attempt to find a 'panacea' to international development challenges. Often, FBOs are brought in as partners in order to 'fix' shortcomings and deal with development problems that previous so-called 'missing ingredients' have failed to do. Others note that there is a dark side to the inclusion of religion, particularly those FBOs of a missionary nature, which have been known to be a rallying point for conflict rather than a salve for peace, due to discriminatory behaviour towards fellow believers and insensitive attempts at conversion (James, 2011). The aim of this chapter is to survey the emergent literature on religion and development to assess these claims for and against its inclusion. In particular we focus on the issue of proselytism and its potential to cause schisms, the apparent value of cultural proximity and trust, and what role FBOs can play in mitigating conflict on account of this trust, and lastly, their effectiveness in post-conflict situations. Thus, to begin we examine the case for religion in development and then step through each of these areas in turn.

PERCEIVED STRENGTHS OF FBOs

Concomitant with the increased interest by governments in FBOs there has been an upsurge of literature by practitioners and academics arguing that FBOs are better placed to provide aid than their secular counterparts. The most common perceived benefits are:

- greater commitment to the cause;
- better access to communities via established networks/cultural proximity;
- greater credibility/trust;
- holistic care;
- less conflict.

Greater Commitment: Flexible Funding and Compassion

It is widely understood that a key factor in successful development projects is sustainability, which requires ongoing funding and commitment. However, there are many obstacles to achieving both ends. By far the biggest obstacle is the donors. Those who give money, be they individuals or organizations, like to see the impact that their contribution is making to the betterment of the community in question. As such, aid organizations are, more often than not, accountable to the donors in terms of how the money is spent. Further, because donors like to be able to ascertain the benefit of their contribution they tend to opt for discrete projects that are pre-planned and contain definite markers of achievement before they sign off on the funds, as opposed to giving fungible or discretionary funds (Garber and Jenden, 1993; Fisher, 1997; World Bank, 1998). There is also the issue of funding predictability. Often Western NGOs raise a significant portion of their funds from governments through offering themselves as intermediaries, contractors and/or project partners between national governments and local NGOs/civil society organizations. This long chain of relations often removes the donor from the consequences of their actions and can reduce incentives to continue funding. For example, Danish aid to Malawi was withdrawn in 2004 after three months due to a change of government in Denmark. All the village health care projects ceased immediately and new ones had to be renegotiated (Barber and Bowie, 2008).

This unpredictability, coupled with the often discrete nature of projects, sees development practitioners and their projects finish up after a short stint, and move on to the next job, despite there being much more work to be done. As Lancaster (2009) notes, it is much sexier to build new roads than to maintain existing ones. However, Flannigan (2008) found that FBOs, particularly those of a Christian background, feel they are largely immune from this problem. Because they obtain their funds from religious sources they feel it gives them greater security and flexibility and allows them to keep going when others cannot. As one practitioner explained:

> We are fortunate that we are able to raise money from people in (our home country), many of whom are Catholic. That's a benefit that we get from being a Catholic organization, and we try to use that money wisely. It's nice, it gives us a little more flexibility. For example, my salary is paid by (our NGO), so I don't have to go out and fundraise for my salary. I can spend more time on things like partnerships with the local Catholic organizations instead of working solely on, for example, a reconstruction project funded by the Dutch government. I can allocate my time in a much more flexible manner, and we can put more of our donor money into the direct implementation of projects. It's a nice situation. There are some organizations that ran their projects here on grant money only, and so when their grant money ran out, they had to close their doors. (Flanigan, 2008, p. 14)

Alongside this greater sense of security and capability, on account of more independent and flexible funding, there is also the factor of compassion. It is widely recognized now amongst development practitioners and scholars that the Abrahamic faiths have at their core empathy for those less fortunate and contain a host of mechanisms to assist the poor that are tied to the divine (Anderson and Woodrow, 1998; Tyndale, 2000; Krafess, 2005; Barber and Bowie, 2008; Deneulin and Bano, 2009; Clarke, 2011). In Islam there is the religious obligation, *zakat* – one of the five pillars of Islam – which directs Muslims to give at least 2.5 per cent of their income as alms for the poor. As the Qur'an points out 'Establish the prayer in conformity with its conditions, and pay the Prescribed Purifying Alms, and obey the messenger so that you may be shown mercy' (24: 56). Moreover, not only is it a religious obligation for believers, but also a right of the poor, as the Qur'an states: 'And in their wealth, the poor (who had to beg) and the destitute (who did not beg out of shame) had due share (a right they gladly honoured)' (51: 19). In Islam there is also the practice of *sadaka* (voluntary giving), which is another means of spreading wealth. The giver is promised rewards many times over the amount given both temporally and in the afterlife. A typical form of this kind of giving is *sadaka jariya* (permanent alms), which can take the form of a *waqf* (pious foundation) and serves the community (Krafess, 2005; Deneulin and Bano, 2009). Similarly, in Judaism there is the concept of *tzedakah*, which is regularly translated as 'charity', but in fact, is closer to the terms justice and righteousness; and the highest form of giving in the Jewish tradition is to give to those that do not have the means to earn their own living. Lastly, the Christian tradition insists that the world was made for the good of everyone, and that everyone needs to use what they have in a responsible way, as inequity is not God's plan. This is expressed well in John's Letters (3: 10): 'The children of God and the children of the devil are revealed in this way: all who do not do what is right are not from God, nor are those who do not love their brothers and sisters' (Tyndale, 2000; Bradley, 2005). In other words, Muslims, Jews and Christians are compelled by their respective faiths to help others in need.

It is believed that this inbuilt sense of compassion within the major faiths predisposes many FBOs to be more motivated and committed to those they serve (Bornstein, 2002; Ferris, 2005). They are prepared to make self-sacrifices for the sake of divine reward, which, coupled with a more secure funding stream, translates into longer-term projects and community affiliations (in some cases hundreds of years) that create the possibility of long-term poverty relief. A good example of this sort of sacrifice is the fact that qualified staff in FBOs often work below the market wage (Reinikka and Svensson, 2003), and are also able to obtain volunteers with relative ease.

Better Access: Local Networks, Cultural Proximity and Trust

Another oft cited benefit of FBOs is that they have extensive local networks that they can partner with (i.e., churches and mosques), which gives them the capacity to reach into regions that secular Western NGOs cannot or at least provide much deeper networks and community affiliations (Kurti et al., 2004; Nishimuko, 2009; Joshi, 2010). In particular Tyndale suggests that FBOs:

> are more firmly rooted or have better networks in poor communities than the non-religious ones and that religious leaders are trusted more than any others. Faith-based organizations are thus seen as essential agents both for influencing the opinions and attitudes of their followers and for carrying out development work at the grassroots. (Tyndale, 2003, p. 26)

An apparent corollary to the better networks, as noted by Tyndale, is that the local partnerships that FBOs have with fellow religious institutions and religious leaders is that they are able to make use of pre-existing networks of trust, whilst secular NGOs have to spend considerable time building up these networks and trust amongst local populations. FBOs have immediate 'cultural authenticity' (Clarke, 2008) or proximity. It is believed that because an NGO shares the religion of the people that they are servicing, combined with local partnerships, they will naturally draw the community to their services over those of other faith-based and secular NGOs. It also commonly argued by practitioners that cultural proximity not only provides logistical advantages via affinity and trust, but also lends itself to services that are culturally sensitive, thereby ensuring more effective aid delivery (De Cordier, 2009; Palmer, 2011).

Holistic Care

A key component of more culturally sensitive and effective care is that FBOs also provide for the spiritual dimension of care. A study by the World Bank that surveyed over 60 000 people from 60 different countries uncovered that a major aspect of well-being amongst the poor was a sense of connection to the transcendent (Narayan et al., 2000). Similarly, the UN Development Programme has recognized the concept of 'human development' that refers to resources that are beyond the purely material and technocratic to include the spiritual (ter Haar and Ellis, 2006). This recognition is seen as a major breakthrough in understanding well-being, as spirituality and religious observance has been found to function as a coping mechanism that allows disadvantaged people to reconcile with their lack of material wealth/comfort and reach a level of serenity or contentedness that would otherwise elude them (Anderson and Woodrow, 1998). Thus, while not a quantifiable measure, it is argued that FBOs, through their own religious activities, or sensitivity to faith, bring additional strengths to the task of uplifting the poor.

Less Conflict

Flanigan (2010) found in her interviews with members of both Christian and Muslim NGOs that there was a sense that their organizations, because of their faith orientation, led to less conflict both within the organization and the communities served. This was due to the belief that their mutual faith and trust in each other within the NGO created a united, harmonious workplace that ultimately produced a relatively tension-free and thereby safer environment for those being served – particularly with regard to welfare of children. Similarly, Lipsky (2011) notes that FBOs have a comparative advantage in consensus building and reducing conflict because of their moral and ethical standing within certain communities.

Alongside this self-assessment by practitioners, there is an emergent argument amongst scholars that although many conflicts are religious in nature, religion also contains the means to diffuse inter-religious and sectarian conflicts. Chandra Muzzafar (2005) makes the case that religion is not the problem per se. It is not their philosophies, doctrines, practices or rituals that are divisive. Rather, it is our interpretation of these elements that lead to exclusive and sectarian cleavages. Further to this, he explains that all of the major religions – Hinduism, Buddhism, Islam Judaism and Christianity – share the universal values of truth, love, justice and compassion, and that this 'shared moral heritage' needs to be recognized and harnessed. He goes on to argue that the secular, materialistic worldview that has taken centre stage, and has always been uneasy about religion, is totally helpless in the face or religious bigotry and conflict. Likewise, David Little (2005), provides an almost identical argument stating that only 'flawed or bad religion' causes conflict and urges FBOs to follow in the footsteps of peacemakers, such as Sant'Egidio and the Bosnia Herzegovina Interreligious Council. Haynes (2007) too follows the line that the major religions, on account of their values, have a lot to contribute to conflict resolution and cites the same examples, though shies away from the assuredness of Muzaffar and Little by pointing to the historical *ambivalence* of religions on the question of violence. Similarly, the United States Institute of Peace (USIP) is cautiously optimistic about the role that FBOs can play in conflict resolution, stating that moral authority of religious organizations can lead to greater effectiveness than that of secular NGOs if they lead by example and eschew claims to religious superiority:

> Faith-based NGOs can work collaboratively with local religious groups to promote reconciliation, respecting local faith traditions and empowering local groups. By scrupulously avoiding any hint of religious superiority, faith-based NGOs can help repair broken relationships using culturally appropriate processes. (Smock, 2001, p. 7)

Interreligious dialogue and reconciliation as proposed here have precedents and can offer a way of coming together. However, religion can also be used to differentiate and divide populations. Both Christianity and Islam are missionary religions with the latter, in particular, regarding its texts and teachings as the final and perfect religion that will lead all back onto the divine path. Recognition of past prophets in Abraham, Moses and Jesus has not precluded Muslim groups from being hostile towards their fellow Abrahamic faiths (Ghandour, 2003). Nor have the Christian values of charity and compassion prevented Christian development agencies from being caught up in politics and ideology (Diamond, 1989, 1995). Indeed, the recent case for religion in development appears to presuppose that religious agencies will rise above creed, culture, politics, economics and other variables to provide non-partisan, judgement-free services. Yet, there is little evidence to suggest that FBOs are better equipped to do what – theoretically – secular NGOs are already doing, and it is to this quandary that we now turn.

A PANACEA OR SUGAR PILL? REALITIES OF FBOs ON THE GROUND

A recent broadside that has been levelled by Ben Jones and Marie Petersen (2011) at the current state of play of research on development and religion, outlined above, is that it is instrumental in its orientation, and has been artificially introduced to the academic research agenda – and both accusations are problematic for a number of reasons. On the first charge, while much of the literature does tend to examine religion only in terms of how it can positively impact development practice – that is, as the 'missing link' that has been overlooked by normative economically driven development discourse – there is also a growing body of literature that explores the complexities of FBOs on the ground that problematize their operation, which Jones and Petersen have seemingly overlooked. Certainly at this stage there is more material being produced that extols the virtues of religion, which has in part been driven by donor agencies, such as the World Bank, DFID and the Norwegian government. However, to say that the agenda is purely driven by funders, as opposed to academics – a somewhat fraught, or black and white delineation – is specious. Therefore, Jones and Petersen's call for more studies on a case by case basis, while welcome, is behind the times. Indeed, two years prior, Bruno De Cordier noted in his study of Muslim Aid agencies that it would be naive to assume that Islamic identity functions the same way in every Muslim country, stating there is:

> a caveat that one has to take into account when determining the added value of cultural proximity through a Muslim identity: the way in which and the degree to which communities and beneficiaries actually identify themselves with the Islamic religion and the actual role that formal and informal Islamic institutions play in the given society. (De Cordier, 2009, p. 615)

Naturally, De Cordier's observation, by highlighting that cultural proximity is not a given within a particular faith group, also brings into question the issues of access to networks, safety, sensitivity and the possibility of competition in the form of intra-communal (as well as inter-communal) proselytism, with the latter having a negative effect on all other areas.

PROSELYTISM AND ITS ASSOCIATED PROBLEMS

Often, proselytism is understood in very narrow terms of one faith group simply trying to convert individuals from another faith tradition. This is certainly valid and is the most common form of proselytism that takes place, but it is not the only kind. The major world religions are not monoliths, but rather are mosaics that contain a rich variety of schools, traditions and sects that make up a very heterogeneous mix. As such, these substrates of the parent religion also compete with each other for resources (and souls). FBOs operate in this mix and they too are made up of an array of faith traditions, both internally and externally (Benedetti, 2006; Thaut, 2009).

A number of studies have emerged recently that note the problematic nature of internal schisms in international aid amongst both Muslim and Christian FBOs. René Otayek (2009) notes, for example, that the 1990s saw a proliferation of Islamic NGOs that entered the aid arena in sub-Saharan Africa to counteract the dynamism of long-established Catholic and Protestant NGOs, for whom evangelism was a central goal. However, rather than producing a coherent network with the message of one Ummah (Islamic nation), the development saw the introduction of a plurality of Muslim voices from different countries that have their own competing theological traditions and political agendas. This Islamic pluralism in Africa, which has a tendency to work at cross-purposes, is illustrated wonderfully in an account by a Sufi Sheikh in Michael Mumisa's (2002) study of Islamic NGOs in South Africa and Malawi:

> Here in the centre (the youth centre), we are the peasants, the lowest of the low. We are the have-nots. They are the haves, they are the Sunni . . . the ones who support us with food yearly. We have people who support us by paying the electricity, petrol for the cars and all that . . . On Tuesdays you have to be Tablighi and wear a long white kurta and speak about Hadith. Why? Because you need something from that guy. Then the following day you have to change from Tablighism to Sunnism. On Sunday, if it was not a violent day, when the Masjid is full, then you have to go to Soofie Sahib to ask for *dholla* and other rights (to feed the people). If you are not a Soofie he won't give you . . . It's a push. (Mumisa, 2002, p. 293)

Further to this, Mumisa explains that there are also racial dimensions that lead to dissension and conflict. Islam in South Africa is seen as largely an Indian religion, as it was Indian Muslims who first brought it to the region, and at times black converts feel that they are exploited for fund-raising purposes. Indians are reported to use photos of black participants at Iftar dinners (breaking of the fast during Ramadan) to induce funds from wealthy African business people; a practice that has led to protests and a letter to Nelson Mandela. In other words, Muslim solidarity and trust is far from a given. Rather, it is mediated by race and sectarianism and this is neither confined to Africa nor to Islam.

Ferris (2005) notes that the visibility of evangelical Christian NGOs presents a serious challenge to the work of all Christian humanitarian groups as they have the capacity to tar the image of Christian charities as a whole. For example, in Indonesia in 2005, evangelical groups working in tsunami-affected areas were trying to bring the Gospel as well as humanitarian aid, which led to criticism of all Christian aid groups, and caused the Council of Churches in Indonesia to issue a strong statement disassociating them from evangelical organizations. Similarly, in Iraq, Christian churches became targets of anti-Christian sentiment in reaction to foreign evangelical activities. Lastly, Benthall (2008) found in an ironic twist, that some Muslim confessional aid organizations refused to build mosques during disaster reconstruction in Aceh, while some Christian organizations offered to do so, only to be turned down on account of it being *haram* (forbidden). Thus, despite their being networks available on the ground that provide initial access to the region in question, this can be undermined very quickly by attempts at proselytism and by both sectarian and cultural differences. In short, one's apparent 'cultural authenticity or proximity' is not, in itself, a given.

CONCLUSIONS

Faith based organizations are and have been highly influential participants in the domain of international development. Their make up varies just as much as religions vary. Beyond that, the agendas and intentions of FBOs vary just as much again. Some are purely missionary and seek to propel their worldview onto others, whilst some are ecumenical and will help all people, regardless of their religion, background or whether they intend to convert or not. What we hope we have shown in this chapter is that FBOs are neither a panacea nor the meddling agents of God. Whilst FBOs are learning to better portray themselves and tell their story, their intentions and their agendas, the (largely secular) international development sector has begun to embrace religion, at least as a socio-cultural force that deserves more attention – be it in the domain of changing development indices to include spirituality and broader notions of well-being or in the realm of better understanding beliefs and religious identities in communities development practitioners work in. It is here, in the moral and the socio-cultural domains that FBOs are easily reduced to their faith tradition or religious affiliation, but it is also the place where FBOs can do most to dispel myths, empower their communities and work to reduce poverty.

REFERENCES

Anderson, M.B. and P.J. Woodrow (1998), *Rising from the Ashes: Development Strategies in Times of Disaster*, London: IT Publications.

Barber, M. and C. Bowie (2008), 'How international NGOs could do less harm and more good', *Development in Practice*, **18**(6), 748–54.

Barrs, C. (2010), *Preparedness Support: Helping Brace Beneficiaries, Local Staff and Partners for Violence*, Cuny Center, report available at: http://cunycenter.org/content/preparedness-support; accessed 25 July 2012.

BBC News (2008), 'Malaysia detains "dissent" writer' [online], available at: http://news.bbc.co.uk/2/hi/7630789.stm; accessed 25 July 2012.

Benedetti, C. (2006), 'Islamic and Christian inspired relief NGOs: between tactical collaboration and strategic diffidence?', *Journal of International Development*, **18**(6), 849–59.

Benthall, J. (2008), 'Have Islamic aid agencies a privileged relationship in majority Muslim areas? The case of post-tsunami reconstruction in Aceh', *Journal of Humanitarian Assistance*, available at: http://sites.tufts.edu/jha/archives/153; accessed 25 July 2010.

Bornstein, E. (2002), 'Developing faith: theologies of economic development in Zimbabwe', *Journal of Religion in Africa*, **32**(1), 4–31.

Bradley, T. (2005), 'Does compassion bring results? A critical perspective on faith and development', *Culture and Religion*, **6**(3), 337–51.

Clarke, G. (2007), 'Agents of transformation? Donors, faith-based organizations and international development', *Third World Quarterly*, **28**(1), 77–96.

Clark, G. (2008), 'Faith-based organisations and international development: an overview', in Gerard Clarke and Michael Jennings (eds), *Development, Civil Society and Faith-based Organisations*, New York: Palgrave Macmillan.

Clarke, M. (2011), *Development and Religion: Theology and Practice*, Cheltenham, UK and Northampton, MA, USA: Edward Elgar.

De Cordier, B. (2009), 'Faith-based aid, globalisation and the humanitarian frontline: an analysis of Western-based Muslim aid organizations', *Disasters*, **33**(4), 608–28.

De Larrinaga, M. and M.G. Doucet (2008), 'Sovereign power and the biopolitics of human security', *Security Dialogue*, **39**(5), 517–37.

Deneulin, S. and M. Bano (2009), *Religion in Development. Rewriting the Secular Script*, London: New York: Zed Books.

Diamond, S. (1989), *Spiritual Warfare: The Politics of the Christian Right*, Boston: South End Press.

Diamond, S. (1995), *Roads to Dominion: Right-wing Movements and Political Power in the United States*, New York: The Guilford Press.

Ferris, E. (2005), 'Faith-based and secular humanitarian organizations, *International Review of the Red Cross*, **87**(858), 311–25.

Fisher, W.F. (1997), 'Doing good? The politics and antipolitics of NGO practices', *Annual Review of Anthropology*, **26**(1), 439–64.

Flanigan, S.T. (2008), 'The "Added Value" of faith: staff perceptions of the benefits of religion in Buddhist, Christian, and Muslim FBOs', ARNOVA's 37th Annual Conference, Philadelphia.

Flanigan, S.T. (2010), *For the Love of God: NGOs and Religious Identity in a Violent World*, Sterling, VA: Kumarian Press.

Garber, B. and P. Jenden (1993), 'Anthropologists of anthropology? The Band Aid perspective on development projects', in Johan Pottier (ed.), *Practising Development: Social Science Perspectives*, London/New York: Routledge.

Ghandour, A-R. (2003), 'Humanitarianism, Islam and the West: contest or cooperation?', *Humanitarian Exchange Magazine* [online], available at: http://www.odihpn.org/humanitarian-exchange-magazine/issue-25/humanitarianism-islam-and-the-west-contest-or-cooperation; accessed 25 July 2012.

Haynes, J. (2007), *Religion and Development: Conflict or Cooperation?*, Houndmills, Hampshire/New York: Palgrave Macmillan.

James, R. (2011), 'Handle with care: engaging with faith-based organizations in development', *Development in Practice*, **21**(1), 109–17.

Jones, B. and M.J. Petersen (2011), 'Instrumental, narrow, normative? Reviewing recent work on religion and development', *Third World Quarterly*, **32**(7), 1291–306.

Joshi, P. (2010), *Faith-based and Community Organizations' Participation in Emergency Preparedness and Response Activities*, Institute for Homeland Security Solutions.

Krafess, J. (2005), 'The influence of the Muslim religion in humanitarian aid', *International Review of the Red Cross*, **87**(858), 327–42.

Kurti, L., A. Whelan and A. Zwi (2004), 'Faith in international development: evaluating the effectiveness of faith-based NGOs', *Development Bulletin*, No. 65, 72–5.

Lancaster, C. (2009), 'Sixty years of foreign aid: what have we learned?', *International Journal*, **64**(3), 799–810.

Lipsky, A.B. (2011), 'Evaluating the strength of faith: potential comparative advantages of faith-based organizations providing health services in sub-Saharan Africa', *Public Administration and Development*, **31**(1), 25–36.

Little, D. (2005), 'Religion, conflict, and peace', in *Proceedings, Religion, Politics, Conflict and Humanitarian Action: Faith-based Organizations as Political, Humanitarian or Religious Actors Workshop*, 18–19 May, The Graduate Institute of International Studies, Geneva, Switzerland.

Lunn, J. (2009), 'The role of religion, spirituality and faith in development: a critical theory approach', *Third World Quarterly*, **30**(5), 937–51.

Maclellan, N. (2006), *Bridging the Gap Between State and Society: New Directions for the Solomon Islands*, Melbourne: Oxfam Australia and Oxfam New Zealand.

Marshall, K. (2001), 'Development and religion: a different lens on development debates, *Peabody Journal of Education*, **76**(3/4), 339–75.

Mayotte, J.A. (1998), 'Religion and global affairs: the role of religion in development', *SAIS Review*, **18**(2), 65–9.

McDonald, M. (2002), 'Human security and the construction of security', *Global Society*, **16**(3), 277–95.

Mohamad, M. (2010), 'The ascendance of bureaucratic Islam and the secularization of the Sharia in Malaysia', *Pacific Affairs*, **83**(3), 505–20.

Mohd Roslan Mohd Saludin (2007), 'Malaysia's firm stand pays off', *The Star*, 30 January.

Mumisa, M. (2002), 'Islam and proselytism in South Africa and Malawi', *Journal of Muslim Minority Affairs*, **22**(2), 275–98.

Muzaffar, C. (2005), 'Religious conflict in Asia: probing the causes, seeking solutions', in Gerrie ter Haar and James J. Busuttil (eds), *Bridge or Barrier: Religion, Violence, and Visions for Peace*, Leiden: Brill, pp. 57–80.

Narayan, D., R. Patel, K. Schafft, A. Rademacher and S. Koch-Schulte (2000), *Voices of the Poor: Can Anyone Hear Us?*, New York: Published by Oxford University Press for the World Bank.

Nishimuko, M. (2009), 'The role of non-governmental organizations and faith-based organizations in achieving education for all: the case of Sierra Leone', *Compare: A Journal of Comparative and International Education*, **39**(2), 281–95.

Otayek, R. (2009), 'Religion and globalisation: sub-Saharan Islam to conquer new territories', *South African Historical Journal*, **61**(1), 21–37.

Palmer, V. (2011), 'Analysing cultural proximity: Islamic relief worldwide and Rohingya refugees in Bangladesh', *Development in Practice*, **21**(1), 96–108.

Rakodi, C. (2007), 'Understanding the roles of religions in development: the approach of the RaD programme', Religions and Develoment Research Programme Working Paper No. 9, University of Birmingham.

Reinikka, R. and J. Svensson (2003), 'Working for God? Evaluating service delivery of religious not-for-profit health care providers in Uganda', World Bank Policy Research Working Paper No. 3058.

Smock, D. (2001), 'Faith-based NGOs and International Peacebuilding', *Special Report*, Washington, DC: United States Institute of Peace.

ter Haar, G. and S. Ellis (2006), 'The role of religion in development: towards a new relationship between the European Union and Africa', *The European Journal of Development Research*, **18**(3), 351–67.
Thaut, L. (2009), 'The role of faith in Christian faith-based humanitarian agencies: constructing the taxonomy', *Voluntas: International Journal of Voluntary and Nonprofit Organizations*, **20**(4), 319–50.
Tonnessen, A. (2007), 'Faith-based NGOs in international aid: humanitarian agents or missionaries of faith?', *Forum for Development Studies*, **34**(2), 323–42.
Tyndale, W. (2000), 'Faith and economics in "development": a bridge across the chasm?', *Development in Practice*, **10**(1), 9–18.
Tyndale, W. (2003), 'Idealism and practicality: the role of religion in development', *Development*, **46**(4), 22–8.
World Bank (1998), *Assessing Aid: What Works, What Does Not and Why. A World Bank Policy Research Report*, New York: Oxford University Press.

25 Mission, missionaries and development

Steve Bradbury

The continuing existence of the poor is a tremendous challenge to the theological conscience and action of Christians everywhere, and a touchstone of the authenticity of our witness to Jesus.

(J. Andrew Kirk, 1981)

INTRODUCTION

Mission, missionaries, development – simply bringing these words together in the one sentence can be viewed as a provocation by some in both the development and church communities. Within the former, deep-running concerns regarding missionary motivations and agendas persist, while in the latter a long-running theological debate regarding the place and importance of social action and justice in the church's mission responsibility to economically poor communities continues to rumble. Despite all this, and whatever their motivation and in some cases their intent, missionaries from Europe and North America, and the churches that emerged from their endeavours, have had a substantial development impact throughout Asia, Africa and Latin America, and will continue to do so into the future.

From its beginnings, Christianity has been a missionary movement, and, at its best a movement committed to justice and compassion for the poor. The explanation for both these defining characteristics is woven throughout the Christian faith's sacred texts, collated in the Bible, and summarized in a few core texts often referred to as the Great Commandment and the Great Commission. The first of these, and an absolutely fundamental tenet of the Christian faith, is the requirement to love God and to love your neighbour.[1] The Bible makes it clear that these two loves are inseparable, and that any protestation of love for God will fall on divine deaf ears unless integrated with demonstrable, practical and unconditional love for those who are in need. Moreover, the biblical definition of love for your neighbour embraces both compassion and justice, the feeding of the hungry and the challenging of those structures and processes that create conditions of deprivation. The dominant witness of the Bible is that most poverty is the result of the misuse of power, and that this abuse is utterly contrary to the will of God. Sadly, this crucial perspective is invariably muted whenever and wherever the church becomes too comfortable in its association with the powerful, or when church and state become too intimate. As the late South African theologian and missiologist David Bosch once observed:

> Whenever the church is a privileged partner in society, having a say in public life, the real issues become blurred and the essence of the gospel watered down. This means that the church in the catacombs[2] is church in a truer sense of the word than the church of the palaces and the houses of parliament.[3]

According to three of the Bible's New Testament authors, Jesus gave his disciples an instruction of immense significance shortly after his resurrection. It was this foundational instruction that later came to be referred to as the Great Commission:[4] 'Go therefore and make disciples of all nations, baptising them in the name of the Father and of the Son and of the Holy Spirit, and teaching them to obey everything that I have commanded you'.[5] In response to these unequivocal words representatives of the first generation of Jesus' followers ventured far from Galilee, a poor and somewhat disreputable corner of the Roman Empire where their faith was birthed. By the time the last of this generation had died, the Christian movement had established communities throughout much of Southern Europe, North Africa, the Middle East, Ethiopia and even India. By any measure this was a truly remarkable achievement for a movement not allied in any way with society's powerbrokers. Indeed, this rapid early expansion of Christianity was mostly among the poor and disadvantaged, and very probably directly related to the church's application of the founder's radical redefining of neighbour as anyone in need. In every generation since that first wave of missionary endeavour, bearers of this legacy have reached out to share their lives and faith with others. They have done so across borders and beyond the comfort of their own place and culture, often at huge personal cost.

Those more familiar with the history and culture of Western Christendom, and of a church apparently at ease with power and influence, can be forgiven if they are unaware that the Christian faith's origins were at the margins of empire rather than at its heart, and that its 'natural' home is among the lowly and hungry rather than the rich and powerful.[6] This historical reality, however, helps explain a more recent and very significant development in global Christian demography:

> Over the past century . . . the centre of gravity in the Christian world has shifted inexorably southward to Africa, Asia and Latin America. Already today, the largest Christian communities on the planet are to be found in Africa and Latin America. If we want to visualise a 'typical' contemporary Christian, we should think of a woman living in a village in Nigeria or in a Brazilian favela . . . Whatever Europeans or North Americans may believe, Christianity is doing very well indeed in the global south – not just surviving but expanding.[7]

In explaining this phenomenon, Jenkins argues:

> Christianity is flourishing wonderfully among the poor and persecuted while it atrophies among the rich and secure . . . If it is not exactly a faith based on the experiences of poverty and persecution, then at least it regards these things as normal and expected elements of life. That view is not derived from complex theological reasoning, but is rather a lesson drawn from lived experience. Christianity can certainly succeed in other settings, even among peace and prosperity, but perhaps it does become harder, as hard as passing through the eye of a needle.[8]

It is this, perhaps more than anything else, that explains the rapid growth of Christianity in recent decades, and its spread into every corner of the world. As a consequence the church has become 'the only truly global community' and 'it is largely a church of the poor'.[9] This is not to ignore the fraught history of Christianity's association with European imperialism, which will be explored briefly later. But the resilience and strength of Christian churches in the former outposts of European empires, particularly among the poor and vulnerable, long after the demise of imperial power, is testament to the deep indigenization of the faith that has taken place in a myriad of diverse cultures and peoples. To imagine that the churches of Africa, Asia, Latin America and beyond are mere clones of the churches of the former imperial powers is to fail to appreciate the extraordinary diversity and variety that exists, both theologically and structurally, within the global Christian community. Moreover, the flow of missionaries is no longer just from North to South, but also from South to North and from East to West. Catholic priests from Africa minister to parishes in Australia, Filipino missionaries work as development practitioners in Thailand, and Latino theologians teach mission in North American seminaries – all testament to the indigenization that characterizes the global church.

MISSION AND HUMAN WELL-BEING

Setting aside for a moment the controversy surrounding missionary agendas and the even more complex issues associated with the interconnectedness of mission, missionary and empire, has the modern missionary movement had a positive development impact?[10] Has it contributed to human well-being among those it has sought to evangelize? Richard Dowden, Executive Director of the Royal African Society, argues that in the African context the contribution has been huge:

> In most of Africa the Churches have delivered more real development to people than all the governments, the World Bank and aid agencies combined. Africa's network of priests, nuns and Church workers are one of Africa's most effective organizations. When states like Congo, Ghana, Angola, Mozambique and Uganda itself collapsed, the self-sufficient parishes used their moral authority to provide protection. Like the monasteries in Europe in the Dark Ages, they kept civilization going.[11]

Clearly this is a big call. While Dowden's assertion may largely stem from his assessment of the role of the Catholic Church in Africa, there can be little question that the investment of both Catholic and Protestant Churches in health and education – the twin engines of development – has been of critical importance in Africa.[12] Mission schools and hospitals also abounded in many parts of Asia, Latin America and the Pacific. By 1935 'missions were running nearly 57,000 schools throughout the world, including more than one hundred colleges'.[13] Many of these educational institutions played a critical role in the development and training of future leaders for both church and society, including some of those who led successful campaigns of national liberation from imperial overlords. Mission hospitals and health clinics established as curative responses to the obvious health needs of vulnerable communities have gone on to spawn community health initiatives with an emphasis upon prevention, and in some cases far wider community development programmes designed to increase productivity, income and improved nutrition.

Consider, for example, the ground-breaking work of Drs Rajanikant and Mabelle Arole, world-renowned innovators in primary health care for the very poor. The Aroles were graduates of Christian Medical College (CMC), Vellore. This important training institution, founded by American missionary Dr Ida Scudder in 1918 initially to train women doctors, is transparent about its faith foundation. The college's vision is 'to be a witness to the healing ministry of Christ', through the equipping of women and men, 'in the spirit of Christ for service in the relief of suffering and in the promotion of health' and the development and training of 'compassionate, professionally excellent, ethically sound individuals who will go out as servant-leaders of health teams and healing communities'.[14] In 1970, after completing the masters of public health programme at Johns Hopkins University, the Aroles returned to India and co-founded the Comprehensive Rural Health Project (CRHP) at Jamkhed. The CMC vision was given arms and legs in their work as they epitomized what it means to love God and neighbour. According to Jon Rohde, a former UNICEF representative in India:

> While they had faith in a higher being, they realised that the only hands that being has on earth to do good works were theirs – they spent their lives in that endeavour. There is no figure of the past 50 years who contributed more, both by innovation and even more as a living example of what primary health care can be as a leavening in an inequitable world, as a means to lift people not only out of poverty, but also out of despair.[15]

By the time of Rajanikant Arole's death in May 2011 (Mabelle died in 1999) their 'social experiment that initially covered eight villages and a population of 10000 villagers' had grown to cover 300 villages and 500000 people, and their achievements have proved beyond doubt that 'many health problems can be prevented and controlled at the village level without the need for expensive equipment and personnel'.[16] In addition to working with these communities to select and train an army of village health workers, CRHP also encouraged the establishment of women's self-help groups. The agendas of the 140 currently active groups reflect the aspirations of the women to improve the well-being of their families and communities. Their achievements across a broad spread of projects – including kitchen gardens, nutrition education, harnessing safe drinking water, reforestation, microcredit schemes and income generation – has done much to increase the status of women in the region.

The impact of the Aroles' pioneering work has reached far beyond the 300 villages encompassed in CRHP's programmes. Increasing numbers of people seeking training and advice from CRHP led it to establish the Jamkhed Institute for Training and Research in Community Health and Population in 1992. Thus far over 2000 international (from over 100 countries) and 9000 national health and development workers from government, non-government and faith-based organizations have been trained in the principles and practices of community-based health and development.[17] CRHP's achievements have been well recognized in India and beyond, and in Dr Rajanikant Arole was awarded the Mother Teresa Memorial National Award for Social Justice in 2005. In a moving eulogy to her father, Dr Shobha Arole demonstrates how closely his vision and motivation reflected that of his Indian alma mater, the Christian Medical College, Vellore:

> Dr Raj worked wholeheartedly with love, enthusiasm and a deep passion for the poor. He was intelligent, wise, hard working and driven with a deep commitment and faith in God and a strong prayer life which gave him the energy and ability to withstand many setbacks and challenges and never waiver from the commitment dear to his heart.[18]

What began as an initiative of an American medical missionary in the early twentieth century produced remarkable fruit many decades later.

Undoubtedly, the extraordinary impact of CRHP Jamkhed is an exemplary example of how missionary initiative and endeavour can result in significant development outcomes in very disadvantaged communities. But it is far from an isolated example. Craig Sorley, an American Baptist missionary in Kenya, is on the frontline in the battle against climate change. It is well recognized that this impending global ecological disaster poses a huge threat to the world's poor, threatening to undo decades of development work as it pushes thousands of vulnerable communities back to and beyond the edge of survival. Moreover, the fact that those who have done least to cause climate change are the ones who will suffer the most from it makes it yet another case of grave global injustice. Sorley, a second-generation missionary whose parents worked as medical missionaries in Ethiopia and Uganda, is passionate about the urgent need to introduce poor Kenyan farmers to cost-effective and ecologically sound farming techniques, knowing this will be critical to their capacity to adapt to climate change. In 2005 he established Care for Creation Kenya (CCK), a small Christian faith-based development NGO. Its purpose: 'to awaken and mobilize the Kenyan Church to develop a God-honouring response to the serious agricultural and environmental challenges facing the nation'.[19] Sorley observes:

> In many parts of the world, and particularly in Africa, countless communities are facing environmental degradation unprecedented in history. Critical problems include deforestation, overgrazing, erosion, loss of biodiversity, a warming and drying climate, and increasing difficulty in obtaining consistent supplies of food and water. These issues come together to cause increased hardship and suffering, perpetuating poverty, hunger, disease and death.[20]

Sorley is deeply disturbed by what he perceives as a growing 'poverty of spirit' threatening to overwhelm Kenya's embattled small-scale farmers. 'It is critical', he writes:

> that we look even deeper to examine the social implications of this crisis. Only then can we understand the gravity of the situation. The physical poverty resulting from a decline in crop yields is accompanied by an equally if not more serious problem . . . Farmers are discouraged, they are experiencing a greater sense of despair and hopelessness, and they lack the necessary vision for restoring their land. Unfortunately, this 'poverty of spirit' is being passed to the next generation, and this holds serious implications for the future of small-scale agriculture in Africa.[21]

CCK's response, while necessarily limited by the size of its operation, is a comprehensive one worthy of emulation. Its in-community workshops train farmers in simple, low-cost sustainable practices called Farming God's Way (FGW). These include: extensive mulching, which stops soil erosion, captures and traps rainfall, minimizes evaporation from the soil, and adds essential organic matter; crop rotation; zero tillage, which not only reduces soil destruction but also frees up precious labour for other tasks such as weeding; and tree planting, which provides food, fuel, fodder, and mulch. FGW methodology is very appropriate for small-scale farmers reliant on erratic rainfall and working with hand-held tools. Yield increases using FGW methodology have been impressive. When rainfall has been good increases are lower, but in drought conditions this method consistently produces much higher yields than current common farming practices. The expected increase in frequency of such weather heightens the need for such innovation if food security is to be strengthened. Water resource development and tree planting are also key components in CCK's programme. The alarming rate of destruction of Kenya's forests and woodlands – government figures indicate that 50 per cent of these disappeared between 1973 and 2003 – means reforestation is critical to the nation's future. The churches in Kenya have the potential to play a significant role in responding to their country's ecological crisis. They have impressive grassroots networks and a considerable capacity for mobilization. Moreover, it is estimated that 80 per cent of Kenya's 35.5 million people are Christian.[22] From a purely development perspective, therefore, CCK's focus on teaching Christians that environmental responsibility is an urgent Christian duty, a core dimension of FGW, could prove to be of great strategic importance. In an interview with the *Guardian* newspaper Wangari Maathai, the world-renowned Kenyan environmentalist and women's rights activist, pondered her own failure to persuade the church in Kenya to champion the environmental cause, and affirmed Sorley's approach:

> People in Kenya are religious, but often in a superficial way. They look at God like he's a magician . . . rather than a God who wants us to use and protect the tools he has given us. Craig was talking about the environment from a biblical perspective, which I never heard anyone doing before. I thought at the time that if we could get that sort of language coming from the pulpit on Sundays then we would start to see all Christians looking to protect the planet.[23]

Such affirmation from the now deceased Nobel Peace Prize winner is high praise.

THEOLOGY AND MISSION

The need to develop a comprehensive and integrated theology that takes seriously the biblical mandate to nurture and care for the environment in order to sustainably harvest its resources is not, of course, restricted to Kenya or Africa. It is a need within the church worldwide as it is within many of its mission agencies. Sorley is acutely aware of this. 'We as missionaries', he writes, 'have an urgent need to be discipled ourselves on this issue. We often lack the biblical foundations and convictions we need to preach, teach and develop Bible studies that offer God-honouring attitudes and behaviours in response to the environmental problems of our day'.[24] He challenges mission agencies to imagine what might be possible if they all 'committed to a Christ-honouring creation stewardship ethic worked hand-in-hand with local communities to restore watersheds and to re-build degraded landscapes in order to prevent hunger or famine from afflicting people'.[25] In a small but encouraging way, the work he and CCK are doing is an important aid to such imagining, a signpost of what could be achieved. CCK has demonstrated that FGW methodology has enormous potential to help Africa's small-scale farmers and rural communities adapt to the challenges of climate change. Despite the magnitude of CCK's mission and its ongoing resource constraints, Sorley is encouraged:

> While the Church has generally neglected this dimension of life in the past, it is beginning to embrace key issues, such as deforestation and poor farming practices. Today there is a growing recognition of the link between environmental degradation and worsening problems of hunger and poverty. It is our conviction that the Church can play a very instrumental role in cultivating a new vision for creation stewardship that will bring fresh hope to hurting people through the healing of broken landscapes.[26]

In the narrow alleyways of the countless squatter communities in the megacities of Asia, Africa and Latin America, Christian missionaries are working in health clinics, vocational training programmes, and micro-enterprise initiatives, and almost always they are striving to bring this practical support to the most marginalized within those communities. Beyond the cities, in the mountains of the Himalayas, the rainforests of the Amazon, the paddy fields of Asia, and in the rural communities of sub-Saharan Africa, missionaries are working in climate change adaptation, agricultural extension, women's literacy, civil society strengthening – the list could go on and on. Many of these women and men are on the development frontline. Embedded in the communities they seek to serve, they wrestle daily with the challenges of participatory, inclusive and sustainable development. In some contexts they are even doing this while navigating the killing fields of civil conflict and terrorism. Inspired and sustained by what they believe it means to love and be loved by God, many have forgone financial security and stepped aside from 'normal' career paths in order to serve the poor. However, in the minds of some within the development community the work of such people, even if good-hearted, is tarnished, perhaps even invalidated because of its integration into a wider transformational agenda.

The broader aspirations and agendas of Christian missionaries have long been a cause of controversy. Well before the emergence of the current concerns within the development community regarding the evangelistic activities of missionaries, anthropologists and historians had critiqued and in some cases condemned the relationship between an earlier generation of missionaries and European imperialism.

There can be little doubt that many of the highly motivated missionaries in the great wave of missionary activity that began in the late eighteenth century and coincided with the expansion of the British Empire were, in a sense, dual evangelists. They were intent on spreading not only the good news of the Gospel but also the good news of British civilization – changing not just the faith of those to whom they were bringing the Gospel, 'but also their mode of dress, hygiene and housing'.[27] In this regard they were very much creatures of their times, reflecting prevailing attitudes, in particular the conviction that humanity had achieved its finest and most godly expression in European and especially British civilization. In their minds, exporting this civilization was a God-given duty that could only benefit humanity. We may well cringe at the more offensive aspects of this cultural and paternalistic imperialism, and hopefully our awareness of their cultural blinkers may serve to make us more circumspect regarding our own. However, the assumption that all change in cultural practice and belief that occurred as a consequence of missionary activity is by definition an imperialistic impact, that is, one resulting from a power differential, is incorrect. It fails to take into account that some change was intrinsically beneficial and embraced for good reason. In light of her studies of missionary activity in South Australia and British Columbia, Peggy Brock raises some important and astute questions. 'Does the spread of ideas, technology and cultural forms necessarily constitute cultural imperialism? Or can it be something more benign, a two-way process in which Indigenous people grasp the opportunity to import new ideas and technologies into their societies?'[28] Brock argues that 'the distinction between change that might be sought out, and change that might be imposed by imperial interests is an important one'.[29] What's more, her research into Aboriginal community histories in South Australia has led her to 'question the assumption that Christianity was forced on people in the first instance',[30] and she concludes that 'it is difficult . . . to argue that all missions were agents of cultural imperialism'.[31]

But what of the role of missionaries in the far more sinister political and economic dimensions of imperialism? Philosopher and theologian Nicholas Wolterstorff describes these dimensions in simple but graphic terms:

> It was guns that induced South American Indians to mine cheap gold for the Spaniards. It was guns that induced Indians to produce cheap textiles for the British. It is guns that induce Salvadorans to produce cheap coffee, and South African blacks to produce cheap gold, for the rest of the world. Behind the concentration of capital in Europe and the U.S. is the use of much gun power, elaborate torture and many prisons.[32]

In some contexts missionaries preceded those guns and in others accompanied them. Some missionaries courageously exposed and opposed the ruthless conquest and exploitation of indigenous populations, while others welcomed the establishment of European control, believing it would provide a more favourable environment in which they could pursue their mission. To stereotype all missionaries as willing or even unwitting partners in the enterprise of imperial conquest is simply unfair, and those who do so are being less than objective. Vinoth Ramachandra, a Sri Lankan theologian and human rights activist writes:

> There are, of course, many shameful stories to be told of Western missionary complicity in colonial practices of domination. But the more typical stories of missionaries and local Christian leaders in India, Africa or the South Pacific who courageously defended native interests and combated racist theories and stereotypes propagated by their fellow countrymen are missing from the anti-Orientalist corpus.[33]

However, it is the place of conversion in the missionary's agenda that causes most offense to twenty-first-century secularists, and is problematic in the eyes of many official development agencies. It is to this we must now turn our attention and scrutiny.

PERSONAL MOTIVATION

At the very heart of most if not all Christian missionary endeavour there resides a powerful and highly motivational conviction – that humans consist of body, soul and spirit, not body alone. Thus, human flourishing requires more than material well-being, and that it is through faith in Jesus Christ that a person can experience 'life in all its fullness'.[34] In other words, if I truly love my neighbours as myself, then I will not only want to do what I can to ensure that they have access to potable water, but also to introduce them to the one who said he could provide the thirsty with the water that 'will become in them a spring of water gushing up to eternal life'.[35] Regardless of how we might view such a belief, it is pertinent to note that missionary commitment to evangelism, in its purest and most biblically shaped manifestations, is motivated by genuine concern for the others' well-being. This is exemplified by the founding objectives of the Church Missionary Society[36] (CMS): the abolition of the slave trade, the reform of British society, and world evangelization. Together they reflect an integrated, holistic understanding of human well-being. Two of CMS's ardent supporters became household names in nineteenth-century Britain: William Wilberforce, who led the decades-long campaign against slavery in the British Parliament, and Lord Shaftesbury who successfully fought to humanize working conditions in the mines and factories. In each case their cause was far from popular when they started, and each had to fight for many years against an entrenched and powerful opposition. Their persistence grew out of their understanding of the radical social implications of the Christian faith.

This same holistic understanding of Christian mission was clearly evident in the work of the man sometimes referred to as the 'father of modern mission'. William Carey, the founder of the Baptist Missionary Society and its first missionary, arrived in India in 1793 where he served until his death in 1834. During this period he translated much of the Bible into over 30 Indian languages, a truly remarkable achievement, testimony to his passion for evangelism. Convinced that education was the key to the evangelization of Indians, he also set about establishing a network of Bengali medium schools. By 1817 there were 103 such schools with nearly 7000 students. In 1818 he established Serampore College, which continues to this day to provide undergraduate and postgraduate programmes in theology, humanities, and the sciences. Concerned about hunger and malnutrition, he established the Agri-Horticultural Society to foster improved agricultural processes – another institution that survives until this day. Carey also campaigned vigorously against two common practices he encountered on arriving in India – infanticide and *sati*.[37] Evangelism and development, hand in hand, integrated ambitions fuelled by the conviction that God's love is concerned with the total well-being of each and every person.

Such integration remains very much part of the DNA of both CMS and BMS today. In its 2010–11 *Annual Review*, CMS-UK described the society's mission as saying, 'Yes to sharing Jesus and changing lives . . . Yes to gospel proclamation, yes to nurturing disciples, yes to meeting the needs of the vulnerable and marginalized, yes to challenging unjust systems, yes to creation care'.[38] This in an all-embracing commitment to integral mission. Currently, CMS-UK has over 150 missionaries working around the world – in the Middle East, Asia, Europe and Latin America. Many of them work in what are primarily evangelistic ministries, and many are employed in training church leaders. More than half of CMS-UK's missionaries, however, are directly engaged in responding to the development needs of the poor, and even the health of the planet. Ranging in scope from educational initiatives for disabled children in Peru to peace and reconciliation work in Burundi and Rwanda, from climate change adaptation programmes in Bangladesh to medical programmes in Argentina and Tanzania, these missionaries are committed to human development and well-being in some of the world's most vulnerable and struggling communities. But more than that, as their current Executive Director explains, they 'still share a vision with those impossible, controversial missionaries of history: to proclaim hope for all peoples and places in Christ'.[39]

Similarly, BMS remains unequivocal in its commitment to evangelism. The current vision statement states: 'As a Christian mission organization we aim to share life in all its fullness with the world's peoples by: enabling them to know Christ, alleviating suffering and injustice, improving the quality of life, with people as our primary agents of change – motivating, training, sending and resourcing them'.[40] The great majority of these 'agents of change' are labouring on the development frontline as community health workers, social workers, teachers, agriculturalists, and even, in one case, as a justice advocate. In all these contexts their hope and prayer is that the people they serve will come 'to a saving faith in Jesus Christ, and an experience of the abundant life that Jesus described'.[41]

This integration of evangelism and development poses a real dilemma for the development establishment, which largely continues to view development as a secular and material enterprise. It is important to examine the reasons for this dilemma and give careful consideration to its implications.

POVERTY REDUCTION AND EVANGELIZATION

There is increasing recognition within the official development community that faith-based organizations, including missionary organizations and those development NGOs that employ missionary development practitioners, are contributing significantly to global efforts to address poverty. Near the end of his ten-year period as President of the World Bank, James Wolfensohn wrote:

> The vast and complex array of institutions that are organized with faith in God or with spiritual goals at their center share with the development institutions a commitment to addressing the problems of poverty. The critical role of faith institutions in the historic development and current provision of both education and health services is a central example, but so too are the remarkable roles that these institutions play in countries and regions wracked by conflict, their capacity to influence land use, and perhaps less remarked, their significant role in directing investment of financial assets.[42]

The authors of the World Bank report in which these observations were published contend that faith-based organizations 'are important players in many spheres of development, with broadly and deeply established roots as key, and sometimes, sole providers of essential services – notably health and education – and community mobilizers'.[43] However, co-existing with this growing acknowledgment of the development contributions of faith-inspired organizations there is an abiding nervousness, even alarm. This uneasy co-existence is described by Rowan Williams, the global head of the Anglican Church, in an insightful speech exploring the complexities that abound along the faith/development interface. 'At best, communities of religious conviction have the potential to be serious and effective allies in the struggle against privation'. However, Williams also acknowledges that:

> There is a long-standing suspicion towards faith in many quarters of the development establishment. There is always going to be the shadow of suspicion that they will favour their own instead of working for universal benefit, or that they are using aid and development as a vehicle for propaganda on behalf of their convictions, a cloak for proselytism.[44]

Herein lies the dilemma. A common response to this dilemma within the secular development world has been to insist upon a clear demarcation between the development and evangelistic agendas, though what that might mean in practice can be very difficult to pin down and legislate for. A quick examination of some attempts to do this may be helpful.

Consider, for example, the current application guidelines for DFID's[45] Civil Society Challenge Fund. These stress that 'projects that contain any element of evangelising or proselytising' will not be considered.[46] In its Global Poverty Action Fund, DFID goes one step further – Guideline 5.2 states quite simply that applications from any organization 'actively involved in proselytising' will not be considered.[47] A reasonable interpretation of this ruling would suggest that a faith-based organization with programmes that included evangelistic aspirations would be ineligible to apply for funding even for projects devoid of explicitly evangelistic or faith-focused ritualistic activities.

Policies governing the operations of the Australian government's overseas development department demonstrate similar concerns. Its Overseas Aid Gift Deduction Scheme, which sets the criteria for tax deductible donations for overseas aid, first defines evangelism and then clearly proscribes it:

> Evangelism (also called proselytism and missionary work) is the practice of attempting to convert people to another religion or faith . . . Tax-deductible funds cannot be used for evangelistic purposes nor for missionary activities. Missionary activities include evangelism but also extend to activities designed to build up the knowledge and faith of believers including theological training and training in and study of works of religious wisdom such as the Koran, Torah or Bible. The building and maintenance of places of worship are also ineligible.[48]

Guidelines governing AusAID's partnership programme with NGOs similarly exclude evangelistic activities: 'Approval will not be provided for activities which subsidise evangelism or missionary outreach'.[49]

The accompanying explanatory notes provide more detail and reflect the depth of concern. They stress that AusAID funds must be used 'to assist in strengthening an organisation's or a community's development capacity or socio-economic situation', and not to strengthen the 'religious witness' of a church or religious organization. While recognizing that 'in many situations this may not be an either/or question', they recommend that in such cases, where there is a mix of objectives, AusAID funds should not be used.[50] Under the very specific sub-heading of 'Evangelical Activities' the explanatory notes state:

> AusAID and NGOs recognise and agree that AusAID funds are not to be used for programming that is designed to convert people from one religious faith or denomination to another or from one political persuasion to another. Nor should AusAID funds be used to build up church, ecclesiastical or political structures except in circumstances where those structures are specifically designed to provide relief and/or development assistance. In this context, church, ecclesiastical and political structures include not just infrastructure, but could also extend to training or organizational activities.[51]

It is important to note that within the conditionality of these regulations faith-based NGOs have successfully applied for funding from AusAID. Indeed, AusAID is a major supporter of many such organizations. Clearly it is fully satisfied that the faith-based agencies participating in its NGO partnership programme are able to ensure that its grants are used solely for development purposes.

The relevant USAID policy similarly insists that its funds must not be used to support inherently religious activities such as worship, religious instruction, or proselytization'.[52] However, it goes on to stress that 'this restriction does not mean that an organization that receives USAID funds cannot engage in inherently religious activities'. What it does mean is that 'faith-based organizations that receive direct financial assistance from USAID must take steps to separate in time or location, their inherently religious activities from the direct USAID-funded services they offer'.[53] This is a notably more nuanced response than that offered by DFID in its Global Poverty Action Fund.

A final example is provided by the Australian Council for International Development (ACFID), Australia's peak body for aid and development NGOs. Clause 2.7 of ACFID's Code of Conduct, a code all members must adhere to, requires that:

> funds and other resources designated for the purpose of aid and development will be used only for those purposes and will not be used to promote a particular religious adherence or to support a political party, or to promote a candidate or organization affiliated to a political party.[54]

In a guidance document attached to the code ACFID elaborates:

> Funds raised for aid and development purposes are only to be used in programs which in no way exploit the people and communities who are vulnerable and do not place any conditions or obligations on recipients in terms of religious or political outcomes that would affect their access to services being offered.

However, it acknowledges 'that applying this clause will be quite difficult in some situations and some level of judgment may be necessary', and urges members to 'apply the spirit and intent of this clause in the conduct of their Development work'.[55] Despite its presence in an Australian document, the phrase 'quite difficult' would seem more an example of classic English understatement. The complexities are enormous, but in the light of these complexities the exhortation to 'apply the spirit and intent' of the Code has a grace and wisdom beyond mere regulation.

In exploring some of these complexities a number of questions emerge. What is evangelism? Is there a difference between evangelism and proselytism, and if so, what is it? Is evangelism in and of itself an evil activity, or does it depend on when and how and to whom it is directed? Is the development context one in which the conditions shaping human intercourse are such that any form of evangelism is inappropriate or even unethical? Or could there be some situations where, in the context of every day informal conversation, it is not unreasonable or exploitative for a missionary development practitioner to share with a client/beneficiary/friend about matters of faith, life experience and world view? Finally, while remaining mindful of issues of dependency and the dangers of manipulation, is it not still possible that an individual or community, having witnessed something in the life and work of a faith-inspired development practitioner, may exercise genuine choice in deciding to adopt that practitioner's faith? Or, more simply, is it indeed unreasonable to assume that every such conversion is evidence of a coercive process?

Dr Brian Stanley, Professor of World Christianity and Director of the Centre for the Study of World Christianity at the University of Edinburgh argues that a fundamentally illiberal perspective underlies at least some of the current opposition to evangelism:

> Beneath the placid surface of the current pluralist orthodoxy in religious studies, currents of an essentially illiberal kind flow. It is assumed that, for the sake of ethnic harmony and mutual human understanding, religious affiliation should, and even must remain confined within the traditional territorial boundaries of particular communities of faith. Missionary or conversionist religions that refuse to acknowledge those boundaries as sacrosanct are deemed guilty of the sins of 'proselytism' and 'intolerance'.[56]

A blanket opposition to all forms of religious evangelism, regardless of context, is illiberal intolerance, as is the denial of any person's right to change their religious adherence.

The latter, in fact, contravenes Article 18 of the International Covenant on Civil and Political Rights, which declares that:

> Everyone shall have the right to freedom of thought, conscience and religion. This right shall include freedom to have or to adopt a religion or belief of his choice, and freedom, either individually or in community with others and in public or private, to manifest his religion or belief in worship, observance, practice and teaching.[57]

Not withstanding this, faith-inspired development practitioners need to understand that the particular context in which they work requires them to exercise special care to ensure that evangelistic intent does not stray into coercive practice. All development and humanitarian programmes necessarily involve transactions between people of greater or lesser dependence on the one side, and those who are the conduit for essential resources or services on the other. Within the context of these transactional relationships there is an inevitable imbalance of power, regardless of how much care is exercised, and regardless of the humility or otherwise of the development or aid workers. Given this, the potential for misunderstanding and manipulation, even unintentional, is considerable.[58] For this reason faith-inspired development practitioners, whose commitment to justice and compassion for the poor and marginalized is a practical expression of a broader theology of human well-being, must exercise considerable sensitivity in sharing this understanding with those they serve.

Micah Network

The Micah Network, a loose global alliance of evangelical Christian development NGOs, has been grappling with this issue in the particular context of humanitarian relief programmes. A paper on proselytizing produced as part of this process provides a useful insight into fundamental convictions and concerns commonly though not universally held by evangelical Christians working in aid and development. First it differentiates between evangelism and proselytism, defining and condemning the latter as the 'unjustified manipulation or use of coercive techniques or force to achieve conversion'.[59] Notably, it unequivocally affirms the evangelistic 'longing to see people coming to a personal faith in Jesus Christ', while at the same time utterly rejecting 'manipulative or coercive proselytism as a way of propagating the Christian faith'. The paper argues that engagement in humanitarian relief should never be a means to an evangelistic end: 'We are not involved in giving relief to the needy so that we can evangelise, but because it is our Christian calling to give relief to the needy'. Using the strongest possible language it stresses that: 'It is absolutely abhorrent to us to exploit people's vulnerability in order to put pressure on them to convert to our religion'. Moreover, it recognizes that 'conversions gained in this way are often superficial and bring no credit to the converts or the Christian faith in general'. Indeed! The people who are truly compromised in such circumstances are not the exploited who convert, but those who wittingly or unwittingly take advantage of human vulnerability to push a conversion agenda.

The Micah Network's insistence that there is a difference between proselytism and evangelism is shared by many other faith-inspired Christian development practitioners and missionaries. Reverend Tim Dakin, Executive Director of the Church Missionary Society-UK argues:

> Evangelism is not proselytism. The spirit of proselytism is coercion. The spirit of evangelism is kindness. Coercive evangelism may impose a way of life, but a person's fundamental view of reality may not change. Evangelism in the spirit of kindness is about sharing (that is, receiving as well as giving) Christ's love on other people's terms, across frontiers, in the depths of their identity and context.[60]

In its 'Ministry Policy on Witness to Jesus Christ',[61] World Vision, one of the world's largest development NGOs, also draws this distinction between Christian witness and proselytizing. 'Witness to Jesus Christ is an integrating principle in all that we do', it declares, and this witness will 'be expressed in holistic ways through its ministries of relief, development, advocacy and public awareness'. It notes that its 'support of religious freedom requires that we do not proselytise', and very specifically observes that 'proselytism takes place whenever assistance is offered on condition that people must listen or respond to a message, or as an inducement to leave one and join another part of the Christian church and/or one religion to join another religion'. The policy categorically declares that out of respect for 'the dignity of those with whom we work' World Vision will 'not exploit vulnerability or use the power of development and humanitarian programs to coerce conversion'.

Clearly, the abuse of development interventions and humanitarian aid in order to give greater leverage to an evangelistic agenda – sugar for the evangelistic pill – is utterly unacceptable, not just to secularists but also to many, though sadly not all, faith-inspired Christian development practitioners. This creates a real opportunity for fruitful discussion between such practitioners and representatives of the development establishment. The substantial commitment and contribution to development made by these practitioners and the faith communities that stand behind them is added reason to do so. Open-minded dialogue carefully examining 'the intention and nuance behind religiously inspired definitions of mission and human development',[62] has the potential to reduce suspicion regarding the inappropriate misuse of official development funds in the pursuit of evangelistic ends. A commitment by faith-based development NGOs and missionary organizations to conscientiously examine the ethics of evangelism within the context of relief and development would undoubtedly enhance such discussions. A document released in early 2011 provides a useful aid for such examination.

Christian Witness in a Multi-Religious World: Recommendations for Conduct is a joint-produced statement of the World Council of Churches, the Pontifical Council for Interreligious Dialogue, and the World Evangelical Alliance (WEA) – three major global Christian bodies.[63] The World Evangelical Alliance's participation in the development of this brief but thoughtful document ought to be sufficient encouragement for missionaries, development practitioners and development NGOs within the evangelical wing of the church to take its recommendations seriously.[64] The statement urges 'churches, church councils and mission agencies to reflect on their current practices and to use the recommendations in this document to prepare, where appropriate, their own guidelines for their witness and mission among those of different religions and among those who do not profess any particular religion'. It specifically affirms that 'acts of service, such as providing education, health care, relief services and acts of justice and advocacy are an integral part of witnessing to the gospel', but stresses that 'the exploitation of situations of poverty and need has no place in Christian outreach', and therefore, 'Christians should denounce and refrain from offering all forms of allurements, including financial incentives and rewards, in their acts of service'. Clearly, as is recognized in the statement, a lot more work needs to be done to determine what all this means in the nitty-gritty detail of day-to-day work in the development arena. As a gathering point for many hundreds of evangelical Christian development practitioners, the Micah Network is ideally placed to significantly contribute to such work, as is World Evangelical Alliance's own Mission Commission.

CONCLUSION

In the past, missionaries have been too often lampooned and pilloried as agents of imperialism, destroyers of indigenous cultures, ideologically driven manipulators of vulnerable natives. While there were a few to whom such descriptions might legitimately be attached, such generalizations wither under the scrutiny of more detailed historical study. A fairer and certainly more generous assessment is provided by the African Bishop and Nobel Peace Prize recipient Desmond Tutu – undoubtedly one of the greatest and most loved justice champions of our times. He is also, of course, a global leader in a global church, one whose roots and heart are in the global South. In a country where one expression of church fearfully and heretically provided theological legitimacy to racism, dispossession and exploitation, another nurtured and trained this man of prayer, a man whose faith has fuelled an immense courage and informed an unshaken mission for peace and justice. It seems appropriate to conclude with his words: 'The God of Exodus is subversive of all situations of injustice', he once declared, 'and the Bible is the most revolutionary, the most radical book there is. If any book should be banned by those who rule unjustly . . . it is the Bible'.[65] And of the missionaries who brought this book he said:

> You know the old story of how when the missionaries came to Africa, we had the land and they had the Bible. Then they said, 'Let us pray', and we dutifully shut our eyes, and when we said 'Amen' at the end and opened our eyes, why they had the land and we had the Bible. That seems to have been a bad bargain. But we are forever indebted to those indomitable men and women from across the seas who brought us the glorious gospel of God's love for us and who helped educate us in their schools and colleges and who helped to improve our health with the clinics and hospitals and health care they provided. We are forever grateful to them.[66]

NOTES

1. Luke 10: 27–28.
2. A reference to the persecuted church.
3. Bosch (1983, p. 276).
4. Also known as the Universal Commission or Christ's Commission.
5. Matthew 28: 19–20. Other versions appear in Mark 16: 15 and John 20: 21.
6. According to Luke's Gospel, written some time in the first century after Jesus' birth, his own mother predicted this would be the case – see Luke 1: 46–55.
7. Jenkins (2002, p. 2).
8. Ibid., p. 220.
9. Ramachandra (2005, p. 487).
10. The contemporary Protestant missionary movement traces its origins to the sudden wave of missionary activity that began with the establishment of three British missionary organizations: Baptist Missionary

Society (1792), London Missionary Society (1795) and Church Missionary Society (1799). Within 100 years 'every nominally Christian country and almost every denomination had begun to take its share in the support of the missionary cause' (Neil, 1964, p. 252).

11. Dowden (2008, p. 16).
12. Nürnberger (2003, p. 508).
13. Robert (2000, p. 51).
14. http://www.cmch-vellore.edu/MissionStatement/tabid/298/Default.aspx; accessed 2 November 2011.
15. Cited by Pincock (2011, p. 24).
16. Ibid.
17. http://www.jamkhed.org/TrainingandResearch.shtml; accessed 4 November 2011.
18. http://www.future.org/sites/future.org/files/Raj%20Arole%20Obituary.pdf; accessed 2 November 2011).
19. Personal email, 13 August 2010.
20. Sorley (2011, p. 137).
21. Personal email, 17 November 2011.
22. www.state.gov/g/drl/rls/irf/2008/108374.htm; accessed 25 July 2012.
23. www.guardian.co.uk/environment/2009/jun/07/eco-evangelist-craig-sorley; accessed 25 July 2012.
24. Sorley (2011, p. 138).
25. Ibid.
26. Personal email, 13 August 2010.
27. Ferguson (2004, p. 122).
28. Brock (2008, p. 23), available at: http://www.msp.unimelb.edu.au/missions/index.php/missions/article/viewFile/3/27; accessed 25 July 2012.
29. Ibid., p. 24.
30. Ibid., p. 25.
31. Ibid., p. 29.
32. Wolterstorff(1983, p. 32).
33. Ramachandra (2008, p. 247).
34. Relevant biblical texts include John 10: 10 and Matthew 4: 4.
35. John 4: 14.
36. Founded in 1799.
37. A ritual in which widows were burned alive on the cremation pyres of their dead husbands. Carey first made a thorough examination of the Hindu scriptures and could demonstrate that they did not require this practice.
38. *Annual Review 2010–2011*, CMS-UK, available at: http://www.cms-uk.org/Whoweare/Whatwedo/AnnualReview/tabid/227/language/en-GB/Default.aspx; accessed 25 October 2011.
39. http://www.cms-uk.org/Whoweare/Values/Evangelistic/tabid/173/language/en-GB/Default.aspx; accessed 17 November 2011.
40. http://www.bmsworldmission.org/about-us/mission-statement; accessed 21 November 2011.
41. http://www.bmsworldmission.org/node/1459; accessed 21 November 2011.
42. Marshall and Keough (2004, p. xii).
43. Ibid, p. 1.
44. Williams (2009).
45. Department for International Development, the British government's overseas development arm.
46. http://www.dfid.gov.uk/Documents/funding/CSCF-application-guidelines-2010.pdf, p. 6; accessed 23 November 2011.
47. http://www.dfid.gov.uk/Documents/funding/gpaf/GPAF-Innovation-Guidelines.pdf; accessed 24 November 2011.
48. http://www.dfid.gov.uk/documents/funding/gpaf/gpaf-innovation-guidelines.pdf; accessed 27 July 2012.
49. http://www.ausaid.gov.au/ngos/documents/ancp_guidelines.pdf, p. 4; accessed 26 July 2012.
50. Ibid p. 5.
51. Ibid.
52. http://transition.usaid.gov/our_work/global_partnerships/fbci/rule.html; accessed 27 July 2012.
53. Ibid.
54. www.acfid.asn.au/acfid/code-of-conduct/acfid-code-of-conduct, p. 4; accessed 23 November 2011.
55. Ibid., p. 12; accessed 23 November 2011.
56. Stanley (2003, p. 316).
57. http://www2.ohchr.org/english/law/ccpr.htm#art18; accessed 27 July 2012.
58. Bradbury (2012).
59. http://www.micahnetwork.org/library/disaster-management/proselytism-policy-statement; accessed 27 July 2012.

60. http://www.cms-uk.org/Whoweare/AboutCMS/Values/Evangelistic/tabid/173/language/en-GB/Default.aspx; accessed 1 August 2012.
61. https://sites.google.com/site/vmbgoverno/Home/politicas/fins/policy-on-witness-to-jesus-christ; accessed 27 July 2012.
62. Williams (2009).
63. Available at http://www.oikoumene.org/fileadmin/files/wcc-main/2011pdfs/ChristianWitness_recommendations.pdf; accessed 29 November 2011.
64. World Vision and Micah Network are two of WEA's global partners.
65. Sparks and Tutu (2011, p. 86).
66. Ibid, p. 87.

REFERENCES

Bosch, David J. (1983), 'Evangelism and social transformation', in Tom Sine (ed.), *The Church in Response to Human Need*, Monrovia: CA: MARC.

Bradbury, Steve (2012), 'The Micah mandate: an evangelical view', in Matthew Clarke (ed.) *Mission and Development: God's Work or Good Works?*, London and New York: Continuum.

Brock, Peggy (2008), 'Negotiating colonialism: the life and times of Arthur Wellington Clah', in *Evangelists of Empire?: Missionaries in Colonial History*, Amanda Barry, Joanna Cruickshank, Andrew Brown-May and Patricia Grimshaw (eds) [online] Melbourne: University of Melbourne eScholarship Research, available at: http://www.msp.unimelb.edu.au/missions/index.php/missions/article/viewFile/3/27.

Dowden, Richard (2008), *Africa: Altered States Ordinary Miracles*, London: Portobello Books Ltd.

Ferguson, Nial (2004), *Empire: How Britain Made the Modern World*, London: Penguin Books.

Jenkins, Philip (2002), *The Next Christendom: The Coming of Global Christianity*, Oxford/New York: Oxford University Press.

Kirk, Andrew, J. (1981), 'The kingdom, the church and a distressed world', *Evangelical Review of Theology*, **5**(1), 74–93. Reprinted from *Churchman*, **94**(1980).

Marshall, K. and L. Keough (eds) (2004), *Mind, Heart and Soul in the Fight Against Poverty*, Washington, DC: World Bank.

Neil, Stephen (1964), *A History of Christian Missions*, Middlesex, UK: Harmondsworth/New York: Penguin.

Nürnberger, Klaus (2003), 'God's mission in practice: the struggle for liberation, dignity and justice in African societies', *International Review of Mission*, **XCII**(367), 498–520.

Pincock, Stephen (2011), 'Rajanikant Arole', *The Lancet*, **378**(9785), 24.

Ramachandra, Vinoth (2005), 'Global religious transformations, political vision and Christian witness', *International Review of Mission*, **94**(375), 477–92.

Ramachandra, Vinoth (2008), *Subverting Global Myths: Theology and the Public Issues Shaping Our World*, Downers Grove, IL: InterVarsity Press.

Robert, Dana L. (2000), 'Shifting southward: global Christianity since 1945', *International Bulletin of Missionary Research*, **24**(2), 50–58.

Sorley, Craig (2011), 'Christ, creation stewardship and missions: how discipleship into a biblical worldview on environmental stewardship can transform people and their Land', *International Bulletin of Missionary Research*, **35**(3), 137–43.

Sparks, Allister and Mpho A. Tutu (2011), *Tutu: The Authorised Portrait*, Sydney: Hachette Australia in association with PQ Blackwell.

Stanley, Brian (2003), 'Conversion to Christianity: the colonization of the mind?', *International Review of Mission*, **XCII**(366), 315–31.

Williams, Rowan (2009), 'New perspectives on faith and development', lecture available at: http://www.archbishopofcanterbury.org/articles.php/768/new-perspectives-on-faith-and-development; accessed 22 November 2011.

Wolterstorff, Nicholas (1983), *Until Justice and Peace Embrace*, Grand Rapids, MI: Eerdmans.

26 Why Western-based, Pentecostal mission organizations undertake community development in South East Asia

Vicki-Ann Ware, Anthony Ware, Matthew Clarke and Grant Buchanan

INTRODUCTION

There are as many as 524 million Pentecostal/Charismatic believers globally, representing just over a quarter of all professing Christians (Barrett et al., 2001, p. 4). The global Pentecostal movement was founded a century ago as a missionary movement with a strong emphasis on evangelism and reaction against what they saw as liberal Christianity's abandonment of evangelism for social justice action. Pentecostals have always been strong on providing practical assistance to people around them in need, yet this has largely been ad hoc and seen as an aspect of Christian moral responsibility rather than being considered an aspect of legitimate Christian mission, which has been exclusively focused on evangelism.

This research stems from personal observations and anecdotal evidence that Western-based, Pentecostal mission organizations working in mainland South East Asia (Thailand, Laos, Cambodia, Vietnam and Burma/Myanmar) have shifted the emphasis of their activities over the last two decades, to increasingly become involved in community development, social justice and practical assistance alongside more traditional Pentecostal mission emphases of evangelism, starting new churches and training leaders for those churches.

Such a change would be significant as it would indicate not just a change of practice but also a change in their religious understanding of mission. This research therefore seeks to explore any recent shift in Pentecostal understanding of mission in the literature, empirically verify the anecdotal observation of a shift in mission activities in mainland South East Asia, and then explore any such change in the understanding of mission by practitioners in the region. It does so by exploring the motivations of key leaders within Pentecostal mission agencies in the region for any increased engagement in community development activities alongside traditional mission priorities, in particular exploring the extent to which community development and practical activities are seen by these respondents as a strategy for the traditional priority of proselytization, or are conducted out of what could be seen as a more genuine humanitarian motivation.

This chapter is divided into five sections. The next section reviews the literature, placing Pentecostal organizations within the scope of faith-based organizations and discussing the origins and distinctives of the Pentecostal movement, particularly in relation to their understanding of mission. The third section details the methodology for the fieldwork undertaken to examine the research questions, as well as the research participants.

The fourth details the findings of the empirical research, while the fifth section offers a discussion of the implications of these findings.

FAITH-BASED ORGANIZATIONS IN DEVELOPMENT

Pentecostal mission agencies engaged in aid and development work are one subset of an increasingly prominent, but poorly understood, group of faith-based organizations working in the development field. Organized religions have long played an important role in enhancing the welfare of local communities. While religious teaching is primarily concerned with providing spiritual leadership, an interest in the physical welfare of their communities has also been a core activity for some religious organizations working within poor communities. This concern with physical welfare is often expressed and delivered through affiliated faith-based organizations that operationalize this outreach (see work by Clarke, 2008; Harb, 2008; Clarke and Jennings, 2008; Clarke et al., 2011).

The term faith-based organization (FBO) is used to describe a particular niche within the voluntary and/or charitable sector. 'Generally, but by no means exclusively, faith-based organizations are philanthropic in nature, constituted as charities or non-profit organizations, and aligned with one of the world's major religions'.[1] Certainly, FBOs play a significant role in the delivery of development interventions within the Asia-Pacific region (Marshall and Saanen, 2007).

Whilst the existence of organizations with religious affiliations working to improve the well-being of the disadvantaged is not necessarily recent, the term faith-based organization *is* relatively recent and has been coined to distinguish those organizations that are 'sectarian' in nature (James, 2009):

> For many years, FBOs have played major roles in society, delivering a variety of services to the public, such as caring for the infirm and elderly, advocating justice for the oppressed and playing a major role in humanitarian aid and international development efforts. In this context they are perhaps closer in terms of organizational set up, structure and administration to other twentieth-century civil society organizations than to more traditional and historic religious organizations.[2]

Whilst, FBOs share the same basic characteristics of 'secular' NGOs: independence, being not-for-profit, voluntary, and altruistic (Ball and Dunn, 1996), they are further distinguished through their affiliation with a religious structure, doctrine or congregation.

Given the weak consideration of religion within development (Clarke, 2011), it is not surprising therefore that FBOs themselves have also long been invisible in discussions of community development (Marshall and Saanen, 2007). This apparent invisibility though should not be mistaken as non-existence. More correctly, their invisibility reflects a blindness of the development sector itself in failing to recognize the importance of religion within the development sector. This may be partly explained by FBOs being embedded within communities and being less external agents and more 'organic' to the community. It can also be explained by organized religions choosing to position themselves outside the development sector when working to improve the material lives of their congregation (Clarke, 2008).

In recent years, the presence of FBOs in community development work has gradually become increasingly recognized, both within the development sector and within FBOs themselves. Both sectors have begun to recognize that there is importance and synergy to be gained by being aware of one another and incorporating an understanding of religion more purposely into the development domain (Harb, 2008). As participatory community-focused models of development have become increasingly dominant in recent years, religious organizations and FBOs have become increasingly 'attractive' as agents or key stakeholders in the development process due to their strong links to local communities. Moreover, religious bodies themselves have also begun to initiate contact with aid donors to seek increased involvement (and funding) in community development interventions (Clarke and Jennings, 2008).

Missionary organizations may also be considered FBOs if their mission work involves aspects of traditional community development intervention focusing on improving material well-being of local communities. Indeed, many mission organizations have long histories of being 'development' agencies even though this is not the language used to describe their activities (see Clarke and Donnelly, 2008; Rae and Clarke, 2010). However, not all mission organizations have had such an explicit 'development' aspect to their engagement with local communities, with Pentecostal missionaries being such an example.

One important contribution therefore of this chapter is to show how Pentecostal missionaries have made significant contributions to aid and development work, and how this is now becoming a more explicit and integral focus of their work in developing and underdeveloped nations.

HISTORY AND ORIGINS OF PENTECOSTALS

Some would argue that there have always been 'Pentecostals' in the church since the Day of Pentecost (Nichol, 1966, pp. 18–9). However, the modern Pentecostal movement of the twentieth century is a new phenomenon and grew out of several significant movements during the late 1800s. The first of these was the Holiness Movement, and in particular the Wesleyan teaching about a 'second blessing' subsequent to salvation, to enable the believer to live a holy life. The language used by holiness preachers progressively began to refer to this second experience being like tongues of fire, or like a baptism in the Holy Spirit (McGee, 2004, p. 16), which led to the practice of seeking a personal encounter with the Holy Spirit (Moreau et al., 2004, p. 148). It also emphasized the Holy Spirit as the source of power for evangelism and healings (McGee, 2004, pp. 74–5).

The second movement feeding into the growth of the modern Pentecostal movement was a spate of revivalism in Western nations toward the end of the nineteenth century, in which people were heard 'speaking in languages unknown to those who heard the ecstatic utterances' (Nichol, 1966, p. 18). Revivalist practices also emphasized miraculous healing of disease (Macchia, 1999, p. 19). The slow progress in medical knowledge and practice of the 1800s, coupled with rampant outbreaks of deadly disease and poor hygiene, led to a distrust of the medical profession and a greater reliance upon prayer for the sick and faith in God for divine intervention (McGee, 2004, p. 18).

As a third trend, pessimism began to grow about a perceived decline in the moral climate of Western society. A belief developed in some parts of the church that the world would get worse before Christ's return, thus the moral decline was interpreted by some as a sign of Christ's imminent return (ibid., pp. 24–5), providing renewed impetus for giving a much higher priority to evangelism (Anderson, 2004, pp. 178–9). This also fuelled growth in the belief of millennialism, the idea that Christ's return would herald a 1000-year reign on earth in which Christ would restore that which was dysfunctional in the world and liberate the poor. By prioritizing evangelism, more could therefore partake of the fruits of the coming restoration.

Fourth, the established Protestant churches became increasingly middle class during the late nineteenth and early twentieth centuries. As large numbers of poor new converts began to pour in as a result of the holiness movement and renewed emphasis on evangelism, they were not well supported by the middle class and were frequently ostracized, to the point where they began to separate out into holiness churches (ibid., pp. 27, 62). Holiness churches, including the early Pentecostal church, embraced a second post-conversion experience, faith healing and the urgency of evangelism, and were formed largely by the poor, socially marginalized believers of the day.

In this way, the Pentecostal movement was founded primarily as a social movement amongst the poor, and largely remains so in much of the world today (Nichol, 1966, p. 57; Anderson, 2004, p. 227). One distinctive of this is that the Pentecostal church saw the Gospel as the power to heal and the means to endure difficult life circumstances, more than as a means to escape poverty (Anderson, 2004, p. 216).

More recently, beginning in the 1970s and 1980s in the West, many more middle class Christians identifying similar experiences and theology have stayed within existing denominations in what became known as the Charismatic renewal movement, and these Christians as Charismatics (Wagner, 1973). One significant impact of this movement has been the increasing acceptability of the Pentecostal movement within mainstream Christianity, and thus an increase in communication and the sharing of ideas.

Distinctives of Pentecostals

The modern Pentecostal movement grew out of earlier evangelical Protestant denominations, which were themselves in part a reaction against liberalism, formalism and modernism in established Protestant churches. Liberal Christianity places less emphasis on miracles than on the teachings of Jesus, leading to emphasis on moral teaching and social justice over evangelism, thus both evangelicals and Pentecostals have had a long-standing distrust of social justice (Anderson, 2004, p. 27), and point to a number of formerly faith-based organizations that now operate from an entirely secular ideology as a result of adopting a liberal theological agenda.

Nonetheless, the early Pentecostal movement had quite a few characteristics distinct from other evangelical and Protestant denominations. For example, given the origins of Pentecostal churches in the largely uneducated, poor lower classes it is perhaps not surprising that they rejected many facets of evangelical practice. In the early days of the movement they reacted strongly against any sense of institutionalized control or establishment (Nichol, 1966, p. 95): 'The fact that Pentecostals were isolated, rejected and ridiculed by established churches, especially by fundamentalists, eventually resulted in an anti-ecumenical attitude' (Anderson, 2004, p. 62).

They also had little time for education, perhaps given the urgency they perceived around evangelizing the world prior to Christ's imminent return. Indeed, Nichol suggests that in the early days, 'too many of its early leaders tenaciously held to a view "that those who were filled with the Spirit needed no one to instruct them"' (Nichol, 1966, pp. 77–8). The earliest Bible colleges were set up primarily to facilitate the rapid training of pastors and evangelists, and the curriculum focused on mastery of Bible passages for preaching and training new converts, and had 'little time to establish prospective ministers in sound doctrine' (ibid., pp. 97, 109). Perhaps it is not surprising, then, that whereas evangelicals tend towards a set liturgy and derive their theology primarily from didactic passages of the Bible, Pentecostals have a largely oral tradition and a narrative (storytelling) teaching style (Nichol, 1966, p. 16): 'A spontaneous liturgy, which unlike that of most older churches is mainly oral and narrative, carries an emphasis on direct experience of God through the Spirit' (Anderson, 2004, pp. 212–3).

Closely linked to this is the practice of deriving theology from narrative passages of the Bible in preference to didactic passages (Clark, 1997): 'the essence of Pentecostalism cannot be understood through "dogma and doctrines" but through the experience of God, a "narrative theology whose central expression is the testimony" . . . this emphasis on experience is "so total that it shatters the cognitive packaging"' (Anderson, 2004, p. 61).

It therefore follows that Pentecostals avoid intellectualizing about their faith and are thus more pragmatic in their approach to evangelism and helping those in need (Anderson, 2004, p. 223; Moreau, et al., 2004, p. 148).

Traditional Views on Meeting Physical, Social, Emotional and Spiritual Needs

Pentecostals often appear to others as unconcerned with meeting the needs of those living in abject poverty (Miller and Yamamori, 2007, p. 2). However, this reflects a shallow understanding of Pentecostal beliefs and practices, how they have traditionally perceived poverty and injustice, and how their response to it is shaped by theology. In actual fact, Pentecostals have traditionally seen and been very concerned with poverty and injustice in this life. Yet they have viewed its causes and cures through three concurrent sets of lenses, each consisting of a different time horizon, which have fundamentally shaped the way in which they have traditionally responded.

Short term

In the short term, Pentecostals have traditionally been concerned with getting on with the urgent task of evangelism in preparation for Christ's imminent return. McGee observed that 'Firmly believing in the imminent return of Christ, little time remained for church members to evangelize. The clock of prophetic fulfilment was ticking loudly' (McGee, 1994, p. 11). 'Their belief in the imminence of the end has meant that there is little time for matters of social concern, as it is more important to get "souls saved"' (Anderson, 2004, p. 219). The Gospel 'is the only answer to man's every need, complete for body, soul, spirit, and for eternity' (Nichol, 1966, p. 121), and theological reflection has been seen as less important (Warrington, 2008, p. 253).

However, this does not mean there is no practical assistance given to those in need. Accounts of Pentecostal history throughout the late nineteenth and the twentieth centuries are full of stories of missionaries and preachers taking in orphans and widows, feeding the hungry, and providing for the practical needs of the 'destitute' (McGee, 1994, p. 13; Anderson, 2004, p. 69). The difference is that these efforts tended to be ad hoc, based on immediate need presented by new converts, with little or no thought given to a broader poverty alleviation strategy (McGee, 2004, pp. 491–3). Where Pentecostals had limited physical, social and economic means and could not provide practical assistance themselves, they turned to prayer to seek a miracle. Early Pentecostal literature is full of testimonies of divine healings and miraculous provision for immediate needs (Nichol, 1966, p. 16).

Thus, whilst there was little articulation of a priority on meeting the immediate, physical needs of the people around them, Pentecostals in practice were actively involved in this space, albeit in an ad hoc sense and relying on divine intervention, particularly where their resources ran short.

Medium term

In the medium term, Pentecostals had an expectation that conversion would lead to personal change, and that as new believers began to live with greater self-discipline and holiness they would cease bad or sinful habits that robbed them of time, money and opportunity, and thereby their life circumstances would automatically begin to improve. As they learned to behave more courteously and respectfully, and as they lived their lives with greater discipline, it was expected that their access to more lucrative employment opportunities would also improve, bringing with it greater economic benefits. This phenomenon was first described by Donald McGavran (1955, 1970), an evangelical missionary and missions historian who coined the term 'redemption and lift'. This has been adopted into Pentecostal thinking and has been observed and documented in a range of contexts (Wagner, 1973, pp. 71, 92–100).

Some of the most common themes of Pentecostal teaching are the ideas that believers should 'run the race [of life] with the discipline of an athlete' and with hard work (1 Corinthians 9: 24; Hebrews 12: 1; 2 Timothy 4: 7); that one's life should be transformed through studying and applying the truths of the Bible (Rom 12: 1–2); and that one should develop the 'fruits of the Spirit' (Gal 5: 22–23). Likewise, whilst immediate help was available in the short term, ongoing spiritual development in the life of the believer brings the expectation of increasing self-help, as seen in passages that suggest that 'if you refuse to work, you should not eat' (2 Thessalonians 3: 8–10; Proverbs 14: 23).

Long term

In the longer term, the lens of Christ's imminent return meant that for Pentecostals world evangelization must remain the overriding priority (Anderson, 2004, p. 175). They believed that when Christ returned, He would restore all things to their rightful place for those who believed, so the priority was conversion so that the maximum number of people could enjoy Christ's liberation: 'Early Pentecostal eschatology was apocalyptic in the sense that the kingdom of God was understood as soon to break in and miraculously to transform the entire cosmos. This eschatological fervour may have hindered a vision among Pentecostals for long-term social transformation' (Macchia, 1999, p. 23).

The priority in the minds of Pentecostals traditionally was clearly to bring people into God's kingdom, so that they could benefit from the restoration and liberation of the poor, which would be heralded in by the millennial reign. With the expectation that Christ would return within the current believers' lifetimes, there was little incentive to engage in social or political transformation that would be of most benefit to future generations, that is, the millennial reign would rectify these structural issues before future generations came into being (ibid., pp. 8, 13).

The Pentecostal church therefore strongly supported mission activities, both locally and in other cultures and countries (McGee, 2004, p. 37). These usually consisted of preaching for conversion and offering to pray for miracles, particularly divine healing, which were seen as the primary means of meeting people's needs (Nichol, 1966, pp. 203, 9, 22). Starting new churches and training more workers were also top priorities.

A RECENT SHIFT

A number of authors have documented a recent shift in Pentecostal thinking and theology, which appears to date from about the mid-1990s (Fee, 1991; Anderson, 2004; McGee, 2004; Miller and Yamamori, 2007). They suggest that over the late twentieth century, there was a move away from millennialism and the reliance upon miracles in everyday practice (Anderson, 2004, p. 233), as the church has become more middle class – a trend that has provided it with greater resources to engage in broad social programmes (Miller and Yamamori, 2007, p. 3). Nichol suggests that for the generation of Pentecostals after World War II, 'The stress on the future, on preparing for the next world, has given way very largely to a principle of accommodation to the surrounding culture' (Nichol, 1966, p. 237). By the end of the twentieth century, the North American Pentecostal churches were primarily white and middle class, and had 'lost a degree of [their] eschatological fervour during [their] gradual move from the urban poor to the suburban middle class' (Macchia, 1999, p. 23). This trend was mirrored in the church in other Western nations such as Australia.

Some authors suggest that over the late twentieth century, there was also a move away from millennialism and the reliance upon miracles in everyday practice (Anderson, 2004, p. 233). As the church became more middle class, it also had greater resources to engage in broad social programmes (Miller and Yamamori, 2007, p. 3). Further, a range of important global issues have impacted on all mission initiatives including a greater global awareness and rise of poverty, injustice and violence, massive human migration, a changing deterritorialization of culture, culture shock, and political resistance to traditional missionary activity (Daniels, 2011, p. 132).

In an attempt to regain some of their former fervour, the largest Pentecostal denomination, the Assemblies of God, declared 1990–2000 to be a global Decade of Harvest, aiming to double the rate at which churches were started and people converted (McGee, 2004, p. 464). They also began re-assessing their approach to world evangelization:

> Assemblies of God biblical scholars . . . and missiologists . . . began to explore the meaning of the kingdom of God (the rule of God in the hearts and behaviours of believers) as a present reality for the mission of the Church , but without discounting the future millennial reign of Christ in His restored kingdom. (Ibid., p. 483)

As early as 1991, key Pentecostal missions thinkers, such as Gordon Fee, began to re-assess what that 'harvest' would look like, in statements such as the following:

> Our Gospel is not simply that of 'saving soul'; it is rather, as with Jesus, the bringing of wholeness to broken people in every kind of distress. Mission simply cannot be divided between 'spiritual' and 'physical'. To do one is to do the other, and both constitute the global mission of the church. (Fee, 1991, p. 17)

This shift has been further taken up in a desire for the maturing Pentecostal movement to engage in theological reflection on what their missional focus should be and how this should redirect motivations and practical engagement in social concerns. This is seen not as the means to another end, but as a central part of the actual mission. As Klaus notes, 'the realities of poverty, injustice and violence will certainly require fresh and critical theologising on the nature of Pentecostal Mission' (Klaus, 2011, pp. 132; see also p. 6). Likewise, Daniels suggests that 'acknowledging the theological, moral, and socio-political reality that prompts Pentecostal-Charismatic ministries to embrace social engagement is an initial step in their incorporating social ministry as vital to a Pentecostal-Charismatic understanding of the church' and hence mission (Daniels, 2011, p. 343).

Sociologist Michael Wilkinson takes this shift and realignment one step further, highlighting the dynamic way in which recent studies of FBOs reflect a far broader engagement is occurring among Pentecostal FBOs where community and service is balancing the more traditional Pentecostal gospel proclamation. Wilkinson suggests that this is due to the fact that 'a Pentecostal theology of the Kingdom of God' is outworked in these FBOs in both 'word and deed', where social engagement is done alongside a religious focus of 'providing meaning and making sense of the world in spiritual terms' (Wilkinson, 2007, p. 77). However, as our empirical evidence suggests below, such academic dialogue is not the primary source of changed theology and praxis amongst missions practitioners.

MOVING GOALS

The fieldwork research for this chapter seeks to verify the anecdotal observation that there has been a shift in the balance of mission activities undertaken by Western-based Pentecostal mission organizations working in mainland South East Asia, and then understand the motivation behind such a shift as expressed by these fieldworkers.

Given the relatively small number of qualified informants for this study, purposeful selection of key long-term field leaders from Pentecostal Western-based mission organizations was considered the most appropriate means of sampling (Maykut and Morehouse, 1994, p. 45). Any change in their activities was explored through a survey of the activities they were currently involved in, as contrasted to those they were undertaking 15–20 years ago, and was followed by a phenomenological exploration of the subjective personal perceptions these information-rich informants held of the changes they described (Patton, 1990, p. 169; Denzin and Lincoln, 2000, pp. 484–6). 'Any attempt to understand social reality has to be grounded in people's experiences of that social reality' (Gray, 2009, p. 22). Given these participants are all articulate leaders, an elite of foreign non-government organization leaders, semi-structured interviews is the preferred research methodology (Odendahl and Shaw, 2001). Indeed, interviews are the preferred methodology for most phenomenological research (Peräkylä, 2008, p. 351).

Surveys and semi-structured interviews were conducted with 12 key long-term field-workers from nine Pentecostal movements, originating from five Western nations (four predominantly English-speaking). All were engaged in some mix of both traditional missionary activities (such as evangelism or starting new churches) together with development or practical assistance activities in mainland South East Asia (Thailand, Laos, Cambodia, Vietnam and Burma/Myanmar). Most respondents were country or regional directors of mission organizations, all but three having personally been active on the field for at least 15–20 years. In a small number of cases they were newer staff reflecting on organizational experience.

Mullings (1999) found that research with elites is best conducted by those who can occupy 'shared positional spaces' and can present themselves as insiders who understand the concerns of participants. Leaders within mission organizations comprise a foreign elite (Odendahl and Shaw, 2001), and their roles in some contexts in the region result in them holding a range of defensive concerns. It is therefore appropriate that most of the interview participants were personally known to two of the authors as former colleagues (Platt, 1981). In interviewing peers, the interview methodology was informed by an understanding that interviews are conversations within a context (Denzin and Lincoln, 2000), and that to generate candid and natural responses interviewers should interact with participants based on personal rapport and shared meaning (Fontana and Frey, 2008).

Interviews were around 45 minutes each in length, and guided by a schedule of questions enquiring first about the activities they are currently engaged in within the region, contrasting this with the activities they (or their organization) were engaged in 15–20 years ago, and then exploring the motivations they perceive they, their organization, and their donors have in any shift that has occurred to engage in development and practical assistance work alongside the more traditional Pentecostal mission activities.

Interviews were conducted by Skype or phone during March–April 2011, to reduce fieldwork time and costs and generate better response rates (Shuy, 2001). While it is generally regarded that the quality of data obtained through telephone interviews may be slightly lower than that from in-person interviewing, due to a 'contextual naturalness', greater mutual interaction, and slower, more thoughtful responses when face to face, the additional visual interaction afforded by Skype video-calling overcame much of this disadvantage with most participants.

Most interviews were conducted by one researcher while a second researcher transcribed written notes. Because some of the participants work in sensitive contexts and fear misinterpretation of their responses, all interview responses are treated entirely anonymously.

These key informant interviews yielded rich and remarkably consistent data documenting: (1) a significant shift in the nature of mission activities being undertaken by Pentecostal fieldworkers in the region today, as contrasted with those undertaken 15–20 years ago; (2) the timing and reasons they suggest as being behind the shift; and (3) their stated motivations for engaging in development and practical assistance activities alongside more traditional Pentecostal mission emphases. The consistency in responses was remarkable given the number of different movements and home nationalities these fieldworkers represent.

Shift in the Nature of Activities

The interview responses clearly demonstrate that there has indeed been a major shift in the nature of Pentecostal mission activities undertaken by these agencies within the region today, as compared with activities undertaken 15–20 years ago. Ten of the 12 respondents indicated that 15–20 years ago they and their organization were almost exclusively engaged in traditional spiritual emphases of preaching, evangelism, starting new churches and training new leaders for the church, and conducted few formal development or practical assistance programmes beyond meeting ad hoc needs. One of the two exceptions indicated that he had personally adopted a holistic mission perspective during his theological education more than two decades ago, but for a long time found himself at odds with his organization's priorities. He notes, however, that there was a shift within the organization about a decade ago. The other exception might actually be better described as representing a Charismatic evangelical organization than a Pentecostal agency, and this respondent indicated they began their work in the region over 20 years ago with an equal emphasis on practical assistance in areas including drug rehabilitation, microfinance, and children's education.

By contrast, the ten respondents who described a change noted the significance of the shift in their mission activities. Two respondents indicated they had no development or practical assistance programmes at all 15–20 years ago, while the remainder indicated they were engaged in one (or at most, two) of the following activities at that time: running an orphanage (two agencies, one being for AIDS orphans), running a preschool, offering student scholarships, feeding children, providing health care in refugee camps and a small-scale microfinance project. It is interesting to note the extent to which the focus of the activities that were undertaken at that time was primarily on housing and education of children. Beyond this, the agencies and fieldworkers interviewed were at that time only involved in meeting the immediate needs of their members as they arose, in an ad hoc fashion.

This picture is in stark contrast with the current mission activities of these same fieldworkers and agencies. Today, interviewees report, they are engaged in formal activities across almost all community development sectors, in conjunction with (not replacing) traditional Pentecostal spiritual mission emphases. Almost all respondents reported that they or their agency are directly involved in each of these major areas of development (numbers in brackets represent number of respondents indicating current work in this area):

- *Health* (11) – WASH (water, sanitation and hygiene) (9), primary and preventative health care (9), disability (4), drug rehabilitation (4), AIDS training and/or care (3), surgical operations (2), and hospital construction (1);
- *Education* (11) – student scholarships (8), construction and/or running of preschools (7) and primary/secondary schools (3), children's clubs and tutoring programmes (5), young adult job-skill training (7), and language schools (2);

- *Livelihood* (11) – training and assistance to start small businesses (7), microfinance (5), agriculture (7), animal husbandry (4), and other food security (2);
- *Advocacy* (7) – human trafficking (4), equitable access to state services (2), ethnic, religious or political discrimination (2), peacemaking (2), and corruption (1);
- *Other* (10) – orphanage (7), crisis food distribution (6), crisis housing (4), sex industry rescue (5).

Respondents were sometimes hesitant to describe their work using this development terminology. It is not completely clear whether that was hesitation at being too closely associated with NGO development or because the comparatively low level of funding per fieldworker meant most were running programmes on a smaller scale and were less well organized than the major international development NGOs. Several respondents repeatedly clarified the small scale and funding of their programmes, to avoid misinterpretation. It was also clear that respondents had rarely done any formal training in development studies beyond their theological training, and were imitating or experimenting.

Of the above list, advocacy stands out as being something that Pentecostal missions would normally be expected to be less engaged in. This perceived hesitancy of being involved in advocacy may stem from a historical legacy of Pentecostals themselves being from more marginalized groups unaccustomed to being able to influence the decisions of those in power. It may also be due to an orientation to action over discussion and negotiation. Or it may relate to negative views about power resulting in a historical aversion to political involvement. It is interesting to note that the one fieldworker directly engaged in an anti-corruption campaign has a holistic spiritual-plus-physical view of corruption, combining a programme of direct engagement and advocacy with officials with regular prayer meetings seeking divine intervention on this issue as well.

Those advocating on other issues also indicated prayer for miraculous intervention was an equal component in pursuing structural power change. Of the seven respondents that did self-identify as engaging in advocacy, they did so through privately engaging with officials or key leaders on behalf of people rather than promoting an active citizenship in which people educated about their rights make a public stand or hold officials accountable. Human trafficking was an area that four respondents were involved in advocacy work as this directly linked to their work rescuing victims from the sex trade. One respondent reported running a deliberate anti-corruption advocacy programme, while two reported occasional ad hoc advocacy work with local authorities on behalf of communities with which they worked, to help them gain equitable access to state services or just decision-making. Likewise, two of the 12 agencies reported directly working in peacemaking and in promoting ethnic, religious or political equity.

Motivations for Engaging in Development

Respondents were all asked to describe in their own words their motivation for now engaging in development activities rather than maintaining a strict focus on more traditional Pentecostal mission activities. Their responses were informative, speaking of holistic ideas of mission and of following Jesus' example:

> You cannot eat prayer and the Word of God. Practical assistance is one aspect of holistic mission.

> I want to see the whole community transformed. It is holistic. I want to see total health in the community, physically, socially, emotionally, physically, spiritually and environmentally.

> Jesus ministered to people in body, soul and spirit.

> We have to treat people as wholes. It comes out of God's demonstration in Jesus' ministry. We can't bifurcate people.

> I am just following Jesus' example.

> Jesus fed the 5000 and did not take an altar call afterwards [i.e., did not ask anyone to convert].

> The Gospels show God's heart is to feed the hungry and clothe the naked. Salvation is not just limited to people's souls.

> Our motivation comes from the Bible. Jesus told us to give water to the thirsty, to feed the poor, and to preach the Gospel. These are two sides of our calling.

A couple of respondents argued that Pentecostals have long been engaged in these activities, if in a different form:

> We have been doing this for years, but have only recently labelled it as development.

> Pentecostals have always been involved in helping people in tangible ways, but have been rhetorically opposed. We got around it by saying, 'The Holy Spirit led me' to act in an ad hoc compassionate manner – for example, housing orphans.

One of the most interesting observations from the interview research data was that nine of the ten respondents who noted a significant shift in their mission activities date that change to sometime between 1998 and 2001. The tenth pointed to experiencing the impact of the 2004 Boxing Day tsunami.

To clarify their responses, respondents were all asked what had led to their shift in thinking and activities. Respondents pointed to three key factors: being influenced by the ideas and practice of other organizations, seeing human need in a new way, and a re-evaluation of 'what Jesus did' as a model for contemporary action. This latter point correlates closely with the Pentecostal hermeneutic, which emphasizes narrative scriptural passages over didactic ones, and therefore is indicative of a shift in the theology of mission held by these Pentecostals and their agencies. Their responses to the question of what prompted the shift included:

> Cross-pollination with other organizations and ideas.

> We were frustrated that what we were doing was not working, and someone suggested [a particular] training. We were not interested, but we finally went and our eyes were opened.

> We were in the middle of getting AusAID accreditation [to try to access tax deductibility and government funding], when we realized this accreditation was not about meeting our needs but

> about theirs. Thinking through the AusAID criteria, and why they had been set, completely changed my way of thinking.
>
> The Bible is clear we need to be concerned with the whole of life. The trigger was re-reading the Bible, and seeing the example of other people embracing a more holistic approach.
>
> Seeing people die! I could see the difference giving people hope for tomorrow made, and this might touch on the joy of the Lord and so on – but that does not put food on the table or stop people dying of disease.
>
> Visiting some very isolated and needy people, and discovering that a few months earlier a third of the village had died of dysentery for a lack of clean water. For me, that was a paradigm shift, recognizing that ministry was not just teaching and words but has got to be practical.
>
> Became aware that the Bible shows that we need to be concerned with the whole of life.
>
> Understanding that Jesus commands us to preach the Gospel to the poor. It is very important to me to have a scriptural base for all our activity.

To further clarify motives and priorities, respondents were all asked to first rank on a scale of 1 to 10 how important they consider traditional Pentecostal mission activities – such as evangelism, conversion and starting new churches – and then asked to contrast this with a similar rank for how important they consider practical assistance and development activities. Respondents almost all resisted this question, articulating concern as expressing a view about one aspect of mission in isolation to the other. Most attempted to avoid the answer altogether, and then when they did answer quickly added a qualifier to their responses, such as:

> . . . as part of . . . but not in isolation, the two must be integrated.
>
> . . . but I do both, all the time.
>
> You can't separate them. I can't box them like I used to.
>
> It needs a holistic approach – don't separate them

Ultimately, with prodding, respondents gave a cumulative score of 113/120 to the importance of the traditional activities, and 110/120 to development/practical assistance. Five respondents ranked traditional activities as being marginally more important than development/practical assistance, five ranked both of being of equal importance, and two ranked development/practical assistance as marginally more important. Where slightly greater importance was given to traditional spiritual activities over practical assistance, the reason was consistently along the lines that 'Eternity is longer than here'.

Respondents were then asked to explain the difference they see in their motivation for traditional spiritual activities and practical assistance. Directly asking them for a difference was a deliberate ploy to see how consistent their expression of holism was, or whether at a more fundamental level they really perceived a distinction. Their responses expressed a strong concept of holism:

> They are one and the same. It is like a marriage. These are two arms that need to work together.

> They are part of the one, whole package. The transformation process includes inner, social, family, psychological and physical change.

> They are connected; the same. We can't separate them. We have to do both. . . . practical development goes hand in hand with traditional mission stuff.

> We are strongly motivated for both, but the motivation behind relief and development is still spiritual.

> They have to go hand in hand. There is always a tension between the two.

Corroborating their responses on this point, several respondents expanded on their answers without prompting to explain the extent to which they arrange specific prayer for divine assistance as a means to empower the effectiveness of their practical community development work. One responded discussed raising funds and implementing projects while praying for miracles. Another stated:

> We try, and then bathe it in prayer and hope God moves.

At this point respondents were asked the most direct question of the interview, probing at the core issue behind their motivation. Respondents were directly asked whether practical assistance and development work was a strategy for evangelism, or came from other motives. While the responses showed some variation in understanding at this point, these responses do demonstrate a significant level of change in motivation from traditional Pentecostal priorities.

For some, development activities are clearly part of a strategy:

> We do our humanitarian work to build relationships and trust on behalf of the church.

> Practical help creates goodwill and opens lots of doors. It creates a platform and receptivity for spiritual help, and brings relationships we would not have developed any other way.

> We earn the right to speak into people's lives by reaching them at their point of need.

The motivations behind this need to be recognized:

> Bringing people into the kingdom encompasses every area of society and all of life. So evangelism is extremely important, but it is not always the first thing people are ready to tackle. Once God is in your life, you are going to receive benefits of salvation in spirit, but also improvements in other aspects of life. It is the doorway into the rest of the kingdom of God.

> If it was family you were helping, you would never distinguish between practical help and evangelism. Evangelism would flow from a natural relationship. We hang out and be in their lives, and have a natural concern for sharing Jesus and for practical help.

> There is a principle that as you bless people you change the spiritual environment. You meet needs, and evangelism occurs. Blessing people is very important because it changes your attitude towards them. It is NOT a strategy for church planting, although I use to think that way. It is true that if people do not have enough food or water, they are not interested. That is why Jesus fed the 5000. Now I see that you do the whole lot simply because they need it.

For others, development and evangelism are both priorities, but one is not the strategy for the other:

> Compassion for humanitarian needs is not just a strategy.

> Our motivation is not to convert people, but it is to allow them to see the difference in our lives. Before, we were using programmes as bait, to reel people in. Now we don't want something to be bait, we want to bless and love others out of obedience to Christ rather than pressure them to convert. We have had a big shift in our thinking.

> If we do social service as a tool to entice people to change their religion, they know it. That is not the way Jesus operated.

One respondent bemoaned that he had recently left his former Pentecostal organization because they saw doing development as 'almost 100 percent' a strategy for evangelism and church growth, but he disagreed. This disagreement over motivations had led to his change of organizations.

These responses clearly show mixed opinion about whether community development activities are a strategy for evangelism or an important concern of their own. Part of this vacillation appears to stem from a strong view that holistic mission requires both, but that ultimate assistance must also include the spiritual dimension, since, 'eternity is longer than here'. But these responses also show a real change in motivation for many, embracing a genuinely humanitarian concern for the proximal needs and the priorities of the people they work alongside, and a genuine respect for their freedom of choice.

> We have to help the poor [even when] they are not interested and do not accept Christ.

There is also a growing appreciation of the power dynamic at play in a development relationship that leads many secular commentators to have grave concerns about proselytization activities in conjunction with development projects. This issue was not raised directly in the interviews; nonetheless several respondents felt the need to explain their position. The most clearly articulated comment was:

> As we relate to people, we do so because of God's love for all people. It is not conditional on them buying into our worldview. God said to love our neighbours. I have a deep commitment to not acting with a carrot and stick. Therefore I am very upfront about who I am, and I don't attach incentives to any activities. I always ensure the 'classical spiritual stuff' happens outside these events.

In almost all cases, the majority of funding is derived from churches and individual donors (almost always individuals) in their home countries. The final questions of the interview enquired about the reactions and motivations of these donors, and the extent to which they have initiated, supported or resisted the shift to include community development and practical assistance work alongside more traditional activities promoting evangelism and starting new churches. The respondents were uniform in suggesting that donors were lagging behind the understanding of fieldworkers:

> We are ahead of our donors, bringing them on a journey with us.

> Our long-term Christian donors are way behind us. They are slowly being educated.

> Donor churches are playing catch-up with what is happening on-field. They still haven't got a strong, holistic paradigm. It is still piecemeal, not thought through. They see a need here and there and want to help, but there is no comprehensive strategy.

> Donors are slower. They are not catching up as fast – our missionaries are on the cutting edge, but our home base is not. They are taking longer to catch on.

Respondents did suggest a significant disconnect between church leaders and many of the individual donors within their churches. Church leaders were perceived as being motivated more by evangelism and starting new churches, with development being perceived primarily as a strategy:

> The motivation of our movement to engage in development is as a strategy for souls to be saved, and for them to be seen as relevant to their members and the public.

> The majority of churches, particularly the church leaders and big church congregations, love the heart throb stories of children or stories of bricks and mortar projects they can be involved in themselves, particularly where church planting is the end goal. For them it is a strategy to see people saved, as opposed to being for their benefit, full stop. And it is a marketing technique to their home churches.

> The leaders of our movement are keen to publish the number of new churches started and the number of salvations, so we have a problem with them still seeing conversion as the priority. But they are now also giving airplay to the dollars raised for orphanages, child support, etc.

> People love to give to something that helps 'down-and-outers'. But for Pentecostals there is a disconnect. They are concerned that it is not just about social justice, but want to see church planting and development come together into something of eternal value. They want something more holistic, but are scared of the new forms.

Individual Christian donors in those churches, however, are increasingly motivated by holistic humanitarian concerns:

> Today there is a shift in motivation. People respond to compassion and humanitarian need, and churches are particularly generous in giving to crisis situations. They give out of a humanitarian spirit, not to see people saved but because they see people suffering in the media and have compassion for those suffering.

> People who are older in the churches are more motivated by the spiritual side, and helping children. But younger people are increasingly motivated by giving to other things, often the latest hot topic driven by the news media.

> Lots of donors don't see a difference between practical assistance and evangelism. Jesus fed the 5000 and then preached to them.

> Christian donors in general like to hear stories of the underdog who does not have the resources or education to break the poverty cycle, but with the assistance of an outside donor they can break that cycle. The motivation is both humanitarian and for salvation, but the emphasis is now more on meeting humanitarian need.

> There is a full spectrum of views. Some, still a minority, want to do development simply for the benefit of the poor. But there are many more now; it is a gradual shift. The tsunami in 2004 was a trigger.

CONCLUSION

Pentecostals have always been strong on providing practical assistance to people in need, yet there has clearly been a significant, quantifiable shift in Pentecostal mission activities and understanding in mainland South East Asia over the past few decades. Most of this shift would appear to have occurred between about 1998 and 2001. Change within aid agencies over time is not uncommon. Korten (1990), for example, proposed a typology that arranges non-government organizations into four generations, thereby suggesting that relief and welfare services typically evolve into community development, into sustainable development, and eventually into people movements.

While Korten's typology has been widely accepted, its empirical base has not been tested and it remains simply a classification based on observation of a limited cohort of NGOs operating in relation to USAID during the 1980s. Rae and Clarke (2010) tested Korten's approach against a number of Australian faith-based agencies and found that whilst the demarcation between these typologies was not as stark but that there was a demonstrable shift towards more participatory and community based development interventions over time. The shift that has now been identified within Pentecostal missions in South East Asia raises the questions of what has actually changed, and why.

From this research, this shift in activities appears to be connected with underlying changes. The theological articulation of the nature of Christian mission by fieldworkers in the region has changed, to now clearly include practical assistance through things like community development as an integral aspect of mission. Mission is expressed in far more holistic terms, in terms of bringing salvation to people in the here-and-now as well as bringing salvation for eternity. This is a clear shift in Pentecostal theological interpretation, and it would be interesting to see how widespread this is beyond our small sample group.

The result is an articulation of mission in which practical assistance and development are now expressed as a fundamental aspect of mission of approximately equal priority to spiritual ministries of evangelism, starting churches, and so on. But the important conclusion is that the motivation for practical assistance and for evangelism are not separable, and the motivation of field workers (as opposed possibly to some donors) is not to use development as a strategy for evangelism, but to offer either or both unconditionally out of humanitarian concern to help people holistically. Both are seen as aspects of what Jesus did, and of the salvation people need. The one motivation is behind both. This shift in theological thinking has resulted in a far more deliberate organization and planning for development activity within mission by these groups.

We can only speculate on the underlying causes of this shift in theology and practice. This change has clearly occurred first and more clearly amongst the fieldworkers, with many of the leaders of home church who are significant donors only slowly catching up with this change. This change has been driven from the field in at least this instance. Triggers have been cross-pollination from other Christian organizations, resulting in a re-evaluation of what Jesus did and seeing human need and poverty through fresh eyes.

So what brought about this shift? It would be tempting to suggest that the success of campaigns such as Make Poverty History and the like in popularizing the need to address third world poverty, particularly within the Western church, was a factor. However, our field data has shown that this change has been driven from the field. Does this simply reflect growing acceptability of Pentecostals in the eyes of other Christian groups together with reaching a critical mass of workers in the field? Does it relate to a re-evaluation of mission as Pentecostals approached the end of the Decade of Harvest (1990–2000)? Or is it in some way connected with the renewed impetus to incorporate religious organizations into mainstream development brought about by the formation of the World Faith Development Dialogue in 1999 by the Archbishop of Canterbury and the President of the World Bank (Marshall and Keough, 2004)? Identifying the significance of this date would make for interesting follow-up research. However, it does appear to be clearly linked with a change in theological understanding of the nature of mission and changed eschatology. A recent move away from millennialism and less confidence in the imminence of the return of Christ have resulted in devising more deliberate strategies about assisting the poor in the mid-long term.

In conclusion, Pentecostalism is known as a missionary movement, fast growing and driven by an imperative for evangelism and conversion. Practical assistance has always been a part of the movement's work, but has been ad hoc, out of a humanitarian concern for helping people as needs arise, but has theologically been subjugated to the imperative for evangelism because of the reality and proximity of eternity. Pentecostal practical assistance for people outside their group has often been perceived, both by those inside and outside the group, as being primarily a strategy to entice conversion.

The data from this research challenges such preconceived notions about the motivations behind Pentecostal mission workers in mainland South East Asia, who are increasingly implementing community development programmes alongside their more traditional mission activities of evangelism, starting new churches and training leaders for those churches.

What is clear is that for most of these key fieldworkers, doing development work without a spiritual dimension lacks motivation, since the motivation is holistic practical-plus-spiritual. Any regulatory requirements to separate development from evangelism would impose a false division that contravenes the motivation driving these Pentecostal fieldworkers today.

NOTES

1. Religions and Development Research Programme *Key Terms*, available at: http://web.archive.org/web/20080102021101/http://www.rad.bham.ac.uk/index.php?section=24; accessed 30 July 2012.
2. Ibid.

REFERENCES

Anderson, A. (2004), *An Introduction to Pentecostalism: Global Charismatic Christianity*, Cambridge: Cambridge University Press.

Ball, C. and L. Dunn (1996), 'NGOs defined', in T.C. Foundation (ed.), *Non-government Organisations: Guidelines for Good Policy and Practice*, London: The Commonwealth Foundation.

Barrett, D.B., G.T. Kurian and T.M. Johnson (2001), *World Christian Encyclopedia: A Comparative Survey of Churches and Religions in the Modern World*, vol. 1 (2nd edition), New York: Oxford University Press.

Clark, M.S. (1997), 'An investigation into the nature of a viable pentecostal hermeneutic', DTh thesis, University of South Africa.

Clarke, G. (2008), 'Faith based organisations and international development', in G. Clarke and M. Jennings (eds), *Development, Civil Society and Faith-based Organisations*, London: Palgrave Macmillan.
Clarke, M. (2011), *Development and Religion: Theology and Practice*, Cheltenham, UK and Northampton, MA, USA: Edward Elgar.
Clarke, M. and J. Donnelly (2008), 'Learning from missionaries: lessons for secular development practitioners', paper presented to Christian Mission in the Public Square Conference, Australian Association of Missionary Studies, Canberra, 2–5 October.
Clarke, G. and M. Jennings (eds) (2008), *Development, Civil Society and Faith-based Organisations: Bridging the Sacred and the Secular*, Basingstoke: Palgrave Macmillan.
Clarke, M., S. Charnley and J. Lumbers (2011), 'Churches, mosques and condoms: understanding successful faith-based organisations', HIV and AIDS interventions', *Development in Practice*, **21**(1), 3–17.
Daniels, D.I. (2011), 'Future issues is social and economic justice', in V. Synan (ed.), *Spirit-empowered Christianity in the Twenty-first Century*, Lake Mary, FL: Charisma House, pp. 339–55.
Denzin, N.K. and Y.S. Lincoln (eds) (2000), *Handbook of Qualitative Research*, Los Angeles: SAGE Publications.
Fee, G.D. (1991), 'The kingdom of God and the church's global mission', in M.A. Dempster, B.D. Klaus and D. Petersen (eds), *Called and Empowered: Global Mission in Pentecostal Perspective*, Peabody, MA: Hendrickson Publishers.
Fontana, A. and J.H. Frey (2008), 'The interview: from neutral stance to political involvement', in N.K. Denzin and Y.S. Lincoln (eds), *Collecting and Interpreting Qualitative Materials*, Los Angeles: SAGE Publications.
Gray, D.E. (2009), *Doing Research in the Real World*, Los Angeles: SAGE Publications.
Harb, M. (2008), 'Faith-based organisations as effective development partners? Hezbollah and post-war reconstruction in Lebanon', in G. Clarke and M. Jennings (eds), *Development, Civil Society and Faith-based Organisations*, London: Palgrave Macmillan.
James, R. (2009), *What is Distinctive About FBOs? How European FBOs Define and Operationalize their Faith*, Oxford: INTRAC.
Klaus, B. (2011), 'Reflection on Pentecostal mission for the twenty-first century', in V. Synan (ed.), *Spirit-empowered Christianity in the Twenty-first Century*, Lake Mary, FL: Charisma House, pp. 129–40.
Korten, D. (1990), *Getting to the 21st Century: Voluntary Action and the Global Agenda*, West Hartford, CT: Kumarian Press.
Macchia, F.D. (1999), 'The struggle for global witness: shifting paradigms in Pentecostal theology', in M.W. Dempster, B.D. Klaus and D. Petersen (eds), *The Globalization of Pentecostalism: A Religion Made to Travel*, Oxford: Regnum Books International, pp. 8–29.
Marshall, K. and L. Keough (2004), *Mind, Heart and Soul in the Fight Against Poverty*, Washington, DC: World Bank.
Marshall, K. and M.V. Saanen (2007), *Development and Faith: Where Mind, Heart and Soul Work Together*, Washington, DC: World Bank.
Maykut, P. and R. Morehouse (1994), *Beginning Qualitative Research: A Philosophic and Practical Guide*, London/Washington, DC: Falmer Press.
McGavran, D.A. (1955), *The Bridges of God: A Study in the Strategy of Missions*, New York: Friendship.
McGavran, D.A. (1970), *Understanding Church Growth*, Grand Rapids: Eerdmans Publishing Company.
McGee, G.B. (1994), 'Saving souls or saving lives? The tension between ministries of word and deed in assemblies of God missiology', *PARACLETE*, **28**(4), 11–23.
McGee, G.B. (2004), *People of the Spirit; The Assemblies of God*, Springfield: Gospel Publishing House.
Miller, D.E. and T. Yamamori (2007), *Global Pentecostalism: The New Face of Christian Social Engagement*, Berkeley: University of California Press.
Moreau, A.S., G.R. Corwin and G.B. McGee (2004), *Introducing World Missions: A Biblical, Historical and Practical Survey*, Grand Rapids: Baker Academic.
Mullings, B. (1999), 'Insider or outsider, both or neither: some dilemmas of interviewing in a cross cultural setting', *Geoforum*, **30**(4), 337–50.
Nichol, J.T. (1966), *Pentecostalism*, New York: Harper and Row.
Odendahl, T. and A.M. Shaw (2001), 'Interviewing elites', in J.F. Gubrium and J.A. Holstein (eds), *Handbook of Interview Research: Context and Method*, Thousand Oaks, CA: SAGE Publications, pp. 299–316.
Patton, M. (1990), *Qualitiative Evaluation and Research Methods*, London: SAGE Publications.
Peräkylä, A. (2008), 'Analysing talk and text', in N.K. Denzin and Y.S. Lincoln (eds), *Collecting and Interpreting Qualitative Materials*, Los Angeles: SAGE Publications.
Platt, J. (1981), 'On interviewing one's peers', *British Journal of Sociology*, **32**(1), 75–91.
Rae, L. and M. Clarke (2010), 'The evolution of faith-based organisations: reconsidering Korten's four generations', paper presented to the Conference, Religion Shaping Development: Inspirational, Inhibiting, Institutionalized?, University of Birmingham, 21–23 July.

Shuy, R.W. (2001), 'In-person versus telephone interviewing', in J.F. Gubrium and J.A. Holstein (eds), *Handbook of Interview Research: Context and Method*, Thousand Oaks, CA: SAGE Publications, pp. 537–55.
Wagner, C.P. (1973), *Look Out! The Pentecostals are Coming*, Illinois: Creation House.
Warrington, K. (2008), *Pentecostal Theology: A Theology of Encounter*, New York/London: T&T Clark.
Wilkinson, M. (2007), 'Faith-based social services: some observations for assessing Pentecostal social action', *Transformation: An International Journal of Holistic Mission Studies*, **24**(2), 71–9.

PART IV

CASE STUDIES

27 Religion, development and politics in Nigeria*

Insa Nolte

INTRODUCTION

The growing interest in the contribution of religion to development emerges from the neoliberal debate on the role of the state in economic and social provision in divergent ways. While the support of development activities with and through religious groups and organizations[1] reflects the general belief that non-state institutions can provide many state services more efficiently than the state, it also transcends the notion that all forms of social progress are measurable in economic terms, or through the quantifiable parameters of good governance. The rise of religion in development discourse also reflects the rise of public religion in a number of developed and developing countries since the late 1970s, which was strengthened by the growth of identity politics – and the decline of secular liberation ideologies – after the collapse of state-based socialism and the democratic transitions of many developing countries in the 1980s and 1990s (Clarke, 2006, pp. 838–9; Nolte et al., 2009, p. 6). Finally, the vocal engagement of religious organizations in the development debate in the USA and Europe, for example in the debate about the Millennium Development Goals and debt relief, has raised awareness of the potential relevance of religious contributions to development (Clarke, 2007, pp. 79–81).

In the context of African development, this debate has received further impetus by the concerns of the international community over failing, weak or fragile states. Compared with religious groups, which are often accountable to their members as well as able to raise funds more efficiently than state bureaucracies, states riddled by patrimonialism and corruption do not look like ideal agents of development to some observers (cf. Kelsall, 2008, p. 638). While not much detailed research on the topic has been carried out, the hopes associated with the demand for a greater role for religion in development focus on a number of different areas. Several authors have suggested that religious groups provide forms of meaning that are important to development practice, both in order to improve the understanding by development professionals of what people want and to improve the practice and discipline of development itself (cf. Marshall, 2005, p. 3; Deneulin and Bano, 2009, Lunn, 2009).

Beyond the religious engagement with development as a discipline and process, religious groups provide useful and efficient services, especially in health and education, to a section of the population that includes the poor. While estimates on the amount of religious participation in these sectors vary dramatically, some observers have suggested that religious groups constitute up to half of the service providers in some African countries (Marshall, 2005, p. 2; Clarke, 2007, p. 88). And finally, religious groups have been described as the providers of social capital and leadership at the grassroots, and thus as an important sector of a civil society that both supports and corrects the state (Clarke, 2006; see also Ter Haar and Ellis, 2006). Thus, the inclusion of religion in development has been envisaged both as a process of moral, spiritual and intellectual reform of development discourse and practice and as an empowerment of people at the grassroots level that contributes to greater social inclusion and, by implication, democracy.

The fact that religion is understood as a largely unproblematic category in most of these arguments has attracted some criticism, and some commentators have pointed out that the prioritization of religion as a determinant of development in Africa detracts from other forms of social difference (Frances Stewart, 21 July 2010).[2] Moreover, the assumption that religion – and, by implication, its moral values – informs practice in a direct way is problematic. Most anthropologists and sociologists would suggest that social praxis and belief are intrinsically linked, and that the question that beliefs and attitudes are highlighted in a particular social constellation depends on a wide range of factors, including class as well as age, gender and ethnicity. In an insightful reflection on the role of religion in Africa, Maia Green has argued that religion is usually only influential where it is embedded within social institutions (Green, 2006, p. 641). In order to assess in what way the relationship between religion and development affects wider social aims, it is therefore important not only to focus on the potential transformation of development by religion, but also to assess the way in which the engagement in development itself situates religious institutions within the wider political and economic landscape.

In more practical terms, the work of religious organizations who only support their own members, or whose teachings contribute to the increase of religious bias and intolerance, would clearly detract from inclusive development goals (Winkler, 2008, p. 2111; De Kadt, 2009; Lunn, 2009, p. 945). While this is a concern that could be addressed by donor stipulations, it also points to the fragmentation of the religious landscape especially in Africa. Winkler (2008) further suggests that it would be naive to assume that religious organizations, simply by virtue of their shared religiosity, comprise a unified 'faith sector', whose members share common values and mutual respect for each other. While she does not explore the uptake of development offers by members of other religious groups, this is obviously a concern in religiously polarized countries, such as Nigeria.

This chapter provides such an exploration by examining the political context in which Muslim and Christian organizations in Nigeria engage in development.[3] Interviews were carried out among the leaders of religious organizations and government officials in three of Nigeria's 36 states, that is, Anambra, Kano and Oyo States.[4] In this way they covered states with a predominantly Christian, predominantly Muslim and mixed Muslim–Christian majority population respectively. Almost all organizations targeted were engaged in health care, mainly in the field of HIV/AIDS prevention, treatment and counselling, as well as education, usually including primary and secondary schools, but in some cases groups also ran, or were planning to run, universities.

Exploring the context in which these organizations provided development, the chapter also reflects on the wider implications of the dynamics of their engagement for social inclusion. By analysing key dynamics between religious institutions and the political sphere, the chapter reflects on development both as a concern shared by a wide range of institutions, and as a practice embedded in specific relationships of power. While it aims at shedding light on the way in which local ideals, concerns and practices affect social relations, it does not analyse the performance or efficiency of religious groups in development. Rather, it is concerned with the impact of religious development on social inclusion in the specific context of Nigerian politics.

The first part of the chapter illustrates that the general context in which religious groups provide development is characterized by a close engagement, even an inclusion of religion into the administration in all the states examined. Beyond this, the chapter focuses on four areas relevant for a deeper understanding of the relationship between religious institutions and development in terms of social inclusion. These include the material and non-material notions of development held by different organizations, as well as the implications of these ideas for the notion of a unified 'faith sector' in Nigeria. Using the example of education, the chapter also explores the possibility and implications of religiously provided development that aims to be inclusive across religious boundaries. The chapter then examines the relationship between religious organizations and the state governments that are tasked with the provision of the services offered by the religious groups in order to reflect on the links between religion, politics and development. And finally, the chapter explores the relationships of religious organizations with each other, again with a view to assessing the potential impact of religiously provided development on social cohesion.

The findings drawn from the case studies are illustrative of the complex relationship between religion and development. On the one hand, widely shared visions of development among Christian and Muslim groups suggest that these groups are indeed united by jointly held values. Religious groups even provide, as assumed in debates about Africa's 'civil society', both criticism and guidance to the state sector. However, reflecting the strong competition that characterizes relations between Christians and Muslims in Nigeria, these shared values divide rather than unite religious groups in their development activities. Thus, where religious groups offer to open their provision of development to non-members, especially across the Muslim–Christian divide, such offers are viewed with suspicion and might even contribute to conflict.

Moreover, existing religious competition appears to be fuelled not only by Muslim–Christian relations at the central level, but also by the nature of the groups' links to the state governments. The relationships between state governments and religious organizations are characterized not only by very different approaches on both sides, but also by mutual distrust. Successful cooperation between the two sectors is not the norm but rather the result of an incorporation of specific religious groups into the state for political reasons. The practice of politically motivated incorporation has follow-on effects, as excluded groups suspect those who have close ties to government of corruption and even lack of religiosity. Thus, the shared engagement in development by religious groups does not reflect a shared identity which could provide a consistent counterbalance to the state but may even lead to a deepening of religious divisions. As a result, religious competition itself needs to be addressed in order to provide development through religious organizations that is successful and inclusive on a social rather than a project level.

RELIGION AND POLITICS IN KANO, ANAMBRA AND OYO STATES

With at least 140 million inhabitants, Nigeria is Africa's most populous country (Federal Republic of Nigeria, 2006), as well as a regional power of economic, political and military influence. Despite a strong and centralized central government, Nigeria is a religiously and ethnically heterogeneous country. In northern Nigeria, Islam played an important role in many precolonial states, and it continued to be linked to political power under colonial rule, even though significant minorities of traditionalists, and later also Christians, existed. Meanwhile, southern Nigeria is mostly Christian with some traditional worshippers, even though the Yoruba ethnic group in the southwest is almost evenly divided between Muslims and Christians. In this complex constellation, religious conflict has included rivalry between Islam and Christianity as well as violent conflicts between different Muslim groups. Religious intrigue has also affected relationships between Christian denominations and between monotheists and traditionalists.

Muslim–Christian conflict has played a role in Nigerian national politics since the centralization of the political system in the 1970s (Falola, 1998), and it has become increasingly important in Nigerian politics because of the political liberalization associated with the return to civilian rule in 1999. Both religious groups have challenged institutions of common interest provided by the state. Reformulating the local importance of Islam, a critique of secular law has led to the introduction of Shari'a penal law in 12 northern Nigerian states since 1999 (Last, 2003). Meanwhile, building on the fact that Christian missionary activity and education were often closely linked, Christian demands for a re-privatization of former mission schools currently under state control might further emphasize Muslim disadvantage in the educational sector (cf. Hackett, 1999). At the central level, the attempts to give Muslims and Christians equal representation include the even-handed treatment of Christians and Muslims in most central government appointments, as well as the creation of the Nigeria Inter-Religious Council (NIREC) in 2000 as a space for Muslim–Christian dialogue and state–religion interaction. However, although religious difference has been managed mostly peacefully at the central level, religious rivalry, including conflict between different Muslim groups, continues to play an important role in the politics of Nigeria's 36 states and several hundred local governments (cf. Human Rights Watch, 2001, 2005).

The three states of Kano, Anambra and Oyo, in which members and leaders of religious groups were interviewed about their views on and experiences of development activities are located in northern, (south-)eastern and (south-) western Nigeria respectively. The three states have had different historical experiences before, during and even after colonial rule, and they reflect different religious and ethno-regional compositions. As pointed out above, Kano is a mainly Muslim state with Shari'a family and penal law, Anambra is a predominantly Christian state and Oyo a mixed Muslim–Christian state. As a result of these different histories, the local religious organizations experienced different forms of access to the state, which in turn affected their ability to make use of their resources for development. Nonetheless, in all three case studies, state governments had established formal ways of managing their relationships with religious organizations and of co-opting especially important groups, especially since the return to civilian rule in 1999 (Nolte, et al., 2009; see also Obadare, 2007).

Kano State is centred on Kano city, the capital of an old Hausa kingdom and one of the historic centres of West African Islam. In Kano, the emir, a traditional Muslim ruler, continues to hold strong political influence, and a close historical association of religion and power means that religious difference continues to be closely linked to communal and especially ethno-regional boundaries. The majority of the population of Kano State is Muslim, and Christianity is closely associated with immigrant status. However, there are Hausa Christians as well, and for the past two decades, disagreements between Muslim and Christian groups have, occasionally, led to violent conflict (Ludwig, 2008). However, even Muslim immigrants from the south often belong to very different religious networks or institutions than those indigenous to Kano. Moreover, the Muslim networks within Kano are loosely divided between those of the local aristocracy and political elite and those more closely identified with commoners and the poor. It is likely that the high level of conflict between different Muslim groups that the state has experienced also reflects this fact.

Since the introduction of Shari'a penal law in 2000, state policy has reflected greater religious solidarity between elite and commoner as well as local and immigrant Muslim groups, and a larger range of Muslim communities has been able to develop close contacts with the state administration and its representatives. However, Muslim groups potentially critical of the existing political elite were nonetheless marginalized, as were all Christian groups, including 'indigenous' ones, suggesting a clear pattern of primarily religious rather than ethnic exclusion at the political level.[5] While both Muslim and Christian organizations were engaged in the fields of education, sometimes in addition to health-related, microcredit or vocational training activities, the Christian groups often had slightly greater resources in this area for historical reasons. But at the same time, Christian groups were systematically subjected to restrictions while most Muslim groups received government support at different levels (Nolte et al., 2009, pp. 26–44).

Anambra State, located in south-eastern Nigeria, is a predominantly Igbo state with a large Christian majority, some traditionalists and very few Muslim immigrants. While the state has experienced a high degree of political violence in the past decade, this was not linked to religion, and religious conflicts have been rare and tended to reflect ethnic tensions between (Christian) Igbos and (Muslim) Hausa-speaking immigrants. However, these conflicts reflect a primarily ethnic bias, and they usually followed on from northern Nigerian violence in which Igbo Christians came to harm. However, local anti-northern sentiments are mediated by the fact that since the Civil War (1967–70), local leadership has relied on the patronage of northern Nigerian leaders. As a result, Anambra State politics have been dominated by powerful patronage networks.

As a result of the predominance of patrimonial politics, religious organizations experienced little discrimination on the basis of religion, and the principle of religious balance in official appointments is generally accepted. However, reflecting the majority faith as well as their historical association with mission activity and investment, the Christian organizations had a much stronger presence in the fields of education and health than the Muslim organizations, which were mainly concerned with community support. All the same, the ability of all religious organizations to contribute to development was clearly influenced by their proximity to power, and the association of Hausa-speaking Muslims was, perhaps in reflection of the locally established ties to the north, well represented at government level and included in state-sponsored HIV/AIDS outreach schemes. The main Christian denominations in the state – Anglicanism and Roman Catholicism – were loosely associated with competing patronage networks, thus encouraging religious competition as part of the sectional struggle for political power (Nolte et al., 2009, pp. 64–76).

In the Nigerian south-west the mainly Yoruba-speaking Oyo State is dominated by the city of Ibadan, which has a population of both Muslims and Christians.[6] It is also home to traditionalists and a sizeable immigrant community, again of both Muslims and Christians. Due to a historical association with ethnic 'opposition' politics that only ended after 1999, Oyo has only recently developed large-scale patronage networks linking local political factions to the central government. The state has experienced some political violence, most of which was linked to patrimonial politics. It has experienced a low degree of religious violence, some of the 'retaliation' kind experienced in Anambra State, and some linked to conflicts between locals and the northern Nigerian immigrant community, which tends to worship separately from the local Muslim population (cf. Cohen ([1969] 2004).

Perhaps in reflection of a long local history of Muslim–Christian cooperation, both Muslim and Christian groups engaged in similar areas, including health care and HIV/AIDS education, microcredit and training as well as education up to university level. As the notion of balanced religious appointments was widely accepted in state politics, there was very little evidence of religious discrimination among local religious groups in Oyo State. However, religious organizations had differential access to politics on the basis of their position within local politics. Moreover, where religious and ethnic boundaries coincided, such as within the Muslim community, the religious groups of northern Nigerians tended to be excluded from access to government (Nolte et al., 2009, pp. 45–63).

As a result, a first assessment of the religious sector in Nigeria must emphasize its close links to the state, not only at the central level but also at the level of state politics and administration. The integration of religious groups and FBOs into government has advanced furthest in Kano State. Here, religious leaders discuss political, legal and more general concerns with each other and members of the political elite in the Islamic institutions of the state, which were created after the introduction of Shari'a penal law in 2000 (Wakili, 2009). While the exclusion of critical Muslim and Christian groups is most pronounced, sometimes to the degree of hindering their activities, many Muslim organizations are supported in their attempts to play an active part in providing grassroots development activities.

The two southern Nigerian states of Oyo and Anambra have not instituted formal religious participation in government. However, the widespread acceptance of religious proportionalism in state appointments, in reflection of the strength of denominations within the state, ensures the inclusion of different denominations through personal appointments. It is through the links created by personal appointments, as well as public visits, presents and donations, that state governments interact with religious groups (cf. Obianyo, 2008 for Anambra). However, in these southern states, the boundaries between locals and immigrants, expressed in a debate about local belonging, are often a basis for exclusion. Especially in Oyo State, which is, like Kano, home to many in-migrants but also located in a part of the country long dominated by ethno-nationalist politics, some organizations that are closely identified with in-migrant groups were excluded from access to government.

In conclusion, the incorporation of the religious sector into the state is not limited to the central level, and it is likely to be a national trend even at the state level. The political debates and practices in the states suggest that this trend is not primarily driven by a concern over development but by political considerations. These are, at least in Kano and other northern Nigerian states, complemented by religious concerns. But while the locally dominant religious groups seem to be included in politics in all states, other groups – most clearly Christians in Kano, but also non-locals in Oyo, and, to a lesser degree, Anambra State – remain excluded.

SHARED CONCERNS ABOUT INFRASTRUCTURE, HEALTH AND EDUCATION

While the inclusion of religious leaders into the state administration did not take place with a view to improving development provision, it may have contributed to the shared views on development offered by the majority of our respondents. It is, however, striking that even groups that have experienced a strong degree of exclusion share the views that were put forward in all three states. In Kano State, representatives of both Muslim and Christian organizations understood development in a very similar fashion. Most interview partners perceived development as a combination of different forms of infrastructural provision, including electricity and roads, and often also including health, education and security, which would allow people to rise beyond urban poverty or subsistence agriculture. Thus, a female Christian leader from the Kano State chapter of the Christian Association of Nigeria (CAN) argued:

> You know the difference between lantern and electricity, so you will prefer the electricity to the lantern. So by bringing electricity, you are bringing development to the people. Even education, there will be awareness among your children, instead of everybody being farmers they will read and write, they can communicate. (Interview 4 January 2008, Mrs Funmilayo Osho)

Her views on development were echoed by the comments of a male member of the reformist Muslim Izala group in Kano, who explained that:

> Development means . . . the absence of poverty and the presence of good roads, good hospitals, good schools, good markets, good houses, good clothes to wear, and plenty of food, when there is constant electricity, good security of lives and property. (Interview 13 May 2008, Mallam Ali)

Similar sentiments were also voiced by leaders of religious groups in Oyo and Anambra State, where, despite the complex mixture of religious and ethnic relations, all interviewed groups shared views of development that focused on infrastructure and education but also emphasized other values.[7] Thus, the notions of development espoused by the majority of religious groups who participated in this research included infrastructural, education and health provision in a manner that echoed secular and primarily economic notions of development. While the different groups often provided such services primarily for their own members and constituencies, none of our respondents suggested that they perceived development as a right or requirement only for their religious constituency, or, more generally, for a (religiously or otherwise defined) section of the population.

Thus, despite the real difference in the working contexts of the groups interviewed, most respondents understood development in a way that reflected international concerns. Moreover, by avoiding, at least at the rhetorical level, an explicitly sectional discourse, it appeared that many religious groups considered development as a concern and even right shared by all Nigerians.[8] In reflection of this shared concern, it seems possible that the engagement of religious organizations in development could also contribute to greater social inclusion and cohesion.

DEMANDS FOR MORAL VALUES AND CRITIQUES OF CORRUPTION

A rhetorical commitment to the common good was also in evidence when respondents spoke about non-economic aspects of development, which have been considered a potentially important contribution of development initiatives by religious groups (Deneulin and Rakodi, 2011). Several respondents from both Christian and Muslim religious groups pointed out that development also included non-material aspects. In some cases, comments reflected the political experience of exclusion. The comments by Reverend Bwamche, who represents Kano State's Evangelical Church of West Africa (ECWA), which has a mainly northern Nigerian base, emphasized the importance of religious freedom. His comment should not be taken only to reflect frustration over the treatment of Christians in northern Nigeria, as similar comments were also made by respondents from other states:

> Development is the services, the essential services that is [sic] being rendered. . . . And development is when we can dialogue with one another, living harmoniously and respecting our rights . . . you respect the person's rights and the person's opinion. I look at this as development, [but] we are very far from that. (Interview 6 January 2008, Reverend Bwamche)

While the ability to dialogue and respect another's rights are not exclusively moral values, this and similar responses suggest that our respondents were framing these values within a religious context. This may, of course, reflect the fact that respondents in this case were members of religious groups and FBOs, who likely perceived such abstract values as grounded in their faith. But even where comments referred clearly to the Bible or the Qur'an, they were used in a general way, and often addressed at the prevailing political culture of impunity, where those in power often appropriate public resources destined for the general population for individual or sectional benefit. Another response from the Pentecostal Redeemed Christian Church of God (RCCG) in Oyo State illustrates this point:

> [The biblical King] David said, let them that lead in the midst of man be fair and just. When you are fair and just in managing the resources of the community for the welfare of the community, essentially you have good governance. (Interview January 2008, Pastor Peter Adagbada)

The expression of such – essentially political – criticism through religious discourse illustrates that religious visions of economic development are closely linked to concerns about the political culture. In this context, several respondents referred to the lack of a fear of God or Allah among politicians or in the general population. Concerns about impunity were expressed explicitly by some of the organizations that offered a more radical critique of government. Thus, Mallam Ali of the Izala in Kano linked his expectations of development both to religion and the political realm:

> [The Izala preaches] to the political class to govern with the fear of Allah by taking care of the needs of the people, especially the poor. We preach against stealing and looting of public funds, we preach against bad governance and its consequences. (Interview 13 May 2008, Mallam Ali)

A similar critique of the government and the political class came from the Catholic Justice, Development and Peace Commission (JDPC) in Anambra State, whose respondent had asserted earlier that his organization was founded upon the belief that 'religion preaches for the general welfare of the human community'. He explained that:

> Care-free and sit-tight leaders have, most of the time, been there. They have not been interested in the masses they are representing. Imagine, how would somebody win the governorship ticket and . . . not do anything about the people's welfare nor pay the work force? (Interview January 2008, C.J. Onyenze)

Not all religious groups adopted such radical critiques of the political sphere, but while a few groups confirmed their good relations with the state government, many stated that they existed at a distance from it, even if relations were in reality positive. Thus, for example, Pastor Orji of the RCCG in Anambra State pointed out:

> We may have some members who are in government but there is no direct contact or influence from either us or from them. (Interview January 2008, Pastor Orji)

He then explained that:

> the Scripture told us to pray for our leaders. Any policy that is not too good to the populace, we go to God in prayer for a reversal of such a policy, we pray for our leaders, for God to guide them in their policy formulation and implantation. (Interview January 2008, Pastor Orji)

Thus, many of the respondents from the religious sector saw their organizations as contributing to development by playing a role as moral critics and advisers, who used advice, prayer, sermons and other public activities to reprimand or rein in politicians for the greater good. In our responses, the language and main messages of Muslim and Christian leaders were closely related, suggesting that these religions share, at least on the surface, a broadly similar set of values (Haynes, 2009, p. 60). Moreover, it is possible that the religious discourse on development, in which members of different faiths participate, contributes further to a shared moral and political vocabulary.

All the same, it seems important to note that this vocabulary, even when employed by religious leaders, is not only religious. While some comments referred to explicitly religious images such as the fear of Allah or God, others were concerned with values that might also be considered secular, including personal honesty and morality and the acceptance of general human rights. Thus, while the demands of religious organizations are intelligible across linguistic, cultural and geographical divides, they are also compatible with the demands of non-religious groups and organizations able to frame their concerns and hopes for the future in ways that are clear and appealing to their fellow citizens.

CHRISTIAN SCHOOLS FOR MUSLIM CHILDREN?

Beyond their ability to form or participate in larger religious or civic debates, religious groups also provide development, and it is important to assess how relevant the shared concern for Nigerian and Nigerians is at the practical level. In the states where we carried out research, the religious groups translated their shared development concerns into actions in different ways. But while all groups primarily catered for their own constituencies, some groups were proud to provide services beyond their immediate denominational or even religious constituency. This universal reach suggests that not all religiously provided development is inherently biased towards a limited constituency (Winkler, 2008, p. 2111). However, development is not only produced by provision but also by demand and acceptance. This section explores the impact of attempts to reach beyond a religiously constituted constituency.

The relative dominance of Christian groups in the education sector reflects the fact that, historically, Christian missions have provided much of Nigeria's education, while Muslims have attempted to catch up on this original advantage. Even though many mission schools were taken over by the states during the 1970s in order to facilitate greater access to education for Muslims and other non-Christians, a Christian advantage in access to education in many parts of Nigeria is still noticeable. Overall, Nigerian Christians still tend to be better educated than non-Christians, and Christian groups still control a larger share of private schools than non-Christian groups (Clarke, 1978). As a result of their structural advantage in this area, many Christian groups understand their ability to offer education and charity as a way of putting their universal values to practice and of benefiting the country as a whole.

By offering scholarships to students from backgrounds outside their own community – whether they are from other Christian denominations, Muslim, traditionalist or other minority groups – most Christian groups believe that they are demonstrating selfless charity based on an acknowledgement of the shared humanity of all those able to appreciate education. This is illustrated by the comments from the RCCG in Oyo, which has a mixed Muslim–Christian population:

> we have people who are not even Redeemed [Christian Church of God] members who have children here [in our school], we try to make sure that we empathize and sympathize with them when they have difficulties making up the fees . . . when parents have difficulties in paying and you will be surprised, we have a lot of people coming in here, even Muslims, they have their children here. (Interview 3 January 2008, Pastor Peter Adagbada)

Reverend Joshua Bwamche, the senior pastor of ECWA in the overwhelmingly Muslim Kano State also explained:

> it is not only Christian children that are trained [in our schools]; some Muslims bring their children to those schools. (Interview 6 January 2008, Reverend Joshua Bwamche)

However, the offer of Christian organizations to bring Western knowledge and education to Muslim children in their states, and even the financial commitment by such organizations to support those Muslim children through scholarships, has not created a sense of shared engagement in national development among Muslims.

Instead, it has alarmed and even offended many Muslim groups. As a Muslim scholar comments:

> The covert methods used by these missionaries, including enticement of vulnerable and poor people (especially women and children) with certain material benefits, such as scholarship[s] or health benefits, are . . . considered by many as objectionable, if not immoral. (Ahmad, 2005, p. 24)

The Muslim perception of Christian methods of proselytization reflects both historical and contemporary practice. Despite the shared commitment to education, many Muslims perceive the offer of Christian education for their children as a form of covert aggression and even, if it leads to conversion, as immoral and threatening. Ahmad's comment also suggests that the Christian outreach to the poor, which reflects, at least in part, shared development concerns about the exclusion of vulnerable groups, is perceived as particularly perfidious. As a result, the Christian attempt to be inclusive is understood not as charity but as a form of dominance by many Muslims (Sodiq, 2009, pp. 656–8).[9]

It is perhaps not surprising that the Muslim association of Christian education with conversion to Christianity has created some political pressure in states like Kano. Here, state schools only provide Islamic education while Christian schools are subject to close regulation. Unlike Muslim private schools, Christian schools in Kano receive no support from the state. Instead, these schools are required to pay regular dues to the Kano State Ministry of Education. Moreover, as Reverend Bwamche explained, the ECWA school was put under some pressure to provide Islamic studies, even though it was eventually successful in avoiding this:

> At a point when we first built the school the state decided . . . we must employ an Islamic [religion] teacher in [our] Christian school. But our predecessor said no. (Interview 6 January 2008, Reverend Joshua Bwamche)

Similar divisions affected religious provision in the health sector, again most pressingly in northern Nigeria, although in this sector historical rivalry appeared to be less pronounced. We did not come across an example in which Christians rejected the Muslim provision of services in a similar way, but there are similar dynamics of mutual engagement in which Muslims feel that they contribute to social or individual progress and Christians reject this. For example, many Nigerian Muslims believe that the introduction of Shari'a law has improved the lives of the majority of the people by providing a higher degree of security, accountability and education. As a result, they see Shari'a as a form of local development that has also benefited Christians (Harnischfeger, 2008, p. 97; Liman, 2009, pp. 170–73). But in contrast to this view, both the Nigerian and the international debates on this development suggest that the introduction of Shari'a law has been perceived as aggressive and threatening by many Christians.[10] While Christian fears of the Shari'a process clearly go beyond proselytization, suspicions that it is ultimately directed at encouraging conversion to Islam have been voiced (Harnischfeger, 2004, p. 438).

These dynamics suggest that despite the widely shared concerns of Muslims and Christians for the common good, and despite the attempts of some groups to give others beyond their constituency access to the benefits they are able to offer, the gap between most Christian and Muslim organizations is so wide that it makes a sharing of resources across denominational divides difficult. Clearly, fears of proselytization and other forms of dominance characterize the practical relationships between the groups, and it is difficult not to understand these forms of competition as a reflection of the wider political competition between Muslims and Christians at the level of national and state politics.

This suggests that even where the development activities of religious groups are explicitly aimed at creating social inclusivity, they are not likely to be successful where they take place in a context of historical and ongoing rivalry. Paradoxically, this environment creates a situation where many religious groups may be committed to providing development to all Nigerians, but where they refuse to accept the development offered by those not of their religion (or even denomination). Thus, the dominance of religious groups in the Nigerian educational sector means that education might be refused, for religious reasons, by those most in need of it. The solution – a multiplication of educational institutions – is currently taking place across Nigeria, but this is unlikely to be economical.

This process implies that a number of assumptions about religion and development must be examined in more detail. Clearly, Nigeria's religious sphere is deeply divided in practice, and its ability to act as a backbone of a civil society concerned with the good of all Nigerians is more limited than first assumed on the basis of more general statements (above). While a critical assessment of the notion of an African civil society is beyond the concern of this chapter, it is important to note at this juncture that neither Islam nor Christianity constitute a coherent bloc either (cf. Obadare, 2007). This illustrates that the assumption that religious politicization could be prevented simply by donor stipulations is clearly not valid: as long noted in other contexts, the intended provision of development to all does not mean that it will be accepted in this way.

STATE GOVERNMENTS ENCOURAGE RELIGIOUS COMPETITION

As the engagement of Kano State in the education sector suggests, the concerns associated with the provision of development by religious groups were neither acknowledged nor addressed in an impartial manner by state governments. Instead of encouraging the emergence of a more cohesive 'faith sector', state governments were involved in perpetuating the differential access of religious groups to the state. This was also based on the fact that state officials did not seem to think that religious groups and organizations constituted a sphere that could complement the state in the area of development. The most positive acknowledgement of religious groups' developmental contributions from the government's side came from an official at the Anambra State Women Advocacy and Empowerment Agency, who commented:

> Apart from a few, maybe one or two, universities, hospitals and the rest of them, built by the churches, they [religious groups and FBOs] do not really come into governance. (Interview May 2008, Anonymous)

Even in the particular environment of Kano State, where the most important Muslim groups were represented in the new institutions associated with the introduction of

Shari'a penal law, the ability of these religious groups to provide development was, from the state officials' point of view, linked primarily to their ability to mobilize the population. Mallam Danyaro from the Kano State Ministry of Information explained that:

> if government is talking about transparency and accountability, social re-orientation, the . . . religious movements are involved because they have influence over the people too. You know they have followers and therefore, whatever message you want to carry to the people you have to go through them. (Interview 13 May 2008, Mallam Danyaro)

The gap between the perceptions of state officials and religious leaders may partly reflect different rationalities and values, but it also clearly points to one of the strengths of the Nigerian state, namely its control of a significant central income from crude oil export, part of which is allocated to the states. As a result of this distribution policy, most Nigerian states have budgets that exceed their locally raised income by five times or (much) more, and which are, at least in part, available for development expenditure (Suberu, 2001). State officials are therefore not directly dependent on the services provided by faith-based organizations. Instead, state budgets allow state officials to adopt what Deneulin and Bano (2009) describe as an instrumental approach to religion in the pursuit of development.

But the existence of centrally augmented state budgets creates an instrumental logic beyond the sphere of development, because state governments have been, especially since the return to civilian rule in 1999, dependent on political support in order to remain in control of these resources. This logic is reflected in a widespread concern over political influence at the grassroots, especially during the run up to elections. Thus, the above quoted respondent from Anambra also revealed that from the government's point of view, the importance of religious groups was not limited to the dissemination of policy and extended to political purposes:

> You know when someone is at the pulpit you do not question the person or whatever the person says. They subtly tell their congregations what to do or who to vote for. (Interview May 2008, Anonymous)

These comments suggest that the development activities provided by many religious groups, such as their almost universal engagement in education and health provision, are perceived as secondary to their political influence by state governments. Thus, religious groups are perceived mainly as organizations through which government can connect with specific groups, at best in order to deliver a kind of development that reflects government policy, and at worst simply in order to provide political traction. As a result, state governments have little direct interest in supporting a socially inclusive development process by strengthening mutual trust and understanding among religious groups. Instead, they ignore some religious groups and focus on other, usually locally important, organizations in order to create and maintain political constituencies.

The fact that many groups are happy to build on such ties with political leaders or networks rather than to seek agreements with other religious groups means that they are not exempt from the criticism frequently levelled at the state (and states). Not every government official felt as generous towards religious groups as the respondents quoted above. Chief Akanbi Atoyebi, a Director in the Ministry of Women Affairs, Social Development and Children's Welfare, Oyo State, reversed some of the accusations and concerns made – directly or indirectly – by many respondents from the religious sector. Explaining that religious organizations' greed for donations and contributions meant that they did not make a positive contribution to development or public morality, Chief Ayotebi argued:

> I am sorry to say this, I hate to be guilty of heresy but let me be honest with you, the churches and the mosques are paying lip service to moral sanctity in our society. They preach well, they say don't do this or that, but when it comes to the issue of donations, people with questionable integrity would go to the Church and the Mosque and make huge donations, yet the clerics will collect it and they [the donors] would be eulogized . . .
>
> So these are the issues, they [the religious organizations] are culpable in the issue of corruption rampaging the Nigerian Society [sic]. (Interview 25 May 2008, Chief Atoyebi)

These responses suggest not only a wide gap in the mutual perception between state officials and religious leaders, but also a concern over the close links between parts of the political and the religious sector. By stating that religious groups themselves were not immune from corruption, Chief Atoyebi suggested that the close cooperation of state governments with some religious groups had created the opportunity for some groups to participate in the corrupt practices widely attributed to politicians (cf. Smith, 2007).

The collaboration between the political and the religious sector not only undermined the religious groups' claims to moral authority but also their presumed independence from the state and its problems. On the basis of these comments, suggestions that religious organizations, even if divided among themselves, constituted a substantive part of an independent civil society capable of providing a counterbalance to the state's flawed forms of public engagement must be examined more carefully. Moreover, as state governments were closely involved in maintaining and producing forms of competition in which religious groups were involved, it is unlikely that they could provide the kind of support to religious groups that might encourage the emergence of a less divided non-state sector of society, whether based on faith or civic commitment.

RELIGIOUS GROUPS MISTRUST EACH OTHER

The obvious engagement of many religious groups in political struggles means that the suspicion that religious groups are themselves corrupt is not limited to state officials. Fears of political corruption among religious groups are also expressed in popular debate, and a number of scandals involving corrupt practices by religious leaders or organizations have been reported by the press. But perhaps most importantly, concerns over political co-optation and corruption exist among religious groups themselves. The following reflections by Alhaji Abduljeleel from Oyo State suggested that he was aware of the instrumentalization of religious groups by some politicians:

> our [NASFAT] members in government are also the same with them [politicians more generally]. Some came because they know that NASFAT has a large following/membership and want

> to use us to win elections. That is why many belong to NASFAT. (Interview 6 January 2008, Alhaji Abduljeleel)

As a result of this insight, he was careful to emphasize his own distance from the sphere of politics, and pointed out that:

> During my tenure here [as the chairman of NASFAT in Oyo State], I did not entertain politicians, I did not go to them, because I know what they will demand from me, I may not be able to give them. The moment you believe in money and go to them, you will dance to their tune because money dictates a lot of things. (Interview 6 January 2008, Alhaji Abduljeleel)

When religious groups had a close relationship with the government, other groups perceived them as acting in a morally objectionable way, especially if they were critical of the state's politics. Pastor Peter Adagbada from the RCCG in Oyo State argued:

> even some of these [religious] organizations do give their platform for preaching, where they say, okay please, these are the persons you should vote for, without looking at the credibility of the person, the person's past records, antecedents, and what the person stands for. (Interview 3 January 2008, Pastor Peter Adagbada)

In some contexts, especially where minority groups encountered large majorities that dominated politics, such perceptions intensified the tension between different religious groups. This is illustrated by a comment by Mrs Osho from the Kano State chapter of CAN, whose comment suggests that the engagement of religious groups in politics could undermine their religious as well as their moral credibility:

> People use religion to seek after their own selfish interest, they don't care and they make promises that they don't keep. . . . I don't know much of their [Muslim groups'] religion, I only know of mine, but what I know is that if they have the fear of God there will be no religious riots. (Interview 4 January 2008, Mrs Funmilayo Osho)

While the sharpness of this comment undoubtedly reflects both the strong discrimination of Christians as well as the prevalence of religious conflict in Kano State, other respondents made similar assertions, though often more diplomatically, about the religious credentials of rival groups. It is important to note that these accusations were not always addressed by Muslims to Christians and vice versa, and that they also reflected mistrust between different groups of the same religion. Emphasizing again the lack of religiousness of those who manipulate religion for political reasons, Alhaji Garba Haruna, the leader of the Muslim Hausa-speaking community in the predominantly Christian Anambra State, pointed out:

> We all know . . . bad people have also used religion to do other things. This category of people will tell you about religion but they deceive other people with it. (Interview January 2008, Alhaji Garba Haruna)

The last two comments emphasize that rival religious groups, especially those close to powerful political networks, were discredited by this association, especially in the eyes of those excluded from such access. Clearly these respondents understood rival groups not only as morally corrupt, but also as spiritually compromised, of lacking the fear of God, and of using religion to deceive others. They therefore perceived their own exclusion not only as a political fact, but as a result of their moral integrity and spiritual superiority. It is very likely that the political as well as the religious competition between religious groups has increased as a result of such perceptions. Thus, the close engagement between the state governments and some religious groups, which includes, but is not limited to the provision of development, has actually contributed to the deepening of divisions within the religious sphere.

Exploring the public engagement of religious groups from the angle of state politics, it appears that instead of constituting or being part of a sphere of activity that supports and corrects the state, religious groups are actively divided by their engagement with the state. While the political cooperation with and integration into the state of individual groups empowers these individually, it produces political rivalry and thus undermines the shared interests and concerns that exist in the area of development and especially educational and health provision. As a result, the ability of religious groups to contribute to a form of development that reflects their own universalist ideals and increases social peace and cohesion remains severely limited.

CONCLUSION

This chapter has explored a number of conceptual challenges at the heart of faith-based development on the basis of the Nigerian example, and it has illustrated the complex relationship between religion and development. While this chapter does not provide exact numbers about the development provision or its efficiency by religious organizations in these sectors, it confirms, supported by more general estimates, that religious groups provide a large and significant part of Nigeria's health and education services. However, these activities are part of wider social dynamics, in which the shared interests of religious groups play as much of a role as historical differences and ongoing political competition. The interaction between these different trends in turn affects the nature of the wider development process, and especially its social and political cohesion.

As demonstrated, many religious groups are united by their critique of the failure of the central and state governments to deliver welfare to Nigerian citizens. This shared concern suggests that they could be important participants in a national dialogue about the country's future. But without underestimating this shared rhetorical engagement, the practical provision of development is divisive in different ways and illustrates that the assumption of a unified 'faith sector' as part of a cohesive civil society is problematic. In education but also in health care, religious development activities reflects unequal resource bases, which have been used historically by some groups to press their advantage vis-à-vis others, and are therefore viewed with suspicion. And finally, the growing political relevance of religious groups since 1999, and their unequal inclusion into politics at the state level, actually contributed to the deepening of political – and religious – divisions.

As religious competition derives to a large extent from the unequal inclusion of different religious groups into the state for political reasons, the state itself needs to reconsider its techniques of engagement with religious groups below the national level. But a strict separation between religious groups and the state would not be in line with democratic principles as they are currently understood in Nigeria, and it would be politically impossible for religious reasons even under a non-democratic dispensation at least in northern Nigeria.

As a result, the only way to address the unequal participation of religious groups in politics – and thus to reduce religious competition – would be through a process that involves a wide range of religious groups, including minority and politically excluded groups as well as the state. The creation of formal and informal spaces for regular encounters between state governments and different religious (and other) groups might contribute to the emergence of compromises and mutual trust that could increase the efficiency of religiously provided development as well as increasing social cohesion. If donors remain committed to working with religious institutions – and given the dominance of these institutions in the health and education sectors, perhaps they should be – they must support the emergence of a more integrated and less competitive 'faith sector' through the provision of such spaces.

NOTES

* I am grateful to a number of people who have discussed this research, including Surinder Jodhka, Carole Rakodi and Gurharpal Singh. An earlier version of the chapter was also presented on 2 April 2010 at the School of Advanced International Studies (SAIS), Johns Hopkins University, Washington.

1. The term faith-based organization or FBO is not used in this chapter for various reasons, but mainly because in the Nigerian context it is not well established and has only been used very recently, while Muslim and Christian religious groups have been linked to development activity since the precolonial period.
2. Frances Stewart of CRISE, Department of International Development, University of Oxford presented a public address on the topic 'Is religion relevant to debates about development?' on 21 July 2010 during the RaD Conference 2010 on 'Religion shaping development: inspirational, inhibiting, institutionalised?', 21–23 July 2010 at the University of Birmingham.
3. No research was carried out among traditional religious institutions, even though they continue to play an important role in many Nigerian contexts. The main reason for this was that these institutions tend not to be recognized at the state or central level. Also, traditional religious identities have not been subject to the same degree of politicization as Muslim and Christian ones.
4. Interviews were carried out by Uchenna Chester Azubuike, Nathaniel Danjibo and Abubakar Oladeji in Anambra, Kano and Oyo States respectively.
5. These findings contrast with Casey's (2008) article, which suggests that ethnic and religious discrimination were closely linked under the rule of the Governor Kwankwaso (1999–2003). However, it is possible that changes are recent and associated with the more forceful implementation of Shari'a under Kwankwaso's successor Shekarau (2003–11).
6. The state has a Muslim majority, but Christians tend to be overrepresented among the educated and professional classes.
7. As the chairman of the local Muslim organization NASFAT explained, development included infrastructural development as well as psychological or spiritual development: 'what the people need is development starting from good roads, schools, electricity, water, good health and a lot of things' (interview 6 January 2008, Alhaji Abduljeleel). The comment from the Catholic Justice, Development and Peace Commission (JDPC) Anambra State below illustrates that most responses from this south-eastern state also echoed the concern with infrastructural development: 'In development, we look up to and also contribute to the infrastructural aspect of the development by building roads, building schools' (interview January 2008, C.J. Onyenze).
8. Only one of our respondents (from the Yoruba Muslim community in Anambra State) was very critical of the notion of infrastructural or economic development. Imam Ologbonoke emphasized that material wealth was nothing without spiritual well-being and asked, 'Development for all of us in the state? Do you mean for everybody to become rich? Well, it is only God that can take society and the people to a better kind of living. Development is acting according to the will of God for the bettering of mankind' (interview January 2008, Imam Ologbonoke). The comment is a useful reminder that both world

religions, at least potentially, can also constitute the basis for a non- or even anti-materialistic view of the world (and nation).
9. It is important to note that many individual Muslims nonetheless appreciate such offers.
10. However, some Christians have accepted the Muslim argument for Shari'a at least in part (cf. McCain, 2005, pp. 18–19).

REFERENCES

Ahmad, Ali (2005), 'Extension of Shari'ah in Northern Nigeria: human rights implications for non-Muslim minorities', *Muslim World Journal of Human Rights*, **2**(1), 1–36.
Casey, Conerly (2008), '"Marginal Muslims": politics and the perceptual bounds of Islamic authenticity in Northern Nigeria', *Africa Today*, **54**(3), 67–92.
Clarke, Gerard (2006), 'Faith matters: faith-based organisations, civil society and international development', *Journal of International Development*, **18**(6), 835–48.
Clarke, Gerard (2007), 'Agents of transformation? Donors, faith-based organisations and international development', *Third World Quarterly*, **28**(1), 77–96.
Clarke, Peter B. (1978), 'Islam, education and the developmental process in Nigeria', *Comparative Education*, **14**(2), 133–41.
Cohen, Abner ([1969] 2004), *Custom and Politics in Urban Africa: A Study of Hausa Migrants in Yoruba Towns*, London: Routledge.
De Kadt, Emanuel (2009), 'Should God play a role in development?', *Journal of International Development*, **21**(6), 781–6.
Deneulin, Séverine with Masooda Bano (2009), *Religion in Development: Rewriting the Secular Script*, London and New York: Zed Books.
Deneulin, Séverine and Carole Rakodi (2011), 'Revisiting religion: development studies thirty years on', *World Development*, **39**(1), 45–54.
Falola, Toyin (1998), *Violence in Nigeria. The Crisis of Religious Politics and Secular Ideologies*, Rochester, NY: The University of Rochester Press.
Federal Republic of Nigeria (2006), *Population Census*, available at: http://www.nigerianstat.gov.ng/Connections/Pop2006.pdf; accessed 22 July 2009.
Green, Maia (2006), 'Confronting categorical assumptions about the power of religion in Africa', *Review of African Political Economy*, No. 110, 635–50.
Hackett, Rosalind (1999), 'Conflict in the classroom: educational institutions as sites of religious tolerance/intolerance in Nigeria', *Brigham Young University Law Review*, **1999**(2), 537–60.
Harnischfeger, Johannes (2004), 'Sharia and control over territory: conflicts between "settlers" and "indigenes" in Nigeria', *African Affairs*, **103**(412), 431–52.
Harnischfeger, Johannes (2008), *Democratization and Islamic Law. The Sharia Conflict in Nigeria*, Frankfurt and New York: Campus Verlag.
Haynes, Jeffrey (2009), 'Conflict, conflict resolution and peace-building: the role of religion in Mozambique, Nigeria and Cambodia', *Commonwealth & Comparative Politics*, **47**(1), 52–75.
Human Rights Watch (HRW) (December 2001), 'Jos: a city torn apart', available at: http://www.hrw.org/sites/default/files/reports/nigeria1201_1.pdf; accessed 20 July 2009.
Human Rights Watch (HRW) (May 2005), 'Revenge in the name of religion. The cycle of violence in Plateau and Kano States', available at: http://www.hrw.org/reports/2005/nigeria0505/nigeria0505text.pdf; accessed 13 July 2009.
Kelsall, Tim (2008), 'Going with the grain in African Development?', *Development Policy Review*, **26**(6), 627–55.
Last, Murray (2003), 'La charia dans le Nord-Nigeria', *Le Monde Diplomatique*, No. 6/2003, 141–52.
Liman, Sa'adatu Hassan (2009), 'Shari'a and politics: crises, conflicts, and resolutions', in Julius O. Adekunle (ed.), *Religion in Politics. Secularism and National Integration in Modern Nigeria*, Trenton, NJ: Africa World Press, pp. 159–75.
Ludwig, Frieder (2008), 'Christian–Muslim relations in Northern Nigeria since the introduction of Shari'ah in 1999', *Journal of the American Academy of Religion*, **76**(3), 602–37.
Lunn, Jenny (2009), 'The role of religion, spirituality and faith in development: a critical theory approach', *Third World Quarterly*, **30**(5), 937–51.
Marshall, Katherine (2005), 'Africa: how and why is faith important and relevant for development?', The World Bank Dialogue on Values and Ethincs (HDNDE) Working Paper, available at: http://www.vanderbilt.edu/csrc/PDFs%20and%20Jpgs/marshall-africa.pdf; accessed 29 July 2010.

McCain, Danny (2005), 'Which road leads beyond the Shari'ah controversy? A Christian perspective on Shari'ah in Nigeria', in Philip Ostien, Jamila A. Nasir and Franz Kogelmann (eds), *Comparative Perspectives on Shari'ah in Nigeria*, Ibadan: Spectrum Books, pp. 7–26.

Nolte, Insa with Nathaniel Danjibo and Oladeji Abubakar (2009), 'Religion, politics and governance in Nigeria', Religions and Development Working Paper No. 39, published by the International Development Department of the University of Birmingham for the Department for International Development (DfID).

Obadare, Ebenezer (2007), 'Religious NGOs, civil society and the quest for a public sphere in Nigeria', *African Identities*, **5**(1), 135–53.

Obianyo, Nkolika E. (2008), 'Behind the curtains of state power: religious groups and the struggle for ascendancy in Nigerian public institutions: a critical appraisal', paper presented at CODESRIA 12th General Assembly 'Governing the African Public Sphere', available at: http://www.codesria.org/IMG/pdf/Nkolika_E-_Obianyo.pdf; accessed 28 July 2012.

Smith, Daniel Jordan (2007), *A Culture of Corruption. Everyday Deception and Popular Discontent in Nigeria*, Princeton: Princeton University Press.

Sodiq, Yushau (2009), 'Can Muslims and Christians live together peacefully in Nigeria?', *The Muslim World*, **99**(4), 646–88.

Suberu, Rotimi (2001), *Federalism and Ethnic Conflict in Nigeria*, Washington, DC: United States Institute of Peace Press.

Ter Haar, Gerrie and Stephen Ellis (2006), 'The role of religion in development: towards a new relationship between the European Union and Africa', *The European Journal of Development Research*, **18**(3), 351–67.

Wakili, Haruna (2009), 'Islam and the political arena in Nigeria: the Ulama and the 2007 elections', Institute for the Study of Islamic Thought in Africa (ISITA) Working Paper Series, Working Paper No. 09-004, March 2009.

Winkler, Tanja (2008), 'When God and poverty collide: exploring the myths of faith-sponsored community development', *Urban Studies*, **45**(10), 2099–126.

INTERVIEWS

Abduljeleel, Alhaji Opeyemi Abuliazeez, Chairman South-west Zone 4 of the Nasrul-Lahi-Il-Fathi Society of Nigeria (NASFAT), Oyo State, interviewed 6 January 2008.

Adagbada, Pastor Peter, Area Pastor of the Redeemed Christian Church of God (RCCG), New Bodija, Ibadan, Oyo State, interview 3 January 2008.

Ali, Mallam, Secretary to Mallam Abdullahi Pakistan, leader of the Izala movement in Kano State, interview 13 May 2008.

Anonymous, senior government official in the Directorate of the Women Advocacy and Empowerment Agency, Anambra State, May 2008.

Atoyebi, Chief Akanbi, Director in the Ministry of Women Affairs, Social Development and Children's Welfare, Oyo State, interview 25 May 2008.

Bwamche, Reverend Joshua, Senior Pastor, Evangelical Church of West Africa (ECWA), Kano State, interview 6 January 2008.

Danyaro, Mallam Mohammed, Director, Ministry of Internal Affairs, Youth and Social Development, Kano State, 13 May 2008.

Haruna, Alhaji Garba, Head of Northern Muslim community in Awka, Anambra State, interview January 2008.

Ologbonoke, Imam Abdulfatai, Chief Imam of the Muslim Yoruba community in Anambra State, interview January 2008.

Onyenze, C.J., JDPC Project Manager Awka, Anambra State, interviewed January 2008.

Orji, Pastor Richard Ejike, Assistant Provincial Pastor of the Redeemed Christian Church of God (RCCG), Anambra State, interview January 2008.

Osho, Mrs Funmilayo, Secretary Women's Wing Christian Association of Nigeria (CAN), Kano State, interview 4 January 2008.

28 Religion and development in Brazil, 1950–2010
Rowan Ireland

INTRODUCTION

Brazil has long been an important case in the study of religion and development. This is because of its status in development studies for more than half a century, and also by virtue of recognition by scholars that its religions, particularly Catholicism, have been centrally involved, negatively and positively, in its processes of development. Let us consider first Brazil's status in development studies, leaving aside, for the moment, considerations about what development might mean in contemporary Brazil. Geographical and population size, joined with the apparent magnitude of its developmental problems, have guaranteed attention, scholarly and diplomatic. In area, Brazil is by far the largest country in developing Latin America (and the fifth largest in the world, larger than Australia, or the area of the contiguous states of the USA). In the Americas, it is the second largest in population, after the USA. In the six decades noted in this chapter, it has grown from 52 million in 1950 to 195 million in 2010. In world terms, Brazil's economy is very large: just recently it displaced Great Britain to become the sixth largest in the world, and has never been less than ninth over several decades. But over much of that time too, the size of Brazil's developmental problems has kept it in the limelight.

In particular, its inequalities, posing obstacles to sustained economic growth, have been, and remain, dramatic. There are marked regional inequalities of wealth and average living conditions, for example, between the poor, mainly rural northeast compared to the relatively wealthy southeastern industrial hub around São Paulo. There are differences between the social status and life chances of descendents of the African slaves (slavery ended only in 1888) and those of the waves of European migrants who arrived in the later decades of the nineteenth and early twentieth centuries. Then there are the differences between social classes, especially visible in Brazil's great cities where the shining skyscrapers and gated communities spawned by corporate Brazil rub shoulders with the *favelas* (shanty towns) of the poor. These inequalities made Brazil's designation as 'Belgindia'[1] in some of the development literature of the 1980s seem tragically apt. And those inequalities, attributed in part to the legacies of slavery and a colonial primary export economy, were seen as causes and effects of other obstacles to development. They loom large in Brazil's profile of 'persistent underdevelopment in the midst of economic growth' (Baer, 2008, p. 3).

It is not just the size of Brazil's land mass, its economy, its population or its developmental problems that determined its forefront status in development studies. Size in these senses has been important, but always in relation to geopolitics. For more than half of the period examined here, Brazil was the largest unit in the Western hemisphere theatre of the Cold War. As such, resolution of its problems of widespread poverty and pervasive inequality, its dual economy, rampant inflation, and the exhaustion of its import substitution strategy for growth, took on geo-political importance. If these problems, which had been aggregated under the rubric of underdevelopment, were not resolved in Brazil by approved Western means, then the whole Western hemisphere might fall to communist revolution. Or so it was thought in Washington. There, in the early 1960s, it was feared that the 'loss' of Cuba, might well be followed by the loss of Brazil – and so for a while, USAID Northeast Brazil was second only to USAID Vietnam as the recipient of various forms of development aid, including the seeding of development studies.

That long moment when priorities in development studies were shaped by American Cold War concerns has passed, but Brazil has retained its importance in the field. Its changing development profile in the period under review has ensured that. From a start as a political and economic basket case of political and economic obstacles to development, Brazil has emerged by 2011 as one of the BRIC countries (Brazil, Russia, India and China), a 'newly industrialized country' (NIC) supposedly on its way to becoming a power-house in the global economy of the twenty-first century. Later in this chapter we will consider whether Brazil's loss of the soubriquet 'developing country' is apt.

For now, we need only to acknowledge that its passage from urgent basket case to emerging power-house sets agendas in development studies. The issues are grand – all the way from how did it get there, to an issue that will be addressed here, what is development all about? The discrete questions, regarding fact and theory, abound. How did Brazil escape the constraints on its development supposed by dependency theory? In what measure did the military dictatorships (1964–85) through political authoritarianism and modernization programmes, help or hinder later development? Since the later 1970s, how important for subsequent development have been the civil society movements for democracy, urban and rural land rights, the rights of industrial workers, and so on? How important have these movements been, relative to government policy and party politics since the restoration of formal democracy in 1985?

Then the question that is most directly addressed in this chapter: what has been the role of Brazil's religions in the socio-political transformations associated with development that have been observed over the last 60 years? This brings us to the second reason why Brazil is so important in the study of religion and development. It is simply that there is a long and rich history of studies linking religion, and Catholicism in particular, to Brazilian underdevelopment/development and to its concomitant social, political and economic 'modernization'. Forty years ago, Ivan Vallier (1970) traced links between various phases in the modernization of Latin American societies, and changing strategies of the Catholic Church for engagement with powerful elites on the one hand, and the faithful, at the grassroots, on the other. Vallier's necessarily brief profile of the Brazilian case suggested that, by the mid-twentieth century, the Catholic Church was poised between two configurations in these engagements. There was a right wing holding to strategies successfully pursued since the 1930s that had allowed the church to regain a privileged and influential place in Brazil's governing institutions, in return for its provision of public services in education and social welfare. Part of the bargain for the Right was that 'the Church should remain aloof from partisan political involvements and give its attention to traditional religious functions' (Vallier, 1970, p. 131).

To the minority church Left, this non-partisan strategy involved effective endorsement of power structures that enforced unjust distribution of wealth in old rural and new industrial Brazil, and ensured the subordination of the poor majorities in both sectors. By the end of the 1950s, there were 'sizeable groups' of clergy and laity, advocating various means of engaging with the poor in the struggle for social justice and radical structural changes. Emmanuel de Kadt (1970) has told the story of the most important of the attempts to put the Catholic Left's emerging pastoral-political-developmentalist vision for a new church and a new Brazil into practice in the Movement for Grassroots Education (MEB). This project, which aimed to give 'voice to the voiceless', was based on pedagogy later to be made internationally famous in development and education studies when Paulo Freire, in 1970, published English and Spanish translations of his *Pedagogy of the Oppressed.* De Kadt's story ends with the dismemberment of MEB after the military coup of 1964. But that, as we are about to see, was not the end for the Catholic Left and its role in promoting alternative development in Brazil (see Mainwaring, 1986; Ireland, 1989). The stories of the 'progressive church', of the projects expressing the church's 'preferential option for the poor' over the next three decades, and of the study of religion and development in Brazil, unfold in two phases, the classical and the contemporary.

THE CLASSICAL PERIOD

In retrospect, the (roughly) two decades from 1964 to the middle 1980s can be seen as the classical period in the study of religion and development in Brazil. On the side of religion, Brazil, back then, could still be thought of as 'the largest Catholic country' in the world, with the Catholic Church at the heart of Brazil's institutional matrix. Because of this, the focus of religion and development studies remained largely on Catholicism. Significant transformations in Catholicism, already underway in Latin America in the later 1950s and early 1960s, but now under the rubrics of 'the Theology of Liberation' and the 'Grassroots Church Communities' (CEBs), could be seen to herald and embody a model of development for Brazil that was alternative to the prevailing model(s) enforced by the country's military rulers.

For most of the classical period Brazil was ruled by the military. The development models held in place by the dictatorships had several features, against which the development model implicit in the discourse and practices of the CEBs stood in stark contrast. The military models emphasized economic growth over equity as the goal of policy, and justified closing or restricting democratic political institutions for the sake of growth. Growth would be achieved from the top down, by political and economic elites, and the poor, denied agency in development projects, would eventually benefit as wealth 'trickled down'.

The CEBs, at very least symbolically, signalled an alternative model, in two ways. First, they promised a Church less geared to maintaining its place and alliances in Brazil's elitist political institutions (which included the military), and more intent on building a new Church that gave voice to the institutionally excluded or marginalized poor. The fracture of the elitist institutional matrix in this way posed a challenge to the military government's capacity to enforce its own development model. Second, the local projects of the CEBs attempted to enact an alternative development model that emphasized equity, and included the maximization of the agency of the marginalized poor as a prime developmental goal. Both challenges were understood by the government and met with repressive measures.

The connections between the theologically justified practices of the CEBs and national development conceived in secular terms may be seen against the backdrop of what I shall call new development theory (NDT) – though it is no longer so new! The elements of NDT may be garnered from Amartya Sen (1999 and 2001), Peter Evans (1996) and others. Five analytically separable but interacting processes are seen to constitute development in NDT. These are:

1. Increasing engagement of an expanding citizenry (as compared to passive inhabitants) as agents in processes of social choice. This process involves the interaction of increasing capacity for engagement, and actual experience of engagement in the production of public goods.
2. Increasing willingness of citizenry to invest time, energy, and money in public goods (e.g., health and educational services, transportation infrastructure, urban infrastructure, land reform) and to enhance and monitor the delivery of those goods.
3. Consequent enhancement of productivity, contributing to long-term growth.
4. Reduction of violence and corruption as intrinsically valuable and growth enhancing.
5. Enhanced ability of citizens, working with their governments to negotiate challenges and opportunities arising from globalization.

The socio-political dynamics of interaction between these processes includes synergies between social movements acting locally, local and transnational NGOs, and state project administrators to achieve 'embeddedness' and 'complementarity', and thus a 'scaling up' from the local community level to the national-institutional (Evans, 1996; Ireland, 2005). At the local level, the net result of synergies and interactions may be seen in two phenomena that sustain the development processes. The first is the new citizen or 'popular subject' as he or she came to be called in Latin America (Levine, 1993, p. 171). The second is the local autonomous civil association in which citizen-subjects name and prioritize public goods, build bonds of trust, and progressively acquire the confidence and competences that enable collective action.

In the discourse and praxis of the CEBs, many elements of NDT were implicit. In particular, the first two elements of development, as listed above, were integral to the struggle to realize the CEB vision of the Kingdom of God unfolding in the here and now. In the CEBs, new subjects would be formed as the previously voiceless and politically excluded poor learned how to articulate local needs and were moved and motivated to engage in collective projects to meet these needs (e.g., projects to achieve such public goods as land rights, urban infrastructure in the burgeoning shanty towns, and provision of basic education). Engagement in the secular projects of needs articulation, citizen formation, community building, and the struggle for rights, for and among the poor, were seen by those involved in the CEBs as necessary to the living of Catholic faith, and integral to the building of the Kingdom of God. This vision informed action in everyday life, not only among clerical and lay 'organic intellectuals', but, according to some case studies (Ireland, 2005) the likes of shanty town (*favela*) residents engaged in the day-to-day building of a better world.

In the classical period of religion and development studies, this fusion of a Catholic faith movement with a movement of the poor for equity and rights could be seen as, potentially, a crucial contribution to development in Brazil, as seen in NDT terms.

The religion and development literature focused on the Catholic CEBs movement, and the central debates in the literature concerned the scope and effectiveness of the CEBs. Specific issues included: the degree to which the Theology of Liberation-inspired vision of educated clerical and lay 'animators' of the CEBs corresponded to the values and motivations of the Catholic laity from the poorer classes they sought to mobilize; the extent to which the latter really constituted a citizenry independent from the hegemony of elites; the actual extent and impact of the CEBs locally; and the extent of any 'scaling up' from the local. Towards the end of the classical period, debate concerned the fading of the CEBs movement during Brazil's transition to full representative democracy, 1986–90 (e.g., Mainwaring, 1987). Despite questions about the efficacy of the CEBs, however, there could be no doubts about two things by the end of the classical period. First, the Catholic Church had moved away from the positions adopted by the Catholic Right in the 1950s and 1960s – positions that would have left the church as a major institutional bulwark against NDT development. Second, the discourse and models of collective action nurtured in the CEBs, whatever the successes and failures of the CEBs themselves, had entered the public arena. There, the discourse and models not only informed and stirred opposition to the military regime and its development models, but have continued to inspire movements and projects for NDT development in Brazil.

THE CONTEMPORARY SCENE – DEVELOPMENT

By the second decade of the twenty-first century the religion and development landscape of Brazil has changed radically from what it was in the 1960s through the 1980s. That has forced the question of whether the themes and foci in the literature of the classical period are still relevant. At the very least, new substantive issues relating to the five NDT processes have to be considered, and significant new institutional actors have to be factored into the dynamics of development. In this section of the chapter, changes in the landscape will be reviewed and contemporary issues outlined. An argument is mounted that, despite radical changes, some issues of the classical period and modes of address to those issues, remain relevant. However, the effects of economic, political and cultural globalization in Brazil have changed the meaning of citizenship, altered definitions and priorities regarding public goods, and transformed the dynamic interactions between the five processes of development delineated in NDT. We have to ask again, what does development mean in contemporary Brazil?

At the same time, the largest Catholic country has become religiously multicultural Brazil, one of the world's most vibrant religious markets (Chesnut, 2007). Research in religion and development is now geared, necessarily, to tracing a plurality of religion and development dynamics rather than the singular Catholic Church/Theology of Liberation/CEBs dynamic. Further, such research has now to take into account new ideas about what is involved in the social and cultural aspects of development. As a consequence of Brazil's globalization as a political economy, its increasing aggregate prosperity, and its intense multiculturalism, new substantive issues and priorities for development have to be considered.

Let us look first at changes in the Brazilian political economy, in order to raise the question: 'What does development mean in the case of contemporary Brazil?' As one of the BRIC nations in the global marketplace, Brazil might be thought of as already developed, at least in economic terms, in relation to its status in the debt crisis years from 1991 to 1993, the years of stagflation, when GDP increased at an annual rate of just 2.9 per cent and per capita income declined by 6 per cent. Certainly Brazil's is now a dynamic economy, with annual GDP growth rate up around 6 per cent. Baer provides us with a few facts and figures that remind us that Brazil's is no third world economy: over 60 per cent of its exports are industrial products, and it has become the world's fourth largest aircraft manufacturer. Agriculture has not been the leading sector, but 'its growth was substantial' over recent years (Baer, 2008, p. 1). Even the persistent unevenness of wealth distribution, regional and class, which once allowed easy designation as a third world developing political economy, has been modified, though by no means eliminated, during the last two two-term presidencies.

There can be no doubt either, that Brazil has developed politically over the last quarter of a century. Contemporary Brazil must be judged to be one of the world's most stable and least authoritarian political democracies. More than that, the institutionalization of political participation, symbolized by the famous Participatory Budget process in Porto Alegre, would seem to confirm Brazil as one of the most developed democracies in the world (Baiocchi, 2001; Avritzer, 2009). Superficially, Brazil would seem to have moved so far from the economic and political underdevelopment perceived through to the 1980s, that the classical period issues in religion and development would no longer seem relevant. But let us look a little more closely, first at the economy, and then at current Brazilian politics.

Against the backdrop of the elements and dynamics of NDT, as sketched above, Brazil (like many another country considered to be already developed) will be seen as still developing, and in need of further development. Brazil, in this perspective, is undeveloped not only because of the high proportion of the total population still below the poverty line (30 per cent in Baer's estimation), and because of persisting gross inequalities in income and living standards between regions, and social classes. It is undeveloped, also, because so many of its poor are incapacitated as citizens and excluded from the exercise of social choice (i.e., choice regarding public goods) by interacting social, economic and political conditions. Among the signs of this underdevelopment are the growth of *favelas* in the major cities of Brazil, continuing dispossession of the rural poor and the indigenous population, systemic failures in primary education, and the high levels of violence and political corruption, so dramatically evident in the drug wars of Rio de Janeiro.

On the basis of this brief sketch of the contemporary political economy we conclude that, despite enormous changes, the key developmental issues of the classical period remain relevant. In particular, persisting gross inequalities in the distribution of income and resources continue to restrict the processes and interactions that are integral to NDT development. However, when we consider the socio-cultural changes that have taken place in Brazil since the classical period, we arrive quickly at a further set of issues that supplement those connected to economic equity. In evermore multicultural Brazil, the dynamics of development involve not only the political economy set of interactions that link the building of the capacities of citizens to the production of public goods via the reduction of absolute and relative poverty, but another, overlapping set as well.

This second set, which might be called the identity and rights set, links the building of the capacities of Brazilian citizens to effective recognition of the dignity and rights of previously unrecognized and/or marginalized social identities. In contemporary Brazil, the expansion of effective citizenship, as envisaged in NDT, involves not only the progressive inclusion of an undifferentiated mass of the poor, but the inclusion of women, Afro-Brazilians, indigenous Brazilians, and other particular segments of the population, in the negotiation of public goods, and the mediation of the plurality that these segments constitute. For the inquiry into religion and development, this has required a turn toward the study of how religion in contemporary Brazil impinges on diverse struggles for identity and rights. At the same time, that inquiry has had to address vast changes in the religious scene. These were brewing in the classical period, but have in time consolidated, as we are about to see.

THE CONTEMPORARY SCENE – RELIGION

Brazil can no longer be usefully thought of as the largest Catholic country in the world – even if, on the numbers who report themselves Catholic in national surveys and the census, it still is (Birman and Leite, 2000). The Brazilian Catholic Church is no longer dominant institutionally in comparison to other religions – especially the Protestant Pentecostal churches, or more specifically, neo-Pentecostalism in the form of the Universal Church of the Kingdom of God (IURD). In terms of cultural hegemony at the grassroots, Catholicism is no longer the religion of default. At all levels of society, but particularly among the middle classes and the urban poor, a vibrant religious market has developed – varieties of Catholicism compete with one another; Pentecostal churches compete amongst themselves and with the Catholics; hybrid forms of religion, combining elements of New Age, Catholicism, Pentecostalism and the Afro-Brazilian religions, jostle and flourish through ever expanding networks, and in the form of personal religion.

Some trends in the religious marketplace are readily discerned in census and survey data over the years. Between the censuses of 1990 and 2000, the proportion of self-reported Catholics fell from 83.76 per cent to 73.8 per cent of the total population, while the proportion of Protestants (more than two-thirds Pentecostal) rose from 9.05 per cent to 14.45 per cent (Souza, 2007, p. 156). The religious data from the 2010 census were not available at the time of writing, but we may expect continuing rapid change of this kind. The highly respected Datafolha Research Institute Reports from a set of sample surveys conducted over 2006–07 tell us that Catholics were down to 64 per cent, Protestant Pentecostals had jumped to 17 per cent, and non-Pentecostal Protestants stood at 5 per cent. These are extremely rapid rises for the Pentecostals and falls for the Catholics. Over the same period, official statistics record three further items of interest. First, the proportion of the population identifying as Afro-Brazilian spiritists remains small but steady at around 0.4 per cent, while 'White Table' spiritists have risen from 1.1 per cent in the 1991 census to 1.6 per cent in surveys reported by the Fundação Getúlio Vargas (FGV) in 2009. Second, the percentage identifying as other religions, including a profusion of 'Asian religions' has been growing, but remains small at about 3 per cent. Third, the proportion of those stating no religion or atheist has been growing, especially among young, better-educated males, from 4.7 per cent in the 1991 census to 7.4 per cent in 2000 and 6.7 per cent in the FGV 2009 report.

But these statistics do not tell all about the religious marketplace. If anything they understate the public presence of the Pentecostals who are much more active participants in their churches than the Catholics, and worship in neighbourhood chapels or shop-front temples that are much more visible than Catholic parish churches, especially in poorer urban areas. Pentecostals are forcefully present also in the media, with the neo-Pentecostal IURD owning a popular national television network. Other Pentecostal churches are to be heard on myriad pirate and licensed radio stations. Pentecostal 'gospel music' CDs are the biggest and most vital segment of the market for CDs in Brazil. For Brazil's other religious families, we must also look beyond the statistics. The small percentage of Brazilians declaring one or other of the Afro-Brazilian religions as their religion hides the fact that many who declare themselves Catholic will consult a medium more often than they attend Mass. What the IURD incessantly denounces as the Satanic stain of Afro-Brazilian spiritism, spreads well beyond its cult centres and the relatively small number of committed devotees. Moreover, the concentration of those centres in Brazil's largest state capitals lends them a public presence beyond what we would expect from the numbers who identify as adherents. In the case of the alternative religions, small, if rapidly growing memberships of Asian religion and New Age groups, obscure larger numbers who draw from their websites and the social media to construct their own personal or networked hybrid religions.

One obvious conclusion from these considerations and the statistics is that exclusive focus on Catholicism and its transformations is no longer defensible, as it was in the classical period of religion and development studies. Another is that we should examine the consequences of major newer forms of religious life for NDT-type development. This is what is done in the rest of the chapter. One by one, main components of the religious marketplace – Catholicism, Pentecostalism and the Afro-Brazilian religions (more briefly) – are profiled, and questions about the consequences of the religion for development are examined. Some of the questions are specific to a particular component, but all relate to one general question: how do the major religions of Brazil nourish or restrict the engagement of citizens, particularly among historically marginalized segments, in collective processes of effective social choice, as envisaged in NDT? In the reviews of the various forms of religious life, the focus will be on the dynamic links between each form and NDT development.

THE CATHOLIC DYNAMICS

As already noted, two major changes in Brazilian Catholicism have weakened its input to NDT development. The Catholic Church has lost its place at the apex of Brazil's major institutions, and its cultural and political clout as Brazil's default religion has greatly declined, just as the influence of the Pentecostal churches, and particularly the IURD has risen. At the same time, the CEBs, once the main religious vectors of NDT development – in terms of generating motivating vision, community-building practices, and projects for public goods at the grassroots – are no longer central and prioritized in the Church (Vásquez, 1997 and 1998). Groups associated with Catholic Charismatic Renewal (CCR) – more of which below – rather than the CEBs, are now at the centre of contemporary Catholic life. The long-term consequences of that for development are unclear, but in the shorter term, an important Catholic dynamic for NDT development is much diminished.

However, it has by no means disappeared. The CEBs survive in some dioceses, and are kept alive by individual lay and clerical Catholics. Of greater importance is the continuation of CEBs practices and versions of CEBs spirituality in Catholic groups and networks that do not identify as CEBs, and even well beyond the institutional boundaries of the Catholic Church. There is much CEBs-inflected faith and practice without regular Catholic Church belonging or clerical tutelage. Márcia Pereira Leite (2003) helps substantiate the point. She describes the Popular Movement of Favelas (MPF) in Rio de Janeiro, which brought together leaders from 60 *favelas*, with 'militants' from several NGOs active in the *favelas*, to address violence and corruption in the city, and to demand full citizenship rights for *favela* residents. Leite profiles the four of five movement leaders who brought vision, discourse and strategies from their earlier experiences of the CEBs into the movement. She highlights the religious symbols, values and practices, derived from the CEBs that, she argues, came ever more to the fore as the movement went about mobilizing support in the *favelas*.

She found the CEBs-inspired leaders involved in a remaking of the radical and democratic utopia articulated in the Theology of Liberation. The utopia was articulated and expressed in an intense, publicly expressed spirituality. This was especially notable in the instance of Pedro, the founder of the movement. He was estranged from the church in Rio, where the Cardinal-Archbishop had been especially hostile to the CEBs. But he publicly identified as Catholic and announced his continuing engagement with the church pastoral work in which he had been involved since the 1960s (variously, the Workers' Pastoral, the Pastoral of the Favelas, The Afro-Brazilian Pastoral). Another leader (formed in the CEBs, but now unchurched) though convinced that religion was best left in the private sphere, accepted that expressions of the spirituality in prayers and songs, even dress (adornments like scapulars and crosses) were crucial in establishing the identity of the movement and in mobilizing support. Expressions of spirituality helped establish a 'linguistic community' that linked leaders together (including the one Protestant in the leadership group) and with followers in the loosely federated *favela* residents' associations. There the leaders were recognized as Catholic but ecumenically orientated actors open to alliances with secular NGOs, Pentecostal communities and the Afro-Brazilian movements. These were all similarly concerned to combat local drug barons and establish the rights of *favela* residents in confrontations with the police and corrupt politicians, albeit with different constituencies, and employing different strategies.

Leite notes the CEBs phrases employed in the MPF and the secular equivalents with which they were 'fused' (p. 88); and she argues that the fusion helped the MPF to its relative success. The goal of 'full citizenship' became the 'life in abundance' that Jesus had come to bring to us (the phrase comes from John 10: 10). The political struggle for citizenship, equality and other rights was the way taken by the 'people of God' to realize the 'gifts of God' available as the 'Kingdom of God' emerges 'here and now'. Leite's and other studies (e.g., of the Movement of the Landless, or MST) confirm my own observations in the course of a study of residential associations in Brazilian *favelas* over the last 20 years (Ireland, 1999, 2011). The CEBs are certainly not a central feature of the Catholic Church, as they were seen to be in the classical period, but their modus operandi, Theology of Liberation-inflected discourse and spirituality (*mística*) continue to move and motivate a variety of actors for NDT development, especially at the local grassroots. Further, a generation of leaders of trade unions, social movements, and political parties, especially the Workers' Party (PT), who were formed in the CEBs from the 1960s to the 1980s, continue to deploy discourse and values from those years in public arenas (Souza, 2007).

However, there is another Catholic dynamic, arguably negative in its implications for NDT development. This dynamic is evident in a profile of what has become the central feature of the church in place of the CEBs – the Catholic Charismatic Renewal (RCC), or more precisely, the second wave of that Renewal (Clarke, 1999; Souza, 2007). The RCC landed in Brazil from the USA in the 1960s. It was a movement for renewal through cultivation of the gifts of the Holy Spirit in traditional Catholic liturgy and devotions, generally in counterpoint to the CEBs because of its strict focus on individual salvation through spiritual practices, as opposed to the CEBs' focus on collective liberation through journeys to realize the Kingdom of God on earth. It grew by fits and starts as a small movement of Catholic laity, coming to public notice only as the CEBs faded in the 1990s, but even then appearing tiny in comparison to 'the Pentecostal explosion' well underway at the time.

By the end of the decade a second wave of RCC had the British observer Peter B. Clarke (1999) asking whether the 'walkout' from Catholicism to Protestant Pentecostalism might not be coming to an end. A number of young 'pop-star' priests were attracting huge numbers to Catholic liturgies in football stadiums for special festivals, and the likes of converted factories and warehouses for regular Sunday Mass. They stirred ecstatic enthusiasm for RCC spirituality as they sang and danced its messages, reaching millions more through CDs and multimedia appearances. Hymns and devotions to honour the Virgin Mary, and the centrality given to the priestly celebration of the Catholic Mass, distinguished these performances from those of the Protestant Pentecostals, but the emphasis on the direct experience of the Spirit of God, and on the need to express commitment in response to a calling from God to love and worship Him, defined common Pentecostal ground.

Several features of this second wave RCC distinguish it from the first. Where the latter was a small movement led by laity, this huge popular movement for the Spirit is led by the Charismatic priests. The most famous of these, Marcelo Rossi, is renowned for his 'aerobics of the Lord', his TV appearances and catchy hymns are heard in all manner of public places all over Brazil, and most recently (2010) he published a book that, so far, has sold 6 million copies. But he is no one-man band. He is one of several young priests with similar public profiles, and like them, he has earned endorsement from the ecclesiastical establishment. He has had that from the beginning of his ministry from his own bishop, and over time has won over initial doubters in the dominant conservative wing of the Brazilian episcopacy. A second distinguishing feature of the second wave is the up-front use of latest marketing techniques for evangelization – this in common with the IURD. A third feature is the emphasis, one of degree only in comparison with the first wave, on joy, gratitude, and happiness as appropriate expressions of a new Catholic ethos and a renovated church.

It is not hard to find trenchant criticism of the second wave of RCC from defenders of Liberation Theology and the CEBs. The critics dismiss the singing priests as audience rousers who use modern media techniques to deliver simplified and codified teaching to the manipulated masses. In presentations of the 'Renewed Church' on TV Canção Nova (TV New Song) they find the traditional church mode of communication from clerical elites to receptive masses, rather than the open reflections and exchanges promised in the CEBs. They complain about the dualisms embedded in the message – between cultivation of individual spiritual life (prior), and collective action to build community (secondary, and not of direct concern to ministers of the church); between faith and politics, broadly defined. Marcelo Rossi appears to accept main points in the critics' characterization of second wave RCC, once it is purged of the prejudicial language, and the supposed vices are seen as orthodox virtues. The church that he serves does endorse a top-down catechesis, and prioritizes the goal of happiness in the church over fullness of life attained in communal struggle for justice. That church will not be having any direct input into NDT development, and unlike in the classical period, has no pastoral strategy at the grassroots that might provide religious energy for NDT processes.

However, an outline of Catholic development dynamics would be incomplete without noting an unresolved tension or contradiction. The bishops who have stepped back from the Theology of Liberation, presided over the dismantling of the CEBs, and who now endorse second wave RCC, nonetheless continue to issue statements critical of current trends in the political economy, in exactly the terms deployed three decades ago. For example, the declaration issuing from the 44th General Assembly of the Brazilian Conference of Bishops in 2006, argued that inequality and social exclusion, insufficiently addressed in government policy, constitute the greatest long-term challenges to Brazilian development. But there was no call, or means suggested, for the People of God to do anything in particular about it. The contradictions suggested here are well noted by the few remaining members of the progressive church with high public profiles, like Frei Betto. Their critiques of declarations without accompanying pastoral strategy add complexity to the Catholic dynamics.

THE PENTECOSTAL DYNAMICS

Any Pentecostal dynamic for NDT development processes, was rather occluded in the literature of the classical period by the focus on Catholicism. But Emilio Willems (1967) had already traced the lineaments of such a dynamic a quarter of a century before others followed in his footsteps. Willems studied followers of the new faith in Chile and Brazil and found them motivated to active citizenship as they acquired a new sense of dignity and status through experience of the gifts of the Holy Spirit in their converted lives. They felt deeply what Willems described as an incongruity between their high status as worthy, fully participating members in their religious world, and their low status and exclusion as members of the lower classes. Out of this perceived and deeply felt incongruity, Willems argued, arose the Pentecostal citizen, equipped by the participatory skills and confidence acquired in congregational life to strive for 'status congruence' in social, political, and economic life.

Later studies of Pentecostals in Brazil developed these themes. These studies brought the Pentecostal phenomenon to the full attention of scholars of religion and development, and that marked the end of the classical period's exclusive focus on Catholicism.

David Martin (1990) found Pentecostals walking out of the Catholic Church, and away from a Brazilian society in which Catholicism was still the default religion, albeit more honoured in the breach than dominical observance. In their new congregations, as Martin saw it, they created a world apart from the popular culture, the hierarchies, life-styles, and patronage politics of the Catholic-tinged world. Around their congregations, they constructed social, ritual and discursive boundaries protecting new ways of life, new identities, new notions of private and public virtue. In their world apart, self-confident, self-reliant citizens were formed. In Martin's view, a Protestant revolution, of the kind already long since seen in North America, was on the way in Latin America, and in Brazil especially. The Pentecostal citizen would strive for public goods, but not of the socialist kind called for (hopelessly, as Martin saw it) by the Theologians of Liberation. Martin's Pentecostals are more individualistic and attuned to capitalism than the idealized CEB citizen, but they are recognizable, nonetheless, as the sort of citizen called for in NDT.

Case studies of the early 1990s showed some Brazilian Pentecostals, contra stereotypes of them all as world-renouncing mystics, engaged fully and vigorously in local community associations, social movements, trade unions and even the then new Workers' Party (Burdick, 1996). Such engagements were by no means despite Pentecostal faith, these studies showed us, but deeply grounded in Pentecostal religious experience and biblically informed injunctions and worldview. Cecilia Mariz (1992) highlighted the importance of conversion as a liberating experience that counteracted the fatalistic acceptance of the status quo that constrained citizenly engagement in shanty towns of the Brazilian north-east. In a marvellously rich comparison between CEBs participants and Pentecostals to the south, in Duque de Caxias, John Burdick (1996) showed us members of both negotiating their particular faiths and shared experience of harsh material conditions in poor urban neighbourhoods.

He revealed not one, but a complex of Pentecostal-inflected modes of address to those problems. Some modes seemed to confirm stereotype: such a high priority was given to spiritual over material liberation and improvement, that the engagements of citizenship were avoided. But Burdick found a sizable number of Pentecostals of the Assemblies of God impelled by their faith to engage in communal action to right injustices and remedy conditions that undermined 'the Christian life envisaged by the Apostle Paul' (p. 207). This was a way of life centred on 'such worldly relations as marriage, family, work, neighbourhood, and the maintenance of physical health' (p. 207). Poverty might be acceptable, even 'sacralized' but not man-made misery that destroys families and human relationships good in the sight of God. And God expects the Christian to strive for the good and combat evil, even when constituted authority must be challenged in the struggle. Burdick notes that the Pentecostal 'sacralization of poverty carries with it a compelling denial of legitimacy of the rich and the powerful' (p. 214).

Ireland (1999, pp. 124–6) has listed the defining characteristics of the sort of Pentecostalism uncovered by Mariz, Burdick, and others (e.g., Lehmann, 1996), as well as in his own case study of a member of the Assembly of God in a town in the north-east of Brazil (Ireland, 1997). These characteristics amount to a profile of a particular stream of Pentecostal faith that nurtures a distinctive Pentecostal citizen who is disposed by faith and religious experience to seek justice and improvement in community life. Further, this stream of Pentecostalism, seems to call out Pentecostal citizens to act not only for political economic justice but for issues on the identity and rights agenda. Again, Burdick (1999) has led the way, showing how Afro-Brazilian Pentecostals, in a society where there is still much stigmatization and social exclusion of Afro-Brazilians, have come to accept and value their racial identity, and then confidently assume and assert it in their congregations and in everyday life. The religious foundations for this include the constantly celebrated experience of conversion in the Spirit, the relative lack of racial discrimination in congregational life, and deep attention to biblical proclamations of the universal brotherhood of believers. Burdick is at pains to spell out disclaimers – for example, he acknowledges a history of mutual hostility and suspicion between the secular black movement and the Pentecostal churches, and points out how Pentecostal universalism is at odds with ethnic or other group identifications. He is not claiming Pentecostalism as the heart of a black civil rights movement in Brazil, far from it. Rather, what he shows us in the case of Afro-Brazilian believers, is how Pentecostalism enters subtly into what might be called active identity formation, that is, the reflexive construction of the social self rather than the passive assumption of given identity. We see, in individual portraits, a stream of Pentecostalism providing inspiration and resources for the formation of subjects who know who they are, where they have come from, and where they want to go. These are surely at least potential NDT citizens in multi-cultural Brazil.

Researchers like Burdick who have revealed how Pentecostalism may contribute to NDT development, are careful to note divergent Pentecostal streams, some of which would seem to withdraw believers from NDT processes rather than provide inspiration and resources for social engagement. If we include the neo-Pentecostal IURD in the Pentecostal family, the multivalence of the family with respect to development becomes even more pronounced and complex than we have seen so far. Where Burdick and others brought out a positive, if not unequivocal, dynamic for development in Pentecostalism, studies of the IURD suggest a strong negative dynamic. But as always, there are contradictory indications.

On the positive side, followers of the IURD faith appear well armed to sever ties with political, cultural elites that have historically obviated full, independent citizenship among the 'popular classes'. The IURD has mounted aggressive attacks on the Catholic Church as Babylon, fostering idolatrous practices, and it pillories as Satanic the Afro-Brazilian possession religions that the secular intelligentsia and political elites regard benignly as 'a time-honoured element in the construction of Brazilian national identity' (Birman and Lehmann, 1999, p. 3).

Curiously, however, the church appears to mimic much of what it excoriates in other religious groups and in society at large. Its tight, plutocratic hierarchy constitutes an alternative elite, and its own patron–client structures replace those of the old, rejected order. At the same time, the IURD faith, as a Brazilian form of 'prosperity religion', emphasizes the pursuit of individual gain as good in the eyes of God; and it promises to provide its members with the spiritual protection and means to acquire money and material success – all in return for the payment of tithes and other regular fees. The church, and its individual leaders have become immensely rich, and vast sums of money have been spent on the acquisition and running of a national TV network, and the construction of large temples. The church is also involved in politics, especially so its top bishops, and most of all Bishop Edir Macedo who founded the IURD in 1975. The involvement is not for ideological or development goals but for deals that will protect and advance the interests of the church. Members are urged by leadership to vote for politicians who have agreed to promote those interests.

These pieces of information about the IURD might appear decisive indicators of a negative impact on NDT development via the formation given to its members. But we cannot assume that the IURD works like some brainwashing cult, as popularly conceived. Studies of IURD membership show that there is much coming and going as members come from other churches (mainly Pentecostal) when they seek a 'strong' religion to deal with acute problems in life – unemployment, health problems, domestic violence (Birman, 1996; Bonfatti, 2000). Features of the church that have caused it to run afoul of the law, and that scandalize the intelligentsia, appear to be read by its millions of adherents as signs of its strength to protect and deal with the Satanic forces believed to cause all manner of pain and suffering, including the ills of poverty. And IURD strength can be deployed to vanquish the demons causing individual troubles for as long as the dues are paid. Exorcisms from named spirits of the Afro-Brazilian pantheon, conducted by ordained ministers of the church, are central in daily rituals, and what appear to be rituals of financial bargaining with God (I give money to God's church in return for God's protection from evil forces, and His reward of prosperity) are integral experiences of church members.

The exclusive attribution of what Andrew Chesnut (1997) has called 'the pathogens of poverty' to malign spirits, rather than to social causes to be addressed socially in some instances, of itself disposes members of IURD away from engagement in the processes of NDT development. Arguably, the use of money as a form of magic to seal bargains with God completes the turn (Bonfatti, n.d.) The habit of magic, we might reasonably hypothesize, is subversive of the habits of citizenship, to paraphrase Alexis de Tocqueville. A substantial literature has shown other forms of Pentecostalism as a sort of independent variable, working in believers' lives so that they see and address injustice. A smaller literature on members of IURD suggests that this form of neo-Pentecostalism reflects and reproduces the individualism and consumerism of neo-liberal Brazil. Paul Freston sketched an IURD member so involved in the individual struggle to survive and advance in a difficult world as to adopt 'a moralized version of the yuppie gambling ethic, an overnight flight to rapid enrichment' (1993, p. 70).

THE AFRO-BRAZILIAN SPIRITIST DYNAMIC

Case studies and interpretations of the Afro-Brazilian religions suggest that, as with Catholicism and Pentecostalism, there are positive and negative dynamics with respect to development within the tradition. On the whole, in the classical period of religion and development studies, the negative dynamics were most emphasized (Ortiz, 1978; Brown, 1986). Links were drawn between the beliefs and practices of the Afro-Brazilian spiritists and the maintenance of subalternity among the Afro-Brazilian poor. Reginaldo Prandi (1996) drawing on his own studies and reflecting earlier studies, argued that the religions locked their devotees into a time-honoured strategy of survival. This strategy centred on making deals with the powers that be that in effect denied them citizenship, or in contemporary Brazil, limited citizenship to voting for a candidate in exchange for the granting of some favour by the governing elites. The beliefs and practices hallowed a sort of market of magic (involving sacrificial exchanges between the spirits of the African pantheon, and devotees, and between the latter and earthly patrons) in which the aim of individual participants is to harness power, in competition with others, for individual survival or advancement. This, Prandi considers, is 'pre-ethical' religion, altogether lacking any ethic for collective action for public goods, and legitimating the corruption of patrons who deliver the goods. No citizen-subjects or any religious grounding for NDT development here!

But others have seen signs of a more positive dynamic, involving some streams of Afro-Brazilian religion (Ireland, 1991, Chapter 5). Some studies of black identity and civil rights movements in Bahia (Bacelar, 1989; Sansone, 1996) show the important role of Afro-Brazilian religions in them, helping nurture a 'discourse of ethnicity', and encouraging, especially among the young, a sense of identity and collective power derived from ritual connection to mother Africa. Bacelar described effects he observed among young black Bahians of involvement in new carnival groups grounded in the Afro-Brazilian religion Candomblé: 'No longer did they need to distance themselves from their colour: they were given their own spaces and equipped to see that blacks could exercise citizenship' (Bacelar, 1989, p. 96).

CONCLUSION

It is no easy task to consolidate these observations on religion–development dynamics in contemporary Brazil into a coherent picture. It is certainly much harder than it appeared to be in the classical period. However, the roiling of the unruly contemporary scene may be brought to a degree of coherence by framing transformations in the religious landscape over the last 20 years around the central issue set by new development theory. This is the extent to which each of the main religious families disposes and capacitates its members to engage in the pursuit of public goods, broadly conceived. Using that frame, and drawing into it responses to the religion-specific questions reviewed above, we may conclude with a summary of features that must be included in an adequate description of the contemporary religion-and-development scene, albeit those features may be overdrawn and requiring qualification. These features are presented as highlighted propositions regarding Catholicism (linked propositions 1–3), Pentecostalism (4–7), and Afro-Brazilian religions (8–9):

Proposition 1: The Catholic CEBs and the Theology of Liberation are marginal in the contemporary church, in comparison with their status in the classical period. This has meant that the major religious source for the generation of the citizen-subject envisaged in NDT has been depleted.

Proposition 2: However, marginality is not to be mistaken for obliteration. CEBs, as a form of civic association consonant with NDT ideals, are still to be found nurturing local projects for the production of public goods. More important, the values of participatory citizenship and practices for realizing it, once thought to be cultivated almost exclusively in the CEBs, have long since entered into mainstream political and social life. There they continue to contribute to NDT development in Brazil in myriad local development projects, in protest movements contesting large-scale top-down development, and in social movements embodying alternative development. Many personnel in these projects and movements are 'graduates' of CEBs that flourished in the classical period.

Proposition 3: The latter-day transformation of the Catholic Charismatic Renewal (CCR) into the phenomenon of pop-star priests appears to have displaced the CEBs at the centre of church life. The effects of this phenomenon appear negative for NDT development in terms of the form of association CCR engenders and the dispositions it encourages among its devotees. We cannot be sure of long-term impact on devotees or the mooted emergence of hybrid Charismatic-CEBs forms of Catholicism. At present what is clear is that clerical leaders of this new form of CCR remain firmly centre stage, and explicitly reject the CEBs' focus on lay vocations to live Christian faith through collective identification of, and struggle for, public goods. They espouse, perform, and apparently successfully nurture among millions of devotees, a form of Catholicism emphasizing individual spiritual development through Catholic worship and devotions.

Proposition 4: Contrary to stereotypes of the exclusive other-worldly focus of Pentecostals, at least one major stream of Pentecostalism in Brazil equips members with the dispositions and resources to walk into the world of everyday life as NDT citizens. The experiences of conversion and of the transforming power of the Holy Spirit are crucial foundations in the turn to the world. In individual spiritual experience and congregational life, members acquire the confidence, strength, and resources to break out from the old, out-of-control life rooted in popular culture, to life lived as God ordained in the Bible. The rejection of the old life, and focus on fulfilling responsibility to conduct relationships of daily life in a manner required by God, frees and motivates the Pentecostal convert to fight injustice and corruption perpetrated by the powers that be.

Proposition 5: A tributary of the form of Pentecostalism that motivates action for political economic justice at the grassroots, also moves and motivates action on issues of identity and rights. In particular, full inclusion and respect for Afro-Brazilians in church and civil society has become a major concern addressed in many Pentecostal congregations.

Proposition 6: However, there are other forms of Pentecostalism that are close to stereotype. Even in congregations where active Pentecostal citizens are formed and sustained, we find other members (including, sometimes, pastors) opting for radical withdrawal from the world, and justifying the withdrawal in biblical terms. This is the Pentecostalism that prompts members to shelter as much as possible within the safety of the church and private devotions, in a sense abdicating citizenship in the evil world outside to pastors and church authorities.

Proposition 7: The neo-Pentecostal IURD, the fastest growing and most publicly prominent member of the Pentecostal family, appears negative in relation to NDT development. Conversion to IURD does involve a break from Catholic-tinged popular culture, Afro-Brazilian spiritism, and old patron–client ties located in those worlds. But unlike in some other streams in the Pentecostal family, the break does not prepare the way for the exercise of NDT citizenship. Rather, involvement in the business empire of the IURD, unless lightly undertaken, appears to lead to subjection within a new corporate hierarchy. Further, via a demonic soteriology and recourse to a magical cash-based bargaining with God for individual benefit, the IURD member is inserted, passively, into neo-liberal Brazil. There, he or she becomes absorbed as a consumer rather than becoming equipped as a citizen disposed to name, and act for, public goods.

Proposition 8: Like the other religious families, the much smaller Afro-Brazilian family includes divergent tendencies with respect to NDT citizenship. On the one hand, clients of Afro-Brazilian mediums and participating members of ritual groups are inducted into the 'pre-ethical' world of survive-as-best-you-can Brazil. In that world of magical address to the problems of everyday life, and the wheeling and dealing of patron–client politics, there is no space for the cultivation of NDT citizenship.

Proposition 9: However, there are signs that recent cultural ferment in the Afro-Brazilian religious world, has stimulated a new discourse of ethnicity among young Afro-Brazilians, especially in Bahia. New identifications with Afro resistance movements of the past, and transnational resistance and civil rights movements in the present, have inspired a new sense of inclusion and citizenship among young Afro-Brazilians.

On the basis of this resumé, a number of conclusions can be drawn about religion and development in contemporary Brazil. These conclusions are necessarily provisional, given ongoing transformations of the Brazilian political economy, the effects of globalization, and, above all, the complex dynamics of the religious scene. Snapshots of elements in that scene omit developments underway within and between them. For example, some observers of the Pentecostal scene have detected a 'neo-Pentecostalization' of older members of the Pentecostal families in increasing signs of corporation-style restructuring, deployment of modern marketing, and adoption of themes from prosperity theology. Then there are relationships between the listed elements of the religious scene and the new religious movements that have not been addressed in this chapter.

Setting aside these disclaimers it is clear that religion remains enormously important in Brazilian development, especially so if the focus is on developmental processes identified in NDT. This importance of religious factors in development appears set to continue well into the future given the vibrancy of the religious scene in Brazil. Brazilian religions are important in their positive and negative impacts on NDT development in ways identified in the classical period, but also in new ways, involving new religious actors, especially those of the Pentecostal family. Among the many factors bearing on prospects for NDT development, divergent tendencies within each of the religious families, and contestation between the families loom large. It is, though, hard to predict how the contestations will pan out.

There are signs, for example, in the extraordinary florescence of the IURD and the phenomenon of the singing priests, that trends in the Brazilian political economy are favouring movements in the major religious families that are negative for NDT development. These political economic trends include the increasing subordination of social relations to market relations, the relentless commodification of public goods, and generally, the ever-spreading impact of neo-liberal policies on everyday life and social relations.

Indeed, insofar as these developments in the political economy appear to be shaping developments in the religious sphere, we might be seeing some weakening of religion as an independent variable capable of influencing the course of development in Brazil

But we are a long way from the demise of religious factors working in favour of NDT development. It is too early to write off CEBs-type Catholicism, older forms of Pentecostalism, non-Pentecostal Protestantism, and perhaps some forms of the Afro-Brazilian religions in this respect. These diverse strands in multi-religious Brazil have produced, in their different ways, the citizen-subjects and the civil society associations that were conducive to NDT development in the classical period. They continue to do so in constantly changing circumstances in the present, and look set to stimulate 'development as liberation' well into the future.

NOTE

1. The Belg(ium) referred to that segment of Brazil (about 10 per cent of the population) with a level of consumption equal to that of a small industrial country, which was located in a large country of the Third World, like India (at the time), where poverty and deprivation prevail. The decade of the 1980s is often referred to as Brazil's (and Latin America's) lost decade relative to higher levels of economic growth in other decades since 1950.

REFERENCES

Avritzer, L. (2009), *Participatory Institutions in Democratic Brazil*, Baltimore, MD: Johns Hopkins University Press.

Bacelar, J. (1989), *Etnicidade: Ser Negro em Salvador*, Salvador: Inamá, Programa de Estudos do Negro na Bahia (PENBA).

Baer, W. (2008), *The Brazilian Economy: Growth and Development* (6th edition), Boulder, CO: Lynne Rienner Publishers.

Baiocchi, G. (2001), 'Participation, activism and politics: the Porto Alegre experiment and deliberative democratic theory', *Politics and Society*, **29**(1), 43–72.

Birman P. and D. Lehmann (1999), 'Religion and the media in a battle for ideological hegemony: the Universal Church of the Kingdom of God and TV Globo in Brazil', *Bulletin of Latin American Research*, **18**(2), 145–64.

Birman, P. (1996), 'O bispo, o povo e a TV: alguns efeitos, talvez inesperados da presença recente dos pentecostais', *Cadernos de Conjuntura*, **54**, 5–13, Rio de Janeiro: IUPERJ.

Birman, P. and M. Pereira Leite (2000), 'Whatever happened to what used to be the largest Catholic country in the world?', *Daedalus*, **129**(2), 271–91.

Bonfatti, P. (n.d.), 'Sobre as Categorias Universais: Relevantes aspectos observados na Igreja Universal do Reino de Deus', available at: www.rubedo.psc.br/artigosb/cauniver.htm; accessed 28 July 2012

Bonfatti, P. (2000), *A Expressão Popular do Sagrado: Uma Analise Psico-Antropológica da Igreja Universal do Reino de Deus*, São Paulo: Paulinas.

Brown, D. (1986), *Umbanda: Religion and Politics in Brazil*, Ann Arbor: UMI Research Press.

Burdick, J. (1996), *Looking for God in Brazil: The Progressive Catholic Church in Brazil's Religious Arena*, Berkeley and Los Angeles CA: University of California Press.

Burdick, J. (1999), 'What is the colour of the Holy Spirit: Pentecostalism and black identity in Brazil', *Latin American Research Review*, **34**(2), 109–31.

Chesnut, R.A. (1997), *Born Again in Brazil: The Pentecostal Boom and the Pathogens of Poverty*, New Brunswick, NJ: Rutgers University Press.

Chesnut, R.A. (2007), *Competitive Spirits: Latin America's New Religious Economy*, New York: Oxford University Press.

Clarke, P.B. (1999), '"Pop-star" priests and the Catholic response to the "explosion" of evangelical Protestantism in Brazil: the beginning of the end of the "walkout"?', *Journal of Contemporary Religion*, **14**(2), 203–16.

De Kadt, E. (1970), *Catholic Radicals in Brazil*, London: Oxford University Press.
Evans, P. (1996), 'State–society synergy: government action and social capital in development', *World Development*, **24**(6), 1110–32.
Freire, Paulo (1970), *Pedagogy of the Oppressed*, New York: Herder and Herder.
Freston, P. (1993), 'Brother votes for brother: the new politics of Protestantism in Brazil', in V. Garrard-Burnett and D. Stoll (eds), *Rethinking Protestantism in Latin America*, Philadelphia: Temple University Press, pp. 66–110.
Ireland, R. (1989), 'Catholic base communities, spiritist groups, and the deepening of democracy in Latin America', in S. Mainwaring and A. Wilde, *The Progressive Church in Latin America*, Notre Dame: University of Notre Dame Press.
Ireland, R. (1991), *Kingdoms Come: Religion and Politics in Brazil*, Pittsburgh, PA: Pittsburgh University Press.
Ireland R. (1997), 'Pentecostalism, conversions and politics in Brazil', in E.L. Cleary and H.W. Stewart-Gambino (eds), *Power, Politics and Pentecostals in Latin America*, Boulder, CO: Westview Press, pp. 123–37.
Ireland, R. (1999), 'Popular religions and the building of democracy in Latin America: saving the Tocquevillian parallel', in Manuel A. Vásquez (ed.), *Religion in America: Churches, Globalization and Democratization. Special Issue of Journal of Interamerican Studies and World Affairs*, **41**(4), 111–36.
Ireland, R. (2005), 'Fragile synergies for development: the case of Jardim Oratório SP Brazil', in A. Cimadore, H. Dean and J. Siqueira, *The Poverty of the State: Reconsidering the Role of the State in the Struggle Against Global Poverty*, Buenos Aires: CLACSO/CROP, pp. 241–62.
Ireland, R. (2011), 'Citizenship and democracy in Brazil's favelas: the end of the dream?', *Journal of Iberian and Latin American Studies*, **17**(2), 147–62.
Lehmann, D. (1996), *Struggle for the Spirit: Religious Transformation and Popular Culture in Brazil and Latin America*, Princeton: Princeton University Press.
Leite, Márcia Pereira (2003), 'Novas Relações entre Identidade Religiosa e Participação Política no Rio de Janeiro Hoje: O Caso do Movimento Popular de Favelas', in Patricia Birman (ed.), *Religião e Espaço Público*, São Paulo: Attar Editorial, pp. 63–95.
Levine, D. (1993), 'Popular groups, popular culture and popular religion', in D. Levine (ed.), *Constructing Culture and Power in Latin America*, Ann Arbor: University of Michigan Press, pp. 171–225.
Mainwaring, S. (1986), *The Catholic Church and Politics in Brazil*, Stanford CA: Stanford University Press.
Mainwaring, S. (1987), 'Urban popular movements, identity and democracy in Brazil', *Comparative Political Studies*, **20**(2), 131–59.
Mariz, C. (1992), 'Religion and poverty in Brazil: a comparison of Catholic and Pentecostal Communities', *Sociological Analysis*, **53**(S), S63–S70.
Martin D. (1990), *Tongues of Fire: The Explosion of Pentecostalism in Latin America*, Oxford: Basil Blackwell.
Ortiz, R. (1978), *A morte branca do feiticeiro negro – Umbanda: Integração de uma religião numa sociedade de classes*, Petrópolis: Vozes.
Prandi, R. (1996), 'Perto da Magia, Longe da Política', in A. Pierucci and R. Prandi (eds), *A Realidade Social das Religiões no Brasil: Religião, Sociedade e Política*, São Paulo: Hucitec, pp. 93–105.
Rocha, Cristina Moreira da (2006), *Zen in Brazil: The Quest for Cosmopolitan Modernity*, Honolulu: University of Hawaii Press.
Rossi, M. (2010), *Ágape*, São Paulo: Editora Globo.
Sansone, L. (1996), 'The local and the global in today's Afro-Bahia', in T. Salman (ed.), *The Legacy of the Disinherited: Popular Culture in Latin America: Modernity, Globalization, Hybridity and Authenticity*, Amsterdam: CEDLA. pp. 197–219.
Sen, A. (1999), *Development as Freedom*, New York: Alfred A. Knopf.
Sen, A. (2001), 'What development is about', in G. Meir and J. Stiglitz, *Frontiers of Development Economics*, New York: Oxford University Press (for the World Bank).
Souza, André Ricardo de (2007), 'Igreja Católica e mercados: a ambivalência entre a solidariedade e a competição', *Religião e Sociedade*, **27**(1), 156–74.
Vallier, I. (1970), *Catholicism, Social Control, and Modernization in Latin America*, Englewood Cliffs, NJ: Prentice Hall Inc.
Vásquez, M. (1997), 'Structural obstacles to grassroots pastoral practice: the case of a base community in urban Brazil', *Sociology of Religion*, **58**(1), 53–68.
Vásquez, M. (1998), *The Brazilian Popular Church and the Crisis of Modernity*, Cambridge: Cambridge University Press.
Willems, E. (1967), *Followers of the New Faith*, Nashville, TN: Vanderbilt University Press.

29 FBOs in Tanzania

Michael Jennings

INTRODUCTION

In October 2011, protestors campaigning against the extremes of capitalism highlighted by the Global Financial Crisis that began in 2007, camped outside St Paul's Cathedral in London. Invited to stay by the Dean, their presence quickly stirred up a public and surprisingly angry debate about the role of the church in society, a debate that culminated in the resignation of the Dean and the Canon Chancellor of St Paul's. At the heart of the issue was the role the church and its representatives should play in responding to the major social, political and economic issues of the day. Should it be a neutral observer, concentrating on the private soul, or take an active part in the body politic? And if it was to enter public debate, where was such an entrance most appropriate: in defence of the establishment, of law and order, of the financial world in whose epicentre St Paul's Cathedral sits? Or, living up to its symbolic role in Britain having survived as the bombing of the blitz destroyed all around it, speak for the rights of protestors and freedoms to protest?

Whilst in the UK this debate sharpened the rhetorical vitriol on all sides, for outside observers this was perhaps a strange argument to be having in the second decade of the twentieth century. Even within Britain, the idea that the church, in this case the established Anglican Church, should be wary of stepping into the public sphere, had surely been long dissipated by regular clashes between Anglican leaders and the government of the day. Prime Minister Tony Blair's spin doctor in chief may famously have declared of the Labour Administration, 'We don't do God', but the fact that such a statement was regarded as necessary indicated a prevailing sense that a particular brand of Christianity was indeed informing policy decisions. More importantly, even if politicians and their spokespeople wanted to distance themselves from religion, religion in the UK certainly did not agree (and had not over the course of the twentieth century) that it did 'not do politics'. The 1985 Church of England report, *Faith in the City* (Archbishop of Canterbury's Commission on Urban Priority Areas, 1985), lambasted the government's urban policy and denounced it for exacerbating social exclusion and deprivation in inner city areas. The response of the government was equally ferocious, accusing the then Bishop of Liverpool and one of the report's authors, of being a Marxist (perhaps the worst insult the Conservative government of the 1980s could fling at a perceived opponent). The Archbishop of Canterbury, Rowan Williams, criticized the government's decision to go to war in Iraq in the mid-2000s, and in 2011 condemned the new Coalition Government's policies, most notably in health and education, suggesting it had no democratic mandate for them (*BBC News*, 2011; Williams, 2011).

But if the boundaries between the sacred and the secular remain perhaps at their sharpest in Europe, elsewhere the role of faith and religious institutions in politics is perhaps more readily apparent (if no less contested). From the role of evangelical Christianity and the so-called 'Christian Right' in US politics (despite an official separation of church and state), through Hindu nationalism in India, and the growing power of the Muslim Brotherhood under Egypt's new constitution, explicit linkages between politics and faith from the rhetoric of politicians serve to underscore the importance religion continues to play. In South Africa, President Jacob Zuma invoked both Christianity and indigenous belief systems in linking the politics of the ANC and the rewards of faith. 'When you vote for the ANC', Zuma declared, 'you are choosing to go to heaven. When you don't vote for the ANC, you should know you are choosing that man who carries a fork . . . who cooks people'. Membership of the ANC was not just akin to blessed state, it was a passport to the afterlife: 'When you are carrying an ANC card, you are blessed. When you get up there, there are different cards used, but when you have an ANC card, you will be let through to heaven'. In case the message was not clear enough, nor the threat of eternal damnation for those who dared leave the party sufficient, Zuma called upon ancestral spirits in his invocation of the horrors awaiting traitors to the cause: 'You will struggle until you die', Zuma warned those who left the ANC, 'the ancestors of this land . . . will turn their back on you' (*Economist*, 2011).

If the twentieth century was the century that predicted the slow death of God, it seems religion and faith paid little attention to the terminal prognosis. For by the end of the century, and into the twenty-first, world and 'indigenous' religions had become enmeshed in thoroughly globalized webs of faith networks across the world. Religion resurgence, rather than decline, appeared to be one of the dominant historical trends of the past two or so decades.

The recognition of the existence of these globalized faith networks, the permeation of religion, religious language and discourse into politics and social commentary, a more muscular presence of religion and religious leaders at national and international levels, and a focus on identity and identity politics, have contributed to a recognition that religion is far from dead, and is playing a significant role beyond the confines of the private realm of morality and spirituality. But whilst much of the literature (especially political science and international relations) has looked to understand the resurgence of religion in the political crises of the late twentieth and early twenty-first centuries, this chapter questions this fundamental premise that religion has in fact increased its engagement in public and political life. It is, the chapter argues, the literature and secular aid institutions that have shifted their perspectives and started to recognize the role religion has long played in development and humanitarian relief interventions, not that engagement itself. Of course, the precise parameters and forms of engagement, as well as the particular institutional forms through which that engagement is undertaken, have changed over time and place, but not the presence of faith institutions in development itself.

This chapter uses East Africa as a case study in which to anchor the argument, not because it was radically different or particularly extreme in the ways that religious- and faith-based action in welfare delivery and development emerged and evolved, but because context is critical to the analysis of faith-based action in development. The precise contours of the ways in which religion has intersected with development, even for world religions, have been shaped in the crucible of the local. It is self-evident, for example, that the experience of Catholicism reflects both orthodox Catholic teachings and institutional hierarchies, as well as the particular local culture, history and social mores and beliefs in which that experience occurs. Similarly, Islam has shaped and been shaped by the differing national, community and regional contexts in which it has established itself. Indigenous religions and beliefs, too, have adapted as the contextual environment in which they first emerged has changed. But whilst widely acknowledged, the nuance that comes from context has been overshadowed in the literature by a reliance on generalized assumptions that speak for religions, FBOs and state–religion relationships as a whole. If context matters, it is important to look at the general issues through such a lens, in order to recognize that broader experiences may repeat themselves in quite different forms.

RELIGION RESURGENT?

If historians and other analysts of African social life have long recognized the importance of faith, and faith-based organizations, the same is not true of donors and international organizations. Political science too has, until relatively recently, ignored the importance of faith and religion in African political and social life. The surge of Pentecostalism and other evangelical Christian movements across large swathes of sub-Saharan Africa, the rise of Islamic-based movements, and the apparent confrontation between Islam and Christianity in Nigeria and parts of East Africa have caught the imagination of analysts who see in such processes religion resurgent. For 'clash of civilizationists', new and aggressive forms of Islam, the rise of religio-nationalist movements such as the BJP in India, and the spread of Saudi-funded Wahhabi mission activity are both new and alarming. New, because it seems to be turning Weber and Durkheim's predictions on their head. Alarming because it sees in the 'politics of identity' a real threat to the achievements of the 'politics of ideas' (Kaldor, 2006, p. 81).

Whilst the European experience of separating church and state has been presented as a normative experience in the orthodox development of the body politic, experiences from Asia, Africa, Latin America (and even North America) surely raise questions as to the accuracy of early twentieth-century predictions of the death of religion, at least outside the European context in which many were framed. And whilst cosmopolitanism and clash of civilizations discourse both suggest, in their own ways, that the rise in religious identities is fuelling social conflict, these perspectives are based on post-Enlightenment understandings of rationality. If the assumptions of religion as resurgent are wrong – if it is the interest of observers that has resurged rather than the object itself – then the question as to the role of religion in fermenting conflict changes is: why now (if it *is* true – and it is far from clear that it is), and not then?

What has driven this concern over the new and the alarming is a pervading sense in the literature that religion and FBOs have shifted their gaze from concern with the internal and private (care for the soul and spirituality) to a very public engagement with social and political issues. The focus on religion resurgent has, then, been premised to a large extent on assumptions that it has become a stronger and more visible force in the world. José Casanova, for example, argues that religion underwent a fundamental shift in the 1980s, moving from a private realm of activity, into 'the public arena of moral and political contestation' (Casanova, 1994, p. 3). This transformation from agents focused on the inner being to outward facing, socially engaged public actors lies, for those such as Casanova, at the heart of religion's new social role:

> we are witnessing the 'deprivatization' of religion in the modern world. By deprivatization I mean the fact that religious traditions throughout the world are refusing to accept the marginal and privatized role which theories of modernity as well as theories of secularization had reserved for them. (Casanova, 1994, p. 35)

Religions were, he continues, refusing 'to restrict themselves to the pastoral care of individual souls' in their challenge to state and markets (p. 5). Casanova does not suggest that this process was entirely new, but that the resurgence of religion challenged the dominant orthodoxies of secularism in new and wide-ranging ways (p. 6). Toft et al. similarly see something new in religion and its engagement with politics over the past few decades, arguing that 'religion's influence on politics has reversed its decline and become more powerful on every continent and across every major world religion' (2011, p. 3). Secularization theory has, they argue, failed to keep pace with a monumental shift in the place of religion in the world.

Whilst it may be the case that religion's visibility has become more pronounced since the 1970s and 1980s, it is perhaps less a reflection of efforts by religion to reverse an apparent 'decline', but the greater attention paid by scholars to religion itself. The near invisibility of religion in the public realm, as described by Casanova, until the 1980s reflects not the realities of religious engagement with the social and political, but the extent to which it has been written out of, or ignored in, official histories of development, politics and social change during much of the twentieth century. What was occurring in the 1980s – the engagement of the Catholic Church with communism in Eastern Europe, the rise of the Moral Majority and the 'Christian Right' in the United States, the Islamic revolution in Iran, the rise of the Mujahideen in Afghanistan against the Soviet invasion, the Anglican Church's confrontation with Prime Minister Thatcher's government in the UK, and so on – was not new in the sense that religions were moving from a private realm to a public one. Rather, it was part of a broader social and political engagement that has characterized the attempts by world religions in particular to maintain relevance and influence across the whole of the twentieth century. World religions on the global stage, and indigenous religions, cults and prophets on the local, had engaged with questions of social inequality, injustice and the politics of poverty and exclusion throughout the twentieth century. What was perhaps new from the 1980s, was increasingly globalized faith networks linking up with co-religionists and other faith leaders across boundaries and borders. The voice had always been there, but now it was being listened to by analysts, politicians and the world media.

Within the specific field of development, FBOs and religion too has been seen to have adopted a 'new' and more muscular role. This is characterized both by shifts in the internal dynamics of religion (as presented by Casanova), but also by external changes that created new sets of opportunities. The UNFPA's *Guidelines for Engaging FBOs as Agents of Change* argue: 'For many years, international development has been a field dominated by largely "secular" agents of development, with a preference for keeping faith and faith-related matters strictly in the so-called "private" domains'. Indeed, it suggests that, whilst FBOs may have played a role in development, it existed in a separate and parallel sphere of 'faith based . . . development' (UNFPA, 2009, p. 1). That 'dividing line between "public" and "private"' has become, the UNFPA argue, 'increasingly blurred' in an ever more connected and globalized world (ibid.). Mariz Tadros similarly looks to structural and ideological reforms in the 1980s and especially 1990s in seeking to understand why FBOs have a greater presence in development. Whilst Tadros acknowledges the longer history of faith engagement in development, she argues that a number of inter-related factors in play from the 1990s have seen FBOs rise 'to prominence in policy, practice and, increasingly, scholarship':

> the increasing salience of identity-based politics, the impact of neoliberal policies on the demise of the welfare state and the emergence (or re-emergence in some cases) of civil society organizations (CSOs) as service providers, as well as the rise of the New Right and its influence in US domestic and international policy. (Tadros, 2010, p. 3)

Whilst moving away from the assertion that it was a change in the focus of religion itself, and looking instead to broader changes in the environments in which FBOs operate, the narrative is only half right. These factors may have increased the importance of FBOs in certain forms of delivery, but FBOs were not passive actors seizing on opportunities presented by external changes. As this chapter seeks to demonstrate, FBOs and religious engagement in development was driven by internal demands and strategies, as much as prompted and pushed by external elements.

THE HISTORY OF FBO ENGAGEMENT IN DEVELOPMENT IN TANZANIA

Where the role of FBOs in development has been acknowledged, it has largely focused on their role as service providers, especially health and education. There is an implicit suggestion that the shift into development in a wider sense has occurred recently, but as this chapter shows, through the case study of Tanzania, this is not the case. FBOs have been development actors – in the meaningful wider sense, and not in a parallel, isolated 'universe'.

However, service provision was their 'route into' modern development discourses and practices. This is not to argue that FBOs are development actors solely because they provided education, health services, relief during times of famine, a place of refuge during periods of war, and so on. The social ministry of FBOs is not in itself sufficient to make claims of the FBO as development actor. Rather, FBOs became development actors at the point at which they characterized their social activities in discourses that moved beyond the purely religious, the obligation of the faithful. When FBOs sought to ally their efforts with broader objectives that were developmental in type and presentation, when they de-coupled the provision of services from the task of proselytization and conversion and looked to engage with public policy, then their interventions (be it service provision, relief, etc.) moved from the private realm to the public. In part this rests upon a rather narrow definition of 'development' that distinguishes meanings that emerged over the course of the twentieth century from previous iterations and understandings. It sees 'development' as a planned process, consisting of specific interventions designed to achieve particular objectives focused on improving material and social well-being (albeit with different understandings of what that might mean and different emphases over time and place). But whilst perhaps narrow and constrictive, as an analytical tool for understanding the historical role of the FBO as a development actor, it is useful. It allows for comparison with other development actors that emerged in this period, within the same discursive context. It allows for discussion of the extent to which FBO-stated aims and objectives linked up with those of non-faith actors (in other words, the extent to which they shared a 'development universe', or operated in one of their own).

Within the case study of Tanzania, there are two key points at which such shifts can be detected. They were part of longer processes and a continuum of engagement, but reflected changes in the way that engagement was characterized and auctioned. First, the contribution of faith-based actors in the establishment of a formal voluntary sector in the early colonial period, which cemented their engagement in development activities and created a particular set of relationships with the state. Second, a widening of forms of intervention (linked to widening understandings of what 'development' might be) in the early independence period, and the creation of new and development-specific organizations and structures with which to further extend engagement.

FBOS AND DEVELOPMENT IN THE EARLY COLONIAL PERIOD

From the nineteenth century, linked to and inspired by the Protestant evangelical movement, Christian missions looked increasingly to sub-Saharan Africa. Advancing from the littoral, by the end of the century they had established a presence across Southern, Eastern, Western and Central Africa, in many cases before the wars of colonial occupation and formal imposition of the colonial state. Carrying with them ideas about welfare and care for the poor, and in the absence of anything resembling even a basic welfare state (an absence that would last in many areas long after the colonial state had been established), it was these FBOs who provided education and health services for the African communities amongst whom they lived, provided food during periods of famine, provided jobs and training in new skills in order to take advantage of new opportunities opening up, and a place of refuge in times of war and violence. The mission to establish Christianity, civilization and commerce encompassed both religious and broader Western notions about what progress and development meant and should look like.

Initially conceived of primarily in religious terms (following biblical and religious teachings about care for the poor, the sick, the vulnerable), the wider social mission of these FBOs gradually become accepted in its own right (framed, of course, within the language of faith engagement in society, but not necessarily linked directly to the efforts to proselytize and convert). Their efforts were not described formally as 'social development', but in their commitment to introducing Africans to the gains to be made from European and North American 'progress', be it economic, social or political (the three areas caught by Livingstone's rallying call), 'development' was at the heart of what missions were actively doing and seeking to achieve.

What transformed isolated efforts to bring opportunities to local communities into a more substantial 'development' sector, was the growing reliance by colonial authorities on the work of missions in order to be able to demonstrate the secular state's commitment to the self-proclaimed (and at heart dishonest) claims to be holding power in trust until Africans were capable of taking responsibility for governance and development themselves. Without mission involvement in education and health, and the broader range of services they provided, social development in East Africa (and across much of wider sub-Saharan Africa) was a sham. And it was this engagement that turned missions, and the faith sector more widely from independence, into a powerful development sector, capable of engaging with the state from a position of strength.

The reluctance of the state to become involved in education left the field open to the missions, with the result that almost all primary schools, and most of the few secondary schools that existed, were run by missionary organizations. In the field of health service provision, where the colonial state had greater claim to be providing services directly to Africans, missions also had a significant role. And it was in this area that the tussles between colonial state and mission providers over the extent of influence the latter should exercise in the framing of policy, as well as the thorny issue of who should be paying for health service delivery, were most pronounced.

Whilst the scale and reach of mission welfare service provision is important in recognizing the long history of FBO engagement in development processes and services, it was the evolution of individual, isolated and independent mission services into a recognizable voluntary *sector* that transformed FBO development activity into something more powerful, and turned missions into development actors in a more formal sense. Linked into official processes (not running in parallel), helping to shape policy and strategy, and enjoying close relationships with state officials at all levels, this faith-sector entrenched its role and contribution in development. Moreover, it laid the foundation upon which secular NGOs would build when they began to arrive from the 1960s and especially the 1980s (at which point FBOs would gradually become written out of the narrative, even as their contribution and role continued more or less unabated).

In Tanzania, the moment at which one can point to the emergence of the voluntary sector came with the establishment in 1934 of the Tanganyika Mission Council (TMC). Created as an umbrella group representing the main Protestant missions in the territory, its purpose was in part to discuss and debate internal matters of interest between missionary organizations. But it was also intended to act as the voice of Christian (Protestant) mission in discussions with the government. Central to such discussions were issues around service delivery, health and education in particular. In 1936 the Medical Missionary Committee (MMC) was established as a sub-committee of the TMC, meeting directly with the state Medical Department, and negotiating over the thorny question of official funding for mission health facilities and a formal advisory role in the institutions of the colonial state as regards health policy.

Although the TMC (which would later become the Christian Council of Tanganyika, and later still Tanzania) did not represent all mission voices, in the engagement of its sub-committees it rapidly became regarded as the main channel of communication between the state and faith-based voluntary actors in service delivery. The debates over whether the government should be making grants-in-aid to mission health services, negotiations over salaries for teachers in primary schools, the siting of services, and so on, were increasingly centred in these new institutional forms. In the early 1950s, the MMC was reconstituted as the Mission Medical Advisory Committee: a body representing all missions engaged in health delivery, and established to 'advise the Director of Medical Services on all matters relating to or affecting the medical work of Missions in the Territory'.[1]

As a result, by the final decade of Empire, not only had FBOs established themselves as core actors in the development strategies and policies of colonial Tanganyika, they had also in doing so laid the foundations for the broader voluntary sector that would become increasingly significant post-independence. Most importantly, perhaps, they had established they were not bit players in the development of the territory, but vital partners. The social development mandate of the colonial state (always the neglected part of development policy in this period) would have been almost non-existent without the contribution made by missions. FBOs were not pursuing their own vision of 'development', operating in a parallel and disconnected world from the state and other secular actors, they were a key component of a single vision, and (by the early 1950s) were helping to shape as well as deliver that vision. These were certainly not organizations catering solely to the private realm, looking to the care of the soul before that of the body.

And nor was this process confined to Tanganyika. Across sub-Saharan Africa missions and other religious organizations were playing a similarly key role in service provision. The extent to which they were plugged into official institutions differed (and in places such as Northern Nigeria, where missions were excluded for fear of upsetting the largely Muslim population, their role was, of course, more muted or non-existent). Of course, in areas where Islam was dominant, Muslim organizations contributed to the provision of social welfare, albeit less often linked formally to the state. In Uganda, the dominance and quality of hospitals and clinics under the supervision of the Church Missionary Society's Dr Albert Cook, as well as the more political face of missions within that country, placed them more centrally at an earlier date. Less significant in France's African colonies (the colonial state more resistant to diluting its control), mission services nonetheless were an element in meeting social policy needs. Mission medical services played an important role in health provision in the Belgian Congo, dominating the Service Auxiliare de l'Assistance Médicale aux Indigènes that worked alongside the 'official' service (although in this instance the 'official' service was dominated by the non-state Fondation Reine Elisabeth pour l'Assistance Médicale aux Indigènes) (Hailey, 1939, pp. 1178–9).

What was important about the participation with the state in delivering social services was that it reflected an understanding amongst the various FBOs engaged that they were partners in achieving a shared set of objectives. In linking their activities to the state, more, in willingly subsuming individual interests (in this area) to the overall control of the colonial state, these missions were demonstrating their desire to be more than institutions responsible for the care of individuals' souls. They wished to participate in the nation-building exercise of empire.

Not only did the establishment of a 'faith sector', in whichever variation it took across the colonial empire, lead to the establishment of a formal voluntary sector, it also set the parameters of how that voluntary sector would interact with the state – parameters that shaped its interaction throughout much of the post-colonial period and remaining influential today. The reliance of the colonial state on voluntary faith actors for the delivery of social development that formed much of the moral underpinning of the colonial enterprise meant the sector was far closer to the state than was the case in Europe or even North America (where the non-state voluntary sector was always more significant). Moreover, the reliance worked both ways. Even as the state relied on its voluntary partners, FBOs in turn relied upon the state for financial support (an early forerunner of the question of donor dependence that plagued secular NGOs from the 1990s) as well as for being granted access to the corridors of power. FBOs in the colonial period willingly adopted the state's policies and objectives as its own, working with and alongside, rather than challenging, official development discourses. This was to remain the hallmark of FBO engagement as development actors throughout the 1960s and 1970s.

At the close of the colonial period, in 1961, mission health facilities (hospitals, clinics, and dispensaries) treated over 4.5 million out-patients, and provided beds for 152 298 in-patients. State-run facilities treated 160 941 in-patients (having over 1000 less beds than those of the mission sector), and 4.9 million out-patients (GOT, 1962, pp. 12–15, 24). But with the change to a new set of political masters, missions – so intimately linked with Empire – were required to transform themselves in order to meet the new political ecology in which they now found themselves. Development was one key tool for doing this.

BROADENING ENGAGEMENT: FBOS IN POST-COLONIAL TANZANIA[2]

The end of empire did not end the dominance of FBOs and religion's engagement in development, even if it did change the nature of that engagement. In the Mara region, the Catholic Church wrote to the Regional Development Committee with a list of proposed projects, including the establishment of a domestic science school, an agricultural training school, a schools feeding programme and the creation of a community loan fund.[3] The Bishop of Sumbawanga provided funds for road construction.[4] Missions and churches across the country established literacy classes and adult education programmes, helped in the construction and staffing of health clinics, and sought to assist communities develop self-help projects. Secular foreign NGOs coming into Tanzania in the 1960s and 1970s, looking for partners to work with, were confronted with the reality of the ongoing dominance of the faith sector in development practice. Missions and churches, for example, received almost half (47.6 per cent) of all development funds from the British NGO Oxfam between 1968 and 1972. Grants to other voluntary organizations (international and Tanzanian), and contributions to UN agencies, accounted for 41.9 per cent, although a significant proportion of this went to a Tanzanian NGO – the Community Development Trust Fund – that was in practice rather closely linked to the state.[5] When, from the early 1970s, Oxfam sought to move away from faith-based partners to diversify the range of actors it worked with, it found few credible alternatives and was forced to retain its close links with faith-based development activity.[6] It was an experience shared by many secular NGOs, who discovered that outside of the state, the faith sector was the primary indigenous development actor.

Almost from the very moment of independence, faith-based actors, now established rather than missionary in institutional form, underwent another transformation in the ways in which they engaged with development. Having considered themselves 'service providers' (in terms of their engagement in this sector) for much of the colonial period (although this did not reflect the entirety of their work), in the early 1960s a wider development vision began to suffuse the discourses of faith actors, looking to establish a new role in the new political and cultural order. This did not create a new presence in development – that presence had long existed. But the ways in which they engaged with that development were evolving into new forms. Moreover, this evolution mirrored that of their secular non-state counterparts. Building from an understanding that relief activity was palliative rather than a solution to the problem, and in a context where states were increasingly accepting their obligations for service provision, FBOs (without abandoning their service provision work) sought for ways in which the underlying poverty and vulnerability that led to periodic but regular crisis could be tackled. As a result, the language and focus of interventions looked increasingly to poverty reduction, to eliminating the structural, political, economic, social and cultural barriers to escaping from poverty (Jennings, 2008a, pp. 26–7). And in this journey, FBOs progressed alongside, not lagging behind, secular NGOs, international organizations, donors and development 'experts'.

The evolution of FBOs as development actors occurred in two intertwined ways: an institutional shift that saw the creation of specific development-oriented institutions, within the broader religious hierarchy (professionalizing the development work of FBOs, as it were); and a widening of what was understood as the natural arena of FBO engagement in development, as a range of new types of intervention were added to that of the service provision model (Jennings, 2008b).

The institutional response came in two main forms: the establishment, within Tanzanian religious hierarchies, of development-oriented agencies to better operationalize faith-based development thinking and action; and the arrival of faith-based development organizations (FBDOs), which resembled, or could also be seen as, NGOs. The latter was part of the growing presence of, initially, overseas NGOs, but from the 1980s and 1990s also local ones, and reflected the burgeoning of this independent, voluntary non-state sector and its transition into development activity that occurred in this period.

Within Tanzania itself, the establishment of development agencies served to bind the faith sector ever closer to the state (Jennings, 2008a, pp. 65–90), and entrench its position as the leading non-state development actor as Oxfam was to find. Within the Protestant faith, the Relief and Service Division was created within the Christian Council of Tanganyika (CCT)[7] in 1963. Its objectives were to lead the churches' development policy, seeking to provide an overall coherence to the varied projects its members were undertaking. It also sought to act as the liaising authority for Protestant faith development, suggesting (not entirely successfully) it should be the channel through which all funding for church projects should be directed. Within the Catholic Church, the centralized authority of which made it easier to provide greater command and control over the myriad efforts and small parish projects, faith-based development was similarly given a firmer structural shape with the establishment of Caritas as the church's lead development agency.

Engagement in development discourse also evolved in this period, both as a result and as a driver of institutional change. With the arrival of independence, religious leaders and institutions were faced with the delicate question of how to establish relationships with the new governments. This was particularly an issue for the former Christian missions, who had been so closely associated with the colonial enterprise. 'Development' became one mechanism for the forging of this new relationship, and for a public assertion of the importance of religion in the shifting contours of the post-colonial state. In 1962, the CCT's Rapid Social Change Study was established to ask what public role the church should play, highlighting the need to help develop 'a strong wholesome Tanganyika and to banish ignorance, poverty and disease'.[8] In 1965, the CCT presented a report on the role it could play in rural development. By the late 1960s, specific funding streams and projects under a 'community development' rubric had been created. In 1972, for example, the CCT drew up a five-year development plan (to operate alongside the government's own Five Year Development Plan). The Relief and Service Division assisted individual churches in creating their own long-term development plans, which were incorporated into the overall CCT plan.

As the experience of Oxfam showed, this institutional and policy response to both the new political environment of the post-colonial state, and the evolving understanding of 'development' and the role faith institutions could play in it, further entrenched the place of FBOs as development actors in the country. By the late 1960s, CCT member churches were setting up agricultural training projects in the form of farm schools, farm training centres, youth farm schemes, as well as running church farms and running projects in new settlements.[9] New CCT projects seeking funding in 1972 included a livestock management project; a cattle dipping scheme to reduce livestock infections; extensions to hospitals and clinics; several water supply projects, amongst other projects.[10] Projects run by the Catholic Church and supported by the British NGO Oxfam in the early 1970s included: the establishment of an Institute of Social Work; the establishment of a cooperative farm by a group of nuns; the establishment of a poultry unit for training Tanzanians moving into the new Ujamaa villages;[11] training of tractor drivers (again with a view to helping the establishment of Ujamaa villagers); and school-based agricultural schemes.[12]

In addition to making FBOs the leading non-state Tanzanian development actor, it also entrenched another aspect of the formal Tanzanian voluntary sector that had been established in the colonial period: its closeness to, even dependence upon, the state. Faith-based development in this period did not seek to provide alternatives to the government vision, nor challenge some of the more controversial aspects of its national resettlement programme. It was explicitly to support and help drive forward the state's policies and objectives.

As with the role of faith-based development actors in the colonial period, the narrative of faith engagement was not particular to Tanzania, but reflective of broader trends. Whilst the nationalization policy undertaken by the state in that country, drawing back control over schools and health service provision, may have added to the pressure on faith institutions to seek alternative ways to engage in development, that process of redefinition of discourse and structures had begun long before nationalization was pushed forward. To differing degrees, in different ways, FBOs across sub-Saharan Africa retained, or even increased, their presence in development. It is not entirely surprising that this occurred. Outside the state, what other institutions had claim to a presence in almost every village or small settlement? Indeed, in areas where there was no official state presence, there was still likely to be a church, mosque, temple, or combination of these. Where religious institutions were temporal powers, as much as spiritual, engagement in the daily lives of their faith adherents was always likely to involve small-scale development projects and interventions. Able to mobilize resources from global faith networks, as well as offering already established structures and programmes that the newly emerging secular NGOs were looking to partner with, they could command and direct resources in a way no other (or few other) indigenous non-state actors could. Faith-based development was the logical consequence of the narrowness of colonial vision, in restricting alternative sources of political power, patronage and prestige, and those limitations inherited by the post-colonial state.

If the closeness of the relationship between religion and the state was a hallmark of faith-based development actors from the colonial period, as it was to be throughout the 1960s and 1970s, the economic and political crises of the 1980s led to further evolution and change to faith-based development in Tanzania and more widely across sub-Saharan Africa, in particular from the 1990s. As NGOs began to be considered by donors and international organizations as essential components of an effective civil society, faith-based development actors transformed themselves (and were transformed from outside) as civil society organizations, or as external supporters of civil society. The link to the state was broken, not irretrievably, nor completely, as religions sought to champion ideas of human rights, multi-party democracy, challenging the over-mighty opaque state. In West and Central Africa, senior church officials led pro-democracy movements: in Benin, Togo, Congo, and Zaire (now Democratic Republic of Congo) Catholic bishops and archbishops led national conferences demanding political pluralism (Gifford, 1994, p. 513). In Kenya, the National Council of Churches of Kenya pushed for political and constitutional reforms. In Madagascar, the Catholic Archbishop of Antananarivo denounced the government in 1991, calling for the President's resignation, and the Council of Churches was part of the Forces Vives that ousted President Ratsiraka in 1992 (*Africa South of the Sahara*, 2006, pp. 683–4).

The change reflected changing internal debates over the role of religion in the public sphere, as well as recognition of the shifts in power that meant greater authority could perhaps be maintained by distancing from its one-time partner. But whilst the form of engagement changed, as did the nature and type of relationships, the one constant was the determination of religion and FBOs to stay active in that public sphere, to remain development actors. As new secular NGOs emerged in ever greater numbers from the late 1980s and 1990s, the dominance of FBOs was inevitably diluted to some extent, but it did not disappear. As a 2003 World Bank survey of 60 000 people across 60 countries found, FBOs 'emerge frequently in poor people's lists of important institutions', often the 'most important' in rural areas (Narayan et al., 2000, p. 222). They were not seen as perfect or unproblematic, but they were there. They did not 'emerge' in the 1970s or 1980s. Nor had they 'declined' in the decades prior to that. FBOs remained what they always had been: important development actors in their own right and on their own terms.

CONCLUSIONS

When Manji and O'Coill suggested that NGOs were the successors of colonial era missionaries, they were only half right. NGOs did come later to the development space in sub-Saharan Africa previously dominated by these FBOs (2002, p. 569). But they came not to replace, but to work alongside, faith-based development actors. Moreover, they entered (initially at least) a voluntary sector shaped by those FBOs, operating within a framework already established by their faith counterparts. Moreover, when they initially looked for how they might best contribute to development in the countries they had newly entered, NGOs were often forced through lack of alternatives to work closely with FBOs of all types.

The absence of religion and faith-based organizations from the development literature, and efforts (where its presence is acknowledged) to confine it to a separate, largely disconnected sphere of action, do not reflect the realities of faith engagement over the long century of development. Since the last decades of the nineteenth century, and especially from the first of the twentieth – the moment at which 'development' as a concept of planned interventions with the objective of improving the material and social well-being of individuals and communities – religion has been a major development actor. At times its fit with state and international discourses on development has been a close match, at others less so. But its presence, especially in developing countries, has been both sustained and significant.

But this narrative of engagement is not just of important, if forgotten, historical interest. FBOs' and religion's role in development interventions has helped shape the modern development landscape as much as have any other actors, most especially the space occupied by the formal voluntary sector. In many (but not all) parts of sub-Saharan Africa, and to an extent elsewhere in the global South, FBOs laid the foundations for non-state participation in development, welfare and service provision, shaping the environment in which those interventions took place, and setting the terms of the relationship with governments and donors.

This does not make FBOs unproblematic. Their role in development has been, and continues to be, contested, challenged, objected to and scrutinized (as Chapter 22 explores). But whether they *should* be engaged in development – whether the underpinnings of faith create fundamental conflicts with broader developmental objectives – does not change the fact of their involvement. Over the course of the twentieth century, FBOs laid claim to their participation in social and economic development and humanitarian interventions, and an understanding of their evolution as development actors is essential to a broader understanding of the development project of the early twenty-first century.

NOTES

1. *Tanganyika Gazette*, 19 December 1952, TNA 42300.
2. The name Tanzania was adopted in 1965 after the union between Tanganyika and Zanzibar. In this chapter, when referring to the post-colonial period generally, the term Tanzania will be used. Tanganyika will be used when referring to events or policies from the pre-1965 period specifically.
3. Community Development Assistant i/c North Mara, *Annual Report 1963*. Tanzania National Archives SI/III; Community Development Division, Mara Region, *Annual Report 1963*, p. 2, 4. Tanzania National Archives 544 SI/III; RDC minutes, Mara Region, 26 August, 1963. My translation. Tanzania National Archives 544 P/30.
4. Community Development Division Mbeya Region, *Annual Report 1963*, p. 3, 7. Tanzania National Archives 465 D3/18.
5. Toby Gooch, 'Oxfam's assistance to Tanzania, May 1968–December 1972'. Oxfam Archives TAN 64.
6. Interview with Oxfam's East Africa Field Director, 1972–78. 30 April 1966.
7. The Tanganyika Missionary Council became the Christian Council of Tanganyika, re-named in 1966 the Christian Council of Tanzania following the union between Tanganyika and Zanzibar and the renaming of the country.
8. Christian Council of Tanganyika (CCT) Rapid Social Change Study, *Preliminary Report Study Commission A: The Christian Contribution to a Dynamic Society in Tanganyika*, May 1963, p. 24. Christian Aid archives CA/A/6/7.
9. CCT, *Report of the Relief and Service Division to the CCT Annual General Meeting*, 1968. Appendix 1, p. 1 Christian Aid archives CA/A/7/2.

10. CCT, *CCT Five Year Plan, Report on Listed Projects, New Projects*, 30 April 1972. Christian Aid archives CA2/A/26/2.
11. Ujamaa villages were intended to be sites of communal living and communal labour, as living examples of the form of Tanzanian rural socialism (Ujamaa) which underscored Tanzanian development policy in the late 1960s and 1970s.
12. Oxfam Archives, Tan 47, Tan 49 Tan 55, 69, 80.

REFERENCES

Archbishop of Canterbury's Commission on Urban Priority Areas (1985), 'Faith in the city: a call to action by church and nation', London: Church House Publishing.

Africa South of the Sahara (2006), 'Madagascar', London: Europa.

BBC News (2011), 'Archbishop of Canterbury criticizes coalition policies', *BBC News* online, available at: http://www.bbc.co.uk/news/uk-13706710; accessed 29 July 2012.

Casanova, José (1994), *Public Religions in the Modern World*, Chicago and London: University of Chicago Press.

Economist (2011), 'Democracy in South Africa: a step backwards', *Economist*, 10 February 2011, available at: http://www.economist.com/node/18119187; accessed 29 July 2012.

Clarke, Gerard and Michael Jennings (eds) (2008), *Development, Civil Society and Faith-based Organisations: Bridging the Sacred and the Secular*, London: Palgrave Macmillan, pp. 94–116.

Gifford, Paul (1994), 'Some recent developments in African Christianity', *African Affairs*, **93**(373), 513–34.

Government of Tanganyika (GOT) (1962), *Health Division Report, 1961*, Government Printer.

Hailey, Lord (1939), *An African Survey: A Study of Problems Arising in Africa South of the Sahara*, London, New York, Toronto: Oxford University Press.

Jennings, Michael (2008a), *Surrogates of the State: NGOs, Development and Ujamaa in Tanzania*, Bloomfield, CT: Kumarian.

Jennings, Michael (2008b), 'The spirit of brotherhood: Christianity and Ujamaa in Tanzania', in Gerard Clarke and Michael Jennings (eds), *Development, Civil Society and Faith-based Organisations: Bridging the Sacred and the Secular*, London: Palgrave Macmillan, pp. 94–116.

Kaldor, Mary (2006), *New and Old Wars: Organized Violence in a Global Era*, Cambridge: Polity Press.

Manji, Firoze and Carl O'Coill (2002), 'The missionary position: NGOs and development in Africa', *International Affairs*, **78**(3), 567–83.

Narayan, Deepa, Robert Chambers, Meera K. Shah and Patti Petesch (2000), *Voices of the Poor: Crying Out for Change*, New York: Oxford University Press.

Tadros, Mariz (2010), 'Faith-based organizations and service delivery: some gender conundrums', UNRISD Gender and Development Programme Paper No. 11.

Toft, Monica Duffy, Daniel Philpott and Timothy Samuel Shah (2011), *God's Century: Resurgent Religion and Global Politics*, New York: W.W. Norton and Company.

UNFPA (2009), *Guidelines for Engaging Faith-based Organizations (FBOs) as Agents of Change*, available at: http://www.unfpa.org/culture/docs/fbo_engagement.pdf; accessed 29 July 2012.

Williams Rowan (2011), 'Leader: the government needs to know how afraid people are', *New Statesman*, 9 June 2011, available at: http://www.newstatesman.com/uk-politics/2011/06/long-term-government-democracy; accessed 29 July 2012.

30 Partnership through translation: a donor's engagement with religion

Jane Anderson

INTRODUCTION

The place of religion in the field of development cooperation can be mapped in instrumental policy terms, largely through donor funding of faith groups and faith-based organizations as part of civil society, to do development 'better'.[1] In so doing, the need for dialogue to create understanding and opportunities, the need to deal with paradox and ambivalence, and the need for enhanced faith literacy of donor agency staff to appreciate the religious worldviews held by subjects of development have been established.[2] The paradox and ambivalence are located in the potential of 'the religious factor' for violence, power, exclusivity and oppression and in its potential source of energy and motivation for peace, empowerment, inclusivity, and freedom (Ter Haar, 2005; Goldewijk, 2007; Haynes, 2007). This makes donor engagement with religion a potentially risky undertaking. It also sets up a research agenda to which the DFID-funded Religion and Development Research Programme has made a significant contribution, exploring the relationships between several major world religions, development in low-income countries and poverty reduction (Rakodi, 2007, 2011a, 2011b).[3] A Knowledge Centre Religion & Development has been established in the Netherlands for the purpose of providing knowledge about the relationship between religion and development.[4]

In Jones and Petersen's (2011) review of recent research on religion and development, they conclude that the research agenda needs to be broadened beyond its 'instrumental, narrow and normative' interests to include, for example, the effect of the development industry's engagement with religion on religious organizations themselves. Reassessing the treatment of religion in development studies since the special issue of *World Development* on 'Religion and Development' in 1980, Deneulin and Rakodi (2011, p. 51) argue for the importance of adopting an interpretivist method of analysis in development studies research on religion. As a contribution to this agenda, the research presented in this chapter takes 'a non-instrumental, non-normative' approach (Mosse and Lewis, 2006, p. 3) to explore aspects of the Australian government Agency for International Development's (AusAID) engagement with churches in Papua New Guinea (PNG) through Australian faith-based NGOs (ANGOs) in the Church Partnership Program (CPP). Taking up Mosse's concern with the ethnographic question of '*how* development projects work', rather than whether they work (2005, p. 8; emphasis in original; see also Mosse, 2004, p. 646), the chapter analyses how the policy model of partnership works, focusing on the practice of one church's language of development (Arce, 2000; Linden, 2008), and the work of translation (Latour, 1996; Mosse and Lewis, 2006). The chapter draws on eight months of fieldwork in 2010, with three PNG churches in the CPP: the Baptist Union, the Evangelical Lutheran Church, and the United Church.[5]

THE GENESIS OF THE PNG CHURCH PARTNERSHIP PROGRAM

Like other donor agencies, AusAID has engaged in dialogue with faith groups, and includes them under the umbrella of its engagement with civil society.[6] AusAID also provides funding to improve the quality of education in Islamic schools in Indonesia, South Asia and the Philippines (AusAID, 2007), and as well as the PNG CPP, it funds the Vanuatu CPP. A number of studies have contributed to a greater understanding of the role of churches in the development landscape of the Pacific, particularly in relation to service delivery, informing AusAID's engagement (Stein-Holmes, 2003; Hauck et al., 2005; Bird, 2007).

The CPP (A$25 million for Phase 1 2004–09, and A$51 million for Phase 2 2010–16) comprises partnerships between seven Australian faith-based NGOs (ANGOs) and seven mainline churches in PNG, which have a presence in almost every community in the predominantly rural country (see Table 30.1).[7] Historically, the link between each PNG church and the corresponding ANGO varies. For example, although the Lutheran Church of Australia's connections with the Evangelical Lutheran Church in PNG go back many years, the relationship with Australian Lutheran World Service only began with the CPP; the funding mechanism required each church to be partnered with an ANGO. In contrast, Caritas Australia and Anglican Board of Mission have long-established relationships with the Catholic and Anglican Churches in PNG. Unlike other AusAID-funded programmes in PNG administered by managing

Table 30.1 Relationships in the CPP

PNG Church	ANGO Accredited with AusAID	Link Between ANGO and Australian Church
Anglican Church	Anglican Board of Mission (ABM)	Anglican Church organization linking Australian Church with Anglicans around the world
Baptist Union	Baptist World Aid Australia (BWAA)	Activity of and accountable to the Baptist Union of Australia
Evangelical Lutheran Church	Australia Lutheran World Service (ALWS)	Principal channel for overseas aid for the Lutheran Church of Australia governed by an appointed board
Roman Catholic Church	Caritas Australia (CA)	Catholic aid and development agency
Salvation Army	Salvation Army Australian Development Office	Salvation Army Church Development Office
Seventh Day Adventist Church	Adventist Development Relief Agency (ADRA)	Seventh Day Adventist Church Development Relief Agency
United Church	UnitingWorld	Agency of the National Assembly of the Uniting Church in Australia that facilitates the Uniting Church's international partnerships

Source: Adapted from Program Framework (AusAID, 2004, pp. 12–13).

contractors, the CPP utilizes the AusAID NGO Cooperation Program (ANCP), under which ANGOs are accredited, to manage the funding arrangements through its established procedures for financial accountability and audit, programme-level monitoring and evaluation.

The formation of the CPP grew from a nexus of factors. First, relationships between key individuals in ANGOs and AusAID fostered creative discussions, and long-established organizational relationships between some ANGOs and PNG churches created positive synergy for extending support. Second, growing demands on ANGOs for standards of effectiveness by which to evaluate development work led to a peer review of three ANGOs' work in PNG (Nicholls, 2003), the recommendations from which indicated new possibilities. Third, views about PNG as a fragile or failing state prominent in the early 2000s (Hughes, 2003) prompted a consideration of working with structures that were perceived to have strength.[8] Fourth, there was widespread dissatisfaction with the aid programme in both PNG and Australia because of a perceived lack of impact and failure to obtain value for money, prompting an 'appetite for change' for new ideas and approaches (Independent Review Team 2010, p. 1). The CPP represents one of these new ideas, foreshadowing a recommendation that where non-state actors were performing effectively and/or showing potential they should receive increased support, especially making more use of church delivery systems in the health sector (ibid., pp. 5–6).[9] Finally, the development policy model of partnership has become prominent as a modality for development cooperation and as a normative ideal for North–South relations, both for AusAID and internationally (OECD, 1996, 2005; Fowler, 2000b; Abrahamsen, 2004; Brinkerhoff and Brinkerhoff, 2004; Holloway et al., 2011).

The dynamic of relationships in the organizational field of development cooperation created the CPP. These relationships are based on a long-standing commitment to PNG churches by Australian churches and their NGOs. They demonstrate an understanding of the role and influence of churches in the fabric of PNG societies, and a desire to strengthen church networks for the benefit of Papua New Guineans. An opportunity to establish a different kind of development partnership emerged organically out of an astute reading of the political circumstances of the Australia–PNG relationship in the early 2000s, reflecting a more general focus in the development literature and in the field of development cooperation on the importance of civil society actors in development processes (Dickson-Waiko, 1999; Fowler, 2000a; Haley, 2008; Giffen and Judge, 2010) and particularly faith-based organizations in civil society (Clarke and Jennings, 2008; McDuie-Ra and Rees, 2010).

TRANSLATING THE POLICY OF PARTNERSHIP

Latour (1996, pp. 85–6) argues that translation can be understood as enrolling new actors into particular projects, where divergent perspectives are brought together to participate in a shared action. This does not render them unified but rather forms a grouping that remains heterogeneous and it is through the intersection of disparate interests that translation occurs. Mosse and Lewis (2006, p. 13), drawing on Latour (1996) and Mosse (2005), frame translation as the ways in which development projects 'become real through the work of generating and translating interests, creating context by tying in

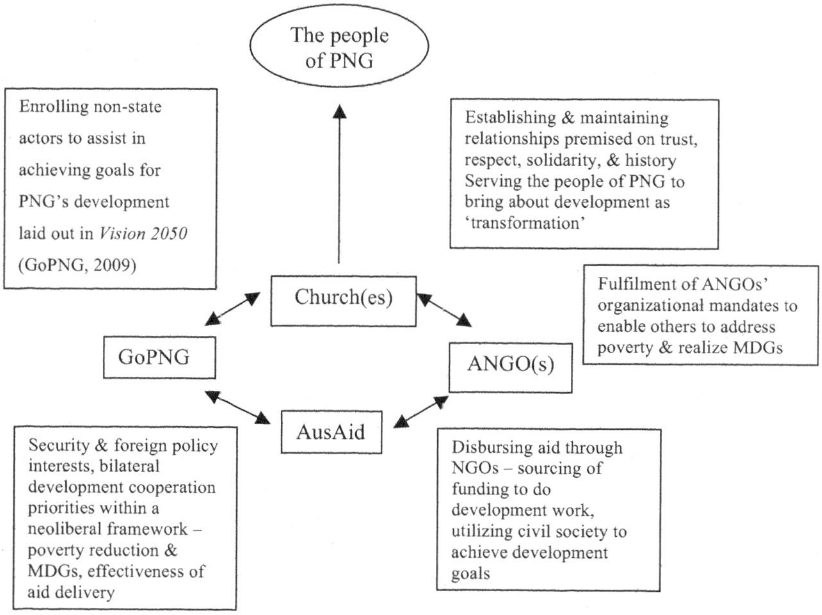

Figure 30.1 Interdependence of organizational interests in the CPP

supporters, and so sustaining interpretations. The concept of "translation" here refers to mutual enrolment and the interlocking of interests that produces project realities'.

The CPP brings together different interests that are instrumental yet interdependent (see Figure 30.1). In bald terms, both AusAID and the Government of PNG (GoPNG) have enrolled churches as civil society organizations to 'do development', building on the churches' long-held role begun during the missionary times as education and health service providers. AusAID cannot fund churches directly because they do not meet NGO accreditation standards and so it disburses funding through accredited ANGOs. Similarly, the ANGOs need organizations in PNG to work with, the churches in this instance, in order to achieve their organizational mandates, and they obtain funding to support their work from AusAID through the ANCP. While the churches have an interest in securing funding for activities that serve the people of PNG, this sits in tension with a strong desire for financial independence:

> I don't want to be pushed by money, so that it satisfies AusAID . . . I don't want us to be seen as a mission field that you [Australians] come to throw this to us and check your objectives and check your goals and all that. I don't like that. (Interview May 2010)

Instead, the data demonstrates a strong interest in establishing and maintaining relationships between people, combining resources in a spirit of solidarity, predicated on an understanding of a Melanesian worldview in which relationships are fundamental (Whiteman, 1984a; Franklin, 2007). In the church–ANGO partnership discourse, the ideal of partnership is a relational one imbued with the moralities of mutuality, equality and solidarity; the relationships are envisaged as continuing beyond the end of any CPP funding.

As a policy document, the *Program Framework* (AusAID, 2004) accomplishes, according to Mosse (2005, p. 21) 'the social tasks of legitimation, persuasion and enrolment, becoming richly encoded with institutional and individual interests and ambitions and optimisms', rather than the task of directing development practice, or implementation. As a written product, it represents the building of a coalition among diverse actors and interests, brought together in an extensive process of consultation. However, in order to manage the amalgamation of interests, policy in the form of a programme design has to contain suitably ambiguous concepts such as 'partnership', 'governance' and 'capacity for development', so that there is flexibility in interpretation and room for manoeuvre on the part of those involved in implementing the policy (Mosse 2005, pp. 25, 26; see also Rottenberg, 2009, p. xx and Mosse and Lewis, 2006, p. 17).

The rationale for the CPP identifies three significant development issues to be addressed, which are translated into programme outcomes or dimensions of change, framed in vague terms (AusAID, 2004, pp. 5 and 30). The first development issue is expressed as: 'the need to strengthen governance in PNG, including increasing participation by civil society in policy dialogue, improving public sector management of service delivery and contributing to strengthening acceptance of the rule of law'. The corresponding outcome is 'enhanced PNG church involvement in improving governance'. The second, about 'the need for more effective service delivery, particularly in health and education to complement government provided services', produces the outcome of 'improved services delivered by PNG churches to local communities'. The third identifies: 'the need for improved governance, in relation to development activities within the churches' own structures, which will also enable them to more effectively address the first two issues'.

This yields the outcome 'strengthened PNG churches' institutional capacity for development'. The stated rationale is that by building the institutional capacity of PNG churches, they will be better able to contribute to strengthening governance in PNG, and improving service delivery. Although suggestions are made about potential activities, processes and areas of focus (ibid., pp. 30–31)[10] the framework does not prescribe how these outcomes are to be achieved other than through a strategy of 'partnership'. Partnership, according to Mosse is one of the 'mobilizing metaphors' generated by policy discourse whose 'vagueness, ambiguity and lack of conceptual precision is *required* to conceal ideological differences, to allow compromise and the enrolment of different interests, to build coalitions, to distribute agency and to multiply criteria of success within project systems' (2004, p. 663; emphasis in the original).

The CPP bears this out. The divergent interests and priorities of the actors involved shaped the framework to make a case for allocating resources to the churches, supporting AusAID's higher policy goals with respect to its aid programme in PNG.[11] For PNG churches, ANGOs and GoPNG, Christianity provides a degree of ideological unity not shared with AusAID, whose development-related objectives are framed within a neo-liberal agenda (Kilby and Olivieri, 2008; Rosser, 2008).[12] However, although the framework does include as a guiding principle and value 'understanding of the holistic nature of development: acknowledging that the development of the whole person is understood to embrace their physical, emotional, spiritual, community and political well-being' (AusAID, 2004, p. 24), this remains vague enough not to alienate the donor constituency. However, the Phase 2 *Design Document* (AusAID, 2009, p. 5) is much more precise, stating that the impact of the programme will be 'improved well-being of men and women, boys and girls, particularly in rural and remote areas', explaining that 'well-being is to be understood in terms of the holistic approach to integral human development embraced by the Constitution of PNG'.

The CPP Phase 2 *Charter* (CPP, 2010) (an agreement between the churches and ANGOs about the operations of partnership to be endorsed by AusAID) uses an unequivocal Christian language of development, articulating a 'CPP Approach to Development'. For example, it begins with a section about Holistic Integral Human Development, and states that the Church Leaders Council, formed at the start of Phase 2, will take a lead role in developing, in consultation with all stakeholders, 'a comprehensive theological position statement on Holistic Integral Human Development' (ibid., p. 4). This reflects perhaps the growing influence and confidence of the churches as the CPP enters its second phase, and a more transparent expression of ANGOs' faith identities. However, this raises a question: whether in trying to articulate a specific theology of development for the CPP and a CPP approach to development, as opposed to churches articulating their own, the vagueness and ambiguity will be lost, making the CPP 'unimplementable' (Mosse, 2004); or whether the proposed theology can retain these characteristics to allow the space for manoeuvre for the different actors to meet their interests and priorities.[13] Given the unique history, identity, and structure of each church, and the agency of the individuals involved, there is resistance to any homogenizing move within the CPP.

The ambiguity attached to the policy of partnership conceals the churches' primary institutional goal: to bring people to know God, to spread the Good News of Jesus Christ as told in the Gospels. The interest that has emerged from the data as most significant for the churches is being better able to practise holistic or integral development to bring about personal and community 'transformation', where people live in 'right relationships with each other and with God'. The churches are translating the policy of partnership to meet this interest expressed through a particular language of development.

A MELANESIAN CHRISTIAN LANGUAGE OF DEVELOPMENT

Arce (2000, pp. 32–3) contends that the term 'development' is located linguistically in three ways to form a 'combined set of linguistic representations and linguistic constructions of how to relate "problems" to "solutions" . . . based on the objectivization of what constitutes development'. First, it is intimately connected 'to theoretical ways of talking about the manifestations and dilemmas of "modernity"'. Second, international development agencies' continual rethinking of policy options for development has influenced the promotion of 'homogeneous models for Third World change from a Western optic'. Third, its use as a political/pragmatic term 'serves to make people aware of the ambiguity of the processes of intervention'. Arce (ibid., p. 33) argues for the necessity of studying 'how people practise the language of development and experience its associated constructions' because '[t]his linguistic set operates against a background of human activities organized through policy actions, technologies and the deployment of specific language strategies'.

The data reveals the practice of a 'Christian language of development' adapted by Papua New Guineans for a Melanesian context. This language travels through global Christian and missionary networks to which churches and ANGOs belong (for example, the World Council of Churches, Council for World Mission and Baptist World Alliance). Alongside is the practice of a 'secular language of development' that moves through transnational development networks (Bebbington and Kothari, 2006) created by the organizational field of development cooperation, to which AusAID and the ANGOs belong (Rottenburg, 2009, p. xiv).[14] These networks are geographically extensive, linking distant places, people, and organizations as well as operating across cultures and languages. The CPP has brought the churches into the transnational development cooperation networks, and in so doing requires them to negotiate another language of development, particularly in relation to gender. Processes of translation are integral to these dual networks, and here translation assumes a different meaning from that in the previous section. For ideas to move from one social world, or frame of reference to another, they are subject to appropriation, adaptation and alteration and are thus translated (ibid., p. xxxi). In multi-lingual PNG, translation also occurs literally between languages. Mosse (2004, p. 647) sees the work of translation as 'the task of skilled brokers (managers, consultants, fieldworkers, community leaders) who read the meaning of a project into the different institutional languages of its stakeholder supporters'. Church leaders, CPP Coordinators in PNG, and ANGO CPP Coordinators in Australia are central in this work of translation; in the tripartite relationship between churches, ANGOs and AusAID, described metaphorically by one interlocutor as being a '*kundu* relationship', they translate the rhythms in the different languages of development used by the partners. The *kundu* is a hand-held drum.

The national church organizations are practising the language of development in holistic or integral terms, and this frames their understanding of contemporary 'problems' in PNG and their 'solutions' based on what they constitute as development. In the case of the United Church, a theology of development (Longgar, 2008) addresses the problem of the processes of development in PNG, questioning how the church across denominations can address and influence these processes, as well as the extent to which Papua New Guineans are the beneficiaries or victims of imposed development models.[15] Adopting a critical standpoint, Longgar assesses the current imposed pattern of development philosophies, strategies and praxis based on foreign principles and ideologies as leading to 'the negation of a holistic approach to development, which in turn, accentuate[s] the destruction of the spiritual, social and cultural values of the people in Papua New Guinea' (ibid., p. 1). A similar criticism was made in the Lutheran Church: Westerners looking at PNG with their eyes see Papua New Guineans as having problems:

> We have a different worldview. Development is a disturbance in the natural world. Even partner churches and donor agencies who have been with us so long don't understand – they look and draw their own judgement. Don't try to help me: sit with me, talk with me and understand. Start with where I am. We are a people interwoven by our culture and our faith. Any donor agency who works with us has to have an integrated view of development. (Meeting with Lutheran Church Leaders, April 2010)

The United Church's theology of development espouses five principles.[16] The first takes 'an incarnational approach to development' derived from the incarnation of God in Jesus Christ identifying with and participating in the struggles of the poor and marginalized, for the purpose of restoring their human dignity and empowering them to 'embrace the radical values of the Kingdom [of God on earth] that would bring about transformation in their lives and society as a whole' (Longgar, 2008, p. 3). In this way, people are believed to become powerful change agents.

The second principle is that of empowering and investing in people such that every person is an equal participator in the processes of development, with the knowledge to be able to make meaningful contributions to their communities, to be personally viable. Personal viability and self-reliance are cornerstones of PNG churches' social action.

The third principle is respect for the dignity of humanity. God created human beings in His own image, and this connotes 'a certain degree of autonomy, because God himself is an autonomous God' (ibid., p. 4). Being autonomous, humans are destined to be productive, to be contributors and responsible stewards of the ecosystem entrusted by God into the care of humans. This is translated into the idea of being destined to engage in sustainable development. It also means that any form of development that results in the creation of a dependent mentality, or is exploitative of human dignity in the name of progress is disrespectful of the God-given gift of being human (ibid.). Similarly, development that creates class systems, threatens people's livelihoods or denies egalitarianism, human equality and the equal distribution of resources and wealth is to be resisted.

The fourth principle is a holistic approach to development. This means development must be inclusive of not only the economic and political aspects of being human, but also the spiritual and social. The good life cannot be lived without spiritual values, the development of the inner spirit. Thus, theologically, development must address all human needs, and must respect Christian values and the traditional religious values of Papua New Guineans.

The fifth principle is transformation, which connotes with the Old Testament concept of *shalom*, meaning harmony, peace, health, well-being and prosperity, and the New Testament image of the Kingdom of God, both in the here and now, and to come:

> Transformation seeks to remove the evil social structures of our world, and to institute through the mission of the church the values of the Kingdom of God . . . In the context of transformation, the United Church perspective of development is not about a better life, but a *better way of living among human beings as whole persons*. (Longgar, 2008, pp. 6–7; emphasis added)

Transformation is thus seen as a better word to use than development. The United Church is using this language of development to construct its 'changing face of mission' that sees and acts upon social issues.

In addition to this interpretation of the 'problem' and the theological 'solution', a situational analysis of contemporary PNG society identified five areas where the Church is being called upon to respond, in a turn to holistic or integral mission through the creation of formal development programmes (Buia, 2007).[17] The first of these is the growing population of young people who are finding themselves 'unemployed, under employed or unemployable' and without a purpose in life. The second is the rapid spread of HIV and AIDS and the related issues of sexual and domestic violence. The third relates to law and order issues – drug abuse, criminality, urban drift and communal conflict, all of which have a significant impact on families. The fourth is the decline in government services, especially in health and education in isolated rural areas. The fifth is poverty. In addition, there are environmental concerns caused by the extractive industries, which are affecting people's lives, especially in areas where there is a strong United Church presence.[18] In its awareness of a changing population/society and the necessity of preparing an appropriate response, the church was asking questions of itself in relation to: how to serve their communities' demographic aspirations and needs in terms of gender, the environment and HIV/health; how to deal with the increasing awareness among congregations (as a result of higher levels of education and better access to information); and how the lay members and the clergy can best work together – 'in the traditional missionary era, all the shots were called by the minister' (Interview September 2010).

In the early 2000s, the 'problem' facing the United Church was two-fold: how to frame its mission, and how to stretch the money raised from its congregations used to finance evangelism and the clergy, to also finance the response to social issues. The 'solution' is framed as partnership with NGOs, donor agencies and government agencies. This partnership is currently restricted to CPP, which is enabling the church to 'have enough strength' to fulfil its wider vision of partnering with other agencies (Interview, September, 2010).

TRANSLATING 'STRENGTHENED INSTITUTIONAL CAPACITY FOR DEVELOPMENT'

Institutional strengthening, referred to as 'another big development vocabulary that we are grappling with' (Seta, 2010, p. 8), is translated as 'building a frame that helps us to stand' (Interview September 2010): the establishment of a Development Unit (DU) is the frame.[19] In addition to the focus on preaching and teaching that nurtures the faith and spiritual life of church members, mission now entails providing a Christian response in the contemporary social context 'by empowering individuals and communities to address social problems and issues that affect them' (Buia, 2007, p. 1). In other words, the Melanesian Christian language of development is lived out through this broader understanding of mission made possible within the frame of the DU. This has meant overcoming resistance from bishops, recruiting lay professionals, developing processes and providing training to make it happen, supported by the necessary information technology. It has also entailed undertaking a strategic planning process that began in 2003 to incorporate all existing and potential funding sources. The CPP contributed to the planning process managed by the DU culminating in the approval of the National Mission and Development Plan 2010–2015 at the General Assembly in October 2010: 'the first lap in the next forty years of ministry. The last forty years have been based on wisdom, intuition, prayer and faith. But the next forty years, with all the technology and experience that's available, let's go into strategic planning' (Interview September 2010).

In 2003 a plan to establish a DU at the Assembly Office had been submitted to the executive, but was shelved due to lack of financial capacity. The start of the CPP enabled the United Church to realize the plan: the creation of a DU was approved by the General Assembly, and came into being at the beginning of 2005. This was achieved despite considerable resistance among the bishops. In one of the meetings, an objection was countered by referring to the church's mission to teach, preach and *live* the Good News. The argument used was reported as follows:

> Yes, we are teaching, preaching but *living*? That's what the theologians call the social Gospel – that's missing. HIV and AIDS – yes we have to [do something]. Poverty – yes we have to. Cutting down of trees, digging up holes in the ground, poisoning the rivers – yes we have to. That's living the Gospel . . . The word people are now using for living the good news is development. (Interview September 2010)

The DU vision and mission statements reflect the church's vision statement:

> DU Vision Statement: to manifest the love of God through empowering and enabling Papua New Guinean people and communities to address their development needs towards sustainable livelihoods.
>
> DU Mission Statement: to promote the mission of the United Church in Papua New Guinea, raise resources for UCPNG development programs, and manage all development programs.
>
> UCPNG Vision Statement: the United Church in Papua New Guinea exists to teach, preach and live the Good News of Jesus Christ in her faith, life and witness; in loving and caring ministries through the united participation of the people of God until He returns. (Buia, 2007, p. 8)

During an induction programme for new staff in the DU it was explained that the vision statement takes into account a verse from the Bible, John 10: 10 – 'I have come so that you may have life, life in all its fullness'. However, staff were informed that for many of the partners the United Church works with:

> the language is not friendly, so we have to change the language to make it user-friendly. So life in all its fullness is sustainable livelihoods . . . Jesus died so that as individuals and as communities and families, we have the potential to reach the highest goal, which is life in all its fullness.

Here, the significance of being in a *kundu* relationship becomes apparent: translation is needed to maintain the relationship and to manoeuvre between discourses of development. The Christian notion of 'life in all its fullness' builds on the core Melanesian value of 'the continuation, protection, maintenance and celebration of Life' (Whiteman, 1984b, p. 91).

A further explanation was given of the DU's approach to empowering individuals and communities:

> We don't solve their problems. We help them to identify those issues that stop them, that limit them from experiencing life in all its fullness – physical, spiritual, financial, intellectual, whatever – we help them to identify that and then we introduce them to ways, and people and organizations including government, how they can use the government system, how they can use people around them, and the resources around them to improve their livelihood . . . It's a very big vision we have and probably too high for us to achieve, but at least that's what guides us, that's the way we do business. (DU Staff Induction, May 2010)

The development programmes managed by the DU include Rural Water Supply and Sanitation, HIV and AIDS, Livelihood and Community Development, Training and Support for the Education and Health Sectors, Planning Monitoring and Evaluation and Strategic Leadership, and Community Peace Building. The process of setting up, naming and managing these programmes borrows from the 'secular language of development', but activities in these programmes are based on a model known as the Four-Square Program (Figure 30.2), which uses the language of holistic development.

Spiritual growth Devotion, knowing Jesus Christ, and making him known to others	*Social growth* Service to others and communities modelled on the life of Jesus, our duty to others
Physical growth Recreation – our culture, everything that gives us our humanity, arts and singing, sports, human expression	*Mental growth* Education – learning and sharing of new ideas and skills

Source: Fieldnotes May 2010.

Figure 30.2 The Four Square Program

Translating the CPP outcome 'strengthened PNG churches' institutional capacity for development' into the establishment of a DU has been achieved by skilful brokers, and provides one example of the work of translation that makes the policy model of partnership work. Living the Good News, or doing development, costs money. The church is now employing suitably qualified and experienced lay professionals to practise its language of development, setting up and running the programmes through which the church conducts its mission. The CPP is one source of funding, but securing ongoing funding resources is a priority, especially as the future of CPP beyond 2016 is unknown. Having begun the process of translating mission to encompass development, churches now have to finance it.

CONCLUSION

Utilizing the concept of translation, this chapter has shown how the policy model of partnership functions by allowing 'compromise and the enrolment of different interests, to build coalitions, [and] to distribute agency' (Mosse, 2004, p. 663), such that the contradiction between the church's institutional goal of spreading the Good News and the policy goals or stated outcomes of the CPP is not a barrier to 'success'. The programme design enables the church actors to practise a Melanesian Christian language of development that expresses their intentions, goals and ambitions alongside the practice of the donor's language of development. What unfolds in the years until 2016, when Phase 2 is due to end, is a matter for further research.

By way of a coda, speeches made at the launch of the CPP Phase 2 affirm the significance attached to the CPP for the Australian Government, and of the importance of the programme in the development landscape of PNG:[20]

> We are celebrating stepping forward in what is a tremendously powerful partnership in development. It's one that is based on mutual trust and it's one that is based on mutual faith. It's a partnership that operates at a number of levels . . . Each partner contributes in different ways, depending on their relative strengths . . . Our recommitment today to the partnership reflects our particular appreciation for the role that churches play in this country . . . A key priority for Phase 2 will be for the CPP to work alongside the Papua New Guinea Government with a view to develop church and state partnerships. (From the speech by the Australian High Commissioner, Phase 2 Launch, CPP Forum October 2010)

In her speech, the AusAID Minister-Counsellor for PNG reflected on the paucity of 'magic bullets' in development and her own experience of what made for successful development. She identified four in evidence where development initiatives had positive outcomes: strong leadership; ensuring a strong role for women in the development process (*met with loud applause*); a strong civil society; and strong partnership. In her assessment, the CPP brings together these four elements. Perhaps when a donor engages with religion through the policy model of partnership with churches, faith is a fifth 'magic bullet'. PNG church workers' practice of holistic development is permeated by their faith, their belief in the divine power, and the power of prayer. They are working to do God's will, to bring about His Kingdom on earth: from their perspective God intervenes to make things happen, and their plans will materialize if God wills it.

NOTES

1. See DFID's White Paper (2009). See also USAID http://transition.usaid.gov/our_work/global_partnerships/ and an Issue Brief on the role of religious leaders and communities in development efforts in Asia and the Middle East (USAID, 2009).
2. See WFFD (1999); Belshaw et al. (2001); Marshall (2001, 2005); Marshall and Keough (2004); Holenstein (2005); Jong (2008a, 2008b); Nordung (2009).
3. See www.rad.bham.ac.uk. The programme was formally completed in March 2011.
4. See http://www.religion-and-development.nl/home. The centre convened two conferences: 'Religion, a source for human rights and development' (Ter Haar, 2006) and 'Transforming development. Exploring approaches to development from religious Perspectives'(van Wensveen, 2008).
5. The fieldwork, conducted as part of my doctoral studies, took place during the transition year between Phase 1 and Phase 2 of the CPP. Data was gathered through participant observation, in-depth semi-structured interviews, and document collection. The thesis is due to be completed in 2012.
6. For example, in 2007 an 'Interfaith dialogue for harmony and peace' convened in Cambodia was premised on the belief that such dialogue is important in building human dignity and security. See Howell (2011) for an analysis of this engagement with civil society.
7. The use of the word church in this chapter refers to the denominational organization centred on a national head office. Each denomination has its own hierarchical structure comprising different groupings and levels of decision-making and authority. The Lutheran and United Churches have an episcopal structure and the Baptist Union a congregational structure.
8. See Douglas (2005) who argues that the church provides an alternative structure to fill the institutional vacuum left by a weak state.
9. AusAID's country programme estimate of funding for PNG is A$436.5 million for 2011–12.
10. Activities excluded from funding are: welfare, evangelism or missionary outreach; partisan political activities; and emergency and disaster relief.
11. See Australia's Partnership for Development with the Government of PNG (AusAID, 2008).
12. The Constitution of PNG pledges the people of PNG 'to guard and pass on to those who come after us our noble traditions and the Christian principles that are ours now'. It also states 'Integral Human Development' as the country's first national goal: 'We declare our first goal to be for every person to be dynamically involved in the process of freeing himself or herself from every form of domination or oppression so that each man or woman will have the opportunity to develop as a whole person in relationship with others' (GoPNG, 1975). However, the extent to which these goals are being met is in doubt.
13. See Fountain (2011, pp. 135–41) for a discussion of theology as policy in the context of the Mennonite Central Committee.
14. I use the term 'secular' as one of convenience to differentiate the language of development used by donor agencies rather than to establish a binary opposition.
15. Dr William Longgar presented the paper at a CPP seminar in 2008, representing the United Church. The late Lutheran Bishop Kigasung also presented a theology of development at the same seminar.
16. These principles find resonance with key concepts within the global Christian network – liberation, theology, 'the Gospel for the poor', 'transformation' and holistic development. See Kim (2007) for an overview of Christian concepts of development. See also Pope Paul VI's Encyclical Populorum Progressio for discussion on integral development (1967, p. 14). For more on liberation theology see Gutierrez (1973);

Hennelly (1990); Rowland (1999). See Clarke (2011, pp. 119–27) and White and Tiongo (1997, Chapter 4) for more on the significance of liberation theology for development thinking. See Samuel and Sugden (1987, 1999) for work on the church and transformation. See articles on transformational development in the journal *Transformation* (Byworth, 2003; Sugden, 2003; Clarke, 2006; Gorlorwulu and Rahschulte, 2010). See Thacker and Hoek (2008) on Micah's Challenge, also Tearfund, www.tearfund.org, and the Micah Declaration on Integral Mission at http://www.micahnetwork.org/sites/default/files/doc/page/mn_integral_mission_declaration_en.pdf; accessed 30 July 2012.

17. The Lutherans and Baptists have similarly identified the same social issues in their reinterpretation of contemporary mission.
18. In an induction for new staff to the DU in May 2010, these issues were presented as those the church was called upon to respond to.
19. The Baptists and Lutherans have their own translations of 'strengthened institutional capacity for development' in the form of strategic plans.
20. There was also considerable coverage of the CPP in the national press at the time the funding for Phase 2 was approved in July 2010 and at the launch: *Gavamani Sivari*, 'Australia provides $50 million to PNG churches', 30 July, 2010; *Post Courier*, 'Church boost', 9 July, 2010; *The National*, 'Australia to provide A$50m for churches', 9 July 2010; *The National*, 'Churches, NGOs and govt unite to deliver services, 14 October, 2010.

REFERENCES

Abrahamsen, R. (2004), 'The power of partnerships in global governance', *Third World Quarterly*, **25**(8), 1453–67.

Arce, A. (2000), 'Creating or regulating development: representing modernities though language and discourse', in A. Arce and N. Long (eds), *Anthropology, Development and Modernities. Exploring Discourses, Counter-tendencies and Violence*, London: Routledge.

AusAID (2004), *PNG Church Partnership Program: Program Framework Final Draft*, Canberra: AusAID.

AusAID (2007), *Better Education. A Policy for Australian Development Assistance in Education*, Canberra: AusAID, available at: http://www.ausaid.gov.au/Publications/Pages/7331_3301_1176_5126_9027.aspx; accessed 15 July 2009.

AusAID (2008), *Partnership for Development between the Government of Australia and the Government of Papua New Guinea*, Canberra: AusAID, available at: http://www.ausaid.gov.au/Publications/Documents/png-partnership08.pdf; accessed 30 July 2012.

AusAID, (2009), *Design Document Church Partnership Program Phase 2 (2009–2016) Draft for Peer Review*, Canberra: AusAID.

Bebbington, A. and U. Kothari (2006), 'Transnational development networks', *Environment and Planning A*, **38**(5), 849–66.

Belshaw, D., R. Caldiseri and C. Sugden (eds) (2001), *Partnership between the World Bank and Churches in Africa*, Oxford and Washington: Regnum Books and the World Bank.

Bird, C. (2007), *Blowing the Conch Shell: A Baseline Survey of Churches Engagement in Service Provision and Governance in the Solomon Islands*, Canberra: AusAID, available at: http://www.ausaid.gov.au/Publications/Pages/8903_1009_8889_1535_8012.aspx; accessed 12 June 2009.

Brinkerhoff, J.M. and D.W. Brinkerhoff (2004), 'Partnerships between international donors and non-governmental development organizations: opportunities and constraints', *International Journal of Administrative Sciences*, **70**(3), 253–70.

Buia, B. (2007), 'Mission and development: the changing face of mission of the United Church in Papua New Guinea', Port Moresby: United Church in Papua New Guinea Assembly Office, unpublished paper.

Byworth, J. (2003), 'World Vision's approach to transformational development: frame, policy and indicators', *Transformation*, **20**(2), 102–14.

Clarke, G. and M. Jennings (eds) (2008), *Development, Civil Society and Faith-based Organisations*, Houndsmills: Palgrave Macmillan.

Clarke, M. (2011), *Development and Religion: Theology and Practice*, Cheltenham, UK and Northampton: Edward Elgar.

Clarke, N. (2006), 'Transformational development as a valid strategy for use in the development of post-tsunami Aceh, Indonesia', *Transformation*, **23**(3), 187–92.

CPP (2010), *Church Partnership Charter: Church Partnership Program II*, Port Moresby: PNG CPP.

Deneulin, S. and C. Rakodi (2011), 'Revisiting religion: development studies thirty years on', *World Development*, **39**(1), 45–54.

DFID (2009), *Eliminating World Poverty: Building Our Common Future*, East Kilbride and London: DFID, available at: http://www.infodev.org/en/Document.671.pdf; accessed 30 July 2012.
Dickson-Waiko, A. (1999), 'Civil society and development, nongovernment organisations and churches', *Development Bulletin* No. 50, October, 44–6.
Douglas, B. (2005), 'Christian custom and the church as structure in "weak states", in Melanesia', paper presented at the international conference 'Civil Society, Religion and Global Governance: Paradigms of Power and Persuasion', Canberra Australia, 1–2 September available at: http://epress.anu.edu.au/kastom/mobile_devices/ch01s05.html; accessed 30 July 2012.
Fountain, P. (2011), 'Translating service: an ethnography of the Mennonite Central Committee', doctoral thesis, School of Archaeology and Anthropology, College of Arts and Social Sciences, Canberra: Australian National University, available at: http://hdl.handle.net/1885/8640; accessed 6 September 2011.
Fowler, A. (2000a), *Civil Society, NGDOs and Social Development: Changing the Rules of the Game*, Geneva: UNRISD.
Fowler, A. (2000b), 'Introduction beyond partnership: getting real about NGO relationships in the aid system', *IDS Bulletin*, **31**(3), 1–13.
Franklin, K. (2007), 'Framework for a Melanesian world view', *Catalyst*, **7**(1), 25–52.
Gavamani Sivarai (2010), 'Australia provides $50 million to PNG churches', 30 July.
Giffen, J. and R. Judge (2010), *Civil Society Policy and Practice in Donor Agencies: An Overview Report Commissioned by DFID*, Oxford: INTRAC.
Goldewijk, B. (ed.) (2007), *Religion, International Relations and Development Cooperation*, Wageningen: Wageningen Academic Publishers.
GoPNG (1975), *Constitution of the Independent State of Papua New Guinea*, Port Moresby: Constitutional Laws Library.
Gorlorwulu, J. and T. Rahschulte (2010), 'Organizational and leadership implications for transformational development', *Transformation*, **27**(3), 199–208.
Gutierrez, G. (1973), *A Theology of Liberation*, Maryknoll, NY: Orbis.
Haley, N. (2008), *Strengthening Civil Society to Build Demand for Better Governance in the Pacific: Literature Review and Analysis of Good Practice and Lessons Learned*, Canberra: SSGM.
Hauck, V., A. Mandie-Filer and J. Bolger (2005), *Ringing the Church Bell: The Role of Churches in Governance and Public Performance in Papua New Guinea*, ECDPM, available at: http://www.ausaid.gov.au/publications/documents/ringing_church_bell.pdf; accessed 7 July 2007.
Haynes, J. (2007), *Religion and Development: Conflict or Cooperation?*, Basingstoke: Palgrave Macmillan.
Hennelly, A. (ed.) (1990), *Liberation Theology: A Documentary History*, Maryknoll, NY: Orbis Books.
Holenstein, A. (2005), 'Role and significance of religion and spirituality in development co-operation', *A Reflection and Working Paper*, Bern: Swiss Agency for Development and Co-operation, available at: http://www.sdc.admin.ch/ressources/resource_en_24892.pdf; accessed 5 June 2009.
Holloway, S., B. Farmer, M. Reid, J. Denton and S. Howes (2011), *Independent Review of Aid Effectiveness*, Canberra: Commonwealth of Australia, available at: http://www.aidreview.gov.au/publications/aidreview.pdf; accessed 1 July 2012.
Howell, J. (2011), *Analysis of Five Cases of AusAID Engagement with Civil Society in Vanuatu, Papua New Guinea and the Philippines*, Canberra: AusAID Office of Development Effectiveness, available at: http://www.ode.ausaid.gov.au/current_work/documents/analysis-civilsociety.pdf; accessed 23 March 2011.
Hughes, H. (2003), 'Aid has failed the Pacific', *Issue Analysis* No. 33, Sydney: Centre for Independent Studies, available at: http://www.cis.org.au/media-information/opinion-pieces/article/1333-aid-has-failed-the-pacific; accessed 30 July 2012.
Independent Review Team (2010), *Review of the PNG-Australia Development Cooperation Treaty (1999)*, Canberra: AusAID, available at: http://www.ausaid.gov.au/Publications/Documents/PNGAustralianAidReview.pdf; accessed 15 January 2011.
Jones, B. and M.J.Petersen (2011), 'Instrumental, narrow, normative? Reviewing recent work on religion and development', *Third World Quarterly*, **32**(7), 1291–306.
Jong, D. (2008a), 'Religion and development policy: an ambiguous relationship', available at: http://www.religion-and-development.nl/publications/18/chapter-2-religion-and-development-policy; accessed 13 September 2011.
Jong, D. (2008b), 'Introduction: religion and development policy', available at: http://www.religion-and-development.nl/documentation-centre/3121/religion-and-development-policy-handout#1141; accessed 13 September 2011.
Kilby, P. and K. Olivieri (2008), 'Gender and Australian aid policy: can women's rights be advanced within a neo-liberal framework?', *Australian Journal of International Affairs*, **62**(3), 319–31.
Kim, K. (2007), 'Concepts of development in the Christian traditions: a religions and development background paper', Birmingham: University of Birmingham, available at: http://epapers.bham.ac.uk/1497/; accessed 30 July 2012.

Latour, B. (1996), *Aramis, or the Love of Technology*, Cambridge, MA: Harvard University Press.
Linden, I. (2008), 'The language of development: what are international development agencies talking about?', in G. Clarke and M. Jennings (eds), *Development, Civil Society and Faith-based Organisations*, Houndsmills: Palgrave Macmillan.
Longgar, W. (2008), 'A theology of development: a United Church perspective', Port Moresby: United Church in Papua New Guinea, unpublished paper.
Marshall, K. (2001), 'Development and religion: a different lens on development debates', *Peabody Journal of Education*, **76**(3), 339–75.
Marshall, K. (2005), 'Faith and development: rethinking development debates', *Development Dialogue on Values and Ethics – Faith and Development*, The World Bank, available at: http://go.worldbank.org/XRHTISAQB0; accessed 15 October 2011.
Marshall, K. and L. Keough (eds) (2004), *Mind, Heart and Soul in the Fight Against Poverty*, Washington, DC: The World Bank.
McDuie-Ra, D. and J. Rees (2010) 'Religious actors, civil society and the development agenda: the dynamics of inclusion and exclusion', *Journal of International Development*, **22**(1), 20–36.
Mosse, D. (2004), 'Is good policy unimplementable? Reflections on the ethnography of aid policy and practice', *Development and Change*, **35**(4), 639–71.
Mosse, D. (2005), *Cultivating Development: An Ethnography of Aid Policy and Practice*, London: Pluto Press.
Mosse, D. and D. Lewis (2006), 'Theoretical approaches to brokerage and translation in development', in D. Lewis and D. Mosse (eds), *Development Brokers and Translators*, Bloomfield, CT: Kumarian Books.
Nicholls, P. (2003), *Report on the Peer Review of Three Australian NGOs Working in PNG*, Canberra: ADRA, ABM, Caritas, ACFOA.
Nordung, N. (2009), *The Role of Religion in Development Cooperation Development Partnership*, Stockholm: Sida, available at: http://www.diakonia.se/documents/public/ABOUT_DIAKONIA/Reports/Report_2009_The_role_of_religion_in_development_cooperation_eng.pdf; accessed 1 September 2011.
OECD (1996), *Shaping the 21st Century: The Contribution of Development Co-operation*, Paris: Organisation for Economic Co-operation and Development, available at: http://www.oecd.org/dataoecd/23/35/2508761.pdf; accessed 20 May 2009.
OECD (2005), *Paris Declaration on Aid Effectiveness*, Paris: DAC/OECD, available at: http://www.oecd.org/dataoecd/11/41/34428351.pdf; accessed 20 June 2009.
Pope Paul VI (1967), *Populorum Progressio: Encyclical of Pope Paul VI on the Development of Peoples*, The Vatican: available at: at http://www.vatican.va/holy_father/paul_vi/encyclicals/documents/hf_p-vi_enc_26031967_populorum_en.html; accessed 10 November 2009.
Post Courier (2010), 'Church boost: churches play key role in development', 9 July.
Rakodi, C. (2007), 'Understanding the roles of religions in development: the approach of the RaD program', *Religions and Development Research Program Discussion Paper*, Birmingham: University of Birmingham.
Rakodi, C. (2011a), 'A guide to analyzing the relationships between religion and development', Birmingham: Religions and Development Research Programme, available at: available at: http://www religionsand development . org / files / resourcesmodule / @random454f80f60b3f4 / 1315399993 _ working _ paper _ 67 ___ complete_for_web.pdf; accessed 14 September 2011.
Rakodi, C. (2011b), 'Inspirational, inhibiting, institutionalized: exploring the links between religion and development', Birmingham: Religions and Development Research Programme available at: http://www.dfid.gov.uk/r4d/Output/187848/Default.aspx; accessed 14 September 2011.
Rosser, A. (2008), 'Neo-liberalism and the politics of Australian aid policy-making', *Australian Journal of International Affairs*, **62**(3), 372–85.
Rottenburg, R. (2009), *Far-fetched Facts: A Parable of Development Aid*, Cambridge, MA: The MIT Press.
Rowland, C. (ed.) (1999), *The Cambridge Companion to Liberation Theology*, Cambridge: Cambridge University Press.
Samuel, V. and C. Sugden (eds) (1987), *The Church in Response to Human Need*, Oxford: Regnum.
Samuel, V. and C. Sugden (eds) (1999), *Mission as Transformation*, Oxford: Regnum.
Seta, B. (2010), 'CPP Phase 2 Year 1 Budget Notes July 2010–June 2011', Port Moresby: United Church in Papua New Guinea Assembly Office Development Unit.
Stein-Holmes, R. (2003), *The Role of Churches in Development in Papua New Guinea*, Canberra: AusAID.
Sugden, C. (2003), 'Transformational development: current state of understanding and practice', *Transformation*, **20**(2), 71–7.
Ter Haar, G. (2005), 'Religion: source of conflict or resource for peace?', in G. Ter Haar and J. Busuttil (eds), *Bridge or Barrier: Religion, Violence and Visions for Peace*, Leiden and Boston, MA: Brill.
Ter Haar, G. (2006), 'Religion: a source for human rights and development cooperation', *Conference Report*, Utrecht: Religion and Development Knowledge Centre, http://www.religion-and-development.nl/publications/26/conference-report-religion-a-source-for-human-rights-and-development-cooperation-april-2006; accessed 13 September 2011.

Thacker, J. and M. Hoek (eds) (2008), *Micah's Challenge. The Church's Responsibility to the Global Poor*, Milton Keynes: Paternoster.

The National (2009), 'Aid "misspent". Rudd admits problems in AusAID programme', 29 April.

The National (2010a), 'Australia to provide A$50m for churches', 9 July

The National (2010b), 'Churches, NGOs and govt unite to deliver services', 14 October.

USAID (2009), 'The role of religious leaders and communities in development efforts in Asia and the Middle East', *Issue Brief*, Washington, DC: USAID, available at: http://transition.usaid.gov/locations/asia/documents/Religion_AME_issue-brief_June-2010.pdf; accessed 30 July 2012.

van Wensveen, L. (2008), 'Transforming development. Exploring approaches to development from religious perspectives', *Conference Report*, Utrecht: Knowledge Centre Religion and Development, available at: http://www.religion-and-development.nl/publications/13/conference-report-transforming-development-exploring-approaches-to-development-from-religious-perspectives-dr-louke-van-wensveen-april-2008; accessed 13 September 2011.

WFFD (1999), 'A different perspective on poverty and development. Comment on the *World Development Report 2000*', Oxford: World Faiths Development Dialogue, available at: http://siteresources.worldbank.org/INTPOVERTY/Resources/WDR/comment.pdf; accessed 13 September 2011.

White, S. and R. Tiongo (1997), *Doing Theology and Development: Meeting the Challenge of Poverty*, Edinburgh: St Andrew Press.

Whiteman, D. (ed.) (1984a), *An Introduction to Melanesian Cultures: A Handbook for Church Workers*, Goroka: The Melanesian Institute.

Whiteman, D. (1984b), 'Melanesian religions: an overview', in E. Mantovani (ed.), *An Introduction to Melanesian Religions: A Handbook for Church Workers*, Goroka: The Melanesian Institute.

31 The (in)visible hand of Muhajirat: a field observation on labour migration, social change and religion in the Vakhsh Valley, Tajikistan

*Bruno De Cordier**

INTRODUCTION

In 2010, labour migration was believed to globally involve some 215 million people and to generate an estimated 440 billion dollars of remittances, of which 325 billion went to so-called developing countries.[1] By comparison, global Official Development Assistance (ODA) that same year amounted to 154.4 billion dollars. While the impact of both labour migration and remittances on economic development and on society in the migrants' countries of origin are well documented, their influence on religion and its evolution remain comparatively under-exposed. This is especially the case when it comes to countries and societies in the former Soviet Union (Eurasia), where labour migration, within as well as outside the region, became a major economic and social dynamic over the last one and half decades. Tajikistan, a majority Muslim country in Southern Eurasia with which the author, having lived and worked there for a while, is personally familiar, offers an interesting case in this regard.

According to official-based international organization data, in 2009, 11.8 per cent of its total official population of 7.53 million was involved in one way or another in labour migration. This does not put it ahead of all of the region's societies. Countries like Ukraine with 13 per cent, Moldova with 18 per cent and Armenia with 27 per cent have larger population shares involved in labour migration. Tajikistan is far ahead though – also globally – when it comes to the share of the Gross Domestic Product (GDP) that comes from remittances. In 2007, for example, remittances to Tajikistan amounted to 45.5 per cent of the country's official GDP. They formed 74.6 per cent of the ODA that the country received that year.[2] More importantly, like elsewhere, remittances are generated at and by the grassroots level. As such, they trickle down much more to that level and revitalized local daily economies more than ODA does, although this can also be explained by the limited share of ODA that is specifically devoted to the grassroots level.[3]

THE GROWTH OF A FINANCIAL LIFELINE

The predominantly rural and agricultural republic of Tajikistan had a peripheral position in the Soviet Union, of which it was part until late 1991. Yet as a border area, it was strategically important. It also received large subsidies from the centre, which by 1988 amounted to 40 per cent of the republic's GDP, and enjoyed the guaranteed markets and the social services of the Soviet system, the disappearance of which deeply affected society. Moreover, in mid-1992, shortly after the end of the USSR, Tajikistan lapsed into a civil war that left up to an estimated 80 000 dead, made some 700 000 refugees and internally displaced, ruined the country's economy and dislocated society for years. The heaviest fighting took place in the Vakhsh, Gharm and Darvaz regions and in the capital Dushanbe. The conflict is often represented as a war between the local Soviet compradore elite and officials who wanted to stay in power, and the United Tajik Opposition (UTO), an umbrella organization of Islamist, nationalist and democratic opposition, that wanted to seize it. Reality, however, was more complex and rooted in the social legacy of Soviet colonialism, a power struggle between micro-regional clans, the manipulation of the tensions by outside actors.[4]

This happened at the same time as the wars in East Slavonia, Bosnia and other parts of the former Yugoslavia. But in contrast to these, the war in Tajikistan largely escaped international media attention. Although a peace and power-sharing agreement was signed by the UTO and the government in mid-1997, the country continued to be plagued by guerrilla actions and coup attempts by renegade commanders from both sides until mid-2001. Few visible traces of this episode remain these days. But psychologically, the deep traumas left by the conflict among the age categories who consciously lived through it, as well as its manipulation by the authorities, give the present authoritarian, secular regime internal legitimacy as a guarantor of stability. The discussion on the real and perceived role of 'religious radicalism' in the conflict continues, up to this day, to be a major ideological stake and carries a lot of weight on the evolution and position of the Islamic religion and of the faith-based identity quest that has occurred among several sectors of society in Tajikistan for several years.

The key sectors in Tajikistan's official economy and GDP are cotton and a large aluminium plant, two sectors that together represent three-quarters of all exports. They are controlled by members of the regime and by inter-personal networks connected to the national and local authorities.[5] The majority of the population relies on coping mechanisms rooted in a daily economy, which is based, in its turn, on small-plot subsistence agriculture, the informal economy, which involves a wide range of sectors and activities and is estimated to represent nearly two-thirds of the country's official GDP in 2005, and remittances from labour migration.[6] In 2006, for example, these represented more than half of the annual income for 91 per cent of the migrant families in the southern region of Kulyab and 58 per cent of those in the Kurgan-Tyube area.[7] The overall significance and evolution of remittances at the country level is shown in Figure 31.1.

Despite a strong culture of attachment to the region of origin, which continues up to this day, seasonal labour migration from the area that is now Tajikistan has been going on for centuries. Like the informal economy, it also existed in the Soviet Union. Yet the present patterns and proportions are a phenomenon that gained momentum between 1999 and 2001 due to the economic growth and labour deficit in Russia, the migrant's main destination, and a labour surplus and economic dislocation in Tajikistan and other Southern Eurasian countries. Estimates on the actual size of labour migration from Tajikistan in 2008, right before the financial crisis, vary widely according to the source. Estimates by governmental institutions and international organizations differ starkly, yet the most realistic bracket is from 630 000 to 800 000 migrants depending on the year.[8] Again according to the year and the region of Tajikistan, between 85 and 95 per cent of these migrants are men of active age. The vast majority is of Sunni Muslim

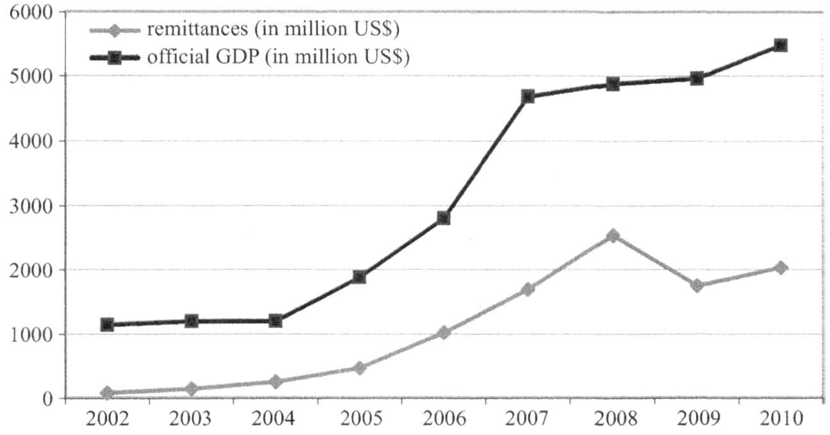

Note: The sudden drop in 2009 is due to the global crisis that also affected Russia and the demand for labour there. See Umarov (2010). The sudden decline in 2008 is due to the global finacnial crisis that also affected Russia (especially the construction sector) and the demand for labour there.

Source: Graphic created by the author on the basis of the Migration Policy Institute, *Remittances Profile of Tajikistan*, MPI Data, www.migrationinformation.org and the World Bank Migration and Remittances Data spreadsheets, econ.worldbank.org (both accessed on 21 September 2011).

Figure 31.1 Remittances vis-à-vis the official GDP in Tajikistan between 2002 and 2010

background. The migrants, most of whom are seasonal and do not intend to stay abroad (at least initially), work in construction, but also in transport, markets, technical services, agriculture and other menial jobs.[9]

MASS MIGRATION AND NICHE MIGRATION

More than international development aid, the impact of remittances at the grassroots level is visible in the form of recent renovation and expansion works at houses and farms, a clear increase in the number of cars and other motorized vehicles of European and newer Russian brands that replaced the worn-out Soviet models that were still prevalent a few years ago, the spread of new communication technologies like mobile phones, parabolic antennas and recently mobile internet, and bazaars with much more on offer, thus indicating more demand, as compared to ten years ago. Based on my personal observations over the last few years, there is also more confidence and much less lethargy among people despite the weariness with the socioeconomic conditions – in the first place, few employment opportunities with any decent salary and substantive impediments to entrepreneurship – that oblige large numbers of men to make a living away from their families.

Almost simultaneous with the strong growth of international labour migration – which in Tajikistan is called by the Arab-Tajik term Muhajirat[10] – comes a clear and visible increase in religiosity in Tajikistan's society. In Soviet Tajikistan, one's cultural identity was generally determined by both a strongly localist traditional environment that included religious elements too, and by Soviet socialism, which included enforced secularization and Russification.[11] The recent increase in religiosity is enhanced by the stark social changes and identity crisis that came with the end of Soviet socialism and the absence of a social base for liberal democracy. It is also a cultural defence reflex against the dislocating affects of neo-liberalism and globalization, and it manifests itself well beyond the geographic areas, social categories and age groups that were traditionally considered to be more religious and 'more conservative' than the rest of society. The growing religiosity is actually visible, at times defying official restrictions. Outward signs include the increase, especially in suburban areas, in the number of young and middle-aged women who wear the Islamic head scarf (which differs from the traditional peasant headscarf) and the increase in grocery shops and small supermarkets that no longer sell alcohol.

Research data on religion and religious observance confirm the trend. According to a survey from 2010, for instance, 71 per cent of respondents claimed that religion played an important role in their lives to a great or to some extent. Daily prayers were said by 63 per cent of the respondents in 2010 compared to 27 per cent in 1996, just like 52 per cent pretended to attend the Salat al-Juma or Friday prayers at the mosque as compared to just 13 per cent one and a half decades earlier.[12] That the growing religious identification, like any social and ideological movement that is difficult to control, makes the Soviet-shaped secular elites in government and other sectors of society not a little nervous, is clear from a number of measures taken over the last ten years to control if not curb religiosity, thereby more often that not raising the spectre of 'radicalism'. Among these were half-baked attempts to construct and promote an official national identity based on pre-Islamic heritage; the prohibition of women and recently also minors on visiting mosques; the imposition of a government-issued list with approved sermon topics for clerics; the closure and demolition of 'unofficial' mosques; the restriction of 'politically correct' Islam to the traditionally dominant Hanafi Sunnism, the government-sanctioned religious scholars council and the 'state imams'; and pressure on independent religious opinion leaders.[13]

The official unease and distrust towards religion is partly ideological and inspired by security concerns. But it especially reflects a social fault wherein elites with vested interests are extremely wary of the masses from 'the province' and of socially mobile sectors of society on a quest for an ideology, which they both consider to be threatening. In 2010 came the obligatory return of hundreds of young Tajiks who went to Egypt, Pakistan, Saudi Arabia and other places to study Islam. This brings us back to the issue of migration and its impact on religion. The students form a numerically tiny but socially and ideologically all but insignificant educational migration, in the sense that it involves young Tajiks who acquired religious knowledge that is often of a higher level than that of the official clergy that is mandated to back the government line, and that of the *muysafedon* – elders who traditionally play a leading religious role at the local level but often have a patchy religious knowledge. As such, they could pose a challenge to their authority.[14] They have also attended educational institutions abroad that are, unlike those at home, not subject to pervasive bribing.

In the meantime, some of these returnee students have been integrated in the official Islamic institute. Many others, however, joined the labour migration to Russia, which

Table 31.1 Labour and religious educational migration from Tajikistan (2008–09)

Labour Migration		Distribution Per Host Country (%)			
Numbers (estimates, 2008)	Population share involved (%)	Russia	Ukraine	Kazakhstan and other ex-USSR	Other (Baltics-EU, Arab countries)
797000	11.8	84.4	5.4	5.4	4.8
Religious Educational Migration		Distribution Per Host Country (estimates %)			
Numbers (estimates, 2009)	Population share involved (%)	Egypt	Saudi Arabia	Iran	Pakistan
1350–2200	0.2–0.3	37–45.5	26.3–31.8	9–14.8	13.6–22.2

Note: Some sources state that more than 3000 Tajiks followed religious courses abroad in 2004; Olimova (2004).

Sources: Table compiled by the author on the basis of Kuddusov (2009, p. 4) and Abramson (2010, pp. 36–43 and 47).

has caused mass (labour) migration and niche (educational) migration somehow to have become intertwined. How do they relate against each other in terms of size and destination? Table 31.1 offers an overview of the situation as it was in 2008 and 2009.

This chapter discusses how the more puritanical Islamic practices from Saudi Arabia that came in the wake of the remittances, consumer goods and the increase in social status of the migrants came to defy and compete with the traditional African Sufism that was long the dominant form of Islam in Wad al-Abbas. Of course, in our case the situation is quite different. To start with, the sociological contexts are completely different. And the labour migration from Tajikistan, or at least the vast majority of it, is not happening between two majority Muslim societies but between one that is by tradition majority Muslim and a majority non-Muslim (Christian and atheist) one.[15] Both have in common that they were part of the Soviet Union. In that respect, Tajikistan is not part of the 'classical' Islamic world. But the chapter's departure point and conclusion, that labour migration, and the social and economic changes that it brings, affect the development of religion in ways other than 'secularization', is valid for the case of Tajikistan as well.

COPING IN THE LAND OF COTTON

The narrow Vakhsh Valley is named after the river that winds its way across the southern part of the country to the Tajik-Afghan border, where it flows into the Panj, the river that forms the border with Afghanistan. The landscape here is predominantly flat and dominated by cotton and cereal fields, and villages surrounded with small family plots and orchards. These once belonged to Soviet collective farms and sometimes villages do still bear typical Soviet names like Oktyabrsk (after the October Revolution) and Chapaev (a Bolshevik commander). In 2009, the official population of the nine districts in the Vakhsh Valley was over 1.1 million.[16] Some 80 000 hectares here were sown with cotton, which is more than one-third of the country's total cotton area. This makes the densely populated Vakhsh Valley one of the core areas of the country's cotton industry, an export-oriented sector that is at once the first non-illicit channel that links this part of Tajikistan to the global economy.[17] Largely cultivated on separate fields rather than large plantations and very labour intensive, it is a highly controversial activity due to the interests of regime-connected groups and middlemen in it, the nominal wages and the practices of exploitation that are legion.

The second non-illicit channel that links the Vakhsh Valley to the global economy is, of course, labour migration. When one strolls in and around the central bazaar of Kurgan-Tyube, the Vakhsh Valley's main urban centre, it is difficult not to see the signs of the prevalence and importance of labour migration and remittances here. Ticket counters advertising flights to two dozen destinations in Russia, and, to a lesser extent, to Kazakhstan, Ukraine, the Gulf and the Baltics are plentiful, just like the money transfer points and wide variety of wiring companies that are often situated in the same offices, the call shops, and the currencies on offer in the money exchange booths. Away from the market, the morning queues of young men at the passport counter and the international status that Kurgan-Tyube's airport has had for quite some years already, suggest the same. According to the official figures, in 2009, close to 68 000 people from the Vakhsh Valley districts were directly involved in this activity.[18] But the actual figure is substantially higher.[19]

Labour migration and displacement are all but new realities in the Vakhsh Valley. Originally, the valley consisted of scarcely populated, semi-arid steppe and marshlands. But in 1924–41 and again in 1946–65, this frontier area became the subject of a large-scale Soviet development scheme that included the layout of an irrigation network and roads, the introduction of cotton cultivation and population resettlement from the republic's mountainous and land-scarce areas to collective farms in the Vakhsh Valley. Beside economic motives, the policy was also driven by security and control. In 1947–49, for example, some 7800 households, and again 20 000 households in 1954–59, were moved under a combination of government pressure, incentives and, in the case of people from localities that were destroyed in the heavy Gharm earthquake of 1949, necessity.[20] Most of the resettled highland Tajiks, who are colloquially called 'Gharmi' after one of their regions of origin, and their descendents still live here. In the 1980s, especially, several personalities of this community played leading roles in the political Islamic underground for reasons that had initially as much to do with identity building as with the social advancement of their community and the widening of the space for the Islamic religion in Soviet society.

The Vakhsh Valley was also one of the main frontlines of the civil war and saw massive displacement, both internal and over the Tajik-Afghan border, and destruction of housing. This brings us to the third non-illicit channel that connects the area to the global economy: relief and development aid. The UN agencies, foreign donors and international non-governmental organizations that started here with relief operations, have now switched the focus of their activity to longer-term programmes like infrastructure rehabilitation, agricultural development, and gender and civil society support. In popular opinion, the relief and reconstruction activities that lasted until around 2001 were certainly essential.[21] Today, there is more cynicism and weariness towards perceived ideological agendas behind aid. Many aid projects are now run by locally recruited cadres who, by not a small part of local opinion, are considered to be a self-serving caste rather than a group advancing society's interests. In terms of infrastructure and social services, foreign aid has partly taken over tasks that the state is supposed to fulfil and indeed fulfilled in the Soviet Union. Yet, due to the temporary nature and budgetary uncertainty of foreign projects, their sustainability is considered questionable by not a small part of popular opinion.

MOBILITY AND IDENTITY

From field observations and interaction with former and recently returned migrants (many of them from Moscow city and province, and from Yekaterinburg), informal and formal authorities, local researchers, opinion leaders and religious figures in both the capital, Dushanbe, and the urban as well as rural Vakhsh Valley, it appears that, as one can expect, migration clearly influences the position and practice of the Islamic religion in several ways.[22] Some are visible straight away. Take mosque attendance, for example. Aside from the migration issue, it has gone up in recent years, yet it differs considerably during and outside the migration season – which runs roughly from spring to late fall – due to the physical absence of many of the men of active age during the season. The imams of the village mosques in the district of Vakhsh who were asked, reported a decrease of one-third to almost two-thirds, increasing again once migrants return home. And indeed, the age category of many of the congregation members who did show up at prayer times, was visibly beyond active age.[23] This seemed to be less the case, though, in the main mosques of the city of Kurgan-Tyube, because as a province capital and market centre, it attracts many internal migrants from rural districts and smaller towns.[24]

More importantly, labour migration affected religious self-identification and the degree of practice in the sense that it gave a new impetus to both. While several respondents state that a minority, which is estimated at 10 to 15 per cent by local researchers, cadres of non-governmental organizations and migrants themselves, become estranged from religion and abandon all religious practice under the influence of the host society once working abroad, a solid majority of the migrants, even among those who practise little at home, tend to do the opposite and rediscover the Islamic part of their background and continue or increase practice to one extent or another.[25] 'One doesn't need to live in Arab countries or in Iran to become more religious any more', a chairperson of a provincial social organization that works on migration issues felt:

> For better or worse, many of our people who go to Russia come back as different people. Many of those who never prayed before, and who were not serious about faith at all, no longer are that way. They stopped drinking alcohol. I also observe that among my own relatives and acquaintances. Once in migration, people start to look for each other for support or company or to get something done. They search for bonds between each other and with the homeland. Tajik culture is by tradition Muslim culture, but the Islamic religion does not stop at the border. As people move they are getting more conscious about these things.[26]

Religion is seen as a continuation of a traditional identity and a cultural defence vis-à-vis a new environment and radical social change both at home and abroad. According to almost all respondents, much depends on the individual himself, the social environment, the informal authority of individual persons, and the *avlod* and *mahalgaroi*. These terms respectively stand for extended kinship networks and for localism, that is, networks of people with a common geographic origin (region, valley, village or town). Both systems, which are key elements of one's identity and social environment, are often intertwined or overlap.[27] Although nowadays the networks tend to diversify and mutate into interpersonal networks, which reach beyond the traditional solidarity spaces, they continue to be the basic unit of migrant networks. Their dynamics and evolution also define the space for the transfer and evolution of religion and religious practices both in migration and in the area of origin. 'Someone who was already a religious person will generally continue to be so over there, and the other way around', said a young migrant who worked in garbage collection and in the meat industry:

> But it's not always like that. Some of the lads change abroad. You see, it's my third year that I have gone to Russia now. I hardly ever practised and prayed here, but started to do it there. How come? Before I went off I was at school and didn't care much. I just lived life; I was younger then. But in Moscow, I lived with 20 people from Tajikistan of which ten or 12 practised regularly. Our foreman, who also lived with us, was from Kulyab. He was not a cleric really, but nonetheless he knew much about religion. He had a positive influence on us. Also, they may not really like us over there. But the Russians do appreciate us as better workers because we don't drink. So that's how it went.[28]

'For me it did not make much difference. I fasted and attended Friday prayers here in Tajikistan and continue to do that when I am away', a skilled construction worker who yearly goes to the Moscow area added. 'The mosque that I attend in Moscow is quite far from where I work. But I do want to go there because one of the imams is a Tajik from a village in Vakhsh district, close by. So we are from the same area'.[29] 'The first time I went to Russia, it was in the company of an older cousin who was at school with me and who is a religious man', told another migrant whose last occupation in migration was that of a porter in a Moscow textile bazaar:

> Thanks to him my religious practice was not interrupted. Then later on, when I went back without him, I somehow always came to live with other migrants who were praying or practising to one extent or another. There was no mosque there at the market, where we lived. But the bloke who ran the workers' canteen, a Tajik from Dushanbe, organized a prayer corner in the canteen's premises. There were people there who were not religious in Tajikistan and became more so abroad, as the other way around. But in my experience, where I was, the first group was more numerous than the second.[30]

'In the 90s, just after the civil war, things were dire here. Everything was in a shambles; there was a lot of unemployment and lots of alcoholics and drug addicts', another migrant respondent told me:

> But since you have the migration and more income, people are different. I felt that every time that I came back. Okay, some got corrupted. But as I see it, there is somehow more sense of responsibility and confidence. Many became more religious when abroad. Where I worked at the Cherkizovskii market in Moscow, the foreman was a Hajji – that's someone who went

> on a pilgrimage to Mecca. Having been in Mecca gives a man a lot of prestige and authority. People respected him for that. But he was also a good organizer and had the authority to get more order and discipline at the work place. And through that personal example, more people became observant.[31]

Some migrants who returned from cities with sizeable Muslim Tatar communities, told me that the presence of these communities' religious infrastructure also encouraged observance. 'There was a Tatar mosque with both Tatar and Tajik clerics close to where we lived', a former construction worker in Nizhnii Novgorod testified:

> Many of us visited it, not because the Tatars asked us to come but because we went by ourselves. The major Islamic holidays we celebrated among ourselves, among Tajiks. But we went to the Tatar mosque for the daily or weekly prayers. As I saw it, many migrants became more observant, not in the beginning, when I first went seven years ago. But later on, they did. Over there, you are a quite isolated community, so it's good to meet people at the mosque. And I experienced it myself: when you stop drinking, you get rewarded. You work better, you get more self-respect somehow.[32]

'I was a construction worker in Kazan and Ufa for ten years. A lot of Tatar Muslims live there. So they know and respect the Islamic religion there. They are also mosques', another respondent said:

> So for me, for my brother and my cousin who were with me there at one time, and for many of the mates, this presence of the Islamic religion certainly gave some hold and continuity. We are Muslims ourselves and so they are at home. So that was encouraging. Probably it inspired others too, because some of the men from our area who came to live with us and who were not observant became so when they were with us. As far as we saw, no one dropped religion altogether there.[33]

Whether the increased religious practice, real as well as relative, of a sizeable percentage of the migrants abroad continues once the migrants return home also depends on the individual and his social environment. 'Whether one becomes more religious or not depends on the group and its influence', an earlier-quoted migrant found:

> There is a difference between those who are religious themselves, and those who become so under group pressure. Basically, 10 per cent take the lead; the rest are followers. These might behave differently once they are back at home or in another group. But a sizeable part of the followers certainly do continue to be more religious even when the leaders and the group are no longer around.[34]

According to an imam of a village mosque, for example:

> nearly half of those who return here remain more religious than they were before their departure, while the rest become again like they were. It differs from person to person really. Over there, you are an alien community, and so identity and a sense of belonging matter more. But once at home, people are back in their own surroundings.[35]

Other sources had similar views. One former student, who attended religious studies in Pakistan for two years before he was called home by presidential order, found that during his absence, many of the men in his village who had worked in Russia had become clearly more observant than they were before. 'It's not that many start to wear Islamic clothes or long beards. Yet men who were drinking vodka before, no longer drink. People who never prayed before, do pray now. They don't do it every day, but they started to do it at least'.[36]

The confrontation with other lifestyles and mentalities and with isolation while abroad, and the increase in income and living standards that are part of the mixed effect of labour migration and the emergence of the remittance economy, definitely affected self-awareness both among labour migrants and in the communities they originate from. In turn, part of this translates into a stronger identification with religion. 'With the money that people send home, living standards are definitely going up here', a former labour migrant who worked in mining in Yakutsk found:

> We are still in the phase that this is the main thing that counts. But slowly, other things start to become important too. You see, people make a lot of sacrifices to feed their families. They don't leave for fun. Life there is not easy. You have to take too many insults, you get estranged from your children and relatives at home and you are confronted with the darker sides of human nature. Some get into all sorts of dubious things, some like to show off their new-found wealth at home, behave as the big man. And for not a few comes a moment when one wonders whether the sacrifices one makes in order to survive and advance in life also mean that you have to take all this, and become like that too. So people look for guidance. That's how many, and more so among the young in my opinion, turn to religion.[37]

Some of the migrants and informal leaders who took the lead in religious observance in migration, also continue to exercise authority once they return home, especially when they acquire higher economic status through the reinvestment of savings and remittances in a business or farm. This brings us to another factor: the social mobility and status of returnee migrants at home. Although the number of labour migrants who settle in Russia or other countries of destination increases, according to a survey from 2010 by the International Labour Organization (ILO) a large majority of 85.1 per cent eventually intend to return and stay in Tajikistan once the circumstances allow.[38] This reflects the views and intentions of my respondents in the Vakhsh Valley. Of course, whether migrants who want to return to stay, and already return home regularly due to the predominantly seasonal nature of labour migration from Tajikistan, can and will do so in the end depends on a set of personal and societal circumstances rather than on what they intend to do. Another ILO study puts the share of migrants who settled in the host country at 16 per cent.[39]

This means that a sizeable part of the migrants will sooner or later settle in Tajikistan, either in their area of origin or in or around the capital or one of the larger cities. According to a survey on Southern Tajikistan including the Vakhsh Valley, in 2006, 81.2 per cent of the interviewees mentioned unemployment and nominal salaries in the home country – that is, sheer necessity – as their reason for doing seasonal work abroad, while hardly anyone mentioned migration plans and the societal and cultural attractiveness of the destination country as a reason to migrate. This also reflects the views of most respondents during this research.[40] 'I think that I speak for most, when I say that I hope that living conditions here in Tajikistan become, as they do bit by bit, decent enough so that no one has to go "over there" to work any more', said one who was a lorry driver in the greater Moscow area.[41] For another to add:

> what else could we do given the circumstances? We need the income, there are no jobs here and we are temporarily needed there. But in fact they hate us. At the end of the day, it's not where we belong and it is also difficult to raise your children as Muslims there.[42]

Although the educational level among labour migrants is gradually decreasing both because of the state of the education sector in Tajikistan and because the demand for unskilled labour abroad offers little incentive to invest in education, the vast majority of the migrants are literate and almost half of the migrants from Southern Tajikistan, including the Vakhsh Valley, in 2006 had a full secondary or higher education that they could not validate abroad. Over three-quarters are also married.[43] In previous research by various international organizations as well as in my interviews and conversations, only a small part declared that they go abroad in order to save capital to invest in a business at home. And while the migrant is absent, the person who is in charge of his responsibilities and manages the money transfers does not often use them to set up a family business or other profit-generating activity.[44]

But once migrants cease their migration activity because of general weariness with life in migration, economic recession and less demand for labour in the host countries (as happened in 2008), family reasons, or because other family members (sons, brothers or cousins) have taken over the seasonal migration duty, they start to look for a steady income-generating activity. About one-third of the former migrants met during this field observation had actually already developed such an activity using migration money. This ranged from farming and livestock breeding, transport services with a car, minivan or small lorry brought from Russia, wholesale and retail trade to eateries and the money exchange and transfer business.[45] Many work with close relatives or with their *avlod* and operate for a large part in the grey zone of the economy. Returnees and migration money thus contribute to the growth of an entrepreneurial segment of society. In turn, it is confronted with frustrating impediments to business development like bureaucratic corruption, heavy official and 'informal' taxation, and hostility from interest groups (connected to the local authorities or others) who do not want such a social segment to become too active and confident.

The fact that in migration, Muslim migrants, despite the practical problems, isolation and the confrontation with xenophobia, generally face less official restrictions on Islamic practice in the majority non-Muslim host society than in majority Muslim Tajikistan, also affects the perception, among many, of the nature of religious policy in the country as well as the level of trust that they have in the 'state imams'. This group is basically stuck between hammer and anvil. Most of these official clerics are part of the local communities and, as such, are confronted with the social reality, the evolution of religion and religiosity and the discontent, at least among part of the population, caused by the humiliating official restrictions on religious observance. Yet their function requires them if not to advocate then at least (to advise the faithful) not to oppose the government line.

Many are also pressured by the state security agency to act as its eyes and ears among the observant. There are indicators that at least in some cases, the authority of state imams erodes fast among returned migrants because of this. 'This migration corrupts people', an offical cleric testified:

> About half of the migrants who attented our mosque before no longer come after they return. Maybe this is because they think that they are 'modern' now and that they no longer have to respect our traditions. But at the same time, many continue to practise Islam at home.[46]

Some imams also resigned in disstisfaction with the regime's religious policy. 'There were some three hundred Muslim workers at the refuse treatment plant close to Moscow where I worked', said a former migrant who used to be an imam at his village mosque after he came back:

> They were not only from Tajikistan, but also from Uzbekistan, from Samarkand in particular. How was that? Part were observant, others not at all. In my experience, those who were not religious at home did not become more so there, save a number who prayed only when they had problems of when they felt homesick. It was hard and dirty work, but the management was basically correct. In any case, alcohol was strictly prohibited at work. In terms of prayers and religious holidays, which I organized being an imam at home, they did not facilitate nor encourage it, but did not obstruct it either. But then, once back in Tajikistan, there were these laws. Now they prohibit children and minors from visiting the mosque. It was then that I stopped being an imam and became a fireman and freelance truck driver. How could I continue to be a mosque imam in such circumstances? Am I supposed to say to people, even minors, who want to come to my mosque that they should stay away? What is this? Even in Russia, a largely Christian country, they did not do that. But in Tajikistan, a Muslim country, they did.[47]

The influence of the *muysafedon* or community elders has been affected in the process too. The elders still have both the traditional position and the physical presence in the communities to look after local affairs. They usually represent a traditionalist and conservative segment of society and are often co-opted as *mahalla* or neighbourhood representatives – that is, including acting as informers – by local government structures who increasingly start to distrust the migrants because of their changing financial situation and their exposure to the outside world. In a number of cases, elders are also engaged in community mobilization activities for international development projects. Yet their authority is no longer automatically taken for granted by young migrants, whose work and remittances assure not only the family's (including the elders') survival but often also brought a new economic impetus to the village or area. Cases of corruption and abuse of power by elders are not unheard of either, especially within the nexus between them and local government.[48]

In the same sphere of changing perception of traditional authorities, and the social structures and practices that they embody, come the costly weddings, dowries and other expenses for life rituals that are part of traditional culture, often said or perceived to be part of Muslim culture but themselves not Islamic at all – more puritanical, non-traditional currents of Islam even explicitly condemn lavish celebrations. In Sarband district, for example, 67.8 per cent of the interviewed migrants in the year 2009 said that dowries and ceremonies, or the reimbursement of family debts made to pay for them, were part of the planned expenses of their migration money.[49] Although still important as social events and a matter of prestige, costly life rituals are increasingly seen as a burden, an unnecessary burden. Hence, theoretically, this changing legitimacy among migrants of traditional authorities and the social structures that they embody, creates a space for a redefinition of identity through religion and non-traditional Islam in particular.[50]

THE 'E-UMMAH' AND RELIGIOUS CIVIL SOCIETY

Another indirect yet, in my view, important influence of labour migration on the development of religion is that migration has created both a large demand and more purchase power for all sorts of new communication technologies like ever more sophisticated mobile phones and portable internet, digital video carriers and parabolic antennas. This happens well beyond the elite niches in the capital and other major cities to which demand for such technology was largely confined until about ten years ago. Mobile internet, for instance, is even promoted in small towns in the Vakhsh Valley these days.

By itself, this development has nothing to do with religion. Yet, the communication channels and media that are used for a wide variety of secular purposes, can also carry religious knowledge and messages and expand their accessibility and audience in Tajikistan as well as in migration. Popular non-governmental religious opinion leaders like the Turajonzoda brothers and Hajji Mirzo Ibronov, who is a former official imam from Kulyab who was sacked after he turned down the list of government-approved sermon topics, now have portal sites where their sermons, opinions and advice are readily accessible for Tajik Muslims in migration.[51] Although these sites are blocked in Tajikistan itself, audio and video files continue to circulate on mobile phones, on audio CDs and DVDs that are sold below the counter, or on proxy sites.

'Migrants to Russia or people who go for business to the Arab emirates also bring back books and videos from further afield with them', a social activist shared

> Most people here can read. Part of these materials are in Russian, others have already been translated into Tajik. There is actually much more religious material in Tajik or in Tajik and Arabic these days, which allows people to know the meaning of what they traditionally learned by heart in Arabic but did not understand. So what we have now is that there is a diversification of Islamic knowledge, beyond the traditional Islam that people grew up with and that was passed on by parents and by the elders. See, before the great migration, people here had hardly ever heard about something like Salafism, or about preachers who say that visiting Sufi shrines and tombs is un-Islamic. But now people do know. There are even several Salafis in the district, and some of them have been labour migrants in Russia and Kazakhstan before.[52]

The influx of remittances seems not yet to have given a serious boost to the emergence of a religious civil society with faith-based charities, social funds and professional associations. Although faith-based charities funded by migration revenue do exist, most of them are informal and not institutionalized in foundations or non-governmental organizations. This is in part because of the strong official scrutiny and clampdowns against religious and faith-based organizations, opposition by the state clergy, which resents competing faith-based structures, but also because due to the Soviet legacy, the pious middle class that often takes the lead in religious civil society is still in the process of forming in Tajikistan.[53] One exception is the social and charitable work of the Hizb-i Nahzat-i Islami or Islamic Renaissance Party, which is Tajikistan's only legal Islamic political group. Part of its original support base is among the Gharmi communities in the Vakhsh Valley and it continues to be quite influential there. Its work is funded through member contributions that are unavoidably also coming from remittances, given the importance of these in the household budgets.[54]

Most charitable and social initiatives, however, are ad hoc, informal and supported by the *avlod*. These initiatives are often, though not exclusively, taken on the occasion of Islamic holidays like Eid Al-Fitr (the end of the fasting month) and Eid-i Qurbon (the feast of sacrifice). They form a continuation of habits and solidarity practices that existed before the migration wave but are now also supported by migration money.

Typical examples that were observed or reported include contributions in cash or in kind by migrants and migrant families for the equipment and repair of village mosques, and Sadaqa or collections to support poorer families in the village. 'Where I worked, we regularly collected donations for the mosques in the villages where we come from', explained a former migrant with a medical background who worked among migrants in Moscow:

> One of the porters' foremen in a big market there was a Hajji from my district. He disptched goods and organized the tasks on commission and managed to earn well, sometimes up to 4000 dollars in one and a half months. He organized the collections for the mosque but also invested some of his savings in modern medical equipment for the provincial hospital where I work now. When I came back, I and his brother rented out this equipment to different physicians here. We made a profit that way. But it was also used for free medical consultations for people who can otherwise not afford it.[55]

'In 1992, we built a mosque in our village but because of the war and lack of means it was long a rudimentary structure', a village imam recalled when we visited his mosque:

> In the late 90s, however, some 40 lads from this village went to work on the same construction site in Moscow. They sent money with which we could build a proper, permanent structure. Three years ago, some migrants who came home from Russia after the season, refurbished it and gave it a fresh coat of paint. Last year, there were floods in Kulyab. The mosque association and some other people here then set up an action to collect aid, to which a number of migrants each contributed (US$50 to 100) or in-kind.[56]

THE CHANGING GENDER REALITIES

Finally, and not least, come the changes that labour migration and the absence of many men brought to the field of labour division between men and women. 'The biggest influence of migration can be felt in the invisible framework in which women are traditionally supposed to live', one local researcher stressed.[57] 'Do not underestimate that. Much work that was traditionally done by men is now done by women, and for that they have to get out of the house more frequently than before'. Observations in the field confirm this. In the fruit and vegetables section of Kurgan-Tyube's central bazaar, for example, more than two-thirds of the vendors were women, which is a clear change compared to the situation, say, ten years ago. A similar situation can be seen in the fields and family plots in and around the villages in the surrounding Vakhsh Valley. Estrangement from spouses and families after a long absence is an issue – according to a previously quoted ILO study this is the case for 40.9 per cent of the migrants surveyed.[58] Outright family abandonment by migrants and informal polygamy – whereby migrants have a wife at home and one in migration or abandoned migrant wives become concubines of a better-off villager as a survival strategy – happen too.

Yet, despite the circulation of lots of anecdotal evidence at the popular level and in the tabloid media, little exact figures about both phenomenon's actual proportions are known. One Tajik researcher who works on gender issues estimated the number of families affected by abandonment at 3 to 5 per cent.[59] Said a former migrant:

> In my village, which has about 1000 inhabitants, some 180 men are in migration. As you can guess, this is pretty much the village's entire active male population. My two sons are among them. Unfortunately, over the last ten years, three men did not come back any more. They left their wives and children, started new lives abroad with other women and stopped sending money. Their first families now have serious problems. I agree that the men who do that are only a few. Yet in our culture and religion, the family is very important. So psychologically, it does have its effect in our village or wherever it also happens.[60]

Yet, despite attempts by secular feminists to diabolize men in general for supposed family abandonment, what happens in the majority of the migrant home communities is, that both the men and the women are becoming support pillars of the extended family – one at home, the other from abroad. Here again, this is, by itself, not a specifically Islamic factor nor even a religious factor. It becomes one, though, when one takes into account two factors. First, given the importance of family matters in the Islamic religion, both in its traditional and non-traditional interpretation and practice, the socio-psychological adaptation and coping process with this new reality is something that cannot be done exclusively or even predominantly through secular ways. The control over the direction that this adaptation process is to take or will take, though, became a stake in an ideological battle between religious and faith-based actors on one hand, and, on the other, neoliberal international gender programmes and the local secular women's organizations that seek to recuperate the issue for the sake of donor funding.

Second, the long seasonal absence of the male head of the household, or male family members of active age in general, affects the transfer of religious knowledge and practice that the male heads of the household are traditionally supposed to do.[61] As a result, and because of the recent prohibition on minors attending the mosque, migrants' wives or mothers or other family members increasingly approach knowledgeable men (or also women) outside of the immediate household to give the children religious education. This certainly opens a space and role for Tajik returnee students who attended Islamic courses abroad. As with the former students of Islam who joined the ranks of the labour migrants to Russia shortly upon their return, the effects of the two forms of migration become intertwined that way. 'Some fear that the students of Islam who had to return to Tajikistan will "contaminate" migrants and youths with radicalism', the previously quoted social activist stressed:

> But the vast majority of these former students are not extremists at all. Many even went abroad on government stipends. What some definitely do find disturbing with them is that they bring in ideas and knowledge of a higher level than what is taught at official Islamic institutes, and that they are less easy to put into line.[62]

CONCLUSION

Labour migration is one of the biggest channels that connect the Vakhsh Valley and the rest of Tajikistan to the global economy. As observed and examined above, its effect on society and religion is clear in a number of ways, and is not so much 'radicalization' as it is social mobility and the (re-) definition of identity that go with it. That process happens on the interface of the traditional identity, the post-Soviet environment and globalization. For the country's powers that be, at whatever level, labour migration and its effects on society, including religion, poses some sort of a 'catch 22' situation. Migration is definitely a big safety valve for the country and especially the ruling elites, as it is a way to 'get rid' of active young men, often from opposition regions or sectors of society. At the same time as it brought living standards beyond the mere survival level, however, migration leads to new expectations and changing perceptions of both one's situation and of authority. This will affect attitudes towards the status quo and lead to social mobilization in one way or another. The result does not necessarily have to be upheaval, only a way society evolves. As public channels and possibilities of religious practice increasingly face restrictions in Tajikistan, migration, along with inter-personal and regional networks and the new media, will gain importance as a framework of increasing religiosity in society.

NOTES

* The author wishes to thank Marc Fumagalli, Yusuf Mahmedov, Suhrob Tavarov, and all those who were were willing to share their stories, impressions and comments.

1. Ratha et al. (2010, pp. 3–4).
2. United Nations Development Programme (2009, Annex, Table E, p. 161); Canagarajah and Kholmatov (2010, pp. 2–3); Kuddusov (2009, p. 4).
3. For an in-depth examination of perceptions and realities of corruption in the international aid sector in Tajikistan, see Mirzoev (2006).
4. For more on the causes and dynamics of the conflict, see Djalili (1995) and Roy (1997, pp. 154–62). Both works exist in English. For a Russian perspective, see Bushkov and Minkulskii (2006a).
5. For in-depth discussions of the personalized control by the political elite and their networks over the key sectors of Tajikistan's economy, see Heathershaw (2011) and Nakaya (2009).
6. Olimov, J. (2007), *Tyenevaya ekonomika v Tadzhikistane*, National Human Development Report series, Dushanbe: United National Development Programme, p. 74.
7. Olimova and Mugal (2006, p. 7).
8. For an overview and discussion of the different estimates of the number of migrants, see Kireyev (2006, p. 7). In informal conversations as well as in popular media, the number often quoted is 1 to 1.5 million, though that probably refers also to those who left the country for good during the war (often minorities like Russians, ethnic Germans, Jews and 'Soviet métis' of mixed ethnic background), as well as to the labour migrants who end up not coming back.
9. International Labour Migration (2010, pp. 14 and 18), Olimova and Bosc (2003, p. 41) and Kuddusov (2009, Annex 3).
10. Tajik, both the majority and official language of Tajikistan, is a Persian language but has absorbed many Arabo-Islamic and Russian terms.
11. For more on the position and evolution of the Islamic religion in the Soviet Union, see Chapters IV and VIII in Roy (1997).
12. Wagner (1997, p. 44) and International Foundation for Election Systems (2010, p. 41). See also Olimova (2007).
13. The ban on women from attending mosques, which was issued by the government-approved religious scholars council in mid-2005 and outraged many, formalized a traditional practice that has long existed in this part of Eurasia and is, according to some, of local pre-Islamic origin and not proper to Hanafi Sunnism for in many other Hanafi Sunni societies women do visit mosques. Other measures, such as the prohibition on minors attending prayer services, also apply to other confessions such as the evangelical Protestants who came to Tajikistan in the 1990s and often use development aid or businesses as a front. Yet they are generally perceived to primarily target Islam and Muslims. Finally, the anchoring of Hanafi Sunnism as the only admissible Islamic school of thought in Tajikistan, was a move to, first, counter the spread of Salafism (a more puritanical Sunni current) and, second, to refute criticism that the regime is anti-Islamic.
14. Abramson (2010).
15. The share of cultural as well as practising Christians in Russia is usually set at about 75 per cent of the population, and the share of atheists, according to source, at 8 to 18 per cent in 2007. Russia has also a native Muslim population segment (mostly Tatars and North Caucasians) whose share was estimated

at 8 per cent of the population in 2007; Statistika – portal statistitsheskih dannyh, *Religia v tsifrah i faktah*, www.statistika.ru; accessed 7 September 2011. In 2003, 96.4 per cent of the labour migrants from Tajikistan considered themselves to be Muslims, and less than 1 per cent atheists. According to data from 2005, only a 0.5 per cent of the population of Tajikistan said that they were atheist as compared to 2 per cent ten years earlier; Olimova and Bosc (2003, p. 131) and Olimova (2007, p. 201).

16. Statistical Agency of the Republic of Tajikistan (2010, p. 20).
17. The Vakhsh Valley – like Southern Eurasia in general – is part of a smuggling corridor and is as such linked to the global economy through an *illicit* sector as well and one that actually follows the same routes as labour migration: the drug trafficking over the Tajik-Afghan border. The United Nations Office on Drugs and Crime (2008) and Mili (2006, pp. 30–45).
18. Spreadsheet of the State Migration Service of the Ministry of Internal Affairs of Tajikistan with district-wise labour migration and destination figures, provided to the author by the International Organization for Migration, Dushanbe, 15 July 2011.
19. See note 8.
20. Bushkov and Minkulskii (2006b). Other groups that were settled here in the process were Tajiks from Kulyab. The original population were predominatly Uzbek Lakai tribes, who still live here too.
21. For an examination of the role of aid in the Vakhsh Valley during the first half of the 1990s, see Harris (1998).
22. The interviews and conversations took place in the city of Kurgan-Tyube and in the districts of Bokhtar, Vakhsh (which covers only a part of the namesake valley) and Sarband. Given the official itchiness over religious issues at times and that the state security agency is watchful due to the recent (2010) upheaval in neighbouring Kyrgyzstan and the Arab Spring, the names of the respondents and the exact locations of the meetings are not given for reasons of privacy and the personal security of the source.
23. Personal observations, and conversations with village imams in three villages in Vakhsh district, 11 and 13 July 2011.
24. Personal observations, and conversations with a local activist and researcher, Kurgan-Tyube, 7 and 13 July 2011.
25. Interviews with a social activist, Bokhtar district, 8 July 2011 and with a member of a social research institute, Dushanbe, 15 July 2011. The increase in religious identification among migrants was already briefly pointed out but not elaborated on in Olimova and Bosc (2003, p. 131).
26. Interview with a leader of a regional social organization that works on migration in Kurgan-Tyube, 11 July 2011.
27. For an examination of the *avlod* (which is also called *qawm*) and other solidarity networks in society in general and in labour migration, see Roy (1996) and Olimova and Bosc (2003, pp. 59–60).
28. Interview with a labour migrant, aged 25, Bokhtar district, 9 July 2011.
29. Interview with a labour migrant, aged 23, Bokhtar district, 7 July 2011.
30. Interview with a labour migrant, aged 25, Bokhtar district, 8 July 2011.
31. Interview with a former labour migrant, aged 42, Vakhsh district, 11 July 2011.
32. Interview with a returned labour migrant, aged 46, Bokhtar district, 9 July 2011.
33. Interview with a former labour migrant, aged 36, Bokhtar district, 8 July 2011.
34. Interview with a returned labour migrant, aged 46, Bokhtar district, 9 July 2011.
35. Interview with an imam of a village mosque, aged 39, Bokhtar district, 9 July 2011.
36. Interview with a former religious student, aged 23, Sarband district, 12 July 2011.
37. Interview with a former labour migrant, aged 50, Bokhtar district, 8 July 2011.
38. International Labour Organization (2010a, p. 18).
39. International Labour Organization (2010b, p. 2).
40. Olimova and Mugal (2006, p. 36).
41. Informal conversation with a former labour migrant, aged 37, Kurgan-Tyube, 11 July 2011.
42. Interview with a labour migrant, aged 32, Bokhtar district, 7 July 2011.
43. Olimova and Mugal (2006, p. 36) and Agence d'Aide à la Coopération Technique et au Développement (2009a, p. 16).
44. International Labour Organization (2010a, pp. 29–30), Agence d'Aide à la Coopération Technique et au Développement (2009a, pp. 10–12) and author's interviews and conversations in the Vakhsh Valley between 6 and 15 July 2011.
45. This is more or less in line with the previously mentioned ILO study, which states that as a national average, 44.3 per cent of returnees had already invested in a business in Tajikistan by 2010. International Labour Organization (2010a, p. 30). Several micro-finance institutions that work in Tajikistan started to get into the returnee migrant niche as well.
46. Interview with a state imam, aged 44, Vakhsh district, 11 July 2011.
47. Interview with a former labour migrant and village imam, aged 41, Bokhtar district, 9 July 2011.

48. For some testimonials and survey data on the relationship between returnee migrants, the local community and the authorities, see International Labour Migration (2010, pp. 35–6).
49. Agence d'Aide à la Coopération Technique et au Développement (2009b, pp. 42–4).
50. In 2007, sensing that lavish celebrations are a cause of debts and the growing popular discontent with them a rallying point for Islamists, Tajikistan's secular president Emomali Rahmon pushed through a law on traditions, celebrations and rituals that limits the number of guests to a maximum of 150 for weddings and 80 for funerals and the duration to half a day instead of several days. This law was generally welcomed among the poorer strata of society, though the extent to which it is implemented differs according to area and sector of society. 'It's a good law', said one respondent in Sarband in a typical reaction. 'Well, mind you, the rich and connected continue to show off as they please. But for others, it makes it easier not to have to spend large amounts of money'.
51. The portal of the Turajonzoda brothers is at www.turajon.com, and that of Hajji Mirzo at hojimirzo.ucoz.com. One of the Turajonzoda brothers, Hajji Akbar, is a former UTO leader and religio-politically influential, while another, Eshoni Nurridinjon, is a popular preacher.
52. Interview with a local activist of a social non-governmental organization, aged 48, Bokhtar district, 8 July 2011.
53. For in-depth case studies on the role of the middle class in faith-based civil society and welfare activities, see Clark (2004).
54. The numbers of the Islamic Renaissance Party's national membership range from over 25000 to 40000 (which makes it the country's third party), of which there are about 5800 members in the Vakhsh Valley districts. Mamedov (2009, Annex II, p. 43) and Dronov (2006).
55. Interview with a former migrant from Vakhsh district, aged 47, Kurgan-Tyube, 11 June 2011.
56. Interview with a village imam, aged 51, Vakhsh district, 11 July 2011.
57. Interview with a cadre and researcher of a non-governmental organization, Dushanbe, 15 June 2011.
58. International Labour Migration (2010, p. 37).
59. Interview with a cadre and researcher of a non-governmental organization, Dushanbe, 15 June 2011. A study from 2009 by the International Organization for Migration gives no clear figures of the phenomenon's proportions either, but some passages suggest 3 per cent for the number of migrants who stopped sending any money home at all. This study tends to extend the category of 'abandoned' to families who do receive remittances but only up to US$500 a year (which, according to this study, is the case for 37 per cent of migrant families that year). International Organization for Migration (2009, pp. 40 and 56).
60. Interview with a former labour migrant, aged 50, Bokhtar district, 8 July 2011.
61. See Olimova (2004, pp. 350–51).
62. Interview with a local activist of a social non-governmental organization, aged 48, Bokhtar district, 8 July 2011.

REFERENCES

Agence d'Aide à la Coopération Technique et au Développement (2009a), *Adding Value to Central Asian Migration. Awareness, Capacity Building and Networking for Maximizing the Impact of Migration on Growth and Development. Baseline Survey*, Document No. 05-AEJ, Dushanbe: ACTED.

Agence d'Aide à la Coopération Technique et au Développement (2009b), *Trends of Labour Migration from Sughd and Khatlon Region, Republic of Tajikistan, Under the Impact of the Global Financial Crisis*, Dushanbe: ACTED.

Bushkov, V.I. and D.V. Minkulskii (2006a), *Anatomiya grazhdanskoi voiny v Tadzhikistane (etno-sotsialnie protsessy i polititsheskaya borba, 1992–95)*, Moscow: Institut etnologii i antropologii Rossiiskaya akademia nauk – Institut prakticheskogo vostokovedenia.

Bushkov, V.I. and Minkulskii, D.V. (2006b), 'Demograficheskaya situatsia v Tadzjikistane. Yestestvennoe i mehanicheskoe dvizhenie naseleniya i ego sotsialnie posledstviya', in *Anatomiya grazhdanskoi voiny v Tadzhikistane (etno-sotsialnie protsessy i polititsheskaya borba, 1992–95)*, Moscow: Institut etnologii i antropologii Rossiiskaya akademia nauk – Institut prakticheskogo vostokovedenia, p. 57.

Canagarajah, S. and M. Kholmatov (2010), *Migration and Remittances in CIS Countries During the Global Economic Crisis*, Europe and Central Asia Knowledge Brief, Volume 16, Washington, DC: The World Bank.

Clark, J.A. (2004), *Islam, Charity, and Activism: Middle-Class Networks and Social Welfare in Egypt, Jordan, and Yemen*, Series in Middle East Studies, Bloomington, IN: Indiana University Press.

David M. Abramson (2010), *Foreign Religious Education and the Central Asian Islamic Revival: Impact and Prospect for Stability*, Central Asia-Caucasus Institute.

Djalili, M.R. (1995), *Le Tadjikistan à l'épreuve de l'indépendance*, Geneva: Institut universitaire de hautes études internationales.

Dronov, V. (2006), *Smert Saida Nuri*, Informatsionni-analititsheskii tsentr po izutsheniyu obshchestvenno-polititshekih protsessov na postsovietskom prostrantstve, www.ia-centr.ru.

Harris, C. (1998), 'Coping with daily life in post-Soviet Tajikistan. The Gharmi villages of Khatlon Province', *Central Asian Survey*, **17**(4), 655–71.

Heathershaw, J. (2011), 'Tajikistan amidst globalization: state failure or state transformation?', Central Asian Survey, **30**(10), 147–68.

International Foundation for Election Systems (2010), *Public Opinion in Tajikistan in 2010*, Washington, DC: IFES.

International Labour Migration (2010), *Migration and Development in Tajikistan. Emigration, Return and Diaspora*, Moscow: ILO Subregional Office for Eastern Europe and Central Asia.

International Labour Organization (2010a), *Migration and Development in Tajikistan. Emigration, Return and Diaspora*, Moscow: ILO Sub-Regional Office for Eastern Europe and Central Asia.

International Labour Organization (2010b), *Migrant Remittances to Tajikistan. The Potential for Savings, Economic Investment and Existing Financial Products to Attract Remittances*, Moscow: ILO Sub-Regional Office for Eastern Europe and Central Asia.

International Organization for Migration (2009), *Broshennye zheny tadzikskih trudovyh migrantov*, Dushanbe: IOM.

Kireyev, A. (2006), 'The macro-economics of remittances. The case of Tajikistan', IMF Working Paper No. 06/2, Policy Development and Review Department.

Kuddusov, J. (2009), *Vliyanie mirovogo finansovo krizisa na trudovyh migrantov iz Tadzhikistana: mneniye migrantov*, Moscow and Dushanbe: International Labour Migration and the Ministry of Labour and Social Protection of Tajikistan.

Mamedov, Y. (2009), *Sostanyanie vnutrennogo nablyudeniya za vyborami co storony polititsheskih partii v Hatlonskoi oblasti*, Kurgan-Tyube: Rushd.

Mili, H. (2006), 'L'Asie centrale, plaque tournante du trafic de drogue', *Le Courrier des pays de l'Est*, 5/2006(1057), 30–45.

Mirzoev, S. (2006), 'Allocative (in)efficiency of grants in Tajikistan: corruption and international organisations', Working Paper No. 050011247, University of Saint-Andrews, School of Economics and Finance.

Nakaya S. (2009), 'Aid and transition from a war economy to an oligarchy in post-war Tajikistan', Central Asian Survey, **28**(3), 259–73.

Olimov, J. (2007), *Tyenevaya ekonomika v Tadzhikistane*, National Human Development Report series, Dushanbe: United National Development Programme.

Olimova, S. (2004), 'Religioznoe obrazovanie v Tadzhikistane v nastoyashee vremya. Obzor situatsii i rekommendatsii', in J.N. Bitter, F. Guérin, D. Rahmonova-Schwartz and A.K. Seifert (2004), *Postroyenie doveri mezhdu islamistami i sekularistami: Tadzhikskii eksperiment*, Dushanbe: Devastish, pp. 346–7.

Olimova, S. (2007), 'La jeunesse du Tadjikistan face à l'islam et l'islamisme', *Cahiers d'Asie Centrale*, **15**(16).

Olimova, S. and A.G. Mugal (2006), *Denezhnie perevodi i ih vliyanie na uroven zhizni v Hatlonskoi oblasti Respubliki Tadzhikistan*, Dushanbe: International Organization for Migration.

Olimova, S. and I. Bosc (2003), *Trudovaya migratsia iz Tadzhikistana*, Dushanbe: International Organization for Migration.

Ratha, D., S. Mohapatra and A. Silwal (2010), *Recueil de statistiques 2011 sur les migrations et les envois de fonds*, Washington, DC: The World Bank-Banque Mondiale: Development Prospects Group – Groupe des perspectives de développement.

Roy, O. (1996), 'Groupes de solidarité au Moyen-Orient et en Asie centrale', *Les Cahiers du CERI*, No. 16.

Roy, O. (1997), *La nouvelle Asie centrale, ou la fabrication des nations*, Paris: Seuil.

Statistical Agency of the Republic of Tajikistan (2010), *Regiony Respubliki Tazdhikistan*, Dushanbe: Statistical Agency of the Republic of Tajikistan.

Umarov, H.M. (2010), *Tadzhikskaya trudovaya migratsia v uslovyah globalnogo finansovo krizisa: pritshiny i posledstviya*, International Organization for Migration, Dushanbe.

United Nations Development Programme (2009), *Human Development Report 2009. Overcoming Barriers: Human Mobility and Development*, New York: United Nations Development Programme, Human Development Report unit.

United Nations Office on Drugs and Crime (2008), *Illicit Drug Trends in Central Asia*, Tashkent: UNODC Regional Office for Central Asia.

Wagner, S. (1997), *Public Opinion in Tajikistan in 1996*, Washington, DC: International Foundation for Election Systems (IFES).

32 Where shadows fall patchwork: religion, violence and human security in Afghanistan

James Astley Connell

INTRODUCTION

There are few places where conflict, violence and human suffering are imagined to cast such long shadows as they do for Afghanistan. Today, 11 years from Operation Enduring Freedom, the country and the international community stand at a crossroads. Pressure for foreign armed forces to withdraw by 2014 comes not only from many Afghanis unhappy with an increasingly heavy-handed military intervention, but also from the electorates of coalition countries, tired of escalating casualties and wary of the mounting costs of building peace and democracy in a country that, it is often perceived, does not desire it. These pressures are exacerbated by a severe global financial crisis and the disquieting recognition that progress towards 'development' in Afghanistan, whether in terms of economic growth, improved governance, better security, or a greater equality of rights for women and minorities, has either failed or rests on thin ice. The Taliban regime, all but eliminated in 2001, has achieved resurgence, and poses a direct threat to Karzai's government (Johnson, 2007). They are not alone. Other groups such as Hezb-e-Islami and al-Qaeda alongside a number of pro-government militias, threaten the well-being of 'ordinary' Afghans. The resurgence of the Taliban has led to questions over their support in Afghanistan, and whether progress made shall prove ephemeral.

A popular narrative frames the pervasive political and social violence in Afghanistan as a consequence of intrinsic resistance to social reform within Afghan culture and society. Proponents underline an inherent and intrinsically bellicose 'tribalism' in Afghan society and culture, one that has earned a mythic reputation for resisting domination and governance, and a mysogonistic religiosity with a tendency towards insurgency. Together these views have contributed to a popular belief that Afghanistan is an unviable, ungovernable, nation (Barfield, 2010) blighted by corruption, religious fundamentalism, and a history of political and social violence – little more than a 'black hole of civic hopelessness' (Bumiller, 2009). Yet is Afghanistan so historically ungovernable? Is violence in the country the fault of culture or religion; and can religion or culture even be understood to determine behaviour in this way? This chapter examines violence in Afghanistan, and the extent to which religion or culture may be seen to inspire it. I focus, in particular, on the well-being of women and children, not because these are the only groups at risk, but because they are often understood to be especially so. Unfortunately, space prevents discussion of other groups, not least the Shi'a Hazara, whose particular experiences of the Afghan conflict demands consideration in its own right.

At heart, it is argued, Afghanistan suffers not from deficiencies in its religious or cultural traditions, but from a crisis of governance and legitimacy. The perpetual nature of violence in the country and the Taliban's resurgence should be seen as resulting from failed development (Johnson, 2007), resentment over increased civilian casualties, and fears over a return to the lawlessness of the 1990s. Poverty, it is additionally argued, forms an equally pernicious threat to the security and well-being of women and children. At the same time, religion and culture, so integral to daily life in Afghanistan, should not be neglected. Drawing on constructivist theory, I explore the ways in which actors such as the Taliban have seized unifying religious, cultural and historical narratives to spiritualize their campaign, and legitimize their authority. Whilst religion is more commonly seen as escalating violence, however, it is argued here to be capable of delegitimizing it and promoting inclusive, equitable development. Such transformation, however, requires trustworthy and legitimate leadership. The impending NATO withdrawal and equivocation over whether to engage the Taliban, local militias, and other insurgent groups in local governance make this distinction critical. Discourses that emphasize the intransigence of Islam or Afghan culture may provide an excuse for prioritizing 'national' over 'human' security, in this regard, but such policies risk the most vulnerable. The inclusion of groups that are at best unaccountable and at worst existentially opposed to human rights and reform, it is argued, will likely prove catastrophic for the security of women, children and minorities in Afghanistan.

THREE DECADES OF CONFLICT

Continued difficulties with pursuing conflict in Afghanistan, concerns of a resurgent Taliban, and reports of the violence faced by Afghans – especially Afghan women – have re-enlivened prejudices of a country that is, and always has been considered otiose, violent, and inherently ungovernable – an incorrigible 'graveyard of empires'. Such notions, reinforced through media reports that portray Afghanistan as the crucible of chaos and terror, excuse the failings of intervention as due to inherent problems of 'mediaeval' Afghan culture, or Islam – a faith of 'bloody borders' (Huntington, 1996), a fundamentally mysogynistic, anti-democratic tradition.

Such analysis, of course, reflects a distorted and selective account of Afghan history and Islam. Whilst Afghanistan has indeed proved resistant to imperialism, and Islam has often formed a unifying force in the country, attempts to frame Afghanistan as a backward, religiously benighted country are more modern contrivance than historical reality. Prior to the Cold War,'Afghans and Americans alike [described] the country as a poor nation, but one that built national roads, stood up an army and defended its borders'. Kabul, was known as 'the Paris of Central Asia' (Bumiller, 2009), where women traded traditional clothing for make-up, high heels and careers (Rashid, 2002). Despite great ethnic diversity, the spectre of ethnic conflict was unknown, and even in 2001, whilst Afghanistan 'may have been a failed-state, it was not a failed nation' (Barfield, 2010, p. 277). Contrary to popular prejudices, Afghanistan has historically been an inclusive, pluralistic society, with a proud but tolerant religious tradition. Discrimination against women was no more prevalent in Afghanistan than elsewhere, and even for the notoriously patriarchal Pashtun, prejudice concerning cultural attitudes is often misplaced: many Pashtun communities, for instance, proudly educated their daughters (Rashid, 2002). Of course problems existed. Minorities such as the Hazara suffered considerable persecution throughout history, and as modernization resculpted the political landscape in the twentieth century, new strands of political Islam were introduced in an attempt to challenge reform. In no way, however, can the brutality of the Taliban regime and the violence that persists in Afghanistan today be understood as an inevitable consequence of Afghan history.

The violence of the Taliban regime and current insurgency instead has root in more recent events, namely the anti-soviet *jihad*, and the internecine conflict that followed it. Memories of the Taliban's brutality often occlude the vicious and largely indiscriminate violence and corruption of the early 1990s. After the Soviet withdrawal in 1989, the alliance that had held the numerous armed factions of the Mujahideen together quickly deteriorated – 'grassroots mobilization' degenerated into 'warlordism' (Guistozzi and Ibrahimi, 2012). Whilst the Soviet-backed Najibullah government afforded some control and security in urban areas, rural communities were subject to torture, murder, extortion and rape. The rural south, in particular, 'became far more dangerous than it had been for years' (Marsden, 1998, p. 37). Kandahar 'experienced virtual anarchy from 1992 until the Taliban takeover as the various Mujahideen commanders fought for control of the streets and reduced much of the city to rubble' (ibid., p. 42). It is in reference to such violence that the Taliban define and justify their origins:

> There was widespread corruption and theft, and there were road-blocks everywhere. Women were being attacked, raped and killed. Therefore, after these incidents, a group of students from religious schools decided to rise against these leaders in order to alleviate the suffering of the residents of Kandahar Province. (Ibid., p. 61)

Raised in foreign madrassahs, and comprised mainly of refugee youth, the Taliban vision was for the creation of an Islamic state based on Shari'a law. Beyond this, they had little interest in governance. '[In] Kabul', argues Kepel (2002, p. 229), 'the Taliban did not so much take control of state institutions as completely eviscerate them, erecting in their stead only three functions: morality, commerce and war'.

The violence of the following years is well documented. On capturing key cities the Taliban established prescriptions regulating personal conduct, imposing brutal punishment for transgression. Strict dress codes were introduced, women were forced from the workplace (resulting in widespread destitution) and music, film, and 'kite-running', were banned. The religious police, operating under the mandate of the regime's one functioning institution, the Ministry for the Promotion of Virtue and the Prevention of Vice, enforced this strict moral code. The suffering of women, confined to a largely shuttered domestic existence, earned particular condemnation. The punishment for so-called 'moral' crimes, including adultery (*zina*), fell hardest on women. Where a woman was suspected of adultery, she would likely face execution, a reality made more disturbing by the regime's failure to distinguish between adultery and rape. Minority groups, particularly the Hazara, were also targeted. 'Representing one of the most brutal strains of puritanical sunnism, the Taliban pursued a virulent anti-shia agenda', notes Brahimi (2010, p. 10). In 1998, 8000 Hazara were massacred during the takeover of Mazar-e-Sharif. According to Brahimi (2010, p. 11), 'the Taliban conducted house-to-house searches for Hazara men, shooting them in the head, chest or testicles, suffocating them to death in shipping containers, or slitting their throats'. The massacre, described as 'genocidal in its ferocity' (Rashid, 2002, p. 73), remains one of the most lamentable episodes of Afghan history.

In October 2001, following the terrorist attacks in New York City, NATO authorized military intervention in Afghanistan to eliminate al-Qaeda and oust the regime that harboured them. Despite predictions to the contrary, forces were welcomed by Afghans. A wave of optimism followed the Bonn Agreement and the introduction of political process, resulting in the mass return of refugees from neighbouring countries. A new government under Hamid Karzai was installed, and a number of wide-reaching social reforms introduced. For the first time in decades peace in Afghanistan seemed a possibility. This was not to last. Widespread corruption and the failure to provide security and development in rural regions – especially in southern Afghanistan – have resulted in a loss of trust in the intervention (Johnson, 2007; Barfield, 2010). Increased civilian casualties have accompanied accusations of civilian mistreatment by armed forces, and by 2006, the Taliban, thought all but eliminated in 2001, had achieved resurgence.

VIOLENCE AGAINST WOMEN IN AFGHANISTAN

The imperative to improve the human rights of women formed – after the removal of the Taliban regime – a principal justification for the invasion and 'rehabilitation' of Afghanistan (Reid, 2009). Unfortunately, despite some progress – most notably with the Law on Elimination of Violence Against Women (EVAW), violence against women remains endemic (Nijhowne and Oates, 2008; Reid, 2009; UNAMA, 2010; HRW, 2012). The evidence is stark. 'Afghan women continue to be among the worst off in the world. Their situation is dismal in every area, including in health, education, employment, freedom from violence, equality before the law, and political participation', notes one report (Reid, 2009, p. 3). Whilst the EVAW law represents progress regarding the criminalization of child marriage, forced marriage, forced self-immolation and a number of other practices (UNAMA, 2011a), implementation of the law, has been limited (ibid.). Many of these practices continue unabated – especially away from urban centres. 'Violence against women in the home', it is reported, 'is so prevalent and so pervasive that practically every Afghan woman will experience it in her lifetime' (Nijhowne and Oates, 2008, p. 1). Furthermore, despite the progress made in terms of the EVAW law and the limited turnout amongst women for elections, both higher political authorities and international policy-makers seem to be losing interest in women's rights for more exigent priorities. The drafting of local militias into the Afghan Local Police (ALP) to bolster rural security has put women and children at considerable risk of sexual exploitation (Reid and Muhammedally, 2011). The enactment of the mysogonistic Shia Personal Law in 2009, proved a further setback for women's rights more broadly. Whilst the law was eventually revised, the attempt reflects the power of conservative influence, and an indication of political non-commitment to women's rights.

In the public sphere, women, their spouses and children are at risk from attacks by insurgents, conservative factions within government, and family members. Recently, a number of prominent women including Lt. Col. Malalai Kakar, head of Kandahar's department for crimes against women, and Safia Amajan, head of the Department for Women's Affairs in Kandahar and a strong advocate of girls' education, have been assassinated, with few arrests or convictions made (Reid, 2009). Whilst assassination forms an obvious peril, the threat alone generates more insidious psychological violence, which is intensified through threats to women's families. In one interview, a female member of government, states: 'I am really afraid for my children because they told me that they will kill my daughters. Every minute I'm afraid. [Any] minute they can kill me. I can never go home, the government cannot protect me there. My old life is over' (Reid, 2009, p. 25).

Perhaps the most notorious campaign of violence against women in public authority, however, against those who advocate and participate in girls' education. Particularly in rural areas, school-building and girls' education has been obstructed by insurgents willing to harm both teachers and children through assassinations, bombings and acid attacks. Attacks are frequently associated with the dissemination of 'night letters' (*shabnameh*) – letters delivered to individuals or institutions as a warning to desist or face the 'consequences':

> You [name removed] teaching at [name removed] School which is a girl's school. You should be afraid of God. We warn you to leave your job as a teacher as soon as possible otherwise we will cut the heads off your children and will set light to your daughter. We will create a situation that you will regret. (Reid, 2010, p. 25)

By inculcating a climate of fear insurgents and their political sympathizers are able to extend their influence beyond their capacity to physically eliminate the broader movement for women's rights. Despite a historic – albeit marginal – precedent of women's participation in public life in Afghanistan, newer regressive forces have stigmatized the activity of women beyond the domestic sphere. As Reid (2009, p. 16) reports, women who take part in public life are often labelled 'infidels' and 'Christians', slurs dangerously suggestive of apostasy, and serve both as 'threats and as a means to shut down the substantive debate about the role of women'.

These problems are worsened by a political and legal system that is resistant or even 'ideologically hostile' to women's rights and freedoms (Reid, 2009). Failure of the police service to investigate or make arrests for crimes against women is common (Amnesty International, 2011b, p. 4), and many women, including some who work within law enforcement, express helplessness at an emerging culture of impunity, and the general lack of protection (Reid, 2009). Human Rights Watch report that women complaining of threats to their lives have often been advised by senior officers 'not to make enemies' especially where their activity is seen to trespass on Shari'a law (ibid.), a domain traditionally – but not exclusively – reserved for men. The combination of such physical and psychological violence have debilitating consequences for women's rights in Afghanistan. 'As a result', note the UNAMA (2009b, p. 1) 'women engage in self-censorship, restrict their movements or discontinue their work'. Women are dissuaded from political participation, standing for public office, or working in public service. This forms a vicious cycle, for without their participation in public life, women's interests cannot be effectively represented. Such politically sanctioned violence forms a fundamental challenge to Afghanistan's future development, and the well-being of its people.

Various sources report high rates of abuse of women by pro-government forces, security organizations, the military, foreign armed forces, and the justice system (UNAMA, 2009a, 2009b; Amnesty International, 2011b; Reid and Muhammedally, 2011; HRW, 2012). The alleged rate of procedural malpractice, as well as the abuse of female detainees by the police, prison and detention officers, for example, is disturbing.

Police corruption is widespread, and respect for the rights of both female victims, and suspected perpetrators of crime variable. Those unable to afford bribes are likely to face detention by exploitative officers (Atabay, 2007). Worse still, officers have been implicated in the abuse of female victims and 'perpetrators' of crime. Atabay (ibid., p. 25) reports a number of such cases, including the sexual assault by four police officers of a child rape victim, and 'persistent' reports documenting the rape of female inmates of the Welayat Kabul Detention Centre. Due to the stigma and fear of repercussions faced by women reporting sexual abuse, these are likely to represent only a small fraction of cases – a problem exacerbated by the number of 'private' prisons across the country, which, according to the Afghan Independent Human Rights Commission (AIHRC), are responsible for some of the most grievous cases of physical and psychological torture. To compound matters, officials frequently violate or neglect procedure, actively delay the legal counsel of women, and take advantage of the illiteracy of many detainees to gain confessions (UNAMA, 2009a). This severely disadvantages the poor, serving to perpetuate poverty, social exclusion, and the mistrust of governance.

The plight of women is worsened by their marginalization within a justice system that largely fails to recognize their equality before the law. Under prevailing interpretations of Shari'a, the testimony of female victims of sexual violence is rarely considered sufficient to prosecute a male accused of assault (Atabay, 2007). Furthermore, the reporting of sexual violence puts women at risk of 'honour-based' retaliation by their accused or other related parties, and leaves them vulnerable to accusations of *zina* (adultery). According to the UNAMA (2009a, p. 7), arbitrary detention and imprisonment for breaches of customary law, so-called 'moral crimes', disproportionately affect women and girls – accounting for 50 per cent of women in detention. *Zina* is illegal under both customary and statutory law in Afghanistan (Atabay, 2007), but the law provides no means of distinguishing between *zina* and rape. As such, all cases of extra-marital sex, consensual or otherwise, are considered adultery, for which both parties may be punished – often involving prison terms of at least five years (ibid.).

Where women fall under customary law – particularly under courts (*shuras* and *jirgas*) run by insurgent groups – conditions are often worse. The Taliban, known for inflicting harsh punishment, subject communities to a largely unaccountable shadow justice system. Punishments, including public execution, torture, and amputations (UNAMA, 2012), are often meted out for crimes ranging from murder to theft, suspected complicity with foreigners, or 'moral crimes' following a cursory trial. Examples of include the stoning of a young couple and a pregnant widow found guilty of 'adultery' in August 2010 (BBC, 2012), and the execution of a woman accused of adultery in Badghis after she was forced to abort her feotus (Amnesty International, 2011a). Evidence points to growing support for Taliban 'justice' – particularly in rural areas where harsh justice is seen to prevent anarchy (Giustozzi and Reuter, 2011).

The lack of accountability within these institutions poses a serious threat to the establishment of an equitable and effective justice system in Afghanistan. The failure in distinguishing between rape and *zina*, and the tenacity of unrecognized parallel penal codes also means that women and girls fleeing forced or abusive marriages, sexual exploitation by their families, or even reporting rape, may be punished unlawfully for 'moral crimes' (UNAMA, 2009a). Although false convictions of *zina* are allegedly falling (Reid, 2009), a report by the UNAMA (2009a, p. 7) found cases where female rape victims were charged with adultery in almost every province of Afghanistan, including cases where child victims of rape had subsequently been convicted.

Sexual violence against women, girls and boys, is prevalent (Reid and Muhammedally, 2011), and access to justice and redress rare (Reid, 2009). 'Women and girls are at risk of rape in their homes and in their communities, in detention facilities and as a result of traditional harmful practices to resolve feuds within the family or community' (UNAMA, 2009b. p. 2). Whilst a threat to the well-being of women globally, the threat of sexual violence is amplified in Afghanistan by widespread impunity and by the precedent of rape as a weapon of war in recent history. It is also facilitated through a number of traditional practices such as *baad*, which involves giving away girls as 'blood-price' to settle communal conflict caused by murder or adultery, and forced marriage (Nijhowne and Oates, 2008). Yet whilst historical and cultural narratives play a role in normalizing the abuse of women, the incidence of sexual violence has also increased through weak governance, and the proliferation of politically connected 'strongmen' throughout rural Afghanistan (Reid and Muhammedally, 2011). In their report on the use of local warlords to reinforce the ALP, Reid and Muhammedally (ibid.) underline the involvement of militias in assassination, torture, abductions, trafficking, rape, and exploitation of local people. 'Several interviewees', it is noted (ibid., p. 31), 'complained that the resurgence of the militias has legitimized the predatory behaviour that used to characterize the *mujahideen* forces'. The deterioration of security in Afghanistan has led many to favour the re-paramilitarization of the police as a means of tackling the insurgency. Whilst advocates insist that safeguards prevent the abuse of power and that care has been taken to engage local communities in selecting recruits, others question whether safeguards are adequate, pointing to widespread armament and ongoing abuses by the ALP in several provinces (Reid and Muhammedally, 2011). The risk of patronage and cronyism further complicates the issue. 'By 2011', note Guistozzi and Isaqzadeh (2011, p. 2), 'the MoI [Ministry of the Interior] was picking individuals deemed to be particularly committed to fighting the insurgents from the same old pool of former comrades in arms and political appointees'. This means militias are usually controlled by men 'whose source of protection extends into the heart of local and national government' (ibid.); they are unaccountable, and often comprise of former insurgents, with little interest in the rights of civilians.

In the private sphere, a number of harmful 'traditional' practices, including forced marriage, *baad* and *baadal*,[1] 'honour' killings, and (forced) self-immolation, threaten the well-being of women. These are compounded by a high rate of domestic violence, poverty, and no access to services such as education and health care. The practice of *baad* forms a most grievous threat to well-being. Whilst illegal and opposed by many Afghans, the practice remains common (UNAMA, 2010). Girls given through *baad* are likely to be at significant threat of abuse.

Both *baad* and forced marriage serve to reinforce and perpetuate related 'traditional' practices of 'honour' killing, and voluntary and forced suicide. The former, a problem that is exclusive to neither Afghanistan or Islam, has earned considerable infamy. 'Honour' killings, whilst illegal under statutory law in Afghanistan, are nevertheless prevalent amongst rural Pashtun communities (ibid.). Justifications for the practice derive from a woman's role as the 'bearer' of family honour. Where the 'immoral' behaviour of a woman compromises family honour, she risks brutal punishment. The boundaries of what constitutes 'moral' offence are expansive, and thousands of women are believed to face murder for fleeing marriage, inappropriate conduct with men, or elopement (ibid.).

Whilst the EVAW law is a positive development for eliminating violence against women, inherent weaknesses within it, political and social obstruction to reform, entrenched discrimination, and widespread poverty and weak governance, frustrate its effectiveness. Whilst conditions vary by province, women in Afghanistan are broadly subject to debilitating levels of physical and psychological violence. Such violence spills over to threaten the future security of children and communities more broadly, and without redress represents a severe threat to the future social, political and economic development of Afghanistan and its people.

VIOLENCE AGAINST CHILDREN

As discussed, insurgents have directly targeted teachers, schools, and children in a campaign to prevent the education of girls and undermine trust in the state. Since 2004, AIHRC (2009) estimate that more than 300 schools have been burned out or shut down as a consequence of attacks or threats by insurgents. The destruction of schools and attacks on teachers have meant that in rural areas children have to travel long, and potentially dangerous, distances to receive education (HRW, 2006). Human Rights Watch document a number of cases where insurgents have directly attacked children, including the poisoning of over 100 girls and women teachers in Kunduz province and Kabul in 2010, and an acid attack on five girls in Kandahar (Reid, 2010). Following the ousting of the Taliban in 2001, tremendous progress has been made with increasing access to education for both boys and girls. The World Bank estimates that child enrolment in school increased from approximately 774000 in the years prior to the Bonn Agreement, to some 5.2 million by 2005. Unfortunately this progress now faces reversal. In southern provinces in particular, the number of girls enrolling in education has started to plateau. A rise in attacks on schools have forced many girls out of education, and where negotiations with the Taliban have been successful, the 'price' has involved replacing 'unacceptable' teachers and curricula with those approved by insurgents (Guistozzi, 2010a).

A number of 'traditional' practices also adversely affect children. Many of these are exacerbated by institutional failure, weak governance and ongoing conflict. Whilst the prevalence of sexual violence suffered by women and girls has been discussed, it is noteworthy that the abuse of both boys and girls is rife, reinforced by under-reporting, misplaced shame, a climate of impunity, and a lack of clear definition within law (UNSC, 2011). For girls and young women, practices such as *baad* and forced marriage increase the risk of sexual exploitation. The sexual abuse of young boys, however, forms an additional and particularly shadowy threat to children (ibid.). The practice of *baccha baazi*, where boys from poor families are used to entertain businessmen or other powerful figures, often involves sexual abuse. Whilst the proliferation of militias in many regions of rural Afghanistan amplifies risk (Reid and Muhammedally, 2011), members of the Afghan National Army and Police Force, have also been implicated (ibid.). Corruption and weak governance fuels a climate of impunity for the politically well connected. The lack of protection from retaliation, and failure to provide support to victims compound matters, deterring the reporting of crimes and forcing the problem underground. Child victims of rape and sexual abuse may also be accused of *zina* and subsequently punished.

Endemic levels of poverty and illiteracy exacerbate these problems. Poverty drives a range of health problems, forms a barrier to education, and increases vulnerability to various forms of exploitation. Furthermore, whilst 'cultural norms' – such as the importance placed on virginity – play a role in practices such as forced marriage, poverty often forms a more direct influence. Aside from the immediate threats to a girl's rights, forced marriage often prevents girls from continuing with education, and is 'the most lasting and destructive of [practices] in the scale of its consequences' (UNAMA, 2010, p. 53). Literacy for people over the age of 15 in Afghanistan stands at 28 per cent, and for women at 12.6 per cent (ibid.). Depriving girls of education not only generates problems for Afghanistan's social and economic development, but also drives deleterious consequences for human security at the individual and broader social level.

Poverty in Afghanistan may also put children at risk of labour exploitation, which is in turn detrimental to health, and limits access to education (World Bank, 2005; IOM, 2008). According to the International Organization for Migration (IOM, 2008), destitution forms a major reason for why some parents in Afghanistan sell their children, and thus forms a significant 'push' factor in human trafficking. Impoverished, illiterate minors – both boys and girls – form a large proportion of trafficking and kidnap victims in Afghanistan, and are frequently used for forced labour or sexual exploitation. Coercive (mis)treatment is common, and may include physical and psychological abuse, confinement and enslavement (IOM, 2008).

RELIGIOUS AND CULTURAL VIOLENCE

A primordialist bias features at the heart of much analysis concerning Afghanistan. For many, this is likely because violence in the country betrays an unmistakable religious or cultural temper. The disproportionate suffering of women, girls and minorities, often justified through appeals to Shari'a, does little to dispel presumptions that religion is less than a key determinant of violence. This, of course, accords with stereotypes framing Islam as a faith with a proclivity for political violence and the marginalization of women. It is a religion, according to Haynes (2009, p. 55) that is seen by some as 'inherently undemocratic or even anti-democratic', and by others as 'vigorously fundamentalist' (Gellner, in Marranci, 2010). 'Within the Western psyche', notes Marsden (1998, p. 57), 'there appears to be an almost paranoid fear of Islam as something wild, mindless and potentially overwhelming'. However misrepresentative such analysis may be, it is strengthened by the fact that much violence in Afghanistan, whether against NATO forces, or civilians, is justified in religious terms. Statements issued by the Taliban and other insurgents are replete with jihadist rhetoric and claims that the intervention is a direct attack on Islam. Johnson (2007), for instance, describes how certain *shabnameh* insinuate a Western agenda to destroy madrassahs and establish secular schools in an attempt to convert Afghan children to Christianity. Broader allusions to the Palestinian issue offer further confirmation of religious inspiration, and echo the rhetoric of the Wahhabis and Islamists. The continued campaign of violence against civilians, including the use of suicide bombers, are accompanied by Qur'anic verses that apparently justify such actions, and Taliban relations with terrorist groups like al-Qaeda entrench the notion that the conflict is one driven by myopic religious fundamentalism.

Arguments that explain violence in Afghanistan as *fundamentally* about religion falter under closer analysis, however. First, as discussed below, the extent to which the Taliban and the ideology they espouse may be seen as products of either Afghanistan's history or Islamic tradition, is limited. Second, relations between the Taliban and global jihadism, are tenuous. Whilst the Taliban provided sanctuary for groups like al-Qaeda, their own vision was a national one, more concerned with Islam in Afghanistan than pan-Islamism (Marsden, 1998) – the rhetoric for which has only recently appeared within insurgent statements (Johnson, 2007). Third, whilst religion plays a fundamental role in Afghanistan, it has traditionally not represented a political force. Certainly, Islam had been drawn on as a means of uniting a diffuse population, but 'Muslim clerics had always been servants of the state, and not its masters' (Barfield, 2010, p. 263). This suggests that the Taliban movement reflected a new, rather than historical, phenomenon. Finally, whilst much has been made of the proclivity to political violence within Islam, this does not reflect the majority of Muslims who emphasize Islam as a religion of peace. Islam is no more inherently violent than any religious tradition. Whilst this forms part of a larger debate with a vast literature, it suffices to note that for every Qur'anic verse that appears to justify violence, another serves to abrogate or condemn it.

Less easy to dismiss, perhaps, is the relationship between religion and the violence experienced by women and girls, particularly given the widespread 'perception of Islam as a religion that is oppressive towards women' (Marsden, 1998, p. 57). The inescapable question, is whether the violence and discrimination experienced by women in Afghanistan is symptomatic of a inherent prejudice towards women within Islam – one merely exacerbated by factors like conflict, weak governance, or poverty. Primordialists are not alone in this concern, 'many, including those who reject religious reductionism, have questioned the compatibility of Islamic philosophy and law with the International Bill of Human Rights in general, and with the principle of gender equity in particular' (Arat, 2000, p. 69). Certainly, the forms of violence detailed above are not unique to Afghanistan, and similar forms of discrimination have precedent within other Islamic societies. Various readings and interpretations of the Qur'an are put forward as evidence for the codified inferiority of women in Islam. Whilst the Qur'an, for instance, emphasizes the equality of men and women in their obligations towards God (Arat, 2000), variant readings of the contested *Surah* 4:34, may suggest men's superiority over women, and legitimizes violence towards them:

> Men are in charge of women by [right of] what Allah has given one over the other and what they spend [for maintenance] from their wealth. So righteous women are devoutly obedient, guarding in [the husband's] absence what Allah would have them guard. But those [wives] from whom you fear arrogance – [first] advise them; [then if they persist], forsake them in bed; and [finally], strike them. But if they obey you [once more], seek no means against them.

The regulation of women's lives through Shari'a law has also received criticism for discriminating against women, and institutionalizing marginalization. Whilst interpretations of Shari'a vary widely, it has been used to justify and enforce policies that restrict women's freedom of movement, their right to work, dress, and regulate even their reproductive rights.

Such arguments, however, neglect the contention within Islam over the interpretation of Qur'anic revelation. Essentializing Islam ignores the reality that it 'is experienced, practiced, and interpreted quite differently over time and space . . . It is fundamentally "plastic"' (Moghadam, 2003, p. 8). For Moghadam, understanding the broader socio-political and economic order in which Islam is practised is infinitely more helpful than whether the Qur'an as a text restricts or emancipates women. Religious texts are also inherently interpretable, and many arguments miss the myriad interpretations of verses such as 4:34. Other parts of the Qur'an, in contrast, expressly vilify forms of violence such as rape. Essentialism also serves to dehistoricize the complex role of women within the religion through a number of normative judgements. As was true in Afghanistan for instance (Marsden, 1998), the veil, often regarded as an instrument of oppression, has also historically served as a symbol of prestige (Moghadam, 2003). Finally, through many periods of history, Islamic countries have been more progressive than Christian ones. 'Islam', notes Moghadam (2003, p. 6) for instance, 'provided women with property rights for centuries, while women in Europe were denied the same rights'. Even today, 'there are marked variations in the legal status, economic conditions, and social positions of women'. The position of Muslim women, therefore, has 'more to do with developmental issues – the extent of urbanization, industrialization and proletarianization, as well as the political ploys of state managers'; 'class', also, plays a key role (ibid.).

Accounts of violence in Afghanistan nevertheless appear to vindicate those that emphasize Islam as the source of gender violence in the country. This appears particularly evident during Taliban rule, where severe policies were often justified through appeals to Islam:

> It is a matter of pride for all Afghanistan that we have kept our women at home . . . The Shari'a has described everyone's way of conduct . . . We have given women the rights that God and his Messenger have instructed, that is to stay in their homes and to gain religious instruction in hejab [seclusion]. (Marsden, 1998, p. 98)

Attempts by foreign human rights workers to improve conditions in the country, were additionally decried as attacks on the faith: 'Let us state what sort of education the UN wants. This is a big infidel policy which gives such obscene freedom to women which would lead to adultery and herald the destruction of Islam' (Rashid, 2002, p. 111).

Further instances, including the persecution of the Shi'a Hazara people – which has led to a number of massacres, including the torture and murder of 11 Hazara men in 2010 (Maley, 2011) – also appear sanctioned under the Taliban's interpretation of the faith: 'Hazaras are not Muslim, they are Shia. They are [*kuffar* – non-believers] . . . wherever you go we will catch you. If you go up, we will pull you down by your feet; if you hide below, we will pull you up by your hair' (Brahimi, 2010, p. 11).

It is important to note that such a severe interpretation of Islam formed an aberration, rather than a continuation, of the Afghan Islamic tradition, however. Certainly, it is undeniable that Islam has been historically fundamental to life in Afghanistan, yet Afghans also consider their interpretation of Islam to be irreproachable (Barfield, 2010), and whilst the Deobandi[2] elements of the Taliban's creed had precedent, much of their radical and conflict-oriented ideology was considered alien. Indeed, rather than proving a source of division, conflict and insurgency, Islam – with some notable exceptions – had served to promote unity and facilitate governance in Afghanistan (Barfield,

2010, p. 337). The Afghan Islamic tradition has also been traditionally tolerant towards other faiths (Brahimi, 2010), and socially progressive. No Afghan ruler, for instance, had ever insisted that women wear the *burqa*, and as Afghanistan started to modernize in the 1950s–1960s, women 'exchanged their traditional clothes for skirts, high heels and make-up'; 40 per cent of women in Kabul held jobs (Rashid, 2002, p. 110). Neither have progressive aspirations disappeared. Surveys indicate that a majority of Afghans wish to educate their daughters, but are constrained by poverty or for fears over their safety. Furthermore:

> history shows that Afghans, women and men, are intuitively conscious of their inherent human rights given that many fundamental rights are espoused in the teachings of Islam. Each time Afghans have been consulted on the issue of justice, they have voted overwhelmingly for a just, free, fair and inclusive society. (UNAMA, 2009b, p. 9)

Despite the incongruities between the Islam practised by the Taliban and that native to the country, it is nevertheless still difficult to entirely dismiss the role of religion as an intervening variable in the violence of the last two decades. Several policies, including the ban imposed on music and film, and attempts made to 'eliminate all images of living things (going so far as to black out pictures of cows on imported cans of dried milk)' (Barfield, 2010, p. 261), are consistent with some conservative interpretations of Islam (Marsden, 1998). Also, whilst discrimination against the Shi'a may reflect ethnic tensions, the broader lack of an ethnic dimension to violence in Afghanistan suggests such persecution is sanctioned in religious terms. It is also difficult to overlook religion considering the way discrimination has become institutionalized via religious pathways such as the Shari'a. Religion, however, needs to be understood as an intervening, rather than an independent variable (Hasenclever and Rittberger, 2000) on violence in Afghanistan, and is ineluctably bound to historical struggles for power and influence.

The similarities in the nature of violence and discrimination experienced by women are nonetheless disquietening, and practices such as forced – and child – marriage, mutilation, and 'honour' killings, suggest some underlying influence. Where religion fails to serve as a reliable explanation, others have suggested that violence, including practices such as 'wife abuse . . . genital mutilation and "honour killings"' may be more due to *culture* (Summary, Douki et al., 2002). Several historians (Montgomery Watt, 1956; Schimmel, 1992) note that much of the violence experienced by women in contemporary Islamic societies, is due not to Islam but to the failed reform of various pre-Islamic cultural traditions (*jahiliyya*) of the region. 'Pre-Islamic Arab women', explains Brown (2009, p. 26), 'endured a hellish existence. If a girl survived to adulthood, she would find herself essentially the property of her father, then her husband, with no economic or social independence or rights'. *Diyyat* – a form of 'blood-payment' (Hallaq, 1997), and the 'disposal' of girl children (Brown, 2009), were also common. The extent to which this analysis is representative of *all* pre-Islamic societies remains questionable (Brown, 2009), but it is generally agreed that for many women Islam brought an *improvement*, rather than a decline, in rights (Montgomery Watt, 1956; Schimmel, 1992).

A focus on local cultural traditions rather than Islam as the 'problem' (Marranci, 2010), has important consequences for understanding violence in Afghanistan, which is often, as noted, attributed to the 'medieval' nature of Afghan culture (Barfield, 2010). Even the UN, in a report on harmful 'traditional' practices such as 'honour' killings, notes: 'Such murders are not based on religion but on deeply rooted cultural beliefs' (UNAMA, 2010, p. 47). Whilst the cultural traditions of other ethnic groups, including those of minorities such as the Hazara, have received criticism for their treatment of women, it is the tribal Pashtun culture, and the historic code of *pashtunwali*, that is more often singled out as the core of Afghan resistance to governance, and as being most detrimental to the well-being of women, children and minority groups. 'Honour' killings, *baachi baazi*, child marriage, and *baad*, are reported as more pervasive amongst the Pashtun than amongst other ethnic groups of Afghanistan (UNAMA, 2010), and the *pashtunwali*, with its focus on *purdah*, is argued to be the source of discrimination against women. It is the Pashtun who are overwhelmingly seen as the source of cultural and kinetic resistance to intervention, a people and region 'steeped in cussedness' (Coll, 2004), inherently incompatible with modernity. As Churchill (1898, p. 17) wrote: 'Their [the Pashtun] system of ethics, which regards treachery and violence as virtues rather than vices, has produced a code of honour so strange and inconsistent that it is incomprehensible to a logical mind'.

Such perspectives have contributed to views that the Taliban itself, having originated in the Pashtun heartland of Kandahar, represent an attempt to reassert Pashtun dominance – a theory disputed by many Pashtun. 'Although they justified their rule in Islamic terms' notes Barfield (2010, p. 279), 'the Taliban were largely Pashtuns who saw all other ethnic groups as enemies'. The notion of the 'revenge of the pashtuns' (Roy, 1998, p. 207):

> [coincided] with a wider sense of frustration among the pashtun population who . . . resented the fact that Kabul was in the hands of non-pashtuns . . . the long beards and turbans which became the Taliban hallmark had long been part of Kandahari culture – in a sense, the Taliban sought to universalize a specifically pashtun custom and enforce its adoption across Afghanistan, as a visible expression of piety but also as a symbol of the Taliban's political monopoly. (Brahimi, 2010, p. 11)

Blaming 'culture' or 'ethnicity' as a driver of violence, whilst an understandable means of avoiding the political minefield of blaming 'religion', is nevertheless as flawed analytically, and for many, as equally offensive. First, it is debateable whether 'religion' and 'culture' may be so easily separated; the very prospect seems to suggest the two are somehow discrete, objectively dissimilar domains. And second, *essentializing* culture – treating it as a coherent, undifferentiated, and inherited condition – is, like religion, theoretically and empirically problematic. This is certainly true for Afghanistan, which, comprising over 55 distinct ethnic groups (Nigel and Allan, 2001) each with different – if related – histories, resists any meaningful generalization (Rashid, 2002). Furthermore, vilification of the Pashtun and the *pashtunwali* also essentializes Pashtun culture, neglecting the difference across the Pashtun community itself. Rashid (2002), for instance, notes that Pashtuns in eastern Afghanistan demonstrate considerable variance in cultural attitudes, and proudly educated their daughters, even under the Taliban. Despite Western prejudices over religious or cultural opposition to girls' education in Afghanistan, it is critical to note that this issue has been de-politicized. Control over schools and curricula has, over the last century, served as a conduit for political ideology, and the exclusion of girls should not be seen as a simple reflection of cultural attitudes towards girl's education – which for the most part, are favourable. Similarly, whilst the *pashtunwali* involves several practices detrimental to well-being, the extent of demonization is troubling, especially given the lack of knowledge concerning it (Rzehak, 2011).

Claims of Pashtun 'nationalism' also face problems (Marsden, 1998; Johnson and Mason, 2007). For one, 'the Taliban have insisted that the movement is open to all Afghans and it is clear that some of the adherents are, indeed, non-Pushtuns' (Marsden, 1998, p. 44; see also Giustozzi, 2010b). Furthermore, aside from the persecution of Hazaras, who are generally vilified in sectarian terms, the Taliban rarely use the inflammatory rhetoric typical of ethnic conflicts. The decline in support following their capture of Afghanistan was no less prevalent in the Pashtun regions than elsewhere, and indeed, the Taliban alienated many Pashtuns, purging village elders, and enforcing unpopular taxation and conscription on communities (Brahimi, 2010). The relationship between insurgency and the Pashtun 'tribes' is complex, and whilst ties exist – due more to the social deprivation of southern Afghanistan (Johnson and Mason, 2007) – it should be noted that many Pashtuns are angered at conflation with a group (Rashid, 2006) that has intimidated communities, and 'devitalized' the *pashtunwali* (Hughes, 2011).

THE 'NEW WAR' IN AFGHANISTAN

The conflict in Afghanistan appears in many ways an archetypal 'new war' (Kaldor, 2002). It is rooted in the disintegration of political legitimacy following the collapse of the Soviet Union, and aggravated by factional 'private' militias, each attempting to capture resources for personal enrichment. The murder, rape and exploitation of civilians as a means of control is widespread, and save for superficial references to Islam there is a distinct absence of ideology. The Taliban, formed largely from the masses of displaced and disillusioned Afghan refugees, were another of these groups. In contrast with the Mujahideen, however, the Taliban structured their legitimacy around the restoration moral order in Afghanistan, and defined themselves against the self-interested excesses of the warlords. Although refugees themselves, the Taliban capitalized on an identity politics built around the vision of decontaminating Afghanistan of foreigners and modern foreign influences. They are an anti-modern movement (Rashid, 2002), exploiting religion as a uniting force, 'a form of political mobilization, a survival tactic' (Kaldor, 2002, p. 82).

New wars theory provides a powerful framework for understanding conflict in Afghanistan – especially with its focus on governance, globalization, and the failures of leaders to maintain legitimacy. Illumination of how elites secure legitimacy and mobilize support from generally conflict-averse citizens through invocation of nostalgia, religion and history correlates well, as does the notion that beyond such mythmaking there is little ideological coherence. As the Taliban increased control over Afghanistan, their inability to govern the country soon became apparent and resulted in the decay of state institutions. Whilst opium production was banned for ordinary Afghans on religious grounds, religious sanction was soon found when needed: the means of corruption, it would seem, were merely captured. The Taliban, like other groups threatened by globalization and 'liberal' state-building, are for new wars theorists no more than a predatory elite. Their appeal to national, cultural and religious values, alongside the laws and social restrictions they put in place, are merely tools allowing them to gain and maintain power. Through violence, and the regulation of access to education and other services, the group are able to maintain the social conditions on which the illusion of their authority depends. Violence, however brutal, serves to maintain power. The use of children as suicide bombers or runners, for instance, is explained not as a result of ideology, but pragmatism: children are simply more cost-efficient and controllable than adults (Boyden and de Berry, 2004).

Yet new wars thesis is not without problems. For one, it tends to depoliticize conflict and endangers stripping actors, and often populations, of their political grievances, reducing them to criminality. This is true of Afghanistan. The criminalization of the Taliban and other insurgents is a common narrative, but understanding of these groups, and their potential grievances, is far from complete. As Marsden (1998, p. 65) notes, for instance, 'there are enormous differences within the ranks of the Taliban as regards gender and other issues, including the relationship with the west. There is the usual spectrum from hard-line to relatively moderate that is to be found in any radical movement'. In essentializing the group, the model neglects differentiation, and the local immaterial forces that influence the behaviour of ordinary people.

At the theoretical level there are also problems with regard to the causes of conflict and nature of violence. Evidence shows that religion, ethnicity and culture are perhaps not as inert as political-economists suppose, and can also serve to constrain elite action. There is an overemphasis of elites, which neglects the probability that conflicts are embedded in broader social relations. The use of rational choice theory in explaining the nature of violence also neglects the fact that actors do not always behave in their own interests. By assuming that they do, theorists often miss the context in which violence takes place and the immaterial factors and narratives that inform behaviour at the local level. This is particularly salient with regard to apparently incomprehensible forms of violence such as that against women. Whilst it has been argued that permissive attitudes towards violence against women may have instrumental value as a means of securing loyalties from male volunteers (Rashid, 2002), explanation for *why* this should be, and why a perceived 're-sexualization' of violence (Mello, 2010) is characteristic of new wars, is not provided. Whilst new wars theory provides a powerful lens through which to view conflict in Afghanistan, material interests alone are unable to wholly explain violence.

TOWARDS UNDERSTANDING

In a country such as Afghanistan, where religion forms a fundamental part of life, it would be disingenuous to dismiss it as merely an 'excuse' for conflict, or to ignore its symbolic role in legitimizing violence. Yet treating religion or culture as unproblematic variables is also empirically unviable, and can lead to fatalism. Constructivists, in contrast, treat phenomena such as religion and ethnicity as discursive, 'inter-subjective structures' capable of 'intervening between a given conflict and the choice of conflict behaviour' (Hasenclever and Rittberger, 2000, p. 649):

> In this way the impact of religious traditions on conflict behaviour is deeply ambiguous: they can make violence more likely, insofar as a reading of holy texts prevails that justifies armed

> combat. On the other hand, they can make violence less likely, insofar as a reading of holy texts prevails that delegitimises the use of violence in a given situation or even generally. (Ibid., pp. 649–50)

Whilst power and interests remain important for understanding elite motivation, constructivists emphasize that 'interests' themselves are determined by identity (Wendt, 1995). 'Constructivists', notes Reus-Smit (2009, p. 221), 'are not opposed to the idea that actors might be self interested', 'but they argue that this tells us nothing unless we understanding how actors define their "selves", and how this informs their "interests"'. Religions serve to condition actors' identities, which in turn inform their material interests and actions (ibid.). 'Through reciprocal interaction', states Wendt (1992, p. 406) 'we create and instantiate the relatively enduring social structures in terms of which we define our identities and interests'. While this means structures are unfixed, it also means that partisan interests can be conflated with religion, and thus institutionalized. They are then difficult to contend without challenging the spiritual, as well as the political, order.

Elites remain important for constructivists.Whilst actors might engage in violence without leaders, it is argued that they will not 'start systematic, sustained campaigns of violence to achieve their goals' (Carnegie Commission, 1997, p. 30). Achieving broader social support for campaigns of violence is crucial for elites, but may be helped through successful appeal to common religious, ideological, or historic narratives (Hasenclever and Rittberger, 2000, p. 649). Through appropriating and distorting common mythologies, leaders may 'lay claim to a single and absolutist religious interpretation at the cost of all others, and they link their interpretation to political power objectives' (Holenstein, 2005, p. 11, in Haynes, 2009). The potential advantage of spiritual legitimacy is great. For one, access to 'spiritual capital' (Verter, 2003) allows actors to engage in 'symbolic politics' (Kaufman, 2006), providing an expedient means of eliminating rivals. 'Identifying the claims of one party with the commands of God or the cosmic order gives them an uncontestestable superiority over competing claims which now appear to be blasphemic having no moral justification at all' (Hasenclever and Rittberger, 2000, pp. 655–66).

Second, invocations of symbols and myths, provided they successfully *resonate* with audiences (Johnson, 2007), appeal emotionally:

> The symbolic politics argument asserts that ordinary people choose emotionally among competing values and leaders by responding to the most evocative symbol presented to them. Symbols are powerful because they simultaneously refer to an interest and to an emotionally laden myth, often framing a conflict of interest as a struggle against hostile, evil, or subhuman forces. (Kaufman, 2006, p. 52)

Myths, or 'narratives', note Johnson (2007, p. 319), reflect foundational beliefs that:

> articulate a group's views towards the world . . . There is ample evidence that such artefacts have an effect on our capacity to recall events, motivate action, modulate our emotional reactions to events, cue certain heuristics and biases, structure our problem-solving capabilities and ultimately influence our very identity.

Where conflicts are thus 'spiritualized', they crystallize around feelings of fear or anger, are framed by leaders as a struggle for basic identity (Juergensmeyer, 2003), and become enmeshed in 'exclusive accounts of the nature of reality' (Kurtz, 1995, in Haynes, 2009, p. 54). Such exclusivity limits the space for dialogue and understanding between groups, severely eroding trust.

Agents, however, should not be understood merely as 'atomistic egoists' but deeply social, their interests conditioned by and contingent on the constitutive social realm. 'Agents and structures, are *mutually* constituted' (Reus-Smit, 2009; emphasis added). The reciprocal process of reconstruction between agents and structures means that actors, their identities, ideologies and actions must be understood within their social context. This also means that elites must be able to convince the community of their interpretation of religion or culture. In Afghanistan, this is helped where people lack the knowledge or resources to challenge interpretations; in other cases, brutality may nudge communities towards compliance. Whilst instrumentalists consider the capacity of actors to exploit structures – or, as Kaufman (2006, p. 55) describes them 'myth-symbol complexes' – as 'virtually unlimited', a key point of dissent for constructivists is that they have a 'life of their own', and may resist exploitation (Hasenclever and Rittberger, 2000). For Kaufman, they are deeply embedded in social relations, and whilst 'malleable to some degree, [typically have] deep roots in history and culture that cannot be easily ignored . . . ' A group's ability to instrumentalize a given myth-symbol complex is therefore 'limited by the cultural context in which they operate' (2006, pp. 50–51). Religion or culture may therefore *constrain* elite action, and delegitimize violence, irrespective of broader economic interests.

An important contribution of constructivist theory is the idea that violence may provide symbolic, as well as strategic, functions. Whilst certain forms of extreme violence or discrimination may lack instrumental value, neither are they entirely irrational. Excessively cruel or ritualistic practices likely bear symbolic value in relation to embedded and 'value-laden' (Hasenclever and Rittberger, 2000) concepts of self and others within society. This is important regarding organized gender violence, argued as an irrational, but inevitable consequence of conflict. As Boyden and de Berry (2004) note drawing on Graca Machel (2000), however, systematic rape and other violent practices may serve to humiliate the enemy or efface religious beliefs. For Kaufman, the reason why violence appears irrational is because conflicts are driven by appeals to emotion, especially fear. Emotions 'help people set priorities among competing goals: fear, for example, causes people to prioritize security over other values such as wealth. Studies have shown that attitudes that originally formed emotionally are more responsive to emotional than to intellectual appeals' (2006, p. 51).

VIOLENCE AND THE TALIBAN

How then, may we understand the apparent perpetuity of violence in Afghanistan, both in terms of conflict, but also in terms of the experiences of women, children and minorities? Does religion 'make a difference' (Hasenclever and Rittberger, 2000), in inspiring or sanctioning violence?

Many reports and analyses of violence in Afghanistan emphasize the threat played by the Taliban and other religious groups to human security (HRW, 2006; UNAMA, 2009b, 2010, 2011a, 2011b; 2012; Reid, 2010; UNSC, 2011; Guistozzi and Ibrahimi,

2012). Whilst other sources of violence are important, the difficulties in restoring peace, stability and human rights to Afghanistan are more often blamed on insurgents. 'Religious' or 'cultural' explanations for these problems rely on groups such as the Taliban being representative of Islam or Afghan culture. It is fair to say that the Taliban do have social roots within the networks of rural madrassahs across Afghanistan. As a social class, village *talibs* (typically poor religious 'students'; *lit.* 'seeker') have been a feature of rural Afghan society throughout history (Johnson, 2007). Links with the Pashtun and Pashtun culture, as noted, are also difficult to dismiss. Furthermore, whilst the degree to which the group were seen as legitimate when they initially rose to power is difficult to estimate, it is certain that some people supported them. In war-torn rural regions, the Taliban promised a return to order, the restoration of morality and justice, and proved capable in this regard (Marsden, 1998).

Yet beyond this, their representativeness falters. Emerging 'as if from nowhere' (ibid.), and comprised largely of refugee youth, the historical and social representativeness of the Taliban is, for one, problematic. Poorly educated:

> many of these young warriors did not even know the history of their own country or the story of the jihad against the Soviets. . . . They had no memories of their tribes, their elders, their neighbours nor the complex ethnic mix of peoples that often made up their villages and their homeland. . . . They were literally the orphans of the war, [and] they admired war because it was the only occupation they could possibly adapt to. (Rashid, 2002, p. 32)

Regarding 'tribal' or 'ethnic' allegiances, whilst the group is predominately made up of Pashtuns it is not exclusively so, and cannot be seen as a simple expression of either Pashtun culture or the *pashtunwali* (Johnson and Mason, 2007; Rashid, 2006). In terms of composition, the Taliban are constituted of myriad elements. Such, notes Barfield (2010, p. 275), were crucial for their success:

> Whilst the Taliban had come close to gaining total control of the country by 2001, it had done so only by increasing the numbers of Pakistanis, Arabs, and other foreign fighters in its ranks. Afghans resented such outside interference in their affairs, particularly the common Pakistani boast that Afghanistan had become its 'fifth province'.

Their eclectic make-up, lack of religious authority, and inexperience in religious law, left the group vulnerable to reactionary and largely foreign ideologies, and suggestions that the Taliban are in any way representative of Islam, or even the Afghan Islamic tradition, has been fiercely contested (Rashid, 2002). The version of Islam and Shari'a espoused by the group is highly idiosyncratic, and historically unpredecented in Afghanistan. Their 'religious ideology was a crude mixture of Salafi Islam and Pashtunwali' (Barfield, 2010, p. 261), and whilst the group's affinity with the Deobandi tradition complemented the Hanafi Islamic tradition of Afghanistan, their interpretation was taken 'to extremes the school's founders would not have recognised' (Johnson and Mason, 2007, p. 75). Indeed, many of the impositions and restrictions introduced into Afghanistan under the guise of religious tradition were 'not local custom at all', the persecution of Sufis, the banning of music and film, and the introduction of punishments such as amputation for theft, or burying homosexuals alive, had not been seen in Afghanistan for generations (Barfield, 2010). Yet the Taliban did not care for criticism – whatever the authority. For Rashid (2002, pp. 87–8), they 'represented nobody but themselves and they recognized no Islam except their own'. Whilst not entirely unfamiliar, the Taliban could be seen as the product of modernity and social dislocation – a synthetic and stray culture.

If the representativeness of the Taliban is in doubt, how then are we to explain their initial rise to power and recent resurgence, including reports (Johnson, 2007) that they are regaining support amongst some communities? One simple explanation, of course, is fear. People recognize that coalition forces will not remain in Afghanistan indefinitely, and the Taliban have made it clear that those who 'collude' with foreigners or the government, will be punished when they return (ibid.). The dissemination of blacklists bearing names of 'traitors', and the brutal mutilation or execution of those tried and found guilty of 'collusion', reinforce this threat. Where security is lax, particularly in rural regions, supporting the Taliban may reflect a prudent judgement that rural areas may once more soon be at the mercy of insurgents.

The diminishing legitimacy of both the NATO intervention and the Karzai government form a second factor. On the one hand this has resulted from broader failures in delivering meaningful development or institutional reform in terms of security, economic growth, or infrastructure to the lives of most people – especially southern Pashtuns (ibid.). Weaknesses in goverance, poor decision-making and chronic underfunding underpin a litany of development failures and endemic levels of corruption. The failures to provide adequate security for rural areas is especially troubling. For many rural Afghans memories of the Mujahideen period remain keen: the 'paramilitarization' of the countryside may prove a strategically expedient measure, but could duly risk undermining rural support. Yet the intervention's legitimacy has also suffered for a series of incidents that anger and alienate ordinary Afghans. The increased use of night-raids and drone attacks have resulted in more civilian casualties. Furthermore, alleged instances of Qur'an burning, and evidence of the abuse of civilians by military personnel plays directly into the hands of insurgents who can justify retaliatory violence as a *defensive* strategy.

Yet it is the Taliban's ability for appropriating religious, cultural and historical narratives that forms the third and most compelling factor in explaining their support. As discussed, narratives and symbols play a crucial role in sustaining myth-symbol complexes. This has been particularly effective with regard to the group's exploitation of fears – particularly within rural areas – of the threats posed by foreign, modern influences and the decay of morality and justice that follows them. The ability to provide security and justice, as Marsden (1998) notes, formed the kernel of the group's original appeal especially in conflict-wracked Kandahar. Prior to the Taliban, the civil war in Afghanistan exposed civilians here to extreme violence, including the widespread rape of women, girls and boys. The notion of 'protection' and even salvation, is one deeply embedded in a number of tales concerning the group's social origins. One is recorded thus:

> On 20 September 1994, a Herati family, while on its way to Kandahar from Herat, was stopped at a check point ninety kilometres short of Kandahar by local *mujahideen* bandits. The men and women were separated. The boys were taken away and molested. The girls were repeatedly raped until they became unconscious. Later all of them were killed and their bodies partially burnt. It was Mullah Omar (sometimes referred to as Mullah Mujahid) who was the first to arrive on the scene. He is reported to have gathered some *talibs* who helped him in collecting the bodies. These were washed and given a decent burial. He then gathered the [religious] students and pledged to start a campaign to get rid of such criminals. (Brahimi, 2010, p. 3)

The re-establishment of law, order and justice to Afghanistan was, for the Taliban, contingent on purification. This was reflected in an effort to eliminate not only the warlords, but also the 'corrupt, western-oriented timeservers' (Marsden, 1998, p. 65), and all traces of modern, foreign influence and ideology. The harshest 'purification' was reserved for the cities. 'The population of Kabul' notes Marsden (ibid.):

> has perhaps been singled out as in need of particular corrective action. [The Taliban] have viewed Kabul as a centre of liberalism, at best, and decadence, at worst. It is also seen as the source of both the socialist and Islamist movements, which, they feel, have brought ruin on Afghanistan.

Through laws stipulating moral conduct, appropriate dress and behaviour, social life was heavily regulated. The ceremonial destruction of music tapes, films, and other vestiges of modernity, served to symbolically reinforce this crusade against corrupting foreign influences. The extent to which the Taliban went in order to ban music, dancing and singing, underscores an aversion to 'culture' that, perhaps, not only reminded the dislocated *talibs* of their social estrangement, but also formed a contested territory, a means of controlling ontological narratives and the elements that constitute broader myth-symbol complexes – a process Kinnvall (2004) labels, 'securitizing subjectivity'.

Narratives of purification and protection are bound with invocations of the sacred, and their role as an Islamic movement forms the core of Taliban legitimacy. From the outset, the Taliban framed themselves as an Islamic reform movement (Rashid, 2002, p. 87). 'It was almost as if', suggests Marsden (1998, p. 71):

> their fixation on the conquest or, in their terms, liberation of Afghanistan, [was] a wish to treat a sick patient, a victim of aggression and civil conflict, who is in danger of rapidly deteriorating if radical action is not taken. The remedy, in this case, [was] Islam.

For the Taliban, curing Afghanistan extended beyond merely ridding the country of the Mujahideen to exorcising the moral corruption that had compromised Afghans themselves – especially in urban areas. Their severe interpretation of Islam and introduction of the Hudud penal code was thus justified as essential for protection, and divinely ordained:

> By the enforcement of Shari'a Hudud, we have made safe the lives and property of millions of people from Herat to Jalabad and Kabul. No one can commit theft or crimes. We have not introduced this law. This is the law that was revealed by God to Muhammad. (Marsden, 1998, p. 63)

The Taliban's role as protectors of Afghanistan, Afghans and Islam is a narrative they continue to espouse. The insurgency is justified as a means of protecting Afghans and their property from the 'infidel occupant forces' (Brahimi, 2010), from the 'crusaders and their domestic servants' who are committing 'atrocities, barbarity and savagery against our innocent brothers' (Johnson, 2007, p. 330). 'Crusader' rhetoric is instructive, evoking historical narratives of attacks on Islam by *kuffar*, to which all Muslims are obliged to respond. 'It proclaims a clash of civilizations' (Johnson, 2007, p. 331), and with it an attempt to frame the insurgency as an identity conflict.

Narratives and symbols have helped the Taliban achieve this religious legitimacy. Through their 'distinctive white turbans and obvious religious fervour and purity', they have cultivated an 'almost supernatural aura' (Marsden, 1998, p. 46). In an especially powerful gesture, Mullah Omar visited the shrine of the Cloak of the Prophet and donned the relic before a large crowd of people in Kandahar's central bazaar (Brahimi, 2010). The message was clear: Omar had assumed the 'mantle' of the Prophet Muhammad, and as such, represented Islam. Johnson (2007), in his exploration of *shabnameh* (night letters), additionally details how such narratives may also serve as effective means of control for people and institutions. He explains that the symbolic effectiveness of *shabnameh* derives from their cultural and historical precedent as instruments of resistance within Afghanistan and Islam more broadly.

Religious legitimacy is necessary for the Taliban, who are acutely aware that Islam is the one narrative capable of '[transcending] all ethnic, political and regional barriers' in Afghanistan (Barfield, 2010, p. 263). The interweaving of religious narratives with those of protection also have historic precedent. A number of accounts detail Afghans being called on to defend creed and country – usually from foreign invasion but sometimes against the government itself. 'Undoubtedly', notes Brahimi, 'the legitimacy sought in Afghanistan is often specifically Islamic'. It was under the banner of 'Islam is in danger' in 1929, for instance, that the modernist and reformist King Amanullah was overthrown. Several decades later Soviet attempts to eliminate Islam resulted in a similar uprising in the form of the Mujahideen (Brahimi, 2010, p. 14). For Brahimi, it is was this recent *jihad* that provided the narrative basis for the Taliban's campaign, serving first to embed the link between Islam and nationalism, second, providing vindication for the notion that only the return to Islam would allow for liberation from foreign invaders, and third, crystallizing in the public imagination the association between atheism and brutality.

At the same time, the Taliban's legitimacy, and the religious authority on which it rests, is fragile. The exploitation of religion in Afghanistan has historically not been straightforward. Despite the supposed vulnerability of people to elite machinations, they do not always yield to such authority, particularly where promises made fail to materialize. This was true for the Islamists, whose inability to address the needs of communities undermined public confidence. 'Speaking in the name of Islam', notes Brahimi (2010, p. 13), 'brought neither unity of ranks nor unconditional popular support'. Similarly, after their rise to power, the Taliban's inability to provide anything but violence quickly undermined their position. An elderly Islamic scholar in Herat told one journalist: 'We are ruled by men who offer us nothing but the Koran, even though many of them cannot read . . . we are in despair'. As Barfield (2010) explains, appeals to Islam and a common Afghan identity also failed to allay ethnic fears. Unable to escape their Pashtun origins, the Taliban provoked fears of a Pashtun attempt at state capture; the killing and persecution of fellow Muslims – wholly denounced by Islam – further shook their legitimacy.

Lessons learned, a number of statements by the Taliban suggest a shift in strategy. Group members continue to portray themselves as 'nationalist actors upholding the undeniable Islamic right to self-defence' (Brahimi, 2010, p. 5), but are also deploying rhetoric that hints at a more progressive social programme, with objectives including 'independence, Islamic social justice, human dignity and national identity' (ibid., p. 9). Does this shift reflect the resistance of Islam to the Taliban's interpretations of the faith? Has religion *constrained* the group's power to exploit Islam beyond its strictures? The introduction in 2006 of the Laheyas – or code of conduct – would appear to suggest that it has, and 'offer an important insight into the neo-Taliban's quest for legitimacy' (ibid., p. 15). The Laheyas stipulate a number of restrictions, compelling members to treat prisoners well, prohibit the persecution or exploitation of civilians, and ban the recruitment of children. Violence, 'is enacted in a moral realm' (ibid.). Civilians should under no circumstance be targeted by *talibs*, and collaborators should be allowed a chance to repent – hence the use of *shabnameh*. The group have cannily appropriated human rights discourses in an attempt to legitimize their actions in this new realm. They note that human rights are an intrinsic part of Islam, and it is the international community, not they, who are guilty of the 'black cloud of atrocities and violations' (ibid.) against the Afghan people.

Gender and Reform

Understanding what the Taliban movement represents, and what purpose the violence they commit – especially that against women – serves, remain divisive questions. Perhaps most convincing are those approaches that frame the Taliban and their support as indicative of broader fears over lawlessness and modernity. As such, the group may be seen as an anti-modern movement; a response to the encroachment of alien value systems into 'traditional' spaces. The introduction of such forces have been theorized to undermine the 'protective framework of the small community' (Giddens, 1990), and threaten pre-existing power relations. Religion, as a source of ontological security (Kinnvall, 2004), plays a crucial role in mediating these threats and mobilizing public support against them. Marsden (1998, p. 59) argues that such religious-political movements could be seen as 'a response to chaos, an attempt to create a tightly defined framework within which society can be contained, a determined effort to hold back a process by which society is gradually being overwhelmed by potentially destructive forces'. Through the symbolic appeal of Islam, the Taliban were able to reinterpret what was a conflict of interest – according to Marsden was the power of the Afghan Ulema) – into a fear-driven conflict for security and protection. Whilst such struggles concern elite power, they also operate at a deeper social level, reflecting broader anxieties over social change.

Such understanding complements those that emphasize the rural–urban dimension of conflict in Afghanistan (Barfield, 2010; Guistozzi and Ibrahimi, 2012). As noted, the Taliban emerged as a grassroots movement, drawing much of their support from the rural southern regions of Afghanistan. Johnson and Mason (2007), have noted that the social 'roots' of the Taliban rest in the networks of rural madrassahs, and for Barfield (2010, p. 261), the Taliban's vision on social policies was rooted more in rural Afghan values than in Islam. As noted, urban areas suffered the brunt of Taliban violence. Kabul, notes Rashid (2010, p. 111), was seen as 'a den of iniquity, a Sodom and Gommorah where women had to beaten into conforming with Taliban standards of behaviour'. This discrimination has been attributed to perceptions that it was urban areas, and particularly through which the socialists and Islamists gained access to Afghanistan, and where most opposition lay (Barfield, 2010). Urban areas are also where the processes of reform and urbanization – processes that threaten rural interests and elites – are rooted (Marsden, 1998).

Whether, as Marsden seems to suggest, such fears over modernity and change are as widespread and salient as this is an important, but currently unanswerable question.

Such a view, whilst perhaps partly true, also belies a somewhat simplistic view of rural social values, as well as white-washing very diverse rural societies in Afghanistan. For rural communities, support from insurgents is likely based on more pragmatic concerns for their own security – as well as issues concerning higher levels of poverty, illiteracy, and a lack of infrastructure that disadvantage communities and leave them more vulnerable. There is clearly, however, a rural–urban dimension to the conflict, and it is likely that the Taliban have been able to enter this space by exploiting fears of rural insecurity and conflating them with processes of reform. This perspective helps illuminate the occurrences of gender violence in Afghanistan, which for Marsden (1998, p. 92), 'need to be looked at in the context of the development of gender-related policies since the beginning of the twentieth century, the use of gender as a key focus of the Mujahideen parties, and the different forms that gender policies have taken within radical Islam'. He draws particular attention to the way in which the issue of gender had, through the twentieth century, become symbolic of reform and a principal point of contention between government and the religious elite. King Amanullah's series of reforms during the 1920s, those of Daoud Khan in the 1950s–60s, and those of the PDPA (People's Democratic Party of Afghanistan), all challenged the traditional restrictions on women in relation to employment, dress, and education. Whilst these reforms may have upset broader social values, they more crucially threatened to undermine the authority, and thus the power and influence, of the religious elite: the Ulema.

This is evident with regard to education, which in Afghanistan has historically been instrumental in propagating political ideology (Marsden, 1998; Guistozzi, 2010a). Schools and curricula are of paramount importance in shaping all societies, but in Afghanistan they also served as a pedagogic political asset. In this light, schools could be seen as a means of ensuring future power, and if girls were educated according to liberal, secular values, the threat posed to the male-dominated Ulema could be an existential one. Whilst the current violence directed at teachers, school children and schools, may therefore reflect genuine concerns over the peddling of 'infidel' curricula, and the conversion of children – especially girl children – to Christianity, it should also be placed in context of the historical role of education as a political instrument. The campaign to frustrate girls' education could be seen to reflect a desperate attempt to capture this instrument, to perpetuate the illiteracy and asymmetrical social relations on which the Taliban thrive, and to safeguard the power base on which religious elite depends.

At the same time genuine concerns over the threats posed by foreigners, foreign influences and modernity should not be dismissed as influences on the group's gender policies, and the violence enacted against women. Women are regarded as bearers of family honour and are responsible for the transmission of Islamic culture.

> There is a concern that girls will be corrupted by anything other than a pure Islamic teaching, consistent with the Taliban interpretation of Islam, and a consequent wish to create an exclusive focus on what is seen as their important role of bringing up the next generation of pure Muslims. (Marsden, 1998, p. 99)

Women, are especially vulnerable to moral corruption. The violence they experienced in urban areas may be understood as part of a process that framed them as in special need of purification. Whilst executions and mutilations for 'moral' crimes, and the imposition of the *burqa*, symbolically reinforce victory over the reformists, and serve strategic functions in creating a climate of fear, they are also symbolic of the campaign to protect women against modernity through the curative power of faith. For Marsden (1998, p. 101), 'the rigidity of the Taliban gender policies could be seen as a desperate attempt to keep out [the world beyond Afghanistan] and to protect Afghan women from influences that could weaken society from within'.

Cultural Violence

The Taliban aside, a number of other sources of violence and discrimination pose pernicious threats to the well-being of women, children and minorities in Afghanistan. As noted, endemic corruption, abuse by officials within institutions and local authorities, and exploitation by local militias, complement and reinforce extreme poverty within the country. A high prevalence of domestic and community-level violence and several harmful traditional practices also threaten well-being. Most are fundamentally the product of ineffective and bad governance – they are simply too pervasive globally to be seen as the product of religion or Afghan culture. But to what extent should harmful traditional practices and the widespread mistreatment of and discrimination against Afghan women and children be attributed to religion or culture?

Prevailing interpretations of religion or culture may serve to both justify and delegitimize harmful and inequitable practices. Whilst religion or cultural 'values' may be 'reinterpreted' to promote a more equitable set of values, the inter-subjective nature of these structures means that specific interpretations and practices (good or bad) that accompany them, may become institutionalized and normalized – especially where they serve elite interests. In Afghanistan, the discrimination and violence enacted against women by the Taliban and other conservative forces in recent history have helped reinforce a several negative cultural narratives concerning women's rights. The difficulties faced by girls in gaining education or accessing health care, their dubious position with regard to the law or in obtaining justice, the risks they face working in positions of public authority, and related problems of poverty and illiteracy, combine to create extraordinary structural resistance to their ability to challenge prevailing norms.

The role of 'culture' in sustaining practices such as 'honour' killings, *baad*, and child marriage across Afghanistan cannot, therefore, be entirely dismissed. Whilst mutable, traditions remain circumscribed to varying degrees, and can present socially entrenched obstacles to women and children's rights. This analysis, however, needs to be tempered with a number of caveats. First, as Rashid (2010) argues, any discussion of cultural 'values' in Afghanistan is frustrated by the great diversity of cultures within the country. This applies equally to considerable intra-ethnic variation, such as it the case with the Pashtun. Second, whilst justifications for practices vary according to cultural context, some – such as child marriage – are not unique to Afghanistan, and may result from more material problems such as poverty. Third, 'culture' should not be seen as a condition, but as a process of mediation between myriad, sometimes contradictory, narratives. Like religion, it needs to be understood as a contested, not given, realm. In Afghanistan, the 'appropriate' treatment of women has historically been subject to intense political contention by elites. According to the UNAMA (2009b, p. 29), many of the problems faced by Afghan women stem from:

> an unholy coalition of conservative political, community and religious leaders, [who] espouse and pursue agendas in the name of Islam or tradition to maintain their own power and influence by attacking and obstructing initiatives designed to tackle deeply engrained discrimination against women.

Lastly, and most importantly, traditions are open to reinterpretation. Given effective, trustworthy and representative leadership, appropriate accountability mechanisms, and institutions that encourage participation, such structures may help facilitate effective, equitable and locally meaningful development.

Governance, Poverty and the Crisis of Legitimacy

Arguments that attribute violence in Afghanistan to religion or culture tend not only to distract from the numerous forms of secular violence that threaten the well-being of women and children, and risk alienating certain groups – such as the Pashtun – but also work to excuse the failures of policy-makers as the fault of Afghans themselves. It is argued here that Afghanistan's current problems are due not to inherent deficiencies within Islam or Afghan 'culture', but to failings of governance, at national and international levels. The current trends in violence [particularly against Afghan women], notes Atabay (2007, p. 12) citing the UN Special Rapporteur on violence against women Yakin Ertürk, 'cannot be solely reduced to culture and tradition without consideration of the conflict and post-conflict situation', including, 'the erosion of protective social mechanisms; the lack of the rule of law; poverty and insecurity'. Effective, representative and legitimate governance can hardly be overated as a fundamental prerequisite for equitable and sustainable development. Unfortunately, governance in Afghanistan is beset by endemic corruption, partisan decision-making, chronic underfunding, foreign meddling, and a series of ill-conceived policy decisions made by the national government and coalition forces. Such conditions undermine the security of women and children and exacerbate violence, insurgency, injustice and impunity.

The view that Afghanistan is, and always has been, inherently 'ungovernable', has 'become an unfortunate conventional wisdom that drives policy decision' (Barfield, 2010, p. 337). Such an assumption is, however, demonstrably false. Despite popular belief to the contrary, most of Afghanistan has, throughout history, been subject to central governance, with relatively few rebellions against the state (Barfield, 2010). Notions of an intrinsic resistance to governance in Afghanistan, then, occlude a more complex set of attitudes towards political authority. Similarly, despite Afghanistan's historic resistance to foreign occupation, Operation Enduring Freedom did not precipitate the mass uprising expected. Indeed, the intervention was welcomed by Afghans tired of violence and willing to 'wait and see' whether foreign intervention would prove beneficial. Afghans, notes Barfield (2010) wanted only peace and protection from anarchy. Unfortunately, however, this comparative advantage was wasted through a number of ill-conceived policies (ibid.). The national government suffers from a lack of legitimacy owing to a proclivity to compromise and a highly centralized approach to rule. 'Far from acting as state builder' notes Barfield (2010, p. 272), 'Karzai adopted a patrimonial model of the state in which its offices and resources were redistributed on a personal basis to buy the support of existing power holders or play them off against one another'. Such an approach has resulted in endemic corruption as well as the compromise of government by powerful conservative interests. This situation perpetuates malpractice and impunity of officials throughout state institutions, and as noted, has blighted women's rights, which are often '"traded" in exchange for political support or leverage in an ever-changing mosaic of alliances' (UNAMA, 2009b. p. 30).

The inability to provide adequate security for rural areas forms a second crucial failing. The provision of effective security across Afghanistan was critical for limiting the power of warlords, preventing the return of the Taliban, and allaying the fears of local people (Johnson, 2007; Barfield, 2010). Unfortunately, chronic underfunding and an initial reluctance of the coalition to engage the outlying provinces of the country – largely because of distractions in Iraq – meant this was not achieved. For Johnson (2007), this failure has not only served to undermine the immediate security of Afghans, but has also impeded development, and is a key reason for the Taliban's successful resurgence. Worse still, attempts to bolster rural security through empowering local strongmen and militias, may appear exigent means of redressing the shortfall in rural security forces, but is insensitive to the historical experiences of rural Afghans and directly threatens their well-being (Reid and Muhammedally, 2011). As private actors, such groups are bound less by duty than by gain, and expect reward for their services. '[A] low level of discipline, professionalism, weak command and control structures, the spread of corruption, and the tendency to live off the population, a trait compounded by the low salaries and payment delays', form further negative consequences of their inclusion (Guistozzi and Ibrahimi, 2012, p. 29).

The failure to provide meaningful development, particularly in southern Afghanistan, perpetuates these problems. Prior to intervention, Afghanistan represented one of the world's least developed countries, suffering chronic poverty, extremely high maternal and infant mortality, and a lack of infrastructure outside urban areas. This remains true today. Whilst poverty is an unreliable indicator for insurgent support or political violence in Afghanistan (Guistozzi and Ibrahimi, 2012), it is a form of violence in its own right, and through illiteracy, and the lack of capacity of the poor to challenge inequitable policies or claim representation, increases vulnerability to insurgents. Poor governance exacerbates poverty, and many decisions taken by the government and the international community have been inept. Aid has been too little too late (Barfield, 2010). Investment in the rural economy, or in providing infrastructure and services to rural areas was largely non-existent. Whilst attempts were made to provide schools for rural children, the lack of security has resulted in their destruction by the Taliban. As noted, whilst parents want their children to receive education, long distances make this impractical at best, and perilous at worst (HRW, 2006). The lack of rural security has exacerbated failures in providing any meaningful improvement in people's lives. For Johnson and Mason (2007, p. 86), this has created 'an angry environment of unfulfilled expectations', fatally undermining the legitimacy of the government and the international coalition.

CONCLUSIONS

Discourses that reinforce the 'ungovernable' nature of Afghanistan and attempt to frame and 'normalize' conflict and violence in the country as owing to inherent problems with its culture or religious tradition, are reductionist and refutable. To claim a nation has proven capable of resisting imperialism is one thing, it is quite another to suggest that a people are disinterested in their own or their children's health, well-being, or freedom from violence. Whilst religion and culture may indeed intervene in justifying and legitimizing violence in Afghanistan, it is argued here that far more significant are failures of governance that have, over the last decade, worked to fatally undermine the legitimacy of the government and the international coalition, and contribute to the resurgence of the Taliban. Such discourses, however, also provide an effective smokescreen for otherwise dubious policy decisions that might prove harmful to the most vulnerable. In light of the coalition's desire to withdraw from Afghanistan and the need to expedite securitization of rural areas, efforts have already been made to engage militias and insurgents in local governance, administration and policing. With knowledge of the lack of accountability amongst these groups, and their historical precedent as serious threats to civilian well-being, the long-term wisdom of this strategy is questioned. Afghanistan's future security, and the well-being of its people, it is argued, depends far more on the establishment of locally relevant, legitimate and trustworthy political leadership committed to the well-being of ordinary Afghans – especially in the desperately poor and historically neglected rural provinces.

A further concern involves the decision of whether to engage the Taliban in negotiations, especially considering the extent of their recent resurgence. Such compromise, it is argued, however, may be similarly disasterous for ordinary people: 'better the devil you know' could prove a Faustian bargain. Despite evidence of a recent 'softening' (Brahimi, 2010), the Taliban 's legitimacy and power rests on a narrow and highly conflict-oriented ideology almost existentially opposed to social reform. For the Taliban and other conservative elements in Afghanistan, rights, and more specifically the rights and well-being of women, have over the last 50 years become a highly contested and politicized field. Gender rights in particular, have come to be recognized as symbolically representative of reform, and for some, of the threat posed to Afghanistan and Islam by immoral, foreign, modern values. Whilst genuine concerns amongst ordinary rural Afghans may be reflected here, this narrative is more likely the product of elites, who understand such reforms as a direct threat to their power and interests. The inclusion and accomodation of the Taliban within Afghan politics is therefore argued here as neither obligatory or wise. Given the proclivity of the Afghan government to compromise and corruption, its illegitimacy in the eyes of Afghans more broadly, and the fatigue of the international coalition in pursuing the conflict, however, such accomodation is likely. As such, the probability that women, children and minority groups will experience a regression in rights and freedoms after the coalition withdraws is high. If religious fundamentalism and violence loom large over the future of Afghanistan, the shadows they cast fall patchwork.

NOTES

1. Whilst *baad* is the use of girls as payment of 'blood-price' to resolve a feud, *baadal* is instead argued to involve the exchange of daughters between families for the purposes of marriage – both, according to the UNAMA (2010) should be considered forms of forced marriage, especially where children are involved).

2. The Deobandi movement is a relatively recent tradition of Sunni Islam, founded in Deoband India during the eighteenth to nineteenth centuries as a reaction against British colonialism, which was believed to be a corrupting influence on the faith. The movement was influenced in part by the Wahhabi movement, and whilst it generally follows the more liberal *hanafi* school of *fiqh* (jurisprudence), it is known for adopting a relatively strict approach to religious practice.

REFERENCES

Afghanistan Independent Human Rights Commission (AIHRC) (2009), *Report on the Situation of Economic and Social Rights in Afghanistan – IV*, Kabul: AIHRC.

Amnesty International (2011a), *Afghanistan Briefing: Don't Trade Away Women's Human Rights*, London: Amnesty International.

Amnesty International (2011b), *Afghanistan Ten Years On: Slow Progress and Failed Promises*, London: Amnesty International.

Arat, Z.F. (2000), 'Women's rights in Islam: revisiting Quranic rights', in A. Pollis and P. Schwab, *Human Rights: New Perspectives, New Realities*, London: Lynne Rienner, pp. 69–94.

Atabay, T. (2007), *Afghanistan: Female Prisoners and their Social Reintegration – Developing Post-release Opportunities for Women and Girl Prisoners*, New York: UNODC.

Barfield, T. (2010), *Afghanistan: A Cultural and Political History*, Princeton, NJ: Princeton University Press.

BBC (16 August 2012), 'Taliban "kill adulterous Afghan couple"', *BBC News South Asia*, available at: http://www.bbc.co.uk/news/world-south-asia-10983494; accessed 5 February 2012.

Boyden, J. and de J. Berry (2004), 'Children and youth on the front line: ethnography, armed conflict and displacement', in J. Boyden and J. de Berry, *Children and Youth on the Front Line: Ethnography, Armed Conflict and Displacement*, Oxford: Berghahn, pp. xi–xxvii.

Brahimi, A. (2010), *The Taliban's Evolving Ideology*, London: London School of Economics Global Governance.

Brown, D. (2009), *A New Introduction to Islam* (2nd edition), Chichester, UK/Malden, MA: Wiley-Blackwell.

Bumiller, E. (17 October 2009), 'Remembering Afghanistan's golden age', *New York Times*, available at: http://www.nytimes.com/2009/10/18/weekinreview/18bumiller.html; accessed 2 March 2012.

Carnegie Commission on Preventing Deadly Conflict (1997), *Preventing Deadly Conflict*, New York: Carnegie Commission.

Churchill, W. (1898), *The Story of the Malakand Field Force: An Episode of Frontier War*, reprinted 2008, Rockville, MD: ArcManor (2008).

Coll, S. (2004), *Ghost Wars: The Secret History of the CIA, Afghanistan, and bin Laden, from Soviet Invasion to September 10, 2001*, New York: Penguin.

Douki, S., F. Nacef, A.Belhadj, A. Bouasker and R. Ghachem (2002), 'Violence against women in Arab and Islamic countries', *Archives of Women's Mental Health*, **6**(3), 165–71.

Giddens, A. (1990), *The Consequences of Modernity*, Stanford: Stanford University Press.

Guistozzi, A. (2010a), *Nation-building is Not for All – The Politics of Education in Afghanistan* Afghanistan Analysis Network.

Giustozzi, A. (2010b), *The Taliban Beyond the Pashtuns*, Ontario: The Centre for International Governance Innovation (CIGI).

Guistozzi, A. and N. Ibrahimi (2012), *Thirty Years of Conflict: Drivers of Anti-government Mobilisation in Afghanistan, 1978–2011*, Kabul: Afghanistan Research and Evaluation Unit.

Guistozzi, M. and M. Isaqzadeh (2011), *Afghanistan's Paramilitary Policing in Context*, Afghanistan Analysts Network.

Giustozzi, A. and C. Reuter (2011), *The Insurgents of the Afghan North – The Rise of the Taleban, the Self-abandonment of the Afghan Government and the Effects of ISAF's 'Capture-and-Kill Campaign'*, Afghanistan Analysts Network.

Hallaq, W.B. (1997), *A History of Islamic Legal Theories*, Cambridge: Cambridge University Press.

Hasenclever, A. and V. Rittberger (2000), 'Does religion make a difference? Theoretical approaches to the impact of faith on political conflict', *Millennium*, **29**(3), 641–74.

Haynes, J. (2009), 'Conflict, conflict resolution and peace-building: the role of religion in Mozambique, Nigeria and Cambodia', *Commonwealth and Comparative Politics*, **47**(1), 52–75.

Holenstein, A. (2005), 'Role and significance of religion and spirituality in development co-operation: a reflection and working paper', Bern: Swiss Agency for Development and Co-operation.

HRW (2006), *Lessons in Terror: Attacks on Education in Afghanistan*, New York: Human Rights Watch.

HRW (2012), *Afghanistan – Country Summary*, New York: Human Rights Watch.

Hughes, M. (24 March 2011), 'Taliban and Karzai regime undermine Pashtun tribal code', *Huffington Post*, available at: http://www.huffingtonpost.com/michael-hughes/pashtun-afghanistan_b_839372.html; accessed 27 February 2012.
Huntington, S. (1996), *The Clash of Civilizations and the Remaking of World Order*, New York: Simon and Schuster.
IOM (2008), *Trafficking in Persons in Afghanistan: Field Survey Report*, Kabul: International Organization for Migration.
Johnson, T. (2007), 'The Taliban insurgency and an analysis of "Shabnamah" (Night Letters)', *Small Wars and Insurgencies*, **18**(3), 317–44.
Johnson, T. and C. Mason (2007), 'Understanding the Taliban and insurgency in Afghanistan', *Orbis*, **51**(1), 71–89.
Juergensmeyer, M. (2003), *Terror in the Mind of God*, Berkeley and Los Angeles: University of California Press.
Kaldor, M. (2002), *New and Old Wars: Organized Violence in a Global Era*, Cambridge: Polity.
Kaufman, S. (2006), 'Symbolic politics or rational choice', *International Security*, **30**(4), 45–86.
Kepel, G. (2002), *Jihad: The Trail of Political Islam*, London: I.B. Taurus.
Kinnvall, C. (2004), 'Globalization and religious nationalism: self, identity and the search for ontological security', *Political Psychology*, **25**(5), 741–67.
Kurtz, L. (1995), *Gods in the Global Village*, Pine Forge: Sage.
Machel, G. (2000), *The Machel Review 1996–2000: A Critical Analysis of Progress Made and Obstacles Encountered in Increasing Protection for War-affected Children*, UNICEF.
Maley, W. (2011), 'On the position of the Hazara minority in Afghanistan', Blue Mountains Refugee Support Group, available at: http://bmrsg.org.au/wp-content/uploads/2011/10/Maley-Hazaras-Opinion-Updated2.pdf; accessed 17 February 2012.
Marranci, G. (2010), 'Sociology and the anthropology of Islam: a critical debate', in B. Turner, *The New Blackwell Companion to the Sociology of Religion*, Oxford: Blackwell, pp. 364–87.
Marsden, P. (1998), *The Taliban: War, Religion and the New Order in Afghanistan*, London: Zed Books.
Mello, P. (2010), 'In search of new wars: the debate about the transformation of war', *European Journal of International Relations*, **XX**(X), 1–13.
Moghadam, V. (2003), *Modernizing Women: Gender and Social Change in the Middle East* (2nd edition), Boulder, CO: Lynne Rienner.
Montgomery Watt, W. (1956), *Muhammad At Medina*, Oxford: Clarendon Press.
Nigel, J. and R. Allan (2001), 'Defining place and people in Afghanistan', *Post-Soviet Geography and Economis*, **42**(8), 545–60.
Nijhowne, D. and L. Oates (2008), *Living with Violence: A National Report on Domestic Abuse in Afghanistan*, Kabul: Global Rights.
Rashid, A. (2002), *Taliban: Islam, Oil and the New Great Game in Central Asia*, London: I.B. Tauris.
Rashid, A. (5 December 2006), 'Pashtuns want an image change', *BBC News*, available at: http://news.bbc.co.uk/1/hi/6198382.stm; accessed 27 February 2012.
Rashid, A. (2010), *Taliban: Militant Islam, Oil and Fundamentalism in Central Asia* (2nd edition), London: IB Taurus.
Reid, R. (2009), *We Have the Promises of the World*, New York: Human Rights Watch.
Reid, R. (2010), *The 'Ten-Dollar Talib' and Women's Rights – Afghan Women and the Risks of Reintegration and Reconciliation*, Human Rights Watch.
Reid, R. and S. Muhammedally (2011), *'Just Don't Call it a Militia' – Impunity, Militias, and the 'Afghan Local Police'*, New York: Human Rights Watch.
Reus-Smit, C. (2009), 'Constructivism', in S. Burchill, *Theories of International Relations* (4th edition), London: Palgrave-Macmillan, pp. 212–36.
Roy, O. (1998), 'Has Islamism a future in Afghanistan?', in W. Maley, *Fundamentalism Reborn? Afghanistan and the Taliban*, London: Hurst and Co.
Rzehak, L. (2011), *Doing Pashto: Pashtunwali as the Ideal of Honourable Behaviour and Tribal Life Among the* Pashtuns, Kabul: Afghanistan Analysts Network.
Schimmel, A. (1992), *Islam: An Introduction*, New York: State University of New York.
UNAMA (2009a), *Arbitrary Detention in Afghanistan – A Call for Action: Volume I – Overview and Recommendations*, Kabul: United Nations.
UNAMA (2009b), *Silence is Violence: End the Abuse of Women in Afghanistan*, Kabul: United Nations.
UNAMA (2010), *Harmful Traditional Practices and Implementation of the Law on Elimination of Violence against Women in Afghanistan*, Kabul: United Nations Assitance Mission in Afghanistan.
UNAMA (2011a), *A Long Way to Go: Implementation of the Elimination of Violence against Women Law in Afghanistan*, Kabul: United Nations Assistance Mission in Afghanistan.
UNAMA (2011b), *Afghanistan – Midyear Report: Protection of Civilians in Armed Conflict*, Kabul: United Nations.

UNAMA (2012), *Afghanistan: Annual Report 2011 – Protection of Civilians in Armed Conflict*, Kabul: United Nations.

UNSC (2011), *Report of the Secretary-General on Children and Armed Conflict in Afghanistan*, United Nations.

Verter, B. (2003), 'Spiritual capital: theorizing religion with Bourdieu against Bourdieu', *Sociological Theory*, **21**(2), 150–74.

Wendt, A. (1992), 'Anarchy is what states make of it: the social construction of power politics', *International Organization*, **46**(2), 391–425.

Wendt, A. (1995), 'Constructing international politics', *International Security*, **20**(1), 71–81.

World Bank (2005), *Afghanistan: National Reconstruction and Poverty Reduction – the Role of Women in Afghanistan's Future*, Kabul: The World Bank.

33 Australian development FBOs and NGOs

Lindsay Rae and Matthew Clarke

INTRODUCTION

Given the weak consideration of religion within development studies and policy, it is not surprising that FBOs themselves have long been invisible in discussions of community development (Marshall and Van Saanen, 2007). This apparent invisibility should not be mistaken for non-existence. More correctly, their invisibility reflects a blindness of the development sector itself in failing to recognize the importance of religion within its area of concern and its tendency to recognize and work with only non-governmental organizations that take a familiar form and operate in familiar ways, often because they have been created in response to donor agendas. Religious organizations, in contrast, may choose to position themselves outside the development sector when working to improve the material lives of their congregations and others. In addition, FBOs are often locally initiated and run, embedded within communities and raise much of their funding from members of the faith body (G. Clarke, 2008).

More recently, however, the presence of FBOs in community development work is gradually becoming recognized. Moreover, there has been recognition both within the development sector and by FBOs themselves that not only is it important but also there is synergy to be gained by being aware of one another and incorporating an understanding of religion more purposely into the development domain (Harb, 2008). As participatory community-focused models of development have become increasingly popular in recent years, religious organizations and FBOs have become increasingly 'attractive' as agents or stakeholders in the development process, due to their strong links to local communities. Moreover, religious bodies themselves have begun to initiate contact with aid donors to seek increased involvement in (and funding for) community development interventions (Clarke et al., 2011). Over the past decade, a number of international forums have been developed that have brought together religious leaders and large international donors to explore how to leverage the experience and expertise that both groups can bring to improving the lives of the poor (see reports emanating from these events, such as Marshall and Keough, 2004 and Clarke and Jennings, 2008).

Faith-based organizations play a prominent, sometimes dominant, role within the non-government development sector. For example, despite Australia being widely understood as a highly secularized society, about 65 per cent of Australian private funds for international development are raised by faith-based agencies. However, the relationship between the faith identity of international development agencies and their development philosophy, practice and outcomes is not always clear. This chapter reports a pilot exercise that constructs a nominal scale that seeks to characterize the development philosophy and practice of 17 Australia-based international development agencies, using ten measures that broadly indicate the agency's position on what may be regarded as an evolutionary path (from welfare-based charity to an emphasis on community development and sustainable development) suggested by David Korten. By differentiating agencies that self-identify as faith-based from those identifying as secular, and also differentiating denominationally based agencies from those claiming faith identity but not affiliated to a specific religious denomination, an attempt is made to establish whether there is a correlation between an organization's faith basis and its development philosophy and practice as understood in Korten's generational typology of aid agencies. The preliminary analysis offered in this chapter finds that FBOs are not necessarily disadvantaged by their faith base in terms of their location compared to secular aid agencies.

The chapter is set out as follows: the next section considers in more detail what faith-based organizations are and their role within the development context, before the subsequent section looks at these organizations within developed nations. The Australian context in which faith-based organizations operate is described, before the Korten typology is discussed. The method for testing organizations in terms of their development thinking is then outlined, before an analysis and comparison of Australian faith-based and secular aid agencies is undertaken.

UNDERSTANDING FAITH-BASED ORGANIZATIONS

The term *faith-based organization* (FBO) is used to describe a particular niche within the voluntary and/or charitable sector, with 'faith-based' often used as an alternative for 'religious'. FBO is increasingly a generic term applied in an undifferentiated way to organizations associated with all faiths. However, Christian FBOs are more numerous than those of other faiths in most developing regions, and these are most often what Western funding agencies have in mind when evaluating the links between the potential roles of religion in development. Religious groups have long played an important role in enhancing the welfare of local communities. While they are primarily concerned with providing spiritual leadership, for many an interest in the physical welfare of their adherents and others has also been a core aspect of their existence. This concern with material welfare is often expressed and enacted through affiliated FBOs that operationalize such outreach (see work by G. Clarke, 2008; Clarke and Jennings, 2008; Harb, 2008; Clarke et al., 2011).

As with many concepts and terms within development (see Cornwall, 2007), it is not surprising that no precise definition of 'faith-based organizations' exists. Vidal (2001) identifies three types of FBO in a United States domestic welfare service provision setting: (1) congregations affiliated with a physical structure for worship or geographical grouping of worshippers; (2) national networks of congregations, including national denominations and their social services affiliates, as well as other networks of related organizations, such as the YMCA and YWCA; and (3) unaligned or freestanding religious organizations that are incorporated separately from congregations and national networks. Vidal's three types do not capture the range of FBOs working in development. Therefore it is necessary that a distinct typology for faith-based international development agencies be developed. For the purposes of this chapter, the following four categories are proposed: (1) FBOs directly linked to a local congregation or religious leader; (2) FBOs directly linked to a religious denomination/sect/branch and formally incorporated within the institutional organization of that religious body; (3) FBOs directly linked to a religious denomination/sect/branch but incorporated separately from that religious body; and (4) FBOs that self-identify as falling within a broad religious tradition from which they draw their motivation.

As noted above, whilst congregations and other organizations with religious affiliations have worked to improve the well-being of the disadvantaged for hundreds of years, the term 'faith-based organization' is relatively recent and has been coined to distinguish specific organizations associated with a faith tradition (James, 2009). Religious organizations delivering a variety of services to the public, such as caring for the infirm and elderly, advocating justice for the oppressed, and playing a major role in humanitarian aid and international development efforts, seem, in terms of their organizational set up, structure and administration, to increasingly resemble other twentieth-century civil society organizations more than traditional and historic religious organizations. Whilst FBOs share the same basic characteristics as 'secular' NGOs – they are autonomous, not-for-profit, voluntary, and altruistic (Ball and Dunn, 1996) – they are distinguished from the latter through their affiliation with a religious structure, doctrine or congregation.

FBOs have traditionally sat outside mainstream development networks either because they are embedded within communities and supposedly more 'organically' linked to them than NGOs and/or because they have chosen to position themselves outside 'the development sector' and remain aligned with the religious body to which they are affiliated. The tendency to exclude FBOs from discussions of community development work, however, seems to have diminished in recent years. Marshall and Van Saanen (2007) note that FBOs are increasingly seeking 'a seat at the policy table, while they are also, in many instances, asking development institutions to work and support faith groups in scaling up their community and social justice operations' (p. 4). Past reticence by donors to be seen to be working with FBOs is arguably now being replaced in the case of some donors by a clearer understanding that FBOs are a legitimate part of civil society, with entrée into local communities, networks across countries and regions, and (often) expertise in community development processes and interventions. In the last decade, there has been a new awareness in 'secular' organizations of the importance of the spiritual dimension in the lives of communities, and of the need to take account of that dimension in plans and programmes for community development.

While religion is often viewed as divisive, dangerous, or defunct, there is now an alternative view suggesting that FBOs, for example, can achieve positive development outcomes. This position is based upon the assumption that FBOs:

- have earned high levels of community trust;
- work directly on development, most significantly in education, the environment and health;
- work through a myriad of peace-making channels, sustaining communities and spearheading the rebuilding and healing process following periods of conflict;
- spur people to grapple with ethical issues, ranging from corruption to equity; and
- promote public support for development assistance (Marshall. 2005).

However, there is little empirical research that has examined the quality of the contribution of faith-based organizations, or indeed the underlying faith/spiritual values and beliefs, to community development.

Despite the lack of evidence as to the 'added value' of FBOs, their recent 'acceptance' by some official development agencies mirrors the 'acceptance' of NGOs during the 1990s by the same agencies. These agencies recognize that enhanced aid effectiveness requires accessing and engaging with local communities and believe that FBOs (like some NGOs) can facilitate this access and engagement. There are consequences though – beyond potential increases in funding – for FBOs that intensify their interaction with multi- and bilateral agencies, as there were for NGOs two or three decades ago. Seeking a seat at the policy table also means greater scrutiny of one's own activities and acceptance of public funding is associated with the expectation that funded interventions will reflect 'best practice' or internationally accepted values and practices in addressing development issues.

Feeny and Clarke (2009) describe the different roles that non-government organizations can play at the micro-, meso-, macro- and supra-macro levels in both advocacy and programming. Like NGOs, FBOs are said to have good national and international organizational networks, but unlike secular NGOs, they are also said to have a 'natural' constituency at the local level. FBOs and their advocates assert that they are uniquely placed within communities but outside the mainstream structures that are perceived to constrain the activities and networking of other civil society groups. Utilizing networks at these different levels by piggy-backing on the existing structures the religious organizations with which FBOs are associated have in place, FBOs claim, enables them to undertake effective community development, aiding their effectiveness and providing them with advantages over secular NGOs.

Another way in which religious organizations are said to be distinctive is in whether and how religious values and beliefs influence their motivation, understanding and practice. According to van Geest (1998), FBOs may understand the links between religion and development in four ways: (1) development is something that is not linked with religious activity; (2) development and evangelism are separate tasks, although the former should be influenced by the values and beliefs that are promoted by the latter; (3) development and evangelism are integral activities, in which development activities accompany and are a way of achieving evangelism, and the values and beliefs underlying each are entirely compatible; and (4) material development can be seen as a precursor and prerequisite for evangelistic activities. In addition to these ways of perceiving the relationship between development activities and evangelism, specific religious values and beliefs may influence the motivations of those involved in donating, advocacy and development activities; the perceptions promoted during fundraising and lobbying on development policy; the choice of partners and beneficiaries; and the choice and design of development activities. These are said to differ between FBOs and NGOs, leading to higher levels of motivation, enhanced empathy and longer-term commitment or, alternatively, social conservatism, patriarchy and opposition to certain behaviours, on the part of the former. While an understanding of these aspects is essential to a full understanding of the similarities and differences between FBOs and NGOs, and may influence where individual organizations are placed in Korten's typology, they are not examined in this chapter.

FBOs IN DEVELOPED NATIONS

Many international organizations engaged in development work are affiliated to religious congregations or identify themselves as faith based. Where they are not structurally linked to a religious denomination, sect or congregation, this generally means they identify religious faith as a motivating factor for their work or that they consider that a specific faith is a factor in the relationships between the agency and either its donors or its beneficiaries. For this reason, consideration of FBOs within developed nations that undertake or financially support development interventions within developing nations is of interest.

A striking feature of Australia-based international development organizations is that, despite Australia being regarded as a generally secularized society in which religious practice has declined substantially (see also below), faith-based NGOs continue to play a prominent, even dominant role, within the development sector. Beyond their market share of the sector, measured by organizational size and reach or financial resources, a question arises about whether these FBOs exhibit distinctive characteristics that impact on their philosophy or approach to development and how they relate to donors and wider communities of supporters or intended beneficiaries. This is not a question of whether FBOs are inherently more or less well equipped to achieve good development outcomes, but rather whether they maximize the potential advantages and minimize the potential advantages that derive from their faith orientation. In order to lay the groundwork for examining this question, it may be useful to first establish whether or not FBOs taken as a category display any distinctiveness in their development approaches when compared with their secular counterparts.

In this pilot study, we examine a sample of 17 development organizations based in Australia. Although necessarily imprecise and to a degree subjective, we attempt to establish whether any correlation exists between their religious or secular orientation and their development approaches. The purpose of this pilot project is to consider if FBOs are distinct from secular NGOs in their ability to 'evolve' from welfare-based charity work to become more focused on sustainable development in line with the generations proposed by Korten (1990). This consideration is important as there is currently little empirical evidence as to how FBOs operate in distinction to NGOs. It is also important when considering the origins of many FBOs sits fairly within welfare charity models (as is discussed below).

The 17 FBOs and NGOs were chosen based on the availability of sufficient information, whether from published sources or from informants, to be able to make at least a subjective assessment of their approaches to development and how their development programmes are organized. In addition, all of these agencies have been operating overseas programmes from an Australian organizational and/or donor base for a period of 20 years or more, albeit with some changes in name or structure in some cases. This allows some judgement to be made about the ways in which the agencies' development approaches have shifted over time. Of these agencies, 11 claim a religious affiliation or identity, and six regard themselves as secular in orientation. All the FBOs are Christian.[2] Of the FBOs, seven have a specific denominational identity and four identify as Christian but are not formally affiliated to any denomination, although all four have their origins in evangelical Protestant traditions. In order to create a reasonably consistent lens for comparing the organizations, we constructed a nominal scale based on characteristics suggested by the four 'generations' of NGOs proposed by Korten (1990 – described below).

Australia: The Social and Religious Context

Australia is a wealthy country with a population of 23 million, occupying a vast land mass. It ranked second only to Norway in the 2010 Human Development Index. It is a long-established and stable liberal democracy with a parliamentary system of government formed in 1901 though the federation of six formerly separate British colonies, all of which had been self-governing since the 1850s. Despite their separate governance, the settler population was remarkably homogeneous across all the colonies. Before 1945, this population was overwhelmingly of British and Irish origin, and levels of formal religious identification were very high. The 1947 national census, for example, showed that about 90 per cent of Australians identified as Christian, 0.4 per cent as Jews, and just 4000 individuals as members of other religions. Of the Christians, about 39 per cent were Anglicans, 35 per cent other Protestants and 25 per cent Catholics. Denominational differences were a powerful shaping force in Australian society and political life from the mid-nineteenth century onwards, due to sectarian division between Catholics, predominantly of Irish heritage, and Protestants.

After World War II, Australia experienced a long period of mass immigration accompanying significant economic expansion. A large proportion of the new immigrants were drawn from non-British sources: from the 1960s onwards increasingly from Asia, the Middle East, Latin America and, even more recently, from Africa. This created a more culturally diverse society and changed the balance of religious denominations. By the 1980s, Catholics had become the largest Christian denomination, based primarily on continuing immigration from Catholic countries. In common with other Western countries, the post-war period also saw the expansion of education, the advent of new media, and a period of considerable change in social attitudes, especially from the 1960s onwards. This included a marked decline in religious participation and, albeit more slowly, religious identification, reflected in successive five-yearly census results.

By 2006 the census revealed that only 64 per cent of Australians still identified as Christian, with Catholicism now by far the largest denomination. Traditional Protestant denominations appear to be in general decline, although there is modest growth in the number of those identifying as Baptists, and fast growth in the number of Pentecostal adherents, albeit from a small base. About 5 per cent identify with other major religions (in descending order, Buddhism, Islam, Hinduism, Judaism and Sikhism). However, other sources suggest that only a small fraction of those professing Christianity in the census actually participate in organized religious activity, with fewer than a tenth of Australians attending church in any given week (8.8 per cent according to the National Church Life Survey, 2001).

Non-government organizations specifically committed to overseas development or relief began to become prominent in the 1960s. However, some organizations undertaking similar work had been in operation for much longer, although they did not define their purpose specifically in those terms. The Australian Red Cross had been formed in 1914 and Save the Children established itself in Australia in 1919. In addition, prior to this date organizations committed to Christian mission had undertaken some similar activities, especially in regard to education and medical work in the Pacific islands (Clarke, 2010).

Food For Peace, an Australian organization specifically concerned with poverty in

Asia, was formed in 1953, at the instigation of the Melbourne Anglican priest Gerard Tucker, also well known as the founder of one of Australia's most significant domestic welfare charities, the Brotherhood of St Laurence. In 1962 Food for Peace changed its name to Community Aid Abroad (CAA), reflecting the evolution of its understanding and approach to international poverty. The Australian Council for the World Council of Churches' Resettlement and Refugee Service, later to evolve into the church-based NGO Act for Peace, was also formed in the early 1950s. In 1959 Australian Quakers formed the Friends Service Council, later to become Quaker Service Australia, although overseas service by Quakers long pre-dated the formation of this organization. Another significant agency, the Australian Freedom From Hunger Campaign, initially supported by affiliated trade unions and community groups, including the Council of Churches, rather than individuals, was created in 1961. CAA and Freedom from Hunger merged in the 1990s and ultimately evolved into Oxfam Australia.

Meanwhile, several international NGOs, both secular and religious, also established operations in Australia, and several of these quickly evolved into substantial and viable organizations in their own right. For example, World Vision Australia commenced with seed funding from the USA in 1966 and Foster Parents Plan (later Plan International) in 1971. These organizations both grew rapidly, significantly expanding the Australian support base for overseas work through child sponsorship programmes.

Another strand of the Australian NGO work grew from volunteering programmes. The largest of these, Overseas Service Bureau, began sending Australians overseas in 1950 and eventually became Australian Volunteers International.

By the middle of the 1960s, the extent of voluntary foreign aid activity in Australia, and concerns about its haphazard nature and how voluntary organizations could interact with government, led to the formation of the Australian Council for Overseas Aid (Kilby, 2008). A further development was the creation of Action for World Development (AWD) in 1971, an organization specifically intended to pursue an advocacy and education agenda in relation to Australian government and community attitudes, along similar lines to the organization with a similar name created in the UK by Oxfam and Christian Aid six years earlier.

From the late 1960s onwards, the sector continued to grow both in the number of agencies and in their size, scale and scope of activity. In line with international trends, this growth in size has been accompanied by expansion in the employment of technical and policy experts, and increased policy and political influence, as well as greater scrutiny by both government and donors, and higher expectations of accountability.

Korten's Typology

Korten's (1990) schema proposing four 'generations' of NGO, characterized by distinctive preferred strategies, argues that the understanding and practice of responding to poverty and suffering of many NGOs evolves over time, based on their experience, and that contemporary NGOs can be categorized according to this typology. It is important to note that Korten's typologies were based on his anecdotal observations and have not been empirically tested. This pilot project seeks to consider this schema for both FBOs and NGOs based in Australia.

Korten notes that many NGOs are initially created with a direct humanitarian relief purpose, such as responding to war or a natural disaster. As a consequence, their initial operating model focuses on material needs as the defining problem, and the time frame for response is immediate. The agency itself is seen as the primary actor and the pressing management task is logistical. Beneficiaries are rarely conceived as communities, rather the focus is on individuals or family units. The appeal to supporters is primarily financial and tends to depend heavily on eliciting an emotional response to stories or images of suffering. The second generation strategies focus more on developing the capacities of communities to become more self-reliant in meeting their own needs. While some agencies display this orientation from the outset, it is more usual for it to evolve from their initial relief-welfare orientation. Implicitly or explicitly, the defining problem is understood not merely as immediate material shortages but as a social inertia or lack of community structures and processes that would enable improvement. The emphasis is not on immediate relief efforts directed to individuals or families, but on projects that enable community self-help. The agency no longer necessarily sees itself as the primary actor, instead understanding the development enterprise as a community concern in which the NGO plays a mobilizing role. The appeal to donors is not based so squarely on emotion and compassion, but also emphasizes respect for the ethic of self-help. Third generation strategies attempt to place the challenges of development in a wider systemic frame, comprehending the significance of policies and institutions for communities. These strategies also reflect a realization that the benefits of short-term interventions can be quickly lost once projects are completed unless systemic change also occurs, as well as the fact that in many places even successful NGO projects do not in and of themselves bring about change on a wide geographic scale. Hence, third generation strategies need to operate on a regional or national scale and generally are conceived as being implemented over a much longer time frame. The NGO cedes much of its role as the implementer or mobilizer of change, acting instead as a catalyst and advocate for change within the structures and systems identified as constraining community improvement. Just as second generation strategies proved insufficient because NGOs were unable to replicate them in countless communities, for Korten third generation strategies also hit their limits. Writing in 1990, Korten's view was that the future required a fourth generation, in which development-oriented NGOs would morph into 'people's movements'. In this manifestation, the NGO would overtly adopt the primary role of activist and educator, with its primary task being to coalesce and energize loosely defined and self-managing networks of people and organizations. No longer bound by project or strategic time frames, these fourth generation strategies would be indefinite in their longevity and conceive of problems primarily in terms of whole systems, within a global thought frame. Drawing on historic examples such as the Chinese literacy movement and the planned parenthood movement, Korten notes the vitality and rapid impact of such movements, even though they remained loosely organized, as well as the subsequent deadening effect of bureaucratization as they developed large budgets and the concomitant organizational systems.

While Korten's typology implies that NGOs ideally 'evolve' through the four generations he identifies, it is more probable that a particular NGO displays characteristics of different generations simultaneously with regard to different aspects of their work, for example, marketing, advocacy and programming. Nor is it necessarily the case – despite Korten's implicit presentation as such – that all aid agencies initially display generation one characteristics before 'evolving' through the second, third and fourth generations. In reality, different aid agencies have different starting places and ending positions. It is also likely that aid agencies will move backwards and forwards between the 'generations' over time.

This pilot study considers the current philosophical and development practice of 17 Australian FBOs and NGOs in order to determine which generational characteristics they most prominently display. Its purpose is to better understand if FBOs are more or less likely than secular NGOs to understand and practise development in a manner consistent with the most 'evolved' generation as posited by Korten.

COMPARING FBOs AND SECULAR NGOs

In order to evaluate the extent to which aid and development organizations can be regarded as having first, second, third or fourth generation characteristics as proposed by Korten, a nominal scale must be created. Determining such criteria required a pragmatic and realistic appreciation of the data that could be used to assess against each criterion. The ten criteria selected reflect to a large extent the essence of his different types. These ten criteria concentrate on the practical and organizational characteristics of agencies, rather than the nature and sources of the values and beliefs that underlie their functioning. Each of the criteria reflect the manner in which each agency understands and practices development in line with Korten's generations. In addition, the criteria are all capable of being assessed by informants with close familiarity with the organizations concerned, or by reference to relevant agency documentation such as mission statements, annual reports and donor communications.

The criteria applied were the extent to which the following characteristics were present in an agency's current policy and practice:

1. *Organizational and programme governance centred in the country of operations and, where relevant, in specific field locations.* Agencies that have decentralized governance structures in which decision making is located as closely as possible to partner communities are more likely to be operating within Korten's fourth generation space than agencies that maintain a centralized structure. This geographical distance reflects a 'distance' of communities and casts them as 'beneficiaries' rather than 'owners'.
2. *Programme managers and staff are predominantly nationals of the country of operations.* Linked to the abilities to hand over responsibilities and controls to local communities above, this criterion reflects agencies' abilities to recognize local capacities and strengths through passing managerial responsibilities to local staff. The increasing involvement of local managers and nationals of the country of operations represents a shift in along the welfare to sustainable development continuum.
3. *Programmes engage with or support local community partners and civil society organizations.* Welfare or charity based activities are less likely to activity engage with local partners – other than as possible distribution points – as agencies focused on achieving sustainable development that requires local civil organizations to

take responsibility for and ownership over development intervention planning and implementation.

4. *Field projects incorporate a high degree of community governance and participation.* As Korten noted in his description of the four generations, relief responses are based on providing material support to those in need and dependent upon the agency for survival. In these instances, community governance and participation is low. However, community governance and participation increases throughout generations and two and three and is almost absolute in generation four
5. *Design, monitoring and evaluation systems are decentralized or participatory.* Ownership of development interventions begins within Korten's second generation where local capacity is noted and built and increases clearly in generation three agencies where much of the control is ceded to the local community and this becomes near complete within agencies operating with generation four characteristics.
6. *Local capacity building is embedded as a primary programme objective.* Understanding capacity within the first generation is based upon a deficit model in which development responses are conceived on the notion that local communities will solely be beneficiaries as they do not have the wherewithal to provide for themselves. Similarly, second generation agencies also see capacity of local communities through the deficit lens, but in contrast to first generation agencies seek to improve what is perceived as missing or flawed. Third and fourth generation agencies though, understand capacity within an appreciative model and seek to build on what is there, culminating in passing complete control to local communities.
7. *System and structural change in relation to policy and institutions is acknowledged as an integral programme objective.* Explicit acknowledgement of moving towards a situation in which the agency's own structures and systems are being reset to not only serve the interests of the local community but are actually being reset by the local community distinguishes agencies who operate in second, third and fourth generation modalities.
8. *The agency's resource allocation is oriented in a way that reflects a movement from relief and welfare towards sustainable development or advocacy.* Fundraising is an important component of an aid agency's operations. Without funds, successful operations cannot exist. Fundraising though also requires dissemination of information regarding the local community. First generation agencies utilize images that project a sense of helplessness and hopelessness of the local community. Classic images of starvation and malnutrition have successfully raised enormous amounts of money. However, as agencies themselves recognize and value the capacities and resources of local communities, they in turn should recast their fundraising activities to also reflect this. Fundraising using these images is more difficult (see M. Clarke, 2008).
9. *The agency formally recognizes, and programme design reflects, rights and/or capability-based approaches to development.* There are numerous ways in which to understand development issues and responses, including rights-based approaches, gender-based approaches, child-focused approaches, and so forth. Korten's fourth generation clearly reflects the principles of the rights- and/or capacity-based approach to development.

10. *Relations with supporters are treated as educational or transformational projects.* As with criterion 8 above, fundraising is a central activity for aid agencies. Agencies that seek to solely raise funds without seeking to educate their supporters display first and second generation characteristics because they do see a relationship between the supporters providing funds and the local communities in which those funds are spent. Agencies though that see the relationship between supporters and local communities will seek to use their fundraising activities as educational or transformative tasks with the transformation of supporters as important as the development interventions taking place in the local community.

As noted, this exercise is a pilot project with the purpose of empirically testing Korten's schema and seeking to determine whether there are inherent biases within faith-based or secular aid agencies with regard to their ability to operate within any of these generations. Having determined the criteria above, the task was to then use a variety of published materials and expert knowledge to determine on a nominal scale how each of the 17 agencies were placed in these regards. Each agency in the sample was scored on a scale of 1 to 5:

5 True in all or almost all instances of current practice or policy
4 True in a majority of instances of current practice or policy
3 True in about half of instances of current practice or policy
2 True in a minority of instances of current practice or policy
1 True in no or almost no instances of current practice or policy

Once assessed and scored, these scores summed and classified into discrete bands aligned with the four generations:

Generation 1 – score of 0–21
Generation 2 – score of 22–31
Generation 3 – score of 32–39
Generation 4 – score of 40+

Using this scale, the 11 faith-based agencies fell fairly clearly into discrete bands. Two were scored as 'Generation 4' (aggregate score of 40 or more), compared to two of the six secular NGOs. Five were scored as 'Generation 3' (a score of 32–39), seven as 'Generation 2' (a score of 21–31) and three as 'Generation 1' (a score of 14–21), compared with three, one and none of the secular NGOs respectively (see Table 33.1). This distribution does not demonstrate any clear difference between organizations with a religious and secular orientation, implying that a similar proportion of both can be said to have the broad characteristics of Korten's third and fourth generation NGOs.

Two key findings emerge from this analysis. The first point to note is that FBOs appear to be as likely as secular NGOs to demonstrate the characteristics of Korten's second, third and fourth generations: the faith-based nature of these organizations, whether denominational or non-denominational, does not (at least in the Australian context) tie them to the charity or welfare provision model of Korten's first generation of NGOs. This is an important finding, as it is often assumed that FBOs are traditional charities

Table 33.1 Classification of FBOs and NGOs according to Korten's 'four generations'

	Generation 1	Generation 2	Generation 3	Generation 4
FBOs (denominational)	1	2	3	1
FBOs (non-denominational)	1	1	1	1
Secular NGOs		2	3	1

with a focus on welfare provision due to their genesis in responding to humanitarian crisis and the charity model that is reflected in nearly all sacred texts and social teaching of the major religions (see Clarke, 2011). Thus, whilst many of these of FBOs did indeed start their operations as welfare and charity oriented first generation organizations, they have followed the trajectory suggested by Korten.

The second point of interpretation from this preliminary analysis is that factors other than faith account for the characteristics of FBOs, although some of these factors may be related to their faith origins. The two key factors are size and constituency. This study suggests that smaller aid agencies (faith-based or secular) are more likely to have the characteristics of second, third or fourth generation organizations than larger agencies and that a clear sense of an organization's constituency aids such a transition. For example, the smaller FBOs in the sample are less likely to be part of large international partnerships and more likely to partner with local organizations that have a similar denominational basis, a commonality that promotes transition towards community engagement, advocacy and ownership by the local partner. A clearly defined constituency also provides freedom for an organization to know more precisely what development issues are acceptable within its governance structure and to its donor base. Small organizations seem to have more clearly defined constituencies than large agencies (secular or religious), which tend to have a broader supporter base. Of course, there are some advantages to absolute size, with larger agencies being able to employ staff with higher qualifications and more experience and invest more resources in design, monitoring and evaluation of programmes. That said, this study indicates that an initial movement from welfare to community development seems to be facilitated by smaller size and smaller support base.

CONCLUSION

The purpose of this preliminary research was to test a method by which to assess the fit between FBOs' characteristics and Korten's characterization of generations of NGO strategies and to determine whether they are less likely to take on the characteristics of his second, third and fourth generation organizations than secular NGOs. The preliminary findings from an analysis of 17 Australian secular and faith-based aid agencies suggest that FBOs, at least in a rich nation, do not appear less likely than secular NGOs to resemble Korten's higher-level generations, suggesting that FBOs' development practice and organizational characteristics can be understood in similar terms to those applied to secular NGOs. This is an important contribution to the (limited but growing) literature surrounding faith-based organizations. This suggests that assessing the effectiveness of FBOs can and should be done in a similar manner to that of secular NGOs and that any distinctiveness between the two (if this exists) will not be a factor of how they operate in terms of Korten's typology.

Thus, this preliminary analysis is not intended to mount an argument that FBOs are as or more effective than their secular counterparts, because many of them demonstrate the characteristics that Korten associates with more effective development agencies. Many of the positive inherent strengths attributed to FBOs, whether these are their ability to raise considerable funds through their affiliation with international and national religious networks or to gain community trust, tackle corruption and advocate on behalf of the poor, are those Korten identifies in his high-level generations as characteristics to which aid agencies should aspire. While this research did not evaluate these claims, if future research finds that they are valid, then it is possible that at least some FBOs can be characterized as effective development organizations.

This chapter presents preliminary evidence that FBOs should, in the first instance, be treated as serious development stakeholders that are not disadvantaged by their faith affiliation in terms of demonstrating the characteristics of NGOs that Korten identifies as associated with positive development outcomes. What is clearly required now is more investigation of how FBOs operate, how their faith identity is reflected in their development practices and whether and how these do indeed translate into different development outcomes from those achieved by their secular counterparts.

NOTE

1. While there are several Muslim international development organizations operating in Australia, they have only existed for a very short time.

REFERENCES

Ball, C. and L. Dunn (1996), 'NGOs defined', in Commonwealth Foundation (ed.), *Non-government Organisations: Guidelines for Good Policy and Practice*, London: The Commonwealth Foundation.

Clarke, G. (2008), 'Faith based organisations and international development', in Gerard Clarke and Michael Jennings (eds), *Development, Civil Society and Faith-based Organisations*, London: Palgrave MacMillan.

Clarke, G. and M. Jennings (eds) (2008), *Development, Civil Society and Faith-based Organisations*, London: Palgrave Macmillan.

Clarke, M. (2008), 'Raising the funds – spending the funds: a case study of the effectiveness of BOTH roles of NGOs', in A. Renzhao (ed.), *Measuring Development Effectiveness*, New York: Nova.

Clarke, M. (2010), 'God i givim ples ya long yumi (God has given us this land): the role of the church in building Pacific nations', presented at the Religion Shaping Development: Inspirational, Inhibiting, Institutionalized? Conference, University of Birmingham, 21–23 July.

Clarke, M. (2011), *Development and Religion: Theology and Practice*, Cheltenham, UK and Northampton, MA, USA: Edward Elgar.

Clarke, M., S. Charnley and J. Lumbers (2011), 'Churches, mosques and condoms: understanding successful faith-based organisations' HIV and AIDS interventions', *Development in Practice*, **21**(1), 3–17.

Cornwall, A. (2007), 'Buzzwords and fuzzwords: deconstructing development discourse', *Development in Practice*, **17**(4–5), 471–84.

Feeny, S. and M. Clarke (2009), *The Millennium Development Goals and Beyond: International Assistance to the Asia-Pacific*, London: Palgrave Macmillan.

Harb, M. (2008), 'Faith-based organisations as effective development partners? Hezbollah and post-war reconstruction in Lebanon', in Gerard Clarke and Michael Jennings (eds), *Development, Civil Society and Faith-based Organisations*, London: Palgrave Macmillan.

James, R. (2009), 'What is distinctive about FBOs? How European FBOs define and operationalise their faith', Praxis Paper No. 22, Oxford: INTRAC.

Kilby, P. (2008,) 'The development of NGO support organizations: the early years of the Australian Council for Overseas Aid', *International Journal of Not-for-Profit Law*, **11**(1), 84–92.

Korten, D. (1990), *Getting to the 21st Century: Voluntary Action and the Global Agenda*, West Hartford, CT: Kumarian Press.

Marshall, K. (2005), 'Rethinking development debates', World Bank, Washington DC, available at: http://web.worldbank.org/WBSITE/EXTERNAL/EXTABOUTUS/PARTNERS/EXTDEVDIALOGUE/0,,contentMDK:20478626~menuPK:64192472~pagePK:64192523~piPK:64192458~theSitePK:537298,00.html; accessed 31 July 2012.

Marshall, K. and L. Keough (2004), *Mind, Heart and Soul in the Fight Against Poverty*, Washington, DC: World Bank.

Marshall, K. and M. Van Saanen (2007), *Development and Faith*, Washington, DC: World Bank.

National Church Life Survey (2001), *National Church Life Survey 2001 First Look Report*, www.ncls.org.au/.

van Geest, W. (1998), 'The relationship between development and religion', *Evangelical Review of Theology*, **22**(1).

Vidal, A. (2001), *Faith-based Organizations in Community Development*, Washington, DC: The Urban Institute.

Index

AACC (All African Conference of Churches) 275
ABC model (HIV/AIDS) 371–2
Abduljeleel, Alhaji 466, 467
abortion 189, 190
Abraham (Judaism) 67
Abu-Nimer, Mohammed 257, 258, 265
Abundant Life *see* Prosperity Gospel
Abuza, Zachary 23
Accelerated Climate Change: Sign of Peril, Test of Faith 211
Aceh 5, 299, 305, 310–20, 321, 322
ACFID (Australian Council for International Development) 424
Acharya, Uddhav 343
Act for Peace 576
Action Against Hunger 262
Adagbada, Pastor Peter 462, 467
Adamu, Fatima 195
Addai, I. 372
Adi Granth (Sikhism) 99
Afghanistan 540–67
  aid 565
  al-Qaeda 543, 549
  assassinations 543–4
  constructivist view 554–6
  education 562
  elites 555–6
  EVAW law 543, 547
  gender and reform 561–4
  governance 564–5
  Haraza massacre 542, 550
  legitimacy 564–5
  night letters 544
  post-Soviet 542
  poverty 564–5
  recent conflict 541–3, 553–4
  religious traditions 554–5
  rural–urban dimension 561, 562
  symbols and myths 555
  Taliban 540, 542, 543, 545, 549–53, 556–65, 566
  tribalism 540, 557
  violence
    against children 547–8, 558
    against women 543–53, 558, 563–4
    cultural 548–53, 563–4
    religious 548–53
    and the Taliban 556–65
Africa South of the Sahara 502
African traditional religions *see* ATR
Afro-Brazilian spiritism 477–8, 479, 484, 485–6, 487–8
Aga Khan Foundation 361
Agai, B. 245, 250
Agarwal, Bina 92
Agri-Horticultural Society 421
ahimsa (Buddhism) 33
Ahl An-Nusrat 393, 395
Ahmad, Ali 463
Ahmed, Habib 290, 293, 294
Ahmed, Leila 191
Ahmed, Sadia 192
AIDS *see* HIV/AIDS
AIDS-Amma shrine 334, 335
AIHRC (Afghan Independent Human Rights Commission) 545, 547
Aitape Catholic Diocese Relief Committee 309
Akal Takhat 100
Al-Azhar 245–6
Al-Fateh Islamic Institute 246
Al-Haramain Islamic Foundation 24, 27
Al-Noor Foundation 246
Al-Qaeda 384, 540
Alberto, Carol 175
Ali, Mallam 460
Ali, N. 240, 241
'alims 241–2
Alkire, S. 58
allegiance, to earth 211
Allen, A.A. 169
Allport, G.W. 232–3
Alolo, Namawu Alhassan 9
alter-globalism 376–96
alternative governance contestation 396
Alternatives Unincorporated: Earth Ethics from the Grassroots 211
Altutmush, Sultan 240
Amajan, Safia 543
Ambedkar, Babasaheb 34
ambivalence of the sacred 252
amorality of delinquency 223
Amritsar 100
An-Nabhani, Taqiuddin 379, 380, 390
Analects of Confucius 126, 127

Anambra state (Nigeria) 455–9, 464
anatta (Buddhism) 32, 33, 37
Andean indigenous resurgence 139
Anderson, Jane 11
Anglican Board of Mission 506
Anglican Church 506
ANGOs (Australian NGOs) 505, 506, 507, 511
Anheier, Helmut J. 360
anti-ascetic/anti-social behaviour 234
anti-conversion movement, Sri Lanka 261–4
anti-corruption programmes 220
Appleby, R.S. 252, 254, 265, 271
ARC (Alliance for Religions and Conservation) 122
Arce, A. 510
Ariyaratne, A.T. 40, 45, 255–6
Arole, Mabelle 415–16
Arole, Rajanikant 415–16
Arole, Shobha 416
as sabiya 293
Asad, T. 270
ascetic Protestantism 103
ASEAN (Association of Southeast Asian Nations) 343
Ashafa, Muhammed Nurayn 260
Assemblies of God 436
Ataturk, Kemal 239, 245
Atoyebi, Chief Akanbi 466
ATR (African traditional religions) 9, 138–61
  ancestors 153
  anthropological studies 143–4
  beliefs 147–50
  common rituals 147
  conflict 153–5
  in contemporary African society 145–51
  crime and justice 155–7
  customs 147–50
  and development 139–41, 151–60
  diversity in 145–6
  enfants sorciers 151
  evil spirits 150–51
  and evolutionary theory 143
  and gender 157–60
  morality 152–3
  muti (medicine) killings 141, 151
  myths of creation 152
  political liberalization 141
  practices 147–50
  sorcery 150–51
  spiritual hierarchy 148–9
  stereotypes 142–3
  study phases 141
  tradition and plurality 145–7
  unity in diversity 145–7
  witchcraft 150–51
AusAID 423, 505, 506, 507, 508, 516
  Design Document 509–10
  development cooperation 511
  Program Framework 509
Australia 11
  FBOs (faith-based organizations) in 570–82
  international NGOs in 576
  post-war immigration 575
  religions in 575
Azharites institute 246
Azusa Street revival 173

Baitul Qiradh 299, 300, 301, 302
Baker, Sir Samuel 142
Bala, Shasha 101
Balchin, Cassandra 193–4
Bandaranayake, S. 343
Bannerman, J.Y. 159
Bano, Masooda 10, 250
Baptist Missionary Society 421
Baptist Union 505, 506
Baptist World Alliance 511
Barfield, T. 560, 564, 565
Barr, M. 5
Barra, G. 159
Barrett, David 171
Bartelink, Brenda 193
Basarke, A. 110
Batson, C.D. 233
Bauer, Peter 103
Baumann, H. 157
Bayes, Jane H. 188
BAZNAS (Badan Amil Zakat Nasional) 299, 300, 301, 302
Beckmann, David 279
Beets, S.D. 221
Beijing women's conference 188
Bellers, Jurgen 21
Bellion-Jourdan, J. 25
Benedict XVI, Pope 58, 62, 63
Benevolence International Foundation 25
Benthall, J. 409
Bercovitch, J. 257–8, 259
Berkley Center for Religion, Peace and World Affairs 12
Berry, Thomas 207
Betto, Frei 482
Bhagavad-Gita 84
Bhai Gurdas 100
Bhave, Vinoba 90–91
Bi, Lijun 9
Bilad Al-Islam 382, 383
BJP Hindu nationalist party 334
Blair, Prime Minister Tony 491
blessing pact 168

BMMI (Baitul Maal Muamalat Indonesia) 297–8, 300, 301, 302
BMT (Baitul Maal wat Tamwil) 296
BMT ONE 299, 301
Boff, Leonardo 211
Bonn Agreement 543
Book of Changes 125
Booth, J.S. 145
Bosch, David 413
Boserup, Ester 12, 183
boundary activation 260
Boyden, J. 556
Bradbury, Steve 11
Brahimi 542, 560, 567
Brain, James 151
Brazil 472–89
  Afro-Brazilian spiritism 477–8, 479, 484, 485–6
  agriculture 477
  Bishops' Conference 482
  as BRIC country 473, 477
  and Catholicism 473–4, 476, 478, 479–82, 486–7
  churches 478
  classical period 474–6, 477
  contemporary development 476–8
  contemporary religion 478–9
  democratic status 477
  human rights 477–8
  IURD (Universal Church of the Kingdom of God) in 478, 478–9, 479, 484, 485
  linguistic community 480
  as NIC 473
  Participatory Budget 477
  Pentecostalism in 482–5, 487
  size of economy 472, 477
  social inequalities 472
  USAID to 473
Bretton Woods 273
Brock, Peggy 419
Broom Goddess 331, 332
Brotherhood of St Lawrence 576
Bubalo, Anthony 28
Buchanan, Grant 11
Buddhism 9, 31–43
anatta 32, 33, 37
  and borrowing 40–41
  dana 33–4
  and debt 40–41
  and development 35–6
  development monks 35, 37–8
  dhamma 32
  and ecology 36–8
  eightfold path 32, 38
  Engaged Buddhism 35, 45
  five precepts 33
  Four Noble Truths 31
  and gender issues 41–4
  heritage tourism 344–8
  kamma 36
  karuna 33
  metta 33
  paramatta sacca 37
  and peace-building 44–5
  philanthropy 33–4
  and poverty 40–41, 43
  sammuti sacca 37
  samsara 32
  sangha 32–3
  social justice 34–5
  sunyata 32, 37
  teachings of 31
  three refuges 32
  Zen 35
Buddhism and poverty 40
Buddhist economics 36–41
Buitelaar, Marjo 193
Burdick, John 483, 484
Burr, J.M. 19, 20, 22, 24, 25
Burton, Sir Richard 142–3
Bush, President George W. 188, 193
Busia, Kofi 144
Bwamche, Reverend Joshua 460, 462, 463

CAA (Community Aid Abroad) 576
CAFOD (Catholic Fund for Overseas Development) 361, 403
Caliphate restoration 376–96
Campo, J.E. 19
CAN (Christian Association of Nigeria) 459
capitalism 4
Carey, William 421
Caritas Australia 506
Caritas in Veritate 58, 59, 62, 63
Casanova, José 493–4
caste 34, 82, 89, 107
Catechism of the Catholic Church 59
Catholic Church
  and abortion 189
  Australia 506
  in Brazil 473–4, 476, 478, 479–82
Catholic social teaching 58, 62
CCK (Care for Kenya) 417–18
CCR (Catholic Charismatic Renewal) 479, 481, 487
CCT (Christian Council of Tanganyika) 500–501
CDA (Chinese Daoist Association) 114, 121–2
CDF (Comprehensive Development Framework) 276–7

CEBs (Grassroots Church Communities) 474–5, 476, 479–82, 483, 486
CEDAW (UN Convention on the Elimination of all forms of Discrimination Against Women) 195
Centesimus Annus 63
CGAP (Consultative Group to Assist the Poor) 290
Chahal, S.K. 107
Chambers, R. 76
Chang, Wen-Chung 120
Charismatic renewal movement 433, 439
Charitable Choice (Welfare Act 1996 USA) 403
Chau, Adam Yuet 118
Chen Duxiu 115
Chesnut, R.A. 485
Chiang Mai University *see* Lampang Temple Project
Chowdry, Kamla 90
Christian Aid 361, 362, 403, 576
Christian Council of Tanganyika 497
Christian language of development (Papua New Guinea) 511
Christian Right 494
Christian Witness in a Multi-Religious World: Recommendations for Conduct 426
Christianity 9, 51–64
  case against 210
  charity 405
  Christian symbolism 203
  Christian traditions 202–3
  the Church 56–7
  common good 59
  communion 52, 59–61
  the creed 52–7
  death and resurrection 55–6
  discipleship 52–3
  divinity and humanity 54–5
  earth-affirming Christianities 210–12
  and ecological degradation 208, 209–10
  and ecological healing 210–16
  faith and community 53
  freedom and responsibility 61
  God the Creator 53–4
  God indwelling 214–15
  neighbour-love as ecological vocation 213–14, 215
  ownership of goods 60
  Pentecostal 164–77
  perspective on international development 57–63
  sin 61–3
  solidarity 60
  structural sin 62
  subsidiarity 59
  Symbol of the Apostles 53
  see also evangelism; missionaries; Pentecostal missions
civic culture and religion 7
Civil Society Challenge Fund (DFID) 422
Clark, Janine Natalya 265
Clark, M.S. 434
Clarke, Gerard 28, 51, 269, 306, 307, 360–61, 364, 403, 406, 431, 570
Clarke, Matthew 5, 8, 9, 10, 11, 307, 348, 351, 431, 446, 573
Clarke, Peter B. 481
clash of civilizations hypothesis 366, 493
Classic of Changes 129
Classic of History 125, 129, 133
Classic of Poetry 129, 133
Classic of Rites 129, 135
Claudill, Steven B. 302
Clean Ganga Campaign 94
climate change 204
climate imperialism 203–4
Clinard, M. 222
CMC (Christian Medical College) 415
CMS (Church Missionary Society) 420
Cold War politics 2
Coleman, S. 170
CollAsia 2010 343
Collier, P. 154
Collins, R.O. 19, 20, 22, 24, 25
Combined Churches Organization 309
The coming anarchy 143
common Africanness 144
community ownership 76
community self governance 40
Complex Political Emergencies 382, 383
concentric circles of influence 240
conflict 10, 252–65
  boundary activation 260
  equity guarantees 261
  faith-based development services 261–4
  polarization 260
  religious roots of 252–3
  see also peacebuilding
Confucian Classics 124
Confucianism 9, 114, 124–36
  Analects 126, 127
  Classics 125, 129, 133, 135
  core teachings of Confucius 125–7
  and cosmology 135
  and development 131–3
  Doctrine of the Mean 129, 133, 136
  and education 130–31
  and environment 133–4
  filial piety 134
  Four Books 129

gender 135
and gender 135
goodness of men 136
Great Learning 129
and health care 134–5
Heaven and man 133–4
Heaven's four functions 133
life of Confucius 125–7
Mencius 127–8, 134, 135
morality 134
Spring and Autumn Annals 125, 129
as state cult 128–30
sustainability 132
Connell, James Astley 9, 11
context
and FBOs 362, 363
and theology 203
Cook, Albert 498
Copeland, Kenneth 169
corruption 10, 220–34, 453, 460–61, 532, 547
anti-corruption programmes 220
and belief in hell 223
cultural explanations for 220
Development Dialogues 222
factors in moral attitudes 223
Indian street vendors 330, 336
levels 225
and moral reasoning 229–33
values and attitudes 229
Cortes, J.B. 223–4
Cosgrave, J. 8
Council of Churches 576
Council for World Mission 511
Couture, D. 188
covenants of purity 117
Coward, Harold G. 91, 252, 254
CPP (Church Partnership Programme) 505–7
CRHP (Comprehensive Rural Health Project) 416, 417
critique of development 204–6
critique and theology 203
Croll, E. 135
Cry of the Earth, Cry of the Poor 211
Cultural Revolution (China) 116, 130
cultural traditions 10

Dakin, Tim 425–6
Dalai Lama 36, 45
Dalforo, A.T. 158
Daly, Herman E. 120–21
dana (Buddhism) 33–4
Daniels, D.I. 437
Danquah, J.B. 144
Danyaro, Mallam 465
Daoism 9, 113–22
and Communism 115
community well-being 116–20
Complete Perfection 114
covenants of purity 117
development 114–16
harmony 114–16
herbal remedies 120
modernity 114–16
Qi (vital energy) 119
sustainability 120–22
Three Pure Ones 113
Dar-ul Uloom Deoband 239, 242
Darling, Malcolm 104, 105
Dars-i-Nizami 243, 244
Dasam Granth 100
Dass, J.R. 103, 104
da'wa 25
Dayanand, Swami 333
De Bary, W.T. 136
De Berry, J. 556
De Cordier, Bruno 11, 308, 408
De Kadt, Emmanuel 474
Deakin University *see* Lampang Temple Project
debt advocacy 280–81
Decade of Harvest 436
Declaration on Global Ecology 121–2
decolonization 308
Delhi Master Plans 329
Delhi street hawking 327–9
Deneulin, Séverine 9, 51
Deng Xiaoping 116
dependency theory 4
deprivatization of religion 307, 494
developing countries 4
development
and economic growth 206–7
and environmental concerns 206–7
holistic approach to 306
development agendas 344–8
Development Dialogues, on corruption 222
development FBOs 360–64
development monks 35, 37–8
deviant behaviour 222–34
devotion (Hinduism) 85
DFID (Department for International Development) 403, 422–3, 505
dhamma (Buddhism) 32
dharma (Hinduism) 81–4, 94
A Different Gospel 169
Dikshit, Sheila 329
Dipavali festival 88
Directorate on Faith 282
disaster counseling failure 318
discourse of ethnicity 486

Divali festival 88
Divine Farmer's Materia Medica 120
doctrine of distinction 107
Doctrine of the Mean 129, 133, 136
dominion controversy 209
Dong Zhongshu 114, 129
donor dependence (secular NGOs) 498
Dowden, Richard 415
dowry 190, 191
drive to maturity modernization stage 3
Duara, Prasenjit 115–16, 122
Dubai, and globalization 386–7
dukkha (suffering) 31, 41
Dunning, J.H. 270
Durga (goddess of power) 330, 331, 336
Duriez, B. 230, 231, 232
Durkheim, E. 6, 252
Dussehra festival 88
Dusuki, Asyraf Wajdi 293
Dwidevi, O.P. 82

Earth Bible 210–11
earth-affirming Christianities 210–12
earth-human relations 207–9
earth-keeping 211
Ebaugh, H. 7
eco-feminism 208
eco-reformation 207
eco-theology 214, 215
ecological destruction 202
ecological issues 206
ecological well-being 212–13
ECWA (Evangelical Church of West Africa) 460, 463
education 10
Eight Year Plan (CDA) 122
eightfold path (Buddhism) 32
Eikerenkoetter, Reverend Ike 170
Ellis, S. 148, 151, 154, 371
embedded Islam 24
empowerment, as buzzword 186
enfants sorciers 151
Engaged Buddhism 35, 45
Engelhardt, Richard 346–7
environment 10, 93–4
environmental racism 204
environmental space 217
equity guarantees 261
Ertürk, Yakin 564
ESCAP (Economic and Social Commission for Asia and the Pacific) 344–8
ethical contestation 396
Evangelical Lutheran Church 505, 506
Evangelii Nuntiandi 54
evangelism 261, 263–4, 372, 420, 430, 434, 491
evangelization 5, 51, 171, 422–7, 435
Evans, Peter 475
Evans-Pritchard, E.E. 142, 144, 151
EVAW (Elimination of Violence Against Women) 543, 547
exorcisms 485

Faith Based and Community Initiative 403
Faith in the City 491
faith engagement, and IFIs 281
faith and IFIs 281
faith loyalty 252
faith-based development services 261–4
faith-based organizations *see* FBOs
family planning 188
Fan Zhongyan 131
Fanany, Ismet 8, 10
Fanany, Rebecca 8, 10
Fang, Xiangshu 9
Farangi Mahall 243, 244
fasting (Hinduism) 87
FBDOs (faith-based development organizations) 364, 500
FBOs (faith-based organizations) 10, 51, 183–4, 192, 193, 194, 195, 262–4, 282, 306, 321, 359–74, 402–10, 431–2
  in Australia 570–82
  categories of 571–2
  commitment 404–5
  cultural proximity 406
  in developed nations 573–8
  in early colonial period 496–9
  flexible funding 404–5
  holistic care 406
  local networks 406
  perceived strengths 404–7
  and social/political issues 493
  in Tanzania 491–503
  trust 406
  see also missionaries; Pentecostal missions
Fealy, Greg 28
Fee, Gordon 437
Feeny, S. 10, 573
female infanticide 109–10, 190
feminism and Hinduism 333–4
feminist studies 183–96
Ferguson, James 205
Ferris, E. 409
festivals (Hinduism) 87–8
FGW (Farming God's Way) 417, 418
Five Year Plans (China) 121
Flanigan, Shawn Teresa 10, 261, 262, 264, 366, 404–5, 406–7
FMG (Friday Morning Group) 279
foeticide 110

Fondation Reine Elisabeth pour l'Assistance Médicale aux Indigiènes 498
Fonrobert, C. 77
Food for Peace 575–6
forced marriage 192
forced religious conversions 263–4
Foster Parents Plan 576
Foucault, Michel 206
Fougier, Eddy 376, 394, 396
Four Books 129
Four Noble Truths (Buddhism) 31
Four Square Program (Papua New Guinea) 514–15
Fox, J. 5
Fraser, C.A. 22, 26
Freedom From Hunger Campaign 576
Freire, Paulo 474
Friends Service Council 576
Frobenius, L. 142
funded research 12

GAD (gender and development) approach 183, 195
  criticism of 185
  and religion 184–6
Gandhi, Mohandas K. 84, 90–92, 94
Gassett, Don 169
GATT (General Agreement on Tariffs and Trade) 272
Gawor, Leszek 376, 377–8, 388, 394, 395
Gebarra, Ivone 211
Geertz, C. 9
gender 9
  in Afghanistan 543–53, 561–3
  in African traditional religions 157–60
  in Buddhism 41–4
  in Confucianism 135
  conservative religious tradition 189
  and development 183–96
  female infanticide 109–10, 190
  in Hinduism 92–3, 333–4
  in indigenous religions 139, 157–60
  inequality and religion 186–94
  in Islam 186
  in Judaism 76–7
  Muslim–Catholic alliance 188
  and Prosperity Gospel 176
  reproductive rights 188–91
  in Sikhism 108–10
  in Tajikistan 534–5
  women bank clients (Islam) 291
Ghosananda, Maha 255
Gibbs, J.L. 156
Giddens, A. 561
Gifford, Paul 172
Gill, Anita 106
Global Financial Crisis (2007–) 491
global gag rule 188
Global Poverty Action Fund (DFID) 422–3
global televangelism 172
globalization
  contestation 396
  ethical framework 271
  faith networks 492
  Islamic 376–96
  and religion 7
Gluckman, M. 154–5, 156
GM (genetically modified crops) 95
God indwelling 214–15
Gold, Ann 90, 92
Gongyang 126
Gongyang Commentary 129
Good, Anthony 330
Gooren, Henri 176
Gorringe, T.J. 335
Gospel of Health and Wealth *see* Prosperity Gospel
Goulet, D. 6, 7, 8
Grace, Sweet Daddy 170
Grameen Bank 26–7, 293
Great Commission 414
Great Learning 129, 131
Greed, Clara 326
Greeley, A. 227, 228
Green, Maia 454
Green, R. 153
Green Seminary Initiative 210
greening Christianity 211
group loyalty 252
group-lending mechanism 291
Guidelines for Engaging FBOs as Agents of Change 494
Gülen, Fethullah 245
Guling 126
gurdwaras (Sikhism) 97, 99
Guru Amar Das 107, 109
Guru Arjan 99–100, 107
Guru Gobind Singh 100
Guru Granth Sahib 99, 100, 107
Guru Nanak 99, 101, 105, 107, 109
Gutierrez, Gustavo 62
Gwassa, C.G.K. 145

Hagin, Kenneth 169, 170
Hahn, Thich Nhat 255
Haiti 5
Hall, Peter 326
Hamas 392
Hanh, Thich Nhat 35
Harcourt, W. 268–9

Hardiman, David 81
Hardin, R. 368
Harris, I. 36
Harris, R.J. 226, 229
Harrison, Milton F. 164, 167
Haruna, Alhaji Garba 467
Harvey, G. 138, 147, 161
Harvey, P. 31, 32, 34, 35, 45
Hasenfeld 261
Hassan, M. Kabir 294
Hastings, Adrian 51
Haynes, Jeffrey 5, 259, 260, 265, 407
HDI (Human Development Index) 270–71
healing revivals 169
Hefferan, T. 370
Hefner, R. 238, 239
Hegel, G. 67
Helmiere, Frederica 10
Help Africa People 27
heritage sites, in South East Asia 338–52
heritage tourism 344–8
Herzegovina Interreligious Council 407
Hezb-ee-Islami 540
Hezbollah 361, 367
Hindu Code Bill 91
Hindu epics 83–4
Hinduism 9, 79–95
  auspicious/inauspicious 90
  basic concepts 81–90
  charity 94
  definition 79–80
  and development 90–94
  devotion 85
  dharma 81–4, 91, 94
  and the environment 93–4
  and equity 91–2
  fasting 87
  festivals 87–8
  gender issues 92–3
  gifts 94
  and GM (genetically modified crops) 95
  gods and goddesses 326–37
  karma 84, 91
  manual labour 103
  moksha 85
  niyamas 83
  oral texts 80
  pilgrimage 88–9
  poverty 94
  practice 85
  puja 86
  purdah 92
  purity/polution 89
  reincarnation 84–5
  renunciation 84–5
  ritual 85
  ritual calendar 86
  ritual practice 86–7
  sacred sites 89
  Sanatana Dharma 80
  seva 86
  sex-selection 190
  social justice 91–2
  and urban development 327–37
  Vedas 80
  yamas 83
HIPC (Heavily Indebted Poor Countries) initiative 280
Hirschi, T. 224–6
HIV/AIDS 8, 33, 43, 193, 334, 366, 371–2, 373, 454, 457, 458, 512
Hizb Ut-Tahrir Al-Islami (Islamic Liberation Party) 378–96
Hizb-i-Nahzat-1 Islami (Islamic Renaissance Party) 533
Hoeffler, A. 154
Hoffman, B. 253
Hoffstaedter, Gerhard 11
Holiness Movement 432
Hollenweger 173
honour killings 192, 546, 551, 563
hostage release 256
Hovland, Ingie 362
HRW (Human Rights Watch) 547
Hulme, David 300
human actions, and sin 52
human behaviour (Sikhism) 101
human development, material and spiritual 57
human dignity 52, 76
human rights 365, 477–8
  and religion 187
human trafficking 440
humanitarian aid 212
humans, as part of nature 215–16
hundred pathologies 119
Huntington, Samuel 366
Hurricane Katrina 310, 321
Hurricane Nigel (1997) 309–10

Ibrahim al-Ibrahim Foundation 27
IBRD (International Bank for Reconstruction and Development) 272
Ibronov, Hajji Mirzo 533
ICCI (Interreligious Coordinating Council in Israel) 257
ICCROM (International Centre for the Study of the Preservation and Restoration of Cultural Property) 339, 343, 344
ICOM (International Council of Museums) 341

ICOREC (International Consultancy on Religion, Education, and Culture) 90
ICSID (International Centre for the Settlement of Investment Disputes) 272
IDC (International Development Association) 272
Idowu, Bolaji 144
IFC (International Finance Corporation) 272
IFEES (Islamic Foundation for Ecology and Environmental Sciences) 24
IFIs (international financial institutions) 268–83
IICDR (International Islamic Council for Da'wa and Relief) 24
IIRO (International Islamic Relief Organization) 23–4, 27
Ikenga-Metuh, E. 143, 144, 147, 148, 150–51, 152, 153
ILO (International Labour Organization) 278
IMF (International Monetary Fund) 4, 206, 272, 402
immanence 214
Indian Constitution 91, 92
indigenous religions 138–61
  alternative terms for 140
  and development 139–41
  gender 139
  muti (medicine) killings 141
  political liberalization 141
  resurgence of 139
INGOs (Islamic non-government organizations) 21–5, 27, 28, 195, 409
Inter-American Development Bank 278, 282
interaction model of religious influence 226
International Covenant on Civil and Political Rights 425
International Network of Engaged Buddhists 35
Introduction to African Traditional Religion 146
IOs (international organizations) 278
IPS (Islam Prochar Samity) 26
irajah 293
IRCSL (Inter-Religious Council of Sierra Leone) 254–5, 258, 265
Ireland, Rowan 11, 483
irrelevance, of religion 3
IRW (Islamic Relief Worldwide) 23
Islam 9, 17–28
  alter-globalism 376–96
  commercial services 295
  core duties 18–20
  da'wa 25
  and development 307–8
  equality within 287–8
  essentialism 550
  feminist Koran interpretations 193
  forced marriage 192
  and gender inequality 186, 188
  globalization 376–96
  honour killings 192
  interest charges 301
  Islamic Khilafah State *see* Hizb Ut-Tahrir
  microfinance institutions 286–302
  Muslim aid recipients 17
  Muslim population 17
  pan-Islamism 376–96
  and poverty alleviation 287–97
  practical nature of 287
  Prescribed Purifying Alms 405
  relief and development 20–21
  religious fundamentalism 191–2
  religious violence (Afghanistan) 548–53
  sadaqa 19
  shalat 317
  social inequality 17–20
  social services 295
  terrorism financing 27–8
  waqf 19
  women bank clients 291
  women and Grameen Bank 26–7, 293
  zakat 18
Islam, S. 9, 10
Islam, Yusuf 24
Islamic aid agencies 21
  and non-Muslim communities 25
Islamic banks 297–9
Islamic Development Bank 20, 21, 307
Islamic education 238–50
  Jamaat-i-Islami 241
  and jihad 238, 241
  madrasa education
    in community 249–50
    financial incentives 249
    reform attempts 244–8
    in South Asia 240–44
    and the state 249–50
    trust of state 249
  madrasas (Islamic schools) 238–9, 241, 561
  muktabs 238
  'ulamas 238, 239, 240, 241, 242, 245, 250
Islamic expansion 381
Islamic extremism 192, 238
Islamic finance instruments 292–3
Islamic finance principles 291–2
Islamic fundamentalism 308
Islamic Gulen movement 370
Islamic Khilafah State *see* Hizb Ut-Tahrir
Islamic Liberation Army *see* Hizb Ut-Tahrir
Islamic microfinance model 286–302
Islamic pluralism 409

Islamic Relief 403
IURD (Universal Church of the Kingdom of God) 478, 478–9, 479, 484, 485
Izala group 459

Jackson, P. 155
Jakobsh, D. 109
Jamaat-i-Islami 241
James, S.P. 35
Jameson, Kenneth 3, 185
Jat Sikhs 97, 98, 108
JDPC (Justice, Development and Peace Commission) 461
Jenkins, Philip 414
Jennings, Michael 11, 360–61
Johl, S.S. 106
John Paul II, Pope 59, 60, 61, 62, 63
Johnson, Luke Timothy 55, 56, 57
Johnson, T. 548, 557, 560, 561, 565
Jones, Ben 408, 505
Jones, L. 232–33
Jubilee 2000 movement 7, 60, 76, 279, 280, 281
Judaism 9, 66–77
  basic beliefs 68–70
  and charity 75–6, 405
  Commandments 69–70
  creation 66
  destruction of mankind 66–7
  and development 70–77
  and gender 76–7
  Holocaust 74
  justice 71–5
  Oral Law 68
  and persecution 71–2
  Pre-Writing Prophets 72–3
  Prophetic Guilds 72
  sacred texts 66–9
  Thirteen Principles of Faith 68
  Writing Prophets 73
Juergensmeyer, M. 3, 5, 253

Kabbani, Muhammed Hisham 27
Kabeer, Naila 366
Kadayifci-Orellana, S.A. 257–8, 259, 265
Kakar, Lt.Col. Malalai 543
Kaldor, M. 154, 553
Kalimullah, N.A. 22, 26
Kalu, Ogbu 173
Kano state (Nigeria) 455–9, 464
Kaplan, Robert 143
Kapp, K.W. 103
karma 84, 101
karuna (Buddhism) 33
Kaufman, S. 556
Kaur, Valerie 103, 104, 109
Kenyatta, Jomo 144
Kenyon, Essek William 169
Keough 280
Khalsa Panth (Sikhism) 100
Khatri Sikhs 98
Khilafah State *see* Hizb Ut-Tahrir
Kilson, M. 159
Kimambo, I.N. 145
King, Ursula 190–91
Kinnvall, C. 559, 561
Kishwar, Madhu 327, 329–30, 331, 332, 334, 336
Klaus, B. 437
Klausner, J. 74
Klenk, Rebecca 91
Knowledge Centre Religion & Development 505
Kohlberg, L. 230, 231
Kohn, Livia 120
Kong Fuzi (Confucius) *see* Confucianism
Korten, David 5, 76, 446, 571, 573, 574, 576–80, 581–2
Kreps, Christina 343–4
Krige, E.J. 152
Krige, J.D. 152
Kronish, Ron 257
Kumar, Satish 91
KUMMM (Komunitas Usaha Mikro Muamalet Berbasis Masjid) 298, 300, 301

labour migration, global 521
Laheyas 560–61
Lakshmi (goddess of wealth) 330, 336
Laliberté, André 118, 119
Lampang Temples Project 338, 339, 342, 343, 344, 348–52
Lancaster, C. 404
Land Alienation Act (1900) 105, 108
Latin America 11
  colonization 51
  and modernization 4
Latour, B. 507
Lawrance, Allan 115
Laws of Manu 81, 82
Le Zoute conference 146
Leaman, O. 67, 71, 76
LEAP (Local Effort in Asia and the Pacific) programme 346
Lefebvre, H. 326
Leite, Márcia Pereira 480
Lenski, G. 226
Levinas, E. 75
Levy, Robert 326
Lewis, Arthur 102–3
Lewis, D. 507

liberalizing policies 402–3
liberation theology *see* Theology of Liberation
Lindsay, Gordon 169
Lipsky, A.B. 407
literacy, religious 8–9
Little, David 252, 254, 265, 407
Lombard, Maurice 381
Loy, David 39, 40
Luanda Declaration 275
Luang Prabang World Heritage Site 347, 348
Lunn, J. 306, 403
Lutheran Church of Australia 506
Lutheran theology 214

MAA (Muslim Aid Australia) 25
Maathai, Wangari 418
Macauliffe, M.A. 101
McConnell, Daniel 169
Macedo, Bishop Edir 168, 484
McGavran, Donald 435
McGee, G.B. 434–5, 436
Machel, Graca 556
MacIntyre, Alisdair 83
McLeod, W.H. 108
McNamara, Robert 274
madrasa education *see* Islamic education
Madrasa-i-Rahimia 244
madrasas (Islamic schools) *see* Islamic education
Magesa, L. 144, 154, 155, 156
Maguire, Daniel 208
Maha Ghosananda 36
Mahabharata epic 83, 94
Mahayana Buddhism 32, 41
Maimonides, M. 75
Mainga, M. 145
Make Poverty History 7, 446
male perspective religion 191
Malik, J. 241
Mandate of Heaven 128
Mani Singh 100
Manji, Firoze 502
Manushi 326, 327, 329–35
Manushi Swachha Narayani Clean Governance 332
Manushi Swachha Narayani (Goddess of Cleanliness) 326, 327, 329–35
Maoshan Declaration (CDA) 122
Mariz, Cecilia 483
market prominence 4
Marquette, Heather 10, 152, 153, 220, 221, 234
Marsden, P. 554, 557, 558, 559, 561, 562
Marshall, Alfred 104
Marshall, K. 275, 278, 280, 305–6, 403, 572
Marshall Plan 2, 280
Martin, David 171, 483
Martin-Schramm, James 211
Marty, Martin E. 253
Maryknoll sisters 201
Mason, C. 561
mass consumption modernization stage 3
mature religiosity 233
Maududi, Maulana 241
May Fourth New Culture Movement 130
Mayer, Jean-François 388
Mayotte, J.A. 403
Mazhabi Sikhs 98
Mbiti, John 142, 144, 145, 146, 147, 148, 152, 157, 158, 159
Mbon 152
MCD (Municipal Corporation of Delhi) 328–9
MDCF (Muslim–Christian Dialogue Forum) 260
MDG (Millenium Development Goals) 296
MEB (Movement for Grassroots Education) 474
Meier, R. 222
Melanesian Christian language of development 510–13
Mencius 127–8
Mencius 127, 135
Mends, E.H. 146, 160
Mennonites 259
Mensah Sarbah, J.H. 144
Mercy Relief International 27
Mesocosm 326
Metcalf, B. 239, 240, 241, 242
metta (Buddhism) 33
Mexico City Policy 188
Meyer, Richard L. 290, 294
MFIs (microfinance institutions) 286–302
Micah Network 425–7
microfinance 10
  conventional/Islamic 294
  graduation model 295
  integrated model 296–7
  Islamic microfinance model 286–302
  problems 291
Middleton, R. 228–9, 234
MIGA (Multilateral Investment Guarantee Agency) 272
Migdal, J. 221
Mihevc, J. 275, 277
militant atheism 402
millenialism 433
Millenium Development Goals 10, 23, 453
Miller, Donald E. 174, 175–6
Miller, James 9, 114, 122

Mills, E.W. 226, 229
Ministry for the Promotion of Virtue and Prevention of Vice (Afghanistan) 542
missionaries 10, 11, 413–27
  Christian 10, 11, 413–15, 418–21, 493
  evangelization 422–7
  and imperialism 420
  Islamic 10, 11
  personal motivation 420–22
  poverty reduction 422–7
  theology and mission 418–20
missionary religions 138
Mitcham, Stephanie 169–70
MMC (Medical Missionary Committee) 497
Model Street Vendors (Protection of Livelihood and Regulation of Street Vending) Bill (2009) 329
modernization, rise of 269
modernization stages 3
Moe-Lobeda, Cynthia 10
Moghadam, V. 550
Mohamed, Yasien 288
moksha (Hinduism) 85
Molyneux, Maxine 365
moral action choices 230–31
moral attitudes, factors in 223
moral development stages 231
moral issues, and religion 222–9
moral majority 232, 494
moral reasoning, and corruption 229–33
moral systems, and applied ethics 234
moral-spiritual power for justice 212–13
morality (Buddhism) 32
More than 100 million women are missing 189
Moser, Caroline 184–5, 186
Moses 67
Mosley, Paul 300
Mosse, D. 507
MPF (Popular Movement of Favelas) 480
MST (Movement of the Landless) 480
mudarabah 292, 296
Muhajirat 523–5
muktabs 238
Mullings, B. 438
Mumisa, Michael 409
murabahah-muajjal 293, 296
musaqat 293
museums, in South East Asia 338–52
Muslim Aid 24–5, 361, 408
Muslim Brotherhood 370, 388, 392
Muslim warfare 382–3
Muslim–Catholic alliance 188
musyarakah 292–3
muti (medicine) killings 141, 151
Muzaffar, Chandra 407
MWL (Muslim World League) 22–3
myth-symbol complexes 556

Nag Panchami festival 87–8
Nair, Kusum 104
Nair, P. 247, 249, 250
Name It and Claim It *see* Prosperity Gospel
Nandy, Asis 333, 336
Nara Document on Authenticity 346
Narayan, D. 369
Narayanan, Yamini 10
NASFAT 466–7
NASVI (National Association of Street Vendors of India) 329
National Commission for Relief and Charity Work Abroad 28
National Mission and Development Plan 513
NDMC (New Delhi Municipal Council) 329
NDT (new development theory) 475, 477, 479–82, 484, 486, 487, 488
neighbour-love, as ecological vocation 213–14, 215
Neo-Pentecostalism *see* Prosperity Gospel
New Thought movement 169
NGOs (non-governmental organizations) 5, 8, 11, 22–5, 27, 28, 37, 44, 260, 261, 262, 276, 360–61, 367–8, 403, 475, 480, 498, 570–82
  characteristics of 578–81
  Korten's generations of 576–8
  secular 578–81
  see also INGOs
Nicea-Constantinople Creed 54
Nichol, J.T. 434, 436
Nichols, J. 252–3
Nigeria 453–69
  Christian schools and Muslim children 462–4
  corruption 460–61
  education 459–60
  health 459–60
  infrastructure 459–60
  inter-religious mistrust 466–8
  missions and Muslim population 498
  moral values 460–61
  Muslim/Christian conflict 455–9
  religion and politics (by state) 455–9
  religious competition 464–6
night letters 544
NIREC (Nigeria Inter-Religious Council) 456
nirodha (end of suffering) 31
Nizam-uddin, Mulla 243
Nizami, F. 240, 241, 243
Noah 66
Nolte, Insa 11
Nomani, Maulana Shibli 243

NORAD 403
Norwegian Research Council 403
Nussbaum, David 223
Nussbaum, Martha 61, 83

Obaidullah, Muhammed 293
Obama, President Barack 188
O'Coill, Carl 502
Octogesima Adveniens 60
ODA (Arab Official Development Assistance) 20–21
Olupona, J.O.K. 138, 140
Omar, Mullah 558, 560
Omari, C.K. 145
Onyenze, C.J. 461
oral culture 80–81
Oral Roberts University 170
Orji, Pastor Richard 461
orthodoxy 74
orthopraxis 74
Osho, Funmilayo 467
Otayek, René 408–9
OTL system 76
Overseas Aid Gift Deduction Fund 423
Overseas Service Bureau 576
Oxfam 501, 576
Oyedepo, Bishop David O. 166
Oyo state (Nigeria) 455–9

Pacific 11
Pakistan development policy 387–8
Pali Canon (Buddhism) 39, 41
Pan Yue 121
pan-Islamism 376–96
panentheism 214
paramatta sacca (Buddhism) 37
Parnwell, M.J.G. 37
Parpart, J. 186
Parsons, T. 224
Participatory Budget 477
partnership policy translation 507–10
The Pastor and the Imam: Responding to Conflict 260
pastoral power 206
pathogens of poverty 485
patrimonialism 453
Patton, Laurie 81
Paul VI, Pope 54, 57, 61
PBI (Peace Brigades International) 256
PDPA (People's Democratic Party of Afghanistan) 562
peacebuilding 252–65
  advocates role 255–6
  educators role 256–7
  faith-based development services 261–4
  herald role 254–5
  hostage release 256
  institution building role 259–60
  negotiators role 257–9
  observers role 256
  and peacemaking 254
  reconciliation role 259–60
  religious actors' roles 253–60
  religious roots of 252–3
Peach, L.J. 43
Pearson, Ruth 184, 365, 366
Pedagogy of the Oppressed 474
Peet, R. 269
Penfold, Peter 258
pengajian groups 317
Pentecostalism
  in Brazil 482–5, 487
  missions 430–47
  in Tanzania 493
Pentecostalization 176
PEPFAR (President's Emergency Plan for AIDS Relief) 193, 366
perceived conformity 225
Peters, R. 19
Petersen, Marie 23–4, 27, 408, 505
Pew Global Attitudes Project 308
Pfanner, T. 269
Pilgrimage of Truth 255
Pincus, J.R. 276
Platvoet, J. 144
PLS (profit and loss sharing) mechanism 292, 298
PNG (Papua New Guinea)
  aid 507
  and AusAID 508
  churches 505, 509
  CPP (Church Partnership Programme) 506–7, 509, 510
  Development Unit (DU) 513–14
  Four Square Program 514–15
  Government (GoPNG) 508
  institutional strengthening 513–15
  Western view of problems 511
Pobee, J.S. 146, 160
political extremism 5
politics of identity 493
Poloma, Margaret 164
Pontifical Council for Interreligious Bodies 426
Populorum Progressio 57, 60, 61
positive confession 164, 167, 168
post-development theory 205
post-disaster aid, and religion 308–10
post-disaster development 305–22
Post-Washington Consensus 4–5

poverty
  Islamic alleviation tools 288–9
  Islamic approach to 288
  and Islamic microfinance 290–97
  Islamic perspective on 287–8
  levels of 286
  and structural injustice 212
PPAs (Programme Partnership Arrangements) 403
Prandi, Reginaldo 485–6
Prasad, Leela 82
pre-take-off modernization stage 3
Pre-Writing Prophets 72–3
Prenatal Diagnostic Act 110
Prescribed Purifying Alms 405
Price, David 155
Price, Frederick 169
pro-democracy movements, sub-Saharan Africa 502
Program Framework 509
Progressio 403
Prophetic Guilds 72
proselytism 408–9, 426
Prosperity Gospel 9, 164–77
  affiliated churches 164
  and African Pentecostalism 171, 173
  Biblical interpretation 165–6
  books on 166
  criticism of 164–5, 168–70, 173–6
  and democratization 175
  development of 168–70
  and gender 176
  global growth 170–74, 177
  global numbers 171
  history of 168–70
  ideas behind 165–8
  key ideas 164
  and oppressive regimes 175
  ostentation of 166
  Pentecostalization 176
  positive confession 164, 167, 168
  proof texts 165
  theology of empowerment/glory 168
  worship 165—8
prosperity religion 484
Prosperity Theology *see* Prosperity Gospel
protectionism 4
The Protestant Ethic and the Spirit of Capitalism 103, 165
Protestant work ethic 3
Protestant World Council of Churches 370
PRSPs (Poverty Reduction Strategy Papers) 280
Pryor, F.L. 39
PT (Workers' Party)(Brazil) 481
PTPA (Parish Twinning Program of the Americas) 370
Pui, H. 261
purdah 92
Puri, B. 45
Puri, Harish 108
Puritanism 4
Putnam, R. 368
Putney, S. 228–9, 234

Qanum Jinayat laws 319
qard hasan 293
Qardhawi, Yusuf 288
Qi (vital energy) 119
Quadragesimo 59
Quaker Service Australia 576
Quakers 258–9
qurd hassan 301, 302

Rabita Bangladesh 22–3, 27
RACHA (Reproductive and Child Health Alliance) 44
radical contestation 396
Rae, Lindsay 411, 446
Raheja, Gloria Goodwin 90
rahitnamas 100, 109
Rakodi, C. 51, 403
Ramachandra, Vinoth 420
Ramayana epic 80, 83–4
Ramgarhia Sikhs 98
Randhawa, M.S. 104
Rao, Govinda M. 106
Rashid, A. 561, 563
Ravidasi Sikhs 98
Ray, B.C. 142, 143, 144, 149, 150, 153
Ray, Niharranjan 101
Raynor-Prince, L. 233
Razavi, Shahra 188, 365
RCCG (Redeemed Christian Church of God) 460, 462, 481
RCG (responsible global capitalism) 270
Reagan, President Ronald 4
rebirth (Buddhism) 31
reconstruction and theology 203
Red Crescent, Turkish 316, 321
Red Cross, Australian 575
Rees, John 10
reformist contestation 396
refugees, Muslim 307
Regnerus, Mark D. 372
reincarnation 84–5
reinterpretation and theology 203
religion
  conceptualizations of 305
  and moral issues 222–9

Religion and Development project (Birmingham) 12
Religion and Development Research programme 505
religiosity and morality 231
Religious Affairs Bureau (China) 116
religious comminity membership 226–7
religious extremism 326
religious feminisms, role of 194–5
religious fundamentalism 191–2
religious resurgence 139–40, 183, 187
religious symbolism 332
religious traditions, and ecological degradation 207
Remenyi, J. 274
Remittances Profile of Tajikistan 523
Renewed Church 482
renunciation 84–5, 104
reproductive rights 188–91
retrieval and theology 203
Reus-Smit, C. 555, 556
reversed sex ratio 189, 190
RFO (responsibility for others) 229
RHEMA Bible College 170
Rhema Ministerial Association International 167
Riddell, Peter 9
Rinehart, Robin 79
Rist, G. 269
Rittberger, V. 273
Robbins, Joel 173
Roberts, Oral 168, 169
Robinson, F. 238, 240, 243, 244
Rohde, Jon 416
Rokeach, M. 229
Romero, Archbishop Oscar 55–6
Rossi, Marcelo 481, 482
Rostow, W.W. 3
Rowlands, Jo 186
Roy, Olivier 384, 388
Roy, Raja Rammohan 333
RSS (Rashtriya Swayamsevak Sangh) 334, 367

Sacks, Jonathan 280
sadaqa 19
Sain, Kanwar 328
St Paul's Cathedral protest 491
Salafism 388–9
Salamon, Lester M. 360
Salvation Army 506
sammuti sacca (Buddhism) 37
Sampson, Cynthia 254
samsara (cycle of rebirths) 32
Sanatana Dharma 80
Sandler, S. 5
Sandrioriva, Qory 320
Sanford, A. Whitney 9
sangha (Buddhism) 32–3, 35
Sanskritization 190
Sant-Egidio 271, 407
Santi Asoke Buddhist Movement 35
Santmire, Paul 210
Sapp, G.L. 232–3
SAPs (Structural Adjustment programmes) 402, 403
SARA (State Administration for Religious Affairs)(China) 114
Saraswati (goddess of learning) 330, 336
Sarvodaya Shramadana Movement 36, 39, 40, 255–6
Saul, J.R. 270
Save the Children (Australia) 575
Scheduled Groups (Sikhism) 107–8
Scheepers, P. 226
Schipper, Kristofer 117
scholar-gentry ideal 131
Schumacher, E.F. 38
Scudder, Ida 415
SD (self-determination) 229
Second Cold War 383
The Secret 169
secular reductionism 307
secular-sacral dichotomy 270
secular-sacral distinction 270–71
secularization 4, 5, 7, 187, 269, 333, 402, 494
securitizing subjectivity 559
security issues 5
Seed-Faith *see* Prosperity Gospel
Segal, E. 70
Seguino, Stephanie 186–7, 192, 194
self-interest morality 227
self-strengthening movement (China) 130
Selinger, L. 305
Sen, Amartya 61, 102, 189, 364, 475
Service Auxiliare de l'Assistance Médicale aux Indigènes 498
Seventh Day Adventist Church 506
Sewa Nagar Model Market 331, 332, 334
SEWA (Self-Employed Women's Association) 328–9
sex workers 8, 43
sex-selective abortion 190
SGPC (Shiromani Gurdwara Parbandhak Committee) 100
shadaqa 288, 289, 290, 298
Shaftesbury, Lord 421
shalat 317
Shanti Sena 256
Sharma, Arvind 103

Sharpe, Matthew 9
Shia Personal Police 543
Shirazi, Fadl Allah 243
Shorter, A. 155, 156
significance methodology 349—50
Sikhism 9, 97—111
  ascetism 99
  beliefs 99–100
  castes 107–8
  debt 105–6
  ecological crisis 106–7
  and economic development 102–4
  four precepts 102
  free meals 99
  gender inequality 108–10
  green revolution 97, 106
  gurdwaras 97, 99
  honest labour 103
  human behaviour 101
  hypocrisy in 109
  Jats 97, 98, 108
  Khalsa Panth 100
  material values 102–3
  Mazhabi Sikhs 98
  Nanak's successors 99–100
  poets 99
  population 98
  poverty 105–6
  practices 99–100
  and Protestant ethic 103
  Ramgarhia Sikhs 98
  Ravidasi Sikhs 98
  sacred book 97
  sects in 98
  SGPC (Shiromani Gurdwara Parbandhak Committee) 100
  sharing earnings 103
  Sikh ethics 100–102
  social crisis 106–7
  social exclusion 107–10
  social groups 107–8
  social life 99
  society 107–10
  spirit of individualism 102
  teachings 99–100
  wealth 105–6
  work ethics 97
  see also Gurus
sin 61–3
Singer, Milton 103
Singh, Avtar 101, 102
Singh, Lakhwinder 106
Sisters of Islam 194
Sivarsksa, Sulak 255, 256, 257, 265
Sklair, Leslie 384
Small is Beautiful: Economics as if People Mattered 38
Smith, D.J. 234
Smith, Gordon S. 252, 254
Smith, H. 68, 72, 73, 74, 75
Social Gospel movement 213
social justice
  Buddhism 34–5
  Hinduism 91–2
social movements and religion 7
social theoretical presuppositions 203–6
sociologization of development studies 402
Soenens, B. 230, 231, 232
Soka Gakkai 35
solidarity 60
Sollicitudo Rei Socialis 60, 61, 62
son preference 189
Sorley, Craig 417, 418
South Africa, ANC politics 492
Southern Eurasia 11
Southwest-Central Asia 11
Spring and Autumn Annals 125, 129, 131
Springs and Autumns of Mr.Lü 119
Sri Lanka, anti-conversion movement 261–4
SSE (steady state economics) 121
Stages of Economic Growth: A Non-Communist Manifesto 3
Stamer, J. 147
Stanley, Brian 424
Stark, R. 224–6, 227
Starkey, Caroline 9
Stations of the Earth 201
sticky/non-sticky trust 368–72
Stiglitz, J.E. 270
strategic gender needs 186
street hawking, Delhi 327–9
structural sin 62
subsidiarity 59
Sukhothai archaeological park 344–5
Suksamran 44
Sulak Sivaraska 35
Sumbawanga, Bishop of 499
Sun Simiao 120
sunyata (Buddhism) 32, 37
Swachha Narayani (Goddess of Cleanliness) 326, 327, 329–35
Swearer, Donald 36, 252
Sweet, Jonathan 10
Symbol of the Apostles 53
symbolic affirmation 231
symbolic disaffirmation 231
Synan, Vinson 175

Tadros, Mariz 365–6, 494–5
Tajikistan 521–36

aid to 526–7
communication technology 532–3
community elders' influence 532
economy of 521–3
education 531
family abandonment 534–5
gender changes 534–5
identity 527–32
Islamic holidays 533
kinship networks 528
migration (Muhajirat) 523–5, 527–9, 531, 533–6
mobility 527–32
religion 528–32
religious civil society 532–4
remittances 523, 533–4
takdir 318
take-off modernization stage 3
Taliban 540, 542, 543, 545, 549–53, 556–65, 566
Tam Wai Lun 117–18
Tamils 261–4
Tanganyike *see* Tanzania
tanha (craving) 31
Tanzania 491–503
early colonial period 496–9
FBO engagement in 495–9
Pentecostalism 493
post-colonial 499–502
religious resurgence 493–5
Tao Hongjing 120
Taoism *see* Daoism
Tatla, Darshan S. 9, 98
TBN (Trinity Broadcasting Network) 172
technical assistance 212
Telford, J. 8
Ter Haar, G. 148, 151, 154, 371
Ter Voert, M. 223, 227, 228
terrorism
financing 27–8
in South Asia 326
Thaplial, Madan 328
Thatcher, Prime Minister Margaret 4
theo-ethical presuppositions 202–3
theological liberalism 214
theology of empowerment/glory 168
Theology of Liberation 205–6, 474, 481–2, 483, 486
therapeutic abortions 189
Theravada Buddhism 32, 33, 39, 41
Thirteen Principles of Faith (Judaism) 68
Thomas, S.M. 270, 278
TI-CPI (Transparency International's Corruption Perception Index) 220, 221
Tittensor, David 11
Tittle, C.R. 224, 225
TMC (Tanganyika Mission Council) 497
Tohidi, Nayreheh 188
Tomalin, Emma 9, 184, 365, 366
tourism 10
traditional modernization stage 3
transcendence 230
transformation 512
Treverton, G. 253
Trinitapoli, J. 372
Truman, President Harry 2
trust
conceptions of 368
and institutions 368–72
tsunami
Aitape (1998) 309
Indian Ocean (2004) 8, 40, 262, 305, 310–20, 321, 322, 409, 441
Tucker, Gerard 576
Tughluq, Firuz Shah 243
Turajonzoda brothers 533
Tutu, Desmond 427
Tyndale, Wendy 90, 269, 406
Tzu-Chi 34, 36

ubiquity of religion 270
'ulamas *see* Islamic education
Ullah, Shah Wali 243, 244
UN Development programme 406
underdevelopment term 4
UNDP *Human Development Reports* 58
UNESCO (United Nations Educational, Scientific and Cultural Organization) World Heritage Sites 338, 340, 342, 344–8
UNFPA (United Nations Population Find) 365–6, 494
United Church 505, 506
development theory principles 511–12
mission argument 513–14
United Nations HDI (Human Development Index) 270–71
United Nations Population and Development Conference (Cairo) 188
Universal Declaration of Human Rights 58, 365, 366
urban planning 10, 326–7, 345
US Embassy bombing (Nairobi) 27
USAID (US Agency for International Development) 205, 206, 403, 473
USIP (United States Institute of Peace) 407
UTO (United Tajik Opposition) 522

Vajrayana Buddhism 32
Vakhsh Valley 521–36
Vallier, Ivan 473

values and attitudes 229
Van den Dungen, P.H.M. 105
Van Der Silk, F. 226
Van Esterik, P. 42
van Geest, W. 573
Van Saanen, M. 275, 279, 572
Varma, P.K. 327, 328
Varnashramadharma (Hinduism) 82
Vedas (Hinduism) 80, 83
Ver Beek, K.A. 269, 305
Vidal, A. 571
Viharn Phra Chao Pun Ong Conservation Project 348
Villanger, Espen 20, 21
vinaya (Buddhism) 33
Vivekananda, Swami 91
Vuola, Elina 188

Wapenhans Report 276
waqf 19, 288, 289, 290, 298
Ware, Anthony 11
Ware, Vicki-Ann 11
Washington Consensus 4
Wat Pongasanuk *see* Lampang Temple Project
The Way and Its Power 121
Way of the Orthodox Unity (Daoism) 116
WBG (World Bank Group) *see* World Bank
WCC (World Council of Churches) 211, 426, 511
WEA (World Evangelical Alliance) 426
Weber, Max 3, 35, 103, 165, 252
Welayat Detention Centre (Afghanistan) 545
Welch, M.R. 224, 225
Welfare Act (1996) (USA) 403
Wendt, A. 555
Wesleyan Methodism 169
White, Lynn 208, 209
White, R.H. 226
WID (women in development) approaches 184–5
Wilber, Charles 3, 185
Wilberforce, William 421
Wildavsky, Aaron 326
Wilkinson, Michael 437
Willems, Emilio 482
Williams, Archbishop Rowan 422, 491
Wills, Jo 10, 349
Winkler, Tanja 454
Winters, J.A. 276
Witness for Peace 256
Wolfensohn, James D. 220, 276, 278–9, 280, 281, 282, 422
Wolterstorff, Nicholas 420
women *see* gender
Women's Role in Economic Development 183
The Word of Faith 167
Word of Faith *see* Prosperity Gospel
World Bank 4, 6, 186, 205, 206, 220, 222, 268, 272–81
  CDF (Comprehensive Development Framework) 276–7
  Directorate on Faith 282
  divisions of 272
  economic dualism 274
  and FBOs 403
  FMG (Friday Morning Group) 279
  integration of religion 276–7
  modernization 274
  policy dynamics 273
  policy on religion in IOs 278
  policy on sacral religion 279
  policy and secular religion 277–8
  poverty eradication 274
  power and influence 272–3
  SAPs (structural adjustment programmes) 275
  secular–sacral distinction 270–71, 281
  structural adjustment 274–6
  subordination of religion 273–4
world conflict, and religion 5
World Development 6
World Faith Development Dialogue 447
World Heritage Sites *see* UNESCO
World Vision Australia 576
World Vision International 366–7
Wuye, James Movel 260

Yarnall, T.F. 35
Yuan Shikai 115
Yueyang Pavilion 131
Yumina, Aimatul 10
Yunus, Muhammed 26–7, 273

Zachariah, George 205, 211
Zadek, S. 39–40
zakat 18, 288, 289, 295, 296, 298, 301, 302
Zaman, M.Q. 238, 239, 240
Zangl, B. 273
Zeghal, M. 245, 250
Zeller, Manfred 290, 294
Zelliot, Eleanor 82, 92
Zen Buddhism 35
Zeng, Chuanhu 116
Zi Gong 132
Zisi (grandson of Confucius) 125
zodiac (China) 114
Zuma, President Jacob 492
Zuo Qiuming 126